FOURTH EDITION INVESTMENT ANALYSIS
AND PORTFOLIO MANAGEMENT

FOURTH EDITION

INVESTMENT ANALYSIS AND PORTFOLIO MANAGEMENT

FRANK K. REILLY
BERNARD J. HANK PROFESSOR OF BUSINESS ADMINISTRATION
UNIVERSITY OF NOTRE DAME

WITH CONTRIBUTIONS BY
DON M. CHANCE
VIRGINIA POLYTECHNIC INSTITUTE AND STATE UNIVERSITY

THE DRYDEN PRESS
HARCOURT BRACE COLLEGE PUBLISHERS

FORT WORTH   PHILADELPHIA   SAN DIEGO   NEW YORK   ORLANDO   AUSTIN
SAN ANTONIO   TORONTO   MONTREAL   LONDON   SYDNEY   TOKYO

Publisher: Elizabeth Widdicombe
Acquisitions Editor: Rick Hammonds
Developmental Editors: Barbara J. C. Rosenberg/Shana Lum
Project Management: Elm Street Publishing Services, Inc.
Compositor: Weimer Graphics, Inc.
Text Type: 10/12 Times Roman
Cover Image: Frank Wing/The Image Bank
Copyright © 1994, 1989, 1985, 1979 by The Dryden Press

Address for Editorial Correspondence
The Dryden Press, 301 Commerce Street, Suite 3700, Fort Worth, TX 76102

Address for Orders
The Dryden Press, 6277 Sea Harbor Drive, Orlando, FL 32887
1-800-782-4479, or 1-800-433-0001 (in Florida)

ISBN: 0-03-097052-0

Library of Congress Catalog Number: 93-26470

CFA Examinations used throughout the text are reprinted with permission from The Institute of Chartered Financial Analysts, Charlottesville, Virginia.

Printed in the United States of America
3 4 5 6 7 8 9 0 1 2 039 9 8 7 6 5 4 3 2 1

The Dryden Press
Harcourt Brace College Publishers

To

MY BEST FRIEND AND WIFE,

THERESE,

AND OUR GREATEST GIFTS AND

SOURCES OF HAPPINESS,

FRANK K. III AND CHARLOTTE,

CLARENCE R. II AND WHITNEY

THERESE B.

EDGAR B. AND MICHELE

The Dryden Press Series in Finance

PREFACE

The pleasure of authoring a textbook comes from writing about a subject that you enjoy and find exciting. As an author, you hope that you can pass on to the reader not only knowledge but also the excitement that you feel for the subject. In addition, writing about investments brings an added stimulant because the subject can affect the reader during his or her entire business career and beyond. I hope what readers derive from this course will help them enjoy better lives through managing their resources properly.

The purpose of this book is to help you learn how to manage your money so that you will derive the maximum benefit from what you earn. To accomplish this purpose, you need to learn about the investment alternatives that are available today and, what is more important, to develop a way of analyzing and thinking about investments that will remain with you in the years ahead when new and different investment opportunities become available.

Because of its dual purpose, the book mixes description and theory. The descriptive material discusses available investment instruments and considers the purpose and operation of capital markets in the United States and around the world. The theoretical portion details how you should evaluate current investments and future opportunities to develop a portfolio of investments that will satisfy your risk-return objectives.

Preparing this fourth edition has been challenging for two reasons. First, many changes have occurred in the securities markets during the last few years in terms of theory, new financial instruments, and trading practices. Second, as mentioned in the prior edition, capital markets have become global. Consequently, very early in the book (in Chapter 2) I present the compelling case for global investing. Subsequently, to ensure that you are prepared to function in this new global environment, almost every chapter discusses how investment practice or theory is influenced by the globalization of investments and capital markets. This completely integrated treatment is to ensure that you leave this course with a completely global mindset on investments that will serve you well into the 21st century.

INTENDED MARKET

This text is addressed to both graduate and advanced undergraduate students who are looking for an in-depth discussion of investments and portfolio management. The presentation of the material is intended to be rigorous and empirical, without being overly quantitative. A proper discussion of the modern developments in investments and portfolio theory must be rigorous. The detailed discussion of numerical empirical studies reflects my personal belief that it is essential for our theories to be exposed to the real world and be judged on the basis of how well they help us understand and explain reality. To make room for the most recent studies and results in this edition, I have condensed or deleted some of the older studies.

MAJOR CHANGES AND ADDITIONS IN THE FOURTH EDITION

The text has been thoroughly updated. In addition to chapter revisions, this edition includes approximately 25 new problems and 15 new CFA Exam questions. By chapter, some specific changes include the following:

- *Chapter 1:* Consideration of the impact of country/political risk on the risk premium; discussion and demonstration of the effects of changes in the market risk premium over time.

- *Chapter 2:* An extensive discussion of why global investing is desirable followed by a description of bonds and equities in the United States and the world.

- *Chapter 3:* An update of new developments in the securities markets in the United States and around the world. An appendix contains a table that lists characteristics of stock exchanges in developed and emerging capital markets.

- *Chapter 4:* Discusses new indexes by Dow Jones & Co. for the domestic market and also a new world stock index. An appendix contains a tabular description of numerous country stock indexes from around the world.

- *Chapter 6:* An extensive update and reorganization of the evidence related to the efficient market hypothesis, including consideration of the growing number of anomalies and the usefulness of the book value/market value ratio.

- *Chapter 8:* Discussion of the arbitrage pricing theory as an asset pricing model. Discussion and demonstration of the impact of a world market portfolio on the measurement of beta and the security market line.

- *Chapter 9:* A new chapter that introduces derivative markets and securities so that these concepts can be used in subsequent discussions of valuation and portfolio management.

- *Chapter 10:* In addition to the DuPont three-way component breakdown of the return on equity, there is a five-way component breakdown considered. Additional use and analysis of cash flow ratios and measures are explained. A discussion of factors to consider when analyzing non-U.S. financial statements, including how these statements differ and the effects of different accounting treatments on various ratios.

- *Chapter 12:* Following the macroanalysis of economies and markets there is an explicit global asset allocation and an example of asset allocation within non-U.S. countries.

- *Chapter 13:* A discussion of the history, growth, and default-adjusted performance of the high-yield bond market.

- *Chapter 14:* A detailed demonstration of factors that influence bond price volatility. A discussion and analysis of the impact of convexity on bond price volatility. An analysis of the effect of a call option on a bond's duration and convexity.

- *Chapter 15:* Expanded discussion of the analysis of high-yield bonds and the new sources of data and analysis for this market.

- *Chapter 16:* This chapter is limited to the microanalysis of the aggregate stock market and contains a more detailed analysis of the income statement components for the aggregate market.

- *Chapter 17:* Considers a new industry (retail drugstore chains) that is consistent with the company analysis (Walgreens). A consideration of Porter's five basic competitive factors that determine the competitive environment and return on capital for an industry. More extensive analysis of factors that influence relative growth of an industry versus the market.

- *Chapter 18:* Employs a new example company (Walgreens). Discussion and analysis of additional measures of relative value for common stocks: the price/book value ratio and the price/cash flow ratio.

- *Chapter 20:* A more detailed and theoretical discussion of the valuation of option contracts.

- *Chapter 21:* A discussion of how the common stock and the bonds of a firm can be viewed as options and how these options affect the yield spread for a risky bond. A discussion of several new index securities related to financial and real assets.

- *Chapter 22:* A more detailed and theoretical discussion of forward and futures contracts. A detailed discussion of alternative approaches to determining the appropriate hedge ratio.

- *Chapter 23:* A new chapter dealing with advanced derivative instruments, including options on futures, currency swaps, interest rate swaps, interest rate floors, caps, and collars. We also consider program trading and the introduction and effect of circuit breakers on the stock exchanges.

- *Chapter 24:* Description of Morningstar Investment Service for evaluating mutual fund performance. Discussion of studies that examine the performance of international funds, bond mutual funds, and specifically high-yield bond funds.

- *Chapter 25:* Considers new tests of the CAPM including a detailed discussion of the recent Fama-French study.

- *Chapter 26:* A discussion and demonstration of the Roll benchmark problem with a global market index. A discussion of customized benchmarks and the important characteristics that any benchmark should possess.

ANCILLARIES

The *Instructor's Manual/Test Bank,* prepared by David Leahigh of King's College, contains the following aids for each chapter: an overview of the chapter; answers to all of the questions and problems; and a test bank of multiple-choice questions. A set of approximately 75 transparency masters is also available to instructors to facilitate the inclusion of key figures and illustrations from the book in classroom lectures.

With this edition, I have prepared a disk containing economic data from U.S. and foreign companies, detailing stock information over a 20-year period. This data disk is offered free to adopters.

A *Computerized Test Bank,* available in both IBM and Macintosh formats, is also free to instructors and contains all the test questions found in the printed *Test Bank.* The computerized test bank program, ExaMaster+ ™, has many features that facilitate exam preparation—random question selection; key-word searches; adding and editing test items; conversion of multiple-choice questions into short-answer questions; and creation of customized exams by question scrambling.

Portfolio Manager for the Personal Computer is a software program developed by Jim Pettijohn and Joe Evans that provides routines for students to apply the concepts and techniques presented in the text, as well as a database of quarterly data from real companies so that students may create a portfolio and perform analyses. This package is available free to adopters.

The Stock Market Simulation, prepared by Peter Bobko of Guilford College, allows students to select a portfolio of securities, track their performance over time, and then observe the effects of diversification. A master disk for duplication is provided free to adopters.

AVAILABLE FOR PURCHASE

A student *Study Guide,* prepared by David Leahigh of King's College, includes the following for each chapter: a detailed outline; extensive exercises, including true-false, fill-in-the-blank, multiple choice, and short-answer questions; a set of problems that provide additional practice; and answers to all of these exercises.

Security Analysis for Portfolio Construction and Management by Wayne E. Boyet of Nicholls State University is a software and workbook package that allows students to input and manipulate data using sophisticated statistical models and programs used in investment analysis. An accompanying manual gives complete instructions for using the disks, with discussions of each program. The package can be used as a supplement to this text.

Managing Investments: A Case Approach, by Michael A. Berry of James Madison University and S. David Young of Tulane University, contains 36 Harvard-style cases and 10 technical notes. Based on real-world problems, the book gives students hands-on experience in applying theoretical principles and models to decisions faced by individual investors and portfolio managers. Adopters of *Managing Investments* have access to a comprehensive *Instructor's Manual,* which includes detailed teaching notes for the cases.

ACKNOWLEDGMENTS

So many people have helped me in so many ways that I hesitate to list them, fearing that I may miss someone. Accepting this risk, I will begin with the University of Notre Dame because of its direct support. Also, I must thank the Bernard J. Hank Family, who have endowed the Chair that helped bring me back to Notre Dame and has provided support for my work. Reviewers for this edition were:

Omar M. Benkato
Ball State University

Susan Block
University of California–Santa Barbara

George Mason
University of Hartford

Katrina F. Sherrera
Association of Investment Management and Research

Kishore Tandon
The City University of New York–Baruch College

I was fortunate to have the following excellent reviewers for earlier editions:

Robert Angell
East Carolina University

George Aragon
Boston College

Brian Belt
University of Missouri–Kansas City

Arand Bhattacharya
University of Cincinnati

Carol Billingham
Central Michigan University

Gerald A. Blum
Babson College

Robert J. Brown
Harrisburg, Pennsylvania

Dosoung Choi
University of Tennessee

John Clinebell
University of Northern Colorado

Eugene F. Drzycimski
University of Wisconsin–Oshkosh

John Dunkelberg
Wake Forest University

Eric Emory
Sacred Heart University

Thomas Eyssell
University of Missouri–St. Louis

James Feller
Middle Tennessee State University

Eurico Ferreira
Clemson University

Michael Ferri
John Carroll University

Joseph E. Finnerty
University of Illinois

Harry Friedman
New York University

R. H. Gilmer
University of Mississippi

Stephen Goldstein
University of South Carolina

Steven Goldstein
Robinson-Humphrey/American Express

Keshav Gupta
Oklahoma State University

Sally A. Hamilton
Santa Clara University

Ronald Hoffmeister
Arizona State University

Ron Hutchins
Eastern Michigan University

A. James Ifflander
Arizona State University

Stan Jacobs
Central Washington University

Kwang Jun
Michigan State University

Jaroslaw Komarynsky
Northern Illinois University

Danny Litt
Century Software Systems/UCLA

Miles Livingston
University of Florida

Christopher Ma
Texas Tech University

Michael McBain
Marquette University

Dennis McConnell
University of Maine

Stephen Mann
University of South Carolina

John Matthys
DePaul University

Jeanette Medewitz
University of Nebraska–Omaha

Jacob Michaelsen
University of California–Santa Cruz

Nicholas Michas
Northern Illinois University

Lalatendu Misra
University of Texas–San Antonio

Michael Murray
LaCrosse, Wisconsin

John Peavy
Southern Methodist University

George Philippatos
University of Tennessee

George Pinches
University of Kansas

Rose Prasad
Central Michigan University

George A. Racette
University of Oregon

Bruce Robin
Old Dominion University

James Rosenfeld
Emory University

Stanley D. Ryals
Investment Counsel, Inc.

Frederic Shipley
DePaul University

Douglas Southard
Virginia Polytechnic Institute

Harold Stevenson
Arizona State University

Donald Thompson
Georgia State University

David E. Upton
Virginia Commonwealth University

E. Theodore Veit
Rollins College

Bruce Wardrep
East Carolina University

Rolf Wubbels
New York University

Valuable comments and suggestions have come from my former graduate students at the University of Illinois: Paul Fellows, University of Iowa; Wenchi Kao, DePaul University; and David Wright, University of Wisconsin–Parkside. Once more, I have been blessed with bright, dedicated research assistants when I needed them the most. This includes Chris Jones and Sumner Weymouth, who were both careful and creative.

Current and former colleagues have been very helpful: Yu-Chi Chang, Bill McDonald, Rick Mendenhall, Bill Nichols, Juan Rivera, and Norlin Rueschhoff, University of Notre Dame; C. F. Lee, Rutgers University; and John M. Wachowicz, University of Tennessee. As always, some of the best insights and most stimulating comments continue to come during my too-infrequent runs with my very good friend, Jim Gentry of the University of Illinois.

I am convinced that a professor who wants to write a book that is academically respectable, relevant, as well as realistic requires help from the "real world." I have been fortunate to develop relationships with a number of individuals (including a growing number of former students) whom I consider my contacts with reality.

I especially want to thank Robert Conway, who was the managing director of the London office of Goldman Sachs & Company, for suggesting several years ago that it was essential to have the book reflect the rapidly evolving global market. This was some of the most important advice I have ever received, and it has had a profound effect on this book over time.

The following individuals have graciously provided important insights and material:

Sharon Athey
Brown Brothers Harriman

Joseph C. Bencivenga
Salomon Brothers

Lowell Benson
Robert A. Murray Partners

David G. Booth
Dimensional Fund Advisors, Inc.

Gary Brinson
Brinson Partners, Inc.

Thomas Coleman
Adler, Coleman and Co. (NYSE)

Robert Conway
Goldman Sachs & Co.

William Cornish
Duff & Phelps

Robert J. Davis
Crimson Capital Co.

Robert J. Davis, Jr.
Goldman Sachs & Co.

Philip Delaney, Jr.
Northern Trust Bank

William Dwyer
Moody's Investors Service, Inc.

Steven Einhorn
Goldman Sachs & Co.

Sam Eisenstadt
Value Line

Paul Feldman
Goldman Sachs & Co.

Kenneth Fisher
Forbes

John J. Flanagan, Jr.
Lawrence, O'Donnell, Marcus & Co.

Martin S. Fridson
Merrill Lynch Pierce Fenner & Smith

Eduardo Haim
Lehman Brothers

William J. Hank
Moore Financial Corporation

Jim Johnson
Options Clearing Corporation

John W. Jordan II
The Jordan Company

Andrew Kalotay
Kalotay Associates

Luke Knecht
Harris Trust & Savings Bank

C. Prewitt Lane
ICH Companies

Martin Leibowitz
Salomon Brothers

Douglas R. Lempereur
Templeton Investment Counsel, Inc.

Robert Levine
Nomura Securities

Richard McCabe
Merrill Lynch Pierce Fenner & Smith

Michael McCowin
Harris Trust & Savings Bank

Terrence J. McGlinn
McGlinn Capital Markets

Scott Malpass
University of Notre Dame

John Maginn
Mutual of Omaha

Robert Milne
Duff & Phelps

Robert G. Murray
First Interstate Bank of Oregon

John J. Phelan, Jr.
New York Stock Exchange

Philip J. Purcell III
Dean Witter Discover

Jack Pycik
Norwest Bank, Indiana

Robert Quinn
Salomon Brothers

Chet Ragavan
Merrill Lynch Pierce Fenner & Smith

John C. Rudolf
Oppenheimer & Co., Inc.

Stanley Ryals
Investment Counsel, Inc.

Ron Ryan
Ryan Labs, Inc.

Sean St. Clair
Duff & Phelps

William Smith
Dean Witter Discover

James Stork
Duff & Phelps

Masao Takamori
Tokyo Stock Exchange

Jeffrey M. Weingarten
Goldman Sachs & Co.

Richard H. Tierney
The Bond Buyer

Thomas V. Williams
Kemper Financial Services

Anthony Vignola
Kidder, Peabody & Co.

Robert Wilmouth
National Futures Association

William M. Wadden
Harris Trust & Savings Bank

Richard S. Wilson
Fitch Investors Service, Inc.

I continue to benefit from the help and consideration of the dedicated people who are or have been associated with the Institute of Chartered Financial Analysts, which is now a part of the Association for Investment Management and Research: Darwin Bayston, Tom Bowman, Whit Broome, Hap Butler, Bob Luck, Pete Morley, Sue Martin, Katie Sherrerd, Donald Tuttle, and everybody's favorite, Peggy Slaughter.

Thankfully, Phyllis Sandfort forgets the pain between editions, so she agreed to type this fourth edition. Her patience, understanding, and willingness to type late at night ensured rapid and accurate turnaround. After she typed five editions of my books, I am happy (and sad) to report that she has gone on to a richly deserved better and less stressful life away from the University. My secretary, Donna Smith, had the unenviable task of keeping the rest of my life in some sort of order. Betsy Webster was the project editor who brought the book from messy manuscript and sloppy exhibits to bound volume with incredible good humor.

As always, my greatest gratitude is to my family—past, present, and future. My parents gave me life and helped me understand love and how to give it. My in-laws created my greatest gift and continuously give through their daughter. Most important is my wife, who provides love, understanding, and support at early morning breakfast and throughout the day and night. We thank God for our children and future grandchildren who ensure that our lives are full of love, laughs, and excitement.

Frank K. Reilly
Notre Dame, Indiana
December 1993

ABOUT THE AUTHOR

Frank K. Reilly is the Bernard J. Hank Professor of Business Administration, and former dean of the College of Business Administration at the University of Notre Dame. Holding degrees from the University of Notre Dame (B.B.A.), Northwestern University (M.B.A.), and the University of Chicago (Ph.D.), Professor Reilly has taught at the University of Illinois, the University of Kansas, and the University of Wyoming in addition to the University of Notre Dame. He has several years of experience as a senior securities analyst as well as experience in stock and bond trading. A Chartered Financial Analyst (CFA), he has been a member of the Council of Examiners, the Council on Education and Research, the grading committee, and is currently on the Board of Trustees of the Institute of Chartered Financial Analysts. Professor Reilly has been president of the Financial Management Association, the Midwest Business Administration Association, the Eastern Finance Association, the Academy of Financial Services, and is currently president of the Midwest Finance Association. He is or has been on the board of directors of the First Interstate Bank of Wisconsin, Norwest Bank of Indiana, the Investment Analysts Society of Chicago, Brinson Global Funds, Fort Dearborn Securities, Greenwood Trust Co., Discover Finance Corporation, NIBCO, Inc., International Board of Certified Financial Planners, and the Association for Investment Management and Research.

As the author of more than one hundred articles, monographs, and papers, his work has appeared in numerous publications including *Journal of Finance, Journal of Financial and Quantitative Analysis, Journal of Accounting Research, Financial Management, Financial Analysts Journal, Financial Review,* and *Journal of Portfolio Management.* In addition to *Investment Analysis and Portfolio Management,* Fourth Edition, Professor Reilly is the author of another textbook, *Investments,* Third Edition (The Dryden Press, 1992).

Professor Reilly was named on the list of *Outstanding Educators in America* and has received the University of Illinois Alumni Association Graduate Teaching Award, the Outstanding Educator Award from the M.B.A. class at the University of Illinois, and the Outstanding Teacher Award from the MBA class at Notre Dame. He also received the C. Stewart Sheppard Award from the Association of Investment Management and Research (AIMR) for his contribution to the educational mission of the Association. He is editor of *Readings and Issues in Investments, Ethics and the Investment Industry,* and *High Yield Bonds: Analysis and Risk Assessment,* and is or has been a member of the editorial boards of *Financial Management, The Financial Review, The Financial Services Review, The Journal of Applied Business Research, Journal of Financial Education,* and *Quarterly Review of Economics and Business.* He is included in *Who's Who in Finance and Industry, Who's Who in America, Who's Who in American Education,* and *Who's Who in the World.*

CONTENTS

xxiv   Contents

THE INVESTMENT BACKGROUND

The chapters in this section will provide a background for your study of investments by answering the following questions:

- Why do people invest?
- How do you measure the returns and risks for alternative investments?
- What investments are available?
- How do securities markets function?
- How and why are securities markets in the United States and around the world changing?
- How can you evaluate the market behavior of common stocks and bonds?
- What are the factors that cause differences among stock and bond market indexes?
- How can you get relevant information to learn about and evaluate potential investments?

In the first chapter we consider why an individual would invest, how to measure the rates of return and risk for alternative investments, and what factors determine an investor's required rate of return on an investment. The latter point will be very important in subsequent analyses when we work to understand investor behavior, the markets for alternative securities, and the valuation of various investments.

To minimize risk, investment theory asserts the need to diversify. To explore investments available to inves-tors, we begin Chapter 2 by making the overpowering case for why investors should invest globally rather than limit choices to only U.S. securities. Building on this premise, we discuss several investment instruments found in global markets. We conclude the chapter with a review of the historical rates of return and measures of risk for a number of alternative asset groups.

In Chapter 3 we examine how markets work in general, and then focus on bond and stock markets specifically. During the 1980s, significant changes occurred in the operation of the securities market, including a trend toward a global market. After discussing these changes and the globalization of these markets, we will envision how global markets will continue to expand available investment alternatives.

This initial section provides the framework for you to understand various securities, the markets where they are bought and sold, and how you might manage a collection of investments in a portfolio. Specific portfolio management techniques are described in later chapters.

Investors, market analysts, and financial theorists often gauge the behavior of securities markets by evaluating changes in various market indexes. We examine and compare a number of stock-market and bond-market indexes for the domestic and global markets in Chapter 4. Chapter 5, the final chapter in this section, describes sources of information for investors seeking to learn more about various investment opportunities.

CHAPTER 1

THE INVESTMENT SETTING

This chapter answers the following questions:

- Why do individuals invest?
- What is meant by an investment?
- How do investors measure the rate of returns on an investment?
- How do investors measure the risk related to alternative investments?
- What factors contribute to the rate of returns that investors require on an investment?
- What macroeconomic and microeconomic factors contribute to *changes* in the required rates of return for individual investments and investments in general?

This initial chapter discusses several topics that are basic to the subsequent chapters. We begin with a consideration of what is an investment and the returns and risks related to investments. This leads to a presentation of how to measure the expected and historical rates of returns for an individual asset or a portfolio of assets. In addition, we consider how to measure the risk not only for an individual investment, but also for an investment that is part of a portfolio.

The third section of the chapter discusses the factors that determine the required rate of return for an individual investment. The factors discussed are those that contribute to an asset's *total* risk. Because most investors have a portfolio of investments, it is necessary to consider how to measure the risk of an asset when it is a part of a large portfolio of assets. The risk that prevails when an asset is part of a portfolio is referred to as its *systematic* risk.

The final section deals with what causes *changes* in an asset's required rate of return over time. Changes occur because of both macro economic events that affect all investment assets and micro events that affect the specific asset.

WHAT IS AN INVESTMENT?

For most of your life, you will be earning and spending money. Rarely, though, will your current money income exactly balance with your consumption desires. Sometimes you may have more money than you want to spend; at other times you may want to purchase more than you can afford. These imbalances will lead you either to borrow or to save to maximize the benefits from your income.

When current income exceeds current consumption desires, people tend to save the excess. They can do any of several things with these savings. One possibility is to put the money under a mattress or bury it in the backyard until some future time when consumption desires exceed current income. When they retrieve their savings from the mattress or backyard, they would have the same amount they saved.

Another possibility is that they can give up the immediate possession of these savings for a future larger amount of money that will be available for future consumption. This tradeoff of *present* consumption for a higher level of *future* consumption is the reason for saving. What you do with the savings to make them increase over time is *investment.*[1]

Those who give up immediate possession of savings (i.e., defer consumption) expect to receive in the future a greater amount than they gave up. Conversely, those who consume more than their current income (i.e., borrow) must be willing to pay back in the future more than they borrowed.

The rate of exchange between *future consumption* (future dollars) and *current consumption* (current dollars) is the *pure rate of interest.* Both people's willingness to pay this difference for borrowed funds and their desire to receive a surplus on their savings give rise to an interest rate referred to as the *pure time value of money.* This interest rate is established in the capital market by a comparison of the supply of excess income available (savings) to be invested and the demand for excess consumption (borrowing) at a given time. If you can exchange $100 of certain income today for $104 of certain income 1 year from today, then the pure rate of exchange on a risk-free investment (i.e., the time value of money) is said to be 4 percent $(104/100 - 1)$.

The investor who gives up $100 today expects to consume $104 of goods and services in the future. This assumes that the general price level in the economy stays the same. This price stability has rarely been the case during the past several decades when inflation rates have varied from 1.1 percent in 1986 to 13.3 percent in 1979, with an average of about 6 percent a year from 1970 to 1992. If investors expect a change in prices, they will require a higher rate of return to compensate for it. For example, if an investor expects a rise in prices (i.e., he or she expects inflation) at the rate of 2 percent during the period of investment, he or she will increase the required interest rate by 2 percent. In our example, the investor would require $106 in the future to defer the $100 of consumption during an inflationary period (a 6 percent interest rate instead of 4 percent).

Further, if the future payment from the investment is not certain, the investor will demand an interest rate that exceeds the pure time value of money plus the inflation rate. The uncertainty of the payments from an investment is the *investment risk.* The excess amount added to the interest rate is called a *risk premium.* In our previous example, the investor would require more than $106 1 year from today to compensate for the uncertainty. As an example, if the required amount were $110, $4, or 4 percent, would be considered a risk premium.

INVESTMENT DEFINED

From our discussion we can specify a formal definition of investment. Specifically, an investment is *the current commitment of dollars for a period of time in order to derive future payments that will compensate the investor for (1) the time the funds are com-*

---

[1] In contrast, when current income is less than current consumption desires, people borrow to make up the difference. Although we will discuss borrowing on several occasions, the major emphasis of this text is how to invest savings.

mitted, (2) the expected rate of inflation, and (3) the uncertainty of the future payments. The "investor" can be an individual, a government, a pension fund, or a corporation. Similarly, this definition includes all types of investments, including investments by corporations in plant and equipment and investments by individuals in stocks, bonds, commodities, or real estate. This text emphasizes investments by individual investors. In all cases the investor is trading a *known* dollar amount today for some *expected* future stream of payments that will be greater than the current outlay.

At this point, we have answered the questions about why people invest and what they want from their investments. They invest to earn a return from savings due to their deferred consumption. They want a rate of return that compensates them for the time, the expected rate of inflation, and the uncertainty of the return. This return, the investor's *required rate of return,* is discussed throughout this book. A central question of this book is how investors select investments that will give them their required rates of return.

The next section of this chapter describes how to measure the expected or historical rate of return on an investment and also how to quantify the uncertainty of expected returns. You need to understand these techniques for measuring the rate of return and the uncertainty of these returns to evaluate the suitability of a particular investment. Although our emphasis will be on financial assets such as bonds and stocks, we will refer to other assets such as art and antiques. Chapter 2 discusses the range of financial assets and also considers some nonfinancial assets.

MEASURES OF RETURN AND RISK

The purpose of this book is to help you understand how to choose among alternative instruments. This selection process requires that you estimate and evaluate the expected risk–return tradeoffs for the alternative investments available. Therefore, you must understand how to measure the rate of return and the risk involved in an investment accurately. To meet this need, in this section we examine ways to quantify return and risk. The presentation will consider how to measure both *historical* and *expected* rates of return and risk.

We consider historical measures of return and risk because this book and other publications provide numerous examples of historical average rates of return and risk measures for various assets, and understanding these presentations is important. In addition, these historical results are often used by investors when attempting to estimate the *expected* rates of return and risk for an asset class.

The first measure is the historical rate of return on an individual investment over the time period the investment is held (i.e., its holding period). Next, we consider how to measure the *average* historical rate of return for an individual investment over a number of time periods. The third subsection considers the average rate of return for a *portfolio* of investments.

Given the measures of historical rates of return, we will present the traditional measures of risk for an historical time series of returns (i.e., the variance and standard deviation).

Following the presentation of measures of historical rates of return and risk we turn to estimating the *expected* rate of return for an investment. Obviously such an estimate contains a great deal of uncertainty, and we present measures of this uncertainty or risk.

MEASURES OF
HISTORICAL
RATES OF RETURN

When you are evaluating alternative investments for inclusion in your portfolio, you will often be comparing investments with very different prices or lives. As an example, you might want to compare a $10 stock that pays no dividends to a stock selling for $150 that pays dividends of $5 a year. To properly evaluate these two investments, you must accurately compare their historical rates of returns. A proper measurement of the rates of return is the purpose of this section.

When we invest we defer current consumption in order to add to our wealth so that we can consume more in the future. Therefore, when we talk about a return on an investment, we are concerned with the change in wealth resulting from this investment. This change in wealth can be due to cash inflows such as interest or dividends, or due to a change in the price of the asset (positive or negative).

If you commit $200 to an investment at the beginning of the year and you get back $220 at the end of the year, what is your return for the period? The period during which you own an investment is called its *holding period,* and the return for that period is the *holding period return (HPR).* In this example, the HPR is 1.10, calculated as follows:

$$\text{HPR} = \frac{\text{Ending Value of Investment}}{\text{Beginning Value of Investment}}$$
$$= \frac{\$220}{\$200} = 1.10$$

This value will always be zero or greater, i.e., it can never be a negative value. A value greater than 1.0 reflects an increase in your wealth, which means that you received a positive rate of return during the period. A value less than 1.0 means that you suffered a decline in wealth, which indicates that you had a negative return during the period. An HPR of zero indicates that you lost all of your money.

Although HPR helps us express the change in value of an investment, investors generally evaluate returns in *percentage terms on an annual basis.* This conversion to annual percentage rates makes it easier to directly compare alternative investments that have very different characteristics. The first step in converting an HPR to an annual percent rate is to derive a percentage return, referred to as the *holding period yield* (HPY). The HPY is equal to the HPR minus 1.

$$\text{HPY} = \text{HPR} - 1$$

In our example:

$$\text{HPY} = 1.10 - 1 = 0.10$$
$$= 10\%$$

To derive an *annual* HPY, you compute an *annual* HPR and subtract 1. Annual HPR is found by:

$$\text{Annual HPR} = \text{HPR}^{1/n}$$

where:

n = number of years the investment is held

Consider an investment that cost $250 and is worth $350 after being held for 2 years:

$$\text{HPR} = \frac{\text{Ending Value of Investment}}{\text{Beginning Value of Investment}} = \frac{\$350}{\$250}$$
$$= 1.40$$
$$\text{Annual HPR} = 1.40^{1/n}$$
$$= 1.40^{1/2}$$
$$= 1.1832$$
$$\text{Annual HPY} = 1.1832 - 1 = 0.1832$$
$$= 18.32\%$$

In contrast, consider an investment of $100 held for only 6 months that earned a return of $12:

$$\text{HPR} = \frac{\$112}{\$100} = 1.12 \ (n = .5)$$
$$\text{Annual HPR} = 1.12^{1/.5}$$
$$= 1.12^2$$
$$= 1.2544$$
$$\text{Annual HPY} = 1.2544 - 1 = 0.2544$$
$$= 25.44\%$$

Note that we made some implicit assumptions when converting the HPY to an annual basis. This annualized holding period yield computation assumes a constant annual yield for each year. In the 2-year investment, we assumed an 18.32 percent rate of return each year, compounded. In the partial year HPR that was annualized, we assumed that the return is compounded for the whole year. That is, we assumed that the rate of return earned during the first part of the year is likewise earned on the value at the end of the first 6 months. The 12 percent rate of return for the initial 6 months compounds to 25.44 percent for the full year.[2]

Remember one final point: The ending value of the investment can be the result of a change in price for the investment alone (e.g., a stock going from $20 a share to $22 a share), income from the investment alone, or a combination of price change and income. Ending value includes the value of everything related to the investment.

COMPUTING MEAN HISTORICAL RETURNS

Now that we have calculated the HPY for a single investment for a single year, we want to consider *mean rates of return* for a single investment and for a portfolio of investments. Over a number of years, a single investment will likely give high rates of return during some years and low rates of return, or possibly negative rates of return, during others. Your analysis should consider each of these returns, but you also want a sum-

---

[2] To check that you understand the calculations, determine the annual HPY for a 3-year HPR of 1.50. (Answer: 14.47 percent.) Compute the annual HPY for a 3-month HPR of 1.06. (Answer: 26.25 percent.)

mary figure that indicates this investment's typical experience, or the rate of return you should expect to receive if you owned this investment over time. You can derive such a summary figure by computing the mean rate of return for this investment over some period of time.

Alternatively, you might want to evaluate a portfolio of investments that might include similar investments (e.g., all stocks, or all bonds) or a combination of investments (e.g., stocks, bonds, and real estate). In this instance, you would calculate the mean rate of return for this portfolio of investments for an individual year or for a number of years.

SINGLE INVESTMENT

Given a set of annual rates of return (HPYs) for an individual investment, there are two summary measures of return performance. The first is the arithmetic mean, the second the geometric mean. To find the *arithmetic mean (AM),* the sum (Σ) of annual yields is divided by the number of years (n) as follows:

$$AM = \Sigma HPY/n$$

where:

ΣHPY = the sum of annual holding period yields

An alternative computation, the *geometric mean (GM),* is the nth root of the product of the HPRs for n years.

$$GM = \pi^{1/n} - 1$$

where:

π = the product of the annual holding period returns as follows:

$$(HPR_1) \times (HPR_2) \ldots (HPR_n)$$

To illustrate these alternatives, consider an investment with the following data:

Year	Beginning Value	Ending Value	HPR	HPY
1	100.0	115.0	1.15	0.15
2	115.0	138.0	1.20	0.20
3	138.0	110.4	0.80	−0.20

$$
\begin{aligned}
AM &= [(.15) + (.20) + (-.20)]/3 \\
&= 0.15/3 \\
&= 0.05 = 5 \text{ percent}
\end{aligned}
$$

$$
\begin{aligned}
GM &= [(1.15) \times (1.20) \times (0.80)]^{1/3} - 1 \\
&= (1.104)^{1/3} - 1 \\
&= 1.03353 - 1 \\
&= 0.03353 = 3.353 \text{ percent}
\end{aligned}
$$

Investors are typically concerned with long-term performance when comparing alternative investments. GM is considered to be a superior measure of the long-term mean rate of return because it indicates the compound annual rate of return based on the ending value of the investment versus its beginning value.[3] Specifically, using the prior example, if we compounded 3.353 percent for 3 years, $(1.03353)^3$, we would get an ending wealth value of 1.104.

Although the arithmetic average provides a good indication of the expected rate of return for an investment during a future individual year, it is biased upward if you are attempting to measure an asset's long-term performance. This is very obvious for a volatile security. Consider, for example, a security that increases in price from $50 to $100 during year 1 and drops back to $50 during year 2. The annual HPYs would be:

Year	Beginning Value	Ending Value	HPR	HPY
1	50	100	2.00	1.00
2	100	50	0.50	−0.50

This would give an arithmetic mean rate of return of:

$$[(1.00) + (-0.50)]/2 = 50/2$$
$$= 0.25 = 25 \text{ percent}$$

This investment brought no change in wealth and therefore no return, yet the arithmetic mean rate of return is computed to be 25 percent.

The geometric mean rate of return would be:

$$(2.00 \times 0.50)^{1/2} - 1 = (1.00)^{1/2} - 1$$
$$= 1.00 - 1 = 0 \text{ percent}$$

This answer of a 0 percent rate of return accurately measures the fact that there was no change in wealth from this investment.

When rates of return are the same for all years, the geometric mean will be equal to the arithmetic mean. If the rates of return vary over the years, the geometric mean will be lower than the arithmetic mean. The difference between the two mean values will depend on the year-to-year changes in the rates of return. Larger annual changes in the rates of return, that is, more volatility, will result in a greater difference between the alternative mean values.

An awareness of both methods of computing mean rates of return is important because published accounts of investment performance or descriptions of financial research will use both the AM and the GM as measures of average historical returns. Also both will be used throughout this book. Currently most studies dealing with long-run historical rates of return include both arithmetic and geometric mean rates of return.

---

[3] Note that the GM is the same whether you compute the geometric mean of the individual annual holding period yields or the annual HPY for a 3-year period, comparing the ending value to the beginning value, as discussed earlier under annual HPY for a multiperiod case.

A PORTFOLIO OF INVESTMENTS

The mean historical rate of return (HPY) for a portfolio of investments is measured as the weighted average of the HPYs for the individual investments in the portfolio, or the overall change in value of the original portfolio. The weights used in computing the averages are the relative *beginning* market values for each investment; this is referred to as dollar-weighted or value-weighted mean rate of return. This technique is demonstrated by the examples in Table 1.1.

The purpose of this section has been to help you understand how you can properly measure the historical rates of return on alternative investments in order to compare them.

Although the analysis of historical performance is very useful, selecting investments for your portfolio requires you to predict the rates of return you *expect* to prevail. The next section discusses how you would derive such estimates of expected rates of return. We will also recognize that there is great uncertainty regarding these future expectations, and we will discuss how one measures this uncertainty that is referred to as the risk of an investment.

CALCULATING EXPECTED RATES OF RETURN

Risk is the uncertainty that an investment will earn its expected rate of return. In the examples in the prior section, we examined *realized* historical rates of return. In contrast, an investor who is evaluating a future investment alternative expects or anticipates a certain rate of return. The investor might say that he or she *expects* the investment will provide a rate of return of 10 percent, but this is really the investor's most likely estimate, also referred to as a *point estimate.* Pressed further, the investor would probably acknowledge the uncertainty of this point estimate return and admit the possibility that, under certain conditions, the annual rate of return on this investment might go as low as -10 percent or as high as 25 percent. The point is, the specification of a larger range of possible returns from an investment reflects the investor's uncertainty regarding the actual return. Therefore, a larger range of returns makes the investment riskier.

An investor determines how certain the expected rate of return on an investment is by analyzing estimates of expected returns. To do this, the investor assigns probability values to all *possible* returns. These probability values range from zero, which means

TABLE 1.1 **Computation of Holding Period Yield for a Portfolio**

Investment	Number of Shares	Beginning Price	Beginning Market Value	Ending Price	Ending Market Value	HPR	HPY	Market Weight	Weighted HPY
A	100,000	$10	$ 1,000,000	$12	$ 1,200,000	1.20	20%	0.05	0.01
B	200,000	20	4,000,000	21	4,200,000	1.05	5%	0.20	0.01
C	500,000	30	15,000,000	33	16,500,000	1.10	10%	0.75	0.075
Total			$20,000,000		$21,900,000				.095

$$HPR = \frac{21,900,000}{20,000,000} = 1.095$$
$$HPY = 1.095 - 1 = .095 = 9.5 \text{ percent}$$

FIGURE 1.1   **Probability Distribution for Risk-Free Investment**

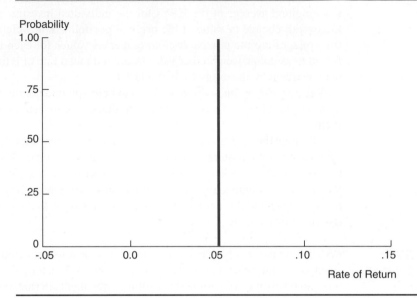

no chance of the return, to 1, which indicates complete certainty that the investment will provide the rate of return. These probabilities are typically subjective estimates based on the historical performance of the investment or similar investments modified by the investor's expectations for the future. As an example, an investor may know that about 30 percent of the time the rate of return on this particular investment was 10 percent. Using this information along with future expectations regarding the economy, one can derive an estimate of what might happen in the future.

The *expected* return from an investment is defined as:

$$\text{Expected Return} = \sum_{i=1}^{n} (\text{Probability of Return})\,(\text{Possible Return})$$

$$E(R_i) = [(P_1)(R_1) + (P_2)(R_2) + (P_3)(R_3) + \ldots + (P_n R_n)]$$

$$E(R_i) = \sum_{i=1}^{n} (P_i)(R_i)$$

Let us begin our analysis of the effect of risk with an example of perfect certainty wherein the investor is absolutely certain of a return of 5 percent. Figure 1.1 illustrates this situation.

Perfect certainty allows only one possible return and the probability of receiving that return is 1.0. Few investments provide certain returns. In the case of perfect certainty, there is only one value for $P_i R_i$:

$$E(R_i) = (1.0)(0.05) = 0.05$$

In an alternative scenario, suppose an investor believed an investment could provide several different rates of return depending on different possible economic conditions.

FIGURE 1.2 **Probability Distribution for Risky Investment with Three Possible Rates of Return**

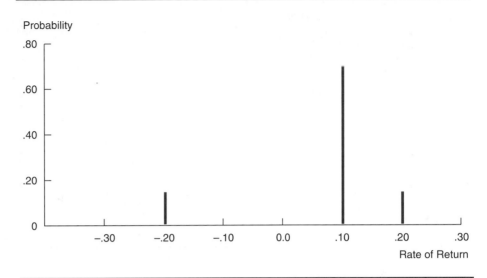

As an example, in a strong economic environment with high corporate profits and little or no inflation, the investor might expect the rate of return on common stocks during the next year to reach as high as 20 percent. In contrast, if there is an economic decline with a higher than average rate of inflation, the investor might expect the rate of return on common stocks during the next year to be a negative 20 percent. Finally, with no major change in the economic environment, the rate of return during next year would probably approach the long-run average of 10 percent.

The investor might estimate probabilities for each of these economic scenarios based on past experience and the current outlook as follows:

Economic Conditions	Probability	Rate of Return
Strong economy, no inflation	0.15	0.20
Weak economy, above average inflation	0.15	−0.20
No major change in economy	0.70	0.10

This set of potential outcomes can be visualized as shown in Figure 1.2
The computation of the expected rate of return [E(R$_i$)] is as follows:

$$E(R_i) = [(0.15)(0.20)] + [(0.15)(-0.20)] + [(0.70)(0.10)]$$
$$= 0.07$$

Obviously, the investor is more uncertain about the expected return from this investment than about the return from the prior investment with its single possible return.

A third example is an investment with ten possible outcomes ranging from −40 percent to 50 percent with the same probability for each rate of return. A graph of this set of expectations would appear as shown in Figure 1.3.

FIGURE 1.3

Probability Distribution for Risky Investment with Ten Possible Rates of Return

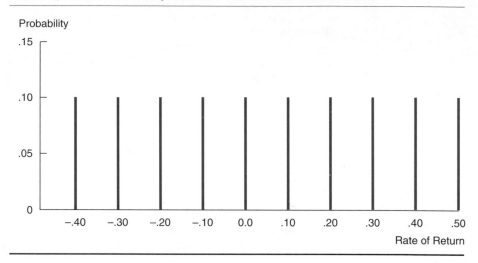

In this case, there are numerous outcomes from a wide range of possibilities. The expected rate of return [$E(R_i)$] for this investment would be:

$$
\begin{aligned}
E(R_i) = {}& (0.10)(-0.40) + (0.10)(-0.30) \\
& + (0.10)(-0.20) + (0.10)(-0.10) \\
& + (0.10)(0.0) + (0.10)(0.10) + (0.10)(0.20) \\
& + (0.10)(0.30) + (0.10)(0.40) + (0.10)(0.50) \\
= {}& (-0.04) + (-0.03) + (-0.02) + (-0.01) \\
& + (0.00) + (0.01) + (0.02) + (0.03) + (0.04) \\
= {}& 0.05
\end{aligned}
$$

The expected rate of return for this investment is the same as the certain return discussed in the first example, but in this case, the investor is highly uncertain about the *actual* rate of return. This would be considered a risky investment because of that uncertainty. We would anticipate that an investor faced with the choice between this risky investment and the certain case would select the certain alternative. This expectation is based on the belief that most investors are *risk averse*, which means that if everything else is the same, they will select the investment with less uncertainty.

MEASURING THE RISK OF EXPECTED RATES OF RETURN

We have shown that we can calculate the expected rate of return and evaluate the uncertainty, or risk, of an investment by identifying the range of possible returns from that investment and assigning each possible return a weight based on the probability that it will occur. Although the graphs help us visualize the dispersion of possible returns, most investors want to quantify this dispersion using statistical techniques. These statistical measures allow you to compare the return and risk measures for alternative investments directly. Two possible measures of risk (uncertainty) have received support in theoretical work on portfolio theory: the *variance* and the *standard deviation* of the estimated distribution of expected returns.

In this section, we demonstrate how variance and standard deviation measure the dispersion of possible rates of return around the expected rate of return. We will work with the examples discussed earlier. The formula for variance is as follows:

$$\text{Variance } (\sigma^2) = \sum_{i=1}^{n} (\text{Probability}) \left(\begin{array}{c} \text{Possible} \\ \text{Return} \end{array} - \begin{array}{c} \text{Expected} \\ \text{Return} \end{array} \right)^2$$
$$= \sum_{i=1}^{n} (P_i)[R_i - E(R_i)]^2$$

VARIANCE

The larger the variance for an expected rate of return, the greater the dispersion of expected returns and the greater the uncertainty, or risk, of the investment. The variance for the perfect-certainty example would be:

$$(\sigma^2) = \sum_{i=1}^{n} P_i[R_i - E(R_i)]^2$$
$$= 1.0(0.05 - 0.05)^2 = 1.0(0.0) = 0$$

Note that in perfect certainty, there is *no variance of return* because there is no deviation from expectations, and therefore *no risk,* or *uncertainty.* The variance for the second example would be:

$$\sigma^2 = \sum_{i=1}^{n} P_i[R_i - E(R_i)]^2$$
$$= [(0.15)(0.20 - 0.07)^2 + (0.15)(-0.20 - 0.07)^2$$
$$+ (0.70)(0.10 - 0.07)^2]$$
$$= [0.010935 + 0.002535 + 0.00063]$$
$$= .0141$$

STANDARD DEVIATION

The standard deviation is the square root of the variance:

$$\text{Standard Deviation} = \sqrt{\sum_{i=1}^{n} P_i[R_i - E(R_i)]^2}$$

For the second example, the standard deviation would be:

$$\sigma = \sqrt{0.0141}$$
$$= 0.11874$$

A RELATIVE MEASURE OF RISK

In some cases, an unadjusted variance or standard deviation can be misleading. If conditions are not similar, that is, if there are major differences in the expected rates of return, it is necessary to use a measure of *relative variability* to indicate risk per unit of return. A relative measure of risk that is widely used is the coefficient of variation, which is equal to:

$$\text{Coefficient of Variation (CV)} = \frac{\text{Standard Deviation of Returns}}{\text{Expected Rate of Return}}$$

$$= \frac{\sigma_i}{E(R)}$$

The CV for the example above would be:

$$CV = \frac{0.11874}{0.07000}$$
$$= 1.696$$

This measure of relative variability and risk is used by financial analysts to compare alternative investments with very different rates of return and standard deviations of returns. As an illustration consider the following two investments:

	Investment A	Investment B
Expected Return	.07	.12
Standard Deviation	.05	.07

Comparing absolute measures of risk, investment B appears to be riskier because it has a standard deviation of 7 percent versus 5 percent for investment A. In contrast, the CV figures show that investment B has less risk per unit of return as follows:

$$CV_A = \frac{0.05}{0.07} = 0.714$$

$$CV_B = \frac{0.07}{0.12} = 0.583$$

RISK MEASURES FOR HISTORICAL RETURNS

To measure the risk for a series of historical rates of returns, we use the same measures as for expected returns (variance and standard deviation) except that we consider the historical holding period yields (HPY) as follows:

$$\sigma^2 = \sum_{i=1}^{n} [HPY_i = E(HPY)]^2/n$$

where:

σ^2 = the variance of the series

HPY_i = the holding period yield during period i

$E(HPY)$ = the expected value of the holding period yield that is equal to the arithmetic mean of the series

n = the number of observations

The standard deviation is the square root of the variance. Both measures indicate how much the individual observations over time deviated from the expected value of the series. An example computation is contained in the appendix to this chapter. As we will see in subsequent chapters where we present historical rates of return for alternative asset classes, presenting the standard deviation as a measure of risk for the series is fairly common.

DETERMINANTS OF REQUIRED RATES OF RETURN

In this section we continue our consideration of factors that you must consider when selecting securities for an investment portfolio. You will recall that this selection process involves finding securities that provide a rate of return that compensates you for the time value of money during the period of investment, the expected rate of inflation during the period, and the risk involved.

The summation of these three components is called the *required rate of return*. This is the minimum rate of return that you should accept from an investment to compensate you for deferring consumption. Because of the importance of the required rate of return to the total investment selection process, this section contains a detailed discussion of the three components and what influences each of them.

The analysis and estimation of the required rate of return is complicated by the behavior of market rates over time. First, a wide range of rates are available for alternative investments at any time. Second, the rates of return on specific assets change dramatically over time. Third, the difference between the rates available on different assets change over time.

The yield data in Table 1.2 for alternative bonds demonstrates these three characteristics. First, even though all of these securities have promised returns based upon bond contracts, the promised annual yields during any year differ substantially. As an example, during 1991 the average yields on alternative assets ranged from 5.38 percent on T-bills to 9.80 percent for Baa corporate bonds. Second, the changes in yields for a specific asset are shown by the 3-month Treasury bill rate that went from 8.11 percent in 1989 down to 3.43 percent in 1992. Third, an example of a change in the difference between yields over time (referred to as a spread) is shown by the Baa–Aaa spread. The yield spread in 1986 was 137 basis points (10.39 − 9.02), but was only 84 basis points in 1992 (8.98 − 8.14) (a basis point is 1/100 of a percent).

Because differences in yields result from the riskiness of each investment, you must understand the risk factors that affect the required rates of return and include them in your assessment of investment opportunities. Because the required returns on all in-

TABLE 1.2	Promised Yields on Alternative Bonds							
Type of Bond	1985	1986	1987	1988	1989	1990	1991	1992
U.S. government 3-month Treasury bills	7.48%	5.97%	5.78%	6.67%	8.11%	7.50%	5.38%	3.43%
U.S. government long-term bonds	10.75	8.14	8.64	8.98	8.58	8.74	8.16	7.52
Aaa corporate bonds	11.37	9.02	9.38	9.71	9.26	9.32	8.77	8.14
Baa corporate bonds	12.72	10.39	10.58	10.83	10.18	10.36	9.80	8.98

Source: *Federal Reserve Bulletin,* various issues.

vestments change over time, and because large differences separate individual invest-ments, you need to be aware of the several components that determine the required rate of return, starting with the risk-free rate.

THE REAL RISK-
FREE RATE

The *real risk-free rate (RFR)* is the basic interest rate, assuming no inflation and no uncertainty about future flows. An investor in an inflation-free economy who knew with certainty what cash flows he or she would receive at what time would demand the real risk-free rate on an investment. Earlier we called this the *pure time value of money,* because the only sacrifice the investor made was deferring the use of the money for a period of time. This real risk-free rate of interest is the price charged for the exchange between current goods and future goods.

Two factors, one subjective and one objective, influence this exchange price. The subjective factor is the time preference of individuals for the consumption of income. When individuals give up $100 of consumption this year, how much consumption do they want a year from now to compensate for that sacrifice? The strength of the human desire for current consumption influences the rate of compensation required. Time preferences vary among individuals, and the market creates a composite rate that in-cludes the preferences of all investors. Although this composite rate changes over time, it does so gradually because it is influenced by all the investors in the economy, whose changes in preferences may offset one another.

The objective factor that influences the real risk-free rate is the set of investment opportunities available in the economy. The investment opportunities are determined in turn by the long-run real growth rate of the economy. When an economy is growing rapidly, there are more and better opportunities to invest funds and experience positive rates of return. A change in the economy's long-run real growth rate causes a change in all investment opportunities and a change in the required rates of return on all investments. Just as investors supplying capital should demand a higher rate of return when growth is higher, those looking for funds to invest should be willing and able to pay a higher rate because of the higher growth rate. Thus, a *positive* relationship exists between the real growth rate in the economy and the RFR.

Three factors influence the real growth rate of the economy: (1) the long-run growth rate of the labor force, (2) the long-run growth rate of the average number of hours worked by the labor force, and (3) the long-run growth in productivity of the labor force (measured by output per hour).[4] Although the long-run real growth rate and therefore the RFR can change over time, these changes will be gradual because the three factors that determine this growth rate (i.e., growth of the labor force, average hours worked, and productivity) change very gradually, sometimes offsetting each other.

FACTORS
INFLUENCING THE
NOMINAL RISK-
FREE RATE

Earlier, we observed that an investor would be willing to forgo current consumption in order to increase future consumption at a rate of exchange called the *risk-free rate of interest.* This rate of exchange was measured in real terms because the investor wanted to increase the actual consumption of actual goods and services rather than

---

[4] For an interesting discussion of the components of real growth and changes in the components over time, see *Economic Report of the President* (Washington, D.C.: U.S. Government Printing Office, 1987). Labor productivity be-came a very popular topic in early 1993 after it was reported that productivity in the United States during all of 1992 (and especially the fourth quarter) was the highest in almost 15 years. For a discussion of the causes and impact, see "Capital Market Report," Kidder Peabody Economics (April 2, 1993).

consuming the same amount that had come to cost more money. Therefore, when we discuss rates of interest, we mean real rates of interest that adjust for changes in the general price level, as opposed to *nominal* rates of interest that are stated in money terms. That is, nominal rates of interest are determined by real rates of interest, plus other factors such as the expected rate of inflation and the monetary environment. It is important to understand these factors.

As noted earlier, the variables that determine the risk-free rate change only gradually over the long term. Therefore, you might expect the required rate on a risk-free investment to be quite stable over time. As discussed in connection with Table 1.2, rates on 3-month T-bills were not stable over the period from 1985 to 1992. This is demonstrated with additional observations in Table 1.3, which contains yields on T-bills for the period 1969 to 1992.

Investors view T-bills as a prime example of a default-free investment because the government has unlimited ability to derive income from taxes or the creation of money from which to pay interest. Therefore, rates on T-bills should change only gradually. In fact, the data show a very erratic pattern. Specifically, there was a sharp decline in 1971, a mammoth increase in 1973, a decline to below 5 percent in 1976, an increase to over 14 percent in 1981 before declining to less than 6 percent in 1986 and 3.43 percent in 1992. In sum, T-bill rates almost tripled in 5 years and then declined by almost 60 percent in 5 years. Clearly, the nominal rate of interest on a default-free investment is not stable in the long run or the short run, even though the underlying determinants of the real RFR are quite stable. The point is, two other factors influence the *nominal* risk-free rate: (1) the relative ease or tightness in the capital markets, and (2) the expected rate of inflation.

CONDITIONS IN THE CAPITAL MARKET
You will recall from prior courses in economics and finance that the purpose of capital markets is to bring together investors who want to invest savings with companies or governments who need capital to expand or to finance budget deficits. The cost of funds at any time (the interest rate) is the price that equates the current supply and demand for capital. A change in the relative ease or tightness in the capital market is a short-run phenomenon caused by a temporary disequilibrium in the supply and demand of capital.

As an example, disequilibrium could be caused by an unexpected change in monetary policy (e.g., a change in the growth rate of the money supply) or fiscal policy (e.g., a change in the federal deficit). Such a change in monetary policy or fiscal policy will produce a change in the risk-free rate of interest, but the change should be short-lived because in the longer run, the higher or lower interest rates will affect capital

TABLE 1.3	**Average Yields on U.S. Government 3-Month Treasury Bills**							
	1969	6.67%	1975	5.80%	1981	14.03%	1987	5.78%
	1970	6.39	1976	4.98	1982	10.61	1988	6.67
	1971	4.33	1977	5.27	1983	8.61	1989	8.11
	1972	4.07	1978	7.19	1984	9.52	1990	7.50
	1973	7.03	1979	10.07	1985	7.48	1991	5.38
	1974	7.84	1980	11.43	1986	5.98	1992	3.43

Source: *Federal Reserve Bulletin,* various issues.

supply and demand. As an example, a decrease in the growth rate of the money supply (a tightening in monetary policy) will reduce the supply of capital and increase interest rates. In turn, this increase in rates will cause an increase in savings and a decrease in the demand for capital by corporations or individuals. These changes will bring rates back to the long-run equilibrium, which is based on the long-run growth rate of the economy.

EXPECTED INFLATION

Up to this point, we have assumed that the rate of return is unaffected by changes in the price level; that is, we have assumed real rates of interest. In discussing the rate of exchange between current and future consumption, we assumed that a 4 percent required rate of return meant that an investor was willing to give up $1 of consumption today to consume $1.04 worth of goods and services 1 year from now. Because this assumed no change in prices, a 4 percent increase in money wealth would mean a 4 percent increase in potential consumption of goods and services.

If, however, investors expected the price level to increase during the investment period, they would require the rate of return to include compensation for the inflation rate. Assume that you require a 4 percent real rate of return on a risk-free investment, but you expect prices to increase by 3 percent during the investment period. In this case, you should increase your required rate of return by this expected rate of inflation to about 7 percent $[(1.04 \times 1.03) - 1]$. If you do not increase your required return, the $104 you receive at the end of the year will represent a real return of only 1 percent, not 4 percent. Because prices have increased by 3 percent during the year, what previously cost $100 now costs $103 so you can consume only about 1 percent more at the end of the year $[(\$104/103) - 1]$. If you had required a 7.12 percent nominal return, your real consumption could have increased by 4 percent $[(\$107.12/103) - 1]$. Therefore, an investor's nominal required rate of return in current dollars on a risk-free investment should be:

$$\text{Nominal RFR} = (1 + \text{Real RFR})(1 + \text{Expected Rate of Inflation}) - 1$$

Rearranging the formula, you can calculate the real risk-free rate of return on an investment as follows:

$$\text{Real RFR} = \left[\frac{(1 + \text{Nominal Risk-Free Rate of Return})}{(1 + \text{Rate of Inflation})} \right] - 1$$

To see how this works, assume that the nominal return on U.S. government T-bills was 9 percent during a given year, when the rate of inflation was 5 percent. In this instance, the real risk-free rate of return on these T-bills was 3.8 percent, as follows:

$$\begin{aligned} \text{Real RFR} &= [(1 + 0.09)/(1 + 0.05)] - 1 \\ &= 1.038 - 1 \\ &= 0.038 = 3.8\% \end{aligned}$$

This discussion makes it clear that the nominal rate of interest on a risk-free investment is not a good estimate of the real RFR, because the nominal rate can change

TABLE 1.4	**Annual Rates of Inflation**						
	(Based on changes in the Consumer Price Index; 1982–1984 = 100.)						
	1969	5.4%	1975	6.2%	1981	10.4%	1987	4.4%
	1970	5.9	1976	5.8	1982	6.1	1988	4.4
	1971	4.3	1977	6.5	1983	3.2	1989	4.6
	1972	3.3	1978	7.7	1984	4.0	1990	6.1
	1973	6.2	1979	11.3	1985	3.8	1991	3.1
	1974	11.0	1980	7.7	1986	1.1	1992	2.9

Sources: *Federal Reserve Bulletin,* various issues; *Economic Report of the President,* various issues.

dramatically in the short run in reaction to temporary ease or tightness in the capital market or because of changes in the expected rate of inflation. The significant changes in the average yield on T-bills shown in Table 1.3 were caused by the large changes in the expected rate of inflation during this period. Table 1.4 shows the volatility of annual rates of inflation.

THE COMMON EFFECT

All the factors discussed thus far regarding the required rate of return affect all investments equally. Whether the investment is in stocks, bonds, real estate, or machine tools, if the expected rate of inflation increases from 2 percent to 6 percent, the investor's required return for *all* investments should increase by 4 percent. Similarly, if there is a decline in the expected real growth rate of the economy that causes a decline in the real RFR of 1 percent, then the required return on all investments should decline by 1 percent.

RISK PREMIUM

A risk-free investment was defined as one for which the investor is certain of the amount and timing of the expected returns. The returns from most investments do not fit this pattern. An investor typically is not completely certain of the income to be received or when it will be received. Investments can range in uncertainty from basically risk-free securities such as T-bills to highly speculative investments such as the common stock of small companies engaged in such high-risk enterprises as oil exploration.

Most investors require higher rates of return on investments to compensate for any uncertainty. This increase in the required rate of return over the nominal risk-free rate is the *risk premium*. Although the required risk premium represents a composite of all uncertainty, it is possible to consider several fundamental sources of uncertainty. In this section we identify and discuss briefly the major sources, including business risk, financial risk (leverage), liquidity risk, exchange rate risk, and country risk, and describe their effects on the required rate of return.

Business risk is the uncertainty of income flows caused by the nature of a firm's business. The more uncertain the income flows of the firm, the more uncertain the income flows to the investor. Therefore, the investor will demand a risk premium that is based on the uncertainty caused by the basic business of the firm. As an example, a firm in an industry such as retail food that has typically experienced very stable sales and earnings growth over time would be considered to have low business risk, and investors would require a lower business risk premium than they would require for a firm in the auto industry, where sales and earnings fluctuate substantially over the business cycle, implying high business risk.

Financial risk is the uncertainty introduced by the method by which the firm finances its investments. If a firm uses only common stock to finance investments, it incurs only business risk. If, in addition to using common stock, a firm borrows money to finance investments, it must pay fixed financing charges (in the form of interest to creditors) prior to providing income to the owners (the holders of common stock). As a result, the uncertainty of returns to the equity investor increases because of the firm's method of financing. This increase in uncertainty because of fixed-cost financing is called *financial risk* or *financial leverage,* and causes the investor to require a financial risk premium.[5]

Liquidity risk is the uncertainty introduced by the secondary market for an investment.[6] When an investor acquires an asset, he or she expects that the investment will mature (as with a bond) or that it will be salable to someone else. In either case, the investor expects to be able to convert the security into cash and use the proceeds for current consumption or other investments. The more difficult it is to make this conversion, the greater the liquidity risk. An investor must consider two questions about liquidity when assessing the liquidity risk of an investment: (1) How long will it take to convert the investment into cash? (2) How certain is the price? Similar uncertainty faces an investor who wants to acquire an asset: How long will it take to acquire the asset? What will the price be?

The ability to buy or sell an investment quickly without a substantial price concession is known as *liquidity.* Greater uncertainty regarding how fast an investment can be bought or sold, or the existence of a large price concession if you want to buy or sell it, increases liquidity risk.

A U.S. government Treasury bill has almost no liquidity risk because it can be bought or sold in minutes at a price almost identical to the quoted price. In contrast, examples of illiquid investment include a work of art, an antique, or a parcel of real estate in a remote area. Such an investment may require a long time to find a buyer, and the selling price could vary substantially from expectations. Investors who are uncertain of their ability to buy or sell investments will increase their required rates of return to compensate for this risk.

Exchange rate risk is the uncertainty of returns to an investor who acquires securities denominated in a currency different from his or her own. The likelihood of incurring this risk is becoming greater as investors buy and sell assets around the world, as opposed to only assets within their own countries. A U.S. investor who buys Japanese stock denominated in yen must consider not only the uncertainty of the return in yen, but also any change in the exchange value of the yen relative to the U.S. dollar. That is, in addition to the foreign firm's business and financial risk as well as the security's liquidity risk, the investor must consider the additional uncertainty of the return when converted from yen to U.S. dollars.

---

[5] For a discussion of financial leverage, see Eugene F. Brigham, *Fundamentals of Financial Management,* 6th ed. (Hinsdale, Ill.: The Dryden Press, 1992), 221–225.

[6] You will recall from prior courses that the overall capital market is composed of the primary market and the secondary market. Securities are initially sold in the primary market and then all subsequent transactions take place in the secondary market. These concepts are discussed in Chapter 3.

As an example of exchange rate risk, assume that you buy 100 shares of Mitsubishi Electric at 1,050 yen when the exchange rate is 135 yen to the dollar. The dollar cost of this investment would be about $7.78 per share (1,050/135). A year later you sell the 100 shares at 1,200 yen when the exchange rate is 150 yen to the dollar. When you calculate the HPY in yen, you find the stock has increased in value by about 14 percent (1,200/1,050), but this is the HPY for a Japanese investor. A U.S. investor receives a much lower rate of return because during this time period the yen has weakened relative to the dollar by about 11 percent (i.e., it requires more yen to buy a dollar—150 versus 135). At the new exchange rate, the stock is worth $8 per share (1,200/150). Therefore, the return to you as a U.S. investor would be only about 3 percent ($8.00/$7.78) versus 14 percent for the Japanese investor. The difference in return for the Japanese investor and U.S. investor is because of the decline in the value of the yen relative to the dollar. Clearly, the exchange rate could have gone in the other direction, the dollar weakening against the yen. In this case, as a U.S. investor you would have experienced the 14 percent return measured in yen, as well as a gain from the exchange rate change.

The more volatile the exchange rate between two countries, the more uncertain you would be regarding the exchange rate, the greater the exchange rate risk, and the larger would be the exchange rate risk premium you would require.[7]

Country risk, also called *political risk,* is the uncertainty of returns caused by the possibility of a major change in the political or economic environment of a country. The United States is acknowledged to have the smallest country risk in the world because its political and economic systems are the most stable. Nations with high country risk include South Africa, with its racial tensions, and China, as a result of the 1989 unrest. On a single day, June 5, 1989, the Hong Kong stock market declined over 20 percent following the student–military confrontations in China.[8] Individuals who invest in countries that have unstable political–economic systems must add a country risk premium when determining their required rates of return.

When investing globally (which will be emphasized throughout the book), investors must consider these additional uncertainties. What will happen to exchange rates during the investment period? What is the probability of a political or economic change that will adversely affect your rate of return? Exchange rate risk and country risk differ among countries. Exchange rate risk will depend on the uncertainty of a given country's exchange rate with the United States (for a U.S. investor). A good measure of exchange rate risk would be the absolute variability of the exchange rate with a composite exchange rate. The analysis of country risk is much more subjective and must be based on the history of the country.

The risk premium on an investment includes the uncertainty of expected returns to the investor from all sources. This value is determined by (1) the variability of operating earnings (business risk), (2) any added uncertainty of returns caused by how the investment is financed (financial risk), and (3) the uncertainty of buying or selling the

[7] A recent article that examines the pricing of exchange rate risk in the U.S. market is Philippe Jorion, "The Pricing of Exchange Rate Risk in the Stock Market," *Journal of Financial Quantitative Analysis* 26, no. 3 (September 1991): 363–376.

[8] Russell Todd and Robert Sherbin, "Hong Kong Stocks Plunge 22% on China Unrest; Other Asia Markets Fall; London Shares Drop," *Wall Street Journal,* June 6, 1989, C10. This country risk for Hong Kong stocks related to events in China is because Hong Kong is scheduled to revert back to China in 1997. During 1993 the uncertainty continued because of political conflicts between the British Governor of Hong Kong and Chinese officials.

investment (liquidity risk). In addition, when investing outside one's own country, one must consider (4) the uncertainty from changing exchange rates (exchange rate risk), and (5) the uncertainty caused by the possibility of a change in the political or economic environment in a foreign country (country risk).

This discussion of risk components can be considered a security's *fundamental risk* because it deals with the intrinsic factors that should affect a security's standard deviation of returns over time. In subsequent discussion, the standard deviation of returns is referred to as the measure of *total risk*.

$$\text{Risk Premium} = f(\text{Business Risk, Financial Risk,}$$
$$\text{Liquidity Risk, Exchange Rate Risk, Country Risk})$$

RISK PREMIUM AND PORTFOLIO THEORY

An alternative view of risk has been derived from extensive work in portfolio theory and capital market theory by Markowitz, Sharpe, and others.[9] These theories are dealt with in greater detail in Chapters 7 and 8, but their impact on the risk premium should be mentioned briefly at this point. This prior work by Markowitz and Sharpe indicated that investors should use an *external market* measure of risk. Under a specified set of assumptions, all rational, profit-maximizing investors want to hold a completely diversified market portfolio of risky assets, and they borrow or lend to arrive at a risk level that is consistent with their risk preferences. Under these conditions, the relevant risk measure for an individual asset is its *comovement with the market portfolio.* This comovement, which is measured by an asset's covariance with the market portfolio, is referred to as an asset's *systematic risk,* the portion of an individual asset's total variance attributable to the variability of the total market portfolio. In addition, individual assets have variance that is not related to the market portfolio but is due to unique features. This nonmarket variance is called *unsystematic* variance or risk. This unsystematic risk is generally considered to be unimportant because it is eliminated in a large, diversified portfolio. Therefore, under these assumptions, *the risk premium for an individual earning asset is a function of the asset's systematic risk with the aggregate market portfolio of risky assets.* The measure of an asset's systematic risk is referred to as its *beta:*

$$\text{Risk Premium} = f(\text{Systematic Market Risk})$$

FUNDAMENTAL RISK VERSUS SYSTEMATIC RISK

Some might expect a conflict between the market measure of risk (systematic risk) and the fundamental determinants of risk (business risk, etc.). A number of studies have examined the relationship between the market measure of risk (systematic risk) and accounting variables used to measure the fundamental risk factors such as business risk, financial risk, and liquidity risk. The authors have generally concluded that *there is a significant relationship between the market measure of risk and the fundamental measures of risk.*[10] Therefore, the two definitions of risk can be complementary. This

---

[9] These works include Harry Markowitz, "Portfolio Selection," *Journal of Finance* 7, no. 1 (March 1952): 77–91; Harry Markowitz, *Portfolio Selection—Efficient Diversification of Investments* (New Haven, Conn.: Yale University Press, 1959); and William F. Sharpe, "Capital Asset Prices: A Theory of Market Equilibrium Under Conditions of Risk," *Journal of Finance* 19, no. 3 (September 1964): 425–442.

[10] A brief review of some of the earlier studies is contained in Donald J. Thompson II, "Sources of Systematic Risk in Common Stocks," *Journal of Business* 49, no. 2 (April 1976), 173–188. There is a further discussion of specific variables in Chapter 10.

consistency seems reasonable because, in a properly functioning capital market, the market measure of the risk should reflect the fundamental risk characteristics of the asset. As an example, you would expect a firm that has high business risk and financial risk to have an above-average beta. At the same time, as we will discuss in Chapter 17, a firm that has a high level of fundamental risk and a large standard deviation can have a lower level of systematic risk because its variability of earnings and stock price is not related to the aggregate economy or the aggregate market. Therefore, one can specify the risk premium for an asset as:

$$\text{Risk Premium} = f(\text{Business Risk, Financial Risk,}$$
$$\text{Liquidity Risk, Exchange Rate Risk, Country Risk})$$
$$\text{or}$$
$$\text{Risk Premium} = f(\text{Systematic Market Risk})$$

SUMMARY OF REQUIRED RATE OF RETURN

The overall required rate of return on alternative investments is determined by three variables: (1) the economy's real RFR, which is influenced by the investment opportunities in the economy (i.e., the long-run real growth rate); (2) variables that influence the nominal RFR, which include short-run ease or tightness in the capital market and expected inflation (the first two sets of variables are the same for all investments); and (3) the risk premium on the investment. In turn, this risk premium can be related to fundamental factors including business risk, financial risk, liquidity risk, exchange rate risk, and country risk, or it can be a function of systematic market risk (beta).

MEASURES AND SOURCES OF RISK

In this chapter we have examined both measures and sources of risk arising from an investment. The *measures* of risk for an investment are:

- Variance of rates of return
- Standard deviation of rates of return
- Coefficient of variation of rates of return (standard deviation/means)
- Covariance of returns with the market portfolio (beta)

The *sources* of risk are:

- Business risk
- Financial risk
- Liquidity risk
- Exchange rate risk
- Country risk

RELATIONSHIP BETWEEN RISK AND RETURN

Previously, we showed how to measure the risk and rates of return for alternative investments, and we discussed what determines the rates of return that investors require. This section discusses the risk–return combinations that might be available at a point in time and illustrates the factors that cause *changes* in these combinations.

Figure 1.4 graphs the expected relationship between risk and return. It shows that investors increase their required rates of return as perceived risk (uncertainty) increases. The line that reflects the combination of risk and return available on alternative in-

FIGURE 1.4   **Relationship Between Risk and Return**

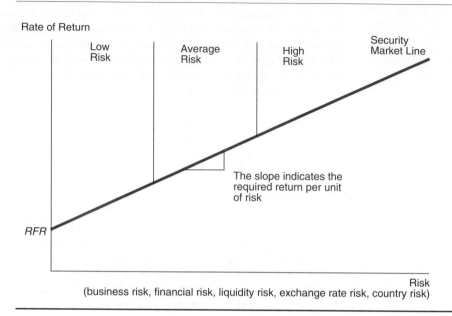

Rate of Return

Low Risk

Average Risk

High Risk

Security Market Line

The slope indicates the required return per unit of risk

RFR

Risk
(business risk, financial risk, liquidity risk, exchange rate risk, country risk)

vestments is referred to as the *security market line (SML)*. It reflects the risk–return combinations available for all risky assets in the capital market at a given time. Investors would select investments that are consistent with their risk preferences; some would consider only low-risk investments, whereas others welcome high-risk investments.

Beginning with an initial security market line, three changes can occur. First, individual investments can change positions on the SML because of changes in their perceived risk. Second, the slope of the SML can change because of a change in the attitudes of investors toward risk; that is, investors can change the returns they require per unit of risk. Third, the SML can experience a parallel shift due to a change in the real RFR or the expected rate of inflation. These three possibilities are discussed in this section.

MOVEMENTS
ALONG THE SML

Investors place alternative investments somewhere along the SML based on their perceptions of the risk of the investment. Obviously, if an investment's risk changes due to a change in one of its risk sources (business risk, etc.), it will move along the security market line. For example, if a firm increases its financial risk by selling a large bond issue that increases its financial leverage, investors will perceive its common stock as riskier and the stock will move up the SML to a higher risk position. Investors will then require a higher rate of return. As the common stock becomes riskier, it changes its position on the SML. Any change in an asset that affects its fundamental risk factors or its market risk (i.e., its beta) will cause the asset to move *along* the SML as shown in Figure 1.5. Note that the SML does not change, only the position of assets on the line.

FIGURE 1.5

Changes in the Required Rate of Return Due to Movements Along the SML

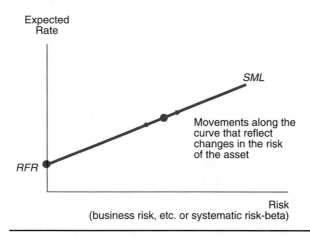

CHANGES IN THE SLOPE OF THE SML

The slope of the security market line indicates the return per unit of risk required by all investors. Assuming a straight line, it is possible to select any point on the SML and compute a risk premium (RP) through the equation:

$$RP_i = R_i - RFR$$

where:

RP_i = risk premium for asset i

R_i = the expected return for asset i

RFR = the expected return on a risk-free asset

If a point on the SML is identified as the portfolio that contains all the risky assets in the market (referred to as the *market portfolio*), it is possible to compute a market risk premium as follows:

$$RP_m = R_m - RFR$$

where:

RP_m = the risk premium on the market portfolio

R_m = the expected return on the market portfolio

RFR = the expected return on a risk-free asset

This market risk premium is *not constant* because the slope of the security market line changes over time. Although we do not understand completely what causes these changes in the slope, we do know that there are changes in the yield differences between assets with different levels of risk even though the risk differences are relatively constant.

FIGURE 1.6   **Time-Series Plot of Moody's Corporate Bond Yield Spreads (Baa–Aaa): Monthly 1964–1992**

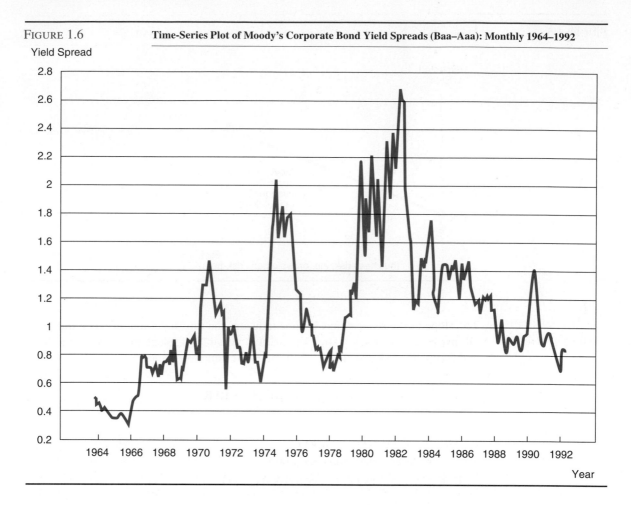

Yield Spread

Year

These differences in yields are referred to as *yield spreads,* and these spreads change over time. As an example, if the yield on a portfolio of Aaa rated bonds is 7.50 percent and the yield on a portfolio of Baa rated bonds is 9.00 percent, we would say that the yield spread is 1.50 percent.[11] This 1.50 percent is referred to as a risk premium because the Baa rated bond is considered to have higher credit risk, that is, greater probability of default. This Baa–Aaa spread is *not* constant over time. For an example of changes in a yield spread, note the substantial difference in yields on Aaa rated bonds and Baa rated bonds shown in Figure 1.6.

Although the underlying risk factors for the portfolio of bonds in the Aaa rated bond index and the Baa rated bond index would probably not change dramatically over time, it is clear from the time-series plot in Figure 1.6 that the difference in yields has

[11] Bonds are rated by rating agencies based upon the credit risk of the securities, that is, the probability of default. Aaa is the top rating Moody's (a prominent rating service) given to bonds with almost no probability of default. (Only U.S. Treasury bonds are considered to be of higher quality.) Baa is a lower rating Moody's gives to bonds of generally high quality that have some possibility of default under adverse economic conditions.

FIGURE 1.7   **Change in Market Risk Premium**

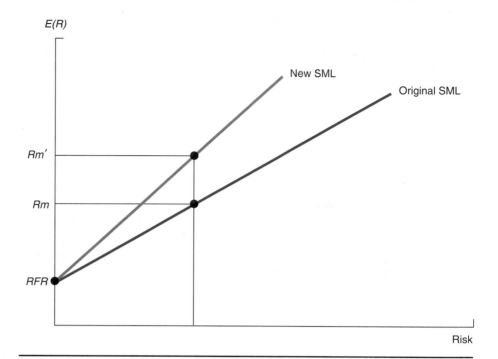

experienced changes of over 100 basis points (1 percent) in a short period of time (e.g., see the increase in 1974–1975 and the dramatic decline in 1983–1984). Such a change in the yield spread during a period where there is no change in the risk characteristics of Baa bonds relative to Aaa bonds would imply a change in the market risk premium. Specifically, although the risk levels of the bonds remain relatively constant, investors have changed the spreads they demand to accept this difference in risk.

This change in the risk premium implies a change in the slope of the security market line. Such a change is shown in Figure 1.7. The figure assumes an increase in the market risk premium, which means that there is an increase in the slope of the market line. Such a change in the slope of the SML will affect the required rate of return for all risky assets. Irrespective of where an investment is on the original SML, its required rate of return will increase, although its individual risk characteristics remain unchanged.

CHANGES IN
CAPITAL MARKET
CONDITIONS OR
EXPECTED
INFLATION

The graph in Figure 1.8 shows what happens to the SML when capital market conditions or the expected rate of inflation changes. Either temporary tightness in the capital market or an increase in the expected rate of inflation could cause the SML to experience a parallel shift upward. The parallel shift occurs because changes in market conditions or a change in the expected rate of inflation affect all investments no matter what their levels of risk.

FIGURE 1.8   **Capital Market Conditions, Expected Inflation, and the Security Market Line**

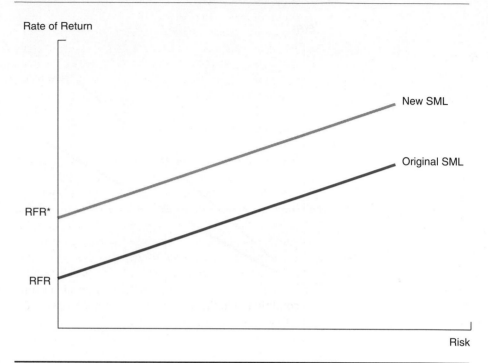

RFR = Nominal risk-free rate.

SUMMARY OF CHANGES IN THE REQUIRED RATE OF RETURN
The relationship between risk and the required rate of return for an investment can change in three ways:

1. A movement *along* the SML demonstrates a change in the risk characteristics of a specific investment, such as a change in its business risk, its financial risk, or its systematic risk (its beta). This change affects only the individual investment.

2. A change in the *slope* of the SML occurs in response to a change in the attitudes of investors toward risk. Such a change demonstrates that investors want either higher or lower rates of return for the same risk. This is also described as a change in the market risk premium (R_m − RFR). A change in the risk premium will affect all risky investments.

3. A *shift* in the security market line reflects a change in market conditions, such as ease or tightness of money, or a change in the expected rate of inflation. Again, such a change will affect all investments.

SUMMARY   The purpose of this chapter is to provide background that can be used in subsequent chapters. To achieve that goal, we covered several topics:

1. We discussed why individuals save part of their income and why they decide to invest their savings. We defined *investment* as the current commitment of these savings for a period of time to derive a rate of return that compensates for the time involved, the expected rate of inflation, and the uncertainty.
2. We examined ways to quantify historical return and risk to help analyze alternative investment opportunities. We considered two measures of mean return (arithmetic and geometric) and applied these to a historical series for an individual investment and to a portfolio of investments during a period of time.
3. We considered the concept of uncertainty and alternative measures of risk (the variance, standard deviation, and relative measure of risk—the coefficient of variation).
4. Prior to discussing the determinants of the required rate of return for an investment, we noted that the estimation of the required rate of return is complicated because the rates on individual investments change over time, because there is a wide range of rates of return available on alternative investments, and because the differences between required returns (e.g., the yield spreads) on alternative investments likewise change over time.
5. We examined the specific factors that determine the required rate of return: (a) the real risk-free rate, which is based on the real rate of growth in the economy, (b) the nominal risk-free rate, which is influenced by capital market conditions and the expected rate of inflation, and (c) a risk premium, which is a function of fundamental factors such as business risk or the systematic risk of the asset relative to the market portfolio (i.e., its beta).
6. We discussed the risk–return combinations available on alternative investments at a point in time (illustrated by the SML) and the three factors that can cause changes in this relationship. First, a change in the inherent risk of an investment (i.e., its fundamental risk or market risk) will cause a movement along the SML. Second, a change in investors' attitudes toward risk will cause a change in the required return per unit of risk, that is, a change in the market risk premium. Such a change will cause a change in the slope of the SML. Finally, a change in capital market conditions or a change in the expected rate of inflation will cause a parallel shift of the SML.

Based on this understanding of the investment environment, you are prepared to consider the numerous alternative investments available in the global market. This is the subject of Chapter 2.

OUTLINE OF THE BOOK

As discussed earlier, Part I of the book provides an investment background by concentrating on why and how individuals invest, the alternative investments that are available, the functioning of the markets for bonds and stocks, and the indexes that track the performance of the major investments.

The second part considers three theoretical topics that are critical to the analysis and investment process. Specifically, there is a discussion of the concept of *efficient markets* and a review of the empirical evidence that supports this theory and some evidence at odds with the theory. Another major development in investment theory is *portfolio theory,* which is at the core of why investors diversify and how they should diversify. Building on this theory several authors have developed an asset pricing theory referred to as the *capital asset pricing model,* which implies a risk measure applicable to all risky assets. The past decade has witnessed explosive growth in *derivative securities,* such as options and futures that allow investors additional risk–return configurations. These instruments and markets are introduced in this section.

Although these topics (efficient markets, portfolio theory, the capital asset pricing model, and derivative securities) are introduced in these chapters, it is important to recognize that these topics are central to the subsequent analysis and portfolio management discussion.

Part III delves into valuation principles and practices. We begin by discussing how to analyze financial statements. Another chapter considers general valuation principles and how these are applied to bonds and stocks. Finally, there is a presentation on macroeconomic analysis and how it might be used to determine how to allocate assets in a global market environment.

The fourth part initiates the detailed analysis of investments beginning with fixed-income securities (bonds) because the valuation process for bonds is easier. Specifically, assuming that the issuer does not default, the investor receives a specified set of income flows and can concentrate on estimating the required rate of return. The first chapter deals with describing the fundamental characteristics and markets for bonds. The second chapter discusses the valuation and analysis of bonds. The final chapter provides a consideration of numerous portfolio strategies including several new techniques introduced for managing a portfolio of bonds.

Part V emphasizes the analysis of common stocks using the top-down, fundamental approach. Specifically, it begins with an analysis of the aggregate stock market and then proceeds to the detailed analysis of various industries and finally to the examination of individual companies within an industry and the stocks of these firms. In contrast to evaluating investments based on fundamental economic factors, some investors feel that the securities market is its own best predictor and, therefore, you need to examine only trends in alternative market series. This approach to investment analysis is called *technical analysis* and it is considered at the end of this section.

Besides the trend toward global markets, the other major development in capital markets has been the creation of new investment instruments. The chapters in Part VI contain descriptions of these alternative investments including options, warrants, convertible securities, and futures contracts as well as a chapter that considers advanced applications of these instruments. We consider how to analyze them and how to use them in a comprehensive investment program. We also consider investment companies (also known as *mutual funds*) as an alternative to direct investment.

The final part contains two chapters that close the loop on the investment process. The first chapter presents an extension on the earlier discussion of portfolio theory and asset pricing theories and reviews the empirical evidence related to alternative theories. The final chapter deals with the very important question of how to evaluate the performance of a portfolio whether you are managing it or someone is managing it for you.

In summary, the purpose of the book is to help you to understand why you invest, what investments are available to you, how you evaluate investments and make investment decisions, how you combine alternative investments into a portfolio, and how you evaluate the performance of your portfolio of investments to determine if it is meeting your objectives.

QUESTIONS

1. Discuss the overall purpose people have for investing. Define investment.

2. As a student, are you saving or borrowing? Why are you doing it?

3. Divide a person's life from ages 20 to 70 into 10-year segments and discuss the likely saving or borrowing patterns during each of these periods.

4. Discuss why you would expect the saving–borrowing pattern to differ by occupation (e.g., for a doctor versus a plumber)?

5. *The Wall Street Journal* reported that the yield on common stocks is about 4 percent, whereas a study at the University of Chicago contends that the annual rate of return on common stocks since 1926 has averaged about 9 percent. Reconcile these statements.

6. Some financial theorists consider the variance of the distribution of expected rates of return to be a good measure of uncertainty. Discuss the reasoning behind this measure of risk and its purpose.

7. Discuss the three components of an investor's required rate of return on an investment.

8. Discuss the two major factors that determine the market nominal risk-free rate (RFR). Explain which of these factors would be more volatile over the business cycle.

9. Briefly discuss the five fundamental factors that influence the risk premium of an investment.

10. You own stock in the Gentry Company, and you read in the financial press that a recent bond offering has raised the firm's debt/equity ratio from 35 percent to 55 percent. Discuss the effect of this change on the variability of the firm's net income stream, other factors being constant. Discuss how this change would affect your required rate of return on the common stock of the Gentry Company.

11. Draw a properly labeled graph of the security market line (SML) and indicate where you would expect the following investments to fall along that line. Discuss your reasoning.
    a. Common stock of large firms
    b. U.S. government bonds
    c. United Kingdom government bonds
    d. Low-grade corporate bonds
    e. Common stock of a Japanese firm

12. Explain why you would change your nominal required rate of return if you expected the rate of inflation to go from zero (no inflation) to 7 percent. Give an example of what would happen if you did not change your required rate of return under these conditions.

13. Assume the long-run growth rate of the economy increased by 1 percent and the expected rate of inflation increased by 4 percent. What would happen to the required rates of return on government bonds and common stocks? Show graphically how the effects of these changes would differ between these alternative investments.

14. You see in *The Wall Street Journal* that the yield spread between Baa corporate bonds and Aaa corporate bonds has gone from 350 basis points (3.5%) to 200 basis points (2%). Show graphically the effect of this change in yield spread on the SML and discuss its effect on the required rate of return for common stocks.

15. Give an example of a liquid investment and an illiquid investment. Discuss why you consider each of them to be liquid or illiquid.

16. *CFA Examination III (1981)* As part of your portfolio planning process, it is suggested that you estimate the real long-run growth potential of the economy.
   a. Identify and explain three major determinants of the economy's real long-run growth. [5 minutes]
   b. Briefly discuss the outlook for each of these three determinants of long-term growth. Present approximate estimates for each of these components and calculate the composite *real* growth potential for the next 5 years. (You should provide a calculation, but emphasize the process rather than specific numbers.) [10 minutes]

PROBLEMS

1. On February 1, you bought some stock for $34 a share and a year later you sold it for $39 a share. During the year you received a cash dividend of $1.50 a share. Compute your HPR and HPY on this stock investment.

2. On August 15, you purchased some stock at $65 a share and a year later you sold it for $61 a share. During the year, you received dividends of $3 a share. Compute your HPR and HPY on this investment.

3. At the beginning of last year you invested $4,000 in 80 shares of the Chang Corporation. During the year Chang paid dividends of $5 per share. At the end of the year you sold the 80 shares for $59 a share. Compute your total HPY on these shares and indicate how much was due to the price change and how much was due to the dividend income.

4. The rates of return computed in Problems 1, 2, and 3 are nominal rates of return. Assuming that the rate of inflation during the year was 4 percent, compute the real rates of return on these investments. Compute the real rates of return if the rate of inflation were 8 percent.

5. During the past 5 years, you owned two stocks that had the following annual rates of return:

Year	Stock T	Stock B
1	0.19	0.08
2	0.08	0.03
3	−0.12	−0.09
4	−0.03	0.02
5	0.15	0.04

   a. Compute the arithmetic mean annual rate of return for each stock. Which is most desirable by this measure?
   b. Compute the standard deviation of the annual rate of return for each stock. (Use the Appendix if necessary.) By this measure, which is the preferable stock?
   c. Compute the coefficient of variation for each stock. (Use the Appendix if necessary.) By this relative measure of risk, which stock is preferable?
   d. Compute the geometric mean rate of return for each stock. Discuss the difference between the arithmetic mean return and geometric mean return for each stock and relate the differences in mean return to the standard deviation of the return for each stock.

6. You are considering acquiring shares of common stock in the Light and Dry Beer Corporation. Your rate of return expectations are as follows:

Possible Rate of Return	Probability
−0.10	0.30
0.00	0.10
0.10	0.30
0.25	0.30

Compute the expected return $[E(R_i)]$ on this investment.

7. A stockbroker calls you and suggests that you invest in the Fast and Powerful Computer Company. After analyzing the firm's annual report and other material, you feel that the distribution of rates of return is as follows:

Possible Rate of Return	Probability
−0.60	0.05
−0.30	0.20
−0.10	0.10
0.20	0.30
0.40	0.20
0.80	0.15

Compute the expected return $[E(R_i)]$ on this stock.

8. Without any formal computations, do you consider Light and Dry Beer in Problem 6 or Fast and Powerful Computer in Problem 7 to present greater risk? Discuss your reasoning.

9. During the past year you had a portfolio that contained U.S. government T-bills, long-term government bonds, and common stocks. The rates of return on each of them were as follows:

U.S. government T-bills	5.50%
U.S. government long-term bonds	7.50
U.S. common stocks	11.60

During the year, the consumer price index, which measures the rate of inflation, went from 160 to 172 (1982–1984 = 100). Compute the rate of inflation during this year. Compute the real rates of return on each of the investments in your portfolio based on the inflation rate.

10. You read in *Business Week* that a panel of economists has estimated that the long-run real growth rate of the U.S. economy over the next 5-year period will average 3 percent. In addition, a bank newsletter estimates that the average annual rate of inflation during this 5-year period will be about 4 percent. What nominal rate of return would you expect on U.S. government T-bills during this period?

11. What would your required rate of return be on common stocks if you wanted a 5 percent risk premium to own common stocks given what you know from Problem 10? If common stock investors became more risk averse, what would happen to the required rate of return on common stocks? What would be the impact on stock prices?

12. Assume that the consensus required rate of return on common stocks is 14 percent. In addition, you read in *Fortune* that the expected rate of inflation is 5 percent and the esti-

mated long-term real growth rate of the economy is 3 percent. What interest rate would you expect on U.S. government T-bills? What approximate risk premium for common stocks do these data imply?

REFERENCES

Fama, Eugene F., and Merton H. Miller. *The Theory of Finance.* New York: Holt, Rinehart and Winston, 1972.

Fisher, Irving. *The Theory of Interest.* New York: Macmillan, 1930; reprinted by Augustus M. Kelley, 1961.

APPENDIX 1A   COMPUTATION OF VARIANCE AND STANDARD DEVIATION

Variance and standard deviation are measures of how actual values differ from the expected values (arithmetic mean) for a given series of values. In this case, we want to measure how rates of return differ from the arithmetic mean value of a series. There are other measures of dispersion, but variance and standard deviation are the best known because they are used in statistics and probability theory. Variance is defined as:

$$\text{Variance } (\sigma^2) = \sum_{i=1}^{n} (\text{Probability}) \left(\begin{array}{c} \text{Possible} \\ \text{Return} \end{array} - \begin{array}{c} \text{Expected} \\ \text{Return} \end{array} \right)^2$$

$$= \sum_{i=1}^{n} (P_i)[R_i - E(R_i)]^2$$

Consider the following example, as discussed in the chapter:

Probability of Possible Return (P_i)	Possible Return (R_i)	P_iR_i
0.15	0.20	0.03
0.15	−0.20	−0.03
0.70	0.10	0.07
		$\Sigma = 0.07$

This gives an expected return [$E(R_i)$] of 7 percent. The dispersion of this distribution as measured by variance is:

Probability (P_i)	Return (R_i)	$R_i - E(R_i)$	$[R_i - E(R_i)]^2$	$P_i[R_i - E(R_i)]^2$
0.15	0.20	0.13	0.0169	0.002535
0.15	−0.20	−0.27	0.0729	0.010935
0.70	0.10	0.03	0.0009	0.000630
				$\Sigma = 0.014100$

The variance (σ^2) is equal to 0.0141. The standard deviation is equal to the square root of the variance:

$$\text{Standard Deviation } (\sigma) = \sqrt{\Sigma P_i [R_i - E(R_i)]^2}$$

Consequently, the standard deviation for the preceding example would be:

$$\sigma_i = \sqrt{0.0141} = 0.11874$$

In this example, the standard deviation is approximately 11.87 percent. Therefore, you could describe this distribution as having an expected value of 7 percent and a standard deviation of 11.87 percent.

In many instances, you might want to compute the variance or standard deviation for a historical series in order to evaluate the past performance of the investment. Assume that you are given the following information on annual rates of return (HPY) for common stocks listed on the New York Stock Exchange (NYSE):

Year	Annual Rate of Return
19__1	0.07
19__2	0.11
19__3	−0.04
19__4	0.12
19__5	−0.06

In this case, we are not examining expected rates of return, but actual returns. Therefore, we assume equal probabilities, and the expected value (in this case the mean value, R) of the series is the sum of the individual observations in the series divided by the number of observations, or 0.04 (0.20/5). The variances and standard deviations are:

Year	R_i	$R_i - \overline{R}$	$(R_i - \overline{R})^2$	
19__1	0.07	0.03	0.0009	$\sigma^2 = 0.0286/5$
19__2	0.11	0.07	0.0049	$= 0.00572$
19__3	−0.04	−0.08	0.0064	
19__4	0.12	0.08	0.0064	$\sigma = \sqrt{0.00572}$
19__5	−0.06	−0.10	0.0110	$= 0.0756$
			$\Sigma = 0.0286$	

We can interpret the performance of NYSE common stocks during this period of time by saying that the average rate of return was 4 percent and the standard deviation of annual rates of return was 7.56 percent.

COEFFICIENT OF VARIATION

In some instances you might want to compare the dispersion of two different series. The variance or standard deviation are *absolute* measures of dispersion. That is, they can be influenced by the magnitude of the original numbers. To compare series with very different values, you need a *relative* measure of dispersion. A measure of relative dispersion is the coefficient of variation, which is defined as:

$$\text{Coefficient of Variation (CV)} = \frac{\text{Standard Deviation}}{\text{Expected Return}}$$

A larger value indicates greater dispersion relative to the arithmetic mean of the series. For the previous example, the CV would be:

$$CV_1 = \frac{0.0756}{0.0400} = 1.89$$

It is possible to compare this value to a similar figure having a very different distribution. As an example, assume you wanted to compare this investment to another investment that had an average rate of return of 10 percent and a standard deviation of 9 percent. The standard deviations alone tell you that the second series has greater dispersion (9 percent versus 7.56 percent) and might be considered to have higher risk. In fact, the relative dispersion for this second investment is much less.

$$CV_1 = \frac{0.0756}{0.0400} = 1.89$$

$$CV_2 = \frac{0.0900}{0.1000} = 0.90$$

Considering the relative dispersion and the total distribution, most investors would probably prefer the second investment.

PROBLEMS

1. Your rate of return expectations for the common stock of Floppy Disc Company during the next year are:

Possible Rate of Return	Probability
−0.10	0.25
0.00	0.15
0.10	0.35
0.25	0.25

   a. Compute the expected return $[E(R_i)]$ on this investment, the variance of this return (σ^2), and its standard deviation (σ).
   b. Under what conditions can the standard deviation be used to measure the relative risk of two investments?
   c. Under what conditions must the coefficient of variation be used to measure the relative risk of two investments?

2. Your rate of return expectations for the stock of Turk Computer Company during the next year are:

Possible Rate of Return	Probability
−0.60	0.15
−0.30	0.10
−0.10	0.05
0.20	0.40
0.40	0.20
0.80	0.10

   a. Compute the expected return $[E(R_i)]$ on this stock, the variance (σ^2) of this return, and its standard deviation (σ).

   b. On the basis of expected return $[E(R_i)]$ alone, discuss whether Floppy Disc or Turk Computer is preferable.

   c. On the basis of standard deviation (σ) alone, discuss whether Floppy Disc or Turk Computer is preferable.

   d. Compute the coefficients of variation (CVs) for Floppy Disc and Turk Computer and discuss which stock return series has the greater relative dispersion.

3. The following are annual rates of return for U.S. government T-bills and United Kingdom common stocks.

Year	U.S. Government T-Bills	United Kingdom Common Stock
19__4	.063	.150
19__5	.081	−.043
19__6	.076	.374
19__7	.090	.192
19__8	.085	−.106

   a. Compute the arithmetic mean rate of return and standard deviation of rates of return for the two series.

   b. Discuss these two alternative investments in terms of their arithmetic average rates of return, their absolute risk, and their relative risk.

   c. Compute the geometric mean rate of return for each of these investments. Compare the arithmetic mean return and geometric mean return for each investment and discuss this difference between mean returns as related to the standard deviation of each series.

CHAPTER 2

SELECTING INVESTMENTS IN A GLOBAL MARKET

This chapter answers the following questions:

- What are the several reasons why investors should have a global perspective regarding their investments?
- What has happened to the relative size of U.S. and foreign stock and bond markets?
- What are the differences in the rates of return on U.S. and foreign securities markets?
- How can changes in currency exchange rates affect the returns that U.S. investors experience on foreign securities?
- Is there an additional advantage of diversifying in international markets beyond domestic diversification?
- What alternative securities are available? What is their cash flow and risk properties?
- What is the historical return and risk characteristics of the major investment instruments?
- What is the relationship among the returns for foreign and domestic investment instruments and what is the implication of these relationships for portfolio diversification?

Individuals are willing to defer current consumption for a range of reasons. Some save for their children's college tuition or their own, others wish to accumulate downpayments for a home, car, or boat, others want to amass adequate retirement funds for the future. Whatever the reason for an investment program, the techniques we used in Chapter 1 to measure risk and return will help you evaluate alternative investments.

But what are those alternatives? Thus far we have said very little about the investment opportunities that are available in financial markets. In this chapter, we address this issue by surveying investment alternatives. This background is needed for later chapters where we analyze in detail several individual investments such as bonds, common stock, and other securities and then consider how to construct and evaluate portfolios of investments.

As an investor in the 1990s, you have an array of investment choices that were not available only a few decades ago. Together, the dynamism of financial markets, technological advances, and new regulations have resulted in numerous new investment instruments and expanded trading opportunities.[1] Improvements in communications and relaxation of international regulations have made it easier for investors to trade in both domestic and global markets. Telecommunications networks enable U.S. brokers to reach security exchanges in London, Tokyo, and other European and Asian cities as easily as those in New York, Chicago, and other U.S. cities. The competitive environment in the brokerage industry and the deregulation of the banking sector have made it possible for more financial institutions to compete for investor dollars. This has spawned investment vehicles with a variety of maturities, risk–return characteristics, and cash flow patterns. In this chapter we will examine some of these choices.

As an investor, you need to understand the differences among investments so you can build a properly diversified *portfolio* that conforms to your objectives. That is, you should seek to acquire a group of investments with different patterns of returns over time. If chosen carefully, such portfolios minimize risk for a given level of return because low or negative rates of return on some investments during a period of time are offset by above-average returns on others. The goal is to build a balanced portfolio of investments with relatively stable overall rates of return. A major goal of this text is to help you understand and evaluate the risk–return characteristics of investment portfolios. An appreciation of alternative security types is the starting point for this analysis.

This chapter is divided into three main sections. In the first section we introduce and briefly describe global capital markets because, as noted earlier, investors can choose securities from financial markets around the world. We look at a combination of reasons why investors should include foreign as well as domestic securities in their portfolios. Taken together these reasons provide a compelling case for global investing. We continue the investigation of where to invest in Chapter 3 when we examine security markets in more detail.

In the second section we discuss securities found in domestic and global markets, describing their main features and cash flow patterns. From this discussion you will see that the varying risk–return characteristics of alternative investments suit the preferences of different investors. Some securities are more appropriate for individuals, whereas others are better suited for financial institutions such as insurance companies and pension funds.

The third and final section contains an assessment of the historical risk and return performance of several investment instruments from around the world and examines the relationship among the returns for many of these securities. An understanding of these relationships will provide further support for the notion of global investing.

THE CASE FOR GLOBAL INVESTMENTS

A description of investment alternatives written 10 years ago would have been much shorter than this one. At that time, the bulk of investments available to individual investors consisted of stocks and bonds sold on U.S. securities markets. Now, however, a call to your broker gives you access to a range of securities sold throughout the world. Currently, you can purchase stock in General Motors or Toyota, U.S. Treasury bonds

---

[1] For an excellent discussion of the reasons for the development of numerous financial innovations and the effect of these innovations on world capital markets, see Merton H. Miller, *Financial Innovations and Market Volatility* (Cambridge, Mass.: Blackwell Publishers, 1991).

or Japanese government bonds, a mutual fund that invests in U.S. biotechnology companies, a global growth stock fund or a German stock fund, or options on a U.S. stock index or the British pound along with innumerable other investments.

Several changes have caused this explosion of investment opportunities. For one, the growth and development of numerous foreign financial markets such as those in Japan, the United Kingdom, and Germany have made them accessible and viable for investors around the world. Numerous U.S. investment firms recognized this opportunity and established and expanded facilities in these countries. This expansion was aided by major advances in telecommunications technology that made it possible to maintain constant contact with offices and financial markets around the world. In addition to the efforts by U.S. firms, foreign firms and investors undertook counterbalancing initiatives with wealth derived from oil sales and foreign exchange provided by surpluses in balances of payments. As a result, investors and investment firms from around the world found it desirable and possible to trade securities worldwide. Thus the range of investment alternatives extends from the traditional U.S. financial markets to security markets around the world.[2]

There are three main or interrelated reasons U.S. investors should think of and work to construct global investment portfolios.

1. When investors compare the absolute and relative sizes of U.S. and foreign markets for stocks and bonds, they will see that ignoring foreign markets reduces their choices to less than 50 percent of available investment opportunities. Because more opportunities broaden your range of risk–return choices, it makes sense to evaluate foreign securities when selecting investments and building a portfolio.
2. The rates of return available on non-U.S. securities often have substantially exceeded those for only U.S. securities. The higher returns on non-U.S. *equities* can be justified by the higher growth rates for the countries where they are issued. These superior results prevail when the returns are risk-adjusted.
3. One of the major tenets of investment theory is that investors should diversify their portfolio. Based on what is the relevant factor when attempting to diversify, diversification with foreign securities can help to substantially reduce portfolio risk.

In this section we will look at each of these reasons in detail to demonstrate why there should be a growing role of foreign financial markets for U.S. investors and to assess the benefits and risks of trading in these markets.

RELATIVE SIZE OF
U.S. FINANCIAL
MARKETS

Prior to 1970, the securities traded in the U.S. stock and bond markets comprised about 65 percent of all the securities available in world capital markets. Therefore, a U.S. investor selecting securities strictly from U.S. markets had a fairly complete range of the investments available. Under these conditions, most U.S. investors probably felt it was not worth the time and effort to expand their investment universe to include investments available in foreign markets. That situation has changed dramatically over

---

[2] In this regard, see Scott E. Pardee, "Internationalization of Financial Markets," Federal Reserve Bank of Kansas City, *Economic Review* (February 1987): 3–7.

FIGURE 2.1   **Total Investable Capital Market: 1969 and 1991**

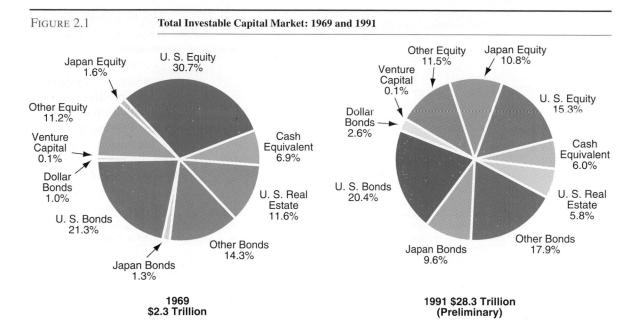

Source: Brinson Partners, Inc., Chicago, Ill.

the last 20 years. Currently, investors who ignore foreign markets limit their investment choices substantially.

Figure 2.1 shows the breakdown of securities available in world capital markets in 1969 and 1991. Not only has the overall value of all securities increased dramatically (from $2.3 trillion to $28.3 trillion), but the composition has also changed. Concentrating on proportions of bond and equity investments, the figure shows that U.S. dollar bond and equity securities made up 52 percent of the total value of all securities in 1969 versus 29.4 percent for nondollar bonds and equity. By 1991, U.S. bonds and equities accounted for 35.7 percent of the total securities market versus 52.4 percent for nondollar bonds and stocks. These data indicate that if you consider only the stock and bond market, the U.S. proportion of this combined market has declined from 63 percent of the total in 1969 to 40 percent in 1991.

Clearly the U.S. security markets have come to include a smaller proportion of the total world capital market, and it is likely that this trend will continue. The faster economic growth of many other countries compared to the U.S. will require foreign companies to issue debt and equity securities to finance this growth. Therefore, U.S. investors should consider investing in foreign securities because of the current and future overall importance of these securities in the world capital markets. Put another way, not investing in foreign stocks and bonds means that you are ignoring 60 percent of the securities that are available to you.

RATES OF RETURN ON U.S. AND FOREIGN SECURITIES

An examination of the rates of return on U.S. and foreign securities not only demonstrates that many non-U.S. securities provide superior rates of return, but also shows the impact of the exchange rate risk discussed in Chapter 1.

TABLE 2.1

International Bond Market Compound Annual Rates of Return: 1978–1989

	Components of Return		
	Total Return in U.S. Dollars	**Total Domestic Return**	**Exchange Rate Effect**
Australia	7.59%	11.07%	−3.13%
Canada	9.92	10.46	−0.49
France	9.46	11.43	−1.77
Germany	8.47	6.58	1.77
Japan	11.65	7.04	4.31
Netherlands	9.39	7.85	1.43
Switzerland	5.73	3.55	2.11
United Kingdom	10.06	11.71	−1.48
United States	9.96	9.96	—

Source: "International Bond Investing and Portfolio Management" in *The Handbook of Fixed Income Securities,* 3d ed., edited by Frank J. Fabozzi, 1991, exhibit 51–6, p. 110. Copyright © 1991 Richard D. Irwin. Reprinted by permission.

GLOBAL BOND
MARKET RETURNS

Table 2.1 reports annual compound rates of return for several major international bond markets for the period 1978 to 1989. You should examine the domestic returns on these bonds and the returns in U.S. dollars. The *domestic return* is the rate of return an investor within the country would earn (e.g., an Australian investor in Australian bonds). In contrast, the return in U.S. dollars is what a U.S. investor would earn after adjusting for the effects of changes in the currency exchange rates during the period.

An analysis of the domestic returns in Table 2.1 indicates that the performance of the U.S. bond market ranked fifth out of the nine countries. When the impact of exchange rates is considered, the U.S. experience was third out of nine. This difference in relative performance for domestic versus U.S. dollar returns means that the exchange rate effect for a U.S. investor was negative for several countries (i.e., the U.S. dollar was strong) and offset superior domestic performance.

As an example, the domestic return on Australian bonds was 11.07 percent compared with the return for U.S. bonds of 9.96 percent. The Australian foreign exchange effect was −3.13 percent, which reduced the return on Australian bonds converted to U.S. dollars to only 7.59 percent, which was below the return for U.S. bonds. Even with these differences, investors in non-U.S. bonds from several countries could experience rates of return close to or above those of investors who limited themselves to the U.S. bond market.

GLOBAL EQUITY
MARKET RETURNS

Table 2.2 contains the compound growth rate of prices in local currencies and in U.S. dollars for 12 major equity markets, four areas of the world, and the total world for the period from 1981 to 1990. The performance in local currency indicated that the U.S. market was ranked thirteenth of the total 17 countries and areas or was the ninth of 12 countries. The performance results in U.S. dollars indicates that the currency effect differed among countries. For example, a U.S. investor experienced a positive currency effect for investments in Germany and Japan (the U.S. dollar was weak relative to these currencies), but the currency effect hurt the U.S. dollar returns for Australia and Italy. Overall, in U.S. dollar returns, the U.S. market was ranked twelfth of the 17 countries and areas or eighth of 12 countries.

TABLE 2.2

FT-Actuaries World Equity Price Performance: Local Currency and U.S. Dollars Compound Growth Rate: 1981–1990

	Local Currency		U.S. Dollars	
	(%)	Rank[a]	(%)	Rank[a]
Australia	7.5	15 (10)	3.1	17 (12)
Canada	4.3	16 (11)	4.6	16 (11)
France	13.6	4 (4)	13.2	7 (5)
Germany	10.6	9 (6)	14.6	4 (3)
Italy	10.1	12 (8)	8.8	14 (9)
Japan	13.4	5 (5)	18.3	2 (2)
Netherlands	10.4	11 (7)	13.9	6 (4)
Spain	14.2	2 (2)	12.5	8 (6)
Sweden	21.1	1 (1)	18.7	1 (1)
Switzerland	3.8	17 (12)	8.1	15 (10)
United Kingdom	13.8	3 (3)	11.5	10 (T)(7)
United States	9.6	13 (9)	9.6	12 (8)
Europe	12.3	6 (T)	12.2	9
Pacific Basin	11.8	8	15.6	3
Europe and Pacific	12.3	6 (T)	14.1	5
North America	9.3	14	9.3	13
World	10.5	10	11.5	10 (T)

[a]Based on rank within 17 countries and areas (rank for only the 12 countries).

Source: "Anatomy of World Markets" (London: Goldman Sachs International, Ltd., October 1991). Reprinted by permission of Goldman Sachs.

Like the bond market performance, these results for equity markets around the world indicate that investors who limited themselves to the U.S. market experienced rates of return below those available in many other countries. This is true for comparisons that considered both domestic returns and rates of return adjusted for exchange rates.

INDIVIDUAL COUNTRY EQUITY RISK AND RETURN

As shown, most countries experienced higher compound price changes on common stock than the United States. A natural question is whether these superior results are attributable to higher levels of risk for common stock in these countries.

Table 2.3 gives figures for return (the compound growth rate of price) and risk for the 12 individual countries, four regions of the world, and the total world for the period from 1981 to 1990. The risk measure is the standard deviation of daily returns as discussed in Chapter 1. Although the risk measure for the U.S. market (16.6) is one of the lowest values, the return is also quite low. A relative measure of performance is derived by dividing the return for each market by its risk measure. These return-to-risk results indicate that the U.S. performance in local currency ranked tenth out of 17. This performance is also shown in Figure 2.2, which plots the annual compound growth rate of domestic price against the standard deviation of daily returns. The results in U.S. dollars in Table 2.3 and Figure 2.3 show similar results. In this case the U.S. performance is ranked ninth of 17.

RISK OF COMBINED COUNTRY INVESTMENTS

Thus far, we have discussed the risk and return results for individual countries. In Chapter 1 we considered the idea of combining a number of assets into a portfolio and noted that it would be desirable to diversify the investments in order to reduce the variability of the returns over time. We discussed how proper diversification reduces

TABLE 2.3

World Equity Long-Term Risk and Return Performance: Local Currency and U.S. Dollars: 1981–1990

	Local Currency			U.S. Dollars		
	Return[a]	Risk[b]	Return/Risk	Return[a]	Risk[b]	Return/Risk
Australia	7.5	25.9	0.29	3.1	31.2	0.10
Canada	4.3	17.6	0.24	4.6	19.5	0.24
France	13.6	22.4	0.61	13.2	25.1	0.53
Germany	10.6	21.0	0.50	14.6	23.2	0.63
Italy	10.1	25.7	0.39	8.8	27.0	0.33
Japan	13.4	20.1	0.67	18.3	25.4	0.72
Netherlands	10.4	18.7	0.56	13.9	18.7	0.74
Spain	14.2	23.8	0.60	12.5	25.6	0.49
Sweden	21.1	24.0	0.88	18.7	24.8	0.75
Switzerland	3.8	18.6	0.20	8.1	20.0	0.41
United Kingdom	13.8	19.6	0.70	11.5	22.5	0.51
United States	9.6	16.6	0.58	9.6	16.6	0.58
Europe	12.3	16.6	0.74	12.2	18.4	0.66
Pacific Basin	11.8	19.3	0.61	15.6	24.0	0.65
Europe and Pacific	12.3	16.3	0.75	14.1	19.6	0.72
North America	9.3	16.4	0.57	9.3	16.5	0.56
World	10.5	14.9	0.70	11.5	15.8	0.73

[a]Compound growth rate of price.

[b]The annualized standard deviation of daily logarithmic returns.

Source: "Anatomy of World Markets" (London: Goldman Sachs International, Ltd., October 1991). Reprinted by permission of Goldman Sachs.

the variability (our measure of risk) of the portfolio because alternative investments have different patterns of returns over time. Specifically, when the rates of return on some investments are negative or below average, other investments in the portfolio will be experiencing above-average rates of return. Therefore, if a portfolio is properly diversified, it should provide a more stable rate of return for the total portfolio (i.e., it will have a lower standard deviation and therefore less risk). Although we will discuss and demonstrate portfolio theory in detail in Chapter 7, we need to consider the concept at this point in order to fully understand the benefits of global investing.

The way to measure whether two investments will contribute to diversifying a portfolio is to compute the correlation coefficient between their rates of return over time. Correlation coefficients can range from +1.00 to −1.00. A correlation of +1.00 means that the rates of return for these two investments move exactly together. Combining investments that move together in a portfolio would not help diversify the portfolio because they have identical rate of return patterns over time. In contrast, a correlation coefficient of −1.00 means that the rates of return for two investments move exactly opposite to each other. When one investment is experiencing above-average rates of return, the other is suffering through similar below-average rates of return of the same magnitude. Combining two investments like this in a portfolio would contribute much to diversification because it would stabilize the rates of return over time, reducing the standard deviation of the portfolio rates of return and hence its risk. Therefore, if you want to diversify your portfolio and reduce your risk, you want an investment that has either *low positive* correlation, *zero* correlation, or, ideally,

FIGURE 2.2   **Plot of Annual Rates of Return and Risk for Major Stock Markets in Local Currency: 1981–1990**

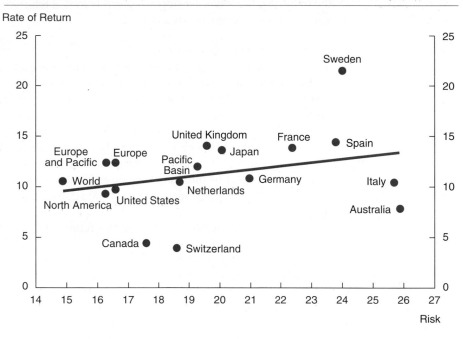

FIGURE 2.3   **Plot of Annual Rates of Return and Risk for Major Stock Markets in U.S. Dollars: 1981–1990**

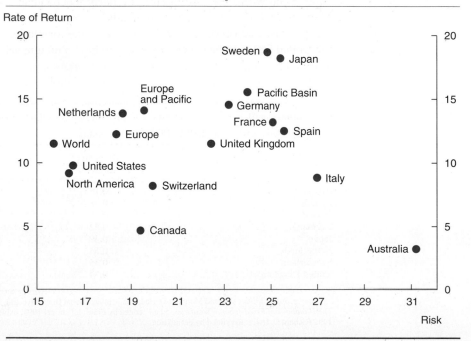

negative correlation with the other investments in your portfolio. With this in mind, the following discussion considers the correlations of returns on U.S. bonds and stocks with returns on foreign bonds and stocks.

GLOBAL BOND PORTFOLIO RISK

Table 2.4 lists the correlation coefficients between domestic rates of return for bonds in the United States and bonds in major foreign markets from 1978 to 1989. Notice that very few correlations between domestic rates of return are above 0.50. For a U.S. investor, the important correlations are between rates of return in U.S. dollars. In this case, all the correlations between returns in U.S. dollars except France are lower than the correlations with domestic returns and only one correlation is above 0.40.

These low positive correlations mean that U.S. investors have substantial opportunities for risk reduction through global diversification of bond portfolios. A U.S. investor in any market except Canada would substantially reduce the standard deviation of the portfolio.

Why do these correlation coefficients for returns between U.S. bonds and those of various foreign countries differ? That is, why is the U.S.–Canada correlation 0.75, whereas the U.S.–Australia correlation is only 0.12? The answer is because the international trade patterns, economic growth, fiscal policies, and monetary policies of the countries differ. We do not have an integrated world economy, but rather a collection of economies that are related to one another in different ways. As an example, the U.S. and Canadian economies are very closely related because of their geographic proximity, similar domestic economic policies, and the extensive trade between them. Each is the other's largest trading partner. In contrast, the United States has much less trade with Australia, and the fiscal and monetary policies of the two countries differ dramatically.

A country between these extremes is Japan. The United States has a strong trade relationship with Japan, but each has a fairly independent set of economic policies. Therefore, the U.S.–Japan correlation falls between those with Canada and Australia. The point is, macroeconomic differences cause the correlation of bond returns between the United States and each other country to have a unique value. These differing cor-

TABLE 2.4

Correlation Coefficients Between Rates of Return on Bonds in the United States and Major Foreign Markets: 1978–1989 (monthly data)

	Domestic Returns	Returns in U.S. Dollars
Australia	0.18	0.12
Canada	0.78	0.72
France	0.25	0.28
Germany	0.52	0.32
Japan	0.39	0.28
Netherlands	0.54	0.37
Switzerland	0.35	0.30
United Kingdom	0.34	0.32

Source: Adam M. Greshin and Margaret D. Hadzima, "International Bond Investing and Portfolio Management," in *The Handbook of Fixed-Income Securities,* 3d ed., edited by Frank J. Fabozzi 1991, exhibit 51–15, p. 1108. Copyright © 1991 Richard D. Irwin. Reprinted by permission.

relations make it worthwhile to diversify with foreign bonds, and the different correlations give guidance regarding which countries will provide the greatest reduction in the standard deviation (risk) of returns for a U.S. investor.

Also, *the correlation of returns between a single pair of countries changes over time,* because the factors influencing the correlations such as international trade, economic growth, fiscal policy, and monetary policy change over time. A change in any of these variables will produce a change in how the economies are related and in the relationship between returns on bonds. As an example, the correlation between bond returns in the United States and Japan before 1980 was quite low, reflecting limited trade and independent economic policies. During the 1980s, international trade between the two countries increased substantially and so did the correlation between returns on bonds.

Figure 2.4 shows what happens to the risk–reward tradeoff when we combine U.S. and foreign bonds. A comparison of a completely non-U.S. portfolio (100 percent foreign) and a 100 percent U.S. portfolio indicates that the non-U.S. portfolio has both a higher rate of return and a higher standard deviation of returns than the U.S portfolio. Combining the two portfolios in different proportions provides a very interesting set of points.

The expected rate of return is a weighted average of the two portfolios. In contrast, the risk (standard deviation) of the combination is not a weighted average, but also depends on the correlation between the two portfolios. In this example, the risk levels of the combined portfolios decline below those of either of the individual portfolios. Therefore, by adding foreign bonds, a U.S. investor is able to not only increase the expected rate of return, but also reduce the risk of a bond portfolio.

GLOBAL EQUITY PORTFOLIO RISK

The correlation of world equity markets resembles that for bonds. Table 2.5 lists the correlation coefficients between monthly equity returns of each country and the U.S. market (in both domestic and U.S. dollars) for the 10-year period from 1981 to 1990. About one-half of the correlations between local currency returns top 0.50. The correlations among rates of return adjusted for exchange rates were always lower; only 4 of the 11 correlations between U.S. dollar returns exceed 0.50, and the average correlation was only 0.44.

These relatively small positive correlations between U.S. stocks and foreign stocks have similar implications to those derived for bonds. Investors can reduce the overall risk of their stock portfolios by including foreign stocks.

Figure 2.5 demonstrates the impact of international equity diversification. These curves demonstrate that as you increase the number of randomly selected securities in a portfolio, the standard deviation will decline due to the benefits of diversification within your own country. This is referred to as domestic diversification. After a certain number of securities (30 to 40), the curve will flatten out at a risk level that reflects the basic market risks for the domestic economy. The lower curve illustrates the benefits of international diversification. Adding foreign securities to a U.S. portfolio to create a global portfolio enables an investor to experience lower overall risk because the non-U.S. securities are not correlated with our economy or our stock market.

To see how this works, consider, for example, the effect of inflation and interest rates on all U.S. securities. As discussed in Chapter 1, all U.S. securities will be affected by

FIGURE 2.4   **Risk–Return Tradeoff for International Bond Portfolios**

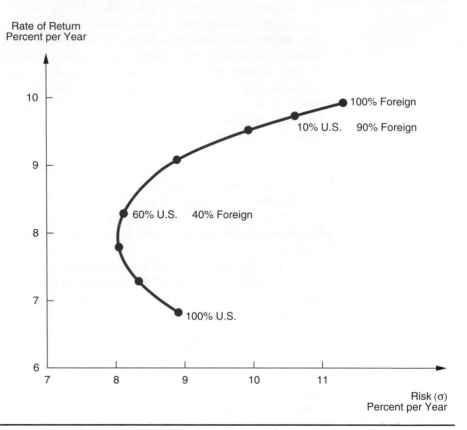

Source: Kenneth Cholerton, Pierre Pieraerts, and Bruno Solnik, "Why Invest in Foreign Currency Bonds?" *Journal of Portfolio Management* 12, no. 4 (Summer 1986): 4–8. Reprinted with permission.

TABLE 2.5   **Correlation Coefficients Between Price Returns on Common Stocks in the United States and Major Foreign Stock Markets: 1981–1990 (Monthly Data)**

	Local Currency Price Returns	U.S. Dollar Price Returns
Australia	0.48	0.40
Canada	0.78	0.75
France	0.52	0.43
Germany	0.44	0.34
Italy	0.33	0.27
Japan	0.39	0.28
Netherlands	0.63	0.57
Spain	0.42	0.33
Sweden	0.46	0.39
Switzerland	0.66	0.52
United Kingdom	0.70	0.56

Source: "Anatomy of World Markets" (London: Goldman Sachs International, Ltd., October 1991). Reprinted by permission of Goldman Sachs.

FIGURE 2.5   **Risk Reduction Through National and International Diversification**

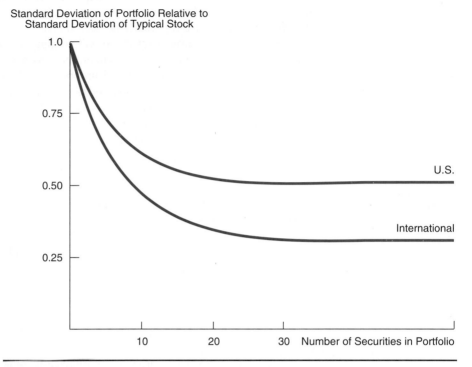

Source: B. H. Solnik, "Why Not Diversify Internationally Rather than Domestically?" *Financial Analyst's Journal* (July–August 1974): 48–54. Reprinted by permission of the Financial Analyst's Journal.

these variables. In contrast, a Japanese stock is mainly impacted by what happens in the Japanese economy and will typically not be affected by changes in U.S. variables. Thus, adding Japanese, German, and French stocks to a U.S. stock portfolio reduces the portfolio risk to a level that reflects only worldwide systematic factors.

SUMMARY ON GLOBAL INVESTING
At this point, we have considered the relative size of the market for non-U.S. bonds and stocks and found that it has grown in size and importance, becoming too big to ignore. We have also examined the rates of return for foreign bond and stock investments and determined that, in most instances, their rates of return per unit of risk were superior to those in the U.S. market. Finally, we discussed constructing a portfolio of investments and the importance of diversification in reducing the variability of returns over time, which reduces the risk of the portfolio. It was noted that successful diversification requires the combination of investments with low positive or negative correlations between rates of return. An analysis of the correlation between rates of return on U.S. and foreign bonds and stocks indicated a consistent pattern of low positive correlations. Therefore, the existence of relatively high rates of return combined with low correlation

coefficients indicate that adding foreign stocks and bonds to a U.S. portfolio can increase the average return and reduce the risk of the portfolio.

As promised, there are several rather compelling reasons for adding foreign securities to a U.S. portfolio. Therefore, developing a global investment perspective is important both because such an approach has been shown to be justified, and also because this current trend in the investment world will continue in the future. Implementing this new global investment perspective will not be easy because it requires an understanding of new terms, instruments (e.g., Eurobonds), and institutions (e.g., the Japanese stock market). Still, the effort is justified because you are developing a set of skills and a way of thinking that will carry you into the next century and beyond.

The next section presents an overview of investment alternatives from around the world, beginning with fixed-income investments and progressing through numerous alternatives.

GLOBAL INVESTMENT CHOICES

This is an important foundation for subsequent chapters where we describe techniques to value individual investments and combine alternative investments into properly diversified portfolios that conform to your risk–return objectives.

The investments are divided by asset classes. Specifically, in the first section, we describe fixed-income investments, which offer contractual payment streams that can include a stated interest payment (or no interest payment) and a specified payment at maturity. This section also considers preferred stock, which involves fixed payments, but does not give the legal protection of bonds. In the second section we discuss equity investments, which do not have specified payments, but involve company ownership. The third section contains a discussion of special equity instruments such as warrants and options, which have characteristics of both fixed-income and equity instruments. In section four we consider futures contracts that allow investors to enter into an agreement for the future delivery of an asset at a specified price. Futures contracts allow for a wide range of return-risk profiles. Many investors are interested in one or several of these investments, but do not want to analyze individual securities. Such individuals should consider investment companies, which are described in the fifth section.

All these investments are called *financial assets* because their payoffs are in money. In contrast, a large set of investments, referred to as *real assets,* include such things as grain or real estate. These assets are considered in the next section. This is followed by a consideration of alternative opportunities in real estate. We conclude with a group of assets that are considered *low liquidity investments* because of the relative difficulty in buying and selling them. This includes art, antiques, coins, stamps, and precious gems.

The purpose of this survey is to briefly introduce each of these investment alternatives so you can appreciate the full spectrum of alternatives. The final section of the chapter describes the historical return and risk patterns for many individual investment alternatives and the correlations among the returns for these investments. Again, the purpose is to provide additional background and a perspective that will help you evaluate individual investments and build a properly diversified portfolio of investments from around the world.

FIXED-INCOME
INVESTMENTS

Fixed-income investments have a contractually mandated payment schedule. Their investment contracts promise specific payments at predetermined times, although the legal force behind the promise varies and this affects their risks and required returns. At one extreme, if the issuing firm does not make its payment at the appointed time, creditors can declare the issuing firm bankrupt. In other cases (e.g., income bond), the issuing firm must make payments only if it earns profits. In yet other instances (e.g., preferred stock), the issuing firm does not have to make payments unless its board of directors votes to do so.

Investors who acquire fixed-income securities (except preferred stock) are really lenders to the issuers. Specifically, you lend some amount of money, called the *principal,* to the borrower. In return, the borrower promises to make periodic interest payments, and at the maturity of the loan, to pay back the principal.

SAVINGS ACCOUNTS

Savings accounts are so familiar you might not think of them as fixed-income investments, yet an individual who deposits funds in a savings account at a bank or savings and loan association (S&L) is really lending money to the institution and, as a result, earning a fixed payment. These investments are generally considered to be convenient, liquid, and very low-risk because almost all are insured. Consequently, their rates of return are generally low compared with other alternatives. Several versions of these accounts have been developed to appeal to investors with differing objectives.

The passbook savings account has no minimum balance, and funds may be withdrawn at any time with very little loss of interest. Due to its flexibility, the promised interest on passbook accounts is relatively low.

For investors with larger amounts of funds who are willing to give up liquidity, banks and S&Ls developed *certificates of deposits (CDs),* which require minimum deposits (typically $500) and have fixed durations (usually 3 months, 6 months, 1 year, 2½ years). The promised rates on CDs are higher than those for passbook savings, and the rate increases with the size and the duration of the deposit. An investor who wants to cash in a CD prior to its stated expiration date must pay a heavy penalty in the form of a much lower interest rate.

Investors with large sums of money ($10,000 or more) can invest in Treasury bills (T-bills), which are short-term obligations (maturing in 3 to 12 months) of the U.S. government. To compete against T-bills, banks and S&Ls issue money market certificates, which require minimum investments of $10,000 and have minimum maturities of 6 months. The promised rate on these certificates fluctuates at some premium over the weekly rate on 6-month T-bills. Investors can redeem these certificates only at the bank of issue, and they incur penalties if they withdraw their funds before maturity.

CAPITAL MARKET INSTRUMENTS

Capital market instruments are fixed-income obligations that trade in the secondary market, which means that you can buy them from and sell them to other individuals or institutions. Capital market instruments fall into four categories that we will discuss in turn: (1) U.S. Treasury securities, (2) U.S. government agency securities, (3) municipal bonds, and (4) corporate bonds.

U.S. TREASURY SECURITIES

All government securities issued by the U.S. Treasury are fixed-income instruments. They may be bills, notes, or bonds depending on their times to maturity. Specifically, bills mature in less than a year, notes in 1 to 10 years, and bonds in over 10 years from time of issue. U.S. government obligations are essentially riskless because there is little chance of default and they are very liquid.

U.S. GOVERNMENT AGENCY SECURITIES

Agency securities are sold by various agencies of the government to support specific programs, but they are not direct obligations of the Treasury. Examples of agencies that issue these bonds include the Federal National Mortgage Association (FNMA or Fannie Mae), which sells bonds and uses the proceeds to purchase mortgages from insurance companies or savings and loans, and the Federal Home Loan Bank (FHLB), which sells bonds and loans the money to its 12 banks, which in turn provide credit to savings and loans and other mortgage-granting institutions. Other agencies are the Government National Mortgage Association (GNMA or Ginnie Mae), Banks for Co-operatives, Federal Land Banks (FLBs), and the Federal Housing Administration (FHA).

Although the securities issued by federal agencies are not direct obligations of the government, they are virtually default-free, because it is inconceivable that the government would allow them to default, and they are fairly liquid. Because they are not officially guaranteed by the Treasury, they are not considered riskless. Also because they are not as liquid as Treasury bonds, they typically provide slightly higher returns than Treasury issues.

MUNICIPAL BONDS

Municipal bonds are issued by local government entities (states, cities, towns, etc.) as either general obligation or revenue bonds. General obligation bonds (GOs) are backed by the full taxing power of the municipality, whereas revenue bonds pay the interest from revenue generated by specific projects (e.g., the revenue to pay the interest on sewer bonds comes from water taxes).

Municipal bonds differ from other fixed-income securities in that they are tax-exempt. The interest earned from them is exempt from taxation by the federal government and by the state that issued the bond, provided the investor is a resident of that state. For this reason, municipal bonds are popular with investors in high tax brackets. For an investor having a marginal tax rate of 30 percent, a regular bond with an interest rate of 8 percent yields a net return after taxes of only 5.60 percent $[0.08 \times (1 - 0.30)]$. Such an investor would prefer a tax-free bond of equal risk with a 6 percent yield. This allows municipal bonds to offer yields that are lower than yields on comparable taxable bonds, generally by about 20 to 30 percent.

CORPORATE BONDS

Corporate bonds are fixed-income securities issued by industrial corporations, public utility corporations, or railroads to raise funds to invest in plant, equipment, or working capital. They can be broken down by issuer, in terms of credit quality (measured by the ratings assigned by an agency on the basis of probability of default), or in terms of maturity (short term, intermediate term, or long term).

All bonds include an *indenture,* which is the legal agreement that lists the obligations of the issuer to the bondholder, including the payment schedule and features such as call provisions and sinking funds. *Call provisions* specify when a firm can issue a call for the bonds prior to their maturity, at which time current bondholders must submit the bonds to the issuing firm, which redeems them (that is, pays back the principal and a small premium). A *sinking fund* provision specifies payments the issuer must make to redeem a given percentage of the outstanding issue prior to maturity.

Corporate bonds fall into various categories based on their contractual promises to investors. They will be discussed in the order of their seniority.

Senior secured bonds are the most senior bonds in a firm's capital structure and have the lowest risk of distress or default. They include various secured issues that differ based on the assets that are pledged. *Mortgage bonds* are backed by liens on specific assets such as land and buildings. In the case of bankruptcy, the proceeds from the sale of these assets are used to pay off the mortgage bondholders. *Collateral trust bonds* are similar except that the assets backing the bonds are financial assets such as stocks, notes, and other high-quality bonds. Finally, *equipment trust certificates* are secured by specific pieces of transportation equipment such as locomotives and box cars for a railroad and airplanes for an airline.

Debentures are promises to pay interest and principal, but they pledge no specific assets (referred to as *collateral*) in case the firm does not fulfill its promise. This means that the bondholder depends on the success of the borrower to make the promised payment. Debenture owners usually have first call on the firm's earnings and any assets that are not already pledged by the firm as backing for senior secured bonds. If the issuer does not make an interest payment, the debenture owners can declare the firm bankrupt and claim any unpledged assets to pay off the bonds.

Subordinated bonds are similar to debentures, but in the case of default, subordinated bondholders have claim to the assets of the firm only after the firm has satisfied the claims of all senior secured and debenture bondholders. That is, the claims of subordinated bondholders are subordinate to those of other bondholders. Within this general category of subordinated issues, you can find senior subordinated, subordinated, and junior subordinated bonds. Junior subordinated bonds have the weakest claim of all bondholders.

Income bonds stipulate interest payment schedules, but the interest is due and payable only if the issuers earn the income to make the payment by stipulated dates. If the company does not earn the required amount, it does not have to make the interest payment and it cannot be declared bankrupt. Instead, the interest payment is considered in arrears and, if subsequently earned, it must be paid off. Because the issuing firm is not legally bound to make its interest payments except when the firm earns it, an income bond is not considered as safe as a debenture or a mortgage bond, so income bonds offer higher returns to compensate investors for the added risk. Although there are a limited number of corporate income bonds, these income bonds are fairly popular with municipalities because municipal revenue bonds are basically income bonds.

Convertible bonds have the interest and principal characteristics of other bonds, with the added feature that the bondholder has the option to turn them back to the firm in exchange for its common stock. As an example, a firm could issue a $1,000 face-value bond and stipulate that owners of the bond could, at their discretion, turn the bond in to the issuing corporation and convert it into 40 shares of the firm's common stock. These bonds are very appealing to investors because they combine the features of a fixed-income security with the option of conversion into the common stock of the firm, should it prosper.

Because of their desirability, convertible bonds generally pay lower interest rates than nonconvertible debentures of comparable risk. The difference in the required interest rate increases with the growth potential of the company, because this increases the value of the option to convert the bonds into common stock. These bonds are almost always subordinated to the nonconvertible debt of the firm, so they are considered riskier and rated lower.

An alternative to convertible bonds is a debenture with warrants attached. A *warrant* allows the bondholder to purchase the firm's common stock from the firm at a specified price for a given time period. The specified purchase price for the stock set in the warrant is typically above the price of the stock at the time the firm issues the bond but below the expected future stock price. The warrant makes the debenture more desirable, which lowers its required yield. The warrant also provides the firm with future common stock capital when the holder exercises the warrant and buys the stock from the firm.

Unlike the typical bond that pays interest every 6 months and its face value at maturity, a *zero coupon bond* promises no interest payments during the life of the bond but only the payment of the principal at maturity. Therefore, the purchase price of the bond is the present value of the principal payment at the required rate of return. As an example, the price of a zero coupon bond that promises to pay $10,000 in 5 years with a required rate of return of 8 percent is $6,756. To find this, assuming semiannual compounding (which is the norm), use the present value factor for 10 periods at 4 percent, which is 0.6756.

INTERNATIONAL BOND INVESTING

As noted earlier, over half of all fixed-income securities available to U.S. investors are issued by firms in countries outside the United States. Investors identify these securities in different ways: by the country or city of the issuer (e.g., United States, United Kingdom, Japan), by the location of the primary trading market (e.g., United States, London), by the home country of the major buyers, and by the currency in which the securities are denominated (e.g., dollars, yens, pounds sterling). We will identify foreign bonds by their country of origin and include these other differences in each description.

A *Eurobond* is an international bond denominated in a currency not native to the country where it is issued. Specific kinds of Eurobonds include Eurodollar bonds, Euroyen bonds, Eurodeutschemark bonds, and Eurosterling bonds. A Eurodollar bond is denominated in U.S. dollars and sold outside the United States to non-U.S. investors. A specific example would be a U.S. dollar bond issued by General Motors and sold in London. These are typically issued in Europe, with the major concentration in London.

Eurobonds can also be denominated in yen or deutschemarks. As an example, Nippon Steel can issue Euroyen bonds for sale in London. Also, if it appears that investors are looking for foreign bonds, a U.S. corporation (e.g., IBM) can issue a Euroyen bond in London.

Yankee bonds are sold in the United States, denominated in U.S. dollars, but issued by foreign corporations or governments. This allows a U.S. citizen to buy a bond of a foreign firm or government but receive all payments in U.S. dollars, eliminating exchange rate risk. An example would be a U.S. dollar-denominated bond issued by British Airways.[3] Similar bonds are issued in other countries, including the Bulldog Market, which involves British sterling-denominated bonds issued in the United Kingdom by non-British firms, or the Samurai Market, which involves yen-denominated bonds issued in Japan by non-Japanese firms.

International domestic bonds are bonds sold by an issuer within its own country in that country's currency. An example would be a bond sold by a Japanese corporation in Japan denominated in yen. A U.S. investor acquiring such a bond would receive maximum diversification, but would incur exchange rate risk.

Preferred stock is classified as a fixed-income security because its yearly payment is stipulated as either a coupon (e.g., 5 percent of the face value) or a stated dollar amount (e.g., $5 preferred). Preferred stock differs from bonds because its payment is legally a dividend and therefore not legally binding. For each period, the firm's board of directors must vote to pay it, similar to a common stock dividend. Even if the firm earned enough money to pay the preferred stock dividend, the board of directors could theoretically vote to withhold it. Because most preferred stock is cumulative, the unpaid dividends would accumulate to be paid in full at a later time.

Although preferred dividends are not legally binding as the interest payments on a bond are, they are considered practically binding because of the credit implications of a missed dividend. Because corporations can exclude 80 percent of intercompany dividends from taxable income, preferred stocks have become attractive investments for financial corporations. As an example, a corporation that owns preferred stock of another firm and receives $100 in dividends, can exclude 80 percent of this amount and pay taxes on only 20 percent of it. Assuming a 40 percent tax rate, the tax would only be $8 or 8 percent versus 40 percent on other investment income. Due to this benefit, the yield on high-grade preferred stock is typically lower than that on high-grade bonds.

EQUITY INSTRUMENTS

This section describes several equity instruments, which differ from fixed-income securities because their returns are not contractual. As a result, you can receive returns that are much better or much worse than what you would receive on a bond. We begin with common stock, the most popular equity instrument and probably the most popular investment instrument.

Common stock represents *ownership* of a firm. Owners of the common stock of a firm share in the company's successes and problems. If, like Wal-Mart Stores, McDonald's, Merck, or Xerox, the company does very well, the investor receives very high rates of return and can become very wealthy. In contrast, the investor can lose money if the firm does not do well or even goes bankrupt, as the once formidable Penn Central, W. T. Grant, and Interstate Department Stores all did. In these instances, the firm is forced to liquidate its assets and pay off all its creditors, and preferred stockholders and common stock owners receive what is left. Investing in common stock entails all the advantages and disadvantages of ownership and is a relatively risky investment compared with fixed-income securities.

---

[3] For a discussion of the growth of this market related to stocks, see Michael Siconolf, "Foreign Firms Step Up Offerings in U.S." *Wall Street Journal,* June 1, 1992, CI, CII.

COMMON STOCK CLASSIFICATIONS

When considering an investment in common stock, people tend to divide the vast universe of stocks into categories based on general business line and by industry within these business lines. The division by business line would give classifications for industrial firms, utilities, transportation firms, and financial institutions. Within each of these business lines, there are industries. The most diverse group—the industrial group—would include such industries as automobiles, industrial machinery, chemicals, and beverages. Utilities would include electrical power companies, gas suppliers, and the water industry. Transportation would include airlines, trucking firms, and railroads. Financial institutions would include several categories of banks, savings and loans, and credit unions.

An alternative classification scheme might separate domestic (U.S.) and foreign common stocks. We will avoid this division because the business line–industry breakdown is more appropriate and useful when constructing a diversified portfolio of common stock investments. With a global capital market, the focus of analysis should be all the companies in an industry viewed in a global setting. As an example, when one is considering the automobile industry, it is necessary to go beyond General Motors, Ford, and Chrysler and also consider auto firms from throughout the world such as Honda Motors, Porsche, Daimler Benz, Nissan, and Fiat.

Therefore, our subsequent discussion on foreign equities concentrates on how you buy and sell these securities because this procedural information has often been a major impediment. Many investors may recognize the desirability of investing in foreign common stock because of the risk and return characteristics, but they may be intimidated by the logistics of the transaction. The purpose of the next section is to alleviate this concern by explaining the alternatives available.

ACQUIRING FOREIGN EQUITIES

Currently, there are several ways to acquire foreign common stock:

1. Purchase or sale of American Depository Receipts (ADRs)
2. Purchase or sale of American shares
3. Direct purchase or sale of foreign shares listed on a U.S. or foreign stock exchange
4. Purchase or sale of international mutual funds

PURCHASE OR SALE OF AMERICAN DEPOSITORY RECEIPTS   The easiest way to acquire foreign shares directly is through *American Depository Receipts (ADRs)*. These are certificates of ownership issued by a U.S. bank, which holds the shares in safekeeping as a convenience to an investor. ADRs can be issued at the discretion of the bank based on the demand for the stock. The shareholder absorbs the additional handling costs of an ADR through higher transfer expenses, which are deducted from dividend payments.

ADRs are quite popular in the United States. As of the end of 1992, 120 foreign companies had stocks listed on the NYSE and 75 of these were available through ADRs, including all the stock listed from Japan, the United Kingdom, Australia, and the Netherlands. In addition, there are 65 foreign firms listed on the AMEX with most of the non-Canadian stocks available through ADRs.

PURCHASE OR SALE OF AMERICAN SHARES   American shares are securities issued in the United States by a transfer agent acting on behalf of a foreign firm. Because of the added effort and expense incurred by the foreign firm, a limited number of American shares are available.

DIRECT PURCHASE OR SALE OF FOREIGN SHARES   The most difficult and complicated foreign equity transaction takes place in the country where the firm is located because it must be carried out in the foreign currency and the shares must then be transferred to the United States. This routine can be cumbersome. A second alternative is a transaction on a foreign stock exchange outside the country where the securities originated. As an example, if you acquired shares of a French auto company listed on the London Stock Exchange (LSE), the shares would be denominated in pounds and the transfer would be swift, assuming your broker has a membership on the LSE.

Finally, you could purchase foreign stocks listed on the NYSE or American Stock Exchange (AMEX). This is similar to buying a U.S. stock, but only a limited number of foreign firms qualify for and are willing to accept the cost of listing. Still, this number is growing. As of the end of 1992, over 35 foreign firms were directly listed on the NYSE, in addition to the firms that were available through ADRs.

PURCHASE OR SALE OF INTERNATIONAL MUTUAL FUNDS   Numerous investment companies invest all or a portion of their funds in stocks of firms outside the United States. The alternatives range from *global funds,* which invest in both U.S. stocks and foreign stocks, to *international funds,* which invest almost wholly outside the United States. In turn, international funds can: (1) diversify across many countries, (2) concentrate in a segment of the world (e.g., the Pacific basin), (3) concentrate in a specific country (e.g., the Japan Fund, the Germany Fund, the Italy Fund, or the Korea Fund) or (4) concentrate in types of markets (e.g., emerging markets such as Thailand, Indonesia, India and China). A mutual fund is a convenient path to global investing, particularly for a small investor, because the purchase or sale of one of these funds is similar to a transaction for a comparable U.S. mutual fund.

SPECIAL EQUITY INSTRUMENTS: OPTIONS

In addition to common stock investments, it is also possible to invest in equity-derivative securities, which are securities that have a claim on the common stock of a firm. This would include *options,* which are rights to buy or sell common stock at a specified price for a stated period of time. The two kinds of option instruments are warrants, and puts and calls.

WARRANTS

As mentioned earlier, a warrant is an option issued by a corporation that gives the holder the right to acquire a firm's common stock from the company at a specified price within a designated time period. The warrant does not constitute ownership of the stock, only the option to buy the stock.

CALL OPTIONS

A call option is similar to a warrant, because it is an option to buy the common stock of a company within a certain period at a specified price called the *striking price.* A call option differs from a warrant because it is not issued by the company but by another investor who is willing to assume the other side of the transaction. Options are also typically valid for a shorter time period than warrants. Call options are generally valid for less than a year, whereas warrants extend for over 5 years.

PUT OPTIONS

The holder of a put option has the right to sell a given stock at a specified price during a designated time period. Puts are used by investors who expect a stock price to decline during the specified period or by investors who own the stock and want protection from a price decline.

FUTURES CONTRACTS	As discussed, options provide the right to buy or sell common stock at a specified price during some time interval. Another instrument that provides an alternative to the purchase of an investment is a *futures contract.* This is an agreement that provides for the future exchange of a particular asset at a specified delivery date in exchange for a specified payment at the time of delivery. Although the full payment is not made until the delivery date, a good faith deposit, called the *margin,* is made to protect the seller. This is typically about 10 percent of the value of the contract.

The bulk of trading on the commodity exchanges is in futures contracts, which are contracts for the delivery of a commodity at some future date, usually within 9 months. The current price of the futures contract is determined by the participants' beliefs about the future for the commodity. In July of a given year, a trader could speculate on the Chicago Board of Trade for wheat in September, December, March, and May of the next year. If the investor expected the price of a commodity to rise, he or she could buy a futures contract on one of the commodity exchanges for later sale. If the investor expected the price to fall, he or she could sell a futures contract on an exchange with the expectation of buying similar contracts later when the price had declined to cover the sale.

There are several differences between investing in an asset through a futures contract and investing in the asset itself. One is the use of borrowed funds to finance the futures purchase, which increases the volatility of returns. Because an investor puts up only a small proportion of the total value of the futures contract (10 to 15 percent), when the price of the commodity changes, the change in the total value of the contract is large compared to the amount invested. Another unique aspect is the term of the investment. Although stocks can have infinite maturities, futures contracts typically expire in less than a year.

FINANCIAL FUTURES

In addition to futures contracts on commodities, a recent innovation has been the development of futures contracts on financial instruments such as T-bills, Treasury bonds, and Eurobonds. For example, it is possible to buy or sell a futures contract that promises future delivery of $100,000 of Treasury bonds on a given day in the future at a set price and yield. Such a contract is available on the Chicago Board of Trade (CBT). These futures contracts allow individual investors, bond portfolio managers, and corporate financial managers to protect themselves against volatile interest rates. There are currency futures that allow individual investors or portfolio managers to speculate on or to protect against changes in currency exchange rates. Finally, there are futures contracts on stock market series such as the S&P (Standard & Poor's) 500, the *Value Line* Index, and the Nikkei Average on the Tokyo Stock Exchange.

INVESTMENT
COMPANIES

The investment alternatives described so far are individual securities that can be acquired from a government entity, a corporation, or another individual. However, rather than directly buying an individual stock or bond issued by one of these sources, you may choose to acquire these investments indirectly by buying shares in an investment company, also called a *mutual fund,* that owns a portfolio of individual stocks, bonds, or a combination of the two. Specifically, an *investment company* sells shares in itself and uses the proceeds of this sale to acquire bonds, stocks, or other investment instruments. As a result, an investor who acquires shares in an investment company is a partial owner of the investment company's portfolio of stocks or bonds. We distinguish investment companies by the types of investment instruments they acquire. Discussions of some of the major types follow.

MONEY MARKET FUNDS

Money market funds are investment companies that acquire high-quality, short-term investments (referred to as *money market* instruments) such as T-bills, high-grade commercial paper (public short-term loans) from various corporations, and large CDs from the major money center banks. The yields on the money market portfolios always surpass those on normal bank CDs, because the investment by the money market fund is larger and the fund can commit to longer maturities than the typical individual. In addition, the returns on commercial paper are above the prime rate. The typical minimum initial investment in a money market fund is $1,000, it charges no sales commission, and minimum additions are $250 to $500. You can always withdraw funds from your money market fund without penalty, and you receive interest to the day of withdrawal.

Individuals tend to use money market funds as alternatives to bank savings accounts because they are generally quite safe (because they typically limit their investments to high-quality, short-term investments), they provide yields above what is available on most savings accounts, and the funds are readily available. Therefore, you might use one of these funds to accumulate funds to pay tuition or for a down payment on a car. Because of relatively high yields and extreme flexibility and liquidity, the total value of these funds has grown to over $250 billion in 1993.

BOND FUNDS

Bond funds generally invest in various long-term government, corporate, or municipal bonds. They differ by the type and quality of the bonds included in the portfolio as assessed by various rating services. Specifically, the bond funds range from those that invest only in risk-free government bonds and high-grade corporate bonds to those that concentrate in lower-rated corporate or municipal bonds, called *high-yield bonds* or *junk bonds.* The expected rate of return from various bond funds will differ, with the low-risk government bond funds paying the lowest returns and the high-yield bond funds expected to pay the highest returns.

COMMON STOCK FUNDS

There are numerous common stock funds that invest to achieve stated investment objectives, which can include aggressive growth, income, precious metals investments, and international stocks. Such funds offer smaller investors the benefits of diversification and professional management. To meet the diverse needs of investors, numerous funds have been created that concentrate in one industry or sector of the economy, such as chemicals, electric utilities, health, housing, and technology. These funds are diversified within a sector or an industry, but they are not diversified across the total market. Investors who participate in a sector or an industry fund bear more risk than an investor in a total market fund because the sectors will tend to fluctuate more than an aggregate market fund that is diversified across all sectors.

Also, there are international funds that invest outside the United States or global funds that invest in the United States and in other countries. These offer opportunities for global investing by individual investors.[4]

BALANCED FUNDS
Balanced funds invest in a combination of bonds and stocks of various sorts depending on their stated objectives.

REAL ESTATE

Like commodities, most investors view real estate as an interesting and profitable investment alternative but believe that it is only available to a small group of experts with a lot of capital to invest. The fact is, some feasible real estate investments do not require detailed expertise or large capital commitments. We will begin by considering low-capital alternatives.

REAL ESTATE INVESTMENT TRUSTS (REIT)
A *real estate investment trust* is basically an investment fund designed to invest in various real estate properties. It is similar to a stock or bond mutual fund except that the money provided by the investors is invested in property and buildings rather than in stocks and bonds. There are several types of REITs.

Construction and development trusts lend the money required by builders during the initial construction of a building. Mortgage trusts provide the long-term financing for properties. Specifically, they acquire long-term mortgages on properties once construction is completed. Equity trusts own various income-producing properties such as office buildings, shopping centers, or apartment houses. Therefore, an investor who buys shares in an equity real estate trust is buying part of a portfolio of income-producing properties.

REITs have experienced periods of great popularity and significant depression in line with changes in the aggregate economy and the money market. Although they are subject to cyclical risks depending on the economic environment, they offer small investors a way to participate in real estate investments.[5]

DIRECT REAL ESTATE INVESTMENTS
The most common type of direct real estate investment is the purchase of a home, which is the largest investment most people ever make. Today, according to the Federal Home Loan Bank, the average cost of a single-family house exceeds $95,000. The purchase of a home is considered an investment because, as the buyer, you initially pay

---

[4] For a study that examines the diversification of individual country funds, see Warren Bailey and Joseph Lim, "Evaluating the Diversification Benefits of the New Country Funds," *Journal of Portfolio Management* 18, no. 3 (Spring 1992): 74–80.

[5] Diane Harris, "Prime REITs for Would-Be Moguls," *Money,* April 1984, 93–96; Jill Bettner, "REITs House Good Value after Recent Price Declines," *Wall Street Journal,* November 28, 1989, C1, C3.

a sum of money either all at once or over a number of years through a mortgage. For most people, who are not in a position to pay cash for a house, the financial commitment includes a down payment (typically 10 to 20 percent of the purchase price) and specific mortgage payments over a 20- to 30-year period that include reducing the loan's principal and also paying interest on the outstanding balance. Subsequently, a homeowner hopes to sell the house for its cost plus a gain.

RAW LAND   Another direct real estate investment is the purchase of raw land with the intention of selling it in the future at a profit. During the period of time that you own the land, you have negative cash flows because it is necessary to make mortgage payments, maintain the property, and pay taxes on it. An obvious risk is the possible difficulty of selling it for an uncertain price. Raw land generally has low liquidity compared to most stocks and bonds. An alternative to buying and selling the raw land is the development of the land into a housing project or a shopping mall as discussed below.

LAND DEVELOPMENT   Typically, land development involves buying raw land, dividing it into individual lots, and building houses on it. Alternatively, buying land and building a shopping mall would also be considered land development. This is a feasible form of investment, but requires a substantial commitment of capital, time, and expertise. Although the risks can be high because of the commitment of time and capital, the rates of return from a successful housing or commercial development can be significant.[6]

RENTAL PROPERTY   Many investors with an interest in real estate investing acquire apartment buildings or houses with low down payments, with the intention of deriving enough income from the rents to pay the expenses of the structure, including the mortgage payments. For the first few years following the purchase, the investor generally has no reported income from the building because of tax-deductible expenses including the interest component of the mortgage payment and depreciation on the structure. Subsequently, rental property provides a cash flow and an opportunity to profit from the sale of the property.[7]

LOW-LIQUIDITY INVESTMENTS   Most of the investment alternatives we have described are traded on securities markets. Except for real estate, most of these securities have good liquidity. Although many investors view the investments that we will discuss in this section as alternatives to financial investments, financial institutions do not typically acquire them because they are considered to be fairly illiquid and have high transaction costs compared to stocks and bonds. Many of these assets are sold at auctions, causing expected prices to vary substantially. In addition, transaction costs are high because there is generally no national market for these investments, so local dealers must be compensated for the added

---

[6] For a review of studies that have examined returns on real estate, see G. Stacey Sirmans and C. F. Sirmans, "The Historical Perspective of Real Estate Returns," *Journal of Portfolio Management* 13, no. 3 (Spring 1987): 22–31. The implications of these return and risk measures for portfolio management are discussed in James R. Webb and Jack A. Rubens, "How Much in Real Estate? A Surprising Answer," *Journal of Portfolio Management* 13, no. 3 (Spring 1987): 10–14.

[7] For a discussion of this alternative, see Diane Harris, "An Investment for Rent," *Money,* April 1984, 87–90.

carrying costs and the cost of searching for buyers or sellers. Given these liquidity risk considerations, many financial theorists view the following low-liquidity investments more as hobbies than investments, even though studies have indicated that some of these assets have experienced substantial rates of return.

ANTIQUES

The investors who earn the greatest returns from antiques are dealers who acquire them at estate sales or auctions to refurbish and sell at a profit. If we gauge the value of antiques based on prices established at large public auctions, it appears that many serious collectors enjoy substantial rates of return. In contrast, the average investor who owns a few pieces to decorate his or her home finds such returns elusive. The high transaction costs and illiquidity of antiques may erode any profit that the individual may earn when selling these pieces. The subsequent discussion of rates of return on various assets will provide some evidence on the returns.

ART

The entertainment sections of newspapers or the personal finance sections of magazines often carry stories of the results of major art auctions, such as when Van Gogh's *Irises* and *Sunflowers* sold for $59 million and $36 million, respectively.

Obviously, these examples and others indicate that some paintings have increased significantly in value and thereby generated large rates of return for their owners. However, investing in art typically requires substantial knowledge of art and the art world, a large amount of capital to acquire the work of well-known artists, patience, and an ability to absorb high transaction costs. For investors who enjoy fine art and have the resources, these can be satisfying investments, but for most small investors, this is a difficult area in which to get returns that compensate for the uncertainty and illiquidity. This was especially true during the period 1989–1992 when there was a bear market in art.[8]

COINS AND STAMPS

Many individuals enjoy collecting coins or stamps as a hobby and also as an investment. The market for coins and stamps is fragmented compared to the stock market, but it is more liquid than the market for art and antiques. Indeed, the volume of coins and stamps traded has prompted the publication of weekly and monthly price lists.[9] An investor can get a widely recognized grading specification on a coin or stamp and, once graded, a coin or stamp can usually be sold quickly through a dealer.[10] It is important to recognize that the difference between the bid price the dealer will pay to buy the

---

[8] For a listing and discussion of art sold at auction, see Jerry E. Patterson, "A Dazzling Year," *Institutional Investor,* International Edition, September 1987, 324–339; John R. Dorfman, "Art of Investing May Mean Avoiding Art," *Wall Street Journal,* June 6, 1989, C1, 25; Peter C. DuBois, "Not a Pretty Picture," *Barron's,* November 12, 1990, 14; Judith H. Dobrzynski, "The Art Market Is Not a Pretty Picture," *Business Week,* November 13, 1990, 57; and Alexandra Peers, "With Spring Auction, Shaky Art Market Faces Flood of Less-than-Stellar Works," *Wall Street Journal,* April 29, 1992, C1, C16.

[9] A weekly publication for coins is *Coin World,* published by Amos Press, Inc., 911 Vandemark Rd., Sidney, OH 45367. There are several monthly coin magazines, including *Coinage,* published by Behn-Miller Publications, Inc., Encino, Calif. Amos Press also publishes several stamp magazines, including *Linn's Stamp News* and *Scott Stamp Monthly.* These magazines provide current prices for coins and stamps.

[10] For an article that describes the alternative grading services, see Diana Henriques, "Don't Take Any Wooden Nickels," *Barron's,* June 19, 1989; 16, 18, 20, 32. For an analysis of experience with commemorative coins, see R. W. Bradford, "How to Lose a Mint," *Barron's,* March 6, 1989, 54, 55.

stamp or coin and the asking or selling price the investor must pay the dealer is going to be fairly large compared to the difference between the bid and ask prices on stocks and bonds.

DIAMONDS

Diamonds can be and have been good investments during many periods. Still, investors who purchase diamonds must realize that: (1) diamonds can be very illiquid, (2) the grading process that determines their quality is quite subjective, (3) most investment-grade gems require substantial investments, and (4) they generate no positive cash flow during the holding period until the stone is sold. In fact, during the holding period the investor must cover costs of insurance and storage. Finally, there are appraisal costs before selling.[11]

In this section, we have described the most common investment alternatives in order to introduce you to the range of investments available. We will discuss many of these in more detail when we consider how you evaluate them for investment purposes. You should keep in mind that new investment alternatives are constantly being created and developed. You can keep abreast of these by reading business newspapers and magazines.

In our final section, we will present some data on historical rates of return and risk measures for a number of these investments to provide some background on their historical return–risk performance. This should give you some feel for the returns and risk characteristics you might expect in the future.

HISTORICAL RISK/RETURNS ON ALTERNATIVE INVESTMENTS

How do investors weigh the costs and benefits of owning investments and make decisions to build portfolios that will provide the best risk–return combinations? To help individual or institutional investors answer this question, financial theorists have examined extensive data and attempted to provide information on the return and risk characteristics of various investments.

Many theorists have studied the historical rates of return on common stocks, and a growing interest in bonds has caused investigators to assess their performance as well. Because inflation has been so pervasive, many studies include both nominal and real rates of return on investments. Still other investigators have examined the performance of such assets as real estate, foreign stocks, art, antiques, and commodities. This section reviews some of the major studies to provide background on the rates of return and risk for these investment alternatives. This should help you to make decisions on which of the alternatives you might want to examine when building your investment portfolio.

STOCKS, BONDS, AND T-BILLS

A set of studies by Ibbotson and Sinquefield (I&S) examined historical nominal and real rates of return for six major classes of assets in the United States: (1) common stocks, (2) small capitalization common stocks,[12] (3) long-term U.S. government

---

[11] For a discussion of problems and opportunities, see "When to Put Your Money into Gems," *Business Week*, March 16, 1981, 158–161.

[12] Small capitalization stocks were broken out as a separate class of asset because several studies have shown that firms with relatively small capitalization (stock with low market value) have experienced rates of return and risk that were very different from those of stocks in general. Therefore, it is felt that they should be considered a unique asset class. We will discuss these studies in Chapter 6 which deals with the efficient markets hypothesis.

bonds, (4) long-term corporate bonds, (5) U.S. Treasury bills, and (6) consumer goods (a measure of inflation).[13] For each asset, the authors calculated total rates of return before taxes or transaction costs.

These investigators computed geometric and arithmetic mean rates of return and computed nine series derived from the basic series. Four of these series were net returns reflecting different premiums: (1) a *risk premium,* which I&S defined as the difference in the rate of return that investors receive from investing in common stocks rather than in risk-free U.S. Treasury bills; (2) a *small stock premium,* which they defined as the return on small capitalization stocks minus the return on total stocks; (3) a *horizon premium,* which they defined as the difference in the rate of return received from investing in long-term government bonds rather than short-term U.S. Treasury bills; and (4) a *default premium,* which they defined as the difference between the rates of return on long-term risky corporate bonds and long-term risk-free government bonds. I&S also computed the real inflation-adjusted rates of return for common stocks, small capitalization stocks, Treasury bills, long-term government bonds, and long-term corporate bonds.

A summary of the rates of return, risk premiums, and standard deviations for the basic and derived series appears in Table 2.6. As discussed in Chapter 1, the geometric means of the rates of return are always lower than the arithmetic means of the rates of return, and the difference between these two mean values increases with the standard deviation of returns.

Over the period from 1926 to 1991, all common stocks returned 10.4 percent a year, compounded annually. To compare this to other investments, the results show that common stock experienced a risk premium of 6.5 percent and inflation-adjusted real returns of 7.0 percent per year. In contrast to all common stocks, the small capitalization stocks (which are represented by the smallest 20 percent of stocks listed on the NYSE measured by market value) experienced a geometric mean return of 12.1 percent, which was a premium compared to all common stocks of 1.5 percent.

Although common stocks and small capitalization stocks experienced higher rates of return than the other asset groups, their returns were also more volatile as measured by the standard deviations of annual returns.

Long-term U.S. government bonds experienced a 4.8 percent annual return, a real return of 1.6 percent, and a maturity premium (compared to Treasury bills) of 1.1 percent. Although the returns on these bonds were lower than those on stocks, they were also far less volatile.

The annual compound rate of return on long-term corporate bonds was 5.4 percent, the default premium compared to U.S. government bonds was 0.5 percent, and the inflation-adjusted return was 2.2 percent. Although corporate bonds provided a higher return, as one would expect, the volatility of corporate bonds was slightly lower than that experienced by long-term government bonds.

The nominal return on U.S. Treasury bills was 3.7 percent a year, whereas the inflation-adjusted return was 0.5 percent. The standard deviation of nominal returns

---

[13] The original study was Roger G. Ibbotson and Rex A. Sinquefield, "Stocks, Bonds, Bills, and Inflation: Year-by-Year Historical Returns (1926–1974)," *Journal of Business* 49, no. 1 (January 1976): 11–47. Although this study was updated in several monographs, the current update is contained in *Stocks, Bonds, Bills, and Inflation: 1992 Yearbook* (Chicago: Ibbotson Associates, 1992).

TABLE 2.6

Basic and Derived Series: Historical Highlights (1926–1991)

Series	Annual Geometric Mean Rate of Return	Arithmetic Mean of Annual Returns	Standard Deviation of Annual Returns
Common stocks	10.4%	12.4%	20.8%
Small capitalization stocks	12.1	17.5	35.3
Long-term corporate bonds	5.4	5.7	8.5
Long-term government bonds	4.8	5.1	8.6
U.S. Treasury bills	3.7	3.8	3.4
Consumer Price Index	3.1	3.2	4.7
Equity risk premium	6.5	8.3	20.5
Small stock premium	1.5	4.5	18.6
Default premium	0.5	0.6	2.9
Maturity premium	1.1	1.3	7.9
Common stock—inflation adjusted	7.0	9.1	20.9
Small capitalization stock— inflation adjusted	8.7	13.9	34.6
Long-term corporate bonds— inflation adjusted	2.2	2.7	9.9
Long-term government bonds—inflation adjusted	1.6	2.1	10.1
U.S. Treasury bills— inflation adjusted	0.5	0.6	4.3

for T-bills was the lowest of the series examined, which reflects the low risk of these securities and is consistent with the lowest rate of return.

This study reported the rates of return, return premiums, and risk measures on various asset groups in the United States. The rates of return were generally consistent with the uncertainty of annual returns as measured by the standard deviations of annual returns.

WORLD PORTFOLIO PERFORMANCE

Expanding this analysis from domestic to global securities, Ibbotson, Siegel, and Love examined the performance of numerous assets, not only in the United States, but in the world.[14] Specifically, for the period from 1960 to 1984 they constructed a value-weighted portfolio of stocks, bonds, cash (the equivalent of U.S. T-bills), real estate, and precious metals from the United States, Northern and Western Europe, Japan, Hong Kong, Singapore, Canada, and Australia. They computed annual returns, risk measures, and correlations among the returns for alternative assets. Table 2.7 shows the geometric and arithmetic average annual rates of return and the standard deviations of returns for that period.

[14] Roger G. Ibbotson, Laurence B. Siegel, and Kathryn S. Love, "World Wealth: Market Values and Returns," *Journal of Portfolio Management* 12, no. 1 (Fall 1985): 4–23.

TABLE 2.7

World Capital Market: Total Annual Returns (1960–1984)

	Compound Return[a]	Arithmetic Mean	Standard Deviation[b]	Coefficient of Variation[c]
Equities				
United States	8.81%	10.20%	16.89%	1.66
Foreign				
Europe	7.83	8.94	15.58	1.74
Asia	15.14	18.42	30.74	1.67
Other	8.14	10.21	20.88	2.04
Equities total	9.08	10.21	15.28	1.46
Bonds				
United States				
Corporate[d]	5.35	5.75	9.63	1.67
Government	5.91	6.10	6.43	1.05
United States total	5.70	5.93	7.16	1.21
Foreign				
Corporate domestic	8.35	8.58	7.26	0.85
Government domestic	5.79	6.04	7.41	1.23
Crossborder	7.51	7.66	5.76	0.75
Foreign total	6.80	7.01	6.88	0.98
Bonds total	6.36	6.50	5.56	0.86
Cash equivalents				
United States	6.49	6.54	3.22	0.49
Foreign	6.00	6.23	7.10	1.14
Cash total	6.38	6.42	2.92	0.45
Real estate[e]				
Business	8.49	8.57	4.16	0.49
Residential	8.86	8.93	3.77	0.42
Farms	11.86	12.13	7.88	0.65
Real estate total	9.44	9.49	3.45	0.36
Metals				
Silver	9.14	20.51	75.34	3.67
Bold	9.08	12.62	29.87	2.37
Metals total	9.11	12.63	29.69	2.35
U.S. market wealth portfolio	8.63	8.74	5.06	0.58
Foreign market wealth portfolio	7.76	8.09	8.48	1.05
World market wealth portfolio				
Excluding metals	8.34	8.47	5.24	0.62
Including metals	8.39	8.54	5.80	0.68
U.S. inflation rate	5.24	5.30	3.60	0.68

[a]Equal to geometric mean.

[b]Standard deviation from arithmetic mean.

[c]Coefficient of variation equals standard deviation/arithmetic mean.

[d]Including preferred stock.

[e]United States only.

Source: Robert G. Ibbotson, Laurence B. Siegel, and Kathryn S. Love, "World Wealth: Market Values and Returns," *Journal of Portfolio Management* 12, no. 1 (Fall 1985): 4–23. Reprinted with permission.

ASSET RETURN AND RISK

The results in Table 2.7 generally confirm the expected relationship between annual rates of return and the risk of these securities. The riskier assets, those that had higher standard deviations, experienced the highest returns. For example, silver had the highest arithmetic mean rate of return (20.51 percent), but also the largest standard deviation (75.34 percent), whereas risk-free U.S. cash equivalents (T-bills) had low returns (6.49 percent) and the smallest standard deviation (3.22 percent). The data amassed by Ibbotson et al. could be used to assess the relative risk of assets in a portfolio, as well as risk and return values for each asset.

RELATIVE ASSET RISK

Calculating the coefficients of variation (CVs), which measure relative variability, Ibbotson et al. found a wide range of values. The lowest CVs were experienced by the cash equivalents (T-bills) and real estate investments. Silver had the highest CV value because of its very large standard deviation, and corporate bonds the next highest because of a relatively small mean return. The CVs for stocks ranged from 1.46 to 2.04, with U.S. stocks about in the middle (1.66). Finally, the world market portfolios had rather low CVs (0.62 and 0.68), demonstrating the benefits of global diversification.

CORRELATIONS BETWEEN ASSET RETURNS

Table 2.8 is a correlation matrix of selected U.S. and world assets. The first column shows that U.S. equities showed reasonably high correlation with European equities (0.640) and other foreign equities (0.807), but low correlation with Asian equities (0.237). Also, U.S. equities showed a negative correlation with U.S. government bonds (-0.006), farm real estate (-0.171), and gold (-0.088). You will recall from our earlier discussion that you can use this information to build a diversified portfolio by combining those assets with low positive or negative correlations.

ART AND ANTIQUES

Unlike financial securities, where the results of transactions are reported daily, art and antique markets are very fragmented and lack any formal transaction reporting system. This makes it difficult to gather data. The best-known series that attempt to provide information about the changing value of art and antiques were developed by Sotheby's, a major art auction firm. These value indexes cover 13 areas of art and antiques and a weighted aggregate series that is a combination of the 13.

Reilly examined these series for the period from 1975 to 1991 and computed rates of return, measures of risk, and the correlations among the various art and antique series.[15] Table 2.9 shows these data and compares them with returns for 1-year Treasury bonds, the Lehman Brothers Government/Corporate Bond Index, the Standard & Poor's 500 Stock Index, and the annual inflation rate.

These results vary to such a degree that it is not possible to generalize about the performance of art and antiques. As shown, the average annual compound rates of return (measured by the geometric means) ranged from a high of 16.8 percent (modern paintings) to a low of 9.99 percent (English silver). Similarly, the standard deviations varied from 21.67 percent (Impressionist–Post Impressionist Paintings) to 8.74 percent (American furniture). The relative risk measures (the coefficients of variation) varied from a high of 1.33 (continental silver) to a low value of 0.71 (English furniture). The annual rankings likewise changed over time.

---

[15] Frank K. Reilly, "Risks and Returns on Art and Antiques: The Sotheby's Indexes," Eastern Finance Association Meeting, April 1987. The results reported are a summary of the study results and have been updated through September 1991.

TABLE 2.8   **Correlation Matrix of World Capital Market Security Returns**

	U.S. Equities	Total U.S. Bonds	Total Real Estate	U.S. Market Portfolio	World Market Including Metals
U.S. equities	1.000	−0.166	0.054	0.917	0.757
Europe equities	0.640	−0.045	0.156	0.605	0.706
Asia equities	0.237	−0.007	0.033	0.209	0.351
Other equities	0.807	−0.160	0.288	0.754	0.753
Foreign total: equities	0.672	−0.074	0.129	0.626	0.732
World total: equities	0.964	0.075	0.083	0.886	0.805
U.S. corporate bonds and preferred stock	0.323	0.962	−0.123	0.393	0.207
U.S. government bonds	−0.006	0.967	−0.040	0.152	−0.023
U.S. total: bonds	0.166	1.000	−0.082	0.284	0.093
Foreign domestic corporation bonds	0.050	0.180	0.164	0.153	0.380
Foreign domestic government bonds	−0.024	0.192	0.303	0.171	0.426
Foreign total: bonds	0.052	0.242	0.256	0.191	0.429
World total: bonds	0.124	0.646	0.172	0.288	0.389
U. S. cash equivalents (T-bills)	0.079	−0.247	0.405	0.130	−0.004
Foreign cash equivalents	−0.386	−0.192	0.399	−0.233	0.105
World total: cash equivalents	−0.238	−0.141	0.529	0.103	0.046
Business real estate	0.164	0.192	0.518	0.394	0.390
Residential real estate	0.125	0.017	0.916	0.442	0.552
Farm real estate	−0.171	−0.274	0.570	−0.019	0.133
U.S. total: real estate	0.054	−0.082	1.000	0.371	0.531
Gold	−0.088	−0.280	0.684	0.104	0.427
Silver	0.116	0.153	0.580	0.291	0.283
World total: metals	−0.086	−0.282	0.696	0.111	0.427
U.S. market wealth portfolio	0.917	0.284	0.371	1.000	0.873
Foreign market wealth portfolio	0.510	0.080	0.177	0.533	0.727
World market wealth portfolio (excluding metals)	0.861	0.231	0.332	0.925	0.924
World market wealth portfolio (including metals)	0.757	0.093	0.531	0.873	1.000

Source: Adapted from Roger G. Ibbotson, Laurence B. Siegel, and Kathryn S. Love, "World Wealth: Market Values and Returns," *Journal of Portfolio Management* 12, no. 1 (Fall 1985) 19–21. Reprinted with permission.

Although there was a wide range of mean returns and risk, the risk–return plot in Figure 2.6 indicates that there was a fairly consistent relationship between risk and return during this 16-year period. Comparing the art and antique results to the bond and stock indexes indicates that the stocks and bonds experienced results in the middle of the art and antique series.

Analysis of the correlation matrix of these assets in Table 2.10 using annual rates of returns reveals several important relationships. First, the correlations among alternative antique and art categories (e.g., paintings and furniture) vary substantially from over 0.90 to some negative correlations. Second, the correlations between rates of return on art/antiques and bonds are generally negative. Third, the correlations of art/antiques with stocks are typically small positive values. Finally, the correlation of art and antiques with percentage changes in the CPI (i.e., the rate of inflation) indicates that several of the categories have been fairly good inflation hedges since they were

TABLE 2.9

Average Annual Rates of Return and Risk Measures for Sotheby's Art and Antique Indexes, Common Stock and Bond Indexes, and Inflation: 1976–1991 (September Year End)

	Mean Rates of Return		Standard	Coefficients
	Arithmetic	Geometric	Deviation	of Variation
Old masters paintings	14.66	13.19	18.50	1.26
19th century European paintings	13.72	12.44	16.91	1.23
Impressionist–post impressionist paintings	18.41	16.25	21.67	1.18
Modern paintings	18.84	16.80	21.29	1.13
American paintings	17.34	16.20	16.07	0.93
Continental art	18.47	16.59	21.38	1.16
Continental ceramics	16.81	12.32	14.20	1.07
Chinese ceramics	10.97	15.50	18.08	1.08
English silver	10.60	9.99	14.27	1.30
Continental silver	10.60	10.76	14.14	1.33
American furniture	11.09	12.39	8.74	0.79
French and continental furniture	12.85	12.39	10.24	0.80
English furniture	15.44	14.92	10.92	0.71
Fixed, weight index	15.79	15.04	12.97	0.82
Unweighted index	19.80	14.31	10.52	0.71
Value weighted index	19.70	14.01	12.24	0.83
1-year Treasury bond	8.17	8.30	2.62	0.32
LBGC bond index	10.91	10.54	9.24	0.85
S&P 500	16.27	14.92	17.57	1.08
Consumer Price Index	5.97	5.93	3.25	0.54

Source: Adapted from Frank K. Reilly, "Risk and Return on Art and Antiques: The Sotheby's Indexes," Eastern Finance Association Meeting, May 1987. (Updated through September 1991).

positively correlated with inflation (e.g., Chinese ceramics), and they were clearly superior inflation hedges compared to bonds and common stocks.[16] This would suggest that a properly diversified portfolio of art, antiques, stocks, and bonds might provide a fairly low-risk portfolio. It is important to reiterate the earlier observation that most art and antiques are considered to be quite illiquid and the transaction costs are fairly high compared to the financial assets we have discussed.

SUMMARY

Investors who want the broadest range of choices in investments must consider foreign stocks and bonds in addition to domestic financial assets. Many foreign securities offer investors higher risk-adjusted returns than domestic securities. In addition, the low positive or negative correlations between foreign and U.S. securities makes them ideal for building a diversified portfolio.

Figure 2.7 summarizes the risk and return characteristics of the investment alternatives described in this chapter. Some of the differences are due to unique factors that we discussed. Foreign bonds are considered riskier than domestic bonds because of

---

[16] These results for stocks are very consistent with several prior studies that likewise found a negative relationship between inflation and rates of return on stocks which indicates that common stocks have generally been very poor inflation hedges. In this regard, see Eugene F. Fama, "Stock Returns, Real Activity, Inflation and Money," *American Economic Review* 71, no. 2 (June 1981): 545–565; and Jeffrey Jaffe and Gershon Mandelker, "The 'Fisher Effect' for Risky Assets: An Empirical Investigation," *Journal of Finance* 31, no. 2 (June 1976): 447–458.

FIGURE 2.6   **Geometric Mean Rates of Return and Standard Deviation for Sotheby's Indexes, S&P 500, Bond Market Series, 1-Year Bonds, and Inflation: 1976–1991**

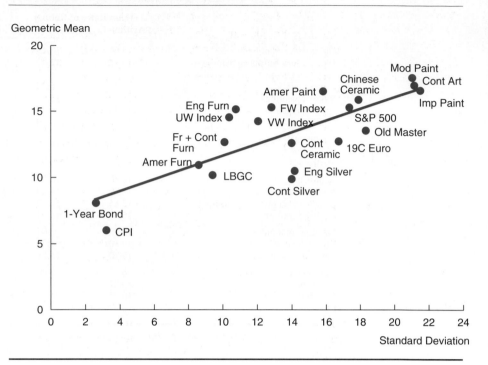

the unavoidable uncertainty due to exchange rate risk and country risk. The same is true for foreign and domestic common stocks. Investments such as art, antiques, coins, and stamps require very heavy liquidity risk premiums. You should divide consideration of real estate investments between your personal home, on which you do not expect as high a return because of nonmonetary factors, and commercial real estate, which requires a higher return due to cash flow uncertainty and illiquidity.

Studies on the historical rates of return for common stocks and other investment alternatives (including bonds, commodities, real estate, foreign securities, and art and antiques) point toward two generalizations:[17]

1. A positive relationship typically holds between the rate of return earned on an asset and the variability of its historical rate of return. This is expected in a world of risk-averse investors, who require higher rates of return to compensate for more uncertainty.

2. The correlation among rates of return for selected alternative investments is typically quite low, especially for U.S and foreign stocks and bonds and between

---

[17] A recent book that provides an excellent discussion of global investing and contains extensive analysis of returns and risks for alternative asset classes, is Roger G. Ibbotson and Gary P. Brinson, *Global Investing* (New York: McGraw-Hill, 1992).

TABLE 2.10 **Correlation Coefficients Among Annual Rates of Return for Art, Antiques, Stocks, Bonds, and Inflation 1976–1991 (September Year End)**

	Old Mast.	19C Euro.	Impr. Pt.-Im.	Mod. Paint.	Cont. Art	Amer. Paint.	Cont. Ceram.	Chin. Ceram.	Engl. Silver	Cont. Silver	Amer. Furn.	Fr.&Cont. Furn.	Engl. Furn.	Fix Wt. Index	Unwtd. Index	Pr. W. Index	1-yr. T Bond	LBGC Bond	S&P 500	CPI
Old masters paintings	*																			
19-century European paintings	0.948	*																		
Impressionist–post impressionist paintings	0.442	0.467	*																	
Modern paintings	0.403	0.473	0.969	*																
Continental art	0.780	0.652	0.566	0.476	*															
American paintings	0.599	0.515	0.464	0.386	0.674	*														
Continental ceramics	0.589	0.584	0.200	0.191	0.227	0.498	*													
Chinese ceramics	0.447	0.419	0.279	0.267	0.279	0.561	0.708	*												
English silver	0.394	0.497	0.117	0.186	0.057	-0.012	0.295	0.098	*											
Continental silver	0.628	0.709	0.354	0.404	0.301	0.054	0.600	0.270	0.729	*										
American furniture	-0.176	-0.204	0.185	0.165	-0.071	0.012	-0.251	-0.167	0.122	-0.168	*									
French and continental furniture	0.648	0.755	0.116	0.192	0.310	0.143	0.622	0.459	0.541	0.764	-0.379	*								
English furniture	0.234	0.328	0.548	0.605	-0.016	0.433	0.471	0.449	0.105	0.222	0.043	0.178	*							
Fixed, weight index	0.817	0.835	0.851	0.838	0.727	0.637	0.536	0.525	0.359	0.622	0.001	0.525	0.550	*						
Unweighted index	0.859	0.872	0.740	0.731	0.700	0.677	0.666	0.611	0.450	0.686	-0.017	0.620	0.540	0.977	*					
Price weighted index	0.828	0.826	0.791	0.776	0.733	0.723	0.610	0.593	0.397	0.611	0.000	0.536	0.555	0.984	0.990	*				
1-year Treasury bond	-0.331	-0.376	-0.089	-0.131	0.159	-0.109	-0.570	-0.269	-0.103	-0.302	0.130	-0.248	-0.612	-0.269	-0.309	-0.258	*			
LBGC bond index	-0.169	-0.182	-0.280	-0.308	-0.173	-0.308	-0.422	-0.318	0.052	-0.210	-0.159	-0.328	-0.351	-0.332	-0.366	-0.359	-0.080	*		
S&P 500	0.038	-0.026	-0.082	-0.134	-0.097	-0.127	-0.041	-0.015	-0.031	-0.058	0.144	-0.113	-0.030	-0.075	-0.080	-0.121	-0.224	0.127	*	
Consumer Price Index	0.008	0.010	0.064	0.056	0.161	0.283	0.290	0.462	0.127	0.085	0.118	0.338	-0.024	0.141	0.224	0.227	0.496	-0.647	-0.322	*

Source: Frank K. Reilly, "Risk and Return on Art and Antiques," (July, 1992).

FIGURE 2.7   **Alternative Investments—Risk and Return Characteristics**

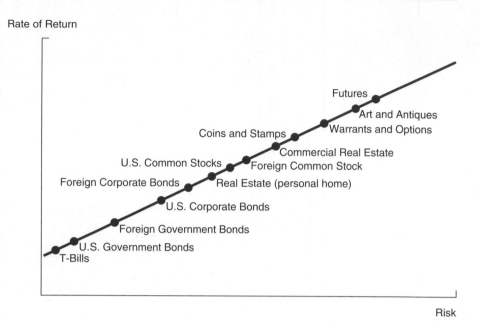

these financial assets and real assets, as represented by art and antiques. This confirms the advantage of diversification among investments.

In addition to describing many direct investments, such as stocks and bonds, we also discussed investment companies that allow investors to buy investments indirectly. These can be very important to investors who want to take advantage of professional management but also want instant diversification with a limited amount of funds. With $10,000, you may not be able to buy many individual stocks or bonds, but you could acquire shares in a mutual fund, which would give you a share of a diversified portfolio that might contain 100 to 150 different stocks or bonds.

Now that we know the range of domestic and foreign investment alternatives, our next task is to learn about the markets in which they are bought and sold. That is the objective of the next chapter. The discussion in Chapter 3 will help us to understand how markets match buyers and sellers of investments. Later chapters will describe how investors evaluate the risk and return characteristics of alternative investments to build diversified portfolios that are consistent with their objectives.

QUESTIONS

1. What are the advantages of investing in the common stock rather than corporate bonds of the same company? Compare the certainty of returns for a bond with those for a common stock. Draw a line graph to demonstrate the pattern of returns you would envision for each of these assets over time.

2. Discuss three factors that cause U.S. investors to consider including global securities in their portfolios.

3. Discuss why international diversification reduces portfolio risk. Specifically, why would you expect low correlation in the rates of return for domestic and foreign securities?

4. Discuss why you would expect a *difference* in the correlation of returns between securities from the United States and from alternative countries (e.g., Japan, Canada, South Africa).

5. Would you expect any *change* in the correlations between U.S. stocks and the stocks for different countries? For example, discuss whether you would expect the correlation between U.S. and Japanese stock returns to change over time.

6. If you wanted to invest only in U.S. bonds, what proportion of the world bond market would you be ignoring?

7. When you invest in Japanese or German bonds, what are the major additional risks you must consider besides yield changes within the country?

8. Some investors believe that international investing introduces additional risks. Discuss these risks and how they can affect your return. Give an example.

9. What alternatives to direct investment in foreign stocks are available to investors?

10. You are a wealthy individual in a high tax bracket. Why might you consider investing in a municipal bond rather than a straight corporate bond, even though the promised yield on the municipal bond is lower?

11. You can acquire convertible bonds from a rapidly growing company or from a utility. Speculate on which convertible bond would have the lower yield and discuss the reason for this difference.

12. What is an REIT? Describe three alternative types of REITs.

13. Compare the liquidity of an investment in raw land with that of an investment in common stock. Be specific as to why and how they differ. (Hint: Begin by defining *liquidity*.)

14. What are stock warrants and call options? How do they differ?

15. Discuss why financial analysts consider antiques and art to be illiquid investments. Why do they consider coins and stamps to be more liquid than antiques and art? What must an investor typically do to sell a collection of art and antiques? Briefly contrast this procedure to the sale of a portfolio of stocks that are listed on the New York Stock Exchange.

16. You have a fairly large portfolio of U.S. stocks and bonds. You meet a financial planner at a social gathering who suggests that you should diversify your portfolio by investing in gold. Discuss whether the correlation results in Table 2.8 support this suggestion.

17. You are an avid collector/investor of American paintings. Based on the results in Table 2.9, describe your risk–return results during the period from 1976 to 1991 compared to U.S. common stocks.

PROBLEMS

1. Calculate the current horizon (maturity) premium on U.S. government securities based on data in *The Wall Street Journal*. The long-term security should have a maturity of at least 20 years.

2. Using a source of international statistics, compare the percentage change in the following economic data for Japan, Germany, Canada, and the United States for a recent year. What were the differences, and which country or countries differed most from the United States?
    a. Aggregate output (GDP)
    b. Inflation
    c. Money supply growth

3. Using a recent edition of *Barron's*, examine the weekly percentage change in the stock price indexes for Japan, Germany, Italy, and the United States. For each of three weeks, which foreign series moved most closely with the U.S. series? Which series diverged most from the U.S. series? Discuss these results as they relate to international diversification.

4. Using published sources (e.g., *The Wall Street Journal, Barron's, Federal Reserve Bulletin*), look up the exchange rate for U.S. dollars with Japanese yen for each of the past 10 years (you can use an average for the year or a specific time period each year). Based on these exchange rates, compute and discuss the yearly exchange rate effect on an investment in Japanese stocks by a U.S. investor. Discuss the impact of this exchange rate effect on the risk of Japanese stocks for a U.S. investor.

5. *CFA Examination 1 (June 1980)* The following information is available concerning the historical risk and return relationships in the U.S. capital markets:

U.S. Capital Markets Total Annual Returns, 1947–1978

Investment Category	Arithmetic Mean	Geometric Mean	Standard Deviation of Return[a]
Common stocks	11.80%	10.30%	18.0%
Preferred stocks	3.30	2.90	9.2
Treasury bills	3.53	3.51	2.1
Long government bonds	2.60	2.40	6.2
Long corporate bonds	2.40	2.20	6.7
Real estate	8.19	8.14	3.5

[a]Based on arithmetic mean.

Source: Adapted from R. G. Ibbotson and C. L. Fall, "The U.S. Market Wealth Portfolio," *Journal of Portfolio Management.*

a. Explain why the geometric and arithmetic mean returns are not equal and whether one or the other may be more useful for investment decision making. [5 minutes]

b. For the time period indicated, rank these investments on a risk-adjusted basis from most to least desirable. Explain your rationale. [6 minutes]

c. Assume the returns in these series are normally distributed.
   1. Calculate the range of returns that an investor would have expected to achieve 95 percent of the time from holding common stocks. [4 minutes]
   2. Suppose an investor holds real estate for this time period. Determine the probability of at least breaking even on this investment. [5 minutes]

d. Assume you are holding a portfolio composed entirely of real estate. Discuss the justification, if any, for adopting a mixed asset portfolio by adding long-term government bonds. [5 minutes]

6. You are given the following long-run annual rates of return for alternative investment instruments:

U.S. government T-bills	6.50%
Common stock	12.50
Long-term corporate bonds	10.00
Long-term government bonds	15.75
Small capitalization common stock	14.60

a. On the basis of these returns, compute the following:
  1. The common stock risk premium
  2. The small firm stock risk premium
  3. The horizon (maturity) premium
  4. The default premium
b. The annual rate of inflation during this period was 5 percent. Compute the real rate of return on these investment alternatives.

REFERENCES

Beidleman, Carl, ed. *The Handbook of International Investing.* Chicago: Probus Publishing, 1987.

Brick, John R., H. Kent Baker, and John A. Haslem, eds. *Financial Markets Instruments and Concepts.* 2d ed. Reston, Va: Reston Publishing, 1986.

Cholerton, Kenneth, Pierre Pieraerts, and Bruno Solnik. "Why Invest in Foreign Currency Bonds?" *Journal of Portfolio Management* 12, no. 4 (Summer 1986).

Elton, Edwin J. and Martin J. Gruber, eds. *Japanese Capital Markets* (New York: Harper & Row Publishers, 1990).

European Bond Commission, *The European Bond Markets* (Chicago: Probus Publishing Company, 1989).

Fabozzi, Frank J., ed. *The Japanese Bond Markets* (Chicago: Probus Publishing Company, 1990).

Fisher, Lawrence, and James H. Lorie, *A Half Century of Returns on Stocks and Bonds.* Chicago: University of Chicago Graduate School of Business, 1977.

Grabbe, J. Orlin. *International Financial Markets.* New York: Elsevier Science Publishing, 1986.

Greshin, Adam M., and Margaret Durasz Hadzima. "International Bond Investing and Portfolio Management." In *The Handbook of Fixed-Income Securities,* 3d ed., edited by Frank J. Fabozzi. Homewood, Ill.: Business One Irwin, 1991.

Ibbotson, Roger G., and Gary P. Brinson. *Investment Markets.* New York: McGraw-Hill, 1989.

Ibbotson, Roger G., and Gary P. Brinson. *Global Investing.* New York: McGraw-Hill, 1992.

Ibbotson, Roger G., Laurence B. Siegel, and Kathryn S. Love. "World Wealth: Market Values and Returns." *Journal of Portfolio Management* 12, no. 1 (Fall 1985).

Lessard, Donald R. "International Diversification." In *The Financial Analyst's Handbook,* 2d ed., edited by Sumner N. Levine. Homewood, Ill.: Dow Jones-Irwin, 1988.

Newton, Brian K., and Paul B. Chan, "Valuation and Risk Analysis of International Bonds." In *Handbook of Fixed-Income Securities,* 3d ed., edited by Frank J. Fabozzi. Homewood, Ill.: Business One Irwin, 1991.

Robinson, Anthony W., and Stephen W. Glover. "International Fixed-Income Markets and Securities." In *The Financial Analyst's Handbook,* 2d ed., edited by Sumner N. Levine. Homewood, Ill.: Dow Jones-Irwin, 1988.

Rosenberg, Michael R. "International Fixed-Income Investing: Theory and Practice." In *The Handbook of Fixed-Income Securities,* 3d ed., edited by Frank J. Fabozzi. Homewood, Ill.: Business One Irwin, 1991.

Siegel, Laurence B. and Paul D. Kaplan, "Stocks, Bonds, Bills, and Inflation Around the World." In Frank J. Fabozzi, ed. *Managing Institutional Assets* (New York: Harper & Row, 1990).

Solnik, Bruno. *International Investments.* 2d ed. Reading, Mass.: Addison-Wesley Publishing, 1991.

Solnik, Bruno, and Bernard Noetzlin. "Optimal International Asset Allocation." *Journal of Portfolio Management* 9, no. 1 (Fall 1982).

Van der Does, Rein W. "Investing in Foreign Securities." In *The Financial Analyst's Handbook,* 2d ed., edited by Sumner N. Levine. Homewood, Ill.: Dow Jones-Irwin, 1988.

Viner, Aron. *Inside Japanese Financial Markets* (Homewood, Ill.: Dow Jones-Irwin, 1988).

Wilson, Richard S. *Corporate Senior Securities.* Chicago: Probus Publishing, 1987.

Wilson, Richard S., and Frank J. Fabozzi. *The New Corporate Bond Market.* Chicago: Probus Publishing, 1990.

APPENDIX 2A	COVARIANCE AND CORRELATION

COVARIANCE

Because most students have been exposed to the concepts of covariance and correlation, the following discussion is set forth in intuitive terms with examples to help the reader recall the concepts.[1]

Covariance is an absolute measure of the extent to which two sets of numbers move together over time, that is, how often they move up or down together. In this regard *move together* means they are generally above their means or below their means at the same time. Covariance between i and j is defined as:

$$COV_{ij} = \frac{\Sigma(i - \bar{i})(j - \bar{j})}{N}$$

If we define $(i - \bar{i})$ as i' and $(j - \bar{j})$ as j', then

$$COV_{ij} = \frac{\Sigma i'j'}{N}$$

Obviously, if both numbers are consistently above or below their individual means at the same time, their products will be positive, and the average will be a large positive value. In contrast, if the i value is below its mean when the j value is above its mean or vice versa, their products will be large negative values, giving negative covariance.

Table 2A.1 should make this clear. In this example the two series generally moved together, so they showed positive covariance. As noted, this is an *absolute* measure of their relationship and, therefore, can range from $+\infty$ to $-\infty$. Note that the covariance of a variable with itself is its *variance.*

CORRELATION

To obtain a relative measure of a given relationship we use the correlation coefficient (r_{ij}), which is a measure of the relationship:

$$r_{ij} = \frac{COV_{ij}}{\sigma_i\sigma_j}$$

---

[1] A more detailed, rigorous treatment of the subject can be found in any standard statistics text, including S. Christian Albright, *Statistics for Business and Economics* (New York: Macmillan, 1987), 63–67.

TABLE 2A.1

Calculation of Covariance

Observation	i	j	$i - \bar{i}$	$j - \bar{j}$	$i'j'$
1	3	8	-4	-4	16
2	6	10	-1	-2	2
3	8	14	$+1$	$+2$	2
4	5	12	-2	0	0
5	9	13	$+2$	$+1$	2
6	11	15	$+4$	$+3$	12
Σ	42	72			34
Mean	7	12			
Cov_{ij}	$= \dfrac{34}{6} = +5.67$				

You will recall from your introductory statistics course that:

$$\sigma_i = \sqrt{\frac{\Sigma(i - \bar{i})^2}{N}}$$

If the two series move completely together, then the covariance would equal $\sigma_i\sigma_j$ and:

$$\frac{COV_{ij}}{\sigma_i\sigma_j} = 1.0$$

The correlation coefficient would equal unity in this case, and we would say the two series are perfectly correlated. Because we know that:

$$r_{ij} = \frac{COV_{ij}}{\sigma_i\sigma_j}$$

we also know that $COV_{ij} = r_{ij}\sigma_i\sigma_j$. This relationship may be useful when computing the standard deviation of a portfolio, because, in many instances, the relationship between two securities is stated in terms of the correlation coefficient rather than the covariance.

Continuing the example given in Table 2A.1, the standard deviations are computed in Table 2A.2, as is the correlation between i and j. As shown, the two standard deviations are rather large and similar, but not exactly the same. Finally, when the positive covariance is normalized by the product of the two standard deviations, the results indicate a correlation coefficient of 0.898, which is obviously quite large and close to 1.00. Apparently, these two series are highly related.

PROBLEMS

1. As a new analyst, you have calculated the following annual rates of return for both Alpha-Omega Corporation and Beta-Tau Industries.

TABLE 2A.2

Calculation of Correlation Coefficient

Observation	$i - \bar{i}$[a]	$(i - \bar{i})^2$	$j - \bar{j}$[a]	$(j - \bar{j})^2$
1	−4	16	−4	16
2	−1	1	−2	4
3	+1	1	+2	4
4	−2	4	0	0
5	+2	4	+1	1
6	+4	16	+3	9
		42		34

$$\sigma_i^2 = 42/6 = 7.00 \qquad \sigma_j^2 = 34/6 = 5.67$$
$$\sigma_i = \sqrt{7.00} = 2.65 \qquad \sigma_j = \sqrt{5.67} = 2.38$$
$$r_{ij} = \mathrm{Cov}_{ij}/\sigma_i\sigma_j = \frac{5.67}{(2.65)(2.38)} = \frac{5.67}{6.31} = 0.898$$

[a]From Table 2A.1.

Year	Alpha-Omega's Rate of Return	Beta-Tau's Rate of Return
1992	5	5
1993	12	15
1994	−11	5
1995	10	7
1996	12	−10

Your manager suggests that because these companies produce similar products, you should continue your analysis by computing their covariance. Show all calculations.

2. You decide to go an extra step by calculating the coefficient of correlation using the data provided in Problem 1 above. Prepare a table showing your calculations and explain how to interpret the results.

CHAPTER 3

ORGANIZATION AND FUNCTIONING OF SECURITIES MARKETS

In this chapter we will answer the following questions:

- What is the purpose and function of a market?
- What are the characteristics that determine the quality of a market?
- What is the difference between a primary and secondary capital market and how do these markets support each other?
- What are the national exchanges and how are the major security markets becoming linked (what is meant by "passing the book")?
- What are regional stock exchanges and the over-the-counter (OTC) market?
- What are the alternative market-making arrangements available on the exchanges and the OTC market?
- What are the major factors that have caused the significant changes in markets around the world during the past 10 to 15 years?
- What are some of the major changes in world capital markets expected over the next decade?

The stock market, the Dow Jones Industrials, and the bond market are part of our everyday experience. Each evening on the television news broadcasts we find out how stocks and bonds fared; each morning we read in our daily newspapers about expectations for a market rally or decline. Yet how the domestic and world capital markets actually function is imperfectly understood by most. To be a successful investor, you must know what financial markets are available around the world and how they operate.

In Chapter 1 we considered why individuals invest and what determines their required rate of return on investments. In Chapter 2 we learned about the numerous alternative investments available and why we should diversify with securities from around the world. This chapter takes a broader view of securities markets and then provides a detailed discussion of how the major stock markets function. We will conclude with a consideration of how global security markets are changing.

We begin with a discussion of securities markets and the characteristics of a good market. There are two components of the capital markets that are described: primary and secondary. Our main emphasis in this chapter is on the secondary stock market. We consider the national stock exchanges around the world and how these markets that are separated by geography and by time zones are becoming linked through a

24-hour market. We also consider regional stock markets and the over-the-counter market and then provide a detailed analysis of how alternative exchange markets operate. The final section considers numerous historical changes in financial markets since the mid-1970s, the additional current changes, and the significant future changes that are expected into the next century. These numerous changes in our securities markets will have a profound effect on what investments are available to you from around the world and how you buy and sell them.

WHAT IS A MARKET?

This section provides the necessary background for understanding different markets around the world and the changes that are occurring. The first part considers the general concept of a market and its function. The second part describes the characteristics that determine how well a particular market will fulfill its function. The third part of the section describes primary and secondary markets and how they interact and depend on one another.

A market is the means through which buyers and sellers are brought together to aid in the transfer of goods and/or services. Several aspects of this general definition seem worthy of emphasis. First, a market need not have a physical location. It is only necessary that the buyers and sellers can communicate regarding the relevant aspects of the transaction.

Second, the market does not necessarily own the goods or services involved. When we discuss what is required for a good market, you will note that ownership is not involved; the important criterion is the smooth, cheap transfer of goods and services. In most financial markets, those who establish and administer the market do not own the assets. They simply provide a physical location or an electronic system that allows potential buyers and sellers to interact, and they help the market to function by providing information and transfer facilities.

Finally, a market can deal in any variety of goods and services. For any commodity or service with a diverse clientele, a market should evolve to aid in the transfer of that commodity. Both buyers and sellers will benefit from the existence of a market. Basically, we take markets for granted because they are vital to a smooth-operating economy.

CHARACTERISTICS OF A GOOD MARKET

Throughout this book we will discuss markets for different investments such as stocks, bonds, options, and futures in the United States and throughout the world. We will refer to these markets using various terms of quality such as strong, active, liquid, or illiquid. The point is, there are many financial markets, but they are not all equal—some are active and liquid, others are relatively inactive, illiquid, and not very efficient in their operations. To appreciate these discussions you should be aware of the characteristics that investors look for when evaluating the quality of a market. In this section, we describe those characteristics.

One enters a market to buy or sell a good or service quickly at a price justified by the prevailing supply and demand. To determine the appropriate price, participants must have timely and accurate information on the volume and prices of past transactions and on all currently outstanding bids and offers. Therefore, one attribute of a good market is *availability of information*.

Another prime requirement, *liquidity* is the ability to buy or sell an asset (1) quickly and (2) at a known price, that is, a price not substantially different from the prices for prior transactions, assuming no new information is available. An asset's likelihood of being sold quickly, sometimes referred to as its *marketability,* is a necessary, but not a sufficient, condition for liquidity. The expected price should also be fairly certain, based on the recent history of transaction prices and current bid–ask quotes.[1]

A component of liquidity is *price continuity,* which means that prices do not change much from one transaction to the next, unless substantial new information becomes available. Suppose no new information is forthcoming, and the last transaction was at a price of $20; if the next trade were at 20⅛, the market would be considered reasonably continuous.[2] A continuous market without large price changes between trades is a characteristic of a liquid market.

A continuous market requires *depth,* which means that numerous potential buyers and sellers must be willing to trade at prices above and below the current market price. These buyers and sellers enter the market in response to changes in supply and/or demand and thereby prevent drastic price changes.

Another factor contributing to a good market is the *transaction cost.* Lower costs (as a percentage of the value of the trade) make for a more efficient market. An individual comparing the cost of a transaction between markets would choose one that charges 2 percent of the value of the trade compared with a market that charges 5 percent. Most microeconomic textbooks define an efficient market as one in which the cost of the transaction is minimal. This attribute is referred to as *internal efficiency.*

Finally, a buyer or seller wants the prevailing market price to adequately reflect all the available supply and demand factors in the market. If such conditions change as a result of new information, the price should change accordingly. Therefore, participants want prices to adjust quickly to new information regarding supply or demand, which means that prices reflect all available information about the asset. This attribute is referred to as *external efficiency* or *informational efficiency.* This attribute is discussed extensively in Chapter 6.

In summary, a good market for goods and services has the following characteristics:

1. Timely and accurate information is available on the price and volume of past transactions and on prevailing supply and demand.

2. It is liquid, meaning an asset can be bought or sold quickly (has marketability) at a price close to the prices for previous transactions, assuming no new information has been received (there is price continuity). In turn, price continuity requires depth, meaning a number of buyers and sellers are willing and able to enter the market at prices above and below current prices.

3. Transaction cost is low (which implies internal efficiency), meaning that all aspects of the transaction entail low costs, including the cost of reaching the market, the actual brokerage cost involved in the transaction, and the cost of transferring the asset.

---

[1]For a more formal discussion of liquidity and the impact of different market systems, see Sanford J. Grossman and Merton H. Miller, "Liquidity and Market Structure," *Journal of Finance* 43, no. 3 (July 1988): 617–633.

[2]The reader should be aware that common stocks are sold in increments of eighths of a dollar, or $0.125. Therefore, 20⅛ means the stock sold at $20.125 per share.

4.   Prices rapidly adjust to new information (which implies external, informational efficiency), meaning that the prevailing price reflects all available information regarding the asset.

ORGANIZATION OF THE SECURITIES MARKET

Before discussing the specific operation of the securities market, you need to understand its overall organization. The principal distinction is between *primary markets,* where new securities are sold, and *secondary markets,* where outstanding securities are bought and sold. Each of these markets is further divided based on the economic unit that issued the security (the federal government, states or municipalities, or corporations). The following discussion considers each of these major segments of the securities market with an emphasis on the individuals involved and the functions they perform.

PRIMARY CAPITAL MARKETS

The primary market is where new issues of bonds, preferred stock, or common stock are sold by government units, municipalities, or companies to acquire new capital.[3]

GOVERNMENT BOND ISSUES

All U.S. government bond issues are subdivided into three segments based on their original maturities. *Treasury bills* are negotiable, non-interest-bearing securities with original maturities of 1 year or less. They are currently issued for 3 months, 6 months, or 1 year. *Treasury notes* have original maturities of 2 to 10 years, and they have generally been issued with 2-, 3-, 4-, 5-, 7-, and 10-year terms. Finally, *Treasury bonds* have original maturities of more than 10 years.

To sell bills, notes, and bonds, the Treasury relies on Federal Reserve System auctions. In an auction held each week, institutions and some individuals submit bids for T-bills at prices below par that imply specific yields. (The bidding process and pricing is discussed in detail in Chapter 13.)

Treasury notes and bonds are likewise sold at auction by the Federal Reserve, but the bids state yields rather than prices. That is, the Treasury specifies how much it wants and when the notes or bonds will mature. After receiving the competitive bid yields, the Treasury determines the stop-out yield bid (the highest yield it will accept) based on the bids received and how much it wants to borrow. The Fed also receives many noncompetitive bids from investors who are willing to pay the average price of the accepted competitive tenders. All noncompetitive bids are accepted.

MUNICIPAL BOND ISSUES

New municipal bond issues are sold by one of three methods: competitive bid, negotiation, or private placement. Competitive bid sales typically involve sealed bids. The bond issue is sold to the bidding syndicate of underwriters that submits the bid with the lowest interest cost in accordance with the stipulations set forth by the issuer. Negotiated sales involve contractual arrangements between underwriters and issuers wherein the underwriter helps the issuer prepare the bond issue and set the price and has the exclusive right to sell the issue. Private placements involve the sale of a bond

---

[3]For an excellent set of studies related to the primary market, see Michael C. Jensen and Clifford W. Smith, Jr., eds., "Symposium on Investment Banking and the Capital Acquisition Process," *Journal of Financial Economics* 15, no. 1/2 (January-February 1986).

issue by the issuer directly to an investor or a small group of investors (usually institutions).

Note that two of the three methods require an underwriting function. Specifically, in a competitive bid or a negotiated transaction, the underwriter typically purchases the entire issue at a specified price, relieving the issuer from the risk and responsibility of selling and distributing the bonds. Subsequently, the underwriter sells the issue to the investing public. For municipal bonds, this underwriting function is performed by both investment banking firms and commercial banks.

The underwriting function can involve three services: origination, risk-bearing, and distribution. Origination involves the design of the bond issue and initial planning. To fulfill the risk-bearing function, the underwriter acquires the total issue at a price dictated by the competitive bid or through negotiation and accepts the responsibility and risk of reselling it for more than the purchase price. Distribution means selling it, typically with the help of a selling syndicate that includes other investment banking firms or commercial banks.

In a negotiated bid, the underwriter will carry out all three services. In a competitive bid, the issuer specifies the amount, maturities, coupons, and call features of the issue and the competing syndicates submit a bid for the entire issue that reflects the yields they estimate for the bonds. The issuer may have received advice from an investment firm on the desirable characteristics for a forthcoming issue, but this advice would have been on a fee basis and would not necessarily involve the ultimate underwriter who is responsible for the risk-bearing and distribution. Finally, a private placement involves no risk-bearing, but an investment banker could assist in locating potential buyers and negotiating the characteristics of the issue.

Municipal bonds are either general obligation (GO) bonds that are backed by the full taxing power of the municipality, or revenue bonds that are dependent on the revenues from a specific project that was funded by the issue such as a toll road, a hospital, or a sewage system. Commercial banks dominate the management of GO bond sales, and investment banking firms dominate revenue bond sales.

The municipal bond market has experienced two major trends during the recent decade. First, it has shifted toward negotiated bond issues versus competitive bids. Currently, about 75 percent of issues are negotiated deals. Second, there has been a shift toward revenue bonds, wherein almost 70 percent of the market is revenue issues. These two trends are related, because revenue issues tend to be negotiated underwritings. Although many states require that GO bond issues be sold through competitive bidding, they seldom impose such a requirement on revenue issues.[4]

CORPORATE ISSUES

Corporate securities include both bond and stock issues. Corporate bond issues are almost always sold through a negotiated arrangement with an investment banking firm that maintains a relationship with the issuing firm. In a global capital market that involves an explosion of new instruments, the origination function is becoming more important because the corporate chief financial officer (CFO) will probably not be completely familiar with the availability and issuing requirements of many new

---

[4]For a further discussion, see David S. Kidwell and Eric H. Sorensen, "Investment Banking and the Underwriting of New Municipal Issues," in *The Municipal Bond Handbook,* ed. by F. J. Fabozzi, S. G. Feldstein, I. M. Pollack, and F. G. Zarb (Homewood, Ill.: Dow Jones-Irwin, 1983).

instruments and the alternative capital markets around the world. Investment banking firms compete for underwriting business by creating new instruments that appeal to existing investors or a new set of investors. In either case, the expertise of the investment banker can help reduce the issuer's cost of new capital.

Once a stock or bond issue is specified, the underwriter will put together a syndicate of other major underwriters and a selling group for its distribution. For common stock, *new issues* are typically divided into two groups. The first and largest group is seasoned new issues that are offered by companies that have outstanding stock with existing public markets. For example, in 1992 General Motors sold a new issue of common stock. There was a large and active market for General Motors common stock, and the company decided to issue new shares, which increased the number of outstanding shares, to acquire new equity capital.

The second major category of new issues is referred to as *initial public offerings (IPOs),* wherein a company decides to sell common stock to the public for the first time. At the time of an IPO offering, there is no existing public market for the stock, that is, the company has been closely held. An example would be an IPO during 1992 by Franklin Quest Company, which prior to the offering had been a very successful privately held firm providing training seminars and products designed to improve time management. The purpose of the offering was to get additional capital to expand its operations into a number of new locations around the country.

New issues (seasoned or IPOs) are typically underwritten by investment bankers, who acquire the total issue from the company and sell the securities to interested investors. The underwriter gives advice to the corporation on the general characteristics of the issue, its pricing, and the timing of the offering. The underwriter also accepts the risk of selling the new issue after acquiring it from the corporation.[5]

RELATIONSHIPS WITH INVESTMENT BANKERS

The underwriting of corporate issues typically takes one of three forms: negotiated, competitive bids, or best-efforts arrangements. As noted, negotiated underwritings are the most common, and the procedure is the same as for municipal issues.

A corporation may also specify the type of securities to be offered (common stock, preferred stock, or bonds) and then solicit competitive bids from investment banking firms. This is rare for industrial firms but is typical for utilities, which may be required to sell the issue via a competitive bid by state laws. Although competitive bids typically reduce the cost of an issue, it also brings fewer services from the investment banker. The banker gives less advice, but still accepts the risk-bearing function by underwriting the issue and the distribution function.

Alternatively, an investment banker can agree to support an issue and sell it on a best-efforts basis. This is usually done with speculative new issues. In this arrangement, the investment banker does not underwrite the issue because it does not buy any securities. The stock is owned by the company, and the investment banker acts as a broker to sell whatever it can at a stipulated price. The investment banker earns a lower commission on such an issue than on an underwritten issue. With any of these arrange-

---

[5]For an extended discussion of the underwriting process, see Richard A. Brealey and Stewart C. Myers, *Principles of Corporate Finance,* 4th ed. (New York: McGraw-Hill, 1991), Chapter 15.

ments, the lead investment banker will typically form an underwriting syndicate of other investment bankers to spread the risk and also help in the sales. In addition, if the issue is very large, the lead underwriter and underwriting syndicate will form a selling group of smaller firms to help in the distribution.

INTRODUCTION OF RULE 415

The typical practice of negotiated arrangements involving numerous investment banking firms in syndicates and selling groups has changed with the introduction of Rule 415. This rule was introduced by the Securities and Exchange Commission (SEC) during 1982 on an experimental basis and subsequently approved on a permanent basis. Rule 415 basically allows large firms to register security issues and sell them piecemeal during the following 2 years. These issues are referred to as *shelf registrations* because after they are registered, the issues lie on the shelf and can be taken down and sold on short notice whenever it suits the issuing firm. As an example, General Electric could register an issue of 5 million shares of common stock during 1994 and sell a million shares in early 1994, another million late in 1994, 2 million shares in early 1995, and the rest in late 1995.

Each such offering can be made with little notice or paperwork by one underwriter or several. In fact, because there may be relatively few shares involved, the lead underwriter often handles the whole deal without a syndicate or will use only one or two other firms. This arrangement has benefited large corporations because it provides great flexibility, reduces registration fees and expenses, and allows firms issuing securities to request competitive bids from several investment banking firms.

On the other hand, some fear that shelf registrations do not allow investors enough time to examine the current status of the firm issuing the securities. Also, the follow-up offerings reduce the participation of small underwriters, because the underwriting syndicates are smaller and selling groups are almost nonexistent. Shelf registrations have typically been used for the sale of straight debentures rather than common stock or convertible issues.[6]

PRIVATE PLACEMENTS AND RULE 144A

Rather than a public sale using one of these arrangements, primary offerings can be sold privately. In such an arrangement, referred to as a *private placement,* the firm, with the assistance of an investment banker, designs an issue and sells it to a small group of institutions. The firm enjoys lower issuing costs, because it does not need to prepare the extensive registration statement required for a public offering. The institution that buys the issue typically benefits, because the issuing firm passes some of these cost savings on to the investor as a higher return. In fact, the institution should require a higher return because of the absence of any secondary market for these securities, which implies higher liquidity risk.

The private placement market has been changed dramatically by the introduction of Rule 144A by the SEC. This rule allows corporations, including non-U.S. firms, to place securities privately with large, sophisticated institutional investors without ex-

[6]For further discussion of Rule 415, see A. F. Ehbar, "Upheaval in Investment Banking," *Fortune,* August 23, 1982, 90; Beth McGoldrick, "Life with Rule 415," *Institutional Investor* 17, no. 2 (February 1983): 129–133; and Robert J. Rogowski and Eric H. Sorensen, "Deregulation in Investment Banking: Shelf Registrations, Structure and Performance," *Financial Management* 14, no. 1 (Spring 1985): 5–15.

tensive registration documents. The SEC intends to provide more financing alternatives for U.S. and non-U.S. firms and possibly increase the number, size, and liquidity of private placements.[7]

SECONDARY FINANCIAL MARKETS

The purpose of this section on secondary financial markets is to introduce this important topic. In this section, we consider the purpose and importance of secondary markets and provide an overview of the secondary markets for bonds, financial futures, and stocks. Next we consider national stock markets around the world. Finally we will discuss regional and over-the-counter stock markets and provide a detailed presentation on the functioning of stock exchanges.

Secondary markets permit trading in outstanding issues; that is, stocks or bonds already sold to the public are traded between current and potential owners. The proceeds from a sale in the secondary market do not go to the issuing unit (i.e, the government, municipality, or company) but rather to the current owner of the security.

WHY SECONDARY MARKETS ARE IMPORTANT

Before discussing the various segments of the secondary market, we must consider its overall importance. Because the secondary market involves the trading of securities initially sold in the primary market, it provides liquidity to the individuals who acquired these securities. After acquiring securities in the primary market, investors want to be able to sell them again in order to acquire other securities, buy a house, or go on a vacation. The primary market benefits greatly from the liquidity provided by the secondary market, because investors would hesitate to acquire securities in the primary market if they felt they could not subsequently sell them in the secondary market. Put another way, without an active secondary market, potential issuers of stocks or bonds would have to provide a much higher rate of return.

Secondary markets are also important to issuers because the prevailing market price of the securities are determined by action there. New issues of outstanding stocks or bonds that are to be sold in the primary market are based on prices and yields in the secondary market. As a result, capital costs for the government, municipalities, and corporations are determined by investor expectations and actions in the secondary market.

SECONDARY BOND MARKETS

The secondary market for bonds distinguishes among bonds issued by the federal government, municipalities, or corporations.

SECONDARY MARKETS FOR U.S. GOVERNMENT AND MUNICIPAL BONDS
U.S. government bonds are traded by bond dealers that specialize in either Treasury bonds or agency bonds. Treasury issues are bought or sold through a set of 35 primary dealers, including large banks in major cities such as New York and Chicago and some of the large investment banking firms (e.g., Merrill Lynch, First Boston, Morgan

---

[7]For a discussion of the rule and private placements, see Michael Siconolfi and Kevin Salwen, "SEC Ready to Ease Private-Placement Rules," *Wall Street Journal,* April 13, 1990, C1, C5. For a discussion of some reactions to Rule 144A, see Ida Picker, "Watch Out for Linda Quinn," *Institutional Investor* 23, no. 8 (July 1989): 77, 78, 83; John W. Milligan, "Two Cheers for 144A," *Institutional Investor* 24, no. 9 (July 1990): 117–119; and Sara Hanks, "SEC Ruling Creates a New Market," *Wall Street Journal,* May 16, 1990, A12.

Stanley). These institutions and other firms also make markets for government agency issues, but there is no formal set of dealers for agency securities.[8]

The major market makers in the secondary municipal bond market are banks and investment firms. Banks are active in municipal bond trading because they are involved in some of the underwriting of general obligation issues and they commit large parts of their investment portfolios to these securities. Also, many large investment firms have municipal bond departments that are active in underwriting and trading these issues.

SECONDARY CORPORATE BOND MARKETS

The secondary market for corporate bonds has two major segments: security exchanges and an over-the-counter (OTC) market. The major exchange for corporate bonds is the New York exchange. As of the end of 1992, almost 1,500 corporate bond issues were listed on this exchange with a combined par value of about $269 billion and a combined market value of approximately $228 billion.[9] On a typical day there are about 2,200 trades with a total volume of about $46 million. In addition, 232 issues are listed on the American Stock Exchange (AMEX) with par value of over $22 billion, a total market value of almost $17 billion, and typical daily trading volume in excess of $3.4 million.

All corporate bonds not listed on one of the exchanges are traded over-the-counter by dealers who buy and sell for their own accounts. In sharp contrast to what occurs for stocks where most of the trading takes place on the national exchanges such as the NYSE, in the United States most corporate bond trades occur on the OTC market. Virtually all large trades are carried out on the OTC market, even for bonds that are listed on an exchange.

The major bond dealers are the large investment banking firms that underwrite the issues such as Merrill Lynch, Goldman Sachs, Salomon Brothers, Kidder Peabody, and Morgan Stanley. Because of the limited trading in corporate bonds compared to the fairly active trading in government bonds, corporate bond dealers do not carry extensive inventories of specific issues. Instead, they hold a limited number of bonds desired by their clients and when someone wants to do a trade, they work more like brokers than dealers.

FINANCIAL FUTURES

In addition to the market for the bonds, recently a market has developed for futures contracts related to these bonds. These contracts allow the holder to buy or sell a specified amount of a given bond issue at a stipulated price. These futures contracts and the futures market are discussed in detail in Chapter 22.

EQUITY MARKETS

The secondary equity market is usually broken down into three major segments: (1) the major national exchanges, including the New York, the American, the Tokyo, and the London stock exchanges; (2) regional exchanges in such cities as Chicago,

---

[8]For a discussion of non-U.S. bond markets, see European Bond Commission, *The European Bond Markets* (Chicago: Probus Publishing, 1989); and Frank J. Fabozzi, ed., *The Japanese Bond Market* (Chicago: Probus Publishing, 1990).

[9]*NYSE Fact Book* (New York: NYSE 1993), 41. If you include U.S. government issues and non-U.S. issues of companies, banks, and governments, there are over 3,300 issues with a par value and market value of over $1,600 billion.

San Francisco, Boston, Osaka and Nagoya in Japan, and Dublin in Ireland; and (3) the over-the-counter market, which involves trading in securities not listed on an organized exchange.

The first two groups, referred to as *listed securities exchanges,* differ only in size and geographic emphasis. Both are composed of formal organizations with specific members and specific securities (stocks or bonds) that have qualified for listing. Although the exchanges typically consider similar factors when evaluating firms that apply for listing, the level of requirement differs (the national exchanges have more stringent requirements). Also, the prices of listed securities are determined via several different trading systems that will be discussed in the next section.

NATIONAL SECURITIES EXCHANGES

As indicated, the secondary stock market is composed of three segments: national stock exchanges, regional stock exchanges and the over-the-counter market. We will discuss each of these separately because they differ in importance within countries and they have different trading systems. As an investor interested in trading global securities, you should be aware of these differences. This section is devoted to a discussion of the major national stock exchanges in the world because they typically are the dominant markets within a country. The next section will consider the regional exchanges and the over-the-counter markets.

Although these exchanges are similar in that only certain stocks can be traded by individuals who are members of the exchange, they can differ in their *pricing systems.* There are two major pricing systems, and an exchange can use one of these or a combination of them. One is a *pure auction process* where interested buyers and sellers submit bid and ask prices for a given stock to a central location where they are matched by a broker who does not own the stock, but who acts as a facilitating agent. In this system shares of stock are sold to the highest bidder and bought from the seller with the lowest selling price.

The other major pricing system is a *dealer market* where individual dealers provide liquidity by buying and selling the shares of stock for themselves. Therefore, in such a market when an investor wants to buy or sell shares of a stock, they must go to a dealer. Ideally, there will be a number of dealers competing against each other to provide the highest bid prices when you are selling and the lowest asking price when you are buying stock. When we discuss the various exchanges, we will indicate the pricing system used.

Two U.S. securities exchanges are generally considered national in scope: the New York Stock Exchange (NYSE) and the American Stock Exchange (AMEX). Outside the United States, each country typically has one national exchange, such as the Tokyo Stock Exchange (TSE), the London Exchange, the Frankfurt Stock Exchange, and the Paris Bourse. These exchanges are considered national because of the large number of listed securities, the reputation of the firms listed, the wide geographic dispersion of the listed firms, and the diverse clientele of buyers and sellers who use the market.

NEW YORK STOCK EXCHANGE (NYSE)   The New York Stock Exchange (NYSE), the largest organized securities market in the United States, was established in 1817 as the New York Stock and Exchange Board. The Exchange dates its founding when the

TABLE 3.1

Listing Requirements for Stocks on the NYSE and the AMEX

	NYSE	AMEX
Pretax income last year[a]	$ 2,500,000	$ 750,000 latest year or
Pretax income last 2 years	2,000,000	2 of last 3 years
Net tangible assets	18,000,000	4,000,000
Shares publicly held	1,100,000	500,000
Market value of publicly held shares[b]	18,000,000	3,000,000[c]
Minimum number of holders of round lots (100 shares or more)	2,000	800

[a]For AMEX, this is *net* income last year.

[b]This minimum required market value varies over time, depending on the value of the NYSE Common Stock Index. For specifics, see the *1993 NYSE Fact Book, 29–30.*

[c]The AMEX only has one minimum.

Source: *NYSE Fact Book* (New York: NYSE, 1993); and *AMEX Fact Book* (New York: AMEX, 1992). Reprinted by permission.

famous Buttonwood Agreement was signed in May 1792 by 24 brokers.[10] The name was changed to the New York Stock Exchange in 1863.

At the end of 1992, 2,089 companies had stock listed on the NYSE, for a total of 2,654 stock issues (common and preferred) with a total market value of over $4.0 trillion. The specific listing requirements for the NYSE as of 1993 appear in Table 3.1.

The average number of shares traded daily on the NYSE has increased steadily and substantially, as shown in Table 3.2. Prior to the 1960s, the daily volume averaged less than 3 million shares, compared with current average daily volume in excess of 200 million shares and record volume of over 600 million shares.

The NYSE has dominated the other exchanges in the United States in trading volume. During the past decade, the NYSE has consistently accounted for about 80 percent of all shares traded on U.S. listed exchanges, as compared with about 10 percent for the American Stock Exchange and about 10 percent for all regional exchanges combined. Because share prices on the NYSE tend to be higher than those on the AMEX, the trading on the NYSE has averaged about 85 percent of the total value of U.S. trades, compared with less than 5 percent for the AMEX and a little over 10 percent for the regional exchanges.[11]

The volume of trading and relative stature of the NYSE is reflected in the price of a membership on the exchange (referred to as a seat). As shown in Table 3.3, the price of membership has fluctuated in line with trading volume and other factors that influence the profitability of membership.

AMERICAN STOCK EXCHANGE (AMEX)   The American Stock Exchange (AMEX) was begun by a group of persons who traded unlisted shares at the corner of Wall and

---

[10]The NYSE considers the signing of this agreement the birth of the Exchange and celebrated its 200th birthday during 1992. For a pictorial history, see *Life,* collector's edition, Spring 1992.

[11]For a breakdown of shares traded and their value, see Securities and Exchange Commission, *Annual Report* (Washington, D.C.: U.S. Government Printing Office, annual); and *NYSE Fact Book* (New York: NYSE, annual). For a discussion of trading volume and membership prices in 1993, see Anita Rashavan, "Stock Boom Doesn't Spur Bull Market in Seats," *Wall Street Journal,* March 24, 1993, C1, C25.

TABLE 3.2

Average Daily Reported Share Volume Traded on Selected National Stock Exchanges (000)

Year	NYSE	AMEX	NASDAQ	TSE
1940	751	171	N.A.	N.A.
1945	1,422	435	N.A.	N.A.
1950	1,980	583	N.A.	2,000
1955	2,578	912	N.A.	8,000
1960	3,042	1,113	N.A.	90,000
1965	6,176	2,120	N.A.	116,000
1970	11,564	3,319	N.A.	144,000
1975	18,551	2,138	5,500	183,000
1980	44,871	6,427	26,500	359,000
1981	46,853	5,310	30,900	377,000
1982	65,052	5,287	33,300	275,000
1983	85,334	8,225	62,900	365,000
1984	91,190	6,107	59,900	361,000
1985	109,169	8,337	82,100	428,000
1986	141,028	11,773	113,600	709,000
1987	188,938	13,858	149,800	962,000
1988	161,461	9,941	122,800	1,035,000
1989	165,470	12,401	133,100	894,000
1990	156,777	13,158	131,900	500,000
1991	178,917	13,309	163,300	380,000
1992	202,266	14,157	190,800	269,000

N.A. = not available.

Sources: *NYSE Fact Book* (New York: NYSE, various issues); *AMEX Fact Book* (New York: AMEX, various issues); *Tokyo Stock Exchange Fact Book* (Tokyo: TSE, various issues). Reprinted with permission.

TABLE 3.3

Membership Prices on the NYSE and the AMEX ($000)

	NYSE		AMEX			NYSE		AMEX	
	High	**Low**	**High**	**Low**		**High**	**Low**	**High**	**Low**
1925	$150	$ 99	$ 38	$ 9	1985	480	310	160	115
1935	140	65	33	12	1986	600	455	285	145
1945	95	49	32	12	1987	1,150	560	420	265
1955	90	49	22	12	1988	820	580	280	180
1960	162	135	60	51	1989	675	420	215	155
1965	250	190	80	55	1990	430	250	170	84
1970	320	130	185	70	1991	440	345	120	80
1975	138	55	72	34	1992	600	410	110	76
1980	275	175	252	95					

Sources: *NYSE Fact Book* (New York: NYSE, various issues); *AMEX Fact Book* (New York: AMEX, various issues). Reprinted by permission of the New York Stock Exchange and the American Stock Exchange.

Hanover Streets in New York. It was originally called the Outdoor Curb Market. In 1910 it established formal trading rules and its name changed to the New York Curb Market Association. The members moved inside a building in 1921 and continued to trade mainly in unlisted stocks (i.e., stocks not listed on one of the registered exchanges) until 1946, when its volume in listed stocks finally outnumbered that in unlisted stocks. The current name was adopted in 1953.

The AMEX is a national exchange, distinct from the NYSE because, except for a short period in the late 1970s, no stocks have been listed on both the NYSE and AMEX at the same time. The AMEX has emphasized listing foreign securities, listing 85 foreign issues in 1992, with trading in these issues constituting about 13 percent of total volume.[12] Warrants were listed on the AMEX for a number of years before the NYSE would list them.

Also, the AMEX has become a major options exchange since January 1975 when it began listing options on stocks. Since then it has added numerous options on stocks and also options on interest rates and stock indexes that are discussed in Chapter 20.

At the end of 1992, 943 stock issues were listed on the AMEX.[13] As shown in Table 3.2, average daily trading volume has fluctuated substantially over time, growing overall from below 500,000 shares to over 14 million shares a day in 1992. Because of the differences between the NYSE and the AMEX, most large brokerage firms are members of both exchanges.

TOKYO STOCK EXCHANGE (TSE)   Of the eight stock exchanges in Japan, those in Tokyo, Osaka, and Nagoya are the largest. The TSE dominates its country's market much as the NYSE does. Specifically, about 87 percent of trades in volume and 83 percent of value occur on the TSE. The market value of stocks listed on the TSE surpassed the NYSE during 1987 but fell below it when Japanese stocks declined during the period 1990–1992.

The Tokyo Stock Exchange Co. Ltd., established in 1878, was replaced in 1943 by the Japan Securities Exchange, a quasi-governmental organization that absorbed all existing exchanges in Japan. The Japan Securities Exchange was dissolved in 1947, and the Tokyo Stock Exchange in its present form was established in 1949. It currently lists about 1,766 companies with a total market value of 377,924 trillion yen (this is equal to about 3.15 trillion dollars at an exchange rate of 120 yen to the dollar). As shown in Table 3.2, average daily share volume has increased by more than 10 times, from 90 million shares per day in 1960 to a peak of over 1 billion shares in 1988 prior to a decline to 269 million shares in 1992. The value of shares traded has increased by almost 50 times from 1960 to 1992 because of the substantial increase in the prices of the shares.

Both domestic and foreign stocks are listed on the Tokyo Exchange. The domestic stocks are further divided between the First and Second Sections. The First Section contains about 1,700 stocks. The 150 most active stocks on the First Section are traded on the trading floor. Trading in all other domestic stocks and all foreign stocks is

---

[12]*AMEX Fact Book* (New York: AMEX, 1992).

[13]The requirements for listing on the AMEX appear in Table 3.1.

TABLE 3.4

Share Volume and Yen Value of Foreign Stocks Listed on the Tokyo Stock Exchange

| Year | Number of Listed Companies at Year-End | Volume (000) | | Value (million Yen) | |
		Total	Daily Average	Daily Total	Average
1982	12	1,271	4	18,257	64
1983	11	4,974	17	126,858	43
1984	11	4,522	15	93,118	324
1985	21	131,424	461	853,336	2,994
1986	52	309,701	1,110	1,151,863	4,128
1987	88	755,203	2,756	3,469,228	12,661
1988	112	216,332	792	795,252	2,913
1989	119	480,193	1,928	2,797,627	11,235
1990	125	256,252	1,042	2,015,601	8,194
1991	125	150,598	614	520,572	2,116
1992	119	86,239	349	157,011	636

Source: *TSE Fact Book* (Tokyo: Tokyo Stock Exchange, various issues).

conducted by computer as follows. From on-line terminals in their offices, member firms enter buy and sell orders that are received at the exchange. A clerk employed by a *Saitori* member, the TSE member firm responsible for this function, matches buy and sell orders for each stock on the electronic book-entry display screen and returns confirmations to the trading parties. The same information is also recorded on the trade-report printer and displayed on all stock-quote screens on the trading floor.

Besides domestic stocks, foreign company stocks are listed and traded on the TSE foreign stock market, which was opened in December 1973. As shown in Table 3.4, only a limited number of foreign companies were listed before 1985. As of the end of 1992 there are 119 foreign companies listed on the TSE. The value of daily average trading in these stocks has fluctuated dramatically. It was very active in 1987 and 1989 (over 11 billion yen), but weak in 1988, 1991, and 1992 (less than 3 billion yen).

LONDON STOCK EXCHANGE (LSE)   The largest established securities market in the United Kingdom, generally referred to as "The Stock Exchange," is the London Stock Exchange. Since 1973 it has served as the stock exchange of Great Britain and Ireland, with operating units in London, Dublin, and six other cities. Both listed securities (bonds and equities) and unlisted securities are traded on the LSE. The listed equity segment involves over 2,600 companies (2,700 security issues) with a market value in excess of 374 billion pounds (approximately $561 billion at an exchange rate of $1.50/pound). Of the 2,600 companies listed on the exchange, about 600 are foreign firms, the largest number on any exchange.

The stocks listed on the LSE are divided into three groups: Alpha, Beta, and Gamma. The Alpha stocks are the 65 most actively traded stocks, and the Betas are the 500 next most active stocks. In Alpha and Beta stocks, market makers are required to offer firm bid–ask quotes to all members of the exchange. For the rest of the stocks, Gamma stocks, market quotations are only indicative and must be confirmed before a trade. All equity trades must be reported to the Stock Exchange Automated Quotation (SEAQ) system within minutes, although only trades in Alpha stocks are reported in full on the screen.

The pricing system on the LSE is competing dealers who communicate via computers in offices away from the stock exchange. This system is very similar to the NASDAQ system used in the OTC market in the United States, which is described in the next section.

OTHER NATIONAL EXCHANGES   Other national exchanges are located in Frankfurt, Toronto, and Paris. In addition, the International Federation of Stock Exchanges was established in 1961. Members include 35 exchanges or national associations of stock exchanges in 29 countries. Located in Paris, the federation's 29 full members and 6 associate members meet every autumn to promote closer collaboration among themselves and to provide the development of securities markets.[14]

One of the newest national stock exchanges is in Shanghai, People's Republic of China. It was established in 1986 in response to the opening up of the Chinese economy. As of 1992, eight stock issues were listed. There is trading in stocks and also bonds on the exchange. The Shanghai People's Bank is authorized to regulate trading on the exchange where all trading is supposed to take place.[15] There was also a stock exchange established in Shenzchen that was subject to off-exchange trading.[16] Also, the first stock exchange in post-communist Eastern Europe opened in Budapest, Hungary, in June 1990.[17]

THE GLOBAL 24-HOUR MARKET   Our discussion of the global securities market will tend to emphasize the three markets in New York, London, and Tokyo because of their relative size and importance, and also because they represent the major segments of a worldwide 24-hour market. You will often hear about a continuous market where investment firms "pass the book" around the world. This means that the major active market in securities moves around the globe as trading hours for these three markets begin and end. Consider the individual trading hours for each of the three exchanges, translated into a 24-hour Eastern Standard clock:

---

[14]For further discussions of equity markets around the world, see Thomas J. Carroll, ed., *International Guide to Security Exchanges* (New York: Peat, Marwick, Mitchell, Co., 1986): David Smyth, *Worldly Wise Investor* (New York: Franklin Watts, 1988); *The Spicer and Oppenheim Guide to Securities Markets around the World* (New York: John Wiley & Sons, 1988); and Bryan de Caires, ed., *The Kidder Peabody Guide to International Capital Markets* (London: Euromoney Publications, 1988). Appendix 3A summarizes information about the major stock exchanges around the world.

[15]Han Guojian, "Shanghai: Stock Market Reestablished," *Beijing Review* (September 24, 1989): 23–29; David Bain, "Shanghai Stock Market Aims to Invigorate Industry," *Far East Business* (October 1989): 25.

[16]Adi Ignatius, "For Chinese Speculators the Streets Offer Better Deals than the Stock Exchange," *Wall Street Journal,* July 6, 1990, A4. Because of the lack of regulation and liquidity on these two exchanges in China, many of the viable Chinese companies that want a public market are applying for listing on the Hong Kong exchange. In this regard, see Marcus Brauchli and Kathy Chen, "Major Chinese Firms May Offer Shares in Hong Kong, but Gripes, Doubts Occur," *Wall Street Journal* (February 12, 1993): C10; Simon Davies, "Chinese Candidates Line Up for HK Listing," *Financial Times* (February 11, 1993): 21.

[17]William Echikson, "Budapest Opens a Regulated Stock Exchange Amid Fanfare, Much Hope and Many Hurdles," *Wall Street Journal,* June 27, 1990, C10.

	Local Time (24-hr. notations)	24-Hour EST
New York Stock Exchange	0930–1600	0930–1600
Tokyo Stock Exchange	0900–1100	2300–0100
	1300–1500	0300–0500
London Stock Exchange	0815–1615	0215–1015

Conceive of trading starting in New York and going until 1600 in the afternoon, being picked up by Tokyo late in the evening and going until 0500 in the morning, and continuing in London (with some overlap) until it begins in New York again (with some overlap) at 0930. Alternatively, it is possible to envision trading as beginning in Tokyo at 2300 hours and continuing until 0500, when it moves to London, then it ends the day in New York. This latter model seems the most relevant because the first question a London trader asks in the morning is "What happened in Tokyo?" and the U.S. trader asks "What happened in Tokyo and what is happening in London?" The point is, the markets operate almost continuously in time and they are certainly related in their response to economic events. Therefore, as an investor you are not dealing with three separate and distinct exchanges, but with one interrelated world market.[18] Clearly, this interrelationship is growing daily because of numerous dual listings and sophisticated telecommunications.

REGIONAL EXCHANGES AND OVER-THE-COUNTER MARKET

Within most countries there are regional stock exchanges that compete with and supplement the national exchanges by providing secondary markets for the stocks of smaller companies. Beyond these exchanges, there is trading off the exchange in what is called the over-the-counter (OTC) market, which includes all stocks that are not listed on one of the formal exchanges, as well as trading in some listed stocks. The size and significance of the regional exchanges versus the OTC market and the relative impact of these to the overall secondary stock markets vary between countries. In the first part of this section, we will discuss the rationale for and operation of regional stock exchanges. The second part of the section describes the OTC market, including heavy emphasis on the OTC market in the United States where it is a large and growing part of the total secondary stock market.

REGIONAL SECURITIES EXCHANGES

Regional exchanges typically have the same operating procedures as the national exchanges in the same countries, but they differ in their listing requirements and the geographic distributions of the listed firms. There are two main reasons for the existence of regional stock exchanges. First, they provide trading facilities for local companies that are not large enough to qualify for listing on one of the national exchanges. Their listing requirements are typically less stringent than are those of the national exchanges, as presented in Table 3.1.

---

[18]For an example of global trading, see "How Merrill Lynch Moves Its Stock Deals All Around the World," *Wall Street Journal,* November 9, 1987, 1, 19; and *Opportunity and Risk in the 24-Hour Global Marketplace* (New York: Coopers & Lybrand, 1987). In response to this trend toward global trading, the International Organization of Securities Commissions (IOSCO) has been established. For a discussion of it, see David Lascelles, "Calls to Bring Watchdogs into Line," *Financial Times,* August 14, 1989, 10.

Second, regional exchanges in some countries list firms that are also listed on one of the national exchanges to give local brokers who are not members of a national exchange access to these securities. As an example, American Telephone & Telegraph and General Motors are listed both on the NYSE and on several regional exchanges. This dual listing allows a local brokerage firm that is not large enough to purchase a membership on the NYSE to buy and sell shares of a dual-listed stock (e.g., General Motors) without going through the NYSE and giving up part of the commission. Currently, between 65 and 90 percent of the volume on regional exchanges is attributable to trading in dual-listed issues. The regional exchanges in the United States are:

- Midwest Stock Exchange (Chicago)
- Pacific Stock Exchange (San Francisco–Los Angeles)
- PBW Exchange (Philadelphia–Baltimore–Washington)
- Boston Stock Exchange (Boston)
- Spokane Stock Exchange (Spokane, Washington)
- Honolulu Stock Exchange (Honolulu, Hawaii)
- Intermountain Stock Exchange (Salt Lake City)

The first three exchanges (Midwest, Pacific, and PBW) account for about 90 percent of all regional exchange volume. In turn, total regional exchange volume is 9 to 10 percent of total exchange volume in the United States.

In Japan there are seven regional stock exchanges that supplement the Tokyo Stock Exchange. The exchange in Osaka accounts for about 10 percent and that in Nagoya for about 2.3 percent of the total volume. The remaining exchanges in Kyoto, Hiroshima, Fukuoto, Niigata, and Sapporo together account for less than 1 percent of volume.

The United Kingdom has one stock exchange in London with operating units in seven cities, including Dublin, Belfast, Birmingham, Manchester, Bristol, Liverpool, and Glasgow. Germany has eight stock exchanges, with its national exchange in Frankfurt where about 50 percent of the trading occurs. There are regional exchanges in Düsseldorf, Munich, Hamburg, Berlin, Stuttgart, Hanover, and Bremen.

Without belaboring the point, each country typically has one national exchange that accounts for the majority of trading and also has several regional exchanges that have less stringent listing requirements to allow trading in smaller firms. Recently, several national exchanges have created second-tier markets that are divisions of the national exchanges to allow smaller firms to be traded as part of the national exchanges.[19] In general, the fortunes of the regional exchanges have fluctuated substantially over time, based on interest in small, young firms and/or institutional interest in dual-listed stocks.

OVER-THE-COUNTER (OTC) MARKET

The over-the-counter (OTC) market includes trading in all stocks not listed on one of the exchanges. It can also include trading in listed stocks, which is referred to as the *third market,* and is discussed in the following section. The OTC market is not a formal

---

[19] An example of these second-tier markets is the second section on the TSE and the Unlisted Stock Market (USM) on the LSE. In both cases, the exchange is attempting to provide trading facilities for smaller firms without changing their listing requirements for the national exchange. Unfortunately, the LSE is planning to eliminate the USM because of the lack of trading. This is discussed further in a subsequent subsection.

TABLE 3.5   **Number of Companies and Issues Trading on NASDAQ: 1974–1992**

Year	Number of Companies	Number of Issues
1974	2,463	2,564
1975	2,467	2,579
1976	2,495	2,627
1977	2,456	2,575
1978	2,475	2,582
1979	2,543	2,670
1980	2,894	3,050
1981	3,353	3,687
1982	3,264	3,664
1983	3,901	4,467
1984	4,097	4,723
1985	4,136	4,784
1986	4,417	5,189
1987	4,706	5,537
1988	4,451	5,144
1989	4,293	4,963
1990	4,132	4,706
1991	4,094	4,684
1992	4,113	4,764

Source: *NASDAQ Fact Book* (Washington, D.C.: National Association of Securities Dealers, 1993). 5.

organization with membership requirements or a specific list of stocks deemed eligible for trading.[20] In theory, any security can be traded on the OTC market as long as someone else is willing to make a market in the security (i.e., willing to buy and sell shares of the stock).

SIZE OF THE OTC MARKET   The U.S. OTC market is the largest segment of the U.S. secondary market in terms of the number of issues traded. It is also the most diverse in terms of quality. As noted earlier, about 2,600 issues are traded on the NYSE and about 1,000 issues on the AMEX. In contrast, almost 2,700 issues are actively traded on the OTC market's NASDAQ National Market System (NMS).[21] Another 2,000 stocks are traded on the NASDAQ system independent of the NMS. Finally, 1,000 OTC stocks are regularly quoted in *The Wall Street Journal* but not included in the NASDAQ system. Therefore, a total of almost 6,000 issues are traded on the OTC market— substantially more than on the NYSE and AMEX combined.

Table 3.5 sets forth the growth in the number of companies and issues on NASDAQ. The growth in average daily trading is shown in Table 3.2 relative to some national exchanges. As of the end of 1992, 261 issues on NASDAQ were either foreign stocks

---

[20]The requirements of trading on different segments of the OTC trading system will be discussed later in this section.

[21]NASDAQ is an acronym for National Association of Securities Dealers Automated Quotations. The system is discussed in detail in a later subsection. A firm on the NMS must have a certain size and trading activity and at least four market makers. A specification of requirements for various components of the NASDAQ system is contained in Table 3.6.

or American Depository Receipts (ADRs). Trading in foreign stocks and ADRs represented over 5 percent of total NASDAQ share volume in 1992. About 250 of these issues trade on both NASDAQ and a foreign exchange such as Toronto. In March 1988 NASDAQ developed a link with the Singapore Stock Exchange that allows 24-hour trading going from NASDAQ in New York to Singapore to a NASDAQ/London link and back to New York.

Although the OTC market has the greatest number of issues, the NYSE has a larger total value of trading. In 1992 the approximate value of equity trading on the NYSE was $1,745 billion, and NASDAQ was $891 billion. Notably, the NASDAQ value exceeded what transpired on the LSE ($532 billion) and on the TSE ($484 billion).

There is tremendous diversity in the OTC market because it imposes no minimum requirements. Stocks that trade on the OTC range from those of small, unprofitable companies to large, very profitable firms. On the upper end, all U.S. government bonds are traded on the OTC market, as are the majority of bank and insurance stocks. Finally, about 100 exchange-listed stocks are traded on the OTC—this is referred to as the third market.

OPERATION OF THE OTC   As noted, any stock can be traded on the OTC as long as someone indicates a willingness to make a market whereby the party buys or sells for his or her own account acting as a dealer.[22] This differs from most transactions on the listed exchanges, where some of the members keep the book and attempt to match buy and sell orders. Therefore, the OTC market is referred to as a *negotiated market,* in which investors directly negotiate with dealers. Several of the major exchanges are continuous auction markets, with some of the members acting as intermediaries (auctioneers).

UNLISTED SECURITIES MARKET (USM)   The Unlisted Securities Market (USM) was started by the LSE in 1980. It handles smaller companies without the sufficiently long trading records required for full listing. As of early 1992, about 500 companies were traded on the USM with a total market value of over 5,000 million pounds. In contrast to the OTC market in the United States, which is completely separate from the exchanges, the USM was established and is supervised by the LSE. In late 1992 a number of market makers in this market withdrew because of the low volume which made it unprofitable for them. There was a resolution to disband the market that was expected to be passed in 1993. The result would be twofold for stocks on this market—either become listed on the main exchange (LSE), or become part of a bulletin board market without market makers.[23]

THE NASDAQ SYSTEM   *The National Association of Securities Dealers Automated Quotation (NASDAQ)* system is an automated, electronic quotation system for the vast OTC market. Any number of dealers can elect to make markets in an OTC stock. The actual number depends on the activity in the stock. The average number of market makers for all stocks on the NASDAQ system was 11.5 in 1992 according to the *NASDAQ Fact Book.*

---

[22]Dealer and market maker are synonymous.

[23]The bulletin board would be a broker market.

Historically, a broker trying to buy or sell an OTC stock for a customer had trouble determining the current quotations by specific market makers. NASDAQ makes all dealer quotes available immediately. The broker can check the quotation machine and call the dealer with the best market, verify that the quote has not changed, and make the sale or purchase. The NASDAQ system works on three levels to serve firms with different needs and interests.

Level 1 provides a single median representative quote for the stocks on NASDAQ. This quote system is for firms that want current quotes on OTC stocks but do not consistently buy or sell OTC stocks for their customers and are not market makers. This composite quote changes constantly to adjust for any changes by individual market makers.

Level 2 provides instantaneous current quotations on NASDAQ stocks by all market makers in a stock. This quotation system is for firms that consistently trade OTC stocks. Given an order to buy or sell, brokers check the quotation machine and call the market maker with the best market for their purposes (highest bid if they are selling, lowest offer if buying) and consummate the deal.

Level 3 is for OTC market makers. Such firms want Level 2, but they also need the capability to change their own quotations, which Level 3 provides.

LISTING REQUIREMENTS FOR NASDAQ   Quotes and trading volume for the OTC market are reported in two lists: a National Market System (NMS) list and a regular NASDAQ list. As of 1993, there were four sets of listing requirements. The first, for initial listing on any NASDAQ system, is the least stringent. The second is for automatic (mandatory) inclusion on the NASDAQ/NMS system. For stocks on this system there is up-to-the-minute volume and last-sale information for the competing market makers as well as end-of-the-day information on total volume and high, low, and closing prices. In addition, two sets of criteria govern voluntary participation on the NMS by companies with different characteristics. Alternative 1 accommodates companies with limited assets or net worth but substantial earnings; Alternative 2 is for large companies that are not necessarily as profitable. The four sets of criteria are set forth in Table 3.6.

A SAMPLE TRADE   Assume you are considering the purchase of 100 shares of Apple Computer. Although Apple is large enough and profitable enough to be listed on a national exchange, the company has never applied for listing because it enjoys a very active market on the OTC. (It is one of the volume leaders with daily volume typically above 500,000 shares and often in excess of 1 million shares.) When you contact your broker, he or she will consult the NASDAQ electronic quotation machine to determine the current dealer quotations for AAPL, the trading symbol for Apple Computer.[24] The quote machine will show that there are about 15 dealers making a market in AAPL. An example of differing quotations might be as follows:

---

[24]Trading symbols are one- to four-letter codes used to designate stocks. Whenever a trade is reported on a stock ticker, the trading symbol appears with the figures. Many are obvious, such as GM (General Motors), F (Ford Motors), GE (General Electric), and T (American Telephone & Telegraph).

TABLE 3.6

Qualification Standards for Inclusion in NASDAQ and NMS

Standard	Initial NASDAQ Inclusion (Domestic Common Stocks)	Mandatory NASDAQ/ NMS Inclusion	Voluntary NASDAQ/NMS Inclusion	
			Alternative 1	**Alternative 2**
Total assets	$2 million		$2 million	$2 million
Net tangible assets	—	$2 million	$4 million	$12 million
Capital and surplus	$1 million	$1 million	$1 million	$8 million
Net income	—	—	$400,000 in latest or last 2 of 3 fiscal years	—
Pretax income	—	—	$750,000 in latest or last 2 of 3 fiscal years	—
Operating history	—	—	—	3 years
Public float (shares)	100,000	500,000	500,000	1 million
Market value of float	—	—	$3 million	$15 million
Minimum bid	—	$10 for 5 business days	$5	$3
Trading volume	—	Average 600,000 shares/month for 6 months	—	—
Shareholders of record	100	300	800	400
Market makers	2	Four for 5 business days	2	2

Source: *NASDAQ Fact Book* (Washington, D.C.: National Association of Securities Dealers, 1993), 37.

Dealer	Bid	Ask
1	55½	55¾
2	55⅜	55⅝
3	55¼	55⅝
4	55⅜	55¾

Assuming that these are the best markets available from the total group, your broker would call either Dealer 2 or 3 because they have the lowest offering prices. After verifying the quote, your broker would give one of these dealers an order to buy 100 shares of AAPL at 55⅝ ($55.625 a share). Because your firm was not a market maker in the stock, the firm would act as a broker and charge you $5,562.50 plus a commission for the trade. If your firm had been a market maker in AAPL with an asking price of 55⅝, the firm would have sold the stock to you at 55⅝ net (without commission). If you had been interested in selling 100 shares of Apple Computer instead of buying, the broker would have contacted Dealer 1, who made the highest bid.

CHANGING DEALER INVENTORY   Let us consider the price quotations by an OTC dealer who wants to change his or her inventory on a given stock. For example, assume Dealer 4, with a current quote of 55⅜ bid–55¾ ask, decides to increase his or her holdings of AAPL. The NASDAQ quotes indicate that the highest bid is currently 55½. Increasing the bid to 55½ would bring some of the business currently going to Dealer 1. Taking a more aggressive action, the dealer might raise the bid to 55⅝ and buy all the stock that is offered, including some from Dealers 2 or 3, who are offering it at 55⅝. In this example, the dealer raises the bid price but does not change the asking price, which was above those of Dealers 2 or 3. This dealer will buy stock but probably not sell any. A dealer that had excess stock would keep the bid below the market (lower than 55½) and reduce the asking price to 55⅝ or less. Dealers constantly change their bid and/or ask prices, depending on their current inventories or changes in the outlook based on new information for the stock.[25]

THIRD MARKET

As mentioned, the term *third market* describes over-the-counter trading of shares listed on an exchange. Although most transactions in listed stocks take place on an exchange, an investment firm that is not a member of an exchange can make a market in a listed stock. Most of the trading on the third market is in well-known stocks such as AT&T, IBM, and Xerox. The success or failure of the third market depends on whether the OTC market in these stocks is as good as the exchange market and whether the relative cost of the OTC transaction compares favorably with the cost on the exchange. This market is very important during the relatively few periods when trading is not available on the NYSE either because trading is suspended or the exchange is closed.[26]

FOURTH MARKET

The term *fourth market* describes direct trading of securities between two parties with no broker intermediary. In almost all cases, both parties involved are institutions. When you think about it, a direct transaction is really not that unusual. If you own 100 shares of AT&T and decide to sell it, there is nothing wrong with simply offering it to your friends or associates at a mutually agreeable price and making the transaction directly.

Investors typically buy or sell stock through brokers because it is faster and easier. Also, you would expect to get a better price for your stock because the broker has a good chance of finding the best buyer. You are willing to pay a commission for these liquidity services. The fourth market evolved because of the substantial brokerage fees charged institutions with large orders. At some point it becomes worthwhile for institutions to attempt to deal directly with each other and save the brokerage fees. Assume an institution decides to sell 100,000 shares of AT&T, which is selling for about $60 a share, for a total value of $6 million. The average commission on such a transaction prior to the advent of negotiated rates in 1975 was about 1 percent of the value of the trade, or about $60,000. This cost made it attractive for a selling institution to spend some time and effort finding another institution interested in increasing its holdings of AT&T and negotiating a direct sale. Currently, such transactions cost about 5 cents a

---

[25]A number of studies have examined the determinants of dealers' bid–ask spreads including, H. R. Stoll, "Inferring the Components of the Bid–Ask Spread: Theory and Empirical Tests," *Journal of Finance* 44, no. 1 (March 1989): 115–134.

[26]Rhonda L. Rundle, "Jefferies 'Third Market' Trading Often Steals Show from Exchanges," *Wall Street Journal,* July 12, 1984, 29; Craig Torres, "Third Market Trading Crowds Stock Exchanges," *Wall Street Journal,* March 8, 1990, C1, C9.

share, which implies a cost of $5,000 for the 100,000 share transactions. This is lower, but still not trivial. Because of the diverse nature of the fourth market and the lack of reporting requirements, no data are available regarding its specific size or growth.

DETAILED
ANALYSIS OF
EXCHANGE
MARKETS

Because of the importance of the listed exchange markets, they must be dealt with at some length. In this section we discuss the several types of membership on the exchanges, the major types of orders, and finally the role and function of the specialist, who is the exchange market maker. These individuals are a critical component of a good exchange market.

EXCHANGE
MEMBERSHIP

Listed U.S. securities exchanges typically offer four major categories of membership: (1) specialist, (2) commission broker, (3) floor broker, and (4) registered trader. Specialists (or exchange market makers), who constitute about 25 percent of the total membership on exchanges, will be discussed after a description of types of orders.

Commission brokers are employees of a member firm who buy or sell for the customers of the firm. When you place an order to buy or sell stock through a brokerage firm that is a member of the exchange, the firm contacts its commission broker on the floor of the exchange. That broker goes to the appropriate post on the floor and buys or sells the stock as instructed.

Floor brokers are independent members of an exchange who act as brokers for other members. As an example, when commission brokers for Merrill Lynch become too busy to handle all of their orders, they will ask one of the floor brokers to help them. At one time these people were referred to as *$2 brokers* because that is what they received for each order. Currently they receive about $4 per 100-share order.

Registered traders are allowed to use their memberships to buy and sell for their own accounts. They therefore save commissions on their own trading, and observers believe they have an advantage because they are on the trading floor. The exchanges and others are willing to allow these advantages because these traders provide the market with added liquidity, but regulations limit how they trade and how many registered traders can be in a trading crowd around a specialist's booth at any time. In recent years, registered traders have become *registered competitive market makers (RCMM),* who have specific trading obligations set by the exchange. Their activity is reported as part of the specialist group.[27]

TYPES OF ORDERS

It is important to understand the different types of orders entered by investors and the specialist as a dealer.

MARKET ORDERS
The most frequent type of order, a *market order,* is an order to buy or sell a stock at the best price currently prevailing. An investor who enters a market sell order indicates a willingness to sell immediately at the highest bid available at the time the order reaches the specialist on the exchange. A market buy order indicates that the investor is willing

---

[27]Prior to the late 1970s, there were also odd-lot dealers who bought and sold to individuals with orders for less than round lots (usually 100 shares). Currently, this function either is handled by the specialist or some large brokerage firm.

to pay the lowest offering price available at the time the order reaches the floor of the exchange. Market orders provide immediate liquidity for someone willing to accept the prevailing market price.

Assume you are interested in General Electric (GE) and you call your broker to find out the current "market" on the stock. The quotation machine indicates that the prevailing market is 95 bid–95¼ ask. This means that the highest current bid on the books of the specialist is 95; that is, $95 is the most that anyone has offered to pay for GE. The lowest offer is 95¼, that is, the lowest price anyone is willing to accept to sell the stock. If you placed a market buy order for 100 shares, you would buy 100 shares at $95.25 a share (the lowest ask price) for a total cost of $9,525 plus commission. If you submitted a market sell order for 100 shares, you would sell the shares at $95 each and receive $9,500 less commission.

LIMIT ORDERS

The individual placing a *limit order* specifies the buy or sell price. You might submit a bid to purchase 100 shares of Coca-Cola stock at $45 a share when the current market is 50 bid–50¼ ask, with the expectation that the stock will decline to $45 in the near future.

You must also indicate how long the limit order will be outstanding. Alternative time specifications are basically boundless. A limit order can be instantaneous ("fill or kill," meaning fill the order instantly or cancel it). It can also be good for part of a day, a full day, several days, a week, or a month. It can also be open-ended, or good until canceled (GTC).

Rather than wait for a given price on a stock, your broker will give the limit order to the specialist, who will put it in a limit order book and act as the broker's representative. When and if the market reaches the limit order price, the specialist will execute the order and inform your broker. The specialist receives a small part of the commission for rendering this service.

SHORT SALES

Most investors purchase stock (i.e., "go long") expecting to derive their return from an increase in value. If you believe that a stock is overpriced, however, and want to take advantage of an expected decline in the price, you can sell the stock short. A *short sale* is the sale of stock that you do not own with the intent of purchasing it back later at a lower price. Specifically, you would borrow the stock from another investor through your broker, sell it in the market, and subsequently replace it at (you hope) a price lower than the price at which you sold it. The investor who lent the stock has the proceeds of the sale as collateral. In turn, this investor can invest these funds in short-term, risk-free securities. Although a short sale has no time limit, the lender of the shares can decide to sell the shares, in which case your broker must find another investor willing to lend the shares.[28]

Three technical points affect short sales. First, a short sale can be made only on an *uptick trade,* meaning the price of the short sale must be higher than the last trade

[28]For a discussion of short selling strategies, see Brett Duval Fromson, "Shortseller in the Bull Market," *Fortune,* August 31, 1987, 52, 53, 54, 56. For a discussion of profitable results, see Gary Putka, "Fortune Smiles on Short Side of Market," *Wall Street Journal,* October 27, 1987, 5.

price. This restriction is because the exchanges do not want traders to be able to force a profit on a short sale by pushing the price down through continually selling short. Therefore, the transaction price for a short sale must be an uptick or, without any change in price, the previous price must have been higher than its previous price (a zero uptick). For an example of a zero uptick, consider the following set of transaction prices: 42, 42¼, 42¼. You could sell short at 42¼ even though it is no change from the previous trade at 42¼ because that was an uptick trade.

The second technical point concerns dividends. The short seller must pay any dividends due to the investor who lent the stock. The purchaser of the short-sale stock receives the dividend from the corporation, so the short seller must pay a similar dividend to the lender.

A final point is that short sellers must post the same margin as an investor who had acquired stock. This margin can be in any unrestricted securities owned by the short seller.

SPECIAL ORDERS

In addition to these general orders, there are several special types of orders. A *stop loss order* is a conditional market order whereby the investor directs the sale of a stock if it drops to a given price. Assume you buy a stock at 50 and expect it to go up. If you are wrong, you want to limit your losses. To protect yourself, you could put in a stop loss order at 45. In this case, if the stock dropped to 45, your stop loss order would become a market sell order, and the stock would be sold at the prevailing market price. The stop loss order does not guarantee that you will get the $45; you can get a little bit more or a little bit less. Because of the possibility of market disruption caused by a large number of stop loss orders, exchanges have, on occasion, canceled all such orders on certain stocks and not allowed brokers to accept further stop loss orders on those issues.

A related type of stop loss tactic for short sales is a *stop buy order.* An investor who has sold stock short and wants to minimize any loss in case the stock begins to increase in value would enter this conditional buy order at a price above that at which the investor sold the stock short. Assume you sold a stock short at 50, expecting it to decline to 40. To protect yourself from an increase, you could put in a stop buy order to purchase the stock using a market buy order if it reached a price of 55. This conditional buy order would hopefully limit any loss on the short sale to approximately $5 a share.

MARGIN TRANSACTIONS

On any type of order, an investor can pay for the stock with cash or borrow part of the cost, leveraging the transaction. Leverage is accomplished by buying or selling *on margin,* which means that the investor pays some cash and borrows the rest through the broker, putting up the stock for collateral.

As shown in Figure 3.1, the dollar amount of margin credit extended by brokers and dealers increased substantially beginning in early 1991 and reached a record level in March 1993. The interest rate charged on these loans by the investment firms is typically 1.50 percent above the rate charged by the bank making the loan. The bank rate, referred to as the *call money rate,* is generally about 1 percent below the prime rate. For example, in April 1993 the prime rate was 6 percent, and the call money rate was 5 percent.

FIGURE 3.1   **Borrowing Against Stocks—Amount of Margin Credit Extended by Brokers and Dealers at End of Month ($ billions)**

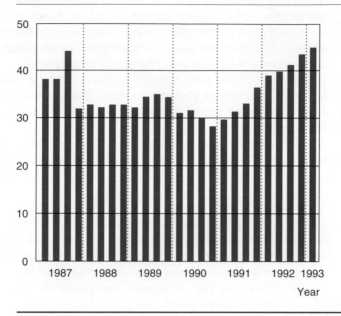

Source: Federal Reserve Board, Washington, D.C., 1993.

Federal Reserve Board Regulations T and U determine the maximum proportion of any transaction that can be borrowed. These regulations were enacted during the 1930s because it was contended that the excessive credit extended for stock acquisition contributed to the stock market collapse of 1929. Since the enactment of the regulations, this *margin requirement* (the proportion of total transaction value that must be paid in cash) has varied from 40 percent (allowing loans of 60 percent of the value) to 100 percent (allowing no borrowing). As of June 1993, the initial margin requirement specified by the Federal Reserve was 50 percent, although individual investment firms can require higher rates.

After the initial purchase, changes in the market price of the stock will cause changes in the *investor's equity,* which is equal to the market value of the collateral stock minus the amount borrowed. Obviously, if the stock price increases, the investor's equity as a proportion of the total market value of the stock increases (that is, the investor's margin will exceed the initial margin requirement).

Assume you acquired 200 shares of a $50 stock for a total cost of $10,000. A 50 percent initial margin requirement allowed you to borrow $5,000, making your initial equity $5,000. If the stock price increases by 20 percent to $60 a share, the total market value of your position is $12,000, and your equity is now $7,000, or 58 percent ($7,000/$12,000). In contrast, if the stock price declines by 20 percent to $40 a share, the total market value would be $8,000, and your equity would be $3,000 or 37.5 percent ($3,000/$8,000).

This example demonstrates that buying on margin provides all the advantages and the disadvantages of leverage. Lower margin requirements allow you to borrow more, increasing the percentage of gain or loss on your investment when the stock price increases or decreases. The leverage factor equals 1/percent margin. Thus, as in this example, if the margin is 50 percent, the leverage factor is 2, that is 1/.50. Therefore, when the rate of return on the stock is plus or minus 10 percent, the return on your equity was plus or minus 20 percent. If the margin declines to 33 percent, you can borrow more (67 percent), and the leverage factor is 3, (1/.33). When you acquire stock or other investments on margin, you are increasing the financial risk of the investment beyond the risk inherent in the security itself. You should increase your required return rate accordingly.[29]

The following example shows how borrowing by using margin affects the distribution of your returns before commissions and interest on the loan. When the stock increased by 20 percent, your return on the investment was as follows:

1. The market value of the stock is $12,000, which leaves you with $7,000 after you pay off the loan.
2. The return on your $5,000 investment is:

$$\frac{7,000}{5,000} - 1 = 1.40 - 1$$
$$= 0.40 = 40\%$$

In contrast, if the stock declined by 20 percent to $90 a share, your return would be as follows:

1. The market value of the stock is $8,000, which leaves you with $3,000 after you pay off the loan.
2. The return on your $5,000 investment is:

$$\frac{3,000}{5,000} - 1 = 0.60 - 1$$
$$= -0.40 = -40\%$$

You should also recognize that this symmetrical increase in gains and losses is only true prior to commissions and interest. Obviously, if we assume a 6 percent interest on the borrowed funds (which would be $5,000 x .06 = $300) and a $100 commission on the transaction, the results would indicate a lower increase and a larger negative return as follows:

---

[29]For a discussion of margin calls following market declines in 1987 and 1990, see Karen Slater, "Margin Calls Create Dilemma for Investors," *Wall Street Journal*, October 23, 1987, 21; William Power, "Stocks' Drop Spurs Margin Calls Less Severe than in Earlier Falls," *Wall Street Journal*, August 15, 1990, C1. For a discussion of the environment in 1993, see Georgette Jasen, "Cheap Margin Loans are Tempting, but Beware," *Wall Street Journal*, April 23, 1993, C1, C21; and Michael Siconolfi, "Does Margin-Loan Binge Signal Stock-Market Top?" *Wall Street Journal*, April 23, 1993, C1, C16.

$$20\% \text{ increase: } \frac{\$12,000 - \$5,000 - \$300 - \$100}{\$5,000} - 1 = \frac{6,600}{5,000} - 1$$
$$= 0.32 = 32\%$$
$$20\% \text{ decline: } \frac{\$8,000 - \$5,000 - \$300 - \$100}{\$5,000} - 1 = \frac{2,600}{5,000} - 1$$
$$= -0.48 = -48\%$$

In addition to the initial margin requirement, another important concept is the *maintenance margin,* which is the required proportion of your equity to the total value of the stock; the maintenance margin protects the broker if the stock price declines. At present, the minimum maintenance margin specified by the Federal Reserve is 25 percent, but, again, individual brokerage firms can dictate higher margins for their customers. If the stock price declines to the point where your equity drops below 25 percent of the total value of the position, the account is considered undermargined, and you will receive a *margin call* to provide more equity. If you do not respond with the required funds in the time allotted, the stock will be sold to pay off the loan. The time allowed to meet a margin call varies between investment firms and is affected by market conditions. Under volatile conditions, the time allowed to respond to a margin call can be shortened drastically.

Given a maintenance margin of 25 percent, you must consider how far the stock price can fall before you receive a margin call. The computation for our example is as follows: If the price of the stock is P and you own 200 shares, the value of the position is 200P and the equity in the account is 200P $-$ \$5,000. The percentage margin is (200P $-$ 5,000)/200P. To determine the price, P, that is equal to 25 percent (0.25), we use the equation:

$$\frac{200P - \$5,000}{200P} = 0.25$$
$$200P - 5,000 = 50P$$
$$P = \$33.33$$

Therefore, when the stock is at \$33.33, the equity value is exactly 25 percent; so if the stock goes below \$33.33, the investor will receive a margin call.

To continue the previous example, if the stock declines to \$30 a share, its total market value would be \$6,000 and your equity would be \$1,000, which is only about 17 percent of the total value (\$1,000/\$6,000). You would receive a margin call for approximately \$667, which would give you equity of \$1,667, or 25 percent of the total value of the account (\$1,667/\$6,667).[30]

EXCHANGE
MARKET MAKERS

Now that we have discussed the overall structure of the exchange markets and the orders that are used to buy and sell stocks, we can discuss the role and function of the market makers on the exchange. These people and the role they play differ among

---

[30]For a further discussion see Jill Bettner, "Brokers Begin Pushing Margin Loans—But Critics Say Borrowers Should Beware," *Wall Street Journal,* August 26, 1987, 17; and Georgette Jasen, "Cheap Margin Loans are Tempting, but Beware," *Wall Street Journal,* April 23, 1993, C1, C21.

exchanges. For example, on U.S. exchanges these people are called *specialists*; on the TSE they are a combination of the *Saitori* and regular members. Most exchanges do not have a single market maker but have competing dealers. On exchanges that have central market makers, these individuals are critical to the smooth and efficient functioning of these markets.

As noted, a major requirement for a good market is liquidity, which depends on how the market makers do their job. Our initial discussion centers on the specialist's role in U.S. markets, followed by a consideration of comparable roles on exchanges in other countries.

U.S. MARKETS

The specialist is a member of the exchange who applies to the exchange to be assigned stocks to handle.[31] The typical specialist will handle about 15 stocks. The capital requirement for specialists changed in April 1988 in response to the October 1987 market crash.[32] Specifically, the minimum capital required of each specialist unit was raised to $1 million or the value of 15,000 shares of each stock assigned, whichever is greater.

FUNCTIONS OF THE SPECIALIST   Specialists have two major functions. First, they serve as *brokers* to match buy and sell orders and also handle limit special orders placed with member brokers. An individual broker who receives a limit order leaves the limit order (or stop loss or stop buy order) with the specialist, who executes it when and if the specified price occurs. For this service, the specialist receives a portion of the broker's commission on the trade.

The second major function of a specialist is to act as a *dealer* to maintain a fair and orderly market by providing liquidity when the normal flow of orders is not adequate. In this capacity, the specialist must buy and sell for his or her own account (like an OTC dealer) when public supply or demand is insufficient to provide a continuous, liquid market.

Consider the following example. If a stock is currently selling for about $40 per share, the current bid and ask in an auction market (without the intervention of the specialist) might be a 40 bid–41 ask. Under such conditions, random market buy and sell orders might cause the price of the stock to fluctuate between 40 and 41 constantly—a movement of 2.5 percent between trades. Most investors would probably consider such a price pattern too volatile; the market would not be considered continuous. Under such conditions the specialist is expected to provide "bridge liquidity" by entering alternative bids and/or asks to narrow the spread and improve the stock's price continuity. In this example, the specialist could enter a bid of 40½ or 40¾ or an ask of 40½ or 40¼ to narrow the spread to one-half or one-quarter point.

---

[31]Most specialists are part of a specialist unit that can be a formal organization of specialists (a specialist firm) or a set of independent specialists who join together to spread the work load and the risk of the stocks assigned to the unit. At the end of 1992 a total of 446 individual specialists made up 53 specialist units (about 8 specialists per unit).

[32]For a detailed presentation on the 1987 crash, see *Report of the Presidential Task Force on Market Mechanisms* (Washington, D.C.: The Superintendent of Documents, U.S. Government Printing Office, January 1988). The Chairman of the Task Force was Nicholas Brady, so there are references to it as "The Brady Report."

Specialists can enter either side of the market, depending on several factors, including the trend of the market. They are expected to buy or sell against the market when prices are clearly moving in one direction. Specifically, they are required to buy stock for their own inventories when there is an excess of sell orders and the market is definitely declining. Alternatively, they must sell stock from their inventories or sell it short to accommodate an excess of buy orders when the market is rising. They are not expected to prevent prices from rising or declining, but only to ensure that the prices change in an orderly fashion (i.e., to maintain price continuity). Evidence that they have fulfilled this requirement is that during recent years NYSE stocks traded unchanged from, or within one-eighth point of, the price of the previous trade about 95 percent of the time.

Another factor affecting a specialists' decision on how to narrow the spread is their current inventory position in the stock. For example, if they have large inventories of a given stock, all other factors being equal, they would probably enter on the ask (sell) side to reduce these heavy inventories. In contrast, specialists who had little or no inventory of shares because they had been selling from their inventories, or selling short, would tend toward the bid (buy) side of the market to rebuild their inventories or close out their short positions.

Finally, the position of the limit order book will influence these actions. Numerous limit buy orders (bids) close to the current market and very few limit sell orders (asks) might indicate a tendency toward higher prices because demand is apparently heavy and supply limited. Under such conditions, a specialist who is not bound by one of the other factors would probably opt to accumulate stock in anticipation of an increase. The specialists on the NYSE have historically participated as a dealer in 10 to 12 percent of all trades.

SPECIALIST INCOME   The specialist derives income from both the broker and dealer functions. The actual breakdown between the two depends on the specific stock. In an actively traded stock such as IBM a specialist has little need to act as a dealer because the substantial public interest in the stock creates a tight market (i.e., a small bid–ask spread). In such a case the main source of income would be maintaining the limit orders for the stock. Notably, the income derived from acting as a broker for a stock such as IBM can be substantial and is basically without risk.

In contrast, a stock with low trading volume and substantial price volatility would probably have a fairly wide bid–ask spread, and the specialist would have to be an active dealer. The specialist's income from such a stock would depend on his or her ability to trade in it profitably. Specialists have a major advantage when trading because of their limit order books. Only specialists are supposed to see the limit order book, which means that they have a monopoly on a source of very important information regarding all limit orders, representing the current supply and demand curve for a stock. This information should allow specialists to profit in the long run on their dealer trades despite being forced to buy or sell against the market for short periods of time.[33]

---

[33]For evidence that the specialists do not fare too badly when they trade against the market, see Frank K. Reilly and Eugene F. Drzycimski, "The Stock Exchange Specialist and the Market Impact of Major World Events," *Financial Analysts Journal* 31, no. 4 (July–August 1975): 27–32. Also, if a major imbalance in trading arises due to new informa-

Most specialists attempt to balance their portfolios between strong broker stocks that provide steady, riskless income and stocks that require active dealer roles. An SEC study done in 1972 indicated substantial returns on investment for all specialist units.[34] It is unlikely that specialists are currently earning returns of such magnitude because the 1972 returns were prior to negotiated commission rates, which affected the fees paid to specialists. Also, as indicated earlier, following the October 1987 market crash, specialists were required to increase their capital positions substantially, which would reduce their return on investment.[35]

TOKYO STOCK EXCHANGE (TSE)

As of 1993, the TSE has a total of 124 "regular members" (99 Japanese members and 25 foreign members) and 1 *Saitori* member (4 *Saitori* firms merged during 1992). A membership currently costs about 1.15 billion yen (about $8 million). For each membership, the firm is allowed several people on the floor of the exchange, depending on its trading volume and capital position (the average number of employees on the floor is 20 per firm for a regular member and about 300 employees for the *Saitori* member). The employees of a regular member are called *trading clerks,* and the employees of the *Saitori* member are called *intermediary clerks.*

Regular members buy and sell securities on the TSE either as agents or principals (i.e., brokers or dealers). *Saitori* members specialize in acting as intermediaries (brokers) for transactions among regular members, and they maintain the books for limit orders. (Stop loss and stop buy orders as well as short selling are not allowed.) Therefore, *Saitori* members have some of the characteristics of the U.S. exchange specialist, because they match buy and sell orders for customers, handle limit orders, and are not allowed to deal with public customers. They *differ* from the specialist on a U.S. exchange in that they do not act as dealers to maintain an orderly market. Only regular members are allowed to buy and sell for their own accounts. Therefore, the TSE is a two-way, continuous auction, order-driven market where buy and sell orders directly interact with one another with the *Saitori* acting as the auctioneer (intermediary between firms submitting the orders).

Also, although there are about 1,700 listed domestic stocks and 125 foreign stocks on the first section, only the largest 150 stocks are traded on the floor of the exchange. All the others are traded through a computer system called CORES, which stands for Computer-assisted Order Routing and Execution System. With CORES after an order is entered into the central processing unit, it becomes part of an electronic "book" which is monitored by a *Saitori* member who matches all buy and sell orders on the

tion, the specialist can request a temporary suspension of trading. For an analysis of what occurs during these trading suspensions, see Michael H. Hopewell and Arthur L. Schwartz, Jr., "Temporary Trading Suspensions in Individual NYSE Securities," *Journal of Finance* 33, no. 5 (December 1978): 1355–1373; and Frank J. Fabozzi and Christopher K. Ma, "The Over-the-Counter Market and New York Stock Exchange Trading Halts," *The Financial Review* 23, no. 4 (November 1988): 427–437.

[34]U.S. House Committee on Interstate and Foreign Commerce, Subcommittee on Commerce and Finance, *Securities Industry Study: Report and Hearings,* 92d Congress, 1st and 2d sessions, 1972: Chapter 12.

[35]For a discussion of the problems facing specialists, see Edward A. Wyatt, "Eye of the Hurricane," *Barron's,* February 19, 1990, 28.

screen in accordance with trading rules. The system also automatically executes all orders for transactions at the last sale price and provides a narrow bid–ask spread within which orders are executed.

TSE membership is available to corporations licensed by the Minister of Finance. Member applicants may request any of four licenses: (1) to trade securities as a dealer, (2) to trade as a broker, (3) to underwrite new securities on secondary offerings, or (4) to handle retail distribution of new or outstanding securities. A firm may have more than one license, but it cannot act as principal and agent in the same transaction. The minimum capital requirements for these licenses vary from 200 million to 3 billion yen ($1.67 million to $25 million) depending on the type of license.

Although Japan's securities laws allow foreign securities firms to obtain membership on the exchanges, the individual exchanges determine whether membership will be granted. Twenty-five foreign firms have become members of the TSE since 1986.[36]

LONDON STOCK EXCHANGE (LSE)

Historically, members on the LSE were either brokers, who could trade shares on behalf of customers, or jobbers, who bought and sold shares as principals. Following a major deregulation (the "Big Bang") on October 27, 1986, brokers are allowed to make markets in various equities and gilts (British government bonds) and jobbers can deal with non-stock-exchange members including the public and institutions.

Membership in the LSE is granted based on experience and competence, and there are no citizenship or residency requirements. Currently, over 5,000 individual memberships are held by 214 broker firms and 22 jobbers. Although individuals gain membership, the operational unit is a firm that pays membership fees based on the number of exchange-approved members it employs during its first year of membership. Subsequently a member firm pays an annual charge equal to 1 percent of its gross revenues.

CHANGES IN THE SECURITIES MARKETS

Since 1965 there have been numerous changes prompted by the significant growth of trading by large financial institutions such as banks, insurance companies, pension funds, and investment companies because the trading requirements of these institutions differ from those of individual investors. Additional changes have transpired because of the globalization of capital markets. In this section we discuss these changes and why they occurred, consider their impact on the market, and speculate about future changes.

EVIDENCE AND EFFECT OF INSTITUTIONALIZATION

The growing impact of large financial institutions is evidenced by data on block trades (transactions involving at least 10,000 shares) and the size of trades, as seen in Table 3.7.

Financial institutions are the main source of large block trades, and the number of block trades on the NYSE has grown steadily from an average of 9 per day in 1965 to

---

[36]Some observers have questioned the pure economics of these memberships, but the firms have defended them as a means of becoming a part of the very lucrative Japanese financial community. In this regard, see Kathryn Graven, "Tokyo Stock Exchange's Broker-Fees Cut Is Seen Trimming Foreign Firms' Profits," *Wall Street Journal,* October 2, 1987, 17; and Marcus W. Brauchli, "U.S. Brokerage Firms Operating in Japan Have Mixed Results," *Wall Street Journal,* August 16, 1989, A1, A8.

TABLE 3.7   **Block Transactions^a and Average Shares per Sale on the NYSE**

Year	Total Number of Block Transactions	Total Number of Shares in Block Trades (000)	Percentage of Reported Volume	Average Number of Block Transactions per Day	Average Shares per Sale
1965	2,171	48,262	3.1%	9	224
1970	17,217	450,908	15.4	68	388
1975	34,420	778,540	16.6	136	495
1980	133,597	3,311,132	29.2	528	872
1981	145,564	3,771,442	31.8	575	1,013
1982	254,707	6,742,481	41.0	1,007	1,305
1983	363,415	9,842,080	45.6	1,436	1,434
1984	433,427	11,492,091	49.8	1,713	1,781
1985	539,039	14,222,272	51.7	2,139	1,878
1986	665,587	17,811,335	49.9	2,631	1,881
1987	970,679	24,497,241	51.2	3,639	2,112
1988	768,419	22,270,680	54.5	3,037	2,303
1989	872,811	21,316,132	51.1	3,464	2,123
1990	843,365	19,681,849	49.6	3,333	2,082
1991	981,077	22,474,382	49.6	3,878	1,670
1992	1,134,832	26,069,383	50.7	4,468	1,684

^aTrades of 10,000 shares or more.

Source: *NYSE Fact Book* (New York: NYSE, various issues). Reprinted by permission.

almost 4,500 a day in 1992. On average, such trades constitute half of all the volume on the exchange. Institutional involvement is also reflected in the average size of trades, which has grown consistently from about 200 shares in 1965 to almost 1,700 shares per trade in 1992.[37]

Several major effects of this institutionalization of the market have been identified:

1. Negotiated (competitive) commission rates
2. The influence of block trades
3. The impact on stock price volatility
4. The development of a National Market System (NMS)

In the following sections, we will discuss each of these effects and how they affect the operation of the U.S. securities market.

NEGOTIATED
COMMISSION
RATES

BACKGROUND

When the NYSE was formally established in 1792, it was agreed that the members would carry out all trades in designated stocks on the exchange, and that they would charge nonmembers on the basis of a *minimum commission schedule* that outlawed price cutting. Because the market was designed for individual investors, the minimum commission schedule was developed to compensate for handling small orders and made no allowance for the trading of large orders by institutions. As a result, institutional

[37]Although the influence of institutional trading is greatest on the NYSE, it is also a major factor on the AMEX, where block trades constituted about 40 percent of share volume in 1992, and on the NASDAQ-NMS, where block trades accounted for almost 45 percent of share volume in 1992.

investors were forced to pay substantially more in commissions than the costs of the transactions justified.

The initial reaction to the excess commissions were give-ups, whereby brokers agreed to pay part of their commissions (sometimes as much as 80 percent) to other brokerage houses or research firms designated by the institution making the trade. These firms provided services to the institution. These commission transfers were referred to as *soft dollars.* Another response was the increased use of the third market, where commissions were not fixed as they were on the NYSE.

The fixed commission structure also fostered the development and use of the fourth market, where two institutions deal directly with one another, saving the full commission. Finally, some institutions became members of one of the regional exchanges (the NYSE and AMEX would not allow institutional members).

IMPOSITION OF NEGOTIATED COMMISSIONS

Beginning in 1970, the SEC began a program of negotiated commissions on large transactions and finally allowed negotiated commissions on all transactions on May 1, 1975 (the event was called May Day).

The effect on commissions charged has been dramatic. Initially, the negotiated commissions were stated in terms of 30 to 50 discounts from pre-May Day fixed rates. Currently, commissions for institutions are in the range of 5 to 10 cents per share irrespective of the price of the stock, which implies a very large discount on high-priced shares. Although individuals initially enjoyed little discounting, currently there are numerous competing discount brokers who charge a straight transaction fee and do not provide research advice or safekeeping services. These discounts vary depending on the size of the trade. Discount brokerage firms advertise extensively in *The Wall Street Journal* and *Barron's.*

The reduced commissions caused numerous mergers and liquidations by smaller investment firms after May Day. Also, with fixed minimum commissions, it was cheaper for most institutions to buy research using soft dollars than to do their own research. When competitive rates reduced excess commissions, the institutions switched to large brokerage firms that had good trading and research capabilities. As a result, many independent research firms either disbanded or merged with full-service brokerage firms.

Regional stock exchanges flourished prior to competitive rates because they helped institutions distribute soft dollars, allowed institutions to become members, and facilitated trading in large blocks. Some observers expected regional exchanges to be adversely affected by competitive rates. Apparently, the unique trading capabilities on these exchanges, including the ability to help cross block trades, prevented this because the relative trading on these exchanges has been maintained.[38]

SUMMARY OF EFFECTS OF NEGOTIATED COMMISSIONS   Total commissions paid have shown a significant decline, and the size and structure of the industry have changed as

---

[38]For a discussion of trading on regional exchanges and the third market, see J. L. Hamilton, "Off-Board Trading of NYSE-Listed Stocks: The Effects of Deregulation and the National Market System," *Journal of Finance* 42, no. 5 (December 1987): 1331–1346.

a result. Although independent research firms and the third market have contracted, regional stock exchanges have felt little impact.

THE IMPACT OF BLOCK TRADES

Because the increase in institutional development has caused an increase in the number and size of block trades, it is important to consider how they influence the market and understand how these blocks trade. These topics are discussed in this section.

BLOCK TRADES ON THE EXCHANGES

The increase in block trading by institutions has strained the specialist system, which had three problems with block trading: capital, commitment, and contacts (the "three Cs."). First, specialists did not have the capital needed to acquire blocks of 10,000 or 20,000 shares. Second, even when specialists had the capital, they may have been unwilling to commit the capital because of the large risks involved. Finally, because of Rule 113 specialists are not allowed to directly contact institutions to offer a block brought by another institution. Therefore, they are cut off from the major source of demand for blocks and are reluctant to take large positions in thinly traded stocks.

BLOCK HOUSES

This lack of capital, commitment, and contacts by specialists on the exchange created a vacuum in block trading that resulted in the development of block houses. *Block houses* are investment firms (also referred to as *upstairs traders* because they are away from the floor of the exchange) that help institutions locate other institutions interested in buying or selling blocks of stock. A good block house has (1) the capital required to position a large block, (2) the willingness to commit this capital to a block transaction, and (3) contacts among institutions.

EXAMPLE OF A BLOCK TRADE

Assume a mutual fund owns 250,000 shares of Ford Motors and decides to sell 50,000 shares. The fund decides to do it through Goldman Sachs & Company (GS&Co.), a large, active block house that is a lead underwriter for Ford and knows institutions interested in the stock. After being contacted by the fund, the traders at Goldman Sachs contact several institutions that own Ford to see if any of them want to add to their position and to determine their bids. Assume that the previous sale of Ford on the NYSE was a $56\frac{3}{4}$ and GS&Co. receives commitments from four different institutions for a total of 40,000 shares at an average price of $56\frac{5}{8}$. Goldman Sachs returns to the mutual fund and bids $56\frac{1}{2}$ minus a negotiated commission for the total 50,000 shares. Assuming the fund accepts the bid, Goldman Sachs now owns the block and immediately sells 40,000 shares to the four institutions that made prior commitments. It also "positions" 10,000 shares; that is, it owns the 10,000 shares and must eventually sell them at the best price possible. Because GS&Co. is a member of the NYSE, the block will be processed ("crossed") on the exchange as one transaction of 50,000 shares at $56\frac{1}{2}$. The specialist on the NYSE might take some of the stock to fill limit orders on the book at prices between $56\frac{1}{2}$ and $56\frac{3}{4}$.

For working on this trade, GS&Co. receives a negotiated commission, but it has committed almost $570,000 to position the 10,000 shares. The major risk to GS&Co. is the possibility of a subsequent price change on the 10,000 shares. If it can sell the 10,000 shares for $56\frac{1}{2}$ or more, it will just about break even on the position and have the commission as income. If the price weakens, it may have to sell the position at 56¼ and take a loss on it of about $2,500, offsetting the income from the commission.

This example indicates the importance of institutional contacts, capital to position a portion of block, and willingness to commit that capital to the block trade. Without all three, the transaction would not take place.

INSTITUTIONS AND STOCK PRICE VOLATILITY

Some observers have speculated that there should be a strong positive relationship between institutional trading and stock price volatility. The reasoning is that institutions trade in large blocks and it is contended that they tend to trade together. Empirical studies of these contentions have examined the relationship between the proportion of trading by large financial institutions and stock price volatility. These studies have never supported the folklore.[39] In a capital market where trading has come to be dominated by institutions, the best environment is one where all institutions are actively involved, because they provide liquidity for one another and for noninstitutional investors.

NATIONAL MARKET SYSTEM (NMS)

The development of a National Market System (NMS) has been advocated by the financial institutions because it is expected to provide greater efficiency, competition, and lower cost of transactions. Although there is no generally accepted definition of an NMS, four major characteristics are generally expected:

1. Centralized reporting of all transactions
2. Centralized quotation system
3. Centralized limit-order book (CLOB)
4. Competition among all qualified market makers.

CENTRALIZED REPORTING

Centralized reporting requires a composite tape to report all transactions in a stock regardless of where the transactions took place. As you watched the tape, you might see a trade in GM on the NYSE, another trade on the Midwest, and a third on the OTC. The intent is to provide full information on all completed trades on the tape.

As of June 1975, the NYSE began operating a central tape that includes all NYSE stocks traded on other exchanges and on the OTC. The volume of shares reported on the consolidated tape is shown in Table 3.8. The breakdown among the seven exchanges and two OTC markets appears in Table 3.9. Therefore, this component of a National Market System (NMS) is available for stocks listed on the NYSE. As shown, the volume of trading is becoming more dispersed among the exchanges and the NASD.[40]

---

[39]In this regard, see Frank K. Reilly and John M. Wachowicz, "How Institutional Trading Reduces Market Volatility," *Journal of Portfolio Management* 5, no. 2 (Winter 1979): 11–17; Neil Berkman, "Institutional Investors and the Stock Market," *New England Economic Review* (November-December 1977): 60–77; and Frank K. Reilly and David J. Wright, "Block Trades and Aggregate Stock Price Volatility," *Financial Analysts Journal* 40, no. 2 (March-April, 1984): 54–60.

[40]For a discussion of these changes, see Craig Torres and William Power, "Big Board is Losing Some of Its Influence Over Stock Trading," *Wall Street Journal,* April 17, 1990, A1, A6; Janet Bush, "Hoping for a New Broom at the NYSE," *Financial Times,* August 16, 1990, 13; William Power, "Big Board, at Age 200, Scrambles to Protect Grip on Stock Market," *Wall Street Journal,* May 13, 1992, A1; A8; Pat Widder, "NYSE in 200th Year as 'Way of Doing Business,' " *Chicago Tribune,* May 17, 1992, Section 7, pp. 1, 4; and Pat Widder, "NASDAQ Has Its Eyes Set on the Next 100 Years," *Chicago Tribune,* May 17, 1992, Section 7, pp. 1, 4.

TABLE 3.8

Consolidated Tape Volume (thousands of shares)

1976	6,281,008	1985	32,988,595
1977	6,153,173	1986	42,478,164
1978	8,147,569	1987	55,472,855
1979	9,254,044	1988	47,390,121
1980	12,935,607	1989	49,794,547
1981	13,679,194	1990	48,188,072
1982	19,203,590	1991	55,294,725
1983	25,362,458	1992	63,064,667
1984	27,455,178		

Source: *NYSE Fact Book* (New York: NYSE, 1993): 24.

TABLE 3.9

Exchanges and Markets Involved in Consolidated Tape with Percentage of Trades During 1992

	Percentage		Percentage
AMEX	0.00%	NASD	10.57%
Boston	3.17	NYSE	65.17
Cincinnati	1.85	Pacific	7.55
Instinet	0.03	Philadelphia	3.31
Midwest	8.34		

Source: *NYSE Fact Book* (New York: NYSE, 1993): 25.

CENTRALIZED QUOTATION SYSTEM

A centralized quotation system would list the quotes for a given stock (e.g., IBM) from all market makers on the national exchanges, the regional exchanges, and the OTC. With such a system, a broker who requested the market for IBM would see the prevailing quotes and should complete the trade on the market with the best quote for the client.

INTERMARKET TRADING SYSTEM   A centralized quotation system is currently available—the Intermarket Trading System (ITS), developed by the American, Boston, Midwest, New York, Pacific, and Philadelphia Stock Exchanges and the NASD. ITS consists of a central computer facility with interconnected terminals in the participating market centers. As shown in Table 3.10, the number of issues included, the volume of trading, and the size of trades have all grown substantially. Of the 2,532 issues included on the system in 1992, 2,100 were listed on the NYSE and 432 were listed on the AMEX and other markets.

With ITS, brokers and market makers in each market center indicate specific buying and selling commitments through a composite quotation display that shows the current quotes for each stock in every market center. A broker is expected to go to the best market to execute a customer's orders by sending a message committing to buy or sell at the price quoted. When this commitment is accepted, a message reports that the transaction has taken place. The following example illustrates how ITS works.

TABLE 3.10   **Intermarket Trading System Activity**

Year	Issues Eligible	Daily Average		
		Share Volume	Executed Trades	Average Size of Trade
1978 (April)	300	235,000	377	623
1979	687	827,600	1,402	590
1980	884	1,565,900	2,868	546
1981	947	2,144,700	3,659	586
1982	1,039	3,264,100	4,697	695
1983	1,120	4,104,000	5,645	727
1984	1,160	4,692,200	5,404	868
1985	1,288	5,669,400	5,867	966
1986	1,278	7,222,100	7,712	987
1987	1,537	8,608,559	8,573	1,004
1988	1,816	7,625,926	7,069	1,079
1989	2,082	9,168,867	8,065	1,137
1990	2,126	9,387,114	8,744	1,075
1991	2,306	10,408,566	9,971	1,044
1992	2,532	10,755,704	10,179	1,057

Source: *NYSE Fact Book* (New York: NYSE, 1993): 26.

A broker on the NYSE has a market order to sell 100 shares of IBM stock. Assuming the quotation display at the NYSE shows that the best current bid for IBM is on the Pacific Stock Exchange (PSE), the broker will enter an order to sell 100 shares at the bid on the PSE. Within seconds, the commitment flashes on the CRT screen and is printed out at the PSE specialist's post, where it is executed against the PSE bid. The transaction is reported back to New York, and reported on the consolidated tape. Both brokers receive immediate confirmation, and the results are transmitted to the appropriate market centers at the end of each day. Thereafter, each broker completes his or her own clearance and settlement procedure.

The ITS system currently provides centralized quotations for stocks listed on the NYSE and specifies whether a bid or ask away from the NYSE market is superior to that on the NYSE. Note, however, that the system lacks several characteristics. It does not have the capability for automatic execution at the best market. Instead you must contact the market maker and indicate that you want to buy or sell, at which time the bid or ask may be withdrawn. Also, it is not mandatory that a broker go to the best market. Although the best price may be at another market center, a broker might consider it inconvenient to transact on that exchange if the price difference is not substantial. It is almost impossible to audit such actions. Still, even with these shortcomings, technical and operational progress on a central quotation system has been substantial.

CENTRAL LIMIT-ORDER BOOK (CLOB)

Substantial controversy has surrounded the idea of a central limit-order book (CLOB) that would contain all limit orders from all exchanges. Ideally, the CLOB would be visible to everyone, and all market makers and traders could fill orders on it. Currently most limit orders are placed with specialists on the NYSE and filled when a transaction on the NYSE reaches the stipulated price. The NYSE specialist receives some part of the commission for rendering this service. The NYSE has opposed a CLOB because its specialists do not want to share this very lucrative business. The technology for a CLOB is available, but it is difficult to estimate when it will become a reality.

COMPETITION AMONG MARKET MAKERS (RULE 390)

Market makers have always competed on the OTC market, but competition has been opposed by the NYSE. The argument in favor of competition among market makers is that it forces dealers to offer better bids and asks, or they will not do any business. Several studies have indicated that competition among a large number of dealers (as in the OTC market) results in a smaller spread. In contrast, the NYSE argues that a central auction market forces all orders to one central location where the orders are exposed to all interested participants and this central auction results in the best market.

To help create a centralized market, the NYSE's Rule 390 requires members to obtain the permission of the exchange before carrying out a transaction in a listed stock off the exchange. This rule is intended to draw all volume to the NYSE, so that the exchange can provide the most complete auction market. The exchange contends that Rule 390 is necessary to protect the auction market, arguing that its elimination would fragment the market, tempting members to trade off the exchange and to internalize many orders (i.e., to match orders from their own customers, which would keep these orders from exposure to the full auction market). Hamilton contends that the adverse effects of fragmentation are more than offset by the benefits of competition.[41] Progress in achieving this final phase of the NMS has been slow because of strong opposition by members of the investment community and caution by the SEC.

NEW TRADING SYSTEMS

As daily trading volume has gone from 5 or 10 million shares to over 200 million shares, it has become necessary to introduce new technology into the trading process. Currently, the NYSE is capable of handling daily volume of over 500 million shares as shown in October 1987. The following discussion considers some technological innovations that assist in the trading process.

SUPER DOT

Super Dot is an electronic order-routing system through which member firms transmit market and limit orders in NYSE-listed securities directly to the posts where the securities are traded or to the member firm's booth. After the order has been executed, a report of execution is returned directly to the member firm office over the same electronic circuit, and the execution is submitted directly to the comparison systems. Member firms can enter market orders up to 2,099 shares and limit orders in round or odd lots up to 30,099 shares. An estimated 80 percent of all market orders enter the NYSE through the Super Dot system.

OPENING AUTOMATED REPORT SERVICE (OARS)

OARS, the opening feature of the Super Dot system, accepts member firm's preopening market orders up to 30,099 shares. OARS automatically and continuously pairs buy

---

[41]James L. Hamilton, "Marketplace Fragmentation Competition and the Efficiency of the Stock Exchange," *Journal of Finance* 34, no. 1 (March 1979): 171–187. For a recent article on this topic, see Hans R. Stoll, "Organization of the Stock Market: Competition or Fragmentation," *Journal of Applied Corporate Finance* 5, no. 4 (Winter 1993): 89–93.

and sell orders and presents the imbalance to the specialist prior to the opening of a stock. This system, which helps the specialist determine the opening price, is now operational for all issues.

MARKET ORDER PROCESSING

Super Dot's postopening market order system is designed to accept member firm's postopening market orders up to 2,099 shares. The system guarantees execution reports within 3 minutes. In fact, during 1992, 98.6 percent were reported within 2 minutes.

INDIVIDUAL INVESTOR EXPRESS DELIVERY SERVICE (IIEDS)

IIEDS provides priority delivery via the Super Dot system of simple round-lot and odd-lot market orders up to 2,099 shares for individual investor orders. The service is initiated on any day when the DJIA moves 25 points up or down from the previous day's close and remains in effect for the rest of the trading day.

LIMIT ORDER PROCESSING

The limit order processing system electronically files orders to be executed when and if a specific price is reached. The system accepts limit orders up to 99,999 shares, appends turnaround numbers, and delivers printed orders to the trading posts or the member firms' booths for storage. Good-until-canceled orders that are not executed on the day of submission are automatically stored until executed or canceled.

ELECTRONIC BOOK

The electronic book system replaces the specialist's handwritten limit order book with electronically generated display screens. It facilitates the researching, execution, and reporting of limit and market orders and helps eliminate processing errors. At the end of 1992, there were 619 electronic books handling 2,218 stocks on the NYSE floor.

GLOBAL MARKET CHANGES

NYSE OFF-HOURS TRADING

One of the major concerns of the NYSE is the continuing erosion of its market share for stocks listed on the NYSE due to global trading. Specifically, the share of trading of NYSE-listed stock has declined from about 80 to 85 percent during the early 1980s to about 60 to 65 percent in 1992. This reflects an increase in trading on the third market, some increase in fourth-market trading, but mainly an increase in trading in foreign markets in London and Tokyo. The NYSE has attempted to respond to this by expanding its trading hours and listing more non-U.S. stocks. The expansion of hours was initiated on May 24, 1991, when the SEC approved a 2-year pilot program of two NYSE crossing sessions. Crossing session I provides the opportunity to trade individual stocks at the NYSE closing prices after the regular session—from 4:15 P.M. to 5:00 P.M. Crossing session II allows crossing multiple stock orders of at least 15 NYSE stocks with a market value of at least $1 million. This session is from 4:00 P.M. to 5:15 P.M. During 1992 the average daily share volume for the two sessions was about 2.1 million shares.

LISTING FOREIGN STOCKS ON THE NYSE   A major goal/concern for the NYSE is the ability to list foreign stocks on the exchange. The NYSE Chairman, William Donaldson, has stated on several occasions that the exchange recognizes that much of the growth in the coming decades will be in foreign countries and their stocks. As a result, the exchange wants to list a number of these stocks. The problem is that current SEC regulations will not allow the NYSE to list these firms because these firms follow less-stringent foreign accounting and disclosure standards. Specifically, many foreign companies issue financial statements less frequently and with less information than what is required by the SEC. As a result, there are currently about 107 foreign firms that trade on the NYSE (mainly through ADRs), but Mr. Donaldson contends that there are 2,000 to 3,000 foreign companies that would qualify for listing on the NYSE except for the accounting rules. The exchange contends that unless the rules are adjusted and the NYSE is allowed to compete with other world exchanges (the LSE lists over 600 foreign stocks), it will eventually become a regional exchange in the global capital market. The view of the SEC is that they have an obligation to ensure that investors receive adequate disclosure. This difference hopefully will be resolved during 1993 in favor of allowing additional foreign listings.[42]

LONDON STOCK EXCHANGE

The London Stock Exchange initiated several major changes on October 27, 1986 in an event referred to as the *Big Bang.* As a result of this event, brokers can act as market makers, jobbers can deal with the public and with institutions, and all commissions are fully negotiable.

The gilt market was restructured to resemble the U.S. government securities market. The Bank of England approved a system whereby 27 primary dealers make markets in U.K. government securities and transact with a limited number of interdealer brokers. This new arrangement has created a more competitive environment.

Trades are reported on a system called *Stock Exchange Automated Quotations (SEAQ) International,* which is an electronic market-price information system similar to NASDAQ. In addition, real-time prices are being shared with the NYSE while the NASD provides certain U.S. OTC prices to the London market. Also, as discussed earlier, 35 U.S. OTC stocks are available for 24-hour trading between New York, Tokyo, Singapore, and London.

There is increased access to membership on the exchange whereby foreign firms are admitted as members, and they can be wholly owned by non-U.K. firms. As a result, some U.S. banks have acquired British stockbrokers, and several major U.S. firms are now members of the exchange.

SOME EFFECTS OF THE BIG BANG   Probably one of the most visually striking changes caused by the big bang occurred on the trading floor of the LSE. Prior to October 1986 the activity on the floor of the LSE was similar to that on the NYSE and the TSE—there were large numbers of people gathered around trading posts and moving between the phones and the posts. Currently, the exchange floor is completely deserted except for some traders in stock options. Once they introduced competitive market makers

---

[42]William Power and Kevin G. Salwen, "Big Board's Donaldson Says SEC Rules Could Cost Exchange Its Global Standing," *Wall Street Journal,* December 12, 1991, C1, C18. The NYSE argument is supported in the following articles: William J. Baumol and Burton Malkiel, "Redundant Regulation of Foreign Security Trading and U.S. Competitiveness," *Journal of Applied Corporate Finance* 5, no. 4 (Winter 1993): 19–27; and Franklin Edwards, "Listing of Foreign Securities on U.S. Exchanges," *Journal of Applied Corporate Finance* 5, no. 4 (Winter 1993): 28–36.

on the floor of the exchange, it was just as easy to buy and sell listed stocks away from the exchange using the quotes on SEAQ.

The rest of the Big Bang's effects can be summarized by the phrase "more business, less profit." Specifically, there is more activity throughout the system, but profit margins have declined or disappeared due to the intense competition. In the process, many firms have merged or been acquired by firms from the United States, Japan, or Germany that have been willing to accept lower returns in order to establish market presence. Also, they have increased their staffs and general overhead leading to small or negative profits. Notably, these difficult conditions were present before the October 1987 crash that affected markets around the world.[43]

TOKYO STOCK EXCHANGE (TSE)

Thus far, changes on the TSE have been minimal, because the exchange has resisted competitive pressures through regulation. Trading commissions are still based on fixed-scale rates that vary by the type and value of the transactions. Most transactions require a fixed charge plus a percentage of the value of the trade.

As of early 1993, 25 foreign firms were members of the TSE. Four Japanese investment firms dominate the Japanese financial market: Nomura, Daiwa, Nikko, and Yamaichi. The equity bases and market values of these firms exceed those of most U.S. firms and all firms from other countries. During 1990–1991 they were becoming major players in both London and the United States and building market share with lower commission rates, especially for fixed-income securities, but also for equities. They were less aggressive during 1992–1993 because of the dramatic slowdown in the Japanese economy and its security market that prompted a call for reform.[44]

PARIS BOURSE

As an example of continuing changes, in January 1988 the relatively small Paris Bourse initiated changes similar to the Big Bang in London. Specifically, the monopoly on stock trading held by the big brokerage houses was opened up to French and foreign banks and some investment firms began to merge with banks to acquire the capital needed to trade in a world market. The Bourse also began moving to a continuous auction market rather than the call market that had been operating for 2 hours a day.[45]

FUTURE DEVELOPMENTS

Besides the expected effects of the NMS and a global capital market, some additional changes are expected. You should understand why they are happening and contemplate their effects.

---

[43]Craig Forman, "Britain's Deregulation Leaves a Casualty Trail in Securities Industry," *Wall Street Journal,* October 14, 1987, 1, 18.

[44]For a further discussion of their impact during the late 1980s, see "Japan on Wall Street," *Business Week,* September 7, 1987, 82–90; and "The Evolution of the Tokyo Capital Market and Nomura Securities," a sponsored section in *Institutional Investor* 22, no. 4 (April 1988): 157–168. For a discussion of the problems in the early 1990s, see Manny Sender, "Why Japan's Financial Crisis is so Scary," *Institutional Investor* (June 1992): 60–66. The call for reform is discussed in Robert Thomson, "New Plea to Japan to Reform Markets," *Financial Times,* February 5, 1993; 17.

[45]Fiona Gleizes, "Paris Bourse Begins Its Own 'Big Bang' in Effort to Rival London's Exchange," *Wall Street Journal,* January 4, 1988, 15.

MORE SPECIALIZED INVESTMENT COMPANIES

Although more individuals want to own stocks and bonds, they have increasingly acquired this ownership through such institutions as investment companies, because most individuals feel that it is too difficult and time-consuming to do their own analysis. This increase in fund sales has caused a proliferation of new funds that provide numerous opportunities to diversify. This includes global stock and bond funds, international stock and bond funds limited to specific countries (e.g., Korea, Spain, Germany) or areas (e.g., Pacific Basin, Europe, Latin America), and sector funds that are limited to an industry (e.g., chemicals, bio-technology) or economic segment (e.g., emerging markets).

This trend toward specialized funds will continue and could include other investment alternatives such as stamps, coins, and art. Because of the lower liquidity of foreign securities, stamps, coins, and art, many of these new mutual funds will be closed-end and trade on an exchange. These funds and their surge in popularity will be discussed in Chapter 24.

CHANGES IN THE FINANCIAL SERVICES INDUSTRY

The financial services industry is experiencing a major change in makeup and operation. Prior to 1960, the securities industry was composed of specialty firms that concentrated in specific investments such as stocks, bonds, commodities, real estate, or insurance. One of the major trends has been the development of financial supermarkets that consider all of these investment alternatives around the world. Prime examples would be Sears Financial Corporation and Merrill Lynch, which have acquired insurance and real estate subsidiaries and would move into banking if allowed. A subset of this includes firms that are truly global in coverage, but limit their product line to mainstream investment instruments such as bonds, stock, futures and options. Firms in this category would include Merrill Lynch, Goldman Sachs, Salomon Brothers, and Morgan Stanley, among others. At the other end of the spectrum, large banks such as Citicorp want to become involved in the investment banking business.[46]

In contrast to financial supermarkets, some firms have decided not to be all things to all people. These firms are going the specialty, or "boutique" route, attempting to provide unique, superior financial products. Examples include discount brokers, investment firms that concentrate on institutional investors, firms that concentrate on working with individual investors, or special research firms that concentrate their research efforts on a single industry such as banking.

It appears that we are moving toward a world with a few large worldwide investment firms that deal in almost all the asset classes available and numerous specialized firms that provide specialized services in unique products.

Beyond these changes related to the individual firms, the advances in technology continue to accelerate and promise to affect how the secondary market will be organized and operate. Specifically, computerized trading has made tremendous inroads during the last 5 years and promises to introduce numerous additional changes into the

[46]Daniel Hertzberg and Tim Carrington, "Controversy Engulfs Banking Industry in Wake of Fed's Latest Nonbank Ruling," *Wall Street Journal*, December 16, 1983, 6.

twenty-first century in markets around the world. The 24-hour market will require extensive computerized trading.

SUMMARY

The securities market is divided into primary and secondary markets. Secondary markets provide the liquidity that is critical for primary markets. The major segments of the secondary markets include listed exchanges (the NYSE, AMEX, TSE, LSE, and regional exchanges), the over-the-counter market, the third market, and the fourth market. Because you will want to invest across these secondary markets within a country as well as these markets among countries, you need to understand how they differ and how they are similar.

Many of the dramatic changes in our securities markets during the last 30 years are due to an increase in institutional trading and to rapidly evolving global markets. It is important to understand what has happened and why it happened because numerous changes have occurred and many more changes are yet to come. You need to understand how these changes will affect your investment alternatives and opportunities. You need to look not only for the best investment, but also for the best market to use for a transaction. This discussion should provide the background to help you make that trading decision.

QUESTIONS

1. Define *market,* and briefly discuss the characteristics of a good market.

2. You own 100 shares of General Electric stock, and you want to sell it because you need the money to make a down payment on a stereo. Assume there is absolutely no secondary market system in common stocks. How would you go about selling the stock? Discuss what you would have to do to find a buyer, how long it might take, and the price you might receive.

3. Define liquidity and discuss the factors that contribute to it. Give examples of a liquid asset and an illiquid asset, and discuss why they are considered liquid and illiquid.

4. Define a primary and secondary market for securities and discuss how they differ. Discuss how the primary market is dependent on the secondary market.

5. Give an example of an initial public offering (IPO) in the primary market. Give an example of a seasoned equity issue in the primary market. Discuss which would involve greater risk to the buyer.

6. Find an advertisement for a recent primary offering in *The Wall Street Journal.* Based on the information in the ad, indicate the characteristics of the security sold and the major underwriters. How much new capital did the firm derive from the offering before paying commissions?

7. Briefly explain the difference between a competitive bid underwriting and a negotiated underwriting.

8. a. How do the two U.S. national stock exchanges differ?
   b. Briefly describe how the TSE differs from the NYSE in size and operation.

9. The figures in Table 3.3 reveal a major difference in the price paid for a membership (seat) on the NYSE compared with one on the AMEX. How would you explain this difference?

10. What are the major reasons for the existence of regional stock exchanges? Discuss how they differ from the national exchanges.

11. List and briefly discuss the differences between the OTC market and the listed exchanges.

12. Which segment of the secondary market (listed exchanges or the OTC) is larger in terms of the number of issues? Which is larger in terms of the value of the issues traded? Discuss which has more diversity in terms of the size of the companies and the quality of the issues.

13. What is the NASDAQ system? Discuss the three levels of NASDAQ in terms of what each provides and who would subscribe to each.

14. a. Define the third market. Give an example of a third-market stock.
     b. Define the fourth market. Discuss why a financial institution would use the fourth market.

15. Briefly define each of the following terms and give an example:
     a. Market order
     b. Limit order
     c. Short sale
     d. Stop loss order

16. Briefly discuss the two major functions of and sources of income for the NYSE specialist.

17. What is the high-risk segment of the specialists' dealer function? Why is it high risk? Discuss the risk involved in the specialists' broker function.

18. Describe the duties of the *Saitori* member on the TSE. Discuss how these duties differ from those of the NYSE specialist.

19. Discuss the overall reason why the secondary equity market in the United States has experienced major changes since 1965.

20. Discuss the empirical evidence for growth in institutional trading.

21. What were give-ups? What are "soft dollars"? Discuss why they existed when there were fixed commissions.

22. What is meant by the term *negotiated commissions?* When was May Day? When was the Big Bang?

23. The discussion of block trades and the specialist noted that the specialist is hampered by the three Cs. Discuss each of the three Cs as it relates to block trading.

24. Describe block houses, and explain why they evolved. Describe what is meant by *positioning* part of a block.

25. Discuss why the market size of an investment is important to an institutional portfolio manager.

26. a. Describe the major attributes of the National Market System (NMS).
     b. Briefly describe the ITS and what it contributes to the NMS. Discuss the growth of the ITS.

27. In the chapter, there is a discussion of expected future changes in world capital markets. Discuss one of the changes suggested in terms of what has been happening or discuss an evolving change that was not mentioned.

PROBLEMS

1. In the section of *The Wall Street Journal* on government bonds with the title "Treasury Bonds, Notes and Bills," what are the current bid and yield figures on the 8½ of 1997?

2. The initial margin requirement is 60 percent. You have $40,000 to invest in a stock selling for $80 a share. Ignoring taxes and commissions, show in detail the impact on your rate of return if the stock rises to $100 a share and also if it declines to $40 a share assuming: (a) you pay cash for the stock, and (b) you buy it using maximum leverage.

3. Shawn has a margin account and deposits $50,000. Assuming that the prevailing margin requirement is 40 percent, commissions are ignored, and The Gentry Shoe Corporation is selling at $35 per share:
    a. How many shares can Shawn purchase using the maximum allowable margin?
    b. What is Shawn's profit (loss) if the price of Gentry's stock
       1. Rises to $45?
       2. Falls to $25?
    c. If the maintenance margin is 30 percent, to what price can Gentry Shoe fall before Shawn will receive a margin call?

4. Suppose you buy a round lot of Maginn Industries stock on 55 percent margin when the stock is selling at $20 a share. The broker charges a 10 percent annual interest rate, and commissions are 3 percent of the total stock value on both the purchase and sale. If at year-end you receive a $0.50 per share dividend and sell the stock for 27⅝, what is your rate of return on the investment?

5. You decide to sell 100 shares of Charlotte Horse Farms short when it is selling at its yearly high of 56¼. Your broker tells you that your margin requirement is 45 percent and that the commission on the purchase is $155. While you are short the stock, Charlotte pays a $2.50 per share dividend. At the end of 1 year you buy 100 shares of Charlotte at 46⅜ to close out your position and are charged a commission of $145 and 8 percent interest on the money borrowed. What is your rate of return on the investment?

REFERENCES

AMEX Fact Book. New York: AMEX, published annually.

Amihad, Y., T. Ho, and Robert Schwartz, *Market Making and the Changing Structure of the Securities Industry.* New York: Lexington-Heath, 1985.

Amihad, Y., and H. Mendelson. "Trading Mechanisms and Stock Returns: An Empirical Investigation," *Journal of Finance* 42, no. 3 (July 1987): 533–553.

Beidleman, Carl, ed. *The Handbook of International Investing.* Chicago: Probus Publishing, 1987.

Berkowitz, S. A., Dennis E. Logue, and E. A. Naser, "The Total Cost of Transactions on the NYSE," *Journal of Finance* 41, no. 1 (March 1988).

Cohen, Kalman, Steven Maier, Robert Schwartz, and David Whitcomb. *The Microstructure of Securities Markets.* Englewood Cliffs, N.J.: Prentice-Hall, 1986.

Cooper, K., J. Groth and William Avera, "Liquidity, Exchange Listing, and Common Stock Performance," *Journal of Economics and Business* 37, no. 1 (March 1985).

deCaires, Bryan, ed. *The GT Guide to World Equity Markets, 1987.* London: Euromoney Publications, 1987.

Fabozzi, Frank J., and Frank G. Zarb, eds. *Handbook of Financial Markets.* 2d ed. Homewood, Ill.: Dow Jones-Irwin, 1986.

Garbade, Kenneth D. *Securities Markets.* New York: McGraw-Hill, 1982.

Glosten, L. R., "Components of the Bid-Ask Spread and the Statistical Properties of Transaction Prices," *Journal of Finance* 42, no. 5 (December 1987).

Grabbe, J. Orlin. *International Financial Markets.* New York: Elsevier, 1986.

Grossman, S. J. and Merton H. Miller, "Liquidity and Market Structure," *Journal of Finance,* 43, no. 2 (June 1988).

Hasbrouck, Joel, "Assessing the Quality of a Security Market: A New Approach to Transaction-Cost Measurement," *The Review of Financial Studies* 6, no. 1 (1993).

Hasbrouck, Joel and R. A. Schwartz, "An Assessment of Stock Exchange and Over-the-Counter Markets," *Journal of Portfolio Management* 14, no. 3 (Spring 1988): 10–17.

Ibbotson, Roger G. and Gary P. Brinson, *Global Investing,* New York: McGraw-Hill, 1992.

Jensen, Michael C., and Clifford W. Smith, eds. "Symposium on Investment Banking and the Capital Acquisition Process." *Journal of Financial Economics* 15, no. 1/2 (January-February 1986).

Loll, Leo M., and Julian G. Buckley. *The Over-the-Counter Securities Markets.* 4th ed. Englewood Cliffs, N.J.: Prentice-Hall, 1981.

Lorie, James H., Peter Dodd, and Mary Hamilton Kimpton. *The Stock Market: Theories and Evidence.* 2d ed. Homewood, Ill.: Richard D. Irwin, 1985.

Madhaven, Ananth. "Trading Mechanisms in Securities Markets." *Journal of Finance* 47, no. 2 (June 1992): 607–642.

NASDAQ Fact Book. Washington, D.C.: National Association of Securities Dealers, published annually.

Nikko Research Center, Ltd. *The New Tide of the Japanese Securities Market.* Tokyo: Nikko Research Center, 1988.

NYSE Fact Book. New York: NYSE, published annually.

Roll, Richard, "A Simple Model of the Implicit Bid-Ask Spread in an Efficient Market," *Journal of Finance* 39, no. 4 (September 1984).

Schwartz, Robert A. *Equity Markets: Structure, Trading, and Performance.* New York: Harper & Row, 1988.

Smyth, David. *Worldly Wise Investor.* New York: Franklin Watts, 1988.

Sobel, Robert. *N.Y.S.E.: A History of the New York Stock Exchange, 1935–1975.* New York: Weybright and Talley, 1975.

Sobel, Robert. *The Curbstone Brokers: The Origins of the American Stock Exchange.* New York: Macmillan, 1970.

Solnik, Bruno. *International Investments.* 2d ed. Reading, Mass.: Addison-Wesley, 1991.

Spicer and Oppenheim Guide to Securities Markets Around the World. New York: John Wiley & Sons, 1988.

Stoll, Hans. *The Stock Exchange Specialist System: An Economic Analysis.* Monograph Series in Financial Economics 1985-2. New York University, 1985.

Stoll, Hans. "Principles of Trading Market Structure." Working Paper 90-31. Vanderbilt University, 1990.

Stoll, Hans, and Robert Whaley. "Stock Market Structure and Volatility." *Review of Financial Studies* 3, no. 1 (1990). 37–71.

Tokyo Stock Exchange Fact Book. TSE, published annually.

U.S. Congress, Office of Technology Assessment. *Trading Around the Clock: Global Securities Markets and Information Technology—Background Paper,* OTA-BP-CIT-66. Washington, D.C.: U.S. Government Printing Office, July 1990.

Viner, Aron. *Inside Japanese Financial Markets.* Homewood, Ill.: Dow Jones-Irwin, 1988.

TABLE 3A   Developed Markets Around the World

Country	Principal Exchange	Other Exchanges	Total Market Capitalization ($ billions)	Available Market Capitalization ($ billions)	Trading Volume ($ billions)	Domestic Issues Listed	Total Issues Listed	Auction Mechanism	Official Specialists	Options/ Futures Trading	Price Limits	Principal Market Indexes
Australia	Sydney	5	82.3	53.5	39.3	N.A.	1496	Continuous	No	Yes	None	All Ordinaries—324 issues
Austria	Vienna	—	18.7	8.3	37.2	125	176	Single	Yes	No	5%	GZ Aktienindex—25 issues
Belgium	Brussels	3	48.5	26.2	6.8	186	337	Mixed	No	Few	10%	Brussels Stock Exchange Index—186 issues
Canada	Toronto	4	186.8	124.5	71.3	N.A.	1208	Continuous	Yes	Yes	None	TSE 300 Composite Index
Denmark	Copenhagen	—	29.7	22.2	11.1	N.A.	284	Mixed	No	No	None	Copenhagen Stock Exchange Index—38 issues
Finland	Helsinki	—	9.9	1.7	5.2	N.A.	125	Mixed	N.A.	N.A.	N.A.	KOP (Kansallis–Osake–Pannki) Price Index
France	Paris	6	256.5	137.2	129.0	463	663	Mixed	Yes	Yes	4%	CAC General Index—240 issues
Germany	Frankfurt	7	297.7	197.9	1003.7	N.A.	355	Continuous	Yes	Options	None	DAX; FAZ (Frankfurter Allgemeine Zeitung)
Hong Kong	Hong Kong	—	67.7	37.1	34.6	N.A.	479	Continuous	No	Futures	None	Hang Seng Index—33 issues
Ireland	Dublin	—	8.4	6.4	5.5	N.A.	N.A.	Continuous	No	No	None	J&E Davy Total Market Index
Italy	Milan	9	137.0	73.2	42.6	N.A.	317	Mixed	No	No	10–20%	Banca Commerziale—209 issues
Japan	Tokyo	7	2754.6	1483.5	1602.4	N.A.	1576	Continuous	Yes	No	10% down	TOPIX—1097 issues; TSE II—423 issues; Nikkei 225

Country	City		Market Capitalization (total)	Market Capitalization (available)	Trading Volume		Number of Issues	Trading				Domestic Share Price Index
Luxembourg	Luxembourg	—	1.5	0.9	0.1	61	247	Continuous	N.A.	N.A.	N.A.	Domestic Share Price Index—9 issues
Malaysia	Kuala Lumpur	—	37.0	14.2	10.6	240	282	Continuous	No	No	None	Kuala Lumpur Composite Index—83 issues
Netherlands	Amsterdam	—	112.1	92.4	80.4	279	569	Continuous	Yes	Options	Variable	ANP—CBS General Index—51 issues
New Zealand	Wellington	—	6.7	5.3	2.0	295	451	Continuous	No	Futures	None	Barclay's International Price Index—40 issues
Norway	Oslo	9	18.4	7.9	14.1	N.A.	128	Single	No	No	None	Oslo Bors Stock Index—50 issues
Singapore	Singapore	—	28.6	15.6	8.2	N.A.	324	Continuous	No	No	None	Straits Times Index—30 issues; SES—32 issues
South Africa	Johannesburg	—	72.7	N.A.	8.2	N.A.	N.A.	Continuous	No	Options	None	JSE Actuaries Index—141 issues
Spain	Madrid	3	86.6	46.8	41.0	N.A.	368	Mixed	No	No	10%	Madrid Stock Exchange Index—72 issues
Sweden	Stockholm	—	59.0	24.6	15.8	N.A.	151	Mixed	No	Yes	None	Jacobson & Ponsbach—30 issues
Switzerland	Zurich	6	128.5	75.4	376.6	161	380	Mixed	No	Yes	5%	Societe de Banque Suisse—90 issues
United Kingdom	London	5	756.2	671.1	280.7	1911	2577	Continuous	No	Yes	None	Financial Times—(FT) Ordinaries—750 issues; FTSE 100; FT 33
United States	New York	6	2754.3	2429.2	1787.1	N.A.	2234	Continuous	Yes	Yes	None	S&P 500; Dow Jones Industrial Average; Wilshire 5000; Russell 3000

NOTES: Market capitalizations (both total and available) are as of December 31, 1990, except for South African market capitalization, which is from 1988. Available differs from total market capitalization by subtracting out crossholdings, closely held and government-owned shares, and takes into account restrictions on foreign ownership. Number of issues listed are from 1988 except for Malaysia which is from 1990. Trading volume data is 1990 except for Switzerland, which is from 1988. Trading institutions data is from 1987. Market capitalizations (both total and available) for all countries except the United States and South Africa are from the Salomon-Russell Global Equity Indices. U.S. market capitalization (both total and available) is from the Frank Russell Company. All trading volume information (except for Switzerland) and Malaysian total issues listed is from the *Emerging Stock Markets Factbook: 1991*, International Finance Corp., 1991. Trading institutions information is from Richard Roll, "The International Crash of 1987," *Financial Analysts Journal*, September/October 1988. South African market capitalization, number of issues listed for all countries (except Malaysia), and Swiss trading volume are reproduced courtesy of Euromoney Books extracted from *The G. T. Guide to World Equity Markets: 1989*, 1988.

Source: Roger G. Ibbotson and Gary P. Brinson, *Global Investing* (New York: McGraw-Hill, 1992): 109–111.

TABLE 3B   Emerging Markets Around the World

Country	Principal Exchange	Other Exchanges	Market Capitalization ($ billions)	Trading Volume ($ billions)	Total Issues Listed	Auction Mechanism	Principal Market Indexes
Argentina	Buenos Aires	4	3.3	0.9	179	N.A.	Buenos Aires Stock Exchange Index
Brazil	São Paulo	9	16.4	6.2	581	Continuous	BOVESPA Share Price Index—83 issues
Chile	Santiago	1	13.6	0.8	215	Mixed	IGPA Index—180 issues
Colombia	Medellín	—	1.4	0.1	80	N.A.	Bogota General Composite Index
Greece	Athens	—	15.2	3.8	145	Continuous	Athens Stock Exchange Industrial Price Index
India	Bombay	14	38.6	27.3	2435	Continuous	Economic Times Index—72 issues
Indonesia	Jakarta	—	8.1	3.9	125	Mixed	Jakarta Stock Exchange Index
Israel	Tel Aviv	—	10.6	5.5	267	Single	General Share Index—all listed issues
Jordan	Amman	—	1.0	0.4	105	N.A.	Amman Financial Market Index
Mexico	Mexico City	—	32.7	11.8	199	Continuous	Bolsa de Valores Index—49 issues
Nigeria	Lagos	—	1.4	N.A.	131	Single	Nigerian Stock Exchange General Index
Pakistan	Karachi	—	3.0	0.2	487	Continuous	State Bank of Pakistan Index
Philippines	Makati	1	5.9	1.2	153	N.A.	Manila Commercial & Industrial Index—25 issues
Portugal	Lisbon	1	9.2	1.6	181	Single	Banco Totta e Acores Share Index—50 issues
South Korea	Seoul	—	110.6	76.0	669	Continuous	Korea Composite Stock Price Index
Taiwan	Taipei	—	100.7	718.0	199	Continuous	Taiwan Stock Exchange Index
Thailand	Bangkok	—	23.9	22.2	214	Continuous	Securities Exchange of Thailand Price Index
Turkey	Istanbul	—	19.1	5.7	110	Continuous	Istanbul Stock Exchange Index—50 issues
Venezuela	Caracas	1	8.4	2.2	66	Continuous	Caracas Stock Exchange Price Index
Zimbabwe	N.A.	—	2.4	0.1	57	N.A.	Reserve Bank of Zimbabwe Industrial Index

NOTES: Market capitalizations, trading volume, and total issues listed are as of 1990. Market capitalization, trading volume, and total issues listed for Brazil and São Paulo only. Trading volume for the Philippines is for both Manila and Makati. Total issues listed for India is Bombay only. Trading institutions information is from 1987 and 1988. Market capitalizations, trading, volume, and total issues listed are from the *Emerging Stock Markets Factbook: 1991*, International Finance Corp., 1991. Trading institutions information is from Richard Roll, "The International Crash of 1987," *Financial Analysts Journal*, September/October 1988. Additional trading institutions information is reproduced courtesy of Euromoney Books extracted from *The G. T. Guide to World Equity Markets: 1989*, 1988.

Source: Roger G. Ibbotson and Gary P. Brinson, *Global Investing* (New York: McGraw-Hill, 1992): 125–126.

CHAPTER 4

SECURITY-MARKET INDICATOR SERIES

In this chapter we will answer the following questions:

- What are some major uses of security market indicator series (indexes)?
- What are the major characteristics that cause alternative indexes to differ?
- What are the major stock market indexes in the United States and globally and what are their characteristics?
- What are the major bond market indexes for the United States and the world?
- What are some of the composite stock-bond market indexes?
- Where can you get historical and current data for all these indexes?
- What is the relationship among many of these indexes in the short-run (daily) or longer-run (monthly and annually)?

A fair statement regarding security-market indicator series—especially those outside the United States—is that everybody talks about them, but few people understand them. Even those investors familiar with widely publicized stock-market series, such as the Dow Jones Industrial Average (DJIA), usually know very little about indexes for the U.S. bond market or for non-U.S. stock markets such as Tokyo or London.

Although portfolios are obviously composed of many different individual stocks, investors typically ask, "What happened to the market today?" The reason for this question is that if an investor owns more than a few stocks or bonds, it is cumbersome to follow each stock or bond individually to determine the composite performance of the portfolio. Also there is an intuitive notion that most individual stocks or bonds move with the aggregate market. Therefore, if the overall market rose, an individual's portfolio probably also increased in value. To supply investors with a composite report on market performance, some financial publications or investment firms have developed stock-market and bond-market indexes.[1]

The initial section discusses several ways that investors use market indicator series. These significant functions provide an incentive for becoming familiar with these series and is why we present a full chapter on this topic. The second section considers what

---

[1] Throughout this chapter and the book we will use indicator series and indexes interchangeably, although indicator series is the more correct specification because it refers to a broad class of series; one popular type of series is an index, but there can be other types and many different indexes.

characteristics cause alternative indexes to differ. In this chapter we will discuss over 20 stock-market and bond-market indexes, each of which is different. You should understand what makes them different and why one of them is preferable for a given task because of its characteristics. The third section presents the most well-known U.S. and global stock-market series separated into groups based on the weighting scheme used. The fourth section considers bond-market indexes, which is a relatively new topic, not because the bond market is new, but because the creation and maintenance of total return bond indexes is new. Again, we consider international bond indexes following the domestic indexes. In section five we consider composite-stock market–bond market series. Our final section examines how these indexes relate to each other over time—daily, monthly, and yearly. This comparison demonstrates the important factors that cause high or low correlation among series. With this background, you should be able to make an intelligent choice of the indicator series that is best for your use.

USES OF SECURITY-MARKET INDEXES

Security-market indexes have at least five specific uses. A primary application is to examine total returns for an aggregate market or some component of a market over a specified time period and use the rates of return computed as a benchmark to judge the performance of individual portfolios. A basic assumption when evaluating portfolio performance is that any investor should be able to experience a rate of return comparable to the "market" return by randomly selecting a large number of stocks or bonds from the total market; hence, a superior portfolio manager should consistently do better than the market. Therefore, *an aggregate stock- or bond-market index can be used to judge the performance of professional money managers.* You should recall from our earlier discussion that you should also analyze the differential risk for the portfolios being judged as compared to the market index.

Indicator series are also used to develop an index portfolio. As we will discuss later, it is difficult for most money managers to consistently outperform specified market indexes on a risk-adjusted basis over time. If this is true, an obvious alternative is to invest in a portfolio that will emulate this market portfolio. This notion led to the creation of *index funds* whose purpose is to track the performance of the specified market series (index) over time—that is, derive similar rates of return.[2] Although the original index fund concept was related to common stocks, the development of comprehensive, well-specified bond-market indexes and similar inferior performance relative to the bond market by most bond portfolio managers has led to a similar phenomenon in the fixed-income area (i.e., the creation of bond index funds).[3]

Securities analysts, portfolio managers, and others use security-market indexes to examine the factors that influence aggregate security price movements (i.e., the indexes are used to measure aggregate market movements). A similar use is to analyze the relationship among stock and bond returns of different countries. An example would be the analysis of the relationship among U.S., Japanese, and German stock price movements.

---

[2]For a discussion of developments in indexing, see "New Ways to Play the Indexing Game," *Institutional Investor* 22, no. 13 (November 1988): 92–98; and Edward A. Wyatt, "Avidly Average," *Barron's* (May 22, 1989): 17, 30.

[3]See Fran Hawthorne, "The Battle of the Bond Indexes," *Institutional Investor* 20, no. 4 (April 1986).

Another group interested in an aggregate market series are "technicians," who believe past price changes can be used to predict future price movements. For example, in order to project future stock price movements technicians would plot and analyze price and volume changes for a stock market series like the Dow Jones Industrial Average.

Finally, work in portfolio and capital market theory has implied that the relevant risk for an individual risky asset is its *systematic risk,* which is the relationship between the rates of return for a risky asset and the rates of return for a market portfolio of risky assets.[4] Therefore, it is necessary when computing the systematic risk for an individual risky asset (security) to relate its returns to the returns for an aggregate market index that is used as a proxy for the market portfolio of risky assets.

DIFFERENTIATING FACTORS IN CONSTRUCTING MARKET INDEXES

Because indicator series are intended to reflect the overall movements of a group of securities, it is necessary to consider which factors are important in computing an index that is intended to represent a total population.

THE SAMPLE

The size of the sample, the breadth of the sample, and the source of the sample used to construct a series are all important.

A small percentage of the total population will provide valid indications of the behavior of the total population if the sample is properly selected. In fact, at some point the costs of taking a larger sample will almost certainly outweigh any benefits of increased size. The sample should be *representative* of the total population; otherwise, its size will be meaningless. A large biased sample is no better than a small biased sample. The sample can be generated by completely random selection or by a nonrandom selection technique that is designed to incorporate the characteristics desired. Finally, the *source* of the sample becomes important if there are any differences between alternative segments of the population, in which case samples from each segment are required.

WEIGHTING OF SAMPLE MEMBERS

Our second concern is with the weight given to each member in the sample. Three principal weighting schemes are used: (1) a price-weighted series, (2) a value-weighted series, and (3) an unweighted series, or what would be described as an equally weighted series.

COMPUTATIONAL PROCEDURE

Our final consideration is with the computational procedure used. One alternative is to take a simple arithmetic average of the various members in the series. Another is to compute an index and have all changes, whether of price or value, reported in terms of the basic index. Finally, some prefer using a geometric average of the components rather than an arithmetic average.

---

[4]This concept and its justification are discussed in Chapters 7 and 8.

STOCK-MARKET
INDICATOR
SERIES

As mentioned in the introduction to this chapter, we hear a lot about what happened to the Dow Jones Industrial Average (DJIA) each day. In addition, you might also hear about other stock indexes, such as the NYSE Composite, the S&P 500 index, the AMEX index, or even the Nikkei Average. If you listened carefully, you would realize that all of these indexes did not change by the same amount. The reason for some of the differences are obvious, such as the DJIA versus the Nikkei Average, but others are not. The purpose of this section is to briefly review each of the major series and point out how they differ in terms of the characteristics discussed in the prior section. As a result, you should come to understand that the movements over time for alternative indexes *should* differ and you will understand why they differ.

The discussion of the indexes is organized by the weighting of the sample of stocks. We begin with the price-weighted series because some of the most popular indexes are in this category. The next group are the value-weighted series, which is the technique being used for most of the recently developed indexes. Finally, we will examine the unweighted series.

PRICE-WEIGHTED
SERIES

A price-weighted series is an arithmetic average of current prices, which means that, in fact, movements are influenced by the differential prices of the components.

DOW JONES INDUSTRIAL AVERAGE

The best-known price series is also the oldest and certainly the most popular stock-market indicator series, the Dow Jones Industrial Average (DJIA). The DJIA is a price-weighted average of 30 large, well-known industrial stocks that are generally the leaders in their industry (blue chips) and are listed on the NYSE. The DJIA is computed by totaling the current prices of the 30 stocks and dividing the sum by a divisor that has been adjusted to take account of stock splits and changes in the sample over time.[5] The adjustment of the divisor is demonstrated in Table 4.1.

$$\text{DJIA}_t = \sum_{i=1}^{30} p_{it}/D_{adj}$$

where:

DJIA_t = the value of the DJIA on day t

p_{it} = the closing price of stock i on day t

D_{adj} = the adjusted divisor on day t

In Table 4.1 three stocks are employed to demonstrate the procedure used to derive a new divisor for the DJIA when a stock splits. When stocks split, the divisor becomes smaller. An idea of the cumulative effect of splits can be derived from the fact that the divisor was originally 30.0, but as of May 1993 was 0.4627.

---

[5]A complete list of all events that have caused a change in the divisor since the DJIA went to 30 stocks on October 1, 1928, is contained in Phyllis S. Pierce, ed., *The Business One Irwin Investor's Handbook* (Homewood, Ill.: Dow Jones Books, annual). Prior to 1992 it was *The Dow Jones Investor's Handbook*.

TABLE 4.1

Example of Change in DJIA Divisor When a Sample Stock Splits

	Before Split	After Three-for-One Split by Stock A	
	Prices	Prices	
A	30	10	
B	20	20	
C	10	10	
	60 ÷ 3 = 20	40 ÷ X = 20	X = 2 (New Divisor)

TABLE 4.2

Demonstration of the Impact of Differently Priced Shares on a Price-Weighted Indicator Series

		Period T + 1	
	Period T	Case A	Case B
A	100	110	100
B	50	50	50
C	30	30	33
Sum	180	190	183
Divisor	3	3	3
Average	60	63.3	61
Percentage change		5.5	1.7

The adjusted divisor ensures that the new value for the series is the same as it would have been without the split. In this case, the pre-split index value was 20. Therefore, after the split, given the new sum of prices, the divisor is adjusted downward to maintain this value of 20. The divisor is also changed if there is a change in the sample makeup of the series, which does not happen very often.

Because the series is price weighted, a high-priced stock carries more weight than a low-priced stock, so as shown in Table 4.2, a 10 percent change in a $100 stock ($10) will cause a larger change in the series than a 10 percent change in a $30 stock ($3). In Case A, when the $100 stock increases by 10 percent, the average rises by 5.5 percent; in Case B, when the $30 stock increases by 10 percent, the average rises by only 1.7 percent.

The DJIA has been criticized over time on several counts. First, the sample used for the series is limited. It is difficult to conceive that 30 nonrandomly selected blue-chip stocks can be representative of the 1,800 stocks listed on the NYSE. Beyond the limited number, the stocks included are, by definition, offerings of the largest and most prestigious companies in various industries. Therefore, it is contended that the DJIA probably reflects price movements for large, mature blue-chip firms rather than for the typical company listed on the NYSE. Several studies have pointed out that the DJIA has not been as volatile as other market indexes and that the long-run returns on the DJIA are not comparable to the other NYSE stock indexes.

In addition, because the DJIA is price weighted, when companies have a stock split, their prices decline, and therefore their weight in the DJIA is reduced—even though they may be large and important. Therefore, the weighting scheme causes a downward bias in the DJIA, because the stocks that have higher growth rates will have higher prices, and because such stocks tend to split, they will consistently lose weight within the index.[6] Regardless of the several criticisms made of the DJIA, there is a fairly close relationship between the *daily* percent changes for the DJIA and comparable price changes for other NYSE indexes as shown in a subsequent section of this chapter. Dow Jones also publishes an average of 20 stocks in the transportation industry and 15 utility stocks. Detailed reports of the averages are contained daily in *The Wall Street Journal* and weekly in *Barron's,* including hourly figures.

NIKKEI-DOW JONES AVERAGE
Also referred to as the Nikkei Stock Average Index, the Nikkei-Dow Jones Average is an arithmetic average of prices for 225 stocks on the First Section of the Tokyo Stock Exchange (TSE). This is the most well-known series in Japan, and it has been used to show stock price trends since the reopening of the TSE. Notably, it was formulated by Dow Jones and Company, and, similar to the DJIA, it is a price-weighted series, so a large dollar change for a small company will have the same impact of a similar price change of a large firm. It is also criticized because the 225 stocks that are included only comprise about 15 percent of all stocks on the First Section. The results for this index are reported daily in *The Wall Street Journal* and *The Financial Times* and weekly in *Barron's.*

VALUE-WEIGHTED SERIES

A value-weighted index is generated by deriving the initial total market value of all stocks used in the series (Market Value = Number of Shares Outstanding x Current Market Price). This figure is typically established as the base and assigned an index value (the most popular beginning index value is 100, but it can vary—e.g., 10, 50). Subsequently, a new market value is computed for all securities in the index, and the current market value is compared to the initial "base" value to determine the percentage of change, which in turn is applied to the beginning index value.

$$Index_t = \frac{\Sigma P_t Q_t}{\Sigma P_b Q_b} \times \text{Beginning Index Value}$$

where:

$Index_t$ = index value on day t

P_t = ending prices for stocks on day t

Q_t = number of outstanding shares on day t

P_b = ending price for stocks on base day

Q_b = number of outstanding shares on base day

A simple example for a three-stock index is shown in Table 4.3. As can be seen,

---

[6]For discussions of these problems, see H. L. Butler, Jr., and J. D. Allen, "The Dow Jones Industrial Average Reexamined," *Financial Analysts Journal* 35, no. 6 (November–December, 1979): 37–45; and E. E. Carter and K. J. Cohen, "Stock Averages, Stock Splits, and Bias," *Financial Analysts Journal* 23, no. 3 (May–June 1967): 77–81.

TABLE 4.3

Example of a Computation of a Value-Weighted Index

Stock	Share Price	Number of Shares	Market Value
December 31, 1993			
A	$10.00	1,000,000	$ 10,000,000
B	15.00	6,000,000	90,000,000
C	20.00	5,000,000	100,000,000
Total			$200,000,000
			Base Value Equal to an Index of 100
December 31, 1994			
A	$12.00	1,000,000	$ 12,000,000
B	10.00	12,000,000[a]	120,000,000
C	20.00	5,500,000[b]	110,000,000
Total			$242,000,000

$$\text{New Index Value} = \frac{\text{Current Market Value}}{\text{Base Value}} \times \text{Beginning Index Value}$$

$$= \frac{\$242,000,000}{\$200,000,000} \times 100$$

$$= 1.21 \times 100$$

$$= 121$$

[a]Stock split two-for-one during year.

[b]Company paid a 10 percent stock dividend during the year.

there is an *automatic adjustment* for stock splits and other capital changes in a value-weighted index because the decrease in the stock price is offset by an increase in the number of shares outstanding. In a value-weighted index, the importance of individual stocks in the sample is dependent on the market value of the stocks. Therefore, a specified percentage change in the value of a large company has a greater impact than a comparable percentage change for a small company. As can be envisioned using the data in Table 4.3, if we begin with a base value of $200 million and assume that the only change is a 20 percent increase in the value of Stock A, which has a beginning value of $10 million, the ending index value would be $202 million, or an index of 101. In contrast, if only Stock C increases by 20 percent from $100 million, the ending value will be $220 million or an index value of 110. The point is, price changes for the large market value stocks in a value-weighted index will dominate changes in the index value over time.

STANDARD & POOR'S INDEXES

The first company to widely employ a market value index was Standard & Poor's Corporation (S&P). Using 1935–1937 as a base period, the firm computed the index for 425 industrial stocks, 50 utilities, 25 transportation firms, and a 500-stock composite index. The base period was subsequently changed to 1941–1943 and the base value to 10. All the S&P series were again changed significantly on July 1, 1976, to: 400 industrials, 40 utilities, 20 transportation, and 40 financial. A number of OTC stocks were added because, as noted in Chapter 3, most of the major banks and insurance companies have been traded on the OTC market. Therefore, to construct a relevant financial index, it was necessary to break the tradition of including only NYSE-listed stocks.[7] S&P has also constructed over 90 individual industry series. Daily figures for the major S&P indexes are carried in *The Wall Street Journal, The Financial Times,* and other newspapers, and weekly data are contained in *Barron's.* S&P has a weekly publication titled *The Outlook* that contains weekly values for all the industry groups. Extensive historical data on all these indexes and other financial series are contained in S&P's annual publication, *Trade and Securities Statistics.*

NEW YORK STOCK EXCHANGE INDEX

In 1966 the NYSE derived five market value indexes (industrial, utility, transportation, financial, and a composite index, which contains the other four) with figures available back to 1940. (The December 31, 1965, figures are equal to 50.) In contrast to other indexes, the various NYSE series are not based on a sample of stocks but include all stocks listed on the exchange. Therefore, questions about the number of stocks in the sample or the breadth of the sample do not arise as long as it is recognized that these indexes are limited to stocks listed on the NYSE. However, because the index is value weighted, the stocks of large companies still control major movements in the index. For example, the 500 stocks in the Standard & Poor's Composite Index represent about 74 percent of the market value of all stocks on the NYSE, although they are only about 28 percent of exchange listings in terms of numbers.[8]

NASDAQ SERIES

A comprehensive set of price indicator series for the OTC market was developed by the National Association of Securities Dealers (NASD). These NASDAQ-OTC Price Indicator Series were released to the public on May 17, 1971, with figures available from February 5, 1971. (The index value was 100 as of February 5.) Through NAS-DAQ, the NASD provides daily, weekly, and monthly sets of stock price indicators for OTC securities in different industry categories. Most domestic OTC common stocks listed on NASDAQ are included in the indexes, and new stocks are included when they are added to the system. As of the end of 1992 there are 4,013 issues contained in the NASDAQ Composite Price Indexes, and they have been divided into seven categories:[9]

1. Composite (4,013 issues)
2. Industrials (2,860 issues)
3. Banks (224 issues)
4. Insurance (106 issues)
5. Other finance (614 issues)
6. Transportation (65 issues)
7. Utilities (144 issues)

---

[7]For a detailed discussion of the computation and potential adjustment of all the series, see *Trade and Securities Statistics* (New York: Standard & Poor's, annual).

[8]For a listing of daily values for each year and a matrix of growth rates in the NYSE Index for the period 1972 to the present, see the annual *NYSE Fact Book* (New York: New York Stock Exchange).

[9]Besides the 4,013 issues in the NASDAQ Composite Price Index, there are 751 issues that are unassigned, bringing the total number on NASDAQ to 4,764.

Because the indexes are value weighted, they are heavily influenced by the largest 100 stocks on the NASDAQ system. Most of the NASDAQ series are reported daily in *The Wall Street Journal* and *The Financial Times* and weekly in *Barron's.* Further descriptive information about the index along with annual high, low, and close figures for all years since 1974 are contained in the *NASDAQ Fact Book & Company Directory,* which is published annually by the NASD.

AMERICAN STOCK EXCHANGE

The AMEX developed a Price Change Index in 1966 but subsequently commissioned the creation of a value-weighted series referred to as the Market Value Index. This new series was released in September 1973 with a base level of 100 as of August 31, 1973, and figures available back to 1969. On July 5, 1983, the Market Value Index was adjusted to one-half its previous level so now it has a base level of 50. The index includes common shares, ADRs, and warrants but does not include rights, preferred stock, or "when-issued" stock. Daily figures for the index are available in *The Wall Street Journal,* weekly data are in *Barron's,* and monthly closing values from 1969 are contained in the annual *AMEX Fact Book.*

DOW JONES EQUITY MARKET INDEX

A relatively new market value weighted index was introduced in October 1988. It is the Dow Jones Equity Market Index that includes nearly 700 stocks in 82 industry groups and has an index value of 100 as of June 30, 1982. Besides being market value weighted rather than price weighted, this index considers stocks from the NYSE, AMEX and the NASDAQ National Market System. Currently these 700 stocks represent about 80 percent of the market value of the total U.S. equity market.

The index is reported daily in *The Wall Street Journal.* Besides providing data for the composite index, there is a table that reports the top five industry groups for the day (e.g., steel, health care) and the strongest stocks in each of these industry groups. There is a similar listing of the five lagging industry groups and the weakest stocks in these groups.

WILSHIRE 5000 EQUITY INDEX

The Wilshire 5000 Equity Index is a value-weighted index published by Wilshire Associates (Santa Monica, California) that derives the dollar value of 5,000 common stocks, including all NYSE and AMEX issues, plus the most active stocks on the OTC market. The specific weighting is about 82 percent NYSE, 4 percent AMEX, and 14 percent OTC, which means that the NYSE has the greatest influence because of its higher market value. The index was created in 1974 with month-end history computed back to December 1970. Beginning December 1979, it was calculated daily. The Wilshire 5000 base is its December 31, 1980, capitalization of $1,404.596 billion. The index currently appears daily in *The Wall Street Journal* and several other major daily papers and has been published weekly in *Barron's* since January 1975.

THE RUSSELL INDEXES

There are three separate but overlapping indexes provided by the Frank Russell Company, a money manager consulting firm in Tacoma, Washington: the Russell 3000, the

Russell 1000, and the Russell 2000. The Russell 3000 consists of the 3,000 largest U.S. stocks by market capitalization and represents 97 percent of the U.S. equity market in terms of market value. The Russell 1000 consists of the 1,000 largest capitalization U.S. stocks. The smallest stock in this index has a market value of $350 million. The Russell 2000 is an index of small stocks and consists of the smallest 2,000 stocks in the Russell 3000 index. The firms in the 2000 series range in size from approximately $350 million to $30 million, and the total value of all the stocks in the Russell 2000 represents about 10 percent of total capitalization.

These indexes are considered pure because they include only U.S. stocks. Also, although the Russell 3000 is more comprehensive than most other U.S. indexes, size differences allow for analysis of the institutional segment (using the Russell 1000) or the small-firm segment (using the Russell 2000), which has become a popular sector based on numerous efficient-market studies that will be discussed in Chapter 6. The Russell 2000 is reported daily in *The Wall Street Journal,* and the three indexes are reported weekly in *Barron's.*

Figure 4.1 shows the "Stock Market Data Bank" from *The Wall Street Journal* of May 3, 1993, which contains values for many of the U.S. stock indexes we have discussed.

FINANCIAL TIMES ACTUARIES SHARE INDEXES

The *Financial Times* Actuaries Share indexes are for stocks listed on the London Stock Exchange (LSE). They relate current market capitalizations of each index to the market capitalization at the base date (April 10, 1962), adjusted for intervening capital changes. The following is a recent breakdown of LSE stocks:

Capital goods	207
Consumer group	186
Other group	93
Industrial group index	486
Oils	14
	500 Share Index
Financial group index	122
Others	78
	700 All-Share Index

The sample is broken down into 34 subsections. The advantages of this index is that it is very broad and therefore reflects the movements of the total London market. Also, because it is a market value weighted series, it can be used to measure long-term market movements and to evaluate portfolio performance. The All-Share Index and all of its components are reported daily in *The Financial Times.*

In addition to the All-Share index, *The Financial Times* has constructed several specialized indexes. The FT-SE 100 (referred to as the "Footsie 100") is a market-value weighted index of the 100 largest publicly traded stocks on the LSE. It was initiated in 1984 and has been used as the underlying asset for futures and options contracts. As a result, it is widely quoted and followed.

FIGURE 4.1   **Stock Market Data Bank**

STOCK MARKET DATA BANK   5/3/93

MAJOR INDEXES

HIGH	LOW (†365 DAY)		CLOSE	NET CHG		% CHG	†365 DAY CHG		% CHG	FROM 12/31		% CHG
DOW JONES AVERAGES												
3478.61	3136.58	30 Industrials	x3446.46	+	18.91	+ 0.55	+	68.33	+ 2.02	+	145.35	+ 4.40
1683.08	1204.40	20 Transportation	x1607.54	+	14.70	+ 0.92	+	226.75	+ 16.42	+	158.33	+ 10.93
247.68	209.69	15 Utilities	x239.98	+	0.62	+ 0.26	+	27.79	+ 13.10	+	18.96	+ 8.58
1322.35	1107.47	65 Composite	x1289.96	+	8.03	+ 0.63	+	94.59	+ 7.91	+	85.41	+ 7.09
432.78	377.00	Equity Mkt. Index	419.66	+	2.09	+ 0.50	+	27.52	+ 7.02	+	6.37	+ 1.54
NEW YORK STOCK EXCHANGE												
251.36	220.61	Composite	244.54	+	1.08	+ 0.44	+	15.12	+ 6.59	+	4.33	+ 1.80
303.16	273.18	Industrials	294.30	+	1.59	+ 0.54	+	7.26	+ 2.53	−	0.09	− 0.03
232.40	193.40	Utilities	224.28	+	0.50	+ 0.22	+	28.08	+ 14.31	+	14.62	+ 6.97
246.81	182.66	Transportation	236.11	+	1.30	+ 0.55	+	27.10	+ 12.97	+	21.39	+ 9.96
223.96	171.44	Finance	211.11	+	0.34	+ 0.16	+	36.44	+ 20.86	+	10.28	+ 5.12
STANDARD & POOR'S INDEXES												
456.33	400.96	500 Index	442.46	+	2.27	+ 0.52	+	25.55	+ 6.13	+	6.75	+ 1.55
524.99	471.36	Industrials	507.64	+	2.94	+ 0.58	+	13.45	+ 2.72	+	0.18	+ 0.04
405.65	307.94	Transportation	386.58	+	3.40	+ 0.89	+	27.05	+ 7.52	+	22.83	+ 6.28
176.23	145.17	Utilities	169.42	+	0.32	+ 0.19	+	21.80	+ 14.77	+	10.96	+ 6.92
46.67	34.15	Financials	43.33	+	0.15	+ 0.35	+	8.51	+ 24.44	+	2.44	+ 5.97
166.77	136.02	400 MidCap	161.49	+	1.04	+ 0.65	+	17.46	+ 12.12	+	0.93	+ 0.58
NASDAQ												
708.85	547.84	Composite	666.71	+	5.29	+ 0.80	+	83.17	+ 14.25	−	10.24	− 1.51
757.05	581.60	Industrials	686.34	+	7.20	+ 1.06	+	49.36	+ 7.75	−	38.60	− 5.32
868.27	608.60	Insurance	837.49	+	4.09	+ 0.49	+	224.22	+ 36.56	+	33.58	+ 4.18
641.57	420.75	Banks	607.91	+	1.60	+ 0.26	+	187.16	+ 44.48	+	74.98	+ 14.07
314.39	242.25	Nat. Mkt. Comp.	294.81	+	2.45	+ 0.84	+	36.56	+ 14.16	−	5.75	− 1.91
303.87	232.48	Nat. Mkt. Indus.	274.42	+	3.01	+ 1.11	+	19.57	+ 7.68	−	16.98	− 5.83
OTHERS												
423.43	364.85	Amex	422.21	+	1.25	+ 0.30	+	30.60	+ 7.81	+	22.98	+ 5.76
281.38	238.81	Value-Line(geom.)	273.07	+	0.89	+ 0.33	+	17.12	+ 6.69	+	6.39	+ 2.40
232.36	185.81	Russell 2000	r223.66	+	0.99	+ 0.44	+	25.90	+ 13.10	+	2.65	+ 1.20
4475.25	3860.55	Wilshire 5000	4336.62	+	20.50	+ 0.47	+	305.27	+ 7.57	+	46.88	+ 1.09

†-Based on comparable trading day in preceding year.

Source: *Wall Street Journal* (May 4, 1993): C2.

In response to the growing interest in smaller companies because of academic research on the performance of these stocks (to be discussed in Chapter 6), *The Financial Times* created a Small Cap Index of stocks with low market value on the exchange. During 1992, *The Financial Times* filled out their index offerings with a FT-SE Mid 250 which included the 250 stocks with market values below the FT-SE 100 and above the small cap sample. Finally, they also report a FT-SE 350 which is a combination of the FT-SE 100 and the FT-SE 250. All of these indexes are reported daily in *The Financial Times* as shown in Figure 4.2.

FIGURE 4.2   ***Financial Times* Actuaries Share Indices**

FT-SE   Actuaries Share Indices   THE UK SERIES

FT-SE 100	**FT-SE MID 250**	**FT-A ALL-SHARE**
2786.8 –10.5	**3110.4 –11.3**	**1377.21 –4.97**

	Apr 29	Day's change %	Apr 28	Apr 27	Apr 26	Year ago	Earnings yield %	Dividend yield %	P/E Ratio	Xd adj ytd
FT-SE 100	2786.8	–0.4	2797.3	2832.7	2822.3	2654.1	6.50	4.09	19.51	36.73
FT-SE Mid 250	3110.4	–0.4	3121.7	3134.3	3133.8	2712.4	6.52	3.74	19.33	31.93
FT-SE-A 350	1390.3	–0.4	1395.5	1410.4	1406.4	1299.1	6.50	4.01	19.47	17.42
FT-SE SmallCap	1585.09	......	1585.75	1584.27	1582.31	–	4.63	3.60	30.94	15.62
FT-SE SmallCap ex Inv Trusts	1596.89	–0.1	1597.89	1596.97	1595.22	–	5.13	3.80	28.86	16.17
FT-A ALL-SHARE	1377.21	–0.4	1382.18	1395.92	1392.17	1282.75	6.38	3.98	19.93	17.02

Source: *Financial Times* (April 30, 1993), p. 35.

TOKYO STOCK EXCHANGE PRICE INDEX (TOPIX)

The price index of the Tokyo Stock Exchange was devised in July 1969 to take account of various defects noted in the Nikkei Stock Average, namely, limited sample and price weighting. TOPIX is a composite index that measures changes in aggregate market value of all common stocks listed on the First Section of the TSE. The base of 100 for the index is the market value at the close on January 4, 1968. Similar to the S&P indexes, the base market value is adjusted to reflect nonprice changes such as new listings, delistings, and mergers.

The composite index is supplemented by subgroup indexes for each of 28 industry groups and three size groups: large (over 200 million shares listed), medium (between 60 and 200 million shares listed), and small (less than 60 million shares listed). The index results are published daily in *The Wall Street Journal* and *The Financial Times.*

UNWEIGHTED PRICE INDICATOR SERIES

In an unweighted index, all stocks carry equal weight regardless of their price and/or their market value. A $20 stock is as important as a $40 stock, and the total market value of the company is not important. Such an index can be used by individuals who randomly select stock for their portfolio. One way to visualize an unweighted series is to assume that equal dollar amounts are invested in each stock in the portfolio (e.g., an equal $1,000 investment in each stock would work out to 50 shares of a $20 stock, 100 shares of a $10 stock, and 10 shares of a $100 stock). In fact, the actual movements in the index are typically based on the arithmetic average of the percent price changes for the stocks in the index. The use of percent price changes means that the price level or the market value of the stock does not make a difference—each percent change has equal weight.

UNIVERSITY OF CHICAGO SERIES

The best-known unweighted (or equal-weighted) stock-market series are those constructed by Lawrence Fisher while at the University of Chicago.[10] These series were used in several studies conducted by Fisher and James Lorie that examined the performance of stocks on the NYSE.[11] They have been used extensively in subsequent empirical studies.

VALUE LINE AVERAGES

The Value Line Composite Average is an index based on an equally weighted geometric average of the percent changes for the approximately 1,700 stocks regularly reviewed in *The Value Line Investment Survey.* The composite index is broken down into the following major categories and 146 subgroups.

	Number of Stocks
Industrials	1,499
Utilities	177
Rails	19
Composite	1,695

More than 80 percent of the stocks comprising the Value Line Averages are listed on the NYSE. The average is computed as follows:

Each market day the closing price of each stock is divided by the preceding day's close, with the preceding day set at an index of 100. The resulting indexes of change for that day are geometrically averaged for the 1,695 stocks. You will recall from Chapter 1 that a *geometric average* is defined as the nth root of the product of N items. In other words, it is the square root of two items, the cube root of three items, and so on. In the *Value Line Average,* it is the 1695th root of the product of the 1,695 ratios. The geometric average of these changes for each day is then multiplied by the value of the Value Line Composite Average on the preceding day to get the latest value. Table 4.4 contains an example of a computation involving three stocks. Note that there is no consideration of the market value for the stocks, and the price level does not have an impact because you are dealing with percentage changes. In contrast to the earlier discussion of how equal-weighted indexes are computed, these indexes are a geometric average of the percent changes rather than an arithmetic average. As a result, the results would be biased downward slightly compared to an unweighted index that used an arithmetic average of the percent changes.

When stock splits or dividends occur, the preceding day is adjusted accordingly, and the index of change computed thereafter. As stocks are added to *The Value Line Investment Survey,* the average is enlarged. Additions and deletions of stocks present no problem to the average because of its large base and method of construction. Daily

---

[10]Lawrence Fisher, "Some New Stock Market Indexes," *Journal of Business* 39, no. 1, Part II (January 1966 supplement): 191-225.

[11]Lawrence Fisher and James H. Lorie, "Rates of Return on Investments in Common Stock," *Journal of Business* 37, no. 1 (January 1964): 1–21; L. Fisher and J. H. Lorie, "Rates of Return on Investments in Common Stock: The Year-By-Year Record, 1926–1965," *Journal of Business* 41, no. 3 (July 1968): 291–316; and Lawrence Fisher, "Outcomes for 'Random' Investments in Common Stock Listed on the New York Stock Exchange," *Journal of Business* 38, no. 2 (April 1965): 149-161.

TABLE 4.4   **Example of a Computation of Value Line Index**

	Share Price		Index of
Stock	T	T + 1	Change
X	10	12	1.20
Y	22	20	.91
Z	44	47	1.07

$$\Pi = 1.20 \times .91 \times 1.07$$
$$= 1.168$$
$$1.168^{1/3} = 1.0531$$

$$\text{Index Value (T)} \times 1.0531 = \text{Index Value (T + 1)}$$

figures for the Value Line (VL) composite average are contained in *The Wall Street Journal,* and weekly data are in *Barron's.*

INDICATOR DIGEST INDEX

All stocks on the NYSE are included in the Indicator Digest Unweighted Index. Compared to value-weighted series that are heavily influenced by large firms, this series is intended to be more representative of all stocks on the exchange. In several instances, it reached a trough earlier than other indexes and continued to be depressed after some of the "popular" market indexes resumed rising during a bull market. Such a difference in performance would indicate that the market increase was heavily influenced by the large, popular stocks contained in the DJIA or the Standard & Poor's series rather than being affected by the numerous small stocks that have equal weight in this index.

FINANCIAL TIMES ORDINARY SHARE INDEX

Sometimes known as the 30-Share Index because it includes 30 heavily traded blue-chip stocks listed on the LSE, *The Financial Times* Ordinary Share Index is similar to the DJIA because it includes a limited number of blue-chip stocks, but it differs from the DJIA because it is an unweighted index (i.e., similar to the Value Line indexes, it is a geometric average of the rates of return for the 30 stocks). The index has an unbroken history back to 1935 with a limited number of changes in the sample over time. Although about half the constituents are unchanged from the beginning, the index includes oil and financial firms, so it is not only an industrial index.

The creators of the index recognize that using a geometric average of the rates of return during a period of time biases the series downward compared to other series. Therefore, although the series reflects the short-term movements ("mood") of the market, it should not be used as a long-term measure of market returns when evaluating portfolio performance. *The Financial Times* All-Share Index described earlier is considered more appropriate for evaluating long-term portfolio performance. Daily figures for this 30-share index are contained in *The Financial Times* and *The Wall Street Journal,* with weekly data in *Barron's.*[12]

---

[12]Appendix 4A contains a table that provides the main characteristics of a number of indexes created and reported within numerous countries.

GLOBAL EQUITY
INDEXES

As noted in footnote 12 and described in Appendix 4A, there are stock-market indexes available for most individual foreign markets similar to those we described for Japan (the Nikkei and TOPIX) and the United Kingdom (the several *Financial Times* indexes). While these local indexes are closely followed within each country, there can be a problem comparing these indexes to one another because there is no consistency among them in sample selection, weighting, or computational procedure. To solve these problems several groups have computed a set of country stock indexes with consistent sample selection, weighting, and computational procedure. As a result, these indexes can be directly compared and they can be combined to create various regional indexes (e.g., Pacific Basin). We will describe five sets of global equity indexes.

FT-ACTUARIES WORLD INDEXES

The FT-Actuaries World Indexes are jointly compiled by The Financial Times Limited, Goldman Sachs & Company, and Wood Mackenzie & Company, Ltd. in conjunction with the Institute of Actuaries and the Faculty of Actuaries. Approximately 2,200 equity securities in 24 countries are measured, covering at least 70 percent of the total value of all listed companies in each country. Actively traded medium and small capitalization stocks are included along with major international equities. All securities included must allow direct holdings of shares by foreign nationals.

The indexes are market value weighted and have a base date of December 31, 1986 = 100. The index results are reported in U.S. dollars, U.K. pound sterling, Japanese yen, German mark, and the local currency of the country. Performance results are calculated after the New York markets close and are published the following day in *The Financial Times*. The 24 countries and the proportion of each in U.S. dollars is as follows (as of June 1992):

Australia	1.29	Hong Kong	0.89	Norway	0.11
Austria	0.08	Ireland	0.10	Singapore	0.13
Belgium	0.60	Italy	2.35	South Africa	0.64
Canada	2.19	Japan	32.17	Spain	0.72
Denmark	0.20	Malaysia	0.06	Sweden	0.36
Finland	1.29	Mexico	0.08	Switzerland	1.42
France	2.21	Netherlands	1.42	United Kingdom	8.79
Germany	4.63	New Zealand	0.26	United States	39.30

In addition to the individual countries and the world index, there are several geographic subgroups as shown in Table 4.5

MORGAN STANLEY CAPITAL INTERNATIONAL (MSCI) INDEXES

The Morgan Stanley Capital International Indexes consist of 3 international, 19 national, and 38 international industry indexes. The indexes consider some 1,375 companies listed on stock exchanges in 19 countries with a combined market capitalization that represents approximately 60 percent of the aggregate market value of the stock exchanges of these countries. All the indexes are market value weighted. Table 4.6 contains the countries included, the number of stocks, and market values for stocks in the various countries and groups.

In addition to reporting the indexes in U.S. dollars and the country's local currency, the following valuation information is available: (1) price-to-book value (P/BV) ratio,

TABLE 4.5   FT-Actuaries World Indexes

NATIONAL AND REGIONAL MARKETS — Figures in parentheses show number of lines of stock	WEDNESDAY APRIL 28, 1993							DOLLAR INDEX		
	U.S. Dollar Index	Day's Change %	Pound Sterling Index	Yen Index	DM Index	Local Currency Index	Local % chg on day	Gross Div. Yield	1993 High	1993 Low	Year ago (approx)
Australia (68)	140.93	−1.6	132.96	100.13	116.21	131.51	+0.0	3.76	144.19	117.39	148.38
Austria (18)	142.02	−1.0	133.98	100.91	117.10	117.11	−0.5	1.77	150.96	131.16	164.42
Belgium (42)	150.21	−0.3	141.71	106.72	123.86	120.76	+0.1	4.69	156.76	131.19	138.18
Canada (110)	125.15	+0.4	118.07	88.91	103.19	115.41	+0.7	2.88	125.97	111.41	126.71
Denmark (33)	214.10	−0.4	201.98	152.12	176.53	177.77	−0.1	1.28	217.26	185.11	229.75
Finland (23)	93.55	−2.5	88.26	66.47	77.14	106.42	−1.4	1.17	95.93	65.50	77.40
France (98)	162.19	+0.3	153.01	115.23	133.72	136.11	+0.6	3.30	167.36	142.72	160.69
Germany (62)	113.87	−1.1	107.43	80.92	93.89	93.89	−0.7	2.27	117.10	101.59	117.56
Hong Kong (55)	277.23	+0.9	261.55	196.97	228.60	275.03	+0.9	3.37	277.23	218.82	222.04
Ireland (15)	164.68	+0.2	155.36	117.01	135.79	150.78	+0.5	3.51	170.40	129.28	162.69
Italy (73)	70.31	−0.2	66.33	49.95	57.97	77.17	−0.6	2.55	70.44	53.78	70.85
Japan (470)	141.57	+0.2	133.56	100.58	116.75	100.58	+1.3	0.83	141.84	100.75	97.61
Malaysia (69)	312.05	−0.2	294.40	221.70	257.30	308.93	−0.2	2.18	312.62	251.66	237.42
Mexico (18)	1569.57	+0.1	1480.77	1115.18	1294.20	5313.85	+0.2	1.27	1725.81	1410.30	1654.78
Netherland (24)	169.38	−0.2	159.79	120.34	139.66	137.76	+0.2	4.02	172.75	150.39	155.21
New Zealand (13)	49.03	+1.1	46.26	34.84	40.43	47.84	+1.6	4.57	49.03	40.56	43.62
Norway (22)	163.38	+1.4	154.14	116.08	134.72	148.47	+1.6	1.78	163.38	137.71	174.83
Singapore (38)	242.48	+0.5	228.76	172.28	199.94	180.52	+0.6	1.86	242.48	207.04	209.49
South Africa (60)	181.45	−0.6	171.18	128.92	149.61	184.02	+0.2	2.72	182.65	144.72	226.11
Spain (45)	132.19	+0.7	124.71	93.92	108.99	116.16	+0.4	5.20	132.82	115.23	148.26
Sweden (36)	172.15	+0.8	162.41	122.32	141.95	184.96	+0.8	1.82	174.66	149.70	183.19
Switzerland (55)	120.18	+0.1	113.38	85.39	99.11	106.81	+0.7	2.04	121.72	108.91	99.97
United Kingdom (218)	178.42	−1.6	168.32	126.75	147.10	168.32	−1.1	4.09	181.99	162.00	189.45
USA (519)	178.75	+0.0	168.63	127.00	147.39	178.75	+0.0	2.85	186.27	175.38	167.89
Europe (764)	146.89	−0.7	138.58	104.37	121.13	131.49	−0.4	3.40	149.02	133.92	149.15
Nordic (114)	163.19	+0.2	153.96	115.95	134.56	154.17	+0.4	1.62	165.12	142.13	171.91
Pacific Basin (713)	145.51	+0.2	137.28	103.39	119.98	106.73	+1.2	1.12	145.51	105.89	103.62
Euro–Pacific (1477)	145.96	−0.2	137.70	103.69	120.34	117.43	+0.5	2.06	146.26	117.26	122.03
North America (629)	175.40	+0.0	165.48	124.64	144.66	174.43	+0.0	2.85	182.38	171.51	165.30
Europe Ex. UK (546)	127.28	−0.2	120.08	90.45	104.97	110.59	+0.1	2.93	128.65	112.51	125.20
Pacific Ex. Japan (243)	184.57	−0.1	174.13	131.16	152.21	167.80	+0.4	3.24	184.84	152.70	162.88
World Ex. US (1665)	146.47	−0.2	138.19	104.08	120.78	119.40	+0.5	2.08	146.75	118.51	124.34
World Ex. UK (1966)	154.18	+0.0	145.46	109.55	127.15	134.65	+0.5	2.19	155.77	134.22	133.25
World Ex. So. Af. (2124)	156.25	−0.1	147.41	111.03	128.85	137.34	+0.3	2.37	157.88	137.29	137.53
World Ex. Japan (1714)	165.92	−0.3	156.53	117.90	136.83	158.20	−0.1	3.05	168.09	157.47	160.71
The World Index (2184)	156.31	−0.1	147.47	111.06	128.90	137.76	+0.3	2.37	157.83	137.32	138.09

Jointly compiled by The Financial Times Limited, Goldman Sachs & Co. and NatWest Securities Limited in conjunction with the Institute of Actuaries and the Faculty of Actuaries.

Source: *The Financial Times* (April 30, 1993), p. 37.

TABLE 4.6 **Market Capitalizations in Morgan Stanley Capital International Indices as of September 30, 1993**

	GDP EAFE	Weights[a] World	COS in Index	U.S. $ Billion	EAFE[b]	World
Austria	1.6	1.1	20	$ 17.2	0.4	0.3
Belgium	1.7	1.1	20	41.6	1.0	0.6
Denmark	1.2	0.8	23	25.8	0.6	0.4
Finland	0.9	0.6	22	13.9	0.3	0.2
Finland (free)	—	—	22	13.6	—	—
France	11.3	7.5	67	246.5	6.0	3.6
Germany	16.3	10.7	66	235.6	6.2	3.8
Ireland	0.4	0.3	12	9.9	0.2	0.1
Italy	9.9	6.5	72	87.0	2.1	1.3
Netherlands	2.8	1.8	21	125.6	3.0	1.9
Norway	0.9	0.6	24	13.9	0.3	0.2
Norway (free)	—	—	18	10.9	—	—
Spain	4.7	3.1	36	78.2	1.9	1.2
Sweden	2.0	1.3	28	59.1	1.4	0.9
Sweden (free)	—	—	28	59.1	—	—
Switzerland	2.1	1.4	57	178.0	4.0	2.6
United Kingdom	7.7	5.0	146	676.8	16.4	10.0
Europe 14 (free)	—	—	608	1,826.0	—	—
Europe 14	63.7	41.6	614	1,829.0	44.3	27.6
Australia	2.5	1.6	52	102.3	2.5	1.5
Hong Kong	0.8	0.6	39	138.3	3.3	2.0
Japan	31.6	20.6	266	1,929.4	46.7	28.5
Malaysia	0.6	0.4	68	75.7	1.8	1.1
New Zealand	0.4	0.3	8	14.2	0.3	0.2
Singapore	0.4	0.3	22	40.5	1.0	0.6
Singapore (free)	—	—	22	49.9	—	—
Pacific	36.3	23.7	463	2,300.3	28.7	24.0
Pacific (free)	—	—	165	2,309.7	—	—
EAFE (free)	—	—	1,073	4,235.7	—	—
EAFE	100.0	65.3	1,079	4,129.2	100.0	61.0
Canada	—	2.7	81	142.0	—	2.1
United States	—	31.9	335	2,484.9	—	36.7
South African Gold Mines	—	—	20	10.1	—	0.1
The World Index (free)	—	—	1,509	6,772.7	—	—
The World Index	—	100.0	1,315	6,766.3	—	100.0
Nordic countries (free)	—	—	91	109.6	—	—
Nordic countries	3.0	3.2	97	112.6	7.7	1.7
Europe 14 ex. UK	56.0	36.6	468	1,152.2	27.9	17.0
Far East	33.5	21.9	405	2,183.5	32.9	32.3
Far East (free)	—	—	405	2,193.3	—	—
EASEA (EAFE ex. Japan)	30.4	44.7	813	2,199.9	53.3	32.8
North America	—	34.7	416	2,626.9	—	36.8
Kokusai (World ex. Japan)	—	79.4	1,249	4,636.5	—	71.5

[a]GDP weight figures represent the initial weights applicable for the first month. They are used exclusively in the MSCI "GDP weighted" indices.

[b]Free indicates that only stocks that can be acquired by foreign investors are included in the index. If the number of companies is the same and the value is different, it indicates that the stocks available to foreigners are priced differently from domestic shares.

Source: Morgan Stanley Capital International (New York: Morgan Stanley & Co., 1993). Reprinted by permission.

(2) price-to-cash earnings (earnings plus depreciation) (P/CE) ratio, (3) price-to-earnings (P/E) ratio, and (4) dividend yield (YLD). These ratios help in analyzing different valuation levels among countries and over time for specific countries. Also, they are available for each of the International Industry Indexes.

FIGURE 4.3   **Listing of Morgan Stanley Capital International Stock Index Values for April 30, 1993**

Here are price trends on the world's major stock markets, as calculated by Morgan Stanley Capital International Perspective, Geneva. To make them directly comparable, each index, calculated in local currencies, is based on the close of 1969 equaling 100. The percentage change is since year-end.

	Apr 30	Apr 29	% This Year
U.S.	410.8	409.8	+ 1.1
Britain	847.9	839.5	+ 0.6
Canada	408.2	405.1	+ 9.4
Japan	954.0	936.6	+ 23.9
France	564.6	559.8	+ 5.1
Germany	245.0	245.6	+ 7.3
Hong Kong	4808.1	4848.7	+ 22.6
Switzerland	265.2	264.4	+ 3.9
Australia	354.0	353.5	+ 5.4
World index	561.1	556.4	+ 12.9

Source: *Wall Street Journal* (May 4, 1993): C12.

The daily and monthly indexes are reported in the *Morgan Stanley Capital International Perspective.* Monthly issues examine recent stock-market performance and compare market valuation factors within countries and international industry groups. Quarterly issues include graphs on 2,000 of the largest companies in the world. Absolute and relative performance compared to the world index is shown for the latest 22 years, together with operating data for the last five years.

Notably, the Morgan Stanley group index for Europe, Australia, and the Far East (EAFE) is being used as the basis for futures and options contracts on the Chicago Mercantile Exchange and the Chicago Board Options Exchange. Several of the MSCI country indexes, the EAFE index, and a world index are reported daily in *The Wall Street Journal* as shown in Figure 4.3.

DOW JONES WORLD STOCK INDEX
In January 1993 Dow Jones introduced its World Stock Index that is composed of over 2,200 companies worldwide organized into 120 industry groups. Initially, the index included 10 countries representing more than 80 percent of the combined capitalization of these countries, with subsequent expansion to 13 countries. In addition to the 13 countries shown in Figure 4.4, the countries are grouped into three regions: Pacific Rim, Europe, and the Americas. The overall organization into industries and broad sectors such as consumer, financial, and utilities is the same as used in the Dow Jones Equity Market Index for the U.S. market. Finally, each country's index is calculated in that country's own currency as well as in the U.S. dollar, British pound, German mark and Japanese yen. The indexes are reported daily in the domestic *Wall Street Journal* and also in *The Wall Street Journal Europe* and *The Asian Wall Street Journal.* It is published weekly in *Barron's.*[13]

---
[13]"Journal Launches Index Tracking World Stocks," *Wall Street Journal* (January 5, 1993), C1.

FIGURE 4.4   **Dow Jones World Stock Index Listing in *The Wall Street Journal* on May 4, 1993**

DOW JONES WORLD STOCK INDEX

Monday, May 3, 1993

REGION/ COUNTRY	DJ EQUITY MARKET INDEX, LOCAL CURRENCY		PCT. CHG.	CLOSING INDEX	CHG.		PCT. CHG.	IN U.S. DOLLARS 12-MO HIGH	12-MO LOW	12-MO CHG.		PCT. CHG.		FROM 12/31		PCT. CHG.	
Americas				106.27	+	0.50	+ 0.48	109.27	95.89	+ 7.60	+	7.71	+	1.99	+	1.91	
Canada	101.55	− 0.40		92.56	−	0.05	− 0.06	94.47	80.90	− 0.04	−	0.04	+	8.25	+	9.78	
U.S.	419.66	+ 0.50		419.66	+	2.10	+ 0.50	432.79	377.00	+ 31.58	+	8.14	+	6.38	+	1.54	
Europe				100.83	+	0.17	+ 0.17	106.23	89.16	− 1.23	−	1.21	+	7.80	+	8.38	
France	110.09	− 0.18		106.44	+	0.20	+ 0.19	110.93	90.15	+ 0.84	+	0.80	+	10.67	+	11.14	
Germany	101.17	− 0.03		97.11	+	0.25	+ 0.26	110.03	86.68	− 3.40	−	3.38	+	8.62	+	9.75	
Italy	107.89	+ 1.28		90.07	+	1.93	+ 2.19	92.37	64.86	− 0.94	−	1.03	+	16.33	+	22.14	
Netherlands	114.67	+ 0.33		110.31	+	0.70	+ 0.64	113.59	97.77	+ 9.31	+	9.22	+	10.29	+	10.29	
Switzerland	127.18	+ 0.99		120.21	+	1.39	+ 1.17	120.90	100.08	+ 20.13	+	20.11	+	9.20	+	8.29	
United Kingdom	closed																
Asia/Pacific				109.24	+	0.20	+ 0.18	109.24	67.91	+ 33.52	+	44.26	+	29.97	+	37.81	
Australia	93.90	− 1.01		92.19	−	0.83	− 0.90	102.96	73.82	− 8.55	−	8.49	+	7.26	+	8.55	
Hong Kong	153.66	− 0.47		156.34	−	0.71	− 0.45	158.07	114.90	+ 29.03	+	22.81	+	29.48	+	23.24	
Japan	closed																
Malaysia	148.93	+ 0.12		157.96	+	0.26	+ 0.16	157.96	109.44	+ 43.62	+	38.15	+	28.04	+	21.58	
Singapore	115.09	+ 0.09		116.16	+	0.10	+ 0.09	116.16	85.46	+ 17.56	+	17.80	+	11.40	+	10.89	
Asia/Pacific (ex. Japan)				124.47	−	0.52	− 0.41	125.31	96.59	+ 13.00	+	11.66	+	19.12	+	18.14	
World (ex. U.S.)				105.64	+	0.18	+ 0.17	105.64	80.48	+ 19.28	+	22.32	+	20.98	+	24.78	
DJ WORLD STOCK INDEX				105.89	+	0.32	+ 0.30	105.89	88.10	+ 14.67	+	16.09	+	13.25	+	14.30	

Indexes based on 6/30/82=100 for U.S., 12/31/91=100 for World.   ©1993 Dow Jones & Co. Inc., All Rights Reserved

Source: *Wall Street Journal* (May 4, 1993): C12.

EUROMONEY–FIRST BOSTON GLOBAL STOCK INDEX

The Euromoney–First Boston Global Stock Index is a market value weighted set of indexes for 17 individual countries and a composite world index. The series was initiated in 1986 with the value on December 31, 1985 set at 100. The results are reported in local currency and also in U.S. dollars. Monthly results for the individual countries are reported in *Global Investor*.

SALOMON-RUSSELL WORLD EQUITY INDEX

A series of indexes for 22 individual countries and the Salomon-Russell World Equity Index were initiated in 1988. This world equity index combines the Russell 1000 with the Salomon-Russell Primary Market Index (PMI), which is a capitalization-weighted index of 600 non-U.S. stocks covering about 65 percent of the market capitalization in each of 22 markets. Stocks were selected based on their adjusted capitalizations (that considered crossownership) and liquidity (trading volume). All indexes are presented in local currency and U.S. dollars with monthly results reported in *Global Investor*.

BOND-MARKET
INDICATOR
SERIES[14]

Although investors may not know a lot about the various stock-market indexes, they know less about the several bond-market series, because these bond series are relatively new and not widely published. Knowledge regarding these bond series is becoming more important because of the growth of fixed-income mutual funds and the consequent need to have a reliable set of benchmarks to use in evaluating performance.[15] Also, because the performance of many fixed-income money managers has not been able to match that of the aggregate bond market, there has been a growing interest in bond index funds, which requires the development of an index to emulate.[16]

Notably, the creation and computation of bond-market indexes is more difficult than a stock-market series for several reasons. First, the universe of bonds is much broader than that of stocks, ranging from U.S. Treasury securities to bonds in default. Also, the universe of bonds is changing constantly because of numerous new issues, bond maturities, calls, and bond sinking funds. Further, the volatility of bond prices changes because it is affected by duration, which is likewise changing constantly because of changes in maturity, coupon, and market yield (see Chapter 14). Finally, there can be significant problems in correctly pricing the individual corporate or mortgage bond issues in an index compared to the current and continuous transactions prices available for most stocks used in stock indexes.

TOTAL RATE OF
RETURN SERIES

This section contains a brief description of the major bond indexes created during the past 10 years. All of them indicate total rates of return for the portfolio of bonds, including price change, accrued interest, and coupon income reinvested. Also most of them are market value weighted using current prices and outstanding par values publicly held.

LEHMAN BROTHERS (LB) INDEXES

The LB indexes were initiated in 1976. Over 4,000 issues are included in the Lehman Brothers (LB) indexes, which are based on the following criteria for inclusion: minimum outstanding principal of $75 million; minimum maturity of 1 year; and issues in the mortgage index must have a minimum of $15 million outstanding. All total returns are market value weighted. Most issues are priced by traders with a few small corporate issues priced using a proprietary algorithm.

MERRILL LYNCH (ML) BOND INDEXES

The Merrill Lynch Bond Indexes track more than 5,000 issues and consist of several corporate and U.S. government master indexes supplemented by more than 150 subindexes segmenting the market by coupon, quality, industry, and maturity.

---

[14]The discussion in this section draws heavily from Frank K. Reilly, Wenchi Kao, and David J. Wright, "Alternative Bond Market Indexes," *Financial Analysts Journal* 48, no. 3 (May–June 1992): 44–58.

[15]For a discussion of what is involved in the evaluation of bond portfolios, see Peter D. Dietz, Russell Fogler, and Anthony U. Rivers, "Duration, Nonlinearity, and Bond Portfolio Performance," *Journal of Portfolio Management* 7, no. 3 (Spring 1981); and Gifford Fong, Charles Pearson, Oldrick Vasicek, and Theresa Conroy, "Fixed-Income Portfolio Performance: Analyzing Sources of Return," in *Handbook of Fixed-Income Securities,* 3d ed., ed. by Frank J. Fabozzi (Homewood, Ill.: Business One Irwin, 1991).

[16]For a discussion of this phenomenon, see Fran Hawthorne, "The Battle of the Bond Indexes," *Institutional Investor* 20, no. 4 (April 1986); and Sharmin Mossavar-Rahmani, *Bond Index Funds* (Chicago: Probus Publishing, 1991).

To qualify for inclusion in the Merrill Lynch indexes, securities must have the following characteristics: be nonconvertible, have a maturity of at least 1 year, have a minimum par value of $10 million, and be rated by Standard & Poor's or Moody's. Prices for U.S. Treasury and agency securities come from Merrill Lynch Government bond traders. Prices of corporate bonds are based on trader-supervised pricing matrices provided by the Merrill Lynch Bond Pricing Service. The indexes provide total rates of return and are market value weighted.

RYAN INDEX

The Ryan Index is a daily total return series derived by computing the equal-weighted average of the daily returns of seven current Treasury auction issues with the following maturities: 2-, 3-, 4-, 5-, 7-, 10- and 30-years. The index level is calculated each day by compounding the previous day's index by the current day's total return. Only Treasury auction issues are used because these are the most active issues with the best pricing.

SALOMON BROTHERS (SB) BOND INDEXES

The Salomon Brothers (SB) indexes were introduced in October 1985, with data available back to 1980. These indexes are market value weighted and include about 3,800 individually priced Treasury/agency, corporate, and mortgage securities with the following criteria: maturity of 1 year or longer, a minimum of $25 million outstanding, all Treasury/agencies except flower bonds, corporate bonds rated BBB or better, and mortgage bonds including conventional pass-throughs. Every issue in the SB Broad Index is trader priced.

MERRILL LYNCH CONVERTIBLE SECURITIES INDEXES

In March 1988 Merrill Lynch introduced a convertible bond index with data beginning in January 1987. This index includes 600 issues in three major subgroups: U.S. domestic convertible bonds, Eurodollar convertible bonds issued by U.S. corporations, and U.S. domestic convertible preferred stocks. The issues included must be public U.S. corporate issues, have a minimum par value of $25 million, and have a minimum maturity of 1 year.

GLOBAL BOND INDEXES

MERRILL LYNCH INTERNATIONAL BOND INDEXES

Merrill Lynch has developed a set of indexes for 11 Eurobond markets, a Eurobond Master Index, and indexes for three foreign bond markets as shown in Table 4.7.

These indexes measure monthly total returns in both local currency and U.S. dollars from December 1985. The Eurodollar Index is available since December 1982. These indexes include all straight bonds in each of the major Eurobond and foreign bond markets with the following criteria: minimum 1-year maturity, 10 million or more in local currency outstanding, and nonconvertible or without warrants (as long as they trade actively, it is not necessary that they be rated). From this universe, a sample is selected with the additional criteria that the issue be publicly traded and have a rating of BBB (Baa) or better if it is rated. The returns are calculated based upon the samples, but the weights are based upon the relative value of the bonds *in the universe*. Therefore,

TABLE 4.7   **Merrill Lynch International Bond Performance Indexes**

	Number of Issues	Amount (local currency)	Amount (U.S. $)	Percentage of Master[a]	Maturity Date	Adjustment for Call	
						Duration	Yield
Eurobond master index	3,039	—	$334.8	100.0%	1993/07/26	4.1	7.3
Nondollar Eurobond master index	2,190	—	190.0	—	1994/02/21	4.3	6.8
Eurobond Indexes							
Eurodollar	849	144.8	144.8	43.8	1992/10/30	3.8	7.78
Euro-Canadian dollar	180	14.1	10.2	3.1	1992/11/04	4.0	9.65
Euroyen	131	4,355.9	27.5	8.1	1993/10/05	4.9	5.87
Eurosterling	118	7.2	10.7	3.1	1993/08/08	4.3	11.03
Eurodeutschemark	562	106.9	55.6	16.4	1993/04/03	4.2	6.01
Euro-Swiss franc	666	78.9	48.9	14.5	1996/10/05	4.5	4.92
Euro-French franc	45	24.4	3.8	1.1	1993/05/31	4.7	9.17
Euroguilder	78	9.9	4.6	1.3	1991/11/22	3.8	6.16
ECU	223	20.3	21.8	6.4	1993/01/07	4.1	8.32
Euro-Australian dollar	138	8.0	5.3	1.6	1990/09/26	2.8	13.89
Euro-New Zealand dollar	49	2.9	1.6 / $334.8	0.5 / 100.0	1989/10/26	2.3	15.56
Foreign Bond Markets							
Samurai	41	5,169.5	32.7	—	1994/02/28	3.5	6.16
Bulldog	27	3.1	4.6	—	2009/12/21	8.2	11.93
Foreign guilder	85	16.5	7.6 / 44.9	—	1995/01/11	5.8	7.35

Note: The sum of the Eurobond indexes ($334.8 billion) uses end-of-month exchange rates, whereas the U.S. dollar amount of the Eurobond Master Index ($330.6 billion) uses beginning-of-month exchange rates.

[a]The shares of the Eurobond Master Index are the actual shares used to calculate the December Master Index values.

Source: Merrill Lynch, reprinted by permission. All rights reserved.

the index reflects the characteristics of the total bond market and not only the specific bonds in the priced sample.

SALOMON BROTHERS INTERNATIONAL BOND AND MONEY MARKET PERFORMANCE INDEXES

These total return indexes were introduced in September 1981 with historical information back to January 1, 1978. For each of eight major countries, there is typically a domestic government bond series, a Euro currency bond, and a domestic money market security in local currency and in U.S. dollars. There is also a market value weighted and unweighted composite world bond index and money market index. The results for these indexes are reported monthly in *Global Investor*.

J. P. MORGAN INTERNATIONAL GOVERNMENT BOND INDEXES

J. P. Morgan has created a comprehensive set of government bond indexes for 12 nations. The indexes are value weighted and begin during the 1970s.

COMPOSITE STOCK–BOND INDEXES

Beyond separate stock indexes and bond indexes for individual countries, a natural step is the development of a composite series that measures the performance of all securities in a given country. A composite series of stocks and bonds makes it possible to examine the benefits of diversifying with a combination of stocks and bonds in addition to diversifying within the asset classes of stocks or bonds.

MERRILL LYNCH–WILSHIRE CAPITAL MARKETS INDEX (MLWCMI)

A market value weighted index called Merrill Lynch–Wilshire Capital Markets Index (MLWCMI) has been created to measure the total return performance of the combined U.S. taxable fixed-income and equity markets. It is basically a combination of the Merrill Lynch fixed-income indexes and the Wilshire 5000 common stock index. As such, it tracks more than 10,000 stocks and bonds. The makeup of the index is as follows (as of June 1992):

Security	$ in Billions	Percent of Total
Treasury bonds	$1,085	20.89%
Agency bonds	166	3.20
Mortgage bonds	467	8.99
Corporate bonds	453	8.72
OTC stocks	331	6.37
AMEX stocks	105	2.02
NYSE stocks	2,586	49.92
	$5,193	100.00

COMPARISON OF INDEXES OVER TIME

This section contains a discussion of price movements in the different series for various daily, monthly, or annual intervals.

CORRELATIONS AMONG DAILY EQUITY PRICE CHANGES

Table 4.8 contains a matrix of the correlation coefficients of the daily percent of price changes for a set of U.S. and non-U.S. equity-market indexes during the 20-year period 1972 through 1991 (4,953 observations). Most of the correlation differences are attributable to sample differences, that is, differences in the firms listed on the alternative stock exchanges. Most of the major series—except the DJIA, the Nikkei Stock Average, the Value Line (VL) series, and the FT Ordinary Share Index—are market value-weighted indexes that include a large number of stocks. Therefore, the computational procedure is generally similar and the sample sizes are large or all-encompassing (except for the DJIA and the FT-30 Share Index). Thus, the major difference between the indexes is that the stocks are from different segments of the stock market or from different countries.

There are high positive correlations (0.94 to 0.98) among the alternative NYSE series (the DJIA, S&P 400, S&P 500, and the NYSE composite). This indicates that, on a short-run basis, even the DJIA, which has been criticized, is a very adequate indicator of price movements on the NYSE.

In contrast, there is significantly lower correlation (about .74) between these NYSE series and the AMEX series or the NASDAQ indexes. These significant differences in correlations suggest the possibility that the U.S. market is segmented.[17] Further, the relationship between the Value Line Index and the other U.S. series is about .80 to .88, which reflects the fact that it includes a sample from all exchanges and has a different weighting (it is unweighted).

---

[17]For studies that consider this notion, see Frank K. Reilly, "Evidence Regarding a Segmented Stock Market," *Journal of Finance* 27, no. 3 (June 1972): 607–625; and Arthur A. Eubank, Jr., "Risk-Return Contrasts: NYSE, AMEX, and OTC," *Journal of Portfolio Management* 3, no. 4 (Summer 1977).

TABLE 4.8   **Correlation Coefficients Among Daily Percentage Price Changes in Alternative Equity Market Indicator Series: January 4, 1972, to December 31, 1991 (4,953 observations)**

	DJIA	S&P 400	S&P 500	NYSE Composite	AMEX Value Index	NASDAQ Industrials	NASDAQ Composite	Value Line	Wilshire 5000	FT 30-Share	FT 500	FT All-Share	Nikkei	TSE Index
DJIA	—													
S&P 400	0.954	—												
S&P 500	0.947	0.978	—											
NYSE Composite	0.946	0.977	0.971	—										
AMEX Value Index	0.703	0.744	0.744	0.771	—									
NASDAQ Industrials	0.747	0.783	0.777	0.811	0.780	—								
NASDAQ Composite	0.751	0.786	0.783	0.820	0.778	0.948	—							
Value Line	0.824	0.851	0.845	0.880	0.808	0.868	0.886	—						
Wilshire 5000	0.902	0.940	0.936	0.946	0.772	0.811	0.810	0.852	—					
FT 30-Share	0.188	0.194	0.197	0.210	0.209	0.264	0.280	0.260	0.313	—				
FT 500	0.215	0.225	0.228	0.240	0.248	0.293	0.313	0.298	0.352	0.889	—			
FT All-Share	0.213	0.220	0.222	0.236	0.246	0.290	0.310	0.296	0.343	0.882	0.959	—		
Nikkei	0.089	0.100	0.096	0.116	0.094	0.196	0.222	0.189	0.151	0.150	0.180	0.186	—	
TSE Index	0.111	0.116	0.120	0.132	0.113	0.200	0.226	0.202	0.168	0.141	0.179	0.186	0.917	—

The correlations among the U.S. series and those from the United Kingdom and Japan support the case for global investing. The relationships among the three *Financial Times* series for the LSE varied from .88 to .96, and the two TSE series were correlated about .92 even though the sample sizes, weightings, and computations differ. These within-country results attest to the importance of the basic sample. In contrast, the U.S.–U.K. correlations, which ranged from .16 to .34, and the U.S.–Japan correlations, which ranged from .08 to .22, confirm the benefits of global diversification because such low correlations reduce the variance of a portfolio.

CORRELATIONS AMONG MONTHLY BOND INDEXES

The correlations among the monthly bond return series are contained in Table 4.9. The correlations ranged from .91 to .99, confirming that although the *level* of interest rates differ due to the risk premium, the overriding factors that cause a change in the interest rates for investment grade bonds over time (which in turn affect the rates of return on the bonds) are *systematic* macroeconomic variables, such as changes in the risk-free rate and inflation expectations.

ANNUAL STOCK PRICE CHANGES

The annual percentage of price changes for the major stock indexes are contained in Table 4.10. One would expect differences among the price changes and measures of risk for the various series due to the different samples. For example, the NYSE series should have lower rates of return and risk measures than the AMEX and OTC series. The results generally confirm these expectations. The lower rate of return for the Value Line series is due to the use of a geometric average in calculating daily changes.

The LSE had higher rates of change and much greater variability than any U.S. series. The TSE likewise had higher average price changes, but its risk measures were also somewhat greater. These results for the Japanese market were significantly impacted by poor results during 1990–1991. Notably, you should recall that the Japanese stock market had relatively low correlation with alternative U.S. stock-market indexes, which indicates that, even though the individual country risk-return results were comparable, Japan would have been a prime source of diversification benefits.

ANNUAL BOND RATES OF RETURN

Table 4.11 contains the annual total rates of return for the Lehman Brothers bond-market indexes.[18] You cannot directly compare the bond and stock results because the bond results are *total* rates of return versus annual percentage price change results for stocks (some of the stock series do not report dividend data).

The major comparison for the bond series should be among the average rate of return and the risk measures, because although the monthly rates of return are correlated, we would expect a difference in the level of return because of the differential risk premiums. The results generally confirm our expectations (i.e., there are lower returns and risk measures for the government series followed by higher returns and risk for corporate bonds and the highest returns and risk for the mortgage series).

---

[18]Because of the high correlations among the monthly rates of return, the results for various bond-market segments (government, corporate, mortgages) are very similar irrespective of the source (Lehman Brothers, Merrill Lynch, Salomon Brothers, Ryan). Therefore, only the Lehman Brothers results are presented.

TABLE 4.9   Correlation Coefficients Among Monthly Bond Rate of Return Series: January 1980 to December 1990 (132 observations)

	MLGC	MLG	MLC	MLD	MLM	LBGC	LBG	LBC	LBM	LBY	LBA	SBB	SBG	SBC	SBM	RYAN
MLGC	—															
MLG	.993	—														
MLC	.981	.954	—													
MLD	.998	.990	.983	—												
MLM	.946	.928	.948	.962	—											
SLGC	.997	.991	.977	.996	.951	—										
SLG	.991	.997	.953	.988	.928	.994	—									
SLC	.979	.954	.992	.983	.962	.982	.955	—								
SLM	.938	.919	.943	.953	.983	.944	.921	.957	—							
SLY	.981	.964	.981	.983	.943	.983	.965	.984	.936	—						
SLA	.994	.986	.980	.997	.965	.998	.988	.987	.962	.984	—					
SBB	.995	.988	.977	.997	.961	.996	.987	.983	.954	.985	.997	—				
SBG	.985	.994	.941	.981	.916	.987	.995	.945	.905	.960	.980	.985	—			
SBC	.977	.950	.992	.980	.950	.976	.949	.993	.944	.982	.979	.980	.939	—		
SBM	.950	.933	.950	.964	.988	.953	.930	.963	.992	.949	.969	.967	.920	.953	—	
RYAN	.986	.988	.955	.985	.937	.988	.990	.959	.929	.965	.985	.987	.987	.952	.940	—

Source: Frank K. Reilly, Wenchi Kao, and David J. Wright, "Alternative Bond Market Indexes," *Financial Analysts Journal* 48, no. 3 (May–June, 1992): p. 49.

TABLE 4.10   Percentage Price Changes in Stock Price Indicator Series: 1972–1991

	DJIA	S&P 400	S&P 500	NYSE Composite	AMEX Value Index	NASDAQ Industrials	NASDAQ Composite	Value Line	Wilshire 5000	FT 30-Share	FT 500	FT All-Share	Nikkei	TSE Index
1972	14.58	16.10	15.63	14.27	10.33	13.63	17.18	0.78	14.86	5.38	9.72	12.11	91.91	101.40
1973	-16.58	-17.38	-17.37	-19.63	-30.00	-36.88	-31.06	-35.46	-20.96	-31.94	-30.84	-31.36	-17.30	-23.71
1974	-27.57	-29.93	-29.72	-30.28	-33.22	-32.44	-35.11	-33.47	-31.49	-53.02	-54.39	-54.34	-11.37	-9.01
1975	38.44	31.92	31.55	31.86	38.40	43.38	29.76	44.35	32.83	132.78	141.35	136.33	19.18	15.99
1976	17.86	18.42	19.15	21.50	31.58	23.68	26.10	32.23	21.69	-5.59	-1.01	-3.87	14.51	18.69
1977	-17.27	-12.53	-11.50	-9.30	16.43	9.30	7.33	0.48	-6.98	36.85	41.45	41.18	-2.51	-5.16
1978	-3.15	2.39	1.06	2.13	17.73	15.92	12.31	4.31	3.96	-2.99	3.92	2.70	23.33	23.48
1979	4.19	12.88	12.31	15.54	64.10	38.10	28.11	24.44	19.28	12.04	2.54	4.30	9.46	2.24
1980	14.93	27.62	25.77	25.68	41.25	49.19	33.88	18.28	27.61	14.56	24.57	27.07	3.33	7.50
1981	-9.23	-11.22	-9.73	-8.67	-8.13	-12.27	-3.21	-4.43	-8.43	11.78	7.88	7.24	7.95	15.42
1982	19.60	14.95	14.76	13.95	6.23	19.32	18.67	15.32	12.86	12.50	27.44	22.07	4.36	4.10
1983	20.27	18.16	17.27	17.46	30.95	18.31	19.87	22.28	18.74	30.00	19.27	23.10	23.42	23.26
1984	-4.33	-0.40	0.81	0.75	-9.07	-20.00	-11.67	-8.97	-1.25	22.84	29.29	26.02	16.66	24.81
1985	27.66	25.86	26.33	26.15	20.50	23.78	31.86	20.72	27.18	18.73	15.20	15.18	13.61	14.89
1986	22.58	17.30	16.87	13.98	7.30	6.06	7.51	5.01	12.48	16.13	22.18	22.34	42.61	48.31
1987	2.26	3.90	0.06	-0.25	-1.42	-3.21	-5.40	-10.69	1.49	4.52	4.59	4.52	21.35	10.89
1988	11.85	12.38	12.40	13.04	17.54	12.03	15.41	21.77	13.29	5.38	5.35	4.52	42.54	36.57
1989	26.96	25.60	27.25	24.82	23.53	10.30	20.44	17.08	26.69	32.38	29.91	30.01	28.67	22.25
1990	-4.34	-5.07	-6.56	-7.46	-18.49	-2.86	-0.98	15.97	-10.61	-12.67	-14.01	-14.31	-38.72	-39.83
1991	20.32	27.18	26.31	27.12	28.22	64.75	57.54	27.22	30.28	13.02	17.30	15.13	-3.63	-1.10
Avg. of annual changes (arithmetic mean)	7.95	8.91	8.63	8.63	12.69	12.00	11.93	7.26	9.18	13.13	15.09	14.48	14.47	14.55
Standard deviation of annual changes	17.04	16.67	16.54	16.61	23.85	25.19	21.58	20.54	17.49	34.32	36.04	35.21	25.91	27.79
Avg. annual compound rate of change (geometric mean)	6.53	7.51	7.26	7.24	9.98	8.89	9.61	5.09	7.63	8.41	9.97	9.49	11.62	11.36

TABLE 4.11   **Annual Percentage Rates of Return; Arithmetic and Geometric Mean Annual Rates of Return and Standard Deviations of Annual and Monthly Rates of Return: 1976–1990**

	Lehman Brothers					
	Government/ Corporate	Government	Corporate	Mortgage- Backed	Yankee Bond	Aggregate Bond
1976	15.59	12.35	19.34	16.31	15.08	15.60
1977	2.98	2.81	3.16	1.90	5.23	3.03
1978	1.19	1.80	.35	2.41	2.91	1.40
1979	2.30	5.40	−2.11	.13	−.43	1.93
1980	3.06	5.19	−2.29	.65	1.93	2.70
1981	7.26	9.36	2.95	.07	3.48	6.25
1982	31.09	27.74	39.21	43.04	35.82	32.62
1983	8.00	7.39	9.27	10.13	9.43	8.35
1984	15.02	14.50	16.63	15.79	16.38	15.15
1985	21.30	20.43	24.06	25.21	25.99	22.11
1986	15.62	15.31	16.53	13.43	16.27	15.26
1987	2.29	2.20	2.56	4.28	1.89	2.76
1988	7.58	7.03	9.22	8.72	8.81	7.89
1989	14.24	14.23	14.09	15.35	15.42	14.53
1990	8.28	8.72	7.05	10.72	7.05	8.96
Arithmetic mean	10.39	10.30	10.67	11.21	11.02	10.57
Standard deviation	8.13	7.00	10.92	11.12	9.69	8.47
Geometric mean	10.10	10.08	10.16	10.70	10.62	10.26
Standard deviation (monthly returns)	2.16	1.92	2.72	2.89	2.63	2.22

Source: Frank K. Reilly, G. Wenchi Kao, and David J. Wright, "Alternative Bond Market Indexes," *Financial Analysts Journal* 48, no. 3 (May–June 1992): p. 48. Reprinted by permission of the Financial Analysts Journal.

SUMMARY

Given the several uses of security-market indicator series, you should know how they are constructed and the differences among them. If you want to use one of the many series to learn how the "market" is doing, you need to be aware of what market you are dealing with so you can select the appropriate index. As an example, are you only interested in the NYSE or do you also want to consider the AMEX and the OTC? Beyond the U.S. market, are you interested in Japanese or U.K. stocks or do you want to examine the total world market?[19]

Indexes are also used to evaluate portfolio performance. In this case, you want to be sure that the index is consistent with your investing universe. If you are investing worldwide, you should not judge your performance relative to the DJIA, which is limited to 30 U.S. blue-chip stocks. For a bond portfolio, you also want the index to match your investment philosophy. Finally, if your portfolio contains both stocks and bonds, you want to evaluate your performance against an appropriate combination of indexes.

Whenever you invest, you will examine numerous market indexes to tell you what has happened and how successful you have been. The selection of the appropriate indexes for information or evaluation will depend on how knowledgeable you are regarding the various series. The purpose of this chapter is to help you understand what to look for and how to make the right decision.

---

[19]For a readable discussion on this topic, see Anne Merjos, "How's the Market Doing?" *Barron's* (August 20, 1990): 18–20, 27, 28.

QUESTIONS

1. Discuss briefly several uses of security-market indicator series.

2. What major factors must be considered when constructing a market index? Put another way, what characteristics differentiate indexes?

3. Explain how a market indicator series is price weighted. In such a case, would you expect a $100 stock to be more important than a $25 stock? Why?

4. Discuss the major criticisms of the Dow Jones Industrial Average and the Nikkei Stock Average.

5. Explain how to compute a value-weighted series.

6. Explain how a price-weighted series and a value-weighted series adjust for stock splits.

7. Describe an unweighted price-indicator series and describe how you would construct such a series. Assume a 20 percent price change in GM ($40/share; 50 million shares outstanding) and Coors Brewing ($25/share and 15 million shares outstanding). Explain which stock's change will have the greater impact on this index.

8. If you correlated percentage changes in the Wilshire 5000 equity index with percentage changes in the NYSE composite, the AMEX index, and the NASDAQ composite index, would you expect a difference in the correlations? Why or why not?

9. There are high correlations among the daily percentage price changes for the alternative NYSE indexes. Discuss the reason for this similarity: size of sample, source of sample, or method of computation?

10. Discuss the historical annual price movements for the various NYSE indexes in terms of average annual price changes and the variability of annual price changes. Discuss whether the differences were consistent with economic theory.

11. Compare stock price indicator series for the three U.S. equity-market segments (NYSE, AMEX, OTC) for the period 1972 to 1991. Discuss whether the results in terms of average annual price change and risk (variability of price changes) were consistent with economic theory.

12. Describe the major difference between the three *Financial Times* indexes. Discuss which series is similar to the S&P 500 Index.

13. Discuss how the Nikkei Stock Average is similar to a specific U.S. stock-market index.

14. Discuss the relationship between the two stock price indexes for the Tokyo Stock Exchange (TSE) and the three indexes for the London Stock Exchange. Do the same for the TSE series and two NYSE series. Explain why these relationships differ.

15. You are informed that the Wilshire 5000 market value-weighted series increased by 16 percent during a specified period, whereas a Wilshire 5000 equal-weighted series increased by 23 percent during the same period. Discuss what this difference in results implies.

16. Briefly discuss the uses for bond-market indexes.

17. Why is it contended that bond-market indexes are more difficult to construct and maintain than stock-market index series?

18. Discuss five alternative subindexes you could construct from a composite corporate bond series.

19. The Wilshire 5000 market value-weighted index increased by 5 percent, whereas the Merrill Lynch–Wilshire Capital Markets Index increased by 15 percent during the same period. What does this difference in results imply?

20. The Russell 1000 increased by 8 percent during the past year, whereas the Russell 2000 increased by 15 percent. Discuss the implication of these results.

21. Based upon what you know about the *Financial Times* (FT) World Index, the Morgan Stanley Capital International World Index, and the Dow Jones World Stock Index, what level of correlation would you expect among monthly rates of return? Discuss the reasons for your answer based upon the factors that affect indexes.

PROBLEMS

1. You are given the following information regarding prices for a sample of stocks:

Stock	Number of Shares	Price	
		T	*T* + 1
A	1,000,000	60	80
B	10,000,000	20	35
C	30,000,000	18	25

a. Construct a *price-weighted* series for these three stocks, and compute the percentage change in the series for the period from T to $T + 1$.

b. Construct a *value-weighted* series for these three stocks, and compute the percentage change in the series for the period from T to $T + 1$.

c. Briefly discuss the difference in the results for the two series.

2. a. Given the data in Problem 1, construct an equal-weighted series by assuming $1,000 is invested in each stock. What is the percentage change in wealth for this portfolio?

b. Compute the percentage of price change for each of the stocks in Problem 1. Compute the arithmetic average of these changes. Discuss how this answer compares to the answer in 2a.

c. Compute the geometric average of the percentage changes in 2b. Discuss how this result compares to the answer in 2b.

3. For the last five trading days, on the basis of figures in *The Wall Street Journal,* compute the daily percentage price changes for the following stock indexes:
   a. DJIA
   b. S&P 400
   c. AMEX Market Value Series
   d. NASDAQ Industrial Index
   e. FT-30 Share Index
   f. Nikkei Stock Price Average

   Discuss the difference in results for a and b, a and c, a and d, a and e, a and f, e and f. What do these differences imply regarding diversifying within the United States versus diversifying between countries?

4.

Company	Price			Shares		
	A	B	C	A	B	C
Day 1	12	23	52	500	350	250
Day 2	10	22	55	500	350	250
Day 3	14	46	52	500	175[a]	250
Day 4	13	47	25	500	175	500[b]
Day 5	12	45	26	500	175	500

[a]Split at close of Day 2
[b]Split at close of Day 3

  a. Calculate a Dow Jones Industrial Average for Days 1 through 5.
  b. What effects have the splits had in determining the next day's index? (Hint: Think of the relative weighting of each stock.)
  c. From a copy of a recent *Wall Street Journal,* find the divisor that is currently being used in calculating the DJIA. (Normally this value can be found on the inside back pages.)

5. Utilizing the price and volume data in Problem 4,
  a. Calculate a Standard & Poor's Index for Days 1 through 5 using a beginning index value of 10.
  b. Identify what effects the splits had in determining the next day's index. (Hint: Think of the relative weighting of each stock.)

6. Using Table 4.10 calculate the average annual rate of change in each of the indexes for the 10-year period 1982 to 1991, using (a) the arithmetic mean and (b) the geometric mean.

REFERENCES

Fisher, Lawrence, and James H. Lorie. *A Half Century of Returns on Stocks and Bonds.* Chicago Graduate School of Business, 1977.

Hawthorne, Fran. "The Battle of the Bond Indexes." *Institutional Investor* 20, no. 4 (April 1986).

Lorie, James H., Peter Dodd, and Mary Hamilton Kimpton. *The Stock Market: Theories and Evidence.* 2d ed. Homewood, Ill.: Richard D. Irwin, 1985.

Reilly, Frank K., Wenchi Kao, and David J. Wright. "Alternative Bond Market Indexes." *Financial Analysts Journal* 48, no. 3 (May–June, 1992).

Williams, Arthur III, and Noreen N. Conwell. "Fixed-Income Indices." In *Handbook of Fixed-Income Securities,* 2d ed., edited by Frank J. Fabozzi and Irving M. Pollack. Homewood, Ill.: Dow-Jones Irwin, 1987.

APPENDIX 4A   FOREIGN STOCK MARKET INDEXES

Index Name	Number of Stocks	Weights of Stocks	Calculation Method	History of Index
ATX-index (Vienna)	All stocks listed on the exchange	Market Capitalization	Value-Weighted	Base year 1967, 1991 began including all stocks (Value = 100)
Swiss Market Index	18 stocks	Capitalization Weighted	Value-Weighted	Base year 1988, stocks selected from the Basle, Geneva, and Zurich Exchanges (Value = 1500)
Stockholm General Index	All stocks (voting) listed on exchange	Market Capitalization	Value-Weighted	Base year 1979, continuously updated (Value = 100)
Copenhagen Stock Exchange Share Price Index	All stocks traded		Value-Weighted	Share price is based on average price of the day.
Oslo SE Composite Index (Sweden)	25 companies			Base year is 1972. (Value = 100)
Johannesburg Stock Exchange Actuaries Index	146 companies			Base year is 1959. (Value = 100)
Mexican Market Index	Variable number, based on capitalization and liquidity		Value-Weighted (adjustment for value of paid-out dividends)	Base year is 1978, high dollar returns in recent years
Milan Stock Exchange MIB	Variable number, based on capitalization and liquidity		Weighted Arithmetic Average	Change base at beginning of each year (Value = 1000)
Belgium BEL-20 Stock Index	20 companies	Market Capitalization	Value-Weighted	Base year is 1991 (Value = 1000)
Madrid General Stock Index	92 stocks	Market Capitalization		Change base at beginning of each year
Hang Seng Index (Hong Kong)	33 companies	Market Capitalization		Started in 1969, accounts for 75 percent of total market.
FT-Actuaries World Indexes	2212 stocks		Value-Weighted	Base year is 1986.
FT-SE 100 Index (London)	100 companies	Market Capitalization	Value-Weighted	Base year is 1983. (Value = 1000)
CAC General Share Index (French)	212 companies	Market Capitalization	Value-Weighted	Base year is 1981. (Value = 100)
Morgan Stanley World Index	1482 stocks	Market Capitalization	Value-Weighted	Base year is 1970. (Value = 100)
Singapore Straits Times Industrial Index				
German Stock Market Index	30 companies (Blue Chips)	Market Capitalization	Value-Weighted	Base year is 1987. (Value = 1000)
Frankfurter Allgemeine Zeitung Index (German)	100 companies (Blue Chips)	Market Capitalization	Value-Weighted	Base year is 1958. (Value = 100)
Australian Stock Exchange Share Price Indices	250 stocks (92 percent) of all shares listed)	Market Capitalization	Price-Weighted	Introduced in 1979.
Dublin ISEQ Index	71 stocks (54 official, 17 unlisted). All stocks traded.	Market Capitalization	Value-Weighted	Base year is 1988. (Value = 1000)
HEX Index (Helsinki)	Varies with different share price indexes.	Market Capitalization	Value-Weighted	Base changes every day.
Jakarta Stock Exchange	All listed shares (148 currently)	Market Capitalization	Value-Weighted	Base year is 1982. (Value = 100)
Taiwan Stock Exchange Index	All ordinary stocks (listed for at least a month)	Market Capitalization	Value-Weighted	Base year is 1966. (Value = 100)
TSE 300 Composite Index (Toronto)	300 stocks (comprised of 14 sub-indexes)	Market Capitalization (adjusted for major shareholders)	Value-Weighted	Base year is 1975. (Value = 1000)
KOSPI (Korean Composite Stock Price Index)	All common stocks listed on exchange	Market Capitalization (adjusted for major shareholders)	Value-Weighted	Base year is 1980. (Value = 100)

CHAPTER 5

Sources of Information on Global Investments

In this chapter we will answer the following questions:

- What are the major sources of information and data for aggregate economic analysis in the United States?
- What are the major sources for non-U.S. economic data including the principal bibliographies?
- What are the major sources of information and data for those interested in aggregate security market analysis? Which sources are available, annually, weekly, or daily?
- What investment firms provide comments and recommendations for global markets?
- What are the major sources of information and data needed for industry analysis?
- What are the major sources of information and data available for individual firm stock and bond analysis?
- What are the major investment magazines and which ones are available monthly, bi-weekly, and weekly?
- What are some of the major academic journals that publish theoretical and empirical studies related to investments?
- What are the major computerized data sources?
- What are the names and addresses for the major sources of investment information?

In the chapters that follow, we will discuss the factors that influence aggregate security prices, the prices for securities issued by various industries, and the unique factors that influence the returns on individual securities. In this chapter we will describe some of the major sources of information needed for these analyses. Relevant information is both important and difficult to obtain especially in the current global capital market. The outline of the presentation follows:

- Aggregate economic analysis
    U.S. government sources
    Bank publications
    Non-U.S. economic data

- Aggregate security-market analysis
     Government publications
     Commercial publications
     Brokerage firm reports
- Industry analysis
     Industry publications
     Industry magazines
     Trade associations
- Individual stock and bond analysis
     Company-generated information
     Commercial publications
     Brokerage firm reports
     Investment magazines
- Theoretical and empirical analysis
     Academic journals
- Computerized data sources
     Data banks
     On-line data bases

AGGREGATE ECONOMIC ANALYSIS

This section is concerned with data used in estimating overall economic changes for the United States and other major countries as contrasted to data regarding the aggregate securities markets (stocks, bonds, etc.).

U.S. GOVERNMENT SOURCES

It should come as no surprise that the main source of information on the U.S. economy is the federal government, which issues a variety of publications on the topic.

Federal Reserve Bulletin is a monthly publication issued by the Board of Governors of the Federal Reserve System. It is the primary source for almost all monetary data, including monetary aggregates, factors affecting member bank reserves, member bank reserve requirements, Federal Reserve open market transactions, and loans and investments of all commercial banks. In addition, it contains figures on financial markets, including interest rates and some stock-market statistics; data for corporate finance, including profits, assets, and liabilities of corporations; extensive nonfinancial statistics on output, the labor force, and the GNP; and a major section on international finance.

Survey of Current Business is a monthly publication issued by the U.S. Department of Commerce that gives details on national income and production figures. It is probably the best source for current, detailed information on all segments of the gross domestic product and national income. It also contains industrial production data for numerous segments of the economy. The *Survey* is an excellent secondary source for labor statistics (employment and wages), interest rates, and statistics on foreign economic development. It also contains data regarding the leading, coincident and lagging economic series published by the Department of Commerce.[1] These series are considered important by those who attempt to project peaks and troughs in the business cycle.

Economic Indicators is a monthly publication prepared for the Joint Economic Committee by the Council of Economic Advisers. It contains monthly and annual data

---

[1]These series are discussed more extensively in Chapter 12 where they are related to stock-market movements.

on output, income, spending, employment, production, prices, money and credit, federal finance, and international economies.

The Quarterly Financial Report (QFR) is prepared by the Federal Trade Commission and contains aggregate statistics on the financial position of U.S. corporations. Based on an extensive quarterly sample survey, the *QFR* presents estimated statements of income and retained earnings, balance sheets, and related financial and operating ratios for all manufacturing corporations. The publication also includes data on mining and trade corporations. The statistical data are classified by industry and, within the manufacturing group, by size.

Business Statistics is a biennial supplement to the *Survey of Current Business* that contains extensive historical data for about 2,500 series contained in the survey. The historical section contains monthly data for the past 4 or 5 years, quarterly data for the previous 10 years, and annual data back to 1947 if available. A notable feature is a section of explanatory notes for each series that describes the series and indicates the original source for the data.

Historical Chart Book is an annual supplement to the *Federal Reserve Bulletin* that contains long-range financial and business series. There is an excellent section on the various series that indicates the source of the data.

Economic Report of the President Each January, the president of the United States prepares the Economic Report of the President, which he transmits to the Congress indicating what has transpired during the past year and discussing the current environment and what he considers to be the major economic problems that will face the country during the coming year. This publication also contains an extensive document entitled "The Annual Report of the Council of Economic Advisers," which generally runs over 150 pages and contains a detailed discussion of developments in the domestic and international economies gathered by the council (the group that advises the president on economic policy). An appendix contains statistical tables relating to income, employment, and production. The tables typically provide annual data from the 1940s and in some instances from 1929.

Statistical Abstract of the United States, published annually since 1878, is the standard summary of statistics on the social, political, and economic organization of the United States. Prepared by the Bureau of the Census, it is designed to serve as a convenient statistical reference and as a guide to other statistical publications and sources. This volume, which currently runs over 900 pages, includes data from many statistical publications, both government and private.

BANK
PUBLICATIONS

In addition to the government material, much data and comments on the economy are published by various banks. These generally appear monthly and are free of charge. They can be categorized as publications of the Federal Reserve Banks or of commercial banks.

PUBLICATIONS OF FEDERAL RESERVE BANKS
The Federal Reserve System is divided into 12 Federal Reserve Districts with a major Federal Reserve Bank in each location as follows:[2]

---

[2]Specific addresses for each of the district banks and names of major personnel are contained in the *Federal Reserve Bulletin,* published monthly by the Federal Reserve Board.

1. Boston
2. New York
3. Philadelphia
4. Cleveland
5. Richmond
6. Atlanta
7. Chicago
8. St. Louis
9. Minneapolis
10. Denver
11. Dallas
12. San Francisco

Each of the Federal Reserve district banks has a research department that issues periodic reports. Although the various bank publications differ, monthly reviews, which are available to interested parties, are published by all district banks. These reviews typically contain one or several articles as well as regional economic statistics. A major exception is the St. Louis Federal Reserve Bank, which publishes statistical releases weekly, monthly, and quarterly containing extensive national and international data in addition to its monthly review.[3]

PUBLICATIONS OF COMMERCIAL BANKS

A number of large banks prepare monthly letters available to interested individuals. These letters generally contain a comment on the current and future outlook of the economy and specific industries or segments of the economy.

NON-U.S. ECONOMIC DATA

In addition to data on the U.S. economy, data on other countries where you might consider investing are also important to acquire. Some of the available sources follow.[4]

The Economic Intelligence Unit (EIU) publishes 83 separate quarterly reviews and an annual supplement covering the economic and business conditions and outlook for 160 countries. For each country the reviews consider the economy, trade and finance, trends in investment and consumer spending, along with comments on its political environment. Tables contain data on economic activity and foreign trade.

The EIU also publishes *European Trends,* which discusses the aggregate economic environment for the overall European community and the world.

The Organization for Economic Cooperation and Development (OECD) publishes semiannual surveys showing recent trends and policies and assesses short-term prospects for each country. An annual volume, *Historical Statistics,* contains annual percent change data for the most recent 20 years.

The Economist prepares country reports on more than 100 countries around the world that contain extensive economic and demographic statistics. Of greater importance is a detailed discussion that critically analyzes the current economic and political environment in the country and considers the future outlook. It is possible to subscribe

---

[3]An individual can request to be put on the mailing list for these publications by writing to Federal Reserve Bank of St. Louis, P.O. Box 442, St. Louis, MO 63166. Most of them are free.

[4]This discussion draws heavily from Daniells, *Business Information Sources,* rev. ed. (Berkeley, Calif.: University of California Press, 1986).

to reports for a selected list of countries or for all of them. The reports are updated twice a year.

Worldwide Economic Indicators is an annual book published by the Business International Corporation that contains data for 131 countries on population, gross domestic product (GDP) by activity, wages and prices, foreign trade, and a number of specific items for the most recent 4 years.

Demographic Yearbook, published by the United Nations, contains statistics on population, births, deaths, life expectancy, marriages, and divorces for about 240 countries.

International Marketing Data and Statistics, published by Euromonitor Publications Inc. of London, is an annual guide that contains data for 132 non-European countries covering population, employment, production, trade, the economy, and other economic data.

United Nations Statistical Yearbook is a basic reference book that contains extensive economic statistics on all UN countries (population, construction, industrial production, etc.).

Eurostatistics, a monthly publication by the *Statistical Office of the European Communities (Luxembourg),* contains statistics for short-term economic analysis in ten European community countries and the United States. There are generally data for 6 years covering industrial production, employment and unemployment, external trade, prices, wages, and finance.

U.S. International Trade Administration, International Economic Indicators, is a quarterly publication of the U.S. Government Printing Office that contains comparative economic indicators and trends in the United States and its seven principal industrial competitors: France, Germany, Italy, Netherlands, United Kingdom, Japan, and Canada. The data are organized in five parts: general indicators, trade indicators, price indicators, finance indicators, and labor indicators. Notably, the sources for the data are contained at the back of the booklet.

International Financial Statistics, a monthly publication (with a yearbook issue) of the International Monetary Fund, is an essential source of current financial statistics such as exchange rates, fund position, international liquidity, money and banking statistics, interest rates (including LIBOR), prices, and production.[5]

International Monetary Fund, Balance of Payments Yearbook is a two-part publication. The first part contains detailed balance-of-payments figures for over 110 countries, and the second part contains world totals for balance-of-payments components and aggregates.

United Nations, Yearbook of International Trade Statistics is an annual report on import statistics over a 4-year period for each of 166 countries. The commodity figures for each country are given by commodity code.

United Nations Yearbook of National Accounts Statistics is a comprehensive source of national account data that contains detailed statistics for 155 countries on domestic product and consumption expenditures, national income, and disposable income for a 12-year period.

---

[5]LIBOR is an acronym for London Interbank Borrowing Rate. It is used as a base rate for many international financial transactions.

Also, some individual countries publish national income studies with detailed break-downs as well as annual statistical reports that contain the more important statistics and include bibliographical sources for the tables. Examples would include Brazil, Great Britain, Japan, and Switzerland.

Similar to the United States, major banks in various countries publish bulletins or letters that contain statistical reviews for the individual countries. Examples include:

- *Bank of Canada Review* (monthly)
- *Bank of England* (quarterly)
- *Bank of Japan* (monthly)
- *National Bank of Belgium* (monthly)
- *Deutsche Bundesbank* (monthly)

In addition to these specific sources of data, you should be aware of the following bibliographies:

G. R. Dicks, ed. *Sources of World Financial and Banking Information.* Westport, Conn.: Greenwood Press, 1981.
 A descriptive list of nearly 5,000 financial and banking sources arranged by country.

David Hoopes, ed. *Global Guide to International Business.* New York: File Publications, 1983.
 A descriptive list by country of source information about individual countries.

Index of International Statistics. Washington, D.C.: Congressional Information Service.
 A monthly descriptive guide and index to statistical publications by the world's major international government organizations.

AGGREGATE SECURITY-MARKET ANALYSIS

Several government publications provide useful data on the stock and bond markets, but the bulk of detailed information is provided by private firms. Some of the government publications discussed earlier (e.g., *Federal Reserve Bulletin* and *Survey of Current Business*) contain financial market data such as interest rates and stock prices.

GOVERNMENT PUBLICATIONS

The main source of data in this area is the Securities and Exchange Commission (SEC), which is the federal agency responsible for regulating the operation of the securities markets and collecting data in this regard. The *Annual Report of the SEC* is published for the fiscal year ending in June. It contains a detailed discussion of important developments during the year and comments on the SEC's disclosure system and regulation of the securities markets. Finally, it includes a statistics section containing historical data on many security-market series.

COMMERCIAL PUBLICATIONS

Considering the numerous advisory services in existence, a section dealing with their publications could become voluminous. Therefore, our intent is to list and discuss only *major* services and allow you to develop your own list of other available sources. An excellent source of advertisements for these services is *Barron's.* A publication that lists and briefly describes these publications is the *Fortune Investment Information Directory.*[6] The order of presentation will be by frequency of publication: annual, weekly, daily.

---

[6]This directory contains extensive listings of print material (newspapers, magazines), audiovisual, electronic (software, data bases), and interpersonal (seminars). It is published by the Dushkin Publishing Group, Inc., Sluice Dock, Guilford, CT 06437.

ANNUAL SECURITY-MARKET PUBLICATIONS

New York Stock Exchange Fact Book is an annual publication of the New York Stock Exchange. The book is an outstanding source of current and historical data on stock and bond activity on the NYSE.

AMEX Fact Book is a comparable data book for the American Stock Exchange. It is published annually and contains pertinent information on the exchange, its membership, administration, and trading activities in stocks, bonds, and derivative products.

NASDAQ Fact Book is a data book for the OTC market. First published in 1983 and now issued annually, it contains extensive data on trading volume and information related to the stocks on the NASDAQ system. It also discusses past growth and future plans for the NASDAQ market system.

Tokyo Stock Exchange Fact Book is an annual publication in English, containing information on the TSE. It is similar to the fact books prepared by U.S. institutions and contains extensive data related to stocks, bond and options trading on the exchange, members of the exchange, and the price action of stocks traded on the TSE and other Japanese exchanges. Copies are available through the New York office of the TSE.

Emerging Stock Markets Factbook is an annual publication of the International Finance Corporation (IFC), which is an international organization established to promote the economic growth of its 130 developing member countries through private sector investments. The *Factbook* contains five sections:

1. A background on the IFC and its emerging markets data base which contains statistics on stock markets in developing countries.
2. Extensive statistical data related to both developed and developing countries.
3. Stock indexes for 52 developing countries. There is a description of the index methodology and an analysis of performance for many of the countries using the IFC index and a commonly used local stock index.
4. A statistical analysis of 33 emerging markets.
5. A directory of pertinent information for more than 50 stock exchanges in developing countries.

American Banker Yearbook is an annual publication by the publisher of *American Banker,* a daily newspaper serving the financial services industry (this newspaper is described later in this section). The *Yearbook* contains a review of the events of the year that affect the banking industry plus an extensive statistical section that includes operating and size data on commercial banks, finance companies, mortgage banking, thrifts, and also international banks (the top 100 banks in the world).

The Bond Buyer Yearbook is an annual publication by the publisher of *The Bond Buyer,* a daily newspaper related to the fixed-income market (this newspaper is described later in this section). In addition to a review of the major events of the year, there are extensive statistics related to the municipal bond market such as the volume of long-term and short-term issues in total by purpose and by states, the interest rates on alternative issues, the top underwriter, and the top counseling firms. This is the major source of data related to the tax-exempt bond market.

The Business One Irwin Investor's Handbook is an annual publication that contains the complete DJIA results for each year along with earnings and dividends for the series since 1939. It also contains data on other U.S. stock indexes. A recent important addition is data for a number of individual foreign stocks and historical data for a number of non-U.S. stock indexes (e.g., Japan, Hong Kong, Singapore, Australia, Philippines, Thailand). Individual reports on common and preferred stocks and bonds listed on the NYSE and AMEX, including high and low prices, volume, dividends, and the year's most active stocks, are also included.[7]

Business and Investment Almanac, published annually by Dow Jones-Irwin and edited by Sumner N. Levine, this almanac contains a wide range of information on the economy, various industries, U.S. and foreign securities markets, and individual investments (stocks, bonds, options, futures, real estate, diamonds, and other collectibles). It concludes with a very helpful business and information directory.

The Wall Street Waltz is a book that contains 90 charts dealing with financial cycles and trends of historical interest put together by Kenneth Fisher. Examples include "Price-to-Book Value Ratios" from 1921; "Stock Prices Abroad"—stock prices for seven foreign countries; and a chart of the South Seas Bubble from 1719 to 1720. It provides excellent historical and current perspectives.

S&P Trade and Security Statistics is a service of Standard & Poor's that includes historical data on various economic and security price series and a monthly supplement that updates the series for the recent period. There are two major sets of data: (1) business and financial and (2) security price index record. Within the business and finance section are long-term statistics on trade, banking, industry, prices, agriculture, and the financial sector.

The security price index record contains historical data for all of the Standard & Poor's indexes. This includes the 500 stocks broken down into 88 individual groups. The four main groups are industrials, rails, utilities, and financial firms. There are also four supplementary group series: capital goods companies, consumer goods, high-grade common stocks, and low-priced common stocks. In addition to the stock price series, Standard & Poor's has derived a quarterly series of earnings and dividends for each of the four main groups. The earnings series includes data from 1946 to the present.

The booklet also contains data on daily stock sales on the NYSE since 1918 and historical yields for a number of corporate and government bond series.

Stocks, Bonds, Bills, and Inflation is published annually by Ibbotson Associates and contains monthly rates of return for seven primary U.S. capital market series and a number of derived series. The primary series are: (1) common stocks, (2) small company stocks, (3) long-term corporate bonds, (4) long-term government bonds, (5) intermediate-term government bonds, (6) U.S. Treasury bills, and (7) inflation. Besides the extensive data (which is also available on disk), there is a detailed discussion of the results over time and consideration of how the data can be used by portfolio managers and regulators.

WEEKLY SECURITY-MARKET PUBLICATIONS

Barron's is a weekly publication of Dow Jones and Company that typically contains about six articles on topics of interest to investors and the most complete weekly listing of prices and quotes for all U.S. financial markets. It provides weekly data on individual stocks and the latest information on earnings and dividends as well as quotes on com-

---

[7]Prior to 1992 this was entitled *The Dow Jones Investor's Handbook* .

modities, stock options, and financial futures. Finally, toward the back (typically the last four pages), there is an extensive statistical section with detailed information on the U.S. securities market for the past week.[8] There is also a fairly extensive set of world security-market indicator series and interest rates around the world as well as an "International Trader" section that discusses price movements in the major global stock markets.

Asian Wall Street Journal is a weekly publication of *The Wall Street Journal* that concentrates on the Asian region. It includes detailed economic news and stock and bond quotes related to this area of the global market.

Credit Markets is a weekly newspaper by the publishers of *The Bond Buyer*. It provides a longer-term overview of the major news items that affect the aggregate Treasury and corporate bond market and also individual bonds. There is an extensive statistical section listing bond calls, redemptions, the long-term future underwriting calendar, along with several security-market series.

Banking World is a weekly newspaper from the publishers of *American Banker*. It contains a summary of all the major news stories from Washington, the Federal Reserve, and all sectors of the financial services industry. There is news on marketing, technology, federal and state regulations, and specific financial firms.

Financial Services Week is a weekly publication from Fairchild Publications that is billed as "The Financial Planner's Newspaper." It contains articles on the overall stock and bond market, insurance, and special features such as "Planning for Dentists" and "Baby Boomers and Financial Services." There is also consideration of tax changes and other legislation of importance to those involved in personal financial planning.

International Financing Review is a weekly magazine that contains stories and data regarding international investment banking firms and the international securities markets. There is an emphasis on fixed-income securities, global economies, and politics. It is published by IFR Publishing Ltd.

Equities International, a weekly magazine that is also produced by IFR Publishing, deals with global markets but concentrates on equity instruments such as common stock, warrants, convertibles, options, and futures. The emphasis is on major trends and events in countries around the world. There is a complete listing of stock-market indexes for major global markets.

Euro Week, billed as "The Euromarket's First Newspaper," contains discussions related to notes, bonds, and stocks throughout Europe as well as longer articles on major news items in individual countries. A capital markets guide provides information on forthcoming securities issues. Finally, there is a listing of market indexes for various countries and a listing every quarter of the top investment banking firms in various categories (Eurobonds, Euro-equities) based on the value of the issues underwritten.

DAILY SECURITY-MARKET PUBLICATIONS

The Wall Street Journal, published by Dow Jones and Company, is a daily national business newspaper published five days a week. It contains complete listings for the NYSE, the AMEX, the NASDAQ-OTC market, U.S. bond markets, options markets,

---

[8]A booklet that discusses many of the features in *Barron's* and how the series are used by technicians is Martin E. Zweig, *Understanding Technical Forecasting.* It is likewise available, free of charge, from *The Wall Street Journal,* Educational Service Bureau, P. O. Box 300, Princeton, NJ 08540.

and commodities quotations. There are also a limited number of quotes for foreign stocks and a few non-U.S. stock market indicator series. It is recognized worldwide as a prime source of financial and business information for the United States.[9]

Investor Daily, billed as "America's Business Newspaper," was initiated in 1984 as competition to *The Wall Street Journal.* It provides much of the same information but also attempts to provide added information related to stock prices, earnings, and trading volume. An extensive set of U.S. general market indexes, including several unique to it, are included. It contains little, however, on non-U.S. markets.

The Financial Times is published five times a week in London with issues printed in New York and Los Angeles. Although it could be considered a British version of *The Wall Street Journal,* it is actually much more because it has a true *world* perspective on the financial news. It does an outstanding job of reporting financial news related not only to England, but also discusses the U.S. economy and security markets including extensive stock and bond quotes and security-market indicator series; it also contains news and data for Japan and other countries. Most important, however, is its global perspective in discussing and interpreting the news, which is critical to those involved in global investing.

The Bond Buyer is a daily newspaper (five days a week) that concentrates on news and quotes related to the overall bond market, with special emphasis on the municipal bond market—its caption reads, "The Authority on Municipal Bonds Since 1891." Besides news stories on events that affect bonds, there are extensive listings of new and forthcoming bond sales, bond calls and redemptions, and information on bond ratings. There are also numerous market indicator series reported with the emphasis on fixed-income series.

The American Banker is referred to as "The Daily Financial Services Newspaper." It contains articles of interest to bankers and others involved in the financial services industry on topics such as legislation and general news of the industry and major banks. There is also a brief summary of the financial markets related to Treasuries, financial futures, and mortgage securities.

BROKERAGE FIRM REPORTS

As a means of competing for investor's business, brokerage firms provide, among other services, information and recommendations on the outlook for securities markets (bonds and stocks). These reports are typically prepared monthly and distributed to customers (or potential customers) of the firm free of charge. In the competition for institutional business, investment firms have generated reports that are quite extensive and sophisticated. Among the brokerage firms issuing these reports are Goldman Sachs & Company; Kidder Peabody & Company; Merrill Lynch, Pierce, Fenner & Smith; Morgan Stanley; and Salomon Brothers.

Beyond these reports on the U.S. security markets, several investment banking firms publish extensive reviews of the world capital markets. The economic outlook for the major countries is discussed along with import/export and exchange rate considerations that culminate in evaluations of the outlook for particular industries specified as *global*

---

[9]A booklet that includes a discussion of many of the features of *The Wall Street Journal* is "A Future Manager's Guide to *The Wall Street Journal.*" Copies are available from *The Wall Street Journal,* Educational Service Bureau, P.O. Box 300, Princeton, NJ 08540.

industries and also recommendations related to world bond and stock markets. Examples of such publications include the following:

- Goldman Sachs International Corporation's monthly publication, *World Investment Strategy Highlights,* begins with world investment factors such as economic activity, monetary conditions, and interest rates and moves to individual country reports for about 12 individual countries and groups. The culmination is a recommended world portfolio strategy that considers individual country expectations and exchange rate forecasts.
- Morgan Stanley Capital International has a monthly publication that provides up-to-date pricing and valuation data on individual stocks and world industries. As an example, it is assumed that an analyst or a portfolio manager would evaluate U.S. chemical firms as part of the global chemical industry, not just the U.S. chemical industry. This set of world data allows the analyst or portfolio manager to examine stocks across industries and countries.

  The firm also has a quarterly publication that provides over 20 years of share price information (adjusted for capital changes) for 1,700 of the largest companies in the world, representing over 75 percent of the world's market capitalization. The most recent balance sheet is provided, along with 5 years of operating data.
- The Fixed Income Group of Kidder Peabody & Company publishes "The International Report," which is a monthly publication that suggests a global investment strategy for the fixed-income market based on world markets. Specifically, it considers global fixed-income returns, yields, and exchange rates, including specific country analyses for the United States, Japan, West Germany, the United Kingdom, and other countries of current interest. It also publishes a weekly "Capital Markets Report" that contains numerous charts on output, demand (consumer spending, personal income), inflation, Federal Reserve data, domestic and international interest rates, and international statistics.
- The Merrill Lynch Capital Markets Group publishes "World Bond Market Monitor," a biweekly analysis of international bond yields, spreads, and yield curves that specifically considers the U.S. dollar bond market, the floating rate note market, U.K. sterling bond market, Japanese yen bond market, Deutschemark (DM) bond market, Dutch guilder bond market, and several other countries along with data on world inflation and yields in currency hedged instruments. It also has a monthly publication entitled "International Fixed Income Strategy," which considers the global perspective for the dollar, the world climate for bonds, and specific market perspectives for the Japanese yen, the sterling bond market, and Deutschemark (DM) bonds. It concludes with a recommended international fixed-income strategy for the coming six months.
- Salomon Brothers Inc. has three interlocking monthly reports: "Global Fixed-Income Investment Strategy," "Global Equity Investment Strategy," and "Global Economic Outlook and Asset Allocation." Based on the outlook for the U.S. and world economies and markets, it makes a recommendation for a total world portfolio, including a global fixed-income-equity allocation that considers the exchange rate outlook.

- Nomura Research Institute (NRI)[10] publishes *Nomura Investment Review,* a monthly publication that analyzes and projects the general investment climate in Japan and the rest of the world. Although the emphasis is on the Japanese economy and its securities markets, there is also an extensive discussion of the world stock markets as well as various sectors (industries). The result is a world portfolio structure recommendation and suggestions for specific stocks.
- Daiwa Securities Company, Ltd. has a quarterly publication, *Tokyo Stock Market Quarterly Review,* that includes an in-depth analysis of the Japanese economy and securities market and also discusses numerous markets around the world.

INDUSTRY ANALYSIS

There are only a few publications with extensive information on a wide range of industries. The major source of data on various industries are industry publications and trade association magazines.

INDUSTRY PUBLICATIONS

Standard & Poor's Industry Survey is a two-volume reference work divided into 34 segments dealing with 69 major domestic industries. Coverage in each area is divided into a basic analysis and a current analysis. The *basic analysis* examines the long-term prospects for a particular industry based on an analysis of historical trends and problems. Major segments of the industry are spotlighted, and a comparative analysis of the principal companies in the industry is included. The *current analysis* discusses recent developments and provides statistics for an industry and specific companies along with appraisals of the industry's investment outlook.

Standard & Poor's Analysts Handbook contains selected income account and balance sheet items along with related financial ratios for the Standard & Poor's industry groups. (It is typically not available until about seven months after year-end.) With these fundamental income and balance sheet series, it is possible to compare the major factors bearing on group stock price movements (e.g., sales, profit margins, earnings, assets, debt). These data are used extensively in the industry analysis chapter. Figure 5.1 is a sample page from the *Handbook.*

Value Line Industry Survey is an integral part of the *Value Line Investment Survey.* The reports for the 1,700 companies included are divided into 91 industries and updated by industry. In the binder containing these reports, the industry evaluation precedes the individual company reports. The industry report contains summary statistics for the industry on assets, earnings, and important ratios similar to what is included for companies. There is also an industry stock price index as well as a table that provides comparative data for all the individual companies in the industry on timeliness rank, safety rank, and financial strength. The discussion considers the major factors affecting the industry and concludes with an investment recommendation for the industry.

INDUSTRY MAGAZINES

The magazines published for various industries are an excellent source of data and general information. Depending on the industry, there can be several publications (e.g., the computer industry has spawned at least five such magazines). Examples of industry publications include the following:

---

[10]The Nomura Research Institute is an independently managed research company affiliated with the Nomura Securities Company, Ltd.

- *Computers*
- *Real Estate Today*
- *Chemical Week*
- *Modern Plastics*
- *Paper Trade Journal*
- *Automotive News*

TRADE ASSOCIATIONS

Trade associations are organizations set up by those involved in an industry or a general area of business to provide information for such topics as education, advertising, lobbying for legislation, and problem solving. Trade associations typically gather extensive statistics for the industry. Examples of such organizations would include:[11]

- Iron and Steel Institute
- American Railroad Association
- National Consumer Finance Association
- Institute of Life Insurance
- American Bankers Association
- Machine Tool Association

INDIVIDUAL STOCK AND BOND ANALYSIS

The most extensive material is available on individual firms' stocks and bonds. The sources of these publications include individual companies; commercial publishing firms, which produce a vast array of material; reports provided by investment firms; and several investment magazines, which discuss the overall financial markets and provide opinions on individual companies and their stocks or bonds. We will discuss each of these sources and specific publications; however, you should keep in mind that many of the prior sources such as *The Wall Street Journal* and *Barron's* also include discussions of individual stocks or bonds.

COMPANY-GENERATED INFORMATION

An obvious source of information about a company is the company itself. Indeed, for some small firms, it may be the only source of information because trading activity in the firm's stock is not sufficient to justify its inclusion in publications of commercial services or brokerage firms.

ANNUAL REPORTS
Every firm with publicly traded stock must prepare and distribute to its stockholders an annual report of financial operations and current financial position. In addition to basic information, most reports discuss what happened during the year and outline future prospects. Most firms also publish quarterly financial reports that include brief income statements for the interim period and, sometimes, a balance sheet. These reports can be obtained directly from the company. To find an address for a company, you should consult Volume 1 of *Standard & Poor's Register of Corporations, Directors,*

---

[11]For a more extensive list, see *Encyclopedia of Associations* (Detroit: Gale Research Company, 1977); and *The World Guide to Trade Associations,* (New York: R. R. Bowker, 1986).

CONTAINERS—METAL and GLASS

Per Share Data — Adjusted to stock price index level. Average of stock price indexes, 1941-1943=10

Year	Sales	Oper. Profit	Profit Margin %	Depr.	Income Taxes	Cash Flow	Earnings Per Share	Earnings % of Sales	Dividends Per Share	Dividends % of Earn.	Prices 1941-1943=10 High	Prices Low	Price/Earn. Ratio High	Price/Earn. Ratio Low	Div. Yields % High	Div. Yields % Low	Book Value Per Share	Book Value % Return	Working Capital	Capital Expenditures
1961	42.56	5.20	12.22	1.50	1.79		1.59	3.74	1.00	62.89	30.22	23.71	19.01	14.91	4.22	3.31	19.93	7.98	10.23	2.05
1962	44.41	5.44	12.25	1.61	1.81		1.70	3.83	1.00	58.82	29.52	23.46	17.36	13.80	4.26	3.39	19.87	8.56	10.32	2.06
1963	44.59	5.41	12.13	1.69	1.77		1.70	3.81	1.02	60.00	28.98	26.80	17.05	15.76	3.81	3.52	20.75	8.19	10.52	2.47
1964	47.18	5.76	12.21	1.78	1.71		2.01	4.26	1.03	51.24	32.14	27.47	15.99	13.67	3.75	3.20	20.52	9.80	9.50	3.00
1965	50.26	6.77	13.47	1.78	2.16		2.56	5.09	1.09	42.58	40.38	31.18	15.77	12.18	3.50	2.70	23.24	11.02	10.59	3.57
1966	55.47	7.51	13.54	1.91	2.42		2.92	5.26	1.23	42.12	42.02	35.48	14.39	12.15	3.47	2.93	25.21	11.58	8.87	5.35
1967	58.55	7.82	13.36	2.08	2.35		2.93	5.00	1.29	44.03	44.96	35.44	15.34	12.10	3.64	2.87	26.35	11.12	9.66	5.25
1968	63.76	8.91	13.97	2.33	3.01		3.11	4.88	1.31	42.12	52.18	36.16	16.78	11.63	3.62	2.51	27.97	11.12	10.16	4.96
1969	71.51	9.83	13.75	2.58	3.42		3.29	4.60	1.35	41.03	52.47	44.60	15.95	13.56	3.03	2.57	29.75	11.06	10.55	4.95
1970	78.67	10.30	13.09	2.90	3.36		3.26	4.14	1.37	42.02	46.83	35.05	14.37	10.75	3.91	2.93	28.90	11.28	10.67	5.68
1971	82.11	9.23	11.24	3.00	2.57		2.76	3.36	1.40	50.72	47.24	31.01	17.12	11.24	4.51	2.96	29.65	9.31	12.99	4.98
1972	88.50	9.52	10.76	3.21	2.54		3.10	3.50	1.42	45.81	37.58	33.10	12.12	10.68	4.29	3.78	28.29	10.96	13.58	4.85
1973	103.04	11.23	10.90	3.63	3.07		3.72	3.61	1.45	38.98	35.46	25.25	9.53	6.79	5.74	4.09	31.12	11.95	14.52	5.89
1974	126.24	13.86	10.98	4.05	3.98		4.82	3.82	1.56	32.37	30.53	23.61	6.33	4.90	6.61	5.11	34.14	14.12	16.15	7.48
1975	133.76	13.01	9.73	4.44	3.18		4.41	3.30	1.62	36.73	33.93	28.87	7.69	6.55	5.61	4.77	36.99	11.92	17.29	R7.55
1976	145.79	14.95	10.25	4.62	3.99		5.13	3.52	1.73	33.72	39.53	34.23	7.71	6.67	5.05	4.38	41.10	12.48	21.28	6.75
1977	152.63	14.23	9.32	4.76	3.60	9.98	5.24	3.43	1.86	35.50	41.33	36.11	7.89	6.89	5.15	4.50	44.37	11.81	20.63	8.95
1978	169.86	15.35	9.04	5.12	3.26	10.47	5.37	3.16	2.05	38.18	41.36	33.57	7.70	6.25	6.11	4.96	46.23	11.62	22.30	9.96
1979	188.94	16.61	8.79	5.64	3.43	12.48	6.86	3.63	2.16	31.49	39.47	33.68	5.75	4.91	6.41	5.47	50.75	13.52	R21.79	11.27
1980	212.56	18.50	8.70	6.60	3.61	13.58	7.00	3.29	2.30	32.86	39.81	31.76	5.69	4.54	7.24	5.78	55.56	12.60	R23.78	11.88
1981	211.91	17.67	8.34	7.09	3.50	13.75	6.66	3.14	2.42	36.34	47.01	37.48	7.06	5.63	6.46	5.15	63.39	10.51	25.67	11.12
1982	201.28	15.13	7.52	7.52	1.38	9.27	1.76	0.87	2.55	144.89	41.45	31.05	23.55	17.64	8.21	6.15	58.31	3.02	18.49	11.80
1983	193.11	13.89	7.19	7.34	1.61	12.46	5.12	2.65	2.62	51.17	57.62	39.34	11.25	7.68	6.66	4.55	59.23	8.64	18.36	10.61
1984	224.09	19.37	8.64	7.34	4.37	15.21	7.88	3.52	2.78	35.28	76.47	54.12	9.70	6.87	5.14	3.64	73.50	10.72	20.10	11.11
1985	199.93	20.66	10.33	7.25	6.56	16.07	8.82	4.41	3.01	34.13	106.91	75.30	12.12	8.54	4.00	2.82	80.38	10.97	20.70	11.16
1986	203.47	29.22	14.36	6.71	7.84	17.37	10.66	5.24	3.39	31.80	160.88	103.18	15.09	9.68	3.29	2.11	87.56	12.17	···	10.15
1987	276.20	35.63	12.90	9.65	10.86	23.68	14.02	5.08	2.33	16.62	216.91	147.29	15.47	10.51	1.58	1.07	93.57	14.98	32.92	19.48
1988	305.17	34.85	11.42	10.62	8.73	23.86	13.24	4.34	2.50	18.88	206.43	156.66	15.59	11.83	1.60	1.21	110.53	11.98	34.78	21.33
1989	326.69	34.21	10.47	11.69	6.78	24.72	13.03	3.99	2.79	21.41	241.03	193.00	18.50	14.81	1.45	1.16	96.77	13.46	23.16	14.97
1990	453.64	49.93	11.01	15.89	9.31	31.37	15.49	3.41	2.54	16.40	268.27	212.90	17.32	13.74	1.19	0.95	131.73	11.76	47.53	16.55
1991	595.06	65.06	10.93	22.55	12.15	40.58	18.03	3.03	2.66	14.75	355.24	221.85	19.70	12.30	1.20	0.75	100.36	17.97	56.81	18.40

176

Source: *Analysts Handbook,* 1992 edition (New York: Standard & Poor's, Inc.). Reprinted by permission of Standard & Poor's Corp.

and Executives, which contains an alphabetical listing, by business name, of approximately 37,000 corporations.

SECURITY PROSPECTUS

When a firm wants to sell securities (bonds, preferred stock, or common stock) in the primary market to raise new capital, the Securities and Exchange Commission (SEC) requires that it file a registration statement describing the securities being offered. It must provide extensive financial information beyond what is required in an annual report as well as nonfinancial information on its operations and personnel. A condensed version of the registration statement, referred to as a *prospectus,* is published by the underwriting firm and contains most of the relevant information. Copies of a prospectus for a current offering can be obtained from the underwriter or from the company. Investment banking firms will often advertise offerings in publications such as *The Wall Street Journal, Barron's,* or *The Financial Times.*

REQUIRED SEC REPORTS

In addition to registration statements, the SEC requires three *periodic* statements from publicly held firms. First, the 8-K form is filed each month, reporting any action that affects the debt, equity, amount of capital assets, voting rights, or other changes that might have a significant impact on the stock.

Second, the 9-K form is an unaudited report filed every six months containing revenues, expenses, gross sales, and special items. It typically contains more extensive information than the quarterly statement.

Finally, the 10-K form is an annual version of the 9-K but is even more complete. The SEC requires that firms indicate in their annual reports that a copy of their 10-K is available from the company upon request without charge.

COMMERCIAL PUBLICATIONS

Numerous advisory services supply information on the aggregate market and individual stocks. A partial list follows.

STANDARD & POOR'S PUBLICATIONS

Standard & Poor's Corporation Records is a set of seven volumes. The first six contain basic information on all types of corporations (industrial, financial) arranged alphabetically. The volumes are in binders and are updated throughout the year. The seventh volume is a daily news volume that contains recent data on all companies listed in all the volumes.

Standard & Poor's Stock Reports are comprehensive two-page reports on numerous companies with stocks listed on the NYSE, AMEX, and traded OTC. They include the near term sales and earnings outlook, recent developments, key income statement and balance sheet items, and a chart of stock price movements. They are in bound volumes by exchange and are revised every three to four months. A sample page is shown in Figure 5.2.

Standard & Poor's Stock Guide is a monthly publication that contains, in compact form, pertinent financial data on more than 5,000 common and preferred stocks. A separate section covers over 400 mutual fund issues. For each stock, the guide contains information on price ranges (historical and recent), dividends, earnings, financial

FIGURE 5.2   Sample Pages from *Standard & Poor's Stock Reports*

Int'l Business Machines   1210

NYSE Symbol IBM Options on CBOE (Jan-Apr-Jul-Oct) In S&P 500

Price	Range	P–E Ratio	Dividend	Yield	S&P Ranking	Beta
Sep. 3'93	1993					
45¾	57⅛–40⅝	NM	1.00	2.2%	B	0.60

Summary

IBM is the world's dominant manufacturer of mainframe computers and is also a major supplier of minicomputers, computer peripheral equipment, personal computers, networking products and system software. Results continue to be penalized by a user shift from mainframes toward smaller, nonproprietary computers, intense competition and general economic weakness. An $8.9 billion restructuring charge was recorded in the 1993 second quarter, and the dividend was slashed 54%.

Current Outlook

A loss of $0.65 a share, excluding restructuring charges, is projected for 1993, versus 1992's loss of $12.03, which included a restructuring charge of $14.51. Earnings of $0.75 are possible for 1994. The quarterly dividend was slashed 54%, to $0.25, with the September 1993 payment.

Results for the balance of 1993 will be hurt by ongoing fundamental changes in the computer industry and continued economic weakness. Users are moving away from proprietary mainframe-based computing toward network-based processing that uses lower priced (and hence less profitable) nonproprietary PCs, workstations and midrange computers. Although IBM has begun to focus on the faster growing software and services segments, it will take time until these areas are large enough to allow for a resumption of growth. Total revenues for 1993 are estimated at 5% below 1992 levels.

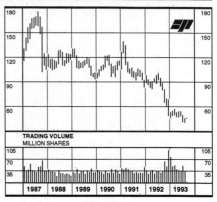

TRADING VOLUME
MILLION SHARES

1987 | 1988 | 1989 | 1990 | 1991 | 1992 | 1993

Revenues (Billion $)

Quarter:	1993	1992	1991	1990
Mar.	13.06	14.04	13.55	14.19
Jun.	15.52	16.22	14.73	16.50
Sep.	E14.00	14.70	14.43	15.28
Dec.	E18.70	19.56	22.08	23.06
	E61.28	64.52	64.79	69.02

Revenues in the six months ended June 30, 1993, decreased 5.6%, year to year, as declines in hardware sales, maintenance and rentals and financing outweighed gains for software and services. Gross margins narrowed sharply on the lower volume and a shift in product mix. Despite 9.2% lower operating expenses, a pretax loss replaced pretax income. Results were penalized by an $8.9 billion restructuring charge. Despite tax credits of $1.1 billion, versus taxes at 35.7%, a loss of $8.3 billion ($14.60 a share) replaced income of $1.4 billion ($2.41). Results in the 1992 interim exclude a credit of $3.33 a share from accounting changes.

Capital Share Earnings ($)

Quarter:	1993	1992	1991	1990
Mar.	d0.50	1.12	0.93	1.81
Jun.	d14.10	1.29	0.20	2.45
Sep.	Ed0.50	d4.87	0.30	1.95
Dec.	E0.43	d9.57	d2.42	4.30
	Ed14.67	d12.03	d0.99	10.51

Important Developments

Jul. '93— IBM said a net charge of $8.9 billion ($14.02 a share) recorded in the 1993 second quarter will cover reductions of 35,000 in its worldwide work force, and cuts in manufacturing capacity and office space. When fully implemented, these actions are expected to save $4 billion annually. The company expects to employ 255,000 at the end of 1993 and 225,000 at the end of 1994.

Next earnings report expected in mid-October.

Per Share Data ($)

Yr. End Dec. 31	1992	¹1991	1990	1989	¹1988	1987	1986	1985	1984	1983
Tangible Bk. Val.	47.86	64.39	74.29	66.33	65.78	62.81	55.40	50.60	41.79	38.02
Cash Flow	d3.63	8.02	17.88	13.76	15.80	14.57	13.23	15.64	16.02	15.02
Earnings²	d12.03	d0.99	10.51	6.47	9.27	8.72	7.81	10.67	10.77	9.04
Dividends	4.84	4.84	4.84	4.73	4.40	4.40	4.40	4.40	4.10	3.71
Payout Ratio	NM	NM	46%	72%	47%	50%	56%	41%	38%	41%
Prices—High	100⅞	139¾	123⅛	130⅞	129½	175⅞	161⅞	158¾	128½	134¼
Low	48¾	83½	94½	93⅜	104¼	102	119¼	117⅜	99	92¼
P/E Ratio—	NM	NM	12–9	20–14	14–11	20–12	21–15	15–11	12–9	15–10

Data as orig. reptd. 1. Refl. acctg. change. 2. Bef. spec. items of +3.33 in 1992, -3.96 in 1991, +0.53 in 1988. d-Deficit. E-Estimated. NM-Not Meaningful.

Standard NYSE Stock Reports
Vol. 60/No. 176/Sec. 5

September 13, 1993
Copyright © 1993 Standard & Poor's Corp. All Rights Reserved

Standard & Poor's Corp.
25 Broadway, NY, NY 10004

International Business Machines Corporation

Income Data (Million $)

Year Ended Dec. 31	Revs.	Oper. Inc.	% Oper. Inc. of Revs.	Cap. Exp.	Depr.	Int. Exp.	[2]Net Bef. Taxes	Eff. Tax Rate	[3]Net Inc.	% Net Inc. of Revs.	Cash Flow
1992	64,523	8,199	12.7	4,751	4,793	1,461	d9,026	NM	d6,865	NM	d2,072
[1]1991	64,792	9,489	14.6	6,502	5,149	1,566	121	566.1%	d564	NM	4,385
1990	69,018	15,249	22.1	6,548	4,217	1,446	10,203	41.0%	6,020	8.7	10,237
1989	62,710	13,553	21.6	6,410	4,240	1,118	6,645	43.4%	3,758	6.0	7,998
[1]1988	59,681	12,617	21.1	5,431	3,871	802	9,033	39.2%	5,491	9.2	9,362
1987	54,217	11,269	20.8	4,304	3,527	619	8,609	38.9%	5,258	9.7	8,785
1986	51,250	11,175	21.8	4,620	3,316	604	8,389	42.9%	4,789	9.3	8,105
1985	50,056	14,281	28.5	6,430	3,051	443	11,619	43.6%	6,555	13.1	9,606
1984	45,937	14,446	31.4	5,473	3,215	408	11,623	43.4%	6,582	14.3	9,797
1983	40,180	13,216	32.9	4,930	3,627	390	9,940	44.8%	5,485	13.7	9,112

Balance Sheet Data (Million $)

Dec. 31	Cash	Assets	Curr. Liab.	Ratio	Total Assets	% Ret. on Assets	Long Term Debt	Common Equity	Total Cap.	% LT Debt of Cap.	% Ret. on Equity
1992	5,649	39,692	36,737	1.1	86,705	NM	12,853	27,624	42,507	30.2	NM
1991	5,151	40,969	33,624	1.2	92,473	NM	13,231	37,006	52,164	25.4	NM
1990	4,551	38,920	25,276	1.5	87,568	7.3	11,943	42,832	58,636	20.4	14.8
1989	4,961	35,875	21,700	1.7	77,734	5.0	10,825	38,509	52,614	20.6	9.8
1988	6,123	35,343	17,387	2.0	73,037	8.1	8,518	39,509	52,650	16.2	14.2
1987	6,967	31,020	13,377	2.3	63,688	8.7	3,858	38,263	47,271	8.2	14.6
1986	7,257	27,749	12,743	2.2	57,814	8.7	4,169	34,374	43,067	9.7	14.5
1985	5,622	26,070	11,433	2.3	52,634	13.7	3,955	31,990	39,595	10.0	22.4
1984	4,362	20,375	9,640	2.1	42,808	16.4	3,269	26,489	31,815	10.3	26.4
1983	5,536	17,270	9,507	1.8	37,243	15.6	2,674	23,219	26,606	10.1	25.2

Data as orig. reptd.; finance subs. consol. aft. 1987. **1.** Refl. acctg. change. **2.** Incl. equity in earns. of nonconsol. subs. **3.** Bef. spec. items. d-Deficit. NM-Not Meaningful.

Business Summary

IBM is the largest manufacturer of data processing equipment and systems. Industry segment contributions to revenues in recent years were:

	1992	1991
Processors	22%	23%
Workstations	16%	18%
Peripherals	14%	16%
Software/maint./services	41%	36%
Financing & other	7%	7%

Hardware sales provided 52% of revenues in 1992, software, maintenance and services 41%, and rentals 7%. Foreign operations contributed 62% of revenues in 1992.

Processors include high-end and midrange products. Workstations include personal systems processors, technical workstations, and other terminals. Peripherals include printers, and storage and telecommunication devices. Software includes applications and systems software. Maintenance represents separately billed maintenance services. Services include consulting, education, systems integration, systems operations and network services. Financing and other is comprised of financing revenue and products not otherwise classified.

Dividend Data

Dividends have been paid since 1916. A dividend reinvestment plan is available.

Amt. of Divd. $	Date Decl.	Ex-divd. Date	Stock of Record	Payment Date
1.21	Oct. 27	Nov. 5	Nov. 12	Dec. 10'92
0.54	Jan. 26	Feb. 4	Feb. 10	Mar. 10'93
0.54	Apr. 26	May 6	May 21	Jun. 10'93
0.25	Jul. 27	Aug. 5	Aug. 11	Sep. 10'93

Finances

In July 1993, directors authorized the issuance of up to 15 million common shares for contribution to a retirement plan. They also approved a plan to issue stock for an ESOP, financing authority for up to $1 billion of debt issuance, and up to $1 billion of asset securitization.

Net restructuring charges totaled $8.3 billion in 1992 ($14.51 a share) and $2.9 billion in 1991 ($5.03), reflecting actions taken to cut costs and capacity.

Capitalization

Long Term Debt: $14,563,000,000 (6/93).

Preferred Stock: $1,091,000,000.

Capital Stock: 571,045,309 shs. ($1.25 par). Institutions hold 39%.
Shareholders of record: 764,630 (12/92).

Office—Old Orchard Rd., Armonk, NY 10504. **Tel**—(914) 765-1900. **Chrmn & CEO**—L. V. Gerstner, Jr. **Vice Chrmn**—J. D. Kuehler. **Vice Chrmn & CFO**—P. J. Rizzo. **Secy**—J. E. Hickey. **Investor Contact**—J. H. Clippard, Jr. **Stockholder Relations Dept**—Tel: (914-765-7777). **Dirs**—H. Brown, J. E. Burke, T. F. Frist, Jr., F. Gerber, L. V. Gerstner, Jr., J. R. Hope, N. O. Keohane, C. F. Knight, J. D. Kuehler, R. W. Lyman, F. A. Metz, T. S. Murphy, J. R. Opel, P. J. Rizzo, H. Sihler, J. B. Slaughter, L. C. van Wachem, E. S. Woolard, Jr. **Transfer Agent & Registrar**— First Chicago Trust Co. of New York, NYC. **Incorporated** in New York in 1911. **Empl**—301,542.

Information has been obtained from sources believed to be reliable, but its accuracy and completeness are not guaranteed. Neeraj K. Vohra position, institutional holdings, and a ranking for earning and dividend stability. It is a very useful quick reference for almost all actively traded stocks, as is shown by the example in Figure 5.3.

Standard & Poor's Bond Guide is a monthly publication that contains the most pertinent comparative financial and statistical information on a broad list of bonds including domestic and foreign bonds (about 3,900 issues), 200 foreign government bonds, and about 650 convertible bonds.

The Outlook is a weekly publication of Standard & Poor's Corporation that advises investors about the general market environment and specific groups of stocks or industries (e.g., high-dividend stocks, stocks with low price-to-earnings ratios, high-yielding bonds, stocks likely to increase their dividends). Weekly stock index figures for 88 industry groups and other market statistics are included.

Daily Stock Price Records is published quarterly by Standard & Poor's, with individual volumes for the NYSE, the AMEX, and the OTC market. Each quarterly book is divided into two parts. Part 1, "Major Technical Indicators of the Stock Market," is devoted to market indicators widely followed as technical guides to the stock market and includes price indicator series, volume series, and data on odd lots and short sales. Part 2, "Daily and Weekly Stock Action," gives daily high, low, close, and volume information as well as monthly data on short interest for individual stocks, insider trading information, a 200-day moving average of prices, and a weekly relative strength series. The books for the NYSE and AMEX are available from 1962 on; the OTC books begin in 1968.

MOODY'S PUBLICATIONS

Moody's Industrial Manual resembles the Standard & Poor's Corporation records service except this service is organized by type of corporation (i.e., industrial, utility, etc.). The two-volume service is published once a year and covers industrial companies listed on the NYSE, the AMEX, and regional exchanges. One section concentrates on international industrial firms. Like all Moody's manuals, there is a news report volume that covers events that occurred after publication of the basic manual.

Moody's OTC Industrial Manual is similar to the *Moody's Industrial Manual* of listed firms but is limited to stocks traded on the OTC market.

Moody's has manuals for various industries as well. *Moody's Public Utility Manual* provides information on public utilities, including electric and gas, gas transmission, telephone, and water companies. *Moody's Transportation Manual* covers the transportation industry, including railroads, airlines, steamship companies, electric railway, bus and truck lines, oil pipe lines, bridge companies, and automobile and truck leasing companies. *Moody's Bank and Finance Manual* covers the field of financial services represented by banks, savings and loan associations, credit agencies of the U.S. government, all phases of the insurance industry, investment companies, real estate firms, real estate investment trusts, and miscellaneous financial enterprises.

Moody's Municipal and Government Manual contains data on the U.S. government, all the states, state agencies, and over 13,500 municipalities. It also includes some excellent information and data on foreign governments and international organizations.

Moody's International Manual provides financial information on about 3,000 major foreign corporations.

FIGURE 5.3 **Example from *Standard & Poor's Stock Guide***

62 DAN-DEL

Standard & Poor's Corporation

¶ S&P 500
\# MidCap 400
• Options

Index	Ticker Symbol	Name of Issue (Call Price of Pfd. Stocks)	Market	Com. Rank. & Pfd. Rating	Par Val.	Inst. Hold Cos	Inst. Hold Shs. (000)	Principal Business	Price Range 1971-91 High	1971-91 Low	1992 High	1992 Low	1993 High	1993 Low	Feb. Sales in 100s	February, 1993 Last Sale Or Bid High	Low	Last	%Div Yield	P-E Ratio
1•[1]	DNKG	✓Danek Group	NMS	NR	No	74	5667	Mfr spinal implant devices	28¼	7½	44¾	21½	45	25¾	54884	39¼	25¾	28¾	...	39
2	DAN	✓Daniel Indus	NY,M,Ph	B	1¼	51	6149	Measure, contr fluid devices	25½	1 3/16	15⅞	10½	12¾	10¾	2538	12¾	11½	12⅛	1.5	30
3	DHC	❖Danielson Holding	AS,M	NR	10¢	20	1686	Investment co/insurance	4½	2⅜	4⅜	2½	4⅜	3⅜	1989	4¼	3⅞	4⅛	...	d
4	DANKY	Danka Business Systems ADR[53]	NMS	NR	[53]..	6	2700	Dstr office equip,east'n U.S.	....	....	20⅝	17⅜	38¼	20¼	29061	38¼	31¼	37¼	0.8	16
5	DANS	Danskin Inc	NMS	NR	1¢	22	1120	Mfr women's clothing,hosiery	....	....	14	6½	8¼	7	3306	8¼	7	7¼	...	..
6	DARTA	✓Dart Group Cl'A'	NMS	B–	1	37	822	Discount book&auto parts strs	178½	3⅝	78	62¾	87	73	218	87	80	81⅜	0.2	16
7	DDL	❖Data-Design Labs	NY,P,Ph	C	33⅓¢	11	705	Mfrs printed circuit boards	13⅛	5/16	1⅞	9/16	1⅜	⅞	9801	1⅜	15/16	1	...	d
¶8•[2]	DGN	✓Data General	NY,B,M,P,Ph	C	1¢	163	21590	General purpose computers	76	3⅛	18⅛	7⅛	12¾	10⅞	45120	12¾	11⅜	12⅜	...	d
9	DAIO	✓Data I/O	NMS	B–	No	32	2775	Programming sys & equip	24¼	2	8⅝	3	5	4	4379	4⅞	4⅛	4⅝	...	12
10	DMCB	❖Data Measurement	NMS	C	1¢	8	172	Mfr/svc electronic instr/sys	18	1	5¾	1	7½	4¾	363	7½	6¼	6¾	...	8
11	RACE	Data Race	NMS	NR	No	6	286	Mfr portable computer comun pd	....	....	27½	13	30¾	16¼	44716	30	16¼	19	...	19
12	DRAI	✓Data Research Associates	NMS	NR	1¢	9	444	Provides library automat'n sys	....	....	12¼	7	13	10½	2076	12½	11½	11½	...	17
13	DASW	✓Data Switch	NMS	C	1¢	18	3399	Mfr switching & control sys	41	1½	3⅜	⅞	3⅜	2 3/16	12958	3⅜	2¾	3	...	d
14	DATX	❖Data Translation	NMS	↓C	1¢	11	563	Mfr microcomputer products	25	2⅝	9¾	3	9¼	6½	915	8¾	6½	7¼	...	d
15	DTLN	Data Transmission Ntwk	NMS	NR	.001	21	885	Agricultural market info svc	22½	5½	15	11¼	14¾	13½	804	14¾	13½	14	...	34
16	DFLX	✓Dataflex Corp	NMS	B	No	23	1470	Sell/lease data terminals	17	3/16	16¾	4	6½	4¾	1166	6¼	4¾	5	...	14
17	DKEY	Datakey Inc	NMS	B–	5¢	8	589	Mfrs electronic access keys	12	3	6¼	2¾	4	3	651	4	3	3B	...	38
18	DC	❖Datametrics Corp	AS	B–	1¢	4	86	Dvlp/mfr computer periph'ls	10⅝	1/16	1¾	1	2¾	1¼	4671	2 5/16	1 11/16	1 15/16	...	7
19	DPT	❖Datapoint Corp	NY,B,M,P,Ph	C	25¢	24	2236	Mfr data process'g systems	67½	¾	4¾	1⅜	6	3⅜	21779	6	4½	5⅞	...	d
20	DTM	❖Dataram Corp	AS,B,Ph	B–	1	14	299	Minicomputer related products	7⅜	1/64	19¾	4¾	12½	7½	6545	12⅛	7½	9	...	13
#21•[3]	DSCP	✓Datascope Corp	NMS	B	1¢	83	9007	Electronic medical instru't'n	39⅛	9/16	41¾	17¾	26½	15¼	53857	22¼	15¼	18¾	...	34
22	DSCC	❖Datasouth Computer	NMS	C	1¢	5	416	Mfr computer printers & prod	12	1	3⅜	1¾	3¾	2⅜	1666	3¾	2⅝	3⅛	...	28
23	DTSI	✓Datron Systems	NMS	B	1¢	17	957	Satellite commun/radar sys	17½	2	14¼	4½	6¼	4½	497	5¾	4½	4¾	...	d
24	DATM	❖Datum Inc	NMS	B	25¢	8	537	Mfr tim'g/frequency devices	16¾	½	4⅜	2⅛	3½	2⅜	598	3⅛	2⅜	2⅜	...	d
#25	DAPN	✓Dauphin Deposit	NMS	A	5	95	5438	Comm'l bkg,Pennsylvania	18¾	3	25¼	17⅝	25½	22½	6707	25¼	23½	24½	3.3	13
26	DWW	✓Davis Water & Waste	NY,M,Ph	B–	1¢	15	761	Sewage/water treat,pump eq	25⅝	½	7⅞	5	7¼	6	296	7	6¼	6⅜	...	d
27•[4]	DVS	❖Davstar Industries 'A'	AS	NR	No	5	298	Mfr,mkt medical products	4⅛	2⅜	13¾	3	9⅝	6	22137	9⅝	6¾	7⅞	...	d
28	WS	Wrrt(Pur 1 Cl'A' com at $5)	AS	....	..	1	11		....	....	8¾	15/16	5¼	2¾	5387	4¾	3¼	3⅝	...	..
29	DWSN	❖Dawson Geophysical	NMS	B–	33⅓	16	721	Seismic data for oil/gas ind	19½	3	5½	4	7⅜	5⅛	1168	7⅜	6¼	7	...	16
30	DXR	❖Daxor Corp	AS	B	1¢	10	320	Operates human sperm bank	37	1/16	17¼	2⅜	8	6¼	1921	8	6⅜	6½	...	8
31	DAYR	Day Runner	NMS	NR	No	27	1412	Mfr personal organizer prd	....	....	21¾	7½	12¾	8⅝	10978	12¾	11½	12¼	...	16
¶32•[5]	DH	✓Dayton Hudson	NY,B,M,P,Ph	A	1	474	58662	Depart/disc/spec stores	80¼	1⅝	79¼	58	85	73⅞	51015	85	77	77⅛	2.1	16
33	DBAS	DBA Systems	NMS	B–	10¢	9	253	Aerospace sys analysis	27¼	3/16	6⅛	3¼	4⅝	4⅛	2212	4⅝	4⅛	4⅜	...	7
34	DDIX	DDI Pharmaceuticals	NMS	B–	50¢	7	350	Drug devel:human/veter	43¼	1½	8⅜	2 1/16	4⅛	3	2567	4⅛	3	3⅜	...	d
#35•[6]	DF	✓Dean Foods	NY,M	A	1	132	13004	Milk & dairy: food items	33½	⅜	31½	22¾	29¼	26⅝	7374	29¼	27⅜	28⅝	2.1	19
36	DWD	Dean Witter, Discover & Co	NY	NR	1¢	..	...	Provides financial svcs/prod	....	....	....	....	33⅛	27	145029	33⅛	27	33⅛	1.2	13
37	GVT	Dean Witter Gvt Income SBI	NY,M,Ph	NR	1¢	23	569	Closed-end investment co	10	8⅜	9¾	8¾	9¼	8⅞	19268	9¼	9	9¼	7.5	..
38	DEBS	✓Deb Shops	NMS	B+	1¢	24	1949	Women's apparel stores	21⅞	4⅜	11¾	6⅛	9	8	578	8¾	8	8¾	2.3	22
39	DBRSY	DeBeers Cons Mns ADR[64]	NSC	NR	r5	31	6108	Diamond mining	32⅝	2⅛	29⅛	9⅞	16½	11⅝	58336	16½	14⅜	15⅛	7.3	5
40	DII	❖Decorator Indus	AS	B–	20¢	6	33	Mfr & dstr of draperies	19	13/16	18⅛	2¼	19	14¼	1782	19	14⅜	18⅛	...	11
¶41•[7]	DE	✓Deere & Co	NY,B,C,M,P,Ph	B	1	445	60688	Lgst mfr farm eq:constr mchy	78⅜	9⅞	54	36¾	52¼	42⅜	72479	52¼	45	52	3.8	..
42	ENRGB	✓DEKALB Energy'B'[65]	NMS	B–	No	51	3870	Oil & Natural gas expl,prod	63	12	15¾	10¼	12½	10¾	1586	12½	11	12¼	...	d
43	SEEDB	✓DEKALB Genetics'B'	NMS	NR	No	60	2773	Agricultural genetic R & D	44¾	12	34½	23½	32	25¼	2205	32	28¼	32	2.5	20
44	DEL	✓Del Electronics Corp	AS,M	B–	10¢	11	396	Mfr hi-voltage pwr supplies	8⅝	1/16	8⅛	5	7⅜	5⅞	1471	6⅞	6⅛	6¾	...	16
45	DLI	❖Del Laboratories	AS	B+	1	12	243	Drugs and cosmetics	26¾	1 13/16	24⅜	19	24⅝	22⅝	296	24⅝	22¾	23⅜B	1.3	13
46	DVL	❖Del-Val Fin'l	NY,M	NR	1	10	194	Mortgage loans: R.E.	22	¼	1¼	5/16	2⅝	⅝	9020	2⅝	1⅛	1⅜	...	d
47	DLCH	Delchamps Inc	NMS	B+	1¢	32	2199	Gulf coast food supermkts	30½	9¾	25	16⅝	27½	21½	3310	27½	23¾	27½	1.6	17
#48•[8]	DELL	✓Dell Computer Corp	NMS	NR	1¢	164	17596	Dvlp/mfr IBM compatible PC's	24⅛	3⅛	48⅜	15	49⅞	29⅛	567024	49⅛	29⅛	32⅛	...	15

Uniform Footnote Explanations-See Page 1. Other: [1]CBOE:Cycle 3. [2]P:Cycle 3. [3]AS,P,Ph:Cycle 3. [4]AS:Cycle 1. [5]P:Cycle 1. [6]P:Cycle 2. [7]ASE:Cycle 3. [8]Ph:Cycle 2. [51]Incl curr amounts. [52]19 Wk Dec'90. [53]Ea ADR rep 4 ord,5p. [54]Approx. [55]®$2.45,'91. [56]Special div. [57]®$0.22,'92. [58]Stk dstr of Intelogic Trace Inc. [59]Accum on pfd. [60]®$0.79,'92. [61]If com'A'price exceeds $7.50for30trad days. [62]®$3.72,'92. [63]®$0.61,'92. [64]ADR equal DeBeers/Centenary linked unit. [65]Before tax country of origin. [66]®$1.68,'92. [67]As reported incl finance subsid. [68]Non-vtg. [69]Incl curr amts.

Source: *Standard & Poor's Stock Guide* (New York: Standard & Poor's Corp., 1992). Reprinted by permission of Standard & Poor's Corp.

FIGURE 5.3 **Example from *Standard & Poor's Stock Guide***

Common and Convertible Preferred Stocks

DAN-DEL 63

Index (Splits ◆)	Cash Divs. Ea. Yr. Since	Dividends – Latest Payment – Period $	Date	Ex. Div.	Total $ So Far 1993	Ind. Rate	Paid 1992	Financial Position Mil-$ – Cash& Equiv.	Curr. Assets	Curr. Liab.	Balance Sheet Date	Capitalization – Lg Trm Debt Mil-$	Shs. 000 Pfd.	Com.
1◆	....	None Since Public			...	Nil	....	18.9	34.4	7.93	12-31-91	0.05	...	17094
2	1948	Q0.04½	3-26-93	3-1	0.04½	0.18	0.18	29.2	112	34.1	9-30-92	17.1	...	11969
3	....	None Since Public			...	Nil	....	Equity per shr $3.11			9-30-92	[51]3.50	...	15113
4◆	1993	[54]0.091	2-4-93	12-4	[54]0.091	0.30	....	2.73	98.5	80.0	9-30-92	19.8	...	37820
5	....	None Since Public			...	Nil	....	2.28	58.6	28.1	9-26-92	15.7	...	6000
6	1965	Q0.033	12-18-92	11-25	...	0.133	0.133	204	500	219	10-31-92	106	...	±1749
7	....	0.06	4-4-89	3-13	...	Nil	....	2.57	21.9	16.1	9-30-92	35.2	...	6863
8	....	None Paid			...	Nil	....	216	684	328	9-26-92	162	...	33553
9	....	[56]4.15	3-8-89	3-9	...	Nil	....	0.71	27.0	17.3	9-24-92	....	...	7021
10	....	None Paid			...	Nil	....	0.78	15.9	5.40	9-30-92	7.86	...	1208
11	....	None Since Public			...	Nil	....	0.22	12.9	6.66	9-30-92	0.72	p...	★4064
12	....	None Since Public			...	Nil	....	7.35	15.7	4.74	9-30-92	0.26	...	3647
13	....	None Since Public			...	Nil	....	0.63	42.8	14.9	9-30-92	20.2	...	11991
14	....	None Since Public			...	Nil	....	7.11	16.9	5.13	8-31-92	....	...	2090
15	....	None Since Public			...	Nil	....	0.20	2.65	5.23	9-30-92	10.9	...	3301
16◆	....	5%Stk	7-5-89	6-15	...	Nil	....	8.16	27.7	7.60	12-31-92	....	...	3359
17	....	None Paid			...	Nil	....	8.11	9.99	0.68	9-25-92	....	196	2762
18	....	7½%Stk	3-21-80	2-26	...	Nil	....	0.07	8.30	3.44	10-25-92	0.03	2129	3701
19◆	....	h[58]....	8-12-85	8-13	...	[59]Nil	....	16.3	117	83.8	10-31-92	66.1	1784	13897
20◆	....	None Since Public			...	Nil	....	5.02	19.5	4.59	10-31-92	....	...	3808
21◆	....	None Paid			...	Nil	....	35.3	116	23.4	12-31-92	....	...	16030
22	....	None Since Public			...	Nil	....	10.2	14.4	1.03	9-30-92	....	...	5691
23	....	None Since Public			...	Nil	....	0.08	33.4	19.4	12-31-92	11.3	...	2472
24	....	None Since Public			...	Nil	....	0.24	12.8	6.02	9-30-92	0.49	...	2505
25◆	1910	Q0.20	4-16-93	3-22	0.40	0.80	0.76	Book Value $14.25			9-30-92	93.3	...	29704
26	....	0.05	10-4-91	9-16	...	Nil	....	2.09	63.9	22.8	10-31-92	27.4	...	3258
27	....	None Since Public			...	Nil	....	5.56	6.78	1.19	9-30-92	....	...	10599
28	....	Terms&trad. basis should be checked in detail						Wrrts expire 3-20-97				....	...	140
29	....	None Since Public			...	Nil	....	5.63	9.17	2.28	12-31-92	1.58	...	2970
30	....	None Since Public			...	Nil	....	28.3	29.0	8.27	9-30-92	....	...	5157
31	....	None Since Public			...	Nil	....	0.81	34.6	14.7	9-30-92	0.11	...	5226
32	1965	Q0.40	3-10-93	2-12	0.40	1.60	1.52	160	4919	3612	10-31-92	★4938	...	71347
33	....	None Paid			...	Nil	....	3.66	16.8	4.88	9-30-92	5.27	...	3866
34	....	None Since Public			...	Nil	....	3.91	4.55	0.29	9-30-92	....	...	4983
35◆	1941	Q0.15	3-15-93	2-12	0.30	0.60	0.57	24.2	469	266	11-30-92	154	...	39509
36	....	Plan qtly div			...	0.40	....	Equity per shr $15.49			12-31-92	....	...	★165675
37	1988	0.05¾	3-19-93	3-1	0.17¼	0.69	0.73½	Net Asset Val $9.64			2-19-93	....	...	57819
38	1984	Q0.05	2-15-93	1-25	0.05	0.20	0.20	45.5	92.8	14.3	10-31-92	2.04	.5	15590
39	1941	[66]0.244	11-20-92	9-14	...	1.10	[68]1.098	715	2004	953	j12-31-91	45.0	3667	±380141
40	....	0.08	12-27-80	12-15	...	Nil	....	3.38	7.61	3.74	9-26-92	0.85	...	911
41	1937	Q0.50	5-3-93	3-25	1.00	2.00	2.00	Equity per shr $30.30			10-31-92	[67]2473	...	76321
42◆	....	0.08	4-12-91	3-22	...	Nil	....	1.00	124	102	9-30-92	84.5	...	±9641
43	1989	Q0.20	3-12-93	2-22	0.20	0.80	0.80	5.30	251	169	11-30-92	91.2	...	±5125
44◆	....	6%Stk	12-17-92	11-27	...	Stk	6%Stk	0.74	15.1	4.24	10-31-92	4.11	...	2988
45◆	1973	Q0.075	1-5-93	11-2	0.075	0.30	0.30	4.44	62.3	25.9	9-30-92	36.7	...	1641
46	....	0.16	10-1-90	9-18	...	Nil	....	Equity per shr $1.05			6-30-92	[69]75.1	...	6912
47	1984	Q0.11	2-17-93	1-28	0.11	0.44	0.44	10.4	120	86.1	12-26-92	39.1	...	7114
48◆	....	None Since Public			...	Nil	....	122	767	424	11-01-92	48.7	...	36576

Index	Earnings $ Per Shr. – Years End	1988	1989	1990	1991	1992	Last 12 Mos.	Interim Earnings – Period	$ per Shr. 1991	1992	Index
1	Dc	0.05	0.12	0.20	0.40	P0.74	0.74				1
2	Sp	d0.33	0.60	0.78	d0.18	0.70	0.41	3 Mo Dec	0.26	d0.03	2
3	Dc	...	...	[52]d0.08	0.01	....	d0.02	9 Mo Sep	0.05	0.02	3
4	Mr	□0.92	1.37	□1.62	□2.04	....	2.30	6 Mo Sep	0.91	1.17	4
5	Mr	...	...	...	*p0.68	....	....	9 Mo Dec	n/a	d0.02	5
6	Ja	Δ14.16	□6.27	Δ4.36	□3.46	E5.25	4.98	9 Mo Oct	□1.34	□2.86	6
7	Je	*0.96	Δ□d1.69	Δd0.89	Δd3.03	d3.34	d0.78	6 Mo Dec	d2.96	Δd0.40	7
8	Sp	d0.55	■d4.10	d4.65	[56]2.62	d1.91	d2.01	3 Mo Dec	0.12	0.02	8
9	Dc	0.61	0.19	0.39	0.44	P□0.40	0.40				9
10	Dc	Δ0.16	d1.66	d1.18	0.02	....	0.88	9 Mo Sep	d0.52	0.34	10
11	Je	*0.02	*0.04	*0.02	*0.08	0.70	1.01	6 Mo Dec	0.27	0.58	11
12	Sp	0.19	0.34	0.47	0.60	0.75	0.66	3 Mo Dec	0.15	0.06	12
13	Dc	0.30	Δd0.10	Δ0.28	Δd2.76	Pd0.08	d0.08				13
14	Nv	0.86	0.78	d0.12	d0.51	Pd1.18	d1.18				14
15	Dc	d0.05	0.16	0.42	0.43	P0.41	0.41				15
16	Mr	0.66	1.00	1.33	1.09	....	0.35	9 Mo Dec	0.93	0.19	16
17	Dc	*0.60	*0.81	0.62	0.45	P0.08	0.08				17
18	Oc	*0.34	d0.61	*0.04	0.13	[57]0.30	0.30				18
19	Jl	*d0.55	*d3.88	Δd9.72	*Δd0.42	*d1.62	d1.40	3 Mo Oct	*d0.28	*d0.06	19
20	Ap	0.05	0.27	0.48	0.38	[60]0.80	0.71	9 Mo JanΔ	0.52	0.43	20
21	Je	0.73	0.69	0.60	0.55	0.47	0.56	6 Mo Dec	0.25	0.34	21
22	Dc	d0.05	0.02	d0.20	d0.03	P0.11	0.11				22
23	Mr	1.15	1.45	0.87	1.32	....	d3.24	9 Mo Dec	1.16	d3.40	23
24	Dc	Δ0.36	0.50	d0.40	Δ0.22	....	d0.13	9 Mo Sep	Δ0.17	d0.18	24
25	Dc	1.57	1.71	1.78	1.83	P1.92	1.92				25
26	Ap	0.76	1.05	0.32	d0.38	d0.26	d0.18	6 Mo Oct	d0.08	ΔNil	26
27	Je	d0.05	d0.02	d0.08	d0.15	d0.34	d0.36	3 Mo Sep	d0.06	d0.08	27
28	Je	...	...	...	....	....	....	Callable at 25¢[61]			28
29	Sp	*d0.81	*d0.22	d0.22	*0.11	*0.31	0.44	3 Mo Dec	d0.02	*0.11	29
30	Dc	0.63	d0.09	0.56	d0.35	....	0.81	9 Mo Sep	d0.42	0.74	30
31	Dc	0.14	Δ0.57	0.58	0.72	P0.77	0.77				31
32	Ja	3.45	5.37	Δ5.41	[62]3.86	E4.80	4.22	9 Mo Oct	1.26	1.62	32
33	Je	1.57	0.50	d4.01	Δd0.35	[63]0.68	0.62	6 Mo Dec	0.35	0.29	33
34	Dc	0.03	0.15	0.17	d0.04	....	d0.05	9 Mo Sep	d0.02	*d0.03	34
35	My	1.07	1.52	1.53	1.79	1.53	1.54	6 Mo Nov	0.81	0.82	35
36	Dc	...	...	...	....	p□2.65	2.65				36
37	Sp	...	§9.31	§9.32	§9.70	§9.72	....				37
38	Ja	0.89	1.14	0.88	0.55	....	0.39	9 Mo Oct	0.23	0.07	38
39	Dc	3.29	4.22	Δ3.47	Δ2.83	....	2.83	No interim report			39
40	Dc	0.13	0.08	0.21	d0.12	P[66]1.68	1.68				40
41	Oc	Δ4.06	5.06	5.42	d0.27	0.49	0.39	3 Mo JanΔ	d0.26	d0.36	41
42	Dc	□1.25	2.48	2.62	d6.51	Pd7.30	d7.30				42
43	Au	1.48	2.14	2.72	2.84	1.94	1.58	3 Mo Nov	0.51	0.15	43
44	Jl	0.25	0.26	0.32	0.42	0.41	0.42	3 Mo Oct	0.09	0.10	44
45	Dc	1.88	d0.85	1.27	1.32	P1.81	1.81				45
46	Dc	1.80	1.86	d9.29	d2.00	....	d0.67	9 Mo Sep	d1.91	d0.58	46
47	Je	Δ1.29	1.71	2.02	2.14	0.81	1.64	6 Mo Dec	0.09	0.92	47
48	Ja	0.53	0.18	0.91	1.41	....	2.22	9 Mo Oct	1.00	1.81	48

◆**Stock Splits & Divs By Line Reference Index** [1]2-for-1,'92. [4]To split 2-for-1,ex Mar 4. [16]Adj to 5%,'89. [19]No adj for Intelogic spinoff'85. [20]3-for-1,'92. [21]3-for-1,'92. [25]Adj for 5%,'89:2-for-1,'92. [35]3-for-2,'91. [42]No adj for stk dstr,'88. [44]Adj to 6%,'92. [45]4-for-3,'91. [48]3-for-2,'92.

Source: *Standard & Poor's Stock Guide* (New York: Standard & Poor's Corp., 1992). Reprinted by permission of Standard & Poor's Corp.

VALUE LINE PUBLICATIONS

The Value Line Investment Survey is published in two parts. Volume 1 contains basic historic information on about 1,700 companies including a number of analytical measures of earnings stability, growth rates, a common stock safety factor, and a timing factor rating. A number of studies have examined the usefulness of the timing factor ratings for investment purposes. The results of these studies will be discussed in the efficient markets chapter.

The *Investment Survey* also includes extensive two-year *projections* for the given firms and three-year *estimates* of performance. As an example, in early 1994 it will include an earnings projection for 1994, 1995, and 1996–1998. The second volume includes a weekly service that provides general investment advice and recommends individual stocks for purchase or sale. An example of a Value Line company report is shown in Figure 5.4.

The Value Line OTC Special Situations Service is published 24 times a year. It serves the experienced investor who is willing to accept high risk in the hope of realizing exceptional capital gains. Each issue discusses past recommendations and presents eight to ten new stocks for consideration.

BROKERAGE FIRM REPORTS

Besides the products of these information firms, many brokerage firms prepare reports on individual companies and their securities. Some of these reports are rather objective and contain only basic information, but others make specific recommendations.

INVESTMENT MAGAZINES

Many periodicals cover the securities industry for the benefit of professionals and individual investors. As noted earlier, although many of these publications emphasize individual companics and their stocks, they also discuss the overall financial markets and industries. Again, the order of presentation will be based on frequency of publication: monthly, biweekly, weekly.

MONTHLY MAGAZINES

Money, a monthly publication of Time Inc., deals specifically with topics of interest to individual investors, including articles on individual companies and general investment suggestions (e.g., "How to Determine Your Net Worth" "The Why and How of Investing in Foreign Securities"). Also, each issue presents a financial planning discussion with an individual or couple.

Institutional Investor is a monthly publication of Institutional Investors Systems aimed at professional investors and portfolio managers. It emphasizes events in the investment industry as they relate to corporate finance, pensions, money management, portfolio strategy, and global stock markets. A popular annual feature is an "All-American Analysts Team" selected by the major institutional investment firms.

Financial Planning, a monthly publication billed by its publisher, Financial Services Information Company, as "The Magazine for Financial Service Professionals," is intended for individuals involved in financial planning. It contains feature articles on alternative investment products and procedures, important regulatory information affecting financial planning (e.g., tax legislation), various industries, and specific classes of investments (e.g., mutual funds, real estate, equipment leasing).

OTC Review is a monthly publication devoted to the analysis and discussion of stocks traded on the OTC market. It usually analyzes an industry that is dominated by

FIGURE 5.4   Sample Listing from *Value Line*

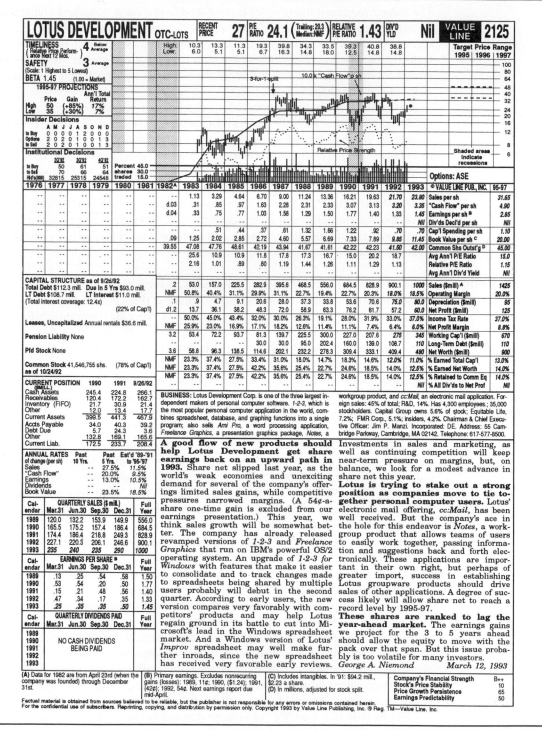

Source: *The Value Line Investment Survey* (New York: Arnold Bernhard & Company, 1992). Reprinted by permission of Value Line Services Publishing.

184

OTC companies and discusses three or four individual firms. In addition, there are numerous earnings reports on OTC firms, name changes, stock exchange listings, and price and volume statistics on OTC stocks.

Global Finance, a monthly magazine published by Global Information, Inc., contains a number of articles on trends around the world. It is an international version of *Institutional Investor,* because it is written for the practicing money manager or investment professional. It also contains regular columns on such topics as venture capital, hedging, and investment strategies.

Global Investor is published monthly (but it produces combined issues for July/August and December/January) by Euromoney Publications PLC. Like *Global Finance,* it contains articles on various markets, international instruments, and specific money management firms. It contains regular columns on the overall bond and stock markets and an extensive section on international bond and stock indexes.

BIWEEKLY MAGAZINES

Forbes is published twice monthly and contains 12 to 14 articles on individual companies, industries, and the market. Several regular columnists discuss the economy, the aggregate money and stock markets, and the commodity markets and make specific stock recommendations.

Fortune, published biweekly by Time Inc., provides extensive articles on the economy, politics, individual companies, securities markets, and personal investing. The magazine is well-known for its special annual reports on the *Fortune 500* and the *Fortune 1000* largest industrial firms in the country. The magazine also publishes a listing of large nonindustrial firms and major foreign companies. The importance of this information on non-U.S. firms is growing with the increase in globalization.

Financial World, which is published twice a month, generally contains about six articles on companies, industries, and the overall market along with several regular features on taxes and options. A separate section reports market data.

Pension and Investment Age is a biweekly newspaper of corporate and institutional investing. It is intended for those who invest in pension fund assets either as corporate managers or money managers. The paper emphasizes stories and interviews related to pension fund management. There is substantial consideration of personnel changes.

WEEKLY MAGAZINES

Business Week is published weekly by McGraw-Hill. Although not strictly an investment magazine, it contains numerous articles on companies and industries, as well as several features of importance to investors including a weekly production index and a leading economic index. The magazine also has initiated several special issues compiling lists such as the Top 1000 U.S. firms and the top 500 global firms.

The Economist is a weekly magazine published in London and New York by The Economist Newspaper, Inc. It is directed to worldwide reporting similar to what *The Financial Times* does on a daily basis. Beyond a set of articles dealing with the major events around the world, the magazine contains two major sections. The first is on "World Politics and Current Affairs," which is divided into subsections on American Survey, Asia, International, Europe, and Britain. The second section is entitled, "Business, Finance and Science," with subsections on business, finance, and science and technology. There is also an excellent set of economic and financial indicators from around the world. Similar to *The Financial Times,* this magazine is required reading for a global investor.

The Wall Street Transcript is published weekly as a composite of sources of information other than market quotations. It contains texts of speeches made at analysts' meetings, copies of brokerage house reports on companies and industries, and interviews with corporate officials. It includes discussions of forthcoming new stock issues.

The Media General Financial Weekly features a series of articles and columns. Of primary interest is a comprehensive set of financial and statistical information on 3,400 common stocks, including every common stock listed on the NYSE and the AMEX and over 700 OTC issues. It also presents charts on 60 major industry groups.

THEORETICAL AND EMPIRICAL ANALYSIS

The material in academic journals differs from that in investment magazines in timeliness and general orientation. Investment magazines are concerned with the *current* investment environment and with providing advice for current action. The material is generally nonquantitative. In contrast, academic journals contain longer, more theoretical, and more quantitative articles that are typically not intended to be immediately applicable. These journals typically contain theoretical or empirical studies related to investments that could have long-run implications.

ACADEMIC JOURNALS

Journal of Finance is a quarterly published by the American Finance Association. The articles are almost all by academicians and are rather theoretical and empirical. The typical issue includes 15 articles, notes and comments, and book reviews.

Journal of Financial Economics is published quarterly by North Holland Publishing Company in collaboration with the Simon Graduate School of Management of the University of Rochester. It publishes academic research in the areas of consumption and investment decisions under uncertainty, portfolio analysis, efficient markets, and the normative theory of financial management.

The Review of Financial Studies is published quarterly by Oxford University Press for the Society for Financial Studies. Its purpose is to publish new research in financial economics balanced between theoretical and empirical research. Although the subject matter appears similar to that of the *Journal of Financial Economics,* it places a stronger emphasis on the theoretical treatment of topics.

Journal of Financial and Quantitative Analysis is a quarterly published by the University of Washington. Almost all of its articles are by academicians and deal with topics in investments and corporate finance.

Financial Analysts Journal is published six times a year by the Association of Investment Management and Research (AIMR). Each issue contains six or seven articles of interest to practicing financial analysts and portfolio managers, a regular feature on securities regulation, and book reviews. The articles are authored by either academicians or practitioners.

Journal of Portfolio Management is published quarterly by Institutional Investors Systems as a forum for academic research of interest to the practicing portfolio manager. Over half the articles are written by academicians, but they are written for the practitioner. Many articles are less technical and mathematical versions of studies previously published in heavily academic journals.

Journal of Fixed Income is published quarterly by Institutional Investor, Inc., as a forum for academic research related to fixed-income securities that can be understood and read by professional analysts and portfolio managers. The topics range from credit analysis and interest rates forecasting to various bond portfolio management strategies.

Financial Management, published quarterly by the Financial Management Association, is intended for executives and academicians interested in the financial management of a firm. It contains investment-related articles on such topics as stock splits, dividend policy, mergers, initial public offerings, and stock listings when it is shown that such events are important to the financing decisions of a firm.

The Financial Review is a quarterly journal sponsored by the Eastern Finance Association. About half of its articles are concerned with capital markets, investments, and portfolio management.

Journal of Financial Research is a joint quarterly publication of the Southern Finance Association and the Southwestern Finance Association. It contains articles on financial management, investments, financial institutions, capital market theory, and portfolio theory.

Financial Services Review is a quarterly journal sponsored by the Academy of Financial Services and published by JAI Press, Inc. It is a journal devoted to publishing academic research on individual financial management, which involves examining the application and effect of all facets of finance on the financial planning decisions made by individuals.

The C.F.A. Digest is published quarterly by the Institute of Chartered Financial Analysts (which is a subsidiary of the Association of Investment Management and Research). Its purpose is to provide, as a service to members of the investment community, about 20 abstracts a quarter of published articles from a wide variety of academic and nonacademic journals that are of interest to financial analysts and portfolio managers.

There are a number of general business and economics journals that include articles on finance and some specifically on investments. One of the foremost is the *Journal of Business,* published by the University of Chicago, which has contained some outstanding articles in the area of investments. Other journals to consider include: *Quarterly Review of Economics and Finance* (University of Illinois), *International Review of Economics and Finance* (JAI Press, Inc.), *Review of Business and Economic Research* (University of New Orleans), *Journal of Business Research* (North Holland Publishing), *American Economic Review* (American Economic Association), *Journal of Political Economy* (University of Chicago), and *Rand Journal of Economics* (American Telephone and Telegraph), and *The Continental Bank Journal of Applied Corporate Finance* (Continental Bank).

COMPUTERIZED DATA SOURCES

In addition to the numerous published sources of data, some financial service firms have developed computerized data sources. The discussion considers (1) major data banks and (2) the well-known on-line data systems. Space limitations restrict the discussion to major sources.

DATA BANKS

Compustat is a computerized bank of financial data developed by Standard & Poor's and currently handled by a subsidiary, Investors Management Services. The Compustat tapes contain 20 years of data for approximately 2,220 listed industrial companies, 1,000 OTC companies, 175 utilities, 120 banks, and 500 Canadian firms. Quarterly tapes contain 20 years of quarterly financial data for over 2,000 industrial firms and 12 years of quarterly data for banks and utilities. The financial data on the annual tapes include almost every possible item from each firm's balance sheet and income statement as well as stock-market data (stock prices and trading volume).

Value Line Data Base contains historical annual and quarterly financial and market data for 1,600 industrial and finance companies beginning in 1954. It also provides quarterly data from 1963. In addition to historical data, it gives estimates of dividends and earnings for the coming year and the Value Line opinion regarding stock price stability and investment timing.

Compact Disclosure is a data base on a compact disk with information on over 4,000 public companies filing with the SEC. It is available from Disclosure Information Group of Bethesda, Maryland.

University of Chicago Stock Price Tapes is a set of monthly and daily stock price tapes developed by the Center for Research in Security Prices (CRSP) at the University of Chicago Graduate School of Business. The monthly tapes contain month-end prices from January 1926 to the present (updated annually) for every stock listed on the NYSE. Stock prices are adjusted for all stock splits, dividends, and any other capital changes. They added monthly AMEX data beginning from July 1962 to the NYSE monthly file to create the current NYSE/AMEX monthly file with information on approximately 6,100 securities.

The daily stock price tape contains the daily high, low, close, and volume figures since July 1962 for every stock listed on the NYSE and AMEX (approximately 5,600 securities). In 1988 the CRSP developed its NASDAQ historical data file with daily price quotes, volume, and information about capitalization and distributions to shareholders for over 9,600 common stocks traded on the NASDAQ system since December 14, 1972. These tapes are updated at the end of each calendar year and supplied to subscribers each spring.

The *Media General Data Bank,* compiled by Media General Financial Services, Inc., includes current price and volume data plus major corporate financial data on 2,000 major companies. In addition, it contains 10 years of daily price and volume information on over 8,000 issues of approximately 4,000 firms on the NYSE, the AMEX, and the OTC market. Finally, it includes price and volume data on several major market indexes.

ISL Daily Stock Price Tapes are prepared by Interactive Data Corporation. They contain the same information as the *Daily Stock Price Records,* published by Standard & Poor's that we discussed earlier.

ON-LINE DATA BASES

Bi Data includes international statistical data including national accounts, labor statistics, foreign trade, consumption, prices, and production. It is produced by Business International Corp. and sold by General Electric Information Service.

Commodities Market Data Bank provides statistical data on all traded commodities. The producer and vendor is Data Resources Inc. (DRI).

CompuServe, Inc. provides references, statistical data, and full text retrieval of information on numerous topics, including financial and investment data from Compustat and the Value Line data bases. The producer and vendor is CompuServe, Inc.

Quick Quote provides current price quotations, trading volume information, and high–low data for the securities of U.S. public corporations. The producer and vendor is CompuServe, Inc.

Dow Jones News/Retrieval Service supplies texts of articles appearing in major financial publications including *The Wall Street Journal* and *Barron's.* The *Stock Quote Reporter* service provides quotes on stocks, bonds, and mutual funds. The producer and vendor of both is Dow Jones & Company.

DRI Capsule/EEI Capsule services provides over 3,700 U.S. social and economic statistical time series on topics such as population, income, money supply, and interest rates. The producer is DRI and the vendor is Business Information Services.

The GTE Financial System One Quotation Service provides current quotations and statistical data on U.S. and Canadian stocks, bonds, options, and commodities along with other market data. The producer and vendor is GTE Information Systems, Inc.

The Information Bank provides extensive information on current affairs based on abstracts from numerous English-language publications. The producer and vendor is the New York Times Information Service.

Quotron 800 provides up-to-the-minute quotations and statistics for a broad range of stocks, bonds, options, and commodities. The producer and vendor is Quotron Systems, Inc.[12]

SUMMARY

As an investor you must be aware of sources of information on the U.S. and world economies, the securities markets around the globe, alternative industries, and individual firms. You should use the information in this chapter as a *starting* point and spend time in a university library examining these and the many other sources available. Six books that would help in this regard are:

Paul Wasserman, ed. *Encyclopedia of Business Information Sources.* 3d ed. Detroit: Gale Research Co., 1976.

P. M. Daniells. *Business Information Sources.* 2d ed. Berkeley: University of California Press, 1986.

Sylvia Michanie. *Course Syllabus for Information Sources of Business and Economics.* Brooklyn, N.Y.: Pratt Institute School of Library and Information Science, 1977.

Fortune Investment Information Directory. Guilford, Conn.: The Dushkin Publishing Group, Inc. 1986. This booklet contains a listing and brief description of numerous newspapers, magazines, investment letters, and books. There is also an excellent listing of software and data bases of interest to investors in stocks, bonds, futures, and options.

Encyclopedia of Information Systems and Services. Detroit: Gale Research Co., 1988.

Guide to American Directories. Coral Springs, Fla.: B. Klein Publications, 1987.

QUESTIONS

1. Name at least three sources of information on the gross domestic product for the past 10 years.

2. Name two sources of information on rates of exchange with major foreign countries.

---

[12]An excellent source for additional computer data bases and software as well as general information on business and economics is *The Dow Jones-Irwin Business and Investment Almanac,* edited by Sumner W. Levine (Homewood, Ill.: Dow Jones-Irwin, annual).

3. Assume you want to compare production in the steel and auto industry to industrial production for the economy. Discuss how you would do it, what data you would use, and where you would get the data.

4. You are told that a relationship exists between the growth rate of the money supply and stock price movements. Where would you obtain the data to test this relationship?

5. You are an analyst for Growth Stock Investment Company. The head of research tells you about a tip on an OTC firm, the Shamrock Corporation. He wants data on the company's sales, earnings, and recent stock price movements. Discuss several sources for this information. (One source is insufficient because the company may not be big enough to be included in some of them.)

6. The head of your research department indicates that the investment committee has decided to become involved in global investing. To get started, the committee wants you to recommend two sources of macroeconomic data for various countries, two sources of industry information, and two sources of company data. Discuss your recommendations.

7. As an individual investor, discuss four publications to which you believe you should subscribe (besides *The Wall Street Journal*). Indicate what each publication can give you and why it is appropriate for you as an individual investor. Be sure that at least two of these sources relate to global investing.

8. As the director of a newly established investment research department at a money management firm, discuss the first four investment services to which you will subscribe, and justify each selection.

9. Select one company each from the NYSE, the AMEX, and the OTC, and look up the name and address of the financial officers you would contact at each firm to obtain recent financial reports.

SOURCES OF INVESTMENT INFORMATION

American Banker-Bond Buyer, A division of International Thomson Publishing Corporation, One State Street Plaza, New York, NY 10004.

American Stock Exchange, 86 Trinity Place, New York, NY 10006.

Business One Irwin, Investor's Handbook is available from Business One Irwin, Homewood, IL 60430.

Business Statistics is obtained from Superintendent of Documents, U.S. Government Printing Office, Washington, DC 20402.

Center for Research in Security Prices, Graduate School of Business, University of Chicago, Chicago, IL 60637.

CompuServe, Inc., 5000 Arlington Centre Boulevard, Columbus, OH 43220.

Data Resources, Inc. (DRI), 29 Hartwell Avenue, Lexington, MA 02173.

Dow Jones & Co., 200 Burnett Road, Chicopee, MA 01021.

Economic Indicators is available from Superintendent of Documents, U.S. Government Printing Office, Washington, DC 20402.

Economic Report of the President may be obtained from Superintendent of Documents, U.S. Government Printing Office, Washington, DC 20402.

The Economist can be subscribed to through a U.S. subscription office: P.O. Box 58524, Boulder, CO 80322–8524.

Euromoney Publications PLC, Nestor House, Playhouse Yard, London ECUV 5EX. The address for North American subscriptions: Reed Business Publishing, 205 East 42nd Street, New York, NY 10017.

Federal Reserve Bulletin is available from the Division of Administrative Services, Board of Governors of the Federal Reserve System, Washington, DC 20551.

Financial Times is available from Bracken House, Cannon Street, London EC4P 4BY England. There is a U.S. office: 44 East 60th Street, New York, NY 10022.

Global Information, Inc., 55 John Street, New York, NY 10038.

GTE Information Systems, Inc., East Park Drive, Mount Laurel, NJ 08054.

Ibbotson Associates, 225 North Michigan Ave., Chicago, IL 60601-7676.

IFR Publishing Ltd., 97 Middlesex Street, London EL 7EZ.

Institutional Investor Systems, Inc., 488 Madison Avenue, New York, NY 10022.

Interactive Data Corporation, 122 E. 42nd Street, New York, NY 10017.

International Finance Corporation, 1818 H Street, N.W., Washington, D.C. 20433.

Investors Management Services, P. O. Box 239, Denver, CO 80201.

London Stock Exchange, Trogmorton Street, London EG2N 1HP, England.

Media General Financial Services, Inc., P. O. Box 26991, Richmond, VA 23261.

Moody's Investor's Services, Inc., 99 Church Street, New York, NY 10007.

National Association of Securities Dealers, Inc. (NASD), 1735 K Street, N.W., Washington, DC 20006

New York Stock Exchange, 11 Wall Street, New York, NY 10005.

New York Times Information Services, Inc., 1719-A Route 10, Parsippany, NJ 07054.

Quarterly Financial Report is available from Superintendent of Documents, U.S. Government Printing Office, Washington, DC 20402.

Quotron Systems, Inc., 5454 Beethoven Street, Los Angeles, CA 90066.

Securities and Exchange Commission, 450 5th Street, N.W., Washington, DC 20549.

Standard & Poor's Corporation, 345 Hudson Street, New York, NY 10014.

Statistical Abstract of the United States is available from the Superintendent of Documents, U.S. Government Printing Office, Washington, DC 20402.

Statistical Bulletin is available from the Superintendent of Documents, U.S. Government Printing Office, Washington, DC 20402.

Survey of Current Business is available from Superintendent of Documents, U.S. Government Printing Office, Washington, DC 20402.

Tokyo Stock Exchange. The Exchange has an office in New York: TSE, New York Research Office, 100 Wall Street, New York, NY 10005.

Value Line Services is available from Arnold Bernhard and Company, Inc., 5 East 44th Street, New York, NY 10017.

PART II

DEVELOPMENTS IN INVESTMENT THEORY

The chapters in Part I provided background on why individuals invest their funds and what they expect to derive from this activity. We also argued very strongly for a global investment program, described the major instruments and capital markets in a global investment environment, and showed the relationship among these instruments and markets. Finally, we discussed where you can get relevant information on these instruments and markets.

At this point, we are ready to discuss how to analyze and value the various investment instruments available. In turn, valuation requires the estimation of expected returns (cash flows) and a determination of the risk involved in the securities. Before we can begin the analysis, we need to understand several major developments in investment theory that have influenced how we specify and measure risk in the valuation process. The purpose of the four chapters in this part is to provide this background on risk and asset valuation.

Chapter 6 describes the concept of efficient capital markets which hypothesizes that security prices reflect the effect of all information. This chapter considers why markets should be efficient, discusses how one goes about testing this hypothesis, describes the results of the tests, and discusses the implications of the results for those engaged in technical and fundamental analysis, as well as portfolio management.

Chapter 7 provides an introduction to portfolio theory which was developed by Harry Markowitz. This theory provided the first rigorous measure of risk for investors and showed how one selects alternative assets in order to diversify and to reduce the risk of a portfolio. Markowitz also derived a risk measure for individual securities within the context of an efficient portfolio.

Subsequent to the development of the Markowitz portfolio model, William Sharpe and several other academicians extended the Markowitz model into a general equilibrium asset pricing model that included an alternative risk measure for all risky assets. Chapter 8 contains a detailed discussion of these developments and an explanation of the relevant risk measure implied by this valuation model, referred to as the *capital asset pricing model* (CAPM). We introduce the CAPM at this early point in the book because the risk measure implied has been used extensively in various valuation models.

Chapter 8 also contains a discussion of an alternative asset pricing model referred to as the *arbitrage pricing theory* (APT). This theory was developed by Steve Ross in response to criticisms of the CAPM because of its restrictive assumptions and the difficulty in testing it. The fundamental differences between the CAPM and the APT models is that APT requires fewer assumptions and is considered a multivariate risk model compared to the CAPM, which is referred to as a single risk variable model (beta).

In addition to the development of asset pricing models, another major development has been the creation and development of new markets and instruments beyond stocks and bonds. The greatest growth and development has been in the area referred to as *derivatives,* which includes options and futures. These instruments create a wider range of risk-return opportunities for investors. Chapter 9 provides an initial description of these instruments, including an understanding of the fundamental principles that determine their prices. Again, these derivative pricing principles can and should be applied to other assets including stocks, but especially bonds.

CHAPTER 6

EFFICIENT CAPITAL MARKETS

In this chapter we will answer the following questions:

- What is meant by the concept that capital markets are efficient?
- Why *should* capital markets be efficient?
- What are the specific factors that contribute to an efficient market?
- Given the overall efficient market hypothesis, what are the three sub-hypotheses and what are the implications of each of them?
- How do you test the weak-form efficient market hypothesis (EMH) and what are the results of the tests?
- How do you test the semistrong-form EMH and what are the test results?
- How do you test the strong-form EMH and what are the test results?
- For each set of tests, which results support the hypothesis and which results indicate an anomaly related to the hypothesis?
- What are the implications of the results for:
  - technical analysis?
  - fundamental analysis?
  - portfolio managers with superior analysts?
  - portfolio managers with inferior analysts?
- What is the evidence related to the EMH for markets in foreign countries?

An *efficient capital market* is one in which security prices adjust rapidly to the arrival of new information and, therefore, the current prices of securities reflect all information about the security. Some of the most interesting and important academic research over the past 20 years has analyzed whether our capital markets are efficient. This extensive research is important because its results have significant real-world implications for investors and portfolio managers. In addition, the efficiency of capital markets is one of the most controversial areas in investment research because opinions regarding the efficiency of capital markets differ widely.

Because of its importance and the controversy, you need to understand the meaning of the terms *efficient capital markets* and *efficient market hypothesis (EMH)*. You should understand the analysis performed to test the EMH and the results of studies that either support or contradict the hypothesis. Finally, you should be aware of the implications of these results when you analyze alternative investments and work to construct a portfolio.

We are considering the topic of efficient capital markets at this point for two reasons. First, the discussions in previous chapters have given you an understanding of how the capital markets function, so now it seems natural to consider the efficiency of the market in terms of how prices react to new information. Second, the overall evidence on capital market efficiency is best described as mixed; some studies support the hypothesis and others do not. The implications of these diverse results are important for you as an investor involved in analyzing securities and working to build a portfolio.

There are four major sections in this chapter. The first discusses why we would expect capital markets to be efficient and the factors that contribute to an efficient market where the prices of securities reflect available information.

The single efficient market hypothesis has been divided into three subhypotheses to facilitate testing. The second section describes these three subhypotheses and the implications of each of them.

Section three is the largest section because it contains a discussion of the tests used to examine the three subhypotheses and reviews the results of numerous studies. This review of the research reveals that a large body of evidence supports the EMH, but a growing number of other studies do not support the hypotheses.

The final section discusses what these results mean for an investor who uses either technical analysis or fundamental analysis or for a portfolio manager who has access to superior or inferior analysts. We conclude with a brief discussion of the evidence for markets in foreign countries.

As noted, we will discuss numerous empirical studies of efficient markets in this chapter. Because space limitations preclude dealing with them in depth, we encourage you to consult the literature cited in the reference section at the end of this chapter.

WHY SHOULD CAPITAL MARKETS BE EFFICIENT?

As noted earlier, in an efficient capital market, security prices adjust rapidly to the infusion of new information, and, therefore, current security prices fully reflect all available information. To be absolutely correct, this is referred to as an *informationally efficient market.* Although the idea of an efficient capital market is relatively straightforward, we often fail to consider *why* capital markets *should* be efficient. What set of assumptions imply an efficient capital market?

An initial, and very important, premise of an efficient market requires that *a large number of profit-maximizing participants analyze and value securities,* each independently of the others.

A second assumption is that *new information regarding securities comes to the market in a random fashion,* and the timing of one announcement is generally independent of others.

The third assumption is especially crucial: *Investors adjust security prices rapidly to reflect the effect of new information.* Although the price adjustment may be imperfect, it is unbiased. This means that sometimes the market will overadjust, and other times it will underadjust, but you cannot predict which will occur at any given time. Security prices adjust rapidly because many profit-maximizing investors are competing against one another.

The combined effect of (1) information coming in a random, independent fashion and (2) numerous competing investors adjusting stock prices rapidly to reflect this new information means that one would expect price changes to be independent and random. You can see that the adjustment process requires a large number of investors following the movements of the security, analyzing the impact of new information on its value, and buying or selling the security until its price adjusts to reflect the new information. This scenario implies that informationally efficient markets require some minimum amount of trading and that more trading by numerous competing investors should cause a faster price adjustment, making the market more efficient. We will return to this need for trading and investor attention when we discuss some anomalies of the EMH.

Finally, because security prices adjust to all new information, these security prices should reflect all information that is publicly available at any point in time. Therefore, the security prices that prevail at any time should be an unbiased reflection of all currently available information, including the risk involved in owning the security. Therefore, in an efficient market *the expected returns implicit in the current price of the security should reflect its risk.*

ALTERNATIVE EFFICIENT MARKET HYPOTHESES

Most of the early work related to efficient capital markets was based on the *random walk hypothesis,* which contended that changes in stock prices occurred randomly. This early academic work contained extensive empirical analysis without much theory behind it. An article by Fama attempted to formalize the theory and organize the growing empirical evidence.[1] Fama presented the efficient market theory in terms of a *fair game model.*

EXPECTED RETURN OR FAIR GAME MODEL[2]

Unlike work done under the random walk hypothesis, which dealt with price movement over time, the fair game model deals with price at a specified point in time. It assumes that the price of a security fully reflects all available information at that point in time. The model requires that the price-formation process be specified in enough detail so that it is possible to indicate what is meant by "fully reflect." Most of the available models of equilibrium prices formulate prices in terms of rates of return that are dependent on alternative definitions of risk. All such expected return theories of price formation can be described notationally as follows:

$$E(\overline{P}_{j,t+1} \mid \phi_t) = [1 + E(\overline{r}_{j,t+1} \mid \phi_t)]P_{j,t}, \tag{6.1}$$

where:

E = **expected value operator**
$P_{j,t}$ = **price of security** j **at time** t
$\overline{P}_{j,t+1}$ = **price of security** j **at time** $t + 1$

[1]Eugene F. Fama, "Efficient Capital Markets: A Review of Theory and Empirical Work," *Journal of Finance* 25, no. 2 (May 1970): 383–417.

[2]This section is drawn from Fama, *ibid.*

$r_{j,t+1}$ = **the one period percent rate of return for security** j **during period**
$t + 1$

ϕ_t = **the set of information that is assumed to be "fully reflected" in**
the security price at time t

Equation 6.1 indicates that the expected price of security j, given the full set of information available at time $t(\phi_t)$, is equal to the current price times 1 plus the expected
return on security j, given the set of available information. This expected future return
should reflect the set of information available at t, which includes the state of the world
at time t, including all current and past values of any relevant variables such as inflation,
interest rates, earnings, GDP, and so forth. In addition, it is assumed that this information set includes knowledge of *all the relevant relationships among variables*—that
is, it considers how alternative economic series relate to each other and how they relate
to security prices.

If equilibrium market prices can be stated in terms of expected returns that "fully
reflect" the information set ϕ_t, this implies that it is not possible to derive trading
systems or investment strategies based on this current very encompassing information
set and experience returns beyond what should be expected on the basis of an asset's
risk. Thus, let us define $x_{j,t+1}$ as the difference between the actual price in $t + 1$ and
the expected price in $t + 1$:

$$x_{j,t+1} = p_{j,t+1} - E(p_{j,t+1} \mid \phi_t) \tag{6.2}$$

Equation 6.2 can be described as a definition of *excess market value* for security j,
because it is the difference between the actual price and the expected price projected
at t on the basis of the information set ϕ_t. In an efficient market:

$$E(\bar{x}_{j,t+1} \mid \phi_t) = 0 \tag{6.3}$$

This equation indicates that the market reflects a "fair game" with respect to the
information set ϕ. This means that investors can be confident that *current prices fully
reflect all available information and are consistent with the risk involved.*

Beyond articulating the efficient market (EM) theory in terms of a fair game model,
in his original article, Fama divided the overall efficient market hypothesis (EMH) and
the empirical tests of the hypotheses into three subhypotheses depending on the
information set involved: (1) weak-form EMH, (2) semistrong-form EMH, and
(3) strong-form EMH.

In a 1991 review article, Fama again divided the empirical results into three groups,
but shifted empirical results between the prior categories.[3] Basically, the weak-form
category was broadened to include numerous studies previously considered in the semistrong-form category. Although there is logic in the new division, it is felt that the
initial division is more intuitive. Therefore, the following discussion uses the original
categories but organizes the presentation of results in the semistrong section using the
new categories.

---

[3]Eugene F. Fama, "Efficient Capital Markets: II," *Journal of Finance* 46, no. 5 (December 1991): 1575–1617.

In the remainder of this section we describe the three hypotheses and the implications of each of them. In the following section, we describe how researchers have tested each of these hypotheses and briefly discuss the results of these tests.

WEAK-FORM
EFFICIENT
MARKET
HYPOTHESIS

The *weak-form EMH* assumes that current stock prices fully reflect all *security-market information,* including the historical sequence of prices, rates of return, trading volume data, and other market-generated information, such as odd-lot transactions, block trades, and transactions by exchange specialists or other unique groups. Because it assumes that current market prices already reflect all past returns and any other security-market information, this hypothesis implies that past rates of return and other market data should have no relationship with future rates of return (i.e., rates of return should be independent). Therefore, you should gain little from any trading rule that decides whether to buy or sell a security based on past rates of return or any other past market data.

SEMISTRONG-
FORM EFFICIENT
MARKET
HYPOTHESIS

The *semistrong-form EMH* asserts that security prices adjust rapidly to the release of *all public information;* that is, current security prices fully reflect all public information. The semistrong hypothesis encompasses the weak-form hypothesis, because all the market information considered by the weak-form hypothesis, such as stock prices, rates of return, and trading volume, is public. Public information also includes all nonmarket information, such as earnings and dividend announcements, price-to-earnings (P/E) ratios, dividend-yield (D/P) ratios, book value–market value (BV/MV) ratios, stock splits, news about the economy, and political news. This hypothesis implies that investors who base their decisions on important new information *after it is public* should not derive above-average profits from their transactions, considering the cost of trading, because the security price already reflects all such new public information.

STRONG-FORM
EFFICIENT
MARKET
HYPOTHESIS

The *strong-form EMH* contends that stock prices fully reflect *all information from public and private sources.* This means that no group of investors has monopolistic access to information relevant to the formation of prices. Therefore, no group of investors should be able to consistently derive above-average profits. The strong-form EMH encompasses both the weak-form and the semistrong-form EMH. Further, the strong-form EMH extends the assumption of efficient markets, in which prices adjust rapidly to the release of new public information, to assume perfect markets, in which all information is cost-free and available to everyone at the same time.

TESTS AND
RESULTS OF
ALTERNATIVE
EFFICIENT
MARKET
HYPOTHESES

Now that you understand the three components of the EMH and what each of them implies regarding the effect on security prices of different sets of information, we can consider how a person doing research in this area tests to see whether the hypotheses are supported by the data. Therefore, in this section we discuss the specific tests used to gauge support for the hypotheses and we summarize the results of these tests.

Like most hypotheses in finance and economics, the evidence on the EMH is mixed. Some studies have supported the hypotheses and indicate that capital markets are efficient. Other studies have revealed some anomalies related to these hypotheses, raising questions about support for them.

WEAK-FORM
HYPOTHESIS:
TESTS AND
RESULTS

Researchers have formulated two groups of tests of the weak-form EMH. The first category involves statistical tests of independence between rates of return. The second entails a comparison of risk–return results for trading rules that make investment decisions based on past market information and results from a simple buy-and-hold policy, which assumes that you buy stock at the beginning of a test period and hold it to the end.

STATISTICAL TESTS OF INDEPENDENCE

As discussed earlier, the EMH contends that security returns over time should be independent of one another because new information comes to the market in a random, independent fashion, and security prices adjust rapidly to this new information. Two major statistical tests have been employed to verify this independence.

First, *autocorrelation tests* of independence measure the significance of positive or negative correlation in returns over time. Does the rate of return on day t correlate with the rate of return on day $t - 1, t - 2,$ or $t - 3$?[4] Those who believe that capital markets are efficient would expect insignificant correlations for all such combinations.

Several researchers have examined the serial correlations among stock returns for several relatively short time horizons including 1 day, 4 days, 9 days, and 16 days.[5] The results typically indicated insignificant correlation in stock returns over time. The typical range of correlation coefficients was from $+.10$ to $-.10$, and these were typically not statistically significant. Some recent studies that considered portfolios of stocks of different size have indicated that the autocorrelation is stronger for portfolios of small stocks.[6] Therefore, although the older results tend to support the hypothesis, the more recent studies cast doubt on it for portfolios of small firms, although these results could be affected by nonsynchronous trading for small-firm stocks.

The second statistical test of independence is the *runs test*.[7] Given a series of price changes, each price change is either designated a plus $(+)$ if it is an increase in price or a minus $(-)$ if it is a decrease in price. The result is a set of pluses and minuses as follows: $+ + + - + - - + + - - + +$. A run occurs when two consecutive changes are the same; two or more consecutive positive or negative price changes constitutes one run. When the price changes in a different direction, such as when a negative price change is followed by a positive price change, the run ends and a new run may begin. To test for independence, you would compare the number of runs for a given series to the number in a table of expected values for the number of runs that should occur in a random series.

Studies that have examined stock price runs have confirmed the independence of stock price changes over time. The actual number of runs for stock price series consistently fell into the range expected for a random series. Therefore, these statistical

[4]For a discussion of tests of independence, see S. Christian Albright, *Statistics for Business and Economics* (New York: Macmillan Publishing, 1987), 515–517.

[5]Eugene F. Fama, "The Behavior of Stock Market Prices," *Journal of Business* 38, no. 1 (January 1965): 34–105; Eugene Fama and James MacBeth, "Risk, Return and Equilibrium: Empirical Tests," *Journal of Political Economy* 81, no. 3 (May-June 1973): 607–636.

[6]Jennifer Conrad and Gantam Kaul, "Time Variation in Expected Returns," *Journal of Business* 61, no. 4 (October 1988): 409–425; Andrew W. Lo and A. Craig MacKinley, "Stock Market Prices Do Not Follow Random Walks: Evidence from a Simple Specifications Test," *Review of Financial Studies* 1, no. 1 (Spring 1988): 41–66.

[7]For the details of a runs test, see Albright, *Statistics for Business and Economics,* 695–699.

tests have likewise confirmed the independence of stock price changes over time. These statistical tests of independence have been repeated for stocks traded on the OTC market, and the results likewise supported the EMH.[8]

Although short horizon stock returns have generally supported the weak-form EMH, several studies that examined price changes for individual *transactions* on the NYSE found significant serial correlations. Notably, none of these studies attempted to show that the dependence of transaction price movements could be used to earn above-average, risk-adjusted returns. Apparently, the significant correlation among individual transaction returns is due to the market-making activities of the specialist, but investors probably cannot use this small imperfection to derive excess profits after considering the trading rule's substantial transaction costs.[9]

TESTS OF TRADING RULES

The second group of tests of the weak-form (EMH) were developed in response to the assertion that the prior statistical tests of independence were too rigid to identify the intricate price patterns examined by technical analysts. As we will discuss in Chapter 19, technical analysts do not accept a set number of positive or negative price changes as a signal of a move to a new equilibrium in the market. They typically look for a general consistency in the price trend over time. Such a trend might include both positive and negative changes. For this reason technical analysts felt that their trading rules were too sophisticated and complicated to be simulated by rigid statistical tests.

In response to this objection, investigators attempted to examine alternative technical trading rules through simulation. Advocates of an efficient market hypothesized that investors could not derive profits above a buy-and-hold policy, or abnormal profits, using any trading rule that depended solely on any past market information about factors such as price, volume, odd-lot sales, or specialist activity.

The trading rule studies compared the risk–return results derived from such a simulation, including transactions costs, to the results from a simple buy-and-hold policy. Three major pitfalls can negate the results of a trading rule study:

1. The investigator should *use only publicly available data* in the decision rule. As an example, the earnings for a firm as of December 31 may not be publicly available until April 1, so you should not factor in an earnings report until then.
2. When computing the returns from a trading rule, you should *include all transactions costs* involved in implementing the trading strategy because most trading rules involve many more transactions than a simple buy-and-hold policy.
3. You must *adjust the results for risk* because a trading rule might simply select a portfolio of high-risk securities that should experience higher returns.

Researchers have encountered two operational problems in carrying out these tests of specific trading rules. First, some trading rules require too much subjective interpretation of data to simulate mechanically. Second, the almost infinite number of po-

[8]Robert L. Hagerman and Richard D. Richmond, "Random Walks, Martingales and the OTC," *Journal of Finance* 28, no. 4 (September 1973): 897–909.

[9]Victor Niederhoffer and M. F. Osborn, "Market-Making and Reversal on the Stock Exchange," *Journal of American Statistical Association* 61, no. 316 (December 1966): 897–916; Kenneth Carey, "A Model of Individual Transactions Stock Prices" (Ph.D. dissertation, University of Kansas, 1971).

tential trading rules makes it impossible to test all of them. As a result, only the better-known technical trading rules have been examined.

Another factor that you should recognize is that some studies have been somewhat biased. Specifically, the operational problems noted above have restricted the studies to relatively simple trading rules, which many technicians contend are rather naive.

In addition, these studies typically employ readily available data from the NYSE, which is biased toward well-known, heavily traded stocks that certainly should trade in efficient markets. Because markets should be more efficient with higher numbers of aggressive, profit-maximizing investors attempting to adjust stock prices to reflect new information, market efficiency depends on trading volume. Specifically, *more trading in a security should promote market efficiency.* Alternatively, for securities with relatively few stockholders and little trading activity, the market could be inefficient because fewer investors would be analyzing the effect of new information and this limited interest would result in insufficient trading activity to move the price of the security quickly to a new equilibrium value that would reflect the new information. Therefore, using only active, heavily traded stocks in the trading rule tests could bias the results toward finding efficiency.

RESULTS OF SIMULATIONS OF SPECIFIC TRADING RULES

In the most popular trading technique, *filter rules,* an investor trades a stock when the price change exceeds a filter value set for it. As an example, an investor using a 5 percent filter would envision a positive breakout if the stock were to rise 5 percent from some base, suggesting that the stock price would continue to rise. A technician would acquire the stock to take advantage of the expected continued rise. In contrast, a 5 percent decline from some peak price would be considered a breakout on the downside, and the technician would expect a further price decline and would sell any holdings of the stock, and possibly even sell the stock short.

Studies of this trading rule have used a range of filters from 0.5 percent to 50 percent. The results indicated that small filters would yield above-average profits *before* taking account of trading commissions. However, small filters generate numerous trades and, therefore, substantial trading costs. When these trading commissions were considered, all the trading profits turned to losses. Alternatively, larger filters did not yield returns above those of a simple buy-and-hold policy.[10]

Researchers have simulated other trading rules that used past market data other than stock prices.[11] Trading rules have been devised that use odd-lot figures, advanced-decline ratios, short sales, short positions, and specialist activities. These simulation tests have generated mixed results. Most of the early studies suggested that these trading rules generally would not outperform a buy-and-hold policy on a risk-adjusted basis after taking account of commissions, while a couple of recent studies have indicated support for specific trading rules.[12] Therefore, most evidence from simulations of

---

[10]Eugene Fama and Marshall Blume, "Filter Rules and Stock Market Trading Profits," *Journal of Business* 39, no. 1 (January 1966 Supplement): 226–241.

[11]Many of these trading rules are discussed in Chapter 19 on technical analysis.

[12]George Pinches, "The Random Walk Hypothesis and Technical Analysis," *Financial Analysts Journal* 26, no. 2 (March-April 1970): 104–110. Two studies have indicated support for some technical trading rules that use a three-part filter or adjust relative strength for the January effect; see John S. Brush, "Eight Relative Strength Models Compared," *Journal of Portfolio Management* 13, no. 1 (Fall 1986): 21–28; and Stephen W. Pruitt and Richard E. White, "Who Says Technical Analysis Can't Beat the Market?" *Journal of Portfolio Management* 14, no. 3 (Spring 1988): 55–58.

specific trading rules indicates that these trading rules have not been able to beat a buy-and-hold policy. These results support the weak-form EMH.

SEMISTRONG-FORM HYPOTHESIS: TESTS AND RESULTS

Recall that the semistrong-form EMH asserts that security prices adjust rapidly to the release of all public information; that is, security prices fully reflect all public information. Adapting the Fama organization, studies that have tested the semistrong-form EMH can be divided into the following sets of studies:

1. Studies to predict future rates of return using available public information beyond the pure market information such as prices and trading volume considered in the weak-form tests. These studies can involve either *time-series analysis* of returns or the *cross-section distribution* of returns for individual stocks. Those who believe in the EMH would contend that it would not be possible to predict *future* returns using past returns or to predict the distribution of future returns using public information.

2. Event studies that examine how fast stock prices adjust to specific significant economic events. A corollary approach would be to test whether it is possible to invest in a security after the public announcement of a significant event and experience significant abnormal rates of return. Again, advocates of the EMH would expect security prices to adjust very rapidly, such that it would not be possible for investors to experience superior risk-adjusted returns by investing after the public announcement and paying normal transactions costs.

ADJUSTMENT FOR MARKET EFFECTS

For any of these tests, you need to adjust the security's rates of return for the rates of return of the overall market during the period considered. The point is, a 5 percent return in a stock during the period surrounding an announcement is not meaningful until you know what the aggregate stock market did during the same period and how this stock normally acts under such conditions. If the market had experienced a 10 percent return during this period, the 5 percent return for the stock may be lower than expected.

Authors of studies undertaken prior to 1970 generally recognized the need to make such adjustments for market movements. They typically assumed that the individual stocks should experience returns equal to the aggregate stock market. This assumption meant that the market adjustment process simply entailed subtracting the market return from the return for the individual security to derive its *abnormal rate of return,* as follows:

$$AR_{it} = R_{it} - R_{mt}$$

where:

AR_{it} = **abnormal rate of return on security** i **during period** t

R_{it} = **rate of return on security** i **during period** t

R_{mt} = **rate of return on a market index during period t**

In the example where the stock experienced a 5 percent increase while the market increased 10 percent, the stock's abnormal return would be minus 5 percent.

Some authors have adjusted the rates of return for securities by an amount different from the market rate of return, recognizing that all stocks do not change by the same amount as the market; that is, some stocks are more volatile than the market, and some are less volatile. These possibilities mean that you must determine an *expected* rate of return for the stock based on the market rate of return *and* the stock's relationship with the market. As an example, suppose a stock is generally 20 percent more volatile than the market. In such a case, if the market experiences a 10 percent rate of return, you would expect this stock to experience a 12 percent rate of return. Therefore, you would determine the abnormal return by computing the difference between the stock's actual rate of return and its *expected rate of return* as follows:

$$AR_{it} = R_{it} - E(R_{it})$$

where:

$E(R_{it})$ = the expected rate of return for stock i during period
  t based on the market rate of return and the stock's
  normal relationship with the market (its beta)

Continuing with the example, if the stock that was expected to have a 12 percent return (based on a market return of 10 percent and a stock beta of 1.20) had only a 5 percent return, its abnormal rate of return during the period would be minus 7 percent. Over the normal long-run period, you would expect the abnormal returns for a stock to sum to zero. Specifically, during one period the returns may exceed expectations, and in the next period they may fall short of expectations.

To summarize, there are two sets of tests of the semistrong-form EMH. In the first set, investigators attempt to predict the future rates of return for individual stocks or the aggregate market (i.e., predict the time series) using public information, such as the aggregate dividend yield or the risk premium spread for bonds. Alternatively, analysts look for public information regarding individual stocks that will allow them to predict the cross-sectional distribution of risk-adjusted rates of return (i.e., test whether it is possible to use variables such as the earnings-price ratio, market value size, book-value/market value ratio, or the dividend yield to predict which stocks will experience above-average or below-average risk-adjusted rates of return). In the second set of tests (event studies), they examine abnormal rates of return for the period immediately after an announcement of a significant economic event to determine whether it is possible for an investor to derive above-average risk-adjusted rates of return by investing after the release of public information.

In both sets of tests, the emphasis is on the analysis of abnormal rates of returns that deviate from long-term expectations, or returns that are adjusted for a stock's specific risk characteristics and overall market rates of return during the period.

RESULTS OF RETURN PREDICTION STUDIES

The *time-series tests* assume that in an efficient market the best estimate of *future* rates of return will be the long-run *historical* rates of return. The point of the tests is to determine whether there is any public information that will provide superior estimates of returns for a short-run horizon (1 to 6 months) or a long-run horizon (1 to 5 years).

The results of these studies have indicated that there is limited success in predicting short-horizon returns, but the analysis of long-horizon returns have been quite successful. Rozeff and Shiller postulated that the aggregate dividend yield (D/P) was a proxy for the risk premium on stocks.[13] Their results indicated a positive relationship between the D/P and future stock-market returns. An analysis and explanation of this relationship for long horizons of 2 to 4 years is contained in papers by Fama and French, which show that the predictive power increases with the horizon.[14] A subsequent study by Balvers, Cosimano, and McDonald provides a theoretical model to explain the phenomenon.[15] Their model and test results show that within an efficient market framework, stock prices do not have to follow a random walk and *long-run* returns on stocks can be predicted as long as you can predict aggregate output.

Several studies have considered not only dividend yield, but also two variables related to the term structure of interest rates: (1) a *default spread,* which is the difference between the yields on lower-grade and Aaa-rated long-term corporate bonds (this spread has been used in earlier chapters of this book as a proxy for a market risk premium), and (2) the *term structure spread,* which is the difference between the long-term Aaa yield and the yield on 1-month Treasury bills.[16] These studies find that these variables can be used to predict stock returns and bond returns. These U.S. variables have even been found to be useful for predicting returns for foreign common stocks.[17]

The reasoning for these empirical results is that when the two most significant variables—the dividend yield (D/P) and the default spread—are high, it implies that investors are expecting or requiring a high return on stocks and bonds, and this occurs when the economic environment has been poor, as reflected in the growth rate of output. Such a poor economic environment also means that there is a low wealth environment and that investors perceive higher risk for investments, which means that to invest and shift consumption from the present to the future investors will require a high rate of return.

QUARTERLY EARNINGS REPORTS   These are an important set of studies that could be considered part of the times-series analysis. These studies question whether it is possible to predict future returns for a stock based on publicly available quarterly earnings reports.

Numerous studies by Latané and associates on the usefulness of quarterly reports consistently have failed to support the semistrong EMH.[18] A study by Joy, Litzenberger,

[13]Michael Rozeff, "Dividend Yields on Equity Risk Premiums," *Journal of Portfolio Management* 11, no. 1 (Fall 1984): 68–75; and Robert Shiller, "Stock Prices and Social Dynamics," *Brookings Papers on Economic Activity* 2, (1984):457–510.

[14]Eugene F. Fama and Kenneth R. French, "Dividend Yields and Expected Stock Returns," *Journal of Financial Economics* 22, no. 1 (October 1988): 3–25; and Eugene F. Fama and Kenneth R. French, "Business Conditions and Expected Returns on Stocks and Bonds," *Journal of Financial Economics* 25, no. 1 (November 1989): 23–49.

[15]Ronald J. Balvers, Thomas F. Cosimano, and Bill McDonald, "Predicting Stock Returns in an Efficient Market," *Journal of Finance* 45, no. 4 (September 1990): 1109–1128.

[16]Donald B. Keim and Robert F. Stambaugh, "Predicting Returns in Stock and Bond Markets," *Journal of Financial Economics* 17, no. 2 (December 1986): 357–390; John Y. Campbell, "Stock Returns and the Term Structure," *Journal of Financial Economics* 18, no. 2 (June 1987): 373–399; and Nai-fu Chen, "Financial Investment Opportunities and the Macroeconomy," *Journal of Finance* 46, no. 2 (June 1991): 529–594.

[17]Harvey Campbell, "The World Price of Covariance Risk," *Journal of Finance* 46, no. 1 (March 1991): 111–157.

[18]Representative studies in the area are H. A. Latané, O. Maurice Joy, and Charles P. Jones, "Quarterly Data, Sort-Rank Routines, and Security Evaluation," *Journal of Business* 43, no. 4 (October 1970): 427–438; and C. Jones and R. Litzenberger, "Quarterly Earnings Reports and Intermediate Stock Price Trends," *Journal of Finance* 25, no. 1 (March 1970): 143–148.

and McEnally (JLM) examined firms that experienced unanticipated changes in quarterly earnings using three categories based upon how actual earnings deviated from expectations: (1) any deviation from expectations, (2) a deviation of plus or minus 20 percent, and (3) a deviation of at least 40 percent.[19] They examined abnormal price changes from 13 weeks prior to the announcement to 26 weeks following it. The abnormal price movements for the "any deviation" category for companies with earnings above expectations was about 1 to 2 percent during the period compared to transactions costs of 2 to 3 percent, indicating a lack of profit opportunities. For the 20-percent-above-expectations category, the post-announcement gain was about 4 percent. Finally, there were 5 to 6 percent gains when actual earnings were 40-percent-above-expectations. These latter abnormal returns exceeded transaction costs. The price adjustment to unfavorable earnings performance was more rapid, and there were no abnormal returns for any category.

These results suggest that favorable information contained in quarterly earnings reports is not instantaneously reflected in stock prices and that a significant relationship exists between the size of the unexpected earnings performance and the post-announcement stock price change.

In reviewing these studies, Joy and Jones noted problems in several of the earlier studies that they believed were remedied in the more recent ones.[20] Acknowledging some possibility of debate on minor points, they stated,

> We conclude from the array of studies we have reviewed that market inefficiencies exist with respect to earnings reports.[21]

Ball reviewed 20 studies of price reaction to earnings announcements and found that the post-announcement risk-adjusted abnormal returns are consistently positive, which is inconsistent with market efficiency.[22] In contrast to Joy and Jones, he contended that the abnormal returns are due to problems with the capital asset pricing model (the CAPM that is discussed in Chapter 8) used to derive expected returns, not market inefficiencies. Watts found significant abnormal returns even after making all the adjustments suggested by Ball.[23] He explicitly showed that the abnormal returns were due to market inefficiencies rather than the CAPM, but noted that the abnormal returns were small and not completely consistent over time.

The more recent earnings announcement studies have employed the concept of *standardized unexpected earnings (SUE)*.[24] Rather than examine the percentage differences between actual and expected, this technique normalizes the difference

---

[19]O. Maurice Joy, Robert H. Litzenberger, and Richard W. McEnally, "The Adjustment of Stock Prices to Announcements of Unanticipated Changes in Quarterly Earnings," *Journal of Accounting Research* 15, no. 2 (Autumn 1977): 207–225.

[20]O. Maurice Joy and Charles P. Jones, "Earnings Reports and Market Efficiencies: An Analysis of Contrary Evidence," *Journal of Financial Research* 2, no. 1 (Spring 1979): 51–63.

[21]Ibid., 62.

[22]Ray Ball, "Anomalies in Relationships Between Securities' Yields and Yield-Surrogates," *Journal of Financial Economics* 6, no. 2/3 (June-September 1978): 103–126.

[23]Ross L. Watts, "Systematic 'Abnormal' Returns After Quarterly Earnings Announcements," *Journal of Financial Economics* 6, no. 2/3 (June-September 1978): 127–150.

[24]These include Henry A. Latané and Charles P. Jones, "Standardized Unexpected Earnings—A Progress Report," *Journal of Finance* 32, no. 5 (December 1977): 1457–1465; and Henry A. Latané and Charles Jones, "Standardized Unexpected Earnings: 1971–1977," *Journal of Finance* 34, no. 3 (June 1979): 717–724.

between actual and expected earnings for the quarter by the standard error of estimate from the regression used to derive the expected earnings figure. Therefore, the SUE is:

$$\frac{\text{Reported EPS}_t - \text{Predicted EPS}_t}{\text{Standard Error of Estimate for the Estimating Regression Equation}}$$

The predicted earnings are estimated by a time-series model that considers the earnings during the prior 20 quarters and includes quarterly dummy variables that adjust for any seasonal factors. Therefore, the SUE indicates how many standard errors the reported EPS figure is above or below the predicted EPS figure. The typical categories are greater than 4.0, between 4.0 and 3.0, between 3.0 and 2.0, and so on, all the way to less than minus 4.0.

An extensive analysis by Rendleman, Jones, and Latané (RJL) using a very large sample and daily returns provided evidence that large SUEs were accompanied by significant abnormal stock price changes.[25] These results contrasted with the earlier findings by Reinganum that the abnormal returns between high and low SUE portfolios were not statistically different from zero.[26] The RJL results were confirmed for the time period examined by Reinganum (1975–1977), but also for the longer period of 1971 to 1980. RJL also examined the impact of different risk adjustments or no risk adjustment (implicitly assuming that the various SUE portfolios have comparable risk levels) and concluded that the results were not sensitive to the risk adjustments. The analysis of daily data from 20 days before a quarterly earnings announcement to 90 days after the announcement indicated that 31 percent of the total response in stock returns came before the announcement, 18 percent on the day of the announcement, and 51 percent afterwards.

Foster, Olsen, and Shevlin examined several reasons for the earnings drift following earnings announcements and confirmed the prior results using different earnings expectations models.[27] The unexpected earnings explained over 80 percent of the subsequent stock price drift for the total time period and during several subperiods. Mendenhall and later Bernard and Thomas review the prior studies and attempt to explain this pervasive drift.[28]

In summary, these results indicate that the market has not adjusted stock prices to reflect the release of quarterly earnings surprises as fast as expected by the semistrong EMH. As a result, it appears that earnings surprises can be used to predict returns for individual stocks.[29]

[25]Richard J. Rendleman, Jr., Charles P. Jones, and Henry A. Latané, "Empirical Anomalies Based on Unexpected Earnings and the Importance of Risk Adjustments," *Journal of Financial Economics* 10, no. 3 (November 1982): 269–287; and C. P. Jones, R. J. Rendleman, Jr., and H. A. Latané, "Earnings Announcements: Pre- and Post-Responses," *Journal of Portfolio Management* 11, no. 3 (Spring 1985): 28–32.

[26]Marc R. Reinganum, "Misspecification of Capital Asset Pricing," *Journal of Financial Economics* 9, no. 1 (March 1981): 19–46.

[27]George Foster, Chris Olsen, and Terry Shevlin, "Earnings Releases, Anomalies, and the Behavior of Security Returns," *Accounting Review* 59, no. 4 (October 1984): 574–603.

[28]Richard R. Mendenhall, "An Investigation of Anomalies Based on Unexpected Earnings" (Ph.D. dissertation, Indiana University, 1986); and Victor L. Bernard and Jacob K. Thomas, "Post-Earnings-Announcement Drift: Delayed Price Response or Risk Premium?" *Journal of Accounting Research* 27, Supplement (1989).

[29]Academic studies such as these that have indicated the importance of earnings surprises have led *The Wall Street Journal* to publish a section on "earnings surprises" in connection with regular quarterly earnings reports.

The final set of studies that attempted to predict rates of return are the *calendar studies*. These studies questioned whether there are some regularities in the rates of return during the calendar year that would allow investors to predict returns on stocks. These studies include numerous studies on "The January Anomaly" and studies that consider a variety of other daily and weekly regularities.

THE JANUARY ANOMALY   Several years ago Branch proposed a unique trading rule for those interested in taking advantage of tax selling.[30] Investors tend to engage in tax selling toward the end of the year to establish losses on stocks that have declined. After the new year, there is a tendency to reacquire these stocks or to buy other stocks that look attractive. This scenario would produce downward pressure on stock prices in late November and December and positive pressure in early January. Those who believe in efficient markets would not expect such a seasonal pattern to persist; it should be eliminated by arbitrageurs who would buy in December and sell in early January.

Dyl supported the tax selling hypothesis when he found that December trading volume was abnormally high for stocks that had declined during the previous year and that volume was abnormally low for stocks that had experienced large gains.[31] He found significant abnormal returns during January for stocks that had experienced losses during the prior year.

Roll confirmed the price pattern on the last day of December and the first four days of January.[32] Stocks with negative returns during the prior year had higher returns around January 1 and 2. The results also indicated that smallness had an effect beyond volatility and tax selling. To examine the impact of transaction costs, Roll assumed a purchase on the second-to-last day of the year and a sale on the fourth day of the new year. This trading rule generated returns of 6.89 percent for the NYSE and 14.2 percent for the AMEX. Applying the 6.77 percent commissions estimated by Stoll and Whaley for small firms, they still had excess returns of 3.94 percent for the NYSE and 10.3 percent for the AMEX. Assuming a purchase at the high price for the second-to-last trading day and sales at the low price on the fourth day of the new year, and also adding commissions, there was no profit on the NYSE, but there was still an excess return on the AMEX. Roll concluded that because of transaction costs, arbitrageurs must not be eliminating the January tax selling anomaly.

Keim analyzed the relation between abnormal returns and market value during each month of the year. Overall he found a negative relationship between size and abnormal returns, but the strongest relationship was always in January, where nearly 50 percent of the overall size effect occurred.[33] In fact, more than 50 percent of the January effect was concentrated in the first week of trading, particularly on the first day of the year.

---

[30]Ben Branch, "A Tax Loss Trading Rule," *Journal of Business* 50, no. 2 (April 1977): 198–207. These results were generally confirmed in Ben Branch and Kyun Chun Chang, "Tax-Loss Trading—Is the Game Over or Have the Rules Changed?" *The Financial Review* 20, no. 1 (February 1985): 55–69.

[31]Edward A. Dyl, "Capital Gains Taxation and Year-End Stock Market Behavior," *Journal of Finance* 32, no. 1 (March 1977): 165–175.

[32]Richard Roll, "Vas Ist Das?" *Journal of Portfolio Management* 9, no. 2 (Winter 1983): 18–28.

[33]Donald B. Keim, "Size-Related Anomalies and Stock Return Seasonality," *Journal of Financial Economics* 12, no. 1 (June 1983): 13–32.

Following the earlier work by Rozeff and Kinney,[34] Reinganum found large abnormal returns at the beginning of January, consistent with tax-loss selling.[35] Still, small firms that did very well the prior year also experienced large abnormal returns in early January, which is not consistent with the tax selling hypothesis.

Brown, Keim, Kleidon, and Marsh examined the January effect using Australian data, because the year-end for tax purposes in Australia is June 30, making the seasonal tax effect occur in July.[36] The results indicated the largest seasonals in January and July. Although the results for July support the tax selling hypothesis, the January impact cannot be thus explained. The authors conclude that the January tax effect may be more a case of correlation than causation. Berges, McConnell, and Schlarbaum document the January effect using Canadian data for the period 1951–1980, but Canada did not introduce the capital gains tax until 1973.[37] Therefore, the tax-loss hypothesis cannot explain the January effect. Also they did not find the small-firm effect in January.

Chang and Pinegar indicate support for the tax-loss selling hypothesis based on an analysis of long-term government and corporate bonds, with most of the support coming from lower-rated bonds (BB and B).[38] Still, they also derived January gains that could not be explained by tax selling. This leads them to acknowledge that tax-loss selling is probably not the only cause of January gains.

Tinic and West highlighted the January effect by examining the seasonality of the relationship between expected return and risk.[39] Consistent with some prior studies, the risk–return relationship for the total period was fairly weak, but there was a very strong seasonal in the relationship. Specifically, there was no significant risk–return relationship in any single month except January, nor during the other eleven months combined.

Keim analyzed dividend yields and stock returns overall and found a nonlinear relationship in January.[40] Specifically, the zero dividend securities had the largest return, and for the rest of the groups there was a positive relationship between the dividend yield and the stock returns. He likewise found a strong seasonal pattern because the dividend yield–stock return relationship only existed during January.

Lakonishok and Smidt found a year-end effect in trading volume for small firms, the most active day being the last day of the year with above-normal trading activity continuing in January.[41]

---

[34]Michael S. Rozeff and William R. Kinney, Jr., "Capital Market Seasonality: The Case of Stock Returns," *Journal of Financial Economics* 3, no. 4 (December 1976): 379–402.

[35]Marc R. Reinganum, "The Anomalous Stock Market Behavior of Small Firms in January: Empirical Tests for Tax-Loss Selling Effects," *Journal of Financial Economics* 12, no. 1 (January 1983): 89–104.

[36]Philip Brown, Donald B. Keim, Allan W. Kleidon, and Terry A. Marsh, "Stock Return Seasonalities and the Tax-Loss Selling Hypothesis," *Journal of Financial Economics* 12, no. 1 (June 1983): 105–127.

[37]Angel Berges, John J. McConnell, and Gary G. Schlarbaum, "The Turn-of-the-Year in Canada," *Journal of Finance* 39, no. 1 (March 1984): 185–192.

[38]Eric C. Chang and J. Michael Pinegar, "Return Seasonality and Tax-Loss Selling in the Market for Long-Term Government and Corporate Bonds," *Journal of Financial Economics* 17, no. 2 (December 1986): 391–415.

[39]Seha M. Tinic and Richard R. West, "Risk and Return: January vs. the Rest of the Year," *Journal of Financial Economics* 13, no. 4 (December 1984): 561–574.

[40]Donald B. Keim, "Dividend Yields and Stock Returns: Implications of Abnormal January Returns," *Journal of Financial Economics* 14, no. 3 (September 1985): 473–489; Donald B. Keim, "Dividend Yields and the January Effect," *Journal of Portfolio Management* 12, no. 2 (Winter 1986): 54–60.

[41]Josef Lakonishok and Seymour Smidt, "Volume and Turn-of-the-Year Behavior," *Journal of Financial Economics* 13, no. 3 (September 1984): 435–455; and Josef Lakonishok and Seymour Smidt, "Trading Bargains in Small Firms at Year-End," *Journal of Portfolio Management* 12, no. 3 (Spring 1986): 24–29.

In summary, the January anomaly is intriguing because it is so pervasive. Its relationship with the small-firm effect is fascinating because of the apparent speed of impact. This seasonal impact also influences the dividend yield effect and trading volume, and a tax-loss explanation of this anomaly has received mixed support. Despite numerous studies, the January anomaly poses as many questions as it answers.[42]

OTHER CALENDAR EFFECTS   Although not as significant as the January anomaly, several other "calendar" effects have been examined, including a monthly effect, a weekend/day-of-the-week effect, and an intraday effect. Ariel found a significant monthly effect wherein all the market's cumulative advance occurred during the first half of trading months.[43]

The weekend effect has been documented by French and by Gibbons and Hess.[44] French examined daily returns from 1953 to 1977 and found that the mean return for Monday was significantly negative in each of the 5-year subperiods and during the full period. In contrast, the average return for the other 4 days was positive. Gibbons and Hess examined daily returns for the period 1962–1968 and for several subperiods and had results that were consistent with French. They also found negative returns on Monday for individual stocks and Treasury bills. Keim and Stambaugh found negative Monday results back to 1928 for individual exchange-listed stocks and for active OTC stocks.[45] They also found that the effect is similar for different size firms that were exchange-traded or on the OTC.

Rogalski decomposed the Monday effect that is typically measured from Friday close to Monday close into a *weekend effect* from Friday close to Monday open, and a *Monday trading effect* from Monday open to the Monday close.[46] He showed that the negative Monday effect found in prior studies occurs from the Friday close to the Monday open (i.e., it is really the weekend effect). After adjusting for the weekend effect, the Monday trading effect was positive. When the day-of-the-week returns were segmented into January and the rest of the year, he found that the Monday effect and the nontrading effect were on average positive in January and negative for all other months. Also the size effect only existed in January.

Two studies have examined this question using intraday observations. Smirlok and Stacks examined hourly observations between 1963 and 1983 for the total period and three subperiods.[47] They found a change in the pattern of returns before and after 1974. The results for the period 1974–1983 were consistent with Rogalski wherein the Monday effect is concentrated in the weekend effect. In contrast, before 1974 the Monday

[42]An article that reviews these studies and others is Donald B. Keim, "The CAPM and Equity Return Regularities," *Financial Analysts Journal* 42, no. 3 (May-June 1986): 19–34.

[43]Robert A. Ariel, "A Monthly Effect in Stock Returns," *Journal of Financial Economics* 18, no. 1 (March 1987): 161–174.

[44]Kenneth R. French, "Stock Returns and the Weekend Effect," *Journal of Financial Economics* 8, no. 1 (March 1980): 55–70; and Michael R. Gibbons and Patrick Hess, "Day of the Weak Effects and Asset Returns," *Journal of Business* 54, no. 4 (October 1981): 579–596. For a subsequent note, see Josef Lakonishok and Maurice Levi, "Weekend Effects on Stock Returns: A Note," *Journal of Finance* 37, no. 2 (June 1982): 883–889.

[45]Donald B. Keim and Robert F. Stambaugh, "A Further Investigation of the Weekend Effect in Stock Returns," *Journal of Finance* 39, no. 3 (July 1984): 819–835.

[46]Richard J. Rogalski, "New Findings Regarding Day-of-the-Week Returns Over Trading and Non-Trading Periods: A Note," *Journal of Finance* 39, no. 5 (December 1984): 1603–1614.

[47]Michael Smirlock and Laura Stacks, "Day-of-the-Week and Intraday Effects in Stock Returns," *Journal of Financial Economics* 17, no. 1 (September 1986): 197–210.

effect occurred during the Monday trading period. These two sets of results imply a shift in the timing of the weekend effect. The hourly results indicated that recently the negative effect is during the weekend. Notably, the Monday trading effect has turned positive because the negative Monday morning effect is swamped by positive Monday afternoon returns.

Harris examined the NYSE transactions data between December 1, 1981 and January 31, 1983, which allowed an analysis across firms and over time.[48] The analysis of the close-to-close returns into trading and nontrading returns indicated that for *large firms,* the negative Monday effect occurred before the market opened (it was a weekend effect), whereas for smaller firms most of the negative Monday effect occurred during the day on Monday (it was a Monday trading effect). Examining 15-minute intervals during the day, the author found that the only differences occurred during the first 45 minutes of the day—on Monday mornings prices tended to drop, whereas on other weekday mornings they increased. Otherwise price patterns during the day were similar. Finally, prices tended to rise on the last trade of the day.

PREDICTING CROSS-SECTIONAL RETURNS

Assuming an efficient market, all securities should lie along a security-market line that relates the expected rate of return to an appropriate risk measure. Put another way, *all securities should have equal risk-adjusted returns* because security prices should reflect all public information that would influence the security's risk. Therefore, studies in this category attempt to determine if it is possible to predict the future distribution of risk-adjusted rates of return (i.e., what stocks will enjoy above-average, risk-adjusted returns, and which will experience below-average, risk-adjusted returns?).

These studies typically examine the usefulness of alternative measures of size or quality as a tool to rank stocks in terms of risk-adjusted returns. The reader should be forewarned that all of these tests involve *a joint hypothesis* because they consider not only the efficiency of the market, but also are dependent on the asset pricing model that provides the measure of risk used in the test. Specifically, if a test determines that it is possible to predict future risk-adjusted returns, these results could occur because the market is not efficient, *or* they could be because the measure of risk is faulty and, therefore, the measures of risk-adjusted returns are wrong.

PRICE-EARNINGS RATIOS AND RETURNS   Basu tested the EMH by examining the relationship between the historical price-earnings (P/E) ratios for stocks and the returns on the stocks.[49] Some have suggested that low P/E stocks will outperform high P/E stocks because growth companies enjoy high P/E ratios, but the market tends to overestimate the growth potential and thus overvalues these growth companies, while undervaluing low-growth firms with low P/E ratios. A relationship between the historical P/E ratios and subsequent risk-adjusted market performance would constitute evidence

[48]Lawrence Harris, "A Transaction Data Study of Weekly and Intradaily Patterns in Stock Returns," *Journal of Financial Economics* 16, no. 1 (May 1986): 99–117.

[49]S. Basu, "Investment Performance of Common Stocks in Relation to Their Price-Earnings Ratios: A Test of the Efficient Market Hypothesis," *Journal of Finance* 32, no. 3 (June 1977): 663–682; and S. Basu, "The Information Content of Price-Earnings Ratios," *Financial Management* 4, no. 2 (Summer 1975): 53–64.

against the semistrong EMH, because it would imply that investors could use publicly available P/E ratios to predict future abnormal returns.

Basu divided the stocks into five P/E classes and determined the risk and return for portfolios of high and low P/E ratio stocks. The average annual rates of return ranged from 9 percent for high P/E ratio stocks to 16 percent for the low P/E ratio group. An unexpected result was that the low P/E ratio group also had lower risk. Performance measures that consider both return and risk indicated that low P/E ratio stocks experienced superior results relative to the market, whereas high P/E ratio stocks had significantly inferior results.[50] Subsequent analysis indicated some impact of taxes and transaction costs, but it was concluded that publicly available P/E ratios possess valuable information. Obviously, these results are not consistent with semistrong efficiency.

Peavy and Goodman examined P/E ratios with adjustments for firm size, industry effects, and infrequent trading.[51] They attempted to eliminate the size problem by considering only firms with a market value above $100 million and to control the industry effect by examining only firms within three industries (electronics, paper/ container, and food). To overcome the infrequent trading problem, they used quarterly intervals for stocks with an average monthly trading volume exceeding 25,000 shares. They found that the risk-adjusted returns for stocks in the lowest P/E ratio quintile for all three industries were superior to those in the highest P/E ratio quintile.

THE SIZE EFFECT   Two authors examined the impact of size (measured by total market value) on the risk-adjusted rates of return.[52] All stocks on the NYSE (Banz) or on the NYSE and the AMEX (Reinganum) were ranked by market value and divided into ten equally weighted portfolios. The risk-adjusted returns for extended periods (10 to 15 years) indicated that the small firms consistently experienced significantly larger risk-adjusted returns than the larger firms. They contended that it was really the size, not the P/E ratio, that caused the Basu results. Subsequently, Basu reexamined Reinganum's results using a different sample period and different portfolio creation techniques and found that the highest risk-adjusted returns were in portfolios that contained both small firms and low P/E ratios.[53]

Recall that these studies on market efficiency are dual tests of the EMH *and* the CAPM. Abnormal returns may occur because the markets are not efficient, or because the market model is not properly specified and therefore does not provide correct estimates of expected returns. Reinganum contended that the abnormal returns were because the simple one-period CAPM is an inadequate description of the real-world capital markets. [54]

[50]Composite performance measures are discussed in Chapter 24.

[51]John W. Peavy, III, and David A. Goodman, "The Significance of P/Es for Portfolios Returns," *Journal of Portfolio Management* 9, no. 2 (Winter 1983): 43–47.

[52]R. W. Banz, "The Relationship Between Return and Market Value of Common Stocks," *Journal of Financial Economics* 9, no. 1 (March 1981): 3–18; and Marc R. Reinganum, "Misspecification of Capital Asset Pricing: Empirical Anomalies Based on Earnings Yield and Market Values," *Journal of Financial Economics* 9, no. 1 (March 1981): 19–46.

[53]S. Basu, "The Relationship Between Earnings Yield, Market Value, and Return for NYSE Common Stocks," *Journal of Financial Economics* 12, no. 1 (June 1983): 129–156.

[54]Marc R. Reinganum, "Abnormal Returns in Small Firm Portfolios," *Financial Analysts Journal* 37, no. 2 (March-April 1981): 52–57.

Roll suggested that the riskiness of the small firms was improperly measured.[55] Because small firms are traded less frequently, this causes an increase in serial correlation of prices over time and a decrease in the variance of returns, which also means that the covariance of returns for the stock with the market portfolio is reduced, so the stock's beta is lower. Earlier, Dimson suggested adding lagged and leading market returns to the market model and summing the coefficients to arrive at the beta for infrequently traded stocks.[56] Reinganum computed betas for the alternative market value portfolios using the standard *ordinary least squares (OLS) model* and using Dimson's *aggregated coefficients model* and found a substantial difference in the estimated betas (e.g., the smallest firm portfolio beta was 0.75 using OLS and 1.69 using the aggregated coefficients method).[57] The difference between betas narrowed with size until the largest firm portfolio beta was 0.98 with OLS and 0.97 with aggregated coefficients. The results supported Dimson and Roll regarding the underestimation of risk for small firms. Still, Reinganum's test of whether these larger betas could explain the large differences in rates of return indicated that the difference in beta did not account for the very large difference in rates of return.

Chan, Chen, and Hsich employed a multifactor pricing model with several risk variables and found the difference in returns between the top and bottom groups was only about 1 or 2 percent, compared with about 12 percent before the multifactor adjustment for risk.[58] The authors contend that these results imply that most of the difference in size-related returns can be explained by *complete measures of risk*.

Stoll and Whaley confirmed that total market value varies inversely with risk-adjusted returns but also found a strong positive correlation between average price per share and market value; firms with small market value have low stock prices.[59] Because transaction costs vary inversely with price per share, they must be considered when examining the small-firm effect. Transaction costs include both the dealer's bid–ask spread and the broker's commission. Specifically, when using a market order, you would buy at the ask price and sell at the bid price and also have a broker's commission on the transaction. Both the proportional bid–ask spread and the commission vary inversely with price. Specifically, the proportional bid–ask spread varied from 2.93 percent for small-value stocks to 0.69 percent for large-value stocks, and the broker's commission was 3.84 percent for small firms and 2.02 percent for large firms. This indicates a total difference in transaction cost of 4.06 percent between large and small firms, a combined cost of 2.93 plus 3.84 (6.77 percent) for small firms and 0.69 plus 2.02 (2.71 percent) for large firms. This differential in transaction cost, with frequent trading, can have a significant impact on the results. Assuming daily transactions, the original small-firm effects are reversed, whereas with less trading, the original abnor-

---

[55]Richard Roll, "A Possible Explanation of the Small Firm Effect," *Journal of Finance* 36, no. 4 (September 1981): 879–888.

[56]Elroy Dimson, "Risk Measurement When Shares Are Subject to Infrequent Trading," *Journal of Financial Economics* 7, no. 2 (June 1979): 197–226.

[57]Marc R. Reinganum, "A Direct Test of Roll's Conjecture on the Firm Size Effect," *Journal of Finance* 37, no. 1 (March 1982): 27–35.

[58]K. C. Chan, Nai-fu Chen, and David A. Hsich, "An Exploratory Investigation of the Firm Size Effect," *Journal of Financial Economics* 14, no. 3 (September 1985): 451–471.

[59]Hans R. Stoll and Robert E. Whaley, "Transactions Costs and the Small Firm Effect," *Journal of Financial Economics* 12, no. 1 (June 1983): 57–80.

mal returns recur. The point is, subsequent size effect studies must consider realistic transaction costs and specify holding period assumptions.

Reinganum investigated a buy-and-hold strategy for longer periods of time and had results that were similar to an annual trading strategy.[60] Two holding period strategies were considered: a one-year holding period, with rebalancing every year, and a buy-and-hold strategy from 1963 through 1980. With *annual* rebalancing, the small-firm portfolio grew from $1 in 1963 to over $46 without commissions, whereas $1 in the largest-firm portfolio grew to about $4. With *no* rebalancing, a dollar in the small-firm portfolio grew to about $11, whereas $1 in the large-firm portfolio again grew to over $4. He did not consider transaction costs with annual rebalancing because the differential returns were so large that any reasonable transaction costs could not overcome this return superiority. In summary, the small firms outperformed the large firms after considering risk and transaction costs, assuming annual rebalancing.

Most studies on size effect employed large data bases and long time periods (30 to 50 years) to show that this phenomenon has existed for many years. In contrast, Brown, Kleidon, and Marsh examined the performance over various intervals of time and concluded that *the small firm effect is not stable.*[61] During some periods they found the negative relationship derived by others, but during others (e.g., 1967 to 1975), they found a positive relationship where large firms outperformed the small firms. Incidentally, analysis of some recent returns indicates that this positive relationship held during the 4-year period of 1984–1987 and also during 1989–1990. A recent study by Reinganum acknowledges this instability, but contends that the small-firm effect is still a long-run phenomenon.[62]

NEGLECTED FIRMS AND TRADING ACTIVITY   Arbel and Strebel considered an additional influence beyond size—attention or neglect.[63] They measured attention in terms of the number of analysts who regularly follow a stock and divided the stocks into three groups: (1) highly followed, (2) moderately followed, and (3) neglected. They confirmed the small-firm effect but also found a neglected-firm effect caused by the lack of information and limited institutional interest. The neglected-firm concept applied across size classes.

James and Edmister examined the impact of trading volume by considering the relationship between returns, market volume, and trading activity.[64] They confirmed the relationship between size and rates of return and then considered the impact of trading volume as an alternative explanation because of a strong positive correlation between size and trading activity. A relationship between return and trading activity would justify the excess return for small stocks on the basis of a liquidity premium.

[60]Marc R. Reinganum, "Portfolio Strategies Based on Market Capitalization," *Journal of Portfolio Management* 9, no. 2 (Winter 1983): 29–36.

[61]Philip Brown, Allen W. Kleidon, and Terry A. Marsh, "New Evidence on the Nature of Size-Related Anomalies in Stock Prices," *Journal of Financial Economics* 12, no. 1 (June 1983): 33–56.

[62]Marc R. Reinganum, "A Revival of the Small Firm Effect," *The Journal of Portfolio Management* 18, no. 3 (Spring 1992): 55–62.

[63]Avner Arbel and Paul Strebel, "Pay Attention to Neglected Firms!" *Journal of Portfolio Management* 9, no. 2 (Winter 1983): 37–42.

[64]Christopher James and Robert Edmister, "The Relation Between Common Stock Returns, Trading Activity, and Market Value," *Journal of Finance* 38, no. 4 (September 1983): 1075–1086.

The results indicated no significant difference between the mean returns of the highest and lowest trading activity portfolios, and there was not the hypothesized inverse relationship between trading activity and mean daily returns. A test on firms with comparable trading activity confirmed the size effect. In summary, the size effect could not be explained by differential trading activity.

Barry and Brown hypothesized that firms with less information require higher returns.[65] Using the period of listing as a proxy for information, they found a negative relationship between returns and the period of listing after adjusting for firm size and the January effect.

In summary, firm size has emerged as a major predictor of future returns and an anomaly in the efficient markets literature. There have been numerous attempts to explain the anomaly in terms of superior risk measurements, transaction costs, analysts' attention, trading activity, and differential information. In general, no single study has been able to explain these very unusual results. Apparently, the two strongest explanations are the risk measurements and the higher transaction costs. Depending on the frequency of trading these two factors may account for much of the differential. Given these results, it is not surprising that Dimson and Marsh warn that the size effect must be considered in any event study that uses long intervals and contains sample firms with significantly different market values.[66]

BOOK VALUE–MARKET VALUE RATIO   This ratio that relates the book value (BV) of a firm's equity to the market value (MV) of its equity was initially suggested by Rosenberg, Reid, and Lanstein as a predictor of stock returns.[67] They found a significant positive relationship between this ratio and future stock returns and contended that this relationship was evidence against the EMH.

The strongest support for the importance of this ratio was provided by a recent study by Fama and French that evaluated the joint effects of market beta, size, E/P ratio, leverage, and the BV/MV ratio on the cross-section average returns on the NYSE, AMEX, and NASDAQ stocks.[68] Although the analysis is mainly for the period 1963–1990, additional analysis considers earlier periods and subperiods within the total period. They analyzed in detail the hypothesized positive relationship between beta and expected returns. They concluded that the positive beta–rate of return relationship found in empirical studies for the period pre-1969 disappeared during the period 1963–1990. In contrast, the negative relationship between size and average return was significant by itself and also significant after inclusion of other variables.

In addition, they found a significant positive relationship between the BV/MV ratio and average return that persisted even when other variables are included. Most importantly, *both* size and the BV/MV ratio are significant when included together and they

[65]Christopher B. Barry and Stephen J. Brown, "Differential Information and the Small Firm Effect," *Journal of Financial Economics* 13, no. 2 (June 1984): 283–294.

[66]Elroy Dimson and Paul Marsh, "Event Study Methodologies and the Size Effect: The Case of UK Press Recommendations," *Journal of Financial Economics* 17, no. 1 (September 1986): 113–142.

[67]Barr Rosenberg, Kenneth Reid, and Ronald Lanstein, "Persuasive Evidence of Market Inefficiency," *Journal of Portfolio Management* 11, no. 3 (Spring 1985): 9–17.

[68]Eugene F. Fama and Kenneth R. French, "The Cross-Section of Expected Stock Returns," *Journal of Finance* 47, no. 2 (June 1992): 427–465.

TABLE 6.1

Average Monthly Returns on Portfolios Formed on Size and Book-to-Market Equity; Stocks Sorted by ME (Down) and then BE/ME (Across); July 1963 to December 1990

In June of each year t, the NYSE, AMEX, and NASDAQ stocks that meet the CRSP-COMPUSTAT data requirements are allocated to 10 size portfolios using the NYSE size (ME) breakpoints. The NYSE, AMEX, and NASDAQ stocks in each size decile are then sorted into 10 BE/ME portfolios using the book-to-market ratios for year $t - 1$. BE/ME is the book value of common equity plus balance-sheet deferred taxes for fiscal year $t - 1$, over market equity for December of year $t - 1$. The equal-weighted monthly portfolio returns are then calculated for July of year t to June of year $t + 1$.

Average monthly return is the time-series average of the monthly equal-weighted portfolio returns (in percent).

The All column shows average returns for equal-weighted size decile portfolios. The All row shows average returns for equal-weighted portfolios of the stocks in each BE/ME group.

	Book-to-Market Portfolios									↓
	All	**Low**	**2**	**3**	**4**	**5**	**6**	**7**	**8**	**9**	**High**
All	1.23	0.64	0.98	1.06	1.17	1.24	1.26	1.39	1.40	1.50	1.63
Small-ME →	1.47	0.70	1.14	1.20	1.43	1.56	1.51	1.70	1.71	1.82	1.92
ME-2	1.22	0.43	1.05	0.96	1.19	1.33	1.19	1.58	1.28	1.43	1.79
ME-3	1.22	0.56	0.88	1.23	0.95	1.36	1.30	1.30	1.40	1.54	1.60
ME-4	1.19	0.39	0.72	1.06	1.36	1.13	1.21	1.34	1.59	1.51	1.47
ME-5	1.24	0.88	0.65	1.08	1.47	1.13	1.43	1.44	1.26	1.52	1.49
ME-6	1.15	0.70	0.98	1.14	1.23	0.94	1.27	1.19	1.19	1.24	1.50
ME-7	1.07	0.95	1.00	0.99	0.83	0.99	1.13	0.99	1.16	1.10	1.47
ME-8	1.08	0.66	1.13	0.91	0.95	0.99	1.01	1.15	1.05	1.29	1.55
ME-9	0.95	0.44	0.89	0.92	1.00	1.05	0.93	0.82	1.11	1.04	1.22
Large-ME	0.89	0.93	0.88	0.84	0.71	0.79	0.83	0.81	0.96	0.97	1.18

Source: Eugene F. Fama and Kenneth French, "The Cross-Section of Expected Stock Returns," *Journal of Finance* 47, no. 2 (June, 1992): p. 446.

dominate other ratios. Specifically, although leverage and the E/P ratio were significant by themselves or when considered with size, they become insignificant when *both* size and the BV/MV ratio are considered.

A demonstration of the significance of both size and the BV/MV ratio can be seen from the results in Table 6.1, which shows the separate and combined effect of the two variables. As shown, going across the Small-ME row, BV/MV captures strong variation in average returns (0.70 to 1.92 percent), whereas controlling for the BV/MV ratio leaves a size effect in average returns (the high BV/MV results decline from 1.92 to 1.18 percent). These positive results for the BV/MV ratio were replicated by Chan, Hamao, and Lakonishok for returns on Japanese stocks.[69]

In summary, the tests of publicly available ratios that can be used to predict the cross-section of expected returns for stocks have provided substantial evidence in conflict with the semistrong-form EMH. Significant results were found for E/P ratios, market value size, neglected firms, leverage, and BV/MV ratios. The latest work has indicated that the optimal combination appears to be size and the BV/MV ratio.

[69]Louis K. Chan, Yasushi Hamao, and Josef Lakonishok, "Fundamentals and Stock Returns in Japan," *Journal of Finance* 41, no. 5 (December 1991): 1739–1789.

RESULTS OF EVENT STUDIES

The use of event studies to test the EMH has been a major growth sector during the past 20 years. You will recall that the intent of these studies is to examine how abnormal rates of return react to significant economic information. Those who advocate the EMH would expect returns to adjust very quickly to announcements of new information such that it is not possible for investors to experience positive abnormal rates of return by acting after the announcement. Because of space constraints, it is not possible to consider the many studies, but only to summarize the results for some of the more popular events considered.

Because numerous studies have examined the price reaction to specific events, the discussion of results is organized by event or item of public information. Specifically, we will review the results of event studies that examined the price movements and profit potential surrounding stock splits, sale of initial public offerings, exchange listings, unexpected world or economic events, and the announcement of significant accounting changes. We will see that the results for most of these studies have supported the semistrong-form EMH.

STOCK SPLIT STUDIES   One of the more popular economic events to examine is stock splits. Some believe that the prices of stocks that split will increase in value because the shares are priced lower, which increases demand for them. In contrast, advocates of efficient markets would not expect a change in value, reasoning that the firm has simply issued additional stock and nothing fundamentally affecting the value of the firm has occurred.

A well-known test of the semistrong hypothesis is the FFJR study, which hypothesized that stock splits alone should not cause higher rates of return because they add nothing to the value of a firm.[70] Therefore, there should be no significant price change following a split. Any relevant information (e.g., earnings growth) that caused the split would have already been discounted.[71]

One reason for expecting a price increase is that companies typically raise their dividends when they split their stock. The dividend change has an information effect because it indicates that management is confident that it will have a new, higher level of earnings in the future, which will justify a higher level of dividends. Therefore, any price increase that accompanies a dividend increase is not caused by the dividend itself, but by the expected earnings information it transmits.

To adjust for the market effect, FFJR derived unique parameters for each stock relative to the market and computed abnormal returns for the period 20 months before and after the stock split. Consistent positive abnormal returns surrounding splits would indicate the presence of good information and vice versa. The analysis was intended to determine whether the positive effects took place before or after the split. The total sample was divided into two groups: stocks that split and increased their dividend rate, and those that split but did not increase their dividend rate.

---

[70]E. F. Fama, L. Fisher, M. Jensen, and R. Roll, "The Adjustment of Stock Prices to New Information," *International Economic Review* 10, no. 1 (February 1969): 1–21.

[71]For a detailed analysis of why firms split their stock, see Josef Lakonishok and Baruch Lev, "Stock Splits and Stock Dividends: Why, Who and When," *Journal of Finance* 42, no. 4 (September 1987): 913–932.

Both groups experienced positive abnormal price changes prior to the split. Stocks that split but did *not* increase their dividend experienced abnormal price declines following the split and within 12 months lost all their accumulated abnormal gains. In contrast, stocks that split and also increased their dividend experienced no abnormal returns after the split.

These results, which indicated that stock splits do not result in higher rates of return for stockholders, support the semistrong EMH because they indicate that investors cannot gain from the information on a split after the public announcement. Hausman, West, and Largay confirmed that conclusion when they examined monthly data.[72] Reilly and Drzycimski also found strong support for the EMH using daily price and volume data for the period surrounding the split announcement.[73] In contrast, Grinblatt, Masulis, and Titman reported positive results on the day of the announcement and subsequent days.[74]

In summary, most studies attribute no short-run or long-run positive impact on security returns because of a stock split, although the results are not unanimous.[75]

INITIAL PUBLIC OFFERINGS   During the past 20 years a number of closely held companies have gone public by selling some of their common stock. Determining the appropriate price for an initial public offer (IPO) is a difficult task. Because of uncertainty about the price and the risk involved in underwriting such issues, it has been the prevailing hypothesis that the underwriters would tend to underprice these new issues.[76]

Given this general expectation of underpricing, the studies in this area have generally considered three sets of questions: (1) How great is the underpricing on average, does the underpricing vary over time, and if so why? (2) What factors cause different amounts of underpricing for alternative issues? (3) How fast does the market adjust the price for the underpricing?

The answer to the first question seems to be an average underpricing of about 16 percent, but it varies over time as shown by the results in Table 6.2.[77] Numerous factors have been suggested for the differential underpricing of alternative issues, but the major variables seem to be various risk measures, the size of the firm, the prestige of the

---

[72]W. H. Hausman, R. R. West, and J. A. Largay, "Stock Splits, Price Changes, and Trading Profits: A Synthesis," *Journal of Business* 44, no. 1 (January 1971): 69–77.

[73]Frank K. Reilly and Eugene F. Drzycimski, "Short-Run Profits from Stock Splits," *Financial Management* 10, no. 3 (Summer 1981): 64–74.

[74]Mark S. Grinblatt, Ronald W. Masulis, and Sheridan Titman, "The Valuation Effects of Stock Splits and Stock Dividends," *Journal of Financial Economics* 13, no. 4 (December 1984): 461–490.

[75]Another question of interest related to stock splits is the impact on the liquidity and volatility of the stocks involved. For a study on this question, see Ohlson and Penman, "Volatility Increases Subsequent to Stock Splits," *Journal of Financial Economics* 14, no. 2 (June 1985): 251–266.

[76]For a discussion of these reasons, see Frank K. Reilly and Kenneth Hatfield, "Investor Experience with New Stock Issues," *Financial Analysts Journal* 25, no. 5 (September-October 1969): 73–80.

[77]Example studies that measured these returns include Roger G. Ibbotson, "Price Performance of Common Stock New Issues," *Journal of Financial Economics* 2, no. 3 (September 1975): 235–272; Dennis E. Logue, "On the Pricing of Unseasoned New Issues, 1965–1969," *Journal of Financial and Quantitative Analysis* 8, no. 1 (January 1973): 91–103; Frank K. Reilly, "Further Evidence on Short-Run Results for New Issue Investors," *Journal of Financial and Quantitative Analysis* 8, no. 1 (January 1973): 83–90; Frank K. Reilly, "New Issues Revisited," *Financial Management* 6, no. 4 (Winter 1977): 28–42; and B. M. Neuberger and C. A. Lachapelle, "Unseasoned New Issue Price Performance on Three Tiers: 1975–1980," *Financial Management* 12, no. 3 (Autumn 1983): 23–28.

TABLE 6.2

Number and Average Initial Return of Initial Public Offerings: 1960–1987

	Number of Offerings[a]	Average Initial Return[b]
1960	269	17.83%
1961	435	34.11
1962	298	−1.61
1963	83	3.93
1964	97	5.32
1965	146	12.75
1966	85	7.06
1967	100	37.67
1968	368	55.86
1969	780	12.53
1970	358	−0.67
1971	391	21.16
1972	562	7.51
1973	105	−17.82
1974	9	−6.98
1975	14	−1.86
1976	34	2.90
1977	40	21.02
1978	42	25.66
1979	103	24.61
1980	259	49.36
1981	438	16.76
1982	198	20.31
1983	848	20.79
1984	516	11.52
1985	507	12.36
1986	953	9.99
1987	630	10.39
Total	8,668	16.37

[a]The number of offerings excludes Regulation A offerings (small issues, raising less than $1.5 million currently). Data are from Ibbotson and Jaffe (1975) for 1960–70, Ritter (1984) for 1971–82, *Going Public: The IPO Reporter* for 1983–85, and *Venture* magazine for 1986–87. The authors have excluded real estate investment trusts (REITs) and closed-end mutual funds.

[b]Initial returns are computed as the percentage return from the offering price to the end-of-the-calendar-month bid price, less the market return, for offerings in 1960–76. For 1977–87, initial returns are calculated as the percentage return from the offering price to the end-of-the-first-day bid price, without adjusting for market movements. Data are from Ibbotson and Jaffe (1975) for 1960, Ritter (1984) for 1971–82, and prepared by the authors for 1983–87. The latter numbers have been prepared with the assistance of Choo-Huang Teoh, using data supplied by Robert E. Miller.

Source: Roger G. Ibbotson, Jody L. Sindelar, and Jay R. Ritter, "Initial Public Offerings," *Journal of Applied Corporate Finance* 1, no. 2 (Summer 1988): 41. Reprinted by permission of the Journal of Applied Corporate Finance.

underwriter, and the status of the firm's accounting firms.[78] Finally, on the question of direct interest to the EMH, the more recent results indicate that the price adjustment takes place within one day after the offering.[79]

---

[78]See Randolph Beatty and Jay Ritter, "Investment Banking, Reputation, and the Underpricing of Initial Public Offerings," *Journal of Financial Economics* 15, no. 1 (March 1986): 213–232; J. R. Ritter, "The 'Hot' Issue Market of 1980," *Journal of Business* 57, no. 2 (April 1984): 215–240; and K. Rock, "Why New Issues Are Underpriced," *Journal of Financial Economics* 15, no. 1 (March 1986): 187–212.

[79]In this regard, see Robert E. Miller and Frank K. Reilly, "An Examination of Mispricing, Returns, and Uncertainty for Initial Public Offerings," *Financial Management* 16, no. 2 (January 1987): 33–38; and Andrew J. Chalk and John W. Peavy, III, "Initial Public Offerings: Daily Returns, Offering Types, and the Price Effect," *Financial Analysts Journal* 43, no. 5 (September-October 1987): 65–69. For an excellent overall review of the research on this topic, see Roger G. Ibbotson, Jody L. Jindelar, and Jay R. Ritter, "Initial Public Offerings," *Journal of Applied Corporate Finance* 1, no. 2 (Summer 1988): 37–45.

EXCHANGE LISTING   Another significant economic event for a firm and its stock is the decision to become listed on a national exchange, especially the NYSE. Such a listing is expected to increase the market liquidity of the stock and add to its prestige. Two questions are important. First, does an exchange listing permanently increase the value of the firm? Second, can an investor derive abnormal returns from investing in the stock when a new listing is announced or around the time of the actual listing? Although the results differed slightly, the overall consensus is that listing on a national exchange does not cause a permanent change in the long-run value of a firm.[80] The results about abnormal returns from investing in such stocks were mixed. All the studies agreed that the stocks' prices increased before any listing announcements and that stock prices consistently declined after the actual listing. The crucial question is, what happens between the announcement of the intent to apply for listing and the actual listing (a period of 4 to 6 weeks)? Although the evidence varies, the more recent studies point toward profit opportunities immediately after the announcement that a firm is applying for listings, and there is also the possibility of excess returns from price declines after the actual listing.[81] Finally, studies that have examined the impact of listing on the risk of the securities found no significant change in systematic risk or the firm's cost of equity.[82]

In summary, these studies on exchange listings indicate no long-run effects on value or risk. They do, however, give some evidence of short-run profit opportunities. This implies profit opportunities from public information, which does not support the semi-strong-form EMH.

UNEXPECTED WORLD EVENTS AND ECONOMIC NEWS   The results of several studies that examined the response of security prices to world or economic news have supported the semistrong-form EMH. Reilly and Drzycimski examined the reaction of stock prices to unexpected world events, such as the Eisenhower heart attack and the Kennedy assassination, and found that prices adjusted to the news before the market opened or before it reopened after the announcement.[83] Pierce and Roley examined the response to announcements about money supply, inflation, real economic activity, and the discount rate and found either no impact or an impact that did not persist beyond the announcement day.[84] When Jain analyzed hourly stock returns and trading volume response to surprise announcements about money supply, prices, industrial production, and the unemployment rate, he found that unexpected information about money supply and prices had an impact that was reflected in about one hour.[85]

[80]In this regard, see James C. VanHorne, "New Listings and Their Price Behavior," *Journal of Finance* 25, no. 4 (September 1970): 783–794; Waldemar M. Goulet, "Price Changes, Managerial Actions, and Insider Trading at the Time of Listing," *Financial Management* 3, no. 1 (Spring 1974): 30–36.

[81]See Gary Sanger and John McConnell, "Stock Exchange Listings Firm Value and Security Market Efficiency: The Impact of NASDAQ," *Journal of Financial and Quantitative Analysis* 21, no. 1 (March 1986): 1–25; John J. McConnell and Gary Sanger, "A Trading Strategy for New Listings on the NYSE," *Financial Analysts Journal* 40, no. 1 (January-February 1989): 38–39.

[82]Frank J. Fabozzi, "Does Listing on the AMEX Increase the Value of Equity?" *Financial Management* 10, no. 1 (Spring 1981): 43–50; Kent Baker and James Spitzfaden, "The Impact of Exchange Listing on the Cost of Equity Capital," *The Financial Review* 17, no. 3 (September 1982): 128–141.

[83]Frank K. Reilly and Eugene F. Drzycimski, "Tests of Stock Market Efficiency Following Major World Events," *Journal of Business Research* 1, no. 1 (Summer 1973): 57–72.

[84]Douglas Pierce and Vance Roley, "Stock Prices and Economic News," *Journal of Business* 59, no. 1 (Summer 1985): 49–67.

[85]Prom C. Jain, "Response of Hourly Stock Prices and Trading Volume to Economic News," *Journal of Business* 61, no. 2 (April 1988): 219–231.

ANNOUNCEMENTS OF ACCOUNTING CHANGES   Numerous studies have analyzed the impact of announcements of accounting changes on stock prices. In efficient markets, security prices should react quickly and predictably to announcements of accounting changes. An announcement of an accounting change that affects the economic value of the firm should cause a rapid change in stock prices. An accounting change that affects reported earnings, but has no economic significance, should not affect stock prices. As an example, consider what should happen when a firm changes its depreciation accounting method for reporting purposes from accelerated to straight-line. In this case, the firm should experience an increase in reported earnings, but this change has no economic consequence. An analysis of stock price movements surrounding this accounting change in depreciation method generally supported the EMH because there was no indication of positive price changes following the change, and there were some negative effects because it was postulated that firms making accounting changes are typically performing poorly.[86]

During periods of high inflation, many firms will change their inventory method from first-in, first-out (FIFO) to last-in, first-out (LIFO). Such a change causes a decline in reported earnings but benefits the firm because it reduces its taxable earnings and, therefore, tax expenses. Advocates of efficient markets would expect positive price changes from the tax savings and study results confirmed this expectation. Although reported earnings were lower than they would have been with FIFO, stock prices generally increased for firms that made such changes in their inventory methods.[87] In this regard, there is some evidence that the U.S. market is more efficient than some foreign markets.[88]

Therefore, these studies indicate that the securities markets react quite rapidly to accounting changes and also adjust security prices as one would expect on the basis of the true value (i.e., analysts are able to pierce the accounting veil and value securities on the basis of economic events).[89]

CORPORATE EVENTS   An area that has received substantial analysis during the last few years is corporate finance events such as mergers and acquisitions, reorganizations, and various security offerings (common stock, straight bonds, convertible bonds). Again there are two general questions of interest: (1) What is the market impact of these alternative events? (2) How fast does the market react to these events and adjust the security prices?

On the question of the reaction to corporate events, the answer is almost unanimous that prices react as one would expect based on the underlying economic impact of the action. An example would be the reaction to mergers where the stock of the firm being acquired increases in line with the premium offered by the acquiring firm, whereas the

---

[86]Examples of such studies include T. Ross Archibald, "Stock Market Reaction to the Depreciation Switch-Back," *Accounting Review* 47, no. 1 (January 1972): 22–30, and Robert S. Kaplan and Richard Roll, "Investor Evaluation of Accounting Information: Some Empirical Evidence," *Journal of Business* 45, no. 3 (April 1972): 225–257.

[87]For a study that examined this change, see Shyam Sunder, "Stock Price and Risk Related to Accounting Changes in Inventory Valuation," *The Accounting Review* 50, no. 3 (April 1975): 305–315.

[88]Robert A. Haugen, Edgar Ortiz, and Enrique Arjona, "Market Efficiency: Mexico versus the U.S.," *Journal of Portfolio Management* 33, no. 1 (Fall 1985): 28–33.

[89]For an extensive review of studies directed to this contention, see William H. Beaver, *Financial Reporting: An Accounting Revolution* (Englewood Cliffs, N.J.: Prentice-Hall, Inc., 1981), especially Chapter 6.

stock of the acquiring firm declines or experiences no change because of the concern that they overpaid for the firm. On the question of speed of reaction, the evidence indicates fairly rapid adjustment, with the time period shortening as shorter interval data is analyzed (i.e., using daily data, most studies find that the price adjustment is completed in about 3 days). Numerous studies related to financing decisions are reviewed by Smith.[90] The rapidly growing number of studies on corporate control that consider mergers and reorganizations are reviewed by Jensen and Warner.[91]

SUMMARY ON THE SEMISTRONG FORM EMH

Clearly, the evidence from tests of the semistrong EMH is mixed. The hypothesis receives strong and almost unanimous support from the numerous event studies on a range of events including stock splits, initial public offerings, world events and economic news, accounting changes, and a variety of corporate finance events. About the only mixed results come from exchange listing studies.

In sharp contrast, the numerous studies on predicting rates of return over time or for a cross-section of stocks presented evidence that indicated markets were not semistrong efficient. This included time-series studies on dividend yields, risk premiums, calendar patterns, and quarterly earnings surprises. Equally pervasive were the anomalous results for cross-sectional predictors such as size, the BV/MV ratio, E/P ratios, and neglected firms.

STRONG-FORM HYPOTHESIS: TESTS AND RESULTS

The strong-form EMH contends that stock prices fully reflect *all information,* public and private. This implies that no group of investors has access to *private information* that will allow them to consistently experience above-average profits. This extremely rigid hypothesis requires not only that stock prices must adjust rapidly to new public information, but also that no group has access to private information.

Tests of the strong-form EMH have analyzed returns over time for different identifiable investment groups to determine whether any group consistently received above-average risk-adjusted returns. To consistently earn positive abnormal returns, the group must have access to important private information or an ability to act on public information before other investors. Such results would indicate that security prices were not adjusting rapidly to *all* new information.

Investigators interested in testing this form of the EMH have analyzed the performance of four major groups of investors. First, several researchers have analyzed the returns experienced by *corporate insiders* from their stock trading. Another group of studies analyzed the returns available to *stock exchange specialists.* The third group of tests examined the ability of the group of *security analysts* at Value Line and elsewhere to select stocks that will outperform the market. Finally, a number of studies have examined the overall performance of *professional money managers.* The analysis of money managers' performance emphasized the risk-adjusted returns experienced by mutual funds because of the availability of data. Recently, these tests have been replicated for pension plans and endowment funds.

---

[90]Clifford W. Smith, Jr., "Investment Banking and the Capital Acquisition Process," *Journal of Financial Economics* 15, no. 1/2 (January/February 1986): 3–29.

[91]Michael C. Jensen and Jerald B. Warner, "The Distribution of Power Among Corporate Managers, Shareholders, and Directors," *Journal of Financial Economics* 20, no. 1/2 (January/March 1988): 3–24.

CORPORATE INSIDER TRADING

Corporate insiders are required to report to the SEC each month their transactions (purchases or sales) in the stock of the firm for which they are insiders. Insiders include major corporate officers, members of the board of directors, and owners of 10 percent or more of any equity class of securities. About 6 weeks after the reporting period, this insider trading information is made public by the SEC. These insider trading data have been used to identify how corporate insiders have traded and determine whether they bought on balance before abnormally good price movements and sold on balance before poor market periods for their stock.[92] The results of these studies have generally indicated that corporate insiders consistently enjoyed above-average profits especially on purchase transactions. This implies that many insiders had private information from which they derived above-average returns on their company stock.

Pratt and DeVere and also Jaffe found that *public* investors who consistently traded with the insiders based on announced insider transactions would have enjoyed excess risk-adjusted returns (after commissions).[93] Kerr tested this trading rule using 1976 data and concluded that the market had eliminated this inefficiency.[94] Trivoli contends that you can substantially increase the returns from using insider trading information by combining it with key financial ratios.[95] Nunn, Madden, and Gombola contend that you should consider what group of insiders (board chair, officers, directors versus other insiders) is doing the buying and selling.[96] Seyhun confirmed that insiders purchase stock prior to abnormal price increases and sell before abnormal declines and confirmed the Nunn, Madden, Gombola findings that some insiders such as officer-directors are better at predicting prices.[97] He also agreed with Kerr that the realizable return to investors who attempt to act on insider reports was not positive after considering total transactions costs.

Overall, these results provide mixed support for the EMH. Although several studies indicate the ability for insiders to experience abnormal profits, several recent studies indicate it is not possible for the noninsider to use this information to receive excess returns. Lee and Solt found it is not possible to use *aggregate* insider trading activity as a guide to market timing.[98] Notably, because of investor interest in these data as a result of academic research, *The Wall Street Journal* currently publishes a monthly column entitled "Inside Track" that discusses the largest insider transactions.

---

[92]The major studies on this topic are James H. Lorie and Victor Niederhoffer, "Predictive and Statistical Properties of Insider Trading," *Journal of Law and Economics* 11, (April 1968): 35–53; Shannon P. Pratt and Charles W. DeVere, "Relationship Between Insider Trading and Rates of Return for NYSE Common Stocks, 1960–1966," in *Modern Developments in Investment Management,* 2d ed., eds. James Lorie and Richard Brealey (New York: Praeger Publishers, 1978), 259–272; Joseph E. Finnerty, "Insiders and Market Efficiency," *Journal of Finance* 31, no. 4 (September 1976): 1141–1148; and Joseph E. Finnerty, "Insiders Activity and Inside Information: A Multivariate Analysis," *Journal of Financial and Quantitative Analysis* 11, no. 2 (June 1976): 205–215.

[93]Pratt and DeVere, "Relationship Between Insider Trading and Rates of Return"; and Jeffrey F. Jaffe, "Special Information and Inside Trading," *Journal of Business* 47, no. 2 (April 1974): 410–428.

[94]Halbert Kerr, "The Battle of Insider Trading and Market Efficiency," *Journal of Portfolio Management* 6, no. 4 (Summer 1980): 47–50. These results are supported by Michael S. Rozeff and Mir A. Zaman, "Market Efficiency and Insider Trading: New Evidence," *Journal of Business* 61, no. 1 (January 1988):25–44.

[95]George W. Trivoli, "How to Profit from Insider Trading Information," *Journal of Portfolio Management* 6, no. 4 (Summer 1980): 51–56.

[96]Kenneth P. Nunn, Jr., Gerald P. Madden, and Michael J. Gombola, "Are Some Insiders More 'Inside' Than Others?" *Journal of Portfolio Management* 9, no. 3 (Spring 1982): 18–22.

[97]H. Nejat Seyhun, "Insiders' Profits, Costs of Trading, and Market Efficiency," *Journal of Financial Economics* 16, no. 2 (June 1986): 189–212.

[98]Wayne Y. Lee and Michael E. Solt, "Insider Trading: A Poor Guide to Market Timing," *Journal of Portfolio Management* 12, no. 4 (Summer 1986): 65–71.

STOCK EXCHANGE SPECIALISTS

Several studies examining the function of stock exchange specialists have determined that specialists have monopolistic access to certain very important information about unfilled limit orders. One would expect specialists to derive above-average returns from this information. This expectation is generally supported by the data. Specialists seem to generally make money because they typically sell shares at higher prices than they purchase shares. Also, they apparently make money when they buy or sell after unexpected announcements and when they trade in large blocks of stock.

An SEC study in the early 1970s examined the rates of return earned on capital by the specialists.[99] The results indicated that these rates of return were substantially above normal, which would not support the strong-form EMH. In fairness to current specialists, the prevailing environment differs substantially from that in the early 1970s. More recent results indicate that specialists are experiencing much lower rates of return following the introduction of competitive rates and other trading practices that have reduced specialists' fees.

SECURITY ANALYSTS

Several tests have been done to consider whether it is possible to identify a set of analysts who have the ability to select stocks that are undervalued. The analysis involves determining whether, after their selection is made known, there is a significant abnormal return available to those who follow their recommendation. These studies and those that follow regarding money managers are more realistic and relevant than those that considered corporate insiders and stock exchange specialists because these analysts and money managers are full-time investment professionals with no obvious advantage except emphasis and training. If anyone should be able to select undervalued stocks, it should be these "pros." The first group of tests examine Value Line rankings, followed by an analysis of how investors react to revelations of recommendations by individual analysts.

THE VALUE LINE ENIGMA   Value Line (VL) is a large well-known advisory service that publishes financial information on approximately 1,700 stocks. Included in its report is a timing rank, which indicates Value Line's expectation regarding a firm's common stock performance over the coming 12 months. A rank of 1 is the most favorable performance and 5 the worst. This ranking system, initiated in April 1965, assigns numbers based on four factors:

1. An earnings and price rank of each security relative to all others
2. A price momentum factor
3. Year-to-year relative changes in quarterly earnings
4. A quarterly earnings "surprise" factor (i.e., actual quarterly earnings compared with VL estimated earnings)

The firms are ranked based on a composite score for each firm. The top and bottom 100 are ranked 1 and 5 respectively, the next 300 from the top and bottom are ranked 2 and 4, and the rest (approximately 900) are ranked 3. Rankings are assigned every

[99]*Report of the Special Study of the Security Markets* (Washington, D.C.: Securities and Exchange Commission, 1963): Part 2, 54.

week based on the latest data. Notably, all the data used to derive the four factors is public information.

The preliminary ranking is made every Wednesday, and the final ranking is sent to the printer on Friday (there are typically about five or six changes between Wednesday and Friday due to unusual new information). The new rankings are ready to be distributed on the following Wednesday, and Value Line attempts a staggered mailing so that everyone should receive the weekly *Survey* on Friday.

Several years after the ranking was started, Value Line indicated that the performance of the stocks in the various ranks differed substantially. Specifically, it was contended that the stocks rated 1 substantially outperformed the market, and the stocks rated 5 seriously underperformed the market (the performance figures did not include dividend income but also did not charge commissions).

Black tested the Value Line system over the period 1965–1970 by constructing portfolios grouped by rank and revised the portfolios monthly.[100] He concluded that rank-1 firms outperformed rank-5 firms by 20 percent per year on a risk-adjusted basis and that even with round-trip transaction costs of 2 percent, the net rate of return for a long position in rank-1 stocks would have been positive. Holloway examined the top 100 stocks in rank and concluded that if you consistently owned these stocks and adjusted your portfolio weekly, the returns would be superior *before* transaction costs but not after.[101] Alternatively, if you assumed annual portfolio revisions, the strategy generated abnormal returns after transaction costs.

Copeland and Mayers found that the abnormal returns were consistent with the rankings, but only the returns for rank 5 were significantly negative, implying that VL has the ability to select underperformers.[102] An analysis of a strategy of buying upgraded stocks and selling short those downgraded indicated significant negative abnormal returns for down-ranked stocks, but only limited significance for stocks that were upgraded. Finally, although the negative abnormal returns for the rank-5 portfolios were *statistically* significant, the trading rules were not profitable after transaction costs.

Stickel found that although all rank changes effect stock prices, the most significant impact occurs when stocks go from rank 2 to 1.[103] Other changes in rank were followed by statistically significant changes that were much smaller than for a move from 2 to 1. Stickel contends that the price movements require three days, but he counts Thursday as Day 0 because some people might receive the *Value Line Survey* on Thursday. Clearly, after Monday, there is no significant impact. Also smaller firms experienced a larger reaction to changes in rank and the change requires several days. However, acting on the rank change from 2 to 1 for the smallest firms would not be profitable due to the large transaction costs of small firms. Therefore, although evidence shows that there is information content in VL rank changes and that the price adjustment is

[100]Fischer Black, "Yes, Virginia, There Is Hope: Tests of the Value Line Ranking System," *Financial Analysts Journal* 29, no. 5 (September-October 1973): 10–14.

[101]Clark Holloway, "A Note on Testing an Aggressive Investment Strategy Using Value Line Ranks," *Journal of Finance* 36, no. 3 (June 1981): 711–719.

[102]Thomas E. Copeland and David Mayers, "The Value Line Enigma (1965–1978): A Case Study of Performance Evaluation Issues," *Journal of Financial Economics* 10, no. 3 (November 1982): 289–321.

[103]Scott E. Stickel, "The Effect of Value Line Investment Survey Changes on Common Stock Prices," *Journal of Financial Economics* 14, no. 1 (March 1985): 121–143.

not instantaneous, the absolute price change is *not* large enough to generate excess returns after transaction costs.

Huberman and Kandel examined the relationship between the VL recommendation and firm size to see if the VL record is because of the firm size phenomenon.[104] Although the VL-based excess returns declined as size increased, which is consistent with Stickel's results, the overall results imply no relationship between the VL rankings and size, because the VL record does not diminish when you control for size. Also, even though the VL investment service favors large firms, the system appears to be better at predicting the relative returns on small-firm stocks.

Peterson examined the daily price changes around the release of initial reviews and consequent new rankings of stocks.[105] The analysis considers the day before official release, the release day, and the following day (typically Thursday, Friday, and Monday). The portfolio returns for stocks ranked 1 were significant on Days -1, 0, and $+1$, individually and combined. The results for Day -1 are apparently due to leakage or early arrival of the *Value Line Survey*. The results for Days 0 and $+1$ could be due to the late arrival of the survey or a lag in adjustment. In general, there were no other significant abnormal returns for stocks assigned any other ranking, which implies that these other rankings contain very little information. Notably, there were no significant price changes after Day $+1$. It is concluded that there is information in some of the rankings (mainly rank 1), but the market is fairly efficient in adjusting to them.

Finally, as noted previously, one of the four factors considered when ranking firms is quarterly earnings "surprises," and it appears that this is a very important factor. Because of this impact, Affleck-Graves and Mendenhall contend that the longer-term abnormal returns from the VL ranking is really caused by the quarterly post-earnings announcement drift discussed earlier.[106] Put another way, the authors contend that this VL anomaly is caused by the quarterly earnings anomaly.

In summary, the several studies on the Value Line enigma indicate that there is information in the VL rankings (especially either rank 1 or 5) and in changes in the rankings (especially going from 2 to 1). Although these changes in rank have a larger effect on smaller firms, there is no direct relationship between the VL rankings and the size anomaly. Further, most of the recent evidence indicates that the market is fairly efficient, because the abnormal adjustments appear to be complete by Day $+2$. An analysis of study results over time indicates a faster adjustment to the rankings during recent years. In fact, a study by Hulbert indicates weaker performance for rank-1 stocks after 1983.[107] Also, although there are statistically significant price changes, there is mounting evidence that it is not possible to derive abnormal returns from these announcements after considering realistic transaction costs. Some of the strongest evidence in this regard is the fact that Value Line's Centurion Fund, which concentrates on rank-1 stocks, has consistently underperformed the market over the past decade.

---

[104]Gur Huberman and Shmuel Kandel, "Value Line Rank and Firm Size," *Journal of Business* 60, no. 4 (October 1987): 577–589; and Gur Huberman and Schmuel Kandel, "Market Efficiency and Value Line's Record," *Journal of Business* 63, no. 2 (April 1990): 187–216.

[105]David R. Peterson, "Security Price Reactions to Initial Reviews of Common Stock by the Value Line Investment Survey," *Journal of Financial and Quantitative Analysis* 22, no. 4 (December 1987): 483–494.

[106]John Affleck-Graves and Richard R. Mendenhall, "The Relation Between the Value Line Enigma and Post-Earnings-Announcement Drift," *Journal of Financial Economics* 31, no. 1 (February 1992):75–96.

[107]Mark Hulbert, "Proof of Pudding," *Forbes* (December 10, 1990): 316.

ANALYSTS' RECOMMENDATIONS   There is evidence in favor of the existence of superior analysts who apparently possess private information. This evidence is provided in studies by Lloyd-Davies and Canes and also by Lin, Smith, and Syed. In both studies the authors found that the prices of stocks mentioned in *The Wall Street Journal* column "Heard on the Street" experience a significant change on the day that the column appears.[108]

PERFORMANCE OF PROFESSIONAL MONEY MANAGERS

The studies of professional money managers are more realistic and widely applicable than the analysis of insiders and specialists because money managers typically do not have monopolistic access to important new information. Still, they are highly trained professionals who work full time at investment management. Therefore, if any "normal" set of investors should be able to derive above-average profits, it should be this group. Also, if any noninsider should be able to derive inside information, professional money managers should, because they conduct extensive management interviews.

Most studies on the performance of money managers have examined mutual funds because performance data is readily available on them. Only recently have data been available for bank trust departments, insurance companies, and investment advisers. The original mutual fund studies indicated that most funds were not able to match the performance of a buy-and-hold policy.[109] When risk-adjusted returns were examined *without* considering commission costs, slightly more than half of the money managers did better than the overall market. When commission costs, load fees, and management costs were considered, approximately two-thirds of the mutual funds did not match aggregate market performance. Also, Klemkosky found that funds were inconsistent in their performance.[110]

More recent studies by Henriksson and by Chang and Lewellen provided similar results on performance.[111] In contrast, Ippolito found that funds during the period 1965–1984 were able to beat the market after research and transaction costs.[112] Finally, Elton, Gruber, Das and Aklarka use a three-factor model to measure risk and find that during the Ippolito period the abnormal returns using more extensive risk measurement were negative.[113] Therefore, the vast majority of money manager studies support the

[108]Peter Lloyd-Davies and Michael Canes, "Stock Prices and the Publication of Second-Hand Information," *Journal of Business* 51, no. 1 (January 1978): 43–56; and Pu Lin, Stanley D. Smith, and Axmat A. Syed, "Security Price Reaction to the *Wall Street Journal's* Securities Recommendations," *Journal of Financial and Quantitative Analysis* 25, no. 3 (September 1990): 399–410.

[109]Notable studies include William F. Sharpe, "Mutual Fund Performance," *Journal of Business* 39, no. 1 (January 1966 Supplement): 119–139; Michael Jensen, "The Performance of Mutual Funds in the Period 1945–1964," *Journal of Finance* 23, no. 2 (May 1968): 389–416; and Jack L. Treynor, "How to Rate Management of Investment Funds," *Harvard Business Review* 43, no. 1 (January-February 1965): 63–75. These studies and others on this topic are reviewed in Chapter 26.

[110]Robert C. Klemkosky, "How Consistently Do Managers Manage?" *Journal of Portfolio Management* 3, no. 2 (Winter 1977): 11–15.

[111]Roy T. Henriksson, "Market Timing and Mutual Fund Performance: An Empirical Investigation," *Journal of Business* 57, no. 1, part 1 (January 1984): 73–96; and Eric C. Chang and Wilber G. Lewellen, "Market Timing and Mutual Fund Investment Performance," *Journal of Business* 57, no. 1, part 1 (January 1984): 57–72.

[112]Richard A. Ippolito, "Efficiency with Costly Information: A Study of Mutual Fund Performance, 1965–84," *Quarterly Journal of Economics* 104, no. 1 (March 1989): 1–23.

[113]Edwin Elton, Martin J. Gruber, Sanjiv Das, and Matt Aklarka, "Efficiency with Costly Information: A Reinterpretation of Evidence from Managed Portfolios."

TABLE 6.3   **Annualized Rates of Return during Alternative Periods Ending December 31, 1992**

	1 Year	2 Years	4 Years	6 Years	8 Years	10 Years
U.S. Equity Broad Universe Medians						
Equity accounts	9.0	20.6	15.8	13.7	16.3	15.7
Equity pooled accounts	7.7	19.5	15.8	13.6	15.9	15.3
Equity oriented separate accounts	9.7	21.0	15.9	13.9	16.6	16.5
Special equity pooled accounts	15.7	32.4	18.5	15.9	16.3	15.8
Mutual Fund Universe Medians						
Balanced mutual funds	7.9	15.7	12.2	11.2	13.4	13.5
Equity mutual funds	9.3	21.9	14.7	12.7	15.1	14.0
U.S. Equity Style Universe Medians						
Earnings growth accounts	7.5	28.0	22.3	17.0	19.1	16.5
Small capitalization accounts	15.4	32.8	18.2	15.8	16.9	16.2
Price-driven accounts	13.5	20.7	13.6	12.9	15.7	15.9
Market-oriented accounts	8.9	19.8	16.3	14.5	17.0	16.5
S&P 500 Index	7.7	18.6	15.6	14.0	16.6	16.0
Number of Universes with Returns above the S&P 500	9	9	7	4	4	4

Source: Frank Russell Company, Tacoma, WA. Reprinted by permission.

EMH with results that indicate mutual fund managers generally cannot beat a buy-and-hold policy.

As noted, recently it has been possible to get performance data for pension plans and endowment funds. Given this data, a study by Brinson, Hood, and Beebower as well as several other studies have documented that the performances of pension plans did not match that of the aggregate market.[114] Finally, Berkowitz, Finney, and Logue documented that the performance of endowment funds were likewise not able to beat a buy-and-hold policy.[115]

The figures in Table 6.3 provide a rough demonstration of these results for a recent period. These data are collected by Frank Russell Analytical Services as part of its performance evaluation service. Table 6.3 contains the mean rates of return for several investment groups compared to the Standard & Poor's 500 Index.[116]

Looking at the long-term, 10-year results, the first set of universes are banks that generally never experienced returns above the Standard & Poor's 500 during any of the periods. The exception was the equity-oriented separate accounts which did slightly better. The mutual funds did not have superior results. Finally, three of the four equity style universes did better. In summary, four of the ten universes beat the market. Notably, these results are *not* adjusted for risk. As stated, these results are generally consistent with the mutual fund results that would support the strong-form EMH.

---

[114]Gary P. Brinson, Randolph Hood, and Gilbert Beebower, "Determinants of Portfolio Performance," *Financial Analysts Journal* 43, no. 4 (July-August 1986): 39–44; Alicia Munnell, "Who Should Manage the Assets of Collectively Bargained Pension Plans?" *New England Economic Review* (July-August 1983): 18–30; and Richard A. Ippolito and John A. Turner, "Turnover Fees and Pension Plan Performance," *Financial Analysts Journal* 43, no. 6 (November-December, 1987): 16–26.

[115]Stephen A. Berkowitz, Louis D. Finney, and Dennis E. Logue, *The Investment Performance of Corporate Pension Plans* (New York: Quorum Books, 1988).

[116]The results for these individual accounts have an upward bias because they consider only accounts retained (e.g., if a firm or bank does a poor job on an account and the client leaves, those results would not be included).

CONCLUSIONS REGARDING THE STRONG-FORM EMH

The tests of the strong-form EMH generated mixed results, but the bulk of relevant evidence supported the hypothesis. The results for two unique groups of investors (corporate insiders and stock exchange specialists) did not support the hypothesis because both groups apparently have monopolistic access to important information and use it to derive above-average returns.

Tests to determine whether there are any analysts with private information concentrated on the Value Line rankings and publications of analysts' recommendations. The results for Value Line rankings have changed over time and currently tend toward support for the EMH. Specifically, the adjustment to rankings and ranking changes is fairly rapid, and it appears that trading is not profitable after transactions costs. Also there is a question whether the Value Line anomaly is really due to the quarterly earnings surprise anomaly. Alternatively, analysts recommendations seem to contain significant information.

Finally, the performance by professional money managers provided support for the strong-form EMH. The vast majority of money manager performance studies have indicated that the investments by these highly trained, full-time investors could not consistently outperform a simple buy-and-hold policy on a risk-adjusted basis. This has been true for mutual funds, pension plans, and endowment funds. Because money managers are similar to most investors who do not have consistent access to inside information, these latter results are considered more relevant to the hypothesis. Therefore, it appears that there is substantial support for the strong-form EMH as applied to most investors.

IMPLICATIONS OF EFFICIENT CAPITAL MARKETS

Overall, the results of numerous studies indicate that the capital markets are efficient as related to numerous sets of information. At the same time, studies have uncovered a substantial number of instances where the market apparently does not adjust rapidly to public information. Given these mixed results regarding the existence of efficient capital markets, it is very important to consider the implications of this contrasting evidence of market efficiency for several groups: technical analysts, investment analysts, and portfolio managers. The following discussion will consider the implications of both the evidence that supports the EMH (what techniques probably will not work), and the evidence that does not support the EMH (what information should be given special attention when attempting to derive superior investment results).

EFFICIENT MARKETS AND TECHNICAL ANALYSIS

The assumptions of technical analysis directly oppose the notion of efficient markets. A basic premise of technical analysis is that stock prices move in trends that persist.[117] Technicians believe that when new information comes to the market, it is not immediately available to everyone but is typically disseminated from the informed professional to the aggressive investing public and then to the great bulk of investors. Also, technicians contend that investors do not analyze information and act immediately. This process takes time. Therefore, they hypothesize that stock prices move to a new

---

[117]Chapter 19 contains an extensive discussion of technical analysis.

equilibrium after the release of new information in a gradual manner, which causes trends in stock price movements that persist for certain periods.

Technical analysts feel that nimble traders can develop systems to detect the beginning of a movement to a new equilibrium (called a "breakout"). Hence, they hope to buy or sell the stock immediately after its breakout to take advantage of the subsequent price adjustment.

The belief in this pattern of price adjustment directly contradicts advocates of the EMH who believe that security prices adjust to new information very rapidly. These EMH advocates do not contend, however, that prices adjust perfectly, which means there is a chance of overadjustment or underadjustment. Still, because it is not certain whether the market will over- or underadjust at any time, you cannot derive abnormal profits from adjustment errors.

If the capital market is efficient and prices fully reflect all relevant information, no technical trading system that depends only on past trading data can have any value. By the time the information is public, the price adjustment has taken place. Therefore, a purchase or sale using a technical trading rule should not generate abnormal returns after taking account of risk and transactions costs.

EFFICIENT MARKETS AND FUNDAMENTAL ANALYSIS

As you know from our prior discussion, fundamental analysts believe that, at any time, there is a basic intrinsic value for the aggregate stock market, various industries, or individual securities and that these values depend on underlying economic factors. Therefore, you determine the intrinsic value of an investment asset at a point in time by examining the variables that determine value such as current and future earnings, interest rates, and risk variables. If the prevailing market price differs from the intrinsic value by enough to cover transaction costs, you should take appropriate action: you buy if the market price is substantially below intrinsic value and sell if it is above. Investors who engage in fundamental analysis believe that occasionally market price and intrinsic value differ, but eventually investors recognize the discrepancy and correct it.

If you can do a superior job of *estimating* intrinsic value, you can consistently make superior market timing (asset allocation) decisions or acquire undervalued securities and generate above-average returns. Fundamental analysis involves aggregate market analysis, industry analysis, company analysis, and portfolio management. The EMH has important implications for all of these components.

AGGREGATE MARKET ANALYSIS WITH EFFICIENT CAPITAL MARKETS

Chapter 11 makes a strong case that intrinsic value analysis should begin with aggregate market analysis. Still, the EMH implies that if you examine only *past* economic events, it is unlikely to help you outperform a buy-and-hold policy because the market adjusts very rapidly to known economic events. Evidence suggests that the market experiences long-run price movements, but to take advantage of these movements in an efficient market you must do a superior job of *estimating* the relevant variables that cause these long-run movements. Put another way, if you only use historical data to estimate future values and invest on the basis of these estimates, you will not experience superior risk-adjusted returns.

INDUSTRY AND COMPANY ANALYSIS WITH EFFICIENT CAPITAL MARKETS

The wide distribution of returns from different industries and companies clearly justifies industry and company analysis. Again, the EMH does not contradict the value of such analyses but implies that you need to (1) understand the relevant variables that affect rates of return, and (2) do a superior job of *estimating* movements in these valuation variables. To demonstrate this, Malkiel and Cragg developed a model that did an excellent job of explaining past stock price movements using historical data. When this model was employed to project *future* stock price changes using *past* company data, however, the results were consistently inferior to a buy-and-hold policy.[118] This implies that, even with a good valuation model, you cannot select stocks using only past data.

Another study showed that the crucial difference between the stocks that enjoyed the best and worst price performance during a given year was the relationship between expected earnings of professional analysts and actual earnings (i.e., it was earning surprises). Specifically, stock prices increased if actual earnings substantially exceeded expected earnings and fell if actual earnings did not reach expected levels.[119] Thus, if you can do a superior job of projecting earnings and your expectations *differ from the consensus,* you will probably have a superior stock selection record.

In the quest to be a superior analyst, there is some good news and some suggestions. The good news is related to the strong-form tests that indicated the likely existence of superior analysts. It was shown that the rankings by Value Line contained information value, even though it might not be possible to profit from it after transactions costs. Also, the price adjustments to the publication of analyst recommendations also points to the existence of superior analysts.

The suggestions for those involved in fundamental analysis are based on the studies that considered the cross-section of future returns. As noted, these studies indicated that E/P ratios, size, and the BV/MV ratios were able to differentiate future return patterns with size and the BV/MV ratio appearing to be the optimal combination. Therefore, these factors should be considered when selecting a universe or analyzing firms. In addition, neglected firms also should be given extra consideration.

HOW TO EVALUATE ANALYSTS OR INVESTORS

If you want to determine if an individual is a superior analyst or investor, you should examine the performance of numerous securities that this analyst or investor recommends over time in relation to the performance of a set of randomly selected stocks of the same risk class. The stock selections of a superior analyst or investor should *consistently* outperform the randomly selected stocks. The consistency requirement is crucial because you would expect a portfolio developed by random selection to outperform the market about half the time.

CONCLUSIONS ABOUT FUNDAMENTAL ANALYSIS

A text on investments can indicate the relevant variables that you should analyze and describe the important techniques, but actually estimating the relevant variables is as much an art and a product of hard work as it is a science. If the estimates could be done

---

[118]Burton G. Malkiel and John G. Cragg, "Expectations and the Structure of Share Prices," *American Economic Review* 60, no. 4 (September 1970): 601–617.

[119]Gary A. Benesh and Pamela P. Peterson, "On the Relation Between Earnings Changes, Analysts' Forecasts and Stock Price Fluctuations," *Financial Analysts Journal* 41, no. 6 (November-December 1986).

on the basis of some mechanical formula, you could program a computer to do it, and there would be no need for analysts. Therefore, the superior analyst or successful investor must understand what variables are relevant to the valuation process and have the ability to do a superior job of *estimating* these variables.

EFFICIENT MARKETS AND PORTFOLIO MANAGEMENT

As noted, a number of studies have indicated that professional money managers cannot beat a buy-and-hold policy on a risk-adjusted basis. One explanation for this generally inferior performance is that there are no superior analysts and the cost of research forces the results of merely adequate analysis into the inferior category. Another explanation, which is favored by the author and has some empirical support from the Value Line and recommendation results, is that money management firms employ both superior and inferior analysts and the gains from the recommendations by the few superior analysts are offset by costs and the poor results due to the recommendations of the inferior analysts.

This raises the question, should a portfolio be managed actively or passively? A portfolio manager with superior analysts or an investor who feels that he or she has the time and expertise to be a superior investor can manage a portfolio actively, looking for undervalued securities and trading accordingly. In contrast, without superior analysts or the time and ability to be a superior investor, you should manage passively and assume that all securities are properly priced based on their levels of risk.

PORTFOLIO MANAGEMENT WITH SUPERIOR ANALYSTS

A portfolio manager with superior analysts who have unique insights and analytical ability should follow their recommendations. The superior analysts should make investment recommendations for a certain proportion of the portfolio, ensuring that the risk preferences of the client are maintained.

Also, the superior analysts should be encouraged to concentrate their efforts in the second tier of stocks. These stocks possess the liquidity required by institutional portfolio managers, but because they do not receive the attention given the top-tier stocks, the markets for these neglected stocks may be less efficient than the market for large well-known stocks.[120]

Recall that capital markets are expected to be efficient because many investors receive new information and analyze its effect on security values. If the number of analysts following a stock differ, one could conceive of differences in the efficiency of the markets. New information on top-tier stocks is well publicized and rigorously analyzed so the price of these securities should adjust rapidly to reflect the new information. In contrast, middle-tier firms receive less publicity and fewer analysts follow these firms, so prices might be expected to adjust less rapidly to new information. Therefore, the possibility of finding temporarily undervalued securities among these neglected stocks are greater. Again, in line with the cross-section study results, these analysts should pay particular attention to neglected firms, to the BV/MV ratio, and to the size of stocks being analyzed.[121]

---

[120]Recall the discussion in Chapter 4 on tiered markets.

[121]The strongest evidence in this regard is contained in Eugene F. Fama and Kenneth French, "The Cross-Section of Expected Stock Returns," *Journal of Finance* 47, no. 2 (June 1992): 427–465.

If you do not have access to superior analysts, your procedure should be as follows. First, you should *measure your risk preferences* or those of your clients. Then build a portfolio to match this risk level by investing a certain proportion of the portfolio in risky assets and the rest in a risk-free asset as discussed in the following two chapters.

You must *completely diversify* the risky asset portfolio on a global basis so it moves consistently with the world market. In this context, proper diversification means eliminating all unsystematic (unique) variability. In our prior discussion, we estimated the number of securities needed to gain most of the benefits (over 90 percent) of a completely diversified portfolio at about 15 to 20 securities. More than 100 stocks are required for complete diversification. To decide how many securities to actually include in your global portfolio, you must balance the added benefits of complete worldwide diversification against the costs of research for the additional stocks.

Finally, you should *minimize transaction costs*. Assuming that the portfolio is completely diversified and is structured for the desired risk level, excessive transaction costs that do not generate added returns will detract from your expected rate of return. Three factors are involved in minimizing total transaction costs.

1. Minimize taxes. Methods of accomplishing this objective vary, but it should receive prime consideration.
2. Reduce trading turnover. You should trade only to liquidate part of the portfolio or to maintain a given risk level.
3. When you trade, minimize liquidity costs by trading relatively liquid stocks. To accomplish this, you should submit limit orders to buy or sell several stocks at prices that approximate the specialist's quote. That is, you would put in limit orders to buy stock at the bid price or sell at the ask price. The stock that is bought or sold first is the most liquid one; all other orders should be withdrawn.

In summary, if you do not have access to superior analysts, you should do the following:

1. Determine and quantify your risk preferences.
2. Construct the appropriate portfolio by dividing the total portfolio between risk-free assets and risky assets.
3. Diversify completely on a global basis to eliminate all unsystematic risk.
4. Maintain the specified risk level by rebalancing when necessary.
5. Minimize total transaction costs.

THE RATIONALE AND USE OF INDEX FUNDS

As the prior discussion indicates, efficient capital markets and a lack of superior analysts imply that many portfolios should be managed so that their performance matches that of the aggregate market, minimizing the costs of research and trading. In response to this desire, several institutions have introduced *market funds,* also referred to as *index funds,* which are security portfolios designed to duplicate the composition, and therefore the performance, of a selected market index series.

Three major investment services started equity index funds in the early 1970s: American National Bank and Trust Company of Chicago; Batterymarch Financial Management Corporation of Boston; and Wells Fargo Investment Advisors, a division of Wells Fargo Bank in San Francisco. All these firms designed equity portfolios to match the performance of the S&P 500 Index. Analysis by the author has documented that the correlation of quarterly rates of return for the index funds and the S&P 500 from 1975 to 1991 exceeded .98. This shows that these index funds generally fulfill their stated goal of matching market performance.

Although these initial funds were only available to institutional investors, there are currently at least five index mutual funds available to individuals. In addition, this concept has been extended to other areas of investments. Index bond funds attempt to emulate the bond-market indexes discussed in Chapter 5 such as the Lehman Brothers bond indexes. Also, there are index funds that focus on specific segments of the market such as international bond index funds and international stock index funds that target specific countries; there are even index funds that target small capitalization stocks in the United States and Japan.[122] The point is, when portfolio managers decide that they want a given asset class in their portfolio to aid diversification, they often look for index funds to fulfill this need for the asset class. The use of index funds as the best way to get representation may be easier and less costly in terms of research and commissions, and it may provide the same or better performance than what is available from specific security selection.

EFFICIENCY IN EUROPEAN EQUITY MARKETS

With rare exception, the discussion in this chapter has been concerned with the efficiency of U.S. markets. The growing importance of world markets raises a natural question about the efficiency of securities markets outside the United States. Numerous studies have dealt with this set of questions, and a discussion of them would substantially lengthen the chapter. Fortunately, a monograph by Hawawini contains a review of numerous studies that examined the behavior of European stock prices and evaluated the efficiency of European equity markets.[123] The monograph lists over 280 studies covering 14 Western European countries from Austria to the United Kingdom classified by country and within each country into five categories:

1. Market model, beta estimation and diversification
2. Capital asset pricing model and arbitrage pricing model
3. Weak-form tests of market efficiency
4. Semistrong-form tests of market efficiency
5. Strong-form tests of market efficiency

Hawawini offers the following overall conclusion after acknowledging that European markets are smaller and less active than U.S. markets.

> Our review of the literature indicates that despite the peculiarities of European equity markets, the behavior of European stock prices is, with few exceptions, surprisingly similar to that of U.S. common stocks. That is true even for countries with extremely narrow equity markets such as Finland. The view that most European equity markets, particularly those of smaller countries, are informationally inefficient does not seem to be borne out by the data. We will see that most of the results of empirical tests performed on European common stock prices are generally in line with those reported by researchers who used U.S. data.

---

[122]For a discussion of some of these indexes, see James A. White, "The Index Boom: It's No Longer Just the S&P 500 Stock Index," *The Wall Street Journal,* May 19, 1991, C1, C3.

[123]Gabriel Hawawini, *European Equity Markets: Price Behavior and Efficiency,* Monograph 1984-4/5, Monograph Series in Finance and Economics, Salomon Brothers Center for the Study of Financial Institutions, Graduate School of Business, New York University, 1984.

This implies that when one considers securities outside the United States, it is appropriate to assume a level of efficiency similar to that for U.S. markets.

SUMMARY

You need to consider the efficiency of capital markets because of the implications of it for your investment analysis and the management of your portfolio. Capital markets should be efficient because numerous rational, profit-maximizing investors react quickly to the release of new information. Assuming prices reflect new information, they are unbiased estimates of the securities' true, intrinsic value, and the relationship between the return on an investment and its risk should be consistent.

The voluminous research on the EMH has been divided into three segments, which have been tested separately. The weak-form EMH states that stock prices fully reflect all market information, so any trading rule that uses past market data to predict future returns should have no value. The results of most studies consistently supported this hypothesis.

The semistrong-form EMH asserts that security prices adjust rapidly to the release of all public information. The tests of this hypothesis either examine the opportunities to predict future rates of return (either a time series or a cross-section), or they involved event studies in which investigators analyzed whether investors could derive above-average returns from trading on the basis of public information. The test results for this hypothesis were clearly mixed. On the one hand, the results for almost all the event studies related to economic events such as stock splits, initial public offerings, and accounting changes consistently support the semistrong hypothesis. In contrast, several studies that examined the ability to predict rates of return on the basis of unexpected quarterly earnings, P/E ratios, size, neglected stocks, and the BV/MV ratio, as well as several calendar effects generally did not support the hypothesis.

The strong-form EMH states that security prices reflect all information. This implies that nobody has private information so no group should be able to derive above-average returns consistently. Studies that examined the results for corporate insiders and stock exchange specialists do not support the strong-form hypothesis. An analysis of individual analysts as represented by Value Line or by recommendations published in the *Wall Street Journal* give mixed results. The results indicated that the Value Line rankings have significant information but it may not be possible to profit from it, whereas the recommendations by analysts indicated the existence of private information. In contrast, the performance by professional money managers supported the EMH because their risk-adjusted investment performance (whether mutual funds, pension funds, or endowment funds) was typically inferior to results achieved with buy-and-hold policies.

The EMH indicates that technical analysis should be of no value. All forms of fundamental analysis are useful, but they are difficult to implement, because they require the ability to *estimate future values* for relevant economic variables. Superior analysis is possible but is very difficult because it requires superior projections. Those who manage portfolios should constantly evaluate investment advice to determine whether it is superior.

Without access to superior analytical advice, you should run your portfolio like an index fund. In contrast, those with superior analytical ability should be allowed to make decisions, but they should concentrate their efforts on middle-tier (smaller) firms and neglected firms, where there is a higher probability of discovering misvalued stocks. In the analysis, there should be particular concern with alternative firms' BV/MV ratio and size.

This chapter contains some good news and some bad news. The good news is that the practice of investment analysis and portfolio management is not an art that has been lost to the great computer in the sky. Viable professions still await those willing to extend the effort and able to accept the pressures. The bad news is that many bright, hardworking people with extensive resources make the game tough. In fact, those competitors have created a fairly efficient capital market in which it is extremely difficult for most analysts and portfolio managers to achieve superior results.

QUESTIONS

1. Discuss the rationale for expecting an efficient capital market.
2. Several factors contribute to an efficient market. What factor would you look for to differentiate the market for two alternative stocks? Specifically, why should the efficiency of the markets for the stocks differ?
3. Define and discuss the weak-form EMH.
4. Describe the two sets of tests used to examine the weak-form EMH.
5. Define and discuss the semistrong-form EMH.
6. Describe the two sets of tests used to examine the semistrong-form EMH.
7. What is meant by the term *abnormal rate of return*?
8. Describe how you would compute the abnormal rate of return for a stock for a period surrounding an economic event. Give a brief example for a stock with a beta of 1.40.
9. When testing the EMH by comparing alternative trading rules to a buy-and-hold policy, there are three common mistakes that can bias the results against the EMH. Discuss each individually and explain why it would cause a bias.
10. Describe the results of a study that supported the semistrong-form EMH. Discuss the nature of the test and specifically why the results support the hypothesis.
11. Describe the results of a study that did *not* support the semistrong-form EMH. Discuss the nature of the test and specifically why the results reported did not support the hypothesis.
12. For many of the EMH tests, it is noted that it is really a test of a "joint hypothesis." Discuss what is meant by this concept and, in this instance, what are the joint hypotheses being tested?
13. Define and discuss the strong-form EMH. Why do some observers contend that the strong-form hypothesis really requires a perfect market in addition to an efficient market? Be specific.
14. Discuss how you would test the strong-form EMH. Why are these tests relevant? Give a brief example.
15. Describe the results of a study that did *not* support the strong-form EMH. Discuss the test involved and specifically why the results reported did not support the hypothesis.
16. Describe the results of a study that supported the strong-form EMH. Discuss the test involved and specifically why these results support the hypothesis.
17. What does the EMH imply for the use of technical analysis?
18. What does the EMH imply for fundamental analysis? Discuss specifically what it does and does not imply.

19. In a world of efficient capital markets, what do you have to do to be a superior analyst? Be specific.

20. How would you test whether an investor or analyst were truly superior?

21. What advice would you give to your superior analysts in terms of the set of firms to analyze and variables that should be considered in the analysis? Discuss your reasoning for this advice.

22. How should a portfolio manager without any superior analysts run his or her portfolio?

23. Describe an index fund. What are its goals?

24. Discuss the contention that index funds are the ultimate answer in a world with efficient capital markets.

25. At a social gathering you meet the portfolio manager for the trust department of a local bank. He confides to you that he has been following the recommendations of the department's six analysts for an extended period and has found that two are superior, two are average, and two are clearly inferior. What would you recommend that he do to run his portfolio?

26. Discuss whether you were surprised by Hawawini's summary of findings related to the EMH for the European equity markets.

27. Describe a test of the weak-form EMH for the Japanese stock market and indicate where you would get the required data.

PROBLEMS

1. Compute the abnormal rates of return for the following stocks during period t (ignore differential systematic risk):

Stock	R_{it}	R_{mt}
B	11.5%	4.0%
F	10.0	8.5
T	14.0	9.6
C	12.0	15.3
E	15.9	12.4

R_{it} = return for stock i during period t

R_{mt} = return for the aggregate market during period t

2. Compute the abnormal rates of return for the five stocks in Problem 1 assuming the following systematic risk measures (betas):

Stock	i
B	0.95
F	1.25
T	1.45
C	0.75
E	−0.30

3. Compare the abnormal returns in Problems 1 and 2 and discuss the reason for the difference in each case.

4. You are given the following data regarding the performance of a group of stocks recommended by an analyst and set of stocks with matching betas.

Stock	Beginning Price	Ending Price	Dividend
C	43	47	1.50
C-match	22	24	1.00
R	75	73	2.00
R-match	42	38	1.00
L	28	34	1.25
L-match	18	16	1.00
W	52	57	2.00
W-match	38	44	1.50
S	63	68	1.75
S-match	32	34	1.00

Based on the composite results for these stocks (assume equal weights), would you judge this individual to be a superior analyst? Discuss your reasoning.

5. Look up the daily trading volume for the following stocks during a recent 5-day period.

- Abbott Labs
- Anheuser Busch
- Chrysler
- McDonalds
- General Electric

Randomly select five stocks from the NYSE and examine their daily trading volume for the same 5 days.
   a. What are the average daily volumes for the two samples?
   b. Would you expect this difference to have an impact on the efficiency of the markets for the two samples? Why or why not?

REFERENCES

Affleck-Graves, John, and Richard R. Mendenhall. "The Relation Between the Value Line Enigma and Post-Earnings-Announcement Drift." *Journal of Financial Economics* 21, no. 1 (February 1992).

Ariel, Robert A. "A Monthly Effect in Stock Returns." *Journal of Financial Economics* 18, no. 1 (March 1987).

Ball, Ray. "Anomalies in Relationships Between Securities' Yield and Yield-Surrogates." *Journal of Financial Economics* 6, no. 2/3 (June-September 1978).

Balvers, Ronald J., Thomas F. Cosimano, and Bill McDonald. "Predicting Stock Returns in an Efficient Market." *Journal of Finance* 45, no. 4 (September 1990).

Banz, R. W. "The Relationship Between Return and Market Value of Common Stocks." *Journal of Financial Economics* 9, no. 1 (March 1981).

Barry, Christopher B., and Stephen J. Brown, "Differential Information and the Small Firm Effect." *Journal of Financial Economics* 13, no. 2 (June 1984).

Basu, Senjoy. "Investment Performance of Common Stocks in Relation to Their Price-Earnings Ratios: A Test of the Efficient Market Hypothesis." *Journal of Finance* 32, no. 3 (June 1977).

Basu, Senjoy. "The Relationship Between Earnings Yield, Market Value and Return for NYSE Common Stocks." *Journal of Financial Economics* 12, no. 1 (June 1983).

Beatty, Randolph, and Jay Ritter. "Investments Banking, Reputation, and the Underpricing of Initial Public Offerings." *Journal of Financial Economics* 15, no. 1 (March 1986).

Berkowitz, Stephen A., Louis D. Finney, and Dennis Logue. *The Investment Performance of Corporate Pension Plans.* New York: Quorum Books, 1988.

Bernard, Victor L., and Jacob K. Thomas. "Post-Earnings-Announcements Drift: Delayed Price Response or Risk Premium?" *Journal of Accounting Research* 27, Supplement (1989).

Fama, Eugene F. "Efficient Capital Markets: A Review of Theory and Empirical Work." *Journal of Finance* 25, no. 2 (May 1970).

Fama, Eugene F. "Efficient Capital Market: II." *Journal of Finance* 46, no. 5 (December 1991).

Fama, Eugene F., L. Fisher, M. Jensen, and R. Roll. "The Adjustment of Stock Prices to New Information." *International Economic Review* 10, no. 1 (February 1969).

Fama, Eugene F., and Kenneth R. French. "The Cross-Section of Expected Stock Returns." *Journal of Finance* 47, no. 2 (June 1992).

Foster, George, Chris Olsen, and Terry Shevlin. "Earnings Releases, Anomalies, and the Behavior of Security Returns." *Accounting Review* 59, no. 4 (October 1984).

French, Kenneth R. "Stock Returns and the Weekend Effect." *Journal of Financial Economics* 8, no. 1 (March 1980).

Harvey, Campbell. "The World Price of Covariance Risk." *Journal of Finance* 46, no. 1 (March 1991).

Hawawini, Gabriel. *European Equity Markets: Price Behavior and Efficiency,* Monograph 1984-4/5. Monograph Series in Finance and Economics, Salomon Brothers Center for the Study of Financial Institutions, Graduate School of Business, New York University, 1984.

Henriksson, Roy T. "Market Timing and Mutual Fund Performance: An Empirical Investigation." *Journal of Business* 57, no. 1 Part 1 (January 1984).

Huberman, Gur, and Shmuel Kandel. "Market Efficiency and Value Line's Record." *Journal of Business* 63, no. 2 (April 1990).

Ibbotson, Roger G., Judy Sindelar, and Jay R. Ritter. "Initial Public Offerings." *Journal of Applied Corporate Finance* 1, no. 3 (Summer 1988).

Jain, Prom C. "Response of Hourly Stock Prices and Trading Volume to Economic News," *Journal of Business* 61, no. 2 (April 1988).

Keim, Donald B. "The CAPM and Equity Return Regularities." *Financial Analysts Journal* 41, no. 3 (May-June 1986).

Keim, Donald B. "Dividend Yields and Stock Returns: Implications of Abnormal January Returns." *Journal of Financial Economics* 14, no. 3 (September 1985).

Keim, Donald B. "Size-Related Anomalies and Stock Return Seasonality." *Journal of Financial Economics* 12, no. 1 (June 1983).

Keim, Donald B., and Robert F. Stambaugh. "Predicting Returns in Stock and Bond Markets." *Journal of Financial Economics* 17, no. 2 (December 1986).

Lakonishok, Josef, and Seymour Smidt. "Volume and Turn-of-the-Year Behavior." *Journal of Financial Economics* 13, no. 3 (September 1984).

Latané, H. A., and Charles Jones. "Standardized Unexpected Earnings: 1971–1977." *Journal of Finance* 34, no. 3 (June 1979).

Lorie, James H., Peter Dodd, and Mary Hamilton Kimpton. *The Stock Market: Theories and Evidence.* 2d ed. Homewood, Ill.: Richard D. Irwin, 1985.

Malkiel, Burton G. *A Random Walk Down Wall Street.* New York: W. W. Norton, 1990.

Miller, Robert E., and Frank K. Reilly. "Examination of Mispricing, Returns, and Uncertainty for Initial Public Offerings." *Financial Management* 16, no. 2 (January 1987).

Peterson, David R. "Security Price Reactions to Initial Reviews of Common Stock by the Value Line Investment Survey." *Journal of Financial and Quantitative Analysis* 22, no. 4 (December 1987).

Reilly, Frank K., and Eugene F. Drzycimski. "Short-Run Profits from Stock Splits." *Financial Management* 10, no. 3 (Summer 1981).

Reinganum, Marc R. "Misspecification of Capital Asset Pricing: Empirical Anomalies Based on Earnings Yield and Market Values." *Journal of Financial Economics* 9, no. 1 (March 1981).

Reinganum, Marc R. "A Revival of the Small Firm Effect," *Journal of Portfolio Management* 18, no. 3 (Spring 1992).

Rendlemen, Richard J., Charles P. Jones, and Henry A. Latané, "Empirical Anomalies Based on Unexpected Earnings and the Importance of Risk Adjustments." *Journal of Financial Economics* 10, no. 3 (November 1982).

Seyhun, H. Nejat. "Insider Profits, Costs of Trading, and Market Efficiency." *Journal of Financial Economics* 16, no. 2 (June 1986).

Smirlock, Michael, and Laura Stacks. "Day-of-the-Week and Intraday Effects in Stock Returns." *Journal of Financial Economics* 17, no. 1 (September 1986).

Watts, Ross L. "Systematic 'Abnormal' Returns After Quarterly Earnings Announcements." *Journal of Financial Economics* 6, no. 2/3 (June-September 1978).

CHAPTER 7

AN INTRODUCTION TO PORTFOLIO MANAGEMENT

In this chapter, we will answer the following questions:

- What is meant by risk aversion and what evidence is there that investors are generally risk averse?
- What are the basic assumptions behind the Markowitz portfolio theory?
- What is meant by risk and what are some of the alternative measures of risk used in investments?
- How do you compute the expected rate of return for an individual risky asset or a portfolio of assets?
- How do you compute the standard deviation of rates of return for an individual risky asset?
- What is meant by the covariance between rates of return and how do you compute covariance?
- What is the relationship between covariance and correlation?
- What is the formula for the standard deviation for a portfolio of risky assets and how does it differ from the standard deviation of an individual risky asset?
- What happens to the standard deviation of a portfolio when you change the correlation between the assets in the portfolio?
- What is the efficient frontier?
- Is it reasonable for investors to select different portfolios from those on the efficient frontier?
- What determines which portfolio on the efficient frontier is selected by an investor?

One of the major advances in the investment field over the past couple of decades has been the explicit recognition that the creation of an optimum investment portfolio is not simply a matter of combining a lot of unique individual securities that have desirable risk–return characteristics. Specifically, it has been shown that you must consider the relationship *among* the investments if you are going to build the optimum portfolio that will meet your investment objectives. The recognition of what is important in creating a portfolio was demonstrated in the derivation of portfolio theory.

Hence, this chapter explains portfolio theory step by step. This involves introducing you to the basic portfolio risk formula that you must understand when you are combining different assets. When you understand this formula and its implications, you will increase your understanding of not only why you should diversify your portfolio, but also *how* you should diversify. The subsequent chapter introduces asset pricing models and capital market theory with an emphasis on the risk measure for individual assets.

SOME
BACKGROUND
ASSUMPTIONS

Prior to the presentation of portfolio theory, we need to clarify some general assumptions of the theory. This includes not only what is meant by an *optimum portfolio,* but also what is meant by the terms *risk aversion* and *risk.* Therefore, these concepts are considered in this section before the presentation of portfolio theory.

One basic assumption of portfolio theory is that as an investor, you want to maximize the returns from your investments for a given level of risk. To adequately deal with such an assumption, certain ground rules must be laid. First, your portfolio should *include all of your assets and liabilities,* not only your stocks or even your marketable securities, but also such items as your car, house, and less marketable investments such as coins, stamps, art, antiques, and furniture. The full spectrum of investments must be considered because the returns from all these investments interact, and *this relationship between the returns for assets in the portfolio is important.* Hence, a good portfolio is *not* simply a collection of individually good investments.

RISK AVERSION

Portfolio theory also assumes that investors are basically *risk averse,* meaning that, given a choice between two assets with equal rates of return, they will select the asset with the lower level of risk. Evidence that most investors are risk averse is that they purchase various types of insurance, including life insurance, car insurance, and health insurance. Buying insurance basically involves a current certain outlay of a given amount to guard against an uncertain, possibly larger outlay in the future. When you buy insurance, this implies that you are willing to pay the current known cost of the insurance policy to avoid the uncertainty of a potentially large future cost related to a car accident or a major illness. Further evidence of risk aversion is the difference in promised yield (the required rate of return) for different grades of bonds that supposedly have different degrees of credit risk. As you might know from reading about corporate bonds, the promised yield on bonds increases as you go from AAA (the lowest risk class) to AA to A, and so on. This increase in yields means that investors require a higher rate of return in order to accept higher risk.

The foregoing does not imply that everybody is risk averse, or that investors are completely risk averse regarding all financial commitments. The fact is, not everybody buys insurance for everything. Some people have no insurance against anything, either by choice or because they cannot afford it. In addition, some individuals buy insurance related to some risks such as auto accidents and illness, but they also buy lottery tickets and gamble at race tracks or in Las Vegas, where it is known that the expected returns are negative, which means that participants are willing to pay for the excitement of the risk involved. This combination of risk preference and risk aversion can be explained by an attitude toward risk that is not completely risk averse or risk preferring, but is a combination of the two that depends on the amount of money involved. Friedman and Savage speculate that this is the case for people who like to gamble for small amounts (in lotteries or nickel slot machines), but buy insurance to protect themselves against large losses such as fire or accidents.[1]

While recognizing such attitudes, our basic assumption is that most investors committing large sums of money to developing an investment portfolio are risk averse. Therefore, we expect a positive relationship between expected return and expected risk.

DEFINITION OF RISK

Although there is a difference in the specific definitions of *risk* and *uncertainty,* for our purposes and in most financial literature the two terms are used interchangeably. In fact, one way to define risk is as *the uncertainty of future outcomes.* An alternative definition might be *the probability of an adverse outcome.* Subsequently in our discussion of portfolio theory, we will consider several measures of risk that are used when developing the theory.

MARKOWITZ PORTFOLIO THEORY

In the 1950s and early 1960s the investment community talked about risk, but there was no specific measure for the term. To build a portfolio model, however, investors had to quantify their risk variable. The basic portfolio model was developed by Harry Markowitz, who derived the expected rate of return for a portfolio of assets and an expected risk measure.[2] Markowitz showed that the variance of the rate of return was a meaningful measure of portfolio risk under a reasonable set of assumptions, and he derived the formulas for computing the variance of a portfolio. This formula for the variance of a portfolio not only indicated the importance of diversifying your investments to reduce the total risk of a portfolio, but also showed *how* to effectively diversify. The Markowitz model is based on several assumptions regarding investor behavior:

1. Investors consider each investment alternative as being represented by a probability distribution of expected returns over some holding period.
2. Investors maximize one-period expected utility, and their utility curves demonstrate diminishing marginal utility of wealth.
3. Investors estimate the risk of the portfolio on the basis of the variability of expected returns.
4. Investors base decisions solely on expected return and risk, so their utility curves are a function of expected return and the expected variance (or standard deviation) of returns only.
5. For a given risk level, investors prefer higher returns to lower returns. Similarly, for a given level of expected return, investors prefer less risk to more risk.

Under these assumptions, *a single asset or portfolio of assets is considered to be efficient if no other asset or portfolio of assets offers higher expected return with the same (or lower) risk, or lower risk with the same (or higher) expected return.*

---

[1]Milton Friedman and Leonard J. Savage, "The Utility Analysis of Choices Involving Risk," *Journal of Political Economy* 56, no. 3 (August 1948): 279–304.

[2]Harry Markowitz, "Portfolio Selection," *Journal of Finance* 7, no. 1 (March 1952): 77–91; and Harry Markowitz, *Portfolio Selection—Efficient Diversification of Investments* (New York: John Wiley & Sons, 1959).

ALTERNATIVE
MEASURES OF
RISK

One of the best-known measures of risk is the *variance,* or *standard deviation of expected returns.*[3] It is a statistical measure of the dispersion of returns around the expected value whereby a larger variance or standard deviation indicates greater dispersion, all other factors being equal. The idea is that the more disperse the expected returns, the greater the uncertainty of those returns in any future period.

Another measure of risk is the *range of returns.* In this case, it is assumed that a larger range of expected returns, from the lowest to the highest, means greater uncertainty and risk regarding future expected returns.

Instead of using measures that analyze all deviations from expectations, some observers believe that when you invest you should be concerned only with *returns below expectations,* which means that you only consider deviations below the mean value. A measure that only considers deviations below the mean is the *semivariance.* An extension of the semivariance measure only computes expected returns *below zero,* or negative returns. Both of these measures of risk implicitly assume that investors want to *minimize the damage* from below-average returns. Obviously, it is assumed that investors would welcome positive returns or returns above expectations, so these are not considered when measuring risk.

Although there are numerous potential measures of risk, we will use the variance or standard deviation of returns, because (1) this measure is somewhat intuitive, (2) it is a correct and widely recognized risk measure, and (3) it has been used in most of the theoretical asset pricing models.

EXPECTED RATES
OF RETURN

The expected rate of return for *an individual investment* is computed as shown in Table 7.1. The expected return for an individual risky asset with the set of potential returns and an assumption of equal probabilities used in the example would be 11 percent.

The expected rate of return for a *portfolio* of investments is simply the weighted average of the expected rates of return for the individual investments in the portfolio. The weights are the proportion of total value for the investment.

The expected return for a hypothetical portfolio with four risky assets is shown in Table 7.2. The expected return for this portfolio of investments would be 11.5 percent. The effect of adding or dropping any investment from the portfolio would be easy to determine because you would use the new weights based on value and the expected returns for each of the investments. This computation of the expected return for the portfolio [$E(R_{port})$] can be generalized as follows:

$$E(R_{port}) = \sum_{i=1}^{n} W_i R_i$$

where:

W_i = **the percent of the portfolio in asset** *i*

R_i = **the expected rate of return for asset** *i.*

---

[3]We consider the variance and standard deviation as one measure of risk because the standard deviation is the square root of the variance.

TABLE 7.1

Computation of Expected Return for an Individual Risky Asset

Probability	Potential Return (%)	Expected Return (%)
.25	.08	.0200
.25	.10	.0250
.25	.12	.0300
.25	.14	.0350
		$E(R) = .1100$

TABLE 7.2

Computation of the Expected Return for a Portfolio of Risky Assets

Weight (W_i) (Percent of Portfolio)	Expected Security Return (R_i)	Expected Portfolio Return ($W_i \times R_i$)
.20	.10	.0200
.30	.11	.0330
.30	.12	.0360
.20	.13	.0260
		$E(R_{port}) = .1150$

VARIANCE (STANDARD DEVIATION) OF RETURNS FOR AN INDIVIDUAL INVESTMENT

As noted, we will be using the variance or the standard deviation of returns as the measure of risk (recall that the standard deviation is the square root of the variance). Therefore, at this point, we will demonstrate how you would compute the standard deviation of returns for an individual investment. Subsequently, after discussing some other statistical concepts, we will consider the determination of the standard deviation for a *portfolio* of investments.

The variance, or standard deviation, is a measure of the variation of possible rates of return, R_i, from the expected rate of return [$E(R_i)$], as follows:

$$\text{Variance} (\sigma^2) = \sum_{i=1}^{n} [R_i - E(R_i)]^2 P_i.$$

where P_i is the probability of the possible rate of return, R_i.

$$\text{Standard Deviation} (\sigma) = \sqrt{\sum_{i=1}^{n} [R_i - E(R_i)]^2 P_i}.$$

The computation of the variance and standard deviation of returns for the individual risky asset in Table 7.1 is set forth in Table 7.3.

TABLE 7.3

Computation of the Variance for an Individual Risky Asset

Potential Return (R_i)	Expected Return $E(R_i)$	$R_i - E(R_i)$	$[R_i - E(R_i)]^2$	P_i	$(R_i - E(R_i))^2 P_i$
.08	.11	−.03	.0009	.25	.000225
.10	.11	−.01	.0001	.25	.000025
.12	.11	.01	.0001	.25	.000025
.14	.11	.03	.0009	.25	.000225
					.000500

Variance (σ^2) = .00050
Standard Deviation (σ) = .02236

VARIANCE (STANDARD DEVIATION) OF RETURNS FOR A PORTFOLIO

Two basic concepts in statistics, covariance and correlation, must be understood before we discuss the formula for the variance of the rate of return for a portfolio.

COVARIANCE OF RETURNS

In this subsection we discuss what the covariance of returns is intended to measure, give the formula for computing it, and present an example of the computation. *Covariance* is a measure of the degree to which two variables "move together" over time. In portfolio analysis, we usually are concerned with the covariance of *rates of return* rather than prices or some other variable.[4] A positive covariance means that the rates of return for two investments tend to move in the same direction during the same time period. In contrast, a negative covariance indicates that the rates of return for two investments tend to move in different directions during specified time intervals over time. The *magnitude* of the covariance depends on the variances of the individual return series, as well as on the relationship between the series.

Table 7.4 contains the monthly closing prices and dividends for Avon and IBM. You can use this data to compute monthly rates of return for these two stocks during 1991. Figures 7.1 and 7.2 contain a time-series plot of the monthly rates of return for the two stocks during 1991. Although the rates of return for the two stocks moved together during some months, in other months they moved in opposite directions. The covariance statistic provides an *absolute* measure of how they moved together over time.

For two assets, i and j, the covariance of rates of return is defined as

$$Cov_{ij} = E\{[R_i - E(R_i)][R_j - E(R_j)]\}.$$

---

[4]Returns, of course, can be measured in a variety of ways, depending on the type of asset being considered. You will recall that we defined returns (R_i) in Chapter 1 as:

$$R_i = \frac{EV - BV + CF}{BV}$$

where EV is ending value, BV is beginning value, and CF is the cash flow during the period.

TABLE 7.4   **Computation of Monthly Rates of Return**

	Avon			IBM		
Date	Closing Price	Dividend	Rate of Return (%)	Closing Price	Dividend	Rate of Return (%)
12/90	29.375			113.000		
1/91	33.750		14.89	126.750		12.17
2/91	41.750		23.70	128.750		1.58
3/91	44.375	0.35	7.13	113.875	1.21	−10.61
4/91	45.125		1.69	103.000		−9.55
5/91	44.125		−2.22	106.125		3.03
6/91	42.500	0.35	−2.89	97.125	1.21	−7.34
7/91	46.500		9.41	101.250		4.25
8/91	45.375		−2.42	96.875		−4.32
9/91	44.500	0.35	−1.16	103.625	1.21	8.22
10/91	41.000		−7.87	98.250		−5.19
11/91	38.875		−5.18	92.250		−6.11
12/91	46.000	0.35	19.23	89.000	1.21	−2.21
			$E(R_{AVON}) = 4.53$			$E(R_{IBM}) = -1.34$

FIGURE 7.1   **Time-Series Returns for Avon: 1991**

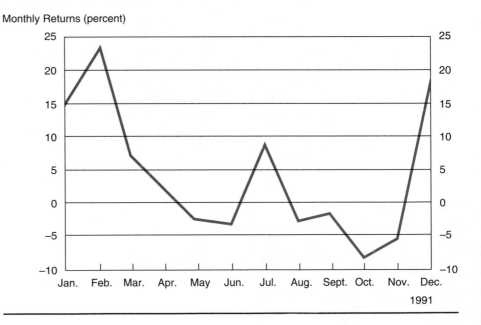

Monthly Returns (percent)

FIGURE 7.2   **Time-Series Returns for IBM: 1991**

Monthly Returns (percent)

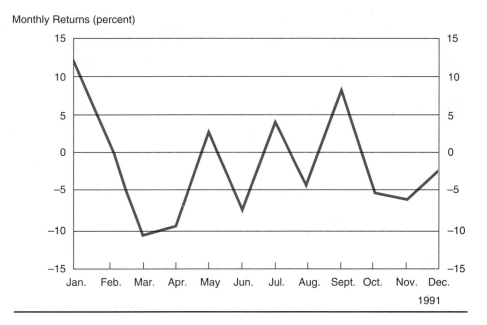

1991

When we apply this formula to the monthly rates of return for Avon and IBM during 1991, it becomes:

$$\frac{1}{12} \sum_{i=1}^{12} [R_i - E(R_i)][R_j - E(R_j)].$$

As can be seen, if the rates of return for one stock are above (below) its mean rate of return during a given period, and the returns for the other stock are likewise above (below) its mean rate of return during this same period, then the *product* of these deviations from the mean is positive. If this happens consistently, the covariance of returns between these two stocks will be some large positive value. If, however, the rate of return for one of the securities is above its mean return while the return on the other security is below its mean return, the product will be negative. If this contrary movement happened consistently, the covariance between the rates of return for the two stocks would be a large negative value.

Table 7.5 contains the monthly rates of return during 1991 for Avon and IBM as computed in Table 7.4. One might expect the returns for the two stocks to have reasonably low covariance because of the differences in the products of these firms (cosmetics and computers). The expected returns $E(R)$ were the arithmetic mean of the monthly returns:

TABLE 7.5		Computation of Covariance of Returns for Avon and IBM: 1991				
	Monthly Return (%)		**Avon**	**IBM**	**Avon**	**IBM**
Date	**Avon (R_i)**	**IBM (R_j)**	$R_i - E(R_i)$	$R_j - E(R_j)$		$[R_i - E(R_i)] \times [R_j - E(R_j)]$
1/91	14.89	12.17	10.36	13.51		140.010
2/91	23.70	1.58	19.17	2.92		55.995
3/91	7.13	−10.61	2.60	−9.27		−24.129
4/91	1.69	−9.55	−2.84	−8.21		23.290
5/91	−2.22	3.03	−6.75	4.37		−29.488
6/91	−2.89	−7.34	−7.42	−6.00		44.498
7/91	9.41	4.25	4.88	5.59		27.299
8/91	−2.42	−4.32	−6.95	−2.98		20.698
9/91	−1.16	8.22	−5.69	9.56		−54.370
10/91	−7.87	−5.19	−12.40	−3.85		47.722
11/91	−5.18	−6.11	−9.71	−4.77		46.297
12/91	19.23	−2.21	14.70	−0.87		−12.784
	$E(R) = $ 4.53	$E(R) = $ −1.34				Sum = 285.038

$$Cov_{ij} = \frac{1}{12} \times 285.038 = 23.75$$

$$E(R_i) = \frac{1}{12} \sum_{i=1}^{12} R_{it}$$

and

$$E(R_j) = \frac{1}{12} \sum_{j=1}^{12} R_{jt}.$$

All figures (except those in the last column) were rounded to the nearest hundreth of 1 percent. As shown in Table 7.4, the average monthly return was 4.53 percent for Avon and −1.34 percent for IBM stock. The results in Table 7.5 show that the covariance between the rates of return for these two stocks was:

$$Cov_{ij} = \frac{1}{12} \times 285.038$$
$$= 23.75.$$

Interpretation of a number like 23.75 is difficult; is it high or low for covariance? We know the relationship between the two stocks is generally positive, but it is not possible to be more specific. Figure 7.3 contains a scatter diagram with paired values of R_{it} and R_{jt} plotted against each other. This plot demonstrates the linear nature and strength of the relationship and shows several instances during 1991 when IBM experienced negative returns when Avon had positive rates of return.

COVARIANCE AND CORRELATION
Covariance is affected by the variability of the two individual return series. Therefore, a number such as the 23.75 in our example might indicate a weak positive relationship if the two individual series were very volatile, but would reflect a strong positive rela-

FIGURE 7.3   **Scatter Plot of Monthly Returns for Avon and IBM: 1991**

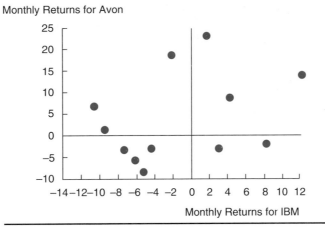

tionship if the two series were very stable. Obviously, you want to "standardize" this covariance measure taking into consideration the variability of the two individual return series, as follows:

$$r_{ij} = \frac{Cov_{ij}}{\sigma_i \sigma_j}$$

where:

r_{ij} = **the correlation coefficient of returns**

σ_i = **the standard deviation of** R_{it}

σ_j = **the standard deviation of** R_{jt}.

Standardizing the covariance by the individual standard deviations yields the *correlation coefficient* (r_{ij}), which can vary only in the range -1 to $+1$. A value of $+1$ would indicate a perfect positive linear relationship between R_i and R_j, meaning the returns for the two stocks move together in a completely linear manner. A value of -1 means that there is a perfect negative relationship between the two return series such that when one stock's rate of return is above its mean, the other stock's rate of return will be below its mean by the comparable amount.

To calculate this standardized measure of the relationship, you need to compute the standard deviation for the two individual return series. We already have the values for $R_{it} - E(R_i)$ and $R_{jt} - E(R_j)$ in Table 7.5. We can square each of these values and sum them as shown in Table 7.6 to calculate the variance of each return series.

$$\sigma_i^2 = \frac{1}{12}(1158.89) = 96.57$$

TABLE 7.6

Computation of Standard Deviation of Returns for Avon and IBM

	Avon		IBM	
Date	$R_i - E(R_i)$	$[R_i - E(R_i)]^2$	$R_j - E(R_j)$	$[R_j - E(R_j)]^2$
1/91	10.36	107.33	13.51	182.52
2/91	19.17	367.49	2.92	8.53
3/91	2.60	6.76	−9.27	85.93
4/91	−2.84	8.07	−8.21	67.40
5/91	−6.75	45.56	4.37	19.10
6/91	−7.42	55.06	−6.00	36.00
7/91	4.88	23.81	5.59	31.25
8/91	−6.95	48.30	−2.98	8.88
9/91	−5.69	32.38	9.56	91.39
10/91	−12.40	153.76	−3.85	14.82
11/91	−9.71	94.28	−4.77	22.75
12/91	14.70	216.09	−0.87	0.76
Sums		1158.89		569.33

$$\sigma^2_{avon} = \frac{1158.89}{12} = 96.57 \qquad \sigma^2_{IBM} = \frac{569.33}{12} = 47.44$$

$$\sigma_{avon} = \sqrt{96.57} = 9.83 \qquad \sigma_{IBM} = \sqrt{47.44} = 6.89$$

and

$$\sigma^2_j = \frac{1}{12}(569.33) = 47.44.$$

The standard deviation for each series is the square root of the variance for each, as follows:

$$\sigma_i = \sqrt{96.57} = 9.83$$
$$\sigma_j = \sqrt{47.44} = 6.89.$$

Thus, based on the covariance between the two series and the individual standard deviations, we can calculate the correlation coefficient between returns for Avon and IBM as

$$r_{ij} = \frac{Cov_{ij}}{\sigma_i\sigma_j} = \frac{23.75}{(9.83)(6.89)} = \frac{23.75}{67.73} = 0.35.$$

STANDARD
DEVIATION OF A
PORTFOLIO

As noted, a correlation of +1.0 would indicate perfect positive correlation, and a value of −1.0 would mean that the returns moved in a completely opposite direction. A value of zero would mean that the returns had no linear relationship, that is, they were uncorrelated statistically. That does *not* mean that they are independent. The value of $r_{ij} = .35$ is significant but not very high. This is not unusual for stocks in diverse industries. Correlations between stocks *within* some industries approach 0.85.

PORTFOLIO STANDARD DEVIATION FORMULA

Now that we have discussed the concepts of covariance and correlation, we can consider the formula for computing the standard deviation of returns for a *portfolio* of assets, our measure of risk for a portfolio. As noted, Harry Markowitz derived the formula for computing the standard deviation of a portfolio of assets.[5]

In Table 7.2 we showed that the expected rate of return of the portfolio was the weighted average of the expected returns for the individual assets in the portfolio; the weights were the percentage of value of the portfolio. Under such conditions, we can easily see the impact on the portfolio's expected return of adding or deleting an asset.

One might assume that it is possible to derive the standard deviation of the portfolio in the same manner, that is, by computing the weighted average of the standard deviations for the individual assets. This would be a mistake. Markowitz derived the general formula for the standard deviation of a portfolio as follows:[6]

$$\sigma_{port} = \sqrt{\sum_{i=1}^{N} W_i^2\, \sigma_i^2 + \sum_{\substack{i=1 \\ }}^{N} \sum_{\substack{j=1 \\ i \neq j}}^{N} W_i W_j Cov_{ij}}$$

where:

σ_{port} = **the standard deviation of the portfolio**

W_i = **the weights of the individual assets in the portfolio, where weights are determined by the proportion of value in the portfolio**

σ_i^2 = **the variance of asset** i

Cov_{ij} = **the covariance between the returns for assets** i **and** j.

Stated in words, this formula indicates that the standard deviation for a portfolio of assets is a function of the weighted average of the individual variances (where the weights are squared), *plus* the weighted covariances between all the assets in the portfolio. The point is, the standard deviation for a portfolio of assets encompasses not only the variances of the individual assets, but *also* the covariances between pairs of individual assets in the portfolio. Further, it can be shown that, in a portfolio with a large number of securities, this formula reduces to the sum of the weighted covariances.

Although the subsequent demonstration will consider portfolios with only two assets, it is important at this point to consider what happens in a large portfolio with many assets. Specifically, what happens when you add a new security to such a portfolio? As shown by the formula, there are two effects. The first is the asset's own variance of returns, and the second is the covariance between the returns of this new asset and the returns of every other asset that is already in the portfolio. The point is,

---

[5]Markowitz, *Portfolio Selection.*

[6]For the detailed derivation of this formula, see Markowitz, *Portfolio Selection.*

the relative weight of these numerous covariances is substantially greater than the asset's unique variance and the more assets in the portfolio, the more this is true. This means that the important factor to consider when adding an investment to a portfolio that contains a number of other investments is *not* the investment's own variance, but *its average covariance with all the other investments in the portfolio.*

In the following examples we will consider the simple case of a two-asset portfolio. We do these relatively simple calculations with two assets to demonstrate the impact of different covariances on the total risk (standard deviation) of the portfolio.

DEMONSTRATION OF THE PORTFOLIO STANDARD DEVIATION CALCULATION

Because of the assumptions used in developing the Markowitz portfolio model, any asset or portfolio of assets can be described by two characteristics: the expected rate of return and the expected standard deviation of returns. Therefore, the following demonstrations can be applied to two *individual* assets with the indicated return-standard deviation characteristics and correlation coefficients, or to two *portfolios* of assets with the indicated return-standard deviation characteristics and correlation coefficients.

EQUAL RISK AND RETURN—CHANGING CORRELATIONS   Consider first the case in which both assets have the same expected return and expected standard deviation of return. As an example, let us assume

$$E(R_1) = .20$$
$$E(\sigma_1) = .10$$
$$E(R_2) = .20$$
$$E(\sigma_2) = .10.$$

To show the effect of different covariances, assume different levels of correlation between the two assets. Consider the following examples where the two assets have equal weights in the portfolio ($W_1 = .50$; $W_2 = .50$). Therefore, the only value that changes in each example is the correlation between the returns for the two assets.

Recall that

$$Cov_{ij} = r_{ij}\sigma_i\sigma_j$$

Consider the following alternative correlation coefficients and the covariances they yield. The covariance will be equal to $r_{1,2}(.10)(.10)$, because both standard deviations are 0.10.

a. $r_{1,2} = 1.00\ Cov_{1,2} = (1.00)(.10)(.10) = .01$
b. $r_{1,2} = .50\ Cov_{1,2} = .005$
c. $r_{1,2} = .00\ Cov_{1,2} = .000$
d. $r_{1,2} = -.50\ Cov_{1,2} = -.005$
e. $r_{1,2} = -1.00\ Cov_{1,2} = -.01.$

Now let us see what happens to the standard deviation of the portfolio under these five conditions. Recall that

$$\sigma_{port} = \sqrt{\sum_{i=1}^{N} W_i^2 \, \sigma_i^2 + \sum_{i=1}^{N} \sum_{\substack{j=1 \\ i \neq j}}^{N} W_i W_j Cov_{ij}}.$$

When this general formula is applied to a two-asset portfolio, it is

$$\sigma_{port} = \sqrt{W_1^2 \, \sigma_1^2 + W_2^2 \, \sigma_2^2 + 2W_1 W_2 r_{1,2}\sigma_1 \sigma_2}$$

or

$$\sigma_{port} = \sqrt{W_1^2 \, \sigma_1^2 + W_2^2 \, \sigma_2^2 + 2W_1 W_2 Cov_{1,2}}.$$

Thus, in Case a,

$$\begin{aligned}
\sigma_{port \, (a)} &= \sqrt{(0.5)^2(0.10)^2 + (0.5)^2(0.10)^2 + 2(0.5)(0.5)(0.01)} \\
&= \sqrt{(0.25)(0.01) + (0.25)(0.01) + 2(0.25)(0.01)} \\
&= \sqrt{0.01} \\
&= 0.10.
\end{aligned}$$

In this case where the returns for the two assets are perfectly positively correlated, the standard deviation for the portfolio is, in fact, the weighted average of the individual standard deviations. The important point is, we get no real benefit from combining two assets that are perfectly correlated; they are like one asset already because their returns move together.

Now consider Case b, where $r_{1,2}$ equals 0.50.

$$\begin{aligned}
\sigma_{port \, (b)} &= \sqrt{(0.5)^2(0.10)^2 + (0.5)^2(0.10)^2 + 2(0.5)(0.5)(0.005)} \\
&= \sqrt{(0.0025) + (0.0025) + 2(0.50)(0.005)} \\
&= \sqrt{0.0075} \\
&= 0.0866
\end{aligned}$$

The only term that changed from Case a is the last term, $Cov_{1,2}$, which changed from 0.01 to 0.005. As a result, the standard deviation of the portfolio declined by about 13 percent, from 0.10 to 0.0866. Note that *the expected return did not change,* because it is simply the weighted average of the individual expected returns; it is equal to 0.20 in both cases.

You should be able to confirm through your own calculations that the standard deviations for Portfolios c and d are as follows:

c. .0707
d. .05.

FIGURE 7.4   **Time Patterns of Returns for Two Assets with Perfect Negative Correlation**

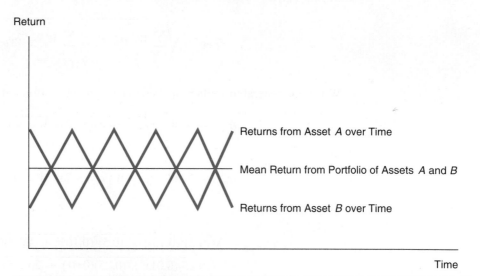

The final case where the correlation between the two assets is -1.00 indicates the ultimate benefits of diversification.

$$\sigma_{port\,(e)} = \sqrt{(0.5)^2(0.10)^2 + (0.5)^2(0.10)^2 + 2(0.5)(0.5)(-0.01)}$$
$$= \sqrt{(0.0050) + (-0.0050)}$$
$$= \sqrt{0}$$
$$= 0.$$

Here, the covariance term exactly offsets the individual variance terms, leaving an overall standard deviation of the portfolio of zero. *This would be a risk-free portfolio.*

Figure 7.4 illustrates a graph of such a pattern. Perfect negative correlation gives a mean combined return for the two securities over time equal to the mean for each of them, so the returns for the portfolio show no variability. Any returns above and below the mean for each of the assets are *completely offset* by the return for the other asset, so there is no variability in total returns, that is, no risk, for the portfolio. This combination of two assets that are completely negatively correlated provides the maximum benefits of diversification—it completely eliminates risk.

Figure 7.5 shows the difference in the risk–return posture for these five cases. As noted, the only impact of the change in correlation is the change in the standard deviation of this two-asset portfolio. Combining assets that are not perfectly correlated does *not* affect the expected return of the portfolio, but it *does* reduce the

FIGURE 7.5

FIGURE 7.5

Risk–Return Plot for Portfolios with Equal Returns and Standard Deviations but Different Correlations

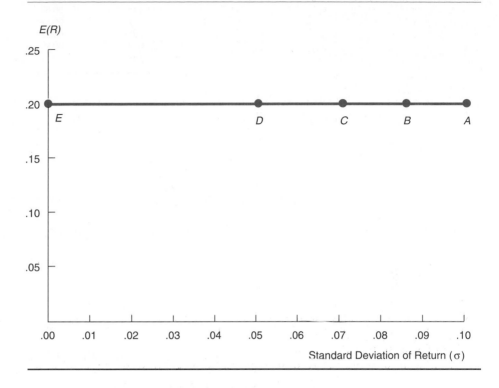

risk of the portfolio (as measured by its standard deviation). When we eventually reach the ultimate combination of perfect negative correlation, risk is eliminated.

COMBINING STOCKS WITH DIFFERENT RETURNS AND RISK   The previous discussion indicated what happens when only the correlation coefficient (covariance) differs between the assets. We now move on to consider two assets (or portfolios) with different expected rates of return and individual standard deviations. We will show what happens when we vary the correlations between them. We will assume two assets with the following characteristics:

Stock	$E(R_i)$	W_i	σ_i^2	σ_i
1	.10	.50	.0049	.07
2	.20	.50	.0100	.10

The previous set of correlation coefficients gives a different set of covariances because the standard deviations are different.

Case	Correlation Coefficient	Covariance $(r_{ij}\,\sigma_i\,\sigma_j)$
a	+1.00	.0070
b	+0.50	.0035
c	0.00	.0000
d	−0.50	−.0035
e	−1.00	−.0070

Because we are assuming the same weights in all cases (.50 − .50), the expected return in every instance will be

$$E(R_{port}) = 0.50\,(0.10) + 0.50\,(0.20)$$
$$= 0.15$$

The standard deviation for Case a will be

$$\sigma_{port\,(a)} = \sqrt{(0.5)^2(0.07)^2 + (0.5)^2(0.10)^2 + 2(0.5)(0.5)(0.0070)}$$
$$= \sqrt{0.007225}$$
$$= 0.085.$$

Again, with perfect positive correlation, the standard deviation of the portfolio is the weighted average of the standard deviations of the individual assets:

$$(0.5)(0.07) + (0.5)(0.10) = 0.085.$$

As you might envision, changing the weights with perfect positive correlation causes the standard deviation for the portfolio to change in a linear fashion. This is an important point to remember when we discuss the capital asset pricing model (CAPM) in the next chapter.

For Cases b, c, d, and e, the standard deviation for the portfolio would be as follows:[7]

$$\sigma_{port\,(b)} = \sqrt{(0.001225) + (0.0025) + (0.5)(0.0035)}$$
$$= \sqrt{0.005475}$$
$$= 0.07399$$
$$\sigma_{port\,(c)} = \sqrt{(0.001225) + (0.0025) + (0.5)(0.00)}$$
$$= 0.0610$$
$$\sigma_{port\,(d)} = \sqrt{(0.001225) + (0.0025) + (0.5)(-0.0035)}$$
$$= 0.0444$$
$$\sigma_{port\,(e)} = \sqrt{(0.003725) + 0.5(-0.00700)}$$
$$= 0.015.$$

---

[7]In all the following examples, we will skip some steps, because you are now aware that only the last term changes. You are encouraged to work out the individual steps to ensure understanding of the computational procedure.

FIGURE 7.6 **Risk–Return Plot for Portfolios with Different Returns, Standard Deviations, and Correlations**

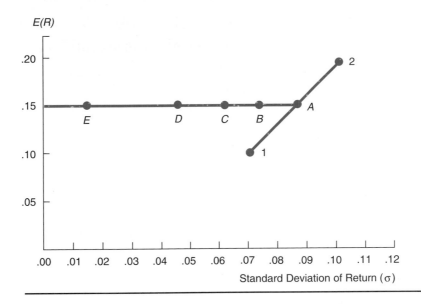

Note that, in this example, with perfect negative correlation the standard deviation of the portfolio is not zero. This is because the different examples have equal weights, but the individual standard deviations are not equal.[8]

Figure 7.6 shows the results for the two individual assets and the portfolio of the two assets assuming the correlation coefficients vary as set forth in Cases a through e. As before, the expected return does not change because the proportions are always set at .50 − .50, so all the portfolios lie along the horizontal line at the return, $R = .15$.

CONSTANT CORRELATION WITH CHANGING WEIGHTS   If we changed the weights of the two assets while holding the correlation coefficient constant, we would derive a set of combinations that trace an ellipse starting at Stock 2, going through the .50 − .50 point, and ending at Stock 1. We can demonstrate this with Case c, in which the correlation coefficient of zero eases the computations. We change the weights as follows:

Case	W_1	W_2	$E(R_i)$
f	.20	.80	.18
g	.40	.60	.16
h	.50	.50	.15
i	.60	.40	.14
j	.80	.20	.12

---

[8]The two appendixes to this chapter show proofs for equal weights with equal variances and the appropriate weights when standard deviations are not equal.

We already know the standard deviation (σ) for Portfolio h. In Cases f, g, i, and j, the standard deviations would be[9]

$$\sigma_{port\,(f)} = \sqrt{(0.20)^2(0.07)^2 + (0.80)^2(0.10)^2 + 2(0.20)(0.80)(0.00)}$$
$$= \sqrt{(0.04)(0.0049) + (0.64)(0.01) + (0)}$$
$$= \sqrt{0.006596}$$
$$= 0.0812$$
$$\sigma_{port\,(g)} = \sqrt{(0.40)^2(0.07)^2 + (0.60)^2(0.10)^2 + 2(0.40)(0.60)(0.00)}$$
$$= \sqrt{0.004384}$$
$$= 0.0662$$
$$\sigma_{port\,(i)} = \sqrt{(0.60)^2(0.07)^2 + (0.40)^2(0.10)^2 + 2(0.60)(0.40)(0.00)}$$
$$= \sqrt{0.003364}$$
$$= 0.0580$$
$$\sigma_{port\,(j)} = \sqrt{(0.80)^2(0.07)^2 + (0.20)^2(0.10)^2 + 2(0.80)(0.20)(0.00)}$$
$$= \sqrt{0.003536}$$
$$= 0.0595.$$

These alternative weights with constant correlations would yield the following risk–return combinations:

Case	W_1	W_2	$E(R_i)$	$E(\sigma_{port})$
f	0.20	0.80	0.18	0.0812
g	0.40	0.60	0.16	0.0662
h	0.50	0.50	0.15	0.0610
i	0.60	0.40	0.14	0.0580
j	0.80	0.20	0.12	0.0595

A graph of these combinations appears in Figure 7.7. You could derive a complete curve by simply varying the weighting by smaller increments.

As noted, the curvature in the graph will depend on the correlation between the two assets or portfolios. With $r_{ij} + 1.00$, the combinations would lie along a straight line between the two assets. With $r_{ij} = -1.00$, the graph would be two straight lines that would touch at the vertical line with some combination. Some specified set of weights would give a portfolio with zero risk.

THE EFFICIENT FRONTIER

If we examined a number of different two-asset combinations and derived the curves assuming all the possible weights, we would have a graph like that in Figure 7.8. The envelope curve that contains the best of all these possible combinations is referred to as the *efficient frontier*. Specifically, *the efficient frontier represents that set of portfolios that has the maximum rate of return for every given level of risk, or the minimum*

___
[9]Again, you are encouraged to fill in the steps we skipped in the computations.

FIGURE 7.7

Portfolio Risk–Return Plot for Different Weights When $r_{ij} = 0.00$

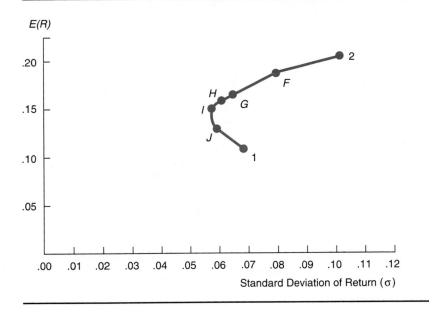

FIGURE 7.8

Numerous Portfolio Combinations of Available Assets

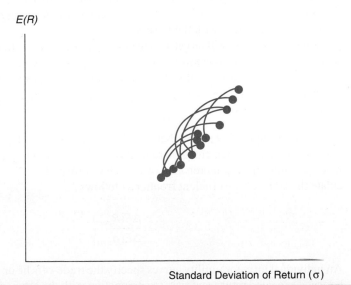

FIGURE 7.9   **Efficient Frontier for Alternative Portfolios**

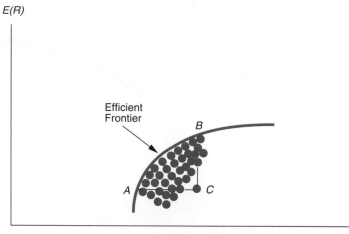

risk for every level of return. An example of such a frontier is shown in Figure 7.9. Every portfolio that lies on the efficient frontier has either a higher rate of return for equal risk or lower risk for an equal rate of return than some portfolio beneath the frontier. Thus, we would say that Portfolio A *dominates* Portfolio C because it has an equal rate of return but substantially less risk. Similarly, Portfolio B dominates Portfolio C because it has equal risk but a higher expected rate of return. Because of the benefits of diversification among imperfectly correlated assets, we would expect the efficient frontier to be made up of portfolios of investments rather than individual securities. Two possible exceptions arise at the end points, which represent the asset with the highest return and that with the lowest risk.

As an investor you will target a point along the efficient frontier based on your utility function and your attitude toward risk. No portfolio on the efficient frontier can dominate any other portfolio on the efficient frontier. All of these portfolios have different return and risk measures, with expected rates of return that increase with higher risk.

THE EFFICIENT
FRONTIER AND
INVESTOR
UTILITY

The curve in Figure 7.9 shows that this slope decreases steadily as you move upward. This implies that adding equal increments of risk as you move up the efficient frontier gives you diminishing increments of expected return. To evaluate this slope, we calculate the slope of the efficient frontier as follows:

$$\frac{\Delta E(R_{port})}{\Delta E(\sigma_{port})}$$

An individual investor's utility curves specify the trade-offs he or she is willing to make between expected return and risk. In conjunction with the efficient frontier these utility curves determine which *particular* efficient portfolio best suits an individual investor.

FIGURE 7.10   **Selecting an Optimal Risky Portfolio**

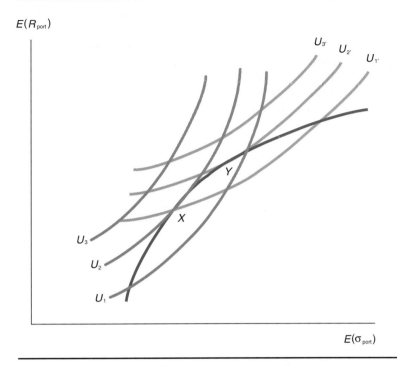

$E(R_{port})$

$U_{3'}$ $U_{2'}$ $U_{1'}$

Y

X

U_3

U_2

U_1

$E(\sigma_{port})$

Two investors will choose the same portfolio from the efficient set only if their utility curves are identical.

Figure 7.10 shows two sets of utility curves along with an efficient frontier of investments. The curves labeled U_1 are for a very risk-averse investor (with $U_3 > U_2 > U_1$). These utility curves are quite steep, indicating that the investor will not tolerate much additional risk to obtain additional returns. The investor is equally disposed toward any $E(R)$, $E(\sigma)$ combinations along a specific utility curve, such as U_1.

The curves labeled $U_{1'}(U_{3'} > U_{2'} > U_{1'})$ characterize a less risk-averse investor. Such an investor is willing to tolerate a bit more risk to get a higher expected return.

The **optimal portfolio** is the efficient portfolio that has the highest utility for a given investor. It lies at *the point of tangency between the efficient frontier and the curve with the highest possible utility*. A conservative investor's highest utility is at point X in Figure 7.10, where the curve U_2 just touches the efficient frontier. A less risk-averse investor's highest utility occurs at point Y, which represents a portfolio with higher expected returns and higher risk than the portfolio at X.

SUMMARY   The basic Markowitz portfolio model derived the expected rate of return for a portfolio of assets and a measure of expected risk, which is the standard deviation of expected rate of return. Markowitz showed that the expected rate of return of a portfolio is the weighted average of the expected return for the individual investments in the portfolio.

The standard deviation of a portfolio is a function not only of the standard deviations for the individual investments, but *also* of the covariance between the rates of return for all the pairs of assets in the portfolio. In a large portfolio, these covariances are the important factors.

Different weights or amounts of a portfolio held in various assets yield a curve of potential combinations. Correlation coefficients are the critical factor you must consider when selecting investments because you can maintain your rate of return while reducing the risk level of your portfolio by combining assets or portfolios that have low positive or negative correlation.

Assuming numerous assets and a multitude of combination curves, the efficient frontier is the envelope curve that encompasses all of the best combinations. It defines the set of portfolios that has the highest expected return for each given level of risk, or the minimum risk for each given level of return. From this set of dominant portfolios, you select the one that lies at the point of tangency between the efficient frontier and your highest utility curve. Because risk–return utility functions differ, your point of tangency and, therefore, your portfolio choice will probably differ from those of other investors.

At this point, we understand that an optimum portfolio is a combination of investments, each having desirable individual risk–return characteristics that also fit together based on their correlations. This deeper understanding of portfolio theory could lead you to reflect back on our earlier discussion of global investing. Because many foreign stock and bond investments provide superior rates of return compared with U.S. securities, *and* have very low correlations with portfolios of U.S. stocks and bonds, including these foreign securities will help you to reduce the overall risk of your portfolio while possibly increasing your rate of return.

QUESTIONS

1. Why do most investors hold diversified portfolios?

2. What is covariance, and why is it important in portfolio theory?

3. Why do most assets of the same type show positive covariances of returns with each other? Would you expect positive covariances of returns between *different* types of assets such as returns on Treasury bills, General Electric common stock, and commercial real estate? Why or why not?

4. What is the relationship between the covariance and the correlation coefficient? Why is the correlation coefficient considered more useful?

5. Explain the shape of the efficient frontier.

6. Draw a properly labeled graph of the Markowitz efficient frontier. Describe the efficient frontier in exact terms. Discuss the concept of dominant portfolios and show an example of one on your graph.

7. Assume you want to run a computer program to derive the efficient frontier for your feasible set of stocks. What information must you input to the program?

8. Why are investor's utility curves important in portfolio theory?

9. Explain how a given investor chooses an optimal portfolio. Will this choice always be a diversified portfolio, or could it be a single asset? Explain your answer.

10. Assume that you and a business associate develop an efficient frontier for a set of investments. Why might the two of you select different portfolios on the frontier?

11. Draw a hypothetical graph of an efficient frontier of U.S. common stocks. On the same graph, draw an efficient frontier assuming the inclusion of U.S. bonds as well. Finally, on the same graph, draw an efficient frontier that includes U.S. common stocks, U.S. bonds, and stocks and bonds from around the world. Discuss the differences in these frontiers.

PROBLEMS

1. Considering the world economic outlook for the coming year and the estimates of sales and earnings for the pharmaceutical industry, you expect the rate of return for Abbott Labs common stock to fall between -20 percent and $+40$ percent with the following range of probabilities:

Probability	Possible Returns
.10	-0.20
.15	-0.05
.20	0.10
.25	0.15
.20	0.20
.10	0.40

Compute the expected rate of return $[E(R_i)]$ for Abbott Labs.

2. Given the following market values of stocks in your portfolio and their expected rates of return, what is the expected rate of return for your common stock portfolio?

Stock	Market Value	$E(R_i)$
Phillips Petroleum	$15,000	0.14
Ford Motor	17,000	-0.04
International Paper	32,000	0.18
Apple Computer	23,000	0.16
Walgreen's	7,000	0.05

3. The following are the monthly rates of return for Coca-Cola and General Electric during a six month-period.

Month	Coca-Cola	General Electric
1	.04	.07
2	.03	$-.02$
3	$-.07$	$-.10$
4	.12	.15
5	$-.02$	$-.06$
6	.05	.02

Compute the following:
   a. Expected monthly rate of return $[E(R_i)]$ for each stock.
   b. Standard deviation for each stock.
   c. Covariance between the rates of return.
   d. The correlation coefficient of rates of return.

What level of correlation did you expect? How did your expectations compare with the computed correlation? Would these two stocks offer a good chance for diversification? Why or why not?

4. You are considering two assets with the following characteristics:

$$E(R_1) = .15 \qquad E(\sigma_1) = .10 \qquad W_1 = .5$$
$$E(R_2) = .20 \qquad E(\sigma_2) = .20 \qquad W_2 = .5$$

Compute the mean and standard deviation of two portfolios if $r_{1,2} = .40$ and $-.60$, respectively. Plot the two portfolios on a risk–return graph. Which would you select? Explain your choice.

5. Given: $E(R_1) = .10$
$$E(R_2) = .15$$
$$E(\sigma_1) = .03$$
$$E(\sigma_2) = .05$$

Calculate the expected returns and expected standard deviations of a two-stock portfolio in which Stock 1 has a weight of 60 percent under the following conditions:
   a. $r_{1,2} = 1.00$
   b. $r_{1,2} = .75$
   c. $r_{1,2} = .25$
   d. $r_{1,2} = .00$
   e. $r_{1,2} = -.25$
   f. $r_{1,2} = -.75$
   g. $r_{1,2} = -1.00$

6. Given: $E(R_1) = .12$
$$E(R_2) = .16$$
$$E(\sigma_1) = .04$$
$$E(\sigma_2) = .06$$

Calculate the expected returns and expected standard deviations of a two-stock portfolio having a correlation coefficient of .70 under the following conditions:
   a. $w_1 = 1.00$
   b. $w_1 = .75$
   c. $w_1 = .50$
   d. $w_1 = .25$
   e. $w_1 = .05$

7. The following are monthly percentage price changes for four market indexes.

Month	DJIA	S&P 400	AMEX	NIKKEI
1	.03	.02	.04	.02
2	.07	.06	.10	−.02
3	−.02	−.01	−.04	.03
4	.01	.03	.03	.02
5	.05	.07	.11	.01
6	−.06	−.04	−.08	.03

Compute the following:
   a. Expected monthly rate of return for each series.
   b. Standard deviation for each series.

c. Covariance between the rates of return for the following indexes:
DJIA—S&P 400
S&P 400—AMEX
S&P 400—NIKKEI
AMEX—NIKKEI
d. The correlation coefficients for the same four combinations.

Based on these results, discuss which combination of domestic series would provide the best diversification. Discuss which domestic–foreign combination is best for diversification. What does this imply regarding international diversification?

REFERENCES

Farrell, James L., Jr. *Guide to Portfolio Management.* New York: McGraw-Hill, 1983.

Harrington, Diana R. *Modern Portfolio Theory, the Capital Asset Pricing Model, and Arbitrage Pricing Theory: A User's Guide.* 2d ed. Englewood Cliffs, N.J.: Prentice-Hall, 1987.

Maginn, John L., and Donald L. Tuttle, eds. *Managing Investment Portfolios: A Dynamic Process.* 2d ed. Sponsored by The Institute of Chartered Financial Analysts. Boston: Warren, Gorham and Lamont, 1990.

Markowitz, Harry. "Portfolio Selection." *Journal of Finance* 7, no. 1 (March 1952).

Markowitz, Harry. *Portfolio Selection: Efficient Diversification of Investments.* New York: John Wiley and Sons, 1959.

APPENDIX 7A

PROOF THAT MINIMUM PORTFOLIO VARIANCE OCCURS WITH EQUAL WEIGHTS WHEN SECURITIES HAVE EQUAL VARIANCE

When $E(\sigma_i) = E(\sigma_2)$, we have:

$$E(\sigma_{port}^2) = W_1^2 E(\sigma_1)^2 + (1 - W_1)^2 E(\sigma_1)^2 + 2 W_1(1 - W_1)r_{12}E(\sigma_1)^2$$
$$= E(\sigma_1)^2[W_1^2 + 1 - 2 W_1 + W_1^2 + 2W_1 r_{12} - 2W_1^2 r_{12}]$$
$$= E(\sigma_1)^2[2 W_1^2 + 1 - 2W_1 + 2 W_1 r_{12} - 2 W_1^2 r_{12}]$$

For this to be a minimum

$$\frac{\partial E(\sigma_{port}^2)}{\partial W_1} = 0 = E(\sigma_1)^2[4 W_1 - 2 + 2r_{12} - 4 W_1 r_{12}]$$

Assuming $E(\sigma_1)^2 > 0$,

$$4 W_1 - 2 + 2r_{12} - 4 W_1 r_{12} = 0$$
$$4 W_1(1 - r_{12}) - 2(1 - r_{12}) = 0$$

from which

$$W_1 = \frac{2(1 - r_{12})}{4(1 - r_{12})} = \frac{1}{2}$$

regardless of r_{12}. Thus, if $E(\sigma_1) = E(\sigma_2)$, $E(\sigma^2_{port})$ will *always* be minimized by choosing $W_1 = W_2 = \frac{1}{2}$, regardless of the value of r_{12}, except when $r_{12} = +1$ (in which case $E(\sigma_{port}) = E(\sigma_1) = E(\sigma_2)$. This can be verified by checking the second-order condition

$$\frac{\partial^2 E(\sigma^2_{port})}{\partial W^2_1} > 0$$

PROBLEMS

The following information applies to Questions 1a and 1b. The general equation for the weight of the first security to achieve minimum variance (in a two-stock portfolio) is given by

$$W_1 = \frac{E(\sigma_2)^2 - r_{1,2}\, E(\sigma_1)\, E(\sigma_2)}{E(\sigma_1)^2 + E(\sigma_2)^2 - 2r_{1,2}\, E(\sigma_1)\, E(\sigma_2)}$$

1a. Show that $W_1 = .5$ when $E(\sigma_1) = E(\sigma_2)$.
1b. What is the weight of Security 1 that gives minimum portfolio variance when $r_{1,2} = .5$, $E(\sigma_1) = .04$, and $E(\sigma_2) = .06$?

APPENDIX 7B

DERIVATION OF WEIGHTS THAT WILL GIVE ZERO VARIANCE WHEN CORRELATION EQUALS -1.00

$$E(\sigma^2_{port}) = W^2_1\, E(\sigma_1)^2 + (1 - W_1)^2 E(\sigma_2)^2 + 2\, W_1(1 - W_1)r_{12}E(\sigma_1)E(\sigma_2)$$

$$= W^2_1 E(\sigma_1)^2 + E(\sigma_2)^2 - 2W_1 E(\sigma_2) + W^2_1 E(\sigma_2)^2$$

$$+ 2\, W_1 r_{12} E(\sigma_1)E(\sigma_2) - 2\, W^2_1 r_{12}E(\sigma_1)E(\sigma_2)$$

If $r_{12} = -1$, this can be rearranged and expressed as

$$E(\sigma^2_{port}) = W^2_1[E(\sigma_1)^2 + 2E(\sigma_1)E(\sigma_2) + E(\sigma_2)^2]$$
$$- 2\, W_1[E(\sigma_2)^2 + E(\sigma_1)E(\sigma_2)] + E(\sigma_2)^2$$
$$= W^2_1[E(\sigma_1) + E(\sigma_2)]^2 - 2\, W_1 E(\sigma_2)$$
$$[E(\sigma_1) + E(\sigma_2)] + E(\sigma_2)^2$$
$$= \{W_1[E(\sigma_1) + E(\sigma_2)] - E(\sigma_2)\}^2$$

We want to find the weight, W_1, which will reduce $E(\sigma^2_{port})$ to *zero;* therefore

$$W_1[E(\sigma_1) + E(\sigma_2)] - E(\sigma_2) = 0$$

which yields

$$W_1 = \frac{E(\sigma_2)}{E(\sigma_1) + E(\sigma_2)}, \text{ and } W_2 = 1 - W_1 = \frac{E(\sigma_1)}{E(\sigma_1) + E(\sigma_2)}$$

CHAPTER 8

An Introduction to
Asset Pricing Models

In this chapter, we will answer the following questions:

- What are the assumptions of the capital asset pricing model?
- What is a risk-free asset and what are its risk–return characteristics?
- What is the covariance and correlation between the risk-free asset and a risky asset or portfolio of risky assets?
- What is the expected return when you combine the risk-free asset and a portfolio of risky assets?
- What is the standard deviation when you combine the risk-free asset and a portfolio of risky assets?
- When you combine the risk-free asset and a portfolio of risky assets on the Markowitz efficient frontier, what does the set of possible portfolios look like?
- Given the initial set of portfolio possibilities with a risk-free asset, what happens when you add financial leverage (i.e., borrow)?
- What is the market portfolio, what assets are included in this portfolio, and what are the relative weights for the alternative assets included?
- What is the capital market line (CML)?
- What do we mean by complete diversification?
- How do we measure diversification for an individual portfolio?
- What are systematic and unsystematic risk?
- Given the capital market line (CML), what is the separation theorem?
- Given the CML, what is the relevant risk measure for an individual risky asset?
- What is the security market line (SML) and how does it differ from the CML?
- What is beta and why is it referred to as a standardized measure of systematic risk?
- How can you use the SML to determine the expected (required) rate of return for a risky asset?
- Using the SML, what is meant by an undervalued and overvalued security and how do you determine whether an asset is undervalued or overvalued?
- What is meant by an asset's characteristic line and how do you compute the characteristic line for an asset?

- What is the impact on the characteristic line when you compute it using different return intervals (e.g., weekly versus monthly) and when you employ different proxies for the market portfolio (e.g., the S&P 500 versus a global stock index)?
- What is the arbitrage pricing theory (APT) and how does it differ from the CAPM in terms of assumptions?
- How does the APT differ from the CAPM in terms of risk measures?

Following the development of portfolio theory by Markowitz, there have been two major theories put forth that employ the theory to derive a model for the valuation of risky assets. In this chapter we will introduce these two models. The background on asset pricing models is important at this point in the book because the risk measures implied by these models are a necessary input for our subsequent discussion on the valuation of risky assets. The bulk of the presentation will be concerned with capital market theory and the capital asset pricing model (CAPM) that was developed almost concurrently by three individuals. More recently, an alternative asset valuation model has been proposed, entitled the arbitrage pricing theory (APT). This theory and the implied pricing model will likewise be introduced and discussed.

CAPITAL MARKET THEORY

Because capital market theory builds on portfolio theory, this chapter begins where the discussion of the Markowitz efficient frontier ended. We assume that you have examined the set of risky assets and derived the aggregate efficient frontier. Further, we assume that you and all other investors want to maximize your utility in terms of risk and return, so you will choose portfolios of risky assets on the efficient frontier at points where your utility maps are tangent to the frontier as shown in Figure 7.10. When you make your investment decision in this manner, you are referred to as a *Markowitz efficient investor.*

Capital market theory extends portfolio theory and develops a model for pricing all risky assets. The final product, the *capital asset pricing model (CAPM)* will allow you to determine the required rate of return for any risky asset.

We begin with the background of capital market theory that includes topics such as the underlying assumptions of the theory and a discussion of the factors that led to its development following the Markowitz portfolio theory. Principal among these factors was the analysis of the effect of assuming the existence of a risk-free asset. This is the subject of the next section.

We will see that assuming a risk-free rate has significant implications for the potential return and risk and also alternative risk–return combinations. This discussion implies a central portfolio of risky assets on the efficient frontier, which we call the *market portfolio*. We discuss the market portfolio in the third section and the implications regarding different types of risk.

The fourth section considers which types of risk are relevant to an investor who believes in capital market theory. Having defined a measure of risk, we can consider how you determine your required rate of return on an investment. You can then compare this required rate of return to your estimate of the asset's expected rate of return during your investment horizon to determine whether the asset is undervalued or overvalued. The section ends with a demonstration of how to calculate the risk measure implied by capital market theory.

The final section discusses an alternative asset pricing model, the arbitrage pricing theory (APT). This model requires fewer assumptions than the CAPM and contends that the required rate of return for a risky asset is a function of multiple factors. This is in contrast to the CAPM, which is a single-factor model. There is a brief demonstration of how to evaluate the risk of an asset and determine its required rate of return using this model.

BACKGROUND FOR CAPITAL MARKET THEORY

When dealing with any theory in science, economics, or finance, it is necessary to articulate a set of assumptions that specify how the world is expected to act. This allows the theoretician to concentrate on developing a theory that explains how some facet of the world will respond to changes in the environment. In the first part of this section, we will consider the main assumptions that underlie the development of capital market theory. The second part of the section considers the major assumptions that allowed theoreticians to extend the portfolio model's techniques for combining investments into an optimal portfolio to a model that explains how to determine the value of those investments (or other assets).

ASSUMPTIONS OF CAPITAL MARKET THEORY

Because capital market theory builds on the Markowitz portfolio model, it requires the same assumptions, along with some additional ones:

1. All investors are Markowitz efficient investors who want to target points on the efficient frontier. The exact location on the efficient frontier and, therefore, the specific portfolio selected, will depend on the individual investor's risk–return utility function.

2. Investors can borrow or lend any amount of money at the risk-free rate of return (RFR). Clearly, it is always possible to lend money at the nominal risk-free rate by buying risk-free securities such as government T-bills. It is not always possible to borrow at this risk-free rate, but we will see that assuming a higher borrowing rate does not change the general results.

3. All investors have homogeneous expectations; that is, they estimate identical probability distributions for future rates of return. Again, this assumption can be relaxed. As long as the differences in expectations are not vast, their effects are minor.

4. All investors have the same one-period time horizon such as 1 month, 6 months, or 1 year. The model will be developed for a single hypothetical period, and its results could be affected by a different assumption. A difference in the time horizon would require investors to derive risk measures that were consistent with their horizons.

5. All investments are infinitely divisible, which means that it is possible to buy or sell fractional shares of any asset or portfolio. This assumption allows us to discuss investment alternatives as continuous curves. Changing it would have little impact on the theory.

6. There are no taxes or transaction costs involved in buying or selling assets. This is a reasonable assumption in many instances. Neither pension funds nor religious groups have to pay taxes, and the transaction costs for most financial

institutions are less than 1 percent on most financial instruments. Again, relaxing this assumption modifies the results, but it does not change the basic thrust.

7.   There is no inflation or any change in interest rates, or inflation is fully anticipated. This is a reasonable initial assumption, and it can be modified.

8.   Capital markets are in equilibrium. This means that we begin with all investments properly priced in line with their risk levels.

You may consider some of these assumptions unrealistic and wonder how useful a theory we can derive with these assumptions. In this regard, two points are important. First, as mentioned, relaxing many of these assumptions would have only minor impacts on the model and would not change its main implications or conclusions. Second, a theory should never be judged on the basis of its assumptions, but rather on how well it explains and helps us predict behavior in the real world. If this theory and the model it implies help us explain the rates of return on a wide variety of risky assets, it is very useful, even if some of its assumptions are unrealistic. Such success implies that the questionable assumptions must not be very important to the ultimate objective of the model, which is to explain the pricing and rates of returns on assets.

DEVELOPMENT OF CAPITAL MARKET THEORY

The major factor that allowed portfolio theory to develop into capital market theory is the concept of a risk-free asset. Following the development of the Markowitz portfolio model, several authors considered the implications assuming the existence of a *risk-free asset,* that is, an asset with *zero variance.* As we will show, such an asset would have zero correlation with all other risky assets and would provide the *risk-free rate of return (RFR).* It would lie on the vertical axis of a portfolio graph.

This assumption allows us to derive a generalized theory of capital asset pricing under conditions of uncertainty from the Markowitz portfolio theory. This achievement is generally attributed to William Sharpe, for which he received the Nobel prize, but Lintner and Mossin derived similar theories independently.[1] Consequently, you may see references to the Sharpe-Lintner-Mossin (SLM) capital asset pricing model.

RISK-FREE ASSET   As noted, the assumption of a risk-free asset in the economy is critical to asset pricing theory. Therefore, this section explains the meaning of a risk-free asset and then shows the effect on the risk and return measures when this risk-free asset is combined with a portfolio on the Markowitz efficient frontier.

We have defined a *risky asset* as one from which future returns are uncertain and we have measured this uncertainty by the variance, or standard deviation of returns. Because the expected return on a risk-free asset is entirely certain, the standard deviation of its return is zero ($\sigma_{RF} = 0$). The rate of return earned on such an asset should be the risk-free rate of return (RFR), which, as we discussed in Chapter 1, should equal the expected long-run growth rate of the economy with an adjustment for short-run liquidity. The next subsections show what happens when we introduce this risk-free asset into the risky world of the Markowitz portfolio model.

---

[1]William F. Sharpe, "Capital Asset Prices: A Theory of Market Equilibrium Under Conditions of Risk," *Journal of Finance* 19, no. 3 (September 1964): 425–442; John Lintner, "Security Prices, Risk and Maximal Gains from Diversification," *Journal of Finance* 20, no. 4 (December 1965): 587–615; and J. Mossin, "Equilibrium in a Capital Asset Market," *Econometrica* 34, no. 4 (October 1966): 768–783.

COVARIANCE WITH A RISK-FREE ASSET

Recall that the covariance between two sets of returns is

$$Cov_{ij} = \sum_{i=1}^{n} [R_i - E(R_i)][R_j - E(R_j)]/n.$$

Because the returns for the risk-free asset are certain, $\sigma_{RF} = 0$, which means $R_i = E(R_i)$ during all periods. Thus, $R_i - E(R_i)$ will also equal zero, and the product of this expression with any other expression will equal zero. Consequently, the covariance of the risk-free asset with any risky asset or portfolio of assets will always equal zero. Similarly, the correlation between any risky asset and the risk-free asset would be zero, because it is equal to

$$r_{rf,i} = Cov_{RF,i}/\sigma_{RF}\, \sigma_i.$$

COMBINING A RISK-FREE ASSET WITH A RISKY PORTFOLIO

What happens to the average rate of return and the standard deviation when you combine a risk-free asset with a portfolio of risky assets such as those that exist on the Markowitz efficient frontier?

EXPECTED RETURN   Like the expected return for a portfolio of two risky assets, the expected rate of return on a portfolio with a risk-free asset is the weighted average of the two returns:

$$E(R_{port}) = W_{RF}(RFR) + (1 - W_{RF})E(R_i)$$

where:

W_{RF} = the proportion of the portfolio invested in the risk-free asset

$E(R_i)$ = the expected rate of return on risky Portfolio i.

STANDARD DEVIATION   Recall from Chapter 7 that the expected variance for a two-asset portfolio is

$$E(\sigma_{port}^2) = W_1^2\sigma_1^2 + W_2^2\sigma_2^2 + 2W_1W_2 r_{1,2}\sigma_1\sigma_2.$$

Substituting the risk-free asset for Security 1, and the risky asset portfolio for Security 2, this formula would become

$$\begin{aligned} E(\sigma_{port}^2) = {} & W_{RF}^2\sigma_{RF}^2 + (1 - W_{RF})^2\sigma_i^2 \\ & + 2W_{RF}(1 - W_{RF})r_{RF,i}\sigma_{RF}\sigma_i. \end{aligned}$$

We know that the variance of the risk-free asset is zero, that is, $\sigma_{RF}^2 = 0$. Because the correlation between the risk-free asset and any risky asset, i, is also zero, the factor $r_{RF,i}$ in the equation above also equals zero. Therefore, any component of the variance formula that has either of these terms will equal zero. When you make these adjustments, the formula becomes

$$E(\sigma^2_{port}) = (1 - W_{RF})^2\sigma_i^2$$

The standard deviation is

$$E(\sigma_{port}) = \sqrt{(1 - W_{RF})^2\sigma_i^2}$$
$$= (1 - W_{RF})\sigma_i.$$

Therefore, the standard deviation of a portfolio that combines the risk-free asset with risky assets is *the linear proportion of the standard deviation of the risky asset portfolio.*

THE RISK–RETURN COMBINATION   Because *both* the expected return *and* the standard deviation of return for such a portfolio are linear combinations, a graph of possible portfolio returns and risks looks like a straight line between the two assets. Figure 8.1 shows a graph depicting portfolio possibilities when a risk-free asset is combined with alternative risky portfolios on the Markowitz efficient frontier.

FIGURE 8.1   **Portfolio Possibilities Combining the Risk-Free Asset and Risky Portfolios on the Efficient Frontier**

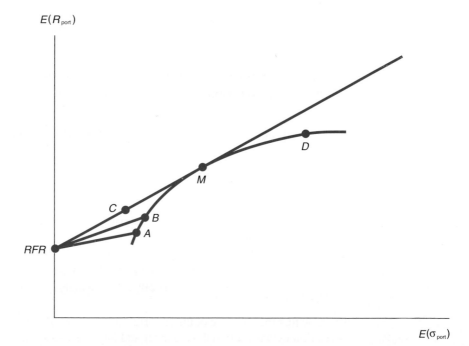

You can attain any point along the straight line *RFR-A* by investing some portion of your portfolio in the risk-free asset W_{RF} and the remainder $(1 - W_{RF})$ in the risky asset portfolio at Point A on the efficient frontier. This set of portfolio possibilities dominates all the risky asset portfolios on the efficient frontier below Point A because some portfolio along Line *RFR-A* has equal variance with a higher rate of return than the portfolio on the original efficient frontier. Likewise, you can attain any point along the Line *RFR-B* by investing in some combination of the risk-free asset and the risky asset portfolio at Point B. Again, these potential combinations dominate all portfolio possibilities on the original efficient frontier below Point B (including Line *RFR-A*).

You can draw further lines from the RFR to the efficient frontier at higher and higher points until you reach the point that is tangent to the frontier, which occurs in Figure 8.1 at Point M. The set of portfolio possibilities along Line *RFR-M* dominates *all* portfolios below Point M. For example, you could attain a risk and return combination between the RFR and Point M (Point C) by investing one-half of your portfolio in the risk-free asset (that is, lending money at the RFR) and the other half in the risky portfolio at Point M.

RISK–RETURN POSSIBILITIES WITH LEVERAGE   An investor may want to attain a higher expected return than is available at Point M in exchange for accepting higher risk. One alternative would be to invest in one of the risky asset portfolios on the efficient frontier beyond Point M such as the portfolio at Point D. A second alternative is to add *leverage* to the portfolio by *borrowing* money at the risk-free rate and investing the proceeds in the risky asset portfolio at Point M. What effect would this have on the return and risk for your portfolio?

If you *borrow* an amount equal to *50 percent* of your original wealth, W_{RF} will not be a positive fraction, but rather a negative 50 percent, $(W_{RF} = -.50)$. The effect on the expected return for your portfolio is

$$
\begin{aligned}
E(R_{port}) &= W_{RF}(RFR) + (1 - W_{RF})E(R_m) \\
&= -0.50(RFR) + [1 - (-0.50)]E(R_m) \\
&= -0.50(RFR) + 1.50E(R_m).
\end{aligned}
$$

The return will increase in a *linear* fashion along the Line *RFR-M,* because the gross return increases by 50 percent, but you must pay interest at the RFR on the money borrowed. As an example, assume that the $E(RFR) = .06$ and $E(R_m) = .12$. The return on your leveraged portfolio would be:

$$
\begin{aligned}
E(R_{port}) &= -0.50(0.06) + 1.5(0.12) \\
&= -0.03 + 0.18 \\
&= 0.15.
\end{aligned}
$$

The effect on the standard deviation of the leveraged portfolio is similar.

$$
\begin{aligned}
E(\sigma_{port}) &= (1 - W_{RF})\sigma_m \\
&= [1 - (-0.50)]\sigma_m = 1.50\sigma_m.
\end{aligned}
$$

FIGURE 8.2   **Derivation of Capital Market Line Assuming Lending or Borrowing at the Risk-Free Rate**

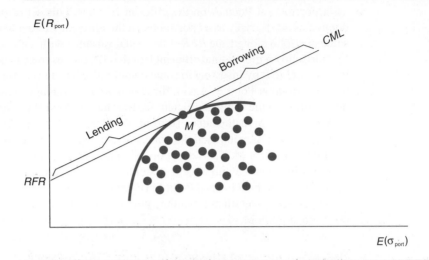

Therefore, *both return and risk increase in a linear fashion along the original Line RFR-M,* and this extension dominates everything below the line on the original efficient frontier. Thus, you have a new efficient frontier: the straight line from the *RFR* tangent to Point M. This line is referred to as the *capital market line (CML)* and is shown in Figure 8.2.

Our discussion of portfolio theory stated that, when two assets are perfectly correlated, the set of portfolio possibilities falls along a straight line. Therefore, because the CML is a straight line, all the portfolios on the CML are perfectly positively correlated. This positive correlation appeals to our intuition because all these portfolios on the CML combine the risky asset Portfolio M and the risk-free asset. You either invest part of your portfolio in the risk-free asset or you borrow at the risk-free rate and invest these funds in the risky asset portfolio. In either case, all the variability comes from the risky asset, M portfolio. The only difference between the alternative portfolios on the CML is the magnitude of the variability caused by the proportion of the risky asset portfolio in the total portfolio.

THE MARKET
PORTFOLIO

Because Portfolio M lies at the point of tangency, it has the highest portfolio possibility line, and everybody will want to invest in it and borrow or lend to be somewhere on the CML. This portfolio must, therefore, include all risky assets. The point is, if a risky asset were not in this portfolio in which everyone wants to invest, it would have no demand and therefore no value.

Because the market is in equilibrium, it is also necessary that all assets are included in this portfolio in *proportion to their market value.* If, for example, an asset accounts for a higher proportion of the M portfolio than its value justifies, excess demand for this asset will increase in price until its relative market value becomes consistent with its proportion in the portfolio.

This portfolio that includes all risky assets is referred to as the *market portfolio.* It includes not only common stocks, but *all* risky assets, such as non-U.S. stocks,

U.S. and non-U.S. bonds, options, real estate, coins, stamps, art, or antiques. Because the market portfolio contains all risky assets, it is a *completely diversified portfolio,* which means that all the risk unique to individual assets in the portfolio is diversified away. The unique risk of any asset is offset by the unique variability of the other assets in the portfolio.

This unique risk is also referred to as *unsystematic risk.* This implies that only *systematic risk,* which is defined as the variability in all risky assets caused by macroeconomic variables, remains in the market portfolio. This systematic risk, measured by the standard deviation of returns of the market portfolio, can change over time with changes in the macroeconomic variables that affect the valuation of all risky assets.[2] Examples of such macroeconomic variables would be variability of growth in the money supply, interest rate volatility, and variability in such factors as industrial production, corporate earnings, and cash flow.

HOW TO MEASURE DIVERSIFICATION

All portfolios on the CML are perfectly positively correlated, which means that all portfolios on the CML are perfectly correlated with the completely diversified market portfolio. This implies a measure of complete diversification.[3] Specifically, a completely diversified portfolio would have a correlation with the market portfolio of + 1.00. This is logical because complete diversification means the elimination of all the unsystematic or unique risk. Once you have eliminated unsystematic risk, only systematic risk is left, which cannot be diversified away. Therefore, completely diversified portfolios would correlate perfectly with the market portfolio because it also has only systematic risk.

DIVERSIFICATION AND THE ELIMINATION OF UNSYSTEMATIC RISK

As discussed in Chapter 7, the purpose of diversification is to reduce the standard deviation of the total portfolio. This assumes imperfect correlations among securities.[4] Ideally, as you add securities, the average covariance for the portfolio declines. An important question is, about how many securities must be included to arrive at a completely diversified portfolio? To discover the answer, you must observe what happens as you increase the sample size of the portfolio by adding securities that have some positive correlation. The typical correlation among U.S. securities is about 0.5 to 0.6.

One set of studies examined the average standard deviation for numerous portfolios of randomly selected stocks of different sample sizes.[5] For example, Evans and Archer computed the standard deviation for portfolios of increasing numbers up to 20 stocks.

---

[2]For an analysis of changes in stock price volatility, see G. William Schwert, "Why Does Stock Market Volatility Change Over Time?" *Journal of Finance* 44, no. 5 (December 1989): 1115–1153; Peter S. Spiro, "The Impact of Interest Rate Changes on Stock Price Volatility," *Journal of Portfolio Management* 16, no. 2 (Winter 1990): 63–68; James M. Poterba and Lawrence H. Summers, "The Persistence of Volatility and Stock Market Fluctuations," *American Economic Review* 76, no. 4 (December, 1981): 1142–1151; R. R. Officer, "The Variability of the Market Factor of the New York Stock Exchange," *The Journal of Business* 46, no. 3 (July 1973): 434–453.

[3]James Lorie, "Diversification: Old and New," *Journal of Portfolio Management* 1, no. 2 (Winter 1975): 25–28.

[4]The discussion in Chapter 7 leads one to conclude that securities with negative correlation would be ideal. Although this is true in theory, it is very difficult to find such assets in the real world.

[5]John L. Evans and Stephen H. Archer, "Diversification and the Reduction of Dispersion: An Empirical Analysis," *Journal of Finance* 23, no. 5 (December 1968): 761–767; Thomas M. Tole, "You Can't Diversify without Diversifying," *Journal of Portfolio Management* 8, no. 2 (Winter 1982): 5–11.

FIGURE 8.3   **Number of Stocks in a Portfolio and the Standard Deviation of Portfolio Return**

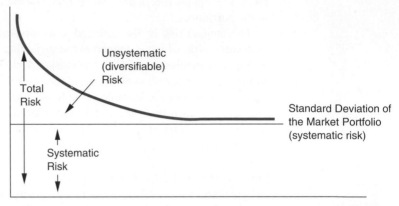

The results indicated a large initial impact with the major benefits of diversification achieved rather quickly. Specifically, about 90 percent of the maximum benefit of diversification was derived from portfolios of 12 to 18 stocks. Figure 8.3 shows a graph of the effect.

A more recent study by Statman compared the benefits of lower risk from diversification to the added transaction costs with more securities. It concluded that a well-diversified stock portfolio must include at least 30 stocks for a borrowing investor and 40 stocks for a lending investor.[6]

By adding stocks to the portfolio that are not perfectly correlated to a portfolio, you can reduce the overall standard deviation of the portfolio, but you *cannot eliminate variability.* The standard deviation of your portfolio will eventually reach the level of the market portfolio, where you will have diversified away all unsystematic risk, but you still have market or systematic risk. You cannot eliminate the variability and uncertainty of macroeconomic factors that affect all risky assets.

THE CML AND THE SEPARATION THEOREM

The CML leads all investors to invest in the same risky asset portfolio, the M portfolio. Individual investors should only differ regarding their position on the CML, which depends on their risk preferences.

In turn, how they get to a point on the CML is based on their financing decisions. If you are relatively risk averse, you will lend some part of your portfolio at the RFR by buying some risk-free securities and investing the remainder in the market portfolio. For example, you might invest in the portfolio combination at Point A in Figure 8.4. In contrast, if you prefer more risk, you might borrow funds at the RFR and invest

---

[6]Meir Statman, "How Many Stocks Make a Diversified Portfolio?" *Journal of Financial and Quantitative Analysis* 22, no. 3 (September 1987): 353–363.

FIGURE 8.4   **Choice of Optimal Portfolio Combinations on the CML**

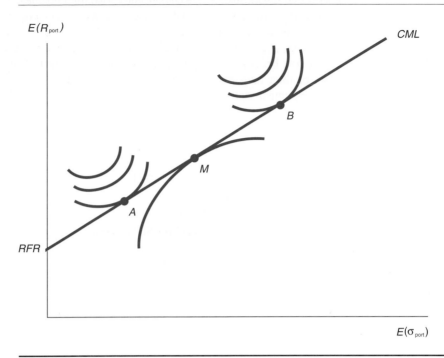

everything (all of your capital plus what you borrowed) in the market portfolio, building the portfolio at Point B. This financing decision provides more risk but greater returns than the market portfolio. As discussed earlier, because portfolios on the CML dominate other portfolio possibilities, the CML becomes the efficient frontier of portfolios, and investors decide where they want to be along this efficient frontier.

Tobin called this division of the investment decision from the financing decision the *separation theorem*.[7] Specifically, to be somewhere on the CML efficient frontier, you initially decide to invest in the market portfolio, M. This is your *investment* decision. Subsequently, based on your risk preferences, you make a separate *financing* decision either to borrow or to lend to attain your preferred point on the CML.

A RISK MEASURE FOR THE CML
In this section we will show that the relevant risk measure for risky assets is *their covariance with the M portfolio,* which is referred to as their systematic risk. The importance of this covariance is apparent from two points of view.

First, in discussing the Markowitz portfolio model, we noted that the relevant risk to consider for a security being added to a portfolio is *its average covariance with all*

[7]James Tobin, "Liquidity Preference as Behavior Towards Risk," *Review of Economic Studies* 25, no. 2 (February 1958): 65–85.

other assets in the portfolio. In this chapter we have shown that *the only relevant portfolio is the M portfolio.* Together, these two findings mean that the only important consideration for any individual risky asset is its average covariance with all the risky assets in the M portfolio, or simply, *the asset's covariance with the market portfolio.* This, then, is the relevant risk measure for an individual risky asset.

Second, because all individual risky assets are a part of the M portfolio, one can describe their rates of return in relation to the returns for the M portfolio using the following linear model:

$$R_{it} = a_i + b_i R_{mt} + \epsilon$$

where:

R_{it} = **return for asset *i* during period *t***

a_i = **constant term for asset *i***

b_i = **slope coefficient for asset *i***

R_{mt} = **return for the M portfolio during period *t***

ϵ = **random error term.**

The variance of returns for a risky asset could be described as

$$\begin{aligned}
Var\,(R_{it}) &= Var\,(a_i + b_i R_{mt} + \epsilon)\\
&= Var\,(a_i) + Var\,(b_i R_{mt}) + Var\,(\epsilon)\\
&= 0 + Var\,(b_i R_{mt}) + Var\,(\epsilon).
\end{aligned}$$

Note that $Var(b_i R_{mt})$ is the variance of return for an asset related to the variance of the market return, or the *systematic variance or risk.* Also, $Var(\epsilon)$ is the residual variance of return for the individual asset that is not related to the market portfolio. This residual variance is the variability that we have referred to as the unsystematic or *unique risk or variance,* because it arises from the unique features of the asset. Therefore:

$$Var\,(R_{it}) = Systematic\ Variance\ +\ Unsystematic\ Variance.$$

We know that a completely diversified portfolio such as the market portfolio has had all the unsystematic variance eliminated. Therefore, the unsystematic variance is not relevant to investors, because they can and do eliminate it when making an asset part of the market portfolio. Therefore, investors should not expect to receive added returns for assuming this unique risk. Only the systematic variance is relevant because it *cannot* be diversified away, because it is caused by macroeconomic factors that affect all risky assets.

THE CAPITAL ASSET PRICING MODEL: EXPECTED RETURN AND RISK

Up to this point, we have considered how investors make their portfolio decisions, including the significant affects of a risk-free asset. The existence of this risk-free asset resulted in the derivation of a capital market line (CML) that became the relevant efficient frontier. Because all investors want to be on the CML, an asset's covariance with the market portfolio of risky assets emerged as the relevant risk measure.

Now that we understand this relevant measure of risk, we can proceed to use it to determine an appropriate expected rate of return on a risky asset. This step takes us into the *capital asset pricing model (CAPM),* which is a model that indicates what should be the expected or required rates of return on risky assets. This transition is important because it helps you to value an asset by providing an appropriate discount rate to use in dividend valuation models. Alternatively, if you have already estimated the rate of return that you think you will earn on an investment, you can compare this estimated rate of return to the required rate of return implied by the CAPM and determine whether the asset is undervalued, overvalued, or properly valued.

To accomplish the foregoing, we demonstrate the creation of a security market line (SML) that visually represents the relationship between risk and the expected or the required rate of return on an asset. The equation of this SML together with estimates for the return on a risk-free asset and on the market portfolio can generate expected or required rates of return for any asset based on its systematic risk. You compare this required rate of return to the rate of return you estimate that you will earn on the investment to determine if the investment is undervalued or overvalued. After demonstrating this procedure, we finish the section with a demonstration of how to calculate the systematic risk variable for a risky asset.

THE SECURITY MARKET LINE (SML)

We know that the relevant risk measure for an individual risky asset is its covariance with the market portfolio (Cov_{im}). Therefore, we draw the risk–return relationship as shown in Figure 8.5 with the systematic covariance variable (Cov_{im}) as the risk measure.

The return for the market portfolio (R_m) should be consistent with its own risk, which is the covariance of the market with itself. Because the covariance of any asset with itself is its variance, $Cov_{ii} = \sigma_i^2$, the covariance of the market with itself is the variance of the market rate of return $Cov_{mm} = \sigma_m^2$. The equation for the risk–return line in Figure 8.5 is

$$E(R_i) = RFR + \frac{R_m - RFR}{\sigma_m^2}(COV_{im})$$

$$= RFR + \frac{Cov_{im}}{\sigma_m^2}(R_m - RFR).$$

Defining Cov_{im}/σ_m^2 as beta (β_i), this equation can be stated:

$$E(R_i) = RFR + \beta_i(R_m - RFR).$$

Beta can be viewed as a *standardized* measure of systematic risk. Specifically, we already know that the covariance of any asset i with the market portfolio Cov_{im} is the relevant risk measure. With beta it is standardized by relating this covariance to the variance of the market portfolio. As a result, the market portfolio has a beta of 1. Therefore, if the β_i for an asset is above 1.0, the asset has higher systematic risk than the market, which means that it is more volatile than the overall market portfolio.

Given this standardized measure of systematic risk, the SML graph can be expressed as shown in Figure 8.6. This is the same graph as in Figure 8.5 except that there is a

FIGURE 8.5 **Graph of SML**

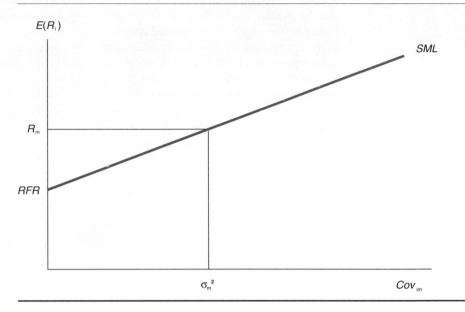

FIGURE 8.6 **Graph of SML with Normalized Systematic Risk**

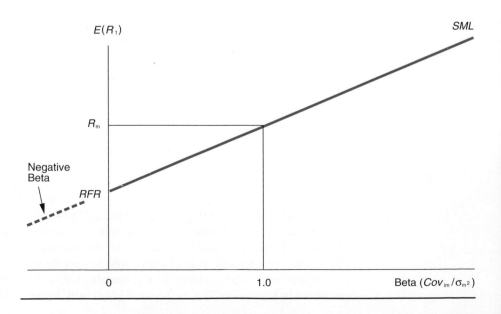

different measure of risk. Specifically, it replaces the covariance of an asset's returns with the market portfolio as the risk measure with the standardized measure of systematic risk (beta), which is the covariance divided by the variance of the market portfolio.

DETERMINING THE EXPECTED RATE OF RETURN FOR A RISKY ASSET

The equation above and the graph in Figure 8.6 tell us that the expected rate of return for a risky asset is determined by the RFR plus a risk premium for the individual asset. In turn, the risk premium is determined by the systematic risk of the asset (β_i), and the prevailing *market risk premium* ($R_m - RFR$). To demonstrate how you would compute the expected or required rates of return, consider the following example stocks assuming you have already computed betas:

Stock	Beta
A	0.70
B	1.00
C	1.15
D	1.40
E	-0.30

Assume that we expect the economy's RFR to be 8 percent (0.08) and the return on the market portfolio (R_m) to be 14 percent (0.14). This implies a market risk premium of 6 percent (0.06). With these inputs, the SML equation would yield the following expected (required) rates of return for these five stocks:

$$E(R_i) = RFR + \beta_i(R_m - RFR)$$
$$E(R_a) = 0.08 + 0.70\,(0.14 - 0.08)$$
$$= 0.122 = 12.2 \text{ percent}$$
$$E(R_b) = 0.08 + 1.00\,(0.14 - 0.08)$$
$$= 0.14 = 14 \text{ percent}$$
$$E(R_c) = 0.08 + 1.15\,(0.14 - 0.08)$$
$$= 0.149 = 14.9 \text{ percent}$$
$$E(R_d) = 0.08 + 1.40\,(0.14 - 0.08)$$
$$= 0.164 = 16.4 \text{ percent}$$
$$E(R_e) = 0.08 + (-0.30)\,(0.14 - 0.08)$$
$$= 0.08 - 0.018$$
$$= 0.062 = 6.2 \text{ percent.}$$

As stated, these are the expected (required) rates of return that these stocks should provide based on their systematic risks and the prevailing SML.

Stock A has lower risk than the aggregate market, so an investor should not expect (require) its return to be as high as the return on the market portfolio of risky assets. You should expect (require) Stock A to return 12.2 percent. Stock B has systematic risk equal to the market's (beta = 1.00), so its required rate of return should likewise be equal to the expected market return (14 percent). Stocks C and D have systematic risk greater than the market's so they should provide returns consistent with this risk. Finally, Stock E has a *negative* beta (which is quite rare in practice) so its required rate of return, if such a stock could be found, would be below the RFR.

In equilibrium, *all* assets and *all* portfolios of assets should plot on the SML. That is, all assets should be priced so that their *estimated rates of return,* which are the actual holding period rates of return that you anticipate, are consistent with their levels of systematic risk. Any security with an estimated rate of return that plots above the SML would be considered underpriced, because it implies that you expect to earn a rate of return on it that is above its required rate of return based on its systematic risk. In contrast, assets with estimated rates of return that plot below the SML would be considered overpriced because this position relative to the SML implies that you expect to receive a rate of return that is below what you should require based on the asset's systematic risk.

In an efficient market in equilibrium, you would not expect any assets to plot off the SML because, in equilibrium, all stocks are expected to provide holding period returns that are equal to their required rates of return. Alternatively, a market that is "fairly efficient" but not completely efficient, may misprice certain assets because not everyone will be aware of all the relevant information for an asset.

As we discussed in Chapter 6 on the topic of efficient markets, a superior investor has the ability to derive value estimates for assets that are consistently superior to the consensus market evaluation. As a result, such an investor will earn better rates of return than the average investor on a risk-adjusted basis.

IDENTIFYING UNDERVALUED AND OVERVALUED ASSETS

Now that we understand how to compute the rate of return one should expect or require for a specific risky asset using the SML, we can compare this *required* rate of return to the asset's *estimated* rate of return over a specific investment horizon to determine whether it would be an appropriate investment. To make this comparison you need an independent estimate of the return outlook for the security based on either fundamental or technical analysis techniques that will be discussed in subsequent chapters. Let us continue the example for the five assets discussed in the previous section.

Analysts in a major trust department have been following these five stocks. Based on extensive fundamental analysis, the analysts provide the price and dividend outlooks contained in Table 8.1. Given these estimates, you can compute the estimated rates of return the analysts would anticipate during this holding period.

Table 8.2 summarizes the relationship between the required rate of return for each stock based on its systematic risk as computed earlier and its *estimated* rate of return based on the current and future prices, and its dividend outlook.

Plotting these estimated rates of return and stock betas on the SML we specified earlier gives the graph shown in Figure 8.7. Stock A is almost exactly on the line, so it is considered properly valued because its estimated rate of return is almost equal to its required rate of return. Stocks B and D are considered overvalued, because their estimated rates of return during the coming period are not consistent with the risk involved as indicated by their positions below the SML. In contrast, Stocks C and E are expected to provide rates of return greater than we would require based on their systematic risk. Therefore, both stocks plot above the SML, indicating that they are undervalued stocks.

TABLE 8.1

Price, Dividend, and Rate of Return Estimates

Stock	Current Price (P_t)	Expected Price (P_{t+1})	Expected Dividend (D_{t+1})	Estimated Future Rate of Return (%)
A	25	27	1.00	12.0
B	40	42	1.25	8.1
C	33	40	1.00	24.2
D	64	65	2.40	5.3
E	50	55	—	10.0

TABLE 8.2

Comparison of Required Rate of Return to Estimated Rate of Return

Stock	Beta	Required Return $E(R_i)$	Estimated Return	Estimated Return minus $E(R_i)$	Evaluation
A	0.70	12.2	12.0	−0.2	Properly valued
B	1.00	14.0	8.1	−5.9	Overvalued
C	1.15	14.9	24.2	9.3	Undervalued
D	1.40	16.4	5.3	−11.1	Overvalued
E	−0.30	6.2	10.0	3.8	Undervalued

FIGURE 8.7

Plot of Estimated Returns on SML Graph

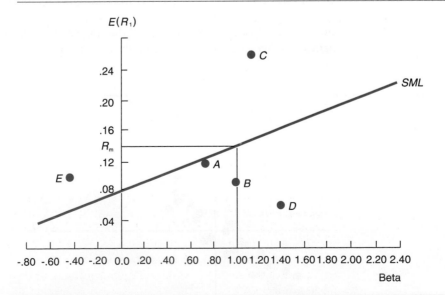

Assuming that you trusted your analyst to forecast estimated returns, you would take no action regarding Stock A, but you would buy Stocks C and E and sell Stocks B and D if you owned them. You might even sell Stocks B and D short if you favored such aggressive tactics.

CALCULATING SYSTEMATIC RISK: THE CHARACTERISTIC LINE

The systematic risk input for an individual asset is derived from a regression model, referred to as the asset's *characteristic line* with the market portfolio:

$$R_{it} + \alpha_i + \beta_i R_{mt} + \epsilon$$

where:

R_{it} = the rate of return for asset i during period t

R_{mt} = the rate of return for the market portfolio during period t

α_i = the constant term, or intercept, of the regression, which equals $\bar{R}_i - \beta_i \bar{R}_m$

β_i = the systematic risk (beta) of asset i equal to Cov_{im}/σ_m^2

ϵ = the random error term.

The characteristic line is the line of best fit through a scatter plot of rates of return for the individual risky asset and for the market portfolio of risky assets over some designated past period, as shown in Figure 8.8.

THE IMPACT OF THE TIME INTERVAL   In practice the number of observations and the time interval vary. Value Line Investment Services derives characteristic lines for common stocks using weekly rates of return for the most recent five years (i.e., 260 weekly observations). Merrill Lynch, Pierce, Fenner & Smith uses monthly rates of return for the most recent five years (60 monthly observations). Because there is no theoretically correct time interval for analysis, we must make a trade-off between enough observations to eliminate the impact of random rates of return and an excessive length of time such as 15 or 20 years over which the subject company may have changed dramatically. Remember that what you really want is the *expected* systematic risk for the

---

FIGURE 8.8   **Scatter Plot of Rates of Return**

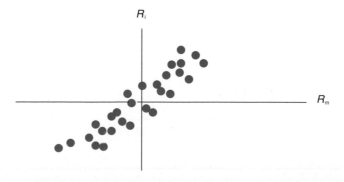

potential investment. In this analysis you are analyzing historical data to help you derive a reasonable estimate.

A couple of studies have considered the impact of the time interval used to compute betas (weekly versus monthly). Statman examined the relationship between Value Line (VL) betas and Merrill Lynch (ML) betas and found a relatively weak relationship.[8] Reilly and Wright examined a larger sample and analyzed the differential effects of return computation, market index, and the time interval and likewise found a weak relationship between VL and ML betas.[9] They showed that the major cause of the significant differences in beta was the use of monthly versus weekly intervals.

They also found that the interval effect depended on the sizes of the firms. The shorter weekly interval caused a larger beta for large firms and a smaller beta for small firms. For example, from 1975 to 1979, the average beta for the smallest decile of firms using monthly data was 1.682, but the average beta for these small firms was only 1.080 using weekly data. The authors concluded that the return time interval makes a difference, and the impact of the interval increases as the size of the firm declines.

THE EFFECT OF THE MARKET PROXY   Also, we must decide which indicator series to use as a proxy for the market portfolio of all risky assets. Obviously, no market series contains all the risky assets in the economy. As a matter of practice, most investigators use the Standard & Poor's 500 Composite Index as a proxy for the market portfolio, because the stocks in this index encompass a large proportion of the total market value of U.S. stocks. Also it is a value-weighted series, which is consistent with the theoretical market series. Still, this series only contains U.S. stocks, most of them listed on the NYSE. You will recall our earlier discussion where it was noted that the theoretically correct market portfolio of all risky assets should include U.S. stocks and bonds, non-U.S. stocks and bonds, real estate, coins, stamps, art, antiques, and any other marketable risky asset from around the world.[10]

EXAMPLE COMPUTATIONS OF A CHARACTERISTIC LINE
The following examples show how you would compute characteristic lines for IBM based on the monthly rates of return during 1991.[11] Twelve is not enough observations, but it should provide a good example. We will provide two examples using two different proxies for the market portfolio. The first is the typical analysis where the S&P 500 is used as the market proxy. In the second example we use the *Financial Times* World Equity Index as the market proxy. Although neither of these indexes are ideal because they only include common stocks, the comparison will allow us to demonstrate the effect of a more complete proxy of stocks.

[8]Meir Statman, "Betas Compared: Merrill Lynch vs. Value Line," *Journal of Portfolio Management* 7, no. 2 (Winter 1981): 41–44.

[9]Frank K. Reilly and David J. Wright, "A Comparison of Published Betas," *Journal of Portfolio Management* 14, no. 3 (Spring 1988): 64–69.

[10]There has been substantial discussion of the market index used and its impact on the empirical results and usefulness of the CAPM. This concern is discussed further and demonstrated in the subsequent section on computing an asset's characteristic line. It is also considered when we discuss the arbitrage pricing theory (APT) in this chapter and in Chapter 25.

[11]These betas are computed using only monthly price changes for IBM, the S&P 500, and the FT World Index (i.e., dividends are not included). This is done for simplicity but is also based on a study indicating that betas derived with and without dividends are correlated 0.99: William Sharpe and Guy M. Cooper, "Risk–Return Classes of New York Stock Exchange Common Stocks," *Financial Analysts Journal* 28, no. 2 (March-April 1972): 35–43.

TABLE 8.3   **Computation of Covariance Between IBM and the S&P 500: 1991**

Date	Month-End Price S&P 500	S&P 500 Return	IBM Return	S&P 500 $R_{MKT} - E(R_{MKT})$	IBM $R_{IBM} - E(R_{IBM})$	S&P 500 $R_{MKT} - E(R_{MKT})$ $\times$ IBM $R_{IBM} - E(R_{IBM})$
12/90	330.22					
1/91	343.93	4.15	12.17	2.09	13.90	29.10
2/91	367.07	6.73	1.58	4.67	3.31	15.44
3/91	375.22	2.22	−11.55	0.16	−9.82	−1.60
4/91	375.35	0.03	−9.55	−2.02	−7.82	15.83
5/91	389.83	3.86	3.03	1.80	4.76	8.56
6/91	371.16	−4.79	−8.48	−6.85	−6.75	46.24
7/91	387.81	4.49	4.25	2.43	5.98	14.51
8/91	395.43	1.96	−4.32	−0.09	−2.59	0.24
9/91	387.86	−1.91	6.97	−3.97	8.70	−34.54
10/91	392.46	1.19	−5.19	−0.87	−3.46	3.02
11/91	375.22	−4.39	−6.11	−6.45	−4.38	28.27
12/91	417.09	11.16	−3.52	9.10	−1.79	−16.32
Average		2.06	−1.73			Total = 108.76
Standard Deviation		4.35	6.97			

$$Cov_{IBM,mkt} = \frac{108.76}{12} = 9.063$$

$$Var_{mkt} = (4.35)^2 = 18.92$$

$$\beta_{IBM} = \frac{9.06}{18.92} = 0.48$$

$$r_{IBM,mkt} = \frac{9.06}{(4.35)(6.97)} = 0.30$$

$$\alpha = \bar{R}_{IBM} - [\beta_{IBM} \times \bar{R}_{mkt}]$$
$$= -1.73 - (.48 \times 2.06)$$
$$= -1.73 - .99$$
$$= -2.72$$

The monthly price changes are computed using the closing prices for the last day of each month. These data for IBM and the S&P 500 are contained in Table 8.3, and a scatter plot of the percent price changes for IBM and the S&P 500 is contained in Figure 8.9. During this 12-month period, IBM had returns that varied when compared with the aggregate market returns as proxied by the S&P 500. Specifically, there were three instances when one series experienced a return above or below its mean while the other series did not do the same. Two of these instances produced fairly large negative products. As a result, the covariance between IBM and the S&P 500 series was positive, but it was not a very large positive value (9.063). The covariance divided by the variance of the market portfolio (18.92) indicates that IBM's beta relative to the S&P 500 was equal to 0.48. This analysis indicates that during this limited time period IBM was substantially less risky than the aggregate market.

When we draw this characteristic line on Figure 8.9, the scatter plots are not very close to the characteristic line, which is consistent with the correlation coefficient of only 0.30.

The computation of the characteristic line for IBM using the FT world index as the proxy for the market is contained in Table 8.4, and the scatter plot is in Figure 8.10.

FIGURE 8.9   **Scatter Plot of IBM and the S&P 500 with Characteristic Line for IBM: 1991**

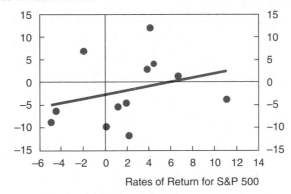

Rates of Return for IBM

Rates of Return for S&P 500

TABLE 8.4   **Computation of Covariance Between IBM and the FT World Index: 1991**

Date	Month-End Price FT World	FT World Return	IBM Return	FT World $R_{MKT} - E(R_{MKT})$	IBM $R_{IBM} - E(R_{IBM})$	FT World $R_{MKT} - E(R_{MKT})$ × IBM $R_{IBM} - E(R_{IBM})$
12/90	129.80					
1/91	134.08	3.30	12.17	1.92	13.90	26.72
2/91	146.18	9.02	1.58	7.65	3.31	25.30
3/91	142.09	−2.80	−11.55	−4.17	−9.82	40.98
4/91	143.66	1.10	−9.55	−0.27	−7.82	2.11
5/91	145.48	1.27	3.03	−0.11	4.76	−0.51
6/91	136.54	−6.15	−8.48	−7.52	−6.75	50.78
7/91	143.04	4.76	4.25	3.39	5.98	20.24
8/91	142.00	−0.73	−4.32	−2.10	−2.59	5.45
9/91	145.84	2.70	6.97	1.33	8.70	11.57
10/91	148.38	1.74	−5.19	0.37	−3.46	−1.27
11/91	141.49	−4.64	−6.11	−6.02	−4.38	26.38
12/91	151.26	6.91	−3.52	5.53	−1.79	−9.92
Average		1.37	−1.73			Total = 197.82
Standard Deviation		4.29	6.97			

$$Cov_{IBM,mkt} = \frac{197.82}{12} = 16.485$$

$$Var_{mkt} = (4.29)^2 = 18.40$$

$$\beta_{IBM} = \frac{16.49}{18.40} = 0.90$$

$$r_{IBM,mkt} = \frac{16.49}{(4.29)(6.97)} = 0.55$$

$$\alpha = \bar{R}_{IBM} - [\beta_{IBM} \times \bar{R}_{mkt}]$$
$$= -1.73 - (.90 \times 1.37)$$
$$= -1.73 - .1.23$$
$$= -2.96$$

FIGURE 8.10   **Scatter Plot of IBM and the FT World Index with Characteristic Line for IBM: 1991**

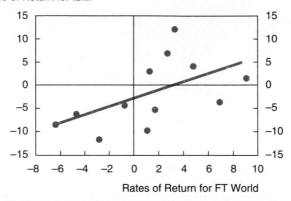

Rates of Return for IBM

Rates of Return for FT World

The results indicate a beta with the world index of 0.90. The fact that the beta with the world index (0.90) is larger than the beta with the S&P 500 (0.48) is inconsistent with expectations because one would normally expect a U.S. firm to have a closer relationship (higher covariance) with a U.S. market index than with a world index. In this case, the covariance with the world index (16.485) was much larger than with the S&P 500 (9.063). Because the market variances for the two market series were almost identical (18.92, S&P 500 vs. 18.40, FT world), the beta relative to the world index reflected the larger covariance.

Although the differences in beta were not consistent with expectations, the fact that they differed is significant and reflects the potential problem that can occur in a global environment where it becomes difficult to select the appropriate proxy for the market portfolio.

ARBITRAGE
PRICING THEORY
(APT)

At this point we have discussed the basic theory of the CAPM, the impact of changing some of its major assumptions, and its dependence on a market portfolio of all risky assets. In addition, the model assumes that investors have quadratic utility functions and that the distribution of security prices is normal—that is, symmetrically distributed, with a variance term that can be estimated.

Some tests of the CAPM that are discussed in Chapter 25 indicate that the beta coefficients for individual securities are not stable, but the beta of portfolios generally were stable assuming long enough sample periods and adequate trading volume. Some studies have also supported a positive linear relationship between rates of return and systematic risk for portfolios of stock. In contrast, a set of papers by Roll criticized the usefulness of the model because of its dependence on a market portfolio of risky assets that is not currently available.[12] When the CAPM is used to evaluate portfolio per-

---

[12]Richard Roll, "A Critique of the Asset Pricing Theory's Tests,"*Journal of Financial Economics* 4, no. 4 (March 1977): 129–176; Richard Roll, "Ambiguity When Performance Is Measured by the Securities Market Line," *Journal of Finance* 33, no. 4 (September 1978): 1051–1069; and Richard Roll, "Performance Evaluation and Benchmark Error II," *Journal of Portfolio Management* 7, no. 2 (Winter 1981): 17–22.

formance, it is necessary to select a proxy for the market portfolio as a benchmark for performance. It has been shown that the results can be changed because of the market proxy used.

Given these questions, the academic community has considered an alternative asset pricing theory that is reasonably intuitive and requires only limited assumptions. This *arbitrage pricing theory (APT),* developed by Ross in the early 1970s and initially published in 1976, has three major assumptions:[13]

1. Capital markets are perfectly competitive.
2. Investors always prefer more wealth to less wealth with certainty.
3. The stochastic process generating asset returns can be represented as a K factor model (to be described).

Equally important, the following major assumptions are *not* required: (1) quadratic utility function, (2) normally distributed security returns, and (3) a market portfolio that contains all risky assets and is mean-variance efficient. Obviously, if such a theory is able to explain differential security prices, it would be considered a superior theory because it is simpler (i.e., it requires fewer assumptions).

As noted, the theory assumes that the stochastic process generating asset returns can be represented as a K factor model of the form

$$R_i = E_i + b_{i\,1}\delta_1 + b_{i\,2}\delta_2 + \cdots + b_{ik}\delta_k + \epsilon_i \text{ for } i = 1 \text{ to } N.$$

where:

R_i = return on asset i during a specified time period
E_i = expected return for asset i
b_{ik} = reaction in asset i's returns to movements in the common factor
δ_k = a common factor with a zero mean that influences the returns on all assets
ϵ_i = a unique effect on asset i's return that, by assumption, is completely diversifiable in large portfolios and has a mean of zero
N = number of assets.

Two terms require elaboration: δ_k and b. As indicated, δ_k terms are the *multiple* factors expected to have an impact on the returns of *all* assets. Examples might include inflation, growth in GNP, major political upheavals, or changes in interest rates. The APT contends there are many such factors, in contrast to the CAPM, where the only relevant variable is the covariance of the asset with the market portfolio.

Given these common factors, the b_{ik} terms determine how each asset reacts to this common factor. To extend the earlier example, although all assets may be affected by growth in GNP, the impact will differ. For example, stocks of cyclical firms will have larger b_{ik} terms for this common factor than noncyclical firms, such as grocery chains. Likewise, you will hear discussions about interest-sensitive stocks: all stocks are affected by changes in interest rates, but some stocks experience larger impacts. It is possible to envision other examples of common factors, such as inflation, exchange

---

[13]Stephen Ross, "The Arbitrage Theory of Capital Asset Pricing," *Journal of Economic Theory* 13, no. 2 (December 1976): 341–360; Stephen Ross, "Return, Risk, and Arbitrage," in *Risk and Return in Finance,* eds. I. Friend and J. Bicksler (Cambridge: Ballinger, 1977), 189–218.

rates, interest rate spreads, and so on. Still, in the application of the theory, *the factors are not identified*. That is, when we discuss the empirical studies, three, four, or five factors that affect security returns will be identified, but *there is no indication of what these factors represent*.

Similar to the CAPM model, it is assumed that the unique effects (ϵ_i) are independent and will be diversified away in a large portfolio. The APT assumes that, in equilibrium, the return on a zero-investment, zero-systematic-risk portfolio is zero when the unique effects are diversified away. This assumption and some theory from linear algebra implies that the expected return on any asset i (E_i) can be expressed as

$$E_i = \lambda_0 + \lambda_1 b_{i1}, + \lambda_2 b_{i2} + \cdots + \lambda_k b_{ik}.$$

where:

λ_0 = **the expected return on an asset with zero systematic risk where $\lambda_0 = E_0$**
λ_1 = **the risk premium related to each of the common factors—e.g., the risk premium related to interest rate risk ($\lambda_i = E_i = E_0$)**
b_i = **the pricing relationship between the risk premium and asset i—i.e., how responsive asset i is to this common factor K.**

Consider the following example of two stocks and a two-factor model.

K_1 = **changes in the rate of inflation. The risk premium related to this factor is 1 percent for every 1 percent change in the rate ($\lambda_1 = .01$).**
K_2 = **percent growth in real GNP. The average risk premium related to this factor is 2 percent for every 1 percent change in the rate ($\lambda_2 = .02$).**
λ_0 = **the rate of return on a zero-systematic-risk asset (zero beta: $b_{0j} = 0$) is 3 percent ($\lambda_0 = .03$).**

The two assets (X,Y) have the following response coefficients to these factors:

b_{x1} = **the response of asset X to changes in the rate of inflation is 0.50 ($b_{x1} = .50$). This asset is not very responsive to changes in the rate of inflation.**
b_{y1} = **the response of asset Y to changes in the rate of inflation is 2.00 ($b_{y1} = 2.00$).**
b_{x2} = **the response of asset X to changes in the growth rate of real GNP is 1.50 ($b_{x2} = 1.50$).**
b_{y2} = **the response of asset Y to changes in the growth rate of real GNP is 1.75 ($b_{y2} = 1.75$).**

These response coefficients indicate that if these are the major factors influencing asset returns, asset Y is a higher risk asset, and therefore its expected return should be greater, as shown below:

$$E_i = \lambda_0 + \lambda_1 b_{i1} + \lambda_2 b_{i2}$$
$$= .03 + (.01)b_{i1} + (.02)b_{i2}.$$

Therefore:

$$E_x = .03 + (.01)(0.50) + (.02)(1.50)$$
$$= .065 = 6.5\%$$

$$E_y = .03 + (.01)(2.00) + (.02)(1.75)$$
$$= .085 = 8.5\%.$$

If the prices of the assets do not reflect these returns, we would expect investors to enter into arbitrage arrangements whereby they would sell overpriced assets short and use the proceeds to purchase the underpriced assets until the relevant prices were corrected. The point is, given these linear relationships, it should be possible to find an asset or a combination of assets with equal risk to the mispriced asset, yet a higher return.

EMPIRICAL TESTS OF THE APT

Studies by Roll and Ross and also by Chen have provided results that support the APT because the model was able to explain different rates of return, in some cases with results that were superior to those of the CAPM.[14] In contrast, results of Reinganum's study do not support the model because it did not explain small-firm results.[15] Finally, Dhrymes and Shanken both questioned the usefulness of the model because it was not possible to identify the factors; under these conditions, is the theory testable?[16]

At this time, the theory is relatively new and will be subject to continued testing. The important points to remember are that the model requires fewer assumptions and considers multiple factors to explain the risk of an asset, in contrast to the single-factor CAPM.[17]

SUMMARY

The assumptions of capital market theory expand on those of the Markowitz portfolio model and include consideration of the risk-free rate of return. The correlation and covariance of any asset with a risk-free asset is zero, so that any combination of an asset or portfolio with the risk-free asset generates a linear return and risk function. Therefore, when you combine the risk-free asset with any risky asset on the Markowitz efficient frontier, you derive a set of straight-line portfolio possibilities.

The dominant line is the one that is tangent to the efficient frontier. This dominant line is referred to as the *capital market line (CML),* and all investors should target points along this line depending on their risk preferences.

Because all investors want to invest in the risky portfolio at the point of tangency, this portfolio, referred to as the market portfolio, must contain all risky assets in proportion to their relative market values. Moreover, the investment decision and the financing decision can be separated, because, although everyone will want to invest in the market portfolio, investors will make different financing decisions about whether to lend or borrow based on their individual risk preferences.

Given the CML and the dominance of the market portfolio, the relevant risk measure for an individual risky asset is its covariance with the market portfolio, that is, its

---

[14]Richard Roll and Stephen A. Ross, "An Empirical Investigation of the Arbitrage Pricing Theory," *Journal of Finance* 35, no. 5 (December 1980): 1073–1103; and Nai-fu Chen, "Some Empirical Tests of Theory of Arbitrage Pricing," *Journal of Finance* 18, no. 5 (December 1983): 1393–1414.

[15]Marc R. Reinganum, "The Arbitrage Pricing Theory: Some Empirical Results," *Journal of Finance* 36, no. 2 (May 1981): 313–321.

[16]Phoebus J. Dhrymes, "The Empirical Relevance of Arbitrage Pricing Models," *Journal of Portfolio Management* 10, no. 4 (Summer 1984): 35–44; Jay Shanken, "The Arbitrage Pricing Theory: Is It Testable?" *Journal of Finance* 37, no. 5 (December 1982): 1129–1140.

[17]For a discussion of how these models relate to each other, see William F. Sharpe, "Factor Models, CAPMs and the APT," *Journal of Portfolio Management* 11, no. 1 (Fall 1984): 21–25.

systematic risk. When this covariance is standardized by the covariance for the market portfolio, we derive the well-known beta measure of systematic risk and a security market line (SML) that relates the expected or required rate of return for an asset to its beta. Because all individual securities and portfolios should plot on this SML, you can determine the expected (required) return on a security based on its systematic risk (its beta).

Alternatively, assuming security markets are not always completely efficient, you can identify undervalued and overvalued securities by comparing your estimate of the rate of return to be earned on an investment to its required rate of return. The systematic risk variable (beta) for an individual risky asset is computed using a regression model that generates an equation referred to as the asset's *characteristic line.*

We concluded the chapter with a discussion of an alternative asset pricing model—the arbitrage pricing theory (APT) model. This included a discussion of the necessary assumptions and the basics of the model as well as an example of its use. We also considered some of the tests of the model that have generated mixed results. Because of the mixed results and the importance of the topic, it is likely that testing of this model will continue.

QUESTIONS

1. Define a risk-free asset.
2. What is the covariance between a risk-free asset and a portfolio of risky assets? Explain your answer.
3. Explain why the set of points between the risk-free asset and a portfolio on the Markowitz efficient frontier is a straight line.
4. What happens to the Markowitz efficient frontier when you combine a risk-free asset with alternative risky asset portfolios on the Markowitz efficient frontier? Draw a graph to show this effect, and explain it.
5. Explain why the line from the RFR that is tangent to the efficient frontier defines the dominant set of portfolio possibilities. Demonstrate it graphically.
6. It has been shown that the capital market line (CML) is tangent to one portfolio (Portfolio M) on the Markowitz efficient frontier. Discuss what risky assets are in Portfolio M and why they are in it.
7. Discuss leverage and its effect on the CML.
8. Why is the CML considered the new efficient frontier?
9. Define complete diversification in terms of capital market theory.
10. Discuss and justify a measure of diversification for a portfolio.
11. What changes would you expect in the standard deviation for a portfolio of stocks between 4 and 10 stocks, between 10 and 20 stocks, and between 50 and 100 stocks?
12. Discuss why the investment and financing decisions are separate when you have a CML.
13. Given the CML, discuss and justify the relevant measure of risk for an individual security.
14. Capital market theory divides the variance of returns for a security into systematic variance and unsystematic or unique variance. Describe what each of these terms means.
15. The capital asset pricing model (CAPM) assumes that there is systematic and unsystematic risk for an individual security. Which is the relevant risk variable and why is it relevant? Why is the other risk variable not relevant?

16. Draw a properly labeled graph of the security market line (SML) and explain it. How does the SML differ from the CML?

PROBLEMS

1. Assume that you expect the economy's rate of inflation to be 3 percent, giving a RFR of 6 percent and a market return (R_m) of 12 percent.
   a. Draw the SML under these assumptions.
   b. Subsequently, you expect the rate of inflation to increase from 3 percent to 6 percent. What effect would this have on the RFR and the R_m? Draw another SML on the graph from part a.
   c. Draw a SML on the same graph to reflect a RFR of 9 percent and a R_m of 17 percent. How does this SML differ from that derived in part b? Explain what has transpired.

2. You expect a RFR of 10 percent and the market return (R_m) of 14 percent. Compute the expected (required) return for the following stocks, and plot them on an SML graph.

Stock	Beta	$E(R_i)$
U	0.85	
N	1.25	
D	−0.20	

3. You ask a stockbroker what the firm's research department expects for these three stocks. The broker responds with the following information:

Stock	Current Price	Expected Price	Expected Dividend
U	22	24	0.75
N	48	51	2.00
D	37	40	1.25

Plot your estimated returns on the graph from Problem 2 and indicate what actions you would take with regard to these stocks. Discuss your decisions.

4. Select a stock from the NYSE and collect its month-end prices for the latest 13 months in order to compute 12 monthly percentage of price changes ignoring dividends. Do the same for the S&P 500 series. Prepare a scatter plot of these series on a graph and draw a visual characteristic line of best fit (the line that minimizes the deviations from the line). Compute the slope of this line from the graph.

5. Given the returns derived in Problem 4, compute the beta coefficient using the formula and techniques employed in Table 8.3. How many negative products did you have for the covariance? How does this computed beta compare to the visual beta derived in Problem 4?

6. Look up the index values and compute the monthly rates of return for either the FT world index or the Morgan Stanley world index.
   a. Compute the beta for your NYSE stock using one of these world stock indexes as the proxy for the market portfolio.
   b. How does this world beta compare to your S&P 500 beta? Discuss the difference.

7. Look up this stock in *Value Line* and record the beta derived by *VL*. How does this *VL* beta compare to the beta you computed? Discuss reasons why the betas might differ.

8. Select a stock that is listed on the AMEX and plot the returns during the last 12 months relative to the S&P 500. Compute the beta coefficient. In general, did you expect this stock to have a higher or lower beta than the NYSE stock? Explain your answer.

9. Given the returns for the AMEX stock in Problem 8, plot the stock returns relative to monthly rates of return for the AMEX Market Value Index and compute the beta coefficient. Does this beta differ from that derived in Problem 8? If so, how can you explain this? Hint: Analyze the specific components of the formula for the beta coefficient. How did the components differ between Problems 7 and 8?

10. Using the data from the prior questions, compute the beta coefficient for the AMEX Index relative to the S&P 500 Index. A priori, would you expect a beta less than or greater than 1.00? Discuss your expectations and the actual results.

11. Based on 5 years of monthly data, you derive the following information for the companies listed.

Company	a_i (Intercept)	σ_i	r_{im}
Apple Computer	0.22	12.10%	0.72
Chrysler	0.10	14.60	0.33
Anheuser Busch	0.17	7.60	0.55
Monsanto	0.05	10.20	0.60
S&P 500	0.00	5.50	1.00

a. Compute the beta coefficient for each stock.

b. Assuming a risk-free rate of 8 percent and an expected return for the market portfolio of 15 percent, compute the expected (required) return for all the stocks and plot them on the SML.

c. Plot the following estimated returns for the next year on the SML and indicate which stocks are undervalued or overvalued.

- Apple Computer—20%
- Chrysler—15%
- Anheuser Busch—19%
- Monsanto—10%

12. Calculate the expected return for each of the following stocks when the risk-free rate is .08 and you expect the market return to be .15.

Stock	Beta
A	1.72
B	1.14
C	0.76
D	0.44
E	0.03
F	0.79

13. Compute the beta for the Golden Computer Company based on the following historic returns:

Year	Golden Computer	General Index
1	37	15
2	9	13
3	−11	14
4	8	−9
5	11	12
6	4	9

14. With the information in Problem 13 compute the following:
    a. The correlation coefficient between Golden Computer and the General Index.
    b. The intercept of the characteristic line.
    c. The equation of the characteristic line.

REFERENCES

Chen, F. N., Richard Roll, and Steve Ross. "Economic Forces and the Stock Market." *Journal of Business* (July 1986).

Hagin, Robert. *Modern Portfolio Theory.* Homewood, Ill.: Dow-Jones-Irwin, 1979.

Hawawini, Gabriel A. "Why Beta Shifts as the Return Interval Changes." *Financial Analysts Journal* 39, no. 3 (May-June 1983).

Lintner, John. "The Valuation of Risk Assets and the Selection of Risky Investments in Stock Portfolios and Capital Budgets." *Review of Economics and Statistics* 47, no. 2 (February 1965).

Mossin, Jan. "Equilibrium in a Capital Asset Market." *Econometrica* 34, no. 4 (October 1966).

Mullins, David. "Does the Capital Asset Pricing Model Work?" *Harvard Business Review* (January-February 1982).

Reilly, Frank K., and David J. Wright. "A Comparison of Published Betas." *Journal of Portfolio Management* 14, no. 3 (Spring 1988).

Rosenberg, Barr, and J. Guy. "Predictions of Beta from Investment Fundamentals." *Financial Analysts Journal* 32, no. 3 (May-June 1976).

Sharpe, William F. "Capital Asset Prices: A Theory of Market Equilibrium Under Conditions of Risk." *Journal of Finance* 19, no. 3 (September 1964).

Statman, Meir. "How Many Stocks Make a Diversified Portfolio?" *Journal of Financial and Quantitative Analysis* 22, no. 3 (September 1987).

CHAPTER 9

AN INTRODUCTION TO DERIVATIVE MARKETS AND SECURITIES

In this chapter, we will answer the following questions:

- What are the basic features of options, forward contracts, and futures contracts?
- What is the terminology employed to describe option contracts?
- What are the similarities and differences between forward and futures contracts?
- How is the price of an option determined?
- What determines the pricing of forward and futures contracts?
- What is the relationship between current prices and expected future spot prices of an asset?
- What are the relationships among the prices of puts, calls, and futures?
- What are some uses of derivatives in investment analysis and portfolio management?
- What is the evidence related to the efficiency of derivative markets?
- What is the empirical evidence regarding the relationship between the derivative market and the spot market?
- What is the empirical evidence regarding the correct pricing of derivatives?

Our financial system has always demonstrated a remarkable tendency to evolve and develop new markets and instruments. In recent years, this tendency has been exhibited most clearly in the rapid development and use of derivative instruments. A *derivative instrument* is one in which the performance is determined by the performance of another instrument. The derivative instrument is said to be "derived" from the other instrument. Early in the book, we briefly described options and futures, which form the basis for nearly all derivative trading. However, many new instruments have been created that possess some of the characteristics of options or futures and indeed some instruments that are like both options *and* futures. The incredible growth in the use of derivatives and the occasional controversy they engender make it all the more important that we develop an early understanding of what derivatives are and what role they play in our financial markets.

Our treatment of derivative instruments in this chapter is focused primarily on understanding the fundamental principles involved in determining their prices. To accomplish this, the initial section considers the general topic of put and call options and reviews the terminology used with these instruments. The second section describes forward and futures contracts and how they relate to each other. Section three deals with the pricing of option contracts using several approaches. The fourth section contains a similar detailed presentation related to the pricing of forward and futures contracts. In section five these pricing concepts are brought together when we discuss the parity relations among puts, calls, and futures. The chapter concludes with a brief section that considers how derivative instruments can be used in investment analysis and portfolio management and a section that reviews the empirical evidence on the efficient pricing of derivative instruments. The institutional characteristics, many of the trading strategies, and a number of advanced pricing principles of these instruments are deferred until Part VI.

Options are instruments that grant to their owners the right to buy or sell something at a fixed price, either on a specific date or any time up to a specific date. Because the owner pays for the option, it is rightly viewed as an asset. However, an option may or may not ever be used to buy or sell the underlying asset. *Forward contracts* are agreements between two parties, the buyer and seller, for the former to purchase an asset from the latter at a specific future date at a price agreed upon up front. No money changes hands between the buyer and seller and, thus, a forward contract itself is not an asset but merely an agreement. Forward contracts are created in an over-the-counter market. *Futures contracts* are somewhat like forward contracts in that they represent an agreement between a buyer and a seller to exchange cash for an asset at a future date. Unlike forward contracts, futures contracts trade on an exchange and are subject to a daily settling-up process, which will be described in more detail later.

To understand the pricing of derivative instruments, it is important to understand the concept of arbitrage, which is one of the most fundamental principles of finance: *two assets offering identical payoffs must sell for the same price.* For example, a share of stock cannot sell simultaneously for different prices on different markets. If it does, investors will "arbitrage," which means that they will buy the lower-priced security and sell the higher-priced security. This activity continues until their prices are equal and a risk-free profit is no longer available. In other words, in efficient markets, there are no arbitrage opportunities. This rule applies to combinations of securities as well. Two portfolios, whose individual compositions may appear to differ greatly, can ultimately produce the same payoffs. In that case, the portfolio values must be equal. A variation of the no-arbitrage rule is that if one security's payoffs are equivalent to those of another in all possible states of the world except one and are higher in that one, it will sell for an equal or higher price. Note that these rules make no statements about investors' feelings about risk; they require only that investors prefer more wealth to less.

OPTIONS

As described above, an option grants the right to buy or sell an asset at a fixed price either at a specific point in time or during a specific period of time. An option to buy an asset is referred to as a *call,* whereas an option to sell an asset is called a *put.* Consider the following examples of calls and puts.

Suppose that a stock is priced at $50 and that there are puts and calls on the stock that expire in 60 days. Consider a call that grants its owner the right to buy the stock during the next 60 days at $45 a share. To obtain this call, one would have to pay about $8. Alternatively, a put that permits the sale of the stock for $45 a share would cost about $1. Buyers of options are said to be "long" and sellers are said to be "short." Now let us familiarize ourselves with a little more terminology.

OPTION
TERMINOLOGY

The price paid for the option itself is the *option premium*. It is what a call buyer must pay for the right to acquire the stock at a given price at some time in the future and what a put buyer must pay for the right to sell the stock at a given price at some time in the future. We will study the determinants of the premium later in this chapter and in more depth in Chapter 20.

The price at which the stock can be acquired or sold is the *exercise price*, or *striking price*. In our example, $45 is the exercise price. The call permits its owner to buy the stock for $45 a share, and the put permits its owner to sell the stock for $45 a share. If the option holder chooses to use the option to buy or sell the stock, he or she is said to be *exercising* the option.

The date on which the option expires, or the last date on which it can be exercised, is the *expiration date*. For options trading on exchanges, the expiration dates are typically specified in terms of a given month. A July option would expire the Saturday following the third Friday in July. However, off the exchanges, options can be created by any two parties and can have any expiration date desired.

Some options permit the holder to exercise them only on the expiration day. These are called *European options*. Those that permit exercise any time up to and including the expiration day are called *American options*. These names have no relationship to where the options are trading. Both European and American options trade extensively on exchanges and in over-the-counter (OTC) markets in both the United States and Europe as well as other parts of the world.

A call option in which the stock price is higher than the exercise price is said to be *in-the-money*. If the stock price is lower than the exercise price, the call is said to be *out-of-the-money*. There is no reason to exercise an out-of-the-money option right now, because the stock can be bought for less in the market. However, an out-of-the-money option can later move in-the-money and vice versa. For puts, in-the-money means that the stock price is less than the exercise price, and out-of-the-money means that the stock price is greater than the exercise price. For both puts and calls, *at-the-money* means that the stock price is approximately equal to the exercise price.

Assuming our options are European, let us consider what happens at the end of 60 days. Suppose the stock price is at $49. Then the holder of the call option will exercise the call, using it to buy the $49 stock for $45. Note that this will occur, even though the call holder originally paid $8 for the call, and, thus, will suffer a loss. As we know, past cash flows are irrelevant; exercise of an in-the-money option at expiration is always the optimal thing to do.[1] If the stock price is below $45 at expiration, the call holder will not exercise the call. A put holder will exercise the put at expiration if the stock price is anywhere below $45, even if it means taking a loss after considering the premium paid.[2]

---

[1] However, in some cases, transaction costs associated with the exercise could make an option that is only slightly in-the-money not worth exercising.

[2] Again, transaction costs might make exercise of a slightly in-the-money put not worthwhile.

Options that trade on exchanges are generally fairly liquid so that they can be sold before expiration. Options that are written privately in the OTC market have no liquid market; however, it is frequently possible for the owner of an option to write a new option with the same terms as the original option, thus, offsetting the original option.

FORWARD AND FUTURES CONTRACTS

Suppose the two parties in our example on options agreed that the first party would buy the stock in 60 days from the second party, paying $62 a share. The amount, $62, is called the *forward price*. The first party is buying the contract and is said to be the buyer who is going long. The second party is selling the contract and is said to be the seller or writer who is going short. The parties have thus entered into a *forward contract*. Of course, each party must trust the other because both are obligated to do something at the expiration in 60 days. Both parties, thus, intend to complete the transaction in 60 days. There is no liquid market for the existing contract; however, the holder of either side of the contract can create a new transaction on the opposite side with the same terms, and, thus, offset the initial position.

Although forward contracts on all types of financial instruments and commodities are traded worldwide, it is difficult to study and understand forward markets because there are no exchanges and forward trading is not publicly reported. Forward contracts are essentially private agreements between parties of relatively high creditworthiness. Transaction sizes tend to be quite large. Fortunately, however, futures markets serve the need for highly liquid agreements similar to forward contracts and permit parties unable to meet the high credit standards of forward markets to construct similar positions.[3]

As noted earlier, futures exchanges are quite similar in structure and operation to stock exchanges. One can buy a futures contract on a futures exchange, which is an agreement to buy the underlying asset at a future date at a price agreed upon today. The other party to the contract, the seller, agrees to sell the underlying asset to the buyer at a future date at the price agreed upon today. That agreed-upon price is called the *futures price*. Like options and forwards, futures have an expiration day. Futures prices fluctuate from day to day, and the buyer of the contract can generally be assured that if he or she wishes to get out of the obligation to buy the asset at the expiration date, he or she can simply sell the contract in the market. Likewise, the seller of a futures contract can buy it back in the market before expiration. The liquidity of futures contracting is an important characteristic distinguishing it from forward contracting. Another important distinction is that futures contracts are standardized, meaning that only contracts with specific terms and conditions created by the exchanges are available for trading. In contrast, forward contracts are created by private individuals or institutions, and their terms are tailored to the specific needs of the participants.

Assume that a buyer and seller agree on a futures price of $62; but at expiration, the underlying asset is priced at $72. The buyer of the futures is quite pleased, knowing that a $72 asset can be acquired for $62. However, the seller of the futures is out $10. In a forward contract, the possibility that a party might default limits trading to the

---

[3]This statement is not meant to suggest that futures market participants are not very creditworthy. Indeed futures markets impose relatively high standards of credit on its participants. However, they use means other than the general reputation of the participants to ensure that all obligations are met.

most creditworthy customers. Futures markets alleviate this risk by settling profits and losses daily. This procedure, called *daily settlement* or *marking-to-market* goes as follows.

The buyer and seller agree on a trade at a futures price of $62. Each contract specifies that a designated amount of money be deposited by both parties in an account with the exchange's clearing corporation, called the *clearinghouse*. This money, which is generally referred to as the *initial margin,* but is more appropriately called a *performance bond,* is fairly small, usually equal to 3 to 6 percent of the price of the contract. Let us say it is $2. At the end of each day, a special exchange committee determines an approximate closing price, called the *settlement price.* Assuming that the next day, the settlement price equals $63, the buyer has made $1 and the seller has lost $1. So $1 is moved from the seller's account, leaving a $1 balance, to the buyer's account, creating a $3 balance. Beyond the first day of a trade, there is a minimum amount that must be maintained in the account, called the *maintenance margin.* If that requirement were $1.25, the seller would be undermargined by $0.25 and would be required to deposit sufficient funds to bring the balance back up, not to $1.25, but all the way to $2, the initial margin. The buyer can withdraw any excess over $2.

This procedure essentially closes out each contract every day and opens up a new one at the current settlement price, which is why it is sometimes called marking the account to market. This process ensures that losses are incurred in small amounts over time, rather than in one large amount at expiration. Parties that cannot deposit the required funds will have their contracts liquidated. In addition, futures markets often have limits on price movements that keep the maximum daily loss approximately equal to the required margin. The cost of these limits is that it prohibits transactions at certain equilibrium prices.

THE PRICING OF OPTIONS

In this section we will learn how an option gets its price. Although nearly all exchange-traded options are American-style, we will focus in this chapter on European options. If you understand the principles of European option pricing, you will be able to grasp the essential elements involved in option pricing. In Chapter 20, we will consider how the early exercise feature of American options affects their pricing.

BASIC CONCEPTS OF VALUE

To assist in understanding option pricing principles, let us construct some examples. Suppose a stock that pays no dividends is selling at $102. There is a call and a put option with an exercise price of $100 and another call and put option with an exercise price of $105. All of the options expire at the same time.

What are the minimum prices of the options? Because the holder cannot be forced to exercise an out-of-the-money option, prices can never be less than zero. Thus, their minimum values are zero.

What are their maximum values? Consider first the calls. If the stock price were at infinity, then the calls would certainly be worth a lot; however, because the calls can be used to buy the stock, they could never exceed the stock price. In fact, regardless of the stock price, the value of the call can never exceed the stock price. Even if the calls had the unusual characteristic of a zero exercise price, they would be worth, at most, the stock price.

Put options would achieve a very high value if the price of the underlying stock were extremely low. Because zero is the lowest the stock could go to, let us assume the firm goes bankrupt and the stock price goes to zero. Then the put holder has the right to sell the worthless stock for the exercise price at the expiration day. The put would then be worth today the present value of the exercise price. Thus, the present value of the exercise price is the put's maximum value.

Now we have established minimum and maximum values for our options:

Option	Minimum Value	Maximum Value
Call	Zero	Stock price
Put	Zero	Present value of exercise price

Although we have now bracketed the option price, unfortunately the range of acceptable prices is rather large. However, we can narrow it down a little more after we consider what the options will be worth at expiration.

Let us now define some symbols that will be helpful. Let time t be today and $S(t)$ be today's stock price. Let time T be the expiration date and $S(T)$ be the stock price at the expiration. Let X be the exercise price. Let $c(t)$ and $p(t)$ be the call and put prices today and $c(T)$ and $p(T)$ be the call and put prices at expiration. What will the options be worth at the expiration? In other words, given a value of $S(T)$, what will $c(T)$ and $p(T)$ be?

If $S(T) > X$, then the call option will expire in-the-money and will be exercised. The call holder will pay X dollars for a stock that can immediately be sold for $S(T)$ dollars. Someone buying the call at the instant of expiration would not pay more than $S(T) - X$. If $c(T)$ were less than $S(T) - X$, then someone could earn a risk-free, arbitrage profit by buying the call and immediately exercising it. Thus, the call price must be exactly $S(T) - X$. If the call expired at-the-money or out-of-the-money, then the call would be worthless because the stock could be bought at an equal or lower price in the market. Thus, we can now define $c(T)$ quite precisely as the maximum of either zero or $S(T) - X$. This is often written as

$$c(T) = Max(0, S(T) - X). \qquad (9.1)$$

Now reconsider the case of $S(T) \geq X$. The put would expire out-of-the-money and would be worthless because the stock could be sold for more in the market. In the case of $S(T) < X$, the put must be worth $X - S(T)$. No one buying the put at the instant of expiration would pay more than $X - S(T)$ because one could only use it to sell a stock worth $S(T)$ for X dollars. If the put were worth less than $X - S(T)$, then a risk-free arbitrage profit could be earned by buying the put and the stock and immediately exercising the put. Thus, given a value of $S(T)$, we can specify the value of the put at expiration as the maximum of zero or $X - S(T)$. This is usually written as

$$p(T) = Max(0, X - S(T)). \qquad (9.2)$$

With this information, we can now establish tighter bounds for current option prices.

TABLE 9.1

The Lower Bound of a European Call

Portfolio	Value Today	Value of Portfolio at Expiration	
		$S(T) \leq X$	$S(T) > X$
A. One share of stock	$S(t)$	$S(T)$	$S(T)$
B. One call	$c(t)$	0	$S(T) - X$
Risk-free discount bound	$\underline{X(1 + r)^{-(T-t)}}$	$\underline{X}$	$\underline{X}$
	$c(t) +$ $X(1 + r)^{-(T-t)}$	X	$S(T)$

Conclusion: B always performs at least as well as A at expiration. Thus, B must be at least as valuable as A today:

$$c(t) + X(1 + r)^{-(T-t)} \geq S(t).$$

Because $c(t)$ can never be less than zero,

$$c(t) \geq Max(0, S(t) - X(1 + r)^{-(T-t)}).$$

LOWER BOUNDS
ON OPTION PRICES

Consider the example of two portfolios illustrated in Table 9.1. Portfolio A consists of one share of stock, currently worth $S(t)$, and at time T, worth $S(T)$. Portfolio B consists of one call, currently worth $c(t)$, and a risk-free pure discount bond with a face value of X, which is currently worth the present value of X, or $X(1 + r)^{-(T-t)}$.[4] We create two columns to identify the option values at expiration. The first column considers the outcome when $S(T) \leq X$. In that case the call expires worthless and the bond pays off its face value of X. In the second column, we consider the outcome that $S(T) > X$. In that case, the call is worth its intrinsic value of $S(T) - X$, and the bond is worth its face value of X. Thus, the portfolio is worth $S(T)$. In the second outcome, both portfolios perform equivalently. In the first case, however, Portfolio B could have a higher terminal value than Portfolio A because it is worth X and A is worth only $S(T)$, and $S(T)$ is less than or equal to X in that case. Portfolio B performs at least as well as Portfolio A in all cases and could outperform A in some cases. Portfolio B is said to dominate A, so it will always be at least as valuable as Portfolio A today. Thus, with regard to their current prices, we can say that $c(t) + X(1 + r)^{-(T-t)} \geq S(t)$. Because we know that $c(t)$ can never be lower than zero, we can establish a lower bound for a call as

$$c(t) \geq Max(0, S(t) - X(1 + r)^{-(T-t)}). \tag{9.3}$$

This is a much tighter boundary than our former range of zero to $S(t)$. Assuming a risk-free rate of 5.13 percent and an expiration of one-half year for our call with $S(t)$ at 102 and X at 100, then $S(t) - X(1 + r)^{-(T-t)} = 102 - 100(1.0513)^{-.5} = 4.47$. Therefore, our call must sell for at least $4.47. Our call with exercise price of 105 would have $S(t) - X(1 + r)^{-.5} = 102 - 105(1.0513)^{-.5} = -.41$. Because this is negative, we set its lower bound at zero.

Table 9.2 illustrates a similar procedure for establishing the lower bound of a put. Portfolio A consists of one share of stock and one put. This portfolio will be worth

---

[4]Note that the exponent reflects the number of years before the option expires. For example, if the option expires in two months, we treat $T - t$ as $2/12 = .167$.

TABLE 9.2

The Lower Bound of a European Put

Portfolio	Value Today	Value of Portfolio at Expiration	
		$S(T) \leq X$	$S(T) > X$
A. One share of stock	$S(t)$	$S(T)$	$S(T)$
One put	$p(t)$	$X - S(T)$	0
	$S(t) + p(t)$	X	$S(T)$
B. Risk-free discount bond	$X(1 + r)^{-(T-t)}$	X	X

Conclusion: A always performs at least as well as B at expiration. Thus, A must be at least as valuable as B today:

$$S(t) + p(t) \geq X(1 + r)^{-(T-t)}.$$

Because $p(t)$ can never be less than zero,

$$p(t) \geq Max(0, X(1 + r)^{-(T-t)} - S(t)).$$

either X or $S(T)$ at expiration; note that X is its lowest possible value at expiration. Portfolio B is a risk-free discount bond with a face value of X at expiration. It will be worth X at expiration. Note that Portfolio A will always perform at least as well as Portfolio B, so its current price must be at least as high as that of Portfolio B, or in other words, $S(t) + p(t) \geq X(1 + r)^{-(T-t)}$. Because $p(t)$ can never be less than zero, we have

$$p(t) = Max(0, X(1 + r)^{-(T-t)} - S(t)). \tag{9.4}$$

This establishes the put's lower bound at the present value of the exercise price minus the stock price, or zero if that figure is negative. For our put with exercise price of 100, we have $X(1 + r)^{-(T-t)} - S(t) = 100(1.0513)^{-.5} - 102 = -4.47$. Thus, its lower bound is set at zero. For the put where the exercise price is 105, we have $105(1.0513)^{-.5} - 102 = .41$ as its lower bound.

These lower bounds tighten the range of possible values for these options. In addition, the time to expiration and exercise prices can affect the option price. Holding everything else constant, options with longer times to expiration will sell for more. However, the exception to this rule is that a European put can, under some circumstances, sell for less the longer the time to expiration. Calls with lower exercise prices will sell for more, and puts with higher exercise prices will sell for more. Next we will discuss exactly how the option is priced.

OPTION PRICING
IN A TWO-STATE
WORLD

Suppose we consider a very simple world in which a stock price today of S can, at some future time, take on a value of either $S+$ or $S-$. We call this a two-state world, and the model is referred to as a two-state model.[5] Corresponding to these stock prices are call prices of c today and either $c+$ or $c-$ one period later, corresponding to whether the stock price goes to $S+$ or $S-$. The exercise price is $45. The calls expire at the end of the period. Figure 9.1 illustrates the tree of stock prices and corresponding

---

[5]The model is also sometimes called a *binomial* model because a binomial process is one in which there are two possible outcomes.

FIGURE 9.1   **One-Period, Two-State Stock Price Process**

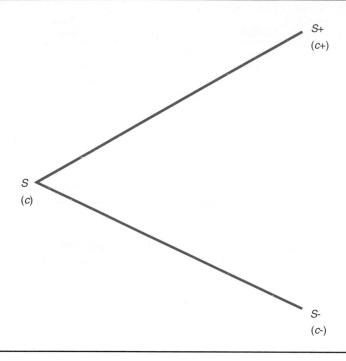

call prices. Suppose that S = \$44, $S+$ = \$52.80, and $S-$ = \$39.60. Now let us form the following portfolio: buy 591 shares of stock and sell 1,000 calls. This portfolio will cost 591(\$44) − 1000(c). We receive 1000c dollars for the calls written, and we leave the value of c, the call price today, unspecified. Since this is the value we are looking for. At expiration, we have the following outcomes:

Assume the stock price goes to $S+$ = 52.80. Then at expiration our call is worth 7.80 and our portfolio will be worth

$$591(\$52.80) - 1000(\$7.80) = \$23,404.$$

Assume the stock price declines to $S-$ = 39.60. Then at expiration the call will expire worthless and the portfolio will be worth

$$591(\$39.60) - 1000(\$0) = \$23,404.$$

Note that the result is the same in both cases. This occurs because the ratio of 591 shares to 1,000 calls, or more precisely, .591 shares per call, is the ratio that forms a perfect hedge between the option and the stock. This ratio is called the *hedge ratio* and is found as

$$\textit{Hedge Ratio } (h) = \frac{c+ \ - \ c-}{S+ \ - \ S-}.$$

Because both outcomes are equivalent, the portfolio is risk free and its current value is the present value of $23,404, using the risk-free rate as the discount rate. Let the risk-free rate, r, be .08. Thus, the current value of the portfolio is

$$\$23,404/1.08 = \$21,670.$$

This is the amount of money the investor needs to construct this portfolio. This must equal the value of 591 shares at the current stock price of $44 a share minus 1,000 calls at their current value of c. Setting this up and solving for c gives

$$591(\$44) - 1,000c = \$21,670$$
$$c = \$4.33.$$

Thus, the call must be worth exactly $4.33. If the call is worth more than $4.33, an investor can sell it, thus, reducing the amount of money the investor must invest. The final value of the portfolio will still be $23,404. Thus, with less money invested and the same final value at expiration, the risk-free return will exceed the risk-free rate of 8 percent. All investors will undertake this transaction until the call price is bid down to $4.33. If the call were priced at less than $4.33, investors would buy the call and sell short the stock until the price were bid up to $4.33.

A somewhat more direct approach to the problem is found by first defining the up and down factors as $u = S+/S = 52.80/44 = 1.2$ and $d = S-/S = 39.60/44 = .9$. Then we calculate a value called ρ as follows:

$$\rho = \frac{(1 + r) - d}{u - d}$$
$$= \frac{1.08 - .9}{1.2 - .9}$$
$$= .6.$$

Because we know $c+$ and $c-$, the option price can be found using the following formula:

$$c = \frac{\rho c+ + (1 - \rho)c-}{1 + r}$$
$$= \frac{.6(7.80) + .4(0)}{1.08}$$
$$= 4.33.$$

Table 9.3 summarizes these two procedures for finding the option price.

Note that in this model the factors that determine the option price are the stock price, exercise price, risk-free rate, and the characteristics of the stock price movements. These stock price movement characteristics, u and d, will reflect the range of possible movements in the stock price and, thus, are an indication of its volatility. Recall from Chapter 7 that the expected return on a stock is a probability-weighted average of the returns in the various states that can occur. Here the stock's return can be either $+20$

TABLE 9.3	**Steps for Finding the Two-State Option Price**

1. Find the hedge ratio:

$$h = \frac{c+ - c-}{S+ - S-} = \frac{7.80 - 0}{52.80 - 39.60} = .591.$$

2. Find the value at expiration (for either $S+$ or $S-$) of h shares and one short call: (Note: You can scale both quantities by 100, 1,000, or whatever, if desired.)

$$For\ S+: .591(52.80) - (1)(7.80) = 23.40$$
$$For\ S-: .591(39.60) = 23.40.$$

3. Find the present value of the value found in Step 2:

$$23.40/(1.08) = 21.67.$$

4. Equate the value today of h shares and one short call to the value found in Step 3:

$$.591(44) - c = 21.67.$$

5. Solve for c:

$$c = 4.33.$$

or

1. Calculate the value of ρ:

$$\rho = \frac{(1 + r) - d}{u - d} = \frac{1.08 - .9}{1.20 - .9} = .6.$$

2. Add the product of ρ and $c+$ to the product of $(1 - \rho)$ and $c-$:

$$\rho c+ + (1 - \rho)c- = .6(7.80) + .4(0) = 4.68.$$

3. Find the present value of the value found in Step 3:

$$4.68/(1.08) = 4.33.$$

percent or -10 percent. However, we do not know the probabilities of these occurrences.[6] Thus, the expected stock price does not enter directly into the formula for the option price. Later we will see that the time to expiration will also affect the option price.

As we have now seen, the option price is derived from its relationship to the stock price; hence, the name "derivative instrument." Forwards and futures are also derivative instruments, and we will now explore their pricing.

THE PRICING OF FORWARD AND FUTURES CONTRACTS

Consider a stock priced at $S(t)$. Suppose there is a forward contract established today at time t, that expires at time T calling for the purchase of the stock at a price of $FO(t,T)$. In addition there is a futures contract, also expiring at time T, that calls for the purchase of the stock at a price of $F(t,T)$. In this section, we will determine how these contracts are priced.

---

[6]Note that ρ and $1 - \rho$ are not the probabilities, though they do behave somewhat like probabilities and will range from zero to one. If investors were risk neutral, these values would be the probabilities of the stock price movements.

BASIC CONCEPTS
OF VALUE

As discussed earlier in the chapter, neither a forward nor a futures contract is an asset. When one party buys a forward or a futures contract from another party, neither party pays the other anything.[7] Thus, the value of both contracts when initially established is zero. This is in sharp contrast to options, stocks, and bonds, for which their prices are their values. Value arises in a forward or futures contract as a result of a price change. Defining $V(t,t,T)$ as the value of a forward contract at time t originally written at time t that expires at time T and $Y(t,t,T)$ as the value of a futures contract at time t originally written at time t that expires at time T, we have

$$V(t,t,T) = 0 \tag{9.5}$$

$$Y(t,t,T) = 0. \tag{9.6}$$

Now consider what happens at expiration. Assume that the stock price at time T is $S(T)$. Then the price of a new forward contract, $FO(T,T)$, written at T and expiring at T, must equal the spot price $S(T)$. If $FO(T,T)$ were less than $S(T)$, one could buy a forward contract, whereupon it would immediately expire and permit the purchase of the stock for $FO(T,T)$, which could be sold for $S(T)$. If $FO(T,T)$ were greater than $S(T)$, then one could buy the stock for $S(T)$, sell a forward contract, and deliver the stock, receiving $FO(T,T)$. Both of these cases would provide a risk-free arbitrage profit. Thus, we can state the following relationship at expiration:

$$FO(T,T) = S(T). \tag{9.7}$$

Because the original forward contract permits the buyer to purchase the stock worth $S(T)$ for a price of $FO(t,T)$ and requires the seller to sell the stock worth $S(T)$ for $FO(t,T)$, the contract has a value at expiration of $S(T) - FO(t,T)$ to the buyer and a value of $FO(t,T) - S(T)$ to the seller. Thus, we have the following for the value at expiration, T, of a forward contract originally written at time t:

$$V(T,t,T) = S(T) - FO(t,T). \tag{9.8}$$

What about the value of a forward contract during its life? Pick a time, t^*, where $t < t^* < T$. Do the following:

At t:

1. Buy a forward contract expiring at T with price $FO(t,T)$. Its value, $V(t,t,T)$, is zero.

At t^*:

1. Sell a new forward contract expiring at T with price $FO(t^*,T)$. Its value is $V(t^*,t,T)$. Now your position consists of a long forward contract at price $FO(t,T)$ and worth $V(t^*,t,T)$ and a short forward contract at price $F(t^*,T)$ and worth $V(t^*,t^*,T)$. Your overall position is worth $V(t^*,t,T) - V(t^*,t^*,T) = V(t^*,t,T)$, because the short forward contract has an initial value of zero.

---

[7]Of course, the futures exchange will require a small margin deposit. In addition, some forward contracts will require that the parties provide evidence of a credit line at a bank.

At T:

1. Use the first forward contract to acquire the stock, paying $FO(t,T)$.
2. Use the second forward contract to deliver the stock, receiving $FO(t^*,T)$.
3. Your net cash flow is $FO(t^*,T) - FO(t,T)$.

At time t^*, the future cash flow at T would be known. This position would, thus, be risk free and would be worth the present value of $FO(t^*,T) - FO(t,T)$ or $[FO(t^*,T) - F(t,T)](1 + r)^{-(T-t^*)}$. So the value at t^* of a combination of a long forward contract allowing you to buy the stock at T for $FO(t,T)$ and a short forward contract requiring you to sell the stock at T for $FO(t^*,T)$ would be worth this amount. Thus,

Value of Combination = Value of Old Long Forward + Value of New Short Forward
= Value of Old Long Forward + Zero

Thus,

$$V(t^*,t,T) = [FO(t^*,T) - FO(t,T)](1 + r)^{-r(T-t^*)}. \qquad (9.9)$$

A futures contract, as noted above, also has a zero initial value. At the end of each day, the futures exchange marks the contract to market and distributes gains and losses in cash. At any time since the last daily settlement, but before the next, the value of the futures is the current futures price minus the last settlement price. As soon as the contract is marked-to-market, its value goes back to zero. This is in keeping with the idea that the daily settlement is equivalent to closing out the futures contract and opening up a new one at the new settlement price every day. At expiration, when the spot price is $S(T)$, the futures price will also converge to the spot price. In other words, if t_1 is the next settlement time after time t and k is any point in the interval t to t_1, then the value of the futures contract at k is

$$Y(k,t,T) = F(k,T) - F(t,T). \qquad (9.10)$$

When $k = t_1$, then we have

$$Y(t_1,t_1, T) = 0. \qquad (9.11)$$

We have talked a lot about the similarities and differences between forward and futures contracts. The big question, however, is whether forward prices are different from futures prices. Cox, Ingersoll, and Ross showed that[8]

1. Prior to the last day of trading (T), the current futures price, $F(t,T)$, need not be equal to the current forward price, $FO(t,T)$. If short-term interest rates are known (deterministic), the current futures price equals the current forward price. On the last day of trading, there are no remaining differences between a futures and a forward contract and, thus, their prices are equal.

---

[8]John Cox, Jonathan Ingersoll, and Stephen Ross, "The Relation Between Forward Prices and Futures Prices," *Journal of Financial Economics* 9, no. 4 (December 1981): 321–346.

2. The futures price is greater (less) than the forward price if the covariance between the percentage changes in the futures price and the price of a default-free pure discount bond is negative (positive). In other words, if futures prices and short-term interest rates are positively (negatively) correlated, futures prices are greater (less) than forward prices.
3. Assume that the underlying asset makes no payouts (such as coupon interest during the life of the contract). If the covariance between percentage changes in the spot price and the price of a default-free pure discount bond is greater (less) than the variance of percentage changes in the default-free pure discount bond, the current forward price is greater (less) than the current futures price.

Typically, the differences between forward and futures prices are relatively small. For our purposes, therefore, we will treat them as equivalent instruments and refer only to futures contracts.

THE RELATIONSHIP BETWEEN CURRENT AND EXPECTED FUTURE SPOT PRICES

The current spot price of an asset is determined by current and expected supply and demand conditions. An expectation of an excess supply of an asset would reduce the inventory of stocks carried and reduce the current spot price. In contrast, an expectation of a shortage would increase inventories, which would exert upward pressure on spot prices. As a result, the current spot price, $S(t)$, and the expected future spot price, $E_t[S(T)]$ are connected by *the cost of carry, C(t,T)*, and a risk premium, *RP*, that compensates for bearing uncertainty about the future spot price. Both the cost of carry and the risk premium are expressed in terms of their values at time T. In broad terms:

$$E_t[S(T)] = S(t) + C(t,T) + RP. \tag{9.12}$$

The cost of carry depends on the type of asset and includes such items as insurance, spoilage, storage, depreciation, and financing costs. The latter are particularly important and reflect the risk-free rate of return that could be earned if the investor put the $S(t)$ dollars in the risk-free asset instead of the commodity. For many commodities, the cost of carry is typically positive. Sometimes, it may be negative because of the *convenience yield,* which represents the benefits of having inventory on hand, wherein inventory is carried even when the expected future spot price is less than the current spot price.[9] For instance, grain merchants and food processors carry stocks from one season to another, even when a bumper crop is expected. They do this to avoid stock-outs and maintain customer goodwill. The convenience yield is inversely related to the size of the inventory. When current inventories are relatively low, the convenience yield may exceed other (positive) components of the cost of carry. However, the expected future spot price could still be above the current spot price, depending on the size of the risk premium.

The cost of carrying financial assets such as debt instruments and foreign currencies is much lower than that of commodities. It includes the cost of financing and

[9]Michael J. Brennan, "The Supply of Storage," *American Economic Review* 47, no. 1 (March 1958): 50–72; Myron S. Scholes, "The Economics of Hedging and Spreading in Futures Markets," *The Journal of Futures Markets* 1, no. 2 (Summer 1981): 265–286.

safekeeping. Furthermore, some financial assets, such as stocks, notes, and bonds, may generate cash distributions such as dividends and coupon payments during the interval (t,T). The net carrying cost is considered fixed over a short period of time, but it becomes stochastic over longer intervals. The last term in Equation 9.12 is the premium for bearing nondiversifiable risk associated with the spot asset. Recall from Chapter 1 that risk premiums are important components of the prices of risky assets. Under some assumptions these risk premiums are determined by the asset's systematic risk. Although we can make that assumption here, we can just as easily leave the source of the risk premium unspecified.

THE
RELATIONSHIP
BETWEEN SPOT
AND FUTURES
PRICES

A futures contract provides a mechanism for locking in today a future spot price for purchase or sale of an asset. The futures price, $F(t,T)$, is fixed today, but the delivery (as well as payment) are deferred until the final settlement date. Hence, the futures contract *eliminates uncertainty* about the future spot price that an individual can expect for an asset at the time of delivery.

As noted above, if one purchases a commodity or financial asset, one incurs storage costs, specified above as $C(t,T)$. These reflect the compound future value of interest lost on the money plus any other costs associated with storage, minus any gains due to a convenience yield or cash flows paid on the asset. The futures price can be shown as follows:

$$F(t,T) = S(t) + C(t,T). \qquad (9.13)$$

If this condition is violated, one could enter into an arbitrage trade that would produce a certain profit in excess of the risk-free rate. One could buy the asset at a price of $S(t)$ and simultaneously sell a futures contract at its price of $F(t,T)$. Then one would store the asset over the period of (t,T). At time T, the accumulated cost of carry would be $C(t,T)$. The asset would be delivered and $F(t,T)$ would be received for certain. This is equivalent to buying an asset for $S(t)$ and selling it later for certain at $F(t,T)$. Because we let $F(t,T)$ exceed the sum of $S(t)$ and $C(t,T)$, the selling price would cover the accumulated storage costs and the interest that could have been earned on the $S(t)$ dollars invested in the risk-free asset. Thus, this risk-free transaction generates an overall return in excess of the risk-free rate which would be attractive and will induce others to engage in the same transaction until the futures price is bid down to $S(t) + C(t,T)$. If the futures price were too low, the transaction is somewhat trickier but can still generally be done if someone holds the asset in his or her portfolio or can sell it short.

In a frictionless market the arbitrage produces a certain gain in excess of the risk-free rate. The recognition of frictions in real-world markets does not invalidate the concept of arbitrage, but it implies that the difference between the right and left sides of Equation 9.13 should not be large enough to exceed costs due to market frictions. Also, because futures contracts are held over a short period of time (generally a few months), the assumption of known storage costs is not unrealistic. However, if the storage costs are unknown, then Equation 9.13 needs to be modified, and the suggested arbitrage would not be risk-free.

TABLE 9.4   **Put-Call Parity**

Portfolio	Value Today	Value of Portfolio at Expiration	
		$S(T) \leq X$	$S(T) > X$
A. One share of stock	$S(t)$	$S(T)$	$S(T)$
One put	$p(t)$	$X - S(T)$	0
	$S(t) + p(t)$	X	$S(T)$
B. One call	$c(t)$	0	$S(T) - X$
Risk-free discount bond	$X(1 + r)^{-(T-t)}$	X	X
	$c(t) +$ $X(1 + r)^{-(T-t)}$	X	$S(T)$

Conclusion: A and B always perform equivalently at expiration so they must have equivalent values today:

$$S(t) + p(t) = c(t) + X(1 + r)^{-(T-t)}.$$

PARITY RELATIONS AMONG PUTS, CALLS, AND FUTURES

Important relationships exist among the prices of puts, calls, and futures. Table 9.4 presents an important result known as *put-call parity*. Suppose we construct Portfolio A, that consists of one share of stock and one put. At expiration of the put, the stock will be worth $S(T)$. We also construct Portfolio B, consisting of one call and one risk-free discount bond with a face value equal to the exercise price. At expiration of the call, the bond matures and is worth X. If, at expiration, $S(T) \leq X$, then the put is worth $X - S(T)$ and the call is worthless. If, at expiration, $S(T) > X$, the put expires worthless and the call is worth $S(T) - X$. As Table 9.4 illustrates, the portfolios produce identical results at expiration. Each is worth the minimum of X or $S(T)$.

Thus, the portfolios must have equivalent values today. Consequently, we can state our result as

$$S(t) + p(t) = c(t) + X(1 + r)^{-r(T-t)}, \qquad (9.14)$$

which is known as *put-call parity*. It expresses the relationship among the put price, the call price, the exercise price, the risk-free rate, and the time to expiration. If we know all but one of these values, we can find the missing value. For example, if we know the call price, the put price is found as

$$p(t) = c(t) - S(t) + X(1 + r)^{-r(T-t)}, \qquad (9.15)$$

which is how put-call parity is often expressed. As you would expect, if these prices are not in line with the above formula, then an arbitrage profit is possible.

The futures price can also be expressed relative to the option prices. Suppose we construct the following portfolios: Portfolio A consists of one long call and one short put. Portfolio B consists of one long futures and a risk-free discount bond with a face value equal to the futures price minus the exercise price on the calls, $F(t) - X$.[10]

---

[10]We will drop the capital T as the second argument for the futures price to make its notation more similar to that of the options.

TABLE 9.5   **Put-Call-Futures Parity**

Portfolio	Value Today	Value of Portfolio at Expiration	
		$S(T) \leq X$	$S(T) > X$
A. One call	$c(t)$	0	$S(T) - X$
One (short) put	$-p(t)$	$-(X - S(T))$	0
	$c(t) - p(t)$	$S(T) - X$	$S(T) - X$
B. One futures	0	$S(T) - F(t)$	$S(T) - F(t)$
Risk-free discount bond	$(F(t) - X)(1 + r)^{-(T-t)}$	$F(t) - X$	$F(t) - X$
	$(F(t) - X)(1 + r)^{-(T-t)}$	$S(T) - X$	$S(T) - X$

Conclusion: A and B always perform equivalently at expiration so they must have equivalent values today:

$$c(t) - p(t) = (F(t) - X)(1 + r)^{-(T-t)}.$$

In both outcomes at expiration, the futures will be worth $S(T) - F(t)$ because $S(T) = F(T)$. As Table 9.5 shows, these portfolios also have the same outcomes at expiration and, thus, should have equivalent values today. Note that because the value of the futures today is zero (it costs nothing to establish), the value of Portfolio B is solely the value of the bond. This leads to put-call-futures parity,

$$c(t) - p(t) = (F(t) - X)(1 + r)^{-(T-t)}, \qquad (9.16)$$

which expresses the relationship between the put and call prices and the futures price, as well as the exercise price, the risk-free rate, and the time to expiration.[11]

Note that the combined results of these two parity equations imply that $F(t) = S(1 + r)^{(T-t)}$. Because the asset is a non-dividend-paying stock, the risk-free interest rate is the only cost of carry. Thus, by grossing up the stock price by the interest rate, we are adding the cost of carry to the stock price to obtain the futures price. This is fundamentally consistent with Equation 9.13, which expresses the futures price as the spot price plus the cost of carry.

THE ROLE OF DERIVATIVE INSTRUMENTS IN INVESTMENT ANALYSIS AND PORTFOLIO MANAGEMENT

At this stage of the book, you need to develop a basic understanding of derivative instruments. We have not discussed the institutional details that characterize derivative instruments and markets. These matters will be covered more thoroughly in Part VI. Our current objective is to acquaint you with these instruments and show you that they play a very important role in the investment world. For example, suppose you were an investment manager who had a very risk-averse client whose primary concern was achieving a minimum overall rate of return. You know from our prior discussion that a combination of a stock and a put can achieve a minimum selling price for the stock equal to the exercise price of the put. Suppose you had another client who was highly risk averse and who believed that interest rates were going to decline. If the client is

---

[11]Technically we are talking about a forward contract but, as discussed earlier, with a constant short-term interest rate, futures prices and forward prices are equal, and we can treat the contracts as equivalent.

not very concerned about the risk of being wrong, you might advise that client to trade an interest rate futures contract. Alternatively, if you have a client who is bearish about the stock market, you might advise him or her to buy a put or sell a call in lieu of selling stock short, because selling short entails rather high margin requirements and must be done on a price increase (up-tick). Other applications that involve derivatives include hedging, arbitrage, and asset allocation strategies. Options and futures open many possibilities that would not exist in a world of only stocks and bonds.

THE EFFICIENCY OF DERIVATIVE MARKETS

In Chapter 6, we examined the theories and evidence on the efficient market hypothesis and concluded that security markets are generally quite efficient. This is good for investors because it permits firms to raise capital cheaply and assures investors that the prices they pay are fair prices. The existence of derivative markets opens up many new questions regarding market efficiency. Besides the obvious one of whether derivative markets are themselves efficient, the interactions between the derivative markets and the stock and bond markets are important to those who study and work in the markets.

DO DERIVATIVES LEAD THE SPOT MARKET?

Derivatives markets are generally expected to respond to movements in the spot market. Our models imply that derivative prices change as a result of a price change in the spot market, all other things constant. However, derivative markets, especially futures, require considerably less capital to trade, and with the exception of the most actively traded stocks, are more liquid than the spot market. Could it be that information is initially impounded into derivative prices and then transmitted into spot market prices? Some people call this the "tail wagging the dog."

This issue has been examined in a number of studies. In options markets, Manaster and Rendleman examined this issue for options traded on the Chicago Board Options Exchange (CBOE) during the period 1973–1976.[12] Using estimates of the information contained in the stock price that would make the observed option prices conform to a theoretical model, they determined that there was about a 24-hour lag in the transmission of information from the options market to the stock market. In other words, they concluded that the options market contains information about future stock prices that is not known by the stock market. A similar study by Bhattacharya using actual transaction prices in the 1977–1978 period found comparable results.[13] Most of the information in the options market did not reach the stock market until the next day.

A more recent study by Stephan and Whaley examined trade-by-trade option prices during the first quarter of 1986 and derived opposite results.[14] Using a sophisticated option pricing model and controlling for numerous complicating factors, they concluded that the stock market leads the option market by up to fifteen minutes.

The issue has been examined more extensively in futures markets. Kawaller, Koch, and Koch examined minute-by-minute stock index futures prices over the 1984–1985

---

[12]Steven Manaster and Richard Rendleman, Jr., "Option Prices as Predictors of Equilibrium Stock Prices," *The Journal of Finance* 37, no. 4 (September 1982): 1043–1057.

[13]Mihir Bhattacharya, "Price Changes of Related Securities: The Case of Call Options and Stocks," *Journal of Financial and Quantitative Analysis* 22, no. 1 (March 1987): 1–15.

[14]Jens A. Stephan and Robert E. Whaley, "Intraday Price Change and Trading Volume Relations in the Stock and Stock Option Markets," *The Journal of Finance* 45, no. 1 (March 1990): 191–220.

period.[15] They found that price movements in the futures market lead price changes in the spot market by about 20 to 45 minutes. Occasionally the spot market led the futures market, but by no more than 1 minute. Stoll and Whaley examined 5-minute returns on stock index futures over the period 1982–1987, and for comparative purposes, the returns on IBM, a very actively traded stock.[16] They found that price changes in the futures market lead price changes in the spot market by about 5 to 10 minutes. The spot market led the futures market only slightly. Moreover, the futures market led the actively traded IBM stock. Chan examined a similar data set and found that the results were similar following bad and good news.[17] Moreover, when there is a strong overall market-wide movement, the futures market reacts faster than the spot market. However, Chan, Chan, and Karolyi found that a change in volatility can originate in either market and is quickly transmitted to the other.[18]

These studies generally show that futures markets absorb information somewhat more rapidly than the spot market. This makes sense because less capital is needed to trade futures. However, most of the research has been done on the stock index spot and futures markets, primarily because the data are more readily available. We do not know whether these results would hold in markets for other commodities and securities. The evidence on options markets is mixed, which is not surprising because options markets require more capital for trading than futures, though less than for the spot market. Does the tail wag the dog? There is evidence of it, particularly for futures. Is this bad? Not really. If futures markets are efficient, then their prices will quickly align with spot market prices so that both markets have fair and orderly prices.

ARE DERIVATIVES
CORRECTLY
PRICED?

The question of whether the option market is efficient has been examined in many studies. The technical issues are quite complex. Bhattacharya found that option prices conform quite rigorously to the boundary condition rules.[19] In other words, there are no quick risk-free profits. Rubinstein, however, found that it is virtually impossible to find an option pricing model that captures the complete behavior of most options.[20] However, Phillips and Smith reviewed a number of studies that examined options market efficiency and concluded that it was virtually impossible to earn option returns that would exceed the transaction costs, particularly the bid–ask spread, of trading options.[21]

One of the difficulties in testing for option market pricing efficiency is that the volatility of the stock is required to derive a price and this is an unobservable variable.

---

[15]Ira G. Kawaller, Paul D. Koch, and Timothy W. Koch, "The Temporal Price Relationship Between S&P 500 Futures and the S&P 500 Index," *The Journal of Finance* 42, no. 5 (December 1987): 1309–1329.

[16]Hans R. Stoll and Robert E. Whaley, "The Dynamics of Stock Index and Stock Index Futures Returns," *Journal of Financial and Quantitative Analysis* 25, no. 4 (December 1990): 441–468.

[17]Kalok Chan, "A Further Analysis of the Lead-Lag Relationship between the Cash Market and Stock Index Futures Market," *Review of Financial Studies* 5, no. 1 (1992): 123–152.

[18]Kalok Chan, K. C. Chan, and G. Andrew Karolyi, "Intraday Volatility in the Stock Index and Stock Index Futures Markets," *Review of Financial Studies* 4, no. 4 (1991): 657—684.

[19]Mihir Bhattacharya, "Transaction Data Tests of Efficiency of the Chicago Board Options Exchange," *Journal of Financial Economics* 12, no. 2 (August 1983): 161–186.

[20]Mark Rubinstein, "Nonparametric Tests of Alternative Option Pricing Models Using All Reported Trades and Quotes on the 30 Most Active CBOE Option Classes From August 23, 1976 Through August 31, 1978," *The Journal of Finance* 40, no. 2 (June 1985): 455–480.

[21]Susan M. Phillips and Clifford W. Smith, Jr., "Trading Costs for Listed Options: The Implications for Market Efficiency," *Journal of Financial Economics* 8, no. 2 (June 1980): 179–201.

As noted earlier in this chapter, the futures pricing model requires only the spot price and an estimate of the cost of carry.

Rendleman and Carabini examined the Treasury bill spot and futures market over the period 1976–1978 and found that most short-term futures contracts were very accurately priced.[22] However, deviations from the fair value existed for more distant contracts. Notably, to take advantage of these deviations one would have to already own the T-bills, because the cost of shorting T-bills would absorb most of the gain. However, Elton, Gruber, and Rentzler in a similar study found numerous arbitrage opportunities that exceeded the cost of exploiting them.[23] These results were corroborated by Hegde and Branch.[24]

Chung examined the pricing of stock index futures over the period 1984–1986 using trade-by-trade prices.[25] He found that, although there were many profitable arbitrage transactions in the early period of trading, as the market matured the number of opportunities faded. Moreover, strategies that were supposed to be riskless actually did incur some risk.

The evidence on the T-bill futures market provides a sharp contrast to the general conclusions regarding futures market efficiency although this market is not nearly as active today as it was many years ago. Most of the trading in short-term interest rates has moved to the Eurodollar futures market and the over-the-counter market. The Eurodollar futures market has not been tested for efficiency and the OTC market does not publicly report prices. It seems unlikely that many arbitrage opportunities could remain in the T-bill futures market or else its volume would increase.

Numerous tests in many other active futures markets have provided generally supportive results and concluded that futures prices conform to the cost of carry model so closely that the differences cannot be economically exploited. Thus, these markets exhibit the efficiency that we observe in the spot market.

SUMMARY

Derivative markets are markets for instruments whose payoffs are determined by the payoffs of other instruments, such as stocks, bonds, and commodities. In recent years, there has been an explosive growth in the use of derivative markets, both on organized exchanges and in over-the-counter markets. The primary derivative assets are options, forwards, and futures. Options grant the right but not the obligation to buy or sell something at a fixed priced either at a specific point in time or during a period of time. An option to buy something is a call and an option to sell something is a put. A forward contract is an agreement between two parties to exchange money for an asset at a future date at a price agreed-upon today. A futures contract is like a forward contract but trades on an organized exchange and is subject to special margin requirements and a daily settling of profits and losses.

---

[22]Richard Rendleman and Christopher Carabini, "The Efficiency of the Treasury Bill Futures Market," *The Journal of Finance* 34, no. 4 (September 1979): 895–914.

[23]Edwin J. Elton, Martin J. Gruber, and Joel Rentzler, "Intra-Day Tests of the Efficiency of the Treasury Bill Futures Market," *The Review of Economics and Statistics* 66, no. 1 (February 1984): 129–137.

[24]Shantaram P. Hegde and Ben Branch, "An Empirical Analysis of Arbitrage Opportunities in the Treasury Bill Futures Market," *The Journal of Futures Markets* 5, no. 3 (Fall 1985): 407–424.

[25]Y. Peter Chung, "A Transactions Data Test of Stock Index Futures Market Efficiency and Index Arbitrage Profitability," *The Journal of Finance* 46, no. 5 (December 1991): 1791–1809.

Options and futures prices conform to several fundamental rules that, if violated, lead to risk-free profits through the process of arbitrage, which is the buying and selling of identical assets at different prices. Option prices are determined by the underlying asset price, the exercise price, the risk-free rate of interest, the time to expiration, and the volatility of the underlying asset. Forward prices are determined by the price of the underlying asset and the cost incurred in purchasing and storing the asset over the life of the contract. Futures contracts are priced in a similar manner to forward contracts and, under some conditions, will have identical prices. Options and futures prices are related through specific parity equations.

Options and futures markets are relatively efficient since they offer few opportunities to earn abnormal profits. In addition, the smaller amount of capital required to trade futures contracts means that futures markets are capable of absorbing information much more rapidly than the spot market. The evidence strongly suggests that futures markets react earlier to new information than does the stock market.

QUESTIONS

1. How are options like forward contracts? How are they different?

2. How do forward contracts differ from futures contracts?

3. Explain what is meant by arbitrage in the context of an investor holding a portfolio containing a derivative instrument.

4. Identify the maximum and minimum prices of puts and calls and explain why they are the maximum and minimum.

5. What is the difference between the price and the value of a futures contract?

6. What is a convenience yield? What kinds of assets are likely to have convenience yields?

7. What are the three values that go into the determination of the current spot price? Explain where they come from.

8. If the price of a stock and a put option exceeded the price of a call option and a risk-free bond with a face value equal to the exercise price, what kind of transaction should you do?

9. Under what conditions are forward and futures prices equivalent?

10. Would you expect that futures markets might reflect information more rapidly than the spot market? What does the empirical evidence say?

PROBLEMS

1. The group of options below expire in 6 months and the risk-free interest rate is 10.52 percent. The current stock price is 56. Find the lower bound of the option prices assuming the following exercise prices.
   a. 55 call
   b. 60 call
   c. 55 put
   d. 60 put

2. Find the value at expiration of the following options if the stock price at expiration is 41.
   a. 40 call
   b. 45 call
   c. 40 put
   d. 45 put

3. Suppose the stock price is currently at 66 and the exercise price of a call option is at 65. The risk-free rate is 8 percent. One period later the stock price can be at either 75 or 60. Compute the value of the call option using the following two methods.
    a. Form a portfolio of 1,000 short calls and a certain number of shares.
    b. Compute the value of the call option directly.

4. A 1-year forward contract is written on a stock priced at $105. The forward price is $110. The risk-free interest rate is 6 percent. Find the following values.
    a. The value of the forward contract today.
    b. The value of the forward contract at expiration if the stock price at expiration is $107.
    c. The value of the forward contract 6 months after it is written if new forward contracts are being written at a price of $99.

5. A futures contract is written at a price of $72. Find the value of the futures contract at the following points in time.
    a. At the time it is written.
    b. Half-way through the day, where the new futures price is $73.50.
    c. At the end of the day, after the contract has been marked-to-market.

6. Suppose the spot price is $35 and the cost of carrying an asset in inventory for 2 months is $2.25. If the futures price is $39 and there are no other transaction costs, what should an investor do?

7. Assume a stock is priced at $82 and the risk-free interest rate is 9 percent. Puts and calls with an exercise price of $80 are available and expire in 3 months. The call is priced at $6.94 and, because you have used a valuation model on the call, you believe this to be a fair price. You believe that at $3.50, the put seems mispriced. How could you verify your hunch?

8. Suppose the risk-free interest rate is 5 percent and puts, calls, and futures are available that expire in 6 months. The exercise price is $55. The calls are priced at $5.32 and the puts are priced at $3.93. If you believe the puts and calls are correctly priced, what should the futures be worth?

REFERENCES

Bhattacharya, Mihir. "Price Changes of Related Securities: The Case of Call Options and Stocks." *Journal of Financial and Quantitative Analysis* 22, no. 1 (March 1987).

Bhattacharya, Mihir. "Transaction Data Tests of Efficiency of the Chicago Board Options Exchange." *Journal of Financial Economics* 12, no. 2 (August 1983).

Brennan, Michael J. "The Supply of Storage." *American Economic Review* 47, no. 1 (March 1958).

Chan, Kalok. "A Further Analysis of the Lead-Lag Relationship Between the Cash Market and Stock Index Futures Market." *The Review of Financial Studies* 5, no. 1 (1992).

Chan, Kalok, K. C. Chan, and G. Andrew Karolyi. "Intraday Volatility in the Stock Index and Stock Index Futures Markets." *Review of Financial Studies* 4, no. 4 (1991).

Chance, Don M. *An Introduction to Options and Futures.* 2d. ed. Fort Worth: The Dryden Press, 1992.

Chung, Y. Peter. "A Transactions Data Test of Stock Index Futures Market Efficiency and Index Arbitrage Profitability." *The Journal of Finance* 46, no. 5 (December 1991).

Cox, John C., and Mark Rubinstein. *Options Markets.* Englewood Cliffs, N.J.: Prentice-Hall, 1985.

Cox, John C., Jonathan E. Ingersoll, Jr. and Stephen A. Ross. "The Relation Between Forward Prices and Futures Prices." *Journal of Financial Economics* 9, no. 4 (December 1981).

Duffie, Darrell. *Futures Markets.* Englewood Cliffs, N.J.: Prentice-Hall, 1989.

Elton, Edwin J., Martin J. Gruber, and Joel Rentzler. "Intra-Day Tests of the Efficiency of the Treasury Bill Futures Market." *The Review of Economics and Statistics* 66, no. 1 (February 1984).

Hegde, Shantaram P., and Ben Branch. "An Empirical Analysis of Arbitrage Opportunities in the Treasury Bill Futures Market." *The Journal of Futures Markets* 5, no. 3 (Fall 1985).

Hull, John. *Options, Futures and Other Derivative Securities.* Englewood Cliffs, N.J.: Prentice-Hall, 1989.

Kawaller, Ira G., Paul D. Koch, and Timothy W. Koch. "The Temporal Price Relationship Between S&P 500 Futures and the S&P 500 Index." *The Journal of Finance* 42, no. 5 (December 1987).

Manaster, Steven, and Richard Rendleman, Jr. "Option Prices as Predictors of Equilibrium Stock Prices." *The Journal of Finance* 37, no. 4 (September 1982).

Phillips, Susan M., and Clifford W. Smith, Jr. "Trading Costs for Listed Options: The Implications for Market Efficiency." *Journal of Financial Economics* 8, no. 2 (June 1980).

Rendleman, Richard, and Christopher Carabini. "The Efficiency of the Treasury Bill Futures Market." *The Journal of Finance* 34, no. 4 (September 1979).

Ritchken, Peter. *Options: Theory, Strategy and Applications.* Glenview, Ill.: Scott-Foresman, 1987.

Rubinstein, Mark. "Nonparametric Tests of Alternative Option Pricing Models Using All Reported Trades and Quotes on the 30 Most Active CBOE Option Classes From August 23, 1976 Through August 31, 1978." *The Journal of Finance* 40, no. 2 (June 1985).

Scholes, Myron S. "The Economics of Hedging and Spreading in Futures Markets." *The Journal of Futures Markets* 1, no. 2 (Summer 1981).

Siegel, Daniel, and Diane F. Siegel. *Futures Markets.* Hinsdale, Ill.: The Dryden Press, 1990.

Stephan, Jens A., and Robert E. Whaley. "Intraday Price Change and Trading Volume Relations in the Stock and Stock Options Markets." *The Journal of Finance* 45, no. 1 (March 1990).

Stoll, Hans R., and Robert E. Whaley. "The Dynamics of Stock Index and Stock Index Futures Returns." *Journal of Financial and Quantitative Analysis* 25, no. 4 (December 1990).

Stoll, Hans R., and Robert E. Whaley. *Futures and Options: Theory and Application.* Cincinnati: South-Western Publishing, 1993.

Valuation Principles and Practices

Based upon the chapters in the first two parts, you know about the numerous investment instruments available on a global basis and you have the background regarding the institutional characteristics of the capital markets. In addition, you are aware of the major developments in investment theory as related to efficient capital markets, portfolio theory, capital asset pricing, and derivative securities. Therefore, at this point you are in a position to consider the theory and practice of estimating the value of various securities, which is the heart of investing. You will recall that the investment decision is based on a comparison of an asset's intrinsic value and its market price.

The major source of information regarding a stock or a bond is the corporation's financial statements. Chapter 10 considers what financial statements are available and what information they provide, followed by a discussion of the financial ratios used to answer several questions about a firm's liquidity, its operating performance, its risk profile, and its growth potential.

Chapter 11 considers the basic principles of valuation and applies these principles to the valuation of bonds, preferred stock, and common stock under several alternative operating scenarios. We conclude by reviewing the basic factors that determine the required rate of return for an investment and the growth rate of earnings and dividends.

Chapter 12 deals with a major question for a global investor—how to allocate assets across countries based on the state of their economies and their security markets. Additionally, within each country it is necessary to make a further allocation among available asset classes including stocks, bonds, and cash.

CHAPTER 10

ANALYSIS OF FINANCIAL STATEMENTS

In this chapter, we will answer the following questions:

- What are the major financial statements that are provided by firms and what is the specific information contained in each of them?
- Why do we use financial ratios to examine the performance of a firm and why is performance relative to the economy and a firm's industry relevant?
- What are the major categories for financial ratios and what questions are being answered by the ratios in these categories?
- What specific ratios are useful to determine a firm's internal liquidity, operating performance, risk profile, growth potential, and external liquidity?
- What are some of the major innovations proposed to analyze the financial risk of a firm?
- What are the various breakdowns proposed for the analysis of a firm's return on equity beyond the traditional DuPont analysis?
- What is involved in the analysis of a company relative to its industry and the aggregate economy?
- What are some of the major differences between U.S. and non-U.S. financial statements and how do these differences impact the financial ratios?
- What are the major financial ratios that have been used to help analysts in the following areas: stock valuation, estimating and evaluating systematic risk, predicting the credit ratings on bonds, and predicting bankruptcy?

Financial statements are the main source of information for major investment decisions, including whether to lend money to a firm (invest in its bonds), to acquire an ownership stake in a firm (buy its preferred or common stock), or to buy warrants or options on a firm's stock. This chapter has 11 sections. The first introduces an example corporation's major financial statements that we will use throughout the chapter. Section two discusses why and how financial ratios are useful. We examine and compute the major financial ratios for our example firm in sections three through eight. In section three there is an outline of the major categories for ratios. In the subsequent five sections we provide example computations of ratios that reflect: internal liquidity, operating performance, risk analysis, growth analysis, and external liquidity. Section nine includes a comparative analysis of the company ratios relative to the firm's industry and the

S&P 400 series. Because you will be dealing with foreign stocks and bonds, section ten contains a discussion of factors that affect the analysis of foreign financial statements. In the final section we address four major areas in investments where financial ratios have been effectively employed.

Our example company is Quaker Oats, a worldwide marketer of consumer grocery products, including cereals, mixes, grain-based snacks, syrup, corn products, edible oils, and pet food. Through its Fisher-Price Division, it was a leading toy maker but it has spun off this division.

MAJOR FINANCIAL STATEMENTS

Financial statements are intended to provide information on the resources available to management, how these resources were financed, and what the firm accomplished with them. The three major accounting statements created to provide this information are the balance sheet, the income statement, and the statement of cash flows.

BALANCE SHEET

The *balance sheet* shows what resources (assets) the firm controls, and how it has financed these assets. Specifically, it indicates the current and fixed assets available to the firm *at a point in time* (the end of the fiscal year or the end of a quarter). In most cases, the firm owns these assets, but some firms lease assets on a long-term basis. How the firm has financed the acquisition of these assets is indicated by its mixture of current liabilities (accounts payable or short-term borrowing), long-term liabilities (fixed debt), and owner's equity (preferred stock, common stock, and retained earnings).

The balance sheet for Quaker Oats in Table 10.1 represents the *stock* of assets and its financing alternatives as of year-end, June 30, 1990, 1991, and 1992.

INCOME STATEMENT

The *income statement* contains information on the efficiency, control, and profitability of the firm during some *period of time* (a quarter or a year). Efficiency is indicated by the sales generated during the period, whereas expenses indicate control, and the earnings derived from these sales indicate profitability. In contrast to the stock concept in the balance sheet, the income statement indicates the *flow* of sales, expenses, and earnings during a period of time. The income statement for Quaker Oats for the years 1990, 1991, and 1992 appears in Table 10.2.

STATEMENT OF CASH FLOW

The *statement of cash flow* integrates the two prior statements. For a given period, it shows the effects on the firm's cash flow of income flows and changes in various items on the balance sheet. The balance sheet effect is indicated by differences in the beginning and ending figures. These changes are combined with relevant data from the income statement to derive a set of cash flow values that you can use to evaluate the risk and return for the firm's bonds and stock. The results show the source of the cash flow (i.e., is it profit from operations or new financing?) that will fund expansion (investing activities) and other requirements, such as dividends, stock acquisition, or debt retirement.[1] The statement of cash flows for Quaker Oats for 1990, 1991, and 1992 appears in Table 10.3.

[1]A complete discussion of this statement and its preparation is contained in Erich Helfert, *Techniques of Financial Analysis,* 7th ed. (Homewood, Ill.: Richard D. Irwin, 1991).

TABLE 10.1

The Quaker Oats Company and Subsidiaries Consolidated Balance Sheet ($ millions)
Years Ended June 30, 1990, 1991, and 1992

	1992	1991	1990
Assets			
Current assets			
Cash and short-term investments	$ 95.2	$ 74.6	$ 69.0
Receivables—net of allowances	575.3	655.6	575.6
Inventories			
Finished goods	302.8	309.1	324.1
Grain and materials	93.7	86.7	110.7
Purchase of materials and supplies	38.8	26.5	39.1
Total inventories	435.3	422.3	473.9
Other current assets (including discontinued operations)	150.4	150.0	414.1
Total current assets	1,256.2	1,302.5	1,532.6
Other receivables and investments	83.0	79.1	63.5
Property, plant, and equipment	2,066.1	1,914.6	1,745.6
Less accumulated depreciation	792.8	681.9	591.5
Properties—net	1,273.8	1,232.7	1,154.1
Intangible assets—net of amortization	427.4	446.2	466.7
Net noncurrent assets of discontinued operations	—	—	160.5
Total assets	$3,039.9	$3,060.6	$3,377.4
Liabilities and Common Shareholders' Equity			
Current liabilities			
Short-term debt	$ 61.0	$ 80.6	$ 343.2
Current portion of long-term debt	57.9	32.9	32.3
Trade accounts payable	420.2	395.3	405.3
Accrued payrolls, pensions, and bonuses	147.0	116.3	106.3
Accrued advertising and merchandising	120.2	105.7	92.6
Income taxes payable	49.7	45.1	36.3
Other accrued liabilities	198.6	195.4	173.8
Total current liabilities	1,054.6	971.3	1,189.8
Long-term debt	688.7	701.2	740.3
Other liabilities	97.7	115.5	100.3
Deferred income taxes	348.9	366.7	327.7
Cumulative convertible preferred stock	100.0	100.0	100.0
Deferred compensation	(92.1)	(95.2)	(98.2)
Common shareholders' equity			
Common stock, $5 par value, 83,989,396 shares issued	420.0	420.0	420.0
Additional paid-in capital	2.9	7.2	12.9
Reinvested earnings	1,162.3	1,047.5	1,164.7
Cumulative exchange adjustment	(24.5)	(52.9)	(29.3)
Deferred compensation	(160.4)	(168.0)	(164.1)
Treasury common stock, at cost	(558.2)	(352.9)	(386.7)
Total common shareholders' equity	842.1	901.0	1,017.5
Total liabilities and common shareholders' equity	$3,039.9	$3,060.5	$3,377.4

Source: Quaker Oats annual reports.

PURPOSE OF
FINANCIAL
STATEMENT
ANALYSIS

Financial statement analysis seeks to evaluate management performance in several important areas, including profitability, efficiency, and risk. Although we will necessarily analyze historical data, the ultimate goal is to allow us to project *future* management performance. Expected future performance determines whether you should lend money to a firm or invest in it.

TABLE 10.2

The Quaker Oats Company and Subsidiaries Consolidated Statement of Income[a]
($ millions) Years Ended June 30, 1990, 1991, and 1992

	1992	1991	1990
Net sales	$5,576.4	$5,491.2	$5,030.6
Cost of goods sold	2,817.7	2,839.7	2,685.9
Gross profit	2,758.7	2,651.5	2,344.7
Selling, general, and administrative expenses	2,213.0	2,121.2	1,844.1
Operating profit margin	545.7	530.3	500.6
Interest expense—net	67.4	86.2	101.8
Other expense	56.8	32.6	16.4
Income from continuing operations before income tax	421.5	411.5	382.4
Provision for income taxes	173.9	175.7	153.5
Net income from continuing operations	247.6	235.8	228.9
Net income from discontinued operations	—	(30.0)	(59.9)
Net income from disposal of discontinued operations	0.0	0.0	0.0
Net income	247.6	205.8	169.0
Preferred dividends	4.2	4.3	4.5
Net income available for common shares	$ 243.4	$ 201.5	$ 164.5
Average number of common shares outstanding (000)	74,881	75,904	76,537
Net income per share from continuing operations	$ 3.25	$ 3.05	$ 2.93
Net income per share available for common shares	$ 3.25	$ 2.65	$ 2.15
Dividend per share	$ 1.72	$ 1.56	$ 1.40

[a]Restated to reflect continuing operations only (Fisher-Price is reflected as a discontinued operation).
Source: Quaker Oats annual reports.

ANALYSIS OF FINANCIAL RATIOS

WHY RATIOS OF FINANCIAL DATA?

Analysts employ financial ratios because numbers in isolation are typically not very meaningful. Knowing that a firm earned net income of $100,000 is less informative than also knowing the sales figure that generated this income ($1 million or $10 million) and the assets or capital committed to the enterprise. Thus, ratios are intended to provide meaningful *relationships* between individual values in the financial statements.

Because the major financial statements report numerous individual items, we can produce numerous potential ratios. Therefore, you want to limit your examination to the most relevant ratios and categorize them into groups that provide information on important economic characteristics of the firm. It is also important to recognize the need for relative analysis.

IMPORTANCE OF RELATIVE FINANCIAL RATIOS

Just as a single number from a financial statement is not very useful, an individual financial ratio has little value except in perspective relative to other ratios. That is, *only relative financial ratios are relevant!* The important comparisons relate a firm's performance to

- The aggregate economy
- The firm's industry or industries
- Its major competitors within the industry
- Its past performance

TABLE 10.3

The Quaker Oats Company and Subsidiaries Consolidated Statement of Cash Flow
($ millions) Years Ended June 30, 1990, 1991, and 1992

	1992	1991	1990
Cash Flows from Operations			
Net income	$ 247.6	$ 205.8	$ 169.0
Adjustments to reconcile net income to net cash flows (used in) provided from operations			
Depreciation and amortization	155.9	177.7	162.5
Deferred income taxes and other items	(22.9)	45.3	15.2
Provision for restructuring charges	(1.0)	10.0	(17.5)
Changes in operating assets and liabilities (used in) provided from continuing operations			
(Increase) decrease in receivables	84.7	(116.6)	(47.5)
(Increase) decrease in inventories	(14.3)	30.7	(2.2)
(Increase) decrease in other current assets	(10.1)	5.1	(22.5)
Increase (decrease) in trade accounts payable	24.0	19.2	28.9
Increase (decrease) in other current liabilities	113.0	43.2	83.4
Other—net	(0.7)	9.5	0.4
Change in payable to Fisher-Price	(29.6)	29.6	—
Decrease in net current assets of discontinued operations	—	66.0	74.9
Net cash flows provided from operations	$ 546.6	$ 525.5	$ 444.6
Cash Flows from Investing Activities			
Additions to property, plant, and equipment	$(176.4)	$(240.6)	$(275.6)
Cost of acquisitions, excluding working capital	—	—	—
Increase in other receivables and investments	(20.0)	(10.7)	(22.6)
Disposal of property, plant, and equipment	39.6	17.9	11.9
Other discontinued operations	—	(19.8)	(58.4)
Cash used in investing activities	$(156.8)	$(253.2)	$(344.7)
Cash Flows from Financing Activities			
Cash dividends	$(132.8)	$(123.0)	$(110.5)
Proceeds from issuance of debt for spin-off	—	141.1	—
Change in deferred compensation	(11.6)	(0.2)	3.5
Net increase (decrease) in short-term debt	(19.6)	(256.6)	(7.2)
Proceeds from long-term debt	1.1	1.8	252.1
Reduction of long-term debt	(46.2)	(39.7)	(34.8)
Proceeds from short-term debt to be refinanced	50.0	—	—
Issuance of common treasury stock	20.3	25.6	12.8
Purchase of common stock	(235.1)	—	(223.2)
Purchase of preferred stock	0.9	(0.7)	—
Cash used in financing activities	$(351.6)	$(251.7)	$(107.3)
Effect of exchange rate changes on cash and cash equivalents	(17.6)	(6.0)	1.6
Net increase (decrease) in cash and cash equivalents	20.6	5.6	$ (5.8)
Cash and cash equivalents—beginning of year	74.6	69.0	74.8
Cash and cash equivalents—end of year	$ 95.2	$ 74.6	$ 69.0

Source: Quaker Oats annual reports.

The comparison to the aggregate economy is important because almost all firms are influenced by the economy's expansions and contractions (recessions) in the business cycle. It is not reasonable to expect an increase in the profit margin for a firm during a recession; a stable margin might be very encouraging under such conditions. In contrast, a small increase in a firm's profit margin during a major business expansion may be a sign of weakness. Comparing a firm's financial ratios relative to a comparable set of ratios for the economy will help you to understand how a firm reacts to the business cycle. This analysis will help you project the future performance of the firm during subsequent business cycles.

Probably the most popular comparison relates a firm's performance to that of its industry.[2] Different industries affect the firms within them differently, but this relationship is always significant. The industry effect is strongest for industries with homogenous products such as steel, rubber, glass, and wood products. All firms within these industries experience coincident shifts in demand. In addition, these firms employ fairly similar technology and production processes. The strong industry impact means that an isolated analysis of an individual firm in such an industry is meaningless. For example, even the best-managed steel firm experiences a decline in sales and profit margins during a recession. In such a case, the relevant question might be, how did the firm perform relative to the other steel firms? As part of this, you should examine an industry's performance relative to aggregate economic activity to understand how the industry responds to the business cycle.

Industry comparisons typically look for a ratio that is not too far above or below the industry norm. As we will demonstrate with several ratios, you probably do not want to see ratios too high above the norm even where higher is better, or too far below the norm even where lower is better.

When comparing a firm's financial ratio to an industry ratio, you may not feel comfortable using the average (mean) industry value when there is wide dispersion of individual firm ratios within the industry. Alternatively, you may believe that the firm being analyzed is not typical and has a unique component. Under these conditions, you should probably compare the firm to several firms within the industry that are comparable in size or clientele. As an example, within the computer industry, you should compare IBM to certain individual firms within the industry such as Burroughs or Unisys rather than total industry data that include numerous small firms that produce unique products or services. If you were analyzing a utility stock, you would probably limit your industry comparison to a set of comparable electric utilities and exclude gas and water utilities. Even within the electric utility segments you should consider firms from the same geographic area with comparable mixes of residential, commercial, and industrial customers.

Finally, you should examine a firm's relative performance over time to determine whether it is progressing or declining. This *time-series analysis* is helpful when estimating future performance. Many investigators calculate the average of a ratio for a 5- or 10-year period without considering the trend. This can result in misleading conclusions. For example, an average rate of return of 10 percent can be based on rates of return that have increased from 5 percent to 15 percent over time, or based on a series that begins at 15 percent and declines to 5 percent. Obviously, the difference in the trend for these series would have a major impact on your estimate for the future.

---

[2]An excellent source of comparative ratios for alternative lines of business is *Industry Norms and Key Business Ratios,* Dun and Bradstreet, Inc., 99 Church Street, New York, New York 10007. Another source is Robert Morris Associates, 1616 Philadelphia National Bank Bldg., Philadelphia, PA 19107.

COMPUTATION OF FINANCIAL RATIOS

RATIO CATEGORIES

The ratios discussed are divided into five major categories that will help us understand the following important economic characteristics of a firm:

1. Internal liquidity (solvency)
2. Operating performance
   a. Operating efficiency
   b. Operating profitability
3. Risk analysis
   a. Business risk
   b. Financial risk
4. Growth analysis
5. External liquidity (marketability)

EVALUATING INTERNAL LIQUIDITY

Internal liquidity (solvency) ratios indicate the ability of the firm to meet future short-term financial obligations. They compare near-term financial obligations, such as accounts payable or notes payable with current assets or cash flows that will be available to meet these obligations.

INTERNAL LIQUIDITY RATIOS

CURRENT RATIO

Clearly the best-known liquidity measure is the current ratio, which examines the relationship between current assets and current liabilities as follows:

$$\text{Current Ratio} = \frac{\text{Current Assets}}{\text{Current Liabilities}}$$

For Quaker Oats, the current ratios were (all ratios are in thousands of dollars):

$$1992: \frac{1,256,200}{1,054,600} = 1.19$$

$$1991: \frac{1,302,500}{971,300} = 1.34$$

$$1990: \frac{1,532,500}{1,189,800} = 1.29$$

These current ratios experienced an overall decline during the 3 years and also are fairly low relative to the "typical" current ratio. Given these ratios, it is important to compare these values with similar figures for the firm's industry and the aggregate market. If the ratios differ from the industry results, it is necessary to determine what causes the difference and what might explain it. This comparative analysis is considered in the next section.

QUICK RATIO

Some observers believe that you should not consider total current assets when gauging the ability of the firm to meet current obligations, because inventories and some other assets included in current assets might not be very liquid. As an alternative, they prefer the quick ratio, which relates current liabilities to only relatively liquid current assets (cash items and accounts receivable) as follows:

$$\text{Quick Ratio} = \frac{\text{Cash} + \text{Receivables}}{\text{Current Liabilities}}$$

This ratio is intended to indicate the amount of very liquid assets available to pay near-term liabilities. Quaker Oats' quick ratios were

1992: $\dfrac{670,500}{1,054,600} = 0.64$

1991: $\dfrac{730,200}{971,300} = 0.76$

1990: $\dfrac{648,600}{1,189,800} = 0.54$

These quick ratios for Quaker Oats were adequate and increased over the 3 years. As before, you should compare these values relative to what happened in the industry and the economy.

CASH RATIO

The most conservative liquidity ratio is the cash ratio, which relates the cash and short-term investments (money market instruments) to current liabilities as follows:

$$\text{Cash Ratio} = \frac{\text{Cash and Short-Term Investments}}{\text{Current Liabilities}}$$

Quaker Oats' cash ratios were:

1992: $\dfrac{95,200}{1,054,600} = 0.09$

1991: $\dfrac{74,600}{971,300} = 0.03$

1990: $\dfrac{69,000}{1,189,900} = 0.06$

The cash ratios during these 3 years have been quite low and would be cause for concern except that the firm has strong lines of credit at various banks. Still, as an investor you would want to know the reason for these low levels.

RECEIVABLES TURNOVER

In addition to examining liquid assets relative to near-term liabilities, it is useful to analyze the quality of the accounts receivables. One way to do this is to calculate how often they turn over, which implies an average collection period. The faster these accounts are paid, the sooner the firm gets the funds that can be used to pay off its own current liabilities. Receivables turnover is computed as follows:

$$\text{Receivables Turnover} = \frac{\text{Net Annual Sales}}{\text{Average Receivables}}$$

Analysts typically derive the average receivables figure from the beginning figure plus the ending value divided by 2. Quaker Oats' receivable turnover ratios were

$$1992: \frac{5{,}576{,}400}{(655{,}600 + 573{,}300)/2} = 9.08$$

$$1991: \frac{5{,}491{,}200}{(575{,}600 + 655{,}600)/2} = 8.92$$

It is not possible to compute a turnover value for 1990 because the tables used do not include a beginning receivables figure for 1990 (i.e., we do not have the ending receivables figure for 1989).

Given these annual receivables turnover figures, you can compute an average collection period as follows:

$$\text{Average Receivables Collection Period} = \frac{365}{\text{Annual Turnover}}$$

$$1992: \frac{365}{9.08} = 40.2 \text{ days}$$

$$1991: \frac{365}{8.92} = 40.9 \text{ days}$$

These results indicate that Quaker Oats currently collects its accounts receivables in about 40 days, on average, and this collection record is fairly stable. To determine whether these account collection numbers are good or bad, they should be related to the firm's credit policy and to comparable numbers for other firms in the industry.

The receivable turnover is one of the ratios where you do not want to deviate too much from the norm. In an industry where the norm is 60 days, a collection period of 100 days would indicate slow-paying customers, which increases the capital tied up in receivables and also the possibility of bad debts. You would want the firm to be somewhat below the norm (e.g., 55 days versus 60 days), but a figure *substantially below* the norm (e.g., 25 days) might indicate overly stringent credit terms relative to your competition, which could be detrimental to sales.

Investors also compute inventory turnover figures to measure the liquidity of the firm's inventory. This inventory ratio can also serve as an operating performance measure, and we will consider it in that category.

WORKING CAPITAL/SALES

The working capital/sales ratio goes beyond the balance sheet and relates the net working capital (current assets minus current liabilities) to the sales of the firm. This reveals the stock of working capital available to meet any need for excess current assets that might arise from the flow of sales.

$$\text{Working Capital/Sales} = \frac{\text{Current Assets} - \text{Current Liabilities}}{\text{Net Sales}}$$

Like many ratios, we have no guideline number for the value. Therefore, you need to examine the percentage over time to determine if there is a trend and compare it with a similar ratio for the industry and the aggregate market. The values for Quaker Oats were

$$1992: \frac{1,256,200 - 1,054,600}{5,576,400} = 3.62\%$$

$$1991: \frac{1,302,500 - 971,300}{5,491,200} = 6.03\%$$

$$1990: \frac{1,532,600 - 1,189,800}{5,030,600} = 6.81\%$$

Generally, a higher percentage for this ratio is better because it indicates more liquidity. These ratios appear to be declining during this period. The real insights will come when we compare these values with those for the industry and the market.

EVALUATING
OPERATING
PERFORMANCE

The ratios that indicate how well the management is operating the business can be divided into two subcategories: (1) operating efficiency ratios and (2) operating profitability ratios. Efficiency ratios examine how the management uses its assets and capital, measured in terms of the dollars of sales generated by various asset or capital categories. Profitability ratios analyze the profits as a percentage of sales and as a percentage of the assets and capital employed.

OPERATING
EFFICIENCY
RATIOS

TOTAL ASSET TURNOVER

The total asset turnover ratio indicates the effectiveness of the firm's use of its total asset base (net assets equal gross assets minus depreciation on fixed assets). It is computed as follows:

$$\text{Total Asset Turnover} = \frac{\text{Net Sales}}{\text{Average Total Net Assets}}$$

Quaker Oats' asset turnover values were

$$1992: \frac{5,576,400}{(3,060,500 + 3,039,900)/2} = 1.83 \text{ times}$$

$$1991: \frac{5,491,200}{(3,377,400 + 3,060,500)/2} = 1.71 \text{ times}$$

You must compare this ratio to that of other firms in an industry, because it varies substantially between industries. Total asset turnover ratios range from about 1 for large capital-intensive industries (e.g., steel, autos, and other heavy manufacturing companies) to over 10 for some retailing operations. It can also be affected by the use of leased facilities.

Again, you should consider a *range* of turnover values. It is poor management to have an exceedingly high turnover relative to your industry because this might imply too few assets for the potential business (sales) or the use of outdated, fully depreciated assets. It is equally poor management to have a very low relative turnover because this implies an excess of assets relative to the needs of the firm.

Beyond the analysis of the total asset base, it is insightful to examine the utilization of some specific assets, such as inventories and fixed assets.

INVENTORY TURNOVER

The inventory turnover ratio indicates the firm's utilization of inventory. It is computed as follows:

$$\text{Inventory Turnover} = \frac{\text{Cost of Sales}}{\text{Average Inventory}}$$

The inventory turnover ratios for Quaker Oats were

$$1992: \frac{2,817,700}{(422,300 + 435,300)/2} = 6.57 \text{ times}$$

$$1991: \frac{2,839,700}{(473,900 + 422,300)/2} = 6.34 \text{ times}$$

Again, the emphasis should be on the firm's performance relative to its industry, because inventory turnover ratios vary widely. As before, you should consider the range. Too low an inventory turnover ratio relative to your competitors probably means capital tied up in excess inventory and possibly some obsolete inventory (especially if the firm is in a high technology industry). Too high an inventory turnover ratio may indicate efficiency, but it can also indicate inadequate inventory for the prevailing sales volume, which can lead to shortages, back orders, and eventually lost sales.

NET FIXED ASSET TURNOVER

The net fixed asset turnover ratio reflects the firm's utilization of fixed assets. It is computed as follows:

$$\text{Fixed Asset Turnover} = \frac{\text{Net Sales}}{\text{Average Net Fixed Assets}}$$

Quaker Oats' fixed asset turnover ratios were

$$1992: \frac{5,576,400}{(1,232,700 + 1,273,300)/2} = 4.45 \text{ times}$$

$$1991: \frac{5,491,200}{(1,154,100 + 1,232,700)/2} = 4.60 \text{ times}$$

These turnover ratios must be compared with those of firms in the same industry and should consider the impact of leased assets. Also remember that in this case, an abnormally low turnover implies capital tied up in excessive assets, while an abnormally high asset turnover ratio can indicate the use of old, fully depreciated equipment that may be obsolete.

EQUITY TURNOVER

In addition to specific asset turnover ratios, it is useful to examine the turnover for alternative capital components. An important one, equity turnover, is computed as follows:

$$\text{Equity Turnover} = \frac{\text{Net Sales}}{\text{Average Equity}}$$

Equity includes preferred and common stock, paid-in capital, and total retained earnings.[3] The difference between this ratio and total asset turnover is that it excludes current liabilities and long-term debt. Therefore, when examining this series, you need to consider the capital ratios for the firm, because the firm can increase its equity turnover ratio by increasing its proportion of debt capital (i.e., a higher debt/equity ratio).

Quaker Oats' equity turnover ratios were

$$1992: \frac{5,576,400}{(901,000 + 842,100)/2} = 6.40 \text{ times}$$

$$1991: \frac{5,491,200}{(1,017,500 + 901,000)/2} = 5.72 \text{ times}$$

Quaker has experienced a fairly consistent increase in this ratio during the past several years and the increase continued in 1992. In our later analysis of sustainable growth,

---

[3]Some investors prefer to only consider *owner's* equity, which would not include preferred stock.

we will examine the variables that affect the equity turnover ratio to understand what caused the increase.

Given some understanding of the firm's record of operating efficiency, as shown by its ability to generate sales from its assets and capital, the next step is to examine its profitability in relation to sales and capital.

OPERATING
PROFITABILITY
RATIOS

The ratios in this category indicate two facets of profitability: (1) the rate of profit on sales (profit margin) and (2) the percentage return on capital employed.

GROSS PROFIT MARGIN

Gross profit equals net sales minus the cost of goods sold. The gross profit margin is computed as

$$\text{Gross Profit Margin} = \frac{\text{Gross Profit}}{\text{Net Sales}}$$

The gross profit margins for Quaker Oats were

$$1992: \frac{2,758,700}{5,576,400} = 49.47\%$$

$$1991: \frac{2,651,500}{5,491,200} = 48.29\%$$

$$1990: \frac{2,344,700}{5,030,600} = 46.61\%$$

This ratio indicates the basic cost structure of the firm. An analysis over time relative to a comparable industry figure shows the firm's relative cost-price position. Quaker Oats has been able to experience an increasing margin over the three years. As always, it is important to compare these margins with industry statistics.

OPERATING PROFIT MARGIN

Operating profit is gross profit minus sales, general, and administrative (SG + A) expenses. The operating profit margin equals

$$\text{Operating Profit Margin} = \frac{\text{Operating Profit}}{\text{Net Sales}}$$

For Quaker Oats the operating profit margins were

$$1992: \frac{545,700}{5,576,400} = 9.79\%$$

$$1991: \frac{530,300}{5,491,200} = 9.66\%$$

$$1990: \frac{500,600}{5,030,600} = 9.95\%$$

The variability of the operating profit margin over time is a prime indicator of the business risk for a firm. For Quaker Oats this margin declined during 1991, but experienced a partial recovery in 1992. As an investor you would want to know what caused these changes. Notably, while the gross profit margin experienced a steady increase, the operating margin was slightly lower in 1992. This implies something about the change in SG + A expenses between 1990 and 1992.

If the firm has other income or expenses (these have been relatively minor for Quaker Oats), these are considered before arriving at the earnings before interest expense and taxes (EBIT).

In some instances investors add back depreciation expense and compute a profit margin that consists of earnings before depreciation, interest expense, and taxes (EBDIT). This alternative operating profit margin reflects all controllable expenses. It can provide great insights regarding the profit performance of heavy manufacturing firms with large depreciation charges. It can also indicate earnings available to pay fixed financing costs. This latter use will be discussed in the section on financial risk.

NET PROFIT MARGIN

This margin relates net income to sales. Net income is earnings after taxes but before dividends on preferred and common stock. This margin is equal to

$$\text{Net Profit Margin} = \frac{\text{Net Income}}{\text{Net Sales}}$$

Quaker Oats' net profit margins based on net income from continuing operations were

$$1992: \frac{247,600}{5,576,400} = 4.44\%$$

$$1991: \frac{235,800}{5,491,200} = 4.29\%$$

$$1990: \frac{228,900}{5,030,600} = 4.55\%$$

This ratio is computed based on sales and earnings from continuing operations, because our analysis seeks to derive insights about *future* expectations. Therefore, results for continuing operations are relevant rather than the profit or loss that considers earnings from discontinued operations or the gain or loss from the sale of these operations.

This focus on continuing operations was important in 1991 when the firm spun off the Fisher-Price Division. The change in the net profit margin during 1991 is important because it reflects the effect of spinning off the Fisher-Price subsidiary. Notably, there was a good recovery in 1992 that provides insights into the future performance of the firm without Fisher-Price.

COMMON SIZE INCOME STATEMENT

Beyond these ratios, an additional technique for analyzing operating profitability is a common size income statement, which lists all expense and income items as a percentage of sales. Analyzing this statement for several years (five at least) will provide very useful insights regarding the trends in cost figures and profit margins.

Table 10.4 shows a common size statement for Quaker Oats for the last three years adjusted for the spin-off. It indicates a steady decline in the percentage of cost of goods and, hence, an increase in the gross profit margin. In contrast, there was a steady increase in selling, general, and administrative (SG + A) expense as a percentage of sales that generally offset the positive trend in the gross profit margin. Finally, there was a consistent decline in interest expense. The cumulative impact of these offsetting changes in expenses on the net profit margin is a very small change in the margin.

Beyond the analysis of earnings on sales, the ultimate measure of the success of management is the profits earned on the assets or the capital committed to the enterprise. Several ratios help us evaluate this important relationship.

RETURN ON TOTAL CAPITAL
The return on total capital ratio relates the firm's earnings to all of the capital involved in the enterprise (debt, preferred stock, and common stock). Therefore, the earnings figure used is the net income from continuing operations (before any dividends) *plus* the interest paid on debt.

$$\text{Return on Total Capital} = \frac{\text{Net Income} + \text{Interest Expense}}{\text{Average Total Capital}}$$

TABLE 10.4   **The Quaker Oats Company and Subsidiaries Consolidated Statement of Income ($ millions) Common Size Analysis**

	1992	Percentage	1991	Percentage	1990	Percentage
Net sales	$5,576.4	100.00	$5,491.2	100.00	$5,030.6	100.00
Cost of goods sold	2,817.7	50.53	2,839.7	51.71	2,685.9	53.39
Gross profit	2,758.7	49.47	2,651.5	48.29	2,344.7	46.61
Selling, general, and administrative expenses	2,213.0	39.69	2,121.2	38.63	1,844.1	36.66
Operating profit margin	545.7	9.79	530.3	9.66	500.6	9.95
Interest expense—net	67.4	1.21	86.2	1.57	101.8	2.02
Other expense	56.8	1.02	32.6	0.59	16.4	0.33
Income from continuing operations before income taxes	421.5	7.56	411.5	7.49	382.4	7.60
Provision for income taxes	173.9	3.12	175.7	3.20	153.3	3.05
Net income from continuing operations	247.6	4.44	235.8	4.29	228.9	4.55
Net income from discontinued operations	0.0	0.00	(0.30)	(0.55)	(59.9)	(1.19)
Net income	247.6	4.44	205.8	3.75	169.0	3.36
Preferred dividends	4.2	0.08	4.3	0.08	4.5	0.09
Net income available for common shares	$ 243.4	4.36	$ 201.5	3.59	$ 164.5	3.27

Source: Quaker Oats annual reports.

Quaker Oats incurred interest expense for long-term and short-term debt. The gross interest expense value used in this ratio differs from the "net" interest expense item in the income statement, which is measured as gross interest expense minus interest income.

Quaker Oats' rate of return on total capital was

$$1992: \frac{243,400 \ + \ 77,000^*}{(3,060,500 \ + \ 3,039,900)/2} = 10.50\%$$

$$1991: \frac{235,800 \ + \ 101,500^*}{(3,377,400 \ + \ 3,060,500)/2} = 10.48\%$$

*Gross interest expense.

This ratio indicates the firm's overall return on all the capital it employed. It should be compared with the ratio for other firms in the industry and with that for the economy. If this rate of return does not match the perceived risk of the firm, one might question if the entity should continue to exist, because the capital involved in the enterprise could be used more productively elsewhere in the economy. For Quaker Oats, the results indicate stability in this return at a fairly respectable level given the firm's risk level.

RETURN ON OWNER'S EQUITY

The return on owner's equity (ROE) ratio is extremely important to the owner of the enterprise (the common stockholder), because it indicates the rate of return that management has earned on the capital provided by the owner after accounting for payments to all other capital suppliers. If you consider all equity (including preferred stock), this return would equal

$$\text{Return on Total Equity} = \frac{\text{Net Income}}{\text{Average Total Equity}}$$

If an investor is concerned only with owner's equity (i.e., the common shareholder's equity), the ratio would be calculated

$$\text{Return on Owner's Equity} = \frac{\text{Net Income} \ - \ \text{Preferred Dividend}}{\text{Average Common Equity}}$$

Quaker Oats generated return on owner's equity of

$$1992: \frac{243,400 \ - \ 4,200}{(901,000 \ + \ 842,000)/2} = 27.45\%$$

$$1991: \frac{235,800 \ - \ 4,300}{(1,017,500 \ + \ 901,000)/2} = 24.13\%$$

The ROE in 1991 of 24.13 percent is a very respectable value compared to all industrial firms. The return in 1992 of 27.45 percent is considered to be quite exceptional relative to the average for all corporations which is about 13 percent.

This ratio reflects the rate of return on the equity capital provided by the owners. It should correspond to the firm's overall business risk, but it should also reflect any financial risk assumed by the common stockholder because of the prior claims of the firm's bondholders.

THE DUPONT SYSTEM

The importance of ROE as an indicator of performance makes it desirable to divide the ratio into several components that provide insights into the causes of a firm's ROE or any changes in it. This breakdown of ROE into component ratios is generally referred to as the DuPont System. To begin, the return on equity (ROE) ratio can be broken down into two ratios that we have discussed—the net profit margin and equity turnover.

$$\text{ROE} = \frac{\text{Net Income}}{\text{Common Equity}} = \frac{\text{Net Income}}{\text{Net Sales}} \times \frac{\text{Net Sales}}{\text{Common Equity}}$$

This breakdown is an identity because we have both multiplied and divided by net sales. To maintain the identity the common equity value used is the year-end figure rather than the average of the beginning and ending value. This identity reveals that ROE equals the net profit margin times the equity turnover. This implies that a firm can improve its return on equity by *either* using its equity more efficiently (i.e., increasing its equity turnover) or by becoming more profitable (i.e., increasing its net profit margin).

As noted previously, a firm's equity turnover is affected by its capital structure. Specifically, a firm can increase its equity turnover by employing a higher proportion of debt capital. We can see this effect by considering the following relationship.

$$\frac{\text{Sales}}{\text{Equity}} = \frac{\text{Sales}}{\text{Total Assets}} \times \frac{\text{Total Assets}}{\text{Equity}}$$

Similar to the prior breakdown, this is an identity because we have both multiplied and divided the equity turnover ratio by total assets. This equation indicates that the equity turnover ratio equals the firm's *total asset turnover* (a measure of efficiency) times the ratio of total assets to equity, which is a measure of financial leverage. Specifically, this latter ratio of total assets to equity indicates the proportion of total assets financed with debt. The point is, all assets have to be financed by either equity or some form of debt (either current liabilities or long-term debt). Therefore, the higher the ratio of assets to equity, the higher the proportion of debt to equity. A total asset/equity ratio of 2, for example, indicates that for every 2 dollars of assets there is a dollar of equity, which means the firm financed one-half of its assets with equity, which implies that it financed the other half with debt. A total asset/equity ratio of 3 indicates that only one-third of total assets was financed with equity, so two-thirds must have been financed with debt. This breakdown of the equity turnover ratio implies that a firm can increase its equity turnover by either increasing its total asset turnover (i.e., becoming more efficient) or by increasing its financial leverage ratio (i.e., financing assets with a higher proportion of debt capital).

Combining these two breakdowns, we see that a firm's ROE is composed of three ratios as follows:[4]

$$\frac{\text{Net Income}}{\text{Common Equity}} = \frac{\text{Net Income}}{\text{Sales}} = \frac{\text{Sales}}{\text{Total Assets}} = \frac{\text{Total Assets}}{\text{Common Equity}}$$

$$= \frac{\text{Profit}}{\text{Margin}} \times \frac{\text{Total Asset}}{\text{Turnover}} \times \frac{\text{Financial}}{\text{Leverage}}$$

As an example of this important set of relationships, the figures in Table 10.5 indicate what has happened to the ROE for Quaker Oats and the components of its ROE during the 15-year period from 1978 to 1992. As noted, these ratio values employ year-end balance sheet figures (assets and equity) rather than the average of beginning and ending data.

These data indicate several important trends. First, prior to 1987, the firm's ROE increased steadily from 14.32 percent in 1978 to over 20 percent in 1986. Analysis of this excellent trend should initially examine the two major ratios—equity turnover and net profit margin. Quaker Oats' profit margin varied over time and was about the same in 1986 as it was in 1978.

The profit margin declined in 1987, then experienced a major recovery in 1990 that has been maintained through 1992. Even with the recovery, for the overall period the margin declined from 4.87 to 4.44 percent. Alternatively, the firm's equity turnover ratio increased steadily from about 3 times in 1978 to over 6.6 times in 1992 (a 124 percent increase). Therefore, the big factor that caused the increase in the ROE for Quaker Oats was an increase in its equity turnover.

What caused this increase in equity turnover? The total asset turnover ratio (sales/total assets) increased consistently from 1978 through 1985, declined in 1986 and 1987, and returned to its peak level in 1991 and 1992. In addition, the financial leverage ratio (total assets/equity) *increased steadily* throughout the period and ended at its high value. It increased from 1.97 to 3.61, over an 83 percent change in the ratio. This increase in the financial leverage ratio implies that the proportion of total assets financed with debt went from about 50 percent in 1978 to over 72 percent in 1992. In summary, given the two components of equity turnover there was a small change in the total asset turnover ratio (up 22 percent), and a substantial increase in financial leverage (up over 72 percent). Therefore, while both components of equity turnover contributed to the increase, the dominant factor was the increase in financial leverage.

A detailed analysis of the firm's performance during 1987 through 1992 is very revealing. During the period 1987 to 1989, the ROE declined from 20 percent to 13 percent because of a decline in both the total asset turnover (from 1.70 to 1.56) and the

---

[4]In contrast to this discussion that considered profit margin and equity turnover, some analysts group the three ratios differently. Specifically, they combine the profit margin times total asset turnover to get return on total assets and multiply this times the leverage ratio to get ROE. Obviously, the final ROE values will be the same since the three ratios are the same and the only change is how they are arranged.

TABLE 10.5

Components of Return on Equity for Quaker Oats Company: 1978–1992[a]

Year	(1) Sales/ Total Assets	(2) Total Assets/ Equity	(3)[b] Sales/ Equity	(4) Net Profit Margin (%)	(5)[c] Return on Equity (%)
1978	1.49	1.97	2.94	4.87	14.32
1979	1.56	2.01	3.14	4.65	14.60
1980	1.63	2.11	3.44	4.36	15.00
1981	1.62	2.21	3.58	4.37	15.64
1982	1.68	2.14	3.60	4.55	16.38
1983	1.71	2.15	3.68	4.57	16.82
1984	1.80	2.38	4.28	4.19	17.93
1985	1.82	2.23	4.06	4.48	18.19
1986	1.70	2.45	4.17	4.83	20.14
1987	1.36	2.99	4.07	4.20	17.09
1988	1.56	2.31	3.60	4.36	15.70
1989	1.56	2.75	4.29	3.05	13.08
1990	1.51	3.26	4.92	4.55	22.39
1991	1.82	3.35	6.10	4.29	26.17
1992	1.83	3.61	6.61	4.44	29.35

[a]Ratios use year-end data for total assets and common equity rather than averages for year.

[b]Column 3 is equal to column 1 times column 2.

[c]Column 5 is equal to column 3 times column 4.

profit margin (from 4.83 to 3.05), although these declines were partially offset by an increase in financial leverage (from 2.45 to 2.75). The firm's ROE reversed in 1990 and rose to a record level in 1992 because of a small increase in the firm's total asset turnover, a good recovery in its profit margin (from 3.05 percent to 4.44 percent), and continuing increases in the firm's financial leverage (from 2.75 to 3.61). The point is, the declines in ROE were mainly attributable to lower asset turnover and profit margins, while the record level in 1992 is due to strong performance in all three components.

Therefore, although the overall performance related to the firm's ROE looks very good, an investor should be concerned about the ability of the firm to increase or maintain this ROE, which is a record for the firm and is substantially above the norm for firms in general (i.e., the average is about 13 percent). To estimate the future ratio you would need to examine the near-term and long-term outlook for each component of ROE. Besides providing insights into the firm's ROE, this analysis implies a large change in Quaker Oats' financial risk, which is analyzed in a subsequent section.

AN EXTENDED DUPONT SYSTEM[5]

Beyond the original DuPont System, some analysts have suggested using an extended DuPont System that provides additional insights into the effect of financial leverage on

[5]The original DuPont System was the three-component breakdown discussed in the prior section. Because this analysis also involves the components of ROE, some still refer to it as the DuPont System. In our presentation, we refer to it as the extended DuPont System to differentiate it from the original system.

the firm and also pinpoints the effect of income taxes on the firm's ROE. Because both financial leverage and tax rates have changed dramatically over the last decade, these additional insights are important.

In the prior presentation we started with the ROE and divided it into components. In contrast, in this presentation we begin with the operating profit margin (earnings before interest and taxes (EBIT) divided by sales) and introduce additional ratios to derive an ROE value. Combining the operating profit margin and the total asset turnover ratio yields the following:

$$\frac{EBIT}{Sales} \times \frac{Sales}{Total\ Assets} = \frac{EBIT}{Total\ Assets}$$

This ratio is the operating profit return on total assets. To consider the negative effects of financial leverage, we examine the effect of interest expense as a percentage of total assets:

$$\frac{EBIT}{Total\ Assets} - \frac{Interest\ Expense}{Total\ Assets} = \frac{Net\ Before\ Tax}{Total\ Assets}$$

We consider the positive effect of financial leverage with the leverage multiplier as follows:

$$\frac{Net\ Before\ Tax\ (NBT)}{Total\ Assets} \times \frac{Total\ Assets}{Common\ Equity} = \frac{Net\ Before\ Tax\ (NBT)}{Common\ Equity}$$

This indicates the pretax return on equity. To arrive at ROE, we must consider the tax rate effect. We do this by multiplying the pretax ROE by a tax retention rate as follows:

$$\frac{Net\ Before\ Tax}{Common\ Equity} \times \left(100\% - \frac{Income\ Taxes}{Net\ Before\ Tax}\right) = \frac{Net\ Income}{Common\ Equity}$$

In summary, we have the following five components:

1. $\dfrac{EBIT}{Sales}$ = Operating Profit Margin

2. $\dfrac{Sales}{Total\ Assets}$ = Total Asset Turnover

3. $\dfrac{Interest\ Expense}{Total\ Assets}$ = Interest Expense Rate

4. $\dfrac{Total\ Assets}{Common\ Equity}$ = Financial Leverage Multiplier

5. $\left(100\% - \dfrac{Income\ Tax}{Net\ Before\ Tax}\right)$ = Tax Retention Rate

To demonstrate the use of this extended DuPont System, Table 10.6 contains the calculations using the five components for the years 1982 through 1992. The first column that contains the firm's operating profit margin indicates that this margin peaked in 1983 and has subsequently generally declined. We know from the prior discussion that the firm's total asset turnover (column 2) has tended to increase and reached a high point in 1992, which helped offset the decline in operating profit margin. As a result, operating return on assets looked fairly good in 1991–1992. The negative impact of leverage in column 4 shows that the relative importance of interest expense as a percent of total assets was greatest in the early 1980s, but also was significant in 1989 and 1991.

Column 5 is interesting because it reflects the firm's operating performance before the positive impact of financing (the leverage multiplier) and any impact of taxes. These results show the strongest performance by the firm during 1983–1986, with a recovery in 1992. Column 6 reflects the significant change in financial leverage and this effect shows up in column 7, where the pretax return on equity is greatest during 1990–1992. Column 8 shows the effect of much lower tax rates during 1988–1990 and a higher overall tax retention rate in 1992 than during the early 1980s. In summary, this breakdown should help you to understand *what* happened to a firm's ROE, but also *why* it happened. The intent is to determine what happened to the firm's internal operating results, its financial leverage, and what was the effect of external government tax policy.

RISK ANALYSIS

Risk analysis examines the uncertainty of income flows for the total firm and for the individual sources of capital (i.e., debt, preferred stock, and common stock). The typical approach examines the major factors that cause a firm's income flows to vary. More volatile income flows mean greater risk (uncertainty) facing the investor.

The total risk of the firm has two components: business risk and financial risk. The next section discusses the concept of business risk: how you measure it, what causes it, and how you measure its individual causes. The following section discusses financial risk and describes the ratios by which you measure it.

BUSINESS RISK[6]

Recall that business risk is the uncertainty of income that is caused by the firm's industry. In turn, this uncertainty is due to the firm's variability of sales due to its products, customers, and the way it produces its products. Specifically, a firm's earnings vary over time because its sales and production costs vary. As an example, the earnings for a steel firm will probably vary more than those of a grocery chain. The reason is twofold. First, over the business cycle, steel sales are more volatile than grocery sales. Second, the steel firm's large fixed production costs makes its earnings vary more than its sales.

Business risk is generally measured by the variability of the firm's operating income over time. In turn, the earnings variability is measured by the standard deviation of the historical operating earnings series. You will recall from Chapter 1 that the standard deviation is influenced by the size of the numbers, so investors standardize this measure

[6]For a further discussion on this general topic, see Eugene Brigham, *Financial Management: Theory and Practice,* 7th ed. (Fort Worth: The Dryden Press, 1994), Chapters 6 and 10.

TABLE 10.6   Extended DuPont System Analysis for Quaker Oats: 1982–1992[a]

Year	(1) EBIT/Sales (Percent)	(2) Sales/Total Assets (times)	(3) EBIT/Total Assets (Percent)[b]	(4) Interest Expense/Total Assets (Percent)	(5) Net Before Tax/Total Assets (Percent)[c]	(6) Total Assets/Common Equity (times)	(7) Net Before Tax/Common Equity (Percent)[d]	(8) Tax Retention Rate	(9) Return on Equity (Percent)[e]
1982	10.5	1.68	17.6	4.6	13.0	2.14	27.8	.57	15.85
1983	10.7	1.71	18.3	3.7	14.6	2.15	31.4	.54	16.96
1984	10.0	1.80	18.0	4.1	13.9	2.38	33.1	.53	17.54
1985	10.4	1.82	18.9	3.7	15.2	2.23	33.9	.54	18.31
1986	10.1	1.70	17.2	2.3	14.9	2.45	36.5	.56	20.44
1987	9.4	1.36	12.8	2.0	10.8	2.99	32.3	.52	16.80
1988	8.4	1.56	13.1	2.4	10.7	2.31	24.7	.62	15.31
1989	6.3	1.56	9.8	3.6	6.2	2.75	17.1	.62	10.60
1990	9.8	1.51	14.8	2.6	12.2	3.26	39.8	.60	23.88
1991	9.2	1.82	16.7	3.4	13.3	3.35	44.6	.57	25.42
1992	8.9	1.83	16.3	2.5	13.8	3.61	49.8	.59	29.38

[a]The percents in this table may not be the same as in Table 10.5 due to rounding of percents.

[b]Column 3 is equal to column 1 times column 2.

[c]Column 5 is equal to column 3 minus column 4.

[d]Column 7 is equal to column 5 times column 6.

[e]Column 9 is equal to column 7 times column 8.

of volatility by dividing it by the mean value for the series (i.e, the average operating earnings). The resulting ratio of the standard deviation of operating earnings divided by the average operating earnings is the familiar coefficient of variation (*CV*):

$$\text{Business Risk} = f(\text{Coefficient of Variation of Operating Earnings})$$

$$= \frac{\text{Standard Deviation of Operating Earnings } (OE)}{\text{Mean Operating Earnings}}$$

$$= \frac{\sqrt{\sum_{i=1}^{n} (OE_i - \overline{OE})^2/N}}{\sum_{i=1}^{n} OE_i/N}$$

The *CV* of operating earnings allows comparisons between standardized measures of business risk for firms of different sizes. To compute the *CV* of operating earnings you need a minimum of 5 years up to about 10 years. Less than 5 years is not very meaningful, and data more than 10 years old are typically out of date. We cannot compute the *CV* of operating earnings for Quaker Oats, because we have data for only 3 years.

Besides measuring overall business risk, we can examine the two factors that contribute to the variability of operating earnings: sales variability and operating leverage.

SALES VARIABILITY

Sales variability is the prime determinant of earnings variability. Operating earnings must be as volatile as sales. Notably, the variability of sales is largely outside the control of management. Specifically, although the variability of sales is affected by a firm's advertising and pricing policy, the major cause is its industry. For example, sales for a firm in a cyclical industry, such as automobiles or steel, will be volatile over the business cycle compared to those of a firm in a noncyclical industry, such as retail food or hospital supplies. Like operating earnings, the variability of a firm's sales is typically measured by the *CV* of sales during the most recent 5 to 10 years. The *CV* of sales equals the standard deviation of sales divided by the mean sales for the period.

$$\text{Sales Volatility} = f(\text{Coefficient of Variation of Sales})$$

$$= \frac{\sqrt{\sum_{i=1}^{n} (S_i - \overline{S})^2/N}}{\sum_{i=1}^{n} S_i/N}$$

OPERATING LEVERAGE

The variability of a firm's operating earnings also depends on its mixture of production costs. Total production costs of a firm with no *fixed* production costs would vary directly with sales, and operating profits would be a constant proportion of sales. In this scenario, the firm's operating profit margin would be constant and its operating profits would have the same relative volatility as its sales. Realistically, firms always have some fixed production costs (e.g., buildings, machinery, or relatively permanent personnel). Fixed production costs cause operating profits to vary more than sales over the business cycle. During slow periods, profits decline by a larger percentage than the percentage sales decline. In contrast, during an economic expansion, profits will increase by more than sales.

The employment of fixed production costs is referred to as *operating leverage.* Clearly, greater operating leverage makes the operating earnings series more volatile relative to the sales series.[7] This basic relationship between operating profit and sales leads us to measure operating leverage as the percentage change in operating earnings relative to the percentage change in sales during a specified period as follows:

$$\text{Operating Leverage} = \frac{\sum_{i=1}^{n} \left| \frac{\%\Delta OE}{\%\Delta S} \right|}{N}$$

We take the absolute value of the percentage changes, because the two series can move in opposite directions. The direction of the change is not important, but the relative size of the change is relevant. The more volatile the operating earnings as compared to sales, the greater the firm's operating leverage.

FINANCIAL RISK

Financial risk, you will recall, is the additional uncertainty of returns to equity holders due to a firm's use of fixed obligation debt securities. This financial uncertainty is in addition to the firm's business risk. The point is, when a firm sells bonds to raise capital, the interest payments on this capital precede the computation of common stock earnings, and these interest payments are fixed obligations. As with operating leverage, during good times the earnings available for common stock will experience a larger percentage increase than operating earnings, whereas during a business decline the earnings available to stockholders will decline by a larger percentage than operating earnings because of these fixed financial costs.

Two sets of financial ratios help you measure financial risk. The first set are balance sheet ratios that indicate the proportion of capital derived from debt securities compared to equity capital (preferred and common stock). The second set of ratios considers the flow of earnings or cash available to pay fixed financial charges.

PROPORTION OF DEBT RATIOS

The proportion of debt ratios indicate what proportion of the firm's capital is derived from debt compared to other sources of capital, such as preferred stock, common stock, and retained earnings. A higher proportion of debt capital compared to equity capital makes earnings more volatile and increases the probability that a firm will not be able to meet the required interest payments and will default on the debt. Therefore, higher proportion of debt ratios indicate greater financial risk.

The acceptable level of financial risk for a firm depends on its business risk. If the firm has low business risk, investors are willing to accept higher financial risk. For example, retail food companies typically have rather stable operating earnings over

---

[7]For a further treatment of this area, see James C. Van Horne, *Financial Management and Policy,* 8th ed. (Englewood Cliffs, N.J.: Prentice-Hall, 1990), Chapter 27.

time and, therefore, relatively low business risk, which means that they can have higher financial risk.

DEBT/EQUITY RATIO   The debt/equity ratio is equal to

$$\text{Debt/Equity Ratio} = \frac{\text{Total Long-Term Debt}}{\text{Total Equity}}$$

The debt figure used includes all long-term fixed obligations including subordinated convertible bonds. The equity is typically the book value of equity and includes preferred stock, common stock, and retained earnings. Some analysts prefer to exclude preferred stock and consider only common equity. Total equity is preferable if some of the firms being analyzed have preferred stock. Alternatively, if the preferred stock dividend is considered an interest payment, you might want to compute a ratio of debt plus preferred stock relative to common equity.

Two sets of debt ratios are computed: *with and without deferred taxes.* Most balance sheets include an accumulated deferred tax figure after long-term debt and other liabilities. There is some controversy regarding whether you should treat these deferred taxes as a liability or as part of permanent capital. Some argue that if the deferred tax has accumulated because of the difference in accelerated and straight-line depreciation, this liability may never be paid. That is, as long as the firm continues to grow and add new assets, this total deferred tax account continues to grow and is never paid off. Alternatively, if the deferred tax account is because of differences in the recognition of income on long-term contracts such as government contracts, there will be a reversal, and this liability must eventually be paid. To resolve this question, you must determine the reason for the deferred tax account and examine its long-term trend.[8]

Quaker Oats' deferred tax account arose because of a depreciation difference, and it has typically grown over time. For demonstration purposes, several of the following ratios are computed with and without deferred taxes as a long-term liability. This dual treatment demonstrates that the impact of this difference can be substantial. The two sets of debt/equity ratios for Quaker Oats were

A. Including Deferred Taxes as Long-Term Debt

1992: $\frac{1{,}135{,}300}{842{,}100} = 134.82\%$

1991: $\frac{1{,}183{,}400}{901{,}000} = 131.34\%$

1990: $\frac{1{,}168{,}300}{1{,}017{,}500} = 114.82\%$

---

[8]For a further discussion of this, see Leopold A. Bernstein, *Financial Statement Analysis: Theory, Application, Interpretation,* 4th ed. (Homewood, Ill.: Richard D. Irwin, 1989), 212–214.

**B. Excluding Deferred
Taxes as Long-Term Debt**

1992: $\dfrac{786,400}{842,100} = 93.39\%$

1991: $\dfrac{816,700}{901,000} = 90.64\%$

1990: $\dfrac{840,600}{1,017,500} = 82.61\%$

These ratios indicate a steady increase in the firm's debt burden over the three-year period. These results are consistent with the trend for the total asset/equity ratio discussed earlier.

LONG-TERM DEBT/TOTAL CAPITAL RATIO   The debt/total capital ratio indicates the proportion of long-term capital derived from long-term debt capital. It is computed as

$$\text{Debt/Total Capital Ratio} = \frac{\text{Total Long-Term Debt}}{\text{Total Long-Term Capital}}$$

The long-term capital would include all long-term debt, any preferred stock, and total equity. Again, the ratios are computed including and excluding deferred taxes from long-term debt and long-term capital. The two sets of debt/total capital ratios for Quaker Oats were

**A. Including Deferred
Taxes as Long-Term Debt**

1992: $\dfrac{1,135,300}{2,077,400} = 54.65\%$

1991: $\dfrac{1,183,400}{2,184,400} = 54.18\%$

1990: $\dfrac{1,168,300}{2,285,800} = 52.11\%$

**B. Excluding Deferred
Taxes from Long-Term
Debt and Long-Term
Capital**

1992: $\dfrac{786,400}{1,728,500} = 45.50\%$

1991: $\dfrac{816,700}{1,817,700} = 44.93\%$

1990: $\dfrac{840,600}{1,958,100} = 42.92\%$

Again, this ratio indicates a small but steady increase in the firm's financial risk. It also shows the large effect of including deferred taxes as both debt and long-term capital.

TOTAL DEBT RATIOS   In some cases it is useful to compare total debt (current liabilities plus long-term liabilities) to total capital (total debt plus total equity). This is especially revealing for a firm that derives substantial capital from short-term borrowing, which Quaker Oats does. The two sets of total debt/total capital ratios for Quaker Oats were

A. Including Deferred Taxes as Long-Term Debt

$$1992: \frac{2,189,900}{3,039,900} = 72.04\%$$

$$1991: \frac{2,154,700}{3,060,500} = 70.40\%$$

$$1990: \frac{2,358,100}{3,377,400} = 69.82\%$$

B. Excluding Deferred Taxes from Long-Term Debt and Long-Term Capital

$$1992: \frac{1,841,000}{2,691,000} = 68.41\%$$

$$1991: \frac{1,788,000}{2,693,800} = 66.37\%$$

$$1990: \frac{2,030,400}{3,049,700} = 66.58\%$$

This ratio indicates that about two-thirds of Quaker Oats' assets are currently financed with debt, which corresponds to the total asset/equity ratio of about 3.0. These ratios should be compared with those of other companies in the industry to evaluate their consistency with the business risk of this industry. Such a comparison would also indicate how much higher this total debt ratio can go. This is important because Quaker Oats has raised its ROE target from 20 percent to 25 percent, and investors need to know how much of the increase in ROE can and should come from additional financial leverage.

EARNING OR CASH FLOW RATIOS

In addition to ratios that indicate the proportion of debt on the balance sheet, investors employ ratios that relate the *flow* of earnings or cash that is available to meet the required interest and lease payments. A higher ratio of earnings or cash flow relative to fixed financial charges indicates lower financial risk.

INTEREST COVERAGE   Interest coverage is computed as follows:

$$\text{Interest Coverage} = \frac{\text{Income Before Interest and Taxes}}{\text{Debt Interest Charges}}$$

$$= \frac{\text{Net Income} + \text{Income Taxes} + \text{Interest Expense}}{\text{Interest Expense}}$$

This ratio indicates how many times the fixed interest charges are earned, based on the earnings available to pay these expenses. Alternatively, 1 minus the reciprocal of the coverage ratio indicates how far earnings could decline before it would be impossible to pay the interest charges from current earnings. For example, a coverage ratio of 5 means that earnings could decline by 80 percent (1 minus $\frac{1}{5}$), and the firm could still pay its fixed financial charges. Quaker Oats' interest coverage ratios (using the gross interest expense) were

$$1992: \frac{247,600 + 173,900 + 77,000}{77,000} = 6.47 \text{ times}$$

$$1991: \frac{235,800 + 175,700 + 101,500}{101,500} = 5.05 \text{ times}$$

$$1990: \frac{228,900 + 153,500 + 120,200}{120,200} = 4.18 \text{ times}$$

The good news is that all the coverage ratios were in excess of 4. In addition, these coverage ratios have increased steadily over the three-year period by over 50 percent. Notably, the trend of Quaker Oats' coverage ratios has not been consistent with its proportion of debt ratios. The fact is, the proportion of debt ratios and the cash flow ratios do not always give consistent results, because the proportion of debt ratios are not sensitive to changes in earnings and cash flow or changes in the interest rates on the debt. As an example, if there is an increase in interest rates or if the firm replaced old debt with new debt that had a higher interest rate, there would be no change in the proportion of debt ratios, but, as you can see from the prior ratio, the interest coverage ratio would decline. Also, the interest coverage ratio is sensitive to an increase or decrease in earnings.

The experience of Quaker Oats during this recent period is a dramatic example of a positive difference. Specifically, although the proportion of debt ratios generally indicated more debt and financial risk, these flow ratios indicated *lower* financial risk because earnings have increased and finance charges have declined due to lower interest rates over this period.

TOTAL FIXED CHARGE COVERAGES   You might want to determine how well earnings cover *total* fixed financial charges including any noncancellable lease payments and any preferred dividends paid out of earnings *after* taxes. If you want to consider preferred dividends, you need to determine the pretax earnings needed to meet these dividend payments, as follows:

$$\frac{\text{Fixed}}{\text{Charge}} = \frac{\text{Income Before Interest, Taxes, and Lease Payments}}{\text{Debt Interest + Lease Payments + (Preferred Dividend/1} - \text{Tax Rate)}}$$

CASH FLOW RATIOS   As an alternative to these earnings coverage ratios, analysts employ several cash flow ratios that relate the cash flow available from operations to either interest expense, total fixed charges, or to the face value of outstanding debt. The first set of cash flow to interest expense or total fixed charges are an extension of the earnings coverage ratios. The second set of cash flow ratios are a combination flow/stock ratio. Specifically, they include the flow of earnings and noncash expenses against the stock of outstanding debt. These cash flow ratios have been significant in numerous studies concerned with predicting bankruptcies and bond ratings.[9]

CASH FLOW/INTEREST EXPENSE   These ratios are an alternative to the earnings coverage return. The motivation is that a firm's earnings and cash flow typically will differ substantially (we will discuss these differences in a subsequent section). In order to have ratios that can be compared to similar values for the industry and the aggregate market, the cash flow value used is the "traditional" measure of cash flow which is equal to net income plus depreciation expense plus deferred taxes (if there was an increase in deferred taxes) for the period (the depreciation and deferred tax values are typically given in footnotes).

Quaker Oats' cash flow/interest expense ratios were

$$1992: \frac{247,600 + 155,900 - 22,900}{77,000} = \frac{380,600}{77,000} = 4.94 \text{ times}$$

$$1991: \frac{235,800 + 177,700 + 45,300}{101,500} = \frac{458,800}{101,500} = 4.52 \text{ times}$$

$$1990: \frac{185,700 + 112,200 + 40,500}{120,200} = \frac{410,000}{120,200} = 3.41 \text{ times}$$

Although these ratios are not quite as large as the earnings coverage ratios, they still indicate growth and strong coverage for Quaker Oats. Also, as we will see, they are consistent with the industry and larger than the market series.

CASH FLOW COVERAGE RATIO   To compute a cash flow coverage ratio that is comparable to the earnings coverage ratio, it is necessary to add back the interest charges to this cash flow value because interest expense was deducted to arrive at net income. The cash flow coverage ratios are:

$$1992: \frac{380,600 + 77,000}{77,000} = 5.94 \text{ times}$$

$$1991: \frac{458,800 + 101,500}{101,500} = 5.52 \text{ times}$$

$$1990: \frac{410,000 + 120,200}{120,200} = 4.41 \text{ times}$$

CASH FLOW/LONG-TERM DEBT RATIO   Beyond relating cash flow to the required interest expense, several academic studies have employed a ratio that relates cash flow to a

---

[9]A list of these studies is included in the references.

firm's outstanding debt as a predictor of bankruptcy and found that the ratio was very good as an explanatory variable in these studies that are listed in the references. The cash flow figure used in most academic studies is the traditional measure used in the prior cash flow coverage ratios. Therefore, the ratios would be computed as

$$\text{Cash Flow/LT Debt} = \frac{\text{Net Income + Depreciation Expense + Deferred Tax}}{\text{Book Value of Long-Term Debt}}$$

For Quaker Oats, these ratios were computed based on net income from continuing operations, plus the depreciation expense and deferred taxes reported in the footnotes. Again, we computed these ratios with and without deferred taxes as follows:

A. Including Deferred Taxes as Long-Term Debt

1992: $\dfrac{380,600}{1,135,300} = 33.52\%$

1991: $\dfrac{458,800}{1,183,400} = 38.77\%$

1990: $\dfrac{410,000}{1,168,300} = 35.09\%$

B. Excluding Deferred Taxes from Long-Term Debt

1992: $\dfrac{380,600}{786,400} = 48.40\%$

1991: $\dfrac{458,800}{816,700} = 56.18\%$

1990: $\dfrac{410,000}{840,600} = 48.77\%$

The values for all three years were relatively stable. Subsequently we will see that they are good relative to comparable ratios for the economy.

CASH FLOW/TOTAL DEBT RATIO   Investors should also consider the relationship of cash flow to total debt to check that a firm has not had a significant increase in its short-term borrowing. For Quaker Oats, these ratios were

A. Including Deferred Taxes as Long-Term Debt

1992: $\dfrac{380,600}{2,189,900} = 17.38\%$

1991: $\dfrac{458,800}{2,154,700} = 21.29\%$

1990: $\dfrac{410,000}{2,358,100} = 17.39\%$

B. Excluding Deferred Taxes from Long-Term Debt

$$1992: \frac{380,600}{1,841,000} = 20.67\%$$

$$1991: \frac{458,800}{1,788,000} = 25.66\%$$

$$1990: \frac{410,000}{2,030,400} = 20.19\%$$

When you compare these ratios to those with only long-term debt, they reflect a high proportion of short-term debt for Quaker Oats due to short-term borrowing and trade accounts payable. As before, it is important to compare these flow ratios with similar ratios for other companies in the industry and with the overall economy to gauge the firm's relative performance.

ALTERNATIVE MEASURES OF CASH FLOW   As noted, these cash flow ratios used the traditional measure of cash flow. The requirement that companies must prepare and report the statement of cash flows to stockholders has raised interest in other, more exact measures of cash flow. The first is the *cash flow from operations,* which is taken directly from the statement of cash flows. A second measure is *free cash flow,* which is a modification of the cash flow from operations.

Cash flow from operations considers the traditional measure of cash flow, which is equal to net income plus depreciation expense and deferred taxes. In the cash flow statement for Quaker Oats, there is also a provision for restructuring charges (see Table 10.3). Beyond these income statement adjustments, you know from your accounting course that to get operating cash flow it is also necessary to adjust for operating (current) assets and liabilities that either use or provide cash. For example, an increase in accounts receivable implies that either the firm is using cash to support this increase or the firm did not collect all the sales reported. In contrast, an increase in a current liability account such as accounts payable means that the firm acquired some assets but has not paid for them, which is a source (increase) of cash flow. These changes in operating assets or liabilities can add to or subtract from the cash flow estimated from the traditional measure of only income plus noncash expenses. The table below compares the cash flow from operations figures (Table 10.3) to the traditional cash flow figures we have been using for Quaker Oats from 1990 to 1992:

	Traditional Cash Flow	Cash Flow from Operations
1992	380.6	546.6
1991	458.8	525.5
1990	410.0	444.6

In all 3 years the cash flow from operations was larger than the traditional cash flow estimate, because the firm increased its trade accounts payable and also its other current liabilities. Therefore, using this more exact measure of cash flow, the Quaker Oats' ratios would have been stronger.

Free cash flow further modifies cash flow from operations to recognize that some investing and financing activities are critical to the ongoing success of the firm. It is assumed that these expenditures must be made before a firm can feel free to use its cash flow for other purposes such as reducing debt outstanding or repurchasing common stock. The two additional expenditures considered are: (1) capital expenditures (an investing expenditure), and (2) dividends (a financing activity). These two items are subtracted from cash flow from operations as follows:

	Cash Flow from Operations	Capital Expenditures	Dividends	Free Cash Flow
1992	546.6	176.4	132.8	237.4
1991	525.5	240.6	123.0	161.8
1990	444.6	275.6	110.5	58.5

For firms involved in leveraged buyouts, this free cash flow number is critical because the new owners typically want to use the free cash flow as funds available for retiring outstanding debt. It is not unusual for this to be a negative value. The free cash flow for Quaker Oats has been positive even assuming fairly heavy capital expenditures and larger dividends.

ANALYSIS OF GROWTH POTENTIAL

IMPORTANCE OF GROWTH ANALYSIS

The analysis of growth potential examines ratios that indicate how fast a firm should grow. Analysis of a firm's growth potential is important for both lenders and owners. Owners know that the value of the firm depends on its future growth in earnings and dividends. In the following chapter, we discuss the dividend discount model, which determines the value of the firm based on its current dividends, your required rate of return for the stock, and the firm's expected growth rate of dividends.

Creditors are also interested in a firm's growth potential because the firm's future success is the major determinant of its ability to pay an obligation, and the firm's future success is influenced by its growth. Some financial ratios used in credit analysis measure the book value of a firm's assets relative to its financial obligations. The rationale for this ratio is that it is assumed that the firm can sell these assets and use the proceeds to pay off the loan in case of default. In fact, selling assets in a forced liquidation will typically yield only about 10 to 15 cents on the dollar. Currently, most analysts recognize that the more relevant analysis measures the ability of the firm to pay off its obligations as an ongoing enterprise, and its growth potential indicates its future status as an ongoing enterprise.

DETERMINANTS OF GROWTH

The growth of a business, like the growth of any economic entity including the aggregate economy, depends on

1. The amount of resources retained and reinvested in the entity
2. The rate of return earned on the resources retained

The more a firm reinvests, the greater its potential for growth. Alternatively, for a given level of reinvestment, a firm will grow faster if it earns a higher rate of return on the resources reinvested. Therefore, the growth of equity earnings is a function of two variables: (1) the percentage of net earnings retained (i.e., the firm's retention rate), and (2) the rate of return earned on the firm's equity capital (i.e., the firm's ROE).

$$g = \text{Percentage of Earnings Retained} \times \text{Return on Equity}$$
$$= RR \times ROE$$

where:

g = **potential growth rate**
RR = **the retention rate of earnings**
ROE = **the firm's return on equity**

The retention rate is a decision by the board of directors based on the investment opportunities available to the firm. Theory suggests that the firm should retain earnings and reinvest them as long as the expected rate of return on the investment exceeds the firm's cost of capital.

As discussed, the firm's ROE is a function of three components:

- Net profit margin
- Total asset turnover
- Financial leverage (total assets/equity)

Therefore, a firm can increase its ROE by increasing its profit margin, by becoming more efficient (increasing its total asset turnover), or by increasing its financial leverage and financial risk. As discussed, you should examine and estimate each of the components when attempting to estimate the ROE for a firm.

The growth potential analysis for Quaker Oats begins with the retention rate (RR):

$$\text{Retention Rate} = 1 - \frac{\text{Dividends Declared}}{\text{Net Income from Continuing Operations}}$$

Quaker Oats' RR figures were

$$1992: 1 - \frac{1.72}{3.25} = 1 - 0.53 = 0.47$$
$$1991: 1 - \frac{1.56}{3.05} = 1 - 0.51 = 0.49$$
$$1990: 1 - \frac{1.40}{2.93} = 1 - 0.48 = 0.52$$

These results indicate that the retention rate for Quaker Oats is lower than it was during the 1980s, and has continued to decline during these 3 years.

Table 10.5 contains the three components of ROE for the period 1978-1992. Table 10.7 contains the two factors that determine a firm's growth potential and the implied

TABLE 10.7

Quaker Oats Company
Components of Growth and the Implied Sustainable Growth Rate: 1978–1992

Year	(1) Retention Rate	(2) ROE[a]	(3)[b] Sustainable Growth Rate
1978	0.69	14.32	9.88
1979	0.69	14.60	10.07
1980	0.69	15.00	10.35
1981	0.67	15.64	10.48
1982	0.68	16.38	11.14
1983	0.64	16.82	10.76
1984	0.66	17.93	11.83
1985	0.66	18.19	12.01
1986	0.66	20.14	13.29
1987	0.66	17.09	11.28
1988	0.59	15.70	9.26
1989	0.36	13.08	4.71
1990	0.52	22.39	11.64
1991	0.49	26.17	12.82
1992	0.47	29.35	13.79

[a]Based on year-end equity.
[b]Column 3 is equal to column 1 times column 2.

growth rate during the last 15 years. Overall, Quaker Oats has experienced an increase in its growth potential, although there were declines in 1988 and especially during 1989 because of a lower ROE and a decline in the RR. This was followed by a consistent recovery during 1990–1992.

This table reinforces our understanding of the importance of the firm's ROE. Quaker Oats' retention rate was quite stable prior to 1988, implying that the firm's ROE determined its growth rate. This analysis indicates that the important consideration is the long-run outlook for the components of sustainable growth. As an investor, you need to *project* changes in each of the components of ROE and employ these projections to estimate an ROE to use in the growth model along with an estimate of the firm's long-run retention rate.

EXTERNAL MARKET LIQUIDITY

MARKET LIQUIDITY DEFINED

In Chapter 1 we discussed market liquidity as the ability to buy or sell an asset quickly with little price change from a prior transaction assuming no new information. AT&T and IBM are examples of liquid common stocks because you can sell them very quickly with little price change from the prior trade. You might be able to sell an illiquid stock quickly, but the price would be significantly different from the prior price. Alternatively, the broker might be able to get a specified price, but it could take several days.

DETERMINANTS OF MARKET LIQUIDITY

Investors should know the liquidity characteristics of securities they currently own or may buy, because it can be important if they want to change the composition of their portfolios. Although the major determinants of market liquidity are reflected in market trading data, several internal corporate variables are good proxies for these market variables. The most important determinant of external market liquidity is the number of, or the dollar value of, shares traded (the dollar value adjusts for different price levels). More trading activity indicates a greater probability that you can find someone to take the other side of a desired transaction. Another measure of market liquidity is the bid–ask spread (a smaller spread indicates greater liquidity). Fortunately, certain internal corporate variables correlate highly with these market trading variables:

1. Total market value of outstanding securities (number of common shares outstanding times the market price per share)
2. Number of security owners

Numerous studies have shown that the main determinant of the bid–ask spread (besides price) is the dollar value of trading.[10] In turn, the value of trading is highly correlated with the market value of the outstanding securities and the number of security holders. This relationship holds because with more shares outstanding, there will be more stockholders to buy or sell at any time for a variety of purposes. Numerous buyers and sellers provide liquidity.

You can estimate the market value of outstanding Quaker Oats' stock as the number of shares outstanding at the year end (adjusted for stock splits) times the average market price for the year (equal to the high price plus the low price divided by two) as follows:

$$1992:\ 74,881,000 \times [(76 + 50)/2] = \$4,717,503,000$$
$$1991:\ 75,904,000 \times [(65 + 42)/2] = \$4,060,864,000$$
$$1990:\ 76,537,000 \times [(69 + 45)/2] = \$4,362,609,000$$

The number of Quaker Oats' stockholders is 33,580, including over 400 institutions that own approximately 50 percent of the outstanding stock.

A final measure, *trading turnover* (the percentage of outstanding shares traded during a period of time) also indicates relative trading activity. During calendar year 1992, there were about 44 million shares of Quaker Oats traded, which indicates turnover of approximately 59 percent (44 mil/74.9 mil). This compares with the average turnover for the NYSE of about 48 percent. These large values for market value, the number of stockholders and institutional holders, and the high trading turnover indicate that there is a very liquid market in the common stock of Quaker Oats.

COMPARATIVE ANALYSIS OF RATIOS

We have discussed the importance of comparative analysis, but so far we have concentrated on the selection and computation of specific ratios. Table 10.8 contains most of the ratios discussed for Quaker Oats, the Food Industry (as derived from the S&P *Analysts Handbook*), and the S&P 400 Index. The 3-year comparison should provide some insights, although you would typically want to examine data for a 5- to 10-year period. It is necessary to do the comparison for the period 1989–1991 because industry and market data from Standard and Poor's was not available for 1992 until very late in 1993.

----

[10]Studies on this topic were discussed in Chapter 4.

TABLE 10.8 Summary of Financial Ratios for Quaker Oats, S&P Food Industry, S&P 400 Index: 1989–1991

	1991			1990			1989		
	Quaker Oats	Food Industry	S&P 400	Quaker Oats	Food Industry	S&P 400	Quaker Oats	Food Industry	S&P 400
Internal Liquidity									
Current ratio	1.34	1.39	1.28	1.29	1.43	1.42	1.84	1.37	1.58
Quick ratio	0.76	0.78	0.96	0.54	0.72	1.01	0.75	0.70	1.12
Cash ratio	0.03	0.19	0.15	0.06	0.19	0.17	0.03	0.20	0.22
Receivables turnover	8.92	9.07	3.75	8.22	9.76	3.84	8.49	11.61	5.26
Average collection period (days)	40.91	40.26	97.35	44.42	37.40	95.05	42.99	31.44	69.39
Working capital/sales	6.03	7.05	9.91	6.81	7.71	13.75	14.26	7.01	17.09
Operation Performance									
Total asset turnover	1.71	1.22	0.93	1.56	1.50	1.00	1.62	1.78	1.09
Inventory turnover (sales)[a]	12.25	7.40	8.63	10.56	8.43	8.99	10.93	9.40	8.49
Working capital turnover	16.29	14.19	10.09	9.69	12.70	6.77	8.77	15.52	8.32
Net fixed asset turnover	4.60	3.15	2.67	4.76	3.90	2.89	5.19	4.63	2.90
Equity turnover	5.72	3.14	2.95	4.67	3.77	3.05	4.09	4.49	3.03
Profitability									
Gross profit margin	48.29	—	—	46.61	—	—	45.58	—	—
Operating profit margin	9.66	13.73	12.98	8.95	12.47	15.08	9.12	11.88	15.49
Net profit margins[b]	4.29	5.71	2.94	4.55	4.24	5.04	3.05	5.10	5.51
Return on total capital[b]	10.48	9.27	5.77	10.82	9.07	8.60	7.48	11.88	10.57
Return on equity[b]	24.13	17.92	8.69	20.83	16.19	15.31	12.47	23.06	16.79
Equity turnover	6.10	3.52	2.98	4.92	3.77	3.05	4.29	4.49	3.03
Financial Risk									
Debt/equity ratio[c]	131.34	64.94	80.80	114.82	77.95	81.69	102.43	56.51	83.39
Long-term debt/long-term capital[c]	54.18	39.37	40.30	53.45	43.80	44.96	50.60	35.24	45.47
Total debt/total capital[c]	70.40	53.36	57.83	69.82	60.96	67.59	63.62	59.43	66.47
Interest coverage[b]	5.05	5.84	2.54	4.18	4.95	3.26	4.15	6.36	3.79
Cash flow/long-term debt[b]	0.39	0.70	0.45	0.35	0.35	0.35	0.38	0.55	0.36
Cash flow/total debt[b]	0.28	0.35	0.20	0.17	0.17	0.14	0.16	0.21	0.15
Growth Analysis[d]									
Retention rate[b]	0.49	0.63	0.27	0.52	0.55	0.55	0.36	0.36	0.54
Return on equity[b]	26.17	20.09	8.77	22.39	17.31	15.09	13.09	21.47	16.16
Total asset turnover	1.82	1.46	1.07	1.51	1.53	0.95	1.56	1.69	0.98
Total asset/equity	3.35	2.41	3.20	3.26	2.56	3.09	2.75	2.46	2.98
Net profit margin[b]	4.29	5.71	2.94	4.55	4.24	5.04	3.05	5.10	5.51
Sustainable growth rate[b]	12.82	12.66	2.37	11.64	9.52	8.30	4.72	7.23	8.73

[a]Computed using sales since cost of sales not available for industry and S&P 400.

[b]Calculated using net income from continuing operations.

[c]Ratios include deferred taxes as long-term debt.

[d]Using year end total asset turnover.

INTERNAL
LIQUIDITY

The three basic ratios (current ratio, quick ratio, and cash ratio) all show changes for Quaker Oats, but relative to the industry and market, Quaker Oats looks about the same in 1991 as in 1989. The firm's receivable turnover and collection period is stable, but the collection period is substantially less than the S&P 400 and slightly longer than the food industry (44 days versus 40 in 1991). Because it is stable, the difference is probably because of its basic credit policy (it may allow more liberal credit terms to its customers than other firms in the industry). Prior to 1992 it also could have been impacted by credit terms for the toy industry. The working capital/sales ratio is slightly lower than the industry and both the company and industry are lower than the market series.

Overall, the comparisons are mixed, but the ratios are generally stable and adequate. A positive factor is the firm's ability to sell high-grade commercial paper and the existence of several major credit lines.

OPERATING
PERFORMANCE

This segment of the analysis considers efficiency ratios (turnovers) and profitability ratios. Given the nature of the analysis, the major comparison is relative to the industry. Quaker Oats' turnover ratios were fairly consistent relative to the food industry. Specifically, in 1990 and 1991 all the turnover ratios for Quaker Oats (except for working capital turnover in 1990) were higher than the comparable industry turnovers.

Profitability from sales is best described as adequate. Operating profit margins were consistently below the aggregate market and industry, while the net profit margin became higher than the market in 1991.

The profit performance related to invested capital was historically strong. The food industry return on total capital was consistently above the S&P 400, and Quaker Oats was above the food industry in 1990 and 1991. The food industry experienced ROEs that were substantially above the market and Quaker Oats attained higher ROEs than its industry in 1990 and 1991.

FINANCIAL RISK

Quaker Oats' financial risk ratios measured in terms of proportion of debt were consistently above those of the industry and the market, indicating a riskier posture. In contrast, the financial risk flow ratios for Quaker Oats were above the market but lower than its industry. These comparisons confirm that Quaker Oats has increased its financial risk position during the last several years. Note that the financial risk ratios in Table 10.8 assume that deferred taxes are long-term debt, which is a very conservative assumption for a firm with a strong growth pattern like Quaker Oats.

GROWTH
ANALYSIS

Except for 1988 and 1989, Quaker Oats has generally maintained a sustainable growth rate similar to its industry, and both Quaker Oats and the industry have outperformed the aggregate market. The major factor causing a difference in growth for the firm and its industry is ROE. Quaker Oats' ROE was 26.17 percent in 1991, which caused the potential growth rate to be slightly higher than its industry.

In sum, Quaker Oats has adequate liquidity and a good operating record. Concern arises due to the added debt and a profit margin that lags its industry. As an investor you would monitor the firm's future ability to service its debt and the trend in its profit margin. Your success as an investor depends on how well you use these historical numbers to derive meaningful *estimates*.

ANALYSIS OF
NON-U.S.
FINANCIAL
STATEMENTS

As noted previously, your portfolio should encompass other economies and markets, as well as numerous global industries, and many foreign firms in these global industries. You should recognize, however, that non-U.S. financial statements will be very different from those in this chapter and a typical accounting course. Accounting conventions differ substantially among countries. Although it is not possible to discuss alternative accounting conventions in detail, we will consider some of the major differences in format and principle.

ACCOUNTING
STATEMENT
FORMAT
DIFFERENCES

Table 10.9 contains examples of balance sheet formats for several countries and indicates some major differences in accounts and the order of presentation. As an example, in the United Kingdom fixed assets are presented above current assets, and current liabilities are automatically subtracted from current assets. In Australia, capital accounts are presented initially, and the current assets are placed below long-term assets. The point is, the balance sheet items are similar to those in the United States, but almost exactly opposite in presentation. Clearly, the accounts and presentation in Canada are very similar to those in the United States. Germany's accounts are also similar except that they have numerous reserve accounts on the liability side. Besides finding similarities to the U.S. firms, you need to consider the techniques used to derive individual items.

TABLE 10.9

Comparative Balance Sheet Formats

United Kingdom
Net assets employed
  Fixed assets
  Subsidiaries
  Associated companies
  Current assets
  Less: current liabilities
  Less: deferred liabilities
Assets represented by
  Share capital
  Reserves

Australia
Share capital and reserves and liabilities
  Share capital and reserves
  Long-term debt and deferred income taxes
  Current liabilities
Assets
  Fixed assets
  Investments
  Current assets

Canada
Assets
  Current assets
  Investments
  Fixed assets
  Other assets
Liabilities and stockholders' equity
  Current liabilities
  Long-term debt
  Deferred income taxes
  Shareholders' equity

Germany
Assets
  Outstanding payments on subscribed share capital
  Fixed assets and investments
  Revolving assets
  Deferred charges and prepaid expenses
  Accumulated net loss (of period)
Liabilities and shareholders' equity
  Share capital
  Open reserves
  Adjustments to assets
  Reserves for estimated liabilities and accrued expenses
  Liabilities, contractually payable beyond 4 years
  Deferred income
  Accumulated net profit (of period)

Source: *Professional Accounting in 30 Countries*, pp. 51, 125–126, 169, 629, 746–749. Copyright © 1975 by the American Institute of Certified Public Accountants, Inc. Reprinted by permission of the AICPA.

The comparative income statement formats in Table 10.10 show that the U.K. statements have much less detail than U.S. statements. This limits your ability to analyze trends in expense items. Although Japanese statements are fairly similar to those of the United States, you should be aware of nonoperating income and expense items. These can be substantial because Japanese firms typically have heavy investments in the common stock of suppliers and customers as a sign of goodwill. The income and gains

TABLE 10.10	**Comparative Income Statement Formats**

United Kingdom
Group turnover
Profit before taxation and extraordinary items
    Less: Taxation based on profit for the year
Profit after taxation and before extraordinary items
    Less: Extraordinary items
Profits attributable to shareholders of parent
    company

Japan
Sales
    Less: Cost of goods sold
Gross profit on sales
    Less: Selling and administrative expenses
Operating income
    Add: Nonoperating revenue
Gross profit for the period
    Less: Nonoperating expenses
Net income for the period

Australia
Sales and revenue
    Less: Cost of sales
Operating profit
    Add: Income from investments
    Less: Interest to other persons
Pretax profit
    Less: Provision for income tax
Net profit before extraordinary items
    Less: Extraordinary items
Net profit after extraordinary items
Unappropriated profits, previous year
Prior year adjustments
Transfer from general reserve
Available for appropriation
Dividends
Transfer to general reserve
Transfer to capital profits reserve
Unappropriated profits, end of year

Germany
Net sales
Increase or decrease of finished and unfinished
    products
Other manufacturing costs for fixed assets
Total output
Raw materials and supplies, purchased goods
    consumed in sale
Gross profit
Income from profit transfer agreements
Income from trade investments
Income from other long-term investments
Other interest and similar income
Income from retirement and appraisal of fixed
    assets
Income from the cancellation of lump allowances
Income from the cancellation of overstated
    reserves
Other income, including extraordinary in the sum
    of DM
Income from loss transfer agreements
Total income
Wages and salaries
Social taxes
Expenses for pension plans and relief
Depreciation and amortization of fixed assets and
    investments
Depreciation and amortization of finance
    investments
Losses by deduction or on retirement of current
    assets
Losses on retirement of fixed assets and
    investments
Interest and similar expenses
Taxes on income and net assets
Other expenses
Profits transferable to parent company under profit
    transfer agreement
Profit or loss for the period
Profit or loss brought forward from preceding year
Release of reserves
Amounts appropriated to reserves out of profit of
    period
Accumulated net profit or loss

Source: *Professional Accounting in 30 Countries,* pp. 52, 350, 351, 630, 750, 753. Copyright © 1975 by the American Institute of Certified Public Accountants, Inc. Reprinted by permission of the AICPA.

(or losses) from these equity holdings can be a substantial permanent component of a firm's net income.

The Australian statements, like the British, combine numerous expense items and include several items concerned with the distribution of the net income. Finally, income statements from Germany are very detailed and contain many unusual income and expense items. These details provide numerous opportunities to control the profit or loss for the period.

DIFFERENCES IN ACCOUNTING PRINCIPLES

Beyond the differences in the presentation format, there are numerous differences in the accounting principles employed to arrive at the income, expense, and balance sheet items. Choi and Bavishi compared accounting standards for ten countries and highlighted the differences.[11] Table 10.11 synthesizes the differences in 32 specific items. Following a discussion of several major areas, the authors conclude:

> Perhaps the major conclusion drawn from analyzing the annual reports of the world's leading industrial firms is that fundamental differences in accounting practices between each of ten countries examined are not as extensive as was initially feared. Major differences observed relate to accounting for goodwill, deferred taxes, long-term leases, discretionary reserves, and foreign-currency translation. Having observed this comforting fact, the user must be cautioned against assuming that consistency and harmonization exists among the annual reports of all foreign companies.[12]

INTERNATIONAL RATIO ANALYSIS

The tendency is to analyze accounting statements using financial ratios similar to those discussed in this chapter. Although this is certainly legitimate, it is important to recognize that the representative ratio values and trends may differ among countries because of local accounting practices and business norms. Choi et al. compared a common set of ratios for a sample of companies in the United States, Japan, and Korea.[13] Table 10.12 compares the mean values for these ratios and the differences among them. These ratios differ substantially for all manufacturing, as well as for specific important industries (chemical, textiles, and transportation). Following an extensive discussion of the ratios the authors conclude:

> On the basis of these findings, institutional, cultural, political and tax considerations in Japan and Korea do indeed cause their accounting ratios to differ from U.S. norms without necessarily reflecting better or worse financial risk and return characteristics being measured. . . .
>
> A major conclusion of our study is that accounting measurements reflected in corporate financial reports represent, in one sense, merely "numbers" that have limited meaning and

[11]Frederick D. S. Choi and Vinod B. Bavishi, "Diversity in Multinational Accounting," *Financial Executive* 50, no. 7 (August 1982): 36–39. This table is also presented and discussed in, Frederick D. S. Choi and Gerhard G. Mueller, *International Accounting* (Englewood Cliffs, N.J.: Prentice-Hall, 1984), 72–76.

[12]Choi and Bavishi, "Diversity in Multinational Accounting," 39. Another comparison of accounting standards for the United States, the United Kingdom, the European Economic Community, and Canada is contained in Thomas G. Evans, Martin E. Taylor, and Oscar Holzmann, *International Accounting and Reporting* (New York: Macmillan, 1985), 106–113.

[13]Frederick D. S. Choi, Hisaaki Hino, Sang Kee Min, Sang Oh Nam, Junichi Ujiie, and Arthur J. Stonehill, "Analyzing Foreign Financial Statements: The Use and Misuse of International Ratio Analysis," *Journal of International Business Studies* (Spring-Summer 1983): 113–131, reprinted in Frederick D. S. Choi and Gerhard G. Mueller, *Frontiers of International Accounting: An Anthology* (Ann Arbor, Mich.: UMI Research Press, 1985).

significance in and of themselves. Meaning and significance come from and depend upon an understanding of the environmental context from which the numbers are drawn as well as the relationship between the numbers and the underlying economic phenomena that are the real items of interest.[14]

USES OF
FINANCIAL
RATIOS

We have discussed the role of financial ratios in credit analysis and security valuation. There are four major areas in investments where financial ratios have been used: (1) stock valuation, (2) the identification of internal corporate variables that affect a stock's systematic risk (beta), (3) assigning credit quality ratings on bonds, and (4) predicting insolvency (bankruptcy) of firms. In this section we discuss how ratios have been used in each of these four areas and the specific ratios found to be most useful.

STOCK VALUATION
MODELS

Most valuation models attempt to derive an appropriate price/earnings ratio for a stock. As discussed in Chapter 11, the earnings multiple is influenced by the expected growth rate of earnings and dividends and the required rate of return on the stock. Clearly, financial ratios can help in making both estimates. The estimate of a growth rate employs the ratios discussed in the growth rate potential section—the retention rate and the return on equity.

When estimating the required rate of return on an investment (k), you will recall from Chapter 1 that it depends on the risk premium for the security, which is a function of business risk, financial risk, and liquidity risk. Business risk is typically measured in terms of earnings variability, financial risk is identified by either the debt proportion ratios or the flow ratios (i.e., the interest coverage ratios or the cash flow ratios), and insights regarding a stock's liquidity risk can be derived from the external liquidity measures discussed.

The typical empirical valuation model has examined a cross section of companies and used a multiple regression model that relates the price/earnings ratios for the sample firms to some of the following corporate variables (the averages generally consider the last 5 or 10 years):[15]

1. Operating earnings variability
2. Average debt/equity ratio
3. Average interest coverage ratio
4. Systematic risk during the last 5 years
5. Average dividend payout ratio
6. Average rate of growth of earnings
7. Average return on equity

FINANCIAL
RATIOS AND
SYSTEMATIC RISK

As discussed in Chapter 8, the capital asset pricing model (CAPM) asserts that the relevant risk variable for an asset should be its systematic risk, which is its beta coefficient related to the market portfolio of all risky assets. In efficient markets, a relationship should exist between internal corporate risk variables and market-determined risk variables such as beta. Numerous studies have tested this relationship by examining

[14]Choi et al., "Analyzing Foreign Financial Statements," 131.

[15]A list of studies in this area appears in the reference section at the end of the chapter.

TABLE 10.11 Synthesis of Accounting Differences

Accounting Principles	United States	Australia	Canada	France	Germany	Japan	Nether-lands	Sweden	Switzer-land	United Kingdom
1. Marketable securities recorded at the lower cost or market?	Yes	Yes	Yes	Yes	Yes	Yes	Yes	Yes	Yes	Yes
2. Provision for uncollectible accounts made?	Yes	Yes	Yes	No	Yes	Yes	Yes	Yes	Yes	Yes
3. Inventory costed using FIFO?	Mixed	Yes	Mixed	Mixed	Yes	Mixed	Mixed	Yes	Yes	Yes
4. Manufacturing overhead allocated to year-end inventory?	Yes	Yes	Yes	Yes	Yes	Yes	Yes	Yes	No	Yes
5. Inventory valued at the lower of cost or market?	Yes	Yes	Yes	Yes	Yes	Yes	Yes	Yes	Yes	Yes
6. Accounting for long-term investments: less than 20 percent ownership: cost method?	Yes	Yes	Yes	Yes*	Yes	Yes	No(K)	Yes	Yes	Yes
7. Accounting for long-term investments: 21–50 percent ownership: equity method?	Yes	No(G)	Yes	Yes*	No(B)	No(B)	Yes	No(B)	No(B)	Yes
8. Accounting for long-term investments more than 50 percent ownership: full consolidation?	Yes	Yes	Yes	Yes*	Yes	Yes	Yes	Yes	Yes	Yes
9. Both domestic and foreign subsidiaries consolidated?	Yes	Yes	Yes	Yes	No**	Yes	Yes	Yes	Yes	Yes
10. Acquisitions accounted for under the pooling of interest method?	Yes	No(C)	No(C)	No(C)	No(C)	No(C)	No(C)	No(C)	No(C)	No(C)
11. Intangible assets goodwill amortized?	Yes	Yes	Yes	Yes	No	Yes	Mixed	Yes	No**	No**
12. Intangible assets: other than goodwill amortized?	Yes	Yes	Yes	Yes	Yes	Yes	Yes	Yes	No**	No**
13. Long-term debt includes maturities longer than 1 year?	Yes	Yes	Yes	Yes	No(D)	Yes	Yes	Yes	Yes	Yes
14. Discount/premium on long-term debt amortized?	Yes	Yes	Yes	No	No	Yes	Yes	No	Yes	No
15. Deferred taxes recorded when accounting income is not equal to taxable income?	Yes	Yes	Yes	Yes	Yes	Yes	Yes	No	No	Yes
16. Financial leases (long-term) capitalized?	Yes	No	Yes	No	No	No	No	No	No	No
17. Company pension fund contribution provided regularly?	Yes	Yes	Yes	Yes	Yes	Yes	Yes	Yes	Yes	Yes
18. Total pension fund assets and liabilities excluded from company's financial statement?	Yes	Yes	Yes	Yes	No	Yes	Yes	Yes	Yes	Yes

(continued)

TABLE 10.11   (*continued*)

Accounting Principles	United States	Australia	Canada	France	Germany	Japan	Netherlands	Sweden	Switzerland	United Kingdom
19. Research and development expensed?	Yes	Yes	Yes	Yes	Yes	Yes	Yes	Yes	Yes	Yes
20. Treasury stock deducted from owner's equity?	Yes	NF	Yes	Yes	No	Yes	Mixed	NF	NF	NF
21. Gains or losses on treasury stock taken to owner's equity?	Yes	NF	Yes	Yes	No	No**	Mixed	NF	NF	NF
22. No general purpose (purely discretionary) reserves allowed?	Yes	Yes	Yes	No	No	No	No	No	No	Yes
23. Dismissal indemnities accounted for on a pay-as-you-go basis?	Yes	Yes	Yes	Yes	Yes	Yes	NF	Yes	NF	Yes
24. Minority interest excluded from consolidated income?	Yes	Yes	Yes	Yes	No	Yes	Yes	Yes	Yes	Yes
25. Minority interest excluded from consolidated owner's equity?	Yes	Yes	Yes	Yes	No	Yes	Yes	Yes	Yes	Yes
26. Are intercompany sales/profits eliminated upon consolidation?	Yes	Yes	Yes	Yes	Yes	Yes	Yes	Yes	Yes	Yes
27. Basic financial statements reflect a historical cost valuation (no price level adjustment)?	Yes	No	Yes	No	Yes	Yes	No**	No	No	No
28. Supplementary inflation adjusted financial statements provided?	Yes	No**	No**	No	No	No	No**	No	No**	Yes
29. Straight-line depreciation adhered to?	Yes	Yes	Yes	Mixed	Mixed	Mixed	Yes	Yes	Yes	Yes
30. No express depreciation permitted?	Yes	No	Yes	No	Yes	Yes	No	No	No	No
31. Temporal method of foreign currency translation employed?	Yes	Mixed	Yes	No(E)	No(E)	Mixed	No(E)	No(L)	No(E)	No(E)
32. Currency translation gains or losses reflected in current income?	Yes	Mixed	Yes	Mixed	Mixed	Mixed	No(J)	Mixed	No(H)	No

Key

Yes—Predominant practice.
Yes*—Minor modifications, but still predominant practice.
No**—Minority practice.
No—Accounting principle in question is not adhered to.
NF—Not found.
Mixed—Alternative practices followed with no majority.
B—Cost method is used.
C—Purchase method is used.
D—Long-term debt includes maturities longer than 4 years.

E—Current rate method of foreign currency translation.
F—Weighted average is used.
G—Cost or equity.
H—Translation gains and losses are deferred.
I—Market is used.
J—Owner's equity.
K—Equity.
L—Monetary/Nonmonetary.

Source: "Diversity in Multinational Accounting" by Frederick D. S. Choi and Vinod B. Bavishi. Reprinted with permission from FINANCIAL EXECUTIVE, August 1982, copyright 1982 by Financial Executives Institute, 10 Madison Avenue, P.O. Box 1938, Morristown, NJ 07962-1938.

TABLE 10.12

Mean Differences in Aggregate Financial Ratios: United States, Japan, Korea (unadjusted)

Enterprise Category	Current Ratio	Quick Ratio	Debt Ratio	Times Interest Earned	Inventory Turnover
All Manufacturing					
Japan (976)	1.15	0.80	0.84	1.60	5.00
Korea (354)	1.13	0.46	0.78	1.80	6.60
United States (902)	1.94	1.10	0.47	6.50	6.80
Difference (U.S.–Japan)	40%	26%	(77%)	75%	26%
Difference (U.S.–Korea)	42%	58%	(66%)	73%	2%
Chemicals					
Japan (129)	1.30	0.99	0.79	1.80	7.10
Korea (54)	1.40	0.70	0.59	2.40	7.10
United States (n.a.)	2.20	1.30	0.45	6.50	6.50
Difference (U.S.–Japan)	42%	22%	(74%)	72%	(8%)
Difference (U.S.–Korea)	36%	45%	(31%)	62%	(9%)
Textiles					
Japan (81)	1.00	0.77	0.81	1.10	6.20
Korea (34)	1.00	0.37	0.83	1.30	4.90
United States (n.a.)	2.30	1.20	0.48	4.30	6.50
Difference (U.S.–Japan)	55%	38%	(70%)	74%	5%
Difference (U.S.–Korea)	55%	70%	(74%)	70%	24%
Transportation					
Japan (85)	1.20	0.86	0.83	1.90	3.90
Korea (14)	0.95	0.40	0.91	1.90	18.60
United States (n.a.)	1.60	0.74	0.52	8.70	5.60
Difference (U.S.–Japan)	21%	(16%)	(61%)	78%	28%
Difference (U.S.–Korea)	40%	46%	(75%)	77%	(234%)

Note: Parentheses indicate foreign ratios greater than U.S. ratios.

Source: Frederick D. S. Choi, Hisaaki Hino, Sang Kee Min, Sang Oh Nam, Junichi Ujiie, and Arthur J. Stonehill, "Analyzing Foreign Financial Statements: The Use and Misuse of International Ratio Analysis," *Journal of International Business Studies* (Spring–Summer 1983): 113–131.

internal corporate variables intended to reflect business risk and financial risk.[16] Some of the significant variables (usually 5-year averages) included were

Financial Ratios

1. Dividend payout
2. Total debt/total assets
3. Cash flow/total debt
4. Interest coverage
5. Working capital/total assets
6. Current ratio

Variability Measures

1. Variance of operating earnings
2. Coefficient of variation of operating earnings
3. Coefficient of variation of operating profit margins
4. Operating earnings beta (company earnings related to aggregate earnings)

---

[16]A list of studies in this area appears in the reference section at the end of the chapter.

TABLE 10.12   (*continued*)

Enterprise Category	Average Collection Period	Fixed Asset Turnover	Total Asset Turnover	Profit Margin	Return on Total Assets	Return on Net Worth
All Manufacturing						
Japan (976)	86	3.10	0.93	.013	.012	.071
Korea (354)	33	2.80	1.20	.023	.028	.131
United States (902)	43	3.90	1.40	.054	.074	.139
Difference (U.S.–Japan)	(102%)	22%	32%	26%	84%	49%
Difference (U.S.–Korea)	24%	29%	9%	57%	62%	6%
Chemicals						
Japan (129)	88	2.80	0.90	.015	.014	.065
Korea (54)	33	1.60	0.90	.044	.040	.100
United States (n.a.)	50	2.80	1.10	.073	.081	.148
Difference (U.S.–Japan)	(75%)	0%	19%	79%	83%	56%
Difference (U.S.–Korea)	34%	44%	19%	39%	50%	32%
Textiles						
Japan (81)	66	3.50	0.92	.003	.003	.017
Korea (34)	30	2.20	1.00	.010	.011	.064
United States (n.a.)	48	5.80	1.80	.027	.049	.094
Difference (U.S.–Japan)	(39%)	40%	50%	87%	93%	82%
Difference (U.S.–Korea)	36%	63%	44%	62%	78%	32%
Transportation						
Japan (85)	116	4.50	0.90	.017	.015	.092
Korea (14)	18	1.10	0.80	.026	.021	.221
United States (n.a.)	31	6.50	1.60	.049	.078	.161
Difference (U.S.–Japan)	278%	30%	44%	65%	80%	43%
Difference (U.S.–Korea)	40%	84%	50%	47%	73%	(37%)

Nonratio Variables

1. Asset size
2. Market value of trading in stock

FINANCIAL RATIOS AND BOND RATINGS

As discussed in Chapter 13, there are four financial services that assign quality ratings to bonds on the basis of the issuing company's ability to meet all its obligations related to the bond. An AAA rating or Aaa indicates very high quality and almost no chance of default, whereas a C rating indicates the bond is already in default. A number of studies have used financial ratios to predict the rating to be assigned to a bond.[17] The major financial ratios considered (again, typically 5-year averages) were as follows:

Financial Ratios

1. Long-term debt/total assets
2. Total debt/total capital
3. Net income plus depreciation (cash flow)/long-term senior debt
4. Cash flow/total debt

---

[17]A list of studies in this area appears in the reference section at the end of the chapter.

Financial Ratios

5. Net income plus interest/interest expense (fixed charge coverage)
6. Market value of stock/par value of bonds
7. Net operating profit/sales
8. Net income/total assets
9. Working capital/sales
10. Sales/net worth (equity turnover)

Variability Measures

1. Coefficient of variation (CV) of net earnings
2. Coefficient of variation of return on assets

Nonratio Variables

1. Subordination of the issue
2. Size of the firm (total assets)
3. Issue size
4. Par value of all publicly traded bonds of the firm

FINANCIAL
RATIOS AND
INSOLVENCY
(BANKRUPTCY)

Analysts have always been interested in using financial ratios to identify which firms might default on a loan or declare bankruptcy. Several studies have attempted to identify a set of ratios for this purpose.[18] The typical study examines a sample of firms that have declared bankruptcy against a matched sample of firms in the same industry and of comparable size that have not failed. The analysis involves examining a number of financial ratios expected to reflect declining liquidity for several years (usually 5 years) prior to the declaration of bankruptcy. The goal is to determine which ratios or set of ratios provide the best predictions of bankruptcy. Some of the models have been able to properly classify over 80 percent of the firms 1 year prior to failure, and some achieve high classification results 3 to 5 years before failure. The financial ratios typically included in successful models were:[19]

1. Cash flow/total debt
2. Cash flow/long-term debt
3. Net income/total assets
4. Total debt/total assets
5. Working capital/total assets
6. Current ratio
7. Cash/current liabilities
8. Working capital/sales

LIMITATIONS OF
FINANCIAL
RATIOS

We must reinforce the earlier point that you should always consider *relative* financial ratios. In addition, you should be aware of other limitations of financial ratios:

1. Are alternative firms' accounting treatment comparable? As you know from prior accounting courses, there are several generally accepted methods for treat-

---

[18]A list of studies on this topic appears in the reference section at the end of the chapter.

[19]In addition to the several studies that have used financial ratios to predict bond ratings and failures, a number of studies have also used cash flow variables or a combination of financial ratios and cash flow variables for these predictions, and the results have been quite successful. These studies are listed in the reference section at the end of the chapter.

ing various accounting items, and the alternatives can cause a difference in results for the same event. Therefore, you should check on the accounting treatment of significant items and adjust the values for major differences. This becomes a critical consideration when dealing with non-U.S. firms.

2. How homogeneous is the firm? Many companies have several divisions that operate in different industries. This may make it difficult to derive comparable industry ratios.

3. Are the implied results consistent? It is important to develop a total profile of the firm and not depend on only one set of ratios (e.g., internal liquidity ratios). As an example, a firm may be having short-term liquidity problems but be very profitable, and the profitability will eventually alleviate the short-run liquidity problems.

4. Is the ratio within a reasonable range for the industry? As noted on several occasions, you typically want a *range* of values for the ratio, because a value that is either too high or too low can be a cause for concern.

SUMMARY

The overall purpose of financial statement analysis is to help you make decisions on investing in a firm's bonds or stocks. Financial ratios should be examined relative to the economy, the industry, the firm's main competitors, and the firm's past ratios.

The specific ratios can be divided into five categories, depending on the purpose of the analysis: internal liquidity, operating performance, risk analysis, growth analysis, and external market liquidity. When analyzing the financial statements for non-U.S. firms, you must consider differences in format and in accounting principles. These differences will cause different values for specific ratios in alternative countries. Four major uses of financial ratios are (1) stock valuation, (2) the identification of internal corporate variables affecting a stock's systematic risk (beta), (3) assigning credit quality ratings on bonds, and (4) predicting insolvency (bankruptcy).

A final caveat: you can envision a very large number of potential financial ratios through which to examine almost every possible relationship. The trick is not to come up with more ratios, but to attempt to limit the number of ratios so you can examine them in a meaningful way. This entails an analysis of the ratios over time relative to the economy, the industry, or the past. Any additional effort should be spent on deriving better comparisons for a limited number of ratios that provide insights into the questions of interest to you (e.g., the firm's operating performance or its financial risk).

QUESTIONS

1. What is the overall purpose of financial statements?
2. Discuss briefly some of the decisions that require the analysis of financial statements.
3. Why do analysts employ financial ratios rather than the absolute numbers?
4. The Murphy Company, which produces polish sausage, earned 12 percent on its equity last year. What does this indicate about the firm's management? What other information do you want and why do you want it?
5. Besides comparing a company's performance to its total industry, what other comparisons should be considered *within* the industry? Justify this comparison.

6. What is the purpose of the internal liquidity ratios? What information do they provide? Who would be most interested in this information?

7. What are the components of operating performance? Discuss each of them, and the purpose of the ratios involved.

8. How might a jewelry store and a grocery store differ in terms of asset turnover and profit margin? Would you expect their return on equity to differ assuming equal risk? Discuss.

9. Describe the components of business risk, and discuss how the components affect the variability of operating earnings.

10. Would you expect a steel company or a retail food chain to have greater business risk? Discuss this expectation in terms of the components of business risk.

11. When examining a firm's financial structure, would you be concerned with the firm's business risk? Why or why not?

12. How does the fixed charge coverage ratio differ from the debt/equity ratio? Which would you prefer and why?

13. Give an example of how a cash flow ratio might differ from a proportion of debt ratio. Assuming these ratios differ for a firm (e.g., the flow ratios indicate high financial risk, the proportion of debt ratio indicates low risk), which ratios would you follow? Justify your choice.

14. Why is the analysis of growth potential important to the common stockholder? Why is it important to the debt-investor?

15. What are the general factors that determine the rate of growth of *any* economic unit? Discuss each of the factors.

16. A firm is earning 24 percent on equity and has low risk. Discuss why you would expect it to have a high or low retention rate.

17. The Orange Company earned 18 percent on equity, whereas the Blue Company earned only 14 percent on equity. Does this mean that Orange is better than Blue? Why?

18. Briefly discuss the two components of external market liquidity. In terms of the components of market liquidity, why do investors consider real estate to be a relatively illiquid asset?

19. Discuss some internal company factors that would indicate the firm's market liquidity.

20. Select one of the four uses of financial ratios, and discuss how you would use financial ratios as an investor.

21. Select one of the limitations of ratio analysis and indicate why you believe it is the major limitation.

PROBLEMS

1. The Whit Vegetable Company has the following results:

Net Sales	$6,000,000
Net total assets	4,000,000
Depreciation	160,000
Net income	400,000
Long-term debt	2,000,000
Equity	1,160,000
Dividends	160,000

a. Compute Whit's ROE directly. Confirm this using the three components.
b. Using the ROE computed in a, what is the expected sustainable growth rate for Whit?
c. Assuming the firm's net profit margin went to .04, what would happen to Whit's ROE?
d. Using the ROE in c, what is the expected sustainable growth rate? What if dividends were only $40,000?

2. Three companies have the following results during the recent period.
   a. Derive for each its return on equity based on the three components.

	A	B	C
Net profit margin	.04	.06	.10
Total assets turnover	2.20	2.00	1.40
Total assets/equity	2.40	2.20	1.50

b. Given the following earnings and dividends, compute the sustainable growth rate for each firm.

Earnings/share	2.75	3.00	4.50
Dividends/share	1.25	1.00	1.00

3. Given the following balance sheet, fill in the ratio values for 1994 and discuss how these results compare with both the industry average and Eddies' past performance.

Eddies Enterprises
Consolidated Balance Sheet
Years Ended December 31

Assets (Dollars in Thousands)

	1994	1993
Cash	$ 100	$ 90
Receivables	220	170
Inventories	330	230
Total current assets	650	490
Property, plant, and equipment	1,850	1,650
Depreciation	350	225
Net properties	1,500	1,425
Intangibles	150	150
Total assets	2,300	2,065

Liabilities and Shareholder's Equity

	1994	1993
Accounts payable	$ 85	$ 105
Short-term bank note	125	110
Current portion of long-term debt	75	—
Accruals	65	85
Total current liabilities	350	300
Long-term debt	625	540
Deferred taxes	100	80
Preferred stock (10%, $100 par)	150	150
Common stock ($2 par, 100,000 issued in 1988 and 1987)	200	200
Additional paid-in capital	325	325
Retained earnings	550	470
Common shareholder's equity	1,075	995
Total liabilities and shareholder's equity	2,300	2,065

Eddies Enterprises

Consolidated Statement of Income

Years Ended December 31, 1993 and 1994

(Dollars in Thousands)

	1994	1993
Net sales	$3,500.7	$2,990.6
Cost of goods sold	2,135.2	1,823.0
Selling, general, and administrative expenses	1,107.3	974.6
Operating profit	258.2	193.0
Net interest expense	62.5	54.0
Income from operations	195.7	139.0
Income taxes	66.5	47.3
Net income	129.2	91.7
Preferred dividends	15.0	15.0
Net income available for common shares	114.2	76.7
Dividends declared	40.0	30.0

	Eddies (1994)	Eddies' Average	Industry Average
Current ratio	_____	2.000	2.200
Quick ratio	_____	1.000	1.100
Receivable turnover	_____	18.000	18.000
Average collection period	_____	20.000	21.000
Total asset turnover	_____	1.500	1.400
Inventory turnover	_____	11.000	12.500
Fixed asset turnover	_____	2.500	2.400
Equity turnover	_____	3.200	3.000
Gross profit margin	_____	.400	.350
Operating profit margin	_____	8.000	7.500
Return on capital	_____	.107	.120
Return on equity	_____	.118	.126

	Eddies (1994)	Eddies' Average	Industry Average
Return on common equity	_____	.128	.135
Debt/equity ratio	_____	.600	.500
Debt/total capital ratio	_____	.400	.370
Interest coverage	_____	4.000	4.500
Fixed charge coverage	_____	3.000	4.000
Cash flow/long-term debt	_____	.400	.450
Cash flow/total debt	_____	.250	.300
Retention rate	_____	.350	.400

REFERENCES

GENERAL

Beaver, William H. *Financial Reporting: An Accounting Revolution.* Englewood Cliffs, N.J.: Prentice-Hall, 1981.

Bernstein, Leopold A. *Financial Statement Analysis: Theory Application, and Interpretation.* 4th ed. Homewood, Ill.: Richard D. Irwin, 1989.

Chen, Kung H., and Thomas A. Shimerda. "An Empirical Analysis of Useful Financial Ratios." *Financial Management* 10, no. 1 (Spring 1981).

Foster, George. *Financial Statement Analysis. 2d ed.* Englewood Cliffs, N.J.: Prentice-Hall, 1978.

Gombola, Michael J., and Edward Ketz, "Financial Ratio Patterns in Retail and Manufacturing Organizations." *Financial Management* 12, no. 2 (Summer 1983).

Heckel, Kenneth S., and Joshua Livnat, *Cash Flow and Security Analysis.* Homewood, Ill.: Business One Irwin, 1992.

Helfert, Erich A. *Techniques of Financial Analysis.* 6th ed. Homewood, Ill.: Richard D. Irwin, 1987.

Johnson, W. Bruce. "The Cross-Sectional Stability of Financial Ratio Patterns." *Journal of Financial and Quantitative Analysis* 14, no. 5 (December 1979).

Page, John R., and Paul Hooper. "Financial Statements for Security Analysts." *Financial Analysts Journal* 35, no. 5 (September-October 1979).

ANALYSIS OF INTERNATIONAL FINANCIAL STATEMENTS

Arpan, Jeffrey S., and Lee H. Rodebaugh. *International Accounting and Multinational Enterprises.* (New York: John Wiley & Co., 1981).

Choi, Frederick D. S., ed. *Multinational Accounting: A Research Framework for the Eighties.* Ann Arbor, Mich.: UMI Research Press, 1981.

Choi, Frederick D. S., and Gerhard G. Mueller. *International Accounting.* Englewood Cliffs, N.J.: Prentice-Hall, 1984.

Choi, Frederick D. S., and Gerhard G. Mueller. *Frontiers of International Accounting: An Anthology.* Ann Arbor, Mich.: UMI Research Press, 1985.

Choi, Frederick D. S., and Vinod B. Bavishi. "Diversity in Multinational Accounting." *Financial Executive* 50, no. 7 (August 1982).

Choi, Frederick D. S., H. Hino, S. K. Min, S. O. Nam, J. Ujiie, and A. I. Stonehill. "Analyzing Foreign Financial Statements: The Use and Misuse of International Ratio Analysis." *Journal of International Business Studies* (Spring-Summer 1983).

Davidson, Sidney, and John M. Kohlmeier. "A Measure of the Impact of Some Foreign Accounting Principles." *International Journal of Accounting* (Fall 1967).

Drury, D. H. "Effects of Accounting Practice Divergence: Canada and the U.S.A." *Journal of International Business Studies* 10 (Fall 1979).

Evans, Thomas G., Martin E. Taylor, and Oscar Holzmann. *International Accounting and Reporting.* New York: Macmillan, 1985).

Fitzgerald, R., A. Stickler, and T. Watts. *International Survey of Accounting Principles and Practices.* Scarborough, Ontario: Price Waterhouse International, 1979.

Gray, S. J., J. C. Shaw, and L. B. McSweeney. "Accounting Standards and Multinational Corporations." *Journal of International Business Studies* 12, no. 1 (Spring-Summer 1981).

Hatfield, H. R. "Some Variations in Accounting Practice in England, France, Germany and the United States." *Journal of Accounting Research* 4, no. 2 (Autumn 1966).

Nair, R. D., and Werner G. Frank. "The Impact of Disclosure and Measurement Practices in International Accounting Classifications." *Accounting Review* 55, no. 3 (July 1980).

FINANCIAL RATIOS AND STOCK VALUATION MODELS

Babcock, Guilford. "The Concept of Sustainable Growth." *Financial Analysts Journal* 26, no. 3 (May-June 1970).

Beaver, William, and Dale Morse, "What Determines Price-Earnings Ratios?" *Financial Analysts Journal* 34, no. 4 (July-August 1978).

Estep, Tony. "Security Analysis and Stock Selection: Turning Financial Information into Return Forecasts." *Financial Analysts Journal* 43, no. 4 (July-August 1987).

Farrell, James L. "The Dividend Discount Model: A Primer," *Financial Analysts Journal* 41, no. 6 (November-December 1985).

Malkiel, Burton G., and John G. Cragg. "Expectations and the Structure of Share Prices." *American Economic Review* 60, no. 4 (September 1970).

Wilcox, Jarrod W. "The P/B-ROE Valuation Model." *Financial Analysts Journal* 40, no. 1 (January-February 1984).

FINANCIAL RATIOS AND SYSTEMATIC RISK (BETA)

Beaver, William H., Paul Kettler, and Myron Scholes. "The Association Between Market-Determined and Accounting-Determined Risk Measures." *Accounting Review* 45, no. 4 (October 1970).

Edelman, Richard B. "Telecommunications Betas: Are They Stable and Unique?" *Journal of Portfolio Management* 10, no. 1 (Fall 1983).

Harrington, Diana. "Whose Beta is Best?" *Financial Analysts Journal* 39, no. 4 (July-August 1983).

Rosenberg, Barr. "Prediction of Common Stock Investment Risk." *Journal of Portfolio Management* 11, no. 1 (Fall 1984).

Rosenberg, Barr. "Prediction of Common Stock Betas." *Journal of Portfolio Management* 11, no. 2 (Winter 1985).

Thompson, Donald J. II. "Sources of Systematic Risk in Common Stocks." *Journal of Business* 49, no. 2 (April 1976).

FINANCIAL RATIOS AND BOND RATINGS

Ang, James S., and A. Kiritkumar. "Bond Rating Methods: Comparison and Validation." *Journal of Finance* 30, no. 2 (May 1975).

Bullington, Robert A. "How Corporate Debt Issues Are Rated." *Financial Executive* 42, no. 9 (September 1978).

Edelman, Richard B. "A New Approach to Ratings on Utility Bonds." *Journal of Portfolio Management* 5, no. 3 (Spring 1979).

Ferri, Michael G., and Charles G. Martin. "The Cyclical Pattern in Corporate Bond Quality." *Journal of Portfolio Management* 6, no. 2 (Winter 1980).

Fisher, Lawrence. "Determinants of Risk Premiums on Corporate Bonds." *Journal of Political Economy* 67, no. 3 (June 1959).

Gentry, James A., David T. Whitford, and Paul Newbold. "Predicting Industrial Bond Ratings with a Probit Model and Funds Flow Components." *The Financial Review* 23, no. 3 (August 1988).

Kaplan, Robert S., and Gabriel Urwitz. "Statistical Models of Bond Ratings: A Methodological Inquiry." *Journal of Business* 52, no. 2 (April 1979).

Pinches, George E., and Kent A. Mingo. "The Role of Subordination and Industrial Bond Ratings." *Journal of Finance* 30, no. 1 (March 1975).

Standard and Poor's Corporation. "Corporation Bond Ratings: An Overview." 1978.

FINANCIAL RATIOS AND CORPORATE BANKRUPTCY

Altman, Edward I. "Financial Ratios, Discriminant Analysis, and the Prediction of Corporate Bankruptcy." *Journal of Finance* 23, no. 4 (September 1968).

Altman, Edward I. *Corporate Financial Distress and Bankruptcy.* 2d ed. New York: John Wiley & Sons, 1993.

Altman, Edward I., Robert G. Haldeman, and P. Narayanan. "Zeta Analysis: A New Model to Identify Bankruptcy Risk of Corporations." *Journal of Banking and Finance* 1, no. 2 (June 1977).

Aziz, A. and G. H. Lawson, "Cash Flow Reporting and Financial Distress Models: Testing of Hypothesis," *Financial Management* 18, no. 1 (Spring 1989).

Beaver, William H. "Financial Ratios as Predictors of Failure." *Empirical Research in Accounting: Selected Studies,* 1966, supplement to vol. 4 *Journal of Accounting Research.*

Beaver, William H. "Market Prices, Financial Ratios, and the Prediction of Failure." *Journal of Accounting Research* 6, no. 2 (Autumn 1968).

Beaver, William H. "Alternative Accounting Measures as Predictors of Failure." *The Accounting Review* 43, no. 1 (January 1968).

Casey, Cornelius, and Norman Bartczak. "Using Operating Cash Flow Data to Predict Financial Distress: Some Extensions." *Journal of Accounting Research* 23, no. 1 (Spring 1985).

Collins, R. B., "An Empirical Comparison of Bankruptcy Prediction Models," *Financial Management* 9, no. 2 (Summer 1980).

Dumbolena, I. G., and J. M. Shulman. "A Primary Rule for Detecting Bankruptcy: Watch the Cash." *Financial Analysts Journal* 44, no. 5 (September-October 1988).

Gentry, James A., Paul Newbold, and David T. Whitford. "Classifying Bankrupt Firms with Funds Flow Components." *Journal of Accounting Research* 23, no. 1 (Spring 1985).

Gentry, James A., Paul Newbold, and David T. Whitford. "Predicting Bankruptcy: If Cash Flow's Not the Bottom Line, What Is?" *Financial Analysts Journal* 41, no. 5 (September-October 1985).

Gombola, M. F., M. E. Haskins, J. E. Katz, and D. D. Williams. "Cash Flow in Bankruptcy Prediction." *Financial Management* 16, no. 4 (Winter 1987).

Largay, J. A., and C. P. Stickney. "Cash Flows Ratio Analysis and the W. T. Grant Company Bankruptcy." *Financial Analysts Journal* 36, no. 4 (July-August 1980).

Menash, Yaw M. "The Differential Bankruptcy Predictive Ability of Specific Price Level Adjustments: Some Empirical Evidence." *The Accounting Review* 58, no. 2 (April 1983).

Moyer, R. Charles. "Forecasting Financial Failure: A Re-Examination." *Financial Management* 6, no. 1 (Spring 1977).

Ohlson, J. A. "Financial Ratios and the Probabalistic Prediction of Bankruptcy." *Journal of Accounting Research* 18, no. 2 (Spring 1980).

Reilly, Frank K. "Using Cash Flows and Financial Ratios to Predict Bankruptcies." In *Analyzing Investment Opportunities in Distressed and Bankrupt Companies.* Charlottesville, Va.: The Institute of Chartered Financial Analysts, 1991.

Scott, J. "The Probability of Bankruptcy: A Comparison of Empirical Predictions and Theoretical Models." *Journal of Banking and Finance* 5 (1981).

Wilcox, Jarrod W. "A Prediction of Business Failure Using Accounting Data." *Empirical Research in Accounting: Selected Studies,* 1973, supplement to vol. 11 *Journal of Accounting Research.*

CHAPTER 11   # INTRODUCTION TO SECURITY VALUATION

In this chapter we will answer the following questions:

- What are the two major approaches to the investment process?
- What are the specifics of the top-down (three-step) approach, what is the logic behind it, and what is the empirical evidence related to its viability?
- When valuing an asset, what are the required inputs?
- Once you have derived a value for an asset, what is the investment decision process?
- How do you determine the value of bonds?
- How do you determine the value of preferred stock?
- What are the alternative techniques available to derive a value for common stock?
- What is the dividend discount model (DDM) and what is its logic?
- How do you apply the DDM assuming a one-period investment horizon and a multiple-year holding period?
- What is the effect of the assumptions of the DDM when you have a growth company?
- How do you apply the DDM to the valuation of a firm that is going to experience temporary supernormal growth?
- How can you use the DDM to develop an earnings multiplier model and what does this model imply are the factors that determine a stock's P/E ratio?
- How do you estimate the major inputs to any of the stock valuation models—the required rate of return and the expected growth rate of earnings and dividends?
- What additional factors do you need to consider when estimating the required rate of return and growth rate for a foreign security?

At the start of this book we defined an investment as a commitment of funds for a period of time to derive a rate of return that would compensate the investor for the time during which the funds are invested, for the expected rate of inflation during the investment horizon, and for the uncertainty involved. From this definition we know that the first step in making an investment is determining your required rate of return.

375

Once you have determined this rate, some investment alternatives such as savings accounts and T-bills are fairly easy to evaluate because they provide stated rates of return. Most investments have expected cash flows and a stated market price (e.g., common stock), and you must evaluate the investment to determine if its market price is consistent with your required return. To do this you must estimate the value of the security based on its expected cash flows and your required rate of return. This is the process of estimating the value of an asset. After you have completed estimating a security's value, you compare this estimated value to the market price to decide whether you want to buy the security.

This investment decision process is similar to what you do when shopping for a suit or dress, a stereo, or a car. In each case, you examine the item and subjectively decide how much you think it is worth to you (i.e., its value). If the price is equal to its estimated value or less, you would buy it. The same technique applies to securities, except that the determination of value is more formal.

We start our investigation of security valuation by discussing the *valuation process.* There are two general approaches to the valuation process: (1) the top-down, three-step approach, or (2) the bottom-up, stock valuation, stock picking approach. Both of these approaches can be implemented by either fundamentalists or technicians. The difference is the perceived importance of the economic and industry influence on individual firms and stocks.

Advocates of the top-down, three-step approach believe that both the economy/ market and the industry effect are very significant parts of the total returns for stocks. In contrast, those who employ the bottom-up, stock picking approach contend that it is possible to find stocks that are undervalued relative to their market price, and these stocks will provide superior returns *irrespective* of the market and industry outlook.

The fact is, both of these approaches have numerous supporters, and advocates of both approaches have been quite successful. In this book we advocate and present the top-down, three-step approach because of its logic and the empirical support for it that we will discuss. Although we believe that a portfolio manager or an investor can be successful using the bottom-up approach, we believe that it is more difficult to be successful because these stock pickers are ignoring substantial information from the market and the firms' industry.

Although we know that the value of a security is determined by its quality and profit potential, we also believe that the economic environment and the performance of a firm's industry influences the value of a security and its rate of return. Because of the importance of these economic and industry factors, we present an overview of the valuation process that describes these influences and explains how they can be incorporated into the analysis of security value. Subsequently, we describe the theory of value and emphasize the factors that affect the value of securities.

Next, we apply these valuation concepts to the valuation of different assets—bonds, preferred stock, and common stock. In this section, we show how the valuation models help investors calculate how much they should pay for these assets. In the final section, we emphasize the estimation of the variables that affect value (the required rate of return and the expected rate of growth). We conclude with a discussion of what additional factors must be considered when we extend our analysis to the valuation of global securities.

AN OVERVIEW
OF THE
VALUATION
PROCESS

Psychologists suggest that the success or failure of an individual can be caused as much by environment as by genetic gifts. Extending this idea to the valuation of securities means that we should consider the economic environment during the valuation process. The point is, regardless of the qualities of an issue or the capabilities of a firm and its management, the economic environment will have a major influence on the realized rate of return on the investment.

As an example, assume you own shares of the strongest and most successful firm producing home furnishings. If you own the shares during a strong economic expansion, the sales and earnings of the firm will increase and your rate of return on the stock should be quite high. In contrast, if you own the same stock during a major economic recession, the sales and earnings of this firm would probably experience a decline and the stock price would be stable or decline. Therefore, when assessing the value of a security, it is necessary to analyze the aggregate economy, the security markets, and the firm's specific industry.

The valuation process is like the chicken-and-egg dilemma. Do you start by analyzing the macroeconomy and various industries before individual stocks, or do you begin with individual securities and gradually combine these firms into industries and the industries into the entire economy? For the reasons discussed in the next section, we contend that the discussion should begin with an analysis of aggregate economies and overall securities markets and progress to different industries with a global perspective. Only after a thorough industry analysis are you in a position to properly evaluate the securities issued by individual firms within the better industries. Thus, we recommend a three-step, top-down valuation process in which you first examine the influence of the general economy on all firms and the security markets, then analyze the prospects for various industries in this economic environment, and finally turn to the analysis of individual firms in the industries and the common stock of these firms.

WHY A
THREE-STEP
VALUATION
PROCESS?

GENERAL
ECONOMIC
INFLUENCES

Monetary and fiscal policy measures enacted by various agencies of national governments influence the aggregate economies of those countries. The resulting economic conditions influence all industries and all companies within the economies.

Fiscal policy initiatives such as tax credits or tax cuts can encourage spending, whereas additional taxes on gasoline, cigarettes, and liquor can discourage spending. Increases or decreases in government spending on defense, on unemployment insurance or retraining programs, or on highways also influence the general economy. All such policies influence the business environment for firms that rely directly on those expenditures. In addition, we know that government spending has a strong *multiplier effect*. For example, increases in road building increases the demand for earthmoving equipment and concrete materials. As a result, in addition to the construction workers, the employees in those industries that supply the equipment and materials have more to spend on consumer goods, which raises the demand for consumer goods, which affects another set of suppliers.

Monetary policy produces similar economic changes. A restrictive monetary policy that reduces the growth rate of the money supply reduces the supply of funds for working capital and expansion for all businesses. This raises market interest rates and, therefore, firms' costs, making goods and services more expensive for individuals.

Monetary policy therefore affects all segments of an economy and that economy's relationship with other economies.

Any economic analysis requires the consideration of inflation. As we have discussed several times, inflation causes differences between real and nominal interest rates and changes the spending and savings behavior of consumers and corporations. In addition, unexpected changes in the rate of inflation make it difficult for firms to plan, which inhibits growth and innovation. Beyond the impact on the domestic economy, differential inflation and interest rates influence the trade balance between countries and the exchange rate for currencies.

In addition to monetary and fiscal policy actions, events such as war, political upheavals in foreign countries, or international monetary devaluations produce changes in the business environment that add to the uncertainty of sales and earnings expectations and, therefore, the risk premium required by investors. For example, the reaction of the Chinese government to the student demonstrations in 1989 caused a significant increase in the risk premium for investors in China and a subsequent reduction in investment and spending in China. In contrast, the reunification of East and West Germany was viewed as a very positive event and led to a significant increase in economic activity across Europe.

In short, it is difficult to conceive of any industry or company that can avoid the impact of macroeconomic developments that affect the total economy. Because aggregate economic events have a profound effect on all industries and all companies within these industries, these macroeconomic factors should be considered before industries are analyzed.

Taking a global portfolio perspective, the asset allocation for a country within a global portfolio will be affected by its economic outlook. If a recession is imminent in a country, you would expect a negative impact on its security prices. Because of these economic expectations investors would be apprehensive about investing in most industries in the country. The best investment decision would probably be a smaller allocation to the country. Specifically, the country will be *underweighted* in portfolios relative to its weight based on its market value. Further, given these expectations any funds invested in the country would be directed to low-risk sectors of the economy.

In contrast, optimistic economic and stock-market outlooks for a given country should lead an investor to increase the overall allocation to this country (*overweight* the country based on its weights determined by relative market value). After allocating funds among countries, the investor looks for outstanding industries in each country. This search for the best industries is enhanced by the economic analysis because the future performance of an industry depends on the country's economic outlook *and* the industry's expected relationship to the economy.

INDUSTRY INFLUENCES

The next step in the valuation process is to identify those industries that will prosper or suffer during the expected aggregate economic environment. Examples of conditions that affect specific industries are strikes within a major producing country, import or export quotas or taxes, a worldwide shortage or an excess supply of some resource, or government-imposed regulations on an industry.

You should remember that alternative industries react to economic changes at different points in the business cycle. For example, firms typically increase capital expenditures when they are operating at full capacity at the peak of the economic cycle. Therefore, the construction industry will typically be affected toward the end of a cycle. In addition, alternative industries have different responses to the business cycle. As an example, cyclical industries such as steel or autos typically do much better than the aggregate economy during expansions, but they suffer more during contractions. In contrast, noncyclical industries such as retail food would not experience a significant decline during a recession, or a strong increase during an economic expansion.

Also, firms that sell in international markets can benefit or suffer as foreign economies shift. An industry with a substantial worldwide market might experience low demand in its domestic market but growing demand in its international market. As an example, much of the growth for Coca-Cola and Pepsi and the fast-food chains like McDonald's and Burger King has come from international expansion in Europe and the Far East.

In general, an industry's prospects within the global business environment determines how well or poorly an individual firm will fare, so industry analysis should precede company analysis. Few companies perform well in a poor industry, so even the best company in a poor industry is a bad prospect for investment. For example, poor sales and earnings in the farm equipment industry during the mid-1980s limited Deere and Co., a very well-managed firm and probably the best firm in its industry, to very poor results. Though Deere performed better than other firms in the industry (some went bankrupt), its earnings and stock performance still fell far short of its past performance and did poorly relative to firms in most other industries.

COMPANY ANALYSIS

After determining that an industry's outlook is good, an investor can analyze and compare individual firms' performance within the entire industry using financial ratios and cash flow values. As discussed in Chapter 10, many ratios for firms are valid only when they are compared to the performance of their industries.

You undertake company analysis to identify the best company in a promising industry. This involves examining not only a firm's past performance, but also its future prospects. After you understand the firm and its outlook, you are in a position to determine its value. In the final step you compare this estimated value to the firm's market price and decide whether its stock or bonds are good investments.

Your final goal is to select the best stock or bonds within a desirable industry and include it in your portfolio based on its relationship (correlation) with all other assets in your portfolio. As we will discuss in more detail in Chapter 18, the best stock or bond may not necessarily be issued by the best company because the stock of the finest company in an industry may be overpriced and a poor investment. You cannot know whether a security is undervalued or overvalued until you have analyzed the company, estimated its value, and compared your estimated value to the market price of the stock.

DOES THE THREE-STEP PROCESS WORK?

Although you might agree with the logic of the three-step investment process, you might wonder how well this process works in selecting investments. Several academic studies have supported this technique. First, studies indicated that most changes in an individual firm's *earnings* could be attributed to changes for all firms and changes in the firm's industry, with the earnings changes by all firms being more important.[1] Although the relative influence of the general economy and the industry varied among individual firms, the results consistently demonstrated that there were significant effects of the economic environment on firm earnings.

Second, several studies have found a relationship between aggregate stock prices and various economic series such as employment, income, or production.[2] These results supported the view that there is a relationship between stock prices and economic expansions and contractions.

Third, an analysis of the relationship between *rates of return* for the aggregate stock market, alternative industries, and individual stocks showed that most of the changes in rates of return for individual stocks could be explained by changes in the rates of return for the aggregate stock market and the stock's industry. Although the importance of the market effect tended to decline over time and the significance of the industry effect varied among industries, the combined market–industry effect on the individual firm's rate of return was still important.[3]

These results from academic studies support the use of the three-step investment process. This investment decision approach implies that the most important decision is the asset allocation decision.[4] The asset allocation specifies: (1) what proportion of your portfolio will be invested in various nations' economies, (2) within each country, how will you divide your assets among stocks, bonds, or other assets, and (3) your industry selections based on which industries are expected to prosper or suffer in the projected economic environment.

Now that we have described and justified the three-step process in which we evaluate the overall economy and market, then alternative industries, and finally individual companies and stocks, we need to consider the theory of valuation. The application of this theory allows us to compute a value for the market, for alternative industries, and for individual firms and stocks. Finally, we will compare these estimated values to current market prices and decide whether we want to make particular investments.

THEORY OF VALUATION

You may recall from your studies in accounting, economics, or corporate finance that the value of an asset is the present value of its expected returns. Specifically, you expect

---

[1]The classic study on this topic was Philip Brown and Ray Ball, "Some Preliminary Findings on the Association Between the Earnings of a Firm, Its Industry, and the Economy," *Empirical Research in Accounting, Selected Studies,* 1967, supplement to volume 5, *Journal of Accounting Research*: 55–77.

[2]Studies that examined this relationship include Julius Shiskin, "Systematic Aspects of Stock Price Fluctuations," reprinted in James Lorie and Richard Brealey, *Modern Developments in Investment Management,* 2nd ed. (Hinsdale, IL.: The Dryden Press, 1978): 640–658; Eugene F. Fama, "Stock Returns, Expected Returns, and Real Activity," *Journal of Finance* 45, no. 4 (September, 1990): 1089–1108; Geoffrey Moore and John P. Cullity, "Security Markets and Business Cycles," in *The Financial Analysts Handbook,* 2nd ed. (Homewood, IL.: Dow Jones-Irwin, 1988); and Jeremy J. Siegel, "Does It Pay Stock Investors to Forecast the Business Cycle?," *Journal of Portfolio Management* 18, no. 1 (Fall 1991): 27–34.

[3]The initial study was Benjamin F. King, "Market and Industry Factors in Stock Price Behavior," *Journal of Business* 39, no. 1, part 2 (January 1966): 139–190. Subsequent studies that examined differential industry effects included Stephen L. Meyers, "A Re-Examination of Market and Industry Factors in Stock Price Behavior," *Journal of Finance* 28, no. 3 (June 1973): 695–705; and Miles Livingston, "Industry Movements of Common Stocks," *Journal of Finance* 32, no. 2 (June 1977): 861–874.

[4]Authors that examine this question generally refer to it as market timing. Studies on this topic include Robert F. Vandell and Jerry L. Stevens, "Evidence of Superior Performance from Timing," *Journal of Portfolio Management* 15, no. 3 (Spring 1989): 38–42; and Jerry Wagner, Steve Shellans, and Richard Paul, "Market Timing Works Where It Matters Most . . . in the Real World," *Journal of Portfolio Management* 18, no. 4 (Summer 1992): 86–90.

an asset to provide a stream of returns during the period of time that you own it. To convert this stream of returns to a value for the security you must discount this stream at your required rate of return. This process of valuation requires estimates of (1) the stream of expected returns, and (2) the required rate of return on the investment.

STREAM OF
EXPECTED
RETURNS

An estimate of the expected returns from an investment encompasses not only the size but also the form, time pattern, and the uncertainty of returns, which affects the required rate of return.

FORM OF RETURNS

The returns from an investment can take many forms, including earnings, dividends, interest payments, or capital gains (i.e., increases in value) during a period. Alternative valuation techniques use different forms of returns. As an example, one common stock valuation model applies a multiplier to a firm's earnings, whereas another valuation model computes the present value of dividend payments. The point is, returns or cash flows can come in many forms, and you must consider all of them to evaluate an investment accurately.

TIME PATTERN OF RETURNS

You cannot calculate an accurate value for a security unless you can estimate when you will receive the returns. Because money has a time value you must know the time pattern of returns from an investment. This knowledge will make it possible to properly value the stream of returns relative to alternative investments with a different time pattern of returns.

REQUIRED RATE
OF RETURN

UNCERTAINTY OF RETURNS

You will recall from Chapter 1 that the required rate of return on an investment is determined by (1) the economy's real risk-free rate of return, plus (2) the expected rate of inflation during the holding period, plus (3) a risk premium that is determined by the uncertainty of returns. All investments are affected by the risk-free rate and the expected rate of inflation because these two variables determine the nominal risk-free rate. Therefore, the factor that causes a difference in required rates of return is the risk premium for alternative investments. In turn, this risk premium depends on the uncertainty of returns on the assets.

We can identify the sources of the uncertainty of returns by the internal characteristics of assets or by market-determined factors. Earlier we subdivided the internal characteristics into business risk (BR), financial risk (FR), liquidity risk (LR), exchange rate risk (ERR), and country risk (CR). The market-determined risk measure is the systematic risk of the asset, its beta or its multiple APT factors.

INVESTMENT
DECISION
PROCESS: A
COMPARISON OF
ESTIMATED
VALUES AND
MARKET PRICES

To ensure that you receive your required return on an investment, you must estimate the value of the investment at your required rate of return, and then compare this estimated investment value to the prevailing market price. You should not buy an investment if its market price exceeds your estimated value because the difference will prevent you from receiving your required rate of return on the investment. In contrast, if the estimated value of the investment exceeds the market price, you should buy the investment. In summary:

- If Estimated Value > Market Price, Buy
- If Estimated Value < Market Price, Don't Buy

Assume, for example, that you read about a firm that produces athletic shoes for running and hiking that has stock listed on the NYSE. Using one of the valuation models we will discuss, and making estimates of earnings and growth based on the company's annual report and other information, you estimate its value using your required rate of return as $20 a share. After estimating this value, you look in the paper and see that the stock is currently being traded at $15 a share. You would want to buy this stock because you think it is worth $20 a share and you can buy it for $15 a share. In contrast, if the current market price were $25 a share, you would not consider buying the stock.

The theory of value discussed provides a common framework for the valuation of all investments. Different applications of this theory generate different estimated values for alternative investments because of the different payment streams and characteristics of the securities. The interest and principal payments on a bond differ substantially from the expected dividends and selling price for a common stock. The initial discussion that follows applies the discounted cash flow method to bonds, preferred stock, and common stock. This presentation demonstrates that the same basic model is useful across a range of investments. Subsequently, because of the difficulty in estimating the value of common stock we consider several additional techniques for evaluating this class of security.

VALUATION OF
ALTERNATIVE
INVESTMENTS

VALUATION OF
BONDS

Calculating the value of bonds is relatively easy, because the size and time pattern of the returns from the bond over its life are known. A bond typically promises

1. Interest payments every 6 months equal to one-half the coupon rate times the face value of the bond.
2. The payment of the principal on the bond's maturity date.

As an example, in 1994 a $10,000 bond due in 2009 with a 10 percent coupon will pay $500 every six months for its 15-year life. In addition, the bond issuer promises to pay the $10,000 principal at maturity in 2009. Therefore, assuming the bond issuer does not default, the investor knows what payments will be made and when they will be made.

Applying the valuation theory, which states that the value of any asset is the present value of its returns, the value of the bond is the present value of the interest payments, which we can think of as an annuity of $500 every 6 months for 15 years, and the present value of the principal payment, which in this case is the present value of $10,000 in 15 years. The only unknown for this asset (assuming the borrower does not default) is the rate of return that you should use to discount the expected stream of payments. If the prevailing nominal risk-free rate is 9 percent, and the investor requires a 1 percent risk premium on this bond because there is some probability of default, the required rate of return would be 10 percent.

The present value of the interest payments is an annuity for 30 periods (15 years every 6 months) at one-half the required return (5 percent).[5]

---

[5]The annuity factors and present value factors are contained in Appendix A, at the end of the book.

$500 \times 15.3725 = \$7,686$ (present value of interest at 10 percent)

The present value of the principal is likewise discounted at 5 percent for 30 periods:[6]

$\$10,000 \times .2314 = \$2,314$ (present value of the principal payment at 10 percent)

This can be summarized as follows:

Present value of interest payments	
$500 × 15.3725	= $ 7,686
Present value of principal payment	
$10,000 × .2314	= 2,314
Total value of bond at 10 percent	= $10,000

This is the amount that an investor should be willing to pay for this bond, assuming that the required rate of return on a bond of this risk class is 10 percent. If the market price of the bond is above this value, the investor should not buy it, because the promised yield to maturity will be less than the required rate of return.

Alternatively, assuming an investor wants a 12 percent return on this bond, its value would be:

$500 × 13.7648	= $6,882
$10,000 × .1741	= 1,741
Total value of bond at 12 percent	= $8,623

This example shows that if you want a higher rate of return, you will not pay as much for an asset; that is, a given stream of returns has a lower value to you. As before, you would compare this computed value to the market price of the bond to determine whether you should invest in it.[7]

VALUATION OF PREFERRED STOCK

The owner of a preferred stock receives a promise to pay a stated dividend, usually each quarter, for an infinite period. Preferred stock is a perpetuity because there is no maturity. As was true with a bond, stated payments are to be made on specified dates although it does not entail the same legal obligation to pay investors as bonds do. Payments are made only after the firm meets its bond interest payments. This increases the uncertainty of returns so investors should require a higher rate of return on a firm's preferred stock than on its bonds. Although this differential in required return should exist in theory, it generally does not exist in practice because of the tax treatment

---

[6]If we used annual compounding this would be 0.239 rather than 0.2314. We use semiannual compounding because it is consistent with the interest payments and also is used in practice.

[7]To test your mastery of bond valuation, check that if the required rate of return were 8 percent, the value of this bond would be $11,729.

accorded dividends paid to corporations. As described in Chapter 2, 80 percent of intercompany preferred dividends are tax-exempt, making the effective tax on them about 6.8 percent, assuming a corporate tax rate of 34 percent. This tax advantage stimulates the demand for preferred stocks, and the yield on them has generally been below that on the highest grade corporate bonds.

Because preferred stock is a perpetuity, its value is simply the stated annual dividend divided by the required rate of return on preferred stock (k_p) as follows:

$$V = \frac{\text{Dividend}}{k_p}$$

Assume that a preferred stock has a $100 par value and a dividend of $8 a year. Because of the expected rate of inflation, the uncertainty of the dividend payment, and the tax advantage to you as a corporate investor, your required rate of return on this stock is 9 percent. Therefore, the value of this preferred stock to you is

$$V = \frac{\$8}{.09}$$
$$= \$88.89.$$

Given this estimated value, you would inquire about the current market price in order to decide whether you would want to buy this stock. If the current market price is $95, you would decide against a purchase, whereas if it is $80, you would buy the stock. Also, given the market price of preferred stock, you can derive its promised yield. Assuming a current market price of $85, it would be

$$k_p = \frac{\text{Dividend}}{\text{Price}} = \frac{\$8}{\$85.00} = .0941.$$

VALUATION OF COMMON STOCKS

The valuation of common stocks is more difficult than bonds or preferred stock because an investor is uncertain about the size of the returns, the time pattern of returns, and the required rate of return (k_e). In contrast, the only unknown for a bond is the required rate of return, which is the prevailing nominal RFR plus a risk premium. For preferred stock the only unknown is the required rate of return on the stock (k_p). Nevertheless, we can find common stock values using the same theory that we applied to bonds and preferred stock.

We can use either dividends or earnings as the stream of returns to be discounted. Some investors prefer to use earnings because they are the source of dividends. Others feel that investors should discount the cash flows that they will receive—dividends. Although we will present models that use both streams, we will introduce the dividend discount model (DDM) first because it is intuitively appealing (dividends *are* the flow received). Also, because the DDM has been used extensively by others, you may be familiar with its reduced form.

THE DIVIDEND DISCOUNT MODEL (DDM)

The dividend discount model assumes that the value of a share of common stock is the present value of all future dividends as follows:[8]

$$V_j = \frac{D_1}{(1 + k)} + \frac{D_2}{(1 + k)^2} + \frac{D_3}{(1 + k)^3} + \cdots \frac{D_\infty}{(1 + k)^\infty}$$

$$= \sum_{t=1}^{\infty} \frac{D_t}{(1 + k)^t}$$

where:

V_j = value of common stock j

D_t = dividend during period t

k = required rate of return on stock j.

An obvious question is, what happens when the stock is not held for an infinite period? A sale of the stock at the end of Year 2 would imply the following formula:

$$V_j = \frac{D_1}{(1 + k)} + \frac{D_2}{(1 + k)^2} + \frac{SP_{j2}}{(1 + k)^2}.$$

The value is equal to the two dividend payments during Years 1 and 2 plus the sale price (SP) for stock j at the end of Year 2. The expected selling price of the stock at the end of Year 2 is simply the value of all remaining dividend payments:

$$SP_{j2} = \frac{D_3}{(1 + k)} + \frac{D_4}{(1 + k)^2} + \cdots \frac{D_\infty}{(1 + k)^\infty}.$$

If SP_{j2} is discounted back to the present by $1/(1 + k)^2$, this equation becomes

$$PV(SP_{j2}) = \frac{\dfrac{D_3}{(1 + k)} + \dfrac{D_4}{(1 + k)^2} + \cdots \dfrac{D_\infty}{(1 + k)^\infty}}{(1 + k)^2}$$

$$= \frac{D_3}{(1 + k)^3} + \frac{D_4}{(1 + k)^4} + \cdots \frac{D_\infty}{(1 + k)^\infty},$$

which is simply an extension of the original equation. The point is, whenever the stock is sold, its value (i.e., the sale price at that time) will be the present value of all future dividends. When this ending value is discounted back to the present, you are back to the dividend discount model.

What about stocks that do not pay dividends? Again, the concept is the same, except that some of the early dividend payments are zero. Notably, there are expectations that

---

[8]This model was initially set forth in J. B. Williams, *The Theory of Investment Value* (Cambridge, Mass.: Harvard, 1938). It was subsequently reintroduced and expanded by Myron J. Gordon, *The Investment, Financing, and Valuation of the Corporation* (Homewood, Ill.: Richard D. Irwin, 1962).

at some point the firm will start paying dividends. If investors did not have such an expectation, nobody would be willing to buy the security. It would have zero value. A firm with a non-dividend-paying stock is reinvesting its capital rather than paying current dividends so that its earnings and dividend stream will be larger and grow faster in the future. In this case, we would apply the dividend discount model as:

$$V_j = \frac{D_1}{(1 + k)} + \frac{D_2}{(1 + k)^2} + \frac{D_3}{(1 + k)^3} + \cdots \frac{D_\infty}{(1 + k)^\infty}.$$

where:

$D_1 = 0$

$D_2 = 0$.

The investor expects that when the firm starts paying dividends in period 3, it will be a large initial amount and dividends will grow faster than those of a comparable stock that had paid out dividends. The stock has value because of these *future* dividends. If we apply this model with several cases having different holding periods, you can see how it works.

ONE-YEAR HOLDING PERIOD   Assume that an investor wants to buy the stock, hold it for one year, and then sell it. To determine the value of the stock, that is, how much the investor should pay for it, using the dividend discount model, we must estimate the dividend to be received during the period, the expected sale price at the end of the holding period, and its required rate of return.

To estimate the dividend for the coming year, adjust the current dividend for expectations regarding the change in the dividend during the year. Assume that the company we are analyzing earned $2.50 a share last year and paid a dividend of $1 a share. Assume further that the firm has been fairly consistent in maintaining this 40 percent payout over time. The consensus of financial analysts is that the firm will earn about $2.75 during the coming year and it will raise its dividend to $1.10 per share.

A crucial estimate is the expected selling price for the stock a year from now. You can estimate this expected selling price by either of two alternative procedures. In the first, you can apply the dividend discount model where you estimate the specific dividend payments for a number of years into the future and calculate the value from these estimates. In the second, the earnings multiplier model, you multiply the future expected earnings for the stock by an earnings multiple, which you likewise estimate, to find an expected sale price. We will discuss this model in a later section of the chapter. For now, assume that you prefer the dividend discount model. Applying this model, you project that the sales price of this stock a year from now will be $22.

Finally, you must determine the required rate of return. As discussed before, the nominal risk-free rate is determined by the real risk-free rate and the expected rate of inflation. A good proxy for this rate is the promised yield on one-year government bonds because your investment horizon (expected holding period) is 1 year. You estimate the stock's risk premium by comparing its risk level to the risk of other potential investments. In later chapters we will discuss how you can estimate this risk. For the moment, assume that one-year government bonds are yielding 10 percent, and you believe that a 4 percent risk premium over the yield of these bonds is appropriate for this stock. Thus, you specify a required rate of return of 14 percent.

In summary, you have estimated the dividend at $1.10 (payable at year end), an ending sale price of $22, and a required rate of return at 14 percent. Given these inputs, you would estimate the value of this stock as follows:

$$
\begin{aligned}
V_1 &= \frac{\$1.10}{(1 + .14)} + \frac{\$22.00}{(1 + .14)} \\
&= \frac{1.10}{1.14} + \frac{22.00}{1.14} \\
&= .96 + 19.30 \\
&= \$20.26.
\end{aligned}
$$

Note that we have not mentioned the current market price of the stock. This is because the market price is not relevant to you as an investor except as a comparison to the independently derived value based on your estimates of the relevant variables. Once we have calculated the stock's value as $20.26, we can compare it to the market price and apply the investment decision rule: If the stock's market price is more than $20.26, do not buy; if it is equal to or less than $20.26, buy.

MULTIPLE-YEAR HOLDING PERIOD   If you anticipate holding the stock for several years and then selling it, the valuation estimate is harder because it is necessary to forecast several future dividend payments and also to estimate the sale price of the stock several years in the future.

The difficulty with estimating future dividend payments is that the future stream can have numerous forms. The exact estimate of the future dividends depends on two projections. The first is your outlook for earnings growth because earnings are the source of dividends. The second projection is the firm's dividend policy, which can take several forms. A firm can have a constant percent payout of earnings each year, which implies a change in dividend each year, or the firm could follow a step pattern in which it increases the dividend rate by a constant dollar amount each year or every 2 or 3 years. The easiest dividend policy to analyze is one where the firm enjoys a constant growth rate in earnings and maintains a constant dividend payout. This set of assumptions implies that the dividend stream will experience a constant growth rate that is equal to the earnings growth rate.

Assume the expected holding period is 3 years, and you estimate the following dividend payments at the end of each year:

Year 1	$1.10/share
Year 2	$1.20/share
Year 3	$1.35/share

The next estimate is the expected sales price (SP) for the stock 3 years in the future. Again, if we use the dividend discount model for this estimate you would need to project the dividend growth pattern for this stock beginning 3 years from now. Assume an estimated sale price of $34.

The final estimate is the required rate of return on this stock during this period. Assuming that the 14 percent required rate is still appropriate, the value of this stock is

$$V = \frac{1.10}{(1 + .14)^1} + \frac{1.20}{(1 + .14)^2} + \frac{1.35}{(1 + .14)^3} + \frac{34.00}{(1 + .14)^3}$$

$$= \frac{1.10}{(1.14)} + \frac{1.20}{(1.30)} + \frac{1.35}{(1.4815)} + \frac{34.00}{(1.4815)}$$

$$= .96 + .92 + .91 + 22.95$$

$$= \$25.74.$$

Again, to make an investment decision you would compare this estimated value for the stock to its market price to determine whether you should buy.

At this point you should recognize that the valuation procedure discussed here is similar to that used in corporate finance when making investment decisions, except that the cash flows are from dividends instead of returns to an investment project. Also, rather than estimating the scrap value or salvage value of a corporate asset, we are estimating the ending sales price for the stock. Finally, rather than discounting cash flows using the firm's cost of capital, we employ the individual's required rate of return. In both cases we are looking for excess present value, which means that the present value of expected cash inflows, that is, the estimated value of the asset, exceeds the present value of cash outflows, which is the market price of the asset.

INFINITE PERIOD MODEL   We can extend the multiperiod model by extending our estimates of dividends 5, 10, or 15 years into the future. The benefits derived from these extensions would be minimal, however, and you would quickly become bored with this exercise. Instead, we will move to the infinite period dividend valuation model, which assumes that investors estimate future dividend payments for an infinite number of periods.

Needless to say, this is a formidable task! As mere mortals, we must make some simplifying assumptions about this future stream of dividends to make the task viable. The easiest assumption is that *the future dividend stream will grow at a constant rate for an infinite period*. This is a rather heroic assumption in many instances, but where it does hold, it allows us to derive a model with which we can value individual stocks, as well as the aggregate market and alternative industries. This model is generalized as follows:

$$V_j = \frac{D_0(1 + g)}{(1 + k)} + \frac{D_0(1 + g)^2}{(1 + k)^2} + \cdots \frac{D_0(1 + g)^n}{(1 + k)^n}$$

where:

V_j = **the value of stock** j
D_0 = **the dividend payment in the current period**
g = **the constant growth rate of dividends**

k = the required rate of return on stock j
n = the number of periods, which we assume to be infinite

In the appendix to this chapter we show that with certain assumptions, this model can be simplified to the following expression:

$$V_j = \frac{D_1}{k - g}.$$

You will probably recognize this formula as one that is widely used in corporate finance to estimate the cost of equity capital for the firm.

To use this model, you must estimate: (1) the required rate of return (k), and (2) the expected growth rate of dividends (g). After estimating g, it is a simple matter to estimate D_1, because it is the current dividend (D_0) times $(1 + g)$.

Consider the example of a stock with a current dividend of $1 a share, which you expect to rise to $1.09 next year. You believe that, over the long run, this company's earnings and dividends will continue to grow at 9 percent; therefore, your estimate of g is 0.09. For the long run, you expect the rate of inflation to decline, so you set your long-run required rate of return on this stock at 13 percent; your estimate of k is 0.13. To summarize the relevant estimates:

$$g = .09$$
$$k = .13$$
$$D_1 = 1.09 \ (\$1.00 \times 1.09)$$
$$V = \frac{1.09}{.13 - .09}$$
$$= \frac{1.09}{.04}$$
$$= \$27.25.$$

A small change in any of the original estimates will have a large impact on V, as shown by the following examples:

1. $g = .09; k = .14; D_1 = \$1.09$. (We assume an increase in k.)

$$V = \frac{\$1.09}{.14 - .09}$$
$$= \frac{\$1.09}{.05}$$
$$= \$21.80$$

2. $g = .10; k = .13; D_1 = \$1.10$. (We assume an increase in g.)

$$V = \frac{\$1.10}{.13 - .10}$$
$$= \frac{\$1.10}{.03}$$
$$= \$36.67$$

These examples show that as small a change as 1 percent in either *g* or *k* produces a large difference in the estimated value of the stock. The crucial relationship that determines the value of the stock is the *spread between the required rate of return (k) and the expected growth rate (g)*. Anything that causes a decline in the spread will cause an increase in the computed value, whereas any increase in the spread will decrease the computed value.

INFINITE PERIOD DDM AND GROWTH COMPANIES

As noted in the Appendix, the infinite period DDM had the following assumptions:

1. Dividends grow at a constant rate.
2. The constant growth rate will continue for an infinite period.
3. The required rate of return (*k*) *is greater than the infinite growth rate (g)*. If it is not, the model gives meaningless results because the denominator becomes negative.

What is the effect of these assumptions if you want to use this model to value the stock of growth companies such as Intel, Merck, Wal-Mart, McDonald's, and Apple Computer? *Growth companies* are firms that have the opportunities and the abilities to earn rates of return on investments that are consistently above their required rates of return.[9] To exploit these outstanding opportunities, these firms generally retain a high percentage of earnings for reinvestment, and their earnings grow faster than the typical firm. Notably, the earnings growth pattern for these firms is inconsistent with the assumptions of the infinite period dividend discount model.

First, the infinite period dividend valuation model assumes that dividends will grow at a constant rate for an infinite period. This assumption seldom holds for companies that are currently growing at above-average rates. As an example, Intel and Wal-Mart have both grown at rates in excess of 30 percent a year for several years. It is unlikely that they can maintain such extreme rates of growth for an infinite period in an economy where other firms will compete with them for these high rates of return.

Second, when these firms are experiencing abnormally high rates of growth, their rate of growth will probably exceed their required rates of return. There is *no* automatic relationship between growth and risk; a high-growth company is not necessarily a high-risk company. In fact, a firm growing at a high but fairly constant rate would have lower risk (less uncertainty) than a low-growth firm with an unstable earnings pattern.

In summary, some firms experience periods of abnormally high rates for some periods of time. The infinite period DDM *cannot* be used to value these firms because these temporary high-growth conditions are inconsistent with the assumptions of the model. In the following section of this chapter and in Chapter 18 we introduce models that can be used to estimate the stock values of growth companies.

---

[9]Growth companies are discussed in Ezra Salomon, *The Theory of Financial Management* (New York: Columbia University Press, 1963) and Merton Miller and Franco Modigliani, "Dividend Policy, Growth, and the Valuation of Shares," *Journal of Business* 34, no. 4 (October 1961): 411–433. They are discussed in Chapter 18.

VALUATION WITH
TEMPORARY
SUPERNORMAL
GROWTH

Thus far, we have considered how to value a firm with different growth rates for short periods of time (1 to 3 years) and how to value a stock with a model that assumes a constant growth rate for an infinite period. Recall that the infinite period DDM assumed a constant growth rate for an infinite period and this growth rate was less than the required rate of return (see Appendix 11A). Although a company cannot permanently maintain a growth rate higher than its required rate of return, certain firms may be able to experience temporary supernormal growth. A firm cannot grow at a supernormal rate for a very long period, because competition will enter this apparently lucrative business, which will reduce the firm's profit margins and, therefore, its ROE and its growth rate. Therefore, after a few years of exceptional growth, a firm's growth rate is expected to decline and to eventually stabilize at a level consistent with the assumptions of the infinite period DDM.

To determine the value of a temporary supernormal growth company, you combine the previous models. During the initial years of exceptional growth, you need to examine each year individually. If there are two or three stages of supernormal growth, then you must examine each year during these stages of growth. When the firm's growth rate stabilizes at a rate below the required rate of return, you can compute the value under constant growth and discount this lump-sum value back to the present. The technique should become clear as you work through the following example.

The Bourke Company has a current dividend (D_0) of $2.00 a share. The following are the expected annual growth rates for dividends.

Year	Dividend Growth Rate
1–3:	25%
4–6:	20
7–9:	15
10 on:	9

The required rate of return for the stock is 14 percent. Therefore, the value equation becomes

$$V_i = \frac{2.00\,(1.25)}{1.14} + \frac{2.00\,(1.25)^2}{(1.14)^2} + \frac{2.00\,(1.25)^3}{(1.14)^3} + \frac{2.00\,(1.25)^3(1.20)}{(1.14)^4}$$
$$+ \frac{2.00\,(1.25)^3(1.20)^2}{(1.14)^5} + \frac{2.00\,(1.25)^3(1.20)^3}{(1.14)^6}$$
$$+ \frac{2.00\,(1.25)^3(1.20)^3(1.15)}{(1.14)^7} + \frac{2.00\,(1.25)^3(1.20)^3(1.15)^2}{(1.14)^8}$$
$$+ \frac{2.00\,(1.25)^3(1.20)^3(1.15)^3}{(1.14)^9} + \frac{\frac{2.00\,(1.25)^3(1.20)^3(1.15)^3(1.09)}{(.14 - .09)}}{(1.14)^9}$$

The specific computations in Table 11.1 indicate that the total value of the stock is $94.36. The difficult part of the valuation is estimating the supernormal growth rates and determining *how long* they will last.

TABLE 11.1

Computation of Value for Stock of Company with Temporary Supernormal Growth

Year	Dividend	Discount Factor (14 percent)	Present Value
1	$ 2.50	0.8772	$ 2.193
2	3.12	0.7695	2.401
3	3.91	0.6750	2.639
4	4.69	0.5921	2.777
5	5.63	0.5194	2.924
6	6.76	0.4556	3.080
7	7.77	0.3996	3.105
8	8.94	0.3506	3.134
9	10.28	0.3075[b]	3.161
10	11.21		
	$224.20[a]	0.3075[b]	68.941
		Total value =	$94.355

[a]Value of dividend stream for Year 10 and all future dividends (i.e., $11.21/(0.14 − 0.09) = $224.20).

[b]The discount factor is the ninth year factor because the valuation of the remaining stream is made at the end of Year 9 to reflect the dividend in Year 10 and all future dividends.

This part of the chapter has demonstrated the application of the valuation model to bonds, preferred stock, and common stock. The valuation of bonds and preferred stock was fairly straightforward, because we knew the amount and timing of the returns and our only estimate was the required rate of return. The bulk of the section dealt with the valuation of common stock, which is more difficult because you do not know the amount of flows, the timing of flows, and the required rate of return. The common stock valuation model considered in this section was the dividend discount model (DDM). We noted that the infinite period DDM cannot be applied to the valuation of stock for growth companies because the flow of earnings for the growth company is inconsistent with the assumptions of the DDM model. We were able to adapt the DDM model to evaluate companies with temporary supernormal growth.

EARNINGS MULTIPLIER MODEL

Rather than concentrate on dividends alone, many investors prefer to derive the value of common stock using an earnings multiplier model. The reasoning for this approach recalls the basic concept that the value of any investment is the present value of future returns. In the case of common stocks, the returns they are entitled to receive are the net earnings of the firm. Therefore, one way investors can derive value is by determining how many dollars they are willing to pay for a dollar of expected earnings (typically represented by the estimated earnings during the following 12-month period). As an example, investors willing to pay 10 times expected earnings, would value a stock they expect to earn $2 a share during the following year at $20. You can compute the prevailing earnings multiplier, also referred to as the *price/earnings (P/E) ratio,* as follows:

$$\text{Earnings Multiplier} = \text{Price/Earnings Ratio} = \frac{\text{Current Market Price}}{\text{Following 12 Month Earnings}}$$

This computation of the current earnings multiplier (P/E ratio) indicates the prevailing attitude of investors toward a stock's value. Investors must decide if they agree with the prevailing P/E ratio (i.e., is the earnings multiplier too high or too low?).

To answer this question we need to consider what influences the earnings multiplier (P/E ratio) over time. In Chapter 16 where we discuss market valuation, it is shown that the aggregate stock market P/E ratio, as represented by the S&P 400 Index, has varied from about 6 times earnings to about 23 times earnings.[10] The infinite period dividend discount model can be used to indicate the variables that should determine the value of the P/E ratio as follows:[11]

$$P_i = \frac{D_1}{k - g}$$

If we divide both sides of the equation by E_1 (expected earnings during the next 12 months), the result is

$$\frac{P_i}{E_1} = \frac{D_1/E_1}{k - g}$$

Thus, the P/E ratio is determined by

1. The expected *dividend payout ratio* (dividends divided by earnings).[12]
2. The required rate of return on the stock (k).
3. The expected growth rate of dividends for the stock (g).

As an example, if we assume a stock has an expected dividend payout of 50 percent, a required rate of return of 13 percent, and an expected growth rate for dividends of 9 percent, we would have the following:

$$D/E = .50; k = .13; g = .09$$
$$P/E = \frac{.50}{.13 - .09}$$
$$= \frac{.50}{.04}$$
$$= 12.5.$$

Again, a small change in either k or g will have a large impact on the multiplier, as shown in the following two examples.

---

[10]When computing historical P/E ratios, the practice is to use earnings for the *last* 12 months rather than expected earnings. Although this will influence the level, it should not affect the changes over time.

[11]In this formulation of the model we use P rather than V (i.e., the value is stated as the estimated price of the stock).

[12]You will recall from Chapter 10 that this is the proportion of earnings paid out to stockholders in dividends. Subtracting this proportion from 1 gives the retention rate (RR) used in the growth rate calculation.

1. $D/E = .50$; $k = .14$; $g = .09$. (In this example, we assume an increase in k.)

$$P/E = \frac{.50}{.14 - .09}$$
$$= \frac{.50}{.05}$$
$$= 10$$

2. $D/E = .50$; $k = .13$; $g = .10$ (In this example, we assume an increase in g and the original k.)

$$P/E = \frac{.50}{.13 - .10}$$
$$= \frac{.50}{.03}$$
$$= 16.7$$

As before, the spread between k and g *is the main determinant of the size of the P/E ratio.* Although the dividend payout ratio has an impact, it is typically rather stable with little effect on year-to-year changes in the P/E ratio (earnings multiplier).

After estimating the earnings multiple, you would apply it to your estimate of earnings for the next year (E_1) to arrive at an estimated value. In turn, E_1 is based on the earnings for the current year (E_0) and your expected growth rate of earnings. Using these two estimates, you would compute an estimated value of the stock and compare this to its market price.

Consider the following estimates for an example firm:

$$D/E = .50$$
$$k = .14$$
$$g = .10$$
$$E_0 = \$2.00$$

Using these estimates, you would compute an earnings multiple of:

$$P/E = \frac{.50}{.14 - .10} = \frac{.50}{.04} = 12.5\times$$

Given current earnings (E_0) of \$2.00 and a g of 10 percent, you would expect E_1 to be \$2.20. Therefore, you would estimate the value (price) of the stock as

$$V = 12.5 \times \$2.20$$
$$= \$27.50$$

As before, you would compare this estimated value of the stock to its market price to decide whether you should invest in it.

ESTIMATING THE INPUTS: THE REQUIRED RATE OF RETURN AND THE EXPECTED GROWTH RATE OF DIVIDENDS

Now that we have considered the valuation models, this section deals with estimating two inputs that are critical to the process: the required rate of return and the expected growth rate of dividends.

We will review these factors and discuss how the estimation of these variables differs for domestic versus foreign securities. Although the valuation procedure is the same for securities around the world, k and g differ among countries. Therefore, we will review the components of the required rate of return for U.S. securities and then consider the components for foreign securities. Following this, we will turn to the estimation of the growth rate of earnings and dividends for domestic stocks and then discuss estimating growth for foreign stocks.

REQUIRED RATE OF RETURN (k)

This discussion reviews the presentation in Chapter 1 dealing with the determinants of the nominal required rate of return on an investment including a consideration of factors for non-U.S. markets. Recall that three factors influence an investor's required rate of return:

1. The economy's real risk-free rate (RFR)
2. The expected rate of inflation (I)
3. A risk premium (RP)

THE ECONOMY'S REAL RISK-FREE RATE

This is the absolute minimum rate that an investor should require. It depends on the real growth rate of the economy because capital invested should grow at least as fast as the economy. It is recognized that the rate can be impacted for short periods of time by temporary tightness or ease in the capital markets.

THE EXPECTED RATE OF INFLATION

Investors are interested in real rates of return that will allow them to increase their rate of consumption. Therefore, if investors expect a given rate of inflation, they should increase their nominal required risk-free rates of return to reflect any expected inflation as follows:

$$\text{Nominal RFR} = [1 + \text{Real RFR}][1 + E(I)] - 1$$

where:

$E(I)$ = **expected rate of inflation**

The two factors that determine the nominal RFR affect all investments, from U.S. government securities to highly speculative land deals. Investors who hope to calculate security values accurately must carefully estimate the expected rate of inflation. Not only does it affect all investments, but its extreme volatility makes its estimation difficult.

THE RISK PREMIUM

The risk premium causes differences in the required rates of return among alternative investments that range from government bonds to corporate bonds to common stocks. This premium also explains the difference in the expected return among securities of the same type. This is the reason corporate bonds with different ratings of Aaa, Aa, or

A, have different yields, and different common stocks have widely varying earnings multipliers despite similar growth expectations.

In Chapter 1 we noted that investors demand a risk premium because of the uncertainty of returns expected from an investment. A measure of this uncertainty of returns was the dispersion of expected returns. We suggested several internal factors that influence the variability of returns, so you can evaluate the risk of an investment by analyzing internal factors such as business risk, financial risk, and liquidity risk. We noted that foreign investments bring additional risk factors including exchange rate risk and country risk. All of these risk factors will be considered in the following section.

VARIABILITY OF THE RISK PREMIUM

Because different securities have different patterns of returns and different guarantees to investors, we expect their risk premiums to differ. In addition, the risk premiums for the same securities can *change over time.* For example, Figure 11.1 graphs the spread

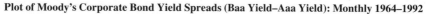

FIGURE 11.1   **Plot of Moody's Corporate Bond Yield Spreads (Baa Yield–Aaa Yield): Monthly 1964–1992**

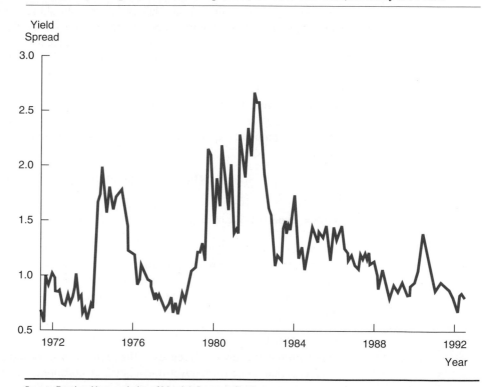

Source: Reprinted by permission of Moody's Investors Service.

between the yields to maturity for Aaa-rated corporate bonds and Baa-rated corporate bonds from 1964 to 1992. This spread, or difference in yield, is a measure of the risk premium for investing in higher-risk bonds (Baa) compared to low-risk bonds (Aaa). As shown, the difference in yield varied from .61 percent to 2.69 percent (less than 1 percent to almost 3 percent).

Figure 11.2 plots the *ratio* of the yields for the same period, which indicates the percentage risk premium of Baa bonds compared to Aaa bonds. You might expect a larger difference in yield between Baa and Aaa bonds if Aaa bonds are yielding 12 percent rather than 6 percent. The ratio in Figure 11.2 adjusts for this size difference. This shows that even adjusting for the size difference, the risk premium varies from about 1.07 to 1.23—a 7 percent premium to a 23 percent premium over the base yield on Aaa bonds. This change in risk premium over time occurs because either investors perceive a change in the level of risk of Baa bonds compared to Aaa bonds, or the

FIGURE 11.2   **Plot of the Ratio of Moody's Corporate Bond Yields (Baa Yield ÷ Aaa Yield): Monthly 1964–1992**

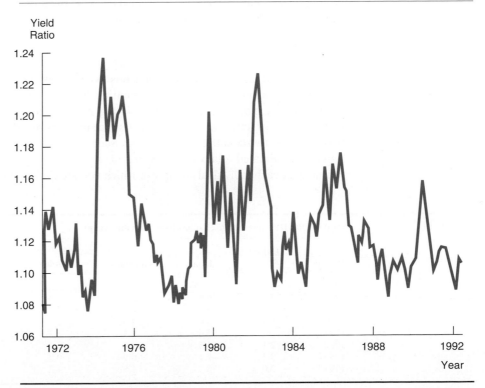

amount of return they require to accept the same level of risk changes. In either case, this change in the risk premium for a set of assets implies a change in the slope of the security market line (SML). This change in the slope of the SML was demonstrated in Chapter 1.

ESTIMATING THE
REQUIRED
RETURN FOR
FOREIGN
SECURITIES

Our discussion of the required rate of return for investments has been limited to the domestic market. Although the basic valuation model and its variables are the same around the world, there are significant differences in the specific variables. This section points out where these differences occur.

FOREIGN REAL RFR

Because the real RFR in other countries should be determined by the real growth rate within the particular economy, the estimated rate can vary substantially among countries due to differences in the three variables that affect an economy's real growth rate: (1) growth rate of the labor force, (2) growth rate of the average number of hours worked, and (3) growth rate of labor productivity. An example of differences in the real growth rate of Gross Domestic Product (GDP) can be seen in Table 11.2. There is a range of estimates for 1994 of 2.5 percent (i.e., 0.7 percent for Italy compared with 3.2 percent for Japan). This difference in the growth rates of real GDP implies a substantial difference in the real RFR for these countries. To estimate the real rates of growth for alternative countries, you must examine the historical values for the three variables that affect each country's real growth.

INFLATION RATE

To estimate the nominal RFR for a country, you must also estimate its expected rate of inflation and adjust the real RFR for this expectation. Again, this rate of inflation typically varies substantially among countries. The price change data in Table 11.3 show that the expected rate of inflation during 1994 varied from 1.7 percent in Japan to 4.3 percent in Italy. This implies a difference in the nominal required rate of return between these two countries of 2.6 percent. Such a difference in k can have a substantial impact on estimated values as demonstrated earlier. Again, you must make a separate estimate for each individual country in which you are evaluating securities.

TABLE 11.2

Real GNP/GDP (percentage changes from previous year)

Period	United States	Japan	Germany	France	United Kingdom	Italy
1987	3.7%	4.6%	1.7%	1.9%	4.5%	3.0%
1988	4.4	5.8	3.6	3.4	4.6	4.2
1989	2.5	4.8	4.0	3.6	1.9	3.2
1990	0.8	5.6	4.6	2.5	1.0	1.9
1991	0.1	3.6	3.3	1.2	−1.2	1.5
1992	2.1	1.5	1.5	1.2	−0.5	1.0
1993[e]	3.3	1.1	−0.9	−0.8	1.5	−0.6
1994[e]	3.0	3.2	1.5	1.2	3.0	0.7

[e]estimate

Source: "World Investment Strategy Highlights" (London: Goldman, Sachs International Ltd., May 1993).

TABLE 11.3 **Consumer or Retail Price (percentage changes from previous year)**

Period	United States	Japan	Germany	France	United Kingdom	Italy
1987	3.7%	0.1%	0.3%	3.3%	4.1%	4.6%
1988	4.1	0.7	1.3	2.7	4.9	5.0
1989	4.8	2.3	2.8	3.4	7.8	6.6
1990	5.4	3.0	2.7	3.4	9.5	6.1
1991	4.7	3.2	3.5	3.1	6.0	6.0
1992	3.0	1.7	4.0	2.8	3.7	5.2
1993[e]	3.2	1.2	3.7	2.3	1.8	4.5
1994[e]	3.0	1.7	3.1	2.1	2.9	4.3

[e]estimate

Source: "World Investment Strategy Highlights" (London: Goldman, Sachs International Ltd., May 1993). Reprinted by permission of Goldman Sachs.

TABLE 11.4 **Estimates of 1994 Nominal RFR for Major Countries**

Country	Real Growth in GNP/GDP[a]	Expected Inflation[b]	Nominal RFR
United States	3.0%	3.0%	6.1%
Japan	3.2	1.7	5.0
Germany	1.5	3.1	4.6
France	1.2	2.1	3.3
United Kingdom	3.0	2.9	6.0
Italy	0.7	4.3	5.0

[a]Taken from Table 11.2.
[b]Taken from Table 11.3.

Source: Reprinted by permission of Goldman Sachs.

To demonstrate the combined impact of differences in real growth and expected inflation, Table 11.4 shows the results of the following computation for the six countries based on the 1994 estimates:

$$\text{Nominal RFR} = (1 + \text{Real Growth})(1 + \text{Expected Inflation}) - 1$$

Given the differences between countries in the two components, the range in the nominal RFR of almost 3 percent is not surprising (6.1 percent for the United States versus 3.3 percent for France). As demonstrated earlier, such a difference in k for an investment will have a significant impact on its value.

RISK PREMIUM

You must also derive a risk premium for the investments in each country. Again, the five risk components differ substantially between countries: business risk, financial risk, liquidity risk, exchange rate risk, and country risk. Business risk can vary because it is a function of the variability of economic activity within a country and of the operating leverage employed by firms within the country. Firms in different countries assume significantly different financial risk as well. For example, Japanese firms employ substantially more financial leverage than U.S. or U.K. firms. Regarding liquidity risk, the U.S. capital markets are acknowledged to be the most liquid in the world, with Japan and London being close behind. In contrast, some small, inactive capital markets are quite illiquid and investors would have to add a significant liquidity risk premium.

When investing globally you must also estimate exchange rate risk. Exchange rate risk is the additional uncertainty of returns caused by changes in the exchange rates for the currency of another country. This uncertainty can range from very small for a country such as Hong Kong where the currency is pegged to the U.S. dollar so there is a negligible effect for a U.S. investor from changes in the exchange rate. In this case, the domestic return in Hong Kong and the return in U.S. dollars is almost identical. In contrast, there are some countries where there is substantial volatility in the exchange rate over time, which means that there will be significant differences in the domestic return for the country and the return in U.S. dollars. The point is, the level of volatility for the exchange rate differs between countries, where the volatility is measured as *the average monthly absolute percentage change in the exchange rate*. The higher the average absolute percentage change, the greater the uncertainty regarding the future changes and the larger the exchange rate risk for the country.

The difference in the exchange rate between countries occurs because of specific trade relations between individual countries. As an example of exchange rate risk, consider the trade imbalances between the United States and Japan during 1985 to 1993 that caused significant fluctuations in the exchange rates between the U.S. dollar and Japanese yen—the exchange rate of yen per dollar went from 250 down to 110, back up to 160 and then down to 103 in mid-1993. When the U.S. dollar weakened relative to the yen during 1986, 1987, and 1993, Japanese investors in U.S. stocks and bonds suffered a significant exchange rate loss. Subsequently, when the U.S. dollar strengthened in 1988 and 1989, U.S. investors in Japanese securities suffered. In contrast, during the first half of 1993, the Japanese stock market experienced a rally *and* the yen strengthened against the dollar so during this period U.S. investors in Japanese stocks experienced very high rates of return.

Beyond the difference in the *level* of exchange rate risk (ERR), investors need to be aware of *changes* in the level of ERR caused by changes in exchange rate volatility. These changes in ERR are caused by internal changes in the economy and political condition in a country and also by changes in the relationship of a country with the United States. Specifically, a country's economy may become more or less stable, or the country can develop a different relationship to the U.S. economy that will influence the volatility of its exchange rate with the United States.

Recall that country risk arises from unexpected events in a country such as upheavals in its political or economic environment. As an example, many investors expect country risk to rise in Hong Kong in 1997 when it changes from a territory of the United Kingdom to a province of China. A past example of country risk would be the violent confrontation between students and the army in Beijing during 1989 that signaled a major change in the political and economic environment in China. Another example would be the continuing anti-apartheid movement in South Africa. Such political unrest or change in the economic environment creates uncertainties that increase the risk of investments in these countries. Before investing in such countries, investors must evaluate the additional returns they should require to accept this increased uncertainty.

Thus, when estimating required rates of return on foreign investments, you must evaluate these differences in fundamental risk factors and assign a unique risk premium for each country.

EXPECTED
GROWTH RATE OF
DIVIDENDS

After arriving at a required rate of return, the investor must estimate the growth rate of earnings and dividends, because the valuation models for common stock depend heavily on good estimates of this value. The procedure that we describe here is similar to the presentation in Chapter 10, where we used financial ratios to measure a firm's growth potential.

The growth rate of dividends is determined by the growth rate of earnings and the proportion of earnings paid out in dividends (the payout ratio). Over the short-run, dividends can grow faster or slower than earnings if the firm changes its payout ratio. Specifically, if a firm's earnings grow at 6 percent a year and it pays out exactly 50 percent of earnings in dividends, then the firm's dividends will likewise grow at 6 percent a year. Alternatively, if a firm's earnings grow at 6 percent a year and the firm increases its payout, then during the period when the payout ratio increases dividends will grow faster than earnings. In contrast, if the firm reduces its payout ratio, dividends will grow slower than earnings for a period of time. Because there is a limit to how long this difference in growth rates can continue, most investors make the long-run assumption that the dividend payout ratio is fairly stable. Therefore, analysis of the growth rate of dividends is really an analysis of the growth rate of equity earnings.

When a firm retains earnings and acquires additional assets, if it earns some positive rate of return on these additional assets, the total earnings of the firm will increase because its asset base is larger. How rapidly earnings increase depends on (1) the proportion of earnings it retains and reinvests in new assets and (2) the rate of return it earns on these new assets. Specifically, the growth rate (g) of equity earnings (i.e., earnings per share) without any external financing is equal to the percentage of net earnings retained (the retention rate, which equals $1 -$ the payout ratio) times the rate of return on equity capital.

$$g = \text{(Retention Rate)} \times \text{(Return on Equity)}$$
$$= \text{RR} \times \text{ROE}$$

Therefore, a firm can increase its growth rate by increasing its retention rate (reducing its payout ratio) and investing these added funds at its historic ROE. Alternatively, the firm can maintain its retention rate but increase its ROE. As an example, if a firm retains 50 percent of net earnings, and consistently has a ROE of 10 percent, its net earnings will grow at the rate of 5 percent a year, as follows:

$$g = \text{RR} \times \text{ROE}$$
$$= .50 \times .10$$
$$= .05.$$

If, however, the firm increases its retention rate to 75 percent and invests this money in internal projects that earn 10 percent, its growth rate will increase to 7.5 percent, as follows:

$$g = .75 \times .10$$
$$= .075.$$

If, instead, the firm continues to reinvest 50 percent of its earnings, but derives a higher rate of return on these investments, say 15 percent, it can likewise increase its growth rate, as follows:

$$g = .50 \times .15$$
$$= .075.$$

BREAKDOWN OF ROE

Although the retention rate is a management decision, you will recall from Chapter 10 that changes in the firm's ROE result from changes in its operating performance or its financial leverage. To see what is required, we divided the ROE ratio into the following three components:

$$\text{ROE} = \frac{\text{Net Income}}{\text{Sales}} \times \frac{\text{Sales}}{\text{Total Assets}} \times \frac{\text{Total Assets}}{\text{Equity}}$$

$$= \frac{\text{Profit}}{\text{Margin}} \times \frac{\text{Total}}{\text{Asset Turnover}} \times \frac{\text{Financial}}{\text{Leverage}}$$

As discussed in Chapter 10, this breakdown allows us to consider the three factors that determine a firm's ROE. Because it is a multiplicative relationship, an increase in any of the three ratios will cause an increase in ROE. Two of the three ratios reflect operating performance and one indicates a firm's financing decision.

The first operating ratio, net profit margin, indicates the firm's profitability on sales. This ratio changes over time for some companies and is very sensitive to the business cycle. For growth companies, this is one of the first ratios to decline as increased competition forces price cutting, reducing profit margins. Also, during recessions profit margins decline because of price cutting or because of higher percentages of fixed costs due to lower sales.

The second component, total asset turnover, is the ultimate indicator of operating efficiency and reflects the asset and capital requirements of the business. Although this ratio varies dramatically by industry, within an industry it is an excellent indicator of management's operating efficiency.

The final component, total assets/equity, does not measure operating performance, but rather financial leverage, which indicates how management has decided to finance the firm. This management decision regarding the financing of assets has financial risk implications for the stockholder.

Knowing this breakdown of ROE, you must examine past results and expectations for a firm and develop *estimates* of the three components and, therefore, an estimate of a firm's ROE. This estimate of ROE combined with the firm's retention rate will indicate its growth potential.

ESTIMATING
DIVIDEND
GROWTH FOR
FOREIGN STOCKS

The procedure for finding the growth rates for foreign stocks is similar to that for U.S. stocks, but the value of the equation's components may differ substantially from what is common in the United States. Remember that these differences in the retention rate or the components of ROE result from differences in accounting practices as well as alternative management performance or philosophy.

RETENTION RATES

The retention rates for foreign corporations differ by company within countries, but there are also differences in the average for all firms in different countries due to differences in the country's investment opportunities. As an example, firms in Japan have a higher retention rate than firms in the United States, whereas the rate of retention in France is much lower. Therefore, you need to examine the retention rates for a number of firms in a country as a background for estimating the standard rate within a country.

NET PROFIT MARGIN

The net profit margin of foreign firms can differ because of different accounting conventions between countries. Foreign accounting rules may allow firms to recognize revenue and allocate expenses differently from U.S. firms. As an example, German firms are allowed to build up large reserves for various reasons. As a result they report very low earnings for tax purposes. Also, different foreign depreciation practices require adjustment of earnings and cash flows.

TOTAL ASSET TURNOVER

Total asset turnover can likewise differ among countries because of different accounting conventions on the reporting of asset value at cost or market values. For example, in Japan a large part of the market values for some firms comes from their real estate holdings and their common stock investments in other firms. These assets are reported at cost, which prior to 1991, substantially understated their true value. This also means that the total asset turnover ratio for these firms is substantially overstated.

TOTAL ASSET/EQUITY RATIO

This ratio, a measure of financial leverage, differs among countries because of differences in economic environments, tax laws, management philosophies regarding corporate debt, and accounting conventions. In several countries, the attitude toward debt is much more liberal than in the United States. A prime example is Japan, where debt as a percentage of total assets is almost 50 percent higher than a similar ratio in the United States. Notably, most corporate debt in Japan entails borrowing from banks at fairly low rates of interest. Balance sheet debt ratios may be higher in Japan than in the United States or other countries, but because of the lower interest rates in Japan, the fixed-charge coverage ratios such as the times interest earned ratio will be similar to those in other countries. The point is, it is important to consider the several cash flow ratios along with the balance sheet debt ratios.

Consequently, when analyzing a foreign stock market or an individual foreign stock, you need to estimate the growth rate for earnings and dividends considering the three components of the ROE just as you would for a U.S. stock. The point of this brief discussion and the discussion in Chapter 10 is that you must recognize that the financial ratios for foreign firms can differ from those of U.S. firms. Subsequent chapters on stock valuation applied to the aggregate market, various industries, and companies contain examples of these differences.

SUMMARY

As an investor, you want to select investments that will provide a rate of return that compensates you for your time, the expected rate of inflation, and the risk involved. To help you find these investments, this chapter considered the theory of valuation by which you derive the value of an investment using your required rate of return. We considered the two investment decision processes, which are the top-down, three-step approach or the bottom-up, stock pickers approach. We argued that a preferable approach is the top-down, three step approach in which you initially consider the aggregate economy and market, then alternative industries, and finally individual firms and their stocks.

We applied the valuation theory to a range of investments including bonds, preferred stock, and common stock. In all instances where we used several different valuation models, the trading rule was always the same: if the estimated value of the investment is greater than the market price, you should buy the investment; if the estimated value of an investment is less than its market price, you should not invest in it.

We concluded with a review of factors that you consider when estimating your required rate of return on an investment and the growth rate of earnings and dividends. Finally, we considered some unique factors that affect the application of these models to foreign stocks.

QUESTIONS

1. Discuss the difference between the top-down and bottom-up approaches. What is the major assumption that causes the difference in these two approaches?
2. What is the benefit of analyzing the market and alternative industries before individual securities?
3. Discuss whether you would expect all industries to have a similar relationship to the economy. Give an example of two industries that have different relationships to the economy.
4. Discuss why estimating the value for a bond is easier than estimating the value for common stock.
5. Would you expect the required rate of return for a U.S. investor in U.S. common stocks to be the same as the required rate of return on Japanese common stocks? What factors would determine the required rate for stocks in these countries?
6. Would you expect the nominal RFR in the United States to be the same as in Germany? Discuss your reasoning.
7. Would you expect the risk premium for an investment in an Indonesian stock to be the same as a stock from the United Kingdom? Discuss your reasoning.
8. Would you expect the risk premium for an investment in a stock from Singapore to be the same as a stock from the United States? Discuss your reasoning.

PROBLEMS

1. What is the value to you of a 14 percent coupon bond with a par value of $10,000 that matures in 10 years if you want a 12 percent return? Use semiannual compounding.

2. What would the value of the bond in Problem 1 be if you wanted a 16 percent rate of return?

3. The preferred stock of the Clarence Biotechnology Company has a par value of $100 and a $9 dividend rate. You require an 11 percent rate of return on this stock. What is the maximum price you would pay for it? Discuss whether you would buy it at a market price of $96.

4. The Bozo Basketball Company (BBC) earned $10 a share last year and paid a dividend of $6 a share. Next year you expect BBC to earn $11 and continue its payout ratio. Assume that you expect to be able to sell the stock for $132 a year from now. If you require 14 percent on this stock, how much would you be willing to pay for it?

5. Given the expected earnings and dividend payments in Problem 4, if you expected a selling price of $110 and required a 10 percent return on this investment, how much would you pay for the BBC stock?

6. Over the very long run you expect dividends for BBC to grow at 8 percent and you require 12 percent on the stock. Using the infinite period DDM, how much would you pay for this stock?

7. Based on new information regarding the popularity of basketball, you revise your growth estimate for BBC to 10 percent. What is the maximum P/E ratio you will apply to BBC and what is the maximum price you will pay for the stock?

8. The Shamrock Dogfood Company (SDC) has consistently paid out 40 percent of its earnings in dividends. The company's return on equity is 16 percent. What would you estimate as its dividend growth rate?

9. Given the low risk in dog food, your required rate of return on SDC is 13 percent. What P/E ratio would you apply to the firm's earnings?

10. What P/E ratio would you apply if you learned that SDC had decided to increase its payout to 50 percent?

11. Discuss three ways a firm can increase its ROE. Make up an example to illustrate your discussion.

12. It is widely known that grocery chains have very low profit margins—on average they earn about 1 percent on sales. How would you explain the fact that their ROE is about 12 percent? Does this seem logical?

13. Compute a recent 5-year average of the following ratios for three companies of your choice (attempt to select diverse firms):
    a. Retention rate
    b. Net profit margin
    c. Equity turnover
    d. Total asset turnover
    e. Total assets/equity.
    Based on these ratios, explain which firm should have the highest growth rate of earnings.

14. You have been reading about the Pear Computer Company (PCC), which currently retains 90 percent of its earnings ($5 a share this year). It earns an ROE of almost 40 percent. Assuming a required rate of return of 16 percent, how much would you pay for PCC on the basis of the earnings multiplier model? Discuss your answer. What would you pay for Pear Computer if its retention rate was 60 percent and its ROE was 19 percent? Show your work.

15. Gentry Can Company's latest annual dividend of $1.25 a share was paid yesterday and maintained its historic 7 percent annual rate of growth. You plan to purchase the stock today because you feel that the dividend growth rate will increase to 8 percent for the

next three years and the selling price of the stock will be $40 per share at the end of that time.

    a. How much should you be willing to pay for the Gentry Can Company stock if you require a 14 percent return?

    b. What is the maximum price you should be willing to pay for the Gentry Can Company stock if you feel that the 8 percent growth rate can be maintained indefinitely and you require a 14 percent return?

    c. If the 8 percent rate of growth is achieved, what will the price be at the end of Year 3 assuming the conditions in Problem 15b?

16. In the *Federal Reserve Bulletin,* find the average yield of AAA and BBB bonds for a recent month. Compute the risk premium (in basis points) and the percentage risk premium on BBB bonds relative to AAA bonds. Discuss how these values compare to those shown in Figures 11.1 and 11.2.

REFERENCES

Beaver, William, and Dale Morse. "What Determines Price-Earnings Ratios?" *Financial Analysts Journal* 34, no. 4 (July-August 1978).

Benesh, Gary A., and Pamela P. Peterson. "On the Relation Between Earnings Changes, Analysts' Forecasts and Stock Price Fluctuations." *Financial Analysts Journal* 42, no. 6 (November-December 1986).

Brown, Philip, and Ray Ball. "Some Preliminary Findings on the Association Between the Earnings of a Firm, Its Industry, and the Economy." *Empirical Research in Accounting: Selected Studies 1967,* supplement to vol. 5. *Journal of Accounting Research.*

Chen, Nui-Fu, Richard Roll, and Stephen A. Ross. "Economic Forces and the Stock Market." *Journal of Business* 59, no. 3 (July 1986).

Farrell, James L. "The Dividend Discount Model: A Primer." *Financial Analysts Journal* 41, no. 6 (November-December 1985).

King, Benjamin F. "Market and Industry Factors in Stock Price Behavior." *Journal of Business* 39, no. 1, Part II (January 1966).

Levine, Sumner N., ed. *The Financial Analysts Handbook.* 2d ed. Homewood, Ill.: Dow Jones-Irwin, 1988.

Moore, Geoffrey and John P. Cullity, "Security Markets and Business Cycles," in *The Financial Analysts Handbook* 2nd ed. (Homewood, Ill.: Dow Jones-Irwin, 1988).

Nagorniak, John J. "Thoughts on Using Dividend Discount Models." *Financial Analysts Journal* 41, no. 6 (November-December 1985).

Reilly, Frank K. "The Misdirected Emphasis in Security Valuation." *Financial Analysts Journal* 29, no. 1 (January-February 1973).

Rie, Daniel, "How Trustworthy Is Your Valuation Model?" *Financial Analysts Journal* 41, no. 6 (November-December 1985).

Shaked, Israel. "International Equity Markets and the Investment Horizon." *Journal of Portfolio Management* 11, no. 2 (Winter 1985).

Shiskin, Julius. "Systematic Aspects of Stock Price Fluctuations." Reprinted in James Lorie and Richard Brealey, *Modern Developments in Investment Management.* 2d ed. Hinsdale, Ill.: The Dryden Press, 1978.

Siegel, Jeremy J. "Does It Pay Stock Investors to Forecast the Business Cycle?" *Journal of Portfolio Management* 18, no. 1 (Fall 1991).

Vandell, Robert F. and Jerry L. Stevens, "Evidence of Superior Performance from Timing." *Journal of Portfolio Management* 15, no. 3 (Spring 1989).

Wagner, Jerry, Steven Shellans and Richard Paul, "Market Timing Works Where It Matters Most . . . in the Real World," *Journal of Portfolio Management* 18, no. 4 (Summer 1992).

APPENDIX 11A   DERIVATION OF CONSTANT GROWTH DIVIDEND DISCOUNT MODEL

The basic model is

$$P_0 = \frac{D_1}{(1+k)^1} + \frac{D_2}{(1+k)^2} + \frac{D_3}{(1+k)^3} + \cdots \frac{D_n}{(1+k)^n}$$

where:

P_0 = current price
D_i = expected dividend in period i
k = required rate of return on asset j.

If growth rate (g) is constant,

$$P_0 = \frac{D_0(1+g)^1}{(1+k)^1} + \frac{D_0(1+g)^2}{(1+k)^2} + \cdots \frac{D_0(1+g)^n}{(1+k)^n}.$$

This can be written

$$P_0 = D_0 \left[\frac{(1+g)}{(1+k)} + \frac{(1+g)^2}{(1+k)^2} + \frac{(1+g)^3}{(1+k)^3} + \cdots \frac{(1+g)^n}{(1+k)^n} \right]. \quad (11A.1)$$

Multiply both sides of Equation 11A.1 by $\dfrac{1+i}{1+g}$:

$$\left[\frac{(1+k)}{(1+g)} \right] P_0 = D_0 \left[1 + \frac{(1+g)}{(1+k)} + \frac{(1+g)^2}{(1+k)^2} + \cdots \frac{(1+g)^{n-1}}{(1+k)^{n-1}} \right]. \quad (11A.2)$$

Subtract Equation 11A.1 from Equation 11A.2:

$$\left[\frac{(1+k)}{(1+g)} - 1 \right] P_0 = D_0 \left[1 - \frac{(1+g)^n}{(1+k)^n} \right]$$

$$\left[\frac{(1+k)-(1+g)}{(1+g)} \right] P_0 = D_0 \left[1 - \frac{(1+g)^n}{(1+k)^n} \right].$$

Assuming $i > g$, as $N \to \infty$, the term in brackets on the right side of the equation goes to 1, leaving:

$$\left[\frac{(1+k)-(1+g)}{(1+g)} \right] P_0 = D_0.$$

This simplies to

$$\left[\frac{1+k-1-g}{(1+g)} \right] P_0 = D_0$$

which equals

$$\left[\frac{k - g}{(1 + g)}\right] P_0 = D_0.$$

This equals

$$(k - g)P_0 = D_0(1 + g)$$
$$D_0(1 + g) = D_1$$

so:

$$(k - g)P_0 = D_1$$
$$P_0 = \frac{D_1}{k - g}.$$

Remember, this model assumes

- A constant growth rate
- An infinite time period
- The required return on the investment (k) is greater than the expected growth rate (g)

CHAPTER 12

The Analysis of Alternative Economies and the Security Markets: The Global Asset Allocation Decision

In this chapter we will answer the following questions:

- What is the expected relationship between economic activity and security markets?
- What is the relationship between the economy and the market implied by the empirical evidence?
- What is meant by a macroeconomic approach to estimating future market returns?
- What are the major macroeconomic approach techniques used to project the securities market?
- What is the leading economic indicator approach, what are its uses and short-comings? Can it be used to predict stock prices?
- What is the expected and actual relationship between the growth of the money supply and stock prices?
- What is meant by excess liquidity, how is it measured, and what is its relationship to stock prices in the United States and around the world?
- What is the expected and empirical relationship between inflation, interest rates, and bond prices?
- What is the expected and empirical relationship between inflation and stock prices?
- When analyzing world security markets, what is the relationship between inflation and interest rates in alternative countries and what is the effect of these variables on exchange rates?
- How do the basic valuation variables differ among countries?
- How do stock price returns among countries correlate when considering domestic returns and when examining returns in U.S. dollars?
- What factors are considered when analyzing the outlook for a foreign economy and its stock and bond market?
- What is the procedure when determining the asset allocation for a global portfolio?
- When doing a world asset allocation, what is meant by normal weighting, underweighting, and overweighting?

FIGURE 12.1   **Overview of the Investment Process**

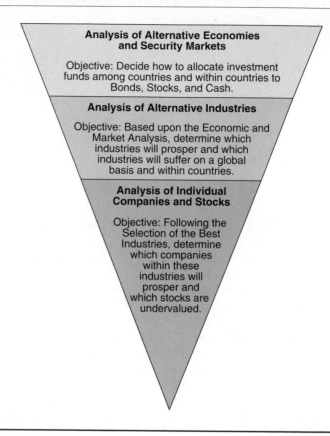

In Chapter 11 we introduced the three-step investment process that begins with economic and market analysis, is followed by industry analysis, and finishes with individual company and stock analysis. Figure 12.1 shows an overview of the process.

We made the point in Chapter 11 that, although we are ultimately interested in securities markets, we analyze economies because of the link between the overall economic environment and the performance of security markets. The point is, *security markets reflect what is going on in an economy.* This is because the value of an investment is determined by its expected cash flows and its required rate of return, and both of these factors are influenced by the economy. Therefore, if you want to estimate cash flows, interest rates, and risk premiums for securities, you need to consider aggregate economic analysis.

From this interrelated economic-market perspective, we initiate discussion of the investment process in this chapter by examining various techniques that relate economic variables to security markets. The first section discusses in detail the relationship between economic activity and the security markets and provides evidence of this relationship. Given this relationship, we consider various techniques used to estimate future market returns based on a macroeconomic approach. Subsequently, we discuss several techniques that are part of this approach, including the use of leading economic indicators and the analysis of money supply growth or other measures of monetary conditions. Following from the analysis of monetary variables, we consider the effect of inflation on interest rates, bond prices, and stock returns.

Although most of the discussion focuses on the U.S. economy, we recognize the need to apply these techniques to other countries. To provide insights into this process, we discuss an example of such an analysis by an investment firm. The culmination of this global analysis is a global asset allocation of all investment funds among countries, and further allocation within countries to specific asset classes: bonds, stocks, and cash equivalents.

In Chapter 11 we discussed the importance of analyzing the general economy as part of arriving at an estimate of future aggregate market values that, in turn, imply future returns from investing in common stocks and/or bonds. There are three major techniques available for analyzing securities markets. A *macroeconomic approach* attempts to project the outlook for securities markets based on an understanding of the underlying relationship between the aggregate economy and the securities markets. The *microanalysis approach* to market analysis involves using the dividend discount model discussed in Chapter 11 to estimate a value for the aggregate stock market. Finally, the *technical analysis approach* assumes that the best way to determine future changes in security market values is to examine past movements in interest rates, security prices, and other market variables.

This chapter deals with the macroeconomic approach to security market analysis and subsequently considers the asset allocation decision that flows from this analysis. Chapter 16 presents the microanalysis of the security markets, and technical analysis techniques are discussed and demonstrated in Chapter 19.

ECONOMIC ACTIVITY AND SECURITY MARKETS

Fluctuations in security markets are related to changes in the aggregate economy. The price of most bonds is determined by the level of interest rates, which in turn are influenced by overall economic activity and Federal Reserve policy. The price of a firm's stock reflects investor expectations about an issuing firm's performance in terms of earnings and cash flow, and that performance is likewise affected by the overall performance of the economy.

In its work monitoring business cycles the National Bureau of Economic Research (NBER) has amassed substantial evidence that supports the relationship between security prices and economic behavior. Based on the relationship of alternative economic series to the behavior of the entire economy, the NBER has classified numerous economic series into three groups: leading, coincident, and lagging indicator series. Further, extensive analysis of the relationship between the economy and the stock market has shown that the consistency of the relationship makes stock prices one of the better leading indicator series.

The evidence indicates a strong relationship between stock prices and the economy, and also shows that stock prices consistently turn *before* the economy does. The data in Table 12.1 document this relationship over the last 30 years. Although this overall leading relationship appears to hold, the data also show several instances of false signals given by the stock market.

TABLE 12.1   **Timing Relationships Between Stock Market and Business Cycle Peaks and Troughs**

I. Stock Market Declines Associated with a Subsequent Recession

Stock Market Cycles[a]				Business Cycles				Lead of Stock Market Over Business Cycle[a]	
Peak		Trough		Peak		Trough		Peak	Trough
Jan.	1953	Sep.	1953	Jul.	1953	May	1954	6.0	8.0
Aug.	1956	Oct.	1957	Aug.	1957	Apr.	1958	11.0	6.0
Aug.	1959	Oct.	1960	Apr.	1960	Feb.	1961	8.0	4.0
Nov.	1968	May	1970	Dec.	1969	Nov.	1970	12.0	6.0
Jan.	1973	Oct.	1974	Nov.	1973	Mar.	1975	10.0	5.0
Feb.	1980	Aug.	1982	Jan.	1980	Nov.	1982	(1.0)	3.0
							Average	7.7	5.3

II. False Signals

Dec.	1961	Jan.	1962
Apr.	1971	Nov.	1971
Sep.	1976	Mar.	1978

III. Stock Market Declines Associated with a Subsequent Growth Recession

Feb.	1966	Mar.	1968

[a]Defined as market declines of approximately 15 percent or more.

Source: Jason Benderly and Edward McKelvey, "The Pocket Chartroom" (Economic Research, Goldman, Sachs & Co., December 1987). Reprinted by permission of Goldman Sachs.

There are two possible reasons why stock prices lead the economy. One is that stock prices reflect *expectations* of earnings, dividends, and interest rates. As investors attempt to estimate these future variables, their stock price decisions reflect expectations for *future* economic activity, not current activity. A second possible reason is that the stock market is known to react to various leading indicator series, the most important being corporate earnings, corporate profit margins, interest rates, and changes in the growth rate of the money supply. Because these series tend to lead the economy, when investors adjust stock prices to reflect these leading economic series, it makes stock prices a leading series as well.

Because stock prices lead the aggregate economy, our macroeconomic approach to market analysis concentrates on economic series that likewise lead the economy by more than stock prices do. First, we will discuss **cyclical indicator approaches** developed by various research groups. These will include the cyclical indicator approach of the National Bureau of Economic Research (NBER) and the *Business Week* leading indicator series, along with several leading series developed by the Center for International Business Cycle Research (CIBCR) at Columbia University. Next we will consider a very popular leading series, the **money supply,** as well as other measures of **monetary liquidity.** Finally, we will discuss the research related to a number of economic series expected to affect security returns (e.g., production, inflation, risk premiums).

CYCLICAL
INDICATOR
APPROACH TO
FORECASTING
THE ECONOMY

The *cyclical indicator approach* to forecasting the economy is based on the belief that the aggregate economy expands and contracts in discernible periods. This view of the economy has been investigated by the National Bureau of Economic Research (NBER), a nonprofit organization that attempts to interpret important economic facts scientifically and impartially. The NBER explains the business cycle as follows:

TABLE 12.2	**Economic Series in NBER Leading Indicator Group**			
		Median Lead (−) or Lag (+) (in months)		
		Peaks	**Troughs**	**All Turns**
	1. Average weekly hours of production workers (manufacturing)	−2	−3	−3
	2. Average weekly initial claims for unemployment insurance (inverted)	−5	−1	−3
	3. Manufacturers' new orders in 1982 dollars, consumer goods and materials	−2	−2	−2
	4. Contracts and orders for plant and equipment in 1982 dollars	−5	+1	$-2\frac{1}{2}$
	5. Index of raw private housing units authorized by local building permits	−9	−6	−7
	6. Index of stock prices, 500 common stocks	−4	−4	−4
	7. M2 money supply in 1982 dollars	−5	−4	−5
	8. Vendor performance (percentage of firms receiving slower deliveries)	−3	−4	−3
	9. Change in sensitive materials, prices smoothed	−4	−8	$-5\frac{1}{2}$
	10. Changes in business and consumer credit outstanding	−4	−6	−5
	11. Changes in manufacturing and trade inventories on hand and on order in 1982 dollars	−2	0	$-1\frac{1}{2}$

Source: Geoffrey H. Moore, "The Leading Indicator Approach—Value, Limitations, and Future," presented at Annual Western Economic Association Meeting (June 1984), revised June 1986; and Marie P. Hertzberg and Barry A. Beckman, "Business Cycle Indicators: Revised Composite Indexes," *Business Conditions Digest* 17, no. 1 (January 1989).

The business cycle concept has been developed from the sequence of events discerned in the historical study of the movements of economic activity. Though there are many cross-currents and variations in the pace of business activity, periods of business expansion appear to cumulate to peaks. As they cumulate, contrary forces tend to gain strength, bringing about a reversal in business activity and the onset of a recession. As a recession continues, forces for an expansion gradually emerge until they become dominant and a recovery begins.[1]

The NBER examined the behavior of hundreds of economic time series in relation to past business cycles. (Recall that a time series reports the values for an economic variable over time, such as the monthly industrial production value for the period 1980–1994.) Based on this analysis, the NBER grouped various economic series into three major categories based on their relationship to the business cycle. The initial list of economic series that could predict turns in the economy was compiled in 1938, and it has undergone numerous revisions over the years. The most recent major revision occurred in 1983 with small modifications in 1987.[2]

CYCLICAL INDICATOR CATEGORIES

The first category, *leading indicators* of the business cycle, includes economic series that usually reach peaks or troughs before corresponding peaks or troughs in aggregate economic activity. The group currently includes the 11 series shown in Table 12.2, which indicates the median lead or lag for each series relative to business cycle peaks or troughs. One of the 11 leading economic series is common stock prices, which has a median lead of 9 months at peaks and 4 months at troughs.[3] Another leading series,

[1]Julius Shiskin, "Business Cycle Indicators: The Known and the Unknown," *Review of the International Statistical Institute* 31, no. 3 (1963): 361–383.

[2]For a discussion of these changes, see Marie P. Hertzberg and Barry A. Beckman, "Business Cycle Indicators: Revised Composite Indexes," *Business Conditions Digest* (January 1989): 291–296.

[3]A detailed analysis of this relationship is contained in Geoffrey H. Moore and John P. Cullity, "Security Markets and Business Cycles," in *The Financial Analysts Handbook,* 2d ed., edited by Sumner N. Levine (Homewood, Ill.: Dow Jones-Irwin, 1988).

TABLE 12.3   **Economic Series in NBER Coincident and Lagging Indicator Series**

	Median Lead ($-$) or Lag ($+$) (in months)		
	Peaks	**Troughs**	**All Turns**
A. Coincident Indicator Series			
1. Employees on nonagricultural payrolls	-2	0	0
2. Personal income less transfer payments in 1982 dollars	0	-1	$-\frac{1}{2}$
3. Index of industrial production	-3	0	$-\frac{1}{2}$
4. Manufacturing and trade sales in 1982 dollars	-3	0	$-\frac{1}{2}$
B. Lagging Indicator Series			
1. Average duration of unemployment in weeks (inverted)	$+1$	$+8$	$+3\frac{1}{2}$
2. Ratio of manufacturing and trade inventories to sales in 1982 dollars	$+2$	$+3$	$+3$
3. Average prime rate charged by banks	$+4$	$+14$	$+5$
4. Commercial and industrial loans outstanding in 1982 dollars	$+2$	$+5$	$+4$
5. Ratio of consumer installment credit outstanding to personal income	$+6$	$+7$	$+7$
6. Labor cost per unit of output in manufacturing, actual data as percentage of trend	$+8\frac{1}{2}$	$+11$	$+10$

Source: Moore, "The Leading Indicator Approach"; and Hertzberg and Beckman, "Business Cycle Indicators."

the money supply in constant (1982) dollars, has a median lead of 10 months at peaks and 8 months at troughs.

The second category, *coincident indicators,* include economic time series that have peaks and troughs that roughly coincide with the peaks and troughs in the business cycle. The bureau uses many of these economic time series to help define the different phases of the cycle.

The third category, *lagging indicators,* are series that experience their peaks and troughs after those of the aggregate economy. A listing and the average timing relationships for the coincident and lagging series are contained in Table 12.3.

A final category, *selected series,* includes economic series that are expected to influence aggregate economic activity but that do not fall neatly into one of the three main groups. This includes such series as U.S. balance of payments, federal surplus or deficit, and military contract awards.

COMPOSITE SERIES AND RATIO OF SERIES

In addition to the individual economic series in each category, a composite time series combines these leading economic series—the *composite leading indicator index.* This composite leading indicator series is widely reported in the press each month as an indicator of the current and future state of the economy. There are also composite coincident and lagging indicator series.

Some analysts have employed a *ratio* of these composite series, contending that the ratio of the composite coincident series divided by the composite lagging series acts like a leading series, in some instances even leading the composite leading series. The rationale for expecting this relationship is that the coincident series should turn before the lagging series, and the ratio of the two series will be quite sensitive to such changes. As a result, this ratio series is expected to lead both of the individual component series.

Although movements for this ratio series tend to be parallel to those of the leading series, its real value comes when it diverges from the pure leading indicator series, because this signals a change in the normal relationship between the indicator series. As an example, if the leading indicator series has been rising for a period of time, you would expect both the coincident and lagging series to be rising also, but the coincident series should be rising faster than the lagging series, so the ratio of the coincident to the lagging series should likewise be rising. In contrast, assume the leading indicator series is rising, but the ratio of coincident to lagging series is flattening out or declining. This change in trend in the ratio series could occur because the coincident series is not rising as fast as the lagging indicator series, or because the coincident series has turned down. Either scenario would indicate a possible end to an economic expansion or at least a less robust expansion.

An example of such a divergence appears in Figure 12.2. The pattern indicates that the coincident and lagging series had been moving at about the same rate, causing the ratio series to run flat and even to decline slightly since 1984 although the leading indicator series continued to increase. Apparently this ratio series signaled a change in the economic environment starting in 1984 that was not confirmed by the leading series until 1989. Investors should note that, despite the divergence between the leading indicator series and the ratio series, stock prices declined prior to a downturn in the leading indicator series.

ANALYTICAL
MEASURES OF
PERFORMANCE

When predicting the future based on an economic series, it is important to consider more than the behavior of the series alone. The NBER has devised certain analytical measures for examining behavior within an alternative economic series.

DIFFUSION INDEXES

As the name implies, *diffusion indexes* indicate how pervasive a given movement is in a series. They are measured by computing the percentage of reporting units in a series that indicate a given result. For example, if 100 companies constitute the sample reporting new orders for equipment, the diffusion index for this series would indicate what proportion of the 100 companies was reporting higher orders during an expansion. In addition to knowing that aggregate new orders are increasing, it is helpful to know whether 55 percent or 95 percent of the companies in the sample are reporting higher orders. This information on the pervasiveness of the increase in new orders would help you project the future length and strength of an expansion.

You would also want to know past diffusion index values to determine the prevailing trend for this index. The diffusion index for a series almost always reaches its peak or trough before the peak or trough in the corresponding aggregate series. Therefore, you can use the diffusion index for a series to predict the behavior of the series itself. Assume that you are interested in the leading series, Manufacturers New Orders in 1982 dollars—Consumer Goods. If the diffusion index for this series drops from 85 percent to 75 percent and then to 70 percent, it indicates a widespread receipt of new orders, but it also indicates a diminishing breadth to the increase and possibly an impending decline in the series itself.

Besides creating diffusion indexes for individual series, the NBER has derived a diffusion index that shows the percentage of the 11 leading indicators rising or falling

FIGURE 12.2   **Indicator Series Performance**

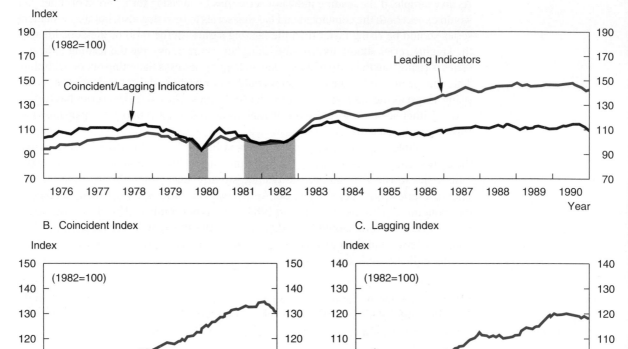

A. Business Cycle Indicators

B. Coincident Index

C. Lagging Index

Source: "Investment Strategy Highlights" (New York: Goldman, Sachs & Co., May 1991). Reprinted by permission of Goldman Sachs.

during a given period. This particular diffusion index is widely reported each month as an indicator of the future state of the economy.

RATES OF CHANGE
Knowing whether a series is increasing is useful, but more helpful is knowing that a 10 percent increase one month followed a 7 percent increase the previous month. Similar to the diffusion index, the rate of change values for a series reaches peaks or troughs prior to the peak or trough in the aggregate series.

DIRECTION OF CHANGE
Direction of change tables show which series rose or fell (indicated by plus or minus signs) during the most recent period and how long the movement in this direction has persisted.

COMPARISON WITH PREVIOUS CYCLES

A set of tables and charts shows the movements of individual series during the current business cycle and compares these movements to previous cycles for the same economic series. This comparison reveals whether a given series is moving slower or faster, or more strongly or weakly, than during prior cycles. This information can be useful because, typically, movements in the initial months of an expansion or contraction indicate their ultimate length and strength.[4]

LIMITATIONS OF THE CYCLICAL INDICATOR APPROACH

The NBER has consistently attempted to improve the usefulness of the cyclical indicators while acknowledging some limitations. The most obvious limitation is false signals. Past patterns might suggest that current indicator values signal a contraction, but then the indicator series turns up again and nullifies previous signals. A similar problem occurs when the indicators show hesitancy that is difficult to interpret. Some economic series may exhibit *high variability,* diminishing confidence in short-run signals as compared to projecting longer-term trends.

Another limitation is *the currency of the data* and *revisions.* The problem is that you might not get the original data very soon and then you have to follow subsequent revisions. Many of the series are seasonally adjusted, so you must also watch for changes in the seasonal adjustment factors.

Also, no series adequately reflects the service sector, which has grown to be a major factor in our economy. Further, no series represents the very important global economy or world securities markets. Finally, as the NBER points out, there are numerous political or international developments that significantly influence the economy, but these factors cannot be incorporated into a statistical system.[5]

LEADING INDICATORS AND STOCK PRICES

We now know that stock prices are part of a composite set of leading indicators. An interesting question is whether we can use the composite series without stock prices to predict stock prices. A study that considered this question specified the decision rule in terms of percentage changes in the composite series.[6] Comparing the results of this decision rule to those of a buy-and-hold policy indicated that as long as the analysts had perfect foresight regarding the correct percentage change to use, they beat a buy-and-hold policy. When they used the trading rule without foresight as to the best percentage change (merely using the percentage change that would have worked during the prior market cycle), they were not able to beat a buy-and-hold policy after subtracting commissions. Therefore, although these leading economic indicator series tend to lead the economy, the composite leading indicator series does not consistently lead its own stock price component in a way that is useful for investment decisions.

OTHER LEADING INDICATOR SERIES

The NBER leading indicator series employs monthly data. The Center for International Business Cycle Research (CIBCR) at the Columbia Graduate School of Business has developed several additional leading indicator series.

---

[4]Monthly presentations of all the series and analytical measures previously appeared in U.S. Department of Commerce publication *Business Conditions Digest.* The government stopped publishing the *Digest* in 1990. The data now appears in the *Survey of Current Business.*

[5]Discussions of these problems are in Evan Koenig and Kenneth Emery, "Misleading Indicators? Using the Composite Leading Indicators to Predict Cyclical Turning Points," Federal Reserve Bank of Dallas *Economic Review* (July 1991): 1–14.

[6]Bryan Heathcotte and Vincent P. Apilado, "The Predictive Content of Some Leading Economic Indicators for Future Stock Prices," *Journal of Financial and Quantitative Analysis* 9, no. 2 (March 1974): 247–258.

BUSINESS WEEK LEADING INDICATOR SERIES

Developed by the CIBCR and published weekly in *Business Week,* the *Business Week Leading Indicator Series* includes seven individual series as shown in Figure 12.3 along with a bar chart for the leading indicator series and a weekly production series along with other weekly data on foreign exchange, prices, and monetary indicators. This composite weekly leading indicator index is meant to help you gauge upswings and declines in general economic activity. Downturns in the index have preceded every recession since 1948, but some downturns in the leading series have been followed only by slowdowns in the economy rather than recessions.

LONG-LEADING INDEX

The CIBCR has also developed its *Long-Leading Index* to provide earlier signals of major turning points in the economy than other leading indexes. It includes the following four series: (1) Dow Jones bond prices (20 bonds by percentage of face value); (2) the ratio of price to unit labor cost in manufacturing (1982 = 100); (3) M2 money supply, deflated (billion 1982 dollars); and (4) new housing building permits (1967 = 100). This index has anticipated recessions by 14 months, on average, and always by at least 7 months.

Monthly data for these series developed and maintained by the CIBCR are available in "The Leading Indicator Press Release." This release is published about the tenth day of each month with data as of 6 weeks prior to its release.

LEADING EMPLOYMENT INDEX

The purpose of the CIBCR's *Leading Employment Index* (1967 = 100) is to forecast future changes in U.S. employment. It includes the following six component series:

1. Average workweek in manufacturing
2. Overtime hours in manufacturing
3. Percentage layoff rate (inverted)
4. Voluntary/involuntary part-time employment
5. Percentage short duration unemployment rate (inverted)
6. Initial claims for unemployment insurance (inverted)

LEADING INFLATION INDEX

The CIBCR *Leading Inflation Index* is intended as a tool for forecasting inflation in the United States. It includes five variables:

1. The percentage employed of the working-age population
2. The growth rate of total debt (including business, consumer, and federal government debt)
3. The growth rate of industrial material prices
4. The growth rate of an index of import prices
5. The percentage of businesspeople anticipating an increase in their selling prices, as determined by a Dun and Bradstreet survey

The leads for this series during the period 1950 to 1991 averaged 7 months at troughs, 4 months at peaks, and 5 months at all turns.

FIGURE 12.3   *Business Week* Index

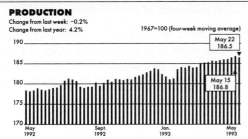

BusinessWeek Index

PRODUCTION

Change from last week: −0.2%
Change from last year: 4.2%

1967=100 (four-week moving average)

May 22
186.5

May 15
186.8

The **production index** fell slightly during the week ended May 22, as the factory sector continues to struggle. On a seasonally adjusted basis, output of trucks, electric power, paperboard, and lumber all declined. Steel, autos, coal, and paper production, plus rail-freight traffic, increased for the week, while crude-oil refining was unchanged. Before calculation of the four-week moving average, the index dropped to 185.2, from 186.2.

BW production index copyright 1993 by McGraw-Hill Inc.

LEADING

Change from last week: 0.3%
Change from last year: 3.7%

May 22
221.8

May 15
221.1r

The **leading index** increased during the week ended May 22 to its highest level since early this year. Higher stock prices and faster growth in M2 helped lift the index. Higher bond yields and deteriorating growth in materials prices and real estate loans hint at trouble ahead. The number of business failures was unchanged. Before calculation of the four-week moving average, the index fell to 222.3, from 223.8 in the previous week.

Leading index copyright 1993 by Center for International Business Cycle Research

PRODUCTION INDICATORS

	Latest week	Week ago	% Change year ago
STEEL (5/29) thous. of net tons	1,902	1,905#	6.9
AUTOS (5/29) units	130,016	142,673r#	16.9
TRUCKS (5/29) units	98,253	104,349r#	28.6
ELECTRIC POWER (5/29) millions of kilowatt-hours	54,152	53,228#	5.2
CRUDE-OIL REFINING (5/29) thous. of bbl./day	13,979	13,733#	1.3
COAL (5/22) thous. of net tons	18,428#	18,142	−2.1
PAPERBOARD (5/22) thous. of tons	802.4#	827.3r	−1.4
PAPER (5/22) thous. of tons	769.0#	736.0r	3.1
LUMBER (5/22) millions of ft.	461.4#	469.9	−8.0
RAIL FREIGHT (5/22) billions of ton-miles	21.4#	21.2	2.9

Sources: American Iron & Steel Institute, Ward's *Automotive Reports*, Edison Electric Institute, American Petroleum Institute, Energy Dept., American Paper Institute, WWPA[1], SFPA[2], Association of American Railroads

FOREIGN EXCHANGE

	Latest week	Week ago	Year ago
JAPANESE YEN (6/2)	107	108	127
GERMAN MARK (6/2)	1.59	1.62	1.60
BRITISH POUND (6/2)	1.54	1.55	1.83
FRENCH FRANC (6/2)	5.38	5.47	5.37
CANADIAN DOLLAR (6/2)	1.27	1.26	1.20
SWISS FRANC (6/2)	1.42	1.45	1.46
MEXICAN PESO (6/2)[3]	3.123	3.127	3.092

Sources: Major New York banks. Currencies expressed in units per U.S. dollar, except for British pound expressed in dollars

PRICES

	Latest week	Week ago	% Change year ago
GOLD (6/2) $/troy oz.	369.000	374.500	9.0
STEEL SCRAP (6/1) #1 heavy, $/ton	106.50	106.50	15.8
FOODSTUFFS (6/1) index, 1967=100	201.8	205.7	−0.1
COPPER (5/29) ¢/lb.	87.6	88.5	−17.0
ALUMINUM (5/29) ¢/lb.	52.5	52.5	−13.2
WHEAT (5/29) #2 hard, $/bu.	3.55	3.57	−8.7
COTTON (5/29) strict low middling 1-1/16 in., ¢/lb.	56.30	58.40	3.7

Sources: London Wednesday final setting, Chicago market, Commodity Research Bureau, Metals Week, Kansas City market, Memphis market

LEADING INDICATORS

	Latest week	Week ago	% Change year ago
STOCK PRICES (5/28) S&P 500	450.58	444.94	8.9
CORPORATE BOND YIELD, Aaa (5/28)	7.46%	7.48%	−9.6
INDUSTRIAL MATERIALS PRICES (5/28)	95.6	95.4	−2.5
BUSINESS FAILURES (5/21)	382	380	−19.6
REAL ESTATE LOANS (5/19) billions	$395.7	$397.7r	−2.7
MONEY SUPPLY, M2 (5/17) billions	$3,471.2	$3,468.8r	1.0
INITIAL CLAIMS, UNEMPLOYMENT (5/15) thous.	340	337	−15.6

Sources: Standard & Poor's, Moody's, *Journal of Commerce* (index: 1980=100), Dun & Bradstreet (failures of large companies), Federal Reserve Board, Labor Dept. CIBCR seasonally adjusts data on business failures and real estate loans

MONTHLY ECONOMIC INDICATORS

	Latest month	Month ago	% Change year ago
PERSONAL INCOME (Apr.) annual rate, billions	$5,262.0	$5,261.0r	4.9
CONSUMER SPENDING (Apr.) billions	$4,282.7	$4,239.2r	6.0
CONSTR. SPENDING (Apr.) annual rate, billions	$444.4	$446.2r	3.9
12 LEADING INDICATORS COMPOSITE (Apr.) index	152.0	151.9r	2.5

Sources: Commerce Dept., Census Bureau

MONETARY INDICATORS

	Latest week	Week ago	% Change year ago
MONEY SUPPLY, M1 (5/17)	$1,068.0	$1,065.2r	12.0
BANKS' BUSINESS LOANS (5/19)	275.1	275.7	−4.1
FREE RESERVES (5/26)	1,077	686r	−19.6
NONFINANCIAL COMMERCIAL PAPER (5/19)	159.0	158.2	9.0

Sources: Federal Reserve Board (in billions, except for free reserves, which are expressed for a two-week period in millions)

MONEY MARKET RATES

	Latest week	Week ago	Year ago
FEDERAL FUNDS (6/1)	3.33%	3.21%	3.85%
PRIME (6/2)	6.00	6.00	6.50
COMMERCIAL PAPER 3-MONTH (6/1)	3.23	3.19	3.97
CERTIFICATES OF DEPOSIT 3-MONTH (6/2)	3.17	3.15	3.91
EURODOLLAR 3-MONTH (5/28)	3.20	3.13	3.91

Sources: Federal Reserve Board, First Boston

#Raw data in the production indicators are seasonally adjusted in computing the BW index (chart); other components (estimated and not listed) include machinery and defense equipment. 1=Western Wood Products Assn.   2=Southern Forest Products Assn.   3=Free market value   NA=Not available   r=revised   NM=Not meaningful

ALTERNATIVE LEADING INDICATOR OF INFLATION

The Wall Street investment banking firm Kidder, Peabody & Company has also suggested a model for predicting inflation composed of the following variables:

1. Rate of capacity utilization (lagged 12 months)
2. The Federal Reserve dollar value index (a trade-weighted index of the value of the dollar against 10 currencies; lagged 14 months)
3. The annual growth rate of the CRB Commodity Spot Index (lagged 8 months)

A graph of the index for the period 1973 to 1987 indicated a strong correlation between inflation and the leading series.[7]

INTERNATIONAL LEADING INDICATOR SERIES

In addition to developing leading indicators for the U.S. economy, the CIBCR has also developed a set of composite leading indicators for eight other major industrial countries: Canada, Germany, France, United Kingdom, Italy, Japan, Australia, and Taiwan (Republic of China). These International Leading Indicator Series are part of an ongoing project to develop an international economic indicator (IEI) system. The series are comparable in data and analysis to the leading series for the United States.[8]

MONETARY
VARIABLES, THE
ECONOMY, AND
STOCK PRICES

Many academic and professional observers hypothesize a close relationship between stock prices and various monetary variables that are influenced by monetary policy. The best-known monetary variable in this regard is the *money supply.* You will recall from your economics course that the money supply can be measured in several ways, including currency plus demand deposits (referred to as the M1 money supply), and the M1 money supply plus time deposits (referred to as the M2 money supply). The government publishes other measures of the money supply, but these are the best known. The Federal Reserve controls the money supply through various tools, the most useful of which is open market operations. In actuality, the money supply influences stock prices as an offshoot of its influence on the aggregate economy.

MONEY SUPPLY
AND THE
ECONOMY

In their classic work on the monetary history of the United States, Friedman and Schwartz thoroughly documented the relationship between changes in the growth rate of the money supply and subsequent changes in the economy.[9] Specifically, they demonstrated that declines in the rate of growth of the money supply have preceded business contractions by an average of 20 months, while increases in the growth rate of the money supply have preceded economic expansions by about 8 months.

Friedman suggests a transmission mechanism through which changes in the growth rate of the money supply affect the aggregate economy. He hypothesizes that, to

---

[7]Steven R. Ricchiute and Stephen W. Gallagher, "Leading Indicators of Inflation," *Money Market Research,* Kidder, Peabody & Co. (January 1988).

[8]For an extended discussion, see Geoffrey H. Moore, "An Introduction to International Economic Indicators," *Business Cycles, Inflation, and Forecasting,* 2d ed. (New York: National Bureau of Economic Research, Studies in Business Cycles, No. 24, 1983).

[9]Milton Friedman and Anna J. Schwartz, "Money and Business Cycles," *Review of Economics and Statistics,* supplement vol. 45, no. 1, part 2 (February 1963): 32–78, reprinted in Milton Friedman, *The Optimum Quantity of Money and Other Essays* (Chicago: Aldine Publishing, 1969), 189–235.

implement planned changes in monetary policy, the Federal Reserve engages in open market operations, buying or selling Treasury bonds to adjust bank reserves and, eventually, the money supply. Because the Fed deals in government bonds, the initial liquidity impact affects the government bond market creating excess liquidity for those who sold bonds to the Fed when the Federal Reserve was buying bonds, or there would be insufficient liquidity when the Federal Reserve sells bonds. Rising or falling government bond prices subsequently filters over to corporate bonds, and subsequently this change in liquidity affects common stocks, and then the real goods market. This liquidity transmission scenario implies that the initial effect of a change in monetary policy appears in financial markets (bonds and stocks) and only later in the aggregate economy.

MONEY SUPPLY AND STOCK PRICES

Numerous studies have tested the relationship suggested by this transmission mechanism. Do changes in the growth of the money supply precede changes in stock prices? The results of these studies have tended to change over time. The initial studies done in the 1960s and early 1970s generally indicated a strong *leading* relationship between money supply changes and stock prices.[10] Such results implied that changes in the growth rate of the money supply could serve as a leading indicator of stock price changes.

More recent studies have questioned these findings.[11] Although these recent studies have likewise typically found a relationship between the money supply and stock prices, the timing of the relationship differs. These studies have found that changes in the growth rate of the money supply consistently *lagged* stock returns by about 1 to 3 months.

The most recent studies have examined the relationship of stock returns to anticipated and unanticipated money supply growth using weekly money supply data.[12] The results indicate that money changes affect stock prices, but the securities markets adjust stock prices very quickly to any expected changes in money supply growth. Therefore, the only way you can enjoy superior returns is to *forecast unanticipated changes* in money supply growth.

EXCESS LIQUIDITY AND STOCK PRICES

Some analysts have looked beyond the growth rate of the money supply. Einhorn contends that *excess liquidity* is the relevant monetary variable that influences stock prices.[13] Excess liquidity is defined as the year-to-year percentage change in the M2

---

[10]Studies that generally support this view include Beryl W. Sprinkel, *Money and Markets: A Monetarist View* (Homewood, Ill.: Richard D. Irwin, 1971); Michael W. Keran, "Expectations, Money, and the Stock Market," Federal Reserve Bank of St. Louis *Review* 53, no. 1 (January 1991): 16–31; and Kenneth Homa and Dwight Jaffee, "The Study of Money and Stock Prices," *Journal of Finance* 26, no. 5 (December 1971): 1015–1066.

[11]These studies include Richard V. L. Cooper, "Efficient Capital Markets and the Quantity Theory of Money," *Journal of Finance* 29, no. 3 (June 1974): 887–908; and M. S. Rozeff, "Money and Stock Prices: Market Efficiency and the Lag Effect of Monetary Policy," *Journal of Financial Economics* 1, no. 3 (September 1974): 245–302.

[12]These studies are Lawrence S. Davidson and Richard T. Froyen, "Monetary Policy and Stock Returns: Are Stock Markets Efficient?" Federal Reserve Bank of St. Louis *Review* 69, no. 3 (March 1982) 3–12; and R. W. Hafer, "The Response of Stock Prices to Changes in Weekly Money and the Discount Rate," Federal Reserve Bank of St. Louis *Review* 68, no. 3 (March 1985). 5–14.

[13]This work is contained in "Investment Strategy Highlights," ed. by Steven G. Einhorn (New York: Goldman, Sachs & Company, monthly).

money supply less the year-to-year percentage change in nominal GNP. It is reasoned that the growth rate of nominal GNP indicates the need for liquidity in the economy. If the money supply growth rate exceeds the GNP growth rate, this indicates that there is excess money (liquidity) in the economy that is available for buying securities. This excess liquidity should lead to higher security prices.

Figure 12.4 shows the relationship between this measure of excess liquidity and stock prices. Although the historical relationship was quite good, recently this relationship has weakened because non-U.S. excess liquidity has been available to acquire U.S. stocks and bonds. Figure 12.5 shows global excess liquidity. These figures reveal positive excess liquidity for the United Kingdom and unified Germany, with negative excess liquidity in Japan. This non-U.S. liquidity helped the U.S. stock market continue to rise in 1993 because it was accompanied by positive excess liquidity in the United States (excess liquidity became positive in the U.S. in late 1990 and has remained positive through May, 1993).

FIGURE 12.4

Relationship of Money, GNP, and Share Prices

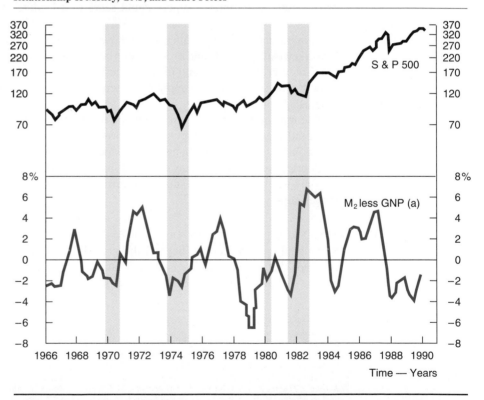

[a]Year-to-year percentage change in M2 growth (as a 6-month moving average) less year-to-year percentage change in nominal GNP.

Note: Shaded areas represent recessions.

Source: "Investment Strategy Highlights" (New York: Goldman, Sachs & Co., February 1990). Reprinted by permission of Goldman Sachs.

FIGURE 12.5

Plot of Excess Liquidity for Selected Countries: 1985–1993

Percent Change, Prior Year

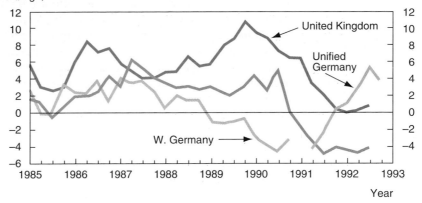

Source: "Investment Strategy Chartbook" (New York: Goldman, Sachs & Co., April 1993). Reprinted by permission of Goldman Sachs.

OTHER ECONOMIC VARIABLES AND STOCK PRICES

Chen, Roll, and Ross examined equity returns relative to a set of macroeconomic variables.[14] They found the following variables to be significant in explaining stock returns:

- Growth in industrial production
- Changes in the risk premium
- Twists in the yield curve
- Measures of unanticipated inflation
- Changes in expected inflation during periods of volatile inflation

The authors did not attempt to predict market returns, but suggested that these variables were important in explaining past returns.

INFLATION, INTEREST RATES, AND SECURITY PRICES

Because this chapter is concerned with the macroeconomic analysis of security markets, we should examine the macroeconomic impact of inflation and interest rates. We have noted throughout the book the critical role of expected inflation and nominal interest rates in determining the required rate of return used to derive the value of all investments. We would expect these variables that are very important in microeconomic valuation, to also affect changes in the aggregate markets.

---

[14]Chen, Nai-Fu, Richard Roll, and Stephen A. Ross, "Economic Forces and the Stock Market," *Journal of Business* 59, no. 3 (July 1986).

INFLATION AND INTEREST RATES

Figure 12.6 contains a plot of long-term interest rates and the year-to-year percentage change in the consumer price index (CPI, a measure of inflation). This graph demonstrates the strong relationship we have discussed between inflation and interest rates. We contended that when investors anticipated an increase in the rate of inflation, they would increase their required rates of return by a similar amount in order to derive constant real rates of return. The time-series graph of the promised yield of AAA corporate bonds and the annual rate of inflation in Figure 12.6 confirm the expected relationship, but also indicate an imperfect relationship between interest rates and inflation. If the relationship was perfect, the difference between the interest rate and the inflation rate (the spread between them) would be fairly constant, reflecting the real return on corporate bonds. The fact is, the spread between these two curves changes over time.

Figure 12.7 plots this spread and demonstrates the following results. Although the two curves move together, in some periods (1975, 1979 to 1980) the inflation rate exceeded the yield on the bonds, which implies that investors received negative real returns on corporate bonds. In contrast, during 1983 to 1985 the real rates of return on these bonds was in the 8 to 10 percent range, which clearly exceeds what most investors would expect on very low risk bonds.

This change in spread does not mean that there is not a relationship between inflation and interest rates; it only shows that *investors are not very good at predicting inflation*. Recall that the relationship is between *expected* inflation and interest rates in contrast to these data that reflect actual inflation. Apparently, investors underestimated inflation during the periods of negative real returns (1975, 1979 to 1980), and overestimated inflation during the periods when there were abnormally high real rates of return.

INTEREST RATES AND BOND PRICES

The relationship between interest rates and bond prices is clearly negative, because the only variable that changes in the valuation model is the discount factor. The expected cash flows from a straight bond would not change. Therefore, an increase in interest rates will cause a decline in bond prices and a decline in interest rates will boost bond prices. For example, if you own a 10-year bond with a coupon of 10 percent, when interest rates go from 10 percent to 12 percent, the price of this bond will go from $1,000 (par) to $885. In contrast, if rates go from 10 percent to 8 percent, the price of the bond will go from $1,000 to $1,136.

The size of the price change will depend on the characteristics of the bond. A longer-term bond will experience a larger price change for a change in interest rates.[15] Therefore, we can anticipate a negative relationship between inflation and bond prices and rates of return on bonds because inflation generally has a direct effect on interest rates, and interest rates have an inverse effect on bond prices and rates of return.

INTEREST RATES AND STOCK PRICES

The relationship between interest rates and stock prices is not so direct. The cash flows from stocks can change along with interest rates, and we cannot be certain whether

---

[15]Chapter 14 contains a detailed discussion of the specific variables that influence bond price volatility.

FIGURE 12.6   **Interest and Inflation: 1975–1992**

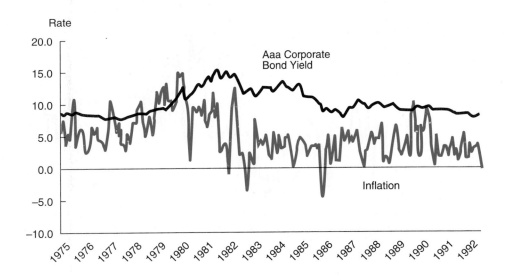

this change in cash flows will augment or offset the change in interest rates. To demonstrate this, consider the following:

1. Interest rates rise due to an increase in the rate of inflation and corporate earnings likewise increase because firms are able to increase prices in line with cost increases. In this case, stock prices might be fairly stable because the negative effect of an increase in the required rate of return is partially or wholly offset by the increase in the growth rate of corporate dividends.
2. Interest rates increase, but expected cash flows change very little because firms are not able to increase prices in response to higher costs. This would cause a decline in stock prices similar to what happens with a bond. The required rate of return (k) would increase, but the growth rate of dividends (g) would be constant, that is, the k–g spread will widen.
3. Interest rates increase while cash flows decline because the factors that cause the rise in interest rates have a negative impact on earnings. For example, during 1981 to 1982 interest rates increased and remained high during a period of economic decline, which caused sales and earnings to decline. Although this set of events does not happen often, its impact can be disastrous. Stock prices will decline significantly because k will increase as g declines, causing a large increase in the k–g spread.

FIGURE 12.7   **Spread Between Interest and Inflation Rates: 1975–1992**

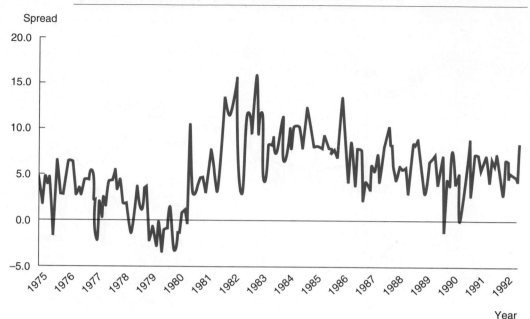

In contrast to these three scenarios, you can envision a comparable set of scenarios when interest rates decline. The point is, the relationship between inflation, interest rates, and stock prices is not as direct or consistent as the relationship between interest rates and bonds. The effect of interest rate changes on stock prices will depend on what caused the change in interest rates and the effect of this cause on the expected cash flows on common stock.

Notably, the actual relationship between inflation, interest rates, and stock prices is an empirical question and the effect varies over time. Therefore, although an inverse relationship has generally held between inflation, interest rates, and the returns on stocks, this is not always true.[16] In addition, even when it is true for the overall market, certain industries or segments of the economy may have earnings and dividends that react positively to inflation and interest rate changes. In such an instance, their stock prices would be positively correlated with inflation and interest rates.[17]

---

[16]A sample of studies on the topic of inflation and common stocks include Frank K. Reilly, Glenn L. Johnson, and Ralph E. Smith, "Inflation, Inflation Hedges and Common Stocks," *Financial Analysts Journal* 26, no. 1 (January–February 1970): 104–110; Frank K. Reilly, "Companies and Common Stocks as Inflation Hedges," New York University, Center for the Study of Financial Institutions, *Bulletin* (April 1975); Jeffrey F. Jaffe and Gershun Mandelker, "The 'Fisher Effect' for Risky Assets: An Empirical Analysis," *Journal of Finance* 31, no. 2 (May 1976): 447–458; Eugene F. Fama, "Stock Returns, Real Activity, Inflation and Money," *American Economic Review* 71, no. 4 (September 1981).

[17]Studies that examined alternative industries as inflation hedges include Stephen P. Ferris and Anil K. Makhija, "A Search for Common Stock Inflation Hedges," *Review of Business and Economic Research* 22, no. 2 (Spring 1987): 27–36; and Frank K. Reilly, "Alternative Industries as Inflation Hedges," Financial Management Association Meeting (October 1987).

SUMMARY OF
MACROECONOMIC
ANALYSIS

There is ample evidence of a strong and consistent relationship between economic activity and the stock market, although stock prices consistently seem to turn from 4 to 9 months before the economy does. Therefore, to project the future direction of the stock market using the macroeconomic approach you must either forecast economic activity about 12 months ahead or examine economic indicator series that lead the economy by more than stock prices do.

The results with the leading indicator series indicated that only with perfect foresight regarding the appropriate change to use with a diffusion index of the leading indicator series could an investor improve on a buy-and-hold policy. The results from studies of the relationship between the money supply and stock prices have indicated a significant relationship, but recent research indicates that stock prices generally turn before the money supply does. Therefore, you *cannot* use the money supply series to develop a mechanical trading rule that will outperform a buy-and-hold policy.

Alternative measures of the monetary environment were also considered, including U.S. and global excess liquidity. Although the historical results with U.S. excess liquidity were interesting, recent results are not as consistent. Some cite global liquidity that has been positive, and this global liquidity has had an impact on the U.S. capital markets. Such a global monetary effect is not surprising in our current environment. These results emphasize the need to consider global macroeconomic variables.

ANALYSIS
OF WORLD
SECURITY
MARKETS

Although we have focused on the U.S. market to demonstrate the macroeconomic approach to forecasting movements in the securities markets, you must also consider a similar analysis for numerous foreign markets including those in Japan, Canada, the United Kingdom, and Germany. It is not feasible to analyze each of these markets in detail, but we can provide an example of such an analysis by reviewing the extensive analysis done by Goldman, Sachs & Co. This analysis is contained in a monthly Goldman, Sachs publication, "World Investment Strategy Highlights," as part of the firm's international research effort. This publication draws on a number of other Goldman, Sachs publications to provide a world portfolio strategy, as well as strategies for several individual countries.[18]

Goldman, Sachs employs a version of the three-step process (also referred to as the *top-down approach*) initially examining a country's aggregate economy and its components that relate to the valuation of securities—GNP, capital investments, industrial production, inflation, and interest rates. Table 12.4 contains the firm's forecast of economic activity for several major countries. Note the fairly substantial differences in outlook for GNP/GDP growth during 1994 (e.g., 0.7 percent for Italy versus 3.2 percent for Japan) and for growth in industrial production (e.g., 0.5 percent for France versus 4.2 percent for the United Kingdom). Obviously, several countries face a flat economic environment, whereas the United States, Japan, the United Kingdom, and Canada are expected to experience significant growth.

---

[18]The other Goldman, Sachs publications used include *The International Economics Analyst, World Markets Monthly, Investment Strategy Highlights, Japan Investment Strategy Highlights,* and *The U.K. Economics Analyst.* The current author benefited from conversations with Jeffrey M. Weingarten, director of international equity research for Goldman, Sachs.

TABLE 12.4

Forecasts for World Economic Activity (percent per annum)

Country	1992	1993E	1994E
United States			
Consumer expenditure	2.2	2.8	2.3
Business fixed investment	3.0	7.0	0.1
GDP	2.1	3.3	3.0
Industrial production	2.0	4.1	3.4
Japan			
Consumer expenditure	1.7	1.0	3.0
Private capital investment	−4.0	−6.5	1.0
Domestic demand	0.6	0.2	3.1
GNP	1.5	1.1	3.2
Industrial production	−6.2	−3.8	4.1
Germany			
Investment	1.7	−2.6	1.3
Domestic demand	1.2	−0.8	1.4
GNP	0.9	−0.9	1.5
Industrial production	−1.4	−4.0	1.5
United Kingdom			
Consumer expenditure	0.2	1.7	1.8
Fixed investment	−0.6	−0.5	2.9
GNP	−0.5	1.5	3.0
Industrial production	−0.3	2.7	4.2
France			
Consumer expenditure	1.5	0.8	0.9
Fixed investment	−1.7	−3.6	0.7
GNP	1.9	−0.8	1.2
Industrial production	−0.6	−1.9	0.5
Italy			
Consumer expenditure	1.9	−0.3	0.5
Fixed investment	−1.0	−3.7	−1.1
GDP	1.0	−0.6	0.7
Industrial production	−1.2	−2.0	1.2
Canada			
Consumer expenditure	1.1	3.0	3.1
Fixed investment	0.8	6.7	6.8
GDP	0.9	2.7	3.5
Industrial production	0.8	3.7	3.8

Source: "World Investment Strategy Highlights" (London: Goldman, Sachs International Corp., May 1993). Reprinted by permission of Goldman Sachs.

INFLATION AND EXCHANGE RATES

An analysis of historical and expected price changes in Table 12.5 also reveals major differences in the outlook for inflation, ranging from 1.7 percent for Japan to 4.3 percent for Italy. These inflation estimates feed into an interest rate forecast for the end of 1993 and mid-1994 in Table 12.6. This combination of forecasts indicates the expected trend in interest rates. The forecast for interest rates were clearly mixed with several increases expected along with several countries where Goldman, Sachs expected declines. The overall range for long rates as of mid-1994 was from 5 percent (Japan) to 8.2 percent (United Kingdom).

Given these differences in inflation and interest rate levels and trends, you can expect major differences in the exchange rates. Table 12.7 presents the firm's forecast for several currencies. The forecasts for 6 months and 12 months imply trends during the year. These figures indicate that Goldman, Sachs expects the U.S. dollar to be stronger

TABLE 12.5

Consumer or Retail Price Changes (percentage changes on previous year)

Period	United States	Japan	Germany	France	United Kingdom	Italy
1988	4.1%	0.7%	1.3%	2.7%	4.9%	5.0%
1989	4.8	2.3	2.8	3.4	7.8	6.6
1990	4.4	3.0	2.7	3.5	9.5	6.1
1991	4.0	2.8	3.8	3.5	7.0	6.0
1992	3.0	1.7	4.0	2.8	3.7	5.2
1993[e]	3.2	1.2	3.7	2.3	1.8	4.5
1994[e]	3.0	1.7	3.1	2.1	2.9	4.3

[e]estimate

Source: "World Investment Strategy Highlights" (London: Goldman, Sachs International Ltd., May 1993.) Reprinted by permission of Goldman Sachs.

TABLE 12.6

Interest Rate Forecasts (percent per annum)

Country	Current Rate[1]	Short Term (1–3 Months)	Medium Term (3–6 Months)	Long Term (12–18 Months)
United States				
90-D commercial paper	3.1	3.1	2.8	3.3
6¼ percent 2003	5.8	5.8	5.5	5.8
Germany				
3M Euro rate	7.8	7.2	6.4	5.8
7⅛ percent 2002	6.6	6.5	6.4	6.8
Japan				
3-month CDs	3.2	3.2	3.1	3.8
No. 145, 5.5 percent	4.2	4.2	4.0	5.0
France				
3M PIBOR	8.4	7.7	6.7	5.9
8½ percent 2003	7.1	6.9	6.7	7.1
United Kingdom				
3M LIBOR	6.0	6.0	6.0	6.0
8 percent 2003	7.8	7.8	7.6	8.2
Canada				
3M T-Bill	5.1	4.8	5.5	5.1
7¼ percent 2003	7.3	7.2	7.3	6.9
Netherlands				
3M Euro rate	7.5	7.2	6.4	5.8
2 percent 2003	6.5	6.5	6.4	6.8

[1]23 April 1993

Source: "World Investment Strategy Highlights" (London: Goldman, Sachs International Ltd., May 1993). Reprinted by permission of Goldman Sachs.

TABLE 12.7

Forecast of Exchange Rates

	U.S. Dollar	Canadian Dollar	Japanese Yen	British Pound	German Mark	French Franc	Swiss Franc	Trade-Weighted
Against U.S. Dollar								**U.S. Dollar**
6 month	—	1.27	113	0.70	1.69	5.95	1.52	68
12 month	—	1.30	111	0.75	1.76	6.16	1.55	70
Against Pound								**Pound**
6 month	1.43	1.82	163	—	2.42	8.51	2.17	78
12 month	1.34	1.74	149	—	2.35	8.25	2.08	76
Against Mark								**Mark**
6 month	0.59	0.75	67	0.41	—	3.52	0.90	124
12 month	0.57	0.74	63	0.43	—	3.50	0.88	121
Against Yen								**Yen**
6 month	113	89	—	162	67	19	74	169
12 month	111	85	—	149	63	18	72	171

Note: All trade-weighted indices are from the Bank of England (1985 = 100).

Source: "World Investment Strategy Highlights" (London: Goldman, Sachs International Ltd., May 1993). Reprinted by permission of Goldman Sachs.

against the British pound and German mark, but be weaker against the Japanese yen during 1993 and 1994.

Based on this analysis of the underlying economies, Table 12.8 estimates corporate earnings and cash flow growth rates for various countries. It also gives estimates of other stock-market variables, including dividend growth, price/earnings ratios, and dividend yield. Again, all series show major differences among countries. The estimated earnings growth rates for 1994 vary from 8 percent expected growth for Germany to over 46 percent for Italy. Likewise, the price/earnings ratio is expected to continue its historical variation ranging in 1993 from less than 13 times for Hong Kong to 68 times for Japan.

CORRELATIONS AMONG RETURNS

These substantial differences in economic performance and major changes in the underlying valuation variables make for fairly low correlations among stock-market returns for alternative countries. The correlation matrix of price changes in local currencies in Table 12.9 shows a fairly high correlation between the United States and Canada, and low correlations between the United States with Italy and Japan. Notably, the U.S.–Japan correlation has increased in recent years as our economies have become more interdependent.

Table 12.10, a similar matrix in U.S. dollars, shows that all of the correlations with the United States decline when one considers the exchange rate effect. Comparisons such as these justify and encourage worldwide diversification of investments.

INDIVIDUAL COUNTRY STOCK PRICE CHANGES

The stock-market impact of exchange rates is shown in Table 12.11, which shows the percentage changes in stock prices both set in the local currency and adjusted for the U.S. dollar. The percentage changes of stock prices in local currency indicate the returns

TABLE 12.8

Comparative Stock Market Statistics

	United States	Japan	Hong Kong	United Kingdom	Germany	France	Italy
Earnings Growth							
1992E	11.5	−34.6	16.9	−2.0	−9.0	−10.4	−34.6
1993F	13.4	7.8	16.0	17.0	−18.5	2.3	18.1
1994F	10.7	26.0	17.6	16.0	8.0	13.2	46.3
Cash Flow Growth							
1992E	8.1	—	—	—	−5.9	—	−1.0
1993F	10.0	—	—	—	−3.7	—	11.8
1994F	8.6	—	—	—	—	—	—
Dividend Growth							
1992E	1.4	1.5	15.1	0.0	−9.0	3.0	−11.0
1993F	3.7	0.5	13.7	2.0	−1.0	3.0	−2.0
1994F	7.5	—	15.4	6.0	1.0	3.0	5.0
Current							
P/E	15.8	68.0	12.9	14.3	19.0	16.7	25.0
D/Y	2.9	1.0	3.3	3.9	2.2	3.3	2.6
Relative							
P/E	94	142	91	134	152	104	168
D/Y	88	64	78	77	74	74	87

Aggregates and multiples for earnings, cash flow, book value and dividend are based on an industrial sample of companies in each country.

Note: Figures for the United States refer to the S&P Industrials Index and pertain to operating earnings.

Source: "World Investment Strategy Highlights" (London: Goldman, Sachs International Ltd., May 1993). Reprinted by permission of Goldman Sachs.

TABLE 12.9

Correlation of Price Returns in Local Currency: 1981–1990

	United States	Japan	Germany	United Kingdom	Canada	France
United States	—					
Japan	0.39	—				
Germany	0.44	0.33	—			
United Kingdom	0.70	0.44	0.49	—		
Canada	0.78	0.34	0.37	0.66	—	
France	0.52	0.42	0.59	0.47	0.42	—
Italy	0.33	0.39	0.43	0.41	0.38	0.49

Source: "Anatomy of World Markets" (London: Goldman, Sachs International Ltd., October 1991). Reprinted by permission of Goldman Sachs.

TABLE 12.10

Correlation of Price Returns in U.S. Dollars: 1981–1990

	United States	Japan	Germany	United Kingdom	Canada	France
United States	—					
Japan	0.28	—				
Germany	0.34	0.37	—			
United Kingdom	0.56	0.46	0.47	—		
Canada	0.75	0.30	0.29	0.62	—	
France	0.43	0.46	0.65	0.48	0.37	—
Italy	0.27	0.43	0.49	0.41	0.34	0.56

Source: "Anatomy of World Markets" (London: Goldman, Sachs International Ltd., October 1991). Reprinted by permission of Goldman Sachs.

TABLE 12.11   **World Stock-Market Performance: 1986–1990 (in local currency and U.S. dollars)**

Country	1986		1987		1988		1989		1990		Average 1986–1990	
	Local Currency	U.S. Dollars	Local Currency	U.S. Dollars	Local Currency	U.S. Dollars	Local Currency	U.S. Dollars	Local Currency	U.S. Dollars	Local Currency	U.S. Dollars
United States	14.2	14.2	0.5	0.5	12.6	12.6	26.4	26.4	−6.8	−6.8	8.8	8.8
Japan	53.9	93.9	8.5	41.4	39.5	35.4	18.6	3.1	−40.4	−36.8	10.5	19.3
Germany	5.6	34.3	−36.8	−22.7	28.3	13.8	34.1	40.7	−20.1	−9.5	−1.7	8.5
United Kingdom	20.2	23.2	4.6	32.5	6.0	2.1	31.6	17.3	−12.8	4.4	8.9	15.3
France	45.2	71.0	−27.8	−13.9	51.5	33.6	29.5	35.6	−25.7	−15.6	8.8	17.6
Italy	73.6	117.1	−32.4	−22.3	22.8	9.4	12.3	15.6	−29.2	−20.4	2.7	11.2
World	29.6	39.3	−0.9	15.0	24.4	21.4	22.8	15.1	−23.6	−19.3	8.4	12.6

Source: "Anatomy of World Markets" (London: Goldman, Sachs International Ltd., October, 1991). Reprinted by permission of Goldman Sachs.

to citizens of the country. The annual averages for 1986 to 1990 range from −1.7 percent for Germany to 10.5 percent for Japan. The percentage changes of stock prices in U.S. dollars indicate the returns to a U.S. investor in each of these countries who converted the domestic returns to U.S. dollars. These changes ranged from 8.5 percent (Germany) to 19.3 percent (Japan).

The significant impact of changes in exchange rates can be seen in a couple of examples. Although the rate of change in Japan stock prices during 1987 was 8.5 percent, the change experienced by a U.S. citizen who invested in Japan during 1987 would have been 41.4 percent because of the significant strength of the yen relative to the dollar. This increase in the rate of return due to the exchange rate changes relative to the U.S. dollar was fairly widespread during 1987. In contrast, during 1988, the U.S. dollar was quite strong, and all percentage stock price changes when converted to U.S. dollars were lower. As an example, the change in Germany during 1988 was over 28 percent in local currency but less than 14 percent in U.S. dollars.

INDIVIDUAL
COUNTRY
ANALYSIS

Goldman, Sachs provides a detailed analysis of major countries that includes the country's economy and equity market, and culminates in a portfolio recommendation for investors in that country. Table 12.12 shows the major economic indicators for Japan reflecting a strong economic recovery (especially in real earnings growth) following its 1991–1992 recession.

An analysis of the country's equity market follows the economic projections. For example, a summary for the United Kingdom appears in Table 12.13. Goldman, Sachs feels that the overall economic outlook for the United Kingdom is moderate but the firm still expects U.K. equities to outperform bonds and short-term bonds (cash) during the next 12 months.

WORLD ASSET
ALLOCATION

The final product of this analysis is a recommendation for an investor's world asset allocation. Table 12.14 begins with a division among bonds, equities, and cash. As of mid-1993 Goldman, Sachs recommended that an investor should be at the upper end of the range for bonds, toward the middle of the equity range, and at the low end of the cash range.

TABLE 12.12   **Economic Outlook for Japan**

	Current Value	Historical Average	Direction of Impact on Stock Return
GDP Growth			
1992	1.5	3.8	−
1993	1.1		−
1994	3.2		−
Real Earnings Growth			
1992	− 36.2	2.0	−
1993	6.6		+
1994	+ 24.3		+
Real Dividend Growth			
1992	− 0.3	0	−
1993	− 0.7		−
Inflation (Consumer Price Index) (Percent)			
1992	1.7		+
1993	1.2		+
1994	1.7		+

Interest Rate Outlook

	Current Rate	1–3 Months	3–6 Months	12–18 Months
3 Month CDs	3.2	3.2	3.1	3.8
No. 145, 5.5 percent	4.3	4.2	4.0	5.0

Source: "World Investment Strategy Highlights" (London: Goldman, Sachs International Ltd., May 1993). Reprinted by permission of Goldman Sachs.

TABLE 12.13   **Recent Stock Market Performance for United Kingdom Relative to World Market and Expected Rates of Return over Next 1, 3, and 12 Months**

	Current Price	Performance (Percent Change)			52-Week Range		Relative to World		
		Last Month	YTD	12 Month	High	Low	Last Month	YTD	12 Month
FT Composite (U.S. dollar)	182.0	7.0	5.6	− 3.3	200.1	161.9	2.5	− 5.1	− 14.7
FT Composite (local currency)	169.7	− 0.8	0.5	7.7	176.6	133.7	− 1.8	− 5.7	− 1.0
FT Industrials (local currency)	170.8	− 1.1	− 1.3	3.9	178.3	140.0	− 2.0	− 6.1	− 1.3
FT All Share	1392.2	− 0.4	2.1	9.1	1438.2	1086.1	− 1.4	− 4.1	0.4
FT–SE 100	2822.3	− 1.1	− 0.9	6.8	2957.3	2281.0	− 2.1	− 7.1	− 1.9

Expected Return (percent)	1 Month	3 Months	12 Months
Equities	− 1.0	4.0	12.0
Bonds	2.8	4.5	7.9
Cash	0.5	1.5	5.9

Source: "World Investment Strategy Highlights" (London: Goldman, Sachs International Ltd., May 1993). Reprinted by permission of Goldman Sachs.

TABLE 12.14   **Asset Allocation—World Portfolios**

	Normal Range (Percent)	Weighting (Percent of Index)	Current Suggested Weighting (Percent)
Bonds	20–40		34
Equities	45–65		56
United States		40.7	35.0
Japan		31.7	32.0
Hong Kong		1.7	1.5
United Kingdom		10.6	12.9
Germany		3.5	1.9
France		3.5	4.4
Italy		1.2	1.2
Netherlands		1.7	2.4
Switzerland		2.1	2.5
Spain		1.0	2.6
Norway		0.1	0.4
Sweden		0.8	1.4
Finland		0.1	0.3
Other Europe		1.4	1.6
		100.0	**100.0**
Cash	0–30		**10**

Source: "World Investment Strategy Highlights" (London: Goldman, Sachs International Ltd., May 1993).

For the equity segment of the portfolio, the firm specified a neutral weighting for each country that is based on its relative market value. The relative market value of a country's equities is their value as a percentage of the total value of all world equities. For example, the market value of U.S. equities is 40.7 percent of the total value of all equities in the world, whereas Japanese equities account for 31.7 percent of the total. A completely neutral portfolio regarding all equity markets would invest a proportion in each country equal to the relative market values of that country's equities. For example, if the value of stocks in a country constituted 10 percent of the value of all stocks in the world, a neutral outlook would lead you to invest 10 percent of your equity portfolio in this country. If you were bullish toward this country relative to other markets, you would *overweight* it, investing more than 10 percent of your equity portfolio there. As of the publication date of this report (May 1993), Goldman, Sachs was slightly bearish on the U.S. stock market due to the Clinton healthcare reform and recommended *underweighting* it (35 percent invested in the United States versus a 40.7 percent market weighting). The firm was about neutral regarding Japan and recommended that you slightly *overweight* Japanese stocks (the recommended weight is 32 percent versus a market weight of 31.7 percent). Alternatively, they are recommending that you overweight the United Kingdom and France (i.e, invest 12.7 percent in the United Kingdom versus a 10.6 percent market weight, and invest 4.4 percent in France versus a 3.5 percent neutral weighting). In contrast, they are bearish on Germany and recommend underweighting the country by investing only 1.9 percent versus a 3.5 percent neutral weighting.

After completing the global market analysis, the next step is to analyze alternative industries worldwide within specified countries. Finally, you should consider alternative firms and their stocks in the preferred industries. This subsequent analysis is the subject of Chapters 17 and 18.

SUMMARY

In earlier chapters we emphasized the importance of analyzing the aggregate markets before beginning any industry or company analysis. You must assess the economic and security-market outlooks and their implications regarding the bond, stock, and cash components of your portfolio. Then you proceed to consider the best industry or company.

Three techniques are used to make the market decision: (1) the macroeconomic technique, which is based on the relationship between the aggregate economy and the stock market, (2) the microeconomic technique, which determines future market values by applying the dividend discount model to the aggregate stock market; and (3) technical analysis, which estimates future returns based on recent past returns. This chapter concentrated on the macroeconomic approach. The microeconomic analysis of equity markets will be considered in Chapter 16 as a prelude to company and stock analysis in Chapter 18, and technical analysis is covered in Chapter 19.

The economy and the stock market have a strong, consistent relationship, but the stock market generally turns before the economy does. Therefore, the best macro-economic projection techniques use economic series that likewise lead the economy, and possibly the stock market. The NBER leading indicator series (which includes stock prices) is one possibility, but the evidence does not support its use as a mechanical predictor of stock prices. Leading series for inflation and for other countries exist, along with a weekly leading indicator series, but none of these series has been examined relative to stock prices.

The money supply has been suggested as a predictor of aggregate market behavior based on its relationship to the economy. Some early studies indicated a strong relationship between the money supply and stock prices, and also suggested that money supply changes turned before stock prices. More recent studies confirmed the link between money supply and stock prices, but they indicated that stock prices turn with or before money supply changes. These recent results imply that, although money supply changes have an important impact on stock price movements, it is not possible to use historical money supply data in a mechanical way to predict stock price changes.

The analysis of excess liquidity indicated an impact on stock prices, but also showed that global liquidity has become important and weakened the relationship of U.S. markets with U.S. liquidity alone. There is also a problem with the appropriate measure of money supply, which appears to change over time.

Although we emphasized the analysis of U.S. markets, we know it is also important to analyze numerous foreign markets. Such an analysis is demonstrated by a Goldman, Sachs' application of the three-step, or top-down approach to major countries. This included an economic analysis and market analysis for each country, including a recommended portfolio strategy for investors in each country. The analysis culminated with a recommendation for a world portfolio allocation among bonds, stocks, and cash. It also recommends an allocation of equity investments among countries in comparison to the country's normal weighting based on its relative market value.

This aggregate market analysis should lead you to a decision as to how much of your portfolio should be committed to bonds, stocks, and cash during the forthcoming investment period. The following three chapters deal with the fixed-income portion of your portfolio. Chapter 13 discusses bond fundamentals, Chapter 14 considers the analysis of individual bonds, and Chapter 15 presents alternative portfolio strategies for bond investors.

QUESTIONS

1. Why would you expect a relationship between economic activity and stock price movements?

2. At a lunch with some business associates you discuss the reason for the relationship between the economy and the stock market. One of your associates believes that stock prices typically turn before the economy does. How would you explain this phenomenon?

3. Define *leading, lagging,* and *coincident economic* indicators. Give an example of an economic series in each category and discuss why you think each series belongs in that particular group.

4. Describe a diffusion index of a leading indicator series. Could it help you predict stock-market movements? Why or why not?

5. Explain the following statements: There is a strong, consistent relationship between money supply changes and stock prices; money supply changes cannot be used to predict stock price movements.

6. How is excess liquidity measured? Discuss the rationale for the relationship of excess liquidity and security prices.

7. You are informed of the following estimates: nominal money supply is expected to grow at a rate of 7 percent, and GDP is estimated to grow at 4 percent. Explain what you think will happen to stock prices during this period and why.

8. The current rate of inflation is 3 percent and long-term bonds are yielding 7 percent. You estimate that the rate of inflation will increase to 6 percent. What do you expect to happen to long-term bond yields? Compute the effect of this change in inflation on the price of a 15-year, 8 percent coupon bond.

9. It is fairly easy to determine the effect of a change in interest rates on the price of a bond. In contrast, some observers contend that it is harder to estimate the effect of a change in interest rates on common stocks. Discuss this contention.

10. Based on the economic projections in Tables 12.5 through 12.8, would you expect the stock prices for the various countries to be highly correlated? Justify your answer with specific examples.

11. You are informed that a well-respected investment firm projects that the rate of return next year for the U.S. equity market will be 10 percent, and returns for German stocks will be 13 percent. Assume that all risks except exchange rate risk are equal and you expect the DM/U.S. dollar exchange rate to go from 1.50 to 1.30 during the year. Given this information, discuss where you would invest and why. Compute the effect if the exchange rate went from 1.50 to 1.90.

PROBLEMS

1. Prepare a table showing the percentage change for each of the last 10 years in (a) the Consumer Price Index (all items), (b) nominal GDP, (c) real GDP (in constant dollars), and (d) the GDP deflator. Discuss how much of nominal growth was due to *real* growth and how much was due to inflation. Is the outlook for next year any different from last year? Discuss.

2. *CFA Examination I* (June 1983)
There has been considerable growth in recent years in the use of economic analysis in investment management. Further significant expansion may lie ahead as financial analysts

develop greater skills in economic analysis and these analyses are integrated more into the investment decision-making process. The following questions address the use of economic analysis in the investment decision-making process.

    a. 1. Differentiate among a leading, lagging, and coincident indicators of economic activity, and give an example of each.

          2. Indicate whether the leading indicators are one of the best tools for achieving above-average investment results. Briefly justify your conclusion. (8 minutes)

    b. Interest rate projections are used in investment management for a variety of purposes. Identify three significant reasons why interest rate forecasts may be important in reaching investment conclusions. (6 minutes)

    c. Assume you are a fundamental research analyst following the automobile industry for a large brokerage firm. Identify and briefly explain the relevance of *three* major economic time series, economic indicators, or economic data items that would be significant to automotive industry and company research. (6 minutes)

3. *CFA Examination III* (June 1985)

A U.S pension plan hired two offshore firms to manage the non-U.S. equity portion of its total portfolio. Each firm was free to own stocks in any country market included in Capital International's Europe, Australia, and Far East Index (EAFE) and free to use any form of dollar and/or nondollar cash or bonds as an equity substitute or reserve. After 3 years had elapsed, the records of the managers and the EAFE Index were as shown below:

Summary: Contributions to Return

	Currency	Country Selection	Stock Selection	Cash/ Bond Allocation	Total Return Recorded
Manager A	(9.0%)	19.7%	3.1%	0.6%	14.4%
Manager B	(7.4)	14.2	6.0	2.8	15.6
Composite of A&B	(8.2)	16.9	4.5	1.7	15.0
EAFE Index	(12.9)	19.9	—	—	7.0

You are a member of the plan sponsor's pension committee, which will soon meet with the plan's consultant to review manager performance. In preparation for this meeting, you go through the following analysis:

    a. Briefly describe the strengths and weaknesses of each manager, relative to the EAFE Index data. (5 minutes)

    b. Briefly explain the meaning of the data in the Currency column. (5 minutes)

4. World Stock Market Indexes are published weekly in *Barron's* in the section labeled "Market Laboratory/Stocks." Consult the latest available issue of this publication and the issue one year earlier to find the following information.

    a. Show the closing value of each index on each date relative to the yearly high for each year.

    b. Name the countries with markets in downtrends. Name those in uptrends.

    c. For the two time periods, calculate the year's change relative to the beginning price. Based on this and the range of annual values, which markets seem the most volatile?

5. Using a source of financial data such as *Barron's* or *The Wall Street Journal*:

    a. Plot the weekly percentage changes in the S&P 400 index (y-axis) versus comparable weekly percentage changes in the M2 money supply figures (x-axis) for the past 10 weeks. Do you see a positive, negative, or zero correlation? (Monetary aggregates will lag the stock-market aggregates.)

    b. Examine the trend in money rates (e.g., federal funds, 90-day T-bills, etc.) over the past 10 weeks. Is there a correlation between these money rates? Estimate the correlation between the individual money rates and percentage changes in M1.

    c. For the past 10 weeks examine the relationship between the weekly percentage changes in the S&P 400 Index and the DJIA. Plot the weekly percentage changes in each index using S&P as the x-axis and DJIA as the y-axis. Discuss your results as they relate to diversification. Do a similar comparison for the S&P 400 and the Nikkei Index and discuss these results.

REFERENCES

Belfer, Nathan. "Economic Indicators and Their Significance." In *The Financial Analysts Handbook,* 2d ed., edited by Sumner N. Levine. Homewood, Ill.: Dow Jones-Irwin, 1988.

Chen, Nai-Fu, Richard Roll, and Stephen A. Ross. "Economic Forces and the Stock Market." *Journal of Business* 59, no. 3 (July 1986).

Davidson, Lawrence S., and Richard T. Froyen. "Monetary Policy and Stock Returns: Are Stock Markets Efficient?" Federal Reserve Bank of St. Louis. *Review* 64, no. 3 (March 1983).

Fogler, H. Russell, and Darwin M. Bayston, eds. *Improving the Investment Decision Process: Quantitative Assistance for the Practitioner and for the Firm.* Charlottesville, VA: The Institute of Chartered Financial Analysts, January 1984.

Friedman, Milton J., and Anna J. Schwartz. "Money and Business Cycles." *Review of Economics and Statistics* 45, no. 1 Supplement (February 1963).

Hafer, R. W. "The Response of Stock Prices to Changes in Weekly Money and the Discount Rate." Federal Reserve Bank of St. Louis. *Review* 68, no. 3 (March 1986).

Hertzberg, Marie P., and Berry A. Beckman. "Business Cycle Indicators: Revised Composite Indicators." *Business Conditions Digest* (January 1989).

Moore, Geoffrey H., and John P. Cullity. "Security Markets and Business Cycles." In *The Financial Analysts Handbook,* 2d ed., edited by Sumner N. Levine. Homewood, Ill.: Dow Jones-Irwin, 1988.

Moore, Geoffrey H., ed. *Business Cycles, Inflation, and Forecasting.* 2d ed. New York: National Bureau of Economic Research, Studies in Business Cycles, no. 24, 1983.

Vertin, James R., ed. *Improving the Investment Decision Process: Applying Economic Analysis to Portfolio Management.* Charlottesville, VA: The Institute of Chartered Financial Analysts, September 1984.

ANALYSIS AND MANAGEMENT OF BONDS

For most investors, bonds are like Rodney Danger-field—"They get no respect!" This is surprising when one considers the fact that the total market value of the bond market in the United States and in most countries of the world is substantially larger than the market value of the stock market. As an example, in the United States as of the end of 1992 the market value of all publicly issued bonds was over $6 trillion, while the market value of all stocks was about $4 trillion. On a global basis, the values are about $14 trillion for bonds versus $10.6 trillion for stocks. Beyond the size factor, bonds have a reputation for low, unexciting rates of return. While this may be true if one goes back 50 or 60 years, it is certainly not true during the past 10 to 15 years. Specifically, the average annual compound rate of return on government/corporate bonds for the period 1976–1991 was slightly over 10 percent versus about 14 percent for common stocks. These rates of return along with corresponding standard deviations (8 percent for bonds versus 13 percent for stocks) indicate that there are substantial opportunities in bonds for individual and institutional investors.

Because of the size and opportunities in bonds, the chapters in this section are intended to provide a basic understanding of bonds and the bond markets around the world, background on analyzing returns and risks in the bond market, and what is involved in either active or passive bond portfolio management.

Chapter 13 on bond fundamentals describes the global bond market in terms of country participation and the makeup of the bond market in the largest countries. Also, the characteristics of bonds in alternative categories such as government, corporate, and municipal are discussed. Because of the credit risk involved in corporate and municipal bonds, there are agencies in many countries that provide credit ratings on bonds that are very important to potential investors. We also discuss the many new corporate bond instruments developed in the United States such as asset-backed securities, zero coupon bonds, and high yield bonds that will eventually be used around the world. Finally, there is a discussion of the information needed by bond investors and where to get it.

Chapter 14 is concerned with the analysis of bonds including a detailed discussion of the alternative rate of return measures for bonds, what factors affect yields on bonds, and what influences the volatility of bond returns. This latter discussion considers the very important concept of bond duration which helps explain bond price volatility, but is also important in active and passive bond portfolio management. There is also a related consideration of the convexity of alternative bonds and the impact of convexity on bond price volatility. We conclude the chapter with a discussion of the effect of the call feature on a bond's duration and convexity. A consideration of the call feature becomes very significant during periods of declining interest rates such as we have experienced during the period 1992–1993.

Chapter 15 considers how to employ the fundamentals and analysis background to create and manage a bond portfolio. There are four major portfolio strategies and each of these are considered in detail. The first is passive strategies that include either a simple buy-and-hold strategy or indexing to one of the major benchmarks. The second is an active management strategy that can involve one or more of five alternatives: interest rate anticipation, valuation analysis, credit analysis, yield spread analysis, or bond swaps. The third strategy category is matched funding, which includes developing dedicated portfolios, classical immunization portfolios, or horizon matching. Finally, there are contingent strategies that are also referred to as structured active management. The major technique in this category is contingent immunization.

The fact that there are three chapters devoted to the study of bonds and the length of the chapters attests to the importance of the topic and the extensive research done in this area. The fact is, during the past 15 years, there have probably been more developments related to the valuation and portfolio management of bonds than of stocks. This growth does not detract from the importance of equities, but certainly enhances the significance of fixed-income securities. A final point that should be kept in mind—this growth in size and sophistication means that there are many more career opportunities in the bond area ranging from trading these securities, credit analysis, and portfolio management, both domestically and globally.

CHAPTER 13

BOND FUNDAMENTALS

In this chapter we will answer the following questions:

- What are some of the basic features of bonds that affect their risk, return, and value?
- What is the current country structure of the world bond market and how has the makeup changed in recent years?
- What are the major components of the world bond market and the international bond market?
- What are bond ratings and what is their purpose? What is the difference between investment grade bonds and high yield (junk) bonds?
- What are the characteristics of bonds in the major bond categories such as governments, agencies, municipalities, and corporates?
- Within each of the major bond categories, what are the differences between major countries such as the United States, Japan, the United Kingdom, and Germany?
- What are the important characteristics of some new corporate bond issues developed in the United States during the past decade, such as mortgage-backed securities, other asset-backed securities, zero coupon and deep discount bonds, and high-yield bonds?
- What is the basic information required by bond investors and what are the sources of this information?
- How do you read the quotes available for the alternative bonds categories (e.g., governments, municipalities, corporates)?

The global bond market is large and diverse, and represents an important investment opportunity. This chapter is concerned with publicly issued, long-term, nonconvertible debt obligations of public and private issuers in the United States and major global markets. In later chapters, we will consider preferred stock and convertible bonds. An understanding of bonds is helpful in an efficient market because U.S. and foreign bonds increase the universe of investments available for the creation of a diversified portfolio.[1]

Material on bonds and world bond markets in this chapter is based on information from "How Big Is the World Bond Market," 1992 update by Rosario Benavides of Salomon Brothers Inc. Copyright 1992 by Salomon Brothers Inc. Reprinted by permission.

[1]Meir Statman and Neal L. Ushman, "Bonds Versus Stocks: Another Look," *Journal of Portfolio Management* 13, no. 3 (Winter 1987): 33–38.

In this chapter we review some basic features of bonds and examine the structure of the world bond market. The bulk of the chapter involves an in-depth discussion of the major fixed-income investments. The chapter ends with a brief review of the data requirements and information sources for bond investors. Chapter 14 discusses the valuation of bonds and considers several factors that influence bond value and bond price volatility.

BASIC FEATURES OF A BOND

Public bonds are long-term, fixed-obligation debt securities packaged in convenient, affordable denominations, for sale to individuals and financial institutions. They differ from other debt, such as individual mortgages and privately placed debt obligations, because they are sold to the public rather than channeled directly to a single lender. Bond issues are considered fixed-income securities because they impose fixed financial obligations on the issuers. Specifically, the issuer agrees to

1. Pay a fixed amount of *interest periodically* to the holder of record.
2. Repay a fixed amount of *principal* at the date of maturity.

Normally, interest on bonds is paid every 6 months, although some bond issues pay in intervals as short as a month or as long as a year. The principal is due at maturity; this *par value* of the issue is rarely less than $1,000. A bond has a specified term to maturity, which defines the life of the issue. The public debt market is typically divided into three segments based on an issue's original maturity:

1. Short-term issues with maturities of 1 year or less. The market for these instruments is commonly known as the *money market*.
2. Intermediate-term issues with maturities in excess of 1 year, but less than 10 years. These instruments are known as *notes*.
3. Long-term obligations with maturities in excess of 10 years, called *bonds*.

The lives of debt obligations change constantly as the issues progress toward maturity. Thus, issues that have been outstanding in the secondary market for any period of time eventually move from long-term to intermediate to short-term. This movement is important, because a major determinant of the price volatility of bonds is the remaining life (maturity) of the issue.

BOND CHARACTERISTICS

A bond can be characterized based on (1) its own intrinsic features, (2) its type, or (3) its indenture provisions.

INTRINSIC FEATURES

The coupon, maturity, principal value, and the type of ownership are important intrinsic features of a bond. The **coupon** of a bond indicates the income that the bond investor will receive over the life (or holding period) of the issue. This is known as *interest income, coupon income,* or *nominal yield.*

The **term to maturity** specifies the date or the number of years before a bond matures (or expires). There are two different types of maturity. The most common is a *term bond,* which has a single maturity date. Alternatively, a **serial obligation** bond issue has a series of maturity dates, perhaps 20 or 25. Each maturity, although a subset of the total issue, is really a small bond issue with, generally, a different coupon. Municipalities issue most serial bonds.

The **principal,** or **par value,** of an issue represents the original value of the obligation. This is generally stated in $1,000 increments from $1,000 to $25,000 or more. Principal value is *not* the same as the bond's market value. The market prices of many issues rise above or fall below their principal values because of differences between their coupons and the prevailing market rate of interest. If the market interest rate is above the coupon rate, the bond will sell at a discount to par. If the market interest rate is below the bond's coupon, it will sell at a premium above par. If the coupon is comparable to the prevailing market interest rate, the market value of the bond will be close to its original principal value.

Finally, bonds differ in their terms of ownership. With a *bearer bond,* the holder, or bearer, is the owner, so the issuer keeps no record of ownership. Interest from a bearer bond is obtained by clipping coupons attached to the bonds and sending them to the issuer for payment. In contrast, the issuers of *registered bonds* maintain records of owners and pay the interest directly to them.

TYPES OF ISSUES

In contrast to common stock, companies can have many different bond issues outstanding at the same time. Bonds can have different types of collateral and be either senior, unsecured, or subordinated (junior) securities. **Secured (senior) bonds** are backed by a legal claim on some specified property of the issuer in the case of default. For example, mortgage bonds are secured by real estate assets, and equipment trust certificates, which are used by railroads and airlines, provide a senior claim on the firm's equipment.

Unsecured bonds (debentures) are backed only by the promise of the issuer to pay interest and principal on a timely basis. As such, they are secured by the general credit of the issuer. **Subordinated (junior) debentures** possess a claim on income and assets that is subordinated to other debentures. Income issues are the most junior type because interest on them is only paid if it is earned. Although income bonds are unusual in the corporate sector, they are very popular municipal issues, referred to as *revenue bonds.* Finally, *refunding issues* provide funds to prematurely retire another issue. They remain outstanding after the refunding operation. A refunding bond can be either a junior or senior issue.

The type of issue has only a marginal effect on comparative yield because it is basically the credibility of the issuer that determines bond quality. A study of corporate bond price behavior found that whether the issuer pledged collateral did not become important until the bond issue approached default.[2] The collateral and security characteristics of a bond influence yield differentials only when these factors affect the bond's quality ratings.

INDENTURE PROVISIONS

The indenture is the contract between the issuer and the bondholder specifying the issuer's legal requirements. A trustee (usually a bank) acting in behalf of the bond-

[2]W. Braddock Hickman, *Corporate Bond Quality and Investor Experience* (Princeton, N.J.: Princeton University Press, 1958).

holders ensures that all the indenture provisions are met, including the timely payment of interest and principal.

FEATURES AFFECTING A BOND'S MATURITY

Investors should be aware of the three alternative call features that can affect the life (maturity) of a bond. One extreme is a *freely callable* provision that allows the issuer to retire the bond at any time with a typical notification period of 30 to 60 days. The other extreme is a *noncallable* provision wherein the issuer cannot retire the bond prior to its maturity.[3] Intermediate between these is a *deferred call* provision, which means the issue cannot be called for a certain period of time after the date of issue (e.g., 5 to 10 years). At the end of the deferred call period, the issue becomes freely callable. Callable bonds have a *call premium,* which is the amount above maturity value that the issuer must pay to the bondholder for prematurely retiring the bond.

A *nonrefunding provision* prohibits a call and premature retirement of an issue from the proceeds of a lower-coupon refunding bond. This is meant to protect the bondholder from a typical refunding, but it is not foolproof. The fact is, an issue with a nonrefunding provision can be called and retired prior to maturity using other sources of funds such as excess cash from operations, the sale of assets, or proceeds from a sale of common stock. This occurred on several occasions during the 1980s and 1990s when many issuers retired previously issued high-coupon issues early because they could get the cash from one of these other sources and felt that this was a good financing decision.

Another important indenture provision that can affect a bond's maturity is the *sinking fund,* which specifies that a bond must be paid off systematically over its life rather than only at maturity. There are numerous sinking-fund arrangements, and the bondholder should recognize this as a feature that can change the stated maturity of a bond. The size of the sinking fund can be a percentage of a given issue or a percentage of the total debt outstanding, or it can be a fixed or variable sum stated on a dollar or percentage basis. Similar to a call feature, sinking fund payments may commence at the end of the first year or may be deferred for 5 or 10 years from date of the issue. The point is, the amount of the issue that must be repaid before maturity from a sinking fund can range from a nominal sum to 100 percent. Like a call, the sinking-fund feature typically carries a nominal premium, but it is generally smaller than the straight call premium (e.g., 1 percent). For example, a bond issue with a 20-year maturity might have a sinking fund that requires that 5 percent of the issue be retired every year beginning in year 10. As a result, by year 20 half of the issue has been retired and the rest is paid off at maturity. Sinking-fund provisions have a small effect on comparative yields at the time of issue, but have little subsequent impact on price behavior.

A sinking-fund provision is an obligation and must be carried out regardless of market conditions. Although a sinking-fund bond issue could be called on a random basis, most of them are retired for sinking-fund purposes through direct negotiations with institutional holders. Essentially, the trustee negotiates with an institution to buy back the necessary amount of bonds at a price slightly above the current market price.

---

[3]Currently most corporate long-term bonds contain some form of call provision.

RATES OF RETURN
ON BONDS

The rate of return on a bond is computed in the same way as the rate of return on stock or any asset. It is determined by the beginning and ending price and the cash flows during the holding period. The major difference between stocks and bonds is that the interim cash flow on bonds (i.e., the interest) is specified, whereas the dividends on stock may vary. Therefore, the holding period return (HPR) for a bond will be

$$\text{HPR}_{i,t} = \frac{P_{i,t+1} + Int_{i,t}}{P_{i,t}}$$

where:

$\text{HPR}_{i,t}$ = **the holding period return for bond *i* during period *t***
$P_{i,t+1}$ = **the market price of bond *i* at the end of period *t***
$p_{i,t}$ = **the market price of bond *i* at the beginning of period *t***
$Int_{i,t}$ = **the interest payments on bond *i* during period *t***

The holding period yield (HPY) is:

$$\text{HPY} = \text{HPR} - 1$$

Note that the only contractual factor is the amount of interest payments. The beginning and ending bond prices are determined by market forces, as discussed in Chapter 14. Notably, the ending price is determined by market forces unless the bond is held to maturity, in which case the investor will receive the par value. These price variations in bonds means that investors in bonds can experience capital gains or losses. Interest rate volatility has increased substantially since the 1960s, and this has caused large price fluctuations in bonds.[4] As a result, capital gains or losses have become a major component of the rates of return on bonds.

THE GLOBAL
BOND-MARKET
STRUCTURE[5]

The market for fixed-income securities is substantially larger than the listed equity exchanges (NYSE, TSE, LSE), because corporations tend to issue bonds rather than common stock. Federal Reserve figures indicate that in the United States during 1992, 20 percent of all new security issues were equity, which included preferred as well as common stock. Corporations issue less common or preferred stock because firms derive most of their equity financing from internally generated funds (i.e., retained earnings). Also, although the equity market is strictly corporations, the bond market in most countries has four noncorporate sectors: the pure government sector (e.g., the Treasury in the United States), government agencies (e.g., FNMA), state and local government bonds (municipals), and international bonds (Yankees and Eurobonds in the United States).

---

[4]The analysis of bond price volatility is discussed in detail in Chapter 14.

[5]For a further discussion of global bond markets and specific national bond markets, see *International Bond Handbook,* International Bond Research Unit, James Capel & Co., London, 1987; and Adam Greshin and Margaret Darasz Hadzima, *"International Bond Investing and Portfolio Management,"* in *The Handbook of Fixed-Income Securities,* 3d ed., edited by Frank J. Fabozzi (Homewood, Ill.: Business One Irwin, 1991).

TABLE 13.1   **Total Debt Outstanding in the 13 Major[a] Bond Markets, by Year (U.S. dollar terms)**

	1987		1989		1991	
	Total Volume ($ billions)	Percentage of Total	Total Volume ($ billions)	Percentage of Total	Total Volume ($ billions)	Percentage of Total
U.S. dollar	$3,717	42.6	$4,950	47.7	$6,238	46.1
Japanese yen	2,033	23.3	1,981	19.1	2,503	18.5
Deutschemark	783	9.0	848	8.2	1,257	9.3
Italian lira	554	6.3	606	5.8	868	6.4
U.K. sterling	310	3.5	303	2.9	376	2.8
French franc	334	3.8	456	4.4	654	4.8
Canadian dollar	228	2.6	283	2.7	361	2.7
Swedish krona	146	1.7	168	1.6	270	2.0
Danish krone	171	2.0	171	1.6	219	1.6
Swiss franc	142	1.6	163	1.6	191	1.4
Dutch guilder	130	1.5	153	1.5	201	1.5
Belgian franc	96	1.1	210	2.0	301	2.2
Australian dollar	91	1.0	79	0.8	88	0.7
Total	**$8,735**	**100.0%**	**$10,371**	**100.0%**	**$13,527**	**100.0%**

[a]Only includes bonds with maturities over 1 year. (Floating rates are excluded.)

Source: For 1987—"Size of the World Bond Markets: 1981–87," Merrill Lynch Capital Markets (February 1988). For 1989, 1991—"How Big is the World Bond Market?," 1990 Update and 1992 Update, Salomon Brothers International Bond Market Analysis (August 29, 1990 and October 1992). Reprinted by permission of Merrill Lynch. All Rights Reserved.

The size of the global bond market and the distribution among countries can be gleaned from Table 13.1, which lists the dollar value of debt outstanding and the percentage distribution for the major bond markets for the years 1987, 1989, and 1991. There has been substantial growth overall including a 55 percent increase in the total in 1991 compared with 1987. Also, the country trends are significant. Specifically, the U.S market went from about 43 percent of the total world market in 1987 to 46 percent in 1991. In contrast, Japan went from about 23 percent to almost 18.5 percent in 1991. The German and Italian markets have maintained a fairly constant percentage of the global bond market during the last several years, whereas the U.K. market has experienced an overall decline from 3.5 to 2.8 percent.

PARTICIPATING ISSUERS

There are generally five different issuers in a country: (1) federal governments (e.g., the U.S. Treasury), (2) agencies of the federal government, (3) various state and local political subdivisions (known as municipalities), (4) corporations, and (5) international issues. The division of bonds among these five types for the three largest markets and the United Kingdom during 1987, 1989, and 1991 is contained in Table 13.2.

GOVERNMENT

The market for government securities is the largest sector in the United States, Japan, and the United Kingdom. It involves a variety of debt instruments issued to meet the growing needs of these governments. In Germany, the government sector is smaller, but it is growing in relative size due to deficits related to the reunification of the country.

TABLE 13.2   **Makeup of Bonds Outstanding in United States, Japan, Germany, United Kingdom: 1987–1991**

	1987		1989		1991	
	Total Volume	Percentage of Total	Total Volume	Percentage of Total	Total Volume	Percentage of Total
A. United States (U.S. dollars in billions)						
Government	1,335.2	28.9	1,514.8	27.3	1,881.3	28.0
Federal agency	1,000.5	21.6	1,233.1	22.2	1,563.4	23.3
Municipal	715.1	15.5	802.4	14.5	893.7	13.3
Corporate	1,140.3	24.7	1,448.5	26.1	1,761.2	26.2
International	434.6	9.4	544.0	9.8	614.2	9.1
Total	4,625.7	100.0	5,542.8	100.0	6,713.8	100.0
B. Japan (yen in billions)						
Government	146,891	49.6	153,957	47.7	161,117	44.6
Government-associated organization	46,656	15.7	49,982	15.5	55,903	15.5
Municipal	20,439	6.9	19,604	6.1	19,431	5.4
Bank debentures	49,941	16.9	58,647	18.2	73,632	20.4
Corporate	19,033	6.4	25,180	7.8	29,600	8.2
International	12,945	4.4	15,120	4.7	21,540	6.0
Total	295,905	100.0	322,490	100.0	361,223	100.0
C. Germany (deutschemarks in billions)						
Government	300.9	23.6	374.6	26.0	493.7	25.9
Agency	54.3	4.3	57.3	4.0	75.1	3.9
State and local	37.1	2.9	37.0	2.6	47.7	2.5
Bank	715.9	56.2	760.7	52.9	1,040.4	54.6
Corporate	2.5	0.2	2.7	0.2	3.2	0.2
International	163.3	12.8	206.4	14.3	245.5	12.9
Total	1,274.0	100.0	1,438.7	100.0	1,905.6	100.0
D. United Kingdom (pounds in billions)						
Government	137.1	77.7	122.7	65.1	120.3	60.0
Agency	—	—	—	—	—	—
Municipal	0.1	0.1	0.1	0.1	0.1	0.1
Corporate	10.3	5.8	15.6	8.3	13.8	6.9
International	28.9	16.4	50.0	26.5	66.7	33.2
Total	176.4	100.0	188.4	100.0	200.9	100.0

Source: "How Big Is the World Bond Market?—1992 Update," Salomon Brothers International Bond Market Analysis, October 1992. Reprinted by permission of Merrill Lynch. All Rights Reserved.

GOVERNMENT AGENCIES

Agency issues have attained and maintained a major position in the U.S. market (over 20 percent), but are a smaller proportion in other countries (e.g., less than 10 percent in Japan, below 4 percent in Germany, and nonexistent in the United Kingdom). These agencies represent political subdivisions of the government although the securities are *not* typically direct obligations of the government. The U.S. agency market has two types of issuers: government-sponsored enterprises and federal agencies. The proceeds of agency bond issues are used to finance many legislative programs. In the United States many of these obligations carry government guarantees although they are not direct obligations of the government. In other countries the relationship of an agency issue to the government varies. In most countries the market yields of agency obligations generally exceed those from pure government bonds. Thus, they represent a way for investors to increase returns with only marginally higher risk.

MUNICIPALITIES

Municipal debt includes issues of states, school districts, cities, or other political sub-divisions. Unlike government and agency issues, the interest income on them is not subject to federal income tax although capital gains is taxable. Moreover, these bonds are exempt from state and local taxes when they are issued by the investor's home state. That is, the interest income on a California issue would not be taxed to a California resident, but it would be taxable to a New York resident. The interest income of Puerto Rican issues enjoys total immunity from federal, state, and local taxes. Also, most U.S. municipal bond issues are serial obligations, which means an investor can select from a number of different maturities from very short (1 or 2 years) to fairly long (20 years).

As shown in Table 13.2, the municipal bond market in most other countries is much smaller than in the United States (less than 3 percent). Also, although each country has unique tax laws, typically the income from a non-U.S. municipal bond would not be exempt for a U.S. investor.

CORPORATIONS

The major nongovernmental issuer of debt is the corporate sector. The importance of this sector differs dramatically among countries. It is a significant factor in the United States; a small but growing sector in Japan, where it is supplemented by bank deben-tures; and a small but constant proportion of the U.K. market. Finally, it is a minuscule part of the German market, because most German firms get their financing through bank loans, which explains the very large percentage of bank debt in Germany.

The market for corporate bonds is commonly subdivided into several segments: industrials, public utilities, transportation, and financial issues. The specific makeup varies between countries. Most U.S. issues are industrials and utilities. Most foreign corporations do not issue public debt but borrow from the banks.

The corporate sector provides the most diverse issues in terms of type and quality. In effect, the issuer can range from the highest investment-grade firm, such as American Telephone and Telegraph or IBM, to a relatively new, high-risk firm that defaulted on previous debt securities.[6]

INTERNATIONAL

The international sector has two components: (1) foreign bonds such as Yankee bonds and Samurai bonds, and (2) Eurobonds including Eurodollar, Euroyen, Eurodeutsche-mark, and Eurosterling bonds.[7] Although the relative importance of the international bond sector varies by country (12.9 percent in Germany, 33 percent in the United Kingdom, 9 percent in the United States, and 6 percent in Japan), it has grown in both absolute and relative terms in all these countries. Although Eurodollar bonds have historically made up over 50 percent of the Eurobond market, the proportion has de-clined as investors have attempted to diversify their Eurobond portfolios. Clearly, the desire for diversification changes with the swings in the value of the U.S. dollar.

---

[6]It is possible to distinguish another sector that exists in the United States but not in other countries—institutional bonds. These are corporate bonds issued by a variety of *private, nonprofit institutions* such as schools, hospitals, and churches. They are not broken out because they are only a minute part of the U.S. market and do not exist elsewhere.

[7]These bonds will be discussed in more detail later in this chapter.

PARTICIPATING INVESTORS

Numerous individual and institutional investors with diverse investment objectives participate in the bond market. Wealthy individual investors are a minor portion because of the market's complexity and the high minimum denominations of most issues. Institutional investors typically account for 90 to 95 percent of the trading, although different segments of the market are more institutionalized than others. For example, institutions are involved heavily in the agency market, whereas they are much less active in the corporate sector.

A variety of institutions invest in the bond market. Life insurance companies invest in corporate bonds and, to a lesser extent, in Treasury and agency securities. Commercial banks invest in the municipal bonds and also government and agency issues. Property and liability insurance companies concentrate on municipal bonds and Treasuries. Private and government pension funds are heavily committed to corporates and also invest in Treasuries and agencies. Finally fixed-income mutual funds have grown in size and their demand spans the full spectrum of the market as they develop bond funds that meet the needs of individual investors. Significant growth has been experienced by municipal bond funds and corporate bond funds (including high-yield bonds).

Alternative institutions tend to favor different issues based on two factors: (1) the tax code applicable to the institution, and (2) the nature of the institution's liability structure. For example, because commercial banks are subject to normal taxation and have fairly short-term liability structures, they favor short- to intermediate-term municipals. Pension funds are virtually tax-free institutions with long-term commitments, so they prefer high-yielding, long-term government or corporate bonds. Such institutional investment preferences can affect the short-run supply and demand of loanable funds and impact interest rate changes.

BOND RATINGS

Agency ratings are an integral part of the bond market because most corporate and municipal bonds are rated by one or more of the rating agencies. The exceptions are very small issues and bonds from certain industries such as bank issues. These are known as *nonrated bonds*. There are four major rating agencies: (1) Duff and Phelps, (2) Fitch Investors Service, (3) Moody's, and (4) Standard & Poor's.

Bond ratings provide the fundamental analysis for thousands of issues.[8] The rating agencies analyze the issuing organization and the specific issue to determine the probability of default and inform the market of their analyses through their ratings.

The primary question in bond credit analysis is whether the firm can service its debt in a timely manner over the life of a given issue. Consequently, the rating agencies consider expectations over the life of the issue, along with the historical and current financial position of the company. Although the agencies have done an admirable job, mistakes happen.[9] A study indicated that the rating services have tended to overestimate the risk of default, which has resulted in unnecessarily high risk premiums given the

---

[8]For a detailed listing of rating classes and a listing of factors considered in assigning ratings, see "Bond Ratings," and "Bond Rating Outlines," in *The Financial Analysts Handbook*, 2d ed., edited by Sumner N. Levine (Homewood, Ill.: Dow Jones-Irwin, 1988), 1102–1138. For a study that examines the value of two bond ratings, see L. Paul Hsueh and David S. Kidwell, "Bond Ratings: Are Two Better Than One?" *Financial Management* 17, no. 1 (Spring 1988): 46–53.

[9]W. Braddock Hickman, *Corporate Bond Quality and Investor Experience* (Princeton, N.J.: Princeton University Press, 1958).

default probabilities.[10] We will consider default estimation further when we discuss high-yield (junk) bonds.

Several studies have examined the relationship between bond ratings and issue quality as indicated by financial variables. The results clearly demonstrated that bond ratings were positively related to profitability, size, and cash flow coverage, and they were inversely related to financial leverage and earnings instability.[11]

The original ratings assigned to bonds have an impact on their marketability and effective interest rate. Generally, the four agencies' ratings agree. When they do not, the issue is said to have a *split rating.* Seasoned issues are regularly reviewed to ensure that the assigned rating is still valid. If not, revisions are made either upward or downward. Revisions are usually done in increments of one rating grade.[12] The ratings are based on both the company and the issue. After an evaluation of the creditworthiness of the total company is completed, a company rating is assigned to the firm's most senior unsecured issue. All junior bonds receive lower ratings based on indenture specifications. Also, an issue could receive a higher rating than justified because of credit-enhancement devices such as the attachment of bank letters of credit, surety, or indemnification bonds from insurance companies.

The agencies assign letter ratings depicting what they view as the risk of default of an obligation. The letter ratings range from AAA (Aaa) to D. Table 13.3 describes the various ratings assigned by the major services. Except for slight variations in designations, the meaning and interpretation is basically the same. The agencies modify the ratings with + and − signs for Duff & Phelps, Fitch, and S&P, or with numbers (1-2-3) for Moody's. As an example, an A+ bond is at the top of the A-rated group.

The top four ratings—AAA (or Aaa), AA (or Aa), A, and BBB (or Baa)—are generally considered to be *investment-grade securities.* The next level of securities is known as *speculative bonds* and include the BB- and B-rated obligations.[13] The C categories are generally either income obligations or revenue bonds, many of which are trading flat. (Flat bonds are in arrears on their interest payments.) In the case of D-rated obligations, the issues are in outright default, and the ratings indicate the bonds' relative salvage values.

ALTERNATIVE BOND ISSUES

At this point, we have described the basic features available for all bonds and the overall structure of the global bond market in terms of the issuers of bonds and investors in bonds. In this section, we provide a detailed discussion of the bonds available from the

---

[10]Gordon Pye, "Gauging the Default Premium," *Financial Analysts Journal* 30, no. 1 (January-February 1974): 49–52.

[11]See, for example, Robert S. Kaplan and Gabriel Urwitz, "Statistical Models of Bond Ratings: A Methodological Inquiry," *Journal of Business* 52, no. 2 (April 1979): 231–262; Ahmed Belkaoui, "Industrial Bond Ratings: A New Look," *Financial Management* 9, no. 3 (Autumn, 1980): 44–52; and James A. Gentry, David T. Whitford, and Paul Newbold, "Predicting Industrial Bond Ratings with a Probit Model and Funds Flow Components," *The Financial Review* 23, no. 3 (August 1988): 269–286.

[12]Bond rating changes and bond-market efficiency are discussed in Chapter 14. Split ratings are discussed in R. Billingsley, R. Lamy, M. Marr, and T. Thompson, "Split Ratings and Bond Reoffering Yields," *Financial Management* 14, no. 2 (Summer 1985): 59–65; L. H. Ederington, "Why Split Ratings Occur," *Financial Management* 14, no. 1 (Spring 1985): 37–47; and P. Liu and W. T. Moore, "The Impact of Split Bond Rating on Risk Premia," *The Financial Review* 22, no. 1 (February 1987).

[13]Marshall E. Blume and Donald B. Keim, "The Risk and Return of Low Grade Bonds: An Update," *Financial Analysts Journal* 47, no. 5 (September/October 1991): 85–89. Increased interest in these bonds is discussed in Constance Mitchell, "Defying Death Certificate, Junk Market Soars," *The Wall Street Journal,* July 1, 1992, 613.

TABLE 13.3

Description of Bond Ratings

	Duff and Phelps	Fitch	Moody's	Standard & Poor's	Definition
High Grade	AAA	AAA	Aaa	AAA	The highest rating assigned to a debt instrument, indicating an extremely strong capacity to pay principal and interest. Bonds in this category are often referred to as *gilt edge securities.*
	AA	AA	Aa	AA	High-quality bonds by all standards with strong capacity to pay principal and interest. These bonds are rated lower primarily because the margins of protection are less strong than those for Aaa and AAA bonds.
Medium Grade	A	A	A	A	These bonds possess many favorable investment attributes, but elements may suggest a susceptibility to impairment given adverse economic changes.
	BBB	BBB	Baa	BBB	Bonds are regarded as having adequate capacity to pay principal and interest, but certain protective elements may be lacking in the event of adverse economic conditions that could lead to a weakened capacity for payment.
Speculative	BB	BB	Ba	BB	Bonds regarded as having only moderate protection of principal and interest payments during both good and bad times.
	B	B	B	B	Bonds that generally lack characteristics of other desirable investments. Assurance of interest and principal payments over any long period of time may be small.
Default	CCC	CCC	Caa	CCC	Poor-quality issues that may be in default or in danger of default.
	CC	CC	Ca	CC	Highly speculative issues that are often in default or possess other marked shortcomings.
	C	C			The lowest-rated class of bonds. These issues can be regarded as extremely poor in investment quality.
		C		C	Rating given to income bonds on which no interest is being paid.

	Duff and Phelps	Fitch	Moody's	Standard & Poor's	Definition
TABLE 13.3					**Description of Bond Ratings** *(continued)*
		DDD, DD, D		D	Issues in default with principal or interest payments in arrears. Such bonds are extremely speculative and should be valued only on the basis of their value in liquidation or reorganization.

Source: *Bond Guide* (New York: Standard & Poor's Corporation, monthly); *Bond Record* (New York: Moody's Investors Services, Inc., monthly); *Rating Register* (New York: Fitch Investors Service, Inc., monthly).

major issuers of bonds. The presentation is longer than you would normally expect because when we discuss each issuing unit such as governments, municipalities, or corporations, we consider the bonds available in several of the major world financial centers such as Japan, Germany, and the United Kingdom.

DOMESTIC GOVERNMENT BONDS

UNITED STATES

As shown in Table 13.2, the U.S. fixed-income market is dominated by U.S. Treasury obligations. The U.S. government with the full faith and credit of the U.S. Treasury issues Treasury bills (T-bills), which mature in less than 1 year, and two forms of long-term obligations: government notes, which have maturities of 10 years or less; and Treasury bonds, with maturities of 10 to 30 years. Current Treasury obligations come in denominations of $1,000 and $10,000. The interest income from the U.S. government securities is subject to federal income tax but exempt from state and local levies. These bonds are popular because of their high credit quality and substantial liquidity.

Short-term T-bills differ from notes and bonds because they are sold at a discount from par to provide the desired yield. The return is the difference between the purchase price and the par at maturity. In contrast, government notes and bonds carry semiannual coupons that specify the nominal yield of the obligations.

Government notes and bonds have some unusual features. First, the period specified for the deferred call feature on Treasury issues is very long and is generally measured relative to the maturity date rather than from date of issue. They generally cannot be called until 5 years prior to their maturity date. Notably, *all* issues since 1989 have been noncallable.

Certain government issues provide a tax break to investors because they can be redeemed at par to pay federal estate taxes. Therefore, an investor can acquire a Treasury bond at a substantial discount, with which his or her estate can pay estate taxes. Such bonds are called *flower bonds*. Although no new flower bonds can be issued, about five such issues are still available in the market. These carry 2¾ to 4½ percent coupons and have maturities that extend to 1998. The lower coupon causes a substantial price discount and more assurance of price appreciation at "time of departure."

Recent estate tax law changes increased the portion of an estate exempt from taxes, thereby reducing the demand for such issues. Also the available supply has declined, because when these flower bonds are used to pay estate taxes, they are retired by the government. Therefore, prices have been maintained, and the yields on flower bonds are consistently below those of other Treasury issues of comparable maturity. As an example, during 1992, when most Treasury bonds were yielding between 7 and 8 percent, the remaining flower bonds were yielding about 3 to 4 percent.

JAPAN[14]

The second largest government bond market in the world is Japan's. It is controlled by the Japanese government and the Bank of Japan (Japanese Central Bank). Japanese government bonds are an attractive investment vehicle for those favoring the Japanese yen, because their quality is equal to that of U.S. Treasury securities (they are guaranteed by the government of Japan) and they are very liquid. There are three maturity segments: medium-term (2, 3, or 4 years), long-term (10 years), and super-long (private placements for 15 and 20 years). Bonds are issued in both registered and bearer form, although registered bonds can be converted to bearer bonds through the registrar at the Bank of Japan.

Medium-term bonds are issued monthly through a competitive auction system similar to that of U.S. Treasury bonds. Long-term bonds are authorized by the Ministry of Finance and issued monthly by the Bank of Japan through an underwriting syndicate consisting of major financial institutions. Most super-long bonds are sold through private placement to a few financial institutions. Government bonds, which are the most liquid of all Japanese bonds, account for more than half of the Japanese bonds outstanding and over 80 percent of total bond trading volume in Japan.

At least 50 percent of the trading in Japanese government bonds will be in the so-called *benchmark issue* of the time. The selection of the benchmark issue is made from among 10-year coupon bonds. (As of mid-1993 the benchmark issue was #145, a 5.5 percent coupon bond maturing in 2002.) The designation of a benchmark issue is intended to assist smaller financial institutions in their trading of government bonds by ensuring these institutions that they would have a liquid market in this particular security. Compared to the benchmark issue, which accounts for about 50 percent of total trading in all Japanese government bonds, the comparable most active U.S. bond within a class accounts for only about 10 percent of the volume.

The yield on this benchmark bond is often as much as 50 or 60 basis points below other comparable Japanese government bonds, reflecting its superior marketability. In the U.S. market, the most liquid bond sells at a yield differential of only 10 basis points. The benchmark issue changes when a designated issue matures or because of a decision by the Bank of Japan. Because of the difference in yield and liquidity, institutions that are interested in buying and holding versus trading, acquire the nonbenchmark issues because of their higher yields. Notably, by taking these nonbenchmark issues out of circulation, these institutions ensure that they will not be traded, which confirms assumptions about their lack of liquidity.

---

[14]For additional discussion, see "International Bond Handbook" (London: James Capel & Co., 1987); Nicholas Sargan, Kermit L. Schoenhotz, Steven Blitz, and Sahar Elhabashi, "Trading Patterns in the Japanese Government Bond Market" (New York: Salomon Brothers, 1986); Aron Viner, *Inside Japanese Financial Markets* (Homewood, Ill.: Dow Jones-Irwin, 1988); Edwin J. Elton and Martin J. Gruber, eds. *Japanese Capital Markets* (New York: Harper & Row, 1990); and Frank J. Fabozzi, ed., *The Japanese Bond Markets* (Chicago: Probus Publishing, 1990).

GERMANY[15]

The third largest bond market in the world is the German market, although the government segment of this market is relatively small. Table 13.2 showed that approximately three-quarters of domestic deutschemark bonds are issued by the major commercial banks, whereas the Federal Republic of Germany issues the remainder through the German Central Bank.

The German capital market is dominated by commercial banks because in Germany there is no formal distinction between investment, merchant, or commercial banks as there is in the United States and the United Kingdom. As a result, firms arrange their financing primarily through bank loans, and these banks in turn raise their capital through public bond issues. Therefore, industrial domestic bonds are substantially less than 1 percent of the total outstanding German bonds.

Bonds issued by the Federal Republic of Germany, referred to as *bund* bonds, are issued in amounts up to DM 4 billion (4 billion deutschemarks) with a minimum denomination of DM 100. Original maturities are normally 10 or 12 years although 30-year bonds have been issued.

Although bunds are issued as bearer bonds, individual bonds do not exist. A global bond is issued and held in safekeeping within the German Securities Clearing System (the *Kassenverein*). Contract notes confirming the terms and ownership of each issue are then distributed to individual investors. Sales are based on these contract notes. Bonds are issued through a fixed quota system by the Federal Bond Syndicate, made up of the Bundesbank and 17 banks including certain resident branches of foreign banks. These government bunds are very liquid because the Bundesbank makes a market at all times. They are also the highest credit quality because they are guaranteed by the German government.

Bunds are quoted net of accrued interest and as a percentage of par on German Stock Exchanges. Daily prices are determined on the exchange floor by the Bundesbank based on their existing order backlog. Market makers use this benchmark level as the basis for trading. Although listed on the exchanges, government bonds are primarily traded over the counter and interest is paid annually.

UNITED KINGDOM[16]

The U.K. government bond market changed dramatically on October 17, 1986 (the day of the Big Bang when the trading rules and organizations in the securities business in the United Kingdom were changed). The roles of jobbers and brokers changed so that broker-dealers could act as principals or agents with negotiated commission structures. In addition, the number of primary dealers in the "gilt" market was expanded from 7 gilt jobbers to 27 primary dealers.

Maturities in this market range from short gilts (maturities of less than 5 years) to medium gilts (5 to 15 years) to long gilts (15 years and longer). Government bonds either have a fixed redemption date or a range of dates with redemption at the option

---

[15]For additional information on the German bond market, see Graham Bishop, "Deutschemark" in *Salomon Brothers International Bond Manual,* 2d ed. (New York: Salomon Brothers, 1987); and *The European Bond Markets* ed. by The European Bond Commission (Chicago: Probus Publishing, 1989).

[16]For further discussion, see Ian C. Collier, "An Introduction to the Gilt-Edged Market" (London: James Capel & Co., 1987); and *The European Bond Markets.*

of the government after giving appropriate notice. Alternatively, some bonds are redeemable on a given date or at any time afterwards at the option of the government. Currently, these bonds have generally passed their first option date and because of the low coupon they have not been redeemed and very likely will not be redeemed in the near future. Government bonds are normally registered, although bearer delivery is available.

Gilts are issued through the Bank of England (the British central bank) using the tender method, whereby prospective purchasers tender offering prices at which they hope to be allotted bonds. The price cannot be less than the minimum tender price stated in the prospectus. If the issue is oversubscribed, allotments are made first to those submitting the highest tenders and continue until a price is reached where only a partial allotment is required to fully subscribe the issue. All successful allottees pay the lowest allotment prices.

These issues are extremely liquid because of the size of the market and the large size of individual issues. They are also highly rated because all payments are guaranteed by the British government. All gilts are quoted and traded net of accrued interest on the London Stock Exchange. Interest is paid semiannually.

GOVERNMENT AGENCY ISSUES

In addition to pure government bonds, the federal government in each country can establish agencies that have the authority to issue their own bonds. The size and importance of these agencies differ among countries. They are a large and growing sector of the U.S. bond market, a much smaller component of the bond markets in Japan and Germany, and nonexistent in the United Kingdom.

UNITED STATES

Agency securities are obligations issued by the U.S. government through various political subdivisions, such as a government agency or a government-sponsored corporation. Six government-sponsored enterprises and over two dozen federal agencies issue these bonds. Table 13.4 lists selected characteristics of the more popular government-sponsored and federal agency obligations, including the recent size of the market, typical minimum denominations, tax features, and the availability of bond quotes.[17] The issues in the table are representative of the wide variety of different obligations that are available.

Generally, agency issues are similar to those of other issuers; that is, interest is usually paid semiannually, and the minimum denominations vary between $1,000 and $10,000. These obligations are not direct issues of the Treasury, yet they carry the full faith and credit of the U.S. government. Moreover, unlike government obligations, some of the issues are subject to state and local income tax, whereas others are exempt.[18]

One agency issue offers particularly attractive investment opportunities: GNMA *(Ginnie Mae)* pass-through certificates, which are obligations of the Government Na-

---

[17]We will no longer distinguish between federal agency and government-sponsored obligations; instead, the term *agency* shall apply to either type of issue.

[18]Federal National Mortgage Association (Fannie Mae) debentures, for example, are subject to state and local income tax, whereas the interest income from Federal Home Loan Bank bonds is exempt. In fact, a few issues are even exempt from federal income tax as well (e.g., public housing bonds).

TABLE 13.4   **Agency Issues: Selected Characteristics**

Type of Security	Minimum Denomination	Form	Life of Issue	Tax Status		How Interest Is Earned
Government-Sponsored						
Banks for Cooperatives (Co-ops)	$ 5,000	B, BE	No longer issued. Longest issue due 1/02/86	Federal: State: Local:	Taxable Exempt Exempt	Semiannual interest, 360-day year
Federal Farm Credit Banks Consolidated Systemwide Notes	50,000	BE	5 to 365 days	Federal: State: Local:	Taxable Exempt Exempt	Discount actual, 360-day year
Consolidated Systemwide Bonds	5,000	BE	6 and 9 months	Federal: State: Local:	Taxable Exempt Exempt	Interest payable at maturity, 360-day year
	1,000	BE	13 months to 15 years	Federal: State: Local:	Taxable Exempt Exempt	Semiannual interest
Federal Home Loan Bank						
Consolidated Discount Notes	100,000	BE	30 to 360 days	Federal: State: Local:	Taxable Exempt Exempt	Discount actual, 360-day year
Consolidated Bonds	10,000[a]	B, BE	1 to 20 years	Federal: State: Local:	Taxable Exempt Exempt	Semiannual interest, 360-day year
Federal Home Loan Mortgage						
Corporation Debentures	10,000[a]	BE	18 to 30 years	Federal: State: Local:	Taxable Taxable Taxable	Semiannual interest, 360-day year
Participation Certificates	100,000	R	30 years (12-year average life)	Federal: State: Local:	Taxable Taxable Taxable	Monthly interest and principal payments
Federal National Mortgage Association Discount Notes	50,000[a]	B	30 to 360 days	Federal: State: Local:	Taxable Taxable Taxable	Discount actual, 360-day year
Debentures	10,000[a]	B, BE	1 to 30 years	Federal: State: Local:	Taxable Taxable Taxable	Semiannual interest, 360-day year
Government National Mortgage Association						
Mortgage-backed Bonds	25,000	B, R	1 to 25 years	Federal: State: Local:	Taxable Taxable Taxable	Semiannual interest, 360-day year
Modified Pass-throughs	25,000[a]	R	12 to 40 years (12-year average)	Federal: State: Local:	Taxable Taxable Taxable	Monthly interest and principal payments
Student Loan Marketing Association Discount Notes	100,000	B	Out to 1 year	Federal: State: Local:	Taxable Exempt Exempt	Discount actual, 360-day year
Notes	10,000	R	3 to 10 years	Federal: State: Local:	Taxable Exempt Exempt	Semiannual interest, 360-day year

TABLE 13.4   **Agency Issues: Selected Characteristics** *(continued)*

Type of Security	Minimum Denomination	Form	Life of Issue	Tax Status		How Interest Is Earned
Floating Rate Notes	10,000[a]	R	6 months to 10 years	Federal: State: Local:	Taxable Exempt Exempt	Interest rate adjusted weekly to an increment over the average auction rate on 91-day Treasury bills and payable quarterly
Tennessee Valley Authority (TVA)	1,000	R, B	5 to 25 years	Federal: State: Local:	Taxable Exempt Exempt	Semiannual interest, 360-day year
U.S. Postal Service	10,000	R, B	25 years	Federal: State: Local:	Taxable Exempt Exempt	Semiannual interest, 360-day year

Notes: Form B = Bearer; R = Registered; BE = Book entry form. Debt issues sold subsequent to December 31, 1982 must be in registered form.
[a]Minimum purchase with increments in $5,000.

Source: "United States Government Securities" (New York: Merrill Lynch Government Securities, Inc., 1985); "Handbook of Securities of the United States Government and Federal Agencies," 31st ed. (New York: First Boston Corporation, 1984).

tional Mortgage Association.[19] These bonds represent an undivided interest in a pool of federally insured mortgages. The bondholders receive monthly payments from Ginnie Mae that include both principal and interest, because the agency "passes through" mortgage payments made by the original borrower (the mortgagee) to Ginnie Mae.

The coupons on these pass-through securities are related to the interest charged on the pool of mortgages. The portion of the cash flow that represents the repayment of the principal is tax-free, but the interest income is subject to federal, state, and local taxes. The issues have minimum denominations of $25,000 with maturities of 25 to 30 years but an average life of only 12 years, because as mortgages in the pool are paid off, payments and prepayments are passed through to the investor. Therefore, unlike most bond issues, the monthly payment is not fixed. In fact, the monthly payment is *very uncertain* because of the prepayment schedule that can and does vary dramatically over time when interest rates change.

There are prepayments on these securities for two reasons. The first is when homeowners pay off their mortgages when they sell their homes. The second occurs because owners refinance their homes when mortgage interest rates decline as they did in 1992 and 1993. A major disadvantage of GNMA issues is that they can be seriously depleted by prepayments, which means that their maturities are very uncertain.

The rates of return on these pass-throughs are relatively attractive compared to corporates. Also, most of the return is tax-free in the later years because the tax-free part of the regular payment that is due to the return of principal is large.

---

[19]For a further discussion of mortgage-backed securities, see *Mortgage-Backed Bond and Pass-Through Sympo-sium,* Charlottesville, Va. (Financial Analysts Research Foundation, 1980), and Gregory Parseghian, "Collateralized Mortgage Obligations," in *The Handbook of Fixed-Income Securities,* 3d ed., edited by Frank J. Fabozzi (Homewood, Ill.: Business One Irwin, 1991).

JAPAN

The agencies in Japan, referred to as *government associate organizations,* account for about 7 to 8 percent of the total Japanese bond market. This agency market includes a substantial amount of public debt, but almost twice as much is privately placed with major financial institutions. Public agency debt is issued like government debt.

GERMANY

The agency market in Germany finances about 4 percent of the public debt. The major agencies are the Federal Railway, which issues *Bahn* or *Bundesbahn* bonds, and the Federal Post Office, which issues *Post* or *Bundespost* bonds. These Bahns and Posts are issued up to DM 2 billion. The issue procedure is similar to that used for regular government bonds, which involves a fixed-quota system by the Federal Bond Syndicate. Bahns and Posts are less liquid than government bunds, but the market is still quite liquid. These agency issues are implicitly, though not explicitly, guaranteed by the government.

UNITED KINGDOM

As shown in Table 13.2, there are no agency bond issues in the United Kingdom.

MUNICIPAL BONDS

Municipal bonds are issued by states, counties, cities, and other political subdivisions. Again, the size of the municipal bond market (referred to as *local authority* in the United Kingdom) varies substantially among countries. It is about 20 percent of the total U.S. market, compared to about 3 percent in Japan and Germany, and less than 1 percent in the United Kingdom. Because of the limited size of this market in other countries, we will discuss only the U.S. municipal bond market.

Municipalities in the United States issue two distinct types of bonds: general obligation bonds and revenue issues. *General obligation bonds (GOs)* are essentially backed by the full faith and credit of the issuer and its entire taxing power. *Revenue bonds,* in turn, are serviced by the income generated from specific revenue-producing projects of the municipality, for example, bridges, toll roads, hospitals, municipal coliseums, and waterworks. Revenue bonds generally provide higher returns than GOs because of their higher default risk. Specifically, should a municipality fail to generate sufficient income from a project designated to service a revenue bond, it has absolutely no legal debt service obligation until the income becomes sufficient.

GO municipal bonds tend to be issued on a serial basis so that the issuer's cash flow requirements will be steady over the life of the obligation. Therefore, the principal portion of the total debt service requirement generally begins at a fairly low level and builds up over the life of the obligation. In contrast, most municipal revenue bonds are term issues, so the principal value is not due until the final maturity date or the last few payment dates.

The most important feature of municipal obligations is that the interest payments are exempt from federal income tax, as well as from taxes in the locality and state in which the obligation was issued. This means that their attractiveness varies with the investor's tax brackets.

You can convert the tax-free yield of a municipal bond selling close to par to an equivalent taxable yield (ETY) using the following equation:

$$ETY = \frac{i}{(1 - t)}$$

where:

ETY = equivalent taxable yield
i = coupon rate of the municipal obligations
t = marginal tax rate of the investor

An investor in the 35 percent marginal tax bracket would find that a 7 percent yield on a municipal bond selling close to its par value is equivalent to a 10.77 percent fully taxable yield according to the following calculation:

$$ETY = \frac{.07}{(1 - .35)} = .1077$$

Because the tax-free yield is the major benefit of municipal bonds, an investor's marginal tax rate is a primary concern in evaluating them. As a rough rule of thumb, using the tax rates expected in 1993, an investor must be in the 28 to 30 percent tax bracket before the lower yields available in municipal bonds are competitive with those from fully taxable bonds. However, although the interest payment on municipals is tax-free, any capital gains are not (which is why the ETY formula is only correct for a bond selling close to its par value).

MUNICIPAL BOND GUARANTEES

A growing feature of the U.S. municipal bond market is *municipal bond guarantees* that provide that a bond insurance company will guarantee to make principal and interest payments in the event that the issuer of the bonds defaults. The guarantees are a form of insurance placed on the bond at date of issue and are *irrevocable* over the life of the issue. The issuer purchases the insurance for the benefit of the investor, and the municipality benefits from lower interest costs due to lower default risk, which in turn causes an increase in the rating on the bond and increased marketability.

As of 1992 approximately 30 percent of all new municipal bond issues were insured. There are four private bond insurance firms as follows: a consortium of four large insurance companies entitled the Municipal Bond Investors Assurance (MBIA), a subsidiary of a large Milwaukee-based private insurer known as American Municipal Bond Assurance Corporation (AMBAC), the Financial Security Assurance, and the Financial Guaranty Insurance Company (FGIC). These firms will insure either general obligation or revenue bonds. To qualify for private bond insurance, the issue must initially carry an S&P rating of BBB or better. Currently, the rating agencies will give a AAA (Aaa) rating to bonds insured by these firms because all of the insurance firms have AAA ratings. Issues with these private guarantees have enjoyed a more active secondary market and lower required yields.[20]

---

[20]For a discussion of municipal bond insurance, see Sylvan Feldstein and Frank J. Fabozzi, "Municipal Bonds," in *Handbook of Fixed-Income Securities,* 3d ed., edited by Frank J. Fabozzi (Homewood, Ill.: Business One Irwin, 1991); and D. S. Kidwell, E. H. Sorenson, and J. M. Wachowicz, "Estimating the Signalling Benefits of Debt Insurance: The Case of Municipal Bonds," *Journal of Financial and Quantitative Analysis* 22, no. 3 (September 1987): 299–313. For a discussion of a problem due to the popularity of insurance, see Constance Mitchell, "Bond Insurers Nearing Their Capacity for Backing Some Municipalities' Debt," *The Wall Street Journal,* June 1, 1992, C1, C7.

CORPORATE
BONDS

Again, the importance of corporate bonds varies across countries. The absolute dollar value of corporate bonds in the United States is substantial and has grown overall and as a percentage of U.S. long-term capital. At the same time, corporate debt as a percentage of total U.S. debt has declined from 18 percent to 12 percent because of the faster increase in government debt caused by large government deficits and the growth of agency (mortgage-backed) debt. The pure corporate sector in Japan is small and declining, whereas bank debentures comprise a significant segment (over 20 percent). The pure corporate sector in Germany is almost nonexistent, whereas bank debentures that are used to finance loans to nonbank corporations are the largest segment. Corporate debt in the United Kingdom is about 6 percent of the total.

U.S. CORPORATE BOND MARKET

Utilities dominate the U.S. corporate bond market. The other important segments include industrials (which rank second to utilities), rail and transportation issues, and financial issues. This market includes debentures, first-mortgage issues, convertible obligations, bonds with warrants, subordinated debentures, income bonds (similar to municipal revenue bonds), collateral trust bonds backed by financial assets, equipment trust certificates, and asset-backed securities (ABS) including mortgage-backed bonds.

If we ignore convertible bonds and bonds with warrants, the preceding list of obligations varies by the type of collateral behind the bond. Most bonds have semiannual interest payments, sinking funds, and a single maturity date. Maturities range from 25 to 40 years, with public utilities generally on the longer end and industrials preferring the 25- to 30-year range. Nearly all corporate bonds provide for deferred calls after 5 to 10 years. The deferment period varies directly with the level of the interest rates. Specifically, during periods of higher interest rates bond issues will typically carry a 7- to 10-year deferment, while during periods of relatively low interest rates, the deferment periods will be much shorter.

On the other hand, corporate notes, with maturities of 5 to 7 years, are generally noncallable. Notes become popular when interest rates are high because issuing firms prefer to avoid long-term obligations during such periods. In contrast, during periods of low interest rates such as 1991 to 1992, most corporate issues did not include a call provision because corporations did not believe that they would be able to use them and did not want to pay the higher yield required to include them.

Generally, the average yields for industrial bonds will be the lowest of the three major sectors, followed by utility returns, with yields on transportation bonds generally being the highest. The difference in yield between utilities and industrials is because utilities have the largest supply of bonds, so yields on their bonds must be higher to increase the demand for these bonds.

Some corporate bonds have unique features or security arrangements that will be discussed in the following subsections.[21]

MORTGAGE BONDS   The issuer of a mortgage bond has granted to the bondholder a first-mortgage lien on some piece of property or possibly all of the firm's property.

---

[21]For a further discussion of corporate bonds, see Frank J. Fabozzi, Harry Sauvain, Richard Wilson, and John Ritchie, "Corporate Bonds," in *The Handbook of Fixed-Income Securities,* 3d ed., edited by Frank J. Fabozzi (Homewood, Ill.: Business One Irwin, 1991).

Such a lien provides greater security to the bondholder and a lower interest rate for the issuing firm. Additional mortgage bonds can be issued, assuming certain protective covenants related to earnings or assets are met by the issuer.

COLLATERAL TRUST BONDS   As an alternative to pledging fixed assets or property, a borrower can pledge stocks, bonds, or notes as collateral. The bonds secured by these assets are termed *collateral trust bonds.* These pledged assets are held by a trustee for the benefit of the bondholder.

EQUIPMENT TRUST CERTIFICATES   Equipment trust certificates are issued by railroads (the biggest issuers), airlines, and other transportation firms with the proceeds used to purchase equipment (freight cars, railroad engines, and airplanes) that serves as the collateral for the debt. Maturities range from 1 to about 15 years. The fairly short maturities reflect the nature of the collateral, which is subject to substantial wear and tear and tends to deteriorate rapidly.

Equipment trust certificates are appealing to investors because of their attractive yields and low default record. Although they lack the visibility of other corporate bonds, they typically are fairly liquid.

COLLATERALIZED MORTGAGE OBLIGATIONS (CMO)[22]   Earlier we discussed mortgage bonds backed by pools of mortgages that pay bondholders proportionate shares of principal and interest paid on the mortgages in the pool. You will recall that the pass-through monthly payments are necessarily both interest and principal and that the bondholder is subject to early retirement if the mortgagees prepay because the house is sold or the mortgage refinanced. As a result, when you acquire the typical mortgage pass-through bond, you receive monthly payments (which may not be ideal), and you would be uncertain about the size and timing of the payments.

Collateralized mortgage obligations (CMOs) were developed to offset some of the problems with the traditional mortgage pass-throughs. The first CMO was issued in June 1983, and the current total issuance exceeds $60 billion. The main innovation of the CMO instrument is the segmentation of irregular mortgage cash flows in order to create securities that are high-quality, short-, medium-, and long-term collateralized bonds. Specifically, CMO investors own bonds that are collateralized by a pool of mortgages or by a portfolio of mortgage-backed securities. The bonds are serviced with the cash flows from these mortgages, but rather than the straight pass-through arrangement, the CMO substitutes a *sequential distribution process* that creates a series of bonds with varying maturities to appeal to a wider range of investors.

The prioritized distribution process is as follows:

- Several classes of bonds are issued against a pool of mortgages, which are the collateral. As an example, let us assume a CMO issue with four classes of bonds. In such a case, the first three (e.g., Class A, B, C) would pay interest at their

---

[22]For a detailed discussion, see Janet Spratlin and Paul Vianna, "An Investor's Guide to CMOs" (New York: Salomon Brothers, 1986); Gregory J. Parseghian, "Collateralized Mortgage Obligations," in *The Handbook of Fixed-Income Securities,* 3d ed., edited by Frank Fabozzi (Homewood, Ill.: Business One Irwin, 1991); and M. D. Youngblood, "The Evolution of CMO Residuals: Economic, Accounting and Tax Issues" (New York: Salomon Brothers, 1987).

stated rates, beginning at their issue date, and the fourth class would be an accrual bond (referred to as a *Z bond*).[23]

- The cash flows received from the underlying mortgages are applied first to pay the interest on the first three classes of bonds, and then to retire these bonds.
- The classes of bonds are retired sequentially. All principal payments are directed first to the shortest-maturity class A bonds until they are completely retired. Then all principal payments are directed to the next shortest-maturity bonds (i.e., the class B bonds). The process continues until all the classes have been paid off.
- During the early periods, the accrual bonds (the class Z bonds) pay no interest, but the interest accrues as additional principal, and the cash flow from the mortgages that collateralize these bonds is used to pay interest on and retire the bonds in the other classes. Subsequently, all remaining cash flows are used to pay off the accrued interest, pay any current interest, and then to retire the Z bonds.

This prioritized sequential pattern means that the A-class bonds are fairly short-term and each subsequent class is a little longer term until the Z-class bond, which is a long-term bond. It also functions like a zero coupon bond for the initial years.

Besides creating bonds that pay interest in a more normal pattern (quarterly or semiannually) and that have more predictable maturities, these bonds are considered very high quality securities (AAA) because of the structure and quality of the collateral. To obtain a AAA rating, CMOs are structured to ensure that the underlying mortgages will always generate enough cash to support the bonds issued, even under the most conservative prepayment and reinvestment rates. The fact is, most CMOs are overcollateralized.

Further, the credit risk of the collateral is minimal, because most are backed by mortgages guaranteed by a federal agency (GNMA, FNMA) or by the FHLMC. Those mortgages that are not backed by agencies carry private insurance for principal and interest and mortgage insurance. Notably, even with this AAA rating, the yield on these CMOs has typically been higher than the yields on AA industrials. This premium yield has, of course, contributed to their popularity and growth.

CERTIFICATES FOR AUTOMOBILE RECEIVABLES (CARS)[24]   A rapidly expanding segment of the securities market is that of *asset-backed securities (ABS),* which involves *securitizing debt.* This is an important concept because it substantially increases the liquidity of these individual debt instruments, whether they be individual mortgages, car loans, or credit card debt. *Certificates for automobile receivables (CARs)* are securities collateralized by loans made to individuals to finance the purchase of cars.

---

[23]The four-class CMO was the typical configuration during the 1980s and is used here for demonstration purposes. By 1992, there were CMOs being issued with 18 to 20 classes. More advanced CMOs are referred to as REMICs which are intended to provide greater certainty regarding the cash flow patterns for various components of the pool or some of those investing in the pool. Discussions of these REMICs include, Robert A. Kulason and Michael Waldman, "Understanding TAC and PAC CMO Structures" (New York: Salomon Brothers, 1988); Mark J. Latimer, "Regarding REMICs," *Secondary Mortgage Markets* (McLean, Va.: Freddie Mac, 1991); Andrew S. Carron, "Understanding CMOs, REMICs, and Other Mortgage Derivatives," *Fixed Income Research* (New York: The First Boston Corp., 1992).

[24]For further discussion, see Thomas Delehanty and Michael Waldman, "Certificates for Automobile Receivables (CARs)" (New York: Salomon Brothers, 1986).

They dominate the asset-backed security market except for mortgage-backed securities.

Auto loans are self-amortizing, with monthly payments and relatively short maturities (i.e., 2 to 5 years). These auto loans can either be direct loans from a lending institution or indirect loans that are originated by an auto dealer and sold to the ultimate lender. CARs typically have monthly or quarterly fixed interest and principal payments, and expected weighted average lives of 1 to 3 years with specified maturities of 3 to 5 years. The expected actual life of the instrument is typically shorter than the specified maturity because of early payoffs when cars are sold or traded in. The cash flows of CARs are comparable to short-term corporate debt. They provide a significant yield premium over General Motors Acceptance Corporation (GMAC) commercial paper, which is the most liquid short-term corporate alternative. The popularity of these collateralized securities makes them important not only by themselves, but also as an indication of the potential for issuing additional collateralized securities backed by other assets and/or other debt instruments.[25]

VARIABLE-RATE NOTES   Introduced in the United States in the mid-1970s, variable-rate notes became popular during periods of high interest rates. The typical variable-rate note possesses two unique features:

1. After the first 6 to 18 months of the issue's life, during which a minimum rate is often guaranteed, the coupon rate floats, so that every 6 months it changes to follow some standard. Usually it is pegged 1 percent above a stipulated short-term rate. For example, the rate might be the preceding 3 weeks' average 90-day T-bill rate.
2. After the first year or two, the notes are redeemable at par, at the *holder's* option, usually at 6-month intervals.

Such notes represent a long-term commitment on the part of the borrower, yet provide the lender with all the characteristics of a short-term obligation. They are typically available to investors in minimum denominations of $1,000. However, although the 6-month redemption feature provides liquidity, the variable rates can cause the issues to experience wide swings in semiannual coupons.[26]

ZERO COUPON AND DEEP DISCOUNT BONDS   The typical corporate bond has a coupon and maturity. In turn, the value of the bond is the present value of the stream of cash flows (interest and principal) discounted at the required yield to maturity (YTM). Alternatively, some bonds do not have any coupons or have coupons that are below the market rate at the time of issue. Such securities are referred to as *zero coupon* or *minicoupon bonds* or *original-issue, discount (OID) bonds.* A zero coupon discount

[25]For an overview of these securities, see K. Jeanne Person, "A Review of Asset-Backed Securities" (New York: Salomon Brothers, 1987); Andrew S. Carron, "Asset-Backed Securities," in *The Handbook of Fixed-Income Securities,* 3d ed., edited by Frank J. Fabozzi (Homewood, Ill.: Business One Irwin, 1991); and Joseph Norton and Paul Spellman, eds., *Asset Securitization* (Oxford, England: Blackwell Finance, 1991). The presentations consider not only CARs but several other asset-backed securities including debt backed by credit card obligations and boat loans. During 1991–1992, the fastest growing segment has been credit card debt.

[26]For an extended discussion, see Richard S. Wilson, "Domestic Floating-Rate and Adjustable-Rate Debt Securities," in *The Handbook of Fixed-Income Securities,* 3d ed., edited by Frank J. Fabozzi (Homewood, Ill.: Business One Irwin, 1991). Adjustable-rate preferred stocks are also discussed in Richard S. Wilson, *Corporate Senior Securities* (Chicago: Probus Publishing, 1987), Chapter 6.

bond promises to pay a stipulated principal amount at a future maturity date, but it does not promise to make any interim interest payments. Therefore, the price of the bond is the present value of the principal payment at the maturity date using the required discount rate for this bond. The return on the bond is the difference between what the investor pays for the bond at the time of purchase and the principal payment at maturity.

Consider a zero coupon, $10,000 par value bond with a 20-year maturity. If the required rate of return on bonds of equal maturity and quality is 8 percent and we assume semiannual discounting, the initial selling price would be $2,082.89, because the present value factor at 8 percent compounded semiannually for 20 years is 0.208289. From the time of purchase to the point of maturity, the investor would not receive any cash flow from the firm. The investor must pay taxes, however, on the implied interest on the bond, although no cash is received. Because an investor subject to taxes would experience severe negative cash flows during the life of these bonds, they are primarily of interest to investment accounts not subject to taxes, such as pensions, IRAs, or Keogh accounts.[27]

A modified form of zero coupon bonds is the original-issue, discount (OID) bond where the coupon is set substantially below the prevailing market rate, for example, a 5 percent coupon on a bond when market rates are 12 percent. As a result, the bond is issued at a deep discount from par value. Again, taxes must be paid on the implied 12 percent return rather than the nominal 5 percent, so the cash flow disadvantage of zero coupon bonds, though lessened, remains.

HIGH-YIELD BONDS   A segment of the corporate bond market that has grown in size, importance, and controversy is *high-yield bonds,* also referred to as *speculative-grade bonds* and *junk bonds.* These are corporate bonds that have been assigned a bond rating by the rating agencies as noninvestment grade, that is, a rating below BBB or Baa. The title of speculative-grade bonds is probably the most objective because bonds that are not rated investment grade are speculative grade. The designation of *high-yield bonds* was by Drexel Burnham Lambert as an indication of the returns available for these bonds relative to Treasury bonds and investment-grade corporate bonds. The *junk bond* designation is obviously somewhat derogatory referring to the quality of the issues.

BRIEF HISTORY OF THE HIGH-YIELD BOND MARKET   Based on a specification that bonds rated below BBB make up the high-yield market, this segment has been in existence for as long as there have been rating agencies. A major difference with this category pre- and post-1980 is that prior to 1980 most of the high-yield bonds were referred to as *fallen angels.* These are bonds that were originally issued as investment grade securities but because of changes in the firm over time, the bonds were downgraded into the high-yield sector (BB and below).

The market changed in the late 1970's when Drexel Burnham Lambert began aggressively underwriting high-yield bonds for two groups of clients: (1) small firms that did not have the financial strength to receive an investment-grade rating by the rating agencies, and (2) large and small firms that issued high-yield bonds in connection with leveraged buyouts (LBOs). The high-yield bond market went from a residual market

---

[27]These bonds will be discussed further in Chapter 15 in the section on duration and immunization. The price volatility of zero coupon bonds in IRA accounts is discussed in Randall Smith, "Zero Coupon Bonds' Price Swings Jolt Investors Looking for Security," *The Wall Street Journal,* June 1, 1984, 19.

TABLE 13.5

High-Yield Bond Issues: Annual Dollar Value, Number, Average Size, and Percentage of All Public Debt Issues ($ millions)

	Total Par Value: New High-Yield Debt Issues			Par Value of Total Corporate Issues	
	Amount	Number	Average Size	Total Value	High Yield as Percentage of Total
1977	1,040	61	17.0	26,314	3.95
1978	1,578	82	19.2	21,557	7.32
1979	1,400	56	25.0	25,831	5.42
1980	1,429	45	31.8	36,905	3.87
1981	1,536	34	45.2	40,784	3.77
1982	2,692	52	51.8	47,209	5.70
1983	7,765	95	81.7	38,373	20.24
1984	15,239	131	116.3	82,492	18.47
1985	15,685	175	89.6	80,477	19.49
1986	33,262	226	147.2	156,051	21.31
1987	30,522	190	160.6	126,134	24.20
1988	31,095	160	194.3	134,792	23.07
1989	28,753	130	221.2	142,791	20.14
1990	1,397	10	139.7	109,284	1.28
1991	9,967	48	207.6	207,301	4.81
1992	39,755	245	162.3	317,606	12.52

Source: Securities Data Company and Martin S. Fridson, "This Year in High Yield," *Extra Credit* (New York: Merrill Lynch & Co., January/February 1993). Reprinted by permission of Merrill Lynch. All Rights Reserved.

that included fallen angels to a new-issue market where bonds were underwritten with below-investment grade ratings.

The individual who is credited with leading the development of this new-issue, high-yield market is Michael Milken, a bond trader/salesman at Drexel Burnham Lambert (DBL). Milken examined the returns and risks related to speculative-grade securities pre-1975 and became convinced that the promised and realized rates of returns on these speculative-grade bonds was higher than justified by their default experience. He convinced a number of institutional investors of the superior risk-adjusted returns available on these bonds, which helped create a demand for them. At the same time, Milken and DBL became active in underwriting a large number of these high-yield bond issues for small firms and LBOs.[28] As a result, the high-yield bond market exploded in size and activity beginning in 1983. As shown in Table 13.5, there were a limited number of new high-yield issues in the late 1970s, and they were not very large issues (the average size was less than $30 million). Therefore, they accounted for only about 4 to 7 percent of all public straight debt issues. Beginning in 1983, more large issues became common (the average size of an issue in 1989 was over $200 million) and high-yield issues became a significant percentage of the total new-issue bond market (between

---

[28]Subsequent to the growth and development of the high-yield bond market, Michael Milken and DBL were indicted for securities law violations. DBL settled with the SEC and paid a fine without admitting guilt. In early 1990 Milken agreed to plea bargain with the SEC that involved a fine and a prison term. It is the author's opinion that observers should separate the development of the high-yield bond market and the securities law violations. While not condoning the security law violations, almost everyone would acknowledge that the development of the high-yield debt market has had a positive impact on the capital-raising ability of the economy. For an analysis of this impact, see Glenn Yago, *Junk Bonds* (New York: Oxford University Press, 1991); and Kevin J. Perry and Robert A. Taggart, Jr., "The Growing Role of Junk Bonds in Corporate Finance," *Journal of Applied Corporate Finance* 1, no. 1 (Spring 1988): 37–45.

TABLE 13.6

Distribution of Ratings for High-Yield Bonds: December 31, 1991 and December 31, 1992

Average S&P Rating	By Par Amount		By Number of Issues	
	1992	1991	1992	1991
BB	32.5%	26.8%	53.9%	51.8%
B	48.7	47.4	31.0	30.5
CCC	18.8	25.8	15.7	17.7

Source: Martin S. Fridson, "This Year in High Yield," *Extra Credit* (New York: Merrill Lynch & Co., January/February 1993). Reprinted by permission of Merrill Lynch. All Rights Reserved.

TABLE 13.7

Distribution of Ownership of High-Yield Bonds: December 31, 1988

	Percentage Ownership
Mutual funds, money managers	30
Insurance companies	30
Pension funds	15
Foreign investors	9
Savings and loans	7
Individuals	5
Corporations	3
Securities dealers	1

Source: "1989 High Yield Market Report" (New York: Drexel Burnham Lambert, March 1989).

15 and 20 percent). Of all the high-yield issues sold since 1978, about 94 percent have been sold since 1983. As of 1992 the total amount of high-yield debt constituted about 20 percent of all public debt in the United States.

An important point bears repeating: Although the high-yield debt market has existed for many years, its real emergence as a significant factor and a major component of the U.S. capital market did not occur until 1983. This is relevant when one considers the liquidity and default experience for these securities.

DISTRIBUTION OF RATINGS   Table 13.6 contains the distribution of ratings for all outstanding high-yield issues as of December 31, 1991 and 1992. As shown, the heavy concentration by par amount is in the B class, which contains almost half of all issues. When measured by the number of issues, the concentration is in the BB class, which implies that the average size of B-rated issues is much larger. A notable change in 1992 was the continuing shift toward higher quality issues—i.e., the proportion of BB issues (par value) went from about 27 percent to almost 33 percent while the CCC component went from about 26 to 19 percent.

OWNERSHIP OF HIGH-YIELD BONDS   As shown in Table 13.7, the major owners of high-yield bonds have been mutual funds, insurance companies, and pension funds. As of the end of 1988, there were almost 100 mutual funds that were either exclusively directed to invest in high-yield bonds, or included such bonds in their portfolio. More recent data on this distribution are not available, but most observers agree that there has been a shift away from insurance companies and savings and loans toward mutual funds.

TABLE 13.8   **Lead Underwriters of New High-Yield Bond Issues: 1991, First Half 1992**

	1991			First Half 1992		
Managers	**Proceeds ($ millions)**	**Market Share (%)**	**Number of Issues**	**Proceeds ($ millions)**	**Market Share (%)**	**Number of Issues**
Merrill Lynch	$ 3,887.9	36.5%	9	$ 2,787.8	14.4%	10
Goldman, Sachs	2,429.8	22.8	22	2,642.1	13.7	15
Morgan Stanley	1,194.1	11.2	6	2,503.8	13.0	12
First Boston	634.1	5.9	5	2,943.2	15.2	16
Salomon Brothers	622.2	5.8	4	1,147.1	5.9	6
Donaldson Lufkin	598.5	5.6	3	2,568.0	13.3	14
Lehman Brothers	346.9	3.3	2	1,506.7	7.8	10
Bankers Trust	299.3	2.8	2	425.0	2.2	2
Wasserstein Perella	200.0	1.9	1	—[a]	—	—
Citicorp	175.0	1.6	1	—	—	—
Bear Stearns	—	—	—	1,186.7	6.1	7
J. P. Morgan	—	—	—	550.0	2.8	3
Industry Total[b]	$10,657.0	—	60	$19,306.6	—	110

[a]Dash indicates manager not in top ten list during this period.

[b]This is the total for the industry, not only for the top 10 underwriters.

This distribution of ownership among a number of groups including institutions willing to trade these bonds is an important contributor to the liquidity of this market. Wider distribution gives bondholders more opportunities to find buyers or sellers.

MAJOR UNDERWRITERS   Table 13.8 lists the major investment banking firms that acted as lead underwriters for high-yield bonds for the year 1991 and the first half of 1992. It demonstrates two important points: (1) the reasonably diverse market share among the major underwriters following the demise of Drexel Burnham, which was evident during 1992 when the market was very active and five underwriters had double-digit market share and the range among the five firms was only 13.0 to 15.2 percent, and (2) the strong recovery of the high-yield market in terms of new issues during 1992 compared to 1990, when there were almost no new issues, and 1991, which initiated the recovery. As shown, the value of new issues during the first half of 1992 was almost double the total for all of 1991. As shown in Table 13.5, the full year total in 1992 was almost $40 billion compared to about $10 billion in 1991.

The point is, although Drexel Burnham Lambert was the major underwriter before it declared bankruptcy in early 1990, a number of other firms have established expertise and a clientele for these securities. Clearly, it is a positive factor for the liquidity of this market that there are more firms involved in underwriting and trading these securities. Therefore, although the market experienced great uncertainty during 1989 and 1990, the market survived and most observers expected it to be a major component of the corporate bond market.

The purpose of this discussion has been to introduce you to high-yield bonds because of the growth in size and importance of this segment of the market for individual and institutional investors. We will revisit this topic in the chapter on bond portfolio management, where we will review the historical rates of return and alternative risk factors including the default experience for these bonds. All of this must be considered by potential investors in these securities.[29]

JAPANESE CORPORATE BOND MARKET

The corporate bond market in Japan is made up of two components: (1) bonds issued by industrial firms or utilities and (2) bonds issued by banks to finance loans to corporations. As noted in connection with Table 13.2, the pure corporate bond sector has declined in relative size over time to less than 4 percent of the total. In contrast, the dollar amount of bank debentures has increased over time to about 20 percent of the total.

Japanese corporate bonds are monitored by the *Kisaikai,* which is the council for the regulation of bond issues. The council is composed of 22 bond-related banks and seven major securities companies. It operates under the authority of the Ministry of Finance (MOF) and the Bank of Japan (BOJ) to determine bond-issuing procedures including conditions for corporate debt. Specifically, the Kisaikai fixes the coupons on corporate bonds in relation to coupons on long-term government bonds to prevent any competition with the government bond market.

Because of numerous bankruptcies during the 1930s depression, the government mandated that all corporate debt be secured, and this was enforced by the Kisaikai. There was pressure by corporations and securities firms during the 1970s and 1980s to relax these requirements. Before this was allowed, domestic Japanese firms began issuing convertible bonds because they were not bound by the collateral rule. Also, foreign firms began issuing Euroyen bonds that were not restricted, and domestic firms began selling straight debt in the Euroyen market. Finally, early in 1987 a large number of firms were allowed to issue unsecured debt. This allowance was broadened in late 1987, and the requirement was abolished during 1988.

The issuance of unsecured debt has led to the birth of bond-rating agencies, which were not needed with completely secured debt. The Japan Bond Research Institute was established in 1979, followed by Mikuni's Credit Rating Company in 1981 and by additional firms in 1985 and 1986: Japan Credit Rating Agency, Ltd.; Nippon Investors Service, Inc.; and Moody's Japan K.K. (a subsidiary of Moody's Investors Service, Inc.).

CORPORATE BOND SEGMENTS   The corporate debt market in Japan is divided into two major segments: bonds issued by electric power supply companies and bonds issued by all other corporations. The nine electric power supply firms receive preferential treatment because they are regulated public utilities. As a result, about 75 percent of all domestic bond issues are public utility bonds. Corporate bonds for other industrial firms are sold in the domestic market and in the Eurobond market.

[29]For additional discussion of these bonds, see Edward I. Altman and Scott A. Nammacher, *Investing in Junk Bonds* (New York: John Wiley & Sons, 1987); Hilary Rosenberg, "The Unsinkable Junk Bond," *Institutional Investor* 23, no. 1 (January 1989): 43–48; Robert Solof, "Historical Perspectives on the Use of High Yield Securities in Corporate Creation: A Hundred Years of 'Junk' " (New York: Drexel Burnham Lambert, February 1989); Edward I. Altman, ed., *The High Yield Debt Market* (Homewood, Ill.: Dow Jones-Irwin, 1990); Frank J. Fabozzi, ed., *The New High Yield Debt Market* (New York: Harper Business, 1990); Martin S. Fridson, *High Yield Bonds* (Chicago: Probus Publishing, 1989); and Frank K. Reilly, ed., *High Yield Bonds: Analysis and Risk Assessment* (Charlottesville, Va.: Institute of Chartered Financial Analysts, 1990).

The Ministry of Finance specifies minimum corporate requirements and issuing requirements, including a stipulation that net corporate assets must exceed 6 billion yen. Also, the ministry controls the month and issuance system that specifies who can issue bonds and when they can be issued. In addition, lead-underwriting managers are predetermined in accordance with a lead manager rotation system that insures balance among the big-four securities firms in Japan (Nomura, Nikko, Daiwa, and Yamaichi Capital Management).

BANK BONDS   The substantial issuance of bank bonds is because of the banking system in Japan, which is segmented into the following rigidly defined components:

- Commercial banks (13 big-city banks and 64 regional banks)
- Long-term credit banks (3)
- Mutual loan and savings banks (6)
- Specialized financial institutions

During the reconstruction after World War II, several banks were permitted to obtain funding by issuing medium- and long-term debentures at rates above yields on government bonds. These funds were used to make mortgage loans to firms in the industrial sector to rebuild plant and equipment. Currently these financial institutions sell 5-year coupon debentures and 1-year discount debentures directly to individual and institutional investors. The long-term credit banks are not allowed to take deposits and thus depend on the debentures to obtain funds. These bonds are traded in the OTC market.[30]

GERMAN CORPORATE BOND MARKET

Germany likewise has a combination sector in corporates that includes pure corporate bonds and bank bonds. Here the contrast is even larger, because the nonbank corporate bonds are almost nonexistent, whereas the bank bonds make up over 60 percent of the total bond market.

Bank bonds may be issued in collateralized or uncollateralized form. For the collateralized bonds the largest categories are mortgage bonds and commercial bonds.

German mortgage bonds are collateralized bonds of the issuing bank backed by mortgage loans registered with a government-appointed trustee. Due to the supervision of these bonds and the mortgage collateral, these bonds are considered to be very high quality. They are issued in bearer or registered form. Most registered bonds are sold to domestic institutions and cannot be listed on a stock exchange because they are not considered to be securities. Alternatively, the bearer bonds, which are transferred by book-entry, are sold in small denominations, traded on the exchanges, and enjoy an active secondary market.

German commercial bonds are subject to the same regulation and collateralization as mortgage bonds. The difference is that the collateral consists of loans to or guarantees by a German public-sector entity rather than a first mortgage. Possible borrowers include the federal government, its agencies (the federal railway or the post office), federal states, and agencies of the European Economic Community (EEC). The credit quality of these loans is excellent. Mortgage and commercial bonds have identical credit standing and trade at very narrow spreads.

---

[30]For further discussion of this market, see Aron Viner, *Inside Japanese Financial Markets* (Homewood, Ill.: Dow Jones-Irwin, 1988), Chapters 5 and 6; and Frank J. Fabozzi, ed., *The Japanese Bond Markets* (Chicago: Probus Publishing, 1990).

Schuldscheindarlehen are private loan agreements between borrowers and large investors (usually a bank) who make the loan but who can (with the borrower's permission) sell them or divide the loans among several investors. These instruments are like a negotiable loan participation. All participants receive a copy of the loan agreement, and a letter of assignment gives the participant title to a share of principal and interest, although the bank acts as the agent. These loan agreements, which come in various sizes, account for a substantial proportion of all funds raised in Germany. There is a large volume of these private loan agreements, but the market is not very liquid. Hence, they are typically used for the investment of large sums to maturity.

U.K. CORPORATE BOND MARKET

Corporate bonds in the United Kingdom are available in three forms: debentures, unsecured loans, and convertible bonds. The values of securities in each class are about equal (about 3 billion pounds). The corporate bond market was fairly inactive prior to the 1980s because of high long-term interest rates, but it experienced a resurgence in the 1980s with lower inflation.

Numerous borrowers offered bonds secured by property or prior calls on the revenue of the issuers. At the same time, many large corporations and banks raised funds through unsecured borrowing. Also, there was significant growth in convertible bonds.

The maturity structure of the corporate bond market is fairly wide. During the 1960s and 1970s most securities were short-term, but this changed during the 1980s when preference shifted toward long maturity bonds. The coupon structure of corporate bonds features low-coupon bonds issued during the 1960s and 1970s and high-coupon bonds issued during the 1980s. The higher end of the coupon range, which goes from 10 to 14 percent, is due to the unsecured segment of this market with convertible bonds having the low coupons. Almost all U.K. corporate bonds are callable term bonds.

Corporate bonds in the United Kingdom have been issued through both public offerings underwritten by investment bankers and private placements. Early in the 1980s, the market tended toward private placements. Since the Big Bang in October 1986, there have been more public offerings through investment banking firms. Prior to the Big Bang, corporate bonds were traded on the stock exchange by brokers and jobbers. Subsequently, a number of primary dealers have begun trading corporate bonds directly with each other. All corporate bonds are issued in registered form.

INTERNATIONAL BONDS

Each country's international bond market has two components. The first, *foreign bonds,* are issues sold primarily in one country and currency by a borrower of a different nationality. An example would be U.S. dollar denominated bonds sold in the United States by a Japanese firm. (These are referred to as *Yankee bonds.*) Second, are *Eurobonds,* which are bonds underwritten by international bond syndicates and sold in several national markets. An example would be Eurodollar bonds that are securities denominated in U.S. dollars, underwritten by an international syndicate, and sold to non-U.S. investors outside the United States. The relative size of these two markets (foreign bonds versus Eurobonds) varies by country.

UNITED STATES

The Eurodollar bond market has been much larger than the Yankee bond market (about $350 billion versus $50 billion). However, because the Eurodollar bond market is heavily affected by changes in the value of the U.S. dollar, it experienced a major setback when the dollar weakened during 1986, 1987, 1991, and 1992. Such periods have created a desire for diversification by investors.

Yankee bonds are issued by foreign firms who register with the SEC and borrow U.S. dollars, using issues underwritten by a U.S. syndicate for delivery in the United States. These bonds are traded in the United States and pay interest semiannually. Over 60 percent of Yankee bonds are issued by Canadian corporations and typically have shorter maturities than U.S. domestic issues. Finally, they typically have longer call protection, which increases their appeal.

The Eurodollar bond market is dominated by foreign investors, and the center of trading is in London. Eurodollar bonds pay interest annually, so it is necessary to adjust the standard yield calculation that assumes semiannual compounding. The Eurodollar bond market historically comprised almost 50 percent of the total Eurobond market.

JAPAN

The Japanese international bond market was historically dominated (over 90 percent) by foreign bonds (Samurai bonds) with the balance in Euroyen bonds. In 1985 the issuance requirements for Euroyen bonds was liberalized. Subsequently, the ratio of issuance by Samurai versus Euroyen has been heavily in favor of Euroyen bonds.

Samurai bonds are yen-denominated bonds issued by non-Japanese issuers and mainly sold in Japan, for example, a yen-denominated bond sold in Tokyo by IBM. The market is fairly small and has limited liquidity, but the bonds are not subject to withholding taxes. The market has experienced very little growth in terms of yen, but substantial growth in U.S. dollar terms because of changes in the exchange rate.

Euroyen bonds are yen-denominated bonds sold in markets outside Japan by international syndicates. As indicated, this market has grown substantially since 1985 because of the liberal issue requirements and favorable exchange rate movements which makes yen-denominated securities desirable.

GERMANY

All deutschemark bonds of foreign issuers can be considered Eurobonds. This is because the stability of the German currency reduces the importance of the distinction between foreign bonds (DM-denominated bonds sold in Germany by non-German firms that are underwritten by domestic institutions) and Euro-DM bonds (DM bonds sold outside Germany and underwritten by international firms). Both types of bonds share the same primary and secondary market procedures, are free of German taxes, and have similar yields.

Recently a Euro-DM bond was issued secured by a Schuldscheindarlehen loan from one of the Federal states (Lander). They have also issued Euro-DM floating-rate notes (FRN) fixed to various rates, including the DM London Inter-Bank Offered Rate (LIBOR).

UNITED KINGDOM

U.K. foreign bonds, referred to as *bulldog bonds,* are sterling-denominated bonds issued by non-English firms and sold in London. Eurosterling bonds are sold in markets outside London by international syndicates.

Similar to other countries, the U.K. international bond market has become dominated by the Eurosterling bonds. By the late 1980s, the ratio of Eurobonds versus foreign bonds had grown to almost five-to-one. The procedure for issuing and trading Eurosterling bonds is similar to that of other Eurobonds.

OBTAINING INFORMATION ON BONDS

As might be expected, the data needs of bond investors are considerably different from those of stockholders. For one thing, there is less emphasis on fundamental analysis because, except for speculative-grade bonds and revenue obligations, most bond investors rely on the rating agencies for credit analysis. An exception would be large institutions that employ in-house analysts to confirm assigned agency ratings or to uncover incremental return opportunities. Because of the large investments by these institutions, the total dollar rewards from only a few basis points can be substantial. As you might expect, the institutions enjoy economies of scale in research. Finally, there are a few private research firms that concentrate on the independent appraisal of bonds.

REQUIRED INFORMATION

In addition to information on the risk of default, bond investors need information on (1) market and economic conditions and (2) intrinsic bond features. Market and economic information allows investors to stay abreast of the general tone of the bond market, overall interest rate developments, and yield-spread behavior in different market sectors. Bond investors also require information on bond indenture provisions such as call features and sinking-fund provisions.

Some of this information is readily available in such popular publications as *The Wall Street Journal, Barron's, Business Week, Fortune*, and *Forbes*, which were discussed in Chapter 5. In addition, two popular sources of bond data are the *Federal Reserve Bulletin* and the *Survey of Current Business*, which were also described in Chapter 5.

In addition, a number of other sources of specific information are important to bond investors. The following are specifically concerned with information and analysis of bonds. Some of them were publications discussed in Chapter 5.

- *Treasury Bulletin* (monthly)
- *Standard & Poor's Bond Guide* (monthly)
- *Moody's Bond Record* (monthly)
- *Moody's Bond Survey* (weekly)
- *Fitch Rating Register* (monthly)
- *Fitch Corporate Credit Analysis* (monthly)
- *Fitch Municipal Credit Analysis* (monthly)
- *Investment Dealers Digest* (weekly)
- *Credit Markets* (weekly)
- *Duff & Phelps Credit Decisions* (weekly)
- *The Bond Buyer* (daily)

SOURCES OF BOND QUOTES

The listed information sources fill three needs of investors: evaluating the risk of default, staying abreast of bond market and interest rate conditions, and obtaining information on specific bonds. Another important data need is current bond quotes and prices.

Unfortunately, many of the prime sources of bond prices are not widely distributed. For example, *Bank and Quotation Record* is a valuable, though not widely circulated, source that provides monthly price information for government and agency bonds, listed and OTC corporate bonds, municipal bonds, and money market instruments. Current quotes on municipal bonds are available only through a fairly costly publication that is used by many financial institutions, called *The Blue List of Current Municipal Offerings.* It contains over 100 pages of price quotes for municipal bonds, municipal notes, and industrial development and pollution-control revenue bonds.

Daily information on all publicly traded Treasury issues, most agency obligations, and numerous corporate issues is published in *The Wall Street Journal.* Similar data are available weekly in *Barron's.* Both publications include corporate bond quotes for bonds listed on the New York and American exchanges that represent a minor portion of the total corporate bond market. You will recall that the majority of corporate bond trading is on the OTC market. Finally, major bond dealers maintain firm quotes on a variety of issues for clients.

INTERPRETING BOND QUOTES

Essentially, all bonds are quoted on the basis of either yield or price. Price quotes are always interpreted as a *percentage of par.* For example, a quote of 98½ is not interpreted as $98.50, but 98½ percent of par. The dollar price is derived from the quote, given the par value. If the par value is $5,000 on a municipal bond, then the price of an issue quoted at 98½ would be $4,925. Actually, the market follows three systems of bond pricing: one system for corporates, another for governments (both Treasury and agency obligations), and a third for municipals.

CORPORATE BOND QUOTES

Figure 13.1 is a listing of NYSE corporate bond quotes that appeared in *The Wall Street Journal* on June 16, 1993. The data pertain to trading activity on June 15. Several quotes have been designated for illustrative purposes. The first issue designated in column one is an IBM issue and is representative of most corporate prices. In particular, the 7¼ 02 indicates the coupon and maturity of the obligation; in this case, the IBM issue carries a 7.25 percent coupon and matures in 2002. The next column provides the *current* yield of the obligation and is found by comparing the coupon to the current market price. For example, a bond with a 7.25 percent coupon selling for 104.625 would have a 6.9 percent current yield. This is *not* the YTM or even necessarily a good approximation to it. Both of these yields will be discussed in Chapter 14.

The next column gives the volume of $1,000 par value bonds traded that day (in this case, 33 bonds were traded). The next column indicates closing quotes, followed by the column for the net change in the closing price from the last day the issue was traded. In this case, IBM closed at 104⅝, which was up ⅜ from the prior day.

The second bond in Column 1 is for the LTV 13⅞ of 02 bond, which has two unique features that make a significant difference. The "vj" in front of all the LTV bonds indicates that the firm is in receivership or bankruptcy. The small letter *"f"* that follows the maturity date of the obligation means that the issue is trading *flat,* which means the issuer is not meeting its interest payments. Therefore, the coupon of the obligation is currently inconsequential, and the dash in the current yield column indicates there are no payments.

The third bond in Column 2 is Marriott zr 06, which refers to a Marriott Corp. zero coupon bond ("zr") due in 2006. As discussed, zero coupon securities do not pay interest but are redeemed at par at maturity. Because there is no coupon, they sell at a deep discount, which implies a yield. Again, since there are no coupon payments, they do not report a current yield.

FIGURE 13.1 **Sample Corporate Bond Quotations**

NEW YORK EXCHANGE BONDS

Quotations as of 4 p.m. Eastern Time
Tuesday, June 15, 1993

Volume $47,000,000

	Domestic Tue.	Domestic Mon.	All Issues Tue.	All Issues Mon.
Issues traded	459	445	462	446
Advances	190	176	192	177
Declines	169	150	169	150
Unchanged	100	119	101	119
New highs	33	28	34	28
New lows	3	3	3	3⅝

SALES SINCE JANUARY 1
(000 omitted)

1993	1992	1991
$5,095,588	$5,768,292	$6,535,732

Dow Jones Bond Averages

–1992– High	–1992– Low	–1993– High	–1993– Low		–1993– Close	–1993– Chg.	–1993– %Yld	–1992– Close	–1992– Chg.
103.89	98.41	107.67	103.49	20 Bonds	107.53	+0.06	6.73	100.08	+ 0.14
103.31	98.45	104.78	102.30	10 Utilities	104.58	+0.05	7.18	99.70	+ 0.06
105.14	97.26	110.86	104.58	10 Industrials	110.48	+0.07	6.29	100.46	+ 0.22

	Bonds	Cur Yld	Vol	Close	Net Chg
	Grace zr06	...	23	37¼	...
	GreyF zr94	...	84	95½	+ ¼
	GrowGp 8½06	cv	13	136	– ½
	Gulfrd 6s12	cv	6	99	– ½
	GlfUSA 10⅞97f	...	72	21	+ ⅞
	GlfUSA 12½04f	...	6	20	+ 1
	Hallb zr06	...	50	46⅞	...
	Hallwd na13½09	...	25	97½	+ ⅝
	HeclMn zr04	...	145	41¾	– ¼
	v|Hills 11s02f	cv	20	5	+ 1
	HmGrp 14⅞99	14.2	57	104½	– ½
	HockV 4½99r	5.0	10	90¼	– ⅜
	HomeDp 4½97	cv	35	131	– 1
	HudFd 8s06	cv	2	100¼	– ¼
	Huffy 7¼14	cv	15	110½	+ ½
	ICN 12⅞98	12.6	59	102⅛	– ¾
	IMC Fer 6¼01	cv	10	79	– 2½
	IllBel 8s04	7.8	5	103⅛	...
	IllBel 8¼16	7.9	5	104¼	– ⅛
	IllPw 8¼07	8.0	10	103	+ ⅞
	Inco 7¾16	7.5	107	103⅞	– ⅞
	IndBel 8⅛17	7.8	49	104½	+ ⅛
	InldStl 9½00	9.4	36	101⅛	– ⅞
	Intlgc 11.99s96f	...	6	90½	...
	IBM 9s98	8.4	39	107½	+ ⅜
	IBM 8⅜19	7.7	125	108½	+ ⅛
	IBM 6⅜97	6.2	120	102½	– ¼
① →	IBM 7¼02	6.9	33	104⅝	+ ⅜
	IBM 7½13	7.5	2226	100	...
	IntTch 9⅜96	9.8	77	95½	– ⅞
	Jamswy 8s05	cv	297	33½	– 23
	v|JonsLI 6¾94f	...	200	8	...
	K mart 8⅛97	8.1	176	100½	– ⅛
	K mart 8⅜17	8.0	35	105	+ ⅜
	KaufB 9⅜03	9.0	121	103¾	+ ⅛
	Kenn 7⅞01	7.8	5	100⅝	– 1⅛
	KerrGp 13s96	12.6	7	103⅛	– ¼
	Kolmrg 8¾09	cv	5	89¾	– ⅛
	Kroger 9s99	8.7	170	103⅜	+ ⅛
	Kroger 6⅜99	cv	5	118½	+ ¼
	v|LTV 5s88mf	...	15	7⅜	...
	v|LTV 11s07f	...	280	7⅛	+ ⅛
② →	v|LTV 13⅞02f	...	70	22¾	– ⅛
	v|LTV 95t f	...	1	7⅞	– ¼
	v|LTV 14s04f	...	10	23½	– ½
	v|LTV 11½97f	...	11	7¼	– ⅛
	v|LTV 7⅞98f	...	8	7	– ⅜
	v|LTV 8¾98f	...	600	7¼	– ⅛
	v|LTV 10⅜99f	...	50	21½	– ½
	v|LTV 15s00f	...	60	22⅜	– ¼
	v|LTV Int 5s88f	cv	70	26	– ¾
	LaFrg 7s13	cv	10	101	– 2
	Leucadia 5¼03	...	5	95½	+ ¼
	Liberte 10½93f	...	23	85½	+ 1 3/16
	LoewCp zr04	...	65	51⅛	...
	LglsLt 11¾94	10.9	50	107½	...
	LglsLt 8.9s19	8.3	5	106¾	+ ½
	LglsLt 8.2s23	8.0	20	102⅛	+ ⅛
	LouN 2⅞03	4.1	6	70¼	– 2¼
	MACOM 9¼06	cv	53	102	+ ⅛

Bonds	Cur Yld	Vol	Close	Net Chg	
MGM Grd 12s02	10.6	10	113⅝	+ ⅞	
MGMUA 13s96f	...	65	101½	– ½	
MfrH 8⅛04	7.9	9	102½	+ 1	
Manvl zr03	...	50	93¼	+ ½	
MarO 9½94	9.2	50	103 5/32	– 1/32	
MarO 9¾99	8.9	41	109⅜	– ⅛	
Marriott zr06	...	38	35½	+ ¼	← ③
Masco 5¼12	cv	4	97½	+ ⅜	
McDInv 8s11	cv	10	110	– ¼	
McDnl zr94	...	140	97 15/16	+ 1/16	
McDnl 8 11	7.7	10	116	– ¾	
McDnlDg 7⅞97	7.8	109	100⅜	– ⅛	
McDnlDg 8⅝97	8.3	92	104⅜	– ¼	
McDnlDg 9¼02	8.9	405	103½	+ ¼	
McDnlDg 9¾12	9.3	433	105	+ ¼	
Mead 6¾12	cv	16	105	– ½	← ④
Medplx 11¾02	11.0	54	107	+ ⅛	
MerLyStkMk 97	...	5	99⅞	– 1⅛	
MerLyGlbl 98	...	30	100½	+ ¾	
MerLyStkMk 99	...	100	99½	...	
MesaC 13½99f	...	739	101⅛	+ ⅞	
MichB 7¾11	7.6	10	102⅜	– ⅛	
MichB 7s12	7.0	25	100⅜	+ ⅛	
MichB 8⅛15	7.8	11	104⅛	– ½	
MKT 5½33f	...	45	56	+ ¾	
Mobil 8⅝21	7.6	60	114	+ 1	
Monog 10s99	10.4	4	96	...	
Monog 11s04	11.2	11	98½	– ½	
Motrla zr09	...	25	77¾	...	
MtSTl 7⅜11	7.2	10	102	– ¾	
MtSTl 7¾13	7.6	27	102⅛	+ ⅜	
MtSTl 8s17	7.7	62	104	+ ⅛	
MtSTl 8⅝cld	...	15	104⅜	...	
NCNB 8⅜99	8.2	20	102⅛	+ ⅛	
NJBTl 7¼11	7.2	5	100⅞	...	
NJBTl 7⅜12	7.2	20	101¾	...	
NJBTl 7¾13	7.5	11	102⅞	...	
NRut 8½98	7.7	5	111	...	
v|NtGyp zr04	...	83	2½	+ ¼	
NInd 10s99	10.0	1	99¾	...	
NtEdu 6½11	cv	22	74½	– ½	
NavFin 11.95s95	11.8	43	101½	+ ⅛	
Navstr 9s04	9.5	27	94¼	– ⅛	
NETelTel 4½02	5.1	4	88⅛	+ 1	
NETelTel 6⅛06	6.4	16	96¼	+ 1¼	
NETelTel 6¼03	6.3	50	99½	+ ⅞	
NYTel 4⅝97	4.8	25	96½	...	
NYTel 7½09	7.4	10	101⅞	+ ¼	
NYTel 7¾06	7.6	2	102½	...	
NYTel 8s08	7.8	46	102½	...	
NYTel 8.3s12	8.0	13	103½	– ¼	
NYTel 8⅝16	8.3	89	103⅝	+ ⅛	
NYTel 8¾23	8.3	23	105	+ ¼	
NoPac 4s97st	4.2	5	95½	+ ⅛	
NorfW 4s96r	4.2	1	96	...	
Novacr 5½2000	cv	10	95¼	+ ¾	
NwnBl 7⅞11	7.7	33	102½	– 1½	
NwnBl 8⅛17	7.9	47	103½	– ¼	
OcciP 11¾11	10.0	20	118	...	
OcciP 10¾98	9.6	12	111½	...	
OcciP 9⅝99	8.7	63	110¼	+ ⅝	
OcciP 10⅛01	8.5	40	119⅛	– 1½	
OhBIT 7½11	7.3	15	102⅜	+ ⅜	
OhBIT 7⅞13	7.6	2	103	...	
OutbM 7s02	cv	183	106	...	
OwIll 10¼99	9.5	421	107½	...	
OwIll 11s03	9.6	3	115⅛	+ ⅛	
OwnIll 10s02	9.4	20	106½	+ ⅛	
OwnIll 9¾04	9.2	60	106	...	
OxyOG 6⅛97	6.2	30	99½	+ ¼	
PNwT 9cld	...	68	104 7/32	...	
PacTT 8⅜17	8.0	25	105¼	...	
PacTT 9s18	8.5	20	106	+ ¼	
PacBell 7½33	7.6	328	99	– ¼	
PacBell 6¼05	6.4	309	98¼	+ ¼	
PacBell 7⅛26	7.3	275	97	– ½	
PGE 8s2003	7.7	10	104	+ ¾	
PacScl 7¾03	cv	16	96½	+ 1	
ParCm 7s03A	7.0	39	99⅞	+ ⅛	
ParCm 7s03B	7.0	1	99⅞	+ ⅛	
Paten 8¼12	cv	15	80	– 1	
PennC 11cld	...	73	106	+ ⅛	

EXPLANATORY NOTES
(For New York and American Bonds)

Yield is Current yield.

cv-Convertible bond. cf-Certificates. cld-Called. dc-Deep discount. ec-European currency units. f-Dealt in flat. il-Italian lire. kd-Danish kroner. m-Matured bonds, negotiability impaired by maturity. na-No accrual. r-Registered. rp-Reduced principal. st, sd-Stamped. t-Floating rate. wd-When distributed. ww-With warrants. x-Ex interest. xw-Without warrants. zr-Zero coupon.

v\|-In bankruptcy or receivership or being reorganized under the Bankruptcy Act, or securities assumed by such companies.

Source: *The Wall Street Journal,* June 16, 1993. Copyright 1993 Dow Jones & Company Inc. Reprinted by permission of The Wall Street Journal. All Rights Reserved Worldwide.

Finally, the fourth bond in Column 2 is a convertible ("cv") bond from Mead Corp. that has a 6.25 coupon and it is due in 2012. The conversion feature means that the bond is convertible into the common stock of the company. If you see a bond with a "dc" before the coupon, it means "deep discount," indicating that the original coupon was set below the going rate at the time of issue. An example of such a bond would be a 5 percent coupon bond when market rates were 9 or 10 percent.

All fixed-income obligations, with the exception of preferred stock, are traded on an *accrued interest basis.* The prices pertain to the value of all *future* cash flows from the bond and exclude interest that has accrued to the holder since the last interest payment date. The actual price of the bond will exceed the quote listed because accrued interest must be added. Assume a bond with a $7\frac{1}{8}$ percent coupon. If two months have elapsed since interest was paid, the current holder of the bond is entitled to $\frac{2}{6}$ or one-third of the bond's semiannual interest payment that will be paid in 4 months. More specifically, the $7\frac{1}{8}$ percent coupon provides semiannual interest income of $35.625. The investor who held the obligation for two months beyond the last interest payment date is entitled to one-third ($\frac{1}{3}$) of that $35.625 in the form of accrued interest. Therefore, whatever the current price of the bond, an accrued interest value of $11.87 will be added.

TREASURY AND AGENCY BOND QUOTES

Figure 13.2 illustrates the quote system for Treasury and agency issues. These quotes resemble those used for OTC securities because they contain both bid and ask prices, rather than high, low, and close. For U.S. Treasury bond quotes, a small *"n"* behind the maturity date indicates that the obligation is a Treasury *note.* A small *"p"* indicates it is a Treasury note on which nonresident aliens are exempt from withholding taxes on the interest.

All other obligations in this section are Treasury bonds. The security identification is different because it is not necessary to list the issuer. Instead, the usual listing indicates the coupon, the month and year of maturity, and information on a call feature of the obligation. For example, quote 1 is an $8\frac{1}{2}$ percent issue that carries a maturity of 1994–1999. This means that the issue has a deferred call feature until 1994 (and is thereafter freely callable), and a (final) maturity date of 1999. The bid–ask figures provided are stated as a percentage of par. The yield figure provided is yield to maturity, or *promised* yield based on the asking price. This system is used for Treasuries, agencies, and municipals.

Quote 2 is an 8 percent obligation of 2001 that demonstrates the basic difference in the price system of government bonds (i.e., Treasuries and agencies). The bid quote is 114:03, and the ask is 114:05. Governments are traded in thirty-seconds of a point (rather than eighths), and the figures to the right of the hyphens indicate the number of thirty-seconds in the fractional bid or ask. In this case, the bid price is actually 114.09375 percent of par. These quotes are also notable in terms of the bid–ask spread which are typically 2 or 3 thirty-seconds, which is about one-half the size of the smallest possible spread for most stocks which is $\frac{1}{8}$. This reflects the outstanding liquidity and low transaction costs for Treasury securities.

The lower section of the first column contains quotes for U. S. Treasury securities that have been "stripped." Specifically, the typical bond that promises a series of coupon payments and its principal at maturity is divided into two separate units. One contains all the coupon interest payments and no principal and is designated as "ci"

FIGURE 13.2 **Sample Quotes for Treasury Bonds, Notes, and Bills**

TREASURY BONDS, NOTES & BILLS

Tuesday, June 15, 1993

Representative Over-the-Counter quotations based on transactions of $1 million or more.

Treasury bond, note and bill quotes are as of mid-afternoon. Colons in bid-and-asked quotes represent 32nds; 101:01 means 101 1/32. Net changes in 32nds. n-Treasury note. Treasury bill quotes in hundredths, quoted on terms of a rate of discount. Days to maturity calculated from settlement date. All yields are to maturity and based on the asked quote. Latest 13-week and 26-week bills are boldfaced. For bonds callable prior to maturity, yields are computed to the earliest call date for issues quoted above par and to the maturity date for issues below par. *-When issued.

Source: Federal Reserve Bank of New York.

U.S. Treasury strips as of 3 p.m. Eastern time, also based on transactions of $1 million or more. Colons in bid-and-asked quotes represent 32nds; 101:01 means 101 1/32. Net changes in 32nds. Yields calculated on the asked quotation. ci-stripped coupon interest. bp-Treasury bond, stripped principal. np-Treasury note, stripped principal. For bonds callable prior to maturity, yields are computed to the earliest call date for issues quoted above par and to the maturity date for issues below par.

Source: Bear, Stearns & Co. via Street Software Technology Inc.

GOVT. BONDS & NOTES

Rate	Maturity Mo/Yr	Bid	Asked	Chg.	Ask Yld.
7	Jun 93n	100:05	100:07	....	0.88
8 1/8	Jun 93n	100:06	100:08	....	1.12
7 1/4	Jul 93n	100:10	100:12	− 1	2.32
6 7/8	Jul 93n	100:14	100:16	....	2.68
8	Aug 93n	100:26	100:28	+ 1	2.54
8 5/8	Aug 93	100:29	100:31	....	2.58
8 3/4	Aug 93n	100:29	100:31	....	2.70
11 7/8	Aug 93n	101:14	101:16	− 1	2.53
6 3/8	Aug 93n	100:21	100:23	....	2.78
6 1/8	Sep 93n	100:26	100:28	....	3.01
8 1/4	Sep 93n	101:14	101:16	....	2.93
7 1/8	Oct 93n	101:08	101:10	....	3.04
6	Oct 93n	100:31	101:01	....	3.15
7 3/4	Nov 93n	101:26	101:28	....	3.10
8 5/8	Nov 93	102:05	102:07	+ 1	3.12
9	Nov 93n	102:10	102:12	....	3.11
11 3/4	Nov 93n	103:15	103:17	....	3.01
5 1/2	Nov 93n	100:31	101:01	+ 1	3.19
5	Dec 93n	100:28	100:30	....	3.22
7 5/8	Dec 93n	102:09	102:11	....	3.18
7	Jan 94n	102:02	102:04	+ 1	3.26
4 7/8	Jan 94n	100:29	100:31	+ 1	3.29
6 7/8	Feb 94n	102:08	102:10	....	3.32
8 7/8	Feb 94n	103:18	103:20	....	3.31
9	Feb 94	103:20	103:22	....	3.34
5 3/8	Feb 94n	101:11	101:13	....	3.34

Rate	Maturity Mo/Yr	Bid	Asked	Chg.	Ask Yld.	
8 1/2	May 94-99	104:07	104:15	+ 1	3.47	← ①
9 1/8	May 99n	118:21	118:23	+ 2	5.39	
6 3/8	Jul 99n	104:27	104:29	+ 3	5.42	
8	Aug 99n	113:08	113:10	+ 3	5.43	
6	Oct 99n	102:25	102:27	+ 3	5.46	
7 7/8	Nov 99n	112:25	112:27	+ 2	5.47	
6 3/8	Jan 00n	104:20	104:22	+ 3	5.52	
7 7/8	Feb 95-00	106:10	106:14	+ 2	3.84	
8 1/2	Feb 00n	116:13	116:15	+ 3	5.51	
5 1/2	Apr 00n	99:20	99:22	+ 1	5.56	
8 7/8	May 00n	118:22	118:24	+ 3	5.57	
8 3/8	Aug 95-00	108:14	108:18	+ 6	4.19	
8 3/4	Aug 00n	118:06	118:08	+ 3	5.62	
8 1/2	Nov 00n	116:29	116:31	+ 4	5.66	
7 3/4	Feb 01n	112:15	112:17	+ 4	5.71	
11 3/4	Feb 01	137:12	137:16	+ 1	5.65	
8	May 01n	114:03	114:05	+ 4	5.75	← ②
13 1/8	May 01	146:18	146:22	+ 4	5.71	
7 7/8	Aug 01n	113:12	113:14	+ 4	5.79	
8	Aug 96-01	109:14	109:18	− 2	4.71	
13 3/8	Aug 01	148:30	149:02	+ 3	5.76	
7 1/2	Nov 01n	110:28	110:30	+ 3	5.84	
15 3/4	Nov 01	165:24	165:28	+ 5	5.76	
14 1/4	Feb 02	156:26	156:30	+ 4	5.80	
7 1/2	May 02n	110:31	111:01	+ 3	5.89	
6 3/8	Aug 02n	103:00	103:02	+ 4	5.94	
11 5/8	Nov 02	140:19	140:23	+ 7	5.92	

U.S. TREASURY STRIPS

Mat.	Type	Bid	Asked	Chg.	Ask Yld.
Aug 93	ci	99:15	99:15	....	3.22
Nov 93	ci	98:22	98:22	+ 1	3.25
Feb 94	ci	97:26	97:27	+ 1	3.33
May 94	ci	96:29	96:30	+ 1	3.44
Aug 94	ci	95:29	95:30	+ 2	3.59
Nov 94	ci	94:29	94:30	+ 2	3.72
Nov 94	np	94:25	94:26	+ 2	3.81
Feb 95	ci	93:24	93:26	+ 2	3.88
Feb 95	np	93:21	93:23	+ 2	3.95
May 95	ci	92:21	92:23	+ 3	4.00
May 95	np	92:21	92:23	+ 3	4.00
Aug 95	ci	91:24	91:25	+ 3	4.00
Aug 95	np	91:21	91:23	+ 3	4.04
Nov 95	ci	90:15	90:17	+ 3	4.17
Nov 95	np	90:14	90:17	+ 3	4.18
Feb 96	ci	89:01	89:03	+ 3	4.39
Feb 96	np	88:31	89:01	+ 3	4.41
May 96	ci	87:21	87:24	+ 4	4.55
May 96	np	87:22	87:24	+ 4	4.54
Aug 96	ci	86:10	86:13	+ 4	4.68
Nov 96	ci	85:01	85:03	+ 4	4.79
Nov 96	np	84:31	85:01	+ 4	4.81
Feb 97	ci	84:00	84:03	+ 2	4.79
May 97	ci	82:20	82:23	+ 2	4.91
May 97	np	82:17	82:20	+ 2	4.94
Aug 97	ci	81:16	81:19	+ 2	4.95
Aug 97	np	81:09	81:12	+ 2	5.01
Nov 97	ci	80:04	80:07	+ 2	5.06
Nov 97	np	79:31	80:03	+ 2	5.10
Feb 98	ci	78:31	79:02	+ 5	5.10
Feb 98	np	78:21	78:24	+ 2	5.19
May 98	ci	77:14	77:17	+ 2	5.25
May 98	np	77:07	77:10	+ 2	5.31

TREASURY BILLS

Maturity	Days to Mat.	Bid	Asked	Chg.	Ask Yld.
Jun 17 '93	0	3.00	2.90	+0.01	0.00
Jun 24 '93	7	2.90	2.80	+0.04	2.84
Jul 01 '93	14	2.90	2.80	....	2.84
Jul 08 '93	21	2.90	2.80	+0.03	2.84
Jul 15 '93	28	2.86	2.76	−0.01	2.80
Jul 22 '93	35	2.88	2.84	−0.01	2.89
Jul 29 '93	42	2.95	2.91	....	2.96
Aug 05 '93	49	2.97	2.93	+0.01	2.98
Aug 12 '93	56	2.98	2.94	+0.01	2.99
Aug 19 '93	63	2.99	2.97	....	3.03
Aug 26 '93	70	2.99	2.97	....	3.03
Sep 02 '93	77	3.02	3.00	−0.01	3.06
Sep 09 '93	84	3.04	3.02	−0.01	3.08
Sep 16 '93	**91**	**3.05**	**3.03**	**−0.01**	**3.10**
Sep 23 '93	98	3.08	3.06	−0.01	3.13
Sep 30 '93	105	3.06	3.04	−0.02	3.11
Oct 07 '93	112	3.07	3.05	−0.01	3.12
Oct 14 '93	119	3.08	3.06	−0.02	3.13
Oct 21 '93	126	3.09	3.07	−0.01	3.15
Oct 28 '93	133	3.09	3.07	−0.02	3.15
Nov 04 '93	140	3.11	3.09	−0.02	3.17
Nov 12 '93	148	3.12	3.10	−0.01	3.18
Nov 18 '93	154	3.14	3.12	−0.01	3.21
Nov 26 '93	162	3.14	3.12	−0.03	3.21
Dec 02 '93	168	3.15	3.13	−0.03	3.22
Dec 09 '93	175	3.15	3.13	−0.03	3.22
Dec 16 '93	**182**	**3.16**	**3.14**	**−0.03**	**3.23**
Jan 13 '94	210	3.19	3.17	−0.04	3.27
Feb 10 '94	238	3.22	3.20	−0.03	3.30
Mar 10 '94	266	3.25	3.23	−0.03	3.34
Apr 07 '94	294	3.27	3.25	−0.03	3.36

Source: *The Wall Street Journal,* June 16, 1993.

(stripped coupon interest), while the other contains only the principal payment and is designated "np" (Treasury note, stripped principal).

The securities listed below the Treasury bond section are for U.S. Treasury bills. Notice that only dates are reported and no coupons. This is because these are pure discount securities, that is, the return is the difference between the price you pay and par at maturity.[31]

MUNICIPAL BOND QUOTES

Figure 13.3 contains municipal bond quotes from *The Blue List of Current Municipal Offerings*. These are ordered according to states and then alphabetically within states. Each issue gives the amount of bonds being offered (in thousands of dollars), the name of the security, the coupon rate, the maturity (which includes month, day, and year), the yield or price, and finally, the dealer offering the bonds. Bond Quote 1 is for $50,000 of Delaware State Health Facilities Authority bonds. The "REG" indicates that they are registered bonds (rather than bearer), and the MBIA indicates that the bonds are guaranteed by this firm as described earlier. They have a 9.250 percent coupon and are due October 1, 2015, but are callable after 1995 at 102. In this instance, the yield to maturity is given (7.20 percent). To determine the price you would either compute it or look up in a yield book the price of a 9.25 percent coupon bond, due in about 7 years (a 1995 call from 1988) to yield 7.20 percent. The dealer offering the bonds is Mooresch. A list in the back of the publication gives the name of the firm and its phone number.

The second bond is a $5,000 Delaware State Housing Authority Revenue bond with an 8 percent coupon. This is somewhat unusual because a price is listed rather than the current yield to maturity—that is, the bond is selling for 103, which is 103 percent of par. These are called *dollar bonds*.

The " + " in the far left column indicates a new item since the prior issue of *The Blue List*. A "#" in the column prior to the yield to maturity or the price indicates that the price or yield has changed since the last issue. It is always necessary to call the dealer to determine the current yield/price, because these quotes are at least one day old when they are published.

SUMMARY

We considered the basic features of bonds: their interest, principal, and maturity. Certain key relationships affect price behavior. Price is essentially a function of coupon, maturity, and prevailing market interest rates. Bond price volatility depends on coupon and maturity. Specifically, bonds with longer maturities and/or lower coupons respond most vigorously to a given change in market rates.

Each bond has unique intrinsic characteristics and can be differentiated by type of issue and indenture provisions. Major benefits to bond investors included high returns for nominal risk, the potential for capital gains, certain tax advantages, and possibly additional returns from active trading of bonds. Aggressive bond investors must consider market liquidity, investment risks, and interest rate behavior. We introduced high-

---

[31]For a discussion on calculating yields, see Bruce D. Fielitz, "Calculating the Bond Equivalent Yield for T-Bills," *Journal of Portfolio Management* 9, no. 3 (Spring 1983): 58–60.

FIGURE 13.3   **Quotes for Municipals**

```
                          CONNECTICUT - CONTINUED
     50 COLCHESTER CONN            *B/B* MBIA    8.000  03/15/91        5.25 ROOSEVLT
     15 DARIEN CONN                              5.750  03/15/91        5.00 ROOSEVLT
   + 25 GUILFORD CONN              *B/B*         4.900  05/15/90         100 OPCOFTL
   + 15 HARTFORD CNTY CONN MET DIST *B/B*        3.000  10/01/91        6.00 ROOSEVLT
   +  5 HARTFORD CNTY CONN MET DIST *B/B*        3.250  11/01/96        6.75 ROOSEVLT
   +  8 HARTFORD CNTY CONN MET DIST *B/B*        3.250  11/01/98        7.00 ROOSEVLT
     95 HEBRON CONN                *B/E* AMBAC   6.400  04/15/90        5.00 CBT
     10 MONTVILLE CONN                           6.700  03/15/02        6.85 ABROWNBO
     70 MONTVILLE CONN                           7.000  03/15/08        7.25 CNB
      5 NEW HAVEN CONN COLISEUM AUTH             5.600  09/01/94        6.00 DWRBOS
     25 NEW HAVEN CONN PKG REV     *B/B*         5.700  09/01/95        6.25 DWRBOS
     65 SIMSBURY CONN                            6.600  04/15/95        5.90 FLEETNTL
    600 SOUTH CENT CONN REGL WTR AUTH P/R @ 102  8.500  08/01/03 C93    6.00 CBT
    750 SOUTH CENT CONN REGL WTR AUTH P/R @ 102  8.500  08/01/03 C93    6.00 WERTHEIM
     25 STAMFORD CONN                            6.500  07/15/95 N/C    5.90 CONNSEC
     15 STONINGTON CONN            *B/E*         6.300  03/15/90        5.05 CBT
     10 WEST HAVEN CONN                          5.700  03/01/00        7.00 FLEETNTL

                              DELAWARE

    115 DELAWARE ST                *B/E* W.I.    6.200  04/01/90        5.10 WHEATPH
     25 DELAWARE ST                              9.600  07/01/90 N/C    5.30 ABROWNBA
     10 DELAWARE ST                              6.250  04/01/93        5.90 WHEATPH
     40 DELAWARE ST                              6.300  04/01/94        6.00 WERTHEIM
     25 DELAWARE ST                P/R @ 103     9.700  07/01/95 C91    5.60 ABROWNBA
     20 DELAWARE ST                *B/E*         7.250  04/01/03 C00     100 PERSH
        (CA @ 100)
     25 DELAWARE RIV & BAY AUTH DEL              3.750  01/01/04          82 BEARSTER
    100 DELAWARE RIV & BAY AUTH DEL              3.750  01/01/04          82 PETERS
     25 DELAWARE ST ECONOMIC DEV AUTH MULTI-FAM 10.750  11/01/14        9.65 WHEELER
     50 DELAWARE ST HEALTH FACS AUTH *REG* MBIA  9.250  10/01/15 C95    7.20 MOORESCH
        (P/C @ 102)
      5 DELAWARE ST HSG AUTH REV                 8.000  01/01/89         103 SMITHB
      5 DELAWARE ST SOLID WASTE AUTH CA @ 103    9.250  07/01/03 C89    6.50 MEYERND
    175 DELAWARE TRANSN AUTH TRANSN &            6.750  07/01/00        7.00 PRUBAPHL
    175 DELAWARE TRANSN AUTH TRANSN &            6.750  07/01/00        7.00 PRUBAPHL
     25 DOVER DEL                                5.500  07/01/92         100 JANNEYPH
     50 DOVER DEL                  BK.QD B/E     5.500  07/01/92         100 NEWBOLDW
     25 DOVER DEL                                5.900  07/01/94         100 JANNEYPH
     15 DOVER DEL                                6.100  07/01/95         100 JANNEYPH
      5 DOVER DEL                  BK.QD B/E     6.250  07/01/96         100 NEWBOLDW
     50 DOVER DEL                                6.250  07/01/96         100 WHEATPH
     25 DOVER DEL                                6.400  07/01/97         100 JANNEYPH
     10 DOVER DEL                                6.550  07/01/98         100 WHEATPH
    250 KENT CNTY DEL              CA @ 100      8.000  06/15/06 C96     7.00 MOORESCH
     20 NEW CASTLE CNTY DEL                      1.875  05/01/89 ETM    6.25 RAMIREZ
    100 NEW CASTLE CNTY DEL        *REG*         8.500  10/15/05 C95    7.00 MOORESCH
        (CA @ 102)
   +300 NORTHERN DEL INDL DEV CORP (PHOENIX)     5.750  11/01/99   #      73 BEARSTER
     10 NORTHERN DEL INDL DEV CORP PHOEN.STL     5.750  11/01/99          65 MABONIDB
     25 NORTHERN DEL INDL DEV CORP PHNX.STL.     5.750  11/01/99      67 1/2 PETERS
     10 NORTHERN DEL INDL DEV CORP               5.750  11/01/99          68 WMBLBONN
     20 WILMINGTON DEL                AMBAC      9.000  03/01/92 C91    5.75 SHEARPHL
        (P/R @ 101)
    200 WILMINGTON DEL                           7.300  08/15/95 N/C    6.60 ABROWNBA

                        DISTRICT OF COLUMBIA

     10 DISTRICT COLUMBIA                        7.750  06/01/91        6.00 BARRBROS
   +850 DISTRICT COLUMBIA             AMBAC      7.900  06/01/98        7.10 PRUBANY
      5 DISTRICT COLUMBIA          SER D         7.100  06/01/00        7.50 IREC
    300 DISTRICT COLUMBIA             MBIA       9.900  12/01/00 C95    6.60 FIRSTCHI
        (P/R @ 102)
    525 DISTRICT COLUMBIA             MBIA       7.650  06/01/03         100 RODMANNY
   +300 DISTRICT COLUMBIA          CA @ 102      7.375  06/01/05 C96    8.10 FMS
     65 DISTRICT COLUMBIA          P/R @ 102     9.750  06/01/05 C95 #  6.75 DREXELPH
   +255 DISTRICT COLUMBIA          CA @ 102      7.875  06/01/06 C96    8.00 FMS
  ..PAGE   8 A          Wednesday May  4, 1988
```

(1) → 50 DELAWARE ST HEALTH FACS AUTH

(2) → 5 DELAWARE ST HSG AUTH REV

Source: *The Blue List of Current Municipal Offerings,* May 4, 1988, p. 8A. The Blue List Division of Standard & Poor's Corp., New York. Reprinted by permission of Standard & Poor's Corp.

yield (junk) bonds because of the growth in size and status of this segment of the bond market.

The global bond market includes numerous countries. The non-U.S. markets have experienced strong relative growth, whereas the U.S. market has been stable, but constitutes less than half the world market. The four major bond markets (the United States, Japan, Germany, and the United Kingdom) have a different makeup in terms of governments, agencies, municipals, corporates, and international issues. The various market sectors are also unique in terms of liquidity, yield spreads, tax implications, and operating features.

To gauge default risk, most bond investors rely on agency ratings. For additional information on the bond market, prevailing economic conditions, and intrinsic bond features, individual and institutional investors rely on a host of readily available publications. While there are extensive up-to-date quotes available on Treasury bonds and notes, trading and price information for corporates and municipals is relatively difficult to find and is expensive.

The world bond market is large, and continuing to grow at a strong rate due to government deficits and the need for capital by corporations. It is also very diverse in terms of country alternatives and issuers within countries. This chapter has provided the background fundamentals that will allow us to consider the valuation of individual bonds in Chapter 14, and the alternative portfolio techniques available in Chapter 15.

QUESTIONS

1. How does a bond differ from other types of debt instruments?

2. Explain the difference between calling a bond and a bond refunding.

3. Identify the three most important determinants of the price of a bond. Describe the effect of each.

4. Given a change in the level of interest rates, what two major factors will influence the relative change in price for individual bonds? What is their impact?

5. Briefly describe two indenture provisions that can affect the maturity of a bond.

6. What factors determine whether a bond is senior or junior? Give examples of each type.

7. What is a bond indenture?

8. Explain the differences in taxation of income from municipal bonds and income from U.S. Treasury bonds and corporate bonds.

9. List several types of institutional participants in the bond market. Explain what type of bond each is likely to purchase and why.

10. Why should investors be aware of the trading volume for a bond in which they are interested?

11. What is the purpose of bond ratings? What are they supposed to indicate?

12. Based on the data in Table 13.1, which is the fastest-growing bond market in the world? Which markets are losing market share?

13. Based on the data in Table 13.2, discuss the makeup of the German bond market and how it differs from the U.S. market. Briefly discuss the reasons for this difference.

14. Discuss why an investor might consider investing in a government agency issue rather than a straight Treasury bond. What is the negative factor for such a bond relative to a Treasury?

15. a. Discuss the distribution of high-yield bond holdings among various groups and how this affected the liquidity of these securities.

b. Discuss the distribution of volume among the major high-yield bond underwriters and the impact of this distribution on the liquidity for the market.

16. Discuss the difference between a foreign bond (e.g., a Samurai) and a Eurobond (e.g., a Euroyen issue).

17. The latter part of this chapter listed and discussed numerous sources of information on bonds. Yet the statement was made earlier that "it is almost impossible for individual investors . . . to keep abreast of the price activity of municipal holdings." Discuss this apparent paradox, explaining how such a condition might exist.

18. Using various sources of information described in the chapter, name at least five bonds rated B or better that have split ratings.

19. Select five bonds that are listed on the NYSE. Using various sources of information, prepare a brief description of each bond, including such factors as its rating, call features, sinking-fund requirements, collateral (if any), interest payment dates, and any refunding provisions.

PROBLEMS

1. An investor in the 28 percent tax bracket is trying to decide which of two bonds to purchase. One is a corporate bond carrying an 8 percent coupon and selling at par. The other is a municipal bond with a 5½ percent coupon, and it, too, sells at par. Assuming all other relevant factors are equal, which bond should the investor select?

2. What would be the initial offering price for the following bonds (assume semiannual compounding):
   a. A 15-year zero coupon bond with a yield to maturity (YTM) of 12 percent.
   b. A 20-year zero coupon bond with a YTM of 10 percent.

3. An 8.4 percent coupon bond issued by the state of Indiana sells for $1,000. What coupon rate on a corporate bond selling at its $1,000 par value would produce the same after-tax return to the investor as the municipal bond if the investor is in
   a. The 15 percent marginal tax bracket?
   b. The 25 percent marginal tax bracket?
   c. The 35 percent marginal tax bracket?

4. The Shamrock Corporation has just issued a $1,000 par value zero coupon bond with an 8 percent yield to maturity, due to mature 15 years from today (assume semiannual compounding).
   a. What is the market price of the bond?
   b. If interest rates remain constant, what will be the price of the bond in 3 years?
   c. If interest rates rise to 10 percent, what will be the price of the bond in 3 years?

5. Complete the information requested for each of the following $1,000 face value, zero coupon bonds, assuming semiannual compounding.

Bond	Maturity (Years)	Yield (Percent)	Price ($)
A	20	12	?
B	?	8	601
C	9	?	350

REFERENCES

Altman, Edward I., ed. *The High Yield Debt Market.* Homewood, Ill.: Dow Jones-Irwin, 1990.

Altman, Edward I., and Scott A. Nammacher. *Investing in Junk Bonds.* New York: John Wiley & Sons, 1987.

Beidleman, Carl, ed. *The Handbook of International Investing.* Chicago: Probus Publishing, 1987.

Belkaoui, Ahmed. "Industrial Bond Ratings: A New Look." *Financial Management* 9, no. 3 (Autumn 1980).

Darst, David M. *The Handbook of the Bond and Money Markets.* New York: McGraw-Hill, 1981.

Douglas, Livingston G. *The Fixed Income Almanac.* Chicago: Probus Publishing Co., 1993.

Elton, Edwin J., and Martin J. Gruber, eds. *Japanese Capital Markets.* New York: Harper & Row, 1990.

European Bond Commission. *European Bond Markets.* Chicago: Probus Publishing, 1989.

Fabozzi, Frank J., ed. *Advances and Innovations in the Bond and Mortgage Markets.* Chicago: Probus Publishing, 1989.

Fabozzi, Frank J., ed. *The Japanese Bond Market.* Chicago: Probus Publishing, 1990.

Fabozzi, Frank J., ed. *The New High Yield Debt Market.* New York: Harper Business, 1990.

Fabozzi, Frank J. *The Handbook of Fixed-Income Securities.* 3d ed. Homewood, Ill.: Business One Irwin, 1991.

Fisher, Lawrence. "Determinants of Risk Premiums on Corporate Bonds." *Journal of Political Economy* 67, no. 3 (June 1959).

Fridson, Martin S. *High Yield Bonds.* Chicago: Probus Publishing, 1989.

Gentry, James A., David T. Whitford, and Paul Newbold. "Predicting Industrial Bond Ratings with Probit Model and Funds Flow Components." *The Financial Review* 23, no. 3 (August 1988).

Grabbe, J. Orlin. *International Financial Markets.* New York: Elsevier, 1986.

Howe, Jane Tripp. *Junk Bonds: Analysis and Portfolio Strategies.* Chicago: Probus Publishing, 1988.

Kaplan, Robert S., and Gabriel Urwitz. "Statistical Models of Bond Ratings: A Methodological Inquiry." *Journal of Business* 52, no. 2 (April 1979).

Perry, Kevin S., and Robert A. Taggart, Jr. "The Growing Role of Junk Bonds in Corporate Finance," *Journal of Applied Corporate Finance* 1, no. 1 (Spring 1988).

Reilly, Frank K., and Michael D. Joehnk. "Association Between Market Determined Risk Measures for Bonds and Bond Ratings." *Journal of Finance* 31, no. 5 (December 1976).

Van Horne, James C. *Financial Market Rates and Flows.* 3d ed. Englewood Cliffs, N.J.: Prentice-Hall, 1988.

Viner, Aron. *Inside Japanese Financial Markets.* Homewood, Ill.: Dow Jones-Irwin, 1988.

Wilson, Richard S. *Corporate Senior Securities.* Chicago: Probus Publishing, 1987.

Wilson, Richard S., and Frank J. Fabozzi. *The New Corporate Bond Market.* Chicago: Probus Publishing, 1990.

Yago, Glenn. *Junk Bonds.* New York: Oxford University Press, 1991.

CHAPTER 14

THE VALUATION OF BONDS

In this chapter we will answer the following questions:

- How do you determine the value of a bond based on the present value formula?
- What are the alternative bond yields that are important to investors?
- How do you compute the following major yields on bonds: current yield, yield to maturity, yield to call, and compound realized (horizon) yield?
- What factors affect the level of bond yields at a point in time?
- What economic forces cause changes in the yields on bonds over time?
- When yields change, what characteristics of a bond cause differential price changes for individual bonds?
- What is meant by the duration of a bond, how do you compute it, and what factors affect it?
- What is modified duration and what is the relationship between a bond's modified duration and its volatility?
- What is the convexity for a bond, how do you compute it, and what factors affect it?
- Under what conditions is it necessary to consider both modified duration and convexity when estimating a bond's price volatility?

In this chapter we apply the valuation principles that were introduced in Chapter 11 to the valuation of bonds. This chapter is concerned with how one goes about finding the value of bonds and understanding the several measures of yields for bonds. It is also important to understand why these bond values and yields change over time. To do this, we begin with a review of value estimation for bonds using the present value model introduced in Chapter 11. This background on valuation allows us to understand and compute the expected rates of return on bonds, which are their yields. We need to measure yields on bonds because they are very important to a bond investor.

After mastering the measurement of bond yields, we consider what factors influence the level of bond yields and what economic forces cause changes in yields over time. We will discuss the effects of various characteristics and indenture provisions that affect the required returns and, therefore, the value of specific bond issues. This includes factors such as time to maturity, coupon, callability, and sinking funds.

With this background we return to the consideration of bond value and examine the characteristics that cause different changes in a bond's price. The point is, when yields change, all bond prices do not change in the same way.

An understanding of the factors that affect the price changes for bonds has become more important during the past several decades because the price volatility of bonds has increased substantially. Before 1950, the yields on bonds were fairly low and both yields and prices were stable. In such an environment, bonds were considered a very safe investment and most investors in bonds intended to hold them to maturity. During the last several decades, the level of interest rates has increased substantially because of inflation, and interest rates have become more volatile because of changes in the rate of inflation and monetary policy. As a result, bond prices and rates of return on bonds have been much more volatile and the rates of return on bond investments have increased. Notably, given these changes, bonds are no longer as safe as they once were.

THE FUNDAMENTALS OF BOND VALUATION

The value of bonds can be described in terms of dollar values or the rates of return that they promise under some set of assumptions. In this section, we describe both the present value model, which computes a specific value for the bond, and the yield model, which computes the promised rate of return based on the bond's current price.

THE PRESENT VALUE MODEL

In our introduction to valuation theory in Chapter 11 we saw that the value of a bond (or any asset) equals the present value of its expected cash flows. The cash flows from a bond are the periodic interest payments to the bondholder and the repayment of principal at the maturity of the bond. Therefore, the value of a bond is the present value of the interest payments plus the present value of the principal payment, where the discount factor is the required rate of return on the bond. We can express this in the following present value formula:

$$P = \sum_{t=i}^{n} C_t \frac{1}{(1 + i_b)^t} \tag{14.1}$$

where:

n = the number of periods in the investment horizon, or the holding period
C_t = the cash flow received in period t
i_b = the required rate of return for this bond issue.

Essentially, any fixed-income security can be valued on the basis of Equation 14.1. The value computed indicates what an investor would be willing to pay for this bond to realize a rate of return, i, that takes into account expectations regarding the RFR, the expected rate of inflation, and the risk of the bond. Many investors assume a holding period is equal to the term to maturity of the obligation. In this case, the number of periods would be the number of years to the maturity of the bond (referred to as its *term to maturity*). In such a case, the cash flows would include all the periodic interest payments and the payment of the bond's par value at the maturity of the bond.

Aggressive bond investors, however, normally do not hold bonds to maturity. They buy bonds with the expectation that they will sell them prior to their maturity. In such a case, the length of time the investor expects to hold the bond determines the number of holding periods. This holding period can range from a few days or weeks to several years, but it would be less than the term to maturity.

Such an investor would estimate the cash flows as the periodic interest payments during the holding period and the expected selling price (SP) at the end of the holding period. Notably, the expected selling price need not be equal to the par value of the bond. The bond can sell at a *discount,* which means that its market price will be less than its par value, or it can sell at a *premium,* that is, at a market price above its par value. For example, a discount bond with a par value of $1,000 might sell for $900, whereas a premium bond with the same par value might have a market price of $1,200. Therefore, when computing the value of a bond that you will sell before maturity, it is necessary to estimate both the holding period and the selling price at the end of the holding period. We will discuss how to do this in an example in the next section.

Whether you intend to hold the bond to maturity or for some shorter time period, you will discount the cash flows at your required rate of return on a bond with the given risk. As discussed in Chapter 11, your investment decision will depend on the relationship of your estimated value of the bond and its market price. If the estimated value of the bond equals or exceeds the market price, you should buy it; if your estimated value of the bond is less than its market price, you should not buy it.

The present value formula implies that the major determinant of changes in the value of a bond is the discount rate because the cash flows are known. Therefore, we will need to discuss what causes differences in discount rates between bonds and over time. That is, why do interest rates change? These questions will be considered in a subsequent section.

THE YIELD MODEL   Instead of determining the value of a bond in dollar terms, investors often price bonds in terms of *yields,* which are the promised rates of return on bonds under certain assumptions. The point is, thus far we have used cash flows and our required rate of return to compute an estimated value for the bond, which we then compared to its market price (P). To compute an expected yield, we use the current market price (P) with the expected cash flows and *compute the expected yield on the bond.* We can express this approach using the present value model as follows:

$$P = \sum_{t=i}^{n} C_t \frac{1}{(1 + i)^t} \qquad (14.2)$$

where:

P = the current market price of the bond
C_t = the cash flow received in period t
i = the discount rate that will discount the cash flows to equal the current market price of the bond.

This i value gives the yield of the bond. We will discuss several types of bond yields that arise from the assumptions of the valuation model in the next section.

Approaching the investment decision stating the bond's value as a yield figure rather than a dollar amount, you consider the relationship of the computed bond yield to your required rate of return on this bond. If the computed bond yield is equal to or greater than your required rate of return, you should buy the bond; if the computed yield is less than your required rate of return, you should not buy the bond.

These approaches to pricing bonds and making investment decisions is similar to the two alternative approaches by which firms make investment decisions. We referred to one approach, the net present value (NPV) method, in Chapter 11. With the NPV approach you compute the present value of the net cash flows from the proposed investment at your cost of capital and subtract the present value cost of the investment to get the net present value (NPV) of the project. If this NPV is positive, you consider accepting the investment; if it is negative, you reject it. This is basically the way we compared the value of an investment to its market price.

The second approach is to compute the *internal rate of return* (*IRR*) on a proposed investment project. The IRR is the discount rate that equates the present value of cash outflows for an investment with the present value of its cash inflows. You compare this discount rate, or IRR (which is also the expected rate of return on the project), to your cost of capital, and accept any investment proposal with an IRR equal to or greater than your cost of capital. We do the same thing when we price bonds on the basis of yield. If the expected yield on the bond is equal to or exceeds your required rate of return on the bond, you should invest in it; if the expected yield is less than your required rate of return on the bond, you should not invest in it.

COMPUTING BOND YIELDS

Bond investors use five types of yields for the following purposes:

Yield Measure	Purpose
Nominal yield	Measures the coupon rate.
Current yield	Measures current income rate.
Promised yield to maturity	Measures expected rate of return for bond held to maturity.
Promised yield to call	Measures expected rate of return for bond held to first call date.
Realized (horizon) yield	Measures expected rate of return for a bond likely to be sold prior to maturity. It considers specific reinvestment assumptions and an estimated sales price. It can also measure the actual rate of return on a bond during some past period of time.

Nominal and current yields are mainly descriptive and contribute little to investment decision making. The last three yields are all derived from the present value model as described in Equation 14.2.

When we present the last three yields based on the present value model, we consider two calculation techniques. First, we consider a fairly simple calculation for the approximate values for each of these yields to provide reasonable estimates. Second, we use the present value model to get accurate values. We provide both techniques because an exact answer with the present value model requires several calculations. In some cases, the approximate yield value is adequate.

To measure an expected realized yield (also referred to as the horizon yield), a bond investor must estimate a bond's future selling price. Following our presentation of bond yields, we will present the procedure for finding these prices. We conclude the section by examining the yields on tax-free bonds.

NOMINAL YIELD

Nominal yield is the coupon rate of a particular issue. A bond with an 8 percent coupon has an 8 percent nominal yield. This provides a convenient way of describing the coupon characteristics of an issue.

CURRENT YIELD

Current yield is to bonds what dividend yield is to stocks. It is computed as

$$CY = C_i/P_m \qquad (14.3)$$

where:

CY = the current yield on a bond
C_i = the annual coupon payment of the bond i
P_m = the current market price of the bond

Because this yield measures the current income from the bond as a percentage of its price, it is important to income-oriented investors who want current cash flow from their investment portfolios. An example of such an investor would be a retired person who lives on this investment income. Current yield has little use for most other investors who are interested in total return because it excludes the important capital gain or loss component.

PROMISED YIELD TO MATURITY

Promised yield to maturity is the most widely used bond yield figure, because it indicates the fully compounded rate of return promised to an investor who buys the bond at prevailing prices, *if two assumptions hold true.* The first assumption is that the investor holds the bond to maturity. This assumption gives this value its shortened name, *yield to maturity* (YTM). The second assumption is implicit in the present value method of computation. Referring back to Equation 14.2, recall that it related the current market price of the bond to the present value of all cash flows as follows:

$$P_m = \sum_{t=i}^{n} C_t \frac{1}{(1 + i)^t}.$$

To compute the YTM for a bond, we solve for the rate i that will equate the current price (P_m) to all cash flows from the bond to maturity. As noted, this resembles the computation of the internal rate of return (IRR) on an investment project. Because it is a present value-based computation, it implies a reinvestment rate assumption because it discounts the cash flows. That is, the equation assumes that *all interim cash flows (interest payments) are reinvested at the computed YTM.* That is why this is referred to as a *promised* YTM because the bond will provide this computed YTM only *if* you meet its conditions:

1. You hold the bond to maturity.
2. You reinvest all the interim cash flows at the computed YTM rate.

If a bond promises an 8 percent YTM, you must reinvest coupon income at 8 percent in order to realize that promised return. If you spend (do not reinvest) the coupon payments or if you cannot find opportunities to reinvest these coupon payments at rates as high as its promised YTM, then the actual realized yield you earn will be less than

FIGURE 14.1

The Effect of Interest-on-Interest on Total Realized Return

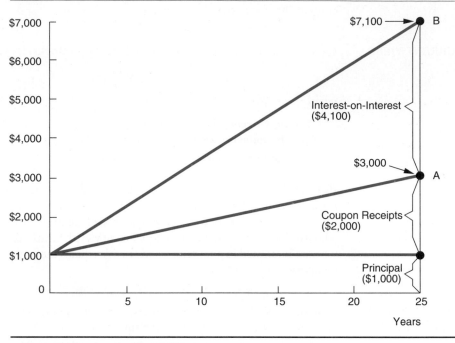

Promised yield at time of purchase: 8.00%

Realized yield over the 25-year investment horizon with no coupon reinvestment (*A*): 4.50%

Realized yield over the 25-year horizon with coupons reinvested at 8% (*B*): 8.00%

the promised yield to maturity. The income earned on this reinvestment of the interim interest payments is referred to as *interest-on-interest.*[1]

The impact of the reinvestment assumption (i.e., the interest-on-interest earnings) on the actual return from a bond varies directly with the bond's coupon and maturity. A higher coupon and/or a longer term to maturity increase the loss in value from failure to reinvest at the YTM. These conditions make the reinvestment assumption more important.

Figure 14.1 illustrates the impact of interest-on-interest for an 8 percent, 25-year bond bought at par to yield 8 percent. If you invested $1,000 today at 8 percent for 25 years and reinvested all the coupon payments at 8 percent, you would have approximately $7,100 at the end of 25 years. We will refer to this money that you have at the end of your investment horizon as your *ending-wealth value.* To prove that you would have an ending-wealth value of $7,100 look up the compound interest factor for 8 percent for 25 years (which is 6.8493) or 4 percent for 50 periods (which assumes semiannual compounding and is 7.1073).

Figure 14.1 shows that this $7,100 is made up of $1,000 principal return, $2,000 of coupon payments over the 25 years ($80 a year for 25 years), and $4,100 in interest

---

[1] This concept is developed in Sidney Homer and Martin L. Leibowitz, *Inside the Yield Book* (Englewood Cliffs, N.J.: Prentice-Hall, 1972), Chapter 1.

earned on the coupon payments reinvested at 8 percent. If you had never reinvested any of the coupon payments, you would have an ending-wealth value of only $3,000. This ending-wealth value of $3,000 derived from the beginning investment of $1,000 gives you an actual (realized) yield to maturity of only 4.5 percent. That is, the rate that will discount $3,000 back to $1,000 in 25 years is 4.5 percent. Reinvesting the coupon payments at some rate between 0 and 8 percent would cause your ending-wealth position to be above $3,000 and below $7,100; therefore, your actual rate of return would be somewhere between 4.5 percent and 8 percent. Alternatively, if you managed to reinvest the coupon payments at rates consistently above 8 percent, your ending-wealth position would be above $7,100, and your actual rate of return would be above 8 percent.

Interestingly, during periods of very high interest rates, you often hear investors talk about "locking in" high yields. Many of these people are subject to *yield illusion,* because they do not realize that attaining the high promised yield requires that they reinvest all the coupon payments at the same very high yields. As an example, if you buy a 20-year bond with a promised yield to maturity of 15 percent, you will actually realize the 15 percent yield *only* if you reinvest all the coupon payments at 15 percent over the next 20 years.

COMPUTING THE PROMISED YIELD TO MATURITY

You can compute the promised yield to maturity in two ways: finding an approximate annual yield, or using the present value model with semiannual compounding.[2] The present value model gives an investor a more accurate result, and it is the technique used by investment professionals.

The approximate promised yield (APY) measure is easy to calculate as follows:

$$APY = \frac{c_t + \dfrac{P_p - P_m}{n}}{\dfrac{P_p + P_m}{2}} \qquad (14.4)$$

$$= \frac{\text{Coupon} + \text{Annual Straight-Line Amortization of Capital Gain or Loss}}{\text{Average Investment}}$$

where:

P_p = **par value of the bond**
n = **number of years to maturity**
c_t = **the bond's *annual* coupon**
P_m = **the current market price of the bond.**

This approximate value for the promised yield to maturity assumes interest is compounded annually, and it does not require the multiple computations of the present

[2] You can compute promised YTM assuming annual compounding, but practitioners use semiannual compounding because the interest cash flows are semiannual. Even when the cash flows are not semiannual, bond analysts use the assumption for calculating the yield. Therefore, all our calculations employ this assumption.

value model. An 8 percent bond with 20 years remaining to maturity and a current price of $900 has an approximate yield of 8.95 percent:

$$\text{APY} = \frac{80 + \dfrac{1000 - 900}{20}}{\dfrac{1000 + 900}{2}} = \frac{80 + 5}{950}$$

$$= 8.95\%.$$

The present value model provides a more accurate yield to maturity value. To be consistent with actual practice, we assume semiannual compounding. Equation 14.5 shows this version of the promised yield valuation model:

$$P_m = \sum_{t=1}^{2n} \frac{C_t/2}{(1 + i/2)^t} + \frac{P_p}{(1 + i/2)^{2n}}. \tag{14.5}$$

All variables are as described previously. This formula reflects the semiannual interest payments. You adjust for these semiannual payments by doubling the number of periods (two times the number of years to maturity) and dividing the annual coupon value in half.

This model is more accurate than the approximate promised yield model, but it is also more complex because the solution requires iteration. The present value equation is a variation of the internal rate of return (IRR) calculation where we want to find the discount rate, i, that will equate the present value of the stream of coupon receipts, (c_t), and principal value, (P_p), with the current market price of the bond (P_m). Using the prior example of an 8 percent, 20-year bond, priced at $900, the equation gives us a semiannual promised yield to maturity of 4.545 percent, which implies an annual YTM of 9.09 percent:[3]

$$900 = 40 \sum_{t=1}^{40} \left(\frac{1}{(1.04545)^t} \right) + 1000 \left(\frac{1}{(1.04545)^{40}} \right)$$

$$= 40(18.2574) + 1000\,(.1702)$$

$$= 900.$$

The values for $1/(1 + i)$ were taken from the present value interest factor tables in the appendix at the back of the book using interpolation.

Comparing the results of Equation 14.5 with those of the approximate promised yield computation, you find a variation of 14 basis points. As a rule, the approximate promised yield tends to understate the present value promised yield for issues selling below par value (i.e., trading at a discount) and to overstate the promised yield for a

---

[3] You will recall from your corporate finance course that you would start with one rate (e.g., 9 percent or 4.5 percent semiannual) and compute the value of the stream. In this example, the value would exceed $900, so you would select a higher rate until you had a present value for the stream of cash flows of less than $900. Given the discount rates above and below the true rate, you would do further calculations or interpolate between the two rates to arrive at the correct discount rate that would give you a value of $900.

bond selling at a premium. The size of the differential varies directly with the length of the holding period. Although the estimated yield value differs, the rankings of yields estimated using the APY formula (Equation 14.4) will generally be identical to those determined by the present value method.

YTM FOR A ZERO COUPON BOND

In several instances we have discussed the existence of zero coupon bonds that only have the one cash inflow at maturity. This single cash flow means that the calculation of YTM is substantially easier as shown by the following example:

Assume a zero coupon bond, maturing in 10 years with a maturity value of $1,000 selling for $311.80. Because you are dealing with a zero coupon bond, there is only the one cash flow from the principal payment at maturity. Therefore, you simply need to determine what is the discount rate that will discount $1,000 to equal the current market price of $311.80 in 20 periods (10 years of semiannual payment). The equation is as follows:

$$\$311.80 = \frac{\$1000}{(1 + i)^{20}}$$

You will see that $i = 6\%$, which implies an annual rate of 12%.

PROMISED YIELD TO CALL

Although investors use promised YTM to value most bonds, they must estimate the return on certain callable bonds with a different measure—the *promised yield to call (YTC)*. Whenever a bond with a call feature is selling for a price above par (i.e., at a premium) equal to or greater than its par value plus one year's interest, a bond investor should value the bond in terms of YTC rather than YTM. The reason is that the marketplace uses the lowest, most conservative yield measure in pricing a bond. When bonds are trading at or above a specified *crossover point,* which approximates the bond's par value plus one year's interest, the yield to call will normally provide the lowest yield measure.[4] The price at the crossover point is important because when the bond rises to this price above par, the computed YTM becomes low enough that it would be profitable for the issuer to call the bond and finance the call by selling a new bond at the prevailing market interest rate.[5] Therefore, the YTC measures the promised rate of return the investor will receive from holding this bond until it is retired at the first available call date, that is, at the end of the deferred call period. Investors need to consider computing the YTC for their bonds after a period when numerous high-yielding, high-coupon bonds have been issued. Following such a period, interest rates will decline, bond prices will rise, and the high coupon bonds will subsequently have a high probability of being called.

---

[4] For a discussion of the crossover point, see Homer and Leibowitz, *Inside the Yield Book,* Chapter 4.

[5] There is extensive literature on the refunding of bond issues, including W. M. Boyce and A. J. Kalotay, "Optimum Bond Calling and Refunding," *Interfaces* (November 1979): 36–49; R. S. Harris, "The Refunding of Discounted Debt: An Adjusted Present Value Analysis," *Financial Management* 9, no. 4 (Winter 1980): 7–12; A. J. Kalotay, "On the Structure and Valuation of Debt Refundings," *Financial Management* 11, no. 1 (Spring 1982): 41–42; and John D. Finnerty, "Evaluating the Economics of Refunding High-Coupon Sinking-Fund Debt," *Financial Management* 12, no. 1 (Spring 1983): 5–10.

COMPUTING PROMISED YIELD TO CALL

Again, there are two methods for computing the promised yield to call: the approximate method and the present value method. Both methods assume that you hold the bond until the first call date. The present value method also assumes that you reinvest all coupon payments at the YTC rate.

Yield to call is calculated using variations of Equations 14.4 and 14.5. The approximate yield to call (AYC) is computed as follows:

$$AYC = \frac{C_t + \dfrac{P_c - P_m}{nc}}{\dfrac{P_c + P_m}{2}} \tag{14.6}$$

where:

AYC = approximate yield to call (YTC)
P_c = call price of the bond (generally equal to par value plus one year's interest)
P_m = market price of the bond
C_t = annual coupon payment
nc = the number of years to first call date.

This equation is comparable to APY, except that P_c has replaced P_p in Equation 14.4, and nc has replaced n.

To find the AYC of a 12 percent, 20-year bond that is trading at 115 ($1,150) with 5 years remaining to first call and a call price of 112 ($1,120), we substitute these values into Equation 14.6.

$$AYC = \frac{120 + \dfrac{1120 - 1150}{5}}{\dfrac{1120 + 1150}{2}} = 10.04\%.$$

This bond's approximate YTC is 10.04 percent, assuming that the issue will be called after 5 years at the call price of 112. To confirm that yield to call is the more conservative and more accurate value for a bond you expect to be called in 5 years, you can compute the approximate promised YTM. Using Equation 14.4 indicates a promised YTM of 10.47 percent.

To compute the YTC by the present value method, we would adjust the semiannual present value equation (Equation 14.5) to give

$$P_m = \sum_{t=1}^{2nc} \frac{C_t/2}{(1 + i/2)^t} + \frac{P_c}{(1 + i/2)^{2nc}} \tag{14.7}$$

where:

P_m = market price of the bond
C_t = annual coupon payment
nc = number of years to first call
P_c = call price of the bond.

Following the present value method, we solve for i, which typically requires several computations or extrapolation to get the exact yield.

REALIZED YIELD

The final measure of bond yield, *realized yield* or *horizon yield,* measures the expected rate of return of a bond that you expect to sell prior to its maturity. In terms of the equation, the investor has a holding period (hp) that is less than n. Realized (horizon) yield can be used to estimate rates of return attainable from various trading strategies. As such it is a very useful measure, but it also requires several additional estimates not required by the other yield measures. Specifically, the investor must estimate the expected future selling price of the bond at the end of the holding period. Also, this measure requires an estimate of the reinvestment rate for the coupon flows prior to the liquidation of the bond. This technique can also help investors measure their actual yields after selling bonds.

COMPUTING REALIZED (HORIZON) YIELD

The realized yields are variations on the promised yield equations (Equations 14.4 and 14.5). The approximate realized yield (ARY) is calculated as follows:

$$\text{ARY} = \frac{C_t + \dfrac{P_f - P_m}{hp}}{\dfrac{P_f + P_m}{2}} \tag{14.8}$$

where:

ARY = **approximate realized yield**
C_t = **annual coupon payment**
P_f = **future selling price of the bond**
P_m = **market price of the bond**
hp = **holding period of the bond in years.**

Again, the same two variables change: the holding period (hp) replaces n, and P_f replaces P_p. Keep in mind that P_f is not a contractual value but is *calculated* by defining the years remaining to maturity as $n - hp$ and by estimating a future market interest rate, i. We describe the computation of the future selling price (P_f) in the next section.

Once we determine hp and P_f, we can calculate the approximate realized yield. Assume that you acquired an 8 percent, 20-year bond for $750. Over the next two years you expect interest rates to decline. As we know, when interest rates decline, bond prices will increase. Suppose that you anticipate that the bond price will rise to $900. The approximate realized yield in this case for the two years would be

$$\text{ARY} = \frac{80 + \dfrac{900 - 750}{2}}{\dfrac{900 + 750}{2}} = 18.79\%.$$

The estimated high realized yield reflects your expectation of a substantial capital gains in a fairly short period of time.

Similarly, the substitution of P_f and hp into the present value model provides the following realized yield model:

$$P_m = \sum_{t=1}^{2hp} \frac{C_t/2}{(1 + i/2)^t} + \frac{P_f}{(1 + i/2)^{2hp}}. \qquad (14.9)$$

Again, this present value model requires that you solve for the i that equates the expected cash flows from coupon payments and the estimated selling price to the current market price. Because of the small number of periods in hp, the added accuracy of this measure is somewhat marginal. It has been suggested that because realized yield measures are based on an uncertain future selling price, the approximate realized (horizon) yield method is appropriate under many circumstances. In contrast, if you are going to use this technique to measure historical performance, you should use the more accurate present value model.

You will note from the present value realized yield formula in Equation 14.9 that the coupon flows are implicitly being discounted at the computed realized (horizon) yield. In many cases, this is an inappropriate assumption because available market rates might be very different from the computed realized (horizon) yield. Therefore, to derive a realistic estimate of the expected realized yield, you should also estimate your expected reinvestment rate during the investment horizon.

Therefore, to complete your understanding of computing expected realized yield for alternative investment strategies, the next section considers the calculation of future bond prices followed by a section on calculating realized return with different reinvestment rates.

CALCULATING FUTURE BOND PRICES

On several occasions we have noted that a bond's price varies with the discount rate. This leads to the very important concept that bond prices move inversely to interest rates. You must keep this in mind when valuing individual bonds or making bond portfolio decisions.

In two instances you will need to calculate dollar bond prices: (1) when computing realized (horizon) yield, you must determine the future selling price (P_f) of a bond, and (2) when issues are quoted on a promised yield basis, as with municipals. You can easily convert a yield-based quote to a dollar price by using Equation 14.7, which does not require iteration. You only need to solve Equation 14.7 for P_m. The coupon (C_t) is given, as is par value (P_p), and the promised YTM, which is used as the discount rate.

Consider a 10 percent, 25-year bond with a promised YTM of 12 percent. You would compute the price of this issue as

$$P_m = 100/2 \sum_{t=1}^{50} \frac{1}{\left(1 + \dfrac{.120}{2}\right)} + 1000 \frac{1}{\left(1 + \dfrac{.120}{2}\right)^{50}}$$

$$= .50(15.7619) + 1000(.0543)$$

$$= \$842.40.$$

In this instance, we are determining the prevailing market price of the bond based on the market YTM. These market figures indicate the consensus of all investors regarding the value of this bond. An investor who has a required rate of return on this bond that differs from the market YTM would estimate a different value for the bond.

In contrast to the current market price, you will need to compute a future price (P_f) when estimating the expected realized (horizon) yield performance of alternative bonds. Investors or portfolio managers who consistently trade bonds for capital gains need to compute expected realized yield rather than promised yield. They would compute P_f through the following variation of the realized yield equation:

$$P_f = \sum_{t=1}^{2n-2hp} \frac{C_t/2}{(1 + i/2)^t} + \frac{P_p}{(1 + i/2)^{2n-2hp}} \tag{14.10}$$

where:

P_f = **estimated future price of the bond**
P_p = **par value of the bond**
n = **number of years to maturity**
hp = **holding period of the bond in years**
c_t = **annual coupon payment**
i = **expected market YTM at the end of the holding period.**

Equation 14.10 is a version of the present value model that calculates the expected price of the bond at the end of the holding period (hp). The term $2n - 2hp$ equals the bond's remaining term to maturity at the end of the investor's holding period. That is, the number of 6-month periods remaining after the bond is sold. Therefore, the determination of P_f is based on four variables: two that are known and two that must be estimated by the investor.

Specifically, the coupon (C_t) and the par value (P_p) are given. The investor must forecast the length of the holding period, and therefore the number of years remaining to maturity at the time the bond is sold ($n - hp$). The investor must also forecast the expected market YTM at the time of sale (i). With this information you can calculate the future price of the bond. The real difficulty (and the potential source of error) in estimating P_f lies in predicting hp and i.

Assume you bought the 10 percent, 25-year bond just discussed at $842, giving it a YTM of 12 percent. Based on an analysis of the economy and the capital market, you expect this bond's market YTM to decline to 8 percent in 5 years. Therefore, you want to compute its future price (P_f) at the end of year 5 to estimate your expected rate of return, assuming you are correct in your assessment of the decline in overall market interest rates. As noted, you estimate the holding period (5 years), which implies a remaining life of 20 years, and the market YTM of 8 percent. A semiannual model gives a future price:

$$P_f = 50 \sum_{t=1}^{40} \frac{1}{(1.04)^t} + 1000 \frac{1}{(1.04)^{40}}$$
$$= 50\,(19.7928) + 1000\,(.2083)$$
$$= 989.64 + 208.30$$
$$= \$1197.94.$$

Based on this estimate of the selling price, you would estimate the approximate realized (horizon) yield on this investment on an annual basis as

$$APY = \frac{100 + \dfrac{1198 - 842}{5}}{\dfrac{1198 + 842}{2}}$$

$$= \frac{100 + 71.20}{1020}$$

$$= .1678$$

$$= 16.78\%.$$

REALIZED YIELD WITH DIFFERENTIAL REINVESTMENT RATES

Equation 14.9 is the standard present value formula with the changes in holding period and ending price. As such, it includes the implicit reinvestment rate assumption that all cash flows are reinvested at the computed i rate. The point is, there may be instances where such an implicit assumption is not appropriate, given your expectations for future interest rates. Assume that current market interest rates are very high and you invest in a long-term bond (e.g., a 20-year, 14 percent coupon) to take advantage of an expected decline in rates from 14 percent to 10 percent over a 2-year period. Computing the future price and using Equation 14.9 to estimate the realized (horizon) yield, we will get the following fairly high realized rate of return:

$$P_m = \$1,000$$

$$hp = 2 \text{ years}$$

$$P_f = \sum_{t=1}^{36} 70\,(1 + .05)^t + \$1,000/(1.05)^{36}$$

$$= \$1,158.30 + \$172.65$$

$$= \$1,330.95$$

$$\$1,000 = \sum_{t=1}^{4} \frac{70}{(1 + i/2)^t} + \frac{1330.95}{(1 + i/2)^4}$$

$$i = 27.5\%.$$

As noted, this calculation assumes that all cash flows are reinvested at the computed i (27.5 percent). However, it is unlikely that during a period when market rates are going from 14 percent to 10 percent you could reinvest the coupon flows at 27.5 percent. It is more appropriate and realistic to estimate the reinvestment rates and calculate the realized yields based on your *ending-wealth position*. This procedure is more precise and realistic and it is easier, because it does not require iteration.

The basic technique calculates the value of all cash flows at the end of the holding period, which is the investor's ending-wealth value. We compare this value to our *beginning-wealth value* to determine the *compound rate of return that equalizes these two values*. Adding to our prior example, assume we have the following cash flows:

$$P_m = \$1,000$$
$$I = \text{interest payments of \$70 in 6, 12, 18, and 24 months}$$
$$P_f = \$1,330.95 \text{ (the ending market value of the bond).}$$

The ending value of the four interest payments is determined by our assumptions regarding specific reinvestment rates. Assume that each payment is reinvested at a different declining rate that holds for its time period (i.e., the first three interest payments are reinvested at progressively lower rates and the fourth interest payment is received at the end of the holding period).

$$
\begin{aligned}
I_1 \text{ at 13\% for 18 months} &= \$70 \times (1 + .065)^3 = \$\ 84.55 \\
I_2 \text{ at 12\% for 12 months} &= \$70 \times (1 + .06)^2 = \quad 78.65 \\
I_3 \text{ at 11\% for \ 6 months} &= \$70 \times (1 + .055) = \quad 73.85 \\
I_4 \text{ not reinvested} &= \$70 \times (1.0) = \quad 70.00 \\
\end{aligned}
$$

$$\text{Future Value of Interest Payments} = \$307.05$$

Therefore, our total ending-wealth value is

$$\$1,330.95 + \$307.05 = \$1,638.00.$$

The compound realized (horizon) rate of return is calculated by comparing our ending-wealth value (\$1,638) to our beginning-wealth value (\$1,000) and determining what interest rate would equalize these two values over a 2-year holding period. To find this, compute the ratio of ending wealth to beginning wealth (1.638). Find this ratio (1.638) in a compound value table for 2 years or 4 periods (assuming semiannual compounding). Table A.3 at the end of the book indicates that the realized rate is somewhere between 12 percent (1.5735) and 14 percent (1.6890). Interpolation gives an estimate of 13.16 percent which indicates an annual rate of 26.32 percent (which compares to an estimate of 27.5 percent when we assume an implicit reinvestment rate of 27.5 percent).

This realized yield specifically states the expected reinvestment rates as contrasted to assuming the reinvestment rate is equal to the computed realized yield. The actual assumption regarding the reinvestment rate can be very important.

A summary of the steps to calculate an expected realized (horizon) yield is as follows:

1. Calculate the ending value of all coupon payments reinvested at estimated rates at the horizon date.
2. Calculate the expected sales price of the bond at your expected horizon date based on your estimate of the required yield to maturity at that time.
3. Sum the values in (1) and (2) to arrive at the total ending-wealth value.
4. Calculate the ratio of the ending wealth value to the beginning value (the purchase price of the bond). Given this ratio and the time horizon, compute the

compound rate of interest that will grow to this ratio over this time horizon

$$\left(\frac{\text{Ending wealth value}}{\text{Beginning value}}\right)^{1/2n}.$$

5. Assuming that all calculations are considered semiannual periods, double the interest rate derived from (4).

PRICE AND YIELD DETERMINATION ON NONINTEREST DATES

So far, we have assumed that the investor buys (or sells) a bond precisely on the date that interest is due, so the measures are accurate only when issues are traded on coupon payment dates. If the approximate yield method is used, sufficient accuracy is normally obtained by extrapolating for transactions on noninterest payment dates. You are already dealing with an approximation, and a bit more is probably acceptable.

However, when the semiannual model is used, and when more accuracy is necessary, another version of the price and yield model must be employed for transactions on noninterest payment dates. Fortunately, the basic models need be extended only one more step, because the value of an issue that trades X years, Y months, and so many days from maturity is found by extrapolating the bond value (price or yield) for the month before and the month after the day of transaction. Thus, the valuation process involves full months to maturity rather than years or semiannual periods.[6]

Using yields to compare bonds and estimate potential returns is a very common practice. In this section we discussed five yields including two (nominal yield and current yield) that are used for description rather than investment decisions. The latter three yields (promised YTM, promised YTC, and realized (horizon) yield) are all based on the present value model and require certain assumptions about the investor's holding period and the reinvestment rate earned on coupon cash flows. These last three yields can be computed by using either an approximate method, which is fairly easy, or by using the present value model, which is more accurate but also requires more computations.

YIELD ADJUSTMENTS FOR TAX-EXEMPT BONDS

Municipal bonds, Treasury issues, and many agency obligations possess one common characteristic: their interest income is partially or fully tax-exempt. This tax-exempt status affects the valuation of taxable versus nontaxable bonds. Although you could adjust each present value equation for the tax effects, it is not necessary for our purposes. We can envision the approximate impact of such an adjustment, however, by computing the fully taxable equivalent yield, which is one of the most often cited measures of performance for municipal bonds.

The *fully taxable equivalent yield (FTEY)* adjusts the promised yield computation for the bond's tax-exempt status. To compute the FTEY, we determine the promised yield on a tax-exempt bond using one of the yield formulas and then adjust the computed yield to reflect the rate of return that must be earned on a fully taxable issue. It is measured as

[6] For a detailed discussion of these calculations, see Frank J. Fabozzi, ed. *The Handbook of Fixed-Income Securities,* 3d ed. (Homewood, Ill.: Business One–Irwin, 1991).

$$\text{FTEY} = \frac{i}{1 - T} \tag{14.11}$$

where:

    i = **promised yield on the tax exempt bond**
    T = **amount and type of tax exemption.**

The FTEY equation has some limitations. It is applicable only to par bonds or current coupon obligations, such as new issues, because the measure considers only interest income, ignoring capital gains. Therefore, we cannot use it for issues trading at a significant variation from par value.

BOND YIELD
BOOKS

Bond value tables, commonly known as *bond books* or *yield books,* can eliminate most of the calculations for bond valuation. Figure 14.2 reproduces a page from a yield book. A bond yield table is like a present value interest factor table in that it provides a matrix of bond prices for a stated coupon rate, various terms to maturity (on the horizontal axis), and promised yields (on the vertical axis). Such a table allows you to determine either the promised yield or the price of a bond.

    The example in the left-hand section indicates that a 17 1/2-year, 8 percent coupon bond yielding 10 percent would be priced at 83.63. Likewise, the example in the right-hand column shows that a 20-year issue priced at 109.54 would have a promised yield to maturity of 7.10 percent. As might be expected, access to sophisticated calculators or computers has substantially reduced the need for and use of yield books.

    To truly understand the meaning of alternative yield measures, however, you must master the present value model and its variations that generate values for promised YTM, promised YTC, realized (horizon) yield, and bond prices.

WHAT
DETERMINES
INTEREST
RATES?

Now that we have learned to calculate various yields on bonds, the question arises as to what causes differences and changes in yields over time. Market interest rates cause these effects because the interest rates reported in the media are simply the prevailing YTMs for the bonds being discussed. For example, when you hear on television that the interest rate on long-term government bonds declined from 8.40 percent to 8.32 percent, this means that the price of this particular bond increased such that the computed YTM at the former price was 8.40 percent, but the computed YTM at the new, higher price is 8.32 percent. Yields and interest rates are the same. They are different terms for the same concept.

    We have discussed the inverse relationship between bond prices and interest rates. When interest rates decline, the prices of bonds increase; when interest rates rise, there is a decline in bond prices. It is natural to ask which of these is the driving force, bond prices or bond interest rates? It is a simultaneous change, and you can envision either factor causing it. Most practitioners probably envision the changes in interest rates as causes because they constantly use interest rates to describe changes. They use interest rates because these rates are comparable across bonds, whereas the price of a bond depends not only on the interest rate, but also on its specific characteristics including its coupon and maturity. The point is, when you change the interest rate (yield) on a bond, you simultaneously change its price in the opposite direction. Later in the chapter

FIGURE 14.2   **A Yield Book**

A   **YEARS and MONTHS**   **8%**

Yield	14-6	15-0	15-6	16-0	16-6	17-0	17-6	18-0
4.00	143.69	144.79	145.88	146.94	147.98	149.00	150.00	150.98
4.20	140.96	141.97	142.97	143.95	144.91	145.84	146.76	147.66
4.40	138.29	139.23	140.14	141.04	141.92	142.78	143.62	144.44
4.60	135.69	136.55	137.39	138.21	139.01	139.80	140.56	141.31
4.80	133.15	133.94	134.71	135.46	136.19	136.90	137.60	138.28
5.00	130.68	131.40	132.09	132.77	133.44	134.09	134.72	135.33
5.20	128.27	128.92	129.55	130.16	130.76	131.35	131.92	132.47
5.40	125.91	126.50	127.07	127.62	128.16	128.69	129.20	129.70
5.60	123.62	124.14	124.65	125.15	125.63	126.10	126.55	127.00
5.80	121.38	121.84	122.30	122.74	123.16	123.58	123.98	124.38
6.00	119.19	119.60	120.00	120.39	120.77	121.13	121.49	121.83
6.10	118.11	118.50	118.87	119.24	119.59	119.93	120.26	120.59
6.20	117.05	117.41	117.76	118.10	118.43	118.75	119.06	119.36
6.30	116.01	116.34	116.67	116.98	117.29	117.58	117.87	118.15
6.40	114.97	115.28	115.58	115.88	116.16	116.43	116.70	116.96
6.50	113.95	114.24	114.51	114.78	115.05	115.30	115.54	115.78
6.60	112.94	113.20	113.46	113.71	113.95	114.18	114.40	114.62
6.70	111.94	112.18	112.42	112.64	112.86	113.07	113.28	113.48
6.80	110.95	111.17	111.39	111.59	111.79	111.99	112.17	112.35
6.90	109.98	110.18	110.37	110.56	110.74	110.91	111.08	111.24
7.00	109.02	109.20	109.37	109.53	109.70	109.85	110.00	110.15
7.10	108.07	108.22	108.38	108.52	108.67	108.80	108.94	109.07
7.20	107.13	107.27	107.40	107.53	107.65	107.77	107.89	108.00
7.30	106.20	106.32	106.43	106.54	106.65	106.75	106.85	106.95
7.40	105.28	105.38	105.48	105.57	105.66	105.75	105.83	105.92
7.50	104.37	104.46	104.54	104.61	104.69	104.76	104.83	104.90
7.60	103.48	103.54	103.61	103.67	103.73	103.78	103.84	103.89
7.70	102.59	102.64	102.69	102.73	102.78	102.82	102.86	102.90
7.80	101.72	101.75	101.78	101.81	101.84	101.87	101.89	101.92
7.90	100.85	100.87	100.88	100.90	100.91	100.93	100.94	100.95
8.00	100.00	100.00	100.00	100.00	100.00	100.00	100.00	100.00
8.10	99.16	99.14	99.13	99.11	99.10	99.09	99.07	99.06
8.20	98.32	98.29	98.26	98.24	98.21	98.18	98.16	98.14
8.30	97.50	97.45	97.41	97.37	97.33	97.29	97.26	97.22
8.40	96.68	96.62	96.57	96.51	96.46	96.41	96.37	96.32
8.50	95.88	95.81	95.74	95.67	95.61	95.55	95.49	95.43
8.60	95.08	95.00	94.91	94.84	94.76	94.69	94.62	94.56
8.70	94.29	94.20	94.10	94.01	93.93	93.85	93.77	93.69
8.80	93.52	93.41	93.30	93.20	93.10	93.01	92.92	92.84
8.90	92.75	92.63	92.51	92.40	92.29	92.19	92.09	92.00
9.00	91.99	91.86	91.73	91.61	91.49	91.38	91.27	91.17
9.10	91.24	91.09	90.96	90.82	90.70	90.57	90.46	90.35
9.20	90.50	90.34	90.19	90.05	89.91	89.78	89.66	89.54
9.30	89.76	89.60	89.44	89.29	89.14	89.00	88.87	88.74
9.40	89.04	88.86	88.69	88.53	88.38	88.23	88.09	87.96
9.50	88.32	88.13	87.96	87.79	87.62	87.47	87.32	87.18
9.60	87.61	87.42	87.23	87.05	86.88	86.72	86.56	86.42
9.70	86.91	86.71	86.51	86.32	86.15	85.98	85.81	85.66
9.80	86.22	86.01	85.80	85.61	85.42	85.24	85.08	84.91
9.90	85.54	85.31	85.10	84.90	84.70	84.52	84.35	84.18
10.00	84.86	84.63	84.41	84.20	84.00	83.81	83.63	83.45
10.20	83.53	83.28	83.05	82.82	82.61	82.41	82.23	82.03
10.40	82.23	81.97	81.72	81.48	81.25	81.04	80.84	80.64
10.60	80.96	80.68	80.42	80.17	79.93	79.71	79.50	79.29
10.80	79.72	79.43	79.15	78.89	78.64	78.41	78.19	77.98
11.00	78.50	78.20	77.91	77.64	77.39	77.14	76.91	76.70
11.20	77.31	77.00	76.71	76.43	76.16	75.91	75.67	75.45
11.40	76.15	75.83	75.52	75.24	74.96	74.70	74.46	74.23
11.60	75.02	74.68	74.37	74.07	73.79	73.53	73.28	73.04
11.80	73.90	73.56	73.24	72.94	72.65	72.38	72.13	71.89
12.00	72.82	72.47	72.14	71.83	71.54	71.26	71.00	70.76

8%   **YEARS and MONTHS**   **B**

Yield	18-6	19-0	19-6	20-0	20-6	21-0	21-6	22-0
4.00	151.94	152.88	153.81	154.71	155.60	156.47	157.32	158.16
4.20	148.54	149.40	150.25	151.08	151.89	152.68	153.46	154.22
4.40	145.24	146.03	146.80	147.56	148.29	149.02	149.72	150.41
4.60	142.05	142.76	143.46	144.15	144.82	145.47	146.11	146.74
4.80	138.95	139.60	140.23	140.85	141.45	142.05	142.62	143.19
5.00	135.94	136.52	137.10	137.65	138.20	138.73	139.25	139.76
5.20	133.02	133.54	134.06	134.56	135.05	135.52	135.99	136.44
5.40	130.18	130.65	131.11	131.56	132.00	132.42	132.84	133.24
5.60	127.43	127.85	128.26	128.66	129.04	129.42	129.79	130.14
5.80	124.76	125.13	125.49	125.84	126.18	126.51	126.84	127.15
6.00	122.17	122.49	122.81	123.11	123.41	123.70	123.98	124.25
6.10	120.90	121.20	121.50	121.78	122.06	122.33	122.59	122.84
6.20	119.65	119.93	120.21	120.47	120.73	120.98	121.22	121.46
6.30	118.42	118.68	118.93	119.18	119.42	119.65	119.87	120.09
6.40	117.21	117.45	117.68	117.91	118.13	118.34	118.55	118.75
6.50	116.01	116.23	116.45	116.66	116.86	117.05	117.24	117.43
6.60	114.83	115.04	115.23	115.42	115.61	115.79	115.96	116.13
6.70	113.67	113.86	114.04	114.21	114.38	114.54	114.70	114.85
6.80	112.53	112.69	112.86	113.01	113.17	113.31	113.46	113.59
6.90	111.40	111.55	111.70	111.84	111.97	112.11	112.23	112.36
7.00	110.29	110.42	110.55	110.68	110.80	110.92	111.03	111.14
7.10	109.19	109.31	109.42	109.54	109.64	109.75	109.85	109.94
7.20	108.11	108.21	108.31	108.41	108.50	108.60	108.68	108.77
7.30	107.04	107.13	107.22	107.30	107.38	107.46	107.54	107.61
7.40	105.99	106.07	106.14	106.21	106.28	106.35	106.41	106.47
7.50	104.96	105.02	105.08	105.14	105.19	105.25	105.30	105.35
7.60	103.94	103.99	104.03	104.08	104.12	104.16	104.20	104.24
7.70	102.93	102.97	103.00	103.04	103.07	103.10	103.13	103.16
7.80	101.94	101.96	101.99	102.01	102.03	102.05	102.07	102.09
7.90	100.96	100.98	100.99	101.00	101.01	101.02	101.03	101.04
8.00	100.00	100.00	100.00	100.00	100.00	100.00	100.00	100.00
8.10	99.05	99.04	99.03	99.03	99.02	99.01	98.99	98.98
8.20	98.11	98.09	98.07	98.05	98.03	98.01	97.99	97.98
8.30	97.19	97.16	97.13	97.10	97.07	97.04	97.01	96.99
8.40	96.28	96.24	96.20	96.16	96.12	96.08	96.05	96.02
8.50	95.38	95.33	95.28	95.23	95.19	95.14	95.10	95.06
8.60	94.49	94.43	94.37	94.32	94.26	94.21	94.16	94.12
8.70	93.62	93.55	93.48	93.42	93.36	93.30	93.24	93.19
8.80	92.76	92.68	92.60	92.53	92.46	92.40	92.33	92.28
8.90	91.91	91.82	91.74	91.66	91.58	91.51	91.44	91.38
9.00	91.07	90.98	90.89	90.80	90.72	90.64	90.56	90.49
9.10	90.24	90.14	90.04	89.95	89.86	89.78	89.70	89.62
9.20	89.43	89.32	89.21	89.11	89.02	88.93	88.84	88.76
9.30	88.62	88.51	88.40	88.29	88.19	88.09	88.00	87.91
9.40	87.83	87.71	87.59	87.48	87.37	87.27	87.17	87.08
9.50	87.05	86.92	86.79	86.68	86.57	86.46	86.36	86.26
9.60	86.27	86.14	86.01	85.89	85.77	85.66	85.55	85.45
9.70	85.51	85.37	85.24	85.11	84.99	84.87	84.76	84.66
9.80	84.76	84.62	84.48	84.34	84.22	84.10	83.98	83.87
9.90	84.02	83.87	83.72	83.59	83.46	83.33	83.21	83.10
10.00	83.29	83.13	82.98	82.84	82.71	82.58	82.45	82.34
10.20	81.86	81.69	81.53	81.38	81.24	81.10	80.97	80.85
10.40	80.46	80.28	80.12	79.96	79.81	79.67	79.54	79.40
10.60	79.10	78.92	78.74	78.58	78.42	78.28	78.13	78.00
10.80	77.78	77.59	77.41	77.24	77.08	76.92	76.78	76.64
11.00	76.49	76.29	76.11	75.93	75.76	75.61	75.46	75.31
11.20	75.23	75.03	74.84	74.66	74.49	74.33	74.17	74.03
11.40	74.01	73.80	73.61	73.42	73.25	73.08	72.93	72.78
11.60	72.82	72.61	72.41	72.22	72.04	71.87	71.71	71.56
11.80	71.66	71.44	71.24	71.05	70.87	70.70	70.53	70.38
12.00	70.53	70.31	70.10	69.91	69.72	69.55	69.39	69.23

Source: Reproduced with permission from Expanded Bond Values Publication #83, pp. 879–880, copyright 1970 Financial Publishing Co., Boston, Mass.

we will discuss the specific price-yield relationship for individual bonds and demonstrate that this price-yield relationship differs among bonds based on their particular coupon and maturity.

Understanding interest rates and what makes them change is necessary for an investor who hopes to maximize returns from investing in bonds. Therefore, in this section we will review our prior discussion of the following topics: what causes overall market interest rates to rise and fall, why do alternative bonds have different interest rates, and why does the difference in rates (i.e., the yield spread) between alternative bonds change over time. To accomplish this, we begin with a general discussion of the influences on interest rates, and then consider the *term structure of interest rates* (shown by yield curves), which relates the interest rates on a set of comparable bonds to their terms to maturity. The term structure is important because it reflects what investors expect to happen to interest rates in the future and it also dictates their current risk attitude. Finally, we turn to the concept of *yield spreads,* which measures the differences in yields between alternative bonds. We will describe various yield spreads and explore changes in them over time.

FORECASTING
INTEREST RATES

As discussed, the ability to forecast interest rates and changes in these rates is critical to successful bond investing. Subsequent presentations consider the major determinants of interest rates, but for now you should keep in mind that interest rates *are the price for loanable funds.* Like any price, they are determined by the supply and demand for these funds. On the one side investors are willing to provide the funds (the supply) at prices based on their required rates of return for a particular borrower. On the other side borrowers need the funds (the demand) to support budget deficits (government), to invest in capital projects (corporations) or to acquire durable goods (cars, appliances) or homes (individuals).

Although the lenders and borrowers have some fundamental factors that determine the supply and demand curves, the prices for these funds (interest rates) are also affected for short time periods by events that shift the curves. Examples include major government bond issues that affect demand, or significant changes in Federal Reserve monetary policy that affect the supply of money.

Our treatment of interest rate forecasting recognizes that you must be aware of the basic determinants of interest rates and monitor these factors. We also recognize that detailed forecasting of interest rates is a very complex task that is best left to professional economists. Therefore, our goal as bond investors and bond portfolio managers is to monitor current and expected interest rate behavior. We should attempt to continuously assess the major factors that affect interest rate behavior but also rely on others, such as economic consulting firms, banks, or investment banking firms, for detailed insights on such topics as the real RFR and the expected rate of inflation.[7] This is precisely the way most bond portfolio managers operate.

FUNDAMENTAL
DETERMINANTS
OF INTEREST
RATES

As shown in Figure 14.3, average interest rates for long-term (10-year) U.S. government bonds during the period from late 1990 to mid-1993 went from 9 percent to 6 percent. These results were midway between the United Kingdom and Japan. UK bonds went from about 12 percent to 8 percent, while the rate on Japanese government bonds declined from about 8.7 percent to about 4.5 percent. As a bond investor you need to understand *why* there are these differences and *why* interest rates changed this way.

As you know from your knowledge of bond pricing, bond prices increased dramatically during periods when market interest rates dropped, and some bond investors experienced very attractive returns. In contrast, some investors experienced substantial losses during several periods when interest rates increased. A casual analysis of this chart, which covers less than 4 years, indicates the need for monitoring interest rates.

---

[7] Sources of information on the bond market and interest rate forecasts would include Merrill-Lynch's *Fixed Income Weekly* and *World Bond Market Monitor*; Goldman, Sach's *Financial Market Perspectives,* and Kidder, Peabody's *Economic Outlook and Chartbook.*

FIGURE 14.3   **International 10-Year Government Bond Yields**

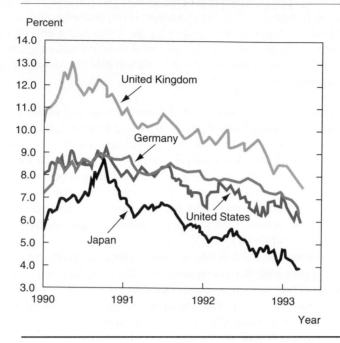

Note: For Japan and Germany, rates on newly issued securities are given until October 1986; secondary market yields are quoted thereafter.

Sources: Federal Reserve Bank, Telerate, *Capital Markets Chartbook* (New York: Kidder, Peabody & Co., June 1993).

Essentially, the factors causing interest rates (i) to rise or fall are described by the following model:

$$i = \text{RFR} + I + \text{RP} \qquad (14.12)$$

where:

   RFR = real risk-free rate of interest
   I = expected rate of inflation
   RP = risk premium.

This relationship should be familiar from our presentations in Chapters 1 and 8. Equation 14.12 is a simple but complete statement of interest rate behavior. It is a more difficult task to estimate the *future* behavior of such variables as real growth, expected inflation, and economic uncertainty. In this regard, interest rates, like stock prices, are extremely difficult to forecast with any degree of accuracy.[8] Alternatively, we can visualize the source of changes in interest rates in terms of the economic conditions and issue characteristics that determine the rate of return on a bond:

[8] For an overview of interest rate forecasting, see Frank J. Jones and Benjamin Wolkowitz, "The Determinants of Interest Rates," and W. David Woolford, "Forecasting Interest Rates," in *Handbook of Fixed-Income Securities,* 3d ed., edited by Frank J. Fabozzi (Homewood, Ill.: Business One–Irwin, 1991).

$$i = f(\text{Economic Forces} + \text{Issue Characteristics})$$
$$= (\text{RFR} + I) + \text{RP}.$$

This rearranged version of Equation 14.12 helps us to isolate the determinants of interest rates.[9]

EFFECT OF ECONOMIC FACTORS

The real risk-free rate of interest (RFR) is the economic cost of money, that is, the opportunity cost necessary to compensate individuals for forgoing consumption. As discussed previously, it is determined by the real growth rate of the economy with short-run effects due to ease or tightness in the capital market.

The expected rate of inflation is the other economic influence on interest rates. We add the expected level of inflation (I) to the real risk-free rate (RFR) to specify the nominal RFR, which is a market rate like the current rate on government T-bills. Given the stability of the real RFR, it is clear that the wide swings in interest rates during the 4 years covered by Figure 14.3 occurred because of expected inflation.[10] Besides the unique country and exchange rate risk that we discuss in the section on risk premiums, differences in the rates of inflation between countries have a major impact on their level of interest rates.

To sum up, one way to estimate the nominal RFR is to begin with the real growth rate of the economy, adjust for short-run ease or tightness in the capital market, and then adjust this real rate of interest for the expected rate of inflation.

Another approach to estimating the nominal rate or changes in the rate is the macroeconomic view, where the supply and demand for loanable funds are the fundamental economic determinants of i. As the supply of loanable funds increases, the level of interest rates declines, other things being equal. Several factors influence the supply of funds. Government monetary policies imposed by the Federal Reserve have a significant impact on the supply of money. The savings pattern of U.S. and non-U.S. investors also affects the supply of funds. Non-U.S. investors have become a stronger influence on the U.S. supply of loanable funds during recent years, as shown by the significant purchases of U.S. securities by non-U.S. investors, most notably the Japanese prior to a pullback in 1992. It is widely acknowledged that this foreign addition to the supply of funds has been very beneficial to the United States in terms of reducing our interest rates and our cost of capital.

Interest rates increase when the demand for loanable funds increases. The demand for loanable funds is affected by the capital and operating needs of the U.S. government, federal agencies, state and local governments, corporations, institutions, and individuals. Federal budget deficits increase the Treasury's demand for loanable funds. Likewise, the level of consumer demand for funds to buy houses, autos, and appliances affects rates, as does corporate demand for funds to pursue investment opportunities.

---

[9] For an extensive exploration of interest rates and interest rate behavior, see James C. Van Horne, *Financial Market Rates and Flows,* 3d ed. (Englewood Cliffs, N.J.: Prentice-Hall, 1989).

[10] In this regard, see R. W. Hafer, "Inflation: Assessing Its Recent Behavior and Future Prospects," Federal Reserve Bank of St. Louis *Review* 65, no. 7 (August-September 1983): 36–41.

The total of all groups determines the aggregate demand and supply of loanable funds and the level of the nominal RFR.[11]

THE IMPACT OF BOND CHARACTERISTICS

The interest rates of a specific bond issue is influenced not only by all these factors that affect the nominal RFR, but also by its unique issue characteristics. These issue characteristics influence the bond's risk premium (RP). The economic forces that determine the nominal RFR affect all securities, whereas issue characteristics are unique to individual securities, market sectors, or countries. Thus, the differences in the yields of corporate and Treasury bonds are not caused by economic forces but rather by different issue characteristics that cause differences in the risk premiums.

Bond investors separate the risk premium into four components:

1. The quality of the issue as determined by its risk of default relative to other bonds
2. The term to maturity of the issue, which can affect yield and price volatility
3. Indenture provisions, including collateral, call features, and sinking-fund provisions
4. Foreign bond risk, including exchange rate risk and country risk

Of the four factors, quality and maturity have the greatest impact on the risk premium for domestic bonds, while exchange rate risk and country risk are important components of risk for non-U.S. bonds.

The credit quality of a bond reflects the ability of the issuer to service outstanding debt obligations. This information is largely captured in the ratings issued by the bond rating firms. As a result, bonds with different ratings have different yields. For example, AAA-rated obligations possess lower risk of default than BBB obligations, so they can provide lower yield.

Notably, the risk premium differences between bonds of different quality levels have changed dramatically over time depending on prevailing economic conditions. When the economy experiences a recession or a period of economic uncertainty, the desire for quality increases, and investors bid up prices of higher-rated bonds, which reduces their yields. This is referred to as the quality spread. It has also been suggested by Dialynas and Edington that this spread is influenced by the volatility of interest rates.[12] This variability in the risk premium over time was demonstrated and discussed in Chapter 11.

Term to maturity also influences the risk premium because it affects an investor's level of uncertainty as well as the price volatility of the bond. In the section on the term structure of interest rates, we will discuss the typical positive relationship between the term to maturity of an issue and its interest rate.

As discussed in Chapter 13, indenture provisions indicate the collateral pledged for a bond, its callability, and its sinking-fund provisions. Collateral gives protection to the

---

[11] For an example of an estimate of the supply and demand for funds in the economy, see *Prospects for Financial Markets in 1993* (New York: Salomon Bros., 1992). This is an annual publication of Salomon Brothers that gives an estimate of the flow of funds in the economy and discusses its effect on various currencies and interest rates, making recommendations for portfolio strategy on the basis of these expectations.

[12] Chris P. Dialynas and David H. Edington, "Bond Yield Spreads: A Postmodern View," *Journal of Portfolio Management,* 19, no. 1 (Fall 1992):68–75.

investor if the issuer defaults on the bond, because the investor has a specific claim on some set of assets in case of liquidation.

Call features indicate when an issuer can buy back the bond prior to its maturity. A bond is called by an issuer when interest rates have declined so it is typically not to the advantage of the investor who must reinvest the proceeds at a lower interest rate. Therefore, more protection against having the bond called reduces the risk premium. The significance of call protection increases during periods of high interest rates. When you buy a bond with a high coupon, you want protection from having it called away when rates decline.[13]

A sinking fund reduces the investor's risk and causes a lower yield for several reasons. First, a sinking fund reduces default risk because it requires the issuer to reduce the outstanding issue systematically. Second, purchases of the bond by the issuer to satisfy sinking-fund requirements provide price support for the bond because of the added demand. These purchases by the issuer also contribute to a more liquid secondary market for the bond because of the increased trading. Finally, sinking-fund provisions require that the issuer retire a bond before its stated maturity, which causes a reduction in the issue's average maturity. The decline in average maturity tends to reduce the risk premium of the bond much as a shorter maturity would reduce yield.[14]

We know that foreign currency exchange rates change over time and that this increases the risk of global investing. Differences in the variability of exchange rates among countries arise because the trade balances and rates of inflation differ among countries. More volatile trade balances and inflation rates in a country make its exchange rates more volatile, which will add to the uncertainty of future exchange rates. These factors increase the exchange rate risk premium.

In addition to the ongoing changes in exchange rates, investors are always concerned with the political and economic stability of a country. If investors are unsure about the political environment or the economic system in a country, they will increase the risk premium they require to reflect this country risk.

TERM STRUCTURE OF INTEREST RATES

The term structure of interest rates (or the *yield curve,* as it is more popularly known) is a static function that relates the term to maturity to the yield to maturity for a sample of bonds at *a given point in time.*[15] Thus, it represents a cross section of yields for a category of bonds that are comparable in all respects but maturity. Specifically, the quality of the issues should be constant, and ideally you should have issues with similar coupons and call features within a single industry category. You can construct different yield curves for Treasuries, government agencies, prime-grade municipals, AAA utilities, and so on. The accuracy of the yield curve will depend on the comparability of the bonds in the sample.

[13] William Marshall and Jess B. Yawitz, "Optimal Terms of the Call Provision on a Corporate Bond," *Journal of Financial Research* 3, no. 3 (Fall 1980): 203–211; and Michael G. Ferri, "Systematic Return Risk and the Call Risk of Corporate Debt Instruments," *Journal of Financial Research* 1, no. 1 (Winter 1978): 1–13,

[14] For a further discussion of sinking funds, see Edward A. Dyl and Michael D. Joehnk, "Sinking Funds and the Cost of Corporate Debt," *Journal of Finance* 34, no. 4 (September 1979): 887–893; A. J. Kalotay, "On the Management of Sinking Funds," *Financial Management* 10, no. 2 (Summer 1981): 34–40; and A. J. Kalotay, "Sinking Funds and the Realized Cost of Debt," *Financial Management* 11, no. 1 (Spring 1982): 43–54.

[15] For a discussion of the theory and empirical evidence, see Richard W. McEnally and James V. Jordan, "The Term Structure of Interest Rates," in *The Handbook of Fixed-Income Securities,* 3d ed., edited by Frank J. Fabozzi (Homewood, Ill.: Business One–Irwin, 1991).

FIGURE 14.4   **Treasury Yield Curves**

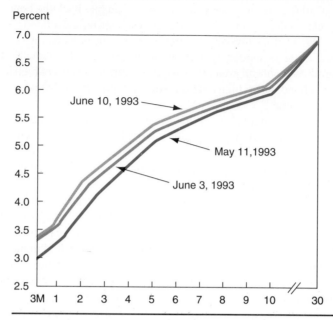

Source: Federal Reserve Bank; *Capital Markets Chartbook* (New York: Kidder, Peabody & Co., June 1993).

As an example, Figure 14.4 shows yield curves for a sample of U.S. Treasury obligations. It is based on the yield to maturity information for a set of comparable Treasury issues from a publication such as the *Federal Reserve Bulletin* or *The Wall Street Journal.* These promised yields were plotted on the graph, and a yield curve was drawn that represents the general configuration of rates. Kidder Peabody collected these data and constructed yield curves at three different points in time to demonstrate the changes in yield levels and in the shape of the yield curve over time.

All yield curves, of course, do not have the same shape as those in Figure 14.4. The point of the example is that, although individual yield curves are static, their behavior over time is quite fluid. As shown, the level of the curve increased from May 11th to June 3rd and then increased slightly to June 10, 1993. Also, the shape of the yield curve can undergo dramatic alterations, following one of the four patterns shown in Figure 14.5. The rising yield curve is the most common and tends to prevail when interest rates are at low or modest levels. The declining yield curve tends to occur when rates are relatively high. The flat yield curve rarely exists for any period of time. The humped yield curve prevails when extremely high rates are expected to decline to more normal levels. Note that the slope of the curve tends to level off after 15 years.

Why does the term structure assume different shapes? Three major theories attempt to explain this: the expectations hypothesis, the liquidity preference hypothesis, and the segmented market hypothesis.

EXPECTATIONS HYPOTHESIS
According to the expectations hypothesis, the shape of the yield curve results from the interest rate expectations of market participants. More specifically, it holds that *any*

FIGURE 14.5   **Types of Yield Curves**

A Rising Yield Curve is formed when the yields on short-term issues are low and rise consistently with longer maturities and flatten out at the extremes.

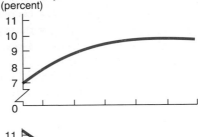

A Declining Yield Curve is formed when the yields on short-term issues are high and yields on subsequently longer maturities decline consistently.

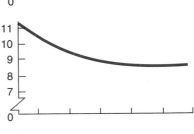

A Flat Yield Curve has approximately equal yields on short-term and long-term issues.

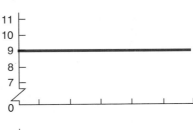

A Humped Yield Curve is formed when yields on intermediate-term issues are above those on short-term issues; and the rates on long-term issues decline to levels below those for the short-term and then level out.

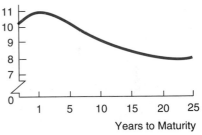

long-term interest rate simply represents the geometric mean of current and future 1-year interest rates expected to prevail over the maturity of the issue. In essence, the term structure involves a series of intermediate and long-term interest rates, each of which is a reflection of the geometric average of current and expected 1-year interest rates. Under such conditions, the equilibrium long-term rate is the rate the long-term bond investor would expect to earn through successive investments in short-term bonds over the term to maturity of the long-term bond.

This relationship can be formalized in a general manner as follows:

$$(1 + {}_tR_n) = [(1 + {}_tR_1)(1 + {}_{t+1}r_1) \ldots (1 + {}_{t+n-1}r_1)]^{1/N} \qquad (14.13)$$

where:

R_n = **actual long-term rate**
N = **term to maturity (in years) of long issue**
R = **current 1-year rate**
$_{t+1}r_1$ = **the expected 1-year yield during some future period, $t + i$ (These future 1-year rates are referred to as *forward rates*.).**

Given the relationship set forth in Equation 14.13, the formula for computing the one-period forward rate beginning at time $t + n$, implied in the term structure at time t is as follows:

$$1 + {}_{t+n}r_{1t} = \frac{(1 + {}_tR_{1t})\ (1 + {}_{t+1}r_{1t})\ (1 + {}_{t+2}r_{1t}) \cdots (1 + {}_{t+n-1}r_{1t})\ (1 + {}_{t+n}r_{1t})}{(1 + {}_tR_{1t})\ (1 + {}_{t+1}r_{1t}) \cdots (1 + {}_{t+n-1}r_{1t})}$$

$$= \frac{(1 + {}_tR_{n+1})^{n+1}}{(1 + {}_tR_n)^n} \tag{14.14}$$

$${}_{t+n}r_{1t} = \frac{(1 + {}_tR_{n+1})^{n+1}}{(1 + {}_tR_n)^n} - 1$$

where $_{t+n}r_{1t}$ is the 1-year forward rate prevailing at $t + n$, using the term structure at time t.

Assume that the 5-year spot rate is 10 percent ($_tR_5 = .10$) and the 4-year spot rate is 9 percent ($_tR_4 = .09$). The forward 1-year rate 4 years from now implied by these spot rates can be calculated as follows:

$$\begin{aligned}
{}_{t+4}r_{1t} &= \frac{(1 + {}_tR_5)^5}{(1 + {}_tR_4)^4} - 1 \\
&= \frac{(1 + .10)^5}{(1 + .09)^4} - 1 \\
&= \frac{1.6105}{1.4116} - 1 \\
&= 1.1409 - 1 = .1409 = 14.09\%
\end{aligned}$$

The term structure at time t implies that the 1-year spot rate 4 years from now (during Year 5) will be 14.09 percent. This concept and formula can be used to derive future rates for multiple years. Thus, the 2-year spot rate that will prevail 3 years from now could be calculated using the 3-year spot rate and the 5-year spot rate. The general formula for computing the j-period forward rate beginning at time $t + n$ as of time t is

$$_{t+n}r_{jt} = \sqrt[j]{\frac{(1 + {}_tR_{n+j})^{n+j}}{(1 + {}_tR_n)^n}} - 1 \tag{14.15}$$

As a practical approximation of Equation 14.13, it is possible to use the *arithmetic* average of 1-year rates to generate long-term yields.

The expectations theory can explain any shape of yield curve. Expectations for rising short-term rates in the future cause a rising yield curve; expectations for falling short-term rates in the future will cause long-term rates to lie below current short-term rates, and the yield curve will decline. Similar explanations account for flat and humped yield curves.

Consider the following explanation by the expectations hypothesis of the shape of the term structure of interest rates using arithmetic averages:

$_1R_1 = 5\frac{1}{2}\%$ the 1-year rate of interest prevailing now (period t)

$_{t+1}r_1 = 6\%$ the 1-year rate of interest expected to prevail next year (period $t + 1$)

$_{t+2}r_1 = 7\frac{1}{2}\%$ the 1-year rate of interest expected to prevail 2 years from now (period $t + 2$)

$_{t+3}r_1 = 8\frac{1}{2}\%$ the 1-year rate of interest expected to prevail 3 years from now (period $t + 3$)

Using these values, and the known rate on a 1-year bond, we compute rates on 2-, 3-, or 4-year bonds (designated R_2, R_3, and R_4) as follows:

$$_1R_1 = 5\ 1/2 \text{ percent}$$
$$_1R_2 = (0.055 + 0.06)/2 = 5.75 \text{ percent}$$
$$_1R_3 = (0.055 + 0.06 + 0.075)/3 = 6.33 \text{ percent}$$
$$_1R_4 = (0.055 + 0.06 + 0.075 + 0.085)/4 = 6.88 \text{ percent}$$

In this illustration (which uses the arithmetic average as an approximation of the geo-metric mean), the yield curve is upward-sloping because, at present, investors expect future short-term rates to be above current short-term rates. This is not the formal method for constructing the yield curve. Rather, it is constructed as demonstrated in Figure 14.3 on the basis of the prevailing promised yields for bonds with different maturities.

The expectations hypothesis attempts to explain *why* the yield curve is upward-sloping, downward-sloping, humped, or flat by explaining the expectations implicit in yield curves with different shapes. The evidence is fairly substantial and convincing that the expectations hypothesis is a workable explanation of the term structure. Be-cause of the supporting evidence, its relative simplicity, and the intuitive appeal of the theory, the expectations hypothesis of the term structure of interest rates is rather widely accepted.

Besides the theory and empirical support, it is also possible to present a scenario wherein investor actions will cause the yield curve postulated by the theory. The ex-pectations hypothesis predicts a declining yield curve when interest rates are likely to fall in the future rather than rise. In such a case, long-term bonds would be considered to be attractive investments, because investors would want to lock in prevailing higher yields (which are not expected to be as high in the future) or they would want to capture the increase in bond prices (as capital gains) that will accompany a decline in rates. By the same reasoning, investors will avoid short-term bonds or sell them and reinvest the funds in long-term bonds. The point is, investor expectations will reinforce the declining shape of the yield curve as they bid up the prices of long-maturity bonds (forcing yields to decline) and short-term bond issues are avoided or sold (so prices decline and yields rise). At the same time, there is confirming action by suppliers of bonds. Specifically, government or corporate issuers will avoid selling long bonds at the current high rates but would want to wait until the rates decline. In the meantime, they will issue short-term bonds if they need to while waiting for lower rates. Therefore, in the long-term market you will have an increase in demand and a decline in the supply and vice versa in the short-term market. These shifts between long- and short-term maturities will continue until equilibrium occurs or expectations change.

LIQUIDITY PREFERENCE HYPOTHESIS

The theory of liquidity preference holds that long-term securities should provide higher returns than short-term obligations, because investors are willing to sacrifice some yields to invest in short-maturity obligations to avoid the higher price volatility of long-maturity bonds. Another way to interpret the liquidity preference hypothesis is to say that lenders prefer short-term loans, and to induce them to lend long term, it is necessary to offer higher yields.

The liquidity preference theory contends that uncertainty causes investors to favor short-term issues over bonds with longer maturities because short-term bonds can easily be converted into predictable amounts of cash should unforeseen events occur. This theory argues that the yield curve should slope upward and that any other shape should be viewed as a temporary aberration.

This theory can be considered an extension of the expectations hypothesis because the formal liquidity preference position contends that the liquidity premium inherent in the yields for longer maturity bonds should be added to the expected future rate in arriving at long-term yields. Specifically, the liquidity premium (L) compensates the investor in long-term bonds for the added uncertainty because of less stable prices. Because the liquidity premium (L) is provided to compensate the long-term investor, it is simply a variation of Equation 14.13 as follows:

$$(1 + {}_tR_N) = [(1 + {}_tR_1)(1 + {}_{t+1}r_1 + L_2) \ldots (1 + {}_{t+N-1}r_1 + L_n)]^{1/N}$$

In this specification the Ls are not the same, but would be expected to increase with time. The liquidity preference theory has been found to possess some strong empirical support.[16]

To see how the liquidity preference theory predicts future yields and how it compares to the pure expectation hypothesis, let us predict future long-term rates from a single set of 1-year rates: 6 percent, 7.5 percent, and 8.5 percent. The liquidity preference theory would suggest that investors would add increasing liquidity premiums to successive rates to derive actual market rates. As an example, they might arrive at rates of 6.3 percent, 7.9 percent, and 9.0 percent.

---

[16] See Reuben A. Kessel, "The Cyclical Behavior of the Term Structure of Interest Rates," Occasional Paper 91, National Bureau of Economic Research, 1965; Phillip Cagan, *Essays on Interest Rates* (New York: Columbia University Press for the National Bureau of Economic Research, 1969); and J. Huston McCulloch, "An Estimate of the Liquidity Premium," *Journal of Political Economy* 83, no. 1 (January-February 1975): 95–119.

As a matter of historical fact, the yield curve shows a definite upward bias, which implies that some combination of the expectations theory and the liquidity preference theory will more accurately explain the shape of the yield curve than either of them alone. Specifically, actual long-term rates consistently tend to be above what is envisioned from the price expectations hypothesis, which implies the existence of a liquidity premium.

SEGMENTED MARKET HYPOTHESIS

Despite meager empirical support, a third theory for the shape of the yield curve is the segmented market hypothesis, which enjoys wide acceptance among market practitioners. Also known as the *preferred habitat*, the *institutional theory*, or the *hedging pressure theory,* it asserts that different institutional investors have different maturity needs that lead them to confine their security selections to specific maturity segments. That is, investors supposedly focus on short-term, intermediate-term, or long-term securities. This theory contends that the shape of the yield curve is ultimately a function of these investment policies of major financial institutions.

Financial institutions tend to structure their investment policies in line with factors such as their tax liabilities, the types and maturity structure of their liabilities, and the level of earnings demanded by depositors. As an example, because commercial banks are subject to normal corporate tax rates, and their liabilities are generally short- to intermediate-term time and demand deposits, they consistently invest in short- to intermediate-term municipal bonds.

The segmented market theory contends that the business environment, along with legal and regulatory limitations, tends to direct each type of financial institution to allocate its resources to particular types of bonds with specific maturity characteristics. In its strongest form, the segmented market theory holds that the maturity preferences of investors and borrowers are so strong that investors never purchase securities outside their preferred maturity range to take advantage of yield differentials. As a result, the short- and long-maturity portions of the bond market are effectively segmented, and yields for a segment depend on the supply and demand *within* that maturity segment.

TRADING IMPLICATIONS OF THE TERM STRUCTURE

Information on maturities can help you to formulate yield expectations by simply observing the shape of the yield curve. If the yield curve is declining sharply, historical evidence suggests that interest rates will probably decline. Expectations theorists would suggest that you need to examine only the prevailing yield curve to predict the direction of interest rates in the future.

Based on these theories, bond investors use the prevailing yield curve to predict the shapes of future yield curves. Using this prediction and knowledge of current interest rates, investors can determine expected yield volatility by maturity sector. In turn, the maturity segments that experience the greatest yield changes give the investor the largest potential price appreciation.[17]

---

[17] Gikas A. Hourdouvelis, "The Predictive Power of the Term Structure During Recent Monetary Regimes," *Journal of Finance* 43, no. 2 (June 1988): 339–356.

YIELD SPREADS

Another technique that can be used to help make good bond investments or profitable trades is the analysis of *yield spreads,* which are the differences in promised yields between bond issues or segments of the market at any point in time. Such differences are specific to the particular issues or segments of the bond market. Thus they add to the rates determined by the basic economic forces ($RFR + I$).

There are four major yield spreads:

1. Different *segments* of the bond market may have different yields. For example, pure government bonds will have lower yields than government agency bonds; and government bonds have much lower yields than corporate bonds.

2. Bonds in different *sectors* of the same market segment may have different yields. For example, prime-grade municipal bonds will have lower yields than good-grade municipal bonds; you will find spreads between AA utilities and BBB utilities, or between AAA industrial bonds and AAA public utility bonds.

3. Different *coupons* or *seasoning* within a given market segment or sector may cause yield spreads. Examples would include current coupon government bonds versus deep-discount governments, or recently issued AA industrials versus seasoned AA industrials.

4. Different *maturities* within a given market segment or sector also cause differences in yields. You will see yield spreads between short-term agency issues and long-term agency issues, or between 3-year prime municipals and 25-year prime municipals.

The differences among these bonds cause yield spreads that may be either positive or negative. More important, *the magnitude or the direction of a spread can change over time.* These changes in size or direction of yield spreads offer profit opportunities. We say that the spread narrows whenever the differences in yield become smaller, and it widens as the differences increase. Table 14.1 contains data on a variety of past yield spreads.

TABLE 14.1

Selected Mean Yield Spreads (Reported in Basis Points)

Comparisons	1984	1985	1986	1987	1988	1989	1990	1991	1992
1. Short Governments—Long Governments[a]	+10	+111	+108	+96	+72	+3	+48	+127	+210
2. Long Governments—Long Aaa Corporates[b]	+72	+62	+88	+74	+73	+68	+58	+61	+62
3. Long Municipals—Long Aaa Corporates[c]	+272	+226	+170	+175	+203	+203	+220	+199	+185
4. Long Aaa Municipals—Long Baa Municipals[d]	+77	+98	+81	+103	+47	+40	+104	+103	+84
5. AA Utilities—BBB Utilities[e]	+88	+90	+70	+76	+74	+42	+41	+46	+31
6. AA Utilities—AA Industrials[e]	−51	−11	+33	+19	−65	−20	−20	−9	−18

[a]Median yield to maturity of a varying number of bonds with 2 to 5 years maturity and more than 10 years, respectively.

[b]Long Aaa corporates based on yields to maturity on selected long-term bonds.

[c]Long-term municipal issues based on Bond Buyer Series, a representative list of high-quality municipal bonds with a 20-year period to maturity being maintained.

[d]General obligation municipal bonds only.

[e]Based on a changing list of representative issues.

Source: Federal Reserve Bulletin, Moody's Bond Guide.

As a bond investor, you should evaluate yield spread changes because these changes influence bond price behavior and comparative return performance. You should attempt to identify (1) any normal yield spread that is expected to become abnormally wide or narrow in response to an anticipated swing in market interest rates, or (2) an abnormally wide or narrow yield spread that is expected to become normal.

Economic and market analysis would help you develop these expectations of potential for yield spread to change. Taking advantage of these changes requires a knowledge of historical spreads and an ability to *predict* not only future total market changes, but also why and when specific spreads will change.[18]

WHAT DETERMINES THE PRICE VOLATILITY FOR BONDS?

In this chapter we have learned about alternative bond yields, how to calculate them, what determines bond yields (interest rates), and what causes them to change. Now that we understand why yields change, we can logically ask, what is the effect of these yield changes on the prices and rates of return for different bonds? We have discussed the inverse relationship between changes in yields and the price of bonds, so we can now discuss *the specific factors that affect the amount of price change for a yield change* in different bonds. This section lists the specific factors that affect bond price changes for a given change in interest rates and demonstrates the effect for different bonds.

The fact is, a given change in interest rates can cause vastly different percentage price changes for alternative bonds. This section will help you understand what causes these differences between price changes. To maximize your rate of return from your knowledge of a decline in interest rates, for example, you need to know which bonds will benefit the most from the yield change. This section will help you make this bond selection decision.

Throughout this section we will talk about bond price changes or bond price volatility interchangeably. A bond price change is measured as the percentage change in the price of the bond, computed as follows:

$$\frac{EPB}{BPB} - 1$$

where:

EPB = the ending price of the bond
BPB = the beginning price of the bond

Bond price volatility is also measured in terms of percentage changes in bond prices. A bond with high price volatility is one that experiences large percentage price changes for a given change in yields.

Bond price volatility is influenced by more than yield behavior alone. Malkiel used the bond valuation model to demonstrate that the market price of a bond is a function of four factors: (1) its par value, (2) its coupon, (3) the number of years to its maturity,

[18] A recent article identifies four determinants of relative market spreads and suggests scenarios when they will change. See Chris P. Dialynas and David H. Edington, "Bond Yield Spreads: A Postmodern View," *Journal of Portfolio Management* 19, no. 1 (Fall 1992): 68–75.

TABLE 14.2

Effect of Maturity on Bond Price Volatility

Term to Maturity	Present Value of an 8 percent Bond ($1,000 Par Value)							
	1 Year		10 Years		20 Years		30 Years	
Discount rate (YTM)	7%	10%	7%	10%	7%	10%	7%	10%
Present value of interest	$ 75	$ 73	$ 569	$498	$ 858	$686	$1,005	$757
Present value of principal	934	907	505	377	257	142	132	54
Total value of bond	$1,009	$980	$1,074	$875	$1,115	$828	$1,137	$811
Percentage change in total value	−2.9		−18.5		−25.7		−28.7	

and (4) the prevailing market interest rate.[19] Malkiel's mathematical proofs showed the following relationships between yield (interest rate) changes and bond price behavior:

1. Bond prices move inversely to bond yields (interest rates).
2. For a given change in yields (interest rates), longer-maturity bonds post larger price changes; thus, bond price volatility is *directly* related to term to maturity.
3. Price volatility (percentage of price change) increases at a diminishing rate as term to maturity increases.
4. Price movements resulting from equal absolute increases or decreases in yield are *not* symmetrical. A decrease in yield raises bond prices by more than an increase in yield of the same amount lowers prices.
5. Higher coupon issues show smaller percentage price fluctuation for a given change in yield; thus, bond price volatility is *inversely* related to coupon.

Homer and Leibowitz showed that the absolute level of market yields also affects bond price volatility.[20] As the level of prevailing yields rises the price volatility of bonds increases, *assuming a constant percentage change in market yields*. It is important to note that if you assume a constant percentage change in yield, the basis-point change will be greater when rates are high. For example, a 25 percent change in interest rates when rates are at 4 percent will be 100 basis points; the same 25 percent change when rates are at 8 percent will be a 200 basis-point change. In the discussion of bond duration, we will see that this difference in basis point change is important.

Tables 14.2, 14.3, and 14.4 demonstrate these relationships assuming semiannual compounding. Table 14.2 demonstrates the effect of maturity on price volatility. In all four maturity classes, we assume a bond with an 8 percent coupon and assume that the discount rate (YTM) changes from 7 to 10 percent. The only difference among the four cases is the maturities of the bonds. The demonstration involves computing the value of each bond at a 7 percent yield and at a 10 percent yield and noting the per-

---

[19] Burton G. Malkiel, "Expectations, Bond Prices, and the Term Structure of Interest Rates," *Quarterly Journal of Economics* 76, no. 2 (May 1962): 197–218.

[20] Sidney Homer and Martin L. Leibowitz, *Inside the Yield Book* (Englewood Cliffs, N.J.: Prentice-Hall, 1972).

TABLE 14.3

Effect of Coupon on Bond Price Volatility

	Present Value of 20-Year Bond ($1,000 par value)							
	0 Percent Coupon		3 Percent Coupon		8 Percent Coupon		12 Percent Coupon	
Discount rate (YTM)	7%	10%	7%	10%	7%	10%	7%	10%
Present value of interest	$ 0	$ 0	$322	$257	$ 858	$686	$1,287	$1,030
Present value of principal	257	142	257	142	257	142	257	142
Total value of bond	$257	$142	$579	$399	$1,115	$828	$1,544	$1,172
Percentage change in total value	−44.7		−31.1		−25.7		−24.1	

centage change in price. As shown, this change in yield caused the price of the 1-year bond to decline by only 2.9 percent, whereas the 30-year bond declined by almost 29 percent. Clearly, the longer-maturity bond experienced the greater price volatility.

Also, price volatility increased at a decreasing rate with maturity. When maturity doubled from 10 years to 20 years, the price increased by less than 50 percent (from 18.5 percent) to 25.7 percent. A similar change occurred when going from 20 years to 30 years. Therefore, this table demonstrates the first three of our price–yield relationships: bond price is inversely related to yields, bond price volatility is positively related to term to maturity, and bond price volatility increases at a decreasing rate with maturity.

It is also possible to demonstrate the fourth relationship with this table. Using the 20-year bond, if you computed the percentage change in price related to an *increase* in rates (e.g., from 7 to 10 percent), you would get the answer reported—a 25.7 percent decrease. In contrast, if you computed the effect on price of a *decrease* in yields from 10 to 7 percent, you would get a 34.7 percent increase in price ($1,115 vs. $828). This demonstrates that prices change more in response to a decrease in rates (from 10 to 7 percent) than to a comparable increase in rates (from 7 to 10 percent).

Table 14.3 demonstrates the coupon effect. In this set of examples, all the bonds have equal maturity (20 years) and experience the same change in YTM (from 7 to 10 percent). The table shows the inverse relationship between coupon rate and price volatility: the smallest coupon bond (the zero) experienced the largest percentage price change (almost 45 percent), versus a 24 percent change for the 12 percent coupon bond.

Table 14.4 demonstrates the yield level effect. In these examples, all the bonds have the same 20-year maturity and the same 4 percent coupon. In the first three cases the YTM changed by a constant 33.3 percent (i.e., from 3 to 4 percent, from 6 to 8 percent, and from 9 to 12 percent). Note that the first change is 100 basis points, the second is 200 basis points, and the third is 300 basis points. The results in the first three columns confirm the statement that when higher rates change by a *constant percentage,* the change in the bond price is larger.

The fourth column shows that if you assume a *constant basis-point change in yields,* you get the opposite results. Specifically, a 100 basis point change in yields from 3 to 4 percent provides a price change of 14.1 percent, while the same 100 basis point change from 9 to 10 percent results in a price change of only 11 percent. Therefore, the yield

TABLE 14.4   **Effect of Yield Level on Bond Price Volatility**

	Present Value of a 20-Year, 4 Percent Bond ($1,000 par value)							
	(1) Low Yields		(2) Intermediate Yields		(3) High Yields		(4) 100 Basis Point Change at High Yields	
Discount rate (YTM)	3%	4%	6%	8%	9%	12%	9%	10%
Present value of interest	$ 602	$ 547	$462	$396	$370	$301	$370	$343
Present value of principal	562	453	307	208	175	97	175	142
Total value of bond	$1,164	$1,000	$769	$604	$545	$398	$545	$485
Percentage change in total value	−14.1		−21.5		−27.0		−11.0	

level effect can differ depending on whether the yield change is a constant percentage change or a constant basis-point change.

Thus, the price volatility of a bond for a given change in yield is affected by the bond's coupon, its term to maturity, the level of yields (depending on what kind of change in yield), and the direction of the yield change. However, although both the level and direction of change in yields affect price volatility, they cannot be used for trading strategies. When yields change, the two variables that have a dramatic effect on bond price volatility are coupon and maturity.

SOME TRADING STRATEGIES

Knowing that coupon and maturity are the major variables that influence bond price volatility, we can develop some strategies for maximizing rates of return when interest rates change. Specifically, if you expect a major *decline* in interest rates, you know that bond prices will increase, so you want a portfolio of bonds with the *maximum price volatility* so that you will enjoy maximum price changes (capital gains) from the change in interest rates. In this situation, the previous discussion regarding the effect of maturity and coupon indicates that you should attempt to build a portfolio of long-maturity bonds with low coupons (ideally a zero coupon bond). A portfolio of such bonds should experience the maximum price appreciation for a given decline in market interest rates.

In contrast, if you expect an *increase* in market interest rates, you know that bond prices will decline, and you want a portfolio with *minimum price volatility* to minimize the capital losses caused by the increase in rates. Therefore, you would want to change your portfolio to short-maturity bonds with high coupons. This combination should provide minimal price volatility for a change in market interest rates.

THE DURATION MEASURE

Because the price volatility of a bond varies inversely with its coupon and directly with its term to maturity, it is necessary to determine the best combination of these two variables to achieve your objective. This effort would benefit from a composite measure that considered both coupon and maturity. Fortunately, such a measure, the *duration of a security*, was developed over 50 years ago by Macaulay.[21] Macaulay showed that

---

[21] Frederick R. Macaulay, *Some Theoretical Problems Suggested by the Movements of Interest Rates, Bond Yields, and Stock Prices in the United States Since 1856* (New York: National Bureau of Economic Research, 1938).

the duration of a bond was a more appropriate measure of time characteristics than the term to maturity of the bond, because duration considers both the repayment of capital at maturity, and the size and timing of coupon payments prior to final maturity. Duration is defined as *the weighted average time to full recovery of principal and interest payments*. Using annual compounding, duration (*D*) is

$$D = \frac{\displaystyle\sum_{t=1}^{n} \frac{C_t(t)}{(1 + i)^t}}{\displaystyle\sum_{t=1}^{n} \frac{C_t}{(1 + i)^t}} \tag{14.16}$$

where:

t = time period in which the coupon or principal payment occurs
C_t = interest or principal payment that occurs in period t
i = yield to maturity on the bond

The denominator in Equation 14.16 is the price of a bond as determined by the present value model. The numerator is the present value of all cash flows *weighted according to the time to cash receipt*. The following example, which demonstrates the specific computations for two bonds, shows the procedure and highlights some of the properties of duration. Consider the following two sample bonds:

	Bond A	Bond B
Face Value	$1,000	$1,000
Maturity	10 years	10 years
Coupon	4%	8%

Assuming annual interest payments and an 8 percent yield to maturity on the bonds, duration is computed as shown in Table 14.5. Duration computed by discounting flows using the yield to maturity of the bond is called *Macaulay duration*. We will use Macaulay duration throughout this chapter.

CHARACTERISTICS OF DURATION
This example illustrates several characteristics of duration. First, the duration of a bond with coupon payments will always be less than its term to maturity, because duration gives weight to these interim payments.

Second, there is *an inverse relationship between coupon and duration*. A bond with a larger coupon will have a shorter duration because more of the total cash flows come earlier in the form of interest payments. As shown in Table 14.5, the 8 percent coupon bond has a shorter duration than the 4 percent coupon bond.

A bond with no coupon payments (i.e., a zero coupon bond or a pure discount bond such as a Treasury bill) will have duration *equal* to its term to maturity. In Table 14.5 if you assume a single payment at maturity, you will see that duration will equal term to maturity because the only cash flow comes in the final (maturity) year.

Third, *a positive relationship generally holds between term to maturity and duration*, but duration increases at a decreasing rate with maturity. Therefore, all else

TABLE 14.5   **Computation of Duration (Assuming 8 Percent Market Yield)**

Bond A

(1) Year	(2) Cash Flow	(3) PV at 8%	(4) PV of Flow	(5) PV as % of Price	(6) (1) × (5)
1	$ 40	.9259	$ 37.04	.0506	.0506
2	40	.8573	34.29	.0469	.0938
3	40	.7938	31.75	.0434	.1302
4	40	.7350	29.40	.0402	.1608
5	40	.6806	27.22	.0372	.1860
6	40	.6302	25.21	.0345	.2070
7	40	.5835	23.34	.0319	.2233
8	40	.5403	21.61	.0295	.2360
9	40	.5002	20.01	.0274	.2466
10	1,040	.4632	481.73	.6585	6.5850
Sum			$731.58	1.0000	8.1193

Duration = 8.12 Years

Bond B

(1) Year	(2) Cash Flow	(3) PV at 8%	(4) PV of Flow	(5) PV as % of Price	(6) (1) × (5)
1	$ 80	.9259	$ 74.07	.0741	.0741
2	80	.8573	68.59	.0686	.1372
3	80	.7938	63.50	.0635	.1906
4	80	.7350	58.80	.0588	.1906
5	80	.6806	54.44	.0544	.2720
6	80	.6302	50.42	.0504	.3024
7	80	.5835	46.68	.0467	.3269
8	80	.5403	43.22	.0432	.3456
9	80	.5002	40.02	.0400	.3600
10	1,080	.4632	500.26	.5003	5.0030
Sum			$1,000.00	1.0000	7.2470

Duration = 7.25 Years

being the same, a bond with longer term to maturity will almost always have a higher duration. Note that the relationship is not direct, because as maturity increases, the present value of the principal declines in value.

As shown in Figure 14.6, the shape of the duration-maturity curve depends on the coupon and the yield to maturity. The curve for a zero coupon bond is a straight line, indicating that duration equals term to maturity. In contrast, the curve for a low coupon bond selling at a deep discount (due to a high YTM) will turn down at long maturities, which means that under these conditions the longer-maturity bond will have lower duration.

Fourth, all else the same, there is an *inverse relationship between YTM and duration*. A higher yield to maturity of a bond reduces its duration. As an example, in Table 14.5, if the yield to maturity had been 12 percent rather than 8 percent, the durations would have been about 7.75 and 6.80 rather than 8.12 and 7.25.[22]

Finally, sinking funds and call provisions can have a dramatic effect on a bond's duration. They can accelerate the total cash flows for a bond and, therefore, significantly

---

[22] These properties are discussed and demonstrated in Frank K. Reilly and Rupinder Sidhu, "The Many Uses of Bond Duration," *Financial Analysts Journal* 36, no. 4 (July-August 1980): 58–72; and Frank J. Fabozzi, Mark Pitts, and Ravi E. Dattatreya, "Price Volatility Characteristics of Fixed Income Securities," in *The Handbook of Fixed-Income Securities,* 3rd ed., edited by Frank J. Fabozzi (Homewood, Ill.: Business One–Irwin, 1991).

FIGURE 14.6   **Duration vs. Maturity**

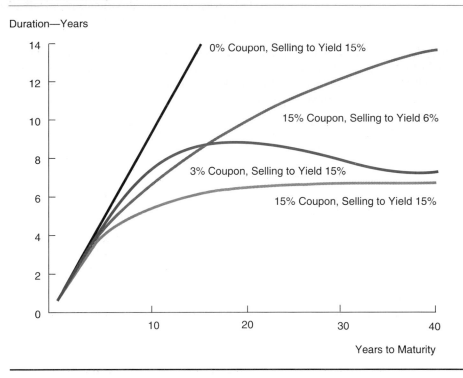

Duration—Years

0% Coupon, Selling to Yield 15%

15% Coupon, Selling to Yield 6%

3% Coupon, Selling to Yield 15%

15% Coupon, Selling to Yield 15%

Years to Maturity

reduce its duration.[23] Between these two factors, the factor that causes the greatest uncertainty is the call feature because it is difficult to estimate when it will be exercised. We will consider this further when we consider the effect of the call feature on the convexity of a bond.

A summary of duration characteristics is as follows:

- The duration of a zero coupon bond will *equal* its term to maturity.
- The duration of a coupon bond will always be less than its term to maturity.
- There is an *inverse* relationship between coupon and duration.
- There is generally a *positive* relationship between term to maturity and duration. Note that duration increases at a decreasing rate with maturity. Also the duration of a deep discount bond will decline at very long maturities (over 20 years).
- There is an *inverse* relationship between yield to maturity and duration.
- Sinking funds and call provisions can cause a dramatic decline in the duration of a bond because of an early payoff (maturity). As noted, the effect of the call feature is discussed in a subsequent section.

The duration measure can be very useful to you as a bond investor because it combines the properties of maturity and coupon to measure the time flow of cash from the

---

[23] An example of the computation of duration with a sinking fund and a call feature is contained in Reilly and Sidhu, "The Many Uses of Bond Duration." The impact of the call feature on duration will be considered farther in the section on convexity.

bond. This is superior to term to maturity, which only considers when the principal will be repaid at maturity. As shown, duration is positively related to term to maturity and inversely related to coupon and to YTM.

DURATION AND
BOND PRICE
VOLATILITY

Duration is more than a superior measure of the time flow of cash from the bond. An adjusted measure of duration called *modified duration* can be used to approximate the price volatility of a bond. Modified duration equals Macaulay duration (computed in Table 14.5), divided by 1, plus the current yield to maturity, divided by the number of payments in a year. As an example, a bond with a Macaulay duration of 10 years, a yield to maturity (i) of 8 percent, and semiannual payments would have a modified duration of

$$D_{mod} = 10 / \left(1 + \frac{.08}{2} \right)$$
$$= 10/(1.04) = 9.62 \text{ years}$$

It has been shown, both theoretically and empirically, that bond price movements *will vary proportionally* with modified duration for *small changes in yields*.[24] Specifically, as shown in Equation 14.17, an estimate of the percentage change in bond price equals the change in yield times modified duration.

$$\frac{\Delta P}{P} \times 100 = -D_{mod} \times \Delta i \qquad (14.17)$$

where:

ΔP = **change in price for the bond**
P = **beginning price for the bond**
$-D_{mod}$ = **the modified duration of the bond**
Δi = **yield change in basis points divided by 100. For example, if interest rates go from 8.00 to 8.50 percent, Δi = 50/100 = 0.50**

Consider a bond with D = 8 years and i = 0.10. Assume that you expect the bond's YTM to decline by 75 basis points (e.g., from 10 percent to 9.25 percent). The first step is to compute the bond's modified duration as follows:

$$D_{mod} = 8 / \left(1 + \frac{.10}{2} \right)$$
$$= 8/(1.05) = 7.62 \text{ years}$$

The estimated percentage change in the price of the bond using Equation 14.17 is as follows:

---

[24] A generalized proof of this is contained in Michael H. Hopewell and George Kaufman, "Bond Price Volatility and Term to Maturity: A Generalized Respecification," *American Economic Review* 63, no. 4 (September 1973): 749–753. The importance of the specification, "for small changes in yields," will become clear when we discuss convexity in the next section.

$$\% \Delta P = -(7.62) \times \frac{-75}{100}$$
$$= (-7.62) \times (-.75)$$
$$= 5.72$$

This indicates that the bond price should increase by approximately 5.72 percent in response to the 75 basis point decline in YTM. If the price of the bond before the decline in interest rates was $900, the price after the decline in interest rates should be approximately $900 × 1.0572 = $951.48.

The modified duration is always a negative value for a noncallable bond because of the inverse relationship between yield changes and bond price changes. Also, you should remember that this formulation provides an *estimate* or *approximation* of the percent change in the price of the bond. The following section on convexity will show that this formula that uses modified duration provides an exact estimate of the percentage price change only for very small changes in yields.

TRADING STRATEGIES USING DURATION

We know from the prior discussion on the relationship between modified duration and bond price volatility that the longest duration security provides the maximum price variation. Table 14.6 demonstrates that there are numerous ways to achieve a given level of duration. The duration measure has become increasingly popular because it conveniently specifies the time flow of cash from a security considering both coupon and term to maturity. Therefore, the following discussion indicates that an active bond investor can use this measure to structure a portfolio to take advantage of changes in market yields.

If you expect a *decline* in interest rates, you should *increase* the average duration of your bond portfolio to experience maximum price volatility. Alternatively, if you expect an *increase* in interest rates, you should *reduce* the average duration of your portfolio to minimize your price decline. Note that the duration of your portfolio is the market value weighted average of the durations of the individual bonds in the portfolio.

BOND CONVEXITY   Modified duration allows us to estimate bond price changes for a change in interest rates. Equation 14.17 is, however, accurate only for *very small changes* in market

TABLE 14.6

Bond Duration in Years for Bond Yielding 6 Percent Under Different Terms

Years to Maturity	Coupon Rates			
	0.02	0.04	0.06	0.08
1	0.995	0.990	0.985	0.981
5	4.756	4.558	4.393	4.254
10	8.891	8.169	7.662	7.286
20	14.981	12.980	11.904	11.232
50	19.452	17.129	16.273	15.829
100	17.567	17.232	17.120	17.064
∞	17.167	17.167	17.167	17.167

Source: L. Fisher and R. L. Weil, "Coping with the Risk of Interest Rate Fluctuations: Returns to Bondholders from Naive and Optimal Strategies," *Journal of Business* 44, no. 4 (October 1971): 418.

TABLE 14.7   **Price–Yield Relationships for Alternative Bonds**

A. 12 Percent 20-Year		B. 12 Percent, 3-Year		C. Zero Coupon 30-Year	
Yield	Price	Yield	Price	Yield	Price
1.0%	$2,989.47	1.0%	$1,324.30	1.0%	$741.37
2.0	2,641.73	2.0	1,289.77	2.0	550.45
3.0	2,346.21	3.0	1,256.37	3.0	409.30
4.0	2,094.22	4.0	1,224.06	4.0	304.78
5.0	1,878.60	5.0	1,192.78	5.0	227.28
6.0	1,693.44	6.0	1,162.52	6.0	169.73
7.0	1,533.88	7.0	1,133.21	7.0	126.93
8.0	1,395.86	8.0	1,104.84	8.0	95.06
9.0	1,276.02	9.0	1,077.37	9.0	71.29
10.0	1,171.59	10.0	1,050.76	10.0	53.54
11.0	1,080.23	11.0	1,024.98	11.0	40.26
12.0	1,000.00	12.0	1,000.00	12.0	30.31

yields. We will see that the accuracy of the estimate of the price change deteriorates with larger changes in yields because the modified duration calculation specified in Equation 14.17 is a *linear* approximation of a bond price change that follows a *curvilinear* (convex) function. To understand the effect of this *convexity,* we must consider the price–yield relationship for alternative bonds.[25]

THE PRICE–YIELD RELATIONSHIP FOR BONDS

Because the price of a bond is the present value of its cash flows at a particular discount rate, if you are given the coupon, maturity, and a yield for a bond, you can calculate its price at a point in time. The price–yield curve provides a set of prices for a specific maturity-coupon bond at a point in time using a range of yields to maturity (discount rates). As an example, Table 14.7 lists the computed prices for a 12 percent, 20-year bond assuming yields from 1 percent to 12 percent. For example, the table shows that discounting the flows from this 12 percent, 20-year bond at a yield of 1 percent, you would get a price of $2,989.47; discounting these same flows at 10 percent gives a price of $1,171.59. The graph of these prices relative to the yields that produced them in Figure 14.7 indicates that the price–yield relationship for this bond is not a straight line but a curvilinear relationship. That is, it is convex.

Two points are important about the price–yield relationship:

1. This relationship can be applied to a single bond, a portfolio of bonds, or any stream of future cash flows.
2. The convex price–yield relationship will differ among bonds or other streams, depending on the nature of the cash flow stream, that is, its coupon and maturity. As an example, the price–yield relationship for a high-coupon, short-term security will be almost a straight line because the price does not change as much for a change in yields (e.g., the 12 percent, 3-year bond in Table 14.7). In contrast, the price–yield relationship for a low-coupon, long-term bond will curve radically (i.e., be very convex), as shown by the zero coupon, 30-year

[25] For a further discussion of this topic, see Mark L. Dunetz and James M. Mahoney, "Using Duration and Convexity in the Analysis of Callable Bonds," *Financial Analysts Journal* 44, no. 3 (May-June 1988): 53–73.

FIGURE 14.7   **Price–Yield Relationship and Modified Duration at 4 Percent Yield**

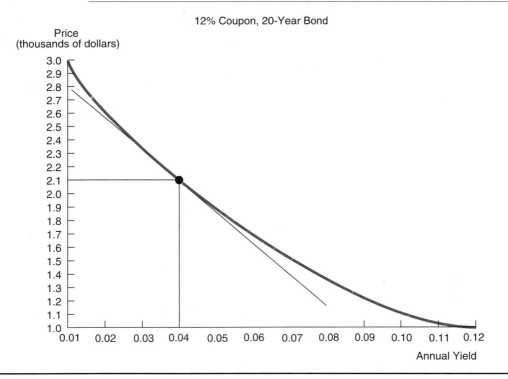

12% Coupon, 20-Year Bond

bond in Table 14.7. These differences in convexity are shown graphically in Figure 14.8. The curved nature of the price–yield relationship is referred to as the bond's *convexity*.

As shown by the graph in Figure 14.8, because of the convexity of the relationship, as yield increases, the rate at which the price of the bond declines becomes slower. Similarly, when yields decline, the rate at which the price of the bond increases becomes faster. Convexity is therefore a desirable trait.

Given this price–yield curve, modified duration is the percentage change in price for a nominal change in yield as follows:[26]

$$D_{mod} = \frac{\dfrac{dP}{di}}{P} \qquad (14.18)$$

Notice that the *dP/di* line is tangent to the price–yield curve *at a given yield* as shown in Figure 14.9. For *small* changes in yields (i.e., from y* to cither y_1 or y_2), this tangent straight line gives a good estimate of the actual price changes. In contrast, for larger changes in yields (i.e., from y* to either y_3 or y_4), the straight line will estimate the new

---

[26] In mathematical terms, modified duration is the first differential of this price–yield relationship with respect to yield.

FIGURE 14.8   **Price–Yield Curves for Alternative Bonds**

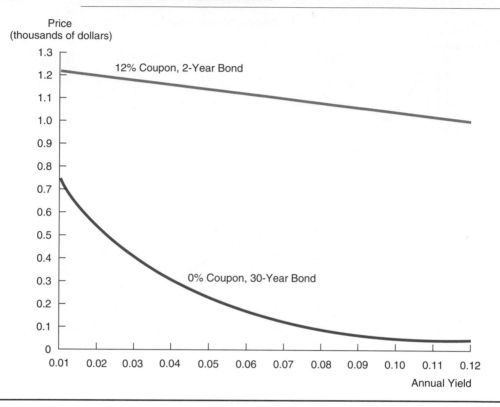

price of the bond at less than the actual price shown by the price–yield curve. This misestimate arises because the modified-duration line is a linear estimate of a curvilinear relationship. Specifically, the estimate using only modified duration will *underestimate* the actual price *increase* caused by a yield decline and *overestimate* the actual price *decline* caused by an increase in yields. This graph, which demonstrates the convexity effect, also shows that price changes are *not* symmetric when yields increase or decrease. As shown, when rates decline, there is a larger price error than when rates increase because when yields decline prices rise at an *increasing* rate, while prices decline at a *decreasing* rate when yields rise.

DETERMINANTS OF CONVEXITY

Convexity is a measure of the curvature of the price–yield relationship. Mathematically, convexity is the second derivative of price with respect to yield (d^2P/di^2) divided by price. Specifically, convexity is the percentage change in dP/di for a given change in yield:

$$\text{Convexity} = \frac{\frac{d^2P}{di^2}}{P} \qquad (14.19)$$

FIGURE 14.9   **Price Approximation Using Modified Duration**

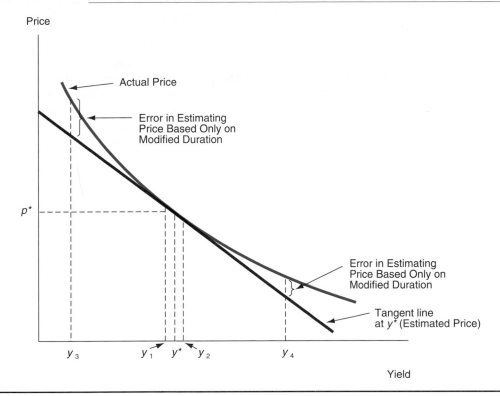

Source: Frank J. Fabozzi, Mark Pitts, and Ravi E. Dattatreya, "Price Volatility Characteristics of Fixed Income Securities," in *Handbook of Fixed Income Securities,* 3rd ed., edited by Frank J. Fabozzi (Homewood, IL: Business One–Irwin, 1991). Reprinted by permission of the publisher.

Convexity is a measure of how much a bond's price–yield curve deviates from the linear approximation of that curve. As indicated by Figures 14.7 and 14.9 for *noncallable* bonds, convexity is always a positive number, implying that the price–yield curve lies above the modified duration (tangent) line. Figure 14.8 illustrates the price–yield relationship for two bonds with very different coupons and maturities. (The yields and prices are contained in Table 14.7.)

These graphs demonstrate the following relationship between these factors and the convexity of a bond.

- There is an *inverse* relationship between coupon and convexity (yield and maturity constant).
- There is a *direct* relationship between maturity and convexity (yield and coupon constant).
- There is an *inverse* relationship between yield and convexity (coupon and maturity constant). This means that the price–yield curve is more convex at its lower-yield (upper left) segment.

Therefore, a short-term, high-coupon bond, such as the 12 percent coupon, 2-year bond in Figure 14.8, has very low convexity—it is almost a straight line. In contrast, the zero coupon, 30-year bond has high convexity.

THE MODIFIED DURATION—CONVEXITY EFFECTS

In summary, the change in a bond's price resulting from a change in yield can be attributed to two sources: the bond's modified duration and its convexity. The relative effect of these two factors on the price change will depend on the characteristics of the bond (i.e., its convexity) and the size of the yield change. For example, if you are estimating the price change for a 300 basis point change in yield for a zero coupon, 30-year bond, the convexity effect would be fairly large, because this bond would have high convexity, and a 300 basis point change in yield is relatively large. In contrast, if you are dealing with only a 10 basis point change in yields, the convexity effect would be minimal because it is a small change. Similarly, the convexity effect would be small for a larger yield change if you are concerned with a bond with small convexity (high coupon, short maturity) because its price–yield relationship is almost a straight line.

In conclusion, modified duration can help you derive an *approximate* percentage bond price change for a given change in interest rates, but you must remember that it is only a good estimate when you are considering small yield changes. You must also consider the convexity effect when you are dealing with large yield changes or when securities or cash flows have high convexity.

COMPUTATION OF CONVEXITY

Again, the formula for computing the convexity of a stream of cash flows looks fairly complex, but it can be broken down into manageable steps. You will recall from Equation 14.19 that

$$\text{Convexity} = \frac{\dfrac{d^2P}{di^2}}{P}$$

In turn,

$$\frac{d^2P}{di^2} = \frac{1}{(1 + i)^2} \left[\sum_t \frac{CF_t}{(1 + i)^t} (t^2 + t) \right]$$

Table 14.8 contains the computations related to this calculation for a 3-year bond with a 12 percent coupon and 9 percent YTM assuming annual flows.

The convexity for this bond is very low, given the short maturity, high coupon, and high yield. Note that *the convexity of a security will vary along the price–yield curve.* You will get a different convexity at a 3 percent yield than at a 12 percent yield. In terms of the computation, the maturity and coupon will be the same, but you will use a different discount rate that reflects where you are on the curve. Remember that *you will also get a different modified duration at different points on the curve,* because the slope varies along the curve. You can also see this mathematically because depending on where you are on the curve, you will be using a different market yield, and the Macaulay duration and the modified duration are inverse to the discount rate.

To compute the price change attributable to the convexity effect after you know the bond's convexity, use this equation:

$$\text{Price Change Due to Convexity} = 1/2 \times \text{Price} \times \text{Convexity} \times (\Delta \text{ in yield})^2$$

TABLE 14.8

Computation of Convexity

$$\text{Convexity} = \frac{d^2P/di^2}{\text{PV of Cash Flows}} = \frac{d^2P/di^2}{\text{Price}}$$

$$\frac{d^2P}{di^2} = \frac{1}{(1+i)^2}\left[\sum_t (t^2 + t)\frac{CF_t}{(1+i)^t}\right]$$

$$\text{Convexity} = \frac{d^2P/di^2}{\text{Price}}$$

Example: 3-Year Bond, 12% Coupon, 9% YTM

(1) Year	(2) CF_t	(3) PV @ 9%	(4) PV CF	(5) $t^2 + t$	(4) × (5)
1	120	.9174	$ 110.09	2	220.18
2	120	.8417	101.00	6	606.00
3	120	.7722	92.66	12	1111.92
3	1000	.7722	772.20	12	9266.40
			$1,075.95		$11,204.50

$$\frac{1}{(1+i)^2} = \frac{1}{(1.09)^2} = \frac{1}{1.19} = .84$$

$$\$11,204.50 \times .84 = \$9,411.78$$

$$\frac{9411.78}{1075.95} = 8.75$$

Table 14.9 shows the change in bond price considering both the duration effect and the convexity effect for an 18-year bond with a 12 percent coupon and 9 percent YTM. For demonstration purposes, we assumed a decline of 100 and 300 basis points (BP) in rates (i.e., 9 percent to 8 percent and 9 percent to 6 percent).

With the 300 BP change, if you considered only the modified-duration effect, you would have *estimated* that the bond went from 126.50 to 158.30 (a 25.14 percent increase), when, in fact, the actual price is closer to 164.41, which is about a *30 percent increase.*

DURATION AND CONVEXITY FOR CALLABLE BONDS

The discussion and presentation thus far have been concerned with noncallable bonds. A callable bond is different because it provides the issuer with an option to call the bond under certain conditions and pay it off with funds from a new issue sold at a lower yield. We noted earlier that the duration of a bond can be seriously affected by a call provision if interest rates decline substantially below a bond's coupon rate. In such a case, the issuer will likely call the bond, which will dramatically change the maturity of the bond and its duration. For example, assume a firm issues a 30-year bond with a 9 percent coupon with a deferred call provision in 6 years at 109 percent of par. If the bond is issued at par, its original *duration to maturity* will be about 10 to 11 years. A year later, if rates decline to about 7 percent, its duration to maturity will still be close to *10 years* because duration is inversely related to yield and yields have declined. Notably, at a yield of 7 percent, this bond will probably trade at *yield to call* because at a 7 percent yield the firm will likely exercise its option and call the bond in 5 years. Notably, the bond's *duration to first call* would be about *4 years.* Clearly, there is a significant difference between duration to maturity and duration to first call.

TABLE 14.9

Analysis of Bond Price Change Considering Duration and Convexity

Example: 18-Year Bond, 12% Coupon, 9% YTM
Price: 126.50
Modified Duration: 8.38 (D*)
Convexity: 107.70
Estimate of Price Change Using Duration:
  Percent Δ Price $= -D^*$ (Δ in YLD/100)
Estimate of Price Change from Convexity:
  Price Change $= \frac{1}{2} \times$ Price $\times$ Convexity $\times$ (Δ in YLD)^2

A. Change in Yield: -100 BP

  Duration Change: $-8.38 \times \left(\dfrac{-100}{100}\right) = +8.38\%$

  $+8.38\% \times 126.50 = +10.60$

  Convexity Change: $\dfrac{1}{2} \times (126.50) \times 107.70 \times (.01)^2$

  $= 63.25 \times 107.70 \times .0001$
  $= 6{,}812.03 \times .0001 = .68$

  Combined Effect: 126.50
  $\underline{+\ 10.60}$ (Duration)
  137.10
  $\underline{+\ .68}$ (Convexity)
  137.78

B. Change in Yield: -300 BP

  Duration Change: $-8.38 \times \left(\dfrac{-300}{100}\right) = +25.14\%$

  $126.50 \times 1.2514 = 158.30\ (+31.80)$

  Convexity Effect: $\dfrac{1}{2} \times (126.50) \times 107.70 \times (.03)^2$

  $6{,}812.03 \times .0009 = 6.11$

  Combined Effect: 126.50
  $\underline{+\ 31.80}$ (Duration)
  158.30
  $\underline{+6.11}$ (Convexity)
  164.41

OPTION-ADJUSTED DURATION[27]

Given these two extreme values of duration to maturity and duration to first call, the investment community derives a duration estimate that is referred to as an option-adjusted or call-adjusted duration based on *the probability that the issuing firm will exercise its call option* for the bond when the bond becomes freely callable. This option-adjusted duration will be somewhere between these two extreme values. When interest rates are substantially above the coupon rate, the probability of the bond being called is very small, and the option-adjusted duration will approach the duration to maturity. In contrast, if interest rates decline to levels substantially below the coupon rate, the probability of the bond being called at the first opportunity is very high and the option-adjusted duration will approach the duration to first call. The point is, it will be some-where between these two extremes with the exact location depending on the level of interest rates relative to the bond's coupon rate.

---

[27] The discussion in this subsection will consider the option-adjusted duration on a conceptual and intuitive basis. For a detailed mathematical treatment see, Dunetz and Mahoney, "Using Duration and Convexity in the Analysis of Callable Bonds."

CONVEXITY OF CALLABLE BONDS

To understand the impact of the call feature on the convexity of a bond, it is important to consider what determines the price of a callable bond. The fact is, a callable bond is really a combination of a noncallable bond plus a *call option* that was *sold to the issuer* that allows the issuer to call the bond under certain conditions discussed earlier. Because the call option is owned by the issuer, it has negative value for the investor in the bond. Thus the bondholder's position is:

Long a Callable Bond = Long a Noncallable Bond + A Short Position in a Call Option

Therefore, the value (price) of a callable bond is equal to:

Callable Bond Price = Noncallable Bond Price − Call Option Price

Given this valuation, anything that increases the value of the call option will reduce the value of the callable bond.

Based upon this background, Figure 14.10 shows what happens to the price of a callable bond versus the value of a noncallable bond when interest rates increase or decline. Starting from yield $y*$ (which is close to the par value yield), if rates increase, the value of the call option declines because at market interest rates that are substantially above the coupon rate, it is unlikely the issuer will want to call the issue, so the call option has very little value and the price of the callable bond will be similar to the price of a noncallable bond. In contrast, when interest rates decline below $y*$ there is an increase in the probability that the issuer will want to use the call option—i.e., the call option begins to have value. As a result, the value of the callable bond will deviate from the value of the noncallable bond—i.e., the price of the callable bond will initially not increase as fast as the noncallable bond price and eventually will almost not increase at all. This is what is shown in the curves a–b.

In the case of the noncallable bond, we indicated that it had *positive convexity* because as yields declined, the price of the bond increased at a *faster* rate. With the callable bond, when rates declined, the price increased at a *slower* rate and eventually does not change at all. This pattern of price–yield change for a callable bond is referred to as *negative convexity.*

Needless to say, this price pattern is one of the risks of a callable bond versus a noncallable bond, especially if there is a chance of declining interest rates.

SUMMARY

The value of a bond equals the present value of all future cash flows accruing to the investor. Cash flows for the conservative bond investor include periodic interest payments and principal return; cash flows for the aggressive investor include periodic interest payments and the capital gain or loss when the bond is sold prior to its maturity. Bond investors can maximize their yields by accurately estimating the level of interest rates, and more importantly, changes in interest rates and yield spreads. Similarly, they must compare coupon rates, maturities, and call features of alternative bonds.

There are five bond yield measures: nominal yield, current yield, promised yield to maturity, promised yield to call, and realized (horizon) yield. The promised YTM and promised YTC equations include the interest-on-interest, or coupon reinvestment assumption. For the realized (horizon) yield computation, the investor estimates the

FIGURE 14.10   **Noncallable and Callable Bond Price/Yield Relationship**

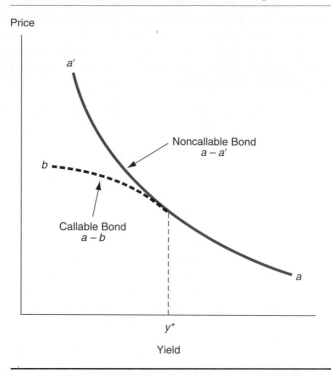

Source: Frank J. Fabozzi, Mark Pitts, and Ravi E. Dattatreya, "Price Volatility Characteristics of Fixed Income Securities," in *Handbook of Fixed Income Securities,* 3rd ed., edited by Frank J. Fabozzi (Homewood, IL: Business One–Irwin, 1991). Reprinted by permission of the publisher.

reinvestment rate and may need to also estimate the future selling price for the bond. The fundamental determinants of interest rates are a real risk-free rate, the expected rate of inflation, and a risk premium.

The yield curve (or the term structure of interest rates) shows the relationship between the yields on a set of comparable bonds and the term to maturity. Yield curves exhibit four basic patterns. Three theories attempt to explain the shape of the yield curve: the expectations hypothesis, the liquidity preference hypothesis, and the segmented market hypothesis.

It is important to understand what causes changes in interest rates and also how these changes in rates affect the prices of bonds. We demonstrated that differences in bond price volatility are mainly a function of differences in yield, coupon, and term to maturity. The duration measure incorporates coupon, maturity and yield in one measure that provides an estimate of the response of bond prices to changes in interest rates. Because modified duration provides a straight-line estimate of the curvilinear price–yield function, you must consider modified duration together with the convexity of a bond for large changes in yields and/or when dealing with securities that have high convexity. Finally, the call feature on a bond can have a significant impact on its duration (the call feature can shorten it dramatically) and on its convexity (the call feature can change the convexity from a positive value to a negative value).

Given the background in valuation and the factors that influence value and volatility, we are ready to consider how to use this background to build a bond portfolio that is consistent with our goals and objectives.

QUESTIONS

1. Why does the present value equation appear to be more useful for the bond investor than for the common stock investor?

2. What are the important assumptions made when you calculate the promised yield to maturity? What are the assumptions when calculating promised YTC?

3. a. Define the variables included in the following model:

$$i = (RFR, I, RP)$$

   b. Assume that the firm whose bonds you are considering is not expected to break even this year. Discuss which factor will be affected by this information.

4. We discussed three alternative hypotheses to explain the term structure of interest rates. Which one do you think best explains the alternative shapes of a yield curve? Defend your choice.

5. *CFA Examination I (June 1982)*
   a. Explain what is meant by the term *structure of interest rates.* Explain the theoretical basis of an upward-sloping yield curve. [8 minutes]
   b. Explain the economic circumstances under which you would expect to see the inverted yield curve prevail. [7 minutes]
   c. Define "real" rate of interest. [2 minutes]
   d. Discuss the characteristics of the market for U.S. Treasury securities. Compare it to the market for AAA corporate bonds. Discuss the opportunities that may exist in bond markets that are less than efficient. [8 minutes]
   e. Over the past several years, fairly wide yield spreads between AAA corporates and Treasuries have occasionally prevailed. Discuss the possible reasons for this. [5 minutes]

6. *CFA Examination III (June, 1982)*
   As the portfolio manager for a large pension fund, you are offered the following bonds:

	Coupon	Maturity	Price	Call Price	Yield to Maturity
Edgar Corp. (new issue)	14.00%	2002	$101.3/4	$114	13.75%
Edgar Corp. (new issue)	6.00	2002	48.1/8	103	13.60
Edgar Corp. (1972 issue)	6.00	2002	48.7/8	103	13.40

Assuming that you expect a decline in interest rates over the next 3 years, identify and justify which of these bonds you would select. [10 minutes]

7. You expect interest rates to decline over the next six months.
   a. Given your interest rate outlook, state what kind of bonds you want in your portfolio in terms of duration and explain your reasoning for this choice.
   b. You must make a choice between the following three sets of noncallable bonds. In each case, select the bond that would be best for your portfolio given your interest rate outlook and the consequent strategy set forth in part a. In each case, briefly discuss why you selected the bond.

	Maturity	Coupon	Yield to Maturity
Case 1: Bond A	15 years	10%	10%
Bond B	15 years	6%	8%
Case 2: Bond C	15 years	6%	10%
Bond D	10 years	8%	10%
Case 3: Bond E	12 years	12%	12%
Bond F	15 years	12%	8%

8. At the present time you expect a decline in interest rates and must choose between two portfolios of bonds with the following characteristics.

	Portfolio A	Portfolio B
Average maturity	10.5 years	10.0 years
Average YTM	7%	10%
Modified duration	5.7 years	4.9 years
Modified convexity	125.18	40.30
Call features	Noncallable	Deferred call features that range from 1 to 3 years

Select one of the portfolios and discuss three factors that would *justify* your selection.

9. The Chartered Finance Corporation has issued a bond with the following characteristics:

Maturity—25 years
Coupon—9%
Yield to Maturity—9%
Callable—after 3 years @109
Duration to maturity—8.2 years
Duration to call—2.1 years

Given this information,
   a. Discuss the concept of call-adjusted duration and indicate the approximate value (range) for it at the present time.
   b. Assuming interest rates increase substantially (i.e., to 13%), discuss what will happen to the call-adjusted duration and the reason for the change.
   c. Assuming interest rates decline substantially (i.e., they decline to 4%), discuss what will happen to the bond's call-adjusted duration and the reason for the change.
   d. Discuss the concept of negative convexity as it relates to this bond.

PROBLEMS

1. Four years ago your firm issued $1,000 par, 25-year bonds, with a 7 percent coupon rate and a 10 percent call premium.
   a. If these bonds are now called, what is the *approximate* yield to call for the investors who originally purchased them?
   b. If these bonds are now called, what is the *actual* yield to call for the investors who originally purchased them at par?
   c. If the current interest rate is 5 percent and the bonds were not callable, at what price would each bond sell?

2. Assume that you purchased an 8 percent, 20-year, $1,000 par, semiannual payment bond priced at $1,012.50 when it has 12 years remaining until maturity. Compute:
   a. Its approximate yield to maturity
   b. Its actual yield to maturity
   c. Its yield to call if the bond is callable in 3 years with an 8 percent premium

3. Calculate the duration of an 8 percent, $1,000 par bond that matures in 3 years if the bond's YTM is 10 percent and interest is paid semiannually.
   a. Calculate this bond's modified duration.
   b. Assuming the bond's YTM goes from 10 percent to 9.5 percent, calculate an estimate of the price change.

4. Two years ago you acquired a 10-year zero coupon, $1,000 par value bond at a 12% YTM. Recently you sold this bond at an 8% YTM. Using semi-annual compounding, compute the annualized horizon return for this investment.

5. A bond for the Webster Corporation has the following characteristics:

Maturity—12 years
Coupon—10%
Yield to Maturity—9.50%
Macaulay duration—5.7 years
Convexity—48
Noncallable

---

   a. Calculate the approximate price change for this bond using only its duration assuming its yield to maturity increased by 150 basis points. Discuss the impact of including the convexity effect in the calculation.
   b. Calculate the approximate price change for this bond (using only its duration) if its yield to maturity declined by 300 basis points. Discuss (without calculations) what would happen to your estimate of the price change if this was a callable bond.

REFERENCES

Dialynas, Chris P., and David H. Edington. "Bond Yield Spreads: A Postmodern View." *Journal of Portfolio Management* 19, no. 1 (Fall 1992).

Dunetz, Mark L., and James M. Mahoney. "Using Duration and Convexity in the Analysis of Callable Bonds." *Financial Analysts Journal* 44, no. 3 (May-June 1988).

Fabozzi, Frank J. "Bond Pricing and Return Measures," in Frank J. Fabozzi, ed. *The Handbook of Fixed Income Securities,* 3rd ed. Homewood, IL: Business One–Irwin, 1991.

Fabozzi, Frank J. *Fixed Income Mathematics.* Chicago: Probas Publishing, 1988.

Fabozzi, Frank J., Mark Pitts, and Ravi E. Dattatreya. "Price Volatility Characteristics of Fixed Income Securities," in Frank J. Fabozzi, ed. *The Handbook of Fixed Income Securities,* 3rd ed. (Homewood, IL: Business One–Irwin, 1991).

Finnerty, John D. "Evaluating the Economics of Refunding High-Coupon Sinking-Fund Debt." *Financial Management* 12, no. 1 (Spring 1983).

Homer, Sidney, and Martin L. Leibowitz. *Inside the Yield Book.* Englewood Cliffs, NJ: Prentice-Hall, 1972.

Kalotay, A. J. "On the Structure and Valuation of Debt Refundings." *Financial Management* 11, no. 1 (Spring 1982).

Kalotay, A. J. "Sinking Funds and the Realized Cost of Debt." *Financial Management* 11, no. 1 (Spring 1982).

Kalotay, Andrew J., and George O. Williams. "The Valuation and Management of Bonds with Sinking Fund Provisions." *Financial Analysts Journal* 48, no. 2 (March-April 1992).

Kritzman, Mark. "What Practitioners Need to Know about Duration and Convexity." *Financial Analysts Journal* 48, no. 6 (November-December 1992).

Macaulay, Frederick R. *Some Theoretical Problems Suggested by the Movements of Interest Rates, Bond Yields, and Stock Prices in the United States Since 1856.* New York: National Bureau of Economic Research, 1938.

Reilly, Frank K., and Rupinder Sidhu. "The Many Uses of Bond Duration." *Financial Analysts Journal* 36, no. 4 (July-August 1980).

Van Horne, James C. *Financial Market Rates and Flows.* 3d ed. Englewood Cliffs, N.J.: Prentice-Hall, 1989.

Winkelmann, Kurt. "Uses and Abuses of Duration and Convexity." *Financial Analysts Journal* 45, no. 5 (September-October 1989).

CHAPTER 15

BOND PORTFOLIO MANAGEMENT STRATEGIES

In this chapter we will answer the following questions:

- What are the four major alternative bond portfolio management strategies available?
- What are the two specific strategies available within the passive portfolio management category?
- What are the five alternative strategies available within the active portfolio management category?
- What is meant by matched-funding techniques and what are the four specific strategies available in this category?
- What is meant by contingent procedures that are also referred to as structured active management strategies?
- What are the major contingent procedure strategies?
- What are the implications of capital market theory for those involved in bond portfolio management?
- What is the evidence on the efficient market hypothesis as it relates to the fixed income markets?
- What are the implications of efficient market studies for those involved in bond portfolio management?

Successful bond portfolio management involves far more than mastering a myriad of technical information. Such information is useful only to the extent that it helps generate higher risk-adjusted returns. In this chapter, we shift attention from the technical dimensions of bond portfolio management to the equally important strategic dimension.

In the first section we will discuss the alternative portfolio management strategies. Next we will consider the implications of capital market theory and the EMH on bond portfolio management. We will then conclude with a discussion of bond market efficiency.

ALTERNATIVE
BOND
PORTFOLIO
STRATEGIES

Bond portfolio management strategies can be divided into four groups:[1]

1. Passive portfolio strategies
   a. Buy and hold
   b. Indexing
2. Active management strategies
   a. Interest rate anticipation
   b. Valuation analysis
   c. Credit analysis
   d. Yield spread analysis
   e. Bond swaps
3. Matched-funding techniques
   a. Dedicated portfolio, exact cash match
   b. Dedicated portfolio, optimal cash match and reinvestment
   c. Classical ("pure") immunization
   d. Horizon matching
4. Contingent procedure (structured active management)
   a. Contingent immunization
   b. Other contingent procedures

We will discuss each of these alternatives because they are all viable for certain portfolios with different needs and risk profiles. Prior to the 1960s, only the first two groups were available, and most bond portfolios were managed on the basis of buy and hold. The 1960s and early 1970s saw growing interest in alternative active bond portfolio management strategies. The investment environment since the late 1970s has been characterized by record-breaking inflation and interest rates, extremely volatile rates of return in bond markets, the introduction of many new financial instruments in response to the increase in return volatility, and the development of several new funding techniques or contingent portfolio management techniques to meet the emerging needs of institutional clients. Several of these new portfolio management techniques have become possible because of the rediscovery of duration in the early 1970s.

PASSIVE BOND
PORTFOLIO
STRATEGIES

There are two specific passive portfolio strategies. First is a *buy-and-hold strategy* in which a manager selects a portfolio of bonds based on the objectives and constraints of the client with the intent of holding these bonds to maturity. In the second passive strategy, *indexing,* the objective is to construct a portfolio of bonds that will equal the performance of a specified bond index such as the Lehman Brothers Government Bond Index.

BUY-AND-HOLD STRATEGY

The simplest portfolio management strategy is to buy and hold. Obviously not unique to bond investors, it involves finding issues with desired quality, coupon levels, term to maturity, and important indenture provisions, such as call feature. Buy-and-hold

---

[1] This breakdown benefited from the discussion in Martin L. Leibowitz, "The Dedicated Bond Portfolio in Pension Funds—Part I: Motivations and Basics," *Financial Analysts Journal* 42, no. 1 (January-February 1986): 61–75.

investors do not consider active trading to achieve attractive returns, but rather look for vehicles whose maturities (or duration) approximate their stipulated investment horizon in order to reduce price and reinvestment risk. Many successful bond investors and institutional portfolio managers follow a modified buy-and-hold strategy wherein an investment is made in an issue with the intention of holding it until the end of the investment horizon, but they still actively look for opportunities to trade into more desirable positions.[2]

Whether the investor follows a strict or modified buy-and-hold approach, the key ingredient is finding investment vehicles that possess attractive maturity and yield features. The strategy does not restrict the investor to accept whatever the market has to offer, nor does it imply that selectivity is unimportant. Attractive high-yielding issues with desirable features and quality standards are actively sought. As an example, these investors recognize that agency issues generally provide incremental returns relative to Treasuries with little sacrifice in quality, that utilities provide higher returns than comparably rated industrials, and that various call features affect the risk and realized yield of an issue. Thus, successful buy-and-hold investors use their knowledge of markets and issue characteristics to seek out attractive realized yields. Aggressive buy-and-hold investors also incorporate timing considerations into their investment decisions using their knowledge of market rates and expectations.

INDEXING STRATEGY

As discussed in the chapter on efficient capital markets, numerous empirical studies have demonstrated that the majority of money managers have not been able to match the risk–return performance of common stock or bond indexes. As a result, many clients have opted to have some part of their bond portfolios indexed, which means that the portfolio manager builds a portfolio that will match the performance of a selected bond-market index such as the Lehman Brothers Index, Merrill Lynch Index, or Salomon Brothers Index. In such a case, the portfolio manager is not judged on the basis of risk and return compared to an index, but by how closely the portfolio *tracks* the index. Specifically, the analysis of performance involves examining the tracking error, which equals the difference between the rate of return for the portfolio and the rate of return for the bond-market index. For example, if the portfolio experienced an annual rate of return of 8.2 percent during a period when the index had a rate of return of 8.3 percent, the tracking error would be 10 basis points.

When initiating an indexing strategy, the selection of the appropriate market index is very important because it will directly determine the client's risk–return results. As such, it is necessary to be very familiar with all the characteristics of the index.[3] For bond indexes, it is also important to be aware of how the aggregate market and the indexes change over time.[4] Reilly, Kao, and Wright demonstrated that the market has

---

[2] Obviously, if the strategy becomes too modified, it would become one of the active strategies.

[3] An article that briefly discusses the indexes is F. Hawthorne, "The Battle of the Bond Indexes," *Institutional Investor* (April 1986). An article that describes a couple of the indexes and discusses how their characteristics affect their performance in different interest rate environments is Chris P. Dialynas, "The Active Decisions in the Selection of Passive Management and Performance Bogeys," in *The Handbook of Fixed-Income Securities,* 3d ed., edited by Frank J. Fabozzi (Homewood, Ill.: Business One-Irwin, 1991).

[4] An article that describes the major indexes, analyzes the relationship among them, and also examines how the aggregate bond market has changed is Frank K. Reilly, Wenchi Kao, and David J. Wright, "Alternative Bond Market Indexes," *Financial Analysts Journal* 48, no. 3 (May-June 1992): 44–58.

experienced significant changes in composition, maturity and duration during the period 1975 to 1991. After the appropriate bond index is selected, there are several techniques available to accomplish the actual tracking.[5]

ACTIVE MANAGEMENT STRATEGIES[6]

There are five active management strategies available that range from interest rate anticipation that involves economic forecasting to valuation analysis and credit analysis that require detailed bond and company analysis. Finally, yield spread analysis and bond swaps require economic and market analysis.

INTEREST RATE ANTICIPATION

Interest rate anticipation is perhaps the riskiest active management strategy because it involves relying on uncertain forecasts of future interest rates. The idea is to preserve capital when an increase in interest rates is anticipated and achieve attractive capital gains when interest rates are expected to decline. Such objectives are usually attained by altering the maturity (duration) structure of the portfolio (i.e., reducing portfolio duration when interest rates are expected to increase and increasing the portfolio duration when a decline in yields is anticipated). Thus, the risk in such portfolio restructuring is largely a function of these duration (maturity) alterations. When maturities are shortened to preserve capital, substantial income could be sacrificed and the opportunity for capital gains could be lost if interest rates decline rather than rise. Similarly, the portfolio shifts prompted by anticipation of a decline in rates are very risky. Specifically, if we assume that we are at a peak in interest rates, it is likely that the yield curve is downward-sloping, which means that bond coupons will decline with maturity. Therefore, the investor is sacrificing current income by shifting from high-coupon short bonds to longer-duration bonds. At the same time, the portfolio is purposely exposed to greater price volatility that could work against the portfolio if there is an unexpected increase in yields. Note that the portfolio adjustments prompted by anticipation of an increase in rates involves less risk of an absolute capital loss. When you reduce the maturity, the worst that can happen is that interest income is reduced and/or capital gains are forgone (opportunity cost).

Once future (expected) interest rates have been determined, the procedure relies largely on technical matters. Assume that you expect an increase in interest rates and want to preserve your capital by reducing the duration of your portfolio. A popular choice would be high-yielding, short-term obligations such as Treasury bills. Although your primary concern is to preserve capital, you would nevertheless look for the best return possible given the maturity constraint. Liquidity is also important, because after interest rates increase, yields may experience a period of stability before they decline, and you would want the ability to shift positions quickly to benefit from the higher income and/or capital gains.

[5] For a detailed discussion of the alternative tracking techniques available, see Sharmin Mossavar-Rahmoni, "Indexing Fixed-Income Assets," in *The Handbook of Fixed-Income Securities,* 3d ed., edited by Frank J. Fabozzi (Homewood, Ill.: Business One-Irwin, 1991); and Sharmin Mossavar-Rahmoni, *Bond Index Funds* (Chicago: Probus Publishing, 1991).
[6] For further discussion on this topic, see H. Gifford Fong, "Active Strategies for Managing Bond Portfolios," in *The Revolution in Techniques for Managing Bond Portfolios,* ed. Donald Tuttle (Charlottesville, Va.: The Institute of Chartered Financial Analysts, 1983), 21–38.

One way to shorten maturities is to use a *cushion bond,* which is a high-yielding, long-term obligation that carries a coupon substantially above the current market rate and that, due to its current call feature and call price, has a market price lower than what it should be given current market yields, so its yield is higher than normal. An example would be a 10-year bond with a 12 percent coupon, currently callable at 110. If current market rates are 8 percent, this bond if it were noncallable would have a price of about 127; but because of its call price, it will stay close to 110, and its yield will be about 10 percent rather than 8 percent. Bond portfolio managers look for cushion bonds when they expect a modest increase in rates, because such issues provide attractive current income *and* protection against capital loss. The point is, because these bonds are trading at an abnormally high yield, market rates would have to rise to that abnormal level before their price would react.

The portfolio manager who anticipates higher interest rates, therefore, has two simple strategies available: shorten the duration of the portfolio and/or look for an attractive cushion bond.[7] In either case, you would want very liquid issues.

A totally different posture is assumed by investors anticipating a decline in interest rates. The significant risks involved in restructuring a portfolio to take advantage of a decline in interest rates are balanced by the potential for substantial capital gains and holding period returns. When you expect lower interest rates, you will recall that you should increase the duration of the portfolio, because the longer the duration, the greater the price volatility. Also, liquidity is important because you want to be able to close out the position quickly when the drop in rates has been completed.

Therefore, high-grade securities should be used, such as Treasuries, agencies, or corporates rated AAA through BAA. Further, because interest rate sensitivity is critical, it is important to recall that the higher the quality of an obligation, the more sensitive it is to interest rate changes. Finally, you want to concentrate on noncallable issues or those with strong call protection because of the substantial call risk discussed in Chapter 14 in connection with the analysis of duration and convexity.

VALUATION ANALYSIS

With valuation analysis, the portfolio manager attempts to select bonds based on their intrinsic value. In turn, the bond's value is determined based on its characteristics and the average value of these characteristics in the marketplace. As an example, a bond's rating will dictate a certain spread relative to comparable Treasury bonds: long maturity might be worth an added 60 basis points relative to short maturity (i.e., the maturity spread); a given deferred call feature might require a higher or lower yield; a specified sinking fund would likewise mean higher or lower required yields. Given all the characteristics of the bond and their normal cost, you would determine the required yield, and therefore, the bond's implied intrinsic value. After you have done this for a number of bonds, you would compare these derived bond values to the prevailing market prices to determine which bonds are undervalued or overvalued. Based on your confidence in the characteristic costs, you would buy the undervalued issues and ignore or sell the overvalued issues.

---

[7] For an extended discussion of cushion bonds, see Sidney Homer and Martin L. Leibowitz, *Inside the Yield Book* (Englewood Cliffs, N.J.: Prentice-Hall, 1972), Chapter 5.

You can appreciate that success in valuation analysis is based on understanding the characteristics that are important in valuation and being able to accurately *estimate* the value of these characteristics over time.

CREDIT ANALYSIS

A credit analysis strategy involves detailed analysis of the bond issuer to determine expected changes in its default risk. This involves attempting to project changes in the quality ratings assigned to bonds by the four rating agencies discussed in Chapter 13. These rating changes are affected by internal changes in the entity (e.g., changes in important financial ratios) and also by changes in the external environment (i.e., changes in the firm's industry and the economy). During periods of strong economic expansion, even financially weak firms may be able to survive and even prosper. In contrast, during severe economic contractions, normally strong firms may find it very difficult or impossible to meet financial obligations. Therefore, historically there has been a strong cyclical pattern to rating changes—typically, downgradings increase during economic contractions, and decline during economic expansions. The period of 1985 to 1989 was an exception because the number of downgradings increased substantially during an economic expansion.[8]

To employ credit analysis as a management strategy, it is necessary to project rating changes prior to the announcement by the rating agencies. As the subsequent discussion on bond-market efficiency notes, the market adjusts rather quickly to bond rating changes—especially downgradings. Therefore, you should acquire bond issues expected to experience upgradings and sell or avoid those expected to be downgraded.

CREDIT ANALYSIS OF HIGH-YIELD (JUNK) BONDS   One of the most obvious opportunities for credit analysis is the analysis of high-yield (junk) bonds. As demonstrated by several studies, the yield differential between junk bonds that are rated below BBB and Treasury securities ranges from about 200 basis points to over 1,000 basis points. Notably, these yield differentials vary substantially over time as shown by a time-series plot in Figure 15.1. Specifically, the average yield spread ranged from a high of almost 1,100 basis points during early 1991 to a low of about 200 basis points in late 1984, and ended in 1992 at 548 basis points.

While the spreads have widened, a study indicated that the average credit quality of high-yield bonds also declined from 1980 to 1988.[9] As an example, interest coverage declined from about 2 times in the period from 1980 to 1982 to 0.71 times in the period from 1987 to 1988. This overall decline in the average ratios for all high-yield bonds is due to two factors.[10] First, the distribution of bonds in rating categories has changed. Specifically, the proportion of BB bonds sold compared to the total declined and the proportion of CCC bonds increased during the period 1983 to 1989 prior to a decline in 1990 and 1991. Second, the credit quality of bonds *within* rating categories has also declined over time. Specifically, the average values of the financial ratios for bonds

---

[8] For a discussion of this pattern, see Frank K. Reilly, "The Growing Importance of Credit Analysis," Working paper, University of Notre Dame (April 1991).

[9] Roger Lowenstein, "Junk Gets Junkier and That May Explain Bonds' Current Ills," *The Wall Street Journal,* November 3, 1989, C1, C2. This article discussed an early draft of Barrie A. Wigmore, "The Decline in Credit Quality of New Issue Junk Bonds," *Financial Analysts Journal* 46, no. 5 (September-October 1990): 53–62.

[10] These changes are demonstrated in Reilly, "The Growing Importance of Credit Analysis."

FIGURE 15.1

Yield Spread (Basis Points) between the Average Yield on the First Boston Composite High Yield Index and the Treasury Index December 1982–December 1992

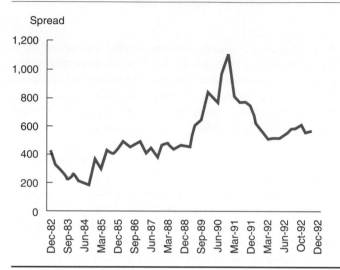

Source: *High Yield Handbook* (New York: High Yield Research Group, First Boston Corp., January 1993).

included in the B or CCC rating classes have declined over time. These two factors explain why overall average credit quality declined during this period. There was a reversal in 1990 and 1991 when very few CCC bonds were issued following the high ratio of defaulted bonds in 1990 and 1991. Therefore, the overall percentage of CCC bonds declined although the ratios for these bonds did not experience much improvement.

These changes in credit quality will make credit analysis of high-yield bonds not only more important, but also more difficult. This means that bond analysts–portfolio managers need to engage in detailed credit analysis to select bonds that will survive. Given the spread in promised yields, if a portfolio manager can, through rigorous credit analysis, avoid bonds with a high probability of default, high-yield bonds will provide substantial rates of return for the investor.

In summary, you can derive substantial rates of return by investing in high-yield bonds assuming that you do the credit analysis required to avoid defaults, which occur with these bonds at substantially higher rates than the overall market. Several recent studies have shown that the average cumulative default rate for high-yield bonds after 10 years is between 30 and 35 percent. Of the high-yield bonds sold in 1980, about 38 percent had defaulted by 1990.[11]

---

[11] Although the details of the analysis differ, the overall results for cumulative defaults are quite consistent. See Edward I. Altman, "Measuring Corporate Bond Mortality and Performance," *Journal of Finance* 44, no. 4 (September 1989): 909–922; Paul Asquith, David W. Mullins, Jr., and Eric D. Wolff, "Original Issue High Yield Bonds: Aging Analysis of Defaults, Exchanges and Calls," *Journal of Finance* 44, no. 4 (September 1989): 929–952; K. Scott Douglass and Douglas J. Lucas, "Historical Default Rates of Corporate Bond Issuers, 1970–1988" (New York: Moody's Investors Services, July 1989). The Altman and Douglass-Lucas studies are updated and discussed in Frank K. Reilly, ed., *High Yield Bonds: Analysis and Risk Assessment* (Charlottesville, Va.: Institute of Chartered Financial Analysts, 1990). Another review of these studies is Edward I. Altman, "Setting the Record Straight on Junk Bonds: A Review of

TABLE 15.1

Average Cumulative Default Rates for Corporate Bonds: 1970–1988

Ratings	Years since Issue		
	5	10	15
Aaa	0.2%	0.8%	2.1%
Aa	0.5	1.4	2.2
A	0.5	1.4	2.7
Baa	1.6	3.7	5.9
Ba	8.3	14.2	18.9
B	22.3	25.3	32.9

Source: K. Scott Douglass and Douglas J. Lucas, "Historical Default Rates of Corporate Bond Issuers, 1970–1988" (New York: Moody's Investors Services, July 1989). Copyright by Moody's Investors Service. Reprinted by permission.

Table 15.1 lists the results for one study that considers the full spectrum of bonds. It shows substantial differences in cumulative default rates for bonds with different ratings for the periods 5, 10, and 15 years after issue. Over 10 years, the holding period that is widely discussed, the default rate for Baa investment grade bonds is only 3.7 percent, but the default rate increases to over 14 percent for Ba and to 25.3 percent for B rated bonds. This analysis does not include Caa issues, which would have even higher default rates.

These default rates do not mean that investors should avoid high-yield bonds, but they do indicate that extensive credit analysis is a critical component for success within this sector. If you can avoid defaults, you can earn substantial rates of return from high-yield bonds. The point is, given the substantial yield spreads over Treasuries, there can be some wonderful opportunities for high returns *if* you can avoid owning bonds that default or are downgraded. The route to avoiding such bond issues is through rigorous, enlightened credit analysis.

The credit analysis of these bonds can employ a statistical model or employ basic fundamental analysis that recognizes some of the unique characteristics of these bonds. The following discussion considers both approaches.

The Altman-Nammacher book suggests that the *Z-score model* used to predict bankruptcy can also be used to predict default for these high-yield bonds or can be used as a gauge of changes in credit quality. The Z-score model combines traditional financial measures with a multivariate technique known as multiple discriminant analysis to derive a set of weights for the specified variables. The result is an overall credit score (zeta score) for each firm.[12] The model is of the form

$$\text{Zeta} = a_0 + a_1 X_1 + a_2 X_2 + a_3 X_3 \ldots a_n X_n$$

where:

Zeta = **overall credit score**

$X_1 \ldots X_n$ = **explanatory variables (ratios and market measures)**

$a_0 \ldots a_n$ = **weightings or coefficients**

the Research on Default Rates and Returns," *Journal of Applied Corporate Finance* 3, no. 2 (Summer 1990): 82–95, and Edward I. Altman, "Revisiting the High-Yield Bond Market," *Financial Management* 21, no. 2 (Summer 1992): 78–92.

[12] Edward I. Altman and Scott A. Nammacher, *Investing in Junk Bonds* (New York: John Wiley & Sons, 1987).

The final model used in this analysis included the following seven financial measures:

X_1 = **profitability: earnings before interest and taxes (EBIT)/total assets**

X_2 = **stability of profitability measure: the standard error of estimate of EBIT/TA (normalized for 10 years)**

X_3 = **debt service capabilities: EBIT/interest charges**

X_4 = **cumulative profitability: retained earnings/total assets**

X_5 = **liquidity: current assets/current liabilities**

X_6 = **capitalization levels: market value of equity/total capital (5-year average)**

X_7 = **size: total tangible assets (normalized)**

The weightings, or coefficients, for the variables were not reported. Using weights derived on a sample of firms that defaulted, the authors contended that during 1985, the zeta model would have anticipated the 13 defaults that they considered. Specifically, in all cases the zeta score was below zero, which was stipulated as the cutoff between healthy and distressed firms.

In contrast to using a model that provides a composite credit score, most analysts and investment houses simply adapt their basic corporate bond analysis techniques to the unique needs of high-yield bonds, which are considered low-quality credits that have characteristics of common stock. Howe claims that the analysis of high-yield bonds is the same as with any bond except that five areas of analysis should be expanded.[13] First, what is the firm's *competitive position* in terms of cost and pricing? This can be critical to a small firm. Second, what is the firm's *cash flow* relative to cash requirements for interest, research, growth, and periods of economic decline? Also, what is the firm's *borrowing capacity* that can serve as a safety net and provide flexibility? Third, what is the *liquidity value of the firm's assets,* and are these assets available for liquidation (are there any claims against them)? In many cases, asset sales are a critical part of the strategy for a leveraged buyout. Fourth, how good is the *total management team,* including general administration, finance, marketing, and production? Are all of them committed and capable of operating in the high-risk environment of this firm? Finally, what is the firm's *financial leverage* on an absolute basis and also on a market-adjusted basis (using market value for equity and debt)?

Hynes suggests that the following four areas require subjective analysis as part of the process of evaluating cash flows when analyzing a leveraged buyout (which typically involves the issuance of high-yield debt).[14]

1. Inherent business risk
2. Earnings growth potential
3. Asset redevelopment potential
4. Refinancing capability

In addition to the potentially higher financial risk, there may be an increase in business risk if the firm sells off some operations that have favorable risk characteristics with

---

[13] Jane Tripp Howe, "Credit Considerations in Evaluating High-Yield Bonds," in *The Handbook of Fixed-Income Securities,* 3d ed., edited by Frank J. Fabozzi (Homewood, Ill.: Business One-Irwin, 1991); Jane Tripp Howe, *Junk Bonds: Analysis and Portfolio Strategies* (Chicago: Probus Publishing, 1988).

[14] Joseph Hynes, "Key Risk Factors for LBOs," *Speculative Grade Debt Credit Review* (New York: Standard & Poor's Corporation, June 15, 1987).

the remaining operations—that is, business risk would increase if the firm sells a division or company that has low correlation of earnings with other units of the firm. In addition, a change in management operating philosophy could have a negative impact on operating earnings. The management of leveraged buyout (LBO) firms are known for making optimistic growth estimates related to sales and earnings, so the analyst should evaluate these very critically with an eye toward the historical record. Asset divestiture plans are often a major element of an LBO, because they provide necessary capital used to reduce the substantial debt taken on as part of the buyout. Therefore, it is important to examine the liquidity of the assets, their estimated selling values, and the timing of these programs. You must ascertain whether the estimated sale prices for the assets are reasonable and whether the timing is realistic. If the schedule is too tight, it could affect the price received and the debt reduction program. At the same time, if the divestiture program is successful in terms of selling prices received (i.e., if the prices received are above normal expectations) or timing (the assets are sold ahead of schedule), this can be grounds for an upgrading of the debt. Finally, it is necessary to constantly monitor the firm's refinancing flexibility. Specifically, what refinancing will be necessary, what does the schedule look like, and does it appear that the bonds and other capital suppliers will be receptive to the refinancing.

HIGH-YIELD BOND RESEARCH   Because of the growth of high-yield bonds, several investment houses have developed specialized high-yield groups that examine high-yield bond issues and also monitor yield spreads in the aggregate junk bond market. Kidder, Peabody & Company has a weekly publication, *High Yield Sector Report,* that typically contains a commentary on the high-yield market and a review of changes in the spreads for bonds in alternative rating groups (e.g., BB, 10-year issues) and industry sectors that issued high-yield debt (e.g., airlines, energy, transportation). Also, a new-issue section discusses recent issues and previews forthcoming issues. Finally, there is a fairly detailed discussion of a specific high-yield issue, the firm, and the overall outlook for the issue.

Merrill Lynch has a monthly publication entitled *High Yield* that provides an overview of the market and reviews several individual industries and firms within these main industries (e.g., retail, steel, building products, and textile). It also contains reports of research done by the firm on general questions on the high-yield market. The firm initiated a high-yield master bond return index in October 1984, and it tracks the yield spreads for high-yield bonds relative to Treasury issues.

Merrill also has a weekly publication entitled *This Week in High Yield*, which discusses current events in the high-yield market. This includes weekly yields and yield spreads for the various sectors of the market and news highlights for specific companies and issues.

Salomon Brothers has a monthly publication entitled *High Yield Market Update* that presents monthly and cumulative long-term returns for their high-yield indexes (long-term and intermediate-term corporates, long-term utilities), as well as spreads between rating categories and relative to appropriate Treasuries. There is also a commentary on a timely topic within the high-yield market (e.g., "Recent Changes in the Airline Industry").

Morgan Stanley & Company provided a substantial amount of the material and data used by Altman and Nammacher in the book discussed earlier. The firm also publishes a monthly review entitled *High Performance.* The publication contains articles on the overall high-yield market, such as "The Anatomy of the High Yield Market," "Group Effect in High Yield Bonds," and "Analyzing Default Risk." It also contains an analysis of individual industries and firms that have issued or are issuing high-yield bonds.

The high-yield research group at First Boston publishes a *Monthly Market Review* related to the high-yield bond market. Beyond a general market review of news and events that affect this market, there is an extensive performance review that examines returns by sectors and industries as well as considering spreads and changing volatility for these bonds. First Boston also publishes an annual *High Yield Handbook* each January that contains a review of annual events and does an extensive performance review that considers every aspect of risk, return, and correlation of high-yield bonds with other asset classes. There is also a very helpful listing of new issues, retirements, and defaults.

In 1992 Lehman Brothers started publishing a weekly review of market trends entitled *High Yield Portfolio Advisor* that reviews the firm's high-yield bond indexes, contains a comment on overall market performance, and has detailed comments on news events that affect alternative industries prominent in the high-yield market. The firm also publishes a monthly *High Yield Bond Market Report* that briefly discusses the returns and new issues for the month and contains extensive data on returns for all components of the HY market (BB, B, CCC, CC-D, non-rated, default) and also contains descriptive statistics regarding bonds in the composite index and various subindexes such as average coupon, maturity, duration to worst, modified adjusted duration, price, and yield.

In addition, several bond rating firms conduct research on these industries and firms to assign the specific ratings. Standard & Poor's has a publication entitled *Speculative Grade Debt Credit Review* that discusses general problems involved in the credit analysis of high-yield bonds (e.g., "Junk Bond Rating Policies Revised," "Junk Bond Rating Change Potential"). The publication also includes a review of several major industries and specific comments on outstanding issues by industry grouping.

Duff & Phelps has three regular publications related to the high-yield bond market. *Credit Comments* is a weekly publication that discusses developments that may influence changes in default rankings or buy/sell/hold recommendations. *Recommendations* is a monthly summary of current recommendations for each bond issue. These summaries include month-end prices, default risk rankings, and yield spreads on more than 400 issues. Finally, *Profiles* is a quarterly bulletin that contains an updated financial profile for each of the companies in the high-yield service. The data include financial ratios, income statement items, a cash flow summary, and the firm's capitalization.

McCarthy, Crisanti and Maffei (MCM), a small bond rating firm that merged with Duff & Phelps was well regarded for its junk bond research.[15] Its approach toward high-yield bond issues was to utilize sound fundamental credit research with a focus on two critical factors: cash flow and financial cushion. Because cash flow is the primary source of funds for debt service, MCM would include a detailed projection of it for 2 years. In addition, it was felt that a firm should have a financial cushion that includes such items as potential asset sales, unused bank lines of credit and discretion-

---

[15] Andrew Marton, "The King of Junk Research," *Institutional Investor* 22, no. 5 (May 1988): 85–87.

ary capital spending. This cushion provides a safety net in case operating results fall below what is needed to meet financial requirements.

In summary, the substantial increase in junk bonds issued and outstanding has been matched by an increase in research and credit analysis. The consensus is that the credit analysis of these bonds is similar to that of investment-grade bonds with an emphasis on the following factors: (1) *the use of cash flows* compared to debt obligations under very conservative assumptions and (2) the detailed analysis of *potential asset sales,* including a conservative estimate of sales prices, the asset's true liquidity, the availability of the assets, and a consideration of the timing of the sales. An in-depth analysis of junk bonds is critical because of the number of such issues, the wide diversity of quality within the junk bond universe (there is "quality" junk and "junk" junk), and the growing complexity of these issues.

YIELD SPREAD ANALYSIS

As discussed in Chapter 14, spread analysis assumes there are normal relationships between the yields for bonds in alternative sectors (e.g., the spread between high-grade versus low-grade industrial or between industrial versus utility bonds). Therefore, a bond portfolio manager would monitor these relationships, and when an abnormal relationship occurs execute various sector swaps. The crucial factor is developing the background to know the normal yield relationship and evaluate the liquidity necessary to buy or sell the required issues quickly enough to take advantage of the supposedly temporary abnormality.

The analysis of yield spreads has been enhanced by a paper by Dialynas and Edington that considers several specific factors that affect the aggregate spread.[16] It is acknowledged that the generally accepted explanation of the spread is that it is related to the economic environment. Specifically, the spread widens during periods of economic uncertainty and recession because investors require larger risk premiums (i.e., larger spreads). In contrast, the spread will decline during periods of economic confidence and expansion. Although not denying the existence of such a relationship, the authors contend that a more encompassing factor is the impact of interest rate (yield) volatility. They contend that yield volatility will affect the spread via three affects: (1) yield volatility and the behavior of imbedded options, (2) yield volatility and transactional liquidity, and (3) the affect of yield volatility on the business cycle. Recall that the value of callable bonds is equal to the value of a noncallable bond minus the value of the call option. Obviously, if the value of the option increases, the value of the callable bond will decline and its yield will increase. The point is, when there is an increase in yield volatility, the value of the call option increases, which causes an increase in the bond's yield and its yield spread relative to Treasury bonds. Similarly, an increase in yield volatility will increase the uncertainty facing bond dealers and cause them to increase their bid–ask spreads that reflect the transactional liquidity for these bonds. This liquidity will have a bigger effect on nongovernment bonds, so their yield spread relative to Treasury bonds will increase. Finally, interest rate volatility causes uncertainty for business executives and consumers regarding their costs of funds. This typically will

---

[16] Chris P. Dialynas and David H. Edington, "Bond Yield Spreads—A Postmodern View," *Journal of Portfolio Management*, 19, no. 1 (Fall, 1992): 60–75.

precede an economic decline that will, in turn, lead to an increase in the yield spread. The main point that is demonstrated is that it is possible to have a change in yield spread that is due not only to economic uncertainty. Put another way, if there is a period a greater yield volatility that is not a period of economic uncertainty, the yield spread will increase due to the imbedded option effect and the transactional liquidity effect. Therefore, when examining yield spreads you should pay particular attention to the relevant interest rate (yield) volatility.

BOND SWAPS

Bond swaps involve liquidating a current position and simultaneously buying a different issue in its place with similar attributes but a chance for improved return. Swaps can be executed to increase current yield, to increase yield to maturity, to take advantage of shifts in interest rates or the realignment of yield spreads, to improve the quality of a portfolio, or for tax purposes. Some are highly sophisticated and require a computer for the necessary calculations. Most, however, are fairly simple transactions, with obvious goals and risk. They go by such names as *profit takeouts, substitution swaps, intermarket spread swaps,* or *tax swaps.* Although many of these swaps involve low risk (such as the pure yield pickup swap), others entail substantial risk (the rate anticipation swap). Regardless of the risk involved, all swaps have one basic purpose: portfolio improvement.

Most swaps involve several different types of risk. One obvious risk is that the market will move against you while the swap is outstanding. Interest rates may move up over the holding period and cause you to incur a loss. Alternatively, yield spreads may fail to respond as anticipated. Another possibility is that the new bond may not be a true substitute and so, even if your expectations and interest rate formulations are correct, the swap may be unsatisfactory because the wrong issue was selected. Finally, if the work-out time is longer than anticipated, the realized yield might be less than expected. You must be willing to accept such risks in order to improve your portfolio. The following subsections consider three of the more popular bond swaps.[17]

PURE YIELD PICKUP SWAP   The pure yield pickup involves swapping out of a low-coupon bond into a comparable higher-coupon bond to realize an automatic and instantaneous increase in current yield and yield to maturity. Your risks are (1) that the market will move against you and (2) that the new issue may not be a viable swap candidate. Also, because you are moving to a higher coupon obligation, there could be greater call risk.

An example of a pure yield pickup swap would be an investor who currently holds a 30-year, Aa-rated 10 percent issue that is trading at an 11.50 percent yield. Assume that a comparable 30-year, Aa-rated obligation bearing a 12 percent coupon priced to yield 12 percent becomes available. The investor would report (and realize) some book loss if the original issue was bought at par but is able to improve current yield and

---

[17] For additional information on these and other types of bond swaps, see Sidney Homer and Martin L. Leibowitz, *Inside the Yield Book* (Englewood Cliffs, N.J.: Prentice-Hall, 1972); Robert W. Kopprasch, John Macfarlane, Janet Showers, and Daniel Ross, "The Interest Rate Swap Market: Yield Mathematics, Terminology, and Conventions," in *The Handbook of Fixed Income Securities,* 3d ed., edited by Frank J. Fabozzi (Homewood, Ill.: Busines One-Irwin, 1991).

TABLE 15.2	**A Pure Yield Pickup Swap**	

Pure Yield Pickup Swap: A bond swap involving a switch from a low-coupon bond to a higher-coupon bond of similar quality and maturity in order to pick up higher current yield and a better yield to maturity.

Example: Currently hold: 30-yr., 10.0% coupon priced at 874.12 to yield 11.5%.
    Swap candidate: 30-yr., Aa 12% coupon priced at $1,000 to yield 12.0%.

	Current Bond	Candidate Bond
Dollar investment	$874.12	$1,000.00[a]
Coupon	100.00	120.00
i on one coupon (12.0% for 6 months)	3.000	3.600
Principal value at year-end	874.66	1,000.00
Total accrued	977.66	1,123.60
Realized compound yield	11.514%	12.0%

Value of swap: 48.6 basis points in one year (assuming a 12.0% reinvestment rate).

The rewards for a pure yield pickup swap are automatic and instantaneous in that both a higher-coupon yield and a higher yield to maturity are realized from the swap.

Other advantages include:
1. No specific work-out period needed because the investor is assumed to hold the new bond to maturity
2. No need for interest rate speculation
3. No need to analyze prices for overvaluation or undervaluation

A major disadvantage of the pure yield pickup swap is the book loss involved in the swap. In this example, if the current bond were bought at par, the book loss would be ($1,000 − 874.12) $125.88.

Other risks involved in the pure yield pickup swap include:
1. Increased risk of call in the event interest rates decline
2. Reinvestment risk is greater with higher-coupon bonds.

[a] Obviously the investor can invest $874.12, the amount obtained from the sale of the bond currently held, and still obtain a realized compound yield of 12.0%.

Swap evaluation procedure is patterned after a technique suggested by Sidney Homer and Martin L. Leibowitz. Source: Adapted from the book *Inside the Yield Book* by Sidney Homer and Martin L. Leibowitz, Ph.D., © 1972, used by permission of the publisher, Prentice-Hall Inc., Englewood Cliffs, NJ and New York Institute of Finance, New York, NY.

yield to maturity simultaneously if the new obligation is held to maturity as shown in Table 15.2.

The investor need not predict rate changes, and the swap is not based on any imbalance in yield spread. The object is simply to seek higher yields. Quality and maturity stay the same, as do all other factors *except coupon*. The major risk is that future reinvestment rates may not be as high as expected, and therefore, the total terminal value of the investment (capital recovery, coupon receipts, and interest-on-interest) may not be as high as expected or comparable to the original obligation. This reinvestment risk can be evaluated by analyzing the results with a number of reinvestment rates to determine the minimum reinvestment rate that would make the swap viable.

SUBSTITUTION SWAP   The substitution swap is generally short term and relies heavily on interest rate expectations. It is subject to considerably more risk than the pure yield pickup swaps. The procedure rests on the existence of a short-term imbalance in yield spreads between issues that are perfect substitutes. The imbalance in yield spread

TABLE 15.3

A Substitution Swap

Substitution Swap: A swap executed to take advantage of temporary market anomalies in yield spreads between issues that are equivalent with respect to coupon, quality, and maturity.

Example: Currently hold: 30-yr., Aa 12.0% coupon priced at $1,000 to yield 12.0%.
       Swap candidate: 30-yr., Aa 12% coupon priced at $984.08 to yield 12.2%
       Assumed work-out period: 1 year
       Reinvested at 12.0%

	Current Bond	Candidate Bond
Dollar investment	$1,000.00	$ 984.08
Coupon	120.00	120.00
i on one coupon (12.0% for 6 months)	3.60	3.60
Principal value at year-end (12.0% YTM)	1,000.00	1,000.00
Total accrued	1,123.60	1,123.60
Total gain	123.60	139.52
Gain per invested dollar	.1236	.1418
Realized compound yield	12.00%	13.71%

Value of swap: 171 basis points in one year.

The rewards for the substitution swap are additional basis point pickups for YTM, and additional realized compound yield, and capital gains that accrue when the anomaly in yield corrects itself.

In the substitution swap, you must realize that any basis point pickup (171 points in this example) will be realized only during the work-out period. Thus, in our example, to obtain the 171 basis point increase in realized compound yield, you must swap an average of once each year and pick up an average of 20 basis points in yield to maturity on each swap.

Potential risks associated with the substitution swap include:
1. A yield spread thought to be temporary may, in fact, be permanent, thus reducing capital gains advantages.
2. The market rate may change adversely.

Swap evaluation procedure is patterned after a technique suggested by Sidney Homer and Martin L. Leibowitz. Source: Adapted from the book *Inside the Yield Book* by Sidney Homer and Martin L. Leibowitz, Ph.D., © 1972, used by permission of the publisher, Prentice-Hall Inc., Englewood Cliffs, NJ and New York Institute of Finance, New York, NY.

is expected to be corrected in the near future. For example, the investor might hold a 30-year, 12 percent issue that is yielding 12 percent and be offered a comparable 30-year, 12 percent bond that is yielding 12.20 percent. Because the issue offered will trade at a price less than $1,000, for every issue sold, the investor can buy more than one of the offered obligations.

You would expect the yield spread imbalance to be corrected by having the yield on the offering bond decline to the level of your current issue. Thus, you would realize capital gains by switching out of your current position into the higher-yielding obligation. This swap is described in Table 15.3.

Although a modest increase in current income occurs as the yield imbalance is corrected, attractive capital gains are possible, causing a differential in *realized yield*. The work-out time will have an important effect on the differential realized return. Even if the yield is not corrected until maturity, 30 years hence, you will still experience a small increase in realized yield (about 10 basis points). In contrast, if the correction takes place in 1 year, the differential realized return is much greater, as shown in Table 15.3.

After the correction has occurred, you would have additional capital for a subsequent swap or other investment. There are several risks involved in this swap. In addition to the pressure of the work-out time, market interest rates could move against you, the yield spread may not be temporary, and the issue may not be a viable swap candidate (i.e., the spread may be because the issue is of lower quality).

TAX SWAP   The tax swap is popular with individual investors because it is a relatively simple procedure that involves no interest rate projections and few risks. Investors enter into tax swaps due to tax laws and realized capital gains in their portfolios. Assume you acquired $100,000 worth of corporate bonds and after 2 years sold the securities for $150,000, implying a capital gain of $50,000. One way to eliminate the tax liability of that capital gain is to sell an issue that has a comparable long-term capital loss.[18] If you had a long-term investment of $100,000 with a current market value of $50,000, you could execute a tax swap to establish the $50,000 capital loss. By offsetting this capital loss and the comparable capital gain, you would reduce your income taxes.

Municipal bonds are considered particularly attractive tax swap candidates, because you can increase your tax-free income and use the capital loss (which is subject to normal federal and state taxation) to reduce capital gains tax liability. To continue our illustration, assume that you own $100,000 worth of New York City, 20-year, 7 percent bonds that you bought at par, but they have a current market value of $50,000. Given this tax loss, you need a comparable bond swap candidate. Suppose you find a 20-year New York City bond with a 7.1 percent coupon and a market value of 50. By selling your New York 7s and instantaneously reinvesting in the New York 7.1s, you would eliminate the capital gains tax from the corporate bond transaction. In effect, you have $50,000 of tax-free capital gains, and you have increased your current tax-free yield. The money saved by avoiding the tax liability can then be used to increase the portfolio's yield, as shown in Table 15.4.

An important caveat is that *you cannot swap identical issues,* such as selling the New York 7s to establish a loss and then buying back the same New York 7s. If it is not a different issue, the IRS considers the transaction a *wash sale* and does not allow the loss. It is easier to avoid wash sales in the bond market than it is in the stock market, because every bond issue, even with identical coupons and maturities, is considered distinct. Likewise, it is easier to find comparable bond issues with only modest differences in coupon, maturity, and quality. Tax swaps are common at year end as investors establish capital losses, because the capital loss must occur in the same taxable year as the capital gain. This procedure differs from other swap transactions in that it exists because of tax statutes rather than temporary market anomalies.

A GLOBAL FIXED-INCOME INVESTMENT STRATEGY

An active management strategy that considers one or several of the techniques discussed thus far should apply these techniques to a global portfolio. The optimum global fixed-income asset allocation must consider three interrelated factors: (1) the local economy in each country that includes the effect of domestic and international demand, (2) the impact of this total demand and domestic monetary policy on inflation and interest rates, and (3) the effect of the economy, inflation, and interest rates on the

---

[18] Although this discussion deals with tax swaps that involve bonds, comparable strategies could be used with other types of investments.

TABLE 15.4   **A Tax Swap**

Tax Swap: A swap undertaken in a situation when you wish to offset capital gains in other securities through the sale of a bond currently held and selling at a discount from the price paid at purchase. By swapping into a bond with as nearly identical features as possible, you can use the capital loss on the sale of the bond for tax purposes and still maintain your current position in the market.

Example: Currently hold: $100,000 worth of corporate bonds with current market value of $150,000 *and* $100,000 in N.Y., 20-year, 7% bonds with current market value of $50,000.
           Swap candidate: $50,000 in N.Y., 20-year, 7.1% bonds.

A. Corporate bonds sold and long-term capital gains profit established	$50,000		
Capital gains tax liability (assume you have 20% capital gains tax rate) ($50,000 × .20)		$10,000	
B. N.Y. 7s sold and long-term capital *loss* established	$50,000		
Reduction in capital gains tax liability ($50,000 × .20)		($10,000)	
Net capital gains tax liability		0	
Tax *savings* realized		$10,000	
C. Complete tax swap by buying N.Y. 7.1s from proceeds of N.Y. 7s sale (therefore, amount invested remains largely the *same*)[a]			
Annual tax-free interest income—N.Y. 7s	$ 7,000		
Annual tax-free interest income—N.Y. 7.1s	$ 7,100		
Net *increase* in *annual* tax-free interest income	$ 100		

[a] N.Y. 7.1s will result in substantial capital gains when liquidated at maturity (because they were bought at deep discounts) and, therefore, will be subject to future capital gains tax liability. The swap is designed to use the capital loss resulting from the swap to offset capital gains from other investments. At the same time, your funds remain in a security almost identical to your previous holding while you receive a slight increase in both current income and YTM.

Because the tax swap involved no projections in terms of work-out period, interest rate changes, etc., the risks involved are minimal. Your major concern should be to avoid potential wash sales.

exchange rates among countries.[19] Based on the evaluation of these factors, a portfolio manager must decide the relative weight for each country. In addition, one might consider an allocation within each country among government, municipal, and corporate bonds. In the examples that follow, most portfolio recommendations concentrate on the country allocation and do not become more specific except in the case of the United States.

Table 15.5 contains the table from a strategy report by Salomon Brothers. In this instance there is no specific percentage breakdown among assets and countries, but rather a specific estimate of what will happen to the yields for various assets relative to equal-duration Treasury issues.

In making your own allocations based on these specific expectations, you would look for U.S. securities in which yields were expected to decline relative to Treasury securities and for foreign securities in countries in which the currency was expected to be strong relative to the United States.

Table 15.6 contains a table from *Currency and Bond Market Trends* published by Merrill Lynch Capital Markets. The discussion likewise analyzes the economies, for-

---

[19] For a detailed discussion of the benefits of international bond investing as well as what is involved in the analysis, see Adam M. Greshin and Margaret Darasz Hadzima, "International Bond Investing and Portfolio Management," and Michael R. Rosenberg, "International Fixed Income Investing: Theory and Practice." Both are included in *The Handbook of Fixed Income Securities*, 3d ed., edited by Frank J. Fabozzi (Homewood, Ill.: Business One–Irwin, 1991).

eign trade, inflation, interest rates, and exchange rates. The portfolio recommendations consider the percentage asset allocation for each of these currency blocs relative to the proportion for each country in the global bond market. The top line in bold is the recommendation, the second line in italics is the global capitalization weights. As an example, the U.S. bond market is 49 percent and the yen market is 23 percent of the total bond market. Given these market proportions, the bold numbers indicate the firm's investment recommendations. As an example, although the U.S. dollar market is 49 percent of the global fixed-income market, Merrill Lynch is recommending that on an unhedged (gross currency position) that you underweight the U.S. market and invest only 39 percent of your bond portfolio in this market versus overweighting the Canadian dollar market by investing 7 percent of your bond portfolio in Canadian bonds, even though this market is only 4 percent of the global bond portfolio. The *net* currency position indicates the firm's recommended exposure to each of the currencies after adjusting the gross currency position for forward currency positions. As shown, assuming 10 percent currency hedging for the United States, the net currency position is equal to the market weight.

The next set of columns indicates Merrill Lynch's recommendations regarding the mix of bonds for each country. As shown, it recommends that 20 percent of the 39 percent for the United States be put into 1–3 year bonds and 19 percent be invested into 7–10 year bonds. This is referred to as a barbell approach that combines short and long bonds. Finally, the average duration for the total U.S. portfolio should be 4.5 years compared to an average duration for the U.S. bond market of 5.0 years. This below-market duration recommendation indicates a desire for low interest rate risk compared to Australia and Europe where they recommend high interest rate risk in anticipation of declining rates in these countries compared to the United States.

In summary, assuming that you want to actively manage a bond portfolio, these examples show alternative approaches to the asset allocation decision on a global scale. Similar to our discussion on equity securities, global asset allocation requires substantially more research because you must evaluate each country individually, and relative to every other country. Finally, your global recommendation must also consider exchange rate changes.

MATCHED-FUNDING TECHNIQUES[20]

As discussed previously, because of an increase in interest rate volatility and the needs of many institutional investors, there has been a growth of the use of matched-funding techniques ranging from pure cash-matched dedicated portfolios to portfolios involved in employing contingent immunization.

DEDICATED PORTFOLIOS

Dedication refers to bond portfolio management techniques that are used to service a prescribed set of liabilities. The idea is that a pension fund has a set of future liabilities, and those responsible for administering these liabilities want a money manager to construct a portfolio of assets with cash flows that will match this liability stream.

<hr>

[20] An overview of these alternative strategies is contained in Martin L. Leibowitz, "The Dedicated Bond Portfolio in Pension Funds—Part I: Motivation and Basics," *Financial Analysts Journal* 42, no. 1 (January-February 1986): 68–75; and Martin L. Leibowitz, "The Dedicated Bond Portfolio in Pension Funds—Part II: Immunization, Horizon Matching, and Contingent Procedures," *Financial Analysts Journal* 42, no. 2 (March-April 1986): 47–57.

TABLE 15.5   **Projected Performance of Major U.S. and International Fixed-Income Sectors, June 30 to December 31, 1988**

	Yield Change versus Comparable Duration Treasury	Currency Change versus U.S.$	Comments
U.S. Dollar Denominated Treasuries			
Coupon	NM		Favor bullets over barbells.
STRIPs	+		Yield spreads are not tight.
Agencies	+		Rising Treasury yields should widen spreads marginally.
Corporates	+		Rising issuance, volatility, and yields point to an increase in spreads.
Industrial	+		Strengthening credit more than offset by restructuring risk and increases in supply.
Telephones	NC		Solid credit prospects, but very tight spreads.
Electric utilities	–		Improving credit prospects among lower-quality electric utilities.
Financials	–		Strong credit prospects.
High yield	–		Relatively high sensitivity to the economy should narrow spreads further.
Mortgages			
Discount coupon (Projects)	–		Option-adjusted spreads have narrowed little relative to other mortgage securities.
Current coupon (New)	+		Technical forces have narrowed spreads artificially.
Current coupon (Seasoned)	–		Wider spreads and shorter effective durations relative to new issues point to superior performance.
Premium coupon	NC		Vigorous demand and absence of supply should sustain performance; if interest rates rise, short effective duration will prove to be attractive.

CMOs			
Principal-only STRIPs	NC		"A" tranche and seasoned issues provide defensive instruments.
	–		Wide spreads and positive convexity of discount instruments provide extraordinary value.
Interest-only STRIPs	NM		Narrow spreads and lagging demand make these securities vulnerable. However, they may have a special value because of their unique negative duration.
ARM pass-throughs	–		Strong demand and limited supply will reinforce returns.
International			
Eurodollar	+		Spreads will widen—in line with domestic corporate spreads—as supply increases and volatility rises.
Yankee	–		Improving credit prospects for many issuers.
Nondollar-Denominated Governments			
Japanese yen	–	6%–7%	Currency should retest the ¥ 120/US$ level, based on strong Japanese economic fundamentals as yields rise only modestly further.
Canadian dollar	NC	1	Maintenance of large short-term interest rate differential, plus lower inflation rate than in the United States lead to continued outperformance.
Australian dollar	–	2	Attractive and narrowing yield spreads. Yield curve likely to remain flat, but volatile conditions will persist. Further modest currency appreciation possible.
British sterling	–	5–6	Yield curve should remain flat; volatility persists at shorter maturities.
Deutschemark	–	5–6	Yield curve remains steep as long yields rise modestly. Current prices already incorporate expected 10 percent withholding tax on interest income.
Dutch guilder	–	5–6	Currency and interest rate linked to Deutschemark. Yield differential reflects effect of German withholding tax.
French franc	–	5–6	Currency linked to Deutschemark. Yield differential versus German bonds should narrow slightly.

Note: Minus sign indicates that yields will decline relative to U.S. Treasuries. Plus sign indicates yields will rise relative to U.S. Treasuries. NC indicates no change in yield spread to U.S. Treasuries. NM indicates not meaningful.

Source: *Global Fixed-Income Investment Strategy* (New York: Salomon Brothers, Inc., 1988). Copyright 1988 by Salomon Brothers, Inc. Reprinted by permission of the authors and Salomon Brothers, Inc.

TABLE 15.6   **Recommended Global Asset Mix (Percentage Breakdown)**

Currency Bloc	Currency Decision — Net Currency Position	Currency Decision — Currency Hedge	Market Decision — Gross Currency Position	Market Decision — Cash	Market Decision — Bonds	Bond Selection Decision — Maturity Structure — 1–3 Years	3–5 Years	5–7 Years	7–10 Years	Long	Portfolio Duration	Portfolio Risk — Currency Risk	Interest Rate Risk
U.S. Dollar	**49** / 49	**10**	**39** / 49	**0**	**39** / 49	**20** / 17	**0** / 8	**0** / 5	**19** / 5	**0** / 14	**4.5** / 5.0	**1.00**	**0.72**
Canadian $	**7** / 4	**0**	**7** / 4	**0**	**7** / 4	**3** / 1	**0** / 1	**0** / 0	**4** / 1	**0** / 1	**4.6** / 4.8	**2.00**	**1.92**
Mexican Peso	**1** / 1	**0**	**1** / 1	**0**	**1** / 1	**1** / 1	**0** / 0	**0** / 0	**0** / 0	**0** / 0	**na**	**1.00**	**na**
Australian $/ New Zealand $	**3** / 1	**0**	**3** / 1	**0**	**3** / 1	**0** / 0	**1** / 0	**0** / 0	**2** / 1	**0** / 0	**5.8** / 3.5	**3.00**	**5.00**
Japanese Yen	**28** / 23	**0**	**28** / 23	**0**	**28** / 23	**0** / 5	**7** / 5	**5** / 5	**15** / 6	**1** / 2	**6.3** / 5.0	**1.22**	**1.53**
Europe	**12** / 22	**–10**	**22** / 22	**0**	**22** / 22	**1** / 4	**2** / 6	**2** / 4	**16** / 5	**1** / 3	**6.4** / 4.6	**0.55**	**1.39**
Total	**100**	**0**	**100**	**0**	**100** / 100	**25** / 28	**10** / 20	**7** / 14	**56** / 18	**2** / 20	**5.6** / 4.9		**1.14**

Source: "Currency and Bond Market Trends," (New York: Merrill Lynch Capital Markets, June 24, 1993).

FIGURE 15.2   **A Prescribed Schedule of Liabilities**

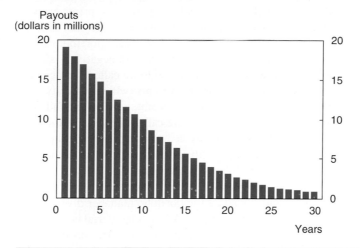

Source: Martin L. Leibowitz, "The Dedicated Bond Portfolio in Pension Funds—Part I: Motivations and Basics," *Financial Analysts Journal* 42, no. 1 (January–February 1986). Reprinted by permission of Financial Analysts Journal.

Such a "dedicated" portfolio can be created in several ways. We will discuss two alternatives.

A *pure cash-matched dedicated portfolio* is the most conservative strategy. Specifically, the objective of pure cash-matching is to develop a portfolio of bonds that will provide a stream of payments from coupons, sinking funds, and maturing principal payments that will exactly match the specified liability schedules. An example of a typical liability stream for a retired-lives component of a pension system is in Figure 15.2.

The goal is to build a portfolio that will generate sufficient funds in advance of each scheduled payment to ensure that the payment will be met. One alternative is to find a number of zero coupon Treasury securities that will exactly cash-match each liability. Such an exact cash-match is referred to as a *total passive* portfolio, because it is designed so that any prior receipts would not be reinvested (i.e., it assumes a zero reinvestment rate).

Dedication with reinvestment is the same as the pure cash-matched technique except it is assumed that the bonds and other cash flows do not have to exactly match the liability stream. Specifically, any inflows that precede liability claims can be reinvested at some reasonably conservative rate. This assumption allows the portfolio manager to consider a substantially wider set of bonds that may have higher return characteristics. In addition, the assumption of reinvestment within each period and between periods will also generate a higher return for the asset portfolio. As a result, the net cost of the portfolio will be lower, with almost equal safety, assuming the reinvestment rate assumption is conservative. An example would be to assume a reinvestment rate of 6 percent in an environment where market interest rates are currently ranging from 7 to 10 percent.

Potential problems exist with both these approaches to a dedicated portfolio. For example, when selecting potential bonds for these portfolios, it is critical to be aware of call/prepayment possibilities (refundings, calls, sinking funds) with specific bonds or mortgage-backed securities. These prepayment possibilities become very important following periods of historically high rates. A prime example was the period 1982 to 1986, when interest rates went from over 18 percent to under 8 percent. Because this substantial change in rates, many dedicated portfolios constructed without adequate concern for complete call protection were negatively affected when numerous bonds were called that were not expected to be called "under normal conditions." For example, bonds selling at deep discounts (which typically provides implicit call protection) when rates were 16 to 18 percent, went to par and above when rates declined to under 10 percent, and they were called. Obviously, the reinvest of these proceeds at the lower rates caused many dedicated portfolios to be underfunded. Therefore, it is necessary to find bonds with complete call protection or consider deep discount bonds under conservative interest rate conditions.

Although quality is also a legitimate concern, it is probably not necessary to invest only in Treasury bonds if the portfolio manager diversifies across industries and sectors. A diversified portfolio of AA or A industrial bonds can provide a current and total annual return of 40 to 60 basis points above Treasuries. This differential over a 30-year period can have a significant impact on the net cost of funding a liability stream.

IMMUNIZATION STRATEGIES

Instead of using a buy-and-hold strategy, one of the active strategies, or one of the dedicated portfolio techniques, a portfolio manager, after client consultation, may decide that the optimal strategy is to immunize the portfolio from interest rate changes. The immunization techniques attempt to derive a specified rate of return (that is generally quite close to the current market rate) during a given investment horizon regardless of what happens to market interest rates.

COMPONENTS OF INTEREST RATE RISK   A major problem encountered in bond portfolio management is deriving a given rate of return to satisfy an ending-wealth requirement at a future specific date—that is, the investment horizon. If the term structure of interest rates were flat and market rates never changed between the time of purchase and the horizon date when funds were required, you could acquire a bond with a term to maturity equal to the desired investment horizon, and the ending wealth from the bond would equal the promised wealth position implied by the promised yield to maturity. Specifically, the ending-wealth position would be the beginning wealth times the compound value of a dollar at the promised yield to maturity. As an example, assume that you acquired a 10-year, $1 million bond with an 8 percent coupon at par (8 percent YTM). If conditions were as specified (there was a flat yield curve and there were no changes in the curve), your wealth position at the end of your 10-year investment horizon (assuming semiannual compounding) would be

$$\$1,000,000 \times (1.04)^{20} = \$1,000,000 \times 2.1911 = \$2,191,100$$

You can get the same answer by taking the $40,000 interest payment every 6 months and compounding it to the end of the period at 8 percent and adding the $1,000,000 principal at maturity. Unfortunately, in the real world, the term structure of interest rates is not typically flat and the level of interest rates is constantly changing. Consequently, the bond portfolio manager faces *interest rate risk* between the time of investment and the future target date. Interest rate risk is the uncertainty regarding the ending-wealth value of the portfolio due to changes in market interest rates between the time of purchase and the target date. It involves two component risks in turn: *price risk* and *coupon reinvestment risk*.

The price risk occurs because if interest rates change before the horizon date and the bond is sold before maturity, the realized market price for the bond will differ from the *expected* price, assuming no change in rates. If rates increased after the time of purchase, the realized price for the bond in the secondary market would be below expectations, whereas if rates declined, the realized price would be above expectations. The point is, because you do not know whether rates will increase or decrease, you are uncertain about the bond's future price.

The coupon reinvestment risk arises because the yield to maturity computation implicitly assumes that all coupon cash flows will be reinvested at the promised yield to maturity.[21] If, after the purchase of the bond, interest rates decline, the coupon cash flows will be reinvested at rates below the promised YTM, and the ending wealth will be below expectations. In contrast, if interest rates increase, the coupon cash flows will be reinvested at rates above expectations, and the ending wealth will be above expectations. Again, because you are uncertain about future rates, you are uncertain about these reinvestment rates.

CLASSICAL IMMUNIZATION AND INTEREST RATE RISK   The price risk and the reinvestment risk caused by a change in interest rates have opposite effects on the ending-wealth position. An increase in interest rates will cause an ending price below expectations, but the reinvestment rate for interim cash flows will be above expectations. A decline in market interest rates will cause the reverse situation. Clearly, a bond portfolio manager with a specific target date (investment horizon) will attempt to eliminate these two interest rate risks. The process intended to eliminate interest rate risk is referred to as *immunization* and was discussed by Redington in the early 1950s.[22] It has been specified by Fisher and Weil as follows:

> A portfolio of investments in bonds is *immunized* for a holding period if its value at the end of the holding period, regardless of the course of interest rates during the holding period, must be at least as large as it would have been had the interest-rate function been constant throughout the holding period.
>
> If the realized return on an investment in bonds is sure to be at least as large as the appropriately computed yield to the horizon, then that investment is immunized.[23]

Fisher and Weil found a significant difference between the *promised* yields and the *realized* returns on bonds for the period 1925 to 1968, indicating the importance of being able to immunize a bond portfolio. They showed that it is possible to immunize a bond portfolio if you can assume that any change in interest rates will be the same

---

[21] This point was discussed in detail in Chapter 14 and also in Homer and Leibowitz, *Inside the Yield Book*, Chapter 1.

[22] F. M. Redington, "Review of the Principles of Life—Office Valuations," *Journal of the Institute of Actuaries,* 78 (1952): 286–340.

[23] Lawrence Fisher and Roman L. Weil, "Coping with the Risk of Interest-Rate Fluctuations: Returns to Bondholders from Naive and Optimal Strategies," *Journal of Business* 44, no. 4 (October 1971): 408–431.

for all, that is, if forward interest rates change, all rates will change by the same amount (i.e., there is a parallel shift of the yield curve). Given this assumption, Fisher and Weil proved that *a portfolio of bonds is immunized from interest rate risk if the duration of the portfolio is always equal to the desired investment horizon.* As an example, if the investment horizon of a bond portfolio is 8 years, in order to immunize the portfolio, the *duration* of the bond portfolio should equal 8 years. To attain a given duration, the weighted average duration (with weights equal to the proportion of value) is set at the desired length following an interest payment, and all subsequent cash flows are invested in securities to keep the portfolio duration equal to the remaining investment horizon.

Fisher and Weil showed that price risk and reinvestment rate risk are affected in opposite directions by a change in market rates and that duration is the time period when these two risks are of equal magnitude but opposite in direction.[24]

APPLICATION OF THE IMMUNIZATION PRINCIPLE   Fisher and Weil simulated the effects of applying the immunization concept (a duration-matched strategy) compared to a naive portfolio strategy where the portfolio's maturity was equal to the investment horizon. They compared the ending-wealth ratio for the duration matched and for the naive strategy portfolios to a wealth ratio that assumed no change in the interest rate structure. In a perfectly immunized portfolio, the actual ending wealth should equal the expected ending wealth implied by the promised yield, so these comparisons should indicate which portfolio strategy does a superior job of immunization. The duration-matched strategy results were consistently closer to the promised yield results, although the results were not perfect. The duration portfolio was not perfectly immunized because the basic assumption did not always hold; that is, when interest rates changed, all interest rates did not change by the same amount.

Bierwag and Kaufman pointed out several specifications of the duration measure.[25] The Macaulay duration measure, which is used throughout this book, discounts all flows by the prevailing yield to maturity on the bond being measured.[26] Alternatively, Fisher and Weil defined duration using future one-period interest rates (forward rates) to discount the future flows.[27] Depending on the shape of the yield curve, the two definitions could give different answers. If the yield curve is flat, the two definitions will compute equal durations. Bierwag and Kaufman computed alternative measures of duration and found that, except at high coupons and long maturities, the values of the alternative definitions were similar, and the Macaulay definition is preferable because it is a function of the yield to maturity of the bond. This means you do not need a forecast of one-period forward rates over the maturity of the bond.[28]

EXAMPLE OF CLASSICAL IMMUNIZATION   Table 15.7 shows the effect of attempting to immunize a portfolio by matching the investment horizon and the duration of a bond

---

[24] This is also noted and discussed in G. O. Bierwag and George G. Kaufman, "Coping with the Risk of Interest Rate Fluctuations: A Note," *Journal of Business* 50, no. 3 (July 1977): 364–370; and G. O. Bierwag, "Immunization, Duration, and the Term Structure of Interest Rates," *Journal of Financial and Quantitative Analysis* 12, no. 5 (December 1977): 725–742.

[25] Bierwag and Kaufman, "Coping with the Risk of Interest Rate Fluctuations," 364–370.

[26] Frederick R. Macaulay, *Some Theoretical Problems Suggested by the Movements of Interest Rates, Bond Yields, and Stock Prices in the United States Since 1856* (New York: National Bureau of Economic Research, 1938).

[27] Fisher and Weil, "Coping with the Risk of Interest Rate Fluctuations," 408–431.

[28] Bierwag and Kaufman, "Coping with the Risk of Interest Rate Fluctuations," 367.

TABLE 15.7 — **An Example of the Effect of a Change in Market Rates on a Bond (Portfolio) that Uses the Maturity Strategy versus the Duration Strategy**

	Results with Maturity Strategy			Results with Duration Strategy		
Year	Cash Flow	Reinvestment Rate	End Value	Cash Flow	Reinvestment Rate	End Value
1	$ 80	.08	$ 80.00	$ 80	.08	$ 80.00
2	80	.08	166.40	80	.08	166.40
3	80	.08	259.71	80	.08	259.71
4	80	.08	360.49	80	.08	360.49
5	80	.06	462.12	80	.06	462.12
6	80	.06	596.85	80	.06	596.85
7	80	.06	684.04	80	.06	684.04
8	$1,080	.06	$1,805.08	$1,120.64[a]	.06	$1,845.72

Expected Wealth Ratio = 1.8509 or $1,850.90.

[a] The bond could be sold at its market value of $1,040.64, which is the value for an 8 percent bond with 2 years to maturity priced to yield 6 percent.

portfolio using a single bond. The portfolio manager's investment horizon is 8 years, and the current yield to maturity for 8-year bonds is 8 percent. Therefore, if we assumed no change in yields, the ending-wealth ratio for an investor should be 1.8509 (1.08^8) with annual compounding.[29] As noted, this should also be the ending-wealth ratio for a completely immunized portfolio.

The example considers two portfolio strategies: (1) the maturity strategy, where the portfolio manager would acquire a bond with a term to maturity of 8 years, and (2) the duration strategy, where the portfolio manager sets the duration of the portfolio at 8 years. For the maturity strategy, the portfolio manager acquires an 8-year, 8 percent bond; for the duration strategy, the manager acquires a 10-year, 8 percent bond that has approximately an 8-year duration (8.12 years), assuming an 8 percent YTM (see Table 14.2). We assume a single shock to the interest rate structure at the end of Year 4, when rates go from 8 percent to 6 percent and stay there through Year 8.

As shown, due to the interest rate change, the wealth ratio for the maturity strategy bond is *below* the desired wealth ratio because of the shortfall in the reinvestment cash flow after Year 4, when the interim coupon cash flow was reinvested at 6 percent rather than 8 percent. Note that *the maturity strategy eliminated the price risk,* because the bond matured at the end of Year 8. Alternatively, the duration strategy portfolio likewise suffered a shortfall in reinvestment cash flow because of the change in market rates. Notably, this shortfall due to the reinvestment risk was partially offset by an *increase* in the ending value for the bond because of the decline in market rates. This second bond is sold at the end of Year 8 at 104.06 of par, because it is an 8 percent coupon bond with 2 years to maturity selling to yield 6 percent. Because of this partial offset due to the price increase, the duration strategy had an ending-wealth value (1845.72) much closer to the expected-wealth ratio (1850.90) than the maturity strategy had (1805.08).

If market interest rates had increased during this period, the maturity strategy portfolio would have experienced an *excess* of reinvestment income compared to the

[29] We use annual compounding to compute the ending-wealth ratio because the example uses annual observations.

expected cash flow, and the ending-wealth ratio for this strategy would have been above expectations. In contrast, in the duration portfolio, the excess cash flow from reinvestment under this assumption would have been partially offset by a *decline* in the ending price for the bond (i.e., it would have sold at a small discount to par value). Although the ending-wealth ratio for the duration strategy would have been lower than the maturity strategy, it would have been closer to the expected-wealth ratio. The point is, although the maturity strategy would have provided a higher than expected ending value for this scenario, the whole purpose of immunization is to *eliminate uncertainty* due to interest rate changes by having the realized-wealth position equal the expected-wealth position. As shown, this is what is accomplished with the duration-matched strategy.

ANOTHER VIEW OF IMMUNIZATION   The prior example assumed that both bonds were acquired and held to the end of the investment horizon. An alternative way to envision what is expected to happen with an immunized portfolio is to concentrate on the specific growth path from the beginning-wealth position to the ending-wealth position and examine what happens when interest rates change.

Assume that the initial-wealth position is $1 million, your investment horizon is 10 years, and the coupon and current YTM is 8 percent. We know from an earlier computation that this implies that the expected ending-wealth value is $2,191,100 (with semiannual compounding). Figure 15.3A shows the compound growth rate path from $1 million to the expected ending value at $2,191,100. In Figure 15.3B, it is assumed that at the end of Year 2, interest rates increase by 2 percent (10 percent). We know that with no prior rate changes, at the end of Year 2 the value of the portfolio would have grown at an 8 percent compound rate to $1,169,900 [$1.04^4 = 1.1699$]. Given the rate change, we know there will be two changes for this portfolio: (1) the price (value of the portfolio) will decline to reflect the higher interest rate, and (2) the reinvestment rate, which is the growth rate, will increase to 10 percent. An important question is, how much will the portfolio value decline? The answer depends on the modified duration of the portfolio when rates change. Fisher and Weil showed that *if the modified duration is equal to the remaining horizon, the price change will be such that at the new growth rate (10 percent), the new portfolio value will grow to the expected-wealth position.* You can approximate the change in portfolio value using the modified duration and the change in market rates (recall that this will not give an exact estimate because of the convexity of the portfolio). The approximate change in price is 16 percent based on a modified duration of 8 years and a 200-basis-point change. This would imply an approximate portfolio value of $982,716 ($1,169,900 × 0.84). In fact, the actual value would be $1,003,743 (recall that the estimated value based on using modified duration is always below the value implied by the price-yield curve). If this new wealth value grows at 10 percent a year for 8 years, the ending-wealth value will be

$$\$1,003,743 \times 2.1829 \text{ (5\% for 16 periods)} = \$2,191,070$$

The difference between the expected value and projected value is due to rounding. This example shows that the price decline is almost exactly offset by the higher reinvestment rate—assuming that the modified duration of the portfolio at the time of the rate change was equal to the remaining horizon.

FIGURE 15.3   **The Growth Path to the Expected Ending-Wealth Value and the Effect of Immunization**

A. Constant 8% Growth Rate

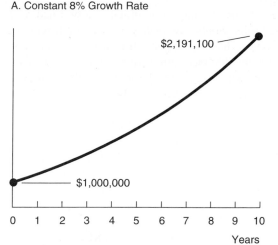

B. Effect of Interest Rate Increase after Two Years with Duration Equal to Investment Horizon

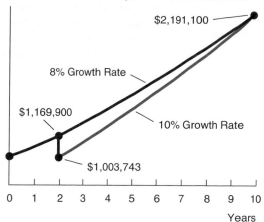

C. Effect of Interest Rate Increase with Duration Greater than Investment Horizon

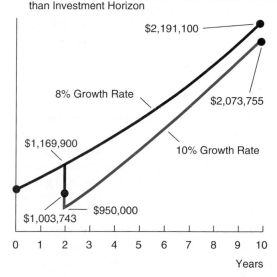

D. Effect of Interest Rate Decline with Duration Greater than Investment Horizon

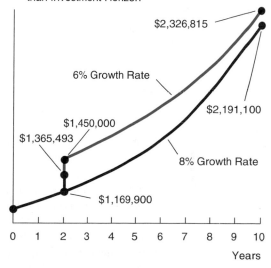

What happens if the portfolio is not properly matched? If the modified duration is greater than the remaining horizon, the price change will be greater. Thus, if interest rates increase, the value of the portfolio after the rate change will be less than $1,003,743. In this case, even if the new value of the portfolio grew at 10 percent a year, it would not reach the expected ending-wealth value. This scenario is shown in Figure 15.3C where it is assumed that the portfolio value declined to $950,000. If this new value grew at 10 percent a year for the remaining 8 years, its ending value would be

$$\$950,000 \times 2.1829 \text{ (5\% for 16 periods)} = \$2,073,755$$

Therefore, the shortfall of $118,000 between the expected-wealth value and the realized-wealth value is because the portfolio was not properly duration matched (immunized) when interest rates changed.

Alternatively, if interest rates had declined, and the modified duration had been longer than 8 years, the new portfolio value would have been greater than the required value of $1,003,743. Figure 15.3D shows what can happen if the portfolio is not properly matched and interest rates decline by 200 basis points to 6 percent. First, if the portfolio *is* properly matched, the value will increase to $1,365,493. If this new portfolio value grows at 6 percent for 8 years, its ending value will be

$$\$1,365,493 \times 1.6047 \text{ (3\% for 16 periods)} = \$2,191,207$$

Again, this deviates slightly from the expected ending-wealth value ($2,191,100) due to rounding. Alternatively, if the modified duration had been above 8 years, the new portfolio value would have been greater than the required value of $1,365,493. Assuming the portfolio value increased to $1,450,000, the ending value would be

$$\$1,450,000 \times 1.6047 \text{ (3\% for 16 periods)} = \$2,326,815$$

In this example, the ending-wealth value would have been greater than the expected-wealth value because you were mismatched and interest rates went in the right direction. The important point is that, when you are not duration matched, you are speculating on interest rate changes, and the result can be very good or very bad. The purpose of immunization is to avoid these uncertainties and ensure the expected ending-wealth value ($2,191,100) irrespective of interest rate changes.

APPLICATION OF CLASSICAL IMMUNIZATION   Once you understand the reasoning behind immunization (i.e., that it is meant to offset the components of interest rate risk) and the general principle (that you need to match duration and the investment horizon), you might conclude that this strategy is fairly simple to apply. You might even consider it a passive strategy; simply match duration and the investment horizon, and you can ignore the portfolio until the end of the horizon period. The following discussion will show that *immunization is neither a simple nor a passive strategy.*

Except for the case of a zero coupon bond, *an immunized portfolio requires frequent rebalancing,* because the modified duration of the portfolio should always be equal to the remaining time horizon. The zero coupon bond is unique because it is a pure discount bond. As such, there is *no reinvestment risk,* because the discounting assumes that the value of the bond will grow at the discount rate. For example, if you discount a future value at 10 percent, the present value factor assumes that the value will grow at a compound rate of 10 percent to maturity. Also, there is *no price risk* if you set the duration at your time horizon, because you will receive the face value of the bond at maturity. Also, recall that the duration of a zero coupon bond is always equal to its term to maturity. In summary, if you immunize by matching your horizon with a zero coupon bond of equal duration, you do not have to rebalance.

In contrast, if you immunize a portfolio using coupon bonds, several characteristics of duration make it impossible to set a duration equal to the remaining horizon at the initiation of the portfolio and ignore it thereafter. First, *duration declines more slowly than term to maturity, assuming no change in market interest rates.* As an example, assume you have a security with a computed duration of 5 years at a 10 percent market yield. A year later, if you compute the duration of the security at 10 percent, you will find that it has a duration of approximately 4.2 years; that is, although the term to maturity has declined by a year, the duration has declined by only 0.8 years. This means that, assuming no change in market rates, the portfolio manager must rebalance the portfolio to reduce its duration to 4 years. Typically, this is not too difficult because cash flows from the portfolio can be invested in short-term T-bills if necessary.

Second, *duration changes with a change in market interest rates.* In Chapter 14 we discussed the inverse relationship between market rates and duration—with higher market rates there will be lower duration and vice versa. Therefore, a portfolio that has the appropriate duration at a point in time can have its duration changed immediately if market rates change. If this occurs, a portfolio manager would have to rebalance the portfolio if the deviation from the required duration becomes too large.

Third, you will recall from our initial discussion of immunization that one of the assumptions is that when market rates change, they will change by the same amount and in the same direction (i.e., there will be a parallel shift of the yield curve). Clearly, if this does not happen, it will affect the performance of a portfolio of diffuse bonds. As an example, assume that you own a portfolio of long- and short-term bonds with a weighted average 6-year duration (e.g., 2-year duration bonds and 10-year duration bonds). If the term structure curve changes such that short-term rates decline and long-term rates *rise* (there is an increase in the slope of the yield curve). In such a case, you would experience a major price decline in the long-term bonds, but would also be penalized on reinvestment, assuming you generally reinvest the cash flow in short-term securities. This potential problem suggests that you should attempt to bunch your portfolio selections close to the desired duration. For example, an 8-year duration portfolio should be made up of 7- to 9-year duration securities to avoid this problem.

Finally, there can always be a problem acquiring the bonds you select as optimum for your portfolio. For instance, can you buy long-duration bonds at the price you consider acceptable? In summary, it is important to recognize that classical immunization is *not a passive strategy* because it is subject to all of these potential problems.[30]

HORIZON MATCHING

Horizon matching is a combination of two of the techniques discussed—cash-matching dedication and immunization. As shown in Figure 15.4, the liability stream is divided into two segments. In the first segment the portfolio is constructed to provide a cash match for the liabilities during this horizon period (e.g., the first 5 years). The second segment is the remaining liability stream following the end of the horizon period—in the example, it is the 25 years after the horizon period. During this second time period, the liabilities are covered by a duration-matched strategy based on immunization principles. As a result, the client receives the certainty of cash matching during the early years and the cost saving and flexibility of duration-matched flows thereafter.

---

[30] Several of these problems are discussed in William L. Nemerever, "Managing Bond Portfolios through Immunization Strategies," *The Revolution in Techniques for Managing Bond Portfolios* (Charlottesville, Va.: The Institute of Chartered Financial Analysts, 1983), 39–65.

FIGURE 15.4   **The Concept of Horizon Matching**

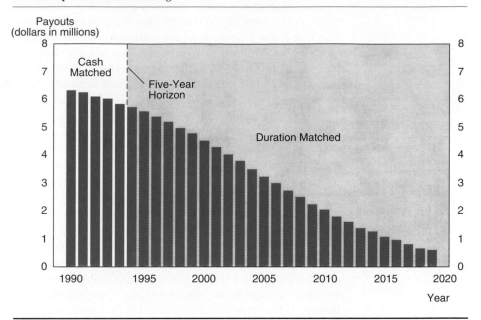

Source: Martin L. Leibowitz, Thomas E. Klaffky, Steven Mandel, and Alfred Weinberger, *Horizon Matching: A New Generalized Approach for Developing Minimum-Cost Dedicated Portfolios* (New York: Salomon Brothers, 1983). Copyright 1983 by Salomon Brothers Inc. Reprinted by permission of the authors and Salomon Brothers Inc.

The combination technique also helps alleviate one of the problems with classical immunization—the potential for nonparallel shifts in the yield curve. Most of the problems related to nonparallel shifts are concentrated in the short end of the yield curve because this is where the most severe curve reshaping occurs. Because the short end is taken care of by the cash matching, these are not of concern and we know that the long end of the yield curve tends toward parallel shifts.

An important decision when using horizon matching is the length of the horizon period. The trade-off when making this decision is between the safety and certainty of cash matching and the cost and flexibility of duration-based immunization. The portfolio manager should provide to the client a set of horizon alternatives and the costs and benefits of each of them and allow the client to make the decision.

It is also possible to consider *rolling out* the cash-matched segment over time. Specifically, after the first year the portfolio manager would restructure the portfolio to provide a cash match during the original Year 6, which would mean that you would still have a 5-year horizon. The ability and cost of rolling out depends on movements in interest rates (ideally, you would want parallel shifts in the yield curve).[31]

---

[31] For a further discussion on this topic, see Martin L. Leibowitz, Thomas E. Klaffky, Steven Mandel, and Alfred Weinberger, *Horizon Matching: A New Generalized Approach for Developing Minimum-Cost Dedicated Portfolios* (New York: Salomon Brothers, 1983).

Contingent procedures are a form of structured active management. The procedure we will discuss here is that of contingent immunization, which entails allowing the portfolio manager some opportunity to actively manage the portfolio with a structure that constrains the portfolio manager if he or she is unsuccessful.

CONTINGENT IMMUNIZATION

Subsequent to the development and application of classical immunization, Leibowitz and Weinberger developed a portfolio strategy entitled *contingent immunization.*[32] Basically, it allows a bond portfolio manager to pursue the highest returns available through active strategies, while relying on classical bond immunization techniques to ensure a given minimal return over the investment horizon. Put another way, it allows active portfolio management with a safety net provided by classical immunization.

To understand contingent immunization, it is necessary to recall our discussion of classical immunization. Recall that when the portfolio duration is equal to the investment horizon, a change in interest rates will cause a change in the dollar value of the portfolio such that when the new asset value is compounded at the new market rate it will equal the desired ending value. This required change in value occurs *only* when the duration of the portfolio is equal to the remaining time horizon, which is why the duration of the portfolio must be maintained at the horizon value.

Consider the following example of this process. Assume that our desired ending-wealth value is $206.3 million. Figure 15.5 shows an example of the required assets with a 5-year horizon and current market rates of 15 percent. Specifically, with five years left, and assuming you can invest funds at 15 percent, you need an initial portfolio worth $100 million to reach $206.3 million ($100 million × 2.063, which is the compound value factor for 10 periods at 7.5 percent). If market rates were lower, you would need more assets; and if market rates were higher, you would need less assets. To extend the example, if rates were 12 percent, you would need beginning assets of $115.2 million, and at 18 percent you would need beginning assets of only $87.14 million.[33] The dotted line in Figure 15.5 indicates that the price sensitivity of a portfolio with a duration of 5 years will have almost exactly the price sensitivity required.

Contingent immunization requires that the client be willing to accept a potential return below the current market return, referred to as a *cushion spread,* which is the difference between the current market return and some floor rate. This cushion spread in required yield provides flexibility for the portfolio manager to engage in active portfolio strategies. As an example, if current market rates are 15 percent, the client might be willing to accept a floor rate of 14 percent. If we assume the client initiated the fund with $100 million, the acceptance of this lower rate will mean that the portfolio

[32] Martin L. Leibowitz and Alfred Weinberger, "Contingent Immunization—Part I: Risk Control Procedures," *Financial Analysts Journal* 38, no. 6 (November-December 1982): 17–32; and Martin L. Leibowitz and Alfred Weinberger, "Contingent Immunization—Part II: Problem Areas," *Financial Analysts Journal* 39, no. 1 (January-February 1983): 35–50. This section draws heavily from these articles.

[33] You derive these required amounts by knowing the desired ending-wealth position (which is $206.3 million in this example) and computing the present value of this amount for the specified time period at the appropriate interest rate (assuming semiannual compounding). Therefore, in these examples we used the present value factor for 6 percent for 10 periods (.5584) and for 9 percent for ten periods (.4224). Given these present values, we know that if we compound them at these rates, we will arrive at our desired ending-wealth value ($206.3 million).

FIGURE 15.5   **Classical Immunization**

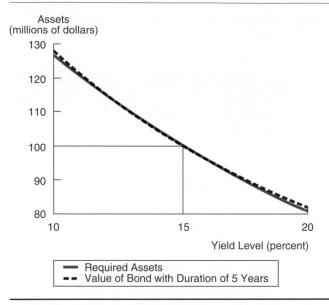

Source: Martin L. Leibowitz and Alfred Weinberger, "Contingent Immunization—Part I: Risk Control Procedures," *Financial Analysts Journal* 38, no. 6 (November–December 1982): 17–32. Reprinted by permission of Financial Analysts Journal.

manager does not have the same ending-asset requirements. Specifically, at 14 percent the required ending-wealth value would be $196.72 million (7 percent for 10 periods) compared to the $206.3 million at 15 percent. Because of this lower floor rate (and lower ending-wealth value), it is possible to experience some declines in the value of the portfolio while attempting to do better than the market through active management strategies.

Figure 15.6 shows the value of assets that are required at the beginning assuming a 14 percent required return and the implied ending-wealth value of $196.72 million. Notably, assuming market rates of 15 percent, the required value of assets at the beginning would be $95.56 million, which is the present value of $196.72 million at 15 percent for 5 years. The difference between the client's initial fund of $100 million and the required assets of $95.56 million is the dollar cushion available to the portfolio manager. As noted, this dollar cushion arises because the client has agreed to a lower investment rate, and therefore a lower ending-wealth value.

At this point, the portfolio manager can engage in various active portfolio management strategies to increase the ending-wealth value of the portfolio above that required at 14 percent. As an example, assume that the portfolio manager believes that market rates will decline. Under such conditions, the portfolio manager might consider acquiring a 30-year bond that has a duration greater than the investment horizon of 5 years and, therefore, has greater price sensitivity to changes in market rates. Hence, if rates decline as expected, the value of the long-duration portfolio will rise above the value stipulated initially. In contrast, if rates increase, the value of the portfolio will decline rapidly. In this latter case, depending on how high rates go, the value of the portfolio

FIGURE 15.6   **Price Behavior Required for Floor Return**

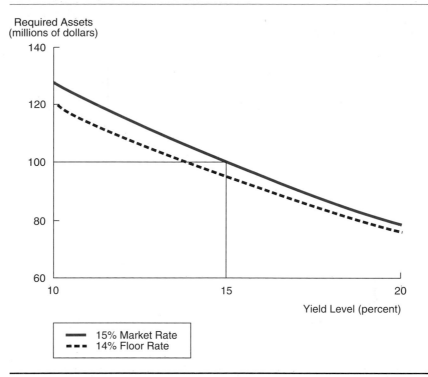

Source: Martin L. Leibowitz and Alfred Weinberger, "Contingent Immunization—Part I: Risk Control Procedures," *Financial Analysts Journal* 38, no. 6 (November–December 1982): 17–32. Reprinted by permission of Financial Analysts Journal.

could decline to a value figure below that needed to reach the desired ending-wealth value of $196.72 million.

Figure 15.7 shows what happens to the value of this portfolio if we assume an instantaneous change in interest rates when the fund is established. Specifically, if rates decline from 15 percent, the portfolio of long duration, 30-year bonds would experience a large increase in value and develop a *safety margin,* which is a portfolio value above the required value. In contrast, if rates increase, the value of the portfolio will decline until you reach the asset value required at 14 percent. When the value of the portfolio reaches this point of minimum return (referred to as a *trigger point*), it is necessary to stop active portfolio management and use classical immunization with the remaining assets to ensure that you attain the desired ending-wealth value (i.e., $196.72 million).

POTENTIAL RETURN   The concept of *potential return* is helpful in understanding the objective of contingent immunization. This is the return the portfolio would achieve over the entire investment horizon if, at any point, the assets in hand were immunized at the prevailing market rate. Figure 15.8 contains the various potential rates of return based on dollar asset values shown in Figure 15.7. If the portfolio were immediately immunized when market rates were 15 percent, it would naturally earn the 15 percent market rate; that is, its potential return would be 15 percent. Alternatively, if yields

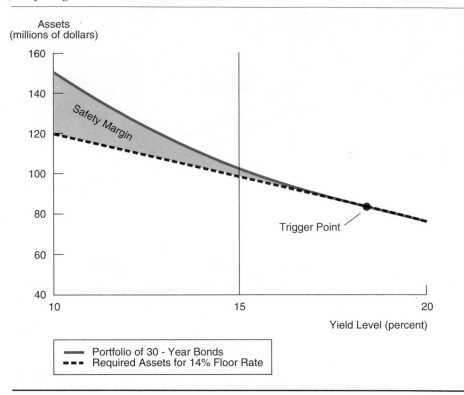

Source: Martin L. Leibowitz and Alfred Weinberger, "Contingent Immunization—Part I: Risk Control Procedures,"
Financial Analysts Journal 38, no. 6 (November–December 1982): 17–32. Reprinted by permission of Financial
Analysts Journal.

declined instantaneously to 10 percent, the portfolio's asset value would increase to
$147 million (see Figure 15.7). If this $147 million portfolio were immunized at the
market rate of 10 percent over the remaining 5-year period, the portfolio would compound at 10 percent to a total value of $239 million ($147 million × 1.6289, which
is the compound growth factor for 5 percent and 10 periods). This ending value of
$239.45 million represents an 18.25 percent realized (horizon) rate of return on the
original $100 million portfolio. Consequently, as shown in Figure 15.8, the portfolio's
potential return would be 18.25 percent. That is, if rates decline by 5 percent, the
potential return for this portfolio at this point in time is 18.25 percent.

In contrast, if interest rates increased, the value of the portfolio will decline substantially and the potential return will decline. For example, if market rates rise to
17 percent (i.e., a yield change of 2 percent), the asset value of the 30-year bond portfolio
will decline to $88 million (see Figure 15.7). If this portfolio of $88 million were
immunized for the remaining 5 years at the prevailing market rate of 17 percent, the
ending value would be $199 million. This ending value implies a potential return of
14.32 percent for the total period.

As Figure 15.7 shows, if interest rates rose to 18.50 percent, the 30-year bonds
would decline to a value of $81.16 million (the trigger point) and the portfolio would

FIGURE 15.8   **The Potential Return Concept**

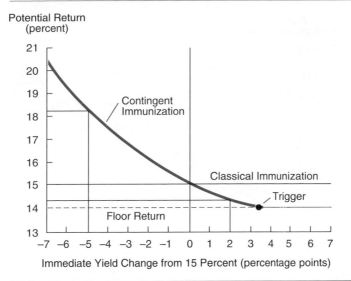

Source: Martin L. Leibowitz and Alfred Weinberger, "Contingent Immunization—Part I: Risk Control Procedures," *Financial Analysts Journal* 38, no. 6 (November–December 1982): 17–32. Reprinted by permission of Financial Analysts Journal.

have to be immunized. At this point, if the remaining assets of $81.16 million were immunized at this current market rate of 18.50 percent, the value of the portfolio would grow to $196.73 million ($81.16 × 2.424, which is the compound value factor for 9.25 percent for 10 periods). This ending value implies that the potential return for the portfolio would be exactly 14 percent as shown in Figure 15.8. Regardless of what happens to subsequent market rates, the portfolio has been immunized at the floor rate of 14 percent. That is a major characteristic of the contingent immunized portfolio; if there is proper monitoring, you will always know your trigger point and can be assured of a return no less than the minimum return specified.

MONITORING THE IMMUNIZED PORTFOLIO   Clearly, a crucial factor in managing a contingent immunized portfolio is monitoring it to ensure that if the asset value falls to the trigger point, it will be detected and the appropriate action taken to ensure that the portfolio is immunized at the floor-level rate. This can be done using a chart as in Figure 15.9. The top line is the current market value of the portfolio over time. The bottom line is the required value of the immunized floor portfolio. Specifically, the bottom line is *the required value of the portfolio* if we were to immunize at *today's rates* to attain the necessary ending-wealth value. This required value is calculated by computing the present value of the promised ending-wealth value at the prevailing market rate.

To demonstrate how this floor portfolio would be constructed, consider our example where we derived a promised ending-wealth value in 5 years of $196.72 million based on an initial investment of $100 million and an acceptable floor rate of 14 percent. If 1 year after the initiation of the portfolio, market rates were 10 percent, you would

FIGURE 15.9   **Contingent Immunization over Time**

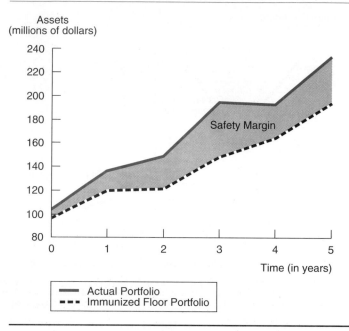

Source: Martin L. Leibowitz and Alfred Weinberger, "Contingent Immunization—Part I: Risk Control Procedures,"
Financial Analysts Journal 38, no. 6 (November–December 1982): 17–32. Reprinted by permission of Financial
Analysts Journal.

need a minimum portfolio value of approximately $133.14 million to get to $196.72
million in 4 years. To compute this minimum required value you multiply the $196.72
million (promised ending-wealth value) times the present value factor for 10 percent
for 4 years, assuming semiannual compounding (.6761). The logic is that $133.14
million invested (immunized) at 10 percent for 4 years will equal $196.72 million.

The point is, if the active manager had predicted correctly that market rates would
decline and had a long-duration portfolio under these conditions, the *actual* value of
the portfolio would be much higher than this *minimum required* value, and there would
be a safety margin. A year later (after year two), you would determine the assets needed
at the rate prevailing at that point in time. Assuming interest rates had increased to
12 percent, you could determine that you would need a floor portfolio of about
$138.69 million. Specifically, this is the present value of the $196.72 million for three
years at 12 percent, assuming semiannual compounding (.7050). Again, you would
expect the actual value of the portfolio to be greater than this required floor portfolio,
so you still have a safety margin. If you ever reached the point where the actual value
of the portfolio was equal to the required floor value, you would stop the active management and immunize what was left *at the current market rate* to ensure that the
ending value would be $196.72 million.

In summary, the contingent immunization strategy encompasses the opportunity
for a bond portfolio manager to engage in various active portfolio strategies if the client
is willing to accept a floor return (and ending-wealth value) that is below what is
currently available. The graph in Figure 15.10 describes the trade-offs involved in

FIGURE 15.10   **Comparison of Return Distributions**

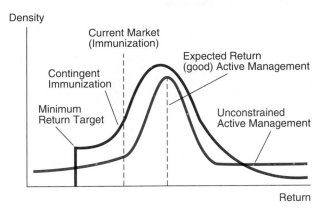

Source: Martin L. Leibowitz and Alfred Weinberger, "Contingent Immunization—Part II: Problem Areas," *Financial Analysts Journal* 39, no. 1 (January–February 1983): 35–50. Reprinted by permission of Financial Analysts Journal.

contingent immunization. Specifically, by allowing for a slightly lower minimum target rate, the client is making it possible to experience a much higher potential return from active management by the portfolio manager.

IMPLICATIONS OF CAPITAL MARKET THEORY AND THE EMH ON BOND PORTFOLIO MANAGEMENT

The high level of interest rates that has prevailed since the latter part of the 1960s has provided increasingly attractive returns to bond investors, and the wide swings in interest rates that have accompanied these high market yields have provided numerous capital gains opportunities for bond portfolio managers. As a result, the average compound rates of return on bonds during the 1980s was the highest of any 10-year period in this century. Specifically, the results contained in Table 15.8 indicate that the annual returns on high-grade bonds during the 1980s ranged from 2.29 percent to 31.10 percent, and the average returns of about 12.50 percent were only moderately lower than the average returns on common stocks of 16.25 percent. When these are compared to the longer-term results reported in Figure 15.12, it appears that it will be difficult to continue such performance. Still, these results indicate that there are some wonderful opportunities available in bonds. An important consideration for portfolio managers, therefore, is the proper role of fixed-income securities when one considers the implications of portfolio theory, capital market theory, and research related to efficient capital markets.

BONDS AND TOTAL PORTFOLIO THEORY

The performance of bonds has improved even more than indicated by returns alone, because bonds offer substantial diversification benefits. In an efficient market, neither stocks nor bonds should dominate a portfolio, but some combination of them should provide a superior risk-adjusted return compared to either one taken alone, assuming low correlation between stocks and bonds. A study by Sharpe confirmed that stock returns were superior to bond yields during the period 1938 to 1971. His results also showed that, due to the favorable covariance between bonds and equities, the

TABLE 15.8

Annual Percentage Rates of Return and Standard Deviations, Lehman Brothers Bond Indexes and the S&P 500 Stock Index, 1980–1990

| | Lehman Brothers | | | | | | S&P |
	Govt./ Corp.	Govt.	Corp.	Mort.	Yank.	Agg.	500
1980	3.06	5.19	−0.29	0.65	1.92	2.71	32.42
1981	7.26	9.36	2.95	0.07	3.48	6.25	−4.91
1982	31.10	27.75	39.20	43.04	35.82	32.62	21.41
1983	7.99	7.39	9.27	10.13	9.43	8.35	22.51
1984	15.02	14.50	16.62	15.79	16.38	15.15	6.27
1985	21.30	20.43	24.06	25.21	26.00	22.10	32.16
1986	15.62	15.31	16.53	13.43	16.27	15.26	18.47
1987	2.29	2.20	2.56	4.29	1.89	2.76	5.23
1988	7.58	7.03	9.22	8.72	8.81	7.89	16.81
1989	14.24	14.23	14.09	15.35	15.42	14.53	31.49
1990	8.28	8.72	7.05	10.72	7.05	8.96	−3.15
Arithmetic Mean							
1980–1990	12.16	12.01	12.84	13.40	12.95	12.42	16.25
Standard Deviation (annual returns)							
1980–1990	8.51	7.41	11.34	12.21	10.58	8.93	13.65
Geometric Mean							
1980–1990	11.88	11.79	12.36	12.85	12.52	12.11	15.50
Standard Deviation (monthly returns)							
1980–1990	2.27	2.04	2.81	3.10	2.78	2.36	4.79

Source: Frank K. Reilly, G. Wenchi Kao, and David J. Wright, "Alternative Bond Market Indexes," *Financial Analysts Journal* 48, no. 3 (May-June 1992): 48.

combination of the securities in a portfolio vastly improved the return per unit of risk.[34]

BONDS AND CAPITAL MARKET THEORY

Capital market theory contends that there should be an upward-sloping market line, meaning that greater return should be accompanied by greater risk. Compared to other market vehicles, fixed-income securities have traditionally been viewed as low risk, and, their rates of return have been accordingly modest—until the late 1960s. At that time, the inflation rate increased, and bond yields likewise increased. Also, during periods of high economic uncertainty, such as the recession of 1981 to 1982, the risk premiums on bonds increased substantially because the risk of default for low-rated obligations increased.[35] As demonstrated earlier in the chapter (Figure 15.1), the risk premium on junk bonds has fluctuated dramatically over time.

Capital market theory also relates the risk–return behavior of fixed-income securities to other financial assets. Because fixed-income securities are considered to be relatively conservative investments, we would expect them to be on the lower end of the capital market line. A study by Soldofsky examined the comparative risk–return

[34] William F. Sharpe, "Bonds vs. Stocks: Some Lessons from Capital Market Theory," *Financial Analysts Journal* 29, no. 6 (November-December 1973): 74–80. The relationship of rates of returns for stocks versus bonds was confirmed in the Reilly, Kao, Wright (RKW) study as shown in Table 15.8. Also, the RKW study confirmed the correlation results for the recent period—i.e., the average correlation between stocks and bonds was about 0.30.

[35] For a detailed discussion on this topic that considers several studies on the subject, see James C. Van Horne, *Financial Market Rates and Flows,* 3d ed. (Englewood Cliffs, N.J.: Prentice-Hall, 1989), Chapter 6.

characteristics of 28 classes of long-term securities.[36] Figure 15.11 shows the basic findings of the study and confirms the a priori expectations. Specifically, government and high-grade corporate bonds were at the low end of the curve, and it progressed to regular preferred stocks, high-quality common stocks, convertible securities, and finally to lower-quality stocks and deep discount bonds. An annual analysis of capital market returns by Ibbotson Associates comparing corporate and government bonds (long- and intermediate-term) to common stocks (total NYSE and small-firm) and Treasury bill obligations indicated similar results. As Figure 15.12 shows, Treasury bills have the least risk and return, followed by government bonds, corporate bonds, total common stocks, and finally small capitalization common stocks. The only results not completely consistent with expectations were the returns for long-term government bonds. These were lower than intermediate government bonds, and yet long governments had a risk measure that was larger than for corporate bonds. It is pointed out in a paper by Reilly and Wright that this inconsistency is caused by the sample used by the authors to construct the long-term government bond index.[37] Basically, they employ a one-bond index and during certain periods the single bond selected experienced abnormally low returns and its volatility was higher because it did not benefit from having a diversified portfolio of bonds like most indexes.

BOND PRICE BEHAVIOR IN A CAPM FRAMEWORK

The capital asset pricing model (CAPM) is expected to provide a framework for explaining realized security returns as a function of nondiversifiable market risk. Bond returns should be linked directly to risk of default and interest rate risk. Although interest rate risk for investment-quality bonds should be nondiversifiable, some evidence exists that default risk is also largely nondiversifiable because default experience is closely related to the business cycle.[38] Therefore, because the major bond risks are largely nondiversifiable, this implies that we should be able to define bond returns in the context of the CAPM. Still, few studies have attempted it because of data-collection problems. Percival found only a modest effect of a computed beta on bond returns.[39] An analysis of beta and its relationship to the bond and issuer characteristics indicated that bond betas were more responsive to the intrinsic characteristics of the bond *issue* (i.e., coupon, maturity, duration, and call features) than of the issuer.

Reilly and Joehnk found that average bond betas had no significant or consistent relationships with agency ratings.[40] It was contended that, because the study involved only investment-grade securities, the major factor affecting bond prices was market interest rate movements. Evidence that high-grade bond risk is almost all systematic risk is found in the Reilly, Kao, Wright study, which shows that the returns among these

[36] Robert M. Soldofsky, "Risk and Return for Long-Term Securities, 1971–1982," *Journal of Portfolio Management* 11, no. 1 (Fall 1984): 57–64.

[37] Frank K. Reilly and David J. Wright, "A New Perspective on Performance in the U.S. Treasury Bond Market," Eastern Finance Association Meeting (April 1993).

[38] W. Braddock Hickman, *Corporate Bond Quality and Investor Experience* (New York: National Bureau of Economic Research, 1958); Thomas R. Atkinson, *Trends in Corporate Bond Quality* (New York: National Bureau of Economic Research, 1967); Dwight M. Jaffee, "Cyclical Variations in the Risk Structure of Interest Rates," *Journal of Monetary Economics* 1, no. 2 (July 1975): 309–325, and Douglas J. Lucas and John G. Lonski, "Changes in Corporate Credit Quality 1970–1990," *Journal of Fixed Income* 1, no. 4 (March 1992): 7–14.

[39] John Percival, "Corporate Bonds in a Market Model Context," *Journal of Business Research* 2, no. 4 (October 1974): 461–467.

[40] Frank K. Reilly and Michael D. Joehnk, "The Association between Market-Determined Risk Measures for Bonds and Bond Ratings," *Journal of Finance* 31, no. 5 (December 1976): 1387–1403.

FIGURE 15.11   **Risk–Return Graph for Long-Term Securities, 1971–1982**

Standard Deviation (σ)

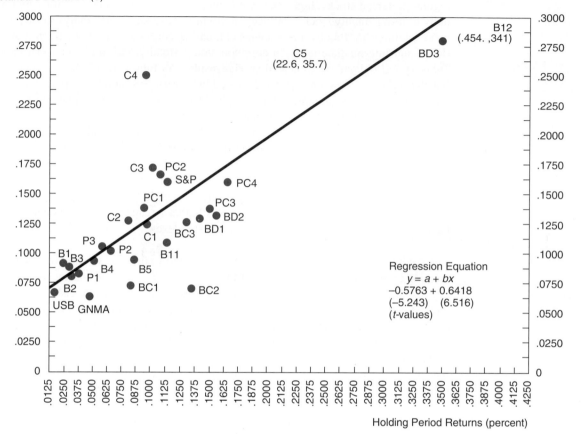

Holding Period Returns (percent)

Risk Class Symbol	Name	#			
			BD1	Discount Bonds—Deep	14
			BD2	Discount Bonds—Very Deep	15
USB	U.S. Government Bonds	1	BD3	Discount Bonds—Extremely Deep	16
GNMA	GNMA Mortgages	2	BI1	Income Bonds—No Breaks in Pyts.	17
B1	Corporate Bonds, Aaa	3	BI2	Income Bonds—Severe Breaks in Pyts.	18
B2	Corporate Bonds, Aa	4	PC1	Preferred Stock, Convert A	19
B3	Corporate Bonds, A	5	PC2	Preferred Stock, Convert BBB	20
B4	Corporate Bonds, Baa	6	PC3	Preferred Stock, Convert BB	21
B5	Corporate bonds, Ba	7	PC4	Preferred Stock, Convert B	22
P1	Preferred Stock High Quality	8	C1	Common Stock Class I	23
P2	Preferred Stock Med. Quality	9	C2	Common Stock Class II	24
P3	Preferred Stock Spec. Quality	10	C3	Common Stock Class III	25
BC1	Convertible Bonds, BBB	11	C4	Common Stock Class IV	26
BC2	Convertible Bonds, BB	12	C5	Common Stock Class V	27
BC3	Convertible Bonds, B	13	S&P	Standard & Poor's 500 Stocks Index	28

* Minimum term to maturity on bonds is 15 years.

Source: Robert M. Soldofsky, "Risk and Return for Long-Term Securities, 1971–1982." *The Journal of Portfolio Management* 11, no. 1 (Fall 1984), p. 60. Reprinted by permission.

FIGURE 15.12   **Mean Rate of Return and Standard Deviation of Returns for Common Stocks, Government and Corporate Bonds, T-Bills, and Inflation: 1926–1992**

Series	Geometric Mean	Arithmetic Mean	Standard Deviation	Distribution
Common Stocks	10.3%	12.4%	20.6%	
Small Company Stocks	12.2	17.6	35.0	
Long-Term Corporate Bonds	5.5	5.8	8.5	
Long-Term Goverment Bonds	4.8	5.2	8.6	
Intermediate-Term Goverment Bonds	5.2	5.3	5.6	
U.S. Treasury Bills	3.7	3.8	3.3	
Inflation	3.1	3.2	4.7	

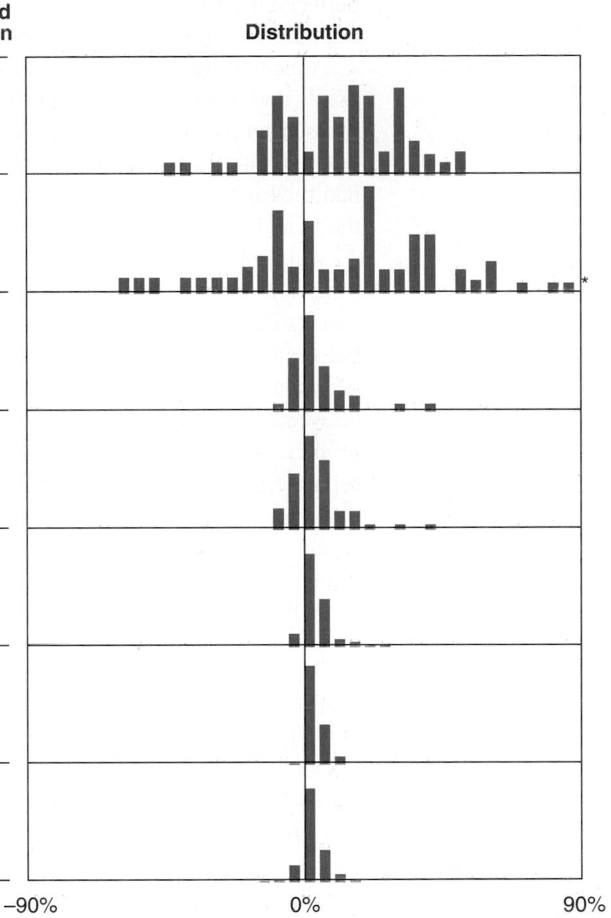

−90%   0%   90%

* The 1933 Small Company Stock Total Return was 142.9 percent.

Source: From *Stocks, Bonds, Bills, and Inflation 1993 Yearbook*™, Ibbotson Associates, Chicago (annually updates work by Roger G. Ibbotson and Rex A. Sinquefield). Used with permission. All Rights Reserved.

bonds irrespective of sector (government, corporate, mortgages) or ratings were correlated .90 to .99.[41] This interest rate risk, which is a market-related, systematic risk factor, has an overpowering effect on price performance and largely negated the effects of differential default risk (which is a company-specific unique risk factor). It is this unique default risk that is reflected in comparative agency ratings. This is compatible with our reasoning in Chapter 14 that interest rate movements are more powerful than yield spreads that are caused by differences in risk of default and agency ratings.

[41] Frank K. Reilly, Wenchi Kao, and David J. Wright, "Alternative Bond Market Indexes," *Financial Analysts Journal* 48, no. 3 (May-June 1992): 44–58.

Notably, the overpowering effect of systematic interest rate risk does *not* prevail when one considers high-yield (junk) bonds. As shown by Reilly and Wright, the correlation between high-yield bonds and investment grade bonds is *lower* than the correlation between high-yield bonds and common stock.[42] This stronger correlation is because both high-yield bonds and common stocks have substantial unsystematic risk.

Alexander examined some of the assumptions of the market model as related to bonds and found two major problems.[43] First, the bond beta results were sensitive to the market index used.[44] Specifically, there were major differences with a pure stock index, a pure bond index, or a composite stock-bond index, and the pure bond index had the biggest problems. Second, the results were sensitive to the time period used; the bond betas increased during periods of high bond yields.

Weinstein computed betas for bonds using several market series and related the betas to term to maturity, coupon, and bond ratings.[45] The results for beta using alternative market indexes (pure stock, pure bond, combined) revealed a very strong correlation between betas from the stock and the combined indexes, a fairly strong relationship between the betas from the bond and the combined indexes, and a weak relationship between the betas from pure stock and bond indexes. Because of some perceived problems with using duration, he examined the relationship with maturity and coupon separately and found a significant positive relationship between beta and term to maturity and a weak negative relationship between the coupon and beta. There was no significant relationship between the betas and bond ratings for the top four classes of ratings (similar to the findings of Reilly and Joehnk), but there was a weak relationship using the top six ratings. The author postulated a nonlinear relationship where the risk of default becomes significant only for low ratings.

In a subsequent study Weinstein computed bond betas and examined their stability over time.[46] He employed a model that allowed the systematic risk to vary consistently with the Black-Scholes-Merton options pricing model. The results indicated that a model that assumes that bond betas change over time has more explanatory power than a constant risk model. Also, he found that the variation in a bond's beta was related to firm characteristics (e.g., debt/equity ratios, variance of rate of return on assets) and to bond characteristics (coupon, term to maturity).

Thus, evidence on the usefulness of the CAPM as related to the bond market is mixed. Specifically, there are obvious problems regarding the appropriate market index to use, the systematic risk measure is unstable, and the risk–return relationship did not hold for the higher-quality bonds. Finally, there appears to be a relationship between the systematic risk measure and some characteristics of the firm. However, it is also impacted by the characteristics of the bond—especially those characteristics such as coupon and maturity that affect the bond's duration and convexity. This is not surprising

---

[42] Frank K. Reilly and David J. Wright, "High Yield Bonds and Segmentation in the Bond Market," Academy of Financial Services Meeting (October 1993).

[43] Gordon J. Alexander, "Applying the Market Model to Long-Term Corporate Bonds," *Journal of Financial and Quantitative Analysis* 15, no. 5 (December 1980): 1063–1080.

[44] This is similar to the well-known work by Roll on market series.

[45] Mark I. Weinstein, "The Systematic Risk of Corporate Bonds," *Journal of Financial and Quantitative Analysis* 16, no. 3 (September 1981): 157–278.

[46] Mark I. Weinstein, "Bond Systematic Risk and the Option Pricing Model," *Journal of Finance* 38, no. 5 (December 1983): 1415–1429.

because we know from Chapter 14 that modified duration is a measure of bond price volatility.

**BOND-MARKET
EFFICIENCY**

Two versions of the efficient market hypothesis (EMH) are examined in the context of fixed-income securities, the weak and the semistrong theories. The weak-form hypothesis contends that security prices fully reflect all market information and maintains that price movements are independent events so historical price information is useless in predicting future price behavior. Studies of weak-form efficiency have examined the ability of investors to forecast interest rates because if you can forecast interest rates you can forecast bond price behavior. Also interest rate expectations are important for bond portfolio management.

Several studies[47] reached the same conclusion: interest rate behavior cannot be consistently and accurately forecast! In fact, one study suggests that the best forecast is no forecast at all. The models developed ranged from a naive approach to fairly sophisticated techniques. Some models used historical information, some ignored it, and one study used the expectations of acknowledged experts. In all cases, the most naive model, or no forecast at all, provided the best measure of future interest rate behavior. Clearly, if interest rates cannot be forecast, then neither can bond prices using historical prices, all of which supports the weak-form EMH.

The semistrong EMH asserts that current prices fully reflect all public knowledge and that efforts to act on such information are largely unproductive. Several studies have examined the informational value of bond rating changes. Katz examined monthly changes in bond yields surrounding ratings changes and found a significant impact of the change.[48] Weinstein examined the behavior of monthly bond returns during and surrounding the announcement of rating changes and found an effect 18 to 7 months before the announcement, but no effect from 6 months before the announcement to 6 months after the announcement.[49]

In contrast, several studies have examined the impact of bond rating changes on stock prices and returns. Pinches and Singleton found very little impact on stock prices due to the ratings change.[50] Griffin and Sanvicente found a significant stock price impact following bond downgradings.[51] Alternatively, they found no impact on stock prices during the month when an upgrading was announced, but there was an impact during the prior 11 months. Holthausen and Leftwich examined daily stock return data surrounding the announcement of bond rating changes and likewise found negative

---

[47] See, for example, Michael J. Prell, "How Well Do the Experts Forecast Interest Rates?" *Monthly Review,* Federal Reserve Bank of Kansas City (September-October 1973): 3–13; William A. Bomberger and W. J. Frazer, "Interest Rates, Uncertainty, and the Livingston Data," *Journal of Finance* 36, no. 3 (June 1981): 661–675; Stephen K. McNees, "The Recent Record of Thirteen Forecasters," *New England Economic Review,* Federal Reserve Bank of Boston (September-October 1981): 3–10; and Adrian W. Throop, "Interest Rate Forecasts and Market Efficiency," *Economic Review,* Federal Reserve Bank of San Francisco (Spring 1981): 29–43.

[48] Steven Katz, "The Price Adjustment Process of Bonds to Rating Reclassifications: A Test of Bond Market Efficiency," *Journal of Finance* 29, no. 2 (May 1974): 551–559.

[49] Mark I. Weinstein, "The Effect of a Rating Change Announcement on Bond Price," *Journal of Financial Economics* 5, no. 3 (December 1977): 329–350.

[50] George E. Pinches and Clay Singleton, "The Adjustment of Stock Prices to Bond Rating Changes," *Journal of Finance* 33, no. 1 (March 1978): 29–44.

[51] Paul A. Griffin and Antonio Z. Sanvicente, "Common Stock Returns and Rating Changes: A Methodological Comparison," *Journal of Finance* 37, no. 1 (March 1982): 103–119.

abnormal returns when bonds were downgraded.[52] There was little evidence of abnormal price changes surrounding the announcement of an upgrading, however.

What does market efficiency imply regarding specific bond-market strategies, such as bond swaps and trading on the basis of yield spreads? By their very nature, bond swaps suggest some market inefficiency, because it is implied that there are some temporary anomalies within or between market segments that afford alert investors the opportunity for above-average returns. The existence of numerous profitable swap opportunities would suggest that underlying price irregularities are neither rare nor random events. Such opportunities may be caused by the institutional nature of the market, which could lead to *market segmentation*. In effect, this would imply that it is largely artificial constraints, regulations, and statutes that lead to the opportunity to execute profitable bond swaps. It is difficult to conduct an empirical study on the success of some of these strategies because of the unavailability of the data for individual firms. As a result, there is no rigorous empirical evidence on the success of these strategies.

In contrast to bond swaps, yield spreads do not necessarily imply inefficiencies. An increase in yield through a quality bond swap that results in a lower agency rating does not imply market inefficiency, because the greater default risk should provide a higher return. The existence of many yield spreads are actually indications of market efficiency, because they reflect equilibrium yield rates based on differential standards of risk, quality, and other issue characteristics. For example, AAA corporates should yield less than A-rated obligations because they possess a different risk profile. The sizes of these spreads are determined in a highly efficient manner, and changes in the yield spreads are likewise rational and rapid. Again, it has not been possible to test whether it is possible to experience abnormal profits by trading on some mechanical yield spread rule.

SUMMARY

During the past decade there has been a significant increase in the number and range of bond portfolio management strategies available. Bond portfolio management strategies include the relatively straightforward buy-and-hold and bond indexing strategies, several alternative active portfolio strategies, dedicated cash matching, classical immunization, horizon matching, and contingent immunization. Although you should understand the alternatives available and how to implement them, you should also recognize that the choice of a specific strategy is based on the needs and desires of the client. In turn, the success of any strategy will depend on the background and talents of the portfolio manager.

The risk–return performance of bonds as a unique asset class has been consistent with expectations. In addition, their inclusion has generally enhanced overall portfolio performance because of their low covariance with other financial assets. The application of CAPM concepts to bonds has been mixed, because it has been difficult to derive acceptable measures of systematic risk, and the risk measures derived have been unstable.

Studies in the bond market have supported the theory of weak-form efficiency. The evidence for semistrong efficiency has been mixed. The results that indicate a lack of

---

[52] Robert W. Holthausen and Richard W. Leftwich, "The Effect of Bond Rating Changes on Common Stock Prices," *Journal of Financial Economics* 17, no. 1 (September 1986): 57–89.

efficiency could be due to the relatively inactive secondary markets for most corporate bonds, which causes pricing and adjustment problems compared to the active markets for equities.

QUESTIONS

1. Explain the difference between a pure buy-and-hold strategy and a modified buy-and-hold strategy.

2. What is meant by an indexing portfolio strategy and what is the justification for using this strategy?

3. Briefly define the following bond swaps: pure yield pickup swap, substitution swap, and tax swap.

4. What are two primary reasons for investing in deep discounted bonds?

5. Briefly describe three techniques that are considered active bond portfolio management strategies.

6. Discuss two variables that you would examine very carefully if you were analyzing a junk bond, and indicate why they are important.

7. What are the advantages of a cash-matched dedicated portfolio? Discuss the difficulties of developing such a portfolio and the added costs.

8. What are the two components of interest rate risk? Describe each of these components.

9. What is meant by bond portfolio immunization?

10. If the yield curve were flat and did not change, how would you immunize your portfolio?

11. You begin with an investment horizon of 4 years and a portfolio with a duration of 4 years with a market interest rate of 10 percent. A year later, what is your investment horizon? Assuming no change in interest rates, what is the duration of your portfolio relative to your investment horizon? What does this imply about your ability to immunize your portfolio?

12. It has been contended that a zero coupon bond is the ideal financial instrument to use for immunizing a portfolio. Discuss the reasoning for this statement in terms of the objective of immunization (i.e., the elimination of interest rate risk).

13. During a conference with a client, the subject of classical immunization is introduced. The client questions the fee charged for developing and managing an immunized portfolio. The client believes that it is basically a passive investment strategy, so the management fee should be substantially lower. What would you tell the client to show that it is not a passive policy and that it requires more time and talent than a buy-and-hold policy?

14. Describe the concept of contingent immunization. What do you give up with this, and what do you gain?

15. *CFA Examination III (June 1983)*
The ability to *immunize* a bond portfolio is very desirable for bond portfolio managers in some instances.
   a. Discuss the components of interest rate risk—assuming a change in interest rates over time, explain the two risks faced by the holder of a bond.
   b. Define immunization and discuss why a bond manager would immunize a portfolio.
   c. Explain why a duration-matching strategy is a superior technique to a maturity-matching strategy for the minimization of interest rate risk.
   d. Explain in specific terms how you would use a zero coupon bond to immunize a bond portfolio. Discuss why a zero coupon bond is an ideal instrument in this regard.

e. Explain how *contingent immunization,* another bond portfolio management technique, differs from *classical immunization.* Discuss why a bond portfolio manager would engage in contingent immunization. [35 minutes]

16. *CFA Exam III (June 1986)*

During the past several years there has been substantial growth in the dollar amount of portfolios managed using *immunization* and *dedication* techniques. Assume a client wants to know the basic differences between (1) classical immunization, (2) contingent immunization, (3) cash-matched dedication, and (4) duration-matched dedication.

a. Briefly describe each of these four techniques.
b. Briefly discuss the ongoing investment action you would have to carry out if managing an *immunized portfolio.*
c. Briefly discuss three of the major considerations involved with creating a *cash-matched dedicated* portfolio.
d. Describe two parameters that should be specified when using *contingent immunization.*
e. Select one of the four alternative techniques that you believe requires the least degree of active management and justify your selection. [20 minutes]

17. *CFA Exam III (June 1988)*

After you have constructed a structured fixed-income portfolio (i.e., one that is dedicated, indexed, or immunized), it may be possible over time to improve on the initial optimal portfolio while continuing to meet the primary goal. Discuss three conditions that would be considered favorable for a restructuring assuming no change in objectives for the investor and cite an example of each condition. [10 minutes]

18. *CFA Exam III (June 1988)*

The use of bond index funds has grown dramatically in recent years.

a. Discuss the reasons you would expect it to be easier or more difficult to construct a bond-market index than a stock-market index.
b. It is contended that the *operational process* of managing a corporate bond index fund is more difficult than managing an equity index fund. Discuss three examples that support this contention. [15 minutes]

19. *CFA Exam III (June 1988)*

Hans Kaufmann is a global fixed-income portfolio manager based in Switzerland. His clients are primarily U.S.-based pension funds. He allocates investments in the following four countries:

United States
Japan
Germany
United Kingdom

His approach is to make investment allocation decisions among these four countries based on his global economic outlook. To develop this economic outlook, Kaufmann analyzes the following five factors for each country: real economic growth; inflation; monetary policy; interest rates; and exchange rates.

When Kaufmann believes that the four economies are equally attractive for investment purposes, he equally weights investments in the four countries. When the economies are not equally attractive, he overweights the country or countries where he sees the largest potential returns.

Tables 1 through 5 present relevant economic data and forecasts.

a. Indicate, before taking into account currency hedging, whether Kaufmann should overweight or underweight investments in each country. Justify your position. [15 minutes]

b. Briefly describe how your answer to part a might change with the use of currency hedging techniques. [5 minutes]

TABLE 1	**Real GNP/GDP** (annual changes)			
	1985	**1986**	**1987**	**1988E**
United States	3.0%	2.9%	2.4%	2.7%
Japan	4.7	2.4	3.2	3.4
West Germany	2.0	2.5	1.5	2.1
United Kingdom	3.4	3.0	3.4	2.3

TABLE 2	**GNP/GDP Deflator** (annual changes)			
	1985	**1986**	**1987**	**1988E**
United States	3.2%	2.6%	3.3%	3.8%
Japan	1.5	2.8	3.0	3.0
West Germany	2.2	3.1	2.5	2.2
United Kingdom	6.0	3.5	4.5	4.8

TABLE 3	**Narrow Money (MI)** (annual changes)			
	1985	**1986**	**1987**	**1988E**
United States	9.2%	13.4%	5.5%	7.0%
Japan	5.0	6.9	9.9	10.0
West Germany	4.3	8.5	7.5	8.5
United Kingdom	17.8	25.6	16.5	12.0

TABLE 4	**Long-term Interest Rates** (annual rates)			
	1985	**1986**	**1987**	**1988E**
United States	10.6%	7.7%	8.8%	9.0%
Japan	6.5	5.2	6.1	6.1
West Germany	6.9	5.9	6.1	7.0
United Kingdom	10.6	9.9	9.8	9.5

TABLE 5

Exchange Rates
(Currency per U.S. $)

	1985	1986	1987	1988E
United States (dollars)	1.00	1.00	1.00	1.00
Japan (yen)	228.08	163.87	141.22	140.09
West German (marks)	2.80	2.08	1.74	1.67
United Kingdom (pounds)	0.74	0.67	0.58	0.59

Sources: *World Economic Outlook,* October 1987, and Kaufmann's estimates.

PROBLEMS

1. You have a portfolio with a market value of $50 million and a Macaulay duration of 7 years (assuming a market interest rate of 10 percent). If interest rates jump to 12 percent, what would be the estimated value of your portfolio using duration? Show all your computations.

2. Answer the following questions assuming that at the initiation of an investment account, the market value of your portfolio is $200 million, and you immunize the portfolio at 12 percent for 6 years. During the first year, interest rates are constant at 12 percent.
   a. What is the market value of the portfolio at the end of Year 1?
   b. Immediately after the end of the year, interest rates *decline* to 10 percent. Estimate the new value of the portfolio assuming you did the required rebalancing (use only modified duration).

3. Compute the Macaulay duration under the following conditions:
   a. A bond with a 5-year term to maturity, a 12 percent coupon (annual payments), and a market yield of 10 percent
   b. A bond with a 4-year term to maturity, a 12 percent coupon (annual payments), and a market yield of 10 percent
   c. Compare your answers to parts a and b, and discuss the implications of this for classical immunization.

4. Compute the Macaulay duration under the following conditions:
   a. A bond with a 4-year term to maturity, a 10 percent coupon (annual payments), and a market yield of 8 percent
   b. A bond with a 4-year term to maturity, a 10 percent coupon (annual payments), and a market yield of 12 percent
   c. Compare your answers to parts a and b. Assuming it was an immediate shift in yields, discuss the implications of this for classical immunization.

5. Answer the following questions about a zero coupon bond with a term to maturity at issue of 10 years (assume semiannual compounding):
   a. What is the duration of the bond at issue assuming a market yield of 10 percent? What is its duration if the market yield is 14 percent? Discuss these two answers.
   b. Compute the initial issue price of this bond at a market yield of 14 percent.
   c. Compute the initial issue price of this bond at a market yield of 10 percent.
   d. A year after issue, the bond in part c is selling to yield 12 percent. What is its current market price? Assuming you owned this bond during this year, what is your rate of return?

6. A major requirement in running a contingent immunization portfolio policy is the need to monitor the relationship between the current market value of the portfolio and the required value of the floor portfolio. In this regard, assume a $300 million portfolio with a horizon of 5 years. The available market rate at the initiation of the portfolio is 14 per-

cent, but the client is willing to accept 12 percent as a floor rate to allow you to use active management strategies. The current market values and current market rates at the end of Years 1, 2, and 3 are as follows:

End of Year	Market Value	Market Yield	Required Floor Portfolio	Safety Margin (deficiency)
1	340.00	.12		
2	375.00	.10		
3	360.20	.14		

a. What is the required ending-wealth value for this portfolio?
b. What is the value of the required floor portfolio at the end of Years 1, 2, and 3?
c. Compute the safety margin or deficiency at the end of Years 1, 2, and 3.

7. Evaluate the following pure yield pickup swap: You currently hold a 20-year, Aa-rated, 9.0 percent coupon bond priced to yield 11.0 percent. As a swap candidate, you are considering a 20-year, Aa-rated, 11 percent coupon bond priced to yield 11.5 percent. (Assume reinvestment at 11.5 percent.)

	Current Bond	Candidate Bond
Dollar investment	_____	_____
Coupon	_____	_____
i on one coupon	_____	_____
Principal value at year end	_____	_____
Total accrued	_____	_____
Realized compound yield	_____	_____

Value of swap: _____ basis points in one year

8. Evaluate the following substitution swap: You currently hold a 25-year, 9.0 percent coupon bond priced to yield 10.5 percent. As a swap candidate, you are considering a 25-year, Aa-rated, 9.0 percent coupon bond priced to yield 10.75 percent. (Assume a 1-year work-out period and reinvestment at 10.5 percent.)

	Current Bond	Candidate Bond
Dollar investment	_____	_____
Coupon	_____	_____
i on one coupon	_____	_____
Principal value at year end	_____	_____
Total accrued	_____	_____
Realized compound yield	_____	_____

Value of swap: _____ basis points in one year

9. *CFA Exam III (June, 1984)*
Reinvestment risk is a major factor for bond managers to consider when determining the most appropriate or optimal strategy for a fixed-income portfolio. Briefly describe each of the following bond portfolio management strategies, and explain how each deals with reinvestment risk:
a. Active management
b. Classical immunization
c. Dedicated portfolio
d. Contingent immunization [20 minutes]

10. *CFA Exam III (June 1985)*

A major requirement in managing a fixed-income portfolio using a contingent immunization policy is the need to monitor the relationship between the current market value of the portfolio and the required value of the floor portfolio. This difference is defined as the *margin of error.* In this regard, assume a $300 million portfolio with a time horizon of 5 years. The available market rate at the initiation of the portfolio is 12 percent, but the client is willing to accept 10 percent as a floor rate to allow use of active management strategies. The current market values and current market rates at the end of Years 1, 2, and 3 are as follows:

End of Year	Market Value ($Mil)	Market Yield	Required Floor Portfolio ($Mil)	Margin of Error ($Mil)
1	$340.9	10%		
2	405.5	8		
3	395.2	12		

Table 1
Present Value (use tables in back of book)

Table 2
Compound Value (use tables in back of book)

Assuming semiannual compounding:

a. Calculate the required ending-wealth value for this portfolio.

b. Calculate the value of the required floor portfolios at the end of Years 1, 2, and 3.

c. Compute the margin of error at the end of Years 1, 2, and 3.

d. Indicate the action that a portfolio manager utilizing a *contingent immunization* policy would take if the margin of error at the end of any year had been zero or negative.

REFERENCES

Alexander, Gordon J. "Applying the Market Model to Long-Term Corporate Bonds." *Journal of Financial and Quantitative Analysis* 15, no. 5 (December 1980).

Altman, Edward I., ed. *The High Yield Debt Market.* Homewood, IL. Dow Jones-Irwin, 1990.

Altman, Edward I., and Scott A. Nammacher. *Investing in Junk Bonds.* New York: John Wiley & Sons, 1987.

Barnes, Tom, Keith Johnson, and Don Shannon. "A Test of Fixed Income Strategies." *Journal of Portfolio Management* 10, no. 2 (Winter 1984).

Beckers, Stan. "Stocks, Bonds, and Inflation in the World Markets: Implications for Pension Fund Investment." *The Journal of Fixed Income* 1, no. 3 (December 1991).

Bierwag, G. O., and George G. Kaufman. "Coping with the Risk of Interest Rate Fluctuations: A Note." *Journal of Business* 50, no. 3 (July 1977).

Bierwag, G. O., George G. Kaufman, and Alden Toevs. "Single Factor Duration Models in a General Equilibrium Framework." *Journal of Finance* 37, no. 2 (May 1982).

Bierwag, G. O., George G. Kaufman, and Alden Toevs, eds. *Innovations in Bond Portfolio Management: Duration Analysis and Immunization.* Greenwich, Conn.: JAI Press, 1983.

Bierwag, G. O., George G. Kaufman, and Alden Toevs. "Immunizing Strategies for Funding Multiple Liabilities." *Journal of Financial and Quantitative Analysis* 18, no. 1 (March 1983).

Bierwag, G. O., George G. Kaufman, and Alden Toevs. "Duration: Its Development and Use in Bond Portfolio Management." *Financial Analysts Journal* 39, no. 4 (July-August 1983).

Bierwag, G. O., George G. Kaufman, and Chulsoon Khang. "Duration and Bond Portfolio Analysis: An Overview." *Journal of Financial and Quantitative Analysis* 13, no. 5 (November 1978).

Bierwag, G. O., George G. Kaufman, Robert L. Schweitzer, and Alden Toevs. "The Art of Risk Management in Bond Portfolios." *Journal of Portfolio Management* 7, no. 3 (Spring 1981).

Cheung, Rayner, Joseph C. Bencivenga, and Frank J. Fabozzi, "Original Issue High-Yield Bonds: Historical Return and Default Experiences, 1977–1989," *The Journal of Fixed Income* 2, no. 2 (September 1992).

Choie, Kenneth S. "A Simplified Approach to Bond Portfolio Management: DDS." *Journal of Portfolio Management* 16, no. 3 (Spring 1990).

Cox, John, Jonathon E. Ingersoll, and Stephen A. Ross. "Duration and Measurement of Basis Risk." *Journal of Business* 52, no. 1 (January 1979).

Fabozzi, Frank J., ed. *The Handbook of Fixed-Income Securities,* 3d ed. Homewood, Ill.: Business One-Irwin, 1991.

Fabozzi, Frank J., ed. *The New High-Yield Debt Market.* New York: Harper Business, 1990.

Fisher, Lawrence, and Roman L. Weil. "Coping with the Risk of Interest-Rate Fluctuations: Returns to Bondholders from Naive and Optimal Strategies." *Journal of Business* 44, no. 4 (October 1971).

Fridson, Martin. *High Yield Bonds: Assessing Risk and Identifying Value in Speculative Grade Securities.* Chicago: Probus Publishing, 1989.

Giberti, Daniela, Marcello Mentini, and Pietro Scabellone, "The Valuation of Credit Risk in Swaps: Methodological Issues and Empirical Results." *The Journal of Fixed Income* 2, no. 4 (March 1993).

Hawawini, Gabriel A., ed. *Bond Duration and Immunization: Early Developments and Recent Contributions.* New York: Garland Publishing, 1982.

Hickman, W. Braddock. *Corporate Bond Quality and Investor Experience.* A study by the National Bureau of Economic Research. Princeton, N.J.: Princeton University Press, 1958.

Homer, Sidney, and Martin L. Leibowitz. *Inside the Yield Book.* Englewood Cliffs, N.J.: Prentice-Hall, 1972.

Howe, Jane Tripp. *Junk Bonds: Analysis and Portfolio Strategies.* Chicago: Probus Publishing, 1988.

Leibowitz, Martin L., and Alfred Weinberger. "Contingent Immunization—Part I: Risk Control Procedures." *Financial Analysts Journal* 38, no. 6 (November-December 1982).

Leibowitz, Martin L., and Alfred Weinberger. "Contingent Immunization—Part II: Problem Areas." *Financial Analysts Journal* 39, no. 1 (January-February 1983).

Leibowitz, Martin L., William S. Krasker, and Ardavan Nozari. "Spread Duration: A New Tool for Bond Portfolio Management." *Journal of Portfolio Management* 16, no. 3 (Spring 1990).

Redington, F. M. "Review of the Principle of Life—Office Valuations." *Journal of the Institute of Actuaries.* 78 (1952).

Reilly, Frank K., ed. *High Yield Bonds: Analysis and Risk Assessment.* Charlottesville, Va.: Institute of Chartered Financial Analysts, 1990.

Reilly, Frank K., and Michael D. Joehnk. "The Association between Market-Determined Risk Measures for Bonds and Bond Ratings." *Journal of Finance* 31, no. 5 (December 1976).

Reilly, Frank K., G. Wenchi Kao, and David J. Wright, "Alternative Bond Market Indexes." *Financial Analysts Journal* 48, no. 3 (May-June 1992).

Tuttle, Donald., ed. *The Revolution in Techniques for Managing Bond Portfolios.* Charlottesville, Va.: The Institute of Chartered Financial Analysts, 1983.

Van Horne, James. *Financial Market Rates and Flows.* 3d. ed. Englewood Cliffs, N.J.: Prentice-Hall, 1989.

Weinstein, Mark I. "The Effect of a Rating Change Announcement on Bond Price." *Journal of Financial Economics* 5, no. 3 (December 1977).

Weinstein, Mark I. "Bond Systematic Risk and the Option Pricing Model." *Journal of Finance* 38, no. 5 (December 1983).

Wilson, Richard S., and Frank J. Fabozzi. *The New Corporate Bond Market.* Chicago: Probus Publishing, 1990.

ANALYSIS OF COMMON STOCKS

In Part III we considered the basic valuation principles and practices applied to all securities and how this was applied to the global asset allocation decision. In Part IV we applied these principles to the analysis and management of bonds. In Part V we will likewise apply these valuation principles and practices to the analysis of common stocks.

You will recall from the discussion in Chapter 11 that successful investing requires several steps beginning with a valuation of the aggregate economy and market, progressing through the examination of various industries, and finally involving the analysis of individual companies and their securities. The globalization of the capital markets has definitely complicated this process. As discussed in Chapter 12, it is now necessary to consider several economies and markets on a worldwide basis followed by the analysis of *world* industries as contrasted to only the U.S. component of an industry. Of course, the number and complexity of companies to be analyzed in an industry is likewise increased.

We begin in Chapter 16 with the first part of the three-step, top-down approach and discuss how to analyze the aggregate stock market using the basic dividend discount model. Chapter 17 contains a discussion of industry analysis. It begins with a review of research related to industry analysis, which provides an incentive for carrying out such research. Subsequently we discuss the specific steps in industry analysis employing the same dividend discount model that was used in the market analysis.

Chapter 18 on company analysis begins with a discussion of the difference between a company and its stock. It is pointed out that in many instances the common stock of a very fine company may not be a good investment, which is why we emphasize that company analysis and stock selection are two separate but dependent activities. Once again, the analysis procedure is

built upon the dividend discount model. In addition, other valuation factors are considered because of the extensive research indicating the importance and usefulness of factors such as corporate size, book value/market value ratio, and price/cash flow ratio. The overall goal of this procedure is to select one of the best companies in a superior industry during a favorable market environment.

It was noted in Chapter 11 that it is not feasible to use the standard dividend discount model to value true growth companies. Therefore, there is a separate discussion in Chapter 18 in which we discuss several valuation models that have been specifically developed for the analysis of growth companies. In all these chapters, we provide examples of how these techniques can and have been applied in a global environment.

Throughout this section, we refer to the semi-strong efficient market hypothesis. You will recall that, although many studies supported this hypothesis, there is growing literature dealing with anomalies related to this hypothesis. The presentation in this section provides a consistent and justifiable valuation technique that can be used to find undervalued securities. You should never forget that the output of alternative valuation models is only as good as the estimated inputs and *the superior analyst is the one who provides the best estimates.*

The final chapter in this section, Chapter 19, deals with technical analysis, an alternative to the fundamental approach discussed in the prior chapters. Rather than attempting to estimate value based upon numerous external variables, the technical analyst contends that the market is its own best estimator. Therefore, he or she believes that it is possible to project future stock price movements based on past stock price changes or other stock market data. Various techniques used by technical analysts for U.S. and world markets are discussed and demonstrated.

CHAPTER 16

STOCK-MARKET ANALYSIS

In this chapter we will answer the following questions:

- How do we apply the basic dividend discount model to the valuation of the aggregate stock market?
- What are the two components involved in the two-part valuation procedure?
- Given the two components in the valuation procedure, which is the more volatile?
- What steps are involved in estimating the earnings per share for an aggregate market series?
- What variables affect the aggregate operating profit margin and how do they affect it?
- What are the variables that determine the level and changes in the market earnings multiplier?
- How do you put together the components to arrive at an expected market value and an expected rate of return for the stock market?
- How do you apply this microanalysis approach to the valuation of stock markets around the world?
- What are some additional factors that must be considered when attempting to evaluate non-U.S. stock markets?
- What are some differences between stock market statistics for the U.S. versus other countries?

Interest in stock-market movements has grown during the past decade. More individuals own stock than ever before, and significant mergers are increasingly frequent. This interest exploded when the stock-market "crash" on October 19, 1987, led to a period of information overload that left few people unaware of the importance of the securities markets in today's world.

In earlier chapters we emphasized the importance of analyzing the aggregate economy and alternative security markets before an industry or a company analysis. It is very important to determine whether the economic and market outlook justifies investing in stocks, bonds, or cash before you consider which is the best industry or company.

There are two techniques for making the security-market decision. The first is macroanalysis, which is based on the strong relationship between the aggregate economy and alternative security markets. The second technique is microanalysis, which applies basic valuation models to the bond or equity markets. Chapter 12 was concerned with the macro techniques and discussed world asset allocation. Chapter 14 discussed the micro valuation of bonds.

This chapter explains the microanalysis of a country's stock market. Your estimate of the future value for the stock market in a country implies an estimate of the rate of return you expect as an investor in the country's stock during the holding period.

This chapter begins the three-step valuation process introduced in Chapter 12. We initiate the fundamental analysis of stocks, which determines value on the basis of sales, earnings, and risk factors. In this chapter we estimate the aggregate market outlook based on the outlook for the economy. This will be followed in Chapter 17 by an analysis of industries, and finally in Chapter 18 we will consider how to estimate the value of an individual firm and its stock.

To determine the future value of the aggregate stock market using microanalysis techniques, we will apply basic valuation theory to the aggregate stock market. We will do this in five sections. The first presents the theoretical background for the two-step multiplier approach. The second section considers the estimation of earnings per share, and the third section deals with estimating the earnings multiplier or the price/earnings ratio. In section four we combine the estimates of earnings per share and the price/earnings ratio to derive a future value for the market. In turn, this future value can be used to estimate the expected rate of return on stocks during the holding period. The final section discusses how to apply this approach to foreign markets.

APPLYING THE VALUATION MODEL TO THE MARKET

In Chapter 11 we worked with a valuation model that equated the value of an investment to

1. The stream of expected returns
2. The time pattern of expected returns
3. The required rate of return on the investment

Using this information, we employed the following dividend discount model (DDM), which estimated the value of the stock (V_j) assuming a constant growth rate of dividends for an infinite period.

$$V_j = \frac{D_0(1 + g)}{(1 + k)} + \frac{D_0(1 + g)^2}{(1 + k)^2} + \cdots \frac{D_0(1 + g)^n}{(1 + k)^n}$$

where:

V_j = **the value of stock** j
D_0 = **the dividend payment in the current period**
g = **the constant growth rate of dividends**
k = **the required rate of return on stock** j
n = **the number of periods, which is assumed to be infinite**

We used this model as the basis for the fundamental analysis of common stock. We can also use it to value a stock-market series. In the appendix to Chapter 11 it was shown that this model can be simplified to the following expression:

$$V_j = P_j = \frac{D_1}{k - g}$$

where:

P_j = **the price of stock j**

D_1 = **dividend in period 1, which is equal to: $D_0 (1 + g)$**

k = **the required rate of return for stock j**

g = **the constant growth rate of dividends**

This model suggests that the parameters to be estimated are (1) the required rate of return (k) and (2) the expected growth rate of dividends (g). After estimating g, it is simple to estimate D_1, because it is the known current dividend (D_0) times $(1 + g)$.

Recall too that we can transform the dividend discount model into an earnings multiplier model by dividing both sides of the equation by E:

$$\frac{P_1}{E_1} = \frac{\dfrac{D_1}{E_1}}{k - g}$$

We call this P/E ratio the *earnings multiplier* or the *price/earnings ratio.* It is determined by

1. The expected dividend payout ratio (D_1/E_1),
2. The required rate of return on the stock (k)
3. The expected growth rate of dividends for the stock (g)

We will see that the estimation of this earning multiplier is important because it varies between stocks and industries. Also the multiplier for the aggregate stock market varies widely over time and has a big impact on changes in the value of the market.

We showed previously that the difficult parameters to estimate are k and g, or more specifically, the *spread* between k and g. Recall that very small changes in either k or g without an offset by the other variable can affect the spread and change the value of the earnings multiplier substantially.

TWO-PART VALUATION PROCEDURE

To find a value for the stock market we use the earnings multiplier version of the dividend discount model because it is a theoretically correct model of value assuming a constant growth of dividends for an infinite time period. These are reasonable assumptions for the aggregate stock market. Also this technique of market valuation or a slight modification of it is consistently used in practice.

Recall that k and g are independent variables because k depends heavily on risk, whereas g is a function of the retention rate and the ROE. Therefore, this spread between k and g can and does change over time. The following equations show that you can derive an estimate of this spread at a point in time by examining the prevailing dividend yield:

$$P_j = \frac{D_1}{k - g}$$
$$P_j/D_1 = 1/k - g$$
$$D_1/P_j = k - g$$

Although the dividend yield gives an estimate of the size of the prevailing spread, it does not indicate the values for the two individual components (k and g). More important it says nothing about the future spread, which is the critical value.

IMPORTANCE
OF BOTH
COMPONENTS
OF VALUE

The ultimate objective of this microanalysis is to estimate the future market value for a major stock-market series, such as the S&P 400. This estimation process has two equally important steps:

1. Estimating the future earnings per share for the stock-market series
2. Estimating a future earnings multiplier for the stock-market series.[1]

Some analysts have concentrated on estimating the earnings for a market series with little consideration of changes in the earnings multiplier for the series. An investor who only considers the earnings for the series and ignores the earnings multiplier implicitly assumes that the earnings multiplier will be relatively constant over time. If this were correct, stock prices would generally move in line with earnings. The fallacy of this assumption is obvious when one examines data for the two components during the period from 1965 to 1992, as shown in Table 16.1.

The earnings figure is the earnings per share during the year for the S&P 400 series, and the next column shows the percentage change from the prior year. The third column is the historical earnings multiplier at the end of the year, which is equal to the year-end value for the S&P 400 series divided by the *historical* earnings for that year. As an example, at the *end of 1965,* the S&P 400 price series was equal to 98.47 and the earnings per share for the firms that made up the series was 5.50 for the 12 months ending 12/31/65. This implies an earnings multiplier of 17.90 (98.47/5.50). Although this may not be the ideal measure of the multiplier, it is constant in its measurement and shows the changes in the relationship between stock prices and earnings over time. An alternative measure is to compute the multiplier using *next* year's earnings (i.e., stock price as of 12/31/65 versus earnings for the 12 months ending 12/31/66). This series likewise reflects large annual changes as shown in the last two columns.

There are numerous striking examples where stock price movements for the S&P 400 series were opposite to earnings changes during the same year:

- 1973 profits *increased* by 30 percent; stock prices *declined* by 17 percent.
- 1974 profits *increased* by 9 percent; stock prices *declined* by almost 30 percent.
- 1975 profits *declined* by 10 percent; stock prices *increased* by 32 percent.
- 1977 profits *increased* by 7 percent; stock prices *declined* by 12 percent.
- 1980 profits *decreased* by 1 percent; stock prices *increased* by over 27 percent.
- 1982 profits *decreased* by 21 percent; stock prices *increased* by 15 percent.
- 1984 profits *increased* by almost 23 percent; stock prices were basically *unchanged.*
- 1985 profits *decreased* by 15 percent; stock prices *increased* by about 26 percent.
- 1986 profits *decreased* by almost 5 percent; stock prices *increased* by over 15 percent.
- 1989 profits were almost *unchanged*; stock prices *increased* by over 25 percent.
- 1991 profits *decreased* by over 32 percent; stock prices *increased* by over 27 percent.

---

[1] Our emphasis will be on *estimating future values.* We will show the relevant variables and provide a procedural framework, but the final estimate depends on the ability of the analyst.

TABLE 16.1   **Annual Changes in Corporate Earnings, the Earnings Multiplier, and Stock Prices for Standard & Poor's 400: 1965–1992**

Year	Earnings per Share	Percentage Change	Year-End Earnings Multiple	Percentage Change	Year-End Stock Prices	Percentage Change	Earnings Multiple t + 1	Percentage Change
1965	5.50	−13.4	17.99	−3.1	98.47	9.9	16.78	3.01
1966	5.87	6.7	14.52	−18.9	85.24	−13.4	15.17	−9.59
1967	5.62	4.3	18.70	28.8	105.11	23.3	17.06	12.46
1968	6.16	9.6	18.35	−1.9	113.02	7.5	18.44	8.09
1969	6.13	−0.5	16.56	−9.8	101.49	−10.2	18.76	1.74
1970	5.41	−11.7	18.65	12.6	100.90	−0.6	16.90	−9.91
1971	5.97	10.4	18.88	1.2	112.72	11.7	16.50	−2.37
1972	6.83	13.9	19.31	2.3	131.87	17.0	14.83	−10.12
1973	8.89	30.9	12.28	−36.4	109.14	−17.2	11.36	−23.40
1974	9.61	8.9	7.96	−35.2	76.47	−29.9	8.91	−21.57
1975	8.58	−10.7	11.62	46.0	100.88	31.9	9.44	5.95
1976	10.69	24.6	11.17	−3.9	119.46	18.4	10.43	10.49
1977	11.45	7.1	9.14	−18.8	104.71	−12.4	8.03	−23.01
1978	13.04	13.9	8.22	10.1	107.21	2.4	6.58	−18.06
1979	16.29	24.9	7.43	−9.6	121.02	12.9	7.51	14.13
1980	16.12	−1.0	9.58	28.9	154.45	27.6	9.23	22.90
1981	16.74	3.8	8.19	−14.5	137.12	−11.2	10.39	12.57
1982	13.20	−21.1	11.96	46.0	157.62	15.0	10.66	2.60
1983	14.78	12.0	12.60	5.4	186.17	18.1	10.28	−3.56
1984	18.11	22.6	10.29	−18.4	186.36	0.1	12.20	18.68
1985	15.28	−15.6	15.35	49.2	234.56	25.9	16.10	31.97
1986	14.57	−4.6	18.53	20.7	269.93	15.1	13.31	−17.33
1987	20.28	37.2	14.09	−24.0	285.85	5.9	10.75	−19.23
1988	26.59	31.1	12.40	−12.8	321.26	12.4	11.97	11.35
1989	26.73	0.9	15.40	24.2	403.49	25.6	16.29	36.09
1990	24.77	−7.7	15.90	3.2	387.42	−4.0	23.17	42.23
1991	16.72	−32.5	25.40	59.7	492.72	27.2	22.40	−3.32
1992(e)	22.00	31.6	23.07	−9.2	507.46	3.0	NA	
With Signs								
Mean	—	6.31		4.38		9.71		2.70
Standard deviation	—	17.16		25.01		14.31		17.76
Coefficient of variability	—	2.72		5.71		1.46		6.58
Without Signs								
Mean	—	14.81		19.79		14.64		14.66
Standard deviation	—	11.71		15.91		8.92		10.88
Coefficient of variability	—	0.72		0.80		0.61		0.71

(e)—estimate.

Source: *Standard & Poor's Analysts Handbook* (New York: Standard & Poor's Corporation, 1992). Reprinted by permission of Standard & Poor's Corp.

FIGURE 16.1

Year-End Earnings Multiplier for S&P 400, Based on Historical Earnings

Earnings Multiplier

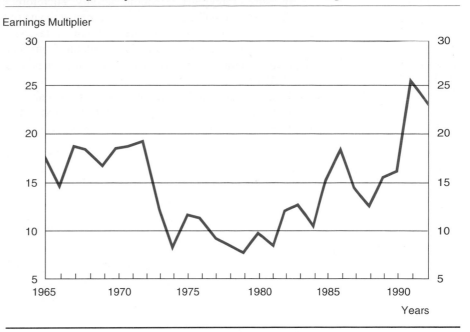

During each of these years, the major influences on stock price movements came from changes in the earnings multiplier during the year. The greater volatility of the multiplier series compared to the earnings per share series can be seen from the summary figures at the bottom of Table 16.1 and from the graph of the earnings multiplier in Figure 16.1. The standard deviation of annual changes for the earnings multiplier series is much larger than the standard deviation of earnings changes (25.01 versus 17.16). The same is true for the relative measures of the coefficient of variability (5.71 versus 2.72). Also, if you consider the mean annual percentage change of the two series without sign, the earnings multiplier series has a larger mean annual percent change value (19.79 versus 14.81) and a larger standard deviation of annual percentage change (15.91 versus 11.71). Therefore, these figures show that, of the two estimates required for market valuation, the earnings multiplier is the more volatile component.

The point is, this calculation of future market value requires two separate estimates and both are important and necessary. Therefore, we will begin by considering a procedure for estimating aggregate earnings. Subsequently we will discuss the factors that should be analyzed when estimating the aggregate market earnings multiplier.

ESTIMATING
EXPECTED
EARNINGS PER
SHARE

The estimate of expected earnings per share for the market series will consider the outlook for the aggregate economy and for the corporate sector. This requires the following distinct steps:

1. Estimate sales per share for a stock-market series such as the S&P 400. This estimate of sales involves a prior estimate of gross national product (GNP)

because of the relationship between the sales of major industrial firms and this measure of aggregate economic activity. Therefore, prior to estimating sales per share, we will consider sources for an estimate of GNP.

2. Estimate the operating profit margin for the series, which equals operating profit divided by sales. Given the data available from Standard & Poor's, we will define operating profit as earnings before depreciation, interest, and taxes (EBDIT).

3. Estimate depreciation per share for the next year.

4. Estimate interest expense per share for the next year.

5. Estimate the corporate tax rate for the next year.

These steps will lead to an estimate of earnings per share that will be combined with an estimate of the earnings multiplier to arrive at an estimate of the ending price for the stock-market series.

ESTIMATING GROSS NATIONAL PRODUCT

GNP is a measure of aggregate economic output or activity. Therefore, one would expect aggregate corporate sales to be related to GNP. We begin our estimate of sales for a stock-market series with a prediction of nominal GNP from one of several banks or financial service firms that regularly publish such estimates.[2] Using this estimate of nominal GNP, we can estimate corporate sales based on the historical relationship between S&P 400 sales per share and aggregate economic activity (GNP).

ESTIMATING SALES PER SHARE FOR A MARKET SERIES

As noted, we will use a sales figure for an existing stock-market series—the S&P 400 Industrial Index.[3] The plot in Figure 16.2 shows the relationship between the annual percentage changes in GNP and S&P 400 sales per share contained in Table 16.2. Except for 1974 there is a strong relationship between the two series whereby a large proportion of the percentage changes in S&P 400 sales per share can be explained by percentage changes in nominal GNP. The equation for the least-squares regression line relating annual percentage changes ($\%\Delta$) in the two series for the period 1965–1991 (without 1974) is

$$\% \, \Delta \text{ S\&P 400 Sales}_t = -2.21 + 1.19 \, (\% \, \Delta \text{ in Nominal GNP}_t)$$
$$\text{Adj. } R^2 = 0.41 \, (-0.85) \quad (4.06) \, F(1,25) = 16.48$$

These results indicate that about 41 percent of the variance in percentage changes in S&P 400 sales can be explained by percentage changes in the nominal GNP. Notably, the -2.21 intercept value is statistically insignificant and can be ignored when using this regression for estimating sales per share. Thus, given an estimate of the expected percentage change in nominal GNP for next year, we can estimate the percentage change in sales for the S&P 400 series and therefore the amount of sales per share. For

---

[2] This would include projections by Standard & Poor's appearing late in the year in *The Outlook*, projections by several of the large investment firms, such as Goldman, Sachs & Company ("The Pocket Chartbook"), and Merrill Lynch, as well as by banks. An example by a Federal Reserve Bank is J. A. Cacy and Richard Roberts, "The U.S. Economy in 1987 and 1988," Federal Reserve Bank of Kansas City, *Economic Review* (December 1987): 3–15.

[3] Sales per share figures are available back to 1945 in Standard & Poor's *Analysts Handbook* (New York: Standard & Poor's Corporation). Because the composite series include numerous companies of different sizes, all data are on a per-share basis. The book is updated annually, and some series are updated quarterly in a monthly supplement.

FIGURE 16.2 **Scatter Plot of Annual Percentage Change in S&P 400 Sales and GNP**

Percent Change in S&P Sales

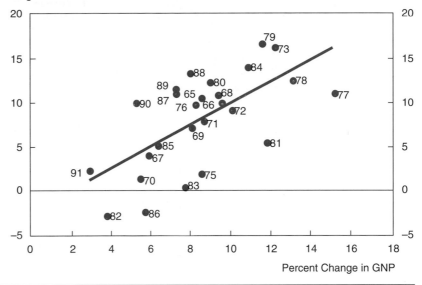

Percent Change in GNP

example, assume that the consensus estimate by economists is that nominal GNP next year will increase by approximately 9 percent (a 5 percent increase in real GNP plus 4 percent inflation). This estimate combined with the regression results implies the following estimated increase in S&P 400 sales:

$$\% \, \Delta \, \text{S\&P 400 Sales} = + \, 1.19 \, (.09)$$
$$= 0.107$$

Notably, this is referred to as a *point estimate of sales* because it is based on a point estimate of GNP. Although we know that there is actually a *distribution* of estimates for GNP, we have used the mean value, or expected value, as our point estimate. In actual practice you would probably consider several estimates and assign probabilities to each of them.

ALTERNATIVE ESTIMATES OF CORPORATE NET PROFITS

Once sales per share for the market series have been estimated, the difficult estimate is the net profit margin. Three alternative procedures are possible depending on the desired level of aggregation.

The first is a direct estimate of the *net* profit margin based on recent trends. As shown in Table 16.3, the net profit margin series is quite volatile because of changes in depreciation, interest, and the tax rate over time. As such, it is the most difficult series to estimate.

The second procedure would attempt to estimate the *net before tax* (NBT) profit margin. Once the NBT margin is derived, a separate estimate of the tax rate is obtained based on recent tax rates and current government tax pronouncements. Examples of

TABLE 16.2   **Nominal GNP and Standard & Poor's Industrial Sales per Share: 1965–1991**

Year	Nominal GNP (Billions of Dollars)	Percentage Change	S&P 400 Sales (Dollar Value of Sales per Share)	Percentage Change
1965	705.1	8.5	80.69	10.2
1966	772.0	9.5	88.46	9.6
1967	816.4	5.8	91.86	3.8
1968	892.7	9.3	101.49	10.5
1969	963.9	8.0	108.53	6.9
1970	1015.5	5.4	109.85	1.2
1971	1102.7	8.6	118.23	7.6
1972	1212.8	10.0	128.79	8.9
1973	1359.3	12.1	149.22	15.9
1974	1472.8	8.3	182.10	22.0
1975	1598.4	8.5	185.16	1.7
1976	1728.8	8.2	202.66	9.5
1977	1990.5	15.1	224.24	10.6
1978	2249.7	13.0	251.32	12.1
1979	2508.2	11.5	292.38	16.3
1980	2732.9	8.9	327.36	12.0
1981	3052.6	11.7	344.31	5.2
1982	3166.0	3.7	333.96	−3.0
1983	3405.7	7.6	334.07	0.1
1984	3772.2	10.8	379.70	13.7
1985	4010.3	6.3	398.42	4.9
1986	4235.0	5.6	388.44	−2.5
1987	4539.9	7.2	430.35	10.8
1988	4900.4	7.9	486.92	13.1
1989	5250.8	7.2	541.38	11.2
1990	5522.2	5.2	574.55	9.8
1991	5677.5	2.8	607.14	2.1
Average		8.4		8.3

Source: Reprinted with permission from Standard & Poor's Corporation, New York, 1992. Reprinted by permission of Standard & Poor's Corp.

critical tax rate estimates were during 1987 and 1988 following the 1986 Tax Reform Act and in 1993–1994 following the Clinton deficit reduction program.

The third method estimates an *operating* profit margin, defined as earnings before depreciation, interest, and taxes as a percentage of sales (EBDIT). Because this measure of operating earnings as a percentage of sales is not influenced by changes in depreciation allowances, interest expense, or tax rates, it should be a stable series compared to either the net profit margin or net before tax margin series.

After we estimate this operating profit margin, we will multiply it by the sales estimate to derive a dollar estimate of operating earnings before depreciation, interest, and taxes (EBDIT). Subsequently, we will derive separate estimates of depreciation

TABLE 16.3   S&P 400 Sales per Share and Components of Operating Profit Margin: 1977–1991

Year	Sales Per Share	EBDIT Per Share	EBDIT Percent of Sales	Depreciation Per Share	Depreciation Percent of Sales	Interest Per Share	Interest Percent of Sales	Income Tax Per Share	Income Tax Tax Rate	Net Income Per Share	Net Income Percent of Sales
1977	223.96	34.54	15.42	8.52	3.80	3.22	1.44	11.15	48.9	11.65	5.20
1978	251.88	38.79	15.40	9.64	3.83	3.81	1.51	12.16	48.0	13.18	5.23
1979	292.38	45.86	15.69	10.81	3.70	4.58	1.57	14.02	46.0	16.45	5.63
1980	327.36	48.30	14.75	12.37	3.78	5.95	1.82	13.67	45.6	16.31	4.98
1981	344.31	51.20	14.87	13.82	4.01	7.49	2.18	12.95	43.3	16.94	4.92
1982	333.86	47.89	14.34	15.30	4.58	8.23	2.47	10.95	45.0	13.41	4.02
1983	334.00	50.48	15.11	15.67	4.69	7.62	2.28	12.12	44.6	15.07	4.51
1984	379.70	57.45	15.13	16.31	4.30	8.54	2.25	14.15	42.7	18.95	4.86
1985	398.42	56.71	14.23	18.19	4.57	9.24	2.32	13.68	46.7	15.60	3.92
1986	387.76	54.96	14.17	19.41	5.01	9.75	2.51	11.01	42.7	14.79	3.81
1987	430.45	64.83	15.06	20.21	4.70	10.14	2.36	13.96	40.5	20.52	4.77
1988	477.85	79.35	16.61	23.34	4.88	14.84	3.11	14.73	35.3	26.94	5.33
1989	541.58	85.56	15.80	24.21	4.47	18.79	3.47	15.73	37.0	26.83	4.96
1990	594.58	87.52	14.72	26.31	4.43	20.17	3.39	16.27	39.6	24.77	4.17
1991	607.14	74.43	12.26	27.05	4.46	18.51	3.05	12.15	42.1	16.72	2.75

EBDIT = Earnings before depreciation, interest, and taxes. This is used as an estimate of operating earnings.
Source: *Standard & Poor's Analysts Handbook* (New York: Standard & Poor's Corporation, 1992). Reprinted by permission of Standard & Poor's Corp.

and interest expenses, which are subtracted from the EBDIT to arrive at earnings before taxes (EBT). Finally, we estimate the expected tax rate (T) and multiply EBT times $(1 - T)$ to get our estimate of net income. The following sections discuss the details of estimating earnings per share beginning with the operating profit margin.

ESTIMATING
AGGREGATE
OPERATING
PROFIT MARGIN

Finkel and Tuttle hypothesized that the following four variables affected the aggregate profit margin.[4]

1.   Capacity utilization rate
2.   Unit labor costs
3.   Rate of inflation
4.   Foreign competition

CAPACITY UTILIZATION RATE

One would expect a positive relationship between the capacity utilization rate and the profit margin because if production increases as a proportion of total capacity, there is a decrease in per-unit fixed production costs and fixed financial costs. The relationship may not be completely linear at very high rates of capacity utilization because operating diseconomies are introduced as firms are forced to employ marginal labor and/or use older plant and equipment to reach the higher capacity. The figures in Table 16.4 indicate that capacity utilization ranged from a peak of over 91 percent in 1966 to slightly above 70 percent during the recession of 1982.

UNIT LABOR COST

The change in unit labor costs is a compound effect of two individual factors: (1) changes in wages per hour and (2) changes in worker productivity. Wage costs per hour typically increase every year by varying amounts depending on the economic environment. As shown in Table 16.4, the annual percentage increase in wages varied from 3.3 percent to about 10.7 percent. If workers did not become more productive, this increase in per-hour wage costs would be the increase in per-unit labor cost. Fortunately, because of advances in technology and greater mechanization, the worker units of output per hour have increased over time—the laborer has become *more productive*. If wages per hour increase by 5 percent and labor productivity increases by 5 percent, there would be no increase in unit labor costs, because the workers would offset wage increases by producing more. Therefore, the increase in *per-unit labor cost* is a function of the percentage change in hourly wages minus the increase in productivity during the period. The actual relationship is typically not this exact due to measurement problems, but it is quite close as indicated by the figures in Table 16.4. During 1965 and 1983 productivity increased by about as much as the hourly compensation did, so there were very small changes in unit labor cost. In contrast, during 1974, wage rates increased by 9.9 percent, productivity *declined* by 2.0 percent because of the recession, and, therefore, unit labor costs increased by 12.1 percent. Because unit labor is the major variable cost of a firm, one would expect a *negative* relationship between the operating profit margin and percentage changes in unit labor cost.

---

[4] Sidney R. Finkel and Donald L. Tuttle, "Determinants of the Aggregate Profits Margin," *Journal of Finance* 26, no. 5 (December 1971): 1067–1075.

TABLE 16.4

Variables that Affect the Aggregate Profit Margin: Capacity Utilization Rate, Percentage Change in Compensation, Productivity, Unit Labor Cost, and Consumer Price Index; 1965–1992

Year	Utilization Rate (Mfg.)	Compensation/ Work Hours[a] Percentage Rate	Output Work Hours[b] Percentage Change	Unit Labor Cost[a] Percentage Change	Rate of Inflation[b]
1965	89.5	3.3	2.3	1.0	1.9
1966	91.1	6.0	2.1	3.8	3.5
1967	86.7	5.8	2.1	3.6	3.0
1968	87.0	7.9	2.9	4.9	4.7
1969	86.7	6.8	.0	6.9	6.1
1970	79.2	7.2	.9	6.2	5.5
1971	77.4	6.4	3.5	2.9	3.4
1972	82.8	6.4	2.7	3.7	3.4
1973	87.0	8.2	2.5	5.7	8.8
1974	82.6	9.9	−2.0	12.1	12.2
1975	72.3	9.9	2.3	7.5	7.0
1976	77.4	8.6	2.7	5.8	4.8
1977	81.4	8.0	1.4	6.5	6.8
1978	84.2	8.9	.7	8.1	9.0
1979	84.6	9.5	−1.4	11.1	13.3
1980	79.3	10.7	−.9	11.7	12.4
1981	78.2	9.6	.9	8.6	8.9
1982	70.3	7.5	.1	7.4	3.9
1983	73.9	3.9	2.4	1.5	3.8
1984	80.5	4.0	2.1	1.9	4.0
1985	80.1	4.2	.8	3.3	3.8
1986	79.7	4.9	1.9	2.9	1.1
1987	81.0	3.4	.8	2.6	4.4
1988	84.0	4.1	.9	3.2	4.4
1989	84.2	3.2	−1.0	4.3	4.6
1990	83.0	5.4	.0	5.4	6.1
1991	79.4	5.2	.5	4.6	3.1
1992[c]	78.7	3.3	2.9	0.4	3.0

[a]Private nonfarm business, 1977 = 100: Source: Department of Labor, Bureau of Labor Statistics.
[b]Percentage Change (December to December) Consumer Price Index, All Items (1982–1984 = 100).
[c]1992 figures are preliminary.
Source: Federal Reserve Board Series, "Total Manufacturing," contained in *Economic Report of the President, 1993* (Washington, D.C.: U.S. Government Printing Office, 1993).

RATE OF INFLATION

The precise effect of inflation on the aggregate profit margin is unresolved. Finkel and Tuttle hypothesized a positive relationship between inflation and the profit margin for several reasons. First, it was contended that a higher level of inflation increases the ability of firms to pass higher costs on to the consumer and thereby raise their profit margin. Second, assuming the classical demand-pull inflation, the increase in prices would indicate an increase in general economic activity, which is typically accompanied by higher margins. Finally, an increase in the rate of inflation might stimulate consumption as individuals attempt to shift their holdings from financial assets to real assets, which would contribute to an expansion.

In contrast, many observers doubt that most businesses can consistently increase prices in line with rising costs. Assume a 5 percent rate of inflation that impacts labor and material costs. The question is whether all firms can *completely* pass these cost increases along to their customers. If a firm increases prices at the same rate as cost increases, the result will be a *constant* profit margin, *not* an increase. Only if a firm can raise prices by *more than* cost increases can it increase its margin. Many firms are not able to raise prices in line with increased costs because of the elasticity of demand for their products.[5] Such an environment will cause the profit margin to decline. Given the three alternatives, it is contended that most firms will not be able to increase their profit margins or even hold them constant. Because many firms will experience lower profit margins during periods of inflation, it is expected that the aggregate profit margin will probably decline when there is an increase in the rate of inflation.

Given the contrasting expectations, one would need to consider the empirical evidence to determine how inflation has tended to affect the operating profit margin.

FOREIGN COMPETITION

Finkel and Tuttle contend that export markets are more competitive than domestic markets so export sales are made at a lower margin. This implies that lower exports by U.S. firms would increase profit margins. In contrast, Gray believed that only exports made by two independent firms should be considered, and they should be examined relative to total output exported.[6] Further, he felt that imports could have an important negative impact on the operating profit margin because they influence the selling price of all competing domestic products. This latter impact of imports has become a major factor since the early 1980s when the U.S. trade balance has become very negative. Therefore, the ultimate effect of foreign trade on the operating profit margin is likewise an empirical question.

The results of the empirical tests by Finkel and Tuttle can be summarized as follows:

- Utilization rate—positive and significant at 0.01 level
- Unit labor cost—negative and significant at 0.01 level
- Inflation—positive and significant at 0.05 level
- Trade surplus—negative and significant at 0.01 level

Analysis of the annual data for the period 1977 to 1991 confirmed that the relationship between the operating profit margin and the capacity utilization rate was always significant and positive, whereas the relationship between the unit labor cost and the operating profit margin was always negative and significant. Alternatively, the rate of inflation and foreign trade variables were never significant in the multiple regression. Finally, the simple correlation between the profit margin and inflation was consistently *negative.*

Therefore, when estimating the operating profit margin, you should concentrate on the capacity utilization rate for the economy and the rate of change in unit labor cost. As an example, consider what will happen at the two extremes of the business cycle.

[5] An extreme example of this inability is regulated industries that may not be able to raise prices at all until after lengthy hearings before regulatory agencies. Even then, the increase in rates may not match the cost increases.

[6] H. Peter Gray, "Determinants of the Aggregate Profit Margin: A Comment," *Journal of Finance* 31, no. 1 (March 1976): 163–165.

At the end of an economic recession, the capacity utilization rate will be very low. Therefore, during the early stages of an economic recovery, there will be a large increase in capacity utilization as firms increase production and sales. At the same time, workers will not be asking for very large wage increases and as production increases, there will be large increases in labor productivity. As a result, unit labor costs will increase very slowly (or could decline). Therefore, the overall impact of an increase in capacity utilization and a very small increase (or a decline) in unit labor cost should be a large increase in the operating profit margin.

At the peak of the business cycle firms will be operating at full capacity, so there will be very small increases or possibly declines in capacity utilization. Also, one would expect a higher rate of inflation, which will prompt demands for large wage increases during a time when you would expect small increases in labor productivity because firms are using marginal labor and production facilities. The effect will be large increases in unit labor cost. Therefore, the overall effect of very small increases or possibly decreases in capacity utilization and large increases in unit labor cost should be a major decline in the operating profit margin at the peak of a business cycle.

How do you use this information to estimate an operating profit margin? The most important estimate is *the direction of the change from current levels.* Assuming that you know the recent operating profit margin, your analysis is concerned with deciding whether the profit margin will increase, decrease, or stay about the same based on your expectation regarding capacity utilization and changes in unit labor cost. The size of the estimated change in the operating profit margin will depend on where the economy is in the business cycle and the direction and size of the expected changes in capacity utilization and unit labor cost.

After estimating the operating profit margin, you can calculate the dollar value of earnings per share before depreciation, interest, and taxes (EBDIT) by applying this operating profit margin estimate to the previously estimated sales per share figure. The next step is to estimate depreciation per share, which we will subtract from operating profits to get earnings before interest and taxes (EBIT). Table 16.3 contains data on the operating earnings components for the period since 1977, which is when S&P began providing this detailed breakdown of the earnings statement.

ESTIMATING DEPRECIATION EXPENSE

As shown in Figure 16.3 the depreciation expense per share series has not declined since 1977 (actually it has not declined since 1946). This is not too surprising, because depreciation expense is an estimate of the fixed cost expense related to the total fixed assets held by the S&P 400 industrial firms. Naturally, this fixed asset base increases over time. Therefore, the relevant question when estimating depreciation expense is *not* whether it will increase or decrease, but by *how much will it increase?*

You can use time series analysis, which involves using the recent trend as a guide to the future increase. Probably the biggest external factor that could influence the rate of growth of the depreciation expense series is recent capital expenditures. If capital expenditures have been above normal, you would expect subsequent depreciation expense to grow at an above average rate. Recently, the average percentage increase in depreciation expense has been in the range of 5 to 8 percent. Based on these several factors you would estimate what you expect for this year. After you have estimated the depreciation expense, you subtract it from the operating profit estimate to get an EBIT estimate.

FIGURE 16.3

Time Series Plot of S&P 400 Depreciation (Per share data, adjusted to stock price index level)

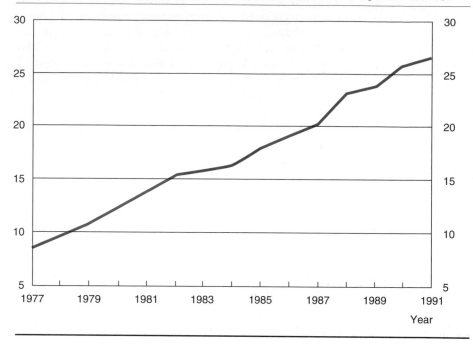

Year

ESTIMATING
INTEREST
EXPENSE

As shown in Table 16.3 interest expense for the companies in the S&P 400 series consistently increased in absolute value (except for 1983 and 1991) and also increased as a percentage of sales from 1.44 percent in 1977 to a peak of 3.47 percent in 1989. This growth in interest expense is consistent with prior discussions, which alluded to the overall increase in debt financing and financial risk assumed by U.S. firms during the past decade. This strong growth of interest expense was reversed after the 1989–1990 recession because of two factors: (1) corporations reduced their debt levels, and (2) interest rates declined. The estimate of interest expense should be based on an estimate of debt outstanding (will it grow and by how much?) and the level of interest rates (do you expect interest rates to rise or decline in the future?).

After you have estimated the interest expense figure, this value is subtracted from the EBIT per share value to estimate the earnings per share before tax (EBT) figure.

ESTIMATING THE
TAX RATE

This is the final step in estimating the earnings per share for the S&P 400 series. As shown in Table 16.3 and Figure 16.4, the average tax rate for the firms in the S&P 400 series during the late 1970s was in the 45 to 50 percent range, whereas during the 1980s it declined to a low point of almost 35 percent (in 1988) following the 1986 Tax Reform Act, then reversed and began to increase in 1989. Subsequently, we will speculate on what will happen in 1993 after the Clinton deficit reduction program takes effect.

Estimating the future tax rate is difficult, because it depends on political action. You must evaluate the current tax rate and recent tax legislation that affects business firms (e.g., tax credits). Once you have estimated the tax rate (T), you multiply one minus

FIGURE 16.4   **Time Series Plot of S&P 400 Tax Rate**

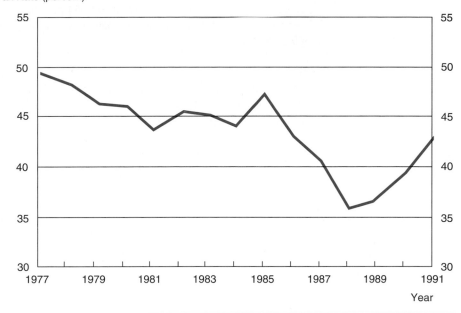

Tax Rate (percent)

this tax rate $(1 - T)$ times the EBT per-share figure to derive an estimate of the net income per share for the S&P 400 series.

At this point we have derived an estimate of sales per share for an aggregate stock-market series and discussed how one estimates an operating profit margin and several specific expense items in order to estimate earnings per share. In the next section we demonstrate this procedure by estimating earnings per share for 1993.

CALCULATING EARNINGS PER SHARE: AN EXAMPLE

The following is a demonstration of the procedure for estimating earnings per share for the year that emphasizes the procedure rather than the actual numbers. An analyst engaged in this exercise would take much longer and be involved in a very detailed analysis. In this example, we are estimating earnings per share for the S&P 400 during 1993 using 1992 data.

STEP 1

Nominal GNP for 1993 is based on an estimate for 1992 of approximately $5,951 billion. In 1992 the economy was in the second year of expansion following a recession that officially spanned the period 1989 to 1990 (1991 was a very weak expansion). In 1993 real GNP is expected to increase by about 2.5 percent and inflation will be approximately 3 percent. Therefore, nominal GNP in 1993 should increase by about 5.5 percent to $6,278 billion.

STEP 2

Corporate sales have had a strong relationship with nominal GNP as shown in Figure 16.2. During 1992, when nominal GNP increased by about 6.5 percent, S&P sales were expected to grow by about 7.74 percent to $654 per share. In 1993, with GNP rising 5.5 percent, this model would indicate that sales should increase by about 6.6 percent to $697 per share.

STEP 3

The operating profit margin increased to about 13.25 percent in 1992, compared to 12.26 percent in 1991. This increase was a function of a higher utilization rate (79.8 percent in 1992 compared to 79.4 percent during 1991), and a lower rate of increase in unit labor cost (4.2 percent in 1992 versus 5.0 percent during 1991). For 1993 the outlook is for a small increase in the operating profit margin because of an increase in the capacity utilization rate (to about 80.5 percent) and a relatively small increase in unit labor cost. Specifically, compensation per hour will likely experience a relatively small increase, but there will be limited gains in productivity during 1993 after the very large increase during 1992. Therefore, the outlook is for a 3 percent increase in unit labor cost. In summary, the outlook is for an increase in the operating profit margin from 13.25 percent in 1992 to 13.75 percent in 1993. Applying this operating profit margin to the sales per share figure ($697) indicates an operating profit (EBDIT) of $95.84 (.1375 × $697).

STEP 4

The depreciation expense during 1992 was approximately $28.50 per share. Although the utilization rate is increasing, the level of utilization is still fairly low (about 80 percent). Therefore, the expectation is for a small increase in capital expenditures of about 4 percent during 1993 and, therefore, an increase in depreciation expense of about 6 percent to $30.20 per share. Thus the estimated earnings before interest and taxes (EBIT) is $65.64 ($95.84 − $30.20).

STEP 5

The interest expense was approximately 2.9 percent of sales in 1992 and is expected to decline further during 1993. During 1992 firms employed more equity financing to reduce the high proportion of debt financing built up during the 1980s. Because of lower leverage *and* lower interest rates in late 1992 and early 1993, the interest expense as a percent of sales is expected to decline to 2.75 percent. Applying this to estimated sales of $697 per share implies interest expense of about $19.17.

When we subtract this interest expense from the EBIT estimate of $65.64, we have an EBT of $46.47.

STEP 6

The corporate tax rate during 1992 was expected to be slightly higher than during 1991. The rate is expected to increase further during 1993 to about 43 percent. Applying a 57 percent rate (1 − .43) to the NBT figure of $46.47 indicates that the net income per share for 1993 will be approximately $26.49. Therefore, the 1993 earnings per share estimate used in future discussions is $26.50 a share.

ESTIMATING
THE EARNINGS
MULTIPLIER
FOR A STOCK-
MARKET SERIES

Given our estimate of earnings per share, the next step is to estimate an earnings multiplier. A combination of the earnings per share estimate times the estimated earnings multiplier will provide an estimate of the future value for the stock-market series. This estimated value for the stock-market series and an estimate of the dividend during the year will be used to compute the expected rate of return for investors who own a portfolio of stocks during this holding period.

Our prior discussion related to Table 16.1 indicated that the earnings multiplier (i.e., P/E ratio) over time has been more volatile than the earnings per share series because the multiplier is very sensitive to changes in the spread between k and g. Earlier we discussed several instances where the changes in the earnings multiplier (P/E ratio) was the dominant factor in stock price changes. Because of the significance of the earnings multiplier, we will examine each of the variables in the P/E ratio equation to determine what determines the value for them and why they change. Given this understanding we can consider the whole P/E ratio equation and demonstrate how an investor would estimate a value for the earnings multiplier.

DETERMINANTS
OF THE EARNINGS
MULTIPLIER

We can recall the variables that influence the earnings multiplier or the P/E ratio by using the equation generated from the dividend discount model:

$$P/E = \frac{D_1/E_1}{k - g}$$

where:

D_1 = dividends expected in period 1, which is equal to $D_0 (1 + g)$
E_1 = earnings expected in period 1
D_1/E_1 = the dividend-payout ratio expected in period 1
k = the required rate of return on the stock
g = the expected growth rate of dividends for the stock

Therefore, the major variables that would affect the earnings multiplier for common stocks in a country are

- The dividend-payout ratio.
- The required rate of return on common stock. Because we are estimating the earnings multiplier for common stocks in a particular country (e.g., the United States, Germany), this would be the required rate of return on the common stocks in the United States or Germany.
- The expected growth rate of dividends. It would be the expected growth rate of dividends for the stocks in the country being analyzed.

Because this equation is derived from the dividend discount model, it assumes constant growth for an infinite period. Also, the required rate of return is the long-term estimate. Therefore, the k and g projections are *long-term estimates*. Thus, although these variables can be impacted by near-term events, they should not experience major changes on a year-to-year basis.

It is easier to discuss the dividend-payout ratio after we have considered both k and g. Therefore, the order of discussion will be

- Estimating k, the required rate of return
- Estimating g, the growth rate of dividends
- Estimating D_1/E_1, the dividend-payout ratio

ESTIMATING THE REQUIRED RATE OF RETURN (k)

The multiplier equation indicates that the earnings multiplier is inversely related to the required rate of return; the higher an investor's required rate of return, the less he or she will pay for a future earnings stream. Our prior discussions indicated that the required rate of return (k) is determined by (1) the economy's risk-free rate (RFR); (2) the expected rate of inflation during the period of investment (I); and (3) the risk premium (RP) for the specific investment.

We combined the first two factors (the RFR and I) into a nominal risk-free rate that affects *all* investments. We saw that the major factor causing changes in the nominal RFR is changes in the expected rate of inflation. Specifically, if the expected rate of inflation changes, investors should increase their nominal required rate of return as follows:

$$\text{Nominal RFR} = (1 + \text{Real RFR})(1 + I) - 1.$$

As an example, if the real RFR were 3 percent, and you expected the rate of inflation during your period of investment to be 4 percent, your nominal required rate of return would be 7.12 percent $[(1.03)(1.04)] - 1$. A good proxy for the nominal RFR rate is the current promised yield to maturity of a government bond that has a maturity equal to your investment horizon. For example, if you had a short horizon, you could use the rate on Treasury bills, whereas you would use longer-term government bond rates if your horizon extended over several years.

The major factor causing differences in required return for alternative investments is the risk premium. A measure of the risk premium for common stocks was calculated by Ibbotson and Sinquefield. They estimated the risk premium on common stocks as the difference in annual rates of return from common stocks and Treasury bills.[7] The geometric mean of this risk premium for the period 1926 to 1991 was 6.7 percent; the arithmetic mean was 8.3 percent. The geometric mean is appropriate for long-run comparisons, whereas the arithmetic mean is what you would want to use if you were estimating the premium for a given year (e.g., the *expected* performance next year). Using this long-run historical estimate, an investor can determine the "normal" expected return by combining this historical risk premium with the nominal RFR. Suppose that the current yield on government T-bills is 6 percent. An investor who considered the current equity-market environment to be fairly typical would estimate that the current required return on common stock should be about 14 percent (6 percent nominal RFR plus an 8 percent common stock risk premium).

Once you have estimated the required rate of return for the current period, you must determine whether the expected rate of inflation or the risk premium on common stock

---

[7] Roger G. Ibbotson and Rex A. Sinquefield, *Stocks, Bonds, Bills, and Inflation: The Past and The Future* (Charlottesville, Va.: Financial Analysts Research Foundation, 1982).

will change during your investment horizon. We know that the fundamental factors that influence the risk premium are business risk (BR), financial risk (FR), liquidity risk (LR), exchange rate risk (ERR), and country risk (CR). These latter two risk components become important when investing in non-U.S. equity.

Alternatively, you can derive a market measure of risk, which is the covariance of an asset with the market portfolio of risky assets. Because a stock-market index is typically used as the market portfolio, the relevant measure of risk for the aggregate market is the variance of returns for stocks. Therefore, when there is a change in the variability of stock prices, one would expect a change in the risk premium on stocks. This assumes that the variability of returns for T-bills is reasonably constant. If you are measuring your risk premium for common stock relative to a longer-term government bond, this risk premium could change, either because common stocks experienced an increase or decrease in volatility or because long-term bonds experienced a change in volatility.[8]

To incorporate these factors into the estimate of k, the required return on common stocks can be expressed as

$$K_e = f(\text{RFR, I, BR, FR, LR, ERR, CR})$$

or

$$K_e = f(\text{RFR, I}, \sigma_m^2)$$

where:

k_e = **the required return on equity**

RFR = **the economy's risk-free rate of return**

   I = **the expected rate of inflation**

BR = **aggregate corporate business risk**

FR = **aggregate corporate financial risk**

LR = **aggregate stock-market liquidity risk**

ERR = **exchange rate risk**

CR = **country risk**

σ^2 = **market risk for common stock measured as the variance of returns**

ESTIMATING THE GROWTH RATE OF DIVIDENDS (g)

The earnings multiple that is applied to next year's earnings must take into account the expected growth rate (g) for common dividends.[9] There is a positive relationship between the earnings multiplier and the growth rate of earnings and dividends; the higher the expected growth rate is, the higher the multiple. When estimating g, you should

---

[8] Several authors have documented changes in stock price volatility over time. This includes Robert Officer, "The Variability of the Market Factor of the New York Stock Exchange," *Journal of Business* 46, no. 3 (July 1973); G. William Schwert, "Why Does Stock Price Volatility Change over Time?" *Journal of Finance* 45, no. 5 (December 1989); G. William Schwert, "Stock Market Volatility," *Financial Analysts Journal* 46, no. 3 (May-June 1990). A number of papers on stock market and bond market volatility is contained in Robert J. Schiller, *Market Volatility* (Cambridge, Mass: The MIT Press, 1989).

[9] You know that the g in the valuation model is the expected growth rate for dividends. In our discussion, we assume a relatively constant dividend-payout ratio (dividend/earnings), so the growth of dividends is dependent on the growth in earnings, and the growth rates are approximately equal.

consider the current expected rate of growth and estimate any *changes* in the growth rate. Such changes in expectations indicate a change in the relationship between k and g and will have a profound effect on the earnings multiplier.

As discussed in Chapters 10 and 11, a firm's growth rate is equal to (1) the proportion of earnings retained and reinvested by the firm, that is, its retention rate (b) times (2) the rate of return earned on investments (ROE). An increase in either or both of these variables causes an increase in the expected growth rate (g) and an increase in the earnings multiplier. Therefore, the growth rate can be stated as

$$g = f(b, \text{ROE})$$

where:

g = expected growth rate
b = the expected retention rate equal to $1 - \dfrac{D}{E}$
ROE = the expected return on equity investments

Therefore, to estimate the growth rate, you need to examine and estimate changes in the retention rate (b) and the return on equity (ROE). The plot in Figure 16.5 shows that the retention rate was relatively high (56 to 63 percent) during the 1970s, declined to the 50 percent range during the early 1980s, increased back to 60 percent in 1988

FIGURE 16.5   **Time Series Plot of S&P 400 Retention Rate**

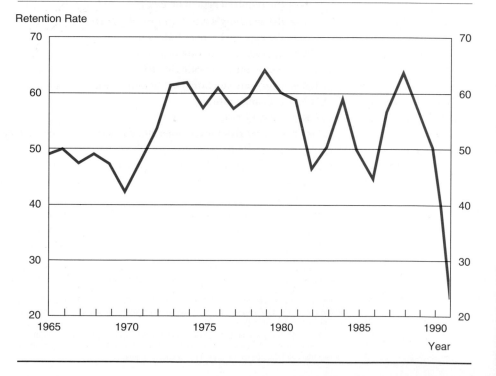

Retention Rate

prior to a significant decline in 1991 when earnings declined but many firms did not cut their dividends. Because the valuation model is a long-run model, you should estimate only relatively permanent changes, although short-run changes can affect expectations. Specifically, while you would acknowledge the decline in 1991, you would recognize that the long-run retention rate has been in the 45–60 percent range and estimate where it will be within this range.

The second variable is changes in the return on equity (ROE) defined as

$$ROE = \frac{Net\ Income}{Equity}$$

You will recall from the discussion in Chapter 10 that ROE can be broken down as follows:

$$\frac{Net\ Income}{Equity} = \frac{Sales}{Total\ Assets} \times \frac{Total\ Assets}{Equity} \times \frac{Net\ Income}{Sales}$$

$$= \frac{Total\ Asset}{Turnover} \times \frac{Financial}{Leverage} \times \frac{Net\ Profit}{Margin}$$

This equation shows that the ROE increases if either the equity turnover or the profit margin increases. In turn, you can increase the equity turnover by increasing either total asset turnover or financial leverage. Because the S&P 400 series includes historical information on total assets for only a few years, we cannot examine this three-component breakdown of ROE. As an alternative, we can examine available data for the Fortune 500. It is reasonable to use this alternative series for demonstration purposes because almost all the companies in the S&P 400 are in the Fortune 500 and the specific data are extremely similar.

As shown in Figure 16.6, the ROE for the Fortune 500 companies experienced very little change over the 35-year period prior to the decline in 1991. An analysis of the three components of ROE indicate what contributed to the overall change (or lack of change) over time. First, the profit margin (Figure 16.7) clearly experienced an overall decline during this period. The second component, total asset turnover (Figure 16.8) increased in the late 1970s, peaked in 1980 and 1981, but declined during the last several years and was much lower in 1991 than in 1956. Therefore, we know by process of elimination that the major variable that must have contributed to no significant change in ROE was the financial leverage ratio (Figure 16.9) that increased from 1.59 to 3.22 in 1991.

All of this shows a need for an investor to estimate the long-term outlook for ROE. In turn, this requires a long-term estimate for each of the three component ratios. Once you have this long-term estimate of ROE, you multiply it by your estimate of b, the retention rate, to calculate an estimate of g. As an example, if you estimate the long-run retention rate of firms will be 60 percent and their ROE at 12 percent, this means that you would expect the long-run growth rate of

$$
\begin{aligned}
g &= b \times ROE \\
&= .60 \times .12 \\
&= .072 = 7.2\%
\end{aligned}
$$

FIGURE 16.6

Fortune 500: Return on Equity and Return on Assets: 1956–1991

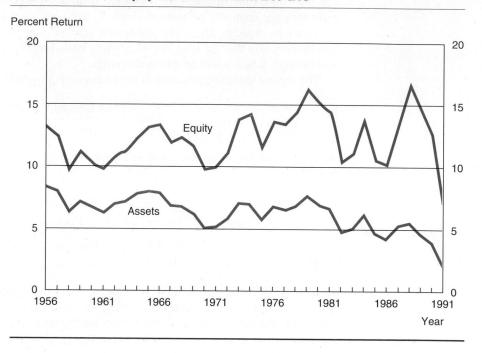

FIGURE 16.7

Fortune 500: Profit Margin: 1956–1991

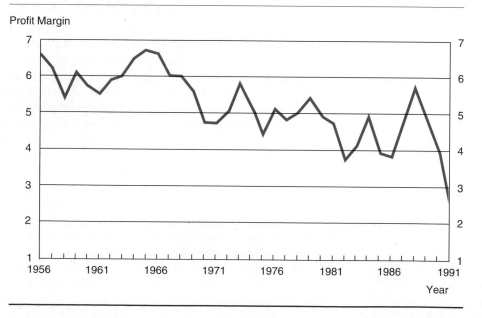

FIGURE 16.8   **Fortune 500: Asset Turnover: 1956–1991**

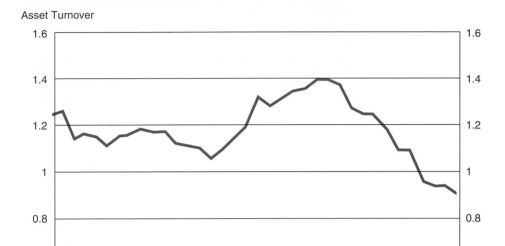

FIGURE 16.9   **Fortune 500: Assets/Equity: 1956–1991**

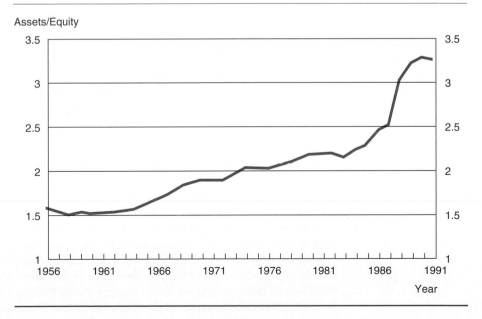

ESTIMATING THE DIVIDEND-PAYOUT RATIO (D_1/E_1)

Based on the P/E equation, there is a positive relationship between payout ratio and the P/E ratio. Therefore, if the k–g spread is constant and this dividend-payout ratio increases, there will be an increase in the earnings multiplier. At the same time, you should recognize that the dividend-payout ratio is equal to one minus the earnings retention rate (b). Therefore, if the dividend payout *increases,* there will be a *decline* in the earnings retention rate (b), which will cause a *decline* in the growth rate (g). Thus, there is a partial offset between changes in the dividend-payout rate and the expected growth rate (g).

In the discussion of the growth rate, we indicated that the retention rate was high in the 1970s, declined in the early 1980s, and increased again during the late 1980s. This implies that the payout ratio has declined recently (prior to 1990–1991).

ESTIMATING AN EARNINGS MULTIPLIER: AN EXAMPLE

There are two ways to estimate the earnings multiplier based on our discussion of the multiplier variables. The first approach begins with the current earnings multiplier and attempts to estimate the direction and amount of any change based on your expectations for changes in the three major components. We will call this approach the *direction of change approach.*

In the second approach, you estimate a specific value for the earnings multiplier by deriving specific estimates for each of the three components in the P/E ratio equation. When using this approach, most analysts derive several estimates based on alternative optimistic or pessimistic scenarios. We will call this the *specific estimate approach.*

THE DIRECTION OF CHANGE APPROACH

You begin with the current earnings multiplier and estimate the direction and extent of change for the dividend payout, and the variables that influence k and g. The direction of the change is more important than its size.

The variables that must be estimated are

1. Changes in the dividend-payout ratio
2. Changes in the real RFR ⎫
3. Changes in the rate of inflation ⎬ Changes in k
4. Changes in the risk premium for common stock ⎭
5. Changes in the earnings retention rate ⎫ Changes in g
6. Changes in the return on equity (ROE) ⎭

The dividend-payout ratio is expected to decline in the near term because the recent values (1991–1992) have been higher than the historical average because of the earnings slow down.

Given the three variables that affect the required rate of return on common stocks (k), there will probably be an increase in the real RFR due to an increase in the rate of real growth caused by higher productivity. The rate of inflation is expected to experience a small increase in 1993 relative to the very low rate in 1992. Finally, the risk premium is expected to experience a small decline for two reasons. First, we are in the middle of a business expansion wherein there is less uncertainty. Second, although there was an increase in stock price volatility during the late 1980s, it has declined in the early 1990s and is expected to remain fairly low. Therefore, given the offsetting trends in the components, overall one would expect no change or a small increase in k during 1993.

The last two factors in the earnings multiplier estimate relate to the growth rate. We expect a small decrease in the payout rate, which implies an increase in the retention rate. The outlook is for a small increase in the aggregate ROE during 1993, because it is a function of the profit margin, total asset turnover, and financial leverage. As noted, the profit margin in 1993 is expected to increase relative to the margin in 1992. Also, there should be a small increase in the total asset turnover at this time in the economic expansion. Finally, there should be a partially offsetting small decline in the financial leverage ratio during 1993 as firms continue to reduce the financial leverage taken on during the late 1980s. The result of a higher profit margin, an increase in asset turnover, and a decline in financial leverage should be a small increase in the ROE during 1993. Therefore, with an increase in the retention rate and a small increase in ROE you would estimate an increase in the expected growth rate.[10] In summary, we expect

- A decrease in the payout ratio
- No change in the required rate of return
- A small increase in the growth rate

Overall, this would imply a *small increase* in the earnings multiple. The earnings multiplier early in 1993 is about 17 times. This discussion would indicate that the multiplier could increase to about 19 times during 1993.

SPECIFIC ESTIMATE APPROACH

This approach derives specific estimates for the earnings multiplier based on a range of estimates for the three variables: dividend payout (D/E), required rate of return (k), and growth (g).

As indicated earlier, the retention rate has fluctuated between 45 and 60 percent during the past 10 years. Therefore, a reasonable dividend-payout ratio (D/E) would be 53 percent.

The required return (k) can be estimated using the interest rate on government bonds plus an estimate of the risk premium for common stocks. An appropriate risk premium could range from 3 percent to 8 percent, depending on the government security used to estimate a nominal risk-free rate. The 8 percent is based on the long-term arithmetic average risk premium as indicated by the Ibbotson-Sinquefield studies for the period 1926 to 1992 using T-bills as the risk-free investment. Notably, during the recent period (1975 to 1992), the risk premium has been in the range of 2.5 to 3.5 percent. In early 1993 the rate on T-bills was about 4 percent, the rate on 5-year government bonds was about 6 percent, and the rate on long-term bonds was 7 percent. Notably, these interest rates are the lowest in over a decade and most observers expect an increase by the end of the year. If there is an adjustment to reflect this, you could conceive of the following possibilities:

---

[10] This is the most reasonable scenario given the economic environment. At the same time, there have been changes in the value of common equity caused by asset write-offs and share repurchases. Both of these events can cause a significant decline in the equity account but have little impact on operating earnings. As a result there may be a higher ROE simply because of a lower equity value.

	Current	Expected at Year-End
A. T-bills	4.0%	6.0%
Historical risk premium	8.0	8.0
Estimated k	12.0%	14.0%
B. 5-year government bonds	6.0%	8.0%
Low risk premium	2.5	2.5
Estimated k	8.5%	10.5%
C. Long-term government bonds	7.0%	9.0%
Medium risk premium	4.0	4.0
Estimated k	11.0%	13.0%

Therefore, the required return (k) could be in the range of 10 to 14 percent.

The estimate of growth should be based on the current and expected return on equity (ROE) and the rate of retention. The graph in Figure 16.6 shows that the ROE for the Fortune 500 was in the 8 to 16 percent range during the period 1981 to 1991. Assuming that 1993 is the midpoint of an economic expansion that officially started in October 1991, a range of 10 to 13 percent for the ROE seems appropriate. As indicated earlier, the retention rate has been between 45 and 60 percent. Therefore, a conservative estimate of the growth rate would combine the 45 percent retention rate and an ROE of 10 percent: $.45 \times .10 = .045$. An optimistic growth rate estimate would combine the 60 percent retention rate and a 13 percent ROE: $.60 \times .13 = .078$. To summarize,

Dividend/earnings	= .400–.550
Government securities	.060–.095
Equity risk premium	.025–.080
Required return (k)	.100–.140
ROE	.100–.130
Sustainable growth	.045–.078

By combining the most optimistic figures we can derive a reasonably generous estimate, or by using the pessimistic estimates we can derive a very conservative estimate. The dividend-payout (D/E) figure should be consistent with the retention rate.

$$\text{High estimate: D/E} = .40$$
$$k = .10$$
$$g = .078 \ (.60 \times .13)$$
$$\text{P/E} = \frac{.40}{.10 - .078} = \frac{.40}{.022} = 18.18\times$$
$$\text{Low estimate: D/E} = .55$$
$$k = .14$$
$$g = .045$$
$$\text{P/E} = \frac{.55}{.14 - .045} = \frac{.55}{.095} = 5.79\times$$

Therefore, these data imply a range of earnings multipliers from about 6 times to 18 times with a midrange of about 12X. The high end of the range is consistent with the expectation of a P/E ratio of 19 derived from the direction of change approach.

CALCULATING AN ESTIMATE OF THE VALUE FOR THE MARKET SERIES

Previously, we estimated the earnings per share for the Standard & Poor's 400 of $26.50. Clearly, it would have been possible to derive additional earnings estimates.

In our work with the P/E we developed several estimates for the price-earnings multiple that varied from about 6 to 19. At this point we can combine these estimates of earnings per share and the earnings multiplier and calculate the following estimates of value for the Standard & Poor's 400 market series:

$$6.0 \times 26.50 = 159.00$$
$$12.0 \times 26.50 = 318.00$$
$$14.0 \times 26.50 = 371.00$$
$$18.0 \times 26.50 = 477.00$$
$$20.0 \times 26.50 = 530.00$$

This example is intended to help you understand the estimation procedure. The estimation of values for D/E, k, and g was fairly complex but it was not as extensive as the process used by professional analysts. In addition, we used a point estimate for earnings per share rather than a range of estimates (pessimistic, optimistic, most likely), which would have been preferable. Our discussion has provided the skeleton of the process that includes the theoretical background that forms the foundation for the fundamental analysis of stocks. It is important to understand *the relevant variables and how they relate to earnings per share and the earnings multiplier.*

CALCULATING THE EXPECTED RATE OF RETURN ON COMMON STOCKS

Having estimated the expected value for the stock-market series, we can estimate the expected rate of return that this ending value implies by using the following equation.

$$E(R_t) = \frac{EV - BV + Div}{BV}$$

where:

$E(R_t)$ = **the expected rate of return during period t. (We will assume a 1-year period.)**

EV = **the ending value for the stock-market series (We will use the several estimates of the ending value of the S&P 400 series derived in this section.)**

BV = **the beginning value for the stock-market series (You would typically use the current value for the stock-market series assuming that you would be investing at this time.)**

Div = **the expected dividend payment on the stock-market series during the investment horizon**

We will compute five rate of return estimates based on the five value estimates for the S&P 400 series. We will always assume the same beginning value for the S&P 400 that prevailed in early 1993 (510.00) and an estimate of the dividend per share during the next 12 months (14.00).[11] Therefore, the five estimates of expected rate of return are

$$1. \quad \frac{159.00 - 510.00 + 14.00}{510.00} = -66.1\%$$

$$2. \quad \frac{318.00 - 510.00 + 14.00}{510.00} = -34.9\%$$

$$3. \quad \frac{371.00 - 510.00 + 14.00}{510.00} = -24.5\%$$

$$4. \quad \frac{477.00 - 510.00 + 14.00}{510.00} = -3.7\%$$

$$5. \quad \frac{530.00 - 510.00 + 14.00}{510.00} = 6.7\%$$

As you would expect, there is a wide range of expected rates of return because of the range of ending values for the S&P 400. At this point, you either select the most reasonable estimate and use this value and the implied rate of return to make the investment decision, or you can assign probabilities to each of the estimates and derive an expected value estimate. In either case, you would compare this *expected* rate of return on common stocks to your *required* rate of return on common stocks. If we use the required k employed in calculating the earnings multiplier, we know that it is somewhere between 10 and 14 percent. Assuming that it is 12 percent, our investment decision would depend on whether the expected return calculated was equal to or greater than 12 percent as follows:

Estimate	Estimated Rate of Return	Required Rate of Return	Investment Decision
1	−66.3%	12%	Do not invest
2	−34.9	12	Do not invest
3	−24.5	12	Do not invest
4	−3.7	12	Do not invest
5	6.7	12	Do not invest

In this case, even the most optimistic estimate does not trigger an investment in the U.S. stock market at this time. Based on the discussion in Chapter 12, we know that this would not cause us to completely disinvest in the U.S. market but would prompt us to *underweight* this market relative to either U.S. bonds or stocks in other markets.

Because these specific market value estimates all generated returns below the required returns, one might want to compute the market value that would provide the desired return as follows:

$$\frac{x + 14.00}{510.00} = 1.12$$

$$x = 557.20.$$

---

[11] This is an approximate estimate based on the expected earnings of $26.50 and a payout ratio of 53 percent.

The question then becomes, is there any combination of reasonable earnings and P/E that would provide such a market value?

ANALYSIS OF WORLD MARKETS

Although we have worked with the U.S. market to demonstrate the procedure for analyzing a country's stock market, investors should perform a similar analysis for non-U.S. markets, especially the major world markets—Japan, Canada, United Kingdom, and Germany. We do not have the space to carry out a detailed analysis of each of these markets, but we can provide an example of the extensive analysis by a major investment firm. Specifically, Goldman, Sachs & Company provides a monthly publication entitled "World Investment Strategy Highlights" that contains a world portfolio strategy as well as a strategy for investors in several individual countries.[12]

Overall, it is a top-down approach in which Goldman, Sachs initially examines the components of a country's economy that relate to the valuation of securities (i.e., GDP, capital investments, industrial production, inflation, and interest rates). In Chapter 12 we discussed the fairly substantial difference in outlook for GDP/industrial production growth during 1993. Likewise, there are major differences in the outlook for inflation and interest rates, which leads to major differences in expectations for exchange rates during 1993.

Given this approach, Table 16.5 contains forecasts for world economic activity (GDP, industrial production) for seven major countries. These data provide insights regarding individual countries in two areas. First is the ability to recover from the recession that affected most countries in 1992. Goldman, Sachs expected most countries—except the United States, the United Kingdom, and Canada—to continue to experience an economic slowdown in 1993. Second, these industrial production data indicate real growth estimates, which varied in 1993 from −2.4 percent (Japan) to 4.6 percent (the United States).

Going from the economy to firm results, Table 16.6 contains comparative results for firms in numerous countries regarding earnings growth, cash flow growth, and dividend growth. The inclusion of cash flow growth is consistent with the increased emphasis on this series in credit analysis and also in equity valuation. Besides being consistent with valuation theory, the cash flow number is less amenable to manipulation by management. Again, the range in results is substantial. For example, expected cash flow growth in 1993 varies from 3.5 percent (Germany) to 33.0 percent (Sweden) and 147.2 percent (Finland).

Because of the importance of interest rates in the valuation process, Table 16.7 contains interest rate forecasts for seven countries that range from the short-term (1 to 3 months) to the long term (12 to 18 months). As one might expect, the range of current short-term rates was greater (3.1 percent to 12.0 percent) than the range of long-term rates (4.4 percent to 8.2 percent).

Putting the earnings growth estimate and interest rates together brings us to market valuation variables including P/E ratios and dividend yields. The prevailing values for various countries contained in Table 16.8 indicate a wide range between countries (e.g.,

[12] The author benefited from conversations with Jeffrey M. Weingarten and Sushil Wadhawani, portfolio strategists with Goldman, Sachs International in London.

TABLE 16.5

Forecasts for World Economic Activity (% per annum)

Country	1992	1993E	1994E
United States			
Consumer expenditure	2.2	2.7	—
Business fixed investment	2.9	5.3	—
GDP	2.0	2.8	—
Industrial production	2.0	4.6	—
Japan			
Consumer expenditure	1.9	2.1	2.6
Private cap. investment	−3.4	−4.9	1.0
Domestic demand	1.0	1.5	2.9
GDP	1.8	2.3	2.9
Industrial production	−6.0	−2.4	3.2
Germany			
Investment	1.2	−2.7	1.3
Domestic demand	1.0	−0.5	1.3
GDP	0.8	−0.5	1.5
Industrial production	−0.8	−1.6	1.5
United Kingdom			
Consumer expenditure	−0.2	1.6	2.0
Fixed investment	−0.8	−0.1	2.9
GDP	−0.6	1.6	3.1
Industrial production	−0.7	3.4	4.1
France			
Consumer expenditure	1.5	0.8	1.4
Fixed investment	−1.7	−2.3	0.9
GDP	1.8	0.0	1.3
Industrial production	−0.8	−1.1	0.5
Italy			
Consumer expenditure	1.9	0.2	0.9
Fixed investment	−0.8	−2.7	−1.5
GDP	1.1	−0.2	0.9
Industrial production	−0.9	−0.5	0.5
Canada			
Consumer expenditure	1.1	3.0	3.1
Fixed investment	0.8	6.7	6.8
GDP	1.4	3.0	3.5
Industrial production	0.9	3.7	3.8

Source: "World Investment Strategy Highlights" (London: Goldman, Sachs International, Ltd., March 1993). Reprinted by permission of Goldman Sachs.

a P/E of 10 in Spain versus 47.5 in Japan. It also provides historical perspective within countries by showing how the current valuation variables compare to historical averages for the particular country (e.g., the current P/E in the United States of 17.4 is about 103 percent of the long-run average of about 16.9 times).

TABLE 16.6   **Comparative Stock-Market Statistics**

	United States	Japan	United Kingdom	Germany	France	Italy	Switzerland	Spain	Sweden	Norway	Finland
Earnings Growth											
1992E	12.9	−35.0	2.0	−9.0	−9.0	−19.5	9.8	2.2	−31.1	−51.0	−41.9
1993F	16.0	5.0	14.0	−10.0	11.2	−5.7	14.0	7.8	78.9	65.7	−147.6
1994F			16.0	10.0	5.0	12.0	15.0	5.4	57.5	30.7	99.5
Cash Flow Growth											
1992E	8.7			4.4		−1.9		2.5	−15.9	−14.5	221.4
1993F	12.2			3.5		5.0		7.4	33.0	17.1	147.2
1994F									29.8	8.3	21.7
Dividend Growth											
1992E	1.4	1.5	0.0	2.5	5.0	−29.6	8.1	5.2	−0.6	17.2	5.5
1993F	7.6	0.5	2.0	−8.0	3.0	−4.0	10.9	5.4	11.9	14.3	27.2
1994F			4.0	3.0	3.0	5.0	10.0	5.0	12.2	14.6	17.9

Aggregates and multiples for earnings, cash flow, book value, and dividend are based on an industrial sample of companies in each country.

E = estimate; F = forecast.

Note: Figures for the United States refer to the S&P Industrials Index and pertain to operating earnings.

Source: "World Investment Strategy Highlights" (London: Goldman, Sachs International Ltd., March 1993). Reprinted by permission of Goldman Sachs.

INDIVIDUAL COUNTRY ANALYSIS

Following the summary of market statistics for the major equity markets, Goldman, Sachs provides a detailed analysis of each of the major countries. This begins with a discussion of the country's economy as part of an analysis of the country's equity market. Table 16.9 contains estimates of the major economic indicators for Germany. These projections reflect a stagnant economy due to the problems involved in reuniting the country. Currently, government authorities are concerned about the slow growth and future competitiveness of German firms in the European community.

Following the discussion of the economy and the projections, there is an analysis of the country's equity market. A summary for Germany is set forth in Table 16.10. Goldman, Sachs feels that the overall investment outlook for Germany is very modest because of the earnings outlook that appears to be deteriorating. Therefore, they recommend underweighting German equities in a global portfolio.

SUMMARY

We have consistently emphasized the importance of analyzing the economies and security markets before analyzing alternative industries or companies. You should determine whether the economic and market outlook indicates an underweighting or overweighting related to investing in stocks, bonds, or cash before you consider which is the best industry or company.

There are two techniques available to help you make the market decision. The first are macro techniques, which are based on the strong relationship between the economy and security markets. These models base their market projections on their outlook for

TABLE 16.7   **Interest Rate Forecasts (% per annum)**

Country	Current Rate[a]	Short Term (1–3 months)	Medium Term (3–6 months)	Long Term (12–18 months)
United States				
90-D Comm Paper	3.1	3.1	3.0	3.5
6⅜% 2002	6.5	6.5	6.5	6.0
Germany				
3M Euro Rate	8.4	8.0	7.5	6.7
7⅛% 2002	7.1	7.0	6.9	7.3
Japan				
3 Month CDs	3.5	3.5	3.4	3.7
No. 145, 5.5%	4.4	4.2	4.5	5.4
France				
3M LIBOR	12.0	10.5	7.0	6.0
8½% 2003	8.0	7.7	7.3	7.2
United Kingdom				
3M LIBOR	6.3	5.5	5.0	4.5
8% 2003	8.2	8.2	8.7	8.4
Canada				
3M T-Bill	6.7	6.5	6.0	5.8
7¼% 2003	8.0	8.0	7.5	7.1
Netherlands				
3M Euro Rate	8.1	8.0	7.5	6.7
8¼% 2002	7.2	7.1	7.0	7.4

[a]28 January 1993.

Source: "World Investment Strategy Highlights" (London: Goldman, Sachs International Ltd., March 1993). Reprinted by permission of Goldman Sachs.

TABLE 16.8   **World Market Valuation Matrix**

	United States	Japan	United Kingdom	Germany	France	Italy	Switzerland	Spain	Sweden	Norway	Finland
Current											
P/E	17.4	47.5	17.7	16.1	11.9	20.0	15.1	10.0	33.1	25.8	NM
Div. Yield	3.0	1.1	4.3	2.4	3.9	3.2	2.2	5.5	3.3	1.8	1.8
Relative											
P/E	103	99	159	129	105	131	97	94	318	226	—
Yield Rel	91	66	84	80	86	114	79	90	113	62	—

Based on Datastream market indices.

U.S. figures refer to S&P Composite Index and pertain to operating earnings. U.K. figures refer to FT-500 Index.

Source: "World Investment Strategy Highlights" (London: Goldman, Sachs International Ltd., March 1993). Reprinted by permission of Goldman Sachs.

TABLE 16.9   **Major German Economic Variables**

	Current Value	Historical Average	Direction of Impact on Stock Return
GNP Growth			
1991	1.5	2.3	−
1992	−0.1	—	−
1993	1.5	—	−
Real Earnings Growth (Industrials)			
1991	−13.0	3.4	−
1992	−13.5	—	−
1993	7.1	—	+
Real Dividend Growth (Industrials)			
1991	−11.0	2.0	−
1992	−11.5	—	−
1993	0.1	—	−
Inflation (Consumer Price Index) (%)			
1991	4.0	3.4	−
1992	3.5	—	−
1993	2.9	—	+

Interest Rate Outlook	Current Rate	1–3 Month	3–6 Months	12–18 Months
3 Month Euro	8.4	8.0	7.5	6.7
7⅛% 2002	7.1	7.0	6.9	7.3

Source: "World Investment Strategy Highlights" (London: Goldman, Sachs International Ltd., March 1993). Reprinted by permission of Goldman Sachs.

the aggregate economy and certain components. The second are micro techniques, which estimate future market values by applying basic valuation models to equity markets. In Chapter 12 we examined the macro techniques and discussed a world asset allocation. This chapter has been devoted to the microanalysis of equity markets in the United States and other countries.

We applied the dividend discount model discussed in Chapter 11 to a stock-market series (the S&P 400) that reflects the U.S. equity market. We estimated earnings per share for this series and generated a set of estimates for the earnings multiplier. Given these two components, we computed an estimate of the future value for the market and used that estimate to derive an expected return for common stocks during the period. It is important to recognize that the procedure generates only a best estimate: it is appropriate to make several estimates that reflect various possible conditions.

This micro technique is best summarized by listing its steps:

I. Estimate expected earnings.
   A. Estimate nominal GNP (or GDP) for the year.
   B. Estimate corporate sales based on the relationship of sales to GNP.

TABLE 16.10   **Stock Indexes for the German Equity Market and Expected Rates of Return**

	Current Price	Performance (% Change)			52-Week Range		Relative to World		
		Last Month	**YTD**	**12 Month**	**High**	**Low**	**Last Month**	**YTD**	**12 Month**
FT Composite (U.S. Dollar)	109.3	4.3	5.1	−8.3	129.7	101.6	4.5	4.6	−3.6
FT Composite (local currency)	89.6	2.4	2.3	−9.4	104.5	81.3	3.2	2.6	−6.8
FT Industrials (local currency)	85.2	3.3	2.8	−12.4	104.0	77.7	4.6	3.6	−9.4
FAZ General	616.3	3.0	2.2	−9.0	725.3	565.6	3.8	2.5	−6.4
DAX	1576.2	3.2	2.0	−5.3	1811.6	1420.3	4.0	2.3	−2.7

Expected Returns (%)

	1 Month	3 Months	12 Months
Equities	3.0	3.0	9.0
Bonds	1.3	2.8	6.6
Cash	0.7	2.1	7.4

Source: "World Investment Strategy Highlights" (London: Goldman, Sachs International Ltd., March 1993). Reprinted by permission of Goldman Sachs.

    C. Estimate the aggregate operating profit margin (NBDIT/sales) based on an analysis of:
       1. Capacity utilization rate
       2. Unit labor cost
          a. Wage/hour increases
          b. Productivity changes
       3. Inflation
       4. Foreign competition
    D. Estimate net profits (earnings per share).
       1. Compute operating profits (operating profit margin times sales).
       2. Subtract estimated depreciation expense.
       3. Subtract estimated interest expense.
       4. Estimate the tax rate (T).
       5. Multiply earnings before taxes (EBT) by $(1 - T)$.
  II. Estimate the expected earnings multiplier.
    A. Estimate changes in the required rate of return (k).
       1. Changes in the risk-free rate (ΔRFR)
       2. Changes in the expected rate of inflation (ΔI)
       3. Changes in the risk premium (ΔRP).
          a. Changes in business risk
          b. Changes in financial risk
          c. Changes in liquidity risk
          d. Changes in exchange rate risk (non-U.S. equity)
          e. Changes in country risk (non-U.S. equity)
            or
          f. Changes in the volatility of the equity market

B. Estimate changes in the expected growth rate of dividends (earnings) (g).
  1. Changes in the aggregate earnings retention rate
  2. Changes in the return on equity (ROE)
    a. Changes in profit margin
    b. Changes in total asset turnover
    c. Changes in financial leverage
C. Estimate changes in the spread between k and g.

III. Estimate the future value of a stock-market series.
  A. Estimated earnings per share times the estimated earnings multiplier.

Finally, although we applied this two-step estimation procedure to the stock market in the United States, we know it is necessary to do a similar analysis for non-U.S. markets. An example of such an analysis by Goldman, Sachs showed how it applied the top-down approach to several major countries.

Following this aggregate market analysis, the next step is industry analysis, which is considered in the following chapter.

QUESTIONS

1. An investor believes that the stock market will experience a substantial increase next year because corporate earnings are expected to rise by at least 12 percent. Do you agree or disagree? Why or why not?

2. In the library find at least three sources of historical information on nominal and real GNP. Attempt to find two sources that provide an estimate of nominal GNP for the coming year or the previous year.

3. To arrive at an estimate of the *net profit margin,* why would you spend time estimating the operating profit margin and working down?

4. You are convinced that capacity utilization next year will decline from 82 percent to about 79 percent. Explain what effect this change will have on the operating profit margin.

5. You see an estimate that hourly wage rates will increase by 6 percent next year. How does this affect your estimate of the operating profit margin? What other information do you need in order to use this estimate of a wage rate increase and why do you need it?

6. You see an estimate that next year hourly wage rates will increase by 7 percent and productivity will increase by 5 percent. What would you expect to happen to unit labor cost? Discuss how this unit labor cost estimate would influence your estimate of the operating profit margin.

7. Assume that each of the following changes are independent (i.e., except for this change, all other factors remain unchanged). In each case, indicate *what* will happen to the earnings multiplier and *why.*
    a. The return on equity increases.
    b. The aggregate debt/equity ratio declines.
    c. Overall productivity of capital increases.
    d. The dividend-payout ratio declines.

8. Based on the economic projections contained in Table 16.7 would you expect the stock prices for the various countries to be highly correlated? Explain and justify your answer with specific examples.

9. You are informed that a well-respected investment firm expects that next year's returns for the U.S. equity market will be 11 percent, and domestic returns in the Germany stock market will be 14 percent. Assume that all risks except exchange rate risk are equal and

you expect the DM/dollar exchange rate to go from 1.70 to 1.45 during the year. Given this information, discuss where you would invest (United States or Germany) and why. What if you expected the exchange rate to go from 1.70 to 2.10?

10. Find a source of the following economic data for the United Kingdom, Germany, and Japan:
    a. Gross domestic product (GDP)
    b. Industrial production
    c. Personal consumption expenditures
    d. Inflation

PROBLEMS

1. Prepare a table for the last 10 years showing the percentage of change each year in (a) the Consumer Price Index (all items), (b) nominal GNP, (c) real GNP (in constant dollars), and (d) the GNP deflator. Discuss what proportion of nominal growth was due to real growth and what part was due to inflation. Is the outlook for the coming year any different from the performance during last year? Discuss.

2. You are told that nominal GNP will increase by about 10 percent next year. Using Figure 16.1 and the regression equation, what increase would you expect in corporate sales? How would this estimate change if you gave more weight to the recent observations?

3. Currently, the dividend-payout ratio (D/E) for the aggregate market is 60 percent, the required return (k) is 13 percent, and the expected growth rate for dividends (g) is 7 percent.
    a. Compute the current earnings multiplier.
    b. You expect the D/E ratio to decline to 50 percent, but you assume there will be no other changes. What will be the P/E?
    c. Starting with the initial conditions, you expect the dividend-payout ratio to be constant, the rate of inflation to increase by 3 percent, and the growth rate to increase by 2 percent. Compute the expected P/E.
    d. Starting with the initial conditions, you expect the dividend-payout ratio to be constant, the rate of inflation to decline by 3 percent, and the growth rate to decline by 1 percent. Compute the expected P/E.

4. *CFA Examination III (1985)*
   A U.S. pension plan hired two offshore firms to manage the non-U.S. equity portion of its total portfolio. Each firm was free to own stocks in any country market included in Capital International's Europe, Australia, and Far East Index (EAFE) and free to use any form of dollar and/or nondollar cash or bonds as an equity substitute or reserve. After 3 years had elapsed, the records of the managers and the EAFE Index were as shown below:

Summary: Contributions to Return

	Currency	Country Selection	Stock Selection	Cash/ Bond Allocation	Total Return Recorded
Manager A	(9.0%)	19.7%	3.1%	0.6%	14.4%
Manager B	(7.4)	14.2	6.0	2.8	15.6
Composite of A&B	(8.2)	16.9	4.5	1.7	15.0
EAFE Index	(12.9)	19.9	—	—	7.0

You are a member of the plan sponsor's pension committee, which will soon meet with the plan's consultant to review manager performance. In preparation for this meeting, you go through the following analysis:

    a. Briefly describe the strengths and weaknesses of each manager, relative to the EAFE Index data. (5 minutes)

    b. Briefly explain the meaning of the data in the "Currency" column. (5 minutes)

5. As an analyst for Middle, Diddle, and O'Leary, you are forecasting the market P/E ratio using the dividend discount model. Because the economy has been expanding for 4 years, you expect the dividend-payout ratio will be at its high of 60 percent and that long-term government bond rates will rise to 8 percent. Because investors are becoming less risk-averse, the equity risk premium will decline to 5 percent. As a result, investors will require a 13 percent return, and the return on equity will be 11 percent.

    a. What is the expected growth rate?

    b. What is your expectation of the market P/E ratio?

    c. What will be the value for the market index if the expectation is for earnings per share of $34.00?

    d. What will be your rate of return if you acquired the index at a value of 500, you sold the index at the value computed in (c), and dividends during the year were $15.00?

6. A table of World Stock Market Indexes are published weekly in *Barron's* in the section labeled "Market Laboratory/Stocks." Based on the analysis of two issues of this publication (the latest edition available and an issue 1 year earlier) in your college library:

    a. Calculate the percentage price change for each index in the table.

    b. Show the closing position of each index on each date relative to the yearly high for each year.

    c. Identify the countries whose markets are in a downtrend.

    d. Calculate the percentage range for the last 12 months (High − Low/High + Low/ 2). Which markets seem the most volatile?

    e. Based on the percentage price change during the year and the percentage range, indicate the three indexes that had the best performance and the two with the poorest performance.

REFERENCES

Copeland, Basil L., Jr. "Inflation, Interest Rates and Equity Risk Premia." *Financial Analysts Journal* 38, no. 3 (May-June 1982).

Fama, Eugene F., and Kenneth French. "Business Conditions and Expected Returns on Stocks and Bonds." *Journal of Financial Economics* 25, no. 1 (November 1989).

Gray, William S. III. "The Anatomy of a Stock Market Forecast." *Journal of Portfolio Management* 16, no. 1 (Fall 1989).

Reilly, Frank K., Frank T. Griggs, and Wenchi Wong. "Determinants of the Aggregate Stock Market Earnings Multiple." *Journal of Portfolio Management* 10, no. 1 (Fall 1983).

Shiller, Robert J., and John Campbell. "Stock Prices, Earnings, and Expected Dividends." *Journal of Finance* 43, no. 3 (July 1988).

Siegel, Jeremy J. "Does It Pay Stock Investors to Forecast the Business Cycle?" *The Journal of Portfolio Management* 18, no. 1 (Fall 1991).

Vandell, Robert F., and George W. Keuter. *A History of Risk-Premia Estimates for Equities: 1944–1978.* Charlottesville, Va.: The Financial Analysts Research Foundation, 1989.

CHAPTER 17

INDUSTRY ANALYSIS

In this chapter we will answer the following questions:

- Is there a difference between the returns for alternative industries during specific time periods and what is the implication of these results?
- Is there consistency in the returns for industries over time and what do these results imply regarding industry analysis?
- Is the performance for firms within an industry consistent and what is the implication of these results for industry analysis?
- Is there a difference in risk among industries and what are the implications of these results for industry analysis?
- What happens to risk for individual industries over time and what does this imply for industry analysis?
- What are the steps involved in estimating earnings per share for an industry?
- What is the industrial life cycle and its stages and how does the life cycle stage affect the sales estimate for an industry?
- How does the estimating procedure for the operating profit margin differ for the aggregate market versus an industry?
- What are the two alternative procedures for estimating an industry earnings multiplier?
- What is involved in a macroanalysis of an industry earnings multiplier?
- What are the steps involved in doing a microanalysis of an industry earnings multiplier?
- When you do a microanalysis of an industry earnings multiplier, how do you determine if the industry's multiplier is relatively high or low?
- What are the five basic competitive forces that determine the intensity of competition in an industry and, thus, its rate of return on capital?
- What are some of the unique factors that must be considered in global industry analysis?

When asked about his or her job, a securities analyst will typically reply that he or she is an oil analyst, a retail analyst, or a computer analyst. A widely read trade publication, *The Institutional Investor* selects an All-American analyst team each year based on industry groups. Investment managers talk about being in or out of the metals, the autos, or the utilities. This constant reference to industry groups is because most professional investors are extremely conscious of differences among alternative industries and organize their analyses and portfolio decisions according to industry groups.

We share this appreciation of the importance of industry analysis as a component of the three-step fundamental analysis procedure initiated in Chapter 12. Industry analysis is the second step as we progress toward selecting specific firms and stocks for our investment portfolio. As the first step, in Chapter 12 we discussed the macro-analysis of the stock market to decide whether the expected rate of return from investing in common stocks was equal to or greater than our required rate of return. Based on this comparison, we would decide to be overweighted, market-weighted, or under-weighted in stocks. We also discussed the microanalysis of the market in Chapter 16 to support the macroanalysis. Following this economic/market decision, we take the second step in this chapter when we analyze different industries to make a similar industry decision. The decision criteria is the same: is the expected rate of return for an industry equal to or greater than our required rate of return for this industry? Based on this relationship we decide how to weight the industry in our stock portfolio. We will take the final step in Chapter 18 when we analyze the individual companies and stocks within the alternative industries.

In the first section we discuss the results of several studies that will help us identify the benefits and uses of industry analysis. Following that, we present a technique for analyzing industries that resembles the process employed in Chapter 16 for analyzing the aggregate stock market. Specifically, we discuss how to estimate earnings per share and an earnings multiplier for an industry, then we combine these two factors to estimate the industry's expected value and its expected rate of return. Another section raises questions that are unique to industry analysis: what is the impact of the competitive environment within an industry and the effect of the intensity of competition on potential industry returns? We conclude the chapter with a demonstration of global industry analysis that recognizes that many industries transcend U.S. borders and compete on a worldwide basis.

WHY DO INDUSTRY ANALYSIS?

Investment practitioners perform industry analysis because they feel it helps them isolate profitable investment opportunities. We likewise have recommended it as part of our three-step, top-down plan for valuing individual companies and selecting stocks for inclusion in our portfolio. What exactly do we learn from an industry analysis? Can we spot trends in industries that make them good investments? Studies of these questions have indicated unique patterns in the rates of return and risk measures over time in different industries. In this section we survey the results of studies that addressed these questions.

In the research we describe, investigators asked a set of questions designed to pinpoint the benefits and limitations of industry analysis. In particular, they wanted answers to the following set of questions:

- Is there a difference between the returns for alternative industries during specific time periods?
- Will an industry that performs well in one period continue to perform well in the future? That is, can we use past relationships between the market and an industry to predict future trends for the industry?
- Is the performance of firms within an industry consistent over time?

Several studies also considered questions related to risk:

- Is there a difference in the risk for alternative industries?
- Does the risk for individual industries vary or remain relatively constant over time?

We consider the results of these studies and come to some general conclusions about the value of industry analysis. This assessment helps us interpret the results of our industry valuation in the next section.

CROSS-SECTIONAL INDUSTRY PERFORMANCE

To find out if the rates of return among different industries varied during a given time period (e.g., 1995), researchers examined the performance of alternative industries during a specific time period and compared them. Completely consistent performance during specific time periods for different industries would indicate that industry analysis is not necessary. As an example, assume that during 1995 the aggregate stock market experienced a rate of return of 10 percent and the returns for *all* industries were bunched between 9 and 11 percent. If this was the result and it persisted for future periods, you might question whether it was worthwhile to conduct an industry analysis to find an industry that would return 11 percent when random selection would provide about 10 percent (the average return).

Studies of the annual industry performance have found that different industries have consistently shown wide dispersion in their rates of return (e.g., a typical range will be from minus 30 percent to plus 50 percent). These results imply that *industry analysis is important and necessary* to uncover performance differences that will help identify both unprofitable and profitable opportunities.[1]

INDUSTRY PERFORMANCE OVER TIME

In another group of investigations, researchers tried to determine whether industries that perform well in one time period would continue to perform well in subsequent time periods or at least outperform the aggregate market in the later time period. In this case, investigators found *almost no association* in industry performance year to year or over sequential rising or falling markets.

These studies imply that past performance alone does not help you project future industry performance. The results do *not,* however, negate the usefulness of industry analysis. They simply confirm that investors must project future industry performance on the basis of future estimates of the relevant variables.

PERFORMANCE OF THE COMPANIES WITHIN AN INDUSTRY

Other studies were designed to determine whether there is consistency in the performance of companies *within* an industry. If all the firms within an industry performed consistently during a specified time period, investors would not need company analysis. In such a case, industry analysis alone would be enough because once you selected a profitable industry, you would know that all the stocks in that industry would do well.

These studies have typically found *wide dispersion* in the performance among companies in most industries. An alternative way to measure this same impact is to examine the industry influence on the returns for individual stocks. Studies that have done such

---

[1] Various financial services provide graphs of *annual* rates of return for alternative industries. These graphical results indicate the substantial variance between industries.

an analysis have showed evidence of an industry effect in specific industries such as oil or autos, but most stocks showed small industry effects, and the industry impact has been declining over time.[2]

IMPLICATIONS OF DISPERSION WITHIN INDUSTRIES

Citing studies such as these, some theorists have contended that industry analysis is useless because all firms in an industry do not move together. Obviously, consistent firm performance in an industry would be ideal, because then you would not need to do company analysis. For industries that have a strong, consistent industry influence such as oil, gold, steel, autos, and railroads, you can reduce the extent of your company analysis after your industry analysis.

The fact is, most analysts do not expect such a strong industry influence, which means that a thorough *company* analysis is still necessary. Even for industries that do not have a strong industry influence, industry analysis is valuable, because it is much easier to select a superior company from a good industry than to find a good company in an unhealthy industry. By selecting the best stocks within an industry with good expectations, you avoid the risk that your analysis and selection of a good company will be offset by poor industry performance.

DIFFERENCES IN
INDUSTRY RISK

Although a number of studies have focused on industry rates of return, few studies have examined industry risk measures. A study by Reilly and Drzycimski investigated two questions: (1) Did risk differ among industries during a given time period? (2) Were industry risk measures stable over time?[3] The study found *a wide range of risk* among different industries and the spreads between risk levels typically widened during rising and falling markets. On a positive note, an analysis of the risk measures over time indicated that they were *reasonably stable over time.*

We can interpret these findings as follows: although risk measures for different industries showed substantial dispersion during a period of time, individual industries' risk measures are stable over time. This means that the analysis of past industry risk is necessary, but this historical analysis can aid your attempt to estimate the future risk for an industry.

SUMMARY OF
RESEARCH ON
INDUSTRY
ANALYSIS

Earlier we noted that several studies have sought answers to questions dealing with industry analysis. The conclusions of the studies are:

- During any time period, returns vary within a wide range, which means that industry analysis can be useful in the process of targeting investments.
- The rates of return for individual industries vary over time, so we cannot simply extrapolate past industry performance into the future.
- The rates of return of firms within industries also vary, so company analysis is a necessary follow-up to industry analysis.

---

[2]For example, see Stephen L. Meyers, "A Re-Examination of Market and Industry Factors in Stock Price Behavior," *Journal of Finance* 28, no. 3 (June 1973): 695–705; and Miles Livingston, "Industry Movements of Common Stocks," *Journal of Finance* 32, no. 2 (June 1977): 861–874.

[3]Frank K. Reilly and Eugene Drzycimski, "Alternative Industry Performance and Risk," *Journal of Financial and Quantitative Analysis* 9, no. 3 (June 1974): 423–446.

- During any time period, different industries' risk levels vary within wide ranges, so we must examine and estimate the risk factors for alternative industries, as well as returns.
- Risk measures for different industries remain fairly constant over time, so the historical risk analysis can be useful when estimating future risk.

The results imply that industry analysis is necessary, both to avoid losses and to find better industries and, subsequently, individual stocks that provide superior risk–return opportunities for investors.

ESTIMATING INDUSTRY RATES OF RETURN

Having determined that industry analysis helps an investor select profitable investment opportunities, how do we go about valuing an industry and estimating the expected rate of return that an investment in it will provide? The procedure for estimating the expected value of an industry is a two-step process similar to the microanalysis of the stock market. First, you estimate the expected earnings per share for the industry and then you estimate the expected industry P/E ratio (earnings multiplier). As before, multiplying the expected earnings per share by the expected earnings multiplier gives the expected ending value for the industry index.

We compute an expected rate of return for the industry by comparing the ending value plus its expected dividend to its beginning value. Comparing this expected rate of return to your required rate of return for this industry allows you to apply the investment decision rule. You would overweight your investment in this industry if the expected rate of return was equal to or greater than your required rate of return.

To demonstrate industry analysis, we will use Standard & Poor's Retail Store-Drug (RSD) index to represent industrywide data and this industry. This retail store-drug index contains three companies as follows: (1) Longs Drug Stores, (2) Rite Aid, and (3) Walgreen Company. This industry was selected because it should be reasonably familiar to most observers, and because it is consistent and useful for the subsequent company analysis that uses Walgreen's as the example company.

ESTIMATING EARNINGS PER SHARE

To estimate earnings per share, you must start by estimating sales per share. The first part of this section describes three techniques that will provide help and insights for the sales estimate. Next we derive an estimate of earnings per share, which implies a net profit margin for the industry. As in Chapter 16 where we estimate earnings per share for a stock market series, we begin with the operating profit margin because it is less volatile and easier to estimate than the net profit margin. Then we subtract estimates of depreciation and interest expenses and apply a tax rate to find the earnings per share.

FORECASTING SALES PER SHARE

Three techniques can be used to derive a sales forecast for an industry:

1. Industrial life cycle
2. Input–Output analysis
3. Industry–aggregate economy relationship

Notably, these techniques are *not* competing alternatives, but complementary and supplementary. All of them together will help you develop a complete picture of the current position and outlook of the industry under a variety of scenarios.

SALES FORECASTING AND THE INDUSTRIAL LIFE CYCLE

We can predict industry sales by viewing the industry over time and dividing its development into stages that are similar to those that humans progress through as they move from birth to adolescence to adulthood to middle age to old age. The number of stages in this *industry life cycle analysis* can vary based on how much detail you want. A five-stage model would include:

1. Pioneering development
2. Rapid accelerating growth
3. Mature growth
4. Stabilization and market maturity
5. Deceleration of growth and decline

Figure 17.1 shows the growth path of sales during each stage. The vertical scale in logs reflects *rates* of growth, whereas the arithmetic horizontal scale has different widths representing different, unequal time periods. To estimate industry sales, you must predict the length of time for each stage. This requires answers to such questions as: How long will an industry grow at an accelerating rate (Stage 2)? How long will it be in a mature growth phase (Stage 3) before its sales growth stabilizes (Stage 4) and then declines (Stage 5)?

Besides sales estimates, this analysis of an industry's life cycle can also provide some insights into profit margins and earnings growth, although these profit measures

FIGURE 17.1	**Life Cycle for an Industry**

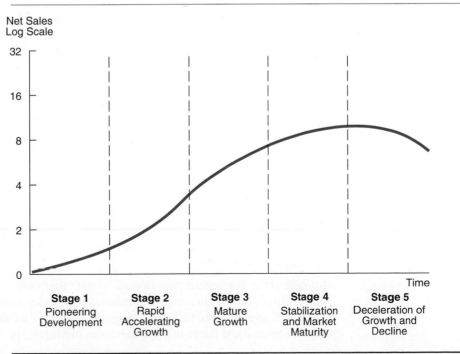

do not necessarily parallel the sales growth. The profit margin series typically peaks very early in the total cycle and then levels off and declines as competition is attracted by the early success of the industry.

To illustrate the contribution of life cycle stages to sales estimates, we will briefly describe these stages and their effects on sales growth and profits:

1. *Pioneering development.* During this start-up stage, the industry experiences modest sales growth and very small or negative profit margins and profits. The market for the industry's product or service during this time is small, and firms incur major development costs.

2. *Rapid accelerating growth.* During this stage, a market develops for the product or service and demand becomes substantial. The limited number of firms in the industry face little competition and individual firms can experience substantial backlogs. The profit margins are very high. The industry builds its productive capacity as sales grow at an increasing rate as the industry attempts to meet excess demand. High sales growth and high profit margins that increase as firms become more efficient cause industry and firm profits to explode. During this phase profits can grow at over 100 percent a year from the low earnings base and because of the rapid growth of sales and net profit margins.

3. *Mature growth.* The success in Stage 2 has satisfied most of the demand for the industry goods or service. The large sales base may keep future sales growth above normal, but it no longer accelerates. As an example, if the overall economy is growing at 8 percent, sales for this industry might grow at a stabilizing rate of 15 to 20 percent a year. Also, the rapid growth of sales and the high historic profit margins attract competitors to the industry and the profit margins stabilize and begin to decline to normal levels.

4. *Stabilization and market maturity.* During this stage, which is probably the longest phase, the industry growth rate matches the growth rate of the aggregate economy or the segment of the economy of which the industry is a part. During this stage, investors can estimate growth easily because sales correlate highly with an economic series. Although sales grow in line with the economy, profit growth varies by industry and by individual firms within the industry because management ability to control costs differs among companies. Competition produces tight profit margins and the rates of return on capital (e.g., return on assets, return on equity) eventually become equal to or slightly below the competitive level.

5. *Deceleration of growth and decline.* At this stage of maturity, the industry's sales growth declines because of shifts in demand or growth of substitutes. Profit margins continue to be squeezed, and some firms experience low profits or even losses. Firms that remain profitable may show very low rates of return on capital and investors begin thinking about alternative uses for the capital tied up in this industry.

Although these are general descriptions of the alternative life cycle stages, they should help you identify the stage your industry is in, which should help you to estimate its potential sales growth. Obviously everyone is looking for an industry in the early phases of Stage 2 and hopes to avoid industries in Stages 4 or 5. Comparing the sales of an industry to activity in the economy should help you identify the industry's stage within the industrial life cycle.

SALES FORECASTING AND INPUT–OUTPUT ANALYSIS

Input–output analysis is another way to gain insights regarding the outlook for an industry by separating industries that supply the input for a specific industry from those that get its output. In other words, we want to identify an industry's suppliers and customers. This will help us identify the future demand from customers, but also the ability of suppliers to provide the goods and services required by the industry. The goal is to determine the long-run sales outlook for both the industry's suppliers and its major customers.[4] To extend this analysis to global industries, we must include worldwide suppliers and customers.

SALES FORECASTING AND THE INDUSTRY–ECONOMY RELATIONSHIP

A third technique that is used extensively to help forecast industry sales is to compare sales for the industry with an aggregate economic series that is related to the goods and services produced by the industry. That is, we try to find a relationship between the industry and the economy. In the following example, we will demonstrate this industry–economy technique for the retail stores-drug industry.

DEMONSTRATING A SALES FORECAST

The retail stores-drug (RSD) industry includes the products of retailers of basic necessities including medicine and many nonmedical products such as cosmetics, snacks, pop, and liquor. Therefore, we want a series that reflects broad consumption expenditures, but also gives weight to the impact of medical expenditures. The economic series we consider are personal consumption expenditures (PCE) and PCE-medical care. Table 17.1 contains the aggregate and per capita values for the two series.

A casual analysis of these time series indicates that although personal consumption expenditures (PCE) have experienced reasonably steady growth of about 8.5 percent a year during this period, PCE-medical care has grown at a faster rate of about 11.7 percent. As a result, as shown in the last column, medical care as a percentage of all PCE has grown from 7.83 percent in 1970 to 14.84 percent in 1991. Obviously, as an analyst, you would hope that retail drug store sales would benefit from this growth in medical expenditures.

The scatter plot in Figure 17.2 indicates a strong linear relationship between retail stores–drug sales per share and PCE-medical care. Although not shown, there is also a good relationship with PCE. Therefore, if you can do a good job of estimating changes in these economic series, you should derive a good estimate of expected sales for the retail drug stores industry.

As the industry becomes more specialized and thus more individualized, you need a more individualized economic series that reflects the demand for the industry's product. There also can be instances where industry sales are dependent on several

[4]For an explanation of input–output analysis, see Howard B. Bonham, Jr., "The Use of Input–Output Economics in Common Stock Analysis," *Financial Analysts Journal* 23, no. 1 (January-February 1967): 27–31.

TABLE 17.1

S&P Retail Store-Drug Sales and Various Economic Series: 1970–1991

Year	Retail Stores-Drug ($/Share)	Personal Consumption Expenditures ($ Billions)	PCE-Medical Care ($ Billions)	Per Capita Personal Consumption Expenditures (Dollars)	Per Capita PCE-Medical Care (Dollars)	Medical Care as a Percentage of PCE
1970	12.46	640.0	50.1	3121	244.3	7.83%
1971	16.79	691.6	56.5	3330	272.0	8.17%
1972	18.58	757.6	63.5	3609	302.5	8.38%
1973	22.43	837.2	71.2	3950	335.9	8.50%
1974	27.61	916.5	80.1	4285	374.5	8.74%
1975	25.89	1012.8	93.0	4689	430.6	9.18%
1976	36.40	1129.3	106.2	5178	487.0	9.41%
1977	43.99	1257.2	122.4	5707	555.6	9.74%
1978	49.87	1403.5	139.7	6304	627.5	9.95%
1979	73.39	1566.8	157.8	6960	701.0	10.07%
1980	84.82	1732.6	181.3	7607	796.2	10.47%
1981	95.50	1915.1	213.6	8320	928.7	11.16%
1982	109.22	2050.7	240.5	8818	1035.7	11.75%
1983	118.85	2234.5	265.7	9516	1133.9	11.92%
1984	135.15	2430.5	290.6	10253	1229.3	11.99%
1985	153.30	2629.0	319.3	10987	1338.7	12.18%
1986	157.74	2797.4	346.4	11588	1439.2	12.42%
1987	191.72	3010.8	384.7	12568	1584.0	12.60%
1988	217.80	3235.1	427.7	13448	1745.1	12.98%
1989	239.68	3470.3	472.2	14219	1908.6	13.42%
1990	265.77	3742.6	523.1	14971	2092.5	13.98%
1991	283.50	3886.8	576.8	15383	2282.9	14.84%
Annual Growth	15.26%	8.55%	11.75%	7.52%	10.69%	

Source: *Analysts Handbook* (New York: Standard & Poor's Corporation, 1992). Reprinted by permission of Standard & Poor's Corp. and Economic Report of the President (Washington, D.C.: U.S. Government Printing Office, 1992).

components of the economy, in which case you would consider a multivariate model that would include two economic series. For example, if you were dealing with the tire industry, you might want to consider new-car production, new-truck production, and a series that would reflect the replacement tire demand.

You should also consider *per capita* personal consumption expenditures—medical care. Although aggregate PCE-medical care increases each year, there is also an increase in the aggregate population, so the increase in the PCE-medical care per capita (the average PCE-medical care for each adult and child) will be less than the increase in the aggregate series. As an example, during 1991 aggregate PCE-medical care increased about 10.3 percent, but per capita PCE-medical care increased only 9.1 percent. Finally, an analysis of the relationship between changes in the economic variable and changes in industry sales will indicate how the two series move together and highlight any changes in the relationship. Using percentage changes provides the following regression model:

$$\% \Delta \text{ Industry Sales} = \alpha + \beta_i (\% \Delta \text{ in Economic Series})$$

The size of the β_i coefficient should indicate how closely the two series move together. Assuming the intercept (α_i) is close to zero, a slope (β_i) value of 1.00 would

FIGURE 17.2   **Scatter Plot of RSD Sales/Share and PCE-Medical Care**

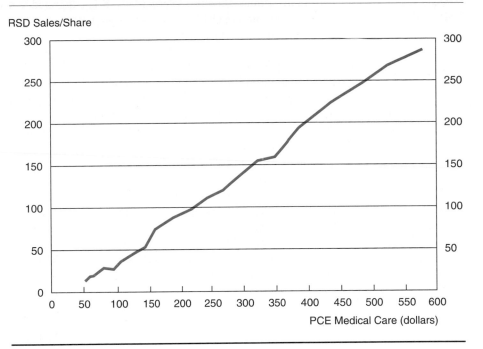

indicate relatively equal percentages of change (e.g., this would indicate that a 10 percent increase in PCE is typically associated with a 10 percent increase in industry sales). A β_i of less than unity would imply that industry sales are not growing as fast as the economy is. This analysis would help you find an economic series that closely reflects the demand for the industry's products and would also indicate the form of the relationship.

As indicated in this analysis, the best relationship was between retail stores-drug and PCE-medical care. The specific regression result was

$$\text{Retail Stores} = -17.45 + 0.53 \ (\text{PCE-Medical Care})$$
$$\text{Drug} \quad (-8.98) \quad (78.01)$$
$$(t\text{-values})$$
$$R^2 = 0.996 \quad F = 6085 \quad DW = 1.53$$

The specific procedure would entail beginning with an estimate of aggregate PCE for the coming year. Given the importance of the PCE series, it should be relatively easy to find one or several estimates. The next step would be to estimate the increase in the proportion of PCE spent on medical care. As noted, this proportion has grown steadily from 7.83 percent to 14.84 percent. Once you estimate this percentage, you apply it to the prior PCE estimate to arrive at an estimate of PCE-medical care, which is then used in the foregoing regression equation to derive a sales estimate for the industry.

INDUSTRY PROFIT
MARGIN
FORECAST

Similar to the aggregate market, the net profit margin is the most volatile and the hardest margin to estimate directly. Alternatively, it is suggested that you begin with the operating profit margin (EBDIT/Sales) and then estimate depreciation expense, interest expense, and the tax rate.

INDUSTRY'S GROSS PROFIT MARGIN

Recall that in the market analysis we analyzed the factors that should influence the economy's operating profit margin, including capacity utilization, unit labor cost, inflation, and net exports. The most important variables were capacity utilization and the unit labor cost. We cannot do such an analysis for most industries because the relevant variables are typically not available for individual industries. We can, however, assume that movements in these industry profit margin variables are related to movements in similar economic variables. As an example, when there is an increase in capacity utilization for the aggregate economy, there is probably a comparable increase in utilization for the auto industry or the chemical industry. The same could be true for unit labor cost and exports. If there is a stable relationship between these variables for the industry and the economy, you would expect a relationship to exist between the profit margins for the industry and the economy. Although it is not necessary that the relationship be completely linear, it is important for the relationship to be generally stable.

The operating profit margin (OPM) for the S&P 400 industrial index and the retail store-drug (RSD) index is presented in Table 17.2. The time-series plot in Figure 17.3 indicates that the S&P 400 OPM has declined over time, and the RSD OPM likewise experienced a decline without the sharp drop in 1991. The analysis of the relationship between the OPM for the market and industry using regression analysis was not very

TABLE 17.2   **Profit Margins and Component Expenses for the S&P 400 and the RSD Industry Index: 1977–1991**

Year	Operating Profit ($)		Profit Margin (%)		Depreciation Expense ($)		Interest Expense ($)		Tax Rate (%)		Net Profit Margin (%)	
	S&P 400	RSD	S&P 400	RSD	S&P 400	RSD	S&P 400	RSD	S&P 400	RSD	S&P 400	RSD
1977	34.54	4.02	15.42	9.14	8.52	0.41	3.22	0.13	48.9	48.6	5.20	4.07
1978	38.79	4.48	15.40	8.98	9.64	0.49	3.81	0.13	48.0	47.9	5.23	4.03
1979	45.86	5.64	15.69	7.68	10.81	0.71	4.58	0.23	46.0	45.7	5.63	3.47
1980	48.30	6.43	14.75	7.58	12.37	0.83	5.95	0.28	45.6	44.7	4.98	3.47
1981	57.20	7.31	14.87	7.65	13.87	1.02	7.49	0.39	43.3	44.2	4.92	3.45
1982	47.89	8.41	14.34	7.70	15.30	1.21	8.23	0.41	45.0	44.6	4.02	3.44
1983	50.40	10.01	15.11	8.42	15.67	1.40	7.62	0.43	44.6	45.0	4.51	3.79
1984	57.45	9.98	15.13	7.38	16.31	1.71	8.54	0.78	42.7	45.1	4.86	3.04
1985	56.71	8.70	14.23	7.45	18.19	2.02	9.24	0.73	46.7	45.9	3.92	2.96
1986	54.96	11.80	14.17	7.48	19.41	2.08	9.75	0.77	42.7	45.1	3.81	3.11
1987	64.83	13.65	15.06	7.12	20.21	2.63	10.14	1.17	40.5	43.9	4.77	2.88
1988	79.35	14.78	16.61	6.79	23.34	3.09	14.84	1.42	35.3	38.6	5.33	2.90
1989	85.56	15.80	15.80	6.59	24.21	3.39	18.79	1.65	37.0	37.8	4.96	2.79
1990	87.52	18.22	14.72	6.86	26.31	4.15	20.17	1.63	39.6	38.3	4.17	2.89
1991	74.43	18.70	12.26	6.60	27.05	4.03	18.51	1.32	42.1	38.1	2.95	2.91

EBDIT—Earnings before depreciation, interest, and taxes. This is used as an estimate of operating earnings.

Source: Standard & Poor's *Analysts Handbook* (New York: Standard & Poor's Corporation, 1992). Reprinted by permission of Standard & Poor's Corp.

FIGURE 17.3   **Time-Series Plot of Operating Profit for RSD Industry and S&P 400**

Operating Profit Margin (percent)

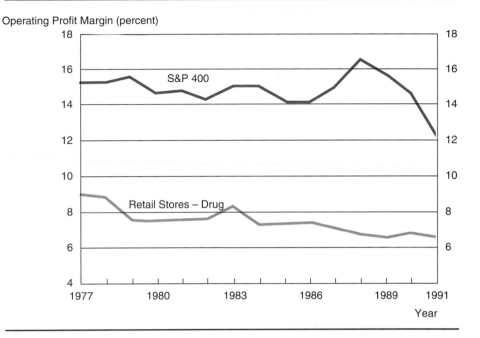

useful so is not discussed. The best estimate can be derived from the OPM time-series plot using what we know about profit trends in the retail drugstore business. It is a matter of judgment for each specific industry whether you use regression analysis or the time-series plot—the empirical relationship will determine the analysis technique.

Either regression analysis or time-series techniques can be useful tools, but *neither technique should be applied mechanically.* You should be aware of any unique factors affecting the specific industry such as price wars, contract negotiations, building plans, or foreign competition. These unique events should be considered as adjustment factors when estimating the final gross profit margin or used in estimating a range of industry profit margins (optimistic, pessimistic, most likely).

Beyond this discussion, which is primarily concerned with an estimate of the near-term OPM, it is also important to consider factors that will affect the long-term profitability of the industry. These long-term influences, which determine the competitive structure of the industry, will be considered in a subsequent section.

INDUSTRY DEPRECIATION

The next step is to estimate industry depreciation, which is typically easier because the series generally is increasing; the only question is by how much. As shown in Table 17.2, except for 1991, the depreciation series for RSD increased every year since 1977. The results in Table 17.2 and the time-series plots in Figure 17.4 relate depreciation for the S&P 400 and the RSD industry. There is not a strong relationship between levels or in terms of growth rates, because the RSD industry started at a lower level and has grown faster over this period. Specifically, depreciation expense for the RSD industry

FIGURE 17.4   **Time-Series Plot of Depreciation for RSD Industry and S&P 400**

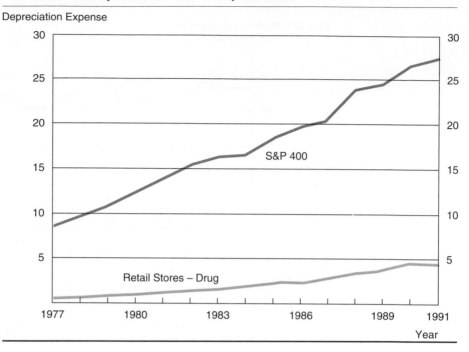

Depreciation Expense

was growing at the rate of about 15 to 20 percent a year prior to the decline in 1991. Therefore, it would probably be best to estimate depreciation based on a time-series analysis of the industry series with some consideration of recent capital expenditures. Subtracting an estimate of depreciation expense from the operating profit figure indicates the industry's net before interest and taxes (EBIT). The next step is estimating the interest expense for the industry.

INDUSTRY INTEREST EXPENSE

An industry's interest expense will be directly related to its financial leverage. As shown in Figure 17.5, interest expense for the RSD industry has always been relatively low when compared to the S&P 400 and did not increase at the same rate during the 1980s. Therefore, looking for a relationship between the two series would not be fruitful. Examining the interest expense series in Table 17.2, it shows steady growth until 1989, a flattening in 1990, and a clear decline in 1991 to a figure lower than what prevailed in 1988. Your estimate for the future would be based on your estimate of any changes in the amount of debt outstanding during the year and your projection of the level of interest rates.

The final step is estimating the tax rate for the industry.

INDUSTRY TAX RATE

As you might expect, tax rates differ between industries. An extreme example would be the oil industry where heavy depletion allowances cause lower taxes. In some in-

FIGURE 17.5   **Time-Series Plot of Interest for RSD Industry and S&P 400**

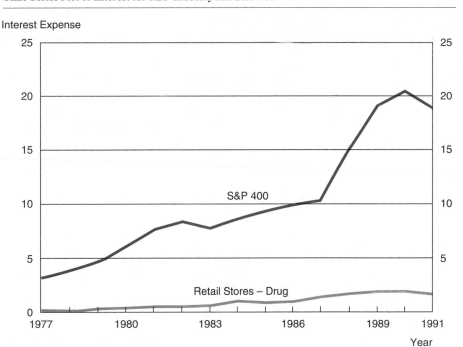

stances, however, you can assume that tax law changes have similar impacts on all industries. To determine the relationship of the industry and the economy, you need to examine the relationship of tax rates over time. This analysis will help you determine if you can use regression analysis or a time-series plot. In either case, you should be aware of unique tax factors for the industry being examined.

As shown in Figure 17.6, the RSD tax rate has historically moved with the economy's tax rate, although the relationship diverged in 1991. Therefore, the time-series plot in Figure 17.6 is fairly informative along with consideration of specific industry factors. Once you have estimated the tax rate, you multiply the EBT per share value by $(1 - \text{tax rate})$ to get your estimate of earnings per share.

In addition to an estimate of earnings per share, you should also derive an estimate of the industry's net profit margin as a check on your EPS estimate. An historical perspective on this series for the industry and the S&P 400 is contained in Figure 17.7, which shows the time series for these two series since 1977. Two important characteristics are notable. First, the S&P 400 net profit margin series is much more volatile than that for retail drugstores. Second, although both profit margin series have experienced an overall decline, the S&P 400 has suffered much more; it has declined from over 5 percent to 3 percent compared to a decline for the RSD industry from 4 percent to 3 percent.

FIGURE 17.6   **Time-Series Plot of Taxes for RSD Industry and S&P 400**

Tax Rates (percent)

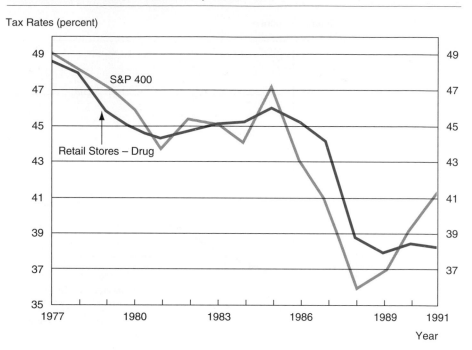

AN EXAMPLE OF
AN INDUSTRY
EARNINGS
ESTIMATE

Now that we have described how to estimate each variable in the equation to help you understand the procedure, the following is an estimate of earnings per share for the retail drugstore industry using the economic forecasts from Chapter 16 and the relationship between the RSD industry and the market derived in this chapter. Our results are not as exact as those of a practicing analyst who would use this example as an *initial* estimate that would be modified based on industry knowledge, current events, and expectations of future unique factors.

The regressions and the plots in Figure 17.2 indicated that the best relationship was between retail drugstore sales and PCE-medical care. The outlook for PCE is for an increase of 4 percent in 1992 and a 5 percent increase in 1993 to $4,244.4 billion. It is further assumed that medical care expenditures will be 15.5 percent of PCE in 1992 and 16 percent in 1993. This implies that PCE-medical care will be about $679 billion in 1993. Using this in the earlier equation indicates that retail drugstore sales in 1993 should be about $342.50, which implies a 20 percent increase over the two years from 1991.

The OPM for retail drugstores was 6.60 in 1991. During 1992 the OPM for the S&P 400 was expected to increase, and retail drugstore margins probably experienced a similar increase to about 6.80. The aggregate OPM was expected to increase again during 1993. Based on the time-series plot in Figure 17.3, this would indicate that retail drugstore margins should increase to about 7 percent, which implies an operating profit per share for the retail drugstore industry of $23.98 (0.07 × $342.50).

FIGURE 17.7   **Time-Series Plot of Net Profit Margin for RSD Industry and S&P 400**

Net Profit Margin (percent)

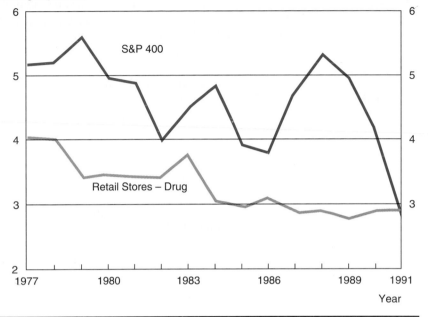

Aggregate depreciation for the S&P 400 series during 1992 was estimated to be $28.00 and expected to grow to $29.30 in 1993. Assuming the retail drugstore industry will reverse the decline in 1991, the depreciation expense is estimated at $4.20 in 1992 and $4.50 in 1993. Therefore, earnings before interest and taxes would be $19.48 (23.98 − 4.50).

As noted, the industry's interest expense declined in 1991 along with the aggregate market. Given the continued decline in yields during 1992 and 1993 along with no major debt financing, we would estimate interest expense of $1.20 for 1992 and $1.00 in 1993. Thus, EBT would be $18.48 (19.48 − 1.00).

The tax rate for the retail drugstore industry has been lower than the aggregate during the last 2 years when the aggregate tax rate increased. The aggregate tax rate was expected to increase slightly in 1992 and also in 1993 as a result of the Clinton deficit reduction program. Therefore, a rate of about 41 percent seems appropriate for the retail drugstore industry. This implies taxes of $7.58 (18.48 × .41) and net income (earnings per share) of $10.90 (18.48 − 7.58). This indicates a net profit margin for the RSD industry of 3.18 percent (10.90/342.50), which is somewhat above the recent experience.

Given an estimate of the industry's net income per share, your next step is to estimate the likely earnings multiplier for this industry. Together the earnings per share and the earnings multiplier provide an estimate of the expected value for the industry index. Given this expected value and an estimate of dividends per share during the holding period, you can compute an expected rate of return from investing in this industry.

ESTIMATING AN
INDUSTRY
EARNINGS
MULTIPLIER

This section discusses how to estimate an industry earnings multiplier using two alternative techniques: macroanalysis and microanalysis. In macroanalysis, you examine the relationship between the multiplier for the industry and the market. In the microanalysis, you estimate the industry earnings multiplier by examining the specific variables that influence it—the dividend-payout ratio, the required rate of return for the industry (k), and the expected growth rate of earnings and dividends for the industry (g).

MACROANALYSIS
OF AN INDUSTRY
MULTIPLIER

Macroanalysis assumes that the major variables that influence the industry multiple are related to similar variables for the aggregate market. In addition, we expect a relationship between changes in k and g for specific industries and for the aggregate market. A similar pattern of changes for these variables (even though they are not the same values) would imply a relationship between changes in the industry P/E ratio and changes in the P/E ratio for the stock market.

An examination of the relationship between the P/E ratios for 71 S&P industries and the S&P 400 index during four partially overlapping 21-year periods indicated a significant positive relationship between percentage changes in P/E ratios for most industries examined.[5] Notably, a difference in the quality of the relationship existed between industries, that is, it was not always significant. Therefore, you must evaluate the quality of the relationship between P/E ratios for an industry and the market before using this technique.

The results in Table 17.3 and Figure 17.8 for the retail drugstore industry during the period 1977 to 1991 indicate a relatively close relationship between the market and the RSD industry with the P/E ratio for drugstores generally above the market P/E ratio. Notably, this changed in 1991 when the market P/E increased to over 25 times, and the P/E for drugstores increased to about 17 times. Also, the industry P/E ratios are less volatile than the market P/E ratios. These results imply that the macroanalysis technique could be considered, but you should also use the microanalysis approach.

MICROANALYSIS
OF AN INDUSTRY
MULTIPLIER

In Chapter 16 we estimated the future earnings multiplier for the stock-market series in two ways. In the first, the direction of change approach, we estimated the changes for the three variables that determine the earnings multiplier—the dividend-payout ratio, the required rate of return, and the expected growth rate of earnings and dividends. Based on the consensus of changes, we estimated a direction of change for the multiplier from its current value. In the second approach, the specific multiplier estimate, we estimated a range of values for the three variables that determine the multiplier and used several individual estimates to derive a range of P/E ratio estimates. These two approaches provided five multiplier estimates that were used with our EPS estimate to compute a range of expected values for the market index that, in turn, provided expected rates of return on common stocks.

Our microanalysis of the industry multiplier could use the same two approaches for each industry. Although this would certainly be legitimate and logical, it would not take advantage of the prior work on the stock-market multiplier. Because the variables

---

[5]Frank K. Reilly and Thomas Zeller, "An Analysis of Relative Industry Price–Earnings Ratios," *The Financial Review* (1974): 17–33.

TABLE 17.3   Earnings Multiplier for the S&P 400 Index and the RSD Industry Index and Influential Variables: 1977–1991

Year	Earnings Multiplier		Retention Rate		Net Profit Margin		Total Asset Turnover		Return on Total Assets		Total Assets/ Equity		Return on Equity	
	S&P 400	RSD	S&P 400	RSD	S&P 400	RSD	S&P 400	RSD	S&P 400	RSD	S&P 400	RSD	S&P 400	RSD
1977	9.55	10.58	56.8	79.9	5.15	4.07	1.27	2.84	6.54	11.56	2.08	1.53	13.93	17.69
1978	8.21	11.05	58.8	76.1	5.19	4.03	1.27	2.81	6.59	11.32	2.15	1.52	14.60	17.19
1979	7.11	8.78	63.7	72.6	5.57	3.47	1.30	3.00	7.24	10.41	2.20	1.65	16.50	17.45
1980	8.44	8.36	59.7	70.8	4.92	3.47	1.31	3.04	6.45	10.55	2.23	1.66	14.88	17.54
1981	8.45	10.52	58.1	69.0	4.86	3.45	1.28	3.03	6.22	10.45	2.25	1.65	14.42	17.20
1982	10.37	11.06	46.0	68.9	3.95	3.44	1.17	2.97	4.62	10.22	2.31	1.66	11.13	16.98
1983	11.84	12.60	50.4	70.7	4.42	3.79	1.15	2.86	5.08	10.84	2.28	1.88	12.07	18.20
1984	9.92	14.22	58.5	62.4	4.77	3.04	1.22	2.65	5.82	8.06	2.39	1.93	14.61	15.18
1985	13.68	16.18	48.5	59.2	3.84	2.96	1.15	2.68	4.42	7.93	2.54	1.88	12.14	15.31
1986	17.48	17.10	44.0	67.1	3.75	3.11	1.07	2.71	4.01	8.43	2.58	1.94	11.64	16.42
1987	16.00	17.89	57.0	68.4	4.77	2.88	1.08	2.80	5.15	8.06	2.62	2.04	13.25	16.50
1988	11.38	14.77	63.1	69.4	5.51	2.90	0.98	2.82	5.40	8.18	3.03	2.07	16.06	16.91
1989	13.59	16.07	55.5	67.7	5.01	2.79	0.97	2.82	4.86	7.87	3.16	2.03	14.87	15.98
1990	14.77	14.94	48.7	68.3	4.26	2.89	0.97	2.82	4.13	8.15	3.27	2.00	13.05	16.26
1991	25.65	16.91	22.8	67.2	2.94	2.91	0.93	2.85	2.73	8.29	3.20	1.83	8.77	15.25
Mean	12.43	13.40	52.8	69.2	4.59	3.28	1.14	2.85	5.28	9.35	2.55	1.82	13.46	16.67

Source: Standard & Poor's *Analysts Handbook* (New York: Standard & Poor's Corp., 1992). Reprinted by permission of Standard & Poor's Corp.

FIGURE 17.8   **Time-Series Plot of Annual Average Multipliers for RSD Industry and S&P 400**

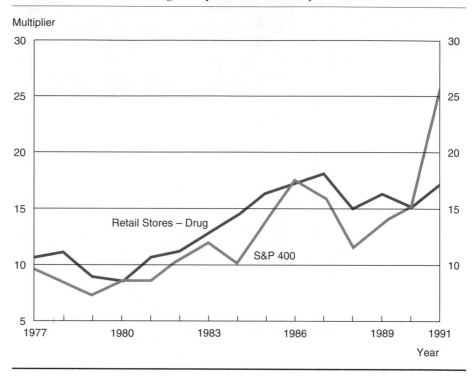

that affect the stock-market multiplier also determine the industry multiplier, it should be possible to compare the two sets of variables.

Therefore, in our microanalysis, we estimate the three variables that determine the industry earnings multiplier and compare them to the comparable values for the market P/E to determine whether the industry earnings multiplier should be above, below, or equal to the market multiplier. Once we feel confident about this relationship, it is easier to derive a specific estimate for the industry P/E ratio. As a first step, we need to recall the long-run relationship between the industry and market P/E ratios.

INDUSTRY MULTIPLIER VERSUS THE MARKET MULTIPLIER

Recall that the mean of the high and low multiplier for the S&P 400 index and the RSD industry is in column 1 of Table 17.3. The P/E ratios for the retail drugstore industry were typically larger than the P/E ratios for the stock market prior to 1991 when the market P/E ratio increased to about 25 times while the RSD multiplier increased to about 17. Obvious questions include: Why do the P/E ratios for this industry and the stock market differ over time? Why were investors in 1991 willing to pay more for a dollar of earnings from the aggregate market than from retail drugstores? Why has the historical relationship that has prevailed between the P/E ratios for this industry and the stock market changed? An analysis of the factors that determine the earnings multiplier should help us answer these questions.

COMPARING DIVIDEND-PAYOUT RATIOS

We can discuss the dividend-payout ratio directly or in terms of the retention rate because the retention rate is one minus the dividend-payout rate. Analyzing the retention rate, we see from the second set of columns in Table 17.3 that the retention rates of retail drugstores have consistently been higher than the retention rates for the market (69.2 versus 52.8). These differences would indicate a higher payout (lower retention rate) for the S&P 400, which implies a higher multiplier for the S&P 400 on the basis of this particular variable.

ESTIMATING THE REQUIRED RATE OF RETURN (k)

Because the required rate of return (k) on all investments is influenced by the risk-free rate and the expected inflation rate, the differentiating factor among assets is the risk premium (in this case the RSD industry and the market). In turn, you will recall that we can discuss the risk premium in terms of fundamental factors including business risk (BR), financial risk (FR), liquidity risk (LR), exchange rate risk (ERR), and country (political) risk (CR). Alternatively, you can derive an estimate of the risk premium based on the CAPM, which implies that the risk premium is a function of the systematic risk (beta) of the asset. Therefore, to derive an estimate of the industry's risk premium, you should examine the BR, FR, LR, ERR, and CR for the industry and compare them to those of the aggregate market. Alternatively, you can compute the systematic risk (beta) for the industry and compare this to the market beta of 1.0.

Business risk is a function of relative sales volatility and operating leverage. We know that the annual percentage changes in retail drugstore sales was less volatile than aggregate sales as represented by PCE. Also the OPM for retail drugstores was less volatile than the S&P 400 OPM. Therefore, because both sales and the OPM for the RSD industry were less volatile than the market, operating profits are substantially less volatile. This implies that the business risk for the RSD industry *is below average.*

The *financial risk* for this industry is difficult to judge because of building leases in the industry. Still, on the basis of the reported data on debt to total capital or interest coverage ratios, the FR for this industry is substantially below the market. Assuming that there are some long-term lease contracts, this industry might have financial risk *about equal* to the market.

To evaluate the *liquidity risk* for an industry, it is necessary to estimate the liquidity risk for all the firms in the industry and derive a composite view. The fact is, there is substantial variation in market liquidity among the firms in this industry. Walgreen's is very liquid, whereas Longs Drug Stores and Rite-Aid are relatively illiquid. A conservative view is that the RSD industry probably has *slightly above-average* liquidity risk.

Exchange rate risk (ERR) is the uncertainty of earnings due to changes in exchange rates faced by firms in this industry that sell outside the United States. The amount of this risk is determined by what proportion of sales is non-U.S. and how these sales are distributed among countries. This risk could range from an industry with very limited international sales (e.g., a service industry that is not involved overseas) to an industry that is clearly worldwide (e.g., the chemical or pharmaceutical industry). For a truly global industry, you need to examine the distribution of sales among specific countries because we know that the exchange rate risk varies among countries based on the volatility of exchange rates with the U.S. dollar. The ERR for the RSD industry would be *quite low* because these firms are almost wholly within the United States.

The existence of *country risk (CR)* is likewise a function of foreign sales and the specific foreign country and the stability of its political/economic system. As noted, there is very little CR in the United Kingdom and Japan, but there can be substantial CR in China, Russia, or South Africa. For the RSD industry, this risk would be very low because of limited foreign sales.

In summary, for the RSD industry, business risk is definitely below average, financial risk is about equal to the market, liquidity risk is slightly above average, and exchange rate risk and country risk are definitely below average. The consensus is that the overall risk for the RSD industry is clearly below the market average on the basis of internal characteristics.

The *systematic risk* for the retail drugstore industry is computed using the market model as follows:

$$\% \, \Delta \, RSD_t = \alpha_i + \beta_i(\% \, \Delta \, \text{S\&P } 500_t)$$

where:

$\% \, \Delta \, RSD_t$ = percentage price change in the retail drugstore (RSD) index during month t

α_i = regression intercept for the RSD industry

β_i = systematic risk measure for the RSD industry equal to $Cov_{i,m}/\sigma^2_m$

To derive an estimate for the RSD industry, the model specified was run with monthly data for the 5-year period 1988 to 1992. The results for this regression are as follows:

$\alpha_i = 0.004$	$R^2 = 0.70$
$\beta_i = 0.50$	$DW = 1.78$
t-value = 8.70	$F = 70.52$

The systematic risk ($\beta = 0.50$) for the retail drugstore industry is clearly below unity indicating a low-risk industry (i.e., risk less than the market). These results are quite consistent with the prior fundamental risk analysis (BR, FR, LR, ERR, CR).

Translating this systematic risk into a required return figure (k) calls for using the security market line model as follows:

$$k_i = \text{RFR} + \beta_i(R_m - \text{RFR})$$

Assuming a nominal risk-free rate during this period of 8 percent (.08), a market return (R_m) of 12 percent, and a beta for the industry of 0.50 indicates the following:

$$k_i = .08 + 0.50(.12 - .08)$$
$$= .10$$
$$= 10 \text{ percent}$$

A micro estimate of fundamental risk below average and a market risk estimate likewise below average implies an industry earnings multiple above the market multiple, all other factors being equal.

ESTIMATING THE EXPECTED GROWTH RATE (*g*)
You will recall that earnings and dividend growth are determined by the retention rate and the return on equity.

$$g = f(\text{Retention Rate and Return on Equity})$$

We have consistently broken down return on equity into the following three components:

$$\frac{\text{Net Profit}}{\text{Equity}} = \frac{\text{Net Income}}{\text{Sales}} \times \frac{\text{Sales}}{\text{Total Assets}} \times \frac{\text{Total Assets}}{\text{Equity}}$$
$$= \frac{\text{Profit}}{\text{Margin}} \times \frac{\text{Total Asset}}{\text{Turnover}} \times \frac{\text{Financial}}{\text{Leverage}}$$

Therefore, we need to examine each of these variables in Table 17.3 to determine if they would imply a difference in expected growth for RSD as compared to the aggregate market (S&P 400).

EARNINGS RETENTION RATE   As noted earlier, the retention rate data in Table 17.3 indicate that the RSD industry had a higher retention (69.2 percent versus 52.8 percent) rate. This means that the RSD industry would have a potentially higher growth rate, all else being the same.

RETURN ON EQUITY   Because the return on equity is a function of the net profit margin, total asset turnover, and a measure of financial leverage, these three variables are examined individually.

Historically, the net profit margin for the S&P 400 series has been consistently higher than the margin for the RSD industry. This is not surprising because retail firms typically have lower profit margins but higher turnover. Notably both series declined over the period, but the market profit margin declined more, to the point that the profit margins were almost equal in 1991.

As noted, one would normally expect the total asset turnover (TAT) for a retail firm to be higher than the average company. This expectation was confirmed because the average TAT for the S&P 400 was 1.14 versus 2.85 for the RSD industry. Beyond the overall difference, the spread between the two series increased over the period—in the early years, the turnovers were about 1.30 versus 2.80, and in the final years, they were about 0.93 versus 2.85. Obviously, this change occurred because the S&P 400 series declined steadily over the period as shown in Figure 17.9. Multiplying these two ratios indicates the industry's return on total assets (ROTA).

$$\frac{\text{Net Income}}{\text{Sales}} \times \frac{\text{Sales}}{\text{Total Assets}} = \frac{\text{Net Income}}{\text{Total Assets}}$$

FIGURE 17.9   **Time-Series Plot of Total Asset Turnover for RSD Industry and S&P 400**

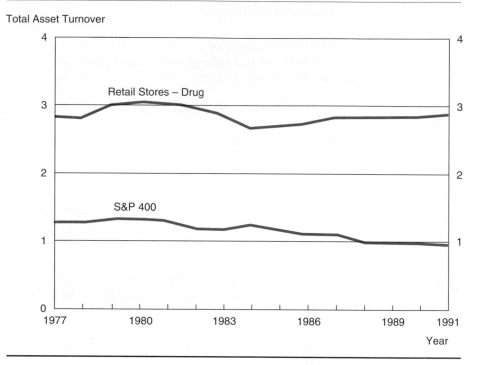

Total Asset Turnover

When we do this for these two series, the results in Table 17.3 indicate that the return on total assets (ROTA) for the S&P 400 series went from 6.54 percent to 2.73 percent and averaged 5.28 percent, whereas the ROTA for the RSD industry went from 11.56 percent to 8.29 percent and averaged 9.35 percent.

The final component is the financial leverage multiplier (total assets/equity). As shown in Table 17.3 and Figure 17.10, the leverage multiplier for the S&P 400 increased fairly steadily from 2.08 to 3.20, whereas the multiplier for the RSD industry went from 1.53 to a high of 2.07 and ended at 1.83. Although this higher financial leverage multiplier implies greater financial risk for the S&P 400 series, it will also contribute to a higher ROE, all else being the same.

This brings us to the final value of ROE, which is the product of the three ratios (profit margin, total asset turnover, and financial leverage); one can also use the product of return on total asset and the financial leverage multiplier. The figures in Table 17.3 and the plot in Figure 17.11 indicate that the ROE for the RSD industry was higher in the beginning and remained higher throughout the period, with a major difference in 1991. The averages were 16.67 percent for the RSD industry versus 13.46 percent for the S&P 400 series. These average percentages are quite consistent with what would be derived from multiplying the averages of the components from Table 17.3 as follows:

FIGURE 17.10   **Time-Series Plot of Assets over Equity for RSD Industry and S&P 400**

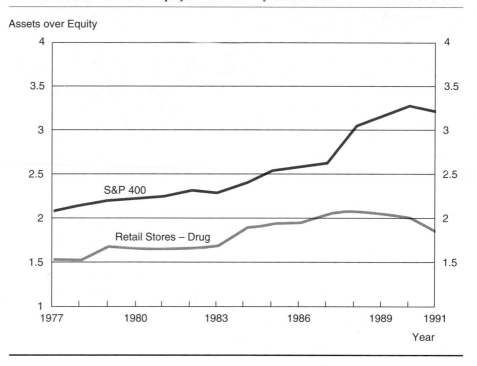

Assets over Equity

	Profit Margin		Total Asset Turnover		Total Assets/ Equity	ROE
S&P 400	4.59	×	1.14	×	2.55	= 13.34
RSD Industry	3.28	×	2.85	×	1.82	= 17.01

Although examining the historical trends and coverage for each of the components is important, you should never lose sight of the fact that it is expectations of *future* performance that will determine value.

ESTIMATING GROWTH   The growth rate is a function of the retention rate times the return on equity. As noted, the RSD industry has consistently had a higher retention rate (all years: 69.2 versus 52.8) and also has experienced a higher return on equity (all years: 16.67 versus 13.46). When these are combined, the estimated long-run growth rates would be

S&P 400	$.528 \times 13.46 =$	7.11%
RSD	$.692 \times 16.67 =$	11.54%

FIGURE 17.11   **Time-Series Plot of Return on Equity for RSD Industry and S&P 400**

Return on Equity

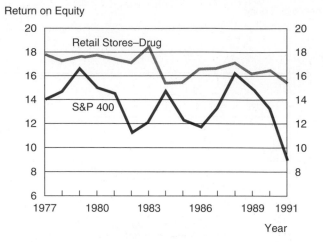

Year

Clearly, the fairly large difference in sustainable growth would favor the RSD series and would indicate that the industry earnings multiplier should be higher, all else being the same.

WHY THE
DIFFERENCE?

Because the earnings multiplier is a function of (1) the dividend-payout ratio, (2) the required rate of return, and (3) the expected growth rate, any differences in P/E ratios should be explained by differences in these variables.

Our initial analysis indicated that the earnings multiplier for the RSD industry was historically higher than the market multiplier, but in 1990 they were almost equal and in 1991 the industry multiple was clearly smaller. The question then becomes: why has the RSD industry lost this premium? There was a small difference in the payout ratio that favored the S&P 400 series. The analysis of risk in terms of fundamental characteristics and a market measure of risk indicated that risk for the RSD industry was lower than the aggregate market risk which would imply a higher industry multiplier.

Finally, an analysis of the growth characteristics of the two series indicated differences in the profit margin, the total asset turnover, and the financial leverage multiplier that resulted in consistently higher returns on equity for the RSD industry. When the return on equity figures were combined with higher RSD retention rates, the implied growth rates clearly favored the RSD industry.

In summary, the payout ratio favored the market multiplier, the risk factor favored the RSD industry, and the growth comparison likewise indicated that the multiplier for the RSD industry should be higher. This would imply that unless investors expected major changes in these relationships, *the RSD industry multiplier should be definitely higher than the market multiplier.*

ESTIMATING THE
FUTURE

Our purpose has been to demonstrate a technique and to indicate the relationships that should exist between an industry and the market so that you will be aware of the important variables. Still, you should never forget that *the past alone is of limited value when projecting the future*, because past relationships may not hold in the future, especially in the short run. As an analyst you need to determine the future values for the relevant variables based on your unique knowledge of the industry.

EXAMPLE OF MULTIPLE ESTIMATE

Ideally you should apply both techniques (macro and micro) to derive fairly consistent estimates of the earnings multiple. In the current case, there was some support for using a macroanalysis approach. The results indicate that the retail drugstore P/E is less volatile than the market P/E. In Chapter 16 it was estimated that the market multiplier would increase slightly during 1993. This would imply a small increase for the retail drugstore industry.

The analysis of individual components indicated that the earnings multiplier for the RSD industry should definitely be higher than for the market. This would imply a multiplier of at least 20 for the RSD industry. In summary, the industry macro P/E estimate is about 18, whereas the microanalysis indicates a multiple of about 20. For our example, we will use the mean value of these two estimates (19).

THE TOTAL ESTIMATE

The net earnings estimate was for $10.90 a share during 1993. This, coupled with a multiple estimate of 19, implied an index value estimate of 207.10 at the end of 1993. Given this index value, you can derive your expected return—$E(R)$—based on the current value of the index and the expected dividend as follows:

$$E\,(R_{rsd}) = \frac{207.10 - \text{Index (Current)} + \text{Dividend}}{\text{Index (Current)}}$$

The RSD industry value as of early 1993 was 185.50. If we use this value and assume a dividend payout of about 30 percent of the $10.50 earnings, it implies a dividend of $3.15. Plugging these values in the equation, we get:

$$E\,(R_{rsd}) = \frac{207.10 - 185.50 + 3.15}{185.50}$$
$$= 13.34\%$$

We would then compare this expected rate of return to our required rate of return of about 10 percent which was based on the industry's beta of 0.50. This comparison would imply an overweighting of this industry.

COMPETITION AND EXPECTED INDUSTRY RETURNS

In this chapter we have demonstrated the two-step approach to estimating the future value for an industry and the expected rate of return based on this future value. This analysis provided a specific estimate of the future industry rate of return based on the industry's historical relationship with the economy and the aggregate stock market. You should realize that other economic forces can influence the likelihood of realizing these returns. One important factor is the intensity of the competition in the industry, as Porter has discussed in a series of books and articles.[6]

Porter's concept of *competitive strategy* is described as the search by a firm for a favorable competitive position in an industry. To create a profitable competitive strategy, a firm must first examine the basic competitive structure of its industry because the potential profitability of a firm is heavily influenced by the inherent profitability of its industry. After determining the competitive structure of the industry, you examine the factors that determine the relative competitive position of a firm within its industry. In this section we consider the competitive forces that determine the competitive structure of the industry. In the next chapter our discussion of company analysis will cover the factors that determine the relative competitive position of a firm within its industry.

BASIC COMPETITIVE FORCES

Porter believes that the *competitive environment* of an industry, the intensity of competition among the firms in that industry, determines the ability of the firms to sustain above-average rates of return on invested capital. He suggests that five competitive forces determine the intensity of competition:

1. Rivalry among existing competitors
2. Threat of new entrants
3. Threat of substitute products
4. Bargaining power of buyers
5. Bargaining power of suppliers

The relative effect of each of these five factors can vary dramatically among industries.

1. *Rivalry among the existing competitors.* For each industry you analyze, you must judge if the rivalry among firms is currently intense and growing, or if it is polite and stable. Rivalry increases when many firms of relatively equal size compete in an industry. When estimating the number and size of firms, be sure to include foreign competitors. Further, *slow growth* causes competitors to fight for market share and increases competition. *High fixed costs* stimulate the desire to sell at the full capacity, which can lead to price cutting and greater competition. Finally, look for *exit barriers,* such as specialized facilities or labor agreements. These can keep firms in the industry despite below-average or negative rates of return.

2. *Threat of new entrants.* Although an industry may have few competitors, you must determine the likelihood of firms entering the industry and increasing competition. *High barriers to entry,* such as low current prices relative to costs, keep the threat of new entrants low. Other barriers to entry include the need to invest large financial resources to compete and the availability of capital. Also, substantial economies of scale give a current industry member an advantage over a new firm. Further entrants might be discouraged if success in the industry requires extensive distribution channels that are hard to build because of exclusive distribution contracts. Similarly, high costs of switching products or brands

---

[6]Michael E. Porter, *Competitive Strategy: Techniques for Analyzing Industries and Competitors* (New York: Free Press, 1980); Michael Porter, "Industry Structure and Competitive Strategy: Keys to Profitability," *Financial Analysts Journal* 36, no. 4 (July-August 1980); and Michael Porter, *Competitive Advantage: Creating and Sustaining Superior Performance* (New York: Free Press, 1985), Chapter 1.

such as those required to change a computer or telephone system keep competition low. Finally, government policy can restrict entry by imposing licensing requirements or limiting access to materials (lumber, coal). Without some of these barriers, it might be very easy for competitors to enter an industry, increasing the competition and driving down potential rates of return.

3. *Threat of substitute products.* Substitute products limit the profit potential of an industry because they limit the prices firms in an industry can charge. Although almost everything has a substitute, you must determine how close the substitute is in price and function to the product in your industry. As an example, the threat of substitute glass containers hurt the metal container industry. Glass containers kept declining in price, forcing metal container prices and profits down. In the food industry consumers constantly substitute between beef, pork, chicken, and fish.

4. *Bargaining power of buyers.* Buyers can influence the profitability of an industry because they can bid down prices or demand higher quality or more services by bargaining among competitors. Buyers become powerful when they purchase a large volume relative to the sales of a supplier. The most vulnerable firm is a one-customer firm that supplies a single large manufacturer, as is common for auto parts manufacturers or software developers. Buyers will be more conscious of the costs of items that represent a significant percentage of the firm's total costs or if the buying firm is feeling cost pressure from its customers. Also, buyers who know a lot about the costs of supplying an industry will bargain more intensely; for example, when the buying firm supplies some of its own needs and also buys from outside.

5. *Bargaining power of suppliers.* Suppliers can alter future industry returns if they increase prices or reduce the quality or services they provide. The suppliers are more powerful if they are few and if they are more concentrated than the industry to which they sell, and if they supply critical inputs to several industries, for which few if any substitutes exist. In this instance the suppliers are free to change prices and services they supply to the firms in an industry. When analyzing supplier bargaining power, be sure to consider labor's power within each industry.

An investor can analyze these competitive forces to determine the intensity of the competition in an industry and assess its long-run profit potential. You should examine each of these factors for every industry and develop a relative competitive profile. You need to update this analysis of an industry's competitive environment over time because an industry's competitive structure can and will change over time.

GLOBAL INDUSTRY ANALYSIS

Because so many firms are active in foreign markets and because the proportion of foreign sales is growing for so many firms, we must expand industry analysis to include the effects of foreign firms on global trade and industry returns. To see why this is so, consider the auto industry. Besides Chrysler, Ford, and General Motors, it includes numerous firms from Japan, Germany, Italy, and Korea, among others. Thus we must extend the analysis described earlier to include additional global factors. This section presents an example of such an analysis for the European chemical industry performed

TABLE 17.4   **Economic Scenario 1992E–1994E (annual percentage changes)[a]**

	GDP			Industrial Output			Chemical Output		
	1992E	1993E	1994E	1992E	1993E	1994E	1992E	1993E	1994E
Germany	1.5	− 0.1	1.5	− 0.8	− 1.6	1.5	1.5	− 0.5	1.0
France	1.8	0.0	1.3	− 0.8	− 1.1	0.5	3.2	1.0	1.0
UK	− 0.6	1.6	3.1	− 0.7	3.4	4.1	0.5	1.5	3.5
Italy	1.1	− 0.2	0.9	− 0.9	− 0.5	0.5	0.8	0.0	1.0
US	2.0	2.8	—	2.0	4.6	—	5.0	5.0	—
Japan	1.8	2.3	2.9	− 6.0	− 2.4	3.2	0.0	0.0	2.0

[a]Goldman Sachs estimates.

Source: Charles K. Brown, Peter Clark, and Mark Tracey, "The Major European Chemicals/Pharm Groups—Testing Times," (London: Goldman Sachs International, February 1993). Reprinted by permission of Goldman Sachs.

TABLE 17.5   **Key Earnings and Financial Statistics for Major Chemical Firms[a]**

		EPS		1991%		P/E	P/CF	P/B
Firm	Currency	1992E	1993E	ROE	ND/Eq	1992E	1991	1991
BASF	DM	12.0	10.0	7	− 8	17.9	2.6	0.8
Bayer	DM	23.0	21.0	11	7	11.6	3.1	1.1
Hoechst	DM	15.5	13.0	9	35	16.5	3.2	1.3
Schering	DM	36.0	40.0	11	− 22	19.1	5.7	1.8
AKZ0	DFL	15.3	14.1	15	56	9.2	3.8	2.4
DSM	DFL	6.3	4.4	12	44	11.4	2.3	0.6
L'Air Liquide	FFr	39.4	41.1	13	13	19.6	7.3	2.6
Rhone-Poulenc	FFr	27.0	42.8	5	131	24.4	5.8	1.3

[a]Goldman Sachs estimates.

Source: Charles K. Brown, Peter Clark, and Mark Tracey, "The Major European Chemicals/Pharm Groups—Testing Times," (London: Goldman Sachs International, February 1993). Reprinted by permission of Goldman Sachs.

by industry analysts at Goldman, Sachs & Company.[7] Although the report discusses individual firms in the industry, we will emphasize the overall chemical industry.

THE EUROPEAN
CHEMICAL
INDUSTRY

Table 17.4 contains the expected economic outlook and chemical production for the major European countries during the period 1992 to 1994. It shows weaknesses or declines in the economies in 1993 and a recovery in 1994. The outlook for European chemical production in 1993 and 1994 is for very slow growth except in the United Kingdom. The outlook for the United States is fairly strong, which is consistent with its earlier recovery from the recession.

PROFIT PERFORMANCE

Table 17.5 shows EPS, ROE, the debt/equity ratio, and several measures of relative value (P/E, P/CF, P/B) for eight major companies, which reflects what happened to

---

[7]Charles K. Brown, Peter Clark, and Mark Tracey, "The Major European Chemical/Pharma Groups—Testing Times,"(London: Goldman Sachs International, February, 1993).

TABLE 17.6   **Exchange Rate Trends 1988–1993E[a]**

		DM Strength		SFr Strength		FFr Strength		DFL Strength		Sterling Strength		
		vs US %	Trade-Weighted %	vs US %	Trade-Weighted %	vs US %	Trade-Weighted %	vs US %	Trade-Weighted %	vs US$ %	vs DM %	Trade-Weighted %
1988	Q1	+9	—	+12	+3	+8	−1	+10	+1	+17	+6	+8
	Q2	+6	—	+5	−1	+4	−1	+6	—	+12	+6	+7
	Q3	−2	−1	−3	−2	−3	−3	−2	−1	+5	+6	+5
	Q4	−4	−2	−7	−4	−5	−3	−4	−2	+2	+6	+4
1989	Q1	−11	−3	−15	−7	−11	−3	−11	−3	−3	+7	+4
	Q2	−13	−2	−19	−7	−13	−2	−14	−2	−11	—	−3
	Q3	−3	—	−6	−3	−3	—	−3	—	−6	−3	−4
	Q4	−2	+2	−7	−3	−2	+2	−2	+1	−11	−10	−9
1990	Q1	+9	+6	+4	+1	+9	+5	+9	+4	−5	−13	−9
	Q2	+13	+6	+15	+7	+14	+6	+13	+4	+3	−11	−5
	Q3	+17	+5	+19	+7	+18	+5	+17	+4	+16	−3	+3
	Q4	+17	+3	+21	+8	+18	+4	+17	+2	+22	+2	+7
1991	Q1	+9	+1	+13	+5	+9	—	+9	+1	+15	+4	+6
	Q2	−3	−2	−2	−1	−4	−3	−3	−2	+2	+5	+3
	Q3	−9	−2	−13	−5	−10	−3	−9	−1	−10	−1	−4
	Q4	−9	−1	−13	−5	−9	−3	−8	−1	−8	−1	−3
1992	Q1	−6	−1	−11	−6	−6	−1	−5	−1	−7	−2	−3
	Q2	+7	+2	−1	−6	+7	+2	+7	+2	+6	−1	+1
	Q3	+16	+5	+14	+2	+16	+5	+16	+4	+13	−5	—
	Q4	+5	+5	+4	+3	+5	+6	+5	+4	−11	−15	−12
1993	Q1E[b]	−1	+6	−4	+2	—	+7	−1	+4	−16	−16	−13
	Q2E[b]	−2	+6	−3	+4	−2	+6	−2	+5	−20	−18	−16
	Q3E[b]	−12	+3	−17	−1	−11	+4	−12	+2	−24	−15	−15
	Q4E[b]	−6	+1	−9	−3	−5	+1	−6	—	−8	−3	−3

[a]Year-on-year percentage changes.

[b]Projections at 1 February 1993 rates of DM1.64/$, SFr1.52/$, FFr5.51$, DFL1.84/$, $1.45/£ and DM2.38/£.

Source: Charles K. Brown, Peter Clark, and Mark Tracey, "The Major European Chemicals/Pharm Groups—Testing Times," (London: Goldman Sachs International, February 1993). Reprinted by permission of Goldman Sachs.

most other firms in this industry. These data indicate that most firms in the industry were expected to experience a decline in profit results during 1993 versus 1992. Also, the ROEs for 1991 were adequate but certainly not robust. Still, the expected P/E ratios were wide ranging, as were the P/CF and P/B ratios. As noted in the financial statement analysis chapter, because of the differences in accounting treatments, it is typically not possible to compare such ratios across countries, but only over time within a country. It was noted that most of these P/E ratios were relatively high on that basis.

The final segment of the analysis examined the currency factors involved in forecasting production for each country, and also the export–import possibilities based on the exchange rate outlook. Table 17.6 lists exchange rate trends for each of the major countries relative to the U.S. dollar and on a trade-weighted basis to all currencies. The main point that comes across from looking at these results for the period 1988–1993E is the cyclical changes—periods of strength followed by periods of weakness, then strength again. It emphasizes the importance of these changes and the need to forecast them.

Overall, the prospects for 1993 were considered flat but not disastrous. The analysts did not expect a collapse in the profitability of major European chemical companies. They envisioned a period of relatively flat performance, with some possibilities of improvement in late 1993 and into 1994, especially if the U.S. dollar gained in strength.

The rest of the report discussed the major chemical firms and made specific recommendations regarding each of them. This segment of the report on individual companies will be considered in our next chapter on company analysis.

SUMMARY

Several studies have examined industry performance and risk. They have found wide dispersion in the performance of alternative industries during specified time periods, implying that industry analysis can help identify superior investments. They also showed inconsistent industry performance over time, implying that looking at only past performance of an industry has little value in projecting future performance. Also, the performance by firms within industries is typically not very consistent, so you must analyze individual companies in an industry following the industry analysis.

The analysis of industry risk indicated wide dispersion in the measures of risk for different industries, but a fair amount of consistency in the risk measure over time for individual industries. These results imply that risk analysis and measurement are useful in selecting industries and that past risk measures may be of some value.

The two-step approach to estimating the value of an industry involves estimating earnings per share beginning with an estimate of sales. We considered three techniques to estimate sales: the industrial life cycle, input–output analysis, and the relationship of the industry sales to alternative economic series. We estimated earnings per share based on an estimate of the operating profit margin, depreciation expense, interest expense, and the industry tax rate. In the second half of the procedure we estimated the earnings multiplier for the industry through macroanalysis and a microanalysis.

An important part of industry analysis is the examination of five factors that determine the intensity of competition in an industry, which in turn affects its long-run profitability.

Global industry analysis must evaluate the effects not only of world supply, demand, and cost components for an industry, but also the impact of exchange rates on the total industry and the firms within it.

QUESTIONS

1. Briefly describe the results of studies that examined the performance of alternative industries during specific time periods and discuss their implications for industry analysis.

2. Briefly describe the results of the studies that examined industry performance over time and discuss their implications for industry analysis. Do these results complicate or simplify industry analysis?

3. Assume that all the firms in a particular industry have consistently experienced rates of return that were similar to the results for the industry. Discuss what this implies regarding the importance of industry and company analysis for this industry.

4. Some observers have contended that differences in the performance of various firms within an industry limit the usefulness of industry analysis. Discuss this contention.

5. Several studies have examined the difference in risk for alternative industries during a specified time period. Describe the results of these studies and discuss their implications for industry analysis.

6. What were the results when risk was examined for different industries during successive time periods? Discuss the implication of these results for industry analysis.

7. Assume that the industry you are analyzing is in the fourth stage of the industrial life cycle. How would you react if your industry–economic analysis predicted that sales per share for this industry would increase by 20 percent? Discuss your reasoning.

8. Discuss at what stage in the industrial life cycle you would like to discover a firm and justify your decision.

9. Discuss an example of input–output analysis to predict the sales for an industry. Discuss how you would use input–output analysis to predict the costs of production for your industry.

10. Discuss an example of the impact of one of the five competitive forces on an industry's profitability.

PROBLEMS

1. Select three industries from the S&P *Analysts Handbook* with different demand factors. For each industry indicate what economic series you would use to help you predict the growth for the industry. Discuss why the economic series selected is relevant for this industry.

2. Prepare a scatter plot for one of the industries in Problem 1 of industry sales per share and observations from the economic series you suggested for this industry. Do this for the most recent 10 years using information available in the *Analysts Handbook*. Based on the results of the scatter plot, discuss whether the economic series was closely related to this industry's sales.

3. Using the S&P *Analysts Handbook*, plot the latest 10-year history of the operating profit margin for the S&P 400 versus the S&P defined industry of your choice. Is there a positive, negative, or zero correlation?

4. Using the S&P *Analysts Handbook*, calculate the means for the following variables of the S&P 400 and the industry of your choice during the last 10 years:
   a. Price/earnings multiplier
   b. Retention rate
   c. Return on equity
   d. Equity turnover
   e. Net profit margin

   Note: Each of these entries is a ratio, so take care when averaging. Briefly comment on how your industry and the S&P 400 differ for each of the variables.

5. Industry information can be found in *Barron's Market Laboratory/Economic Indicators*. Using issues over the past 6 months, plot the trend for
   a. Auto production
   b. Auto inventories (domestic and imports)
   c. Newsprint production
   d. Newsprint inventories
   e. Business inventories

   What tentative conclusions do these data support regarding the current economic environment?

6. Prepare a table listing variables that influence the earnings multiplier for your chosen industry and the S&P 400 series for the most recent 10 years.
   a. Do the average dividend-payout ratio for your industry and the S&P 400 differ? How should the dividend payout influence the difference between the multipliers?
   b. Would you expect the risk for this industry to differ from that for the market? In

what direction, and why? What effect will this difference in risk have on the industry multiplier relative to the market multiplier?

    c. Analyze and discuss the different components of growth (retention rate, total asset turnover, total assets/equity, and profit margin) for your chosen industry and the S&P 400 during the most recent 10 years. Based on this analysis, how would you expect the growth rate for your industry to compare to the growth rate for the S&P 400? How would this difference in expected growth affect the multiplier?

7. Where is your industry in its industrial life cycle? Justify your answer by reference to your prior analysis.

8. Evaluate your industry in terms of the five factors that determine an industry's competitive structure. Discuss your expectations for this industry's long-run profitability.

REFERENCES

Aber, John. "Industry Effects and Multivariate Stock Price Behavior." *Journal of Financial and Quantitative Analysis* 11, no. 5 (November 1976).

Fruhan, William E., Jr. *Financial Strategy.* Homewood, Ill.: Richard D. Irwin, 1979.

Livingston, Miles. "Industry Movements of Common Stocks." *Journal of Finance* 32, no. 3 (June 1977).

Meyers, Stephen L. "A Re-Examination of Market and Industry Factors in Stock Price Behavior." *Journal of Finance* 28, no. 3 (June 1973).

Porter, Michael E. "Industry Structure and Competitive Strategy: Keys to Profitability." *Financial Analysts Journal* 36, no. 4 (July-August 1980).

Porter, Michael E. *Competitive Strategy: Techniques for Analyzing Industries and Competitors.* New York: Free Press, 1980.

Porter, Michael E. *Competitive Advantage: Creating and Sustaining Superior Performance.* New York: Free Press, 1985.

Porter, Michael E. "How to Conduct an Industry Analysis." In *The Financial Analysts Handbook.* 2d ed., edited by Sumner N. Levine. Homewood, Ill.: Dow Jones-Irwin, 1988.

Reilly, Frank K., and Eugene Drzycimski. "Alternative Industry Performance and Risk." *Journal of Financial and Quantitative Analysis* 9, no. 3 (June 1974).

Stewart, Samuel S. "Forecasting Corporate Earnings." In *The Financial Analysts Handbook.* 2d ed., edited by Sumner N. Levine. Homewood, Ill.: Dow Jones-Irwin, 1988.

APPENDIX 17A   PREPARING AN INDUSTRY ANALYSIS

WHAT IS AN INDUSTRY[1]

Identifying a company's industry can be difficult in today's business world. Although airlines, railroads, and utilities may be easy to categorize, what about manufacturing companies with three different divisions and none of them are dominant? Perhaps the best way to test whether a company fits into an industry grouping is to compare the operating results for the company and an industry. For our purposes, an industry is a group of companies with similar demand, supply, and operating characteristics.

    The following is a set of guidelines for preparing an industry appraisal including the topics to consider and some specific items to include.

---

[1]Reprinted and adapted with permission of Stanley D. Ryals, CFA; Investment Council, Inc.; La Crescenta, CA 91214.

CHARACTERISTICS
TO STUDY

1. Price history reveals valuable long-term relationships
    a. Price-earnings ratios
    b. Common stock yields
    c. Price-book value ratios
    d. Price-cash flow ratios
2. Operating data shows comparisons of
    a. Return on total investment (ROI)
    b. Return on equity (ROE)
    c. Sales growth
    d. Trends in operating profit margin
    e. Evaluation of stage in industrial life cycle
    f. Book value growth
    g. Earnings per share growth
    h. Profit margin trends
    i. Evaluation of exchange rate risk from foreign sales
3. Comparative results of industries show
    a. Effects of business cycles on each industry group
    b. Secular trends affecting results
    c. Industry growth compared to other industries
    d. Regulatory changes
    e. Importance of overseas operations

FACTORS IN
INDUSTRY
ANALYSIS

MARKETS FOR PRODUCTS
1. Trends in the markets for the industry's major products, historical and projected
2. Industry growth relative to GDP or other relevant economic series; possible changes from past trends
3. Shares of market for major products among domestic and global producers; changes in market shares in recent years; outlook
4. Effect of imports on industry markets; share of market taken by imports; price and margin changes caused by imports
5. Effect of exports on their markets; trends in export prices and units exported; historical trends and expectations for the exchange rates in major non-U.S. countries

FINANCIAL PERFORMANCE
1. Capitalization ratios; ability to raise new capital; earnings retention rate; financial leverage
2. Ratio of fixed assets to capital invested; depreciation policies; capital turnover
3. Return on total capital; return on equity capital; components of ROE
4. Return on foreign investments; need for foreign capital.

OPERATIONS
1. Degrees of integration; cost advantages of integration; major supply contracts
2. Operating rates as a percentage of capacity; backlogs; new order trends
3. Trends of industry consolidation
4. Trends in industry competition

5. New product development; research and development expenditures in dollars and as a percentage of sales
6. Diversification; comparability of product lines

MANAGEMENT

1. Management depth and ability to develop from within; board of directors; organizational structure
2. Flexibility to deal with product demand changes; ability to identify and eliminate losing operations
3. Record and outlook of labor relations
4. Dividend progression

SOURCES OF INDUSTRY INFORMATION

1. Independent industry journals
2. Industry and trade associations
3. Government reports and statistics
4. Independent research organizations
5. Brokerage house research

CHAPTER 18

COMPANY ANALYSIS AND STOCK SELECTION

In this chapter we will answer the following questions:

- Why is it important to differentiate between company analysis and stock analysis?
- What is the difference between a growth company and a growth stock?
- What techniques are available for estimating company sales?
- What are the steps in estimating the profit margins and earnings per share for a company?
- What are the procedures and factors considered when estimating the earnings multiplier for a firm?
- In addition to the earnings multiplier, what are some other relative valuation ratios that analysts use?
- What are the two specific competitive strategies that a firm can use to cope with the competitive environment in its industry?
- What are some additional factors that should be considered when carrying out company analysis on a global basis?
- What is meant by a true growth company?
- Why is it inappropriate to use the standard dividend discount model to value a true growth company?
- What is meant by a no-growth firm?
- What is the difference between simple growth and dynamic growth?
- What is the growth duration model and what information does it provide to you when analyzing a true growth company and evaluating its stock?
- What is the flexible three-stage growth model and how would you describe the three stages?

At this point you have made two decisions about your investment in equity markets. First, after analyzing the economy and stock markets for several countries, you have decided that you should invest some portion of your portfolio in common stocks. Second, after analyzing a number of industries, you have identified those that offer above-average risk-adjusted performance over your investment horizon. You must now answer the final question in the fundamental analysis procedure: Which are the best companies within these desirable industries and are their stocks underpriced? Specifically, is the value of the stock above its market value or is the expected rate of return on the stock equal to or greater than the required rate of return on it?

We begin this chapter with a discussion of the difference between company analysis and stock selection. We then present an analysis of a company using the technique that was employed in Chapters 16 and 17 to estimate the value of the stock market and an industry. Specifically, we use the dividend discount model to value Walgreen Company shares. Following our valuation example we consider some other valuation measures that you can use to evaluate stock issues. We then discuss some competitive strategies that can help firms maximize returns in an industry's competitive environment. We then present an example of the analysis of foreign stocks. The final section in the chapter discusses the unique features of true growth companies and considers several models that can be used to determine the relative value of these companies.

ANALYSIS OF COMPANIES VERSUS THE SELECTION OF STOCK

The title of this chapter, "Company Analysis and Stock Selection," is meant to convey the idea that *the common stocks of good companies are not necessarily good investments.* In our discussion of the firm value, we will analyze a company and its internal characteristics. The analysis should give you opinions about the quality of the firm and its management, and about its outlook for the future.

Remember, however, that the quality of the company need not reflect the desirability of the company's stock as an investment. As a final step, you must compare the intrinsic value of a stock to its market value to determine if you should invest in it. The point is, the stock of a wonderful firm with superior management and performance measured by sales and earnings growth can be priced so high that the value of the stock is below its market price. Therefore, you would not want to buy the stock of this wonderful company. In contrast, the stock of a company with less success based on its sales and earnings growth may have a stock market price that is below its intrinsic value. In this case, although the company is not as good, its stock could be a good addition to your portfolio.

The classic confusion in this regard concerns growth companies versus growth stocks. The stock of a growth company is not necessarily a growth stock. Recognition of this difference is very important for successful investing.

GROWTH COMPANIES AND GROWTH STOCKS

Growth companies have historically been defined as companies that consistently experience above-average increases in sales and earnings. This definition has some limitations because many firms could qualify due to certain accounting procedures, mergers, or other external events.

In contrast, financial theorists define a growth company as a firm with the management ability and the opportunities to *make investments that yield rates of return greater than the firm's required rate of return.*[1] You will recall from financial management courses that this required rate of return is the firm's average cost of capital. As an example, a growth company might be able to acquire capital at an average cost of 10 percent, and yet have the management ability and the opportunity to invest those funds

---

[1] Ezra Solomon, *The Theory of Financial Management* (New York: Columbia University Press, 1963), 55–68; and Merton Miller and Franco Modigliani, "Dividend Policy, Growth and the Valuation of Shares," *Journal of Business* 34, no. 4 (October 1961): 411–433.

at rates of return of 15 to 20 percent. As a *result* of these investment opportunities, the firm's sales and earnings grow more than those of other firms of equal risk or the overall economy. In addition, a growth company that has above-average investment opportunities should, and typically does, retain a large portion of its earnings to fund these superior investment projects.

Growth stocks are not necessarily shares in growth companies. A *growth stock* is a stock with a higher rate of return than other stocks in the market with similar risk characteristics. The stock achieves this superior return because at some point in time the market undervalued it compared to other stocks. Although the stock market adjusts stock prices relatively quickly and accurately to reflect new information, available information is not always perfect or complete. Therefore, imperfect or incomplete information may cause a given stock to be undervalued or overvalued at a point in time.[2]

If the stock is undervalued, its price should eventually increase to reflect its true fundamental value when the correct information becomes available. During this period of price adjustment, the stock's realized returns will exceed the required returns for a stock with its risk, and it will be considered a growth stock.

Identifying a growth stock as a currently undervalued stock that has a high probability of being properly valued in the near term means that growth stocks are not necessarily limited to growth companies. In fact, if investors recognize a growth company and discount the future earnings stream properly, the current market price of the growth company's stock will reflect its future earnings stream. Thus, those who acquire the stock of a growth company at this *correct* market price will receive a rate of return consistent with the risk of the stock, even when the superior earnings growth is attained. In fact, in many instances investors tend to overprice the stock of a growth company. In turn, investors who acquire the stock of a growth company at such an inflated price will earn a rate of return below the risk-adjusted required rate of return despite the fact that the company fulfills its bright prospects. A future growth stock can be issued by any type of company; the stock need only be undervalued by the market.

The search for a stock that was a growth stock in the past is relatively easy because you only need to examine past rates of return relative to risk. The investor, however, must search for *future* growth stocks. One who uncovers such stocks consistently is, by definition, a superior analyst or investor.[3] A study that examined the stock price performance for a sample of growth companies found an inverse relationship, that is, the stock of growth companies did poorly.[4]

OTHER COMPANY–
STOCK
COMPARISONS

DEFENSIVE COMPANIES AND STOCKS

Defensive companies are those whose future earnings are likely to withstand an economic downturn. One would expect them to have relatively low business risk and not excessive financial risk. Typical examples are public utilities or grocery chains—firms that supply basic consumer necessities.

---

[2] As noted in Chapter 6, an analyst is more likely to find such stocks outside the top tier of companies, because these top-tier stocks are scrutinized by numerous analysts; in other words, look for "neglected" stocks.

[3] See the discussion in Chapter 6 on "Evaluating the Performance of Analysts."

[4] Michael Solt and Meir Statman, "Good Companies, Bad Stocks," *Journal of Portfolio Management* 15, no. 4 (Summer 1989): 39–44. Similar results for "excellent" companies were derived in Michelle Clayman, "In Search of Excellence: The Investor's Viewpoint," *Financial Analysts Journal* 43, no. 3 (May-June 1987): 54–63.

There are two closely related concepts of a defensive stock. First, a defensive stock's rate of return is not expected to decline during an overall market decline, or not decline as much as the overall market. Second, our CAPM discussion indicated that an asset's relevant risk is its covariance with the market portfolio of risky assets, that is, an asset's systematic risk. A stock with low systematic risk (a small beta) would be considered a defensive stock according to this theory.

CYCLICAL COMPANIES AND STOCKS

A cyclical company's sales and earnings will be heavily influenced by aggregate business activity. Such a company will do very well during economic expansions and very poorly during economic contractions. This volatile earnings pattern is typically a function of the firm's business risk and can be compounded by financial risk.

A cyclical stock will experience changes in its rates of return that are greater than changes in overall market rates of return. In terms of the CAPM, these would be stocks that have high betas. The stock of a cyclical company, however, is not necessarily cyclical. A cyclical stock is the stock of any company that has returns that are more volatile than the overall market.

SPECULATIVE COMPANIES AND STOCKS

A speculative company is one whose assets involve great risk, but it also has a possibility of great gain. A good example of a speculative firm is one involved in oil exploration.

A speculative stock possesses a high probability of low or negative rates of return and a low probability of normal or high rates of return. This can be the stock of a speculative company (e.g., a penny mining stock), or it can be the opposite of a growth stock. Specifically, a speculative stock is one that is overpriced, so there is a high probability that during the future period when the market adjusts the stock price to its true value, it will experience either very low or possibly negative rates of return. This might be the case for an excellent growth company whose stock is selling at an extremely high price/earnings ratio.

The point is, you must examine a company to determine its characteristics and derive an estimate of the value for the stock. Then you compare this derived, intrinsic value of the stock to its current market price to determine whether you should acquire it. Specifically, based on a comparison of the stock's estimated intrinsic value and its market price, will the stock provide a rate of return that is consistent with its risk?

ESTIMATING THE VALUE OF A COMPANY

The purpose of this section is to compute a value for a particular company and compare that value to the market price of its stock. To do this, we select a firm and examine its sales and earnings performance, as well as its strategies and policies, relative to its industry and the market. This analysis continues our example from Chapter 16 by evaluating a company in the retail drugstore industry.

We selected the Walgreen Company, the largest retail drugstore chain in the United States. It operates 1,736 drugstores in 29 states and Puerto Rico. General merchandise accounts for 25 percent of total sales and pharmacy generates 44 percent.

Although we limit our demonstration to Walgreen, your complete company analysis would cover all the firms in the retail drugstore industry to determine which stocks should perform the best. The objective is to estimate the expected return and risk for all the individual firms in the industry over the investment horizon.

Similar to the market and industry analysis, you estimate the stock's expected return by estimating its future value. You derive these future values by predicting the stock's earnings per share and expected earnings multiplier.

ESTIMATING COMPANY EARNINGS PER SHARE

Expected earnings per share is a function of the sales forecast and the estimated profit margin.

COMPANY SALES FORECAST

The sales forecast includes an analysis of the relationship of company sales to various relevant economic series and to the retail drugstore industry series. These comparisons tell us how the company is performing relative to the economy and its closest competition. Besides providing background on the company, these relationships can help us develop specific sales forecasts for Walgreen.

Table 18.1 contains data on sales for Walgreen from its annual report, sales per share for the retail drugstore industry, and several personal consumption expenditure (PCE) series for the period 1970 to 1991.

To examine the relationship of Walgreen sales to the economy we considered several alternative series. The series that had the strongest relationship was personal

TABLE 18.1   **Data Used in the Comparative Analysis of Sales for Walgreen Company, the Retail Drugstore Industry, and Various Economic Series: 1970–1991**

Year	Sales Walgreen Company ($ millions)	Retail Drugstore Industry (sales per share)	Personal Consumption Expenditures ($ billions)	Personal Consumption Expenditures per Capita	Personal Consumption Expenditures— Medical Care ($ billions)	PCE- Medical Care/ Total PCE (Percent)
1970	$ 743.6	$ 12.46	$ 646.5	$ 3,152	$ 50.1	7.7%
1971	817.5	16.79	700.3	3,372	56.5	8.1
1972	863.3	18.58	767.8	3,658	63.5	8.3
1973	930.9	22.43	848.1	4,002	71.2	8.4
1974	996.6	27.61	927.7	4,337	80.1	8.6
1975	1,079.1	25.89	1,024.9	4,745	93.0	9.1
1976	1,169.8	36.40	1,143.1	5,241	106.2	9.3
1977	1,223.2	43.99	1,271.5	5,772	122.4	9.6
1978	1,192.9	49.87	1,421.2	6,384	139.7	9.8
1979	1,344.5	73.39	1,583.7	7,035	157.8	10.0
1980	1,530.7	84.82	1,748.1	7,677	181.3	10.4
1981	1,743.5	95.50	1,926.2	8,375	213.6	11.1
1982	2,039.5	109.22	2,059.2	8,868	240.5	11.7
1983	2,360.6	118.85	2,257.5	9,634	265.7	11.8
1984	2,744.6	135.15	2,460.3	10,408	290.6	11.8
1985	3,161.9	153.30	2,667.4	11,184	319.3	12.0
1986	3,660.6	157.74	2,850.6	11,843	346.4	12.2
1987	4,281.6	191.22	3,052.2	12,568	384.7	12.6
1988	4,883.5	217.80	3,296.1	13,448	427.7	13.0
1989	5,380.1	239.68	3,523.1	14,241	471.9	13.4
1990	6,047.5	265.77	3,748.4	14,996	524.9	14.0
1991	6,733.0	283.50	3,887.7	15,384	580.2	14.9

Sources: Walgreen Company annual reports; *Economic Report of the President*, various issues.

FIGURE 18.1   **Scatter Plot of Walgreen Sales and PCE-Medical Care: 1970–1991**

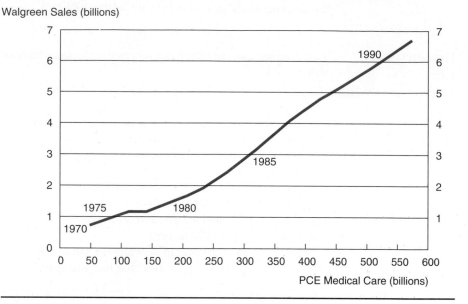

consumption expenditure for medicine (PCE-medical care).[5] The scatter plot of Walgreen sales and the PCE-medical care expenditures contained in Figure 18.1 indicates
a strong linear relationship, even though Walgreen sales have not grown as fast as PCE-
medical care. During the period 1970 to 1991 Walgreen sales increased by about 805
percent compared to an increase in PCE-medical care of 1058 percent. As a result,
Walgreen sales have gone from about 1.61 percent of PCE-medical care to 1.16 percent.

The graph in Figure 18.2 that compares Walgreen sales and sales per share for the
retail drugstore industry does not reflect a very strong relationship because of the
exceptional growth of industry sales.

The figures in the last column of Table 18.1 indicate that during this period, the
proportion of PCE allocated to medical care went from less than 8 percent in 1970 to
almost 15 percent in 1991. The increasing proportion of PCE spent on medical care is
a function of the growing proportion of the population over 65 and the rising cost of
medical care. Although Walgreen sales are not growing as fast as medical expenditures,
these increases should be beneficial for Walgreen sales because 44 percent of sales is
prescriptions. Notably, these increases in medical care expenditures continued during
the economic recessions in 1981 to 1982 and in 1990 to 1991.

As shown in Table 18.2 the internal sales growth for Walgreen resulted from an
increase in the number of stores (from 554 in 1970 to 1,736 in 1992) and an increase
in the annual sales per store because of the upgrading of stores. The net increase in
number of stores includes numerous new, large stores and the closing of many smaller

---

[5] The relationship between Walgreen sales and total PCE or per capita PCE were significant but not as strong as
PCE-medical care.

FIGURE 18.2   **Scatter Plot of Walgreen Sales and RSD Industry Sales: 1970–1991**

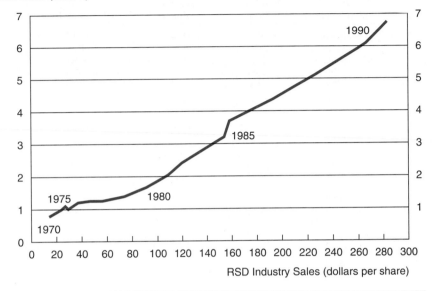

Walgreen Sales (billions)

RSD Industry Sales (dollars per share)

stores. As a result, the average size of stores has increased. More important, the firm has increased its sales per square foot, which is a critical value in the retailing industry.

SAMPLE ESTIMATE OF WALGREEN SALES

The foregoing analysis indicates that you should use the Walgreen–PCE-medical care graph. To estimate PCE-medical care you should initially project total PCE and then determine how much would be included in the medical care component. As noted in Chapter 17 in connection with the industry analysis, economists were forecasting an increase in PCE of 5 percent during 1993, which implied a 1993 estimate of $3,574.4 billion. In addition, it was estimated that the percentage of PCE spent on medical care would increase in 1993 to 16 percent. This implies an estimate for PCE-medical care of $679.1 billion, which is about a 7 percent increase from 1992. Based on the graph in Figure 18.1, which shows the historical relationship between these two variables, this would imply a 6 percent increase in Walgreen sales to about $7.924 billion (7.475 billion × 1.06). Notably, this estimate is below the firm's recent growth in sales.

Firms in this industry provide data on square footage and the number of stores. This allows us to compute an alternative sales estimate using these company data in Table 18.2 to support the prior estimate that was based on macroeconomic data. Assuming an increase in store area during 1993 of about 850,000 square feet (which is approximately what happened in 1990, 1991, and 1992), the firm's total sales area would be about 17.66 million square feet. As noted, sales per square foot have likewise increased. Assuming a continued increase to $460 of sales per square foot implies a sales forecast of about $8,124 million for 1993, an 8.7 percent increase over 1992 sales of $7,475 million.

TABLE 18.2   **Data on Sales, Number of Stores, and Sales Area for Walgreen: 1970–1992**

Year	Sales ($ millions)	Number of Stores	Annual Sales per Store ($ millions)	Store Area (000 square feet)	Average Area per Store (000 square feet)	Sales per Thousand (square feet)
1970	$ 743.6	554	$1.34	N/A	N/A	N/A
1971	817.5	561	1.46	N/A	N/A	N/A
1972	863.3	572	1.51	N/A	N/A	N/A
1973	930.9	569	1.64	N/A	N/A	N/A
1974	996.6	616	1.62	4,963	8.06	$200.81
1975	1,079.1	633	1.70	5,133	8.11	210.81
1976	1,169.8	632	1.85	5,221	8.26	224.06
1977	1,223.2	626	1.95	5,188	8.29	235.77
1978	1,192.9	641	1.86	5,390	8.41	221.32
1979	1,344.5	688	1.95	5,851	8.50	229.79
1980	1,530.7	739	2.07	6,305	8.53	242.78
1981	1,743.5	821	2.12	7,209	8.78	241.85
1982	2,039.5	883	2.31	7,815	8.85	260.97
1983	2,360.6	941	2.51	8.402	8.93	280.96
1984	2,744.6	1,002	2.74	9,002	8.98	304.89
1985	3,161.9	1,095	2.89	10,010	9.14	315.87
1986	3,660.6	1,273	2.88	11,895	9.34	307.74
1987	4,281.6	1,356	3.16	12,844	9.47	333.35
1988	4,883.5	1,416	3.45	13.549	9.57	360.43
1989	5,380.1	1,484	3.63	14,272	9.62	376.97
1990	6,047.5	1,564	3.87	15,105	9.66	400.36
1991	6,733.0	1,646	4.09	15,877	9.65	424.07
1992	7,475.0	1,736	4.31	16,811	9.68	444.65

N/A = Data not available.

Source: Walgreen Company annual reports.

Another internal estimate is possible using the number of stores and sales per store. Walgreen is expected to open at least 130 stores during 1993. Assuming they close 30, this would be a net addition of 100 to the 1,736 at the end of 1992. Assuming sales per store likewise continues to increase from $4.31 million to $4.45 million implies an estimate of $8,170 (1,836 × $4.45 million), which is an increase of 9.3 percent over 1992.

Given the three estimates, the preference is for an estimate close to the high value of 9.3 percent because of the positive economic environment and the company's ability to increase sales by about 11 percent during less prosperous times in 1991 and 1992. Therefore we will assume a 9 percent increase, which implies a final sales forecast for 1993 of $8,148 million.

ESTIMATING THE COMPANY PROFIT MARGIN

The next step in projecting earnings per share is to estimate the firm's net profit margin, which should include two considerations: (1) the internal performance, including general company trends and consideration of any problems that might affect future performance, and (2) the firm's relationship with its industry, which should indicate whether the company's past performance (either good or bad) is attributable to its industry or is unique to the firm. These examinations should help us understand the

TABLE 18.3

Profit Margins for Walgreen Company and the Retail Drugstore Industry: 1970–1991

Year	Walgreen Company			Retail Drugstores		
	Operating Profit Margin	NBT Margin	Net Profit Margin	Operating Profit Margin	NBT Margin	Net Profit Margin
1970	2.57%	2.15%	1.26%	8.83%	7.30%	3.77%
1971	2.62	2.23	1.30	8.46	6.79	3.51
1972	2.63	2.26	1.32	8.93	7.75	4.04
1973	2.97	2.65	1.47	8.87	7.27	3.70
1974	1.58	1.18	0.76	7.57	6.08	3.08
1975	1.78	1.38	0.91	8.65	7.45	3.75
1976	2.97	2.51	1.46	9.18	8.19	4.09
1977	3.11	2.66	1.46	8.96	7.91	4.07
1978	3.86	3.73	2.16	8.78	7.74	4.03
1979	3.86	3.79	2.25	7.24	6.40	3.47
1980	3.56	3.52	2.27	7.07	6.27	3.47
1981	3.40	3.54	2.42	7.17	6.18	3.45
1982	4.32	4.20	2.75	7.30	6.22	3.44
1983	5.16	5.11	2.96	7.98	6.88	3.79
1984	5.57	5.46	3.11	7.19	5.53	3.03
1985	5.63	5.49	2.98	7.00	5.06	2.75
1986	5.37	5.13	2.82	7.37	5.67	3.11
1987	4.92	4.54	2.42	7.08	5.14	2.88
1988	4.59	4.28	2.64	6.70	4.71	2.89
1989	4.71	4.53	2.87	6.71	4.49	2.79
1990	4.70	4.65	2.89	6.71	4.68	2.89
1991	4.77	4.63	2.90	6.52	4.71	2.71
Averages:						
1970–1991	3.85	3.62	2.15	7.74	6.29	3.40
1970–1979	2.79	2.44	1.44	8.55	7.29	3.75
1980–1989	4.72	4.58	2.72	7.16	5.62	3.16

Sources: Walgreen Company annual reports; Standard & Poor's *Analysts Handbook* (New York: Standard & Poor's Corporation, 1992).Reprinted by permission of Standard & Poor's Corp.

firm's past performance, but also provide the background to make a meaningful estimate for the future. In this analysis, we do not consider the company–economy relationship because the significant economywide profit factors are reflected in the industry results.

Profit margin figures for Walgreen and the retail drugstore industry are in Table 18.3. The profit margins for Walgreen increased from 1970 to the mid-1980s followed by a decline through 1988 and a recovery in 1991. In contrast, the margins for the retail drugstore industry experienced a relatively flat pattern during the 1970s, but a steady decline throughout the 1980s and early 1990s. Overall, Walgreen experienced a positive trend in its operating and net profit margins over the past 22 years, which has caused its net profit margin to be about equal to the industry. To predict future values, you need to determine the reason for the overall decline in the industry profit margin and, more important, what factors have caused Walgreen's strong positive performance.

INDUSTRY FACTORS

Industry profit margins have declined over the past two decades due to price discounting by aggressive regional drug chains.[6] The discussion in Chapter 17 suggested this as one of the competitive structure conditions that affect long-run profitability. Industry analysts have observed, however, that price cutting has subsided, and they currently foresee relative price stability. In addition, drugstores have tended toward a more profitable product mix featuring high profit margin items such as cosmetics, and this has positively influenced profit margins.

COMPANY PERFORMANCE

Walgreen's profit margin has showed consistent improvement, and a major reason has been the change in corporate structure. The outlook for profit margins is good because the firm has developed a strong position in the pharmacy business and has invested in service (including mail-order prescriptions) and inventory control technology that will help the firm experience strong margins on this business. The firm has also emphasized other high profit margin items such as greeting cards, photofinishing, and cosmetics.

Specific estimates for Walgreen's future margins would typically begin with an analysis of their relationship with drugstore industry margins using time-series plots such as those in Figure 18.3.[7]

This time-series plot for the period 1970 to 1991 showed good results for Walgreen's versus its industry. Specifically, the net profit margins for the company and industry have come together over time due to steady improvements by Walgreen. You should also consider any unique factors that would influence this long-run relationship, such as any price wars that would be reported in business publications or an abnormal number of store openings or closings as reported by the firm in quarterly or annual earnings reports.

Following a consideration of the long-run company–industry profit margin relationship, you should analyze the firm's common size income statement for several years. As discussed in Chapter 10, the breakdown of the income statement depends on the consistent detail provided by the firm.

Table 18.4 contains a common size income statement for Walgreen during the period 1988 to 1991. An analysis of the main items of interest—cost of goods sold and operating expense—is both encouraging and discouraging. The cost-of-sales percentage increased steadily through 1990, then declined in 1991. In contrast, there was steady decline in the percentage of SG&A expense through 1990 with a small increase in 1991. Interest expense has declined in dollars and percentage through 1991, and interest income increased substantially in 1989 prior to a small decline in 1993. Finally, the tax rate remained at about 37 percent during the last several years.

---

[6] For a more complete discussion, see "Retailing—Drug Stores," *Standard and Poor's Industry Surveys* (New York: Standard & Poor's, 1992).

[7] Both the operating margin and the net before tax margin were analyzed; the results indicated that the net profit margins yielded the best relationships. The long-run relationship cannot be very good because over the total period the industry margin was declining while Walgreen experienced fairly steady increases as shown in Figure 18.3.

FIGURE 18.3   **Time-Series Plot of Net Profit Margin for Walgreen and RSD Industry: 1970–1991**

Net Profit Margin

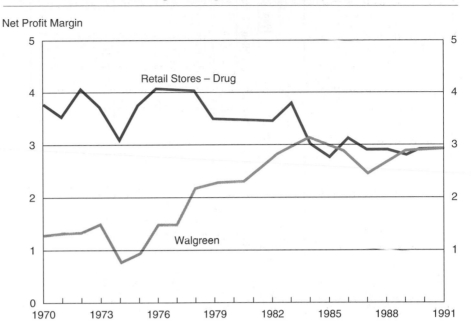

NET PROFIT MARGIN ESTIMATE

The overall industry outlook is encouraging because of stable prices, an increase in mechanization within the industry, and the inclusion of more high profit margin items. Therefore, the industry profit margin is expected to increase during 1993. Because of Walgreen's strong relationship to the industry profit margin and the increase in its margin since 1989 as shown in the common size income statement, it is estimated that the firm will show a further small increase during 1993 to 3 percent.

COMPUTING EARNINGS PER SHARE

This margin estimate, combined with the prior sales estimate of $8,148 million, indicates net income of $244.5 million. Assuming about 123,070 million common shares outstanding, earnings should be about $2.00 per share for 1993, which is an increase of about 12 percent over the earnings of $1.78 per share in 1992.[8] To find the value of Walgreen Company stock, our next step is to estimate its earnings multiplier.

---

[8] The earnings per share for Walgreen for 1992 is noted here because it is available. Still, most of the analysis in the rest of the chapter is limited to 1991 because of the need for comparable industry and market data, which were not available as of mid-1993.

TABLE 18.4   **Walgreen Company Common Size Income Statement**

	1991		1990		1989		1988	
	$ million	Percent	$ million	Percent	$ million	Percent	$ million	Percent
Net sales	$6,733.0	100.0%	$6,047.5	100.0%	$5,380.1	100.0%	$4,883.5	100.0%
Cost of sales	4,829.2	71.7	4,356.4	72.0	3,848.5	71.5	3,469.0	71.0
Gross profit	$1,903.8	28.3	$1,691.1	28.0	$1,531.6	28.5	$1,414.5	29.0
Selling, general, and administrative expense	1,582.7	23.5	1,406.9	23.3	1,278.1	23.8	1,190.3	24.4
Operating profit	$ 321.1	4.5	$ 284.2	4.7	$ 253.5	4.7	$ 224.2	4.6
Interest expense	18.2	0.3	18.8	0.3	18.8	0.3	19.8	0.4
Interest income	13.1	0.2	15.5	0.3	15.3	0.3	4.5	0.1
Extraordinary loss	9.2	0.1	0.0	0.0	6.1	0.1	0.0	0.0
Net before taxes	$ 311.9	4.6	$ 280.9	4.6	$ 243.9	4.5	$ 208.9	4.3
Tax excluding investment credit	117.0	1.7	106.3	1.8	89.6	1.7	79.9	1.6
Net earnings	$ 194.9	2.9	$ 174.6	2.9	$ 154.3	2.9	$ 129.0	2.6
Tax rate	—	37.5		37.8		36.7		38.2
Common shares outstanding (000)	123,071		123,071		123,034		123,028	
Net earnings per share	$ 1.58		$ 1.41		$ 1.26		$ 1.05	

ESTIMATING
COMPANY
EARNINGS
MULTIPLIERS

As in our prior analysis of industry multipliers in Chapter 17, to estimate a company multiplier, we use two approaches. First, we estimate the P/E ratio from the relationships among Walgreen, its industry, and the market. This is the macroanalysis. Second, we estimate a multiplier based on its three components: the dividend-payout ratio, the required rate of return, and the rate of growth. We then resolve the estimates derived from each approach and settle on one estimate.

MACROANALYSIS
OF THE EARNINGS
MULTIPLIER

Table 18.5 and Figure 18.4 show the mean earnings multiple for the company, the retail drugstore industry, and the aggregate market for the period 1970 to 1991. Walgreen's relationship to its industry has changed dramatically over time. During the 1970s and early 1980s, Walgreen's multiplier was consistently below the industry's. After 1983 the Walgreen multiplier has typically exceeded its industry by about 5 to 10 percent, although it was lower than the industry in 1991. Similarly, the Walgreen earnings

TABLE 18.5   **Average Earnings Multiple for Walgreen, the Retail Drugstore Industry, and the Standard & Poor's 400: 1970–1991**

	Walgreen Company			Retail Drugstore				S&P 400	
Year	EPS	Mean Price[a]	Mean P/E	EPS	Mean Price[a]	Mean P/E	Ratio Company/ Industry	Mean P/E	Ratio Company/ Market
1970	1.48	21.500	14.53	0.47	10.28	21.87	.66	16.49	.88
1971	1.59	27.500	17.30	0.59	18.16	30.78	.56	18.02	.96
1972	1.65	27.750	13.79	0.75	28.94	38.59	.36	17.95	.77
1973	1.95	17.625	9.04	0.83	26.00	31.33	.29	13.38	.68
1974	1.11	13.188	11.88	0.85	11.98	14.09	.84	9.43	1.26
1975	1.40	11.938	8.53	0.97	13.92	14.35	.59	10.79	.79
1976	2.05	15.000	7.32	1.49	19.86	13.33	.55	10.41	.70
1977	2.15	16.500	7.67	1.79	18.93	10.58	.73	9.55	.80
1978	3.53	23.250	6.59	2.01	22.2	11.05	.60	8.21	.80
1979	4.14	29.500	7.13	2.55	22.38	8.78	.81	7.11	1.00
1980	4.70	33.813	7.19	2.94	24.57	8.36	.86	8.44	.85
1981	5.53	46.563	8.42	3.29	34.62	10.52	.80	8.45	1.00
1982	3.66	40.313	11.01	3.76	41.58	11.06	1.00	10.37	1.06
1983	2.27	33.188	14.62	4.50	56.70	12.60	1.16	11.84	1.23
1984	2.78	36.938	13.29	4.10	58.30	14.22	.93	9.92	1.34
1985	1.53	25.875	16.91	4.22	68.28	16.18	1.05	13.68	1.23
1986	1.67	31.875	19.09	4.90	83.78	17.10	1.12	17.42	1.10
1987	1.68	34.813	20.72	5.53	98.93	17.89	1.16	20.68	1.00
1988	2.10	32.250	15.36	6.30	93.05	14.77	1.04	11.35	1.35
1989	2.50	40.125	16.05	6.69	107.46	16.06	1.00	13.79	1.16
1990	1.41	22.500	15.96	7.67	114.53	14.93	1.07	15.83	1.01
1991	1.58	23.594	14.93	8.26	139.70	16.91	0.88	25.65	0.58
Means:									
1970–1991	N.M.	N.M.	12.61	N.M.	N.M.	16.61	0.83	12.91	0.99
1970–1980	N.M.	N.M.	10.09	N.M.	N.M.	18.47	0.62	11.79	0.86
1981–1991	N.M.	N.M.	15.12	N.M.	N.M.	14.25	1.06	13.70	1.09

[a]The mean price is the average of the high price and low price for the year.

N.M. = Not meaningful.

Sources: Walgreen Company annual reports; Standard & Poor's *Analyst Handook* (New York: Standard & Poor's, 1992). Reprinted by permission of Standard & Poor's Corp.

FIGURE 18.4

Time-Series Plot of Mean Price/Earnings Ratios for Walgreen, RSD Industry, and S&P400

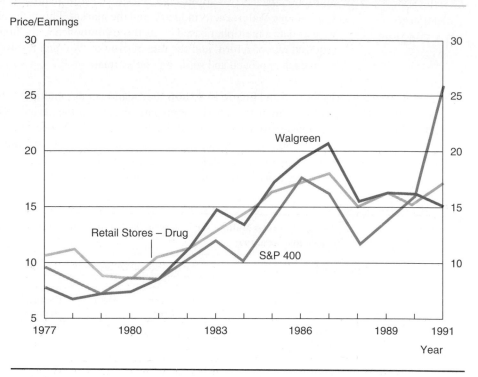

multiplier was typically lower than the market multiplier until 1982; it then began exceeding it until 1991, when it was lower again.

This pattern raises the question, is the premium of the Walgreen P/E relative to both the industry and market that prevailed prior to 1991 justified, or is the current discount relative to the market more appropriate? The microanalyses should provide some insights regarding this question.

MICROANALYSIS OF THE EARNINGS MULTIPLIER

The historical data for the relevant series are contained in Table 18.6. The relevant questions are (1) why was the earnings multiplier for Walgreen's above the market and industry earnings multiplier during most of the 1980s?, and (2) what happened in 1991 that caused this relationship to change? As before, we are looking for estimates of D/E, k, and g to find an earnings multiplier. We will use the historical data in Table 18.6 to determine patterns for the data and develop future projections.

COMPARING DIVIDEND-PAYOUT RATIOS

The dividend-payout ratio for Walgreen has typically been lower than its industry in recent years. The Walgreen–market comparison shows that Walgreen almost always had a lower payout. These results by themselves would produce a P/E ratio for Walgreen that is below the industry and the market P/E ratio.

TABLE 18.6   Variables That Influence the Earnings Multiple for Walgreen, Retail Drugstores, and the Standard & Poor's 400: 1977–1991

Year	Walgreen Company						Retail Drug Stores						S&P 400					
	D/E	TAT	TAE	E/T	NPM	ROE	D/E	TAT	TAE	E/T	NPM	ROE	D/E	TAT	TAE	E/T	NPM	ROE
1977	45.80	3.81	2.39	9.08	1.27	11.56	20.11	2.84	1.53	4.34	4.07	19.14	43.23	1.27	2.15	2.73	5.11	13.93
1978	30.31	3.45	2.34	8.16	2.16	17.65	23.88	2.81	1.52	4.27	4.03	18.39	41.18	1.27	2.22	2.81	5.19	14.60
1979	30.33	3.53	2.30	8.18	2.25	18.43	27.45	3.00	1.68	5.02	3.47	18.28	36.34	1.30	2.28	2.96	5.57	16.50
1980	30.47	3.60	2.16	8.00	2.27	18.20	29.25	3.04	1.66	5.06	3.47	18.25	40.26	1.31	2.30	3.02	4.92	14.88
1981	30.42	3.60	2.08	7.62	2.42	18.40	31.00	3.03	1.65	4.99	3.45	17.83	41.88	1.28	2.32	2.97	4.86	14.42
1982	26.93	3.59	2.06	7.42	2.75	20.40	31.12	2.97	1.66	4.93	3.44	18.13	54.02	1.17	2.40	2.82	3.95	11.13
1983	26.33	3.54	2.04	7.25	2.96	21.44	29.33	2.85	1.68	4.81	3.79	19.28	49.56	1.15	2.37	2.73	4.42	12.07
1984	25.84	3.52	2.03	7.16	3.11	22.30	37.56	2.66	1.88	5.00	3.03	16.26	41.47	1.22	2.52	3.06	4.77	14.61
1985	28.68	3.39	2.16	7.08	2.98	21.03	40.76	2.70	2.04	5.50	2.75	15.73	51.51	1.15	2.75	3.16	3.84	12.14
1986	29.81	3.39	2.16	7.08	2.82	19.97	32.86	2.71	1.96	5.31	3.11	17.67	56.94	1.08	2.88	3.12	3.75	11.70
1987	32.08	3.35	2.19	7.28	2.42	17.61	31.65	2.80	2.04	5.72	2.88	17.96	43.00	1.08	2.97	3.21	4.71	15.11
1988	28.59	3.40	2.12	7.32	2.64	19.34	30.63	2.82	2.07	5.83	2.89	18.39	38.54	0.97	3.59	3.48	5.50	19.13
1989	27.12	3.37	2.04	7.01	2.87	20.08	32.29	2.82	2.22	5.72	2.86	17.90	42.70	0.96	3.18	3.04	4.91	14.92
1990	28.19	3.16	2.02	6.38	2.89	18.43	31.68	2.82	2.16	5.63	2.89	17.60	31.27	0.97	3.27	3.07	4.26	13.05
1991	29.04	3.21	1.94	6.23	2.90	18.03	32.31	2.85	1.95	5.23	2.91	16.17	75.46	0.93	3.20	2.98	2.94	8.77
Means:	31.26	3.46	2.16	7.70	2.58	18.40	30.47	2.85	1.85	5.06	3.27	17.80	44.92	1.14	2.69	2.92	4.56	13.80

D/E = Dividend payout, equal to dividends/earnings.

TAT = Total asset turnover, equal to sales/total assets.

TAE = Leverage ratio, equal to total assets/ equity.

E/T = (Equity turnover) Equity turnover ratio, equal to sales/equity.

NPM = Net profit margin, equal to net income/sales.

ROE = Return on equity, equal to net income/equity.

ESTIMATING THE REQUIRED RATE OF RETURN

To find Walgreen's required rate of return (k), we should analyze the firm's internal risk characteristics (BR, FR, LR, ERR, and CR).

Walgreen should have relatively low business risk due to its stable sales growth compared to its industry and the aggregate economy. Notably, several measures of sales volatility did not support this expectation due to measurement problems. The coefficient of variation of sales that adjusts for absolute size indicated that Walgreen sales were less volatile than its industry, but more volatile than the market. It is necessary to adjust for trend because a high trend will cause a larger standard deviation because of the growth. To adjust for this growth factor, we computed the standard deviation of annual percentage changes. These results indicated that Walgreen was less volatile. Therefore, after adjusting for size and trend, the results indicated that Walgreen sales were less volatile, which indicates lower business risk.

Several financial risk variables for Walgreen, its industry, and the aggregate market are in Table 18.7. The firm's financial leverage ratio (total assets/equity) was about 2.00, which is comparable to the industry and definitely lower than the aggregate market. Walgreen has an interest coverage ratio of almost 15, a cash flow/long-term debt ratio of almost 300 percent, and a cash flow/total debt ratio of about 45 percent. These financial risk ratios indicate that Walgreen has *substantially lower* financial risk than its industry or the aggregate stock market.

The firm's liquidity risk is quite low compared to its industry and the average firm in the market. Indicators of market liquidity are (1) the number of stockholders, (2) the number of shares outstanding, (3) the number of shares traded, and (4) institutional interest in the stock. As of January 1, 1993, Walgreen had 26,400 holders of common stock, which is a relatively large number. At the end of 1992, there were about 123 million common shares outstanding with a market value of almost $4.7 billion. Clearly, Walgreen would qualify as an investment for institutions that require firms with large market value. Walgreen stock has monthly trading volume of almost 1.24 million shares and annual trading turnover of 24 percent. Financial institutions own about 56 million shares of Walgreen, which is about 46 percent of the outstanding shares. Therefore, Walgreen's large number of stockholders, active trading of its stock, and strong institutional interest indicates that Walgreen has very little liquidity risk.

As discussed in Chapter 16, the exchange rate risk for companies depends on what proportion of sales and earnings are generated outside the United States and the volatility of the exchange rates in the specific countries. Walgreen has very little exchange rate risk or country risk because the firm has virtually no non-U.S. sales.

In summary, Walgreen has below-average business risk, very low financial risk, low liquidity risk, and virtually no exchange rate and country risk. This implies that based on fundamental factors the overall risk for Walgreen should be lower than the market.

In addition to the consideration of fundamental factors, one should also consider market-determined risk (beta) based on the CAPM. The stock's beta derived from 5 years of monthly data relative to the S&P 500 for the period 1988 to 1992 is as follows:

$$R_{w,t} = 0.003 + 0.360\,R_{m,t}$$
$$\text{(t-value)} \quad (0.11) \quad\quad (7.45)$$
$$R^2 = 0.49$$

TABLE 18.7   Financial Risk Ratios for Walgreen Company, the Retail Drugstore Industry, and the S&P 400: 1977–1991

Year	Walgreen Company				Retail Drugstores				S&P 400			
	Total Assets/ Equity	Interest Coverage	Cash Flow/ Long-term Debt[a]	Cash Flow/ Total Debt[b]	Total Assets/ Equity	Interest Coverage	Cash Flow/ Long-term Debt[a]	Cash Flow/ Total Debt[b]	Total Assets/ Equity	Interest Coverage	Cash Flow/ Long-Term Debt[a]	Cash Flow/ Total Debt[b]
1977	2.39	6.91	0.36	0.13	1.53	28.9	1.76	0.41	2.08	8.0	0.63	0.22
1978	2.34	7.93	0.43	0.18	1.52	30.9	1.94	0.42	2.15	7.6	0.63	0.22
1979	2.30	8.83	0.50	0.19	1.68	21.2	1.21	0.34	2.20	7.7	0.70	0.22
1980	2.16	9.01	0.60	0.20	1.66	20.1	1.33	0.35	2.23	6.0	0.66	0.21
1981	2.08	10.44	0.91	0.22	1.65	16.2	1.74	0.36	2.25	5.0	0.63	0.21
1982	2.06	13.38	1.40	0.24	1.66	17.4	2.43	0.36	2.31	4.0	0.54	0.18
1983	2.04	19.61	1.76	0.26	1.68	20.2	3.24	0.35	2.28	4.6	0.61	0.19
1984	2.03	25.23	2.14	0.27	1.88	10.6	1.43	0.24	2.34	4.1	0.65	0.19
1985	2.00	28.65	1.79	0.27	2.04	7.8	0.75	0.22	2.54	4.2	0.51	0.16
1986	2.16	17.11	0.90	0.23	2.00	12.7	0.99	0.24	2.59	3.6	0.51	0.15
1987	2.19	11.76	0.94	0.21	2.04	9.4	0.93	0.23	2.57	4.4	0.58	0.17
1988	2.12	11.46	0.99	0.24	2.07	8.2	1.00	0.24	2.99	3.8	0.44	0.15
1989	2.04	13.94	1.21	0.25	2.00	7.5	0.61	0.23	3.09	3.3	0.42	0.14
1990	2.02	11.22	2.26	0.42	2.00	4.7	1.01	0.37	3.27	3.1	0.62	0.19
1991	1.94	14.90	2.95	0.45	1.83	6.3	1.42	0.40	3.20	2.5	0.54	0.16

[a]Long-Term Debt does not include deferred taxes.

[b]Total debt is equal to total assets minus total equity including preferred stock.

These results, which indicate a beta of 0.36, are very consistent with those derived from an analysis of the fundamental factors—both indicate that Walgreen's risk is quite low compared to the aggregate market. This means that the risk premium and the required rate of return for Walgreen stock should be lower than the market. By itself, this would suggest an earnings multiplier above the market multiplier.

ESTIMATING THE EXPECTED GROWTH RATE

Recall that the expected growth rate (g) is determined by the firm's retention rate and its expected return on equity (ROE). We have already noted Walgreen's low dividend payout compared to the industry and the aggregate market. This implies that it has a higher retention rate.

The firm's ROE is determined by the total asset turnover (TAT), financial leverage (total assets/equity), and the net profit margin. As shown in Table 18.6, the TAT for Walgreen has consistently been above its industry and the market. Walgreen's financial leverage ratio has been slightly above the industry, but significantly lower than the market. As a result, Walgreen's equity turnover was above the industry and substantially larger than the market. Walgreen's profit margin has been similar to its industry margin in recent years, but has been consistently lower than the S&P 400 margin (until 1991 when the profit margins were almost equal).

Combining the average values from Table 18.6 for the total asset turnover, leverage, and profit margin indicates the following ROEs for Walgreen, its industry, and the market:

	TAT	Total Assets Equity	Net Profit Margin	ROE
Walgreen	3.46	2.16	2.58	19.28
Retail drugstores	2.85	1.85	3.27	17.24
S&P 400	1.14	2.69	4.58	14.05

The mean ROEs and retention rates in Table 18.8 imply the following growth rates:

	Retention Rate	ROE	Expected Growth Rate
Walgreen	.70	.1840	.1288
Retail drugstores	.69	.1777	.1226
S&P 400	.53	.1380	.0731

Taken alone, these higher expected growth rates for Walgreen would indicate that it should have a higher multiple than its industry and the market.

COMPUTING THE EARNINGS MULTIPLIER

Entering our estimates of D/E, k, and g into the equation for the P/E ratio, we find that Walgreen's earnings multiplier based on the microanalysis should be greater than the multiplier for its industry and the market. The payout ratio points toward a lower

TABLE 18.8 **Expected Growth Rate Components for Walgreen Company, the Retail Drugstore Industry, and the S&P 400: 1977–1991**

	Walgreen Company			Retail Drugstores			S&P 400		
Year	Retention Rate	ROE	Expected Growth Rate	Retention Rate	ROE	Expected Growth Rate	Retention Rate	ROE	Expected Growth Rate
1977	0.54	11.56%	6.27%	0.89	19.14%	15.29%	0.57	13.93%	7.91%
1978	0.70	17.65	12.30	0.76	18.39	13.99	0.59	14.60	8.59
1979	0.70	18.43	12.84	0.73	18.28	13.26	0.64	16.50	10.50
1980	0.70	18.20	12.65	0.71	18.25	12.91	0.60	14.88	8.89
1981	0.70	18.40	12.88	0.69	17.83	12.30	0.58	14.42	8.38
1982	0.73	20.40	14.91	0.69	18.13	12.49	0.45	11.13	5.12
1983	0.74	21.44	15.80	0.71	19.28	13.63	0.50	12.07	6.09
1984	0.74	22.30	16.54	0.62	16.26	10.14	0.59	14.61	8.35
1985	0.71	21.03	15.00	0.59	15.73	9.32	0.48	12.14	5.89
1986	0.70	19.94	13.99	0.68	17.67	11.86	0.44	11.70	5.16
1987	0.68	17.61	11.96	0.68	17.96	12.27	0.57	15.11	8.61
1988	0.71	19.34	13.81	0.63	18.39	11.65	0.61	19.13	11.75
1989	0.73	20.08	14.64	0.68	17.46	11.87	0.57	14.92	8.50
1990	0.72	18.43	13.27	0.68	17.57	11.95	0.47	13.05	6.39
1991	0.71	18.03	12.80	0.67	16.22	10.87	0.25	8.77	2.19
Mean:	0.70	18.40	13.31	0.69	17.77	12.25	0.53	13.80	7.31

multiplier, whereas both the risk analysis and the expected growth rate would indicate a multiplier above that of its industry and the market.

The macroanalysis indicated that Walgreen's multiplier has typically been above that of its industry and the market until 1991. As noted, the microanalysis supported this relationship. Assuming a market multiple of about 18 and a retail drugstore multiplier of about 19, the multiplier for Walgreen should be between 20 and 21, with a tendency toward the upper end of the range. Alternatively, if we inserted specific values for D/E, k, and g into the P/E ratio formula, we would get a multiplier of about 20. Specifically, a payout ratio of .30, a k of about 13.50 percent given current market rates, and an expected growth rate (g) of 12 percent indicate the following

$$P/E = \frac{.30}{.135 - .12}$$

$$= \frac{.30}{.015} = 20X$$

ESTIMATE OF THE FUTURE VALUE FOR WALGREEN

Earlier, we estimated earnings per share for Walgreen of about $2.00 per share. Assuming multipliers of 18-20-21 implies the following estimated future values:

$$18 \times 2.00 = \$36.00$$
$$20 \times 2.00 = \$40.00$$
$$21 \times 2.00 = \$42.00$$

MAKING THE INVESTMENT DECISION

In our prior discussions of valuation we set forth the investment decision in two forms:

1. Compute the estimated value for an investment using your required rate of return as the discount rate. If this estimated value is equal to or greater than the current market price of the investment, buy it.
2. Compute the estimated future value for an investment using your required rate of return as one of the components. Given this future value, compute the expected rate of return that you would receive if you bought the asset at the current market price and held the investment during the future period, which is typically assumed to be a year. If this expected rate of return is equal to or greater than your required rate of return, buy the investment; if the expected return is below your required rate of return, do not buy it.

We can demonstrate how we would apply these two forms of the investment decision to Walgreen's. We estimated three future values for Walgreen assuming a k of 13.5 percent: $36.00, $40.00, and $42.00. For the demonstration we will use $40 a share as the future value and an estimated dividend over the next year of $0.60, which assumes a 30 percent payout of the earnings of $2.00.

COMPARING THE ESTIMATED VALUE TO THE CURRENT MARKET PRICE
Remember that the estimated value we have computed is a future value (at the end of 1 year). To compare it to a current market price, we must discount the ending price ($40) and the expected dividend ($0.60) by our required rate of return of 13.5 percent, which gives a current estimated value of[9]

$$\$40 \times .8811 = \$35.24$$
$$\$0.60 \times .8811 = \underline{0.53}$$
$$\text{Total value} = \$35.77$$

We would compare the current market price of Walgreen stock to this estimated value. As an example, if Walgreen stock were currently priced at $30 a share, you would buy it; if it were currently priced at $40 a share, you would not buy it.

COMPARING THE EXPECTED RATE OF RETURN TO YOUR
REQUIRED RATE OF RETURN
In past demonstrations of this decision rule we have computed an expected rate of return using the expected value and dividend. Although we will again use this technique, we will also introduce another technique for computing an expected rate of return based on the dividend growth model.

We can compute the expected rate of return, $E(R_i)$, based on our expected future value using the formula

$$E(R_i) = \frac{EV - BV + Div}{BV}$$

---

[9] The computation of the value of the dividend payment is simplified and conservative since we have assumed the whole $0.60 is paid at the end of the year rather than $0.15 a quarter, which would have allowed for reinvestment to the end of the year.

where:

> EV = **estimated ending value of the stock**
> BV = **beginning value of the stock (typically its current market price)**
> Div = **the expected dividend per share during the holding period**

In our case, these values would be

$$EV = \$40.00$$
$$BV = (\text{assume } \$35 \text{ a share})$$
$$Div = \$0.60$$

Thus,

$$
\begin{aligned}
E(R) &= \frac{\$40.00 - \$35.00 + \$0.60}{\$35.00} \\
&= \frac{\$ \, 5.60}{\$35.00} \\
&= .16 = 16\%
\end{aligned}
$$

Based on the k of 13.5 percent used in the valuation section, we would buy this stock because its expected rate of return is larger than our required rate of return.

The second technique used to derive an expected rate of return is based on the dividend growth model. You will recall that the dividend growth model states:

$$P_0 = \frac{D_1}{k - g}$$

Solving to estimate k:

$$k_i = \frac{D_1}{P_0} + g$$

In this equation, k serves as an estimate of the required rate of return when you assume that you know the firm's future growth rate. Alternatively, k can be used to estimate the expected rate of return if you are estimating the future dividend and growth rate. For Walgreen, the P_0 would be the current price of the stock, D_1 would be the expected dividend during the investment horizon, and g would be the expected growth rate, as discussed in connection with Table 18.8.

As an example, assume a current price of $35, an expected dividend of $0.60 per share, and a growth rate of 12.8 percent. This would imply the following estimate of your expected rate of return on Walgreen common stock:

$$
\begin{aligned}
k &= \frac{0.60}{35.00} + .128 \\
&= .017 + .128 \\
&= .145 = 14.5\%
\end{aligned}
$$

This computation shows that you would expect a rate of return from investing in Walgreen stock of 14.5 percent. If your required rate of return was 13.5 percent, you would buy this stock.

ADDITIONAL MEASURES OF RELATIVE VALUE

The best-known measure of relative value for common stock is the price/earnings ratio or the earnings multiplier because it is derived from the dividend growth model and has stood the test of time as an accurate measure. Although not rejecting the P/E ratio, analysts have begun to calculate two additional measures of relative value for common stocks—the price/book value ratio and the price/cash flow ratio.

PRICE/BOOK VALUE (P/BV) RATIO

The relationship between the market price of a stock and its book value per share can be used as a relative measure of valuation because, under theoretically ideal conditions, the market value of a firm should reflect its book value. The *price/book value ratio* has been used extensively in the valuation of bank stocks because bank assets often have similar book values and market values. Specifically, bank assets include investments in government bonds, high-grade corporate bonds or municipal bonds, along with commercial, mortgage, or personal loans that are considered to be collectible. Under such ideal conditions, the price/book value (P/BV) ratio should be close to 1. Still, even in the banking industry the range of this ratio has increased. You can envision a P/BV ratio of less than 1 for a bank with a lot of problem loans. In the last few years this might include loans to firms in the oil industry, real estate loans in certain areas of the country, and loans to third-world countries. In contrast, you can envision a P/BV ratio above 1 for a bank with significant growth potential due to its location or merger possibilities. As a result, the P/BV ratios for different individual banks have ranged from 0.4 to over 2.0.

It is easy to see why the P/BV ratio of an industrial firm would exceed 1.0. The book value of assets based on historical cost will almost always be lower than either their current replacement value or the firm's breakup value. (Breakup value is the estimated market value of selling divisions of a firm to others.) An increase in the estimates of breakup value has caused the average P/BV ratio for industrial firms to experience a volatile increase over time. To demonstrate this relationship, the data are contained in Table 18.9. Figure 18.5 is a time-series plot of the historical P/BV ratio for the S&P 400, the retail drugstore industry, and Walgreen. Annual P/BV ratios are equal to the mean annual price/year-end book value.

The P/BV ratio for the S&P 400 was about 1.3 during 1977 through 1982. Subsequently, it increased to about 2.4 prior to the October 1987 crash and declined during 1988 before increasing to record levels in 1990 and 1991.

The retail drugstore industry P/BV ratio has typically followed the S&P P/BV ratio with a premium of about 30 percent. A higher P/BV ratio for the retail drugstore industry appears reasonable because of the industry's higher growth rate of book value. Book value has grown about 5 percent a year for the S&P 400 versus 17.7 percent a year for the retail drugstore industry.

Walgreen's P/BV ratio increased from about 1.60 in 1977 to over 3.5 in the mid-1980s. As a result, the ratio of its P/BV ratio to the market P/BV ratio went from about 1.2 to a peak of over 2.0 in 1981. The company/market relationship has declined steadily since 1985 to the point of equality in 1991. The ratio of Walgreen's P/BV ratio to its

TABLE 18.9   Price/Book Value and Price/Cash Flow Ratios for Walgreen, Retail Drugstores, and the S&P 400: 1977–1991

	Walgreen Company					Retail Drugstore							S&P 400						
Year	Mean Price	Book Value	P/BV	Cash Flow	P/CF	Mean Price	Book Value	P/BV	Company/Industry Ratio	Cash Flow	P/CF	Company/Industry Ratio	Mean Price	Book Value	P/BV	Company/Market Ratio	Cash Flow	P/CF	Company/Market Ratio
1977	2.063	1.31	1.57	0.23	8.97	18.93	9.35	2.02	0.78	2.20	8.60	1.04	109.40	82.21	1.33	1.18	19.94	5.49	1.63
1978	2.906	1.44	2.02	0.32	9.08	22.20	10.93	2.03	0.99	2.50	8.88	1.02	107.12	89.34	1.20	1.68	22.65	4.73	1.92
1979	3.688	1.54	2.25	0.39	9.46	22.38	13.95	1.60	1.40	3.26	6.87	1.38	115.79	98.71	1.17	1.92	27.06	4.28	2.21
1980	4.227	1.86	2.27	0.44	9.61	24.57	16.11	1.53	1.49	3.78	6.50	1.48	136.03	108.33	1.26	1.81	28.45	4.78	2.01
1981	5.820	2.12	2.75	0.50	11.64	34.62	18.45	1.88	1.46	4.31	8.03	1.45	141.48	116.06	1.22	2.25	30.52	4.64	2.51
1982	5.039	2.45	2.06	0.63	8.00	41.58	20.74	2.00	1.03	4.79	8.68	0.92	136.87	118.60	1.15	1.78	28.46	4.81	1.66
1983	5.531	2.87	1.93	0.77	7.18	56.70	23.34	2.43	0.79	5.90	9.61	0.75	174.50	122.32	1.43	1.35	30.41	5.75	1.25
1984	9.235	3.38	2.73	0.90	10.26	58.30	25.21	2.31	1.18	5.81	10.03	1.02	179.62	123.99	1.45	1.89	34.40	5.22	1.97
1985	12.938	3.92	3.30	1.05	12.32	68.28	26.82	2.55	1.30	6.24	10.94	1.13	208.99	125.89	1.66	1.99	33.44	6.25	1.97
1986	15.938	4.50	3.54	1.20	13.28	83.78	27.73	3.02	1.17	6.99	11.99	1.11	253.83	124.87	2.03	1.74	33.91	7.49	1.77
1987	17.407	5.06	3.44	1.28	13.60	98.93	30.79	3.21	1.07	8.16	12.12	1.12	324.30	134.19	2.42	1.42	40.46	8.02	1.70
1988	16.125	5.79	2.78	1.53	10.54	93.05	34.25	2.72	1.03	9.40	9.90	1.06	302.53	139.50	2.17	1.28	50.13	6.04	1.75
1989	20.063	6.69	3.00	1.80	11.15	107.46	38.31	2.81	1.07	11.82	9.09	1.23	364.58	145.34	2.51	1.20	50.02	7.29	1.53
1990	22.500	7.70	2.92	1.99	11.31	114.53	43.65	2.62	1.11	11.98	9.56	1.18	392.12	152.71	2.57	1.14	51.04	7.68	1.47
1991	23.594	8.78	2.69	2.27	10.39	139.70	50.94	2.74	0.98	12.29	11.37	0.91	428.81	157.20	2.73	0.99	43.75	9.80	1.06

FIGURE 18.5   **Time-Series Plot of Price/Book Value for Walgreen, RSD Industry, and S&P400**

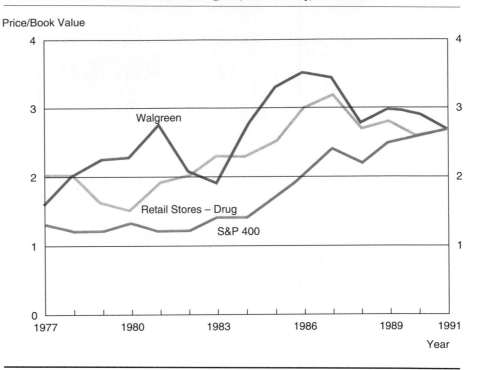

industry P/BV ratio varied from about 0.80 to as high as 1.49. In recent years, it has been about equal to its industry. One can explain the higher P/BV ratio for Walgreen relative to the market based on Walgreen's higher growth rate of book value. Walgreen's premium P/BV ratio relative to its industry's ratio is likewise a function of its higher ROE and higher expected growth rate.

THE P/BV RATIO AS A DECISION RULE

To form this into an investment decision rule, some have suggested that stocks with low P/BV ratios should outperform high P/BV stocks, just as stocks with low P/E ratios outperform stocks with high P/E ratios. A study by Rosenberg, Reid, and Lanstein examined this strategy and found that stocks with low P/BV ratios experienced significantly higher risk-adjusted rates of return than the average stock.[10]

A more recent study by Fama and French provided even greater support for this ratio as a useful measure of relative value.[11] The purpose of their study was to examine alternative variables that would explain the cross section of rates of return on common

---

[10] Barr Rosenberg, Kenneth Reid, and Ronald Lanstein, "Persuasive Evidence of Market Inefficiency," *Journal of Portfolio Management* 11, no. 3 (Spring 1985): 9–17. They examined the inverse of the ratio that is discussed here, that is, BV/P, but the interpretation is comparable; in other words, a high BV/P ratio is comparable to a low P/BV ratio.

[11] Eugene F. Fama and Kenneth R. French, "The Cross-Section of Expected Stock Returns," *Journal of Finance* 47, no. 2 (June 1992): 427–450. They likewise stipulated the ratio as book value/market value, but the interpretation is comparable.

stock. One of the explanatory variables was the well-known beta coefficient. Their results did not provide much support for beta as an explanatory variable, but the results did indicate that both the size of firms and the ratio of book value to market value (BV/MV) of equity were significant explanatory variables. Moreover, they contended that the BV/MV ratio was the single best variable.

The point is, the P/BV ratio has become important as a measure of relative value for stocks. Analysts will discuss the stock's P/BV over time and also examine it relative to a comparable market and industry ratio as we have done and use this information as part of the investment decision. This ratio has also been included as a component in other valuation models.

PRICE/CASH FLOW (P/CF) RATIO

Another measure of relative value, the *price/cash flow ratio* is being used to supplement the P/E ratio because cash flow is typically subject to less accounting manipulation than reported earnings. Also, cash flow has become an important measure of performance, value, and financial strength because numerous academic studies have shown that various cash flow measures can be used to predict both success and future problems.[12] Also, cash flow data have become more accessible because firms currently publish statements of cash flow along with their income statements and balance sheets.

Developing benchmark values for these ratios is important because they are relative measures of value. Therefore, you should understand the comparable values over time for the market as represented by the S&P 400 and the relevant industry. For demonstration purposes, availability of data leads us to define cash flow per share as net income per share plus depreciation expense per share. This traditional measure of cash flow is intended to reflect earnings plus noncash expenses; depreciation is the largest such expense that can be identified.

Historical P/CF ratios are listed in Table 18.9 and plotted in Figure 18.6. These particular ratios are only available beginning in 1977 because the depreciation expense figure for the S&P 400 and individual S&P industries were not reported prior to this time. Again, both the retail drugstore industry and the Walgreen P/CF ratios are consistently higher than the market ratio. As before, this difference is justified by the higher growth rate during the period 1977–1991 of cash flow for the industry versus the market (14.4 versus 6.8 percent), and for the company versus the market (18.3 versus 6.8 percent).

USING THE P/BV AND P/CF RATIOS

As discussed, both of these ratios (P/BV and P/CF) are considered to be good supplements to the P/E ratio when you are engaged in fundamental valuation. Neither has the theoretical base that we have with the P/E ratio, but they can provide additional insights into relative valuation changes for a stock. In both instances you should examine the company ratios over time relative to the same ratio for the market and for the firm's

---

[12]James A. Gentry, David T. Whitford, and Paul Newbold, "Predicting Industrial Bond Ratings with a Profit Model and Funds Flow Components," *The Financial Review* 23, no. 3 (August 1988): 269–286; James A. Gentry, Paul Newbold, and David T. Whitford, "Classifying Bankrupt Firms with Funds Flow Components," *Journal of Accounting Research* 23, no. 1 (Spring 1985): 146–160; and James A. Gentry, Paul Newbold, and David T. Whitford, "Predicting Bankruptcy: If Cash Flows Not the Bottom Line, What Is?" *Financial Analysts Journal* 41, no. 5 (September-October 1985): 47–58. A specific application to selecting common stocks is discussed in Kenneth S. Hackel and Joshua Livnat, *Cash Flow and Security Analysis* (Homewood, Ill.: Business One–Irwin, 1993).

FIGURE 18.6   **Time-Series Plot of Price/Cash Flow for Walgreen, RSD Industry, and S&P400**

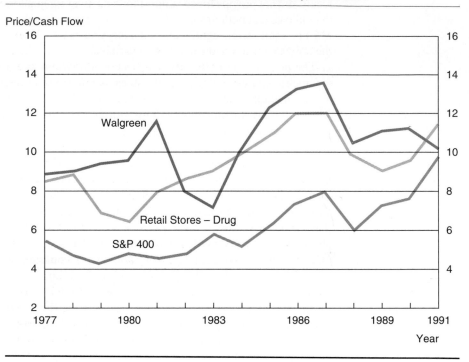

industry. You should look for: (1) relationships that are not justified by the fundamentals, or (2) changes in the normal relationships that are not supported by changes in the fundamentals.

As an example of the first case, assume that a firm's P/BV ratio was 0.8 compared to a market ratio of 2.0 and an industry ratio of 1.9. You would analyze the firm to see if these differences were justified. A difference that was not justified by differences in expected growth and risk might indicate an underpriced stock. As an example of the second case, assume a stock's P/BV ratio had consistently matched the market ratio, but the ratio increased during a period of time by 50 percent relative to the market with no change in fundamentals. You would probably consider this a possible indicator of overvaluation. These examples would be only bits of evidence in a full-scale analysis, but they can be additional indicators of relative valuation.

IDENTIFYING
AND SELECTING
COMPETITIVE
STRATEGIES

In describing competition within industries, we identified five conditions that could affect the competitive structure and profits of an industry. They are (1) current rivalry, (2) threat of new entrants, (3) potential substitutes, (4) bargaining power of suppliers, and (5) bargaining power of buyers. Once you have determined the competitive structure of an industry, you should attempt to identify the *specific competitive strategy* employed by each firm in the industry and evaluate these strategies in terms of the overall competitive structure of the industry. As an investor you must understand the alternatives available, determine each firm's strategy, judge whether the strategy selected by a firm is reasonable for its industry, and finally, evaluate how successfully the firm implements its strategy.

Porter indicates two competitive strategies: *low cost leadership* or *differentiation*.[13] These two competitive strategies dictate how a firm has decided to cope with the five competitive conditions that define an industry's environment. Within each industry the strategies available and the ways of implementing them differ.

LOW-COST STRATEGY

The firm that pursues the low-cost strategy is determined to become *the* low-cost producer and, hence, the cost leader in its industry. Cost advantages will vary by industry and might include economies of scale, proprietary technology, or preferential access to raw materials. To assert cost leadership, the firm must command prices near the industry average, which means that it must differentiate itself about as well as other firms. If the firm discounts price too much, it would erode the superior rates of return available because of its low cost. In the retail business, both Wal-Mart and Kmart are considered low-cost sources. They achieve this by volume purchasing of merchandise and lower-cost operations. As a result, they charge less, but still enjoy higher profit margins and returns on capital than many of their competitors.

DIFFERENTIATION STRATEGY

With the differentiation strategy, a firm seeks to identify itself as unique in its industry in an area that is important to buyers. Again, the possibilities for differentiation vary widely by industry. A company can attempt to differentiate itself based on its distribution system (selling in stores, by mail order, or door-to-door), or some unique marketing approach. A firm employing the differentiating strategy will enjoy above-average rates of return *only* if its price premium based on its differentiation exceeds the extra cost of being unique. Therefore, when you analyze this strategy, you must determine whether the differentiating factor is truly unique, whether it is sustainable, what is its cost, and is the price premium derived from this uniqueness greater than its cost.

FOCUSING A STRATEGY

Whichever strategy it selects, a firm must determine where it will focus this strategy. Specifically, a firm must select a segment or group of segments in the industry and tailor its strategy to serve this specific group. For example, a cost focus would typically exploit cost advantages for certain segments of the industry, such as being the low-cost producer for the expensive segment of the market. Similarly, a differentiation focus would attempt to serve the special needs of buyers in specific segments. For example, in the athletic shoe market, companies have attempted to develop shoes for unique sport segments such as tennis, basketball, aerobics, or walkers and hikers, rather than offering only shoes for runners. Firms thought that individuals involved in these other athletic endeavors needed shoes with different characteristics than those used by joggers. Equally important, they believed that these athletes would be willing to pay a premium for these special shoes. Again, you must ascertain whether these special cost or need possibilities exist, are they not being served by another firm, and can they be priced to generate abnormal returns to the firm.

---

[13] Michael Porter, *Competitive Advantage: Creating and Sustaining Superior Performance* (New York: Free Press, 1985).

Table 18.10

Earnings and Dividends per Share for Major European Chemical Firms

Company	Currency	Earnings per Share		Dividends per Share (1992)	Dividend Payout (1992)
		1992E	1993E		
BASF	DM	12.0	10.0	8.0	0.667
Bayer	DM	23.0	21.0	13.0	0.565
Hoechst	DM	15.5	13.0	10.0	0.645
Ciba	SFr	50.6	52.7	15.0	0.296
AKZO	DFL	15.3[a]	14.1	6.5	0.425
DSM	DFL	6.3[a]	4.4	6.0	0.952
Solvay	BFr	1,016	887	500.0	0.492
L'Air Liquide	FFr	39.4	41.1	14.0	0.355
BOC	BP	48.0	53.9	23.2	0.483
AGA B	SKr	24.5	29.4	9.0	0.367
Rhone-Poulenc	FFr	27.0	42.8	10.5	0.389

[a]Before extraordinary items.

E = Estimate.

Source: Charles K. Brown, Peter Clark, and Mark Tracey, "The Major European Chemicals/Pharma Groups—Testing Times" (London: Goldman, Sachs International Ltd., February 1993). Reprinted by permission of Goldman Sachs.

Next, you must determine which strategy is being pursued and whether the firm is successful at it. Also, can the strategies be sustained? Further, you should evaluate a firm's competitive strategy over time, because strategies will need to change as an industry evolves. The point is, different strategies work during different phases of an industry's life cycle.

GLOBAL COMPANY ANALYSIS

One of our goals in this book is to demonstrate investment techniques. We have shown on several occasions that these techniques can be applied to foreign markets, industries, and companies. The major problem is getting the data required for the analysis.

In this section we will continue the analysis of the European chemical industry that we started in Chapter 17. The objective is to see how to select individual companies and specific stocks for your investment portfolio. As before, we will work with tables assembled by Goldman, Sachs and its global report. The tables contain data on several companies though the desired data is not always available for all the firms.

EARNINGS PER SHARE ANALYSIS

Table 18.10 contains estimated earnings per share values for the major firms for 1992 and 1993 as of February 1993. This two-period comparison shows the outlook for these firms. Most estimates indicate limited or negative growth for 1993. The dividend data indicate a wide range of payouts (i.e., about 30 to 95 percent).

PROFITABILITY AND FINANCIAL STRENGTH

Table 18.11 contains information on profitability as measured by the return on equity (ROE) for the individual firms. The notes to the table caution that the analysis should concentrate on the performance for individual firms over time, because the data are not adjusted for accounting differences between firms and countries. The results for 1991 reflect a decline in 1991 for all the firms relative to the results in 1988. This is probably a result of the economic recession in Europe during the period 1991–1993.

TABLE 18.11

Profitability and Financial Strength for Major European Chemical Firms: 1986, 1988, 1991

	Net Income/Avg. Shareholders' Equity (%)			Net Debt/Shareholders' Equity (%)		
	1986	1988	1991	1986	1988	1991
BASF	8	12	7	−12	−25	−8
Bayer	12	13	11	2	−5	7
Hoechst	15	19	9	−14	28	35
Ciba	9	9	8	−19	−9	6
AKZO	19	21	15	21	63	56
L'Air Liquide	14	14	13	58	34	13
BOC	14	22	16	56	61	52
Rhone-Poulenc	18	14	5	129	57	131

Note: These figures are based on reported results and reflect differing accounting practices; they are intended to set out trends over time for the individual companies rather than provide a basis for comparisons between companies.

Sources: Company Reports, Goldman, Sachs Analysis; Charles K. Brown, Peter Clark, and Mark Tracey, "The Major European Chemicals/Pharma Groups—Testing Times" (London: Goldman, Sachs International Ltd., February 1993). Reprinted by permission of Goldman Sachs.

You should also examine the financial risk of the firms based on their debt/equity ratios. Again, you should limit your analysis to specific firms over time. The discussion makes it clear that the wide range of debt/equity ratios and the changes in these ratios over time reflect operating performance and financial strategy decisions as well as the effects of acquisitions by some firms. There is special mention of Rhone-Poulenc as a very leveraged firm.

COMMON STOCK STATISTICS

Given the prior analysis, Table 18.12 contains measures of stock performance and relative value for the firms in the industry. The absolute P/E ratios show the differences in the earnings multipliers among countries. The table contains some very interesting information on the individual stock P/E ratios relative to the average P/E ratio in the local market. As an example, Bayer's P/E ratio is 11.6, which is only 84 percent of the average of all stocks in Germany. In contrast L'Air Liquide has a P/E ratio of 19.6, which is 145 percent of the average for stocks in France. This shows that two stocks with similar P/E ratios could have different relative valuations in different countries due to variations in accounting conventions or social attitudes. Such a difference in measures of relative valuation among countries might be less in the future as accounting practices among countries become more consistent and global capital markets become more integrated.

The price/book value ratios likewise reflect major differences in relative valuation among countries. Again, these differences could be due to differences in real value or differences in accounting practices. An extreme example is Ciba, where the book values are based on current cost values rather than historical costs that are used in most accounting presentations. As one would expect, the ratio for Ciba is very close to 1.0.

SHARE PRICE PERFORMANCE

Table 18.13 compares the stock price changes for the major chemical firms. Here we can see the impact of exchange rates. Part A shows the stocks' absolute percentage changes and compared to the stock's local market index over 1-, 3- and 5-year time

TABLE 18.12   **Common Stock Statistics for Major European Chemical Firms**

	Currency	Shares Price[a]	12-Month Range		EPS		DPS (1992E)	P/E (1992E)	P/E-Relative (1992E)	P/CF (1991)	P/BV (1991)	Yield (1992E)
			High	Low	(1992E)	(1993E)						
BASF[b]	DM	215	253	201	12.0	10.0	8.0	17.9	130	2.6	0.8	5.8%
Bayer[b]	DM	266	306	242	23.0	21.0	13.0	11.6	84	3.1	1.1	7.6
Hoechst[b]	DM	256	272	218	15.5	13.0	10.0	16.5	120	3.2	1.3	6.1
Ciba[c]	SFr	664	734	602	50.6	52.7	15.0	12.5	72	7.2	1.1	2.4
AKZO	DFL	141	165	125	15.3	14.1	6.5	9.2	74	3.8	2.4	4.6
DSM	DFL	72	116	70	6.3	4.4	6.0	11.4	91	2.3	0.6	5.6
Solvay[d]	BFr	12,975	13,600	11,050	1,016	887	500	12.8	93	3.8	1.0	5.1
L'Air Liquide	FFr	771	800	623	39.4	41.1	14.0	19.6	145	7.3	2.6	2.7
BOC[e]	BP	730	773	584	48.0	53.9	23.2	15.2	101	9.0	2.7	4.2
AGA B	SKr	321	343	247	24.5	29.4	9.0	13.1	39	7.1	2.2	3.1
Rhone-Poulenc	FFr	524	665	487	27.0	42.8	10.5	24.4	183	5.8	1.3	3.0

[a]Prices at 20 October 1992 all per share figures based on this price.

[b]EPS is on DVFA-adjusted basis, undiluted; potential dilution for BASF 7%, Bayer 9%, and Hoechst 2%.

[c]All figures based on current cost values.

[d]Before extraordinary items.

[e]Years to Sept.

E = estimate.

Source: Charles K. Brown, Peter Clark, and Mark Tracey, "The Major European Chemicals/Pharma Groups—Testing Times" (London: Goldman, Sachs International Ltd., February 1993). Reprinted by permission of Goldman Sachs.

TABLE 18.13

Share Price Performance for Major European Chemical Firms

	Absolute Change (%) over Last			Change Relative to Local Market (%) over Last		
	Year	3 Years	5 Years	Year	3 Years	5 Years
A: Domestic Currencies						
ICI	−13	3	7	−24	−13	−31
BASF	−12	−33	−7	−5	−12	−34
Bayer	−10	−19	6	−3	5	−24
Hoechst	3	−18	2	11	7	−27
Ciba	−1	13	133	−18	−7	22
AKZO	6	14	68	4	10	10
Solvay	7	−5	37	10	10	12
L'Air Liquide	23	42	133	27	53	28
BOC	14	39	86	−5	17	21
AGA B	3	40	96	19	26	2
Rhonc-Poulenc PICs	−3	22	91	−1	31	5

	Absolute Change (%) over Last			Change Relative to S&P 500 (%) over Last		
	Year	3 Years	5 Years	Year	3 Years	5 Years
B: U.S. Dollars						
ICI	−30	−11	−13	−36	−35	−51
BASF	−15	−31	−5	−22	−49	−47
Bayer	−14	−18	9	−21	−39	−39
Hoechst	−1	−16	5	−9	−39	−41
Ciba	−8	11	111	−15	−18	18
AKZO	2	17	71	−6	−14	−3
Solvay	3	−3	42	−5	−28	−21
L'Air Liquide	20	46	137	11	8	33
BOC	−9	19	52	−16	−12	−15
AGA B	−20	15	59	−26	−16	−11
Rhone-Poulenc PICs	−6	25	95	−8	−14	9

Source: Charles K. Brown, Peter Clark, and Mark Tracey, "The Major European Chemicals/Pharma Groups—Testing Times" (London: Goldman, Sachs International Ltd., February 1993). Reprinted by permission of Goldman Sachs.

horizons. The results indicate large differences in individual absolute stock performances and also major differences in relative performance. In part B, these stock returns are converted to U.S. dollars to adjust for exchange rate movements and compared to the U.S. market, which shows us the relative performance for a U.S. investor. This latter comparison is critical, because it demonstrates the effect of international diversification and the necessity of considering exchange rate movements when making foreign investments. For example, looking at the results during the most recent year shows that basic exchange rates were a negative factor for most stocks based upon a comparison of domestic returns in part A and U.S. dollar returns in part B. The results deteriorated further when they are compared to the S&P 500. In summary, during this particular period both the U.S. dollar and the U.S. stock market were strong, which hurt these relative comparisons.

TABLE 18.14   **Company and Stock Price Data for Bayer**

Price:	DM266						Price Relative to Market: 1 Month: −5%		
Market Value:	DM17.5bn						3 Months: −4%		
12 Month Range:	DM306-242						1 Year: −3%		
FT-A Germany:	91.4						3 Years: +5%		

Year to December:	Pre-Tax Profit DMm	Net Profit DMm	EPS[a] DM	Net Div Dm	Cash Flow/ Share[b] DM	P/E	P/E Rel %	Price/ Cash Flow	Gross Yield %
1989	4,105	2,083	37.0	13.0	92	7.2	65	2.9	7.6
1990	3,366	1,881	30.0	13.0	84	8.9	72	3.2	7.6
1991	3,206	1,824	28.0	13.0	85	9.5	75	3.1	7.6
1992E	2,550	1,450	23.0	13.0	72	11.6	84	3.7	7.6
1993E	2,300	1,310	21.0	13.0	71	12.7	83	3.7	7.6
1994E	2,700	1,535	25.0	13.0	76	10.6	77	3.5	7.6
1989–94E comp growth %	−8	−6	−8	—	−4				

Options/Convertibles/Warrants:	O/C/W	Reuters: BRr/tO	
Listed ADRs: No		Quotron: BAYR.EU	

[a]DVFA undiluted–dilution approximately 7%.

[b]Undiluted.

Source: Charles K. Brown, Peter Clark, and Mark Tracey, "The Major European Chemical/Pharma Groups—Testing Times" (London: Goldman Sachs International, Ltd. February 1993). Reprinted by permission of Goldman Sachs.

INDIVIDUAL COMPANY ANALYSIS

The report concludes with a summary of the strengths and potential problems of each individual company. Table 18.14 summarizes the results for Bayer, a German firm considered to be one of the world's leading chemical companies. The discussion that accompanies the table considers the poor performance through 1993 with a recovery beginning in 1994. They base this on the outlook for this industry. Also, a stock price chart for Bayer (Figure 18.7) shows the absolute and relative movements for the firm's stock.

ANALYSIS OF GROWTH COMPANIES

Investment literature contains numerous accounts of the rapid growth of companies such as Wal-Mart, Xerox, Merck, and Hewlett-Packard, along with stories about investors who became wealthy because of the timely acquisition of these stocks. These very high rates of return indicate that the proper valuation of true growth companies can be extremely rewarding. At the same time, for every successful Wal-Mart or Hewlett-Packard, there are numerous firms that did not survive. In addition, there are many instances where the stock price of a true growth company overcompensated for the firm's expected growth and the subsequent returns were below expectations. As noted earlier, the common stock of a growth company is *not* always a growth stock!

You are familiar with the dividend discount model and its basic assumptions, that is, that dividends are expected to grow at a constant rate for an infinite time period. As explained in Chapter 11, although these assumptions are reasonable when evaluating the aggregate market and some large industries, they can be very tenuous when analyzing individual securities. The point of this section is, *these assumptions are extremely questionable for a growth company.*

FIGURE 18.7

Bayer Share Price Performance, 1988–1993

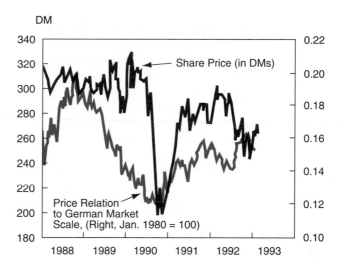

Source: Charles K. Brown, Peter Clark, and Mark Tracey, "The Major European Chemicals/Pharma Groups—Testing Times, (London: Goldman, Sachs & Co., International Research, February 1993). Reprinted by permission of Goldman Sachs.

GROWTH
COMPANY
DEFINED

A growth company has the opportunities and ability to invest capital in projects that generate rates of return greater than the firm's cost of capital. Such a condition is considered to be *temporary* because in a competitive economy, all firms should produce at the point where marginal revenue equals marginal cost, which means that the returns to the producer will exactly compensate for the risks involved. If the returns earned in an industry are below what is expected for the risk involved, some participants will leave the industry. In contrast, if the rates of return for a given industry exceed the returns expected based on the risk involved, other companies will enter the industry, increase the supply, and eventually drive prices down until the rates of return earned are consistent with the risk involved, resulting in a state of equilibrium.

ACTUAL RETURNS
ABOVE EXPECTED
RETURNS

The notion of a firm consistently earning rates of return above its required rate of return requires elaboration. Firms are engaged in business ventures that offer opportunities for investment of corporate capital, and these investments entail some risk. Investors determine their required return for owning a firm based on the risk of its investments compared to the risk of other firms. Consider a firm that produces and sells medical equipment, and assume perfect capital markets. There is some uncertainty about the firm's sales and profits. Investors should compare this composite uncertainty to the uncertainty and rates of returns expected from other investments. Based on the CAPM, one would expect the difference in the required rate of return to be a function of the difference in the stock's systematic risk. This required rate of return is referred to as the firm's cost of equity. If the market is in a state of equilibrium, the rates of return earned on risky investments by the firm should equal the rates of return required by investors. If a firm earns returns above those required for the systematic risk involved, these excess returns are referred to as *pure profits*.

One of the costs of production is the cost of the capital employed. Therefore, in a competitive environment, marginal revenue should equal marginal costs (including capital costs), and there would be no excess returns or pure profits. The point is, excess profits are possible only in a noncompetitive environment. Assume that the medical equipment firm is able to earn 20 percent on its capital, while investors require only 15 percent on such investments because of its systematic risk. The extra 5 percent is defined as pure profit, and numerous companies would enter the medical equipment field to enjoy the excess profits. These competitors would increase the supply of equipment and would reduce the price that producers could charge for the equipment until the marginal returns equaled the marginal costs.

Because many firms have derived excess profits for a number of years, these excess returns are probably not due to a temporary disequilibrium, but rather because of some noncompetitive factors that are allowed to exist such as patents or copyrights that provide a firm or person with monopoly rights to a process or a manuscript for a specified period of time. During this period of protection from competition, the firm can derive above-normal returns without fear of competition. Also, a firm could possess other strategies, such as those discussed by Porter, that provide added profits (e.g., a unique marketing technique or other organizational characteristics). Finally, there may be significant barriers to entry such as capital requirements.

In a purely competitive economy with no frictions, true growth companies would not exist because competition would not allow continuing excess return investments. The point is, pure competition would negate the pure profits and growth. The fact is, our economy is not perfectly competitive (although this is typically the best model to use), because there are a number of frictions that restrict competition. Therefore, it is possible to have *temporary* true growth companies in our economy. The question is, how long can they last?

GROWTH COMPANIES AND GROWTH STOCKS

Recall that a growth stock is expected to experience above-average risk-adjusted rates of return during some future period. This means that any undervalued stock can be a growth stock, regardless of the type of company. Alternatively, the securities of growth companies that are overvalued could be speculative stocks, because the probability of below-normal returns would be very high.

In this section that deals with the analysis of growth companies, we will discuss models that are meant to help you evaluate the unique earnings stream of a growth company. As a result, you should derive a better estimate of the firm's value. In turn, this should help you judge whether the stock of a growth company is (1) a growth stock, (2) a properly valued stock, or (3) a speculative overvalued stock.

GROWTH COMPANIES AND THE DIVIDEND DISCOUNT MODEL

In contrast to the dividend discount model which assumes a constant rate of growth for an infinite time period, we know that it is impossible for a true growth firm to exist for an infinite time period in a relatively competitive economy. Further, even in an economy with some noncompetitive factors, a true growth firm should not be able to exist for very long. Patents and copyrights run out, unusual management practices can eventually be copied, and competitors can enter the industry. Therefore, the constant growth dividend discount growth model is *not* appropriate for the valuation of growth companies, and we must consider special valuation models that allow for the finite periods of abnormal growth and for the possibility of different rates of growth. The rest of the chapter deals with models for valuing growth companies.

ALTERNATIVE GROWTH MODELS[14]

In this section we consider the full range of growth models, from those of no growth and negative growth to dynamic true growth. Knowledge of the full range will help you understand why the dividend growth model is not always applicable. We assume the company is an all-equity firm to simplify the computations.

NO-GROWTH FIRM

The no-growth firm is that mythical company that is established with a specified portfolio of investments that generate a constant stream of earnings (E) equal to r times the value of assets. Earnings are calculated after allowing for depreciation to maintain the assets at their original value. Therefore

$$E = r \times \text{Assets}$$

It is also assumed that all earnings of the firm are paid out in dividends; if b is the rate of retention, $b = 0$. Hence,

$$E = r \times \text{Assets} = \text{Dividends}$$

Under these assumptions, the value of the firm is the discounted value of the perpetual stream of earnings (E). The discount rate (the required rate of return) is specified as k. In this case, it is assumed that $r = k$. The firm's rate of return on assets equals its required rate of return. The value of the firm is

$$V = \frac{E}{k} = \frac{(1 - b)E}{k}$$

In the no-growth case, the earnings stream never changes because the asset base never changes, and the rate of return on the assets never changes. Therefore, the value of the firm never changes, and investors continue to receive k on their investment.

$$k = E/V$$

LONG-RUN GROWTH MODELS

Long-run models differ from the no-growth models because *they assume some of the earnings are reinvested.* The initial case assumes a firm retains a constant dollar amount of earnings and reinvests these retained earnings in assets that obtain a rate of return above the required rate.

---

[14] The discussion in this section draws heavily from Ezra Solomon, *The Theory of Financial Management* (New York: Columbia University Press, 1963), 55–63; and M. Miller and F. Modigliani, "Dividend Policy, Growth, and the Valuation of Shares," *The Journal of Business* 34, no. 4 (October 1961): 411–433.

In all cases it is postulated that the market value (V) of an all-equity firm is the capitalized value of three component forms of returns discounted at the rate k.

- E = the level of (constant) net earnings expected from existing assets, without further net investments.
- G = the growth component that equals the present value of capital gains expected from reinvested funds. The return on reinvested funds is equal to r, which equals mk (m is the relative rate of return operator). If m is equal to one, then $r = k$. If m is greater than 1, the projects that generate these returns are considered true growth investments ($r > k$). If m is less than 1, the investments are generating returns (r) below the cost of capital ($r < k$).
- R = the reinvestment of net earnings (E) and is equal to bE, where b is a percent between zero (no reinvestment) and unity (total reinvestment; no dividends).

SIMPLE GROWTH MODEL

This model assumes that the firm has investment opportunities that provide rates of return equal to r, where r is greater than k (m is above 1). Further, it is assumed that the firm can invest R dollars a year at these rates and that $R = bE$; R is a *constant dollar amount* because E is the constant earnings at the beginning of the period.

The value of G, the capital gain component, is computed as follows: the first investment of bE dollars yields a stream of earnings equal to bEr dollars, and this is repeated every year. Each of these earnings streams has a present value, as of the year it begins, of bEr/k, which is the present value of a constant perpetual stream discounted at a rate consistent with the risk involved. Assuming the firm does this every year, it has a series of investments, each of which has a present value of bEr/k. The present value of *all* these series is $(bEr/k)/k$, which equals bEr/k^2. But because $r = mk$, this becomes

$$\frac{bEmk}{k^2} = \frac{bEm}{k} \quad \begin{array}{l}\text{(Gross Present Value of}\\ \text{Growth Investments)}\end{array} \tag{18.1}$$

To derive these flows, the firm must invest bE dollars each year. The present value of these annual investments is equal to bE/k. Therefore, the *net* present value of growth investments is equal to

$$\frac{bEm}{k} - \frac{bE}{k} \quad \begin{array}{l}\text{(Net Present Value of}\\ \text{Growth Investments)}\end{array} \tag{18.2}$$

The important variable is the value of m, which indicates the relationship of r to k. Combining this growth component with the capitalized value of the constant earnings stream indicates that the value of the firm is

$$V = \frac{E}{k} + \frac{bEm}{k} - \frac{bE}{k} \tag{18.3}$$

This equation indicates that the value of the firm is equal to the constant earnings stream plus a growth component equal to the *net* present value of reinvestment in growth projects. By combining the first and third terms in Equation 18.3, this becomes

$$V = \frac{E(1 - b)}{k} + \frac{bEm}{k} \qquad (18.4)$$

Because $E(1 - b)$ is the dividend, this model becomes

$$V = \frac{D}{k} + \frac{bEm}{k} \quad \begin{array}{l}\text{(Present Value of Constant Dividend} \\ \text{plus the Present Value of Growth Investments)}\end{array} \qquad (18.5)$$

It can be stated as earnings only by rearranging Equation 18.3.

$$V = \frac{E}{k} + \frac{bE(m - 1)}{k} \quad \begin{array}{l}\text{(Present Value of Constant Earnings} \\ \text{plus Present Value of Excess} \\ \text{Earnings from Growth Investments)}\end{array} \qquad (18.6)$$

EXPANSION MODEL
The expansion model assumes a firm retains earnings to reinvest but receives a rate of return on its investments that is equal to its cost of capital ($m = 1$, so $r = k$). The effect of such a change can be seen in Equation 18.2, where the net present value of growth investments would be zero. Therefore, Equation 18.3 would become

$$V = \frac{E}{k} \qquad (18.7)$$

Equation 18.4 would become

$$V = \frac{E(1 - b)}{k} + \frac{bE}{k} = \frac{E}{k} \qquad (18.8)$$

Equation 18.5 is still valid, but the present value of the growth investment component would be smaller because m would be equal to 1. Finally, the last term in Equation 18.6 would disappear.

This discussion indicates that simply because a firm retains earnings and reinvests them, it is not necessarily of benefit to the stockholder *unless the reinvestment rate is above the required rate* ($r > k$). Otherwise, the investor in a tax-free world would be as well off with all earnings paid out in dividends.

NEGATIVE GROWTH MODEL
The negative growth model applies to a firm that retains earnings ($b > 0$) and reinvests these funds in projects that generate rates of return *below* the firm's cost of capital ($r < k$ or $m < 1$). The impact of this on the value of the firm can be seen from Equation 18.2, which indicates that with $m < 1$, the net present value of the growth investments would be negative. Therefore, the value of the firm in Equation 18.3 would be *less* than the value of a no-growth firm or an expansion firm. This can also be seen by examining the effect of $m < 1$ in Equation 18.6. The firm is withholding funds from the investor and investing them in projects that generate returns less than those available from comparable risk investments.

Such poor performance may be difficult to uncover because the firm's asset base will grow since it is retaining earnings and acquiring assets, and the earnings of the firm will increase if it earns *any* positive rate of return on the new assets. The crucial point is, *the earnings will not grow by as much as they should,* so the value of the firm will decline when investors discount this reinvestment stream at the firm's cost of capital.

WHAT DETERMINES THE CAPITAL GAIN COMPONENT?

These equations highlight the factors that influence the capital gain component. All the equations beginning with 18.1 suggest that the gross present value of the growth investments is equal to

$$bEm/k$$

Therefore, three factors influence the size of this capital gain term. The first is b, the percentage of earnings retained for reinvestment. The greater the proportion of earnings retained, the larger the capital gain component. The second factor is m, which indicates the relationship between the firm's rate of return on investments and the firm's required rate of return (i.e., its cost of capital). A value of 1 indicates that the firm is earning only its required return. A firm with an m greater than 1 is a true growth company. The important question is, how much greater than 1 is the return? The final factor is the time period for the superior investments. How long can the firm make these superior return investments? This time factor is often overlooked because we have assumed an infinite horizon to simplify the computations. However, when analyzing growth companies, this time estimate is clearly a major consideration. In summary, the three factors that influence the capital gain component are

1.   The amount of capital invested in growth investments (b)
2.   The rate of return earned on the funds retained (m)
3.   The time horizon for these growth investments

DYNAMIC TRUE GROWTH MODEL

A dynamic true growth model applies to a firm that invests a constant *percentage* of *current* earnings in projects that generate rates of return above the firm's required rate ($r > k$, $m > 1$). As a result, the firm's earnings and dividends will grow at a *constant rate* that is equal to br (the percentage of earnings retained times the return on investments). In the current model, this would equal bmk, where m is greater than 1. Given these assumptions, the dynamic growth model for an infinite time period is the dividend discount model derived in the Appendix to Chapter 11:

$$V = \frac{D_1}{k - g}$$

Applying this model to a true growth company means that earnings and dividends are growing at a constant rate and *the firm is investing larger and larger dollar amounts in projects that generate returns greater than k.* Moreover, the dividend growth model implicitly assumes that the firm can continue to do this for *an infinite time period.* If

TABLE 18.15

Summary of Company Descriptions

	Retention	Return on Investments
No-Growth Company	$b = 0$	$r = k$
Long-Run Growth (assumes reinvestment)		
Negative growth	$b > 0$	$r < k$
Expansion	$b > 0$	$r = k$
Simple long-run growth	$b > 0$ (constant \$)	$r > k$
Dynamic long-run growth	$b > 0$ (constant %)	$r > k$

the growth rate (g) is greater than k, the model blows up and indicates that the firm should have an infinite value. Durand considered this possibility and concluded that, although many firms had current growth rates above the normal required rates of return, very few of their stocks were selling for infinite values.[15] He explained this by contending that investors expected the reinvestment rate to decline or they felt that the investment opportunities would not be available for an infinite time period. Table 18.15 contains a summary of the alternative company characteristics.

THE REAL WORLD

Because these models are simplified to allow us to develop a range of alternatives, several of them are extremely unrealistic. The real world contains companies that combine these models. Unfortunately, most firms have made some investments where $r < k$, and many firms invest in projects that generate returns about equal to their cost of capital. Finally, most firms invest in *some* projects that provide rates of return above the firm's cost of capital ($r > k$). The crucial questions are, how much is invested in these growth projects, and how long do these true growth opportunities last?

Given this understanding of growth companies and what creates their value, the rest of this chapter considers various models that will help you estimate specific values for them.

GROWTH DURATION

The purpose of the growth duration model is to help you *evaluate* the high P/E ratio for the stock of a growth company by relating the P/E ratio to the firm's rate of growth and the duration of growth. A stock's P/E ratio is a function of (1) the firm's expected rate of growth of earnings per share, (2) the stock's required rate of return, and (3) the firm's dividend-payout ratio. Assuming equal risk and no significant difference in the payout ratio for different firms, the principal variable affecting differences in the earnings multiple for two firms *is the difference in expected growth*. Further, the growth estimate must consider the *rate* of growth and how long will it last, that is, the *duration* of expected growth. No company can grow indefinitely at a rate substantially above normal. As an example, Wal-Mart cannot continue to grow at 20 percent a year for an extended period, or it will eventually become the entire economy. The fact is,

---

[15] David Durand, "Growth Stocks and the Petersburg Paradox," *Journal of Finance* 12, no. 3 (September 1957): 348–363.

Wal-Mart or any similar growth firm will eventually run out of high-profit investment projects. Recall that continued growth at a constant rate requires that larger amounts of money be invested in high-return projects. Eventually competition will encroach on these high-return investments, and the firm's growth rate will decline to a rate consistent with the rate for the overall economy. Ascertaining the duration of a firm's high-growth period therefore becomes significant.

COMPUTATION OF GROWTH DURATION

The growth duration concept was suggested by Holt, who showed that if you assume equal risk between a given security and a market security such as the DJIA, you can concentrate on the differential past growth rates for the market and the growth firm as a factor causing the alternative P/E ratios.[16] This allows you to compute the market's *implied growth duration* for the growth firm.

If $E'(0)$ is the firm's current earnings, then $E'(t)$ is earnings in period t according to the expression

$$E'(t) = E(0)(1 + G)^t \tag{18.9}$$

where G is the annual percentage growth rate for earnings. To adjust for dividend payments, it was assumed that all such payments are used to purchase further shares of the stock. This means the number of shares (N) will grow at the dividend rate (D). Therefore

$$N(t) = N(0)(1 + D)^t \tag{18.10}$$

To derive the total earnings for a firm, $E(t)$, the growth rate in per share earnings and the growth in shares are combined as follows:

$$E(t) = E'(t)N(t) = E'(0)[(1 + G)(1 + D)]^t \tag{18.11}$$

Because G and D are small, this expression can be approximated by

$$E(t) \simeq E'(0)(1 + G + D)^t \tag{18.12}$$

Assuming that the growth stock (g) and the nongrowth stock (a) have similar risk and payout, the market should value the two stocks in direct proportion to their earnings in year T, where T is the investor's horizon. In other words, *current prices should be in direct proportion to the expected future earnings ratio that will prevail in year T.* This relationship can be stated

$$\left(\frac{P_g(0)}{P_a(0)}\right) \simeq \left(\frac{E_g(0)(1 + G_g + D_g)^T}{E_a(0)(1 + G_a + D_a)^T}\right) \tag{18.13}$$

---

[16] Charles C. Holt, "The Influence of Growth Duration on Share Prices," *Journal of Finance* 7, no. 3 (September 1962): 465–475.

or

$$\left(\frac{P_g(0)/E_g(0)}{P_a(0)/E_a(0)}\right) \approx \left(\frac{1 + G_g + D_g^T}{1 + G_a + D_a}\right) \tag{18.14}$$

As a result, *the P/E ratios of the two stocks are in direct proportion to the ratio of composite growth rates raised to the Tth power.* You can solve for T by taking the log of both sides as follows:

$$\ln\left(\frac{P_g(0)/E_g(0)}{P_a(0)/E_a(0)}\right) \approx T \ln\left(\frac{1 + G_g + D_g}{1 + G_a + D_a}\right) \tag{18.15}$$

The growth duration model answers the question, how long must the earnings of the growth stock grow at the past rate, relative to the nongrowth stock, to justify its above-average P/E ratio? You must then determine whether the *implied* duration estimate is reasonable in terms of the company's potential.

Consider the following example. The stock of a well-known growth company is selling for $63 a share with expected per share earnings of $3.00 (its earnings multiple is 21). The firm's EPS growth rate during the past 5- and 10-year periods has been 15 percent a year, and its dividend yield has been 3 percent. In contrast, the S&P 400 Industrial Index has a current P/E ratio of 14, an average dividend yield of 4 percent, and an average growth rate of 6 percent. Therefore, the comparison looks as follows:

	S&P 400	Growth Company
P/E ratio	14.00	21.00
Average growth rate	.06	.15
Dividend yield	.04	.03

Inserting these values into Equation 18.15 yields the following:

$$\ln\left(\frac{21.00}{14.00}\right) = T\ln\left(\frac{1 + .15 + .03}{1 + .06 + .04}\right)$$

$$\ln(1.50) = T\ln\left(\frac{1.18}{1.10}\right)$$

$$\ln(1.500) = T\ln(1.073)$$

$$T = \ln(1.500)/\ln(1.073)$$

$$= .1761/.0306 \text{ (log base 10)}$$

$$= 5.75 \text{ years}$$

These results indicate that the market is implicitly assuming that the growth company can continue to grow at this composite rate (18 percent) for almost six more years, after which it is assumed that the growth company will grow at the same rate as the aggregate market (i.e., the S&P 400). You must now ask, can this growth rate be sustained for at least this period? If the implied growth duration is greater than you believe is reasonable, you would advise against buying the stock. If the duration is below your expectations, you would recommend buying the stock.

INTRA-INDUSTRY ANALYSIS

Besides comparing a company to a market series, you can directly compare two firms. For an intercompany analysis, you should compare firms in the same industry because the equal risk assumptions of this model is probably more reasonable.

Consider the following example from the computer software industry:

	Company A	Company B
P/E ratios	21.00	15.00
Average annual growth rate	.1700	.1200
Dividend yield	.0250	.0300
Growth rate plus dividend yield	.1950	.1500
Estimate of T[a]		8.79 years

[a]Readers should check to see that they get the same answer.

These results imply that the market expects Company A to grow at a total rate of almost 20 percent for about 9 years after which it will grow at Company B's rate of 15 percent. If you believe the implied duration is too long, you will prefer Company B; if you believe it is reasonable or low, you will recommend Company A.

AN ALTERNATIVE USE OF T

Instead of solving for T and then deciding whether the figure derived is reasonable, you can use this formulation to compute a reasonable P/E ratio for a security relative to the aggregate market (or another stock) if the implicit assumptions are reasonable for the stock involved. Assume that you estimate the composite growth of a company to be about 20 percent a year compared to the market growth of 11 percent. Further, you believe that this firm can continue to grow at this rate for about 7 years. Using Equation 18.15, this becomes

$$
\begin{aligned}
ln(X) &= 7 \cdot ln\frac{1.20}{1.11} \\
&= 7 \cdot ln(1.081) \\
&= 7 \cdot (.033826) \\
&= .236782
\end{aligned}
$$

To determine what the P/E ratio should be, you must derive the antilog of 0.236782, which is approximately 1.725. Therefore, assuming the market multiple is 14.00, the earnings multiple for this growth company should be about 1.725 times the market P/E ratio, or 24.15.

Alternatively, if you expect that the firm can maintain this differential growth for only 5 years, you would derive the antilog for 0.16913 (5 × .033826). The answer is 1.4761, which implies a P/E ratio of 20.66 for the stock.

FACTORS TO CONSIDER

When employing the growth duration technique, you should remember the following factors: First, the technique assumes equal risk, which may be acceptable when comparing two large, well-established firms or relating them to a market proxy (e.g., General Electric and Standard Oil to each other or to the DJIA). It is probably *not* a valid assumption when comparing a small firm to the aggregate market.

Second, which growth estimate should be used? In the typical case, 5- and 10-year historical growth rates are used. Which time interval is most relevant if historical rates are used? Beyond this, judgment based on analysis is required beyond mere extrapolations. What about using the *expected* rate of growth based on the factors that affect g (i.e., the retention rate and the components of ROE)?

Third, the growth duration technique assumes that stocks with higher P/E ratios have the higher growth rates. In actuality, in many cases the stock with the higher P/E ratio does not have a higher historical growth rate, which generates a useless negative growth duration value. Inconsistency between growth and the P/E ratio could be attributed to one of four factors:

1. A major difference in the risk involved.
2. Inaccurate growth rate estimates. Possibly the firm with the higher P/E ratio is *expected* to grow faster in the future. Consider the historical growth rate employed and whether you expect any changes in it.
3. The stock with a low P/E ratio relative to its growth rate is undervalued. (Before this is accepted, consider the first two factors.)
4. The stock with a high P/E and a low growth rate is overvalued. (Before this is accepted, consider the second factor.)

The growth duration concept is valid, *given the assumptions made,* and can help you evaluate growth investments. It is not universally valid, though, because its answers are only as good as the data inputs (relative growth rates) and the applicability of the assumptions. The answer must be evaluated based on the analyst's knowledge.

The technique is probably most useful for helping spot overvalued growth stocks with very high multiples. The technique will highlight that the company must continue to grow at some very high rate for an extended period of time to justify its high P/E ratio (e.g., 15 to 20 years). Also, it can help you decide between two growth companies in the same industry by comparing each to the market, the industry, or directly to each other. Such a comparison has provided interesting insights wherein the new firms in an industry were growing faster than the large competitor, but their P/E ratios were *substantially* higher and implied that these new firms were going to have to maintain this large growth superiority for *over 10 years.*

A FLEXIBLE
GROWTH STOCK
VALUATION
MODEL

Mao developed an investment opportunities growth model that incorporated some previous work on growth stock valuation by Solomon and by Miller and Modigliani.[17] These authors had recognized the true nature of a growth firm, but they assumed unrealistic infinite growth horizons to simplify the exposition, which meant the models were not applicable to practical problems.

---

[17] James C. Mao, ''The Valuation of Growth Stocks: The Investment Opportunities Approach,'' *Journal of Finance* 21, no. 1 (March 1966): 95–102.

Mao developed a three-stage valuation model that considered (1) *a dynamic growth period* during which the firm invests a constant percentage of current earnings in growth projects, (2) *a simple growth period* during which the firm invests a constant dollar amount in growth opportunities, and finally, (3) *a declining growth period* during which the amount invested in growth investments declines to zero. The model was theoretically correct and realistic but required difficult computations and was somewhat rigid in its assumptions about the parameters b (the retention rate), r (the return on growth investments), and k (the required rate of return on the stock). As a result, the model has not been applied as widely as expected. In this subsection we discuss the flexible growth model, apply it to a growth company, and discuss the effects of varying the parameters.

THE VALUATION MODEL
Mao assumed that the price of the stock is equal to (1) the present value of current earnings, E, discounted to infinity at the required rate of return, k, ($P = E/k$) plus (2) the net present value of growth opportunities assuming three stages of growth.

The dynamic growth stage lasts for n_1 years during which the firm has opportunities to invest a given percentage of current earnings in growth projects where r is greater than k. Because b is a constant percentage of a growing earnings stream, the dollar amount invested in these growth projects grows at an exponential rate. The value of the dynamic investments is given by

$$\left(\frac{r-k}{k}\right)(bE)\sum_{t=1}^{n_1}\frac{(1+br)^{t-1}}{(1+k)^t} \quad \text{(Value of Dynamic Growth Opportunities)} \quad (18.16)$$

The simple growth stage lasts for n_2 years during which the firm invests a constant dollar amount in growth projects ($r > k$). The value of these projects is given by

$$\left(\frac{r-k}{k}\right)(bE)\sum_{t=1}^{n_2}\frac{1}{(1+k)^t} \quad \text{(Value of Simple Growth Opportunities)} \quad (18.17)$$

During the final declining growth stage, which lasts n_3 years, the firm has opportunities to invest in growth projects, but the dollar amount declines steadily from bE to zero. The amount of the decline is steady at $1/n_3$ each year. As an example, if bE equals $100,000, and n_3 is 20, then the amount invested in growth projects would decline by $5,000 a year. The value of this component is

$$\left(\frac{r-k}{k}\right)(bE)\sum_{t=1}^{n_3}\frac{(n_3-t+1)}{n_3(1+k)^t} \quad \text{(Value of Declining Growth Opportunities)} \quad (18.18)$$

The complete model combines the no-growth component (E/k) plus the three growth components. If the final summation term in Equation 18.16 is designated A, the final term in Equation 18.17 is designated B, and the final term in Equation 18.18 is designated C, this formulation can be written as follows:

$$P = \frac{E}{k} + \left(\frac{r-k}{k}\right)(bE)\left[A + \frac{(1+br)^{n_1-1}}{(1+k)^{n_1}}B + \frac{(1+br)^{n_1-1}}{(1+k)^{n_1+n_2}}C\right] \quad (18.19)$$

Tables were provided that contained values for *A* and *C*, given several combinations of the parameters. *B* is simply the present value of an annuity. Even with the tables and no change in the parameters, the computations are rather tedious.

FLEXIBLE PARAMETERS

The Mao model assumes (1) no change in the required rate of return (k), (2) the same rate of return on all growth projects (r), and (3) the same retention rate (b) during the three growth periods. Mao probably assumed constant parameters to avoid complicating a technique that already involved extensive computations. Still, there are indications that investors probably change their required return (k) during different phases of the firm's life cycle. Malkiel contends it is logical to require a higher return on high-growth stocks because the stream of returns is such that these stocks are inherently longer-duration securities.[18] At the other extreme, a firm may become more subject to cyclical variations during its declining years, which indicate higher business risk and a higher required rate of return (k).

Regarding the return on investments (r), it could be too optimistic to assume that during the period of simple growth the firm can continue to earn very high rates, even on a stable dollar amount. Many analysts might prefer a larger n_2 and a somewhat smaller r.

Finally, is it realistic to assume a constant retention rate (b) over the life of a firm? Most observers would expect a high retention rate during the early years when growth opportunities are abundant and capital is scarce, and a lower retention rate during the later years when growth investment opportunities are limited, the level of earnings and cash flow is high, and outside capital is available. The point is, the model would be more useful and realistic if the parameters can be changed.

APPLICATION OF THE MODEL

A computer program that requires three statements for each case allows you to consider several alternative sets of parameters, including most pessimistic, most optimistic, and most likely. For a high P/E stock you should determine the required sets of estimates that justify the prevailing market price. When applying this technique to evaluate growth companies, you should consider the following suggestions:

1. The earnings figure (*E*) is assumed to be the figure for the coming year. A crude estimate is the actual earnings for the most recent year times the growth rate for the past 5 or 10 years. Practicing analysts would use their estimate of future growth.
2. The estimated retention rate (*b*) can be the average retention rate during the last several years.
3. The estimate of the return on investment (*r*) is obviously crucial.[19] You can compute the average ROE during the recent period or estimate the three components (total asset turnover, financial leverage, and the profit margin) and use the product of these three estimates. Alternatively, Mao suggested computing the increase in earnings per share during some period divided by the amount

---

[18] Burton G. Malkiel, "Equity Yields, Growth, and the Structure of Share Prices," *American Economic Review* 53, no. 5 (December 1963): 1004–1031.

[19] An article that discusses the components of growth is Guilford C. Babcock, "The Concept of Sustainable Growth," *Financial Analysts Journal* 26, no. 3 (May-June 1970): 236–242.

of earnings retained over a comparable period with a 1-year lag. For example, the increase in earnings per share for the period 1991 to 1995 divided by the retained earnings for the period 1990 to 1994. This computation attempts to estimate the firm's current return on retained earnings rather than the traditional ROE, which is current net earnings divided by current equity. This average ROE is heavily influenced by past performance and employs historical equity, which can become seriously distorted over time. The Mao estimate is akin to a marginal ROE.

4. The required return estimate (k) could be the actual return derived from all common stocks or the return experienced by the specific stock during some recent period. Alternatively, you could use a required rate based on the CAPM and the stock's beta. Because this model is *extremely sensitive to changes in k,* you definitely should consider a *range* of ks.

AN EXAMPLE

Assume the following for a firm that you consider to be a true growth company:

- Earnings: 1995 $2.50
            1996 (estimated) 2.88 ($2.50 × 1.15)
- Annual growth rate in EPS (1990–1994)   .15
- Retention rate (1990–1994)   .65
- Average return on equity (1990–1994)   .24
- Marginal return on equity (1990–1994)   .26
- Estimated r for analysis   .25

Given these estimates of the major parameters, you can derive a number of stock price values by simply changing the values for the three ns (n_1, n_2, n_3) and consider alternative required returns. You can change the values for each of these parameters for each growth period. In this example they will be constant at these historical values to simplify the presentation. Subsequent estimates should consider alternative parameters. For the example, the initial estimates of the ns are relatively conservative (5, 5, 10) and are changed to more liberal estimates as follows:

A. $n_1 = 5$
    $n_2 = 5$
    $n_3 = 10$
B. $n_1 = 5$
    $n_2 = 10$
    $n_3 = 15$
C. $n_1 = 10$
    $n_2 = 10$
    $n_3 = 15$
D. $n_1 = 15$
    $n_2 = 15$
    $n_3 = 20$

The ks considered ranged from 8 percent to 16 percent in increments of 2 percent. The results in Table 18.16 indicate a wide range of estimated values for this stock. You must select the best estimate of the three time periods and, most important, an estimate of k for this stock based on its systematic risk and the expected security market line (SML).

TABLE 18.16

Estimated Values for Stock Assuming Alternative Time Periods and Required Rates of Return
(E = \$2.88; b = .65; r = .25)

N_1	N_2	N_3	0.08	0.10	0.12	0.14	0.16
5	5	10	91.03	62.79	45.67	34.55	26.96
5	10	15	102.92	68.72	48.72	36.15	27.80
10	10	15	154.15	95.72	63.55	44.46	32.46
15	15	20	242.31	136.49	83.39	54.40	37.48

FIGURE 18.8

Estimated Prices for Flexible Growth Model

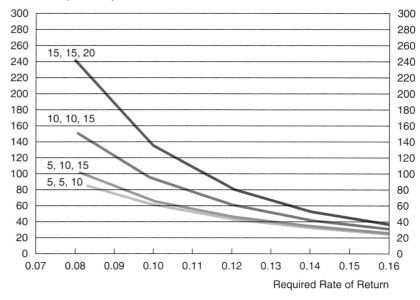

Because almost all growth companies have above-average systematic risk (i.e., betas above 1.00), the required return will typically exceed the expected market return.

Assume the following estimates regarding the SML: RFR = .08; Rm = .12. If the stock has a beta of 1.5, the estimated required return would be

- $k = RFR + (Rm = RFR)$
- $k = .08 + 1.5\,(.12 - .08)$
- $k = .14$

This would indicate further consideration of the .14 percent column and the adjoining columns. Comparing these prices to the current market price will indicate whether the stock should be included in the portfolio.

You can graph the stock values for a given set of n values and different ks. Using several sets of ns will produce a set of curves sloping downward to the right as shown in Figure 18.8. There are two ways to use this graph to examine the model results.

First, compare the current market price to the range of computed values. The prevailing price should be within the total range, and you should get an indication of relative valuation depending on whether the current market price is at the upper or lower end of the valuation range. Second, determine the implied rate of return by drawing the current market price horizontally across the valuation curves. Because the valuation curves generally represent the full range of feasible parameters, the intersection of the current market price line with the curve to the right indicates the highest k that can be expected, with the most liberal parameters, if you buy the stock at the current market price. The curve to the left indicates the lowest k possible if you buy the stock at today's price.

SUMMARY

The purpose of this chapter was to demonstrate how you complete the fundamental analysis process by analyzing a company and deciding whether you should buy its stock. You must realize that this requires a separate analysis of a company and its stock. A wonderful firm can have an overpriced stock, or a mediocre firm can have an underpriced stock.

We demonstrated the dividend discount model using Walgreen Company as an example. We derived an estimate of expected value by computing an earnings per share estimate and the earnings multiplier. The investment decision was based on three comparisons. First, we computed the expected value of the stock discounted to the present and compared it to the prevailing market price. If the present value of the expected price exceeded the market price, we would buy the stock. Second, we computed the expected rate of return during our holding period on the basis of the expected value of the stock and the expected dividend. If this expected rate of return exceeded our required rate of return, we would buy it. Finally, we computed an expected rate of return based on the expected dividend yield plus the expected growth rate and, again, if this expected return exceeded our required rate of return, we would buy the stock.

Subsequently, we considered some additional relative valuation variables that affect the decisions of investors in the United States and abroad. Specifically, we computed and analyzed the price/book value ratio and the price/cash flow ratio for the stock market, the retail drugstore industry, and Walgreen. This analysis provided some historical and current perspective for these ratios and Walgreen's relative position.

We also discussed the strategic alternatives available to firms in response to different competitive pressures in their industries. The alternative strategies include low-cost leadership or differentiation. Either of these should be focused toward alternative segments of the market and, if properly implemented, should help the company attain above-average rates of return.

We continued our example of global analysis by reviewing the company analysis related to the European chemical industry. This demonstration showed the importance of differential demand and cost factors among countries, the significance of different accounting conventions, and finally the impact of exchange rate differences.

We concluded the chapter with a discussion of how true growth companies are unique and temporary in a competitive economy. Because of the abnormal rates of return that are only available for a limited period, it is necessary to use a unique set of valuation models to help make the investment decision. One model used in this analysis is the growth duration model that concentrates on the major question of concern with true growth companies: how long will this superior rate of growth last, and is this expectation consistent with the stock's implied duration? We also considered a three-step growth model that provides a framework that considers the relevant growth variables.

Because of the potential rewards from the superior analysis of growth companies, there is strong competition in the valuation process. The techniques presented in this chapter can help you derive an appropriate value for a growth firm, but *the estimated inputs are crucial.* The superior analyst for true growth companies is the one who derives the best estimates of the rate and duration of growth.

QUESTIONS

1. Define a growth company and a speculative stock.

2. Give an example of a growth company, and discuss why you identify it as such.

3. Give an example of a cyclical stock, and discuss why you have designated it as such. Is it issued by a cyclical company?

4. A biotechnology firm is growing at a compound rate of over 21 percent a year. (Its ROE is over 30 percent, and it retains about 70 percent of its earnings.) The stock of this company is priced at about 65 times next year's earnings. Discuss whether you consider this a growth company and a growth stock.

5. Select a company outside the retail drugstore industry and indicate what economic series you would use for a sales projection. Discuss why this is a relevant series.

6. Select a company outside the retail drugstore industry and indicate what industry series you would use in an industry analysis. (Use one of the industry groups designated by Standard & Poor's.) Discuss why this industry series is appropriate. Were there other possible alternatives?

7. Select a company outside the retail drugstore industry and, based on reading its annual report and other public information, discuss its competitive strategy (i.e., low-cost producer or differentiation). Is the firm successful in implementing this strategy?

8. Discuss a company that is known to be a low-cost producer in its industry and consider what makes it possible for the firm to be a cost leader. Do the same for a firm known for differentiating.

9. What is the rationale for using the price/book value (P/BV) ratio as a measure of relative value?

10. What would you look for to justify a price/book value ratio of 3.0? What would you expect to be the characteristics of a firm with a P/BV ratio of 0.6?

11. Why has the price/cash flow (P/CF) ratio become popular during the recent past? What factors would help explain a difference in this ratio for two firms?

12. You are told that a company retains 80 percent of its earnings, and its earnings are growing at a rate of about 8 percent a year versus an average growth rate of 6 percent for all firms. Discuss whether you would consider this a growth company.

13. It is contended by some that in a completely competitive economy, there would never be a true growth company. Discuss the reasoning behind this contention.

14. Why is it not feasible to use the dividend discount model in the valuation of true growth companies?

15. Discuss the major assumptions of the growth duration model. Why could these assumptions present a problem?

16. You are told that a growth company has a P/E ratio of 10 times and a growth rate of 15 percent compared to the aggregate market, which has a growth rate of 8 percent and a P/E ratio of 11 times. What does this comparison imply regarding the growth company? What else do you need to know to properly compare the growth company to the aggregate market?

17. Define the following:
    a. A negative growth company
    b. An expanding company
    c. A simple growth company
    d. A dynamic growth company

18. Given the terms listed in Question 17, indicate what your label would be for Walgreen Company. Justify your label.

19. Indicate and justify a label for General Motors.

20. What are the variables that must be estimated if you want to use the Mao three-stage growth valuation model?

PROBLEMS

1. Select two stocks in an industry of your choice, and perform a common size income statement analysis over a two-year period.
    a. Discuss which firm is more cost effective.
    b. Discuss the relative year-to-year changes in gross profit margin, operating profit margin, and net profit margin for each company.

2. Select a company outside the retail store industry, and examine its operating profit margin relative to the operating margin for its industry during the most recent 10-year period. Discuss the annual results in terms of levels and percentage changes.

3. Select any industry except chemicals and provide general background information on two *non-U.S.* companies from public sources (see Chapter 5). This background information should include their products, overall size (sales and assets), growth during the past 5 years (sales and earnings), ROE during last 2 years, current stock price, and P/E ratio.

4. Given Hitech's beta of 1.75 and a risk-free rate of 9 percent, what is the expected rate of return assuming
    a. A 15 percent market return?
    b. A 10 percent market return?

5. Select three companies from any industry except retail drugstores.
    a. Compute their P/E ratios using last year's average price (high plus low/2) and earnings.
    b. Compute their growth rate of earnings over the last 5 years.
    c. Look up the most recent beta reported in *Value Line*.
    d. Discuss the relationships between P/E, growth, and risk.

6. What is the implied growth duration of Growth Industries given the following:

	S&P 400	Growth Industries
P/E ratios	16	24
Average growth	.06	14
Dividend yield	.04	.02

7. Modular Industries presently has an 18 percent annual growth rate compared to the market rate of 8 percent. If the market multiple is 14, determine P/E ratios for Modular Industries, assuming its beta is 1.0 and you feel it can maintain its superior growth rate for
   a. The next 10 years.
   b. The next 5 years.

8. You are given the following information about two computer software firms and the S&P 400:

	Company A	Company B	S&P 400
P/E ratio	24.0	20.0	12.0
Average annual growth rate	.18	.15	.07
Dividend yield	.02	.03	.05

   a. Compute the growth duration of each company stock relative to the S&P 400.
   b. Compute the growth duration of Company A relative to Company B.
   c. Given these durations, what must you decide in order to make an investment decision?

9. *CFA Examination II (June 1981)*
   The value of an asset is the present value of the expected returns from the asset during the holding period. An investment will provide a stream of returns during this period, and it is necessary to discount this stream of returns at an appropriate rate to determine the asset's present value. A dividend valuation model such as the following is frequently used.

$$P_i = \frac{D_1}{(k_i - g_i)}$$

where:

P_i = **current price of common stock i**

D_1 = **expected dividend in period 1**

k_i = **required rate of return on stock i**

g_i = **expected constant growth rate of dividends for stock i**

   a. *Identify* the three factors that must be estimated for any valuation model, and *explain* why these estimates are more difficult to derive for common stocks than for bonds. (9 minutes)
   b. *Explain* the principal problem involved in using a dividend valuation model to value
      (1) Companies whose operations are closely correlated with economic cycles.
      (2) Companies that are of giant size and are maturing.
      (3) Companies that are of small size and are growing rapidly.
      Assume all companies pay dividends. (6 minutes)

10. *CFA Examination I (June 1985)*
    Your client is considering the purchase of $100,000 in common stock which pays no dividends and will appreciate in market value by 10 percent per year. At the same time, the client is considering an opportunity to invest $100,000 in a lease obligation that will pro-

vide the annual year-end cash flows listed in Table A. Assume that each investment will be sold at the end of 3 years and that you are given no additional information.

Calculate the present value of each of the two investments assuming a 10 percent discount rate, and state which will provide the higher return over the 3-year period. Use the data in Table A, and show your calculations. (10 minutes)

TABLE A

Annual Cash Flow From Lease

End of Year

1	$ -0-
2 Lease Receipts	15,000
3 Lease Receipts	25,000
3 Sale Proceeds	$100,000

Present Value of $1

Period	6%	8%	10%	12%
1	.943	.926	.909	.893
2	.890	.857	.826	.797
3	.840	.794	.751	.712
4	.792	.735	.683	.636
5	.747	.681	.621	.567

REFERENCES

Babcock, Guilford C. "The Concept of Sustainable Growth." *Financial Analysts Journal* 26, no. 3 (May-June 1970).

Ball, Ray, and Ross Watts. "Some Time Series Properties of Accounting Earnings Numbers." *Journal of Finance* 27, no. 3 (June 1972).

Born, Jeffery, James Moses, and Dennis Officer. "Changes in Dividend Policy and Subsequent Earnings." *Journal of Portfolio Management* 14, no. 4 (Summer 1988).

Clayman, Michelle. "In Search of Excellence: The Investor's Viewpoint," *Financial Analysts Journal* 43, no. 3 (May-June 1987).

Cottle, Sidney, Roger F. Murray, and Frank E. Block. *Graham and Dodd's Security Analysis.* 5th ed. New York: McGraw-Hill, 1988.

Fama, Eugene F., and Kenneth French. "Dividend Yields and Expected Stock Returns." *Journal of Financial Economics* 22, no. 1 (October 1988).

Fama, Eugene F., and Kenneth French. "The Cross-Section of Expected Stock Returns." *Journal of Finance* 47, no. 2 (June 1992).

Gordon, Myron J. *The Investment, Financing, and Valuation of the Corporation.* Homewood, Ill.: Richard D. Irwin, 1962.

Hackel, Kenneth S., and Joshua Livnat. *Cash Flow and Security Analysis* (Homewood, Ill.: Business One–Irwin, 1992).

Hassel, J., and Robert Jennings. "Relative Forecast Accuracy and the Timing of Earnings Forecast Announcements." *The Accounting Review* 61, no. 1 (January 1986).

Imhoff, Eugene, and G. Lobo. "Information Content of Analysts Composite Forecast Revisions." *Journal of Accounting Research* 22, no. 3 (Autumn 1984).

Jaffe, Jeffery, Donald Keim, and Randolph Westerfield. "Earnings Yields, Market Values, Stock Returns." *Journal of Finance 44,* no. 1 (March 1989).

Jennings, Robert. *Reaction of Financial Analysts to Corporate Management Earnings per Share Forecasts.* Financial Analysts Research Foundation, Monograph No. 20, (New York, 1984).

Johnson, R. S., Lyle Fiore, and Richard Zuber. "The Investment Performance of Common Stocks in Relation to Their Price-Earnings Ratios: An Update of the Basu Study." *Financial Review* 24, no. 3 (August 1989).

Levine, Sumner N. *The Financial Analysts Handbook.* 2d ed. Homewood, Ill.: Dow Jones-Irwin, 1988.

Malkiel, Burton G., and John Cragg. "Expectations and the Structure of Share Prices." *American Economic Review* 60, no. 4 (September 1970).

Miller, Merton, and Franco Modigliani. "Dividend Policy, Growth, and the Valuation of Shares." *Journal of Business* 34, no. 4 (October 1961).

Porter, Michael E. "Competitive Strategy: The Core Concepts." In *Competitive Advantage: Creating and Sustaining Superior Performance.* New York: Free Press, 1985.

Solomon, Ezra. *The Theory of Financial Management.* New York: Columbia University Press, 1963.

Waymire, G. "Additional Evidence on the Information Content of Management Earnings Forecasts." *Journal of Accounting Research* 22, no. 3 (Autumn 1984).

CHAPTER 19

TECHNICAL ANALYSIS[1]

In this chapter we will answer the following questions:

- How does technical analysis differ from fundamental analysis?
- What are the underlying assumptions of technical analysis?
- What is the major assumption that causes a difference between technical analysis and the efficient market hypothesis?
- What are the major challenges to the assumptions of technical analysis and its rules?
- What are the major advantages that technical analysts claim compared to fundamental analysis?
- What are the major contrary opinion rules used by technicians and what is the logic for them?
- What are some of the significant rules used by technicians who want to follow the smart money and what is the logic of those rules?
- What are the breadth of market measures and what are they intended to indicate to the technician?
- What are the three types of price movements postulated in the Dow Theory and how are they used by a technician?
- Why is the volume of trading considered important by technicians and how do they use it in their analysis?
- What are support and resistance levels, when do they occur, and how are they used by technicians?
- How are bar charts different from point-and-figure charts?
- What are some uses of technical analysis in foreign security markets?
- How is technical analysis used when analyzing bond markets?

The market reacted yesterday to the report of a large increase in the short interest on the NYSE.

---

[1]The author received very helpful comments and material for this chapter from Richard T. McCabe, Manager of Market Analysis at Merrill Lynch Capital Markets.

Although the market declined today, it was not considered bearish because there was very light volume.

The market declined today after 3 days of increases due to profit taking by investors.

These and similar statements appear daily in the financial news. All of them have as their rationale one of numerous technical trading rules. Technical analysts develop technical trading rules from observations of past price movements of the stock market and individual stocks. This philosophy is in sharp contrast to the efficient market hypothesis that we studied, which contends that past performance has no influence on future performance or market values. It also differs from what we learned about fundamental analysis, which involves making investment decisions based on the examination of fundamental economic and company variables that lead to an estimate of value for an investment, which is then compared to the prevailing market price of the investment. In contrast to the efficient market hypothesis or fundamental analysis, *technical analysis* involves the examination of past market data such as prices and the volume of trading, which leads to an estimate of future price and, therefore, an investment decision. Whereas fundamental analysts use economic data that is usually separate from the market, the technical analyst believes that using data *from the market itself* is a good idea because, "the market is its own best predictor." Therefore, technical analysis is an alternative method of making the investment decision and answering the questions: What securities should an investor buy or sell? When should these investments be made?

Technical analysts see no need to study the multitude of economic and company variables to arrive at an estimate of future value, because past price movements will signal future price movements. Technicians also believe that a change in the price trend may predict a forthcoming change in the fundamental variables such as earnings and risk earlier than it is perceived or anticipated by most fundamental analysts. Are technicians correct? Many investors using these techniques claim to have experienced superior rates of return on many investments. In addition, many newsletter writers base their recommendations on technical analysis. Finally, even the major investment firms that employ a large number of fundamental analysts also employ technical analysts to provide investment advice. The point is, numerous investment professionals as well as individual investors believe in and use technical trading rules to make their investment decisions. Therefore, you should have an understanding of the basic philosophy and reasoning behind these technical approaches. To help you understand technical analysis, we begin this chapter with an examination of the basic philosophy underlying all technical approaches to market analysis and company analysis. Subsequently we consider the advantages and potential problems with the technical approach. Finally, we present and discuss a number of the alternative technical trading rules that are applicable to both the United States market and the foreign securities markets.

UNDERLYING ASSUMPTIONS OF TECHNICAL ANALYSIS

Technical analysts base trading decisions on examinations of prior price and volume data to determine past market trends from which they predict future behavior for the market as a whole and for individual securities. They cite several assumptions that support this view of price movements.

1. The market value of any good or service is determined solely by the interaction of supply and demand for it.

2.   Supply and demand are governed by numerous factors, both rational and irrational. Included in these factors are those economic variables relied on by the fundamental analyst, as well as opinions, moods, and guesses. The market weighs all these factors continually and automatically.

3.   Disregarding minor fluctuations, *the prices for individual securities and the overall value of the market tend to move in trends, which persist for appreciable lengths of time.*

4.   Prevailing trends change in reaction to shifts in supply and demand relationships. These shifts, no matter why they occur, *can be detected sooner or later in the action of the market itself.*[2]

Certain aspects of these assumptions are controversial, leading fundamental analysts and advocates of efficient markets to question their validity. Those aspects are emphasized above.

The first two assumptions are almost universally accepted by technicians and non-technicians alike. Almost anyone who has had a basic course in economics would agree that, at any point in time, the price of a security (or any good or service) is determined by the interaction of supply and demand for it. In addition, most observers would acknowledge that supply and demand are governed by many variables. The only difference in opinion might concern the influence of the irrational factors. A technical analyst might expect this influence to persist for some time, whereas other market analysts would expect only a short-run effect with rational beliefs prevailing over the long-run. Certainly, everyone would agree that the market continually weighs all these factors.

A stronger difference of opinion arises over the technical analysts' third assumption about the *speed of adjustment* of stock prices to changes in supply and demand. Technical analysts expect stock prices to move in trends that persist for long periods because new information that affects supply and demand does not come to the market at one point in time, but rather enters the market *over a period of time.* This pattern of information access occurs because of different sources of information or because certain investors receive the information or perceive fundamental changes earlier than others. As various groups ranging from insiders to well-informed professionals to the average investor receive the information and buy or sell a security accordingly, its price moves toward the new equilibrium. Therefore, technicians do not expect the price adjustment to be as abrupt as fundamental analysts and efficient market supporters do, but expect *a gradual adjustment* to reflect the gradual flow of information.

Figure 19.1 shows this process. The figure shows that new information causes a decrease in the equilibrium price for a security, but the price adjustment is not rapid. It occurs as a *trend* that persists until the stock reaches its new equilibrium. Technical analysts look for the beginning of a movement from one equilibrium value to a new equilibrium value. Technical analysts do not attempt to predict the new equilibrium value. They look for the start of a change so that they can get on the bandwagon early and benefit from the change by buying if the trend is up or selling if the trend is down. A rapid adjustment of prices would keep the ride on the bandwagon very short and thus it would not be worth the effort.

---

[2]These assumptions are summarized in Robert A. Levy, "Conceptual Foundations of Technical Analysis," *Financial Analysts Journal* 22, no. 4 (July-August 1966): 83.

FIGURE 19.1   **Technicians' View of Price Adjustment to New Information**

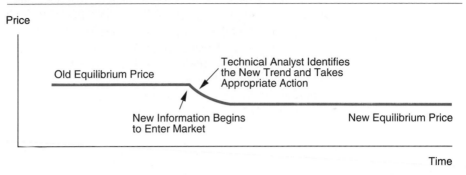

CHALLENGES TO TECHNICAL ANALYSIS

Those who question the value of technical analysis for investment decisions challenge this technique in two areas. First, they challenge some of its basic assumptions. Second, they challenge some of its specific trading rules and their long-run usefulness. In this section, we consider both of these challenges.

CHALLENGES TO TECHNICAL ANALYSIS ASSUMPTIONS

The major challenge to technical analysis is based on the efficient market hypothesis. As discussed in Chapter 6, for technical trading rules to generate superior risk-adjusted returns after taking account of transactions costs, the market would have to be slow to adjust prices to the arrival of new information, that is, when it is inefficient. (This is referred to as the weak-form efficient market hypothesis.) The vast majority of studies that have tested the weak-form efficient market hypothesis have found that prices adjust rapidly to stock market information, which supports the efficient market hypothesis.

As discussed in Chapter 6, these critics acknowledge that there are numerous technical trading rules that have not been or cannot be tested. They raise challenges in addition to those based on efficient market arguments.

CHALLENGES TO TECHNICAL TRADING RULES

An obvious challenge to technical analysis is that the past price patterns or relationships between specific market variables and stock prices may not be repeated. As a result, a technique that previously worked might miss subsequent market turns. This possibility leads most technicians to follow several trading rules and to seek a consensus of all of them to predict the future market pattern.

Other critics challenge that many price patterns become self-fulfilling prophecies. As an example, assume that many analysts expect a stock selling at $40 a share to go to $50 or more if it should rise above its current pattern and "break through" its channel at $45. As soon as it reaches $45, a number of technicians will buy, causing the price to rise to $50, exactly as predicted. In fact, some technicians may place a limit order to buy the stock at such a breakout point. Under such conditions, the increase will probably be only temporary and the price will return to its true equilibrium.

Another problem with technical analysis is that the success of a trading rule will encourage many investors to adopt it. This popularity and the resulting competition will eventually neutralize the value of the technique. If numerous investors focus on a specific technical trading rule, some of them will attempt to anticipate what will happen prior to the completed price pattern and either ruin the expected historical price pattern or eliminate profits for most users of the trading rule by causing the price to change faster than expected. As an example, suppose that it becomes known that technicians who invest on the basis of the amount of short selling have been enjoying very high rates of return. Based on this knowledge, other technicians will likely start using these data and thus affect the stock price pattern following changes in the amount of short selling. As a result, the trading rule that provided high rates of return previously may no longer work after the first few investors react.

Further, as we will see when we examine specific trading rules, *they all require a great deal of subjective judgment.* Two technical analysts looking at the same price pattern may arrive at widely different interpretations of what has happened and, therefore, will come to different investment decisions. This implies that the use of various techniques is neither completely mechanical nor obvious. Finally, as we will discuss in connection with several trading rules, *the standard values that signal investment decisions can change over time.* Therefore, technical analysts must adjust the trading rule or the specified values that trigger investment decisions over time to conform to the new environments.

ADVANTAGES OF TECHNICAL ANALYSIS

Despite these criticisms, technical analysts see benefits in their approach compared to fundamental analysis. Most technical analysts admit that a fundamental analyst with good information, good analytical ability, and a keen sense of information's impact on the market should achieve above-average returns. However, this statement requires qualification. According to technical analysts, the fundamental analysts can experience superior returns *only* if they obtain new information before other investors and process it correctly and quickly. Technical analysts do not believe that the vast majority of investors can consistently get new information before other investors and process it correctly and quickly.

Technical analysts claim that a major advantage of their method is that *it is not heavily dependent on financial accounting statements,* the major source of information about the past performance of a firm or industry. As you know from Chapters 17 and 18, the fundamental analyst evaluates such statements to help project future return and risk characteristics for industries and individual securities. The technician points out several major problems with accounting statements:

1. They do not contain a great deal of information needed by security analysts, such as details on sales and general expenses or sales and earnings by product line and customers.
2. Corporations may choose among several procedures for reporting expenses, assets, or liabilities, and these alternative procedures can produce vastly different values for expenses, income, return on assets, and return on equity. As a result, an investor can have trouble comparing the statements of two firms in the same industry, much less firms in different industries.
3. Many psychological factors and other nonquantitative variables do not appear in financial statements. Examples include employee training and loyalty, customer goodwill, and general investor attitude toward an industry. Investor attitudes could become important when investors become concerned about the risk from restrictions or taxes on products such as tobacco or alcohol or when firms do business in countries that practice repressive policies such as South Africa and China.

Therefore, because technicians are suspicious of financial statements, they consider it advantageous not to depend on them. As we will show, most of the data used by technicians, such as security prices, volume of trading, and other trading information, are derived from the stock market itself.

Also, a fundamental analyst must process new information correctly and *very quickly* to derive a new intrinsic value for the stock or bond before other investors can. Technicians, on the other hand, need only quickly recognize a movement to a new equilibrium value for whatever reason.

Finally, assume a fundamental analyst determines that a given security is under- or overvalued a long time before other investors. He or she still must determine when to make the purchase or sale. Ideally, the highest return would come from making the transaction just before the change in market value occurs. As an example, assume that based on your analysis in February, you expect a firm to report substantially higher earnings in June. Although you could buy the stock in February, you would be better off waiting until about May to buy the stock so your funds would not be tied up for an extra 3 months. Because most technicians do not invest until the move to the new equilibrium is underway, they contend that they are more likely to experience ideal timing compared to the fundamental analyst.

Some technicians buy stocks that have declined to a stable price pattern (referred to as a "bottom" or "base" pattern) despite continued bad news. Subsequently, they wait for the stock price to respond to anticipated positive information. These individuals resemble fundamental analysts.

TECHNICAL TRADING RULES AND INDICATORS

To help you understand the specific technical trading rules, Figure 19.2 shows a typical stock price cycle that could be an example for the overall stock market or for an individual stock. The graph shows a peak and trough along with a rising trend channel, a flat trend channel, a declining trend channel, and indications of when a technical analyst would ideally want to trade.

The graph begins with the end of a declining (bear) market that finishes in a *trough* followed by an upward trend that breaks through the *declining trend channel.* Confirmation that the trend has reversed would be a buy signal. The technical analyst would buy stocks in general or an individual stock that showed this pattern.

The analyst would then look for the development of a *rising trend channel.* As long as the stock price stayed in this rising channel, the technician would hold the stock(s) for the upward ride. Ideally, you want to sell at the peak of the cycle, but you cannot identify a peak until after the trend changes.

If the stock (or the market) begins trading in a flat pattern, it will necessarily break out of its rising trend channel. At this point, some technical analysts would sell, but most would hold to see if the stock will experience a period of consolidation and then break out of the *flat trend channel* on the upside and begin rising again. Alternatively, if the stock were to break out of the channel on the downside, the technician would take this as a sell signal and would expect a declining trend channel. The next buy signal would come after the trough when the price breaks out of the declining channel and establishes a rising trend. Subsequently we will consider the importance of volume in this analysis.

There are numerous technical trading rules and a large number of interpretations for each of them. Almost all technical analysts watch many alternative rules. This

FIGURE 19.2   **Typical Stock Market Cycle**

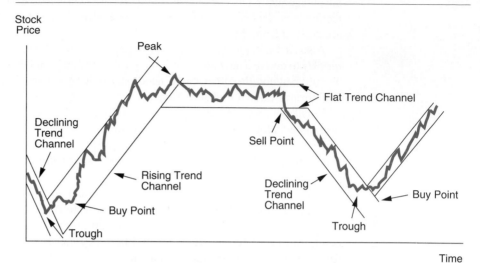

section discusses most of the well-known techniques but certainly not all of them. The presentation is divided into four sections based on the attitudes of technical analysts. The first group includes trading rules used by analysts who like to trade against the crowd using contrary-opinion signals. The second group of rules attempts to emulate very astute investors, that is, the smart money. The next section includes technical indicators that are very popular but not easily classified. The fourth section covers pure price and volume techniques, including the famous Dow Theory. The final subsections describe how these technical trading rules have been applied to foreign securities markets.

CONTRARY-OPINION RULES

Many technical analysts rely on technical trading rules developed from the premise that the majority of investors are wrong most of the time or at least at peaks and troughs. Therefore, these technicians try to determine when the majority of investors is either very bullish or very bearish and then trade in the opposite direction.[3]

THE ODD-LOT SHORT-SALES THEORY

As we know from Chapter 3, investors make short sales when they expect stock prices to decline. Such behavior is pessimistic or bearish. Compared to ordinary purchases of shares for cash, selling short is a fairly high-risk form of investing because it contradicts the long-run upward trend in stock prices and you can lose over 100 percent if the stock increases by over 100 percent.

Most small investors are optimists and would consider short selling too risky. Therefore, they do not engage in short selling except when they feel especially bearish.

---

[3]Prior editions of this book included the percentage of odd-lot purchases and sales as a contrary-opinion rule. It is no longer included because odd-lot volume has become a very small proportion of total trading volume. Thus, odd-lot trading is no longer considered a valid indication of small investor sentiment.

Technical analysts interpret heavy short selling by individuals as a signal that the market is close to a trough because small investors only get pessimistic after a long decline in prices, just when the market is about to turn around.

Technical analysts who translate this into a trading rule contend that a relatively high rate (3 percent or more) of odd-lot short sales as a percentage of total odd-lot sales indicates a very bearish attitude by small investors, which they consider a signal of a near-term trough in stock prices. These technicians would become bullish and begin buying stocks. Alternatively, when the ratio declines below 1 percent, technical analysts interpret small investors' behavior as very bullish and become bearish.

Recent erratic figures for this ratio suggest that it may be necessary to change the investment decision percentages. Specifically, the recent values have very seldom deviated from the 1 percent range so it is difficult to imagine that this series would give a buy signal using the prevailing decision values.

MUTUAL FUND CASH POSITIONS

Mutual funds hold some part of their portfolio in cash for one of several reasons. The most obvious reason is that they need cash to liquidate shares that fundholders sell back to the fund. Another reason is that the money from new purchases of the mutual fund may not have been invested. A third reason might be the portfolio manager's bearish outlook for the market, inspiring a buildup in the fund's defensive cash position.

Mutual funds' ratio of cash as a percentage of the total assets in their portfolios (the *cash ratio* or *liquid asset ratio*) are reported in the press including monthly figures in *Barron's*.[4] This percentage of cash has varied during the last decade from a low point of about 8 percent to a high point near 13 percent, although the range has increased during the last several years.

Contrary-opinion technicians consider the mutual funds to be a good proxy for the institutional investor group. They also feel that mutual funds are usually wrong at peaks and troughs. Thus, they expect mutual funds to have a high percentage of cash near the trough of a market cycle, being bearish exactly at the time that they should be fully invested to take advantage of the impending market rise. At the market peak, technicians expect mutual funds to be almost fully invested with a low percentage of cash. This would indicate a bullish outlook by the mutual funds when they should be selling stocks and realizing gains for some part of their portfolios. Therefore, technicians would watch for the mutual fund cash position to approach one of the extremes and act contrary to the mutual funds. Their trading rule would lead them to buy when the cash ratio approaches 13 percent and sell when the cash ratio approached 8 percent.

Figure 19.3 contains a time-series plot of the Dow Jones Industrial Average (DJIA) and the mutual fund cash ratio. It shows apparent bullish signals in 1970, in late 1974, in 1982, and in late 1990 near market troughs. Bearish signals appeared in 1971, 1972 to 1973, and 1976 prior to market peaks. In contrast, in early 1992 when the ratio was close to 8 percent, the market generally continued to rise.

A high mutual fund cash position can also be considered as a bullish indicator because of potential buying power. Whether the cash balances have built up because of stock sales completed as part of a selling program or because investors have been

---

[4]*Barron's* is a prime source for numerous technical indicators. For a readable discussion of relevant data and its use, see Martin E. Zweig, *Understanding Technical Forecasting* (New York: Dow Jones & Co., 1987).

FIGURE 19.3

FIGURE 19.3   **Time-Series Plot of Dow Jones Industrial Average and Mutual Fund Cash Ratio (Cash/Total Assets)**

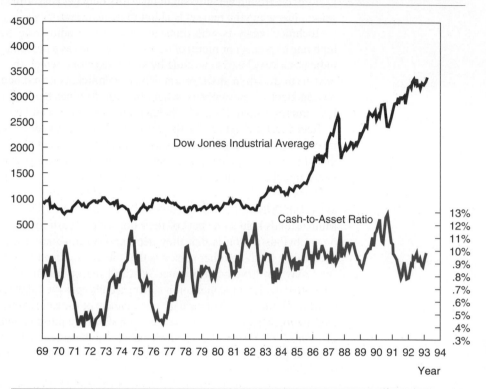

Source: *Where the Indicators Stand* (New York: Merrill Lynch, May 1993. Reprinted by permission of Merrill Lynch. All Rights Reserved.

buying the fund, technicians believe that these funds will eventually be invested and will cause stock prices to increase. Alternatively, a low cash ratio would mean that the institutions have bought heavily and are left with little potential buying power.

A couple of studies have examined this mutual fund cash ratio and its components as a predictor of market cycles. They concluded that the mutual fund liquid asset ratio was not as strong a predictor of market cycles as suggested by technical analysts.[5]

CREDIT BALANCES IN BROKERAGE ACCOUNTS

Credit balances result when investors sell stocks and leave the proceeds with their brokers, expecting to reinvest them shortly. The amounts are reported by the SEC and the NYSE in *Barron's*. Technical analysts view these credit balances as pools of potential purchasing power so they interpret a decline in these balances as bearish because it indicates lower purchasing power as the market approaches a peak. Alternatively, technicians view a buildup of credit balances as an increase in buying power and a bullish signal.

---

[5]Paul H. Massey, "The Mutual Fund Liquidity Ratio: A Trap for the Unwary," *Journal of Portfolio Management* 5, no. 2 (Winter 1979): 18–21; and R. David Ranson and William G. Shipman, "Institutional Buying Power and the Stock Market," *Financial Analysts Journal* 37, no. 5 (September-October 1981): 62–68.

Note that the data used to interpret the market environment is stated in terms of an increase or decline in the credit balance series rather than comparing these balances to some other series. This assumption of an absolute trend could make interpretation difficult as market levels change.

INVESTMENT ADVISORY OPINIONS

Many technicians feel that a large proportion of investment advisory services with a bearish attitude signals the approach of a market trough and the onset of a bull market. It is reasoned that most services tend to be trend followers, so the number of bears is usually greatest when market bottoms are approaching. They develop this trading rule from the ratio of the number of advisory services that are bearish as a percentage of the number of services expressing an opinion.[6] A "bearish sentiment index" of 60 percent indicates a pervasive bearish attitude by advisory services, and contrarians would consider this a bullish indicator. In contrast, a decline of this bearish sentiment index to below 20 percent indicates a pervasive bullish attitude by advisory services, which technicians would interpret as a bearish sign. Figure 19.4 shows a time-series plot of the DJIA and both the bearish sentiment index and the bullish sentiment index.

OTC VERSUS NYSE VOLUME

Prior to the 1970s, the accepted measure of speculative trading activity was the ratio of AMEX volume to NYSE volume. This ratio is no longer considered useful because the relationship between the exchanges has changed dramatically over time. The ratio of AMEX to NYSE volume has gone from about 50 percent in the 1950s and 1960s to about 10 percent or less currently. Instead, technicians currently use the ratio of OTC volume on the NASDAQ system to NYSE volume as a measure of speculative trading. They consider speculative activity high when this ratio gets to 90 percent or more. Speculative trading typically peaks at market peaks. Technicians consider the market to be oversold, which means that investors are too bearish, when this ratio drops below 70 percent. Figure 19.5 contains a time-series plot of the NASDAQ Composite Average and the OTC/NYSE volume ratio.

Notably, the current decision ratios of 90 percent for a peak and 70 percent for an oversold position have changed over the past four years—they were 80 percent and 60 percent in 1990. The reason is that individual investors have started accounting for a higher proportion of trading, and individual investors are more likely to trade the small firms on the OTC market that lack the size and liquidity required by institutions. Also there is a strong tendency for an increase in NASDAQ volume because more firms are being added to this market than to the NYSE. The number of firms listed on the NYSE has been fairly constant over the past 15 years, whereas the number on NASDAQ has increased by about 50 percent (i.e., the firms on NASDAQ have gone from about 3,000 in 1981 to 4,500 in 1993).

THE CHICAGO BOARD OPTION EXCHANGE (CBOE) PUT/CALL RATIO

The CBOE put/call ratio is a relatively new tool of contrary-opinion technicans. They use put options, which give the holder the right to sell stock at a specified price for a

[6]This ratio is compiled by Investors Intelligence, Larchmont, N.Y. 10538.

FIGURE 19.4   **Time-Series Plot of Dow Jones Industrial Average and Bullish and Bearish Sentiment Indexes**

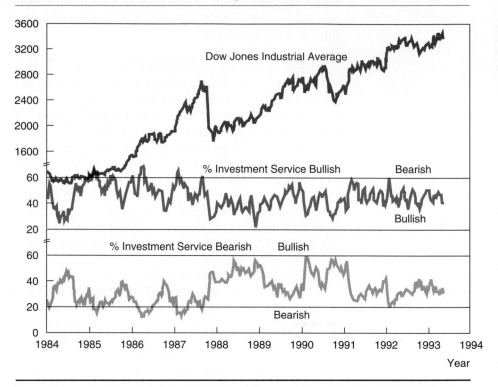

Sources: *Investors' Intelligence,* Larchmont, N.Y. 10538; and *Where the Indicators Stand* (New York: Merrill Lynch, May 1993). Reprinted by permission of Merrill Lynch. All Rights Reserved.

given time period as signals of a bearish attitude. The technicians reason that a higher put/call ratio indicates a more pervasive bearish attitude, which they consider a bullish indicator.

As shown in Figure 19.6 (on page 726), this ratio was historically in the range of 0.35 to 0.80 but is currently in the range of .60 to 1.00. It typically has been substantially less than 1 because investors tend to be bullish and avoid selling short or buying puts. The current decision rule states that a put/call ratio of .90, which means that 90 puts are traded for every 100 calls, is considered bullish. In contrast, a relatively low put/call ratio of .70 or less is considered a bearish sign.

FUTURES TRADERS BULLISH ON STOCK INDEX FUTURES

Another relatively new measure used by contrary-opinion technicians is the percentage of speculators in stock index futures who are bullish. Specifically, an advisory service (Market Vane) surveys other firms that provide advisory services for the futures market along with individual traders involved in the futures market to determine whether these futures traders are bearish or bullish regarding stocks. A plot of the series in Figure 19.7 (on page 727) indicates that these technicians would consider it a bearish sign

FIGURE 19.5   **Time-Series Plot of NASDAQ Composite Average and the Ratio of OTC Volume to NYSE Volume**

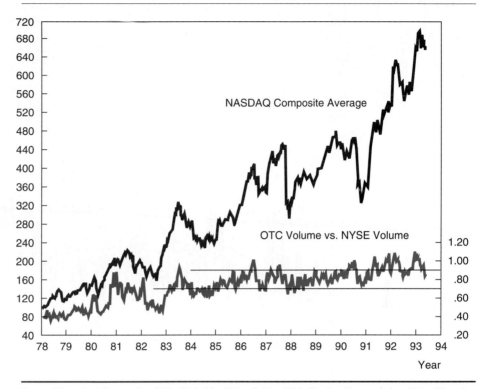

Source: *Where the Indicators Stand* (New York: Merrill Lynch, May 1993). Reprinted by permission of Merrill Lynch. All Rights Reserved.

when over 70 percent of the speculators are bullish. In contrast, if the portion of bullish speculators declines to 30 percent or lower, it is a bullish sign.

As you can see, technicians who seek to be contrary to the market have several series that provide measures of how the majority of investors are investing. They then take the opposite action. They would generally follow several of these series to provide a consensus regarding investors' attitudes.

FOLLOW THE
SMART MONEY

Some technical analysts employ an alternative set of indicators that they expect to indicate the behavior of smart, sophisticated investors. After studying the market, these technicians have created indicators that tell what smart investors are doing and create rules to follow them. In this section, we discuss some of the more popular indicators.

THE CONFIDENCE INDEX
Published by *Barron's,* the Confidence Index is the ratio of *Barron's* average yield on 10 top-grade corporate bonds to the yield on the Dow Jones average of 40 bonds. This index measures the difference in yield spread between high-grade bonds and a large

FIGURE 19.6   **Time-Series Plot of Dow Jones Industrial Average and CBOE Put/Call Ratio**

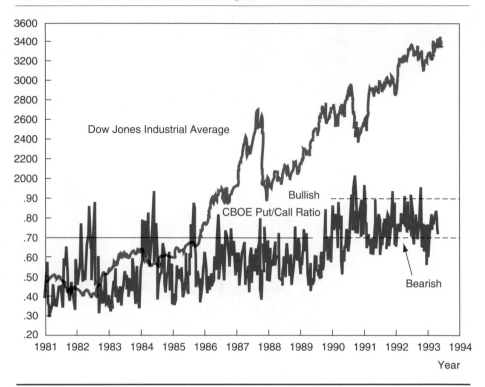

Source: *Where the Indicators Stand* (New York: Merrill Lynch, May 1993). Reprinted by permission of Merrill Lynch. All Rights Reserved.

cross section of bonds.[7] Because the yields on high-grade bonds should always be lower than those on a large cross section of bonds, this ratio should never exceed 100. It approaches 100 as the spread between the two sets of bonds gets smaller.

Technicians feel the ratio is a bullish indicator because during periods of high confidence, investors are willing to invest more in lower-quality bonds for the added yield. This increased demand for lower-quality bonds should cause a decrease in the average yield for the large cross section of bonds relative to the yield on high-grade bonds. Therefore, this ratio of yields, which is the Confidence Index, will increase. In contrast, when investors are pessimistic about the economic and market outlook, there is a flight to quality and investors will avoid investing in low-quality bonds and increase their investments in high-grade bonds. This shift in investment preference increases the yield differential (i.e., the yield spread) between the high-grade bonds and the average bonds, which causes the Confidence Index to decline.

A problem complicates this interpretation of bond investor behavior: it is almost solely demand-oriented. Specifically, it assumes that changes in the yield spread are

---

[7]Historical data for this series is contained in *The Dow Jones Investor's Handbook* (Princeton, N.J.: Dow Jones Books, annual). Current figures appear in *Barron's.*

FIGURE 19.7   **Time-Series Plot of Dow Jones Industrial Average and Percentage of Futures Traders Bullish on Stock Index Futures**

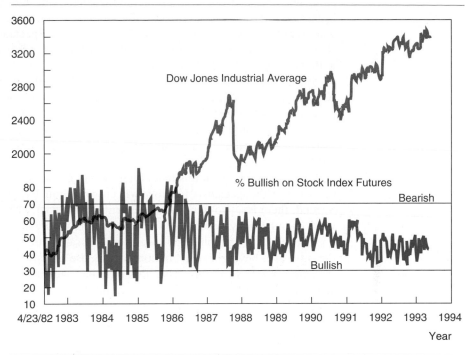

Source: *Market Vane* and *Where the Indicators Stand* (New York: Merrill Lynch, May 1993). Reprinted by permission of Merrill Lynch. All Rights Reserved.

caused almost exclusively by changes in investor demand for different quality bonds. In fact, the yield differences have frequently changed because the supply of bonds in one of the groups increased. As an example, a large issue of high-grade AT&T bonds could cause a temporary increase in yields on all high-grade bonds, which would reduce the yield spread and cause an increase in the Confidence Index without any change in investors' attitudes. Such a change in the supply of bonds can cause the series to generate a false signal of a change in confidence.

Advocates of the index believe that it can be used as an indicator of future stock price movements because it reflects investor attitudes toward financial assets. One may ask, however, why investors in bonds would change their attitude before equity investors. Several studies have found that this index has not been very useful for predicting stock price movements.

T-BILL–EURODOLLAR YIELD SPREAD
As an alternative measure of investor attitude or confidence on a global basis some technicians have suggested using the spread between T-bill yields and Eurodollar rates. It is reasoned that at times of international crisis this spread widens as money flows to safe haven U.S. T-bills. The stock market has tended to reach a trough shortly thereafter.

SHORT SALES BY SPECIALISTS

The NYSE and the SEC report data for total short sales on the NYSE and the AMEX along with those for the specialist on the exchange. This information appears weekly in *Barron's*. It should be no surprise after our discussion in Chapter 3 that technicians who want to follow smart money watch the specialist. Specialists regularly engage in short selling as a part of their market-making function, but they can exercise discretion in this area when they feel strongly about market changes.

The normal ratio of specialists' short sales to the total amount of short sales on the NYSE was about 45 percent prior to 1981.[8] Subsequently, the norm has become approximately 40 percent. Technicians view a decline in this ratio below 30 percent as a bullish sign because it means that specialists are attempting to minimize their participation in short sales. In contrast, an increase in the proportion above 50 percent is a bearish sign.

Note two points about this ratio. First, do not expect it to be a long-run indicator; the nature of the specialists' portfolio will probably limit it to the short-run movements. Second, there is a two-week lag in reporting these data. For example, the data for a week ending Friday, April 7, would be contained in *Barron's* on Monday, April 24.

An analysis of a graph of the specialist short sales ratio indicated some support for the ratio as a buying signal.[9] In contrast, its use as part of a trading rule provided insignificant excess returns. Also, this ratio has become extremely erratic in recent years, possibly because specialists are using stock index futures and/or options to hedge positions.

DEBIT BALANCES IN BROKERAGE ACCOUNTS (MARGIN DEBT)

Debit balances in brokerage accounts represent borrowing by knowledgeable investors from their brokers. Such borrowing is called margin debt. These balances are considered indicators of the attitude of a sophisticated group of investors who engage in margin transactions. Therefore, an increase in debit balances would indicate to technicians an increase in purchasing by this astute group and would be a bullish sign. In contrast, a decline in debit balances would indicate an increase in the supply of stocks as these sophisticated investors liquidate their positions. Alternatively, a decline could indicate less capital available for investing. In either case, this would be a bearish indicator.

Monthly data on margin debt is reported in *Barron's*. A potential problem with this series is that it does not include borrowing by investors from other sources such as banks. Also, it is an absolute value which may be difficult to interpret over time.

OTHER MARKET ENVIRONMENT INDICATORS   In this subsection, we discuss several indicators that are used to make investment decisions related to the aggregate market. These indicators are not considered either contrary-opinion indicators or useful tools to follow the smart money.

---

[8]Notably, during the 1960s and early 1970s the norm for this short sale ratio was about 55 percent. Therefore, this is an example of another technique for which the decision ratio has changed over time.

[9]Frank K. Reilly and David Whitford, "A Test of the Specialists' Short Sale Ratio," *Journal of Portfolio Management* 8, no. 2 (Winter 1982): 12–18.

BREADTH OF MARKET

Breadth of market measures the number of issues that have increased each day and the number of issues that have declined. It helps explain the cause of a change of direction in a composite market series such as the DJIA or the S&P 400 Index. As discussed in Chapter 4, the major stock-market series are either confined to large, well-known stocks or heavily influenced by the stocks of large firms because most indexes are value-weighted. As a result, it is possible that a stock-market series will go up, but the majority of the individual issues will not increase. This divergence between an index and its components causes concern because it means that most stocks are not participating in the rising market. Such a situation can be detected by examining the advance–decline figures for all stocks on the exchange along with the overall market index.

A useful way to specify the advance–decline series for analysis is to create a cumulative series of net advances or net declines. Each day major newspapers publish figures on the number of issues on the NYSE that advanced, declined, or were unchanged. The figures for a 5-day sample, as would be reported in *Barron's*, are shown in Table 19.1. These figures, along with changes in the DJIA at the bottom of the table, indicate a strong market advance to a technician because the DJIA was increasing and the net advance figure was strong, indicating that the market increase was broadly based and extended to most individual stocks. Even the results on Day 3, when the market declined 8 points, were somewhat encouraging. Although the market was down, it was a very small net decline and the individual stocks were split just about 50–50, which points toward a fairly even environment.

An alternative specification of the series, a *diffusion index,* shows the daily total of stocks advancing plus one-half the number unchanged, divided by the total number of issues traded. To smooth the series, Merrill Lynch computes a 5-week moving average of these daily figures as shown in Figure 19.8.

Unusual or extreme readings are used as an indicator of changes in the major trend of the market. For example, assume the major trend in the market has been up. Still, the market has experienced intermediate corrections that were typically accompanied by declines in the advance–decline diffusion index to values of 42 to 45. A subsequent market correction accompanied by a diffusion index value below 42 would suggest that the market's major trend may be turning down. In contrast, assume the major trend in the market had been down and intermediate recoveries typically had been accom-

TABLE 19.1

Daily Advances and Declines on the New York Stock Exchange

Day	1	2	3	4	5
Issues traded	1,608	1,641	1,659	1,651	1,612
Advances	1,010	950	608	961	1,025
Declines	309	350	649	333	294
Unchanged	289	341	402	357	293
Net advances (advances minus declines)	+701	+600	−41	+628	+731
Cumulative net advances	+701	+1,301	+1,260	+1,888	+2,619
Changes in DJIA	+20.47	+13.99	−8.18	+9.16	+15.56

Source: New York Stock Exchange and *Barron's.*

FIGURE 19.8

Time-Series Plot of Dow Jones Industrial and Advance–Decline Diffusion Index

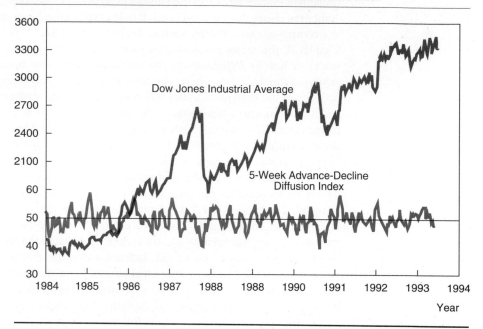

Source: *Where the Indicators Stand* (New York: Merrill Lynch, May 1993). Reprinted by permission of Merrill Lynch. All Rights Reserved.

panied by diffusion index values of 50 to 54. A market recovery with a diffusion index of about 59 would suggest to a technician that the major trend had turned up.

Crossings from below to above 50 indicate the market's intermediate-term trend if the moving average series has turned from down to up. This advance–decline series is also used to measure intermediate trends and to signal overbought or oversold levels if it reaches very low or very high levels.

The usefulness of the advance–decline series is supposedly greatest at market peaks and troughs. At such times the composite value-weighted market series might be moving either up or down, but the advance or decline in the overall market would *not* be broadly based, and the majority of individual stocks might be moving in the opposite direction. As an example, near a peak, the DJIA would be increasing, but the net advance–decline ratio for individual days would become negative, and the cumulative advance–decline series would begin to level off and decline. The *divergence* between the trend for the market index and the cumulative advance–decline series would signal a market peak.

In contrast, as the market approached a trough, the composite market index would be declining, but the daily advance–decline ratio would become positive, and the cumulative advance–decline index would level off and begin to turn up before the aggregate market index.[10] In summary, a technician would look for the advance–decline

---

[10]Ideally the performance of the series should work at both peaks and troughs. In fact, it appears to work best at peaks. Apparently at troughs, the secondary stocks, which make up most of the issues, may remain weak until the low point and keep the advance–decline figures negative.

series to indicate a change in trend before the composite stock-market series. It is considered to be more useful at peaks than at troughs.[11]

SHORT INTEREST

The short interest is the cumulative number of shares that have been sold short by investors and not covered. This means the investor has not purchased the shares sold short and returned them to the investor from whom they were borrowed. Technicians compute a short-interest ratio as the outstanding short interest divided by the average daily volume of trading on the exchange. As an example, if the outstanding short interest on the NYSE was 500 million shares and the average daily volume of trading on the exchange was 170 million shares, the short-interest ratio would be 2.94 (500/170). This means the outstanding short interest equals about 3 days' trading volume.

Technicians probably interpret this ratio contrary to your initial intuition. Because short sales reflect investors expectations that stock prices will decline, one would typically expect an increase in the short-interest ratio to be bearish. On the contrary, technicians consider a high short-interest ratio bullish because it indicates *potential demand* for the stock by those who previously sold short and have not covered the sale.

The ratio fluctuated prior to 1984 between 1.00 and 1.75. Since about 1985 the ratio has increased, seldom falling as low as 1.50. In fact, its typical range in recent years has been between 2.0 to 3.0. The short-interest position is calculated by the stock exchanges and the NASD as of the 20th of each month and is reported about 2 days later in *The Wall Street Journal*.

This is another example of a change in the decision value over time. Recent experience regarding the range of values for this ratio would make a technician bullish when the short-interest ratio approached 3.0 and bearish if it declined toward 2.0.

A number of studies have examined the short-interest series as a predictor of stock price movements with mixed results. For every study that supports the technique, another indicates that it should be rejected.[12] Technical analysts have pointed out that this ratio, and any ratio that involves short selling, has been affected by the introduction of other techniques for short selling such as options and futures.

STOCKS ABOVE THEIR 200-DAY MOVING AVERAGE

Technicians often compute moving averages of a series to determine its general trend. To examine individual stocks, the 200-day moving-average of prices has been fairly popular. From these moving average series for numerous stocks, Media General Financial Services calculates how many stocks are currently trading above their moving-average series as an indicator of general investor sentiment. As shown in Figure 19.9, the market is considered to be *overbought,* which means it is overpriced, when more than 80 percent of the stocks are trading above their 200-day moving average. Technical analysts feel that an overbought market signals a consolidation or a negative correction. In contrast, if less than 20 percent of the stocks are selling above their 200-day moving

---

[11]This series has also been used to evaluate non-U.S. indexes. See Linda Sandler, "Advance–Decline Line, a Popular Indicator, Warns of Correction in Tokyo Stock Market," *The Wall Street Journal,* August 26, 1988, C1.

[12]See Joseph Vu and Paul Caster, "Why All the Interest in Short Interest?" *Financial Analysts Journal* 43, no. 4 (July-August 1987): 77–79.

FIGURE 19.9   **Percentage of NYSE Common Stock above Their 200-Day Moving Average**

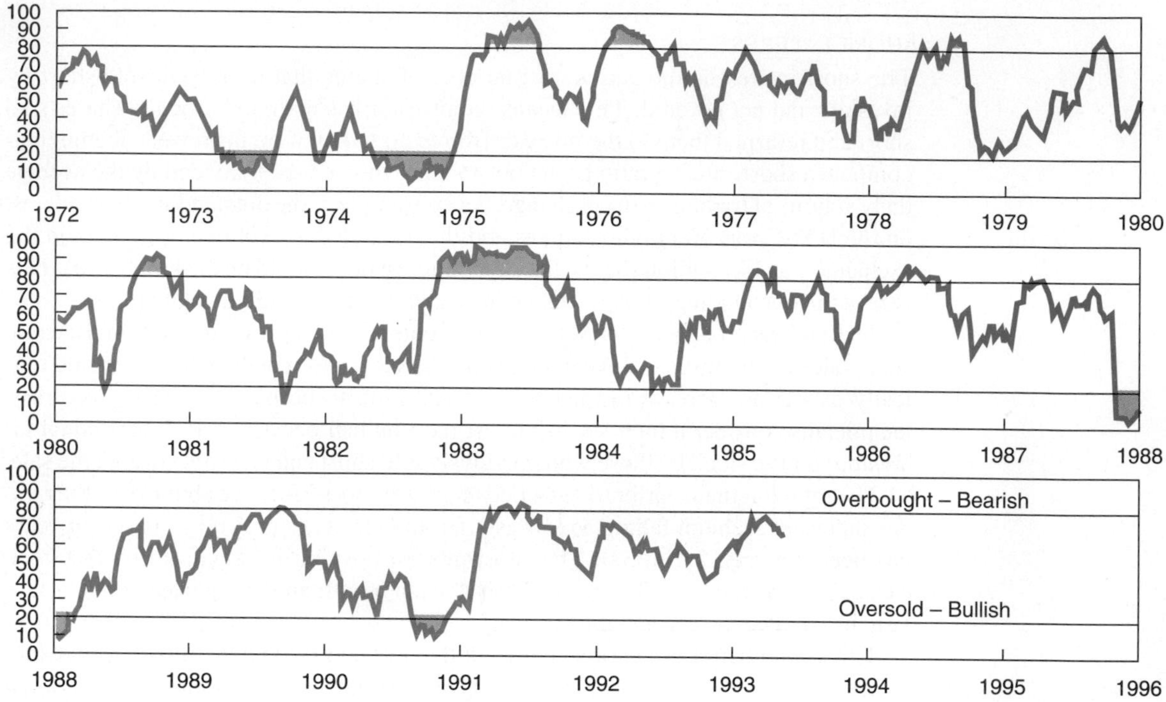

Source: *Where the Indicators Stand* (New York: Merrill Lynch, May 1993). Reprinted by permission of Merrill Lynch. All Rights Reserved.

average, the market is considered as *oversold,* which means that it is underpriced, and investors should be buying stocks in anticipation of positive corrections.

BLOCK UPTICK–DOWNTICK RATIO

As we discussed in Chapter 3, trading in the equity market (especially the NYSE) has become dominated by institutional investors who tend to trade in large blocks. As noted, about 50 percent of NYSE volume comes from block trading by institutions. The exchange can determine whether the price change that accompanied a particular block trade was higher or lower than the price of the prior transaction. If the block trade price is above the prior transaction, it is referred to as an *uptick;* if the block trade price is below the prior transaction price, it is referred to as a *downtick*.

Most observers assume that the price change indicates whether the block trade was initiated by a buyer, in which case you would expect an uptick, or a seller, in which case you would expect a downtick. This line of reasoning led to the development of the *uptick–downtick* ratio, a measure of the number of buyers (uptick transactions) versus the number of sellers (downtick transactions), to indicate institutional investor sentiment. As shown in Figure 19.10, this ratio has generally fluctuated in the range of .70, which reflects a bearish sentiment, to about 1.20, which indicates a bullish sentiment.

FIGURE 19.10   **Time-Series Plot of Dow Jones Industrial Average and NYSE Block Uptick–Downtick Ratio**

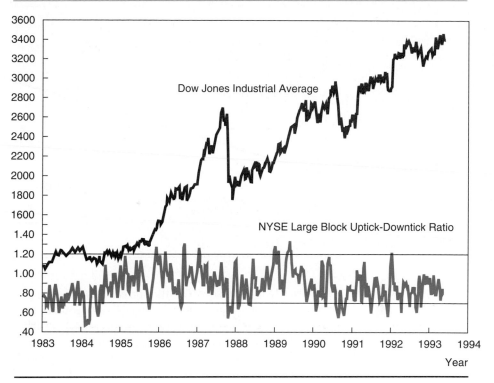

Source: *Where the Indicators Stand* (New York: Merrill Lynch, May 1993). Reprinted by permission of Merrill Lynch. All Rights Reserved.

STOCK PRICE AND
VOLUME
TECHNIQUES

In the introduction to this chapter, we examined a hypothetical stock price chart that demonstrated the market cycle and its peaks and troughs. Also, we considered rising and declining trend channels and breakouts from channels that signal new price trends or reversals of the price trends. Although these price patterns are important, most technical trading rules for the overall market and individual stocks consider *both* stock price movements and corresponding volume movements. Because technicians believe that prices move in trends that persist, they seek to predict future price trends from an astute analysis of past price trends along with changes in the volume of trading.

THE DOW THEORY

Any discussion of technical analysis using price and volume data should begin with a consideration of the Dow Theory because it was some of the earliest work on this topic and it remains the basis for many indicators. In this section we show how Charles Dow combined price and volume information to analyze both individual stocks and the overall stock market.

FIGURE 19.11   **Sample Bullish Price Pattern**

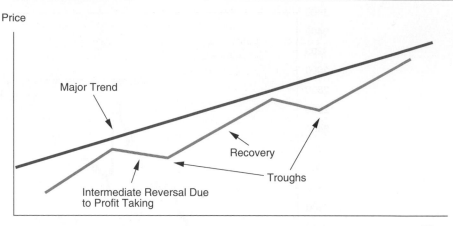

Charles Dow published *The Wall Street Journal* during the late 1800s.[13] Dow described stock prices as moving in trends analogous to the movement of water. He postulated three types of price movements over time: (1) major trends that are like tides in the ocean, (2) intermediate trends that resemble waves, and (3) short-run movements that are like ripples. Followers of the Dow Theory hope to detect the direction of the major price trend (tide), recognizing that intermediate movements (waves) will move in the opposite direction. They recognize that a major market advance does not go straight up, but rather shows deviations including small price declines as some investors decide to take profits.

Figure 19.11 shows the typical bullish pattern. The technician would look for every recovery to reach a new peak above the prior peak, and this price rise should be accompanied by heavy trading volume. Alternatively, each reversal that follows an increase to a new peak should have a trough above the prior trough, with a relatively light volume of trading during the reversals, indicating that only a limited number of investors are interested in profit taking at these levels. When this pattern of price and volume movements changes, the major trend may be entering a period of consolidation or a major reversal. When using the Dow Theory to analyze the overall stock market, technicians also look for confirmation of peaks and troughs in the industrial stock price series by subsequent peaks and troughs in the transportation series. Such an "echo" indicates that the change in direction is occurring across the total market.

IMPORTANCE OF VOLUME

As noted in the description of the Dow Theory, technicians watch volume changes along with price movements as an indicator of changes in supply and demand for

[13]A study that discusses the theory and provides support for it is David A. Glickstein and Rolf E. Wubbels, "Dow Theory Is Alive and Well," *Journal of Portfolio Management* 9 no. 3 (Spring 1983): 28–32.

individual stocks or stocks in general. A price movement in one direction means that the *net* effect on price is in that direction, but the price change alone does not tell us how widespread the excess demand or supply is at that time. A price increase of one-half point on volume of 1,000 shares demonstrates excess demand but little overall interest. In contrast, a one-point increase on volume of 30,000 shares shows a lot of interest and strong demand. Therefore, the technician looks for a price increase on heavy volume relative to the stock's normal trading volume as an indication of bullish activity. Following the same line of reasoning, a price decline with heavy volume is very bearish, because it reflects a strong and widespread desire to sell the stock. A generally bullish pattern would be when price increases are accompanied by heavy volume and small price reversals occur with light trading volume, indicating that there is only limited interest in selling and taking profits.

Technicians also use a ratio of upside–downside volume as an indicator of short-term momentum for the aggregate stock market. Each day the stock exchanges announce the volume of trading that occurred in stocks that experienced an increase divided by the volume of trading in stocks that declined. These data are reported daily in *The Wall Street Journal* and weekly in *Barron's*. Technicians consider this ratio to be an indicator of investor sentiment and use it to pinpoint excesses. Specifically, the ratio typically ranges between a value of 0.50 and 2.00. Technicians feel that a value of 1.50 or more indicates an overbought position and would be a bearish signal. Alternatively, a value of 0.70 and lower would reflect an oversold position and would inspire a bullish attitude.

SUPPORT AND RESISTANCE LEVELS

A *support level* is the price range at which the technician would expect a substantial increase in the demand for a stock. Generally, a support level will develop after the price has increased and the stock has begun to experience a reversal because of profit taking. Technicians reason that, at some price, other investors will buy who did not buy during the first price increase and have been waiting for a small reversal to get into the stock. When the price reaches a support point at which a number of these investors want to buy, demand surges and price and volume begin to increase again.

A *resistance level* is the price range at which the technician would expect an increase in the supply of stock and any price increase to reverse abruptly. A resistance level tends to develop after a stock has experienced a steady decline from a higher price level. In this case, technicians reason that the decline in price leads some investors who acquired the stock at a higher price to look for an opportunity to sell it near their breakeven points. Therefore, the supply of stock owned by these investors is waiting to be sold. Professionals refer to this stock as *overhanging* the market. When the price rebounds to the target price set by these investors, there is a resistance to any further increase because this overhanging supply of stock comes to the market and dramatically reverses the price increase.

MOVING-AVERAGE LINE

Earlier we discussed how technicians use a moving average of past stock prices as an indicator of the long-run trend and how they examine current prices relative to this trend for signals of a change. We also noted that a 200-day moving average is a relatively popular measure for individual stocks and the aggregate market. In this discussion, we want to revisit this moving-average price line and add volume to the analysis.

If the overall price trend of a stock or the market has been down, the moving-average price line would generally lie above current prices. If prices reverse and break through the moving-average line from below accompanied by heavy trading volume, most technicians would consider this a very positive change and expect a reversal of the declining trend. In contrast, if the price of a stock had been rising, the moving-average line would also be rising but would be below current prices. If current prices broke through the moving-average line from above accompanied by heavy trading volume, this would be considered a bearish pattern that would signal a reversal of the long-run rising trend.[14]

RELATIVE STRENGTH

Technicians believe that once a trend begins, it will continue until some major event causes a change in direction. This is also true, they believe, of *relative* performance. If an individual stock or an industry group is outperforming the market, technicians believe it will continue to do so.

Therefore, technicians compute weekly or monthly *relative-strength ratios* for individual stocks and industry groups as the ratio of the price of a stock or an industry index to the value for some stock-market series such as the DJIA or the S&P 400. If this ratio increases over time, it shows that the stock or industry is outperforming the market, and a technician would expect this superior performance to continue. Relative-strength ratios work during declining as well as rising markets. In a declining market, if the price of the stock does not decline as much as the market does, the stock's relative-strength ratio will continue to rise. Technicians believe that if this ratio is stable or increases during a bear market, the stock should do very well during the subsequent bull market.[15]

Merrill Lynch publishes relative-strength charts for stocks and industry groups. Figure 19.12 describes how to read the charts, and Figure 19.13 includes a graph for an industry with strong positive relative strength and one with poor relative strength.

BAR CHARTING

Technicians use charts that show daily, weekly, or monthly time series of stock prices. For a given interval, the technical analyst plots the high and low prices and connects the two points vertically to form a bar. Typically, he or she will also draw a small horizontal line across this vertical bar to indicate the closing price. Finally, almost all bar charts include the volume of trading at the bottom of the chart so that the technical analyst can relate the price and volume movements. A typical bar chart in Figure 19.14 shows data for the DJIA from *The Wall Street Journal* along with volume figures for the NYSE.

---

[14]This technique is tested in J. C. Van Horne and G. C. Parker, "The Random Walk Theory: An Empirical Test," *Financial Analysts Journal* 23, no. 6 (November-December 1967): 57–64.

[15]A study that supports the technique is James Bohan, "Relative Strength: Further Positive Evidence," *Journal of Portfolio Management* 7, no. 1 (Fall 1981): 39–46. A study that rejects the technique is Robert D. Arnott, "Relative Strength Revisited," *Journal of Portfolio Management* 6, no. 3 (Spring 1979): 19–23. Finally, a study that combines it with modern portfolio theory is John S. Brush and Keith Boles, "The Predictive Power in Relative Strength and CAPM," *Journal of Portfolio Management* 9, no. 4 (Summer 1983): 20–23.

FIGURE 19.12   **How to Read Industry Group Charts**

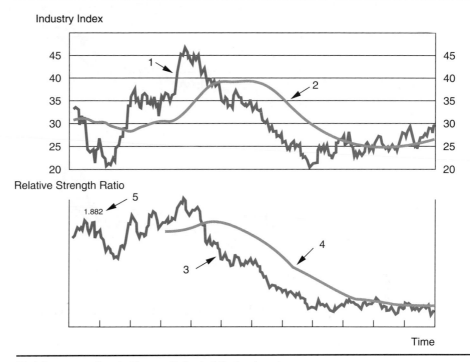

The industry group charts in this report display the following elements:

1. A line chart of the weekly close of the Standard & Poor's Industry Group Index for the last 9½ years, with the index range indicated to the left.
2. A line of the 75-week moving average of the Standard & Poor's Industry Group Index.
3. A relative-strength line of the Standard & Poor's Industry Group Index compared with the New York Stock Exchange Composite Index.
4. A 75-week moving average of relative strength.
5. A volatility reading that measures the maximum amount by which the index has outperformed (or underperformed) the NYSE Composite Index during the time period displayed.

Source: *Technical Analysis of Industry Groups* (New York: Merrill Lynch, monthly). Reprinted by permission of Merrill Lynch. All Rights Reserved.

MULTIPLE INDICATOR CHARTS

The technical analyst might also include a line to show a 200-day moving average for the series, possibly identifying expected resistance and support levels based on past price and volume patterns. Finally, a bar chart for an individual stock might add a relative-strength line. Technicians include as many price and volume series as is reasonable on one chart and, based on the performance of several technical indicators, try to arrive at a consensus about the future movement for the stock.

POINT-AND-FIGURE CHARTS

Another graph that is popular with technicians is the point-and-figure chart.[16] Unlike the bar chart, which typically includes all ending prices and volumes to show a trend,

---

[16]Daniel Seligman, "The Mystique of Point-and-Figure," *Fortune* (March 1962): 113–115.

FIGURE 19.13   **Example of Relative-Strength Charts for Two Industries**

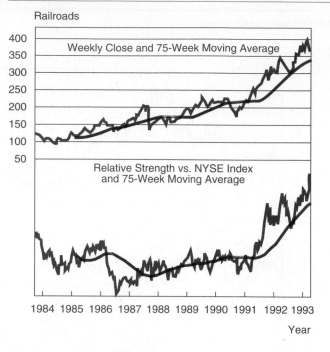

Railroads

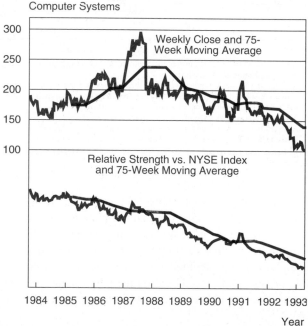

Computer Systems

Top graphs: Railroads: Burlington Northern; Consolidated Rail; CSX; Norfolk Southern; Santa Fe Southern Pacific; Union Pacific. *Bottom graphs:* Computer Systems: Amdahl; Apple Computer; Compaq; Control Data; Cray Research; Data General; Datapoint; Digital Equipment; Intergraph; International Business Machines; Prime Computers; Tandem Computers; Unisys; Wang Laboratories (B).

Source: *Technical Analysis of Industry Groups* (New York: Merrill Lynch, May 1993). Reprinted by permission of Merrill Lynch. All Rights Reserved.

FIGURE 19.14   **A Typical Bar Chart**

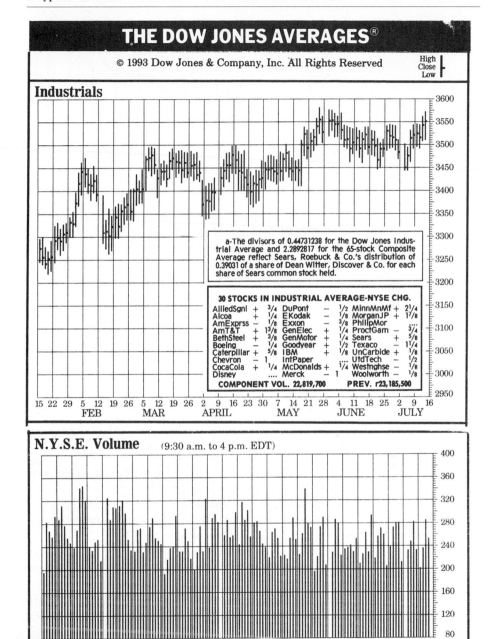

Source: "The Dow Jones Averages," *The Wall Street Journal,* July 16, 1993. Reprinted by permission of *The Wall Street Journal,* © Dow Jones & Company, Inc. 1993. All Rights Reserved.

FIGURE 19.15

Sample Point-and-Figure Chart

50											
48											
46			X								
44			X								
42	X	X	X								
40	X	X	X								
38		X	X								
36		X	X								
34		X	X								
32											
30											

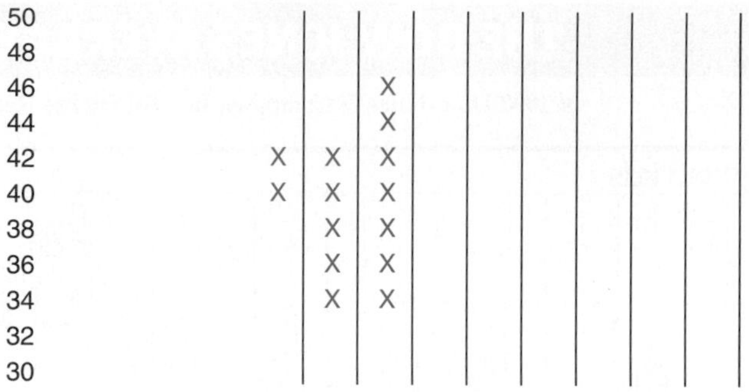

the point-and-figure chart includes only significant price changes, regardless of their timing. The technician determines what price interval to record as significant (one point, two points, etc.) and when to note price reversals.

To demonstrate how a technical analyst would use such a chart, assume that you want to chart a volatile stock that is currently selling for $40 a share. Because of its volatility, you believe that anything less than a two-point price change is not significant. Also, you consider anything less than a four-point reversal, meaning a movement in the opposite direction, quite minor. Therefore, you would set up a chart similar to the one in Figure 19.15, which starts at 40 and progresses in two-point increments. If the stock moves to 42, you would place an X in the box above 40 and do nothing else until the stock rose to 44 or dropped to 38 (a four-point reversal from its high of 42). If it dropped to 38, you would move a column to the right, which indicates a reversal in direction, and begin again at 38 (fill in boxes at 42 and 40). If the stock price dropped to 34, you would enter an X at 36 and another at 34. If the stock then rose to 38 (another four-point reversal), you would move to the next column and begin at 38 going up (fill in 34 and 36). If the stock then went to 46, you would fill in more Xs as shown and wait for further increases or a reversal.

Depending on how fast the prices rise and fall, this process might take anywhere from 2 to 6 months. Given these figures, the technical analyst would attempt to determine trends just as with the bar chart.

As always, you look for breakouts to either higher or lower price levels.[17] A long horizontal movement with many reversals but no major trends up or down would be considered *a period of consolidation.* The technician would speculate that the stock is moving from buyers to sellers and back again with no strong support from either group that would indicate a consensus about its direction. Once the stock breaks out and moves up or down after a period of consolidation, analysts anticipate a major move because previous trading set the stage for it.

Point-and-figure charts differ from bar charts by providing a compact record of movements, because they only consider significant price change for the stock being

---

[17]A study that questions the usefulness of various price patterns is Robert A. Levy, "The Predictive Significance of Five Point Chart Patterns," *Journal of Business* 44, no. 3 (July 1971): 316–323.

analyzed. Therefore, some technicians prefer point-and-figure charts because they are easier to work with and give more vivid pictures of price movements.

This section discussed technical indicators that are widely used and alluded to in the financial press. As noted on several occasions, technical analysts do not generally concentrate on only a few indicators or even general categories, but seek to derive an overall feel for the market or a stock based on a *consensus of numerous technical indicators.*

TECHNICAL ANALYSIS OF FOREIGN MARKETS

Our discussion thus far has concentrated on U.S. markets, but as numerous analysts and firms have discovered, these techniques apply to foreign markets as well. Merrill Lynch, for instance, prepares separate technical analyses publications for individual countries such as Japan, Germany, and the United Kingdom as well as a summary of all world markets. The examples that follow show that many techniques are limited to price and volume data rather than using the more detailed market information described for the U.S. market. This emphasis on price and volume data is necessary because the more detailed information that is available on the U.S. market through the SEC, the stock exchanges, the NASDAQ system, and various investment services is not always available in other countries.

Also, individuals who concentrate on the analysis of foreign markets point out that these markets show a greater tendency toward *group rotation* or major shifts in interest among segments of the market. For example, investors observe shifts among industry groups, such as autos, construction, and electronics, or among major sectors of the market, such as secondary stocks versus large blue-chip stocks. This means that industries or sectors become hot and can cool down very quickly.

FOREIGN STOCK MARKET SERIES

Figure 19.16 contains the time-series plot and moving-average series for the Financial Times Stock Exchange 100 Index (FTSE 100). This chart shows the strong performance by the U.K. market following the significant devaluation of the pound after the U.K. government allowed it to float in September 1992.

In a separate written analysis, the market analysts at Merrill Lynch estimate support and resistance levels for the London Stock Exchange series and comment on the longer-term outlook for the United Kingdom stock market, the British pound, and various U.K. industries.

Figure 19.17 is a similar chart for the Japan Nikkei Stock Average. This chart reflects the end of the significant price decline during 1992 when the Nikkei declined to almost 14,000 and subsequently, in early 1993, rebounded to about 22,000. Also during this period the yen was very strong relative to the dollar. Thus, a U.S. investor in the Japanese stock market experienced outstanding results during this period due to good domestic returns plus the positive exchange rate effect.

Merrill Lynch publishes similar charts and discussions for 10 other countries and a summary release that compares the countries and ranks them by stock and currency performance. The next section discusses the technical analysis of currency markets.

TECHNICAL ANALYSIS OF FOREIGN EXCHANGE RATES

On numerous occasions we have discussed the importance of changes in foreign exchange rates and their impact on the rates of return on foreign securities. Because of

FIGURE 19.16   **FTSE 100 Price Index from June 26, 1992 to June 26, 1993, Daily**

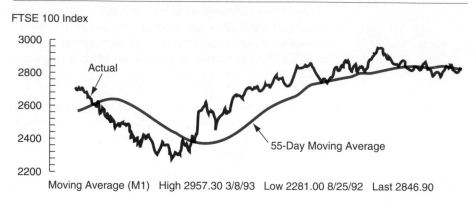

Moving Average (M1)   High 2957.30 3/8/93   Low 2281.00 8/25/92   Last 2846.90

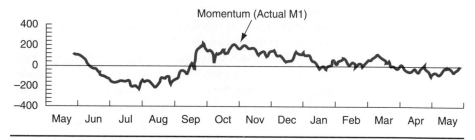

Sources: Datastream; Merrill Lynch Market Analysis/International Research. Reprinted by permission of Merrill Lynch. All Rights Reserved.

the importance of these relationships, technicians who trade bonds and stocks in world markets examine the time-series data of various individual currencies such as the British pound. They also analyze the spread between currencies such as the difference between the Japanese yen (JY) and the German deutschemark (DM).

TECHNICAL
ANALYSIS OF
BOND MARKETS

Thus far we have described technical tools for the analysis of the stock market in the United States and the world. Although we have emphasized the use of technical analysis in stock markets, you should be aware that technicians also apply these techniques to the bond market. The theory and rationale for technical analysis of bonds is the same as for stocks and many of the same trading rules are used. As with stocks, the techniques apply to an individual bond, several bonds, or a bond index. A major difference is that almost no consideration of volume of trading of bonds is possible because these data are not generally available because most bonds are traded OTC, where volume is not reported.

Figure 19.18 contains four sample technical charts for various segments of the bond market. The first chart is the plot of the June Treasury Bond Futures Index, including a 40-week moving-average line to indicate the long-term trend for this index. This classic rising pattern where each peak is above the prior peak and every trough is above the prior trough reflects the fairly consistent decline in long-term bond rates during the period from mid-1991 to mid-1993.

FIGURE 19.17   **Japan Nikkei Stock Average (225) Price Index from May 26, 1992 to May 26, 1993, Daily**

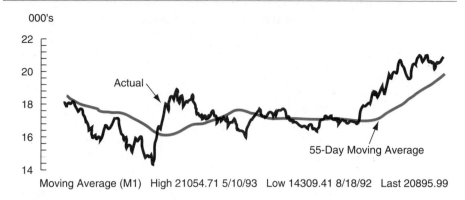

Moving Average (M1)   High 21054.71 5/10/93   Low 14309.41 8/18/92   Last 20895.99

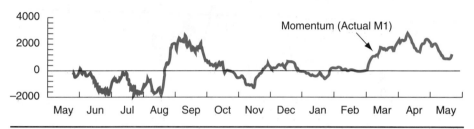

The second chart shows the relationship between the Treasury Bond Futures Index and the yield spread between 10-year Treasury bonds and BAA corporate bonds. This yield spread reflects the required risk premium on corporate bonds, and it tends to increase during periods of economic uncertainty or when there is an increase in interest rate volatility. It is suggested that a further increase in the spread may indicate a peak in bond prices and trough in bond yields.

The third chart shows the prevailing international bond futures index for four major countries (Germany, France, Great Britain, and Japan), that has likewise been increasing in absolute terms, but also in relative terms as shown by the relative strength index. Finally, Chart 4 indicates the relationship between the stock and bond markets in the United States. As shown, during some periods the two markets are highly correlated, whereas the middle time interval indicates clear differences. We know from our discussion of the valuation models that the periods of consistency are when the stock market is being heavily influenced by interest rate changes, whereas the periods of divergence occur when the impact of the economic environment on earnings expectations is a dominant factor.

These examples show how technical analysis can be and is applied to the bond market as well as the stock market.

FIGURE 19.18   **Examples of Technical Analysis Charts for the Fixed-Income Market**

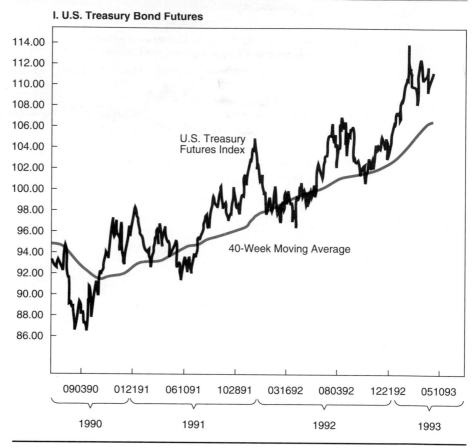

I. U.S. Treasury Bond Futures

Source: *Interest Rates* (New York: Merrill Lynch, May 12, 1993). Reprinted by permission of Merrill Lynch. All Rights Reserved.

SUMMARY

Whether you want to base your investment decisions on fundamental analysis, technical analysis, or a belief in efficient markets, you should be aware of the principles and practice of technical analysis. Numerous investors do believe in and use technical analysis, the large investment houses provide extensive support for technical analysis, and a large proportion of the discussion related to securities markets in the media, whether written or on television, is based on a technical view of the market. Now that you are aware of technical analysis principles, techniques, and indicators, you will recognize this tendency of reporters.

Two main differences separate technical analysts and those who believe in efficient markets. The first, related to the information dissemination process, is concerned with whether one assumes that everybody gets the information at about the same time. The second difference is concerned with how quickly investors adjust security prices to reflect new information. Technical analysts believe that the information dissemination process differs for different people. They believe that news takes time to travel from

FIGURE 19.18 *(continued)*

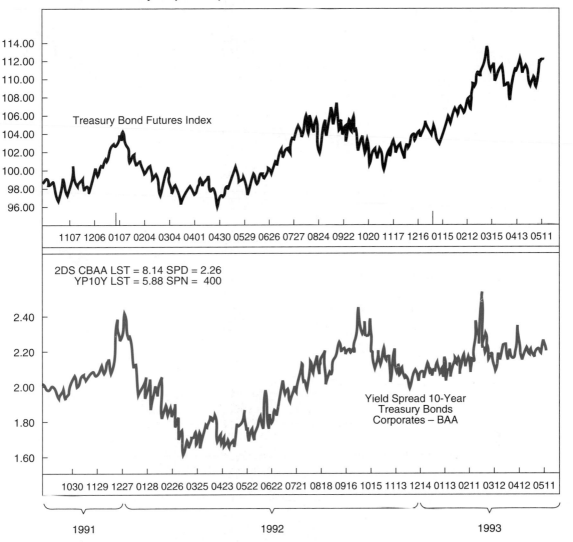

II. Bonds vs. Treasury-Corporate Spread

the insider and expert to the individual investor. They also believe that price adjustments are not instantaneous. As a result, they contend that security prices move in trends that persist and, therefore, past price trends and volume information along with other indicators can help you determine future price trends.

We discussed technical trading rules under four general categories: contrary-opinion rules, follow-the-smart-money tactics, other market indicators, and stock price and volume techniques. These techniques and trading rules can also be applied to foreign markets and to the analysis of currency exchange rates. In addition, technical analysis

FIGURE 19.18   *(continued)*

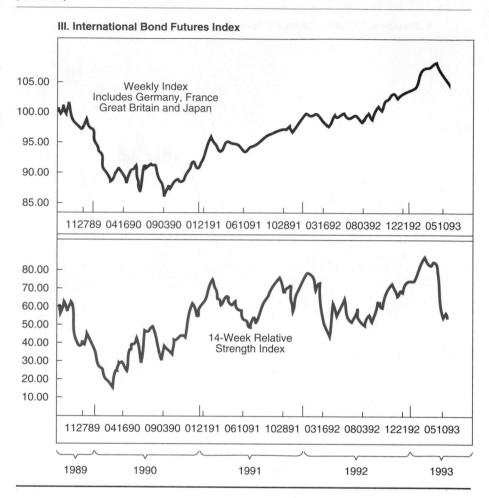

III. International Bond Futures Index

has been used to project interest rates and to determine the prevailing sentiment in the bond market.

Most technicians follow several indicators and decision rules at any point in time and attempt to derive a consensus decision to buy, sell, or do nothing.[18] Many technicians conclude on many occasions to do nothing.

QUESTIONS

1. Technical analysts believe that one can use past price changes to predict future price changes. How do they justify this belief?

2. Technicians contend that stock prices move in trends that persist for long periods of time. What do technicians believe happens in the real world to cause these trends?

---

[18]An analysis using numerous indicators is Jerome Baesel, George Shows, and Edward Thorp, "Can Joe Granville Time the Market?" *Journal of Portfolio Management* 8, no. 3 (Spring 1982): 5–9.

FIGURE 19.18   *(continued)*

IV. Bonds vs. Stocks

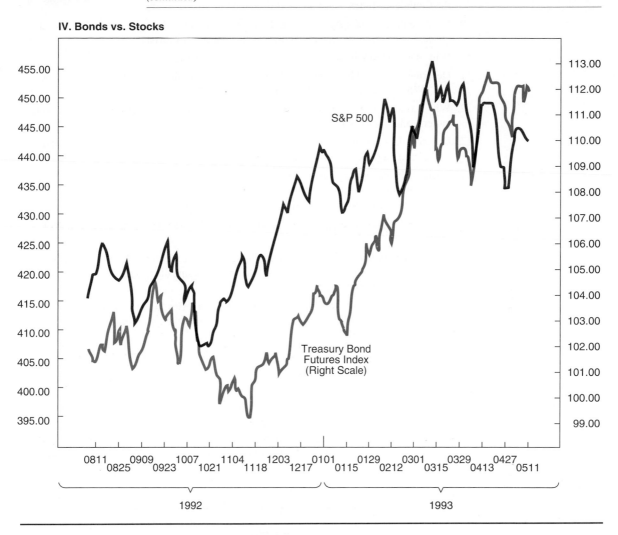

3. Briefly discuss the problems involved with fundamental analysis that are considered to be advantages for technical analysis.

4. Discuss some disadvantages of technical analysis.

5. If the mutual fund cash position were to increase close to 12 percent, would a technician consider this bullish or bearish? Give two reasons why the technical analyst would feel this way.

6. Assume a significant decline in credit balances at brokerage firms. Discuss why a technician would consider this to be bearish.

7. If the bearish sentiment index of advisory service opinions were to increase to 61 percent, would a technician consider this to be bullish or bearish? Discuss the reasoning behind your answer.

8. Define the Confidence Index and describe the reasoning behind it. What problem arises if the Confidence Index is not demand-oriented?

9. Suppose the ratio of specialists' short sales to total short sales increases to 70 percent. Discuss why a technician would consider this bullish or bearish.

10. Why is an increase in debit balances considered bullish?

11. Describe the Dow Theory and its three components. Which component is most important? What is the reason for an intermediate reversal?

12. Why is trading volume important to a technician? Describe a bearish price and volume pattern, and discuss why it is considered bearish.

13. Describe the computation of the breadth of market index. Discuss the logic behind using it to identify a peak in stock prices.

14. During a 10-day trading period, the cumulative net advance series goes from 1,572 to 1,053. During this same period of time, the DJIA goes from 3,257 to 3,407. As a technician, discuss what this set of events would mean to you.

15. Describe a support level and a resistance level. Explain the reasoning behind each of them.

16. What is the purpose of computing a moving-average line for a stock? Describe a bullish pattern using a moving-average line and the stock volume of trading. Discuss why this pattern is considered bullish.

17. Explain how you would construct a relative-strength series for an individual stock or an industry group. What would it mean to say a stock experienced good relative strength during a bear market?

18. Discuss why most technicians follow several technical rules and attempt to derive a consensus.

PROBLEMS

1. Select a stock on the NYSE and construct a daily high, low, and close bar chart for it that includes its volume of trading for 10 trading days.

2. Compute the relative-strength ratio for the stock in Problem 1 relative to the S&P 500 Index, and prepare a table that includes all the data and indicates the computations as follows:

	Closing Price		Relative Strength Ratio
Day	Stock	S&P 500	Stock Price/S&P 500

3. Plot the relative-strength ratio computed in Problem 2 on your bar chart. Discuss whether the stock's relative strength is bullish or bearish.

4. Currently Charlotte Art Importers is selling at $32 per share. Although you are somewhat dubious about technical analysis, you feel that you should know how technicians who use point-and-figure charts would view this stock. You decide to note one-point movements and three-point reversals. You gather the following price information:

Date	Price	Date	Price	Date	Price
4/1	23½	4/18	33	5/3	27
4/4	28½	4/19	35⅜	5/4	26½
4/5	28	4/20	37	5/5	28
4/6	28	4/21	38½	5/6	28¼
4/7	29¾	4/22	36	5/9	28⅛
4/8	30½	4/25	35	5/10	28¼
4/11	30½	4/26	34¼	5/11	29⅛
4/12	32⅛	4/27	33⅛	5/12	30¼
4/13	32	4/28	32⅞	5/13	29⅞

Plot the point-and-figure chart using Xs for uptrends and Os for downtrends. How would a technician evaluate these movements? Discuss why you would expect a technician to buy, sell, or hold.

REFERENCES

Colby, Robert W., and Thomas A. Mayers. *The Encyclopedia of Technical Market Indicators.* Homewood, Ill.: Dow Jones-Irwin, 1988.

Dines, James. *How the Average Investor Can Use Technical Analysis for Stock Profits.* New York: Dines Chart Corporation, 1974.

Edwards, R. D., and John Magee, Jr. *Technical Analysis of Stock Trends.* 5th ed. Springfield, Mass.: John Magee, 1988.

Fosback, Norman G. *Stock Market Logic.* Fort Lauderdale, Fla.: The Institute for Economic Research, 1976.

Grant, Dwight. "Market Timing: Strategies to Consider." *Journal of Portfolio Management* 5, no. 4 (Summer 1979).

Hardy, C. Colburn. *Investor's Guide to Technical Analysis.* New York: McGraw-Hill, 1978.

Levy, Robert A. *The Relative Strength Concept of Common Stock Price Forecasting.* Larchmont, N.Y.: Investors Intelligence, 1968.

Murphy, John J. *Technical Analysis of the Futures Markets.* 2d ed. New York: McGraw Hill, 1985.

Pring, Martin J. *Technical Analysis Explained.* 2d ed. New York: McGraw Hill, 1985.

Shaw, Alan R. "Market Timing and Technical Analysis." In *Financial Analysts Handbook.* 2d ed., edited by Sumner N. Levine. Homewood Ill.: Dow Jones-Irwin, 1988.

Zweig, Martin E. *Winning on Wall Street.* New York: Warner Books, 1986.

PART VI

ANALYSIS OF ALTERNATIVE INVESTMENTS

CHAPTERS   20 Stock Options   23 Advanced Topics on Options and Futures
            21 Warrants and Convertible Securities   24 Investment Companies
            22 Futures

Thus far in the book we have described capital markets, considered how to value assets in general, and then applied these valuation principles to the analysis and management of bonds and subsequently the analysis of common stocks from both a fundamental and technical view. The purpose of the chapters in this section is to consider the analysis of other investment instruments including derivative securities, so-named because the returns on them are derived from the returns experienced by the underlying securities. We will also discuss and analyze *hybrid* securities that are combinations of other securities including stocks and bonds, stocks and options, or bonds and options.

Chapter 20 on Stock Options begins with an historical perspective on the evolution of the secondary options market in the United States, considers its organization and membership, and discusses how it differs from the traditional stock exchanges. The chapter includes a detailed discussion of the rationale and application of the widely used Black-Scholes option pricing model. There is an extensive discussion of the relevant variables in this model and how each of these variables affect the value of an option. The chapter concludes with a consideration of the results of empirical studies that have examined the returns from investing in stocks versus investing in stocks and writing covered call options.

Chapter 21 is mainly concerned with warrants and convertible securities. It begins with a discussion of how our simplest securities such as stocks and bonds can be viewed as an option. The bulk of the chapter deals with the most popular option-like securities, which are warrants and convertible bonds. An extensive discussion of convertible bonds considers the main advantages of these securities to the issuing firm and to investors as well as the valuation of convertible bonds as a combination security involving a straight bond plus a call option on the firm's common stock. After a brief consideration of convertible preferred stock, the chap-

ter concludes with a discussion of new hybrid securities that involve options on various domestic and international stock indexes as well as specific assets.

Chapter 22 is concerned with futures contracts, their characteristics, and alternative strategies for investing and trading these securities. We consider how futures markets are similar and different from stock exchanges and provide a listing of the several futures exchanges and the numerous futures contracts available. We discuss arbitrage as applied to the Treasury bill market and stock indexes and we conclude the chapter with a discussion of the economic functions of futures markets and a review of some empirical studies dealing with the returns experienced by futures traders.

Chapter 23 is concerned with advanced derivative instruments beginning with options on futures including their characteristics, pricing, and how the pricing differs for these options compared to straight exchange traded options. We also consider options on foreign currency, how they are priced, and how they can be used to hedge foreign currency risk. The final topic considered is the circuit breakers introduced on the stock exchange as a result of the crash of 1987.

The final chapter in this section (Chapter 24) considers an alternative to analyzing securities and managing your own portfolio—investment companies. After a basic explanation of the concept of investment companies and a description of the major forms, we examine the numerous types of funds available, including money market funds, REITs, high-growth companies, international stocks and bonds, high-yield (junk) bonds, and option funds. It is demonstrated that almost any investment objective can be met by investing in one or several investment companies. A review of several studies that have examined the performance of funds indicates that on average they are not able to outperform the aggregate market, but they are capable of fulfilling a number of other functions that are important to investors.

STOCK OPTIONS

In this chapter we will answer the following questions:

- How has the secondary options market evolved over the past 25 years?
- What are main features offered by the CBOE relative to the OTC options market?
- What is the organization and membership of the CBOE and how does it differ from the NYSE?
- What are the major options exchanges, how have they grown in volume of trading, and what is the distribution of trading volume among them?
- How do you interpret the quotations for call and put options in the newspaper?
- How do you compute the profit or loss from buying a call option?
- How do you compute the profit or loss from selling a call option? How does the computation differ when selling an uncovered versus a covered call option?
- How do you compute the profit or loss from buying a put option or a protective put?
- What is the profit relationship between buying a put and selling a put option?
- What is a money or vertical spread?
- What is a time or horizontal spread?
- How do you determine the profit or loss from a bullish money spread and a bearish money spread?
- What is the theoretical rationale behind the Black-Scholes option pricing model?
- When implementing the Black-Scholes option pricing model, what are the five variables included and what is the effect of each of them on the price of the option?
- Given the difference between an American and a European option, how does this affect the pricing for an American option?
- What have been the results of empirical studies that have compared investing in stocks versus investing in stocks and writing covered call options?

In Chapter 9, we introduced options as one of the *derivative* instruments, which is an instrument whose payoff is determined by the payoff of another instrument. We learned about the basic principles of valuing options and other derivative instruments. In this chapter, we continue our consideration of options by discussing what types of options trade, where they trade, and their basic characteristics. In addition, we will examine a number of option trading strategies. Finally, our valuation discussion will encompass a more realistic option valuation model, and we will consider the effect of possible early exercise.

RECENT
HISTORY OF
OPTIONS
TRADING

Until 1973 option trading took place exclusively through private contracts involving individuals or institutions. In other words, assume an individual wanted to buy a call on General Motors that would expire in exactly 37 days. If the price of GM was $43.25 and that the investor wanted the option to be at-the-money, that is, have an exercise price of $43.25, the only way an individual could acquire such an option would be to find another individual or institution who was willing to write that particular option. The Put and Call Brokers and Dealers Association existed for the purpose of finding a party willing to take the opposite side of such an option contract. Its member firms worked as brokers, arranging trades between parties. If no counterparty could be found, a member firm might write the option itself, thereby, acting as a dealer. Thus, at any given time, there might be hundreds, perhaps thousands, of outstanding options, each with potentially different terms. The options were meant to be held to expiration because there was a very limited secondary market. What existed was an over-the-counter options market.

Everything changed dramatically in 1973, when the Chicago Board of Trade (CBOT), the largest futures exchange, created a separate exchange called the Chicago Board Options Exchange (CBOE). The CBOE became a centralized facility for trading standardized options contracts. Specifically, the CBOE offered the following features:

1. *The creation of a central marketplace* with regulatory, surveillance, disclosure, and price dissemination capabilities.
2. *The introduction of a Clearing Corporation* as the guarantor of every CBOE option. Standing as the opposite party to every trade, the Clearing Corporation enables buyers and sellers of options to terminate their positions in the market at any time by making an offsetting transaction.
3. *The standardization of expiration dates.* CBOE options have specific expirations. All stocks are classified into one of three cycles: the January cycle (January, April, July, and October), the February cycle (February, May, August, and November), and the March cycle (March, June, September, and December). Each stock's options have an expiration of the current month, the next month, and the next two months in one of these three cycles. The options expire on the Saturday following the third Friday of the month. In recent years, the CBOE has added some long-term options, called LEAPS, that have expirations of 2 to 3 years. Also, its options on stock indexes follow a pattern of expiring over the next several consecutive months.
4. *The standardization of exercise prices.* Options are available with exercise prices that bracket the current stock price. Exercise prices are generally set in $5 intervals. As a stock price moves, additional options with new exercise prices are added.
5. *The standardization of contract size.* Options are traded in units, called contracts, which are standardized at 100. Thus, buying one option is actually buy-

ing 100. Adjustments are made when there are stock splits and stock dividends, which can create odd-lot option contracts.[1]

6. *The creation of a secondary market.* As a result of the standardization of expirations and exercise prices, a secondary market for options is possible. Although an option is a contract guaranteeing the owner the right to buy or sell stock at the agreed-upon price, the majority of option buyers sell their options on the exchange either for a profit or a loss. Before option exchanges were established, the buyers and sellers of OTC options were essentially committed to their positions until the expiration date if the option were not exercised.[2]

Exchange-traded options on stocks are generally American options (i.e., they are exercisable on any day up to and including the expiration). However, some index options are European-style, meaning that they can be exercised only on the expiration day.

Over the years, the CBOE has maintained its basic structure but has added a number of different types of options. Stock index options, which are options on stock indexes, were introduced in 1983 and have been quite popular. The CBOE has also introduced options on U. S. Treasury bonds, but these have experienced limited trading.

Although the CBOE is the only exchange devoted exclusively to options trading, it is not the only exchange on which options trade. The American Stock Exchange (AMEX) got into the business in 1975, followed by the Philadelphia Stock Exchange (PHLX) later that year and the Pacific Stock Exchange (PSE) in 1976. The New York Stock Exchange (NYSE) began trading an index option in 1983, but it did not begin trading options on individual stocks until 2 years later.

Until the late 1980s, it was contended that the over-the-counter (OTC) options market was dead because the standardized exchange-traded options were much cheaper to trade. Over-the-counter options, whose terms and conditions were customized to each trade, were unable to compete, and the OTC market essentially died. However, in recent years, a revival of the OTC options market has occurred, not because of a demand for options by individual investors, but due to corporate demand. A variety of new options and option-like instruments and strategies, combined with greater understanding of the benefits of these instruments, has led many corporations to use options to control their risk. This wave of growth in the OTC options business has coincided with the tremendous globalization of financial markets. Thus, a corporate treasurer in Minneapolis, who wants to use an option to hedge against an increase in the interest rate on a bank loan, would probably turn to a major bank in New York, London, or Tokyo rather than to the CBOE. The additional cost of these tailor-made options over exchange-traded options is simply a cost of doing business in a globally integrated and competitive world.

OPTIONS MARKETS

Readers understand how a market is made on the New York and other U.S. stock exchanges. Specialists are at the center of the stock market and have two functions:

[1]One thing the CBOE did not do was to adjust option contracts when a stock paid dividends. The payment of a dividend on a stock reduces the stock's price and, thus, hurts the call option holder and helps the put option holder. Over-the-counter options made an adjustment to the exercise price. CBOE options make no such adjustment, and this affects how they are priced.

[2]In some cases, it would be possible to create an offsetting position in a new option with identical terms as the original option.

(1) as brokers who maintain the limit-order book and (2) as market makers who buy and sell for their own account to ensure the operation of a fair and orderly market for investors. The specialist has monopoly information from the limit-order book and also a monopoly position as the sole market maker in certain securities. One might, therefore, expect stock specialists to derive above-average returns, which they do.

Apparently the CBOE was aware of the potential problems of the stock specialist arrangement and attempted to avoid them. The limit-order book on the CBOE is handled by an individual, the *order book official* or OBO, who is not a market maker, so the two functions are separate. The OBO handles the limit-order book and accepts only public orders on the book. Unlike the New York Stock Exchange, on the CBOE *the limit-order book is public.* Above the trading post is a video screen that gives figures for the last trade, the best current bid and ask price for limit orders, and the best public market orders. The other major difference from the NYSE is that *there are competing market makers for all options.* On any given day for options of a given stock, these members can trade either for themselves or as a broker for the public, but they cannot do both on the same day.

Each of the market makers is assigned three or four primary options and another three or four options for which they are secondary market makers. They are required to concentrate 50 to 75 percent of their trading activity in their primary issues. Similar to the stock exchange specialist, they are expected to provide liquidity for investors. Given the existence of several market makers for each option, one would expect more funds to be available for trading. One would also expect superior markets because of the added competition.

The third category of CBOE members are *floor brokers* who execute all types of orders for their customers. These floor brokers are very similar to the floor brokers on stock exchanges.

The CBOE's market-maker system, used also by the Pacific Stock Exchange, is slightly different from the AMEX and Philadelphia systems, which have *specialists,* in the more traditional sense of the stock exchange specialist. The options specialist buys and sells options to assist the public in getting orders filled with minimal price changes. The AMEX and Philadelphia exchanges also use *registered options traders,* who are a combination of a broker and a dealer. They buy and sell for themselves and for others but are not obligated to make a market, as is the specialist or the CBOE market maker.

| VOLUME OF TRADING | The CBOE started with options on 16 stocks. This number was gradually increased and today, as indicated in Table 20.1, there are options on almost 1,400 stocks. Table 20.2 provides a description of the index options that also trade on the various exchanges. Index options have special appeal because they involve taking a position on the market as a whole, rather than on individual stocks. As you learned in Chapter 8 regarding capital market theory, the ability to diversify risk should make investors focus more on aggregate market movements. In addition, index options do not actually involve the exchange of cash for a portfolio of stocks that duplicates the index. Rather, they are *cash settled,* meaning that they require a payment representing the difference between the exercise price and the value of the index. For example, if you owned a call option on an individual stock with an exercise price of $100 and decided to exercise it when |

TABLE 20.1

Equity Options Listed on Exchanges (as of June 1993)

Exchange	Starting Date	Number of Stocks
Chicago Board Options Exchange (CBOE)	April 26, 1973	448
American Stock Exchange (AMEX)	January 13, 1975	336
Philadelphia Stock Exchange (PHLX)	June 29, 1975	242
Pacific Stock Exchange (PSE)	April 9, 1976	224
New York Stock Exchange (NYSE)	February 13, 1985	139
Midwest Stock Exchange (MWSE)	December 10, 1976	*
	Total	1,389

*Merged with Chicago Board Options Exchange on June 2, 1980.

TABLE 20.2

Description of Major Index Options (as of July 1992)

Standard & Poor's 100 Index (CBOE). This option, commonly called the OEX after its ticker symbol, is an option on an index of 100 large stocks. It is the most actively traded index option.

Standard & Poor's 500 Index (CBOE). This option, commonly called the SPX after its ticker symbol, is an option on the most widely followed broad-based stock index. Unlike most index options, the S&P 500 option is exercised only on the expiration day. Options are also available with long expirations (2 to 3 years). Trading is fairly active.

New York Stock Exchange Index (NYSE). This option trades on the New York Stock Exchange and is based on the NYSE's index of the 1,500-plus stocks that are listed on the exchange. Trading volume is moderate.

Major Market Index (AMEX). This option is exercisable only on the expiration day. It is based on an index of 20 blue-chip stocks, 15 of which are included in the Dow Jones Industrial Average. The MMI is designed to mimic the Dow Jones Industrial Average. It is the third most active index option. Options are also available with long expirations (2 to 3 years).

Value Line Composite Index (PHLX). This option is based on an index of the approximately 1,700 stocks included in the Value Line Index. The index includes more over-the-counter stocks than most of the other broad-based indexes. Trading volume is light.

S&P Midcap Index (AMEX). This option is based on Standard & Poor's Index of Midcap Stocks. It includes 400 stocks with a capitalization ranging from $170 million to $6 billion, which are considered mid-sized firms. The option is exercisable only on the expiration day. Trading volume is moderate.

Japan Index (AMEX). This option is based on an index of 210 Japanese stocks and is designed to be similar to the Nikkei Index, the most widely quoted index of the Japanese stock market. The option is exercisable only on the expiration day. Trading volume is moderate.

Institutional Index (AMEX). This option is based on an index of 75 stocks with the largest dollar holdings in major institutional portfolios. Trading volume is moderate to light.

Utilities Index (PHLX). This option is based on an index of 120 utility stocks. Trading volume is light.

Gold/Silver Index (PHLX). This option is on an index of seven mining stocks. Trading volume is light.

Financial News Composite Index (PSE). This option is based on an index of 30 stocks of major companies. Trading volume is light.

TABLE 20.3 **Number of Equity Option Contracts Traded and Percentage of Contracts Traded (thousands)**

	CBOE		AMEX		Philadelphia		Pacific		Midwest		NYSE		
Year	Number	Percent	Number	Percent	Number	Percent	Number	Percent	Number	Percent	Number	Percent	Total
1973	1,119	100.0	0	0.0	0	0.0	0	0.0	0	0.0	0	0.0	1,119
1974	5,683	100.0	0	0.0	0	0.0	0	0.0	0	0.0	0	0.0	5,683
1975	14,431	79.7	3,531	19.5	141	0.8	0	0.0	0	0.0	0	0.0	18,103
1976	21,498	66.4	9,036	27.9	1,275	3.9	550	1.7	15	0.1	0	0.0	32,374
1977	24,839	62.7	10,078	25.4	2,195	5.5	1,925	4.9	601	1.5	0	0.0	39,638
1978	34,277	59.9	14,381	25.1	3,270	5.7	3,290	5.6	2,012	3.5	0	0.0	57,230
1979	35,380	55.1	17,467	27.2	4,953	7.7	3,856	6.0	2,609	4.1	0	0.0	64,265
1980	52,917	54.7	29,048	30.0	7,758	8.0	5,487	5.7	1,519	1.6	0	0.0	96,729
1981	57,584	52.6	34,859	31.9	10,010	9.2	6,952	6.4	0	0.0	0	0.0	109,405
1982	75,722	55.2	38,767	28.2	13,467	9.8	9,310	6.8	0	0.0	0	0.0	137,266
1983	71,696	52.9	36,200	26.7	16,608	12.2	11,156	8.2	0	0.0	0	0.0	135,660
1984	58,675	49.3	33,077	27.8	15,982	13.4	11,191	9.4	0	0.0	0	0.0	118,925
1985	57,524	48.5	36,100	30.5	12,068	10.2	12,701	10.7	0	0.0	164	0.1	118,557
1986	64,744	45.6	47,140	33.2	15,055	10.6	13,942	9.8	0	0.0	1,050	0.7	141,931
1987	73,315	44.6	52,771	32.1	18,088	11.0	18,952	11.5	0	0.0	1,306	0.8	164,432
1988	49,393	43.0	37,470	32.6	13,093	11.4	13,069	11.4	0	0.0	1,903	1.7	114,928
1989	61,903	43.6	41,579	29.3	16,769	11.8	17,865	12.6	0	0.0	3,723	2.6	141,839
1990	48,846	43.7	34,198	30.6	12,444	11.1	13,751	12.3	0	0.0	2,547	2.3	111,786
1991	45,255	42.9	32,829	31.1	11,804	11.2	13,781	13.1	0	0.0	1,901	1.8	105,570
1992	44,968	42.2	36,068	33.9	10,409	9.8	12,997	12.2	0	0.0	2,043	1.9	106,485

Source: Chicago Board Options Exchange, *Market Statistics 1992.*

the stock price was $105, you would pay $100 and receive a stock worth $105. If the option were an index option and the index were at 105, you would simply receive $5 in cash. For put index options you would receive cash based on how much lower the index was than the exercise price. Because the stock is never actually handled, this reduces the transaction costs of exercising the option.

As you might expect, the options on individual stocks, called *equity options,* are on stocks of large companies that enjoy active secondary markets. In fact, one of the key criteria for listing an option is the trading activity of the underlying stock. The growth in trading volume has been phenomenal. During the first full month of trading on the CBOE (May 1973), the number of contracts traded totaled about 31,000. In 1992, the total number of equity options traded on the four exchanges was over 106 million, and an additional 83 million index option contracts were traded! The annual totals for equity options are contained in Table 20.3 and the results for index options are in Table 20.4, broken down by exchange.

The CBOE's share of the equity option business was over 50 percent in the early 1980s but has stabilized in the 42 to 43 percent range; the AMEX claims about 34 percent. The Pacific Stock Exchange holds about 12 to 13 percent, and the Philadelphia Stock Exchange has about 10 percent. The New York Stock Exchange, which got in the business quite late, has only around 2 percent of the options business. Incidentally, the Philadelphia Stock Exchange's primary option business is in foreign currency options, where it has 100 percent of the market. These options are discussed in Chapter 21. The CBOE's dominance is particularly evident in the index option business. It currently has over 90 percent of the market and this percent has increased in recent years.

TABLE 20.4   **Number of Index Option Contracts Traded and Percentage of Contracts Traded (thousands)**

	CBOE		AMEX		Philadelphia		Pacific		NYSE		NASD		
Year	Number	Percent	Number	Percent	Number	Percent	Number	Percent	Number	Percent	Number	Percent	Total
1983	10,662	76.1	2,693	19.2	6	0.0	0	0.0	656	4.7	0	0.0	14,017
1984	64,357	85.0	7,006	9.3	127	0.2	175	0.2	4,094	5.4	0	0.0	75,759
1985	90,822	82.5	12,438	11.3	2,321	2.1	93	0.1	4,263	3.9	107	0.1	110,044
1986	114,835	82.9	18,275	13.2	1,399	1.0	134	0.1	3,774	2.7	45	0.0	138,462
1987	108,352	83.5	18,193	14.0	499	0.0	459	0.4	2,193	1.7	0	0.0	129,696
1988	62,250	87.7	7,549	10.6	157	0.2	280	0.4	725	1.0	0	0.0	70,961
1989	64,645	87.5	8,282	11.2	151	0.2	226	0.3	593	0.8	0	0.0	73,897
1990	80,945	91.8	6,618	7.5	219	0.3	130	0.2	271	0.3	0	0.0	88,183
1991	76,385	92.0	5,976	7.2	434	0.5	72	0.1	159	0.2	0	0.0	83,026
1992	76.442	91.8	6,247	7.5	354	0.4	70	0.1	134	0.2	0	0.0	83,247

Source: Chicago Board Options Exchange, *Market Statistics 1992.*

A SAMPLE QUOTATION

Figure 20.1 presents an example of the option quotation page from *The Wall Street Journal.* Suppose you were considering buying a call on Alcoa. Next to Alcoa's name, you'll find the expiration date and exercise (or strike) price, Oct 70 or Sep 75 (a "p" next to the exercise price indicates that the option is a put). The trading volume appears next, followed by the market where the option trades. The fourth and fifth columns give, respectively, today's closing price and the net change from the previous day. The sixth and seventh columns show the closing price of the underlying stock and then the total number of contracts for that specific price and expiration date. If you had done the last trade on the Alcoa October 70 call, the price would have been 5. This is $5 per option. Because each contract is for 100 calls, the total cost would have been $500.00. However, it is important to note two potentially misleading facts about these prices. First, the closing stock price of $73\frac{1}{2}$ and the closing option prices are not necessarily synchronized. The last trade of the day for the stock and the last trade of the day for the options may have occurred at different times.[3] In addition, the prices are not identified as bid or ask prices.[4] Thus, even if the stock and option prices were synchronized and there was no additional information to affect the prices since the last trade, you might have to pay more than $500.00. This is because the price you see may have represented a trade in which an investor sold an option to the CBOE market maker, which means that it would have been the bid price. Thus if you had wanted to purchase an option from a market maker, you would have to pay the ask price, which would be higher.

Figure 20.2 presents an example of *The Wall Street Journal*'s index option quotations. If, for example, you had done the last trade of the day on a September 390 call on the S&P 100, the price would have been $26\frac{7}{8}$, which is a $2,687.50 contract. The index closed at 415.77. Recall, however, that the closing index and option prices are not necessarily synchronized.

---

[3]In fact, the New York Stock Exchange closes at 4:00 P.M. Eastern time, whereas the CBOE closes at 4:15 P.M. Eastern time.

[4]Obviously, this is also true for reported stock price data.

FIGURE 20.1 **Listed Equity Option Quotations from *The Wall Street Journal*, August 4, 1993**

Tuesday, August 3, 1993

Volume, close, net change and open interest of the 1,400 most active equity and 100 most active long-term contracts. Volume figures are unofficial. Open interest is total outstanding for all exchanges and reflects previous trading day. **CB**-Chicago Board Options Exchange. **AM**-American Stock Exchange. **PB**-Philadelphia Stock Exchange. **PC**-Pacific Stock Exchange. **NY**-New York Stock Exchange. **a**-Underlying stock on primary market. **c**-Call. **p**-Put.

MOST ACTIVE CONTRACTS

Option/Strike				Vol	Exch	Last	Net Chg	a-Close	Open Int
Merck	Jan	30	p	4,460	CB	2 3/16	...	31 1/8	13,292
I B M	Aug	45		3,268	CB	7/16	– 5/16	43 3/8	17,627
Abbt L	Nov	25		3,080	PB	1 3/8	...	25	1,073
Merck	Jan	35		2,513	CB	1 1/4	+ 1/16	31 1/8	6,950
Merck	Sep	30		2,500	CB	1 11/16	+ 1/16	31 1/8	7,458
AplMat	Oct	60		2,001	PC	7 1/2	– 3/4	65 1/2	2,057
AplMat	Jan	65		2,001	PC	6 3/4	– 3/4	65 1/2	23
APwrCv	Mar	40	p	2,000	CB	6 5/8	...	41 1/4	...
AT&T	Sep	65		1,913	CB	15/16	– 1/16	63 1/4	305
Merck	Oct	35		1,660	CB	1/2	+ 1/16	31 1/8	12,244
Amgen	Aug	35		1,652	AM	1	+ 1/16	35	5,987
US Surg	Sep	25		1,611	AM	1 1/16	+ 1/8	23 1/2	643
TelMex	Aug	50		1,583	AM	1 1/2	– 3/8	50 3/4	19,919
Intel	Aug	55		1,568	AM	11/16	+ 1/16	53	11,286
TelMex	Aug	50	p	1,500	AM	11/16	+ 1/16	50 3/4	4,565
Motrla	Aug	90		1,378	AM	5 1/4	+ 1/8	94 1/2	4,727
I B M	Jan	40	p	1,369	CB	2 1/8	+ 3/16	43 3/8	3,847
Novell	Nov	20	p	1,350	AM	1 1/2	+ 1/8	20 5/8	4,418
TelMex	Nov	55		1,328	CB	1 3/4	– 1/8	50 3/4	6,683
Motrla	Aug	95	p	1,309	AM	2 3/4	...	94 1/2	567
Merck	Oct	30		1,288	CB	2 1/16	+ 1/16	31 1/8	8,544
Motrla	Oct	90		1,275	AM	7 1/4	– 1/4	94 1/2	2,477
Chryslr	Sep	45	p	1,263	CB	2 5/8	– 1/8	43 7/8	806
EKodak	Oct	55		1,249	CB	2	+ 3/8	54 3/4	6,097
Motrla	Aug	95		1,249	AM	2	...	94 1/2	3,631

-A-B-C-

A M D	Aug	22 1/2	p	94	PC	1/4	– 1/16	25	1,855
A M D	Oct	22 1/2		67	PC	3 1/8	– 1/8	25	1,254
A M D	Oct	22 1/2	p	460	PC	1	...	25	1,783
A M D	Jan	25		92	PC	3	...	25	2,164
A M D	Aug	25		334	PC	3/4	...	25	3,453
A M D	Aug	25	p	62	PC	7/8	– 1/4	25	421
A M D	Sep	25		105	PC	1 1/2	...	25	468
A M D	Oct	25		263	PC	2 1/8	+ 3/16	25	3,945
A M D	Oct	25	p	542	PC	1 7/8	...	25	1,105
A M D	Oct	30		164	PC	9/16	– 1/8	25	2,654
A M P	Aug	65		65	CB	7/8	...	64 5/8	2,981
A M R	Aug	55	p	370	AM	1/8	...	64 3/4	3,284
A M R	Aug	60		170	AM	5 1/8	– 1 1/8	64 3/4	973
A M R	Aug	65		381	AM	1 5/8	– 1/8	64 3/4	3,243
A M R	Sep	70		228	AM	7/8	– 1/4	64 3/4	107
A S A	Feb	50		59	AM	4 3/4	+ 3/8	48 1/2	231
A S A	Aug	50		84	AM	1	– 1/4	48 1/2	3,926
A S A	Nov	50		85	AM	3 1/8	– 5/8	48 1/2	2,912
A S A	Nov	55		99	AM	1 3/4	+ 1/16	48 1/2	1,244
ABrrck	Jan	20		104	AM	8 1/4	– 1/4	27 1/2	931
ABrrck	Jan	22 1/2		75	AM	6 1/2	...	27 1/2	477
ABrrck	Jan	22 1/2	p	110	AM	1	...	27 1/2	895
ABrrck	Oct	22 1/2		108	AM	5 1/2	– 1/2	27 1/2	2,541
ABrrck	Aug	25		65	AM	2 5/8	– 3/4	27 1/2	3,348
ABrrck	Oct	25		706	AM	3 7/8	– 3/8	27 1/2	4,706
ABrrck	Jan	30		105	AM	2 1/2	– 3/8	27 1/2	848
ABrrck	Aug	30		150	AM	3/8	– 1/8	27 1/2	2,060
ABrrck	Sep	30		187	AM	7/8	– 1/4	27 1/2	595
ABrrck	Oct	30		433	AM	1 3/8	– 3/8	27 1/2	3,258
ABrrck	Oct	30	p	62	AM	3 3/8	– 1/8	27 1/2	110
APwrCv	Sep	30	p	110	CB	3/8	+ 3/16	41 1/4	341
APwrCv	Sep	35	p	80	CB	7/8	– 1/2	41 1/4	811
APwrCv	Mar	40	p	2,000	CB	6 5/8	...	41 1/4	...
APwrCv	Aug	40		60	CB	2 3/8	+ 1/4	41 1/4	1,069
ASK	Aug	12 1/2		50	PB	3/16	– 1/16	10 1/2	220
AT&T	Oct	55	p	47	CB	1/4	+ 1/16	63 1/4	3,492
AT&T	Sep	65		1,913	CB	15/16	– 1/16	63 1/4	305
AT&T	Oct	65		124	CB	1 3/8	– 1/4	63 1/4	5,888
Abbt L	Aug	25		123	PB	1/2	– 1/4	25	3,724
Abbt L	Aug	25	p	74	PB	11/16	– 1/16	25	2,350
Abbt L	Nov	25		3,080	PB	1 3/8	...	25	1,073
Adaptc	Oct	25		72	AM	3 5/8	+ 1/2	27 1/4	1,002
AdobeS	Aug	50		261	PC	2 1/2	+ 5/16	51	623
AdobeS	Aug	55		100	PC	5/8	...	51	4,419
Agency	Oct	10		50	AM	3/16	– 1/16	8 1/4	95
Agnico	Aug	12 1/2	p	70	PC	1/2	– 1/8	12 1/2	168
Ahman	Aug	15		100	AM	4 5/8	+ 3/8	19 5/8	547
Ahman	Aug	17 1/2		100	AM	2 1/8	+ 1/4	19 5/8	307
Ahman	Oct	20		50	AM	3/4	– 1/16	19 5/8	685
Alcan	Sep	20		105	AM	1 1/16	+ 3/16	20 1/4	2,147
Alcoa	Oct	70		75	CB	5	– 5/8	73 1/2	583
Alcoa	Sep	75		121	CB	1 3/4	+ 11/16	73 1/2	28
AldSgnl	Aug	70		138	PB	2	– 1/8	71 7/8	3,073
AldSgnl	Sep	70	p	102	PB	1 5/8	– 1/2	71 7/8	58
AldSgnl	Sep	75		176	PB	1 1/8	+ 3/16	71 7/8	322

Source: Listed Options Quotations, *The Wall Street Journal,* August 4, 1993.

OPTION TRADING STRATEGIES

Although options have been around since long before the CBOE, the creation of the CBOE made options more accessible to the general public. The timing of the creation of the CBOE also coincided with the development of *option pricing theory,* the study of the economic processes that determine option prices. Option pricing theory has come a long way since 1973 and remains one of the more popular and sophisticated areas of research in investments. This boom in options research has been accompanied by an increased demand on the part of individuals and institutions for knowledge about options, both the theory and practical aspects. Investors quickly learned that option trading greatly increases the number and complexity of strategies available. In this section, we will not attempt to cover all the strategies but will limit our discussion to the major alternatives. Also, to understand the more sophisticated strategies, you must understand the basic techniques, because the more advanced methods build on these. Some of the end-of-chapter references describe the more sophisticated techniques.

FIGURE 20.2   **Index Option Quotations from *The Wall Street Journal*, August 4, 1993**

INDEX OPTIONS TRADING

Tuesday, August 3, 1993

Volume, close, net change and open interest for all contracts. Volume figures are unofficial. Open interest reflects previous trading day. p-Put c—Call

CHICAGO

Strike	Vol.	Last	Net Chg.	Open Int.
FINTIMES-SE100(FSX)				
Oct 300 c	6	5¼	...	...
Call vol. 6		Open Int............941		
Put vol............. 0		Open Int.........1,121		
RUSSELL 2000(RUT)				
Oct 225 p	8	1¹³/₁₆ −	¼	100
Aug 230 c	100	8⅞ +	1	614
Sep 230 c	10	10⅛ +	⅞	2,025
Aug 235 c	10	4½ +	1	554
Aug 235 p	80	1³/₁₆ −	¹³/₁₆	336
Oct 235 p	15	4 −	⅜	10
Aug 240 p	20	3 −	1⅜	261
Aug 245 c	50	⁵/₁₆ +	¹/₁₆	80
Aug 245 p	100	6¾ +	1¾	30
Call vol. 170		Open Int........ 13,020		
Put vol........... 238		Open Int........ 10,018		
S & P 100 INDEX(OEX)				
Aug 370 p	285	¹/₁₆	...	5,215
Sep 370 p	10	⁷/₁₆	...	2,560
Aug 375 p	36	⅛	...	3,716
Sep 375 p	253	½ −	³/₁₆	1,384
Oct 375 p	314	1	...	993
Aug 380 p	31	⅛ −	¹/₁₆	12,441
Sep 380 p	147	¹¹/₁₆	...	6,088
Oct 380 p	84	1¼ −	⅛	2,755
Nov 380 p	434	2⅜	...	2,768
Aug 385 p	969	³/₁₆	...	12,595
Sep 385 p	2,085	⅞	...	3,707
Oct 385 p	87	1¾ +	¹/₁₆	2,610
Aug 390 c	37	26 +	1⅝	60
Aug 390 p	961	¼ −	¹/₁₆	15,015
Sep 390 c	37	26⅞ +	1⅛	306
Sep 390 p	1,025	1³/₁₆ +	¹/₁₆	15,834
Oct 390 p	81	2¼ +	¹/₁₆	4,555
Nov 390 p	8	3½ −	¼	1,051
Aug 395 c	2,699	⁷/₁₆	...	30,655
Sep 395 p	107	1⁹/₁₆	...	2,615

RANGES FOR UNDERLYING INDEXES

Tuesday, August 3, 1993

	High	Low	Close	Net Chg.	From Dec. 31	% Chg.
S&P 100 (OEX)..........	417.00	414.17	415.77	− 0.90	+ 19.13	+ 4.8
S&P 500 -A.M.(SPX)...	450.43	447.59	449.27	− 0.88	+ 13.56	+ 3.1
S&P 500 -P.M.(NSX)...	450.43	447.59	449.27	− 0.88	+ 13.56	+ 3.1
FT-SE 100 (FSX).......	294.73	294.00	294.50	+ 0.33	+ 9.85	+ 3.5
Russell 2000 (RUT)...	237.82	237.14	237.79	+ 0.63	+ 16.79	+ 7.6
Lps S&P 100 (OEX)..	41.70	41.42	41.58	− 0.09	+ 1.92	+ 4.8
Lps S&P 500 (SPX)...	45.04	44.76	44.93	− 0.09	+ 1.36	+ 3.1
S&P Midcap (MID)...	168.74	168.24	168.74	+ 0.45	+ 8.19	+ 5.1
Major Mkt (XMI)...	362.44	360.38	361.67	− 0.12	+ 14.87	+ 4.3
Leaps MMkt (XLT)..	36.24	36.04	36.17	− 0.01	+ 1.49	+ 4.3
Institut'l -A.M.(XII)...	449.24	445.64	447.37	− 1.29	+ 3.67	+ 0.8
Institut'l -P.M.(PXP)...	449.24	445.64	447.37	− 1.29	+ 3.67	+ 0.8
Eurotop 100 (EUR)...	108.66	108.05	108.62	+ 0.06	+ 21.06	+ 24.1
Japan (JPN)...............			206.12	+ 0.13	+ 34.89	+ 20.4
Pharma (DRG)..........	157.41	156.18	156.82	+ 0.50	− 41.02	− 20.7
Biotech (BTK)...........	106.86	104.47	105.70	− 0.16	− 64.94	− 38.1
NYSE (NYA).............	249.72	248.48	249.25	− 0.28	+ 9.04	+ 3.8
Wilshire S-C (WSX)..	311.88	310.51	311.88	+ 1.28	+ 21.57	+ 7.4
Gold/Silver (XAU)...	128.25	125.46	125.47	− 3.60	+ 54.17	+ 76.0
Value Line (VLE).....	421.65	420.97	421.60	+ 0.44	+ 35.52	+ 9.2
OTC (XOC)................	542.50	539.13	540.31	+ 0.57	+ 9.56	+ 1.8

AMERICAN

Strike	Vol.	Last	Net Chg.	Open Int.
BIO TECH(BTK)				
Aug 100 c	6	7⅛ −	1⅞	...
Aug 105 c	12	3½	...	11
Sep 120 c	49	9⅞ −	⅝	181
Sep 120 p	6	4¼ +	...	33
Oct 120 c	2	11⅞ +	½	28
Oct 120 p	10	5¼ −	...	46
Aug 125 c	54	5 −	1⅝	334
Aug 125 p	64	4 +	⅜	211
Sep 125 c	94	7¼ −	1	402

For the option strategies we shall examine, let us assume that the following options are available for trading.

Exercise Price	Call Price	Put Price
70	6⅛	2¼
75	3½	4¾

The stock price is $73.25. We will ignore taxes and commissions and will treat the options as European options.[5] In addition, we will assume that all strategies are held to expiration. Although this is not required and usually is not done, we cannot under-

---

[5]We will examine American options later in the chapter.

stand how to evaluate option strategies closed out before expiration without a better grasp of option pricing theory.

BUYING CALL OPTIONS

Investors buy call options because they expect the price of the underlying stock to increase during the period prior to the expiration of the option. Given this expectation, the purchase of an option will yield a large return on a small dollar investment. Several alternatives are available in terms of the exercise price relative to the market price. You can purchase an out-of-the-money option, an at-the-money option, or an in-the-money option. An out-of-the-money option costs the least but offers the lowest potential return. An in-the-money option costs the most but offers the highest potential return.

Consider the following example of the purchase of the call option with a $70 exercise price (we will refer to this as the 70 call). You would pay $100 \times \$6.125 = \$612.50$ for this call. At expiration, if the stock price is greater than $70, you will exercise the call, paying $70 and receiving stock worth whatever its price is. Thus, as noted in Chapter 9, we can express the call's value at expiration as $Max[0,S(T) - X]$, where $S(T)$ is the stock price at expiration and X is the exercise price. Thus, the call will be worth zero if the stock price is at $70 or less, and it will be worth the stock price minus the exercise price if the stock price exceeds the exercise price. The profit from the call can be stated as

$$Max[0,S(T) - X] - c(t)$$

where $c(t)$ is the price paid originally for the call, i.e. at time t, which here is 6.125. (We can express these results on a per option basis and then convert later to a per contract basis by multiplying by 100.) Let us say the stock price ends up at $68. Then the profit is $Max(0,68 - 70) - 6.125$. This is -6.125, or a loss of $6.125 per option. If the stock price ends up at $75, the profit is $Max(0,75 - 70) - 6.125$, which is -1.125, or a loss of $1.125 per option. You would break even at a stock price at expiration of $70 + \$6.125$, or $76.125.

Figure 20.3 illustrates these results in the form of a profit graph, which is a visual depiction of the profit from the strategy plotted against the stock price at expiration. You can see that the call buying strategy has a *limited loss* of the option premium, which in this case is $612.50 per contract. There is no limit on the upside because the stock price is unlimited. The leverage inherent in options is quite tempting. For example, assume the stock price rises 20 percent over the life of the option, going from $73.25 to $87.90. Then the option would end up being worth $17.90. Thus, a 20 percent stock price increase led to a 192 percent increase in the option price. On the other hand, if the stock price fell to 70 by expiration, just a 4.44 percent decline, the option value would fall to zero, a 100 percent loss. Even though the loss of 100 percent of the option value is fairly small relative to the stock price (about 8 percent), you should be very careful about interpreting the potential option profits and losses. The lure of potentially large profits with limited dollar losses must be tempered with the fact that the large profits occur quite rarely, whereas the small losses occur quite frequently.

You could have chosen the out-of-the-money option, paying only $3.50 for a call with an exercise price of $75. This option would have limited your overall loss to $350. However, the stock price would have had to have risen to $78.50 at expiration before you would have made money.

FIGURE 20.3   **Profits to Buyer of Call Option**

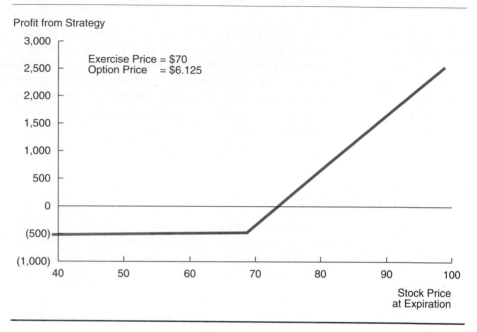

Profit from Strategy

Exercise Price = $70
Option Price   = $6.125

Stock Price
at Expiration

SELLING CALL
OPTIONS

Now let us look at the profits for the individual who sold the 70 call. If we assume the individual does not own the stock, this transaction is referred to as an *uncovered* or *naked* call, for reasons that will become apparent.

The seller of the call will owe the value $Max[0,S(T) - X]$ at expiration, because the seller may have to buy the stock for its market price, $S(T)$, and sell it for X. If $S(T)$ is substantially greater than X, the seller can incur a large loss. In fact, the seller's profits are simply -1 times the buyer's profits.

Figure 20.4 graphs the seller's profits which you should recognize as simply Figure 20.3 inverted. The seller can earn a maximum amount equal to the premium of $612.50, which is retained if the option ends up out-of-the-money. The seller's loss is potentially unlimited.[6]

The risk of great potential loss is why this strategy is referred to as uncovered or naked. The option writer is exposed to unlimited losses. If, however, the writer owns the stock, this is referred to as a *covered* call. If the call is exercised, the covered call writer does not have to buy the stock in the market. He or she simply delivers the stock, effectively selling it for the exercise price.

The profit from a covered call is, thus,

$$-Max[0,S(T) - X] + c(t) + S(T) - S(t)$$

---

[6]Clearly, the seller can be literally "wiped out." For that reason, the seller's broker will generally require that margin money be posted. Another way to reduce the risk of disaster is for the seller to own the stock, a strategy we shall examine next.

FIGURE 20.4   **Profits to Seller of Uncovered Call Option**

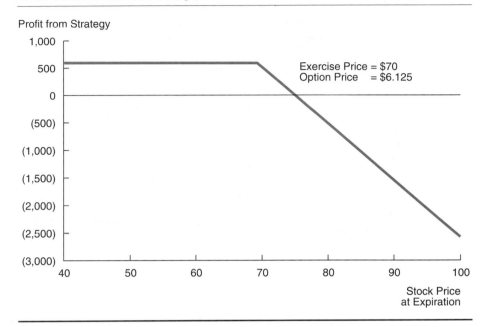

Profit from Strategy

Exercise Price = $70
Option Price   = $6.125

Stock Price
at Expiration

where the writer loses the value of the call at expiration, $Max[0,S(T) - X]$, pays out the price of the stock up front, $S(t)$, receives the price of the call up front, $c(t)$, and receives the value of the stock at expiration, $S(T)$. This specification allows us to break down the profit into the profit on the call, $-Max[0,S(T) - X] + c(t)$, and the profit on the stock, $S(T) - S(t)$. If the call expires out-of-the-money, the writer owes nothing on the call but receives $S(T)$ from the sale of the stock. If the call expires in-the-money, the call is worth $-S(T) + X$ to the writer and the stock is worth $S(T)$. These add up to X. Thus, the covered call writer's profit is

$$X + c(t) - S(t) \qquad \text{if the call expires in-the-money}$$
$$c(t) + S(T) - S(t) \qquad \text{if the call expires out-of-the-money}$$

Figure 20.5 shows the profits of the writer of the covered call, overlayed with the profits of its component strategies, a long position in the stock and an uncovered call. If the stock falls, the covered call writer keeps the premium and the stock, while the premium received cushions against the loss in value of the stock. On the upside, however, the covered call writer's gains are limited because the stock must be sold for the exercise price regardless of how much it is worth in the market.

Covered call writers are often described as the smarter option traders and make money because they capitalize on the public's excessive optimism about potential stock price moves. If the public is indeed overly optimistic, then a covered call writer can collect the premiums, knowing that the stock is unlikely to move high enough to justify the premium. Many covered call writers view this as generating income off of a slow-moving stock. However, you should understand that writing a call option on a stock

FIGURE 20.5

Profits to Seller of Covered Call Option

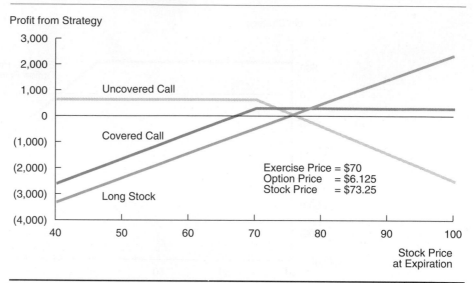

Exercise Price = $70
Option Price   = $6.125
Stock Price   = $73.25

already owned is simply a way of converting the stock's future capital gains to a cash payment up front. If the option buyer is not overly optimistic, then the premium will be a fair payment to the writer for which the buyer benefits from the stock's future capital gains.

BUYING PUT OPTIONS

There are several major reasons for acquiring a put option on a stock. The most obvious is that you expect a particular stock to decline in price and you want to profit from this decline. As will be shown, the purchase of a put option allows you to do this with the benefits of leverage and yet it limits the potential loss if your expectation regarding a price decline in the stock is wrong. Buying put options offers some advantages over selling the stock short, namely, that the losses are limited to the put premium and costly short sale margin requirements are avoided. In addition, put options can be used if you own a stock and do not want to sell it at the present time, although you feel it might decline in the near term. In this latter case, you can buy a put option on the stock you own as a hedge against the decline; if the stock declines, you will offset the decline in the stock with an increase in the value of the put option.

Consider the strategy of purchasing the 70 put for $2.25. The put will be worth $Max[0, X - S(T)]$ at expiration. Thus, the profit from buying the put can be expressed as

$$Max[0, X - S(T)] - p(t)$$

where $p(t)$ is the price originally paid for the put. If the put expires in-the-money, the put holder gets to buy the stock in the market for $S(T)$ and sell it for X, which is greater.[7]

---

[7]As an alternative, the put holder can use the put to sell short the stock.

FIGURE 20.6   **Profits to Buyer of Put Option**

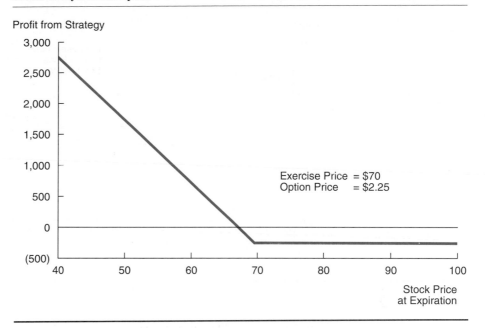

Profit from Strategy

Exercise Price = $70
Option Price   = $2.25

Stock Price
at Expiration

The profit is this amount minus the put premium paid up front. If the put expires out-of-the-money, the put holder simply loses the put premium that was paid up front.

Suppose the stock price ends up at $60. Then the $60 stock can be sold for $70, netting a profit of $10 − $2.25 or $7.75 per option, or $775 per contract. If the stock price ends up at $80, the put holder loses the $225 premium. Figure 20.6 illustrates the profits for the put buyer. As you can see, the put buyer's loss is limited to the premium of $225. The gains are limited because the stock price can never fall below zero. If the company went bankrupt, the stock could theoretically fall to zero and the put buyer would make $70 − $2.25 = $67.75 per option or $6,775 overall. Of course, this extreme case is quite unlikely.

Puts, like calls, also offer enormous leverage. If the stock price falls 20 percent to $58.60, the put price will rise 406.7 percent to $11.40. Because this put is in-the-money, even if it falls to $70, a decrease of only 4.44 percent, the put price will fall 100 percent. However, as with calls, large stock price changes are not very likely and put buyers will often find that they incur a large number of small losses and a small number of large gains. If the put is priced properly, the premium will be adequate compensation to transfer from the writer to the buyer profits from the stock's downward moves.

One of the more attractive strategies employing puts is called the *protective put*. This involves the purchase of a put accompanied by a long position in the stock. The profit from this strategy can be broken down into the profit from the stock, $S(T)$ −

FIGURE 20.7

Profits to Buyer of Protective Put Option

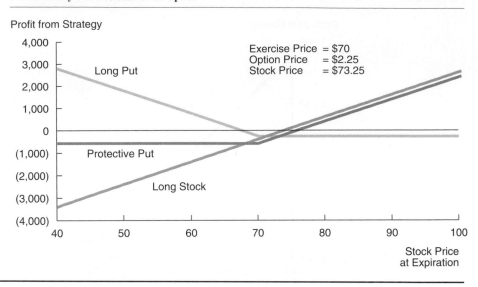

Profit from Strategy

Exercise Price = $70
Option Price   = $2.25
Stock Price   = $73.25

Long Put

Protective Put

Long Stock

Stock Price at Expiration

$S(t)$, plus the profit from the put, $Max[0, X - S(T)] - p(t)$. Thus, the profit from the protective put is

$$S(T) - S(t) + Max[0, X - S(T)] - p(t)$$

If the stock price ends up below the exercise price, the put profit is $X - S(T) - p(t)$. If the stock price ends up above the exercise price, the put profit is $-p(t)$. In both cases, the stock profit is $S(T) - S(t)$. Thus, the protective put profit will be $X - S(t) - p(t)$, if the stock ends up below the exercise price, and it will be, $S(T) - S(t) - p(t)$, if the stock ends up above the exercise price. This breakdown shows that, if the stock price ends up below the exercise price, the investor simply uses the put to sell the stock for the exercise price. Thus, the actual stock price, $S(T)$, does not matter as long as it is below the exercise price. If the stock price is above the exercise price, the put simply expires, not having been used, and the profit of the stock buyer is reduced by the premium paid on the put.

Figure 20.7 illustrates the profits to the protective put holder, overlayed with the profits from the long stock position and the long put position. Notice that the protective put is a lot like a long call. In fact, it is sometimes referred to as a *synthetic call* because the holder of the protective put has limited losses and unlimited gains.

The protective put is also a classic example of how to insure a stock position. The holder of the stock can be viewed as someone holding an asset at risk of losing value. Some investors might be interested in purchasing insurance that would limit the losses on the asset. The put serves as this insurance. By paying the premium up front, the insurer (the put writer) promises to absorb all stock price decreases below the exercise price. If the stock price rises, the put expires worthless, which is equivalent to an insurance policy expiring without having had a claim. The concept of insurance on a

FIGURE 20.8   **Profits to Seller of Put Option**

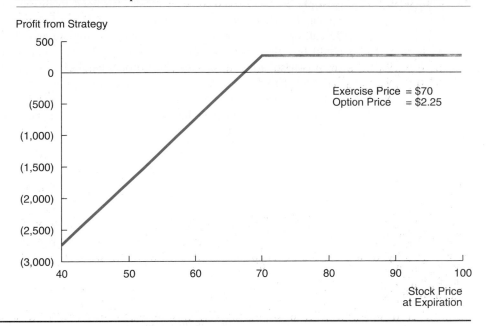

Profit from Strategy

Exercise Price = $70
Option Price   = $2.25

Stock Price
at Expiration

stock can be extended to insuring an entire portfolio. We will cover the subject of portfolio insurance in more detail in Chapter 23.

SELLING PUT
OPTIONS

The seller of the put option, like the seller of the call option, has a profit that can be expressed as simply −1 times the put option buyer's profit. The seller of the put is accepting the premium up front for his or her willingness to purchase the stock at expiration at the exercise price. The put seller's gains are limited, but his or her losses, like the put buyer's gains, are *not* unlimited but can be quite large if the bottom falls out of the stock.

Figure 20.8 illustrates the profits to the seller of the put option. Comparing Figure 20.8 with Figure 20.6, that shows the profits to the buyer of the put, we can see that these two figures are mirror images of each other.

SPREADS

Now let us consider some strategies that combine options with different characteristics. A transaction that combines buying and selling an option is referred to as a *spread*. The purpose is to reduce the risk of a long or short position in the option of a stock.

Buying an option with one exercise price and selling another, identical in all respects except a different exercise price, is called a *money, strike,* or *vertical spread.* Buying an option with one expiration date and selling one with another expiration date is called a *time, calendar,* or *horizontal spread.* Here we will use the terms *money* and *time spreads.* The latter are among the more sophisticated strategies, because they require a better understanding of how option values decrease through time. We will explore only money spreads in this book.

To distinguish our exercise prices, let us designate them as X_1 and X_2. For our example, $X_1 = 70$ and $X_2 = 75$. We also need to distinguish their premiums as $c_1(t)$ and $c_2(t)$, which are 6.125 and 3.5, respectively. Suppose you wanted to sell the 75 call option but are concerned about the unlimited risk. To protect yourself, you could buy the stock *or* you could buy the 70 call. This combination transaction is, of course, a money spread. Your profits would be the profit from *buying* the 70 call, $Max[0,S(T) - X_1] - c_1(t)$, and the profit from selling the 75 call, $-Max[0,S(T) - X_2] + c_2(t)$. The overall profit must be evaluated by considering that the stock price could end up below X_1, at or between X_1 and X_2, or above X_2. Thus, the profit from the money spread will be

If $S(T) < X_1$:
$$-c_1(t) \qquad \text{from the long call}$$
$$+c_2(t) \qquad \text{from the short call}$$

If $X_1 \leq S(T) \leq X_2$:
$$S(T) - X_1 - c_1(t) \qquad \text{from the long call}$$
$$+c_2(t) \qquad \text{from the short call}$$

If $S(T) > X_2$:
$$S(T) - X_1 - c_1(t) \qquad \text{from the long call}$$
$$-S(T) + X_2 + c_2(t) \qquad \text{from the short call}$$
$$= X_2 - X_1 - c_1(t) + c_2(t)$$

Figure 20.9 illustrates the profits to the buyer of the call money spread. Suppose the stock price ends up at $80. Then both calls are in-the-money, and from the above formulas, the spread will generate a profit of $5 - $6.125 + $3.5 = $2.375 per option or $237.50 overall. This will be the profit for any stock price above the higher exercise price. What is happening in effect is the following: the investor exercises the long call, buying the stock for X_1 dollars, and sells the stock for X_2 dollars by delivering it in fulfillment of the exercise of the short call. From the $5 gained off of the stock, we must deduct the $6.125 - $3.5 = $2.625 paid for the spread, which is the excess of the long call's price paid over the short call's price received. If we assume the stock price at expiration is $74, the long call is exercised for a value of $4. From this you must subtract the $2.625 paid for the spread, leaving a total of $1.375, or $137.50. If we assume the stock price ends up at $65, both calls are out-of-the-money, and the profit is simply a loss of $262.50, which is the price paid for the spread.

Obviously the call money spread limits losses and gains. This kind of spread is referred to as a *bull spread* because it makes money in a bull market. A *bear spread* is often constructed using puts. To do this, you buy the 75 put and sell the 70 put (note that in the bear spread you are buying the higher exercise price put, whereas in the bull spread you are buying the lower exercise price call). The profit from the bear spread is the profit from buying the 75 put, $Max[0,X_2 - S(T)] - p_2(t)$ plus the profit from selling the 70 put, $-Max[0,X_1 - S(T)] + p_1(t)$. This can be broken down into the following cases:

FIGURE 20.9   **Profits to Buyer of Call Money Spread**

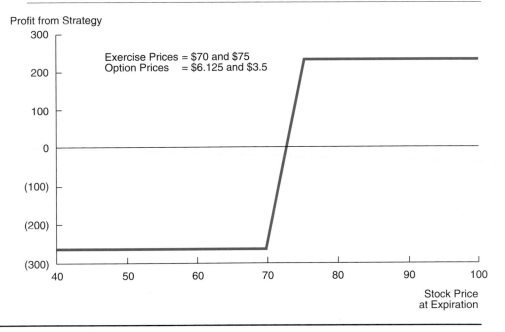

If $S(T) < X_1$:

$-X_1 + S(T) + p_1(t)$	from the short put
$X_2 - S(T) - p_2(t)$	from the long put
$= X_2 - X_1 + p_1(t) - p_2(t)$	

If $X_1 \leq S(T) \leq X_2$:

$p_1(t)$	from the short put
$X_2 - S(T) - p_2(t)$	from the long put

If $S(T) > X_2$:

$+ p_1(t)$	from the short put
$- p_2(t)$	from the long put

Figure 20.10 illustrates the profits from the put money spread. As shown, because it makes money in a bear market, it is called a bear spread. If the stock price ends up at $80, both puts expire out-of-the-money, and the profit is the cost of the spread, which is equal to: $4.75, the premium paid for the long put, minus $2.25, the premium received for the short put, which indicates a total cost of $2.50, or $250 overall. If the stock price ends up at $74, the long put is exercised and generates a profit of $1 minus the cost of the spread, $2.50, or −$1.50. If the stock price ends up at $60, both puts are exercised. In that case, the investor buys the stock for $70 using the short put and sells it for $75 using the long put. Subtracting the cost of the spread of $2.50 leaves a profit

FIGURE 20.10   **Profits to Buyer of Put Money Spread**

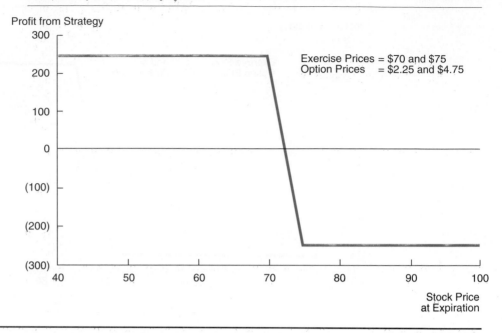

Profit from Strategy

Exercise Prices = $70 and $75
Option Prices   = $2.25 and $4.75

Stock Price
at Expiration

of $2.50, or $250 overall. This is the maximum profit and is achieved if the stock price at expiration is below $70.[8]

VALUATION

In Chapter 9, we discussed the basic principles of valuing options. We learned that European call and put prices must conform to rules that establish minimum and maximum prices. In addition, option prices must be aligned by put-call parity. We also saw that in a simple world in which the stock price can take on only two values when the option expires, we can easily determine the price of the option.

For demonstration purposes, if we divide the option's life into two periods, Figure 20.11 shows what can happen to the stock price (S) and the call option price (C) with this scenario. The stock price (and option price) can go up twice to $S++$, go down twice to $S--$, go up and then down to $S+-$, or go down and then up to $S-+$. The latter two situations lead to identical final prices because the only thing that matters for determining the option price is the stock price at expiration, so how the stock got to $S+-$ or $S-+$ is irrelevant. This property of European options, called *path independency*, is useful because it reduces the four outcomes to three. Unfortunately, for some types of options, including certain American options, the outcomes are *path dependent* which complicates the pricing problem.

---

[8]In this problem the maximum and minimum payoffs are symmetric at +$250 and −$250. This occurs because the cost of the spread is exactly half the spread. However, this is only a special case, and you should not expect the maximum and minimum payoffs from either bull or bear spreads to always be symmetric.

FIGURE 20.11   **Two-Period, Two-State Stock Price Process**

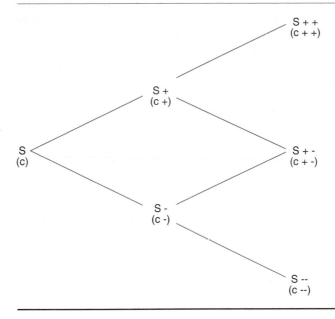

Suppose we consider dividing the option's life into an increasing number of periods. We will need to redefine the up and down returns and the risk-free interest rate discussed in Chapter 9, because the model requires that these be expressed as the per period up and down move and the prevailing risk-free interest rate. Increasing the number of periods will increase the number of outcomes at expiration until eventually we will approximate the real world in which there are an infinite number of outcomes when the option expires. When we have added enough periods, we will be able to calculate the price of the option under realistic conditions. The large number of calculations will necessitate the use of a computer—unless a shortcut can be found. Fortunately, that shortcut was provided by the Black-Scholes option pricing model.

THE BLACK-SCHOLES OPTION PRICING MODEL

Black and Scholes developed a realistic formula for the price of an option in 1973, the same year the CBOE was created.[9] In contrast to the two-state model, which was not discovered until several years later, their model is developed in continuous time. This means that there are an infinite number of periods and trading can occur at all times. The two-state model is a discrete-time model where trading can occur only at specific points in time. However, with a sufficient number of periods, a discrete model approximates a continuous model.

Black and Scholes used some rather sophisticated mathematics to derive their model, but the basic intuition is fairly simple. They reasoned that an investor who holds a stock and sells a call option on the stock gains on the stock and loses on the call when

---

[9]Fischer Black and Myron S. Scholes, "The Pricing of Options and Corporate Liabilities," *Journal of Political Economy* 81, no. 2 (May-June 1973): 637–654.

the stock price rises, and loses on the stock and gains on the call when the stock price declines. A certain number of call options is required so that the option position offsets the stock position. If the proper ratio of calls to stock could be found, they argued that the overall portfolio should earn the risk-free rate. This reasoning is what we used to develop the binomial model. Black and Scholes found the proper number of calls and were then able to solve for the call price. Their formula for the price of a call at time t is

$$c(t) = S(t)N(d_1) - Xe^{-r(T-t)}N(d_2) \tag{20.1}$$

where:

$$d_1 = \frac{\ln(S(t)/X) + (r + (\sigma^2/2))(T - t)}{\sigma\sqrt{(T - t)}}$$
$$d_2 = d_1 - \sigma\sqrt{(T - t)}$$

The expression ln is the natural logarithm, and $N(d_1)$ and $N(d_2)$ are the cumulative normal probabilities for values of d_1 and d_2 as computed in the above formulas. Three of the other terms, S, X, and $T - t$ are already known to us as the stock price, exercise price, and time to expiration in years. The term r is the continuously compounded risk-free rate. The final term, σ, is the standard deviation of the continuously compounded return on the stock over the life of the option. The Black-Scholes model for pricing puts is developed by using put-call parity and recognizing that the present value of the exercise price must now be expressed using continuous discounting:

$$p(t) = Xe^{-r(T-t)}[1 - N(d_2)] - S(t)[1 - N(d_1)] \tag{20.2}$$

IMPLEMENTING THE MODEL

The purpose of using the model is to determine the option's theoretically correct price. If the market price of the option is higher than the option price derived from the model, the option is overvalued. An overvalued call option can be sold and hedged with a long position in the stock to earn a return better than the risk-free rate. If the option were undervalued, it could be bought and hedged with a short position in the stock to earn a return better than the risk-free rate.

Although the formula appears quite complex, almost all of the required inputs are obtainable, and the calculations, though lengthy, are easily done. The stock price and exercise price are, of course, known. The time to expiration is found by simply counting the number of days until expiration and dividing this by 365. Thus, an option with 44 days to go would have $T - t = 44/365 = .1205$. The risk-free rate should correspond to a T-bill rate, which is obtainable from *The Wall Street Journal,* for a maturity that closely matches the option's life. This rate must be expressed as a continuously compounded rate, meaning that the T-bill rate of, say, 5.12 percent, would be expressed as $\ln(1.0512) = .05$.

The cumulative normal probability is found using the Table in Appendix D. Suppose the value of d_1 is 1.25. Then you look down the first column until you find 1.2. Then you move over to the row with 0.05 at the top. The probability is .8943. This is the probability that a standard normal variable will have a value of 1.25 or less. Suppose d_1 is a negative value such as -2.17. Then you simply convert it to a positive 2.17 and find the normal probability for $+2.17$, which is .9850. Then you subtract this value from 1.0, giving .0150. The same procedure is followed for d_2.

The only variable that is not directly observable is the standard deviation, often called the *volatility,* of the continuously compounded return on the stock over the life of the option. This value can be estimated using past returns on the stock, but what you really want is the future volatility of the stock which is quite naturally unknown. Of course, if everyone agreed on the expected volatility, then everyone would agree on the option price. The fact is, it is differences of opinion about the expected volatility that create an incentive for trading options. Although it is difficult to see in the formula, an increase in the volatility will increase the option price. This result should be intuitive, given our treatment of the binomial model in Chapter 9 and the simple fact that larger positive stock price moves and larger negative stock price moves help the option holder without hurting him or her.

An alternative approach used by some traders is to find the volatility that, when plugged into the Black-Scholes formula, produces the actual market price of the option. This volatility is called the *implied volatility.* It says that this is the volatility of the stock that the options market believes is correct. However, it is implicitly assuming that the market price of the option is the theoretically correct price. The implied volatility is viewed by some option traders as an intuitive measure of the option's worth. For example, they might contend that the implied volatility of, say, 25 percent, seems too high, based upon their feelings about the stock's normal volatility. As a result, they expect the option price to fall as the volatility falls.[10]

Notably, volatility is the only variable that option traders are likely to disagree on. In addition, the value of the option is quite sensitive to the volatility estimate. Also, as we saw in the two-state model, the expected return on the stock does not enter into the formula since the stock's expected return is implied by its price, which does appear in the formula.

Table 20.5 illustrates the calculation of the option value for a stock price of \$73.25, an exercise price of \$70, a risk-free rate of 6.5 percent, a time to expiration of 44 days $(T - t = .1205)$, and a volatility of .4. The value of d_1 is found to be .45 and d_2 is .31. The normal probabilities are .6736 for d_1 and .6217 for d_2. Using these values in the formula for the call price in Equation 20.1 gives a value of 6.16.

For puts, the formula utilizes the same variables but in a different way. First we need $1 - N(d_1)$, which is .3264, and $1 - N(d_2)$, which is .3783. Again, using these values in Equation 20.2, the put price is found to be 2.37.

Thus, we see that the five variables that affect an option's price are the stock price, the exercise price, the risk-free rate, the time to expiration, and the expected volatility of the underlying stock. By changing the values of these variables, we can determine the direction of the effect, which is summarized below.

---

[10]Studies of the calculation and use of implied volatility are Henry A. Latané and Richard J. Rendleman, Jr., "Standard Deviations of Stock Price Ratios Implied in Option Prices," *The Journal of Finance* 31, no. 2 (May 1976): 369–381; and Richard Schmalensee and Robert R. Trippi, "Common Stock Volatility Expectations Implied by Option Premia," *The Journal of Finance* 33, no. 1 (March 1978): 129–147.

TABLE 20.5

Calculation of Black-Scholes Option Values

$S(t) = 73.25$, $X = 70$, $r = .065$, $T = 44/365 = .1205$, $\sigma = .4$

$$c(t) = S(t)N(d_1) - Xe^{-r(T-t)}N(d_2)$$
$$p(t) = Xe^{-r(T-t)}(1 - N(d_2)) - S(t)(1 - N(d_1))$$
$$d_1 = \frac{\ln(S(t)/X) + (r + (\sigma^2/2))(T-t)}{\sigma\sqrt{(T-t)}}$$
$$d_2 = d_1 - \sigma\sqrt{(T-t)}$$
$$N(\cdot) = \text{cumulative normal probability}$$

Calls

$$d_1 = \frac{\ln(73.25/70) + (.065 + ((.4)^2/2))(.1205)}{.4\sqrt{.1205}}$$
$$= \frac{.0454 + .0175}{.1389} = .45$$

$N(.45) = .6736$
$$d_2 = .45 - .4\sqrt{.1205} = .31$$
$N(.31) = (.6217)$
$$c(t) = 73.25(.6736) - 70e^{-.065(.1205)}(.6217) = 6.16$$

Puts

$$1 - N(.45) = 1 - .6736 = .3264$$
$$1 - N(.31) = 1 - .6217 = .3783$$
$$p(t) = 70e^{-.065(.1205)}(.3783) - 73.25(.3264) = 2.37$$

	Will cause a higher/lower	
A higher	**call price**	**put price**
stock price	higher	lower
exercise price	lower	higher
risk-free rate	higher	lower
time to expiration	higher	higher or lower
volatility	higher	higher

The stock price effect should be obvious; a higher stock price is good for call holders and bad for put holders. The exercise price effect should also be obvious: a call with a higher exercise price is less likely to end up in-the-money, so the call price would be lower; a put with a higher exercise price is more likely to end up in-the-money, so the put price would be higher. The risk-free rate effect is somewhat difficult to see. Call holders do not have to pay the exercise price until expiration. When interest rates are higher, they earn more interest on the money set aside to pay the exercise price. Put holders, however, have to wait until expiration to receive the exercise price; when interest rates are higher, they are losing interest by waiting to receive the exercise price. A longer time to expiration benefits a call holder, because the call has more time to

FIGURE 20.12   **Call Prices Relative to Stock Prices**

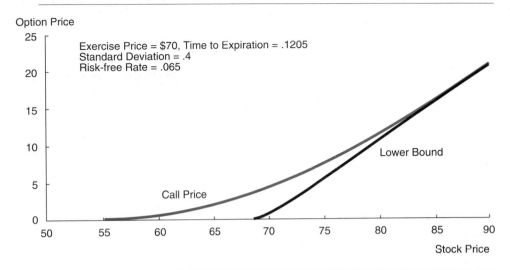

move in-the-money. This is also true for a put holder, but this effect can be offset by the fact that the put holder has to wait longer to receive the exercise price. The Black-Scholes model can be used, however, to determine what combination of inputs will cause the put price to be higher or lower for a longer time to expiration. Finally, both calls and puts are worth more when the stock is expected to be more volatile. Both options have the potential for greater gains due to the volatility, but benefit from limited losses.

Now that we have an option pricing model that should give us accurate prices for a variety of inputs, we can make some calculations of how the option price varies with the stock price. Figure 20.12 presents the call prices for the 70 call for a wide range of stock prices. Also plotted is the lower bound of the call price. Recall from Chapter 9 that the lower bound is the maximum of either zero or the stock price minus the present value of the exercise price. Figure 20.13 presents a comparable graph for put options. The lower bound of the put price is the maximum of zero or the present value of the exercise price minus the stock price. Notice how the option prices, as given by the model, conform to the lower-bound rules. They never fall below the lower bound and are usually above them.

AMERICAN
OPTION PRICING

All the results we have so far developed are for European calls. Although the intuition for European calls is much simpler than for American calls, most actual options are American options. Beginning with our understanding of the principles of European option pricing, we can introduce some ways in which American options are different. Initially we continue to assume no dividends on the stock but drop that assumption later. We will use an upper case C and P for the price of an American call and put. If it is not already obvious, let us state that *an American call is worth at least as much as a European call.* This is because a European call permits exercise only on the

FIGURE 20.13   **Put Prices Relative to Stock Prices**

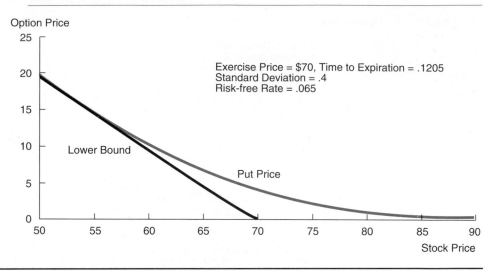

expiration day, while an American call likewise permits exercise on the expiration day and, if desired, any time prior.

First, an American option can be exercised at any time. That means that its price at any time must be worth at least its value if it is exercised. For calls, this means that

$$C(t) \geq Max(0, S(t) - X)$$

If the exercise price were $60, the stock price were $62, and the price of the call option were $1.50, an investor could buy the call and immediately exercise it. This would generate an immediate risk-free profit of $0.50. With all investors doing this, the price of the call would have to rise to at least $2.

The value $Max(0, S(t) - X)$ is called the *intrinsic value*. The remainder of the call price is called the *time value*. The intrinsic value is what could be earned if the call were exercised. The time value is what investors are willing to pay for the right to profit from later stock price increases.

The consequences of this new minimum value, however, are insignificant to the price of the call. The European call lower bound is $Max[0, S(t) - X(1 + r)^{-(T-t)}]$, where r is the discrete risk-free rate. Except at expiration, this European call lower bound value is always greater than $Max[0, S(t) - X]$. The American call price, thus, must adhere to the European lower bound so we can essentially ignore, for now, the American lower bound. Thus,

$$C(t) \geq Max[0, S(t) - X(1 + r)^{-r(T-t)}]$$

Of course at expiration, the European lower bound converges to the intrinsic value, and the American and European call prices will be equal to each other and must equal the intrinsic value.

For American puts, the intrinsic value is $Max[0, X - S(t)]$. Assume the stock price is $53 and the exercise price is $55. If the put is selling for $1.50, an investor can buy the put and the stock and exercise the put, netting a risk-free gain of $0.50. With everyone doing this, the put price must rise to at least $2. Thus, we can say that

$$P(t) \geq Max[0, X - S(t)]$$

In contrast to American puts, the lower bound of the European put, $Max[0, X(1 + r)^{-r(T-t)} - S(t)]$, does *not* dominate the intrinsic value as a minimum. At expiration, the European lower bound converges to the intrinsic value, and the American and European put prices must be equal to each other and must equal the intrinsic value. Prior to expiration, the American put price will contain time value, which is the price the buyer of the put is willing to pay to profit from future stock price decreases.

If an American call were exercised early, the call holder would receive the equivalent of $S(t) - X$. However, as we stated above, the call must sell for at least $S - X(1 + r)^{-r(T-t)}$. This always exceeds the intrinsic value, except at expiration. Thus, an American call will never be exercised early. This is a convenient result, for it permits us to use the Black-Scholes model to price it. An American put, however, can be worth more if exercised. This point can be somewhat difficult to see, but the following simple case should help you to understand the logic: Suppose you own an American put and the firm on whose stock the put is written goes bankrupt. If you hold the put option to expiration, you will receive X dollars for the worthless stock. However, because the option is American, you can exercise it and collect the X dollars today. In general, bankruptcy is not required to induce early exercise of American puts, but the specific conditions that do induce early exercise are complex to identify and are beyond the scope of this book. The point is, we need models more sophisticated than the Black-Scholes model to price American puts.

One useful result regarding American puts that does not always hold for European puts is the fact that a longer time to expiration will always result in a higher American put price. For European puts, the longer time to expiration meant waiting longer to receive the exercise price. For American puts, there is no required waiting period; they can be exercised at any time.

The results thus far all assume that the stock pays no dividends. Although dividends can greatly complicate the pricing of options, we will discuss only their most important implications. Suppose you own an American call where the stock is at $82 and the exercise price is $80. Thus, the intrinsic value of the call option is $2. There is some (unspecified) amount of time value in the call option's price as well. If we assume the stock were about to go ex-dividend we know the stock price will decline by approximately the amount of the dividend. Suppose the dividend is $1.50. By not exercising, you would lose a portion of the call's value resulting from the decline in the stock's price. By exercising, you would throw away the time value, but you would capture the exercise value. If what you throw away is less than what you save, you would be advised to exercise. Thus, with high dividends and low time value (resulting from little time left and/or the call being deep in-the-money), early exercise of American calls would likely occur. For puts, dividends make early exercise less likely. If early exercise occurs at all, it will occur immediately after the stock price decline when the stock goes ex-dividend.

Pricing European options when the stocks pay dividends is fairly straightforward. You simply replace the stock price with the stock price minus the present value of the dividends. Pricing American options on stocks with dividends is far more complex and is beyond the scope of this book.

INVESTOR
EXPERIENCE
WITH OPTIONS

Several studies examined returns from option trading compared to those from trading stocks. Dawson considered some of the problems related to continuous option writing and concluded that both return and risk are reduced.[11] Grube, Panton, and Terrell likewise noted a reduction in the rates of return and variability from investing in covered call options, and also recognized the impact of such investment on turnover and transaction costs.[12] Trennepohl and Dukes examined the performance of several call buying and writing strategies,[13] and Yates and Kopprasch examined the performance of a continuous covered writing strategy.[14] They concluded that writing covered calls is the best overall strategy. Gombola, Roenfeldt, and Cooley examined the performance of option spreading strategies and found that transaction costs are a very heavy burden in spread trading.[15]

Merton, Scholes, and Gladstein reported on the results of a simulation of trading options on 130 stocks as well as a subset consisting of the 30 stocks in the Dow Jones Industrial Average.[16] Their findings generally confirmed that covered call writing was superior to buying calls in markets in which the stock price moved slowly. Their second study compared protective put buying with put writing. They found that protective put buying was a good strategy when put premiums were too low to compensate for the risk the writer is assuming. These results are consistent with expectations.

SUMMARY

Options have increased in popularity, particularly since the development of organized options markets in 1973. Options on individual stocks and options on stock indexes offer a wide range of investment alternatives. Basic option trading strategies include call buying, call writing, put buying, and put writing. Investors desiring to use options to reduce the risk of holding stocks can write covered calls or buy protective puts. In addition, option traders can use spreads, which involve trading options with similar but slightly different characteristics. Although we have covered a number of strategies here, there are many more that involve different combinations of puts, calls, and stock. The

---

[11]Frederic S. Dawson, "Risks and Returns in Continuous Option Writing," *Journal of Portfolio Management* 5, no. 2 (Winter 1979): 58–63.

[12]R. Corwin Grube, Don B. Panton, and J. Michael Terrell, "Risks and Rewards in Covered Call Positions," *Journal of Portfolio Management* 5, no. 2 (Winter 1979): 64–68.

[13]Gary L. Trennepohl and William P. Dukes, "Return and Risk from Listed Option Investments," *Journal of Financial Research* 2, no. 1 (Spring 1979): 37–49.

[14]James W. Yates, Jr., and Robert W. Kopprasch, Jr., "Writing Covered Call Options: Profits and Risks," *Journal of Portfolio Management* 7, no. 1 (Fall 1980): 74–80.

[15]Michael J. Gombola, Rodney L. Roenfeldt, and Philip L. Cooley, "Spreading Strategies in CBOE Options: Evidence on Market Performance," *Journal of Financial Research* 1, no. 1 (Winter 1978): 35–44.

[16]Robert C. Merton, Myron S. Scholes, and Mathew L. Gladstein, "The Returns and Risks of Alternative Call-Option Portfolio Investment Strategies," *Journal of Business* 51 (April 1978): 183–242; and Robert C. Merton, Myron S. Scholes, and Mathew L. Gladstein, "The Returns and Risks of Alternative Put-Option Portfolio Investment Strategies," *Journal of Business* 55 (January 1982): 1–55.

various option strategies produce profit possibilities that were not available from simply trading stocks alone.

The two-state model can be expanded to accommodate a rather large number of periods. When that is done, the model will replicate reality, where there are an infinite number of possible stock prices at expiration. In that case, one can use the Black-Scholes option pricing model, which provides the correct price for European calls and puts on stocks that do not pay dividends. When there are no dividends, American calls will never be exercised early and, thus, will be identical to European calls so the Black-Scholes model can be used to price American calls. When there are dividends, however, an American call might be exercised early and a more sophisticated model is required. For European puts, the Black-Scholes model should give the correct price. For American puts, a far more complex model is required. When there are dividends but the options are still European, the Black-Scholes model with a slight adjustment is appropriate.

QUESTIONS

1. Describe some of the advantages and disadvantages of exchange-traded options in contrast to over-the-counter options.

2. What is the responsibility of the CBOE's market maker? How does it differ from the specialist on the NYSE?

3. Explain how a cash settled call option is exercised, and contrast it with the exercise of a call requiring delivery of a stock.

4. What are the two limitations that you should be aware of when using option prices from *The Wall Street Journal*?

5. What are the advantages and disadvantages of buying a call option over buying the stock, given that you have a strong bullish feeling about the stock?

6. Identify, discuss, and compare two strategies for protecting a long position in a stock.

7. Under what conditions would you use a vertical spread?

8. Name the five variables that affect a call option's price and indicate the direction of the effect. Identify and discuss what you feel is the most critical variable.

9. How are American options different from European options in terms of their lower bounds? Assume no dividends.

10. How do dividends affect call option prices? Put option prices?

PROBLEMS

1. Assume you are bullish on the outlook for the stock market. Look up a 1- to 3-month call option that is approximately at-the-money in *The Wall Street Journal.* Assume the stock increases by 15 percent by the option's expiration. Indicate approximately what will happen to your option, and compute the percentage return on the option purchased.

2. Select a stock option on the CBOE and discuss how you would write a vertical spread assuming you were bullish on the stock.
   a. Describe what will happen if the stock price increases by 20 percent by the option's expiration.
   b. Describe what will happen if the stock price declines by 20 percent by the option's expiration.

3. Select a stock option on the AMEX and discuss how you would enter into a vertical spread assuming you were bearish on the stock.

   a. Describe what will happen if the stock price increases by 25 percent by the option's expiration.
   b. Describe what will happen if the stock price declines by 30 percent by the option's expiration.

4. Assume that you are generally bearish on common stocks and so you buy an S&P 100 put with 3 months to go until expiration. The exercise price is 400 and the index is at 394.05. The put costs 12¾. At expiration the S&P 100 index is at 392.55. What is your profit and rate of return?

5. Use the Black-Scholes model to calculate the theoretical value of the two options below that expire in 90 days. The exercise price is $45 and the stock price is $50. The standard deviation is .6 and the continuously compounded risk-free rate is 6 percent.
   a. A call
   b. A put

6. Ted Westfall was considering the purchase of 100 shares of Stopgap Corporation common stock selling at 32⅜ per share on the last day in October. As an alternative, Len Griffen, Ted's neighbor, suggested that Ted consider a Stopgap option instead. Together they examined the following information that was obtained from their broker.

Exercise Price	Calls	Puts
30	6	2
35	$3\frac{1}{2}$	$4\frac{3}{4}$

   What are Ted's profits and rates of return if he makes the following purchases and subsequently closes his position at expiration given the stock prices as indicated below?
   a. A call with an exercise price of 30. The stock ends up at $41\frac{7}{8}$.
   b. A call with an exercise price of 35. The stock ends up at 33.
   c. A put with an exercise price of 30. The stock ends up at 37.
   d. A put with an exercise price of 35. The stock ends up at 29.

7. Bill Rogers, a colleague of Ted's (see Problem 6) says that he has been making money writing covered calls, whereas Sandy Benson tells Ted that she has been using protective puts to insure her stock positions against a loss. Ted finds these possibilities interesting and wants to try them out. Calculate his profits and returns under the same assumptions as in Problem 6 for
   a. A covered call with exercise price of 30. The stock ends up at $41\frac{7}{8}$.
   b. A covered call with exercise price of 35. The stock ends up at 33.
   c. A protective put with exercise price of 30. The stock ends up at 37.
   d. A protective put with exercise price of 35. The stock ends up at 29.

8. Judy Quackenbush is considering the following alternatives for investing in Swirl Industries, which is now selling for $23 per share:
   (1) Buy 100 shares for cash
   (2) Buy 100 shares on 60 percent margin
   (3) Buy a 6-month call option with an exercise price of $20 for $600

   What are the profits and rates of return for each plan if
   a. The stock reaches $35 in 6 months and all transactions are closed out.
   b. The stock falls to $19 in 6 months and all transactions are closed out.

9. You are given the following information on the prices of Apple Computer options that have 50 days to go until expiration. The stock is at $47\frac{1}{4}$ and the risk-free rate is 3.15 percent.

Exercise Price	Calls	Puts
45	$4\frac{1}{8}$	$1\frac{5}{8}$
50	$1\frac{1}{2}$	$4\frac{1}{4}$

    a. Assuming the options are European, calculate the lower bounds of each option.

    b. How would your answer differ if the options were American?

REFERENCES

Black, Fischer, and Myron S. Scholes. "The Pricing of Options and Corporate Liabilities." *Journal of Political Economy* 81, no. 2 (May-June 1973).

Bookstaber, Richard. *Option Pricing and Strategies in Investing* (New York: Addison-Wesley, 1986).

Chance, Don M. *An Introduction to Options and Futures.* 2d ed. Hinsdale, Ill.: Dryden, 1992.

Cox, John C., and Mark Rubinstein. *Options Markets.* Englewood Cliffs, N.J.: Prentice-Hall, 1985.

Dawson, Frederic S. "Risks and Returns in Continuous Option Writing." *Journal of Portfolio Management* 5, no. 2 (Winter 1979).

Gastineau, Gary L. *The Options Manual.* 3d ed. New York: McGraw-Hill, 1988.

Gombola, Michael J., Rodney L. Roenfeldt, and Philip L. Cooley. "Spreading Strategies in CBOE Options: Evidence on Market Performance." *Journal of Financial Research* 1, no. 1 (Winter 1978).

Grube, R. Corwin, Don B. Panton, and J. Michael Terrell. "Risks and Rewards in Covered Call Positions." *Journal of Portfolio Management* 5, no. 2 (Winter 1979).

Hull, John. *Options, Futures and Other Derivative Instruments.* 2d ed. Englewood Cliffs, N.J.: Prentice-Hall, 1993.

Kolb, Robert W. *Understanding Futures Markets.* 3rd ed. Miami, FL.: Kolb Publishing, 1991.

Latané, Henry A., and Richard J. Rendleman, Jr. "Standard Deviations of Stock Price Ratios Implied in Option Prices." *The Journal of Finance* 31, no. 2 (May 1976).

Macbeth, J., and Larry J. Merville. "Tests of the Black-Scholes and Cox Call Option Valuation Models," *Journal of Finance* 35, no. 2 (May 1980).

Merton, Robert C., Myron S. Scholes, and Mathew L. Gladstein. "The Returns and Risks of Alternative Call-Option Portfolio Investment Strategies." *Journal of Business* 51 (April 1978).

Merton, Robert C., Myron S. Scholes, and Mathew L. Gladstein. "The Returns and Risks of Alternative Put-Option Portfolio Investment Strategies." *Journal of Business* 55 (January 1982).

Rendleman, Richard J., Jr. "Optimal Long-Run Option Investment Strategies." *Financial Management* 10, no. 1 (Spring 1981).

Ritchken, Peter. *Options: Theory, Strategy, and Applications,* Glenview, Ill.: Scott, Foresman, 1988.

Schmalensee, Richard, and Robert R. Trippi. "Common Stock Volatility Expectations Implied by Option Premia." *The Journal of Finance* 33, no. 1 (March 1978).

Slivka, Ronald T. "Risk and Return for Option Investment Strategies," *Financial Analysts Journal* 36, no. 35 (September-October 1980).

Smith, Clifford W., Jr. "Option Pricing: A Review." *Journal of Financial Economics* 3, no. 1, 2 (January-March 1976).

Stoll, Hans R., and Robert E. Whaley. *Futures and Options: Theory and Application.* Cincinnati: South-Western Publishing, 1993.

Trennepohl, Gary L., and William P. Dukes. "Return and Risk from Listed Option Investments." *Journal of Financial Research* 2, no. 1 (Spring 1979).

Yates, James W., Jr., and Robert W. Kopprasch, Jr. "Writing Covered Call Options: Profits and Risk." *Journal of Portfolio Management* 7, no. 1 (Fall 1980).

CHAPTER 21

WARRANTS AND CONVERTIBLE SECURITIES

In this chapter we will answer the following questions:

- How can the common stock of a firm be viewed as an option?
- How can a firm's bond be viewed as an option?
- Given the specification of a bond as an option, what are some factors that affect the yield spread for a risky bond?
- What is a warrant and how does it differ from a listed call option?
- What are the factors that determine the value of a warrant and how is this valuation related to the Black-Scholes option pricing model?
- What are some of the major sources of information on warrants?
- What are currency exchange warrants and how can they be used in global investing?
- What is a convertible security and what are the main characteristics of convertible bonds?
- What are the main advantages of a convertible bond to the issuing firm?
- What are the main advantages of a convertible bond to investors?
- How do you determine the value of a convertible bond that is a combination security?
- What is meant by the terms "conversion premium" and "payback period" and how do you compute these values?
- How does a firm go about forcing the conversion of a convertible bond?
- What are the unique characteristics of convertible preferred stock and what determines its value?
- What are the characteristics of some new hybrid securities such as SPINs, SIGNs, and securities linked to other assets such as oil?

The main focus of this chapter is the discussion and analysis of warrants and convertible securities. In order to properly understand these instruments it is important to recognize that they have many of the same characteristics and valuation properties of call options. Therefore, the first section contains a discussion of how common stock and straight bonds can be viewed as option contracts. Section two discusses the characteristics of warrants including how they differ from the exchange traded call options considered in Chapter 20. We also consider the valuation of warrants and the relation-

TABLE 21.1

Payoffs to Stockholders and Bondholders Given the Value of Assets at Expiration

	$V(T) \leq M$	$V(T) > M$
Bondholders receive	$V(T)$	M
Stockholders receive	0	$V(T) - M$
Total payoffs to security holders	$V(T)$	$V(T)$

ship of warrant valuation to the Black-Scholes option pricing model. This section concludes with a discussion of newly developed warrants on currencies and on various non-U.S. stock price indexes. In section three the discussion shifts to a detailed consideration of convertible bonds including the advantages of these bonds to the issuer and the investor. We also consider the valuation of these combination bond-stock securities and some major valuation factors. Following a brief discussion of convertible preferred stock, the final section considers several new hybrid instruments that include securities where the payments are tied to various stock indexes or to commodity prices.

SIMPLE CORPORATE SECURITIES

In their original article on the option pricing model, Fischer Black and Myron Scholes suggested that their model can be used in a wide variety of situations.[1] One particularly useful one is the valuation of stocks and bonds. This concept was more fully developed by Robert C. Merton.[2]

STOCK AS AN OPTION

One of the remarkable features of modern option theory is its ability to explain many types of financial contracts that had previously been viewed in a totally different light. Shares of common stock for a firm with debt in its capital structure can be viewed as an option. For example, consider the following situation for a firm.

The firm has outstanding only one issue of zero coupon debt, which pays M dollars at its maturity date. The debt's maturity is $T - t$, which as in the previous chapter, is the notation for the maturity of an option. The debt has a market value today of $B(t)$ and the firm's equity is worth $S(t)$. Thus, the firm has assets worth $V(t) = B(t) + S(t)$. The debt is not risk-free. In fact, at the maturity date, the assets may have a value that is less than the face value of the debt, in which case the firm would default on the debt and simply turn the assets over to the bondholders. We will demonstrate that the stock is simply a call option written by the bondholders on the assets of the firm.

Table 21.1 illustrates the payoffs to the stockholders and bondholders for the two possible cases in which the firm either defaults or does not default. On the maturity date of the bond, the firm will owe M dollars to its bondholders. If the value of the assets, $V(T)$, is less than or equal to M, the firm defaults, and the bondholders simply receive what remains of the assets, $V(T)$. The stockholders get nothing. If the value of the assets exceeds M, the bondholders are paid what they are owed, M, and the stockholders receive the excess, $V(T) - M$.

---

[1]Fischer Black and Myron Scholes, "The Pricing of Options and Corporate Liabilities," *Journal of Political Economy* 81, no. 2 (May-June 1973): 637–659.

[2]Robert C. Merton, "On the Pricing of Corporate Debt: The Risk Structure of Interest Rates," *The Journal of Finance* 29, no. 2 (May 1974): 449–470.

The payoffs to the stockholders should resemble those of a call in which the underlying asset is the value of the firm, $V(t)$, the exercise price is M, the expiration is $T - t$. Of course, we know that the risk-free rate of interest, r, is also a factor in valuing the option, and so is the volatility of the underlying asset. If we define σ as the volatility of the assets, we can use the Black-Scholes model to value the stock as a call option.

$$S(t) = V(t)N(d_1) - Me^{-r(T-t)}N(d_2)$$
$$d_1 = \frac{\ln(V(t)/M) + [r + (\sigma^2/2)](T - t)}{\sigma\sqrt{T - t}}$$
$$d_2 = d_1 - \sigma\sqrt{T - t}$$

(21.1)

This is the same Black-Scholes option pricing formula with the notation changed slightly.

Now recall our put-call parity formula in which the call price was expressed as the put price plus the stock price minus the present value of the exercise price. Applying that to the current case, we have

$$S(t) = p(t) + V(t) - Me^{-r(T-t)}$$

(21.2)

This means that a share of stock can be viewed as a long position in both a put and in the assets, and includes the borrowing of M dollars at the risk-free rate. Thus, the stockholders own a put to sell the firm to the bondholders and this put represents the value of the stockholders' right to default. This means that the bondholders are put writers. Now let us consider how the bonds will be valued.

BONDS AS AN OPTION

By definition the bonds are worth $B(t) = V(t) - S(t)$. Because we have a formula (the Black-Scholes model) for the stock, we can substitute for $S(t)$ and obtain a value for $B(t)$. After some algebra, the final result is

$$B(t) = V(t) - S(t) = V(t)[1 - N(d_1)] + Me^{-r(T-t)}N(d_2)$$

(21.3)

Thus, given the value of the stock we can also calculate the value of the bonds. Another way of looking at the bonds is to simply substitute the put-call parity expression for the stock, $S(t)$, into the simple equation $B(t) = V(t) - S(t)$. This gives us

$$B(t) = Me^{-r(T-t)} - p(t)$$

(21.4)

Thus, the holders of this risky debt can be seen as having purchased risk-free debt with face value of M and having written a put on the firm's assets. The credit risk they face is a result of having written the put. In other words, the bondholders agree to give up their claim to M dollars at maturity and accept the value of the assets if that is lower. The right to default is a very valuable option to the stockholders. What you probably have previously referred to as the "limited liability of the stockholders" is, in fact, their right to "put" the firm to the bondholders.

Because the bond is a zero coupon bond, its value can be written as

$$B(t) = Me^{-i(T-t)}$$

(21.5)

FIGURE 21.1    **Value of Stock and Debt by Level of Assets**

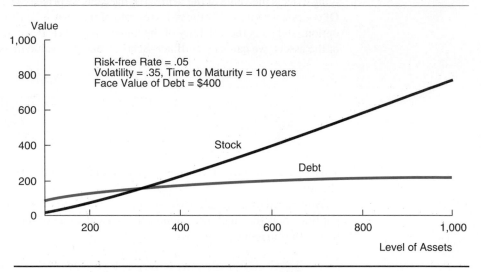

where i is the yield on the bond. Unlike a coupon bond, it is relatively easy to solve for this yield. It is simply

$$i = -\frac{\ln(B(t)/M)}{(T - t)} \tag{21.6}$$

In Chapters 14 and 15, we talked about the default risk of bonds. Now we have a model that explains default risk more thoroughly. Figure 21.1 illustrates how the value of the stock and the debt vary based on the level of assets. It is assumed that the firm has debt with a face value of $400 that is due in 10 years. The risk-free rate is .05, and the volatility of the assets is .35. Note how the value of the stock and the debt change as the assets are varied from $100 to $1,000. At an asset level of $100, the stock is nearly worthless and the debt is not worth much relative to its face value of $400. In fact, the stock is worth only $18.92, and the debt is worth $81.08. The yield on the debt, not shown here, is 15.96 percent. Although this firm is in serious trouble, because there are 10 years before maturity, there is still plenty of time for the firm to turn around. With higher asset values, the value of the debt increases rapidly because the probability of default drops very quickly but the value of the equity increases very slowly. At an asset value of around $400, the value of the debt rises very slowly and the value of the equity begins to increase rapidly. At an asset level of $1,000, the debt is worth $219.28 and the stock is worth $780.72. The debt is now yielding 6.01 percent.

In Chapter 15, we talked about bond yield spreads, which are the difference between the yield on the risky bond and the yield on a reference bond such as a Treasury security.

FIGURE 21.2 **Yield Spread Relative to Volatility**

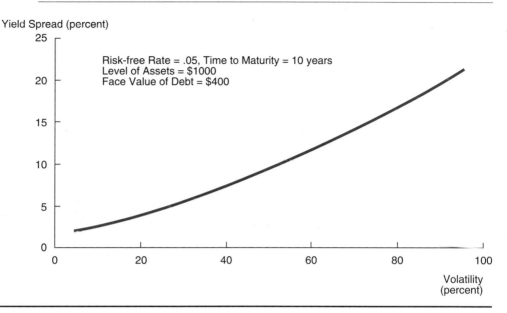

Yield Spread (percent)

Risk-free Rate = .05, Time to Maturity = 10 years
Level of Assets = $1000
Face Value of Debt = $400

Volatility (percent)

Alternatively, we can compute a similar yield spread in terms of the bond yield and the risk-free rate which will be directly related to the probability of default. There are several factors that increase the probability of default. One is the face amount of the debt because the more the firm owes, the higher the probability of default. Another is the volatility of asset values because the more volatile the assets, the greater the chance that the asset value will be below the face value of the debt at maturity. Figure 21.2 presents the yield spread for volatilities of from .05 to .95. As shown, greater volatility commands a greater premium on the part of the bondholders.

Two other variables that affect the yield spread are the size of the assets and the maturity of the debt. Figure 21.3 presents the yield spread relative to the maturity of the debt for two levels of the assets, $250 and $1,000. For assets of $250, the yield spread on very short-term debt is extremely high, well over 40 percent. For longer maturities, however, the spread is much lower because the longer maturity allows more time for the firm's assets to grow, thus reducing its chance of default. For an asset level of $1,000 the likelihood of default is very low for short-term maturities and rises slowly for longer-term securities. The increase in default risk for longer-term securities reflects the fact that the longer term works against the bondholders because it increases the probability that the value of the assets will decline prior to the maturity date.

Unfortunately, few firms have such simple capital structures so the model is not empirically testable. However, it helps explain the characteristics of yield spreads and bond prices. Also it provides intuition about the nature of stockholder and bondholder

FIGURE 21.3   **Yield Spread Relative to Maturity**

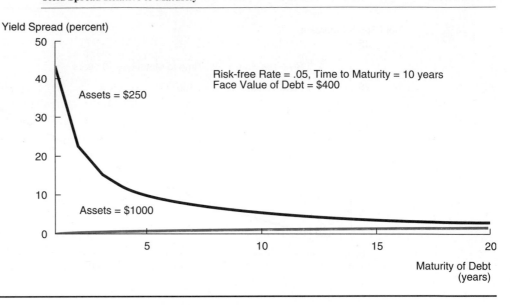

claims and sheds light on the value of the stockholders' right to default which provides their limited liability. Moreover, the model can be used to explain more complex capital structures such as explaining how senior and subordinated debt are also options.[3] Also, since most firms do not issue zero coupon bonds, Geske has shown how coupon bonds can be valued using this framework.[4] The insight gained from looking at corporate securities in this options framework increase our ability to think logically and consistently when analyzing other securities including warrants and convertible securities, which are the subjects of the following sections.

WARRANTS   A *warrant* is an option to buy a stated number of shares of common stock at a specified price at any time during the life of the warrant. Although this definition is quite similar to the description of a call option, there are several important differences. First, when originally issued, the life of a warrant is usually much longer than that of a call option. Although the listed options markets have recently introduced long-term options, the typical exchange-traded call option has a term to expiration that ranges from 3 to 9 months. In contrast, a warrant generally has an original term to maturity of at

---

[3]Fischer Black and John Cox, "Valuing Corporate Securities: Some Effects of Bond Indenture Provisions," *The Journal of Finance* 31, no. 2 (May 1976): 351–368.

[4]The framework requires an understanding of compound options, which are options on options. See Robert Geske, "The Valuation of Compound Options," *Journal of Financial Economics* 3, no. 1 (March 1979): 63–81. The application of compound options to coupon bonds is found in Robert Geske, "The Valuation of Corporate Liabilities as Compound Options," *Journal of Financial and Quantitative Analysis* 12, no. 4 (November 1977): 541–552.

least 2 years, and most are between 5 and 10 years. Some are much longer including a few perpetual warrants.

A second major difference is that warrants are usually issued by the company on whose stock the warrant is written. As a result when the warrant is exercised, the investor buys the stock from the company, and the proceeds from the sale are new capital to the issuing firm.[5]

Because these options could have value if the stock price increases as expected, warrants are often used by companies as sweeteners to make new issues of debt or equity more attractive. When offering a new stock or bond issue, the warrant is often attached and after the initial purchase it can be detached and traded on the stock exchange or the OTC market. At the same time, whenever the warrant is exercised, it provides a major source of new equity capital for the company.

Investors are generally interested in warrants because of the leverage possibilities, as we will discuss. Also, investors should be aware that warrants do not pay dividends and the warrant holder has no voting rights. Further, the investor should be sure that a warrant offers protection to the warrant holder against dilution in the case of stock dividends or stock splits whereby either the exercise price is reduced or the number of shares that can be acquired is increased.

EXAMPLE OF WARRANTS

Consider the following hypothetical example. The Bourke Corporation is going to issue $10 million in bonds but knows that within the next 5 years, it will also need an additional $5 million in new external equity beyond the expected retained earnings. One way to make the bond issue more attractive, and also possibly sell the required stock, is to attach warrants to the bonds. To keep things simple, we shall assume that the warrants are European-style, that is, they cannot be exercised before the expiration.[6] If Bourke common stock is currently selling at $45 a share, the firm may decide to issue 5-year warrants that will allow the holder to acquire the company's common stock at $50 a share. Because the firm wants to raise $5 million, it must issue warrants for 100,000 shares ($5 million/$50). Assuming the bonds will have a par value of $1,000, the company will sell 10,000 bonds, and each bond will have 10 warrants attached to it. Each warrant is for one share. Assume the bond sale is successful, and the market price on the firm's common stock reaches $55 a share at the expiration of the warrants. At this point, the warrants will have an intrinsic value of $5 each ($55 − $50), and all the warrants would be exercised. As a result, the company will sell 100,000 shares of new common stock at $50 a share. The company pays no explicit commission cost but does have administrative costs.

Figure 21.4 provides information on some warrants taken from *Value Line Convertibles,* a weekly publication that evaluates warrants and convertibles. The report provides most of the information needed to evaluate the warrant. Take the British Petroleum warrant shown on line 21. The stock sells on the New York Stock Exchange and is currently priced at $47.50. The next four columns provide information on Value

---

[5]Although most warrants outstanding have been issued in this manner, in recent years there has been an increasing number of warrants issued by firms and foreign governments that are written on other securities or indexes. We will talk about these later.

[6]Most warrants issued by firms on their own shares are American-style, but as we know from Chapter 20, such warrants are more difficult to price and will be exercised early only if sufficiently high dividends are paid.

FIGURE 21.4   **Warrant Information from *Value Line Convertibles***

	V-20 EVALUATION OF COMMON						WARRANT FACTS												
SYMBOL EXCHANGE [1] [2]	PRICE [3]	PERFORMANCE RANK [4]	RELATIVE VOLATILITY (%) [5]	YIELD (%) [6]	LIQUIDITY GRADE [7]	CONVERSION RATIO [8]	EFFECTIVE PER SHARE EXERCISE PRICE [9]	PER SHARE EXERCISE PRICE [10]	TOTAL EXERCISE PRICE [11]	WHEN TERMS CHANGE [12]	EXPIRATION DATE [13]	ISSUE SIZE [14]	LIQUIDITY GRADE RELATIVE SIZE [15]	[16]	DILUTION PROTECTION [17]	PAGE REF [18]	EXCHANGE [19]	SYMBOL [20]	
IATV OTC	1.63	-	185	NIL	d	1.000	6.00	6.00	6.00		5/4/94	850	22%	f	FP		OTC	IATVW	1
ADT NYS	7.63	2	115	NIL	b	1.000	10.00	10.00	10.00		6/30/94	18.000	17	a	FP		NYS	ADTW	2
AM NYS	0.63	-	170	NIL	b	1.000	5.83	5.83	5.83		2/28/97	2.500	5	d	FP	064	ASE	AMLWS	3
BLMP OTC	1.22	-	200	NIL		1.000	1.10	1.10	1.10	8/31/92	2/6/94	5.000	25	d	FP		OTC	BLMPW	4
BLMP OTC	1.22	-	200	NIL		1.000	2.00	2.00	2.00		2/6/95	5.000	25	e	FP		OTC	BLMPW	5
SEMI OTC	1.34	-	120	NIL	b	1.000	1.10	1.10	1.10		6/18/97	1.750	24	c	FP		OTC	SEMIW	6
SEMI OTC	1.34	-	120	NIL	b	1.000	1.50	1.50	1.50		6/18/97	1.750	24	f	FP		OTC	SEMIZ	7
ALU ASE	6.38	-	175	NIL	b	1.000	7.50	7.50	7.50		7/10/94	1.375	34	d	FP	181	ASE	ALUWB	8
ALBM OTC	10.50	-	300	NIL	a	1.000	12.00	12.00	12.00		6/30/95	1.000	14	e	FP		OTC	ALBMZ	9
AZA NYS	46.63	1	120	NIL	a	1.000	15.00	15.00	15.00		12/14/93	6.456	9	a	FP		ASE	AZAWS	10
AU NYS	10.00	-	115	NIL	a	1.000	21.00	21.00	21.00		1/8/96	292.000	397	a	FP		ASE	AUT	11
AXX ASE	2.88	-	280	NIL	a	1.000	2.75	2.75	2.75		1/31/93	2.000	10		FP		ASE	AXWS	12
AAC NYS	3.13	3	195	NIL	a	1.000	1.84	1.84	1.84		11/11/00	6.765	-2	e	FP		OTC		13
AIX ASE	5.00	-	150	NIL	b	1.000	6.00	6.00	6.00		3/31/93	.863	32	c	FP		ASE	AIXWS	14
AZ NYS	4.38	3	130	NIL	b	1.000	15.63	15.63	15.63		NONE	2.030	68	c	FP	278	ASE	AZWS	15
BHI NYS	24.25	3	105	1.9	a	1.000	36.75	36.75	36.75		3/31/95	8.000	7	a	FP	186	OTC	BHICW	16
BPI ASE	1.00	-	165	NIL	e	1.000	3.50	3.50	3.50		12/31/08	1.000	33	f	FP		ASE	BPI W	17
BK NYS	42.13	3	115	3.6	a	1.000	62.00	62.00	62.00		11/29/98	23.500	34	c	FP	178	OTC		18
BAC NYS	42.88	3	110	3.0	a	1.000	17.50	17.50	17.50		10/22/97	7.000	3	c	FP	269	OTC		19
BGEN OTC	22.75	4	170	NIL	a	1.000	20.00	20.00	20.00		6/30/94	.606	3	b	FP		OTC	BGENW	20
BP NYS	47.50	4	70	5.4	a	1.000	80.00	80.00	80.00		1/31/93	21.155	0	b	FP	133	NYS	BPWS	21
BSN ASE	6.13	-	90	2.9	c	1.000	10.75	10.75	10.75		11/14/96	.904	23	e	FP		ASE	BSNWS	22
CAMD OTC	4.00	-	280	NIL	c	1.000	7.48	7.48	7.48		4/16/97	1.000	18	e	FP		OTC	CAMDW	23
CLZR OTC	10.00	-	200	NIL	a	1.000	6.88	6.88	6.88		11/9/00	.300	6		FP		OTC	CLZRW	24
CYNR OTC	2.38	-	145	NIL	b	1.000	3.50	3.50	3.50		12/31/94	3.943	43	e	FP		OTC	CYNRW	25
CTSC OTC	7.75	-	200	NIL	a	1.000	8.00	8.00	8.00		4/12/95	.287	6	c	FP		OTC	CTSCZ	26
CNTO OTC	12.25	5	195	NIL+	a	2.000	11.25	11.25	22.50		12/31/94	2.875	16	d	FP		OTC	CNTOW	27
CHMX OTC	2.75	-	250	NIL	b	1.000	12.00	12.00	12.00		3/31/94	2.669	32		FP		OTC	CHMXL	28
CHMX OTC	2.75	-	250	NIL	b	1.000	6.25	6.25	6.25		10/31/94	2.236	27		FP		OTC	CHMXM	29
CHIP OTC	49.50	4	175	NIL	a	.300	100.00	100.00	30.00		6/30/93	1.500	3	a	FP	013	OTC		30
LEND OTC	4.50	-	150	NIL	c	1.000	5.50	5.50	5.50		4/17/96	.700	100	e	FP		OTC	LENDW	31
DVIC OTC	8.38	-	100	NIL	a	1.000	12.00	12.00	12.00		2/7/96	.500	14	b	FP		OTC		32
DASW OTC	1.44	-	210	NIL	c	1.000	5.00	5.00	5.00		12/31/95	1.000	9	e	FP		OTC	DASWZ	33
DAHI OTC	3.25	-	135	NIL	d	1.000	5.00	5.00	5.00	10/14/93	3/14/96	1.000	16	f	FP		OTC	DAHIW	34
EMBX OTC	4.50	-	200	NIL	d	1.000	10.20	10.20	10.20	11/7/92	11/7/96	2.200	58	f	FP		OTC	EMBXW	35
ENQ NYS	15.88#	-	85	1.0	a	1.000#	17.78	27.78	27.78		7/28/97	35.000	7	c	FP		NYS	ENQW	36
ENZN OTC	7.75	-	250	NIL	b	1.000	18.00	18.00	18.00		10/31/94	3.000	15	d	FP		OTC	ENZNW	37
XTON OTC	1.06	-	240	NIL	b	1.000	1.00	1.00	1.00		12/15/93	4.589	15	d	FP		OTC	XTONW	38
GCO NYS	6.63	3	140	NIL	a	1.000	8.00	8.00	8.00		2/15/93	.738	3		FP	314	OTC		39
GCO NYS	6.63	3	140	NIL	a	1.000	10.65	10.65	10.65		10/15/93	.900	4		FP	226	OTC		40
GENZ OTC	58.31	-	170	NIL	a	1.000	35.92	35.92	35.92		5/31/96	2.100	15	f	FP		OTC	GEMIW	41
GENZ OTC	40.25	-	150	NIL	a	1.000	19.00	19.00	19.00		12/31/94	2.057	13	a	FP	343	OTC	GENZW	42
VCR ASE	2.63	-	150	NIL	b	1.000	8.25	8.25	8.25		3/9/95	2.100	25	c	FP		ASE	VCRWS	43
HAN NYS	19.25	4	75	3.7	a	1.000	18.00	18.00	18.00		9/30/94	26.000	1	b	FP	174	NYS	HANWS	44
	3.85#	3	80	6.7	a	1.000#	5.97	5.97	5.97		9/30/97	$50.000	#	a	FP	174	ASE	HANWB	45
HAS ASE	29.88	2	105	.7+	a	.250	18.91	18.91	4.73		7/12/94	4.000	1	c	FP	272	ASE	HASWS	46
HND ASE	0.19	-	220	NIL	c	1.000	8.00	8.00	8.00		10/31/92	.828	29	f	FP		OTC	HNDIZ	47
HOT NYS	0.94	-	85	NIL	d	1.000	16.95	16.95	16.95	9/13/96	9/14/96	1.860	14	e	FP		ASE	HOTWB	48
HYBD OTC	5.56	-	160	NIL	b	1.000	7.21	7.21	7.21	8/6/93	8/6/97	.500	6	e	FP		OTC	HYBDW	49
IMRE	2.38	-	290	NIL	b	1.000	2.50	2.50	2.50		8/29/96	1.850	13	e	FP		OTC	IMREW	50

Source: *Value Line Convertibles,* September 7, 1992, (New York: Arnold Bernhard & Co., Inc.). Reprinted by permission of Value Line Publishing.

Line's opinion on the stock. The *conversion ratio* in column 8 is the number of shares of stock that can be purchased for each warrant. As you can see, most warrants have a conversion ratio of one share. Column 9 is the exercise price, which is the price at which the stock can be purchased with the warrant. The BP shares can be bought for $80 a share. The expiration date in column 13 indicates that the BP warrants expire January 1, 1993, about 4 months after the date of this publication. The issue size in column 14 (number of warrants in millions) is 21,155,000. The relative size in column 15 (the number of common shares that the warrants can purchase relative to the total number of common shares of the firm) is less than 1 percent. The FP in column 17 indicates that the warrant is fully protected against dilution, meaning that the terms will be adjusted in the event of stock dividends or stock splits.

VALUATION OF WARRANTS

The value of a warrant is determined in a manner similar to that used for call options. However, because the warrant is issued by the firm, the additional shares of stock that are created when the warrant is exercised add a slight wrinkle to the analysis.[7] Let us consider an all equity firm with N_s shares, each worth $S(t)$. Thus, the value of the firm, $V(t)$, equals $N_s S(t)$. Let the firm issue N_w warrants with an exercise price of X and a conversion ratio of 1. For simplicity assume that the warrants are European-style and that the firm uses the proceeds of the warrant to finance a zero net present value project.

Now suppose it is the expiration day and the value of the firm is $V(T)$. If the warrants are exercised, the warrant holders will inject new capital into the firm and the new value of the firm will be

$$V(T)^* = V(T) + N_w X$$

where $V(T)$ is the value of the firm before the warrants are exercised and $V(T)^*$ is the value of the firm immediately after the warrants are exercised. Define $q = N_w/N_s$, which is a measure of the dilution effect from the issuance of new shares. Then we can write $V(T)^*$ as

$$V(T)^* = N_s S(T) + q N_s X$$

After the warrants are exercised, the new stock price will adjust to $S(T)^*$, which is equal to the new value of the firm, $V(T)^*$, divided by the total number of shares, $N_s + N_w$. Substituting for $V(T)^*$, we get

$$S(T)^* = \frac{V(T)^*}{N_w + N_s} = \frac{N_s S(T) + q N_s X}{N_w + N_s}$$

$$= \frac{S(T) + qX}{1 + q}$$

The warrant holder will exercise the warrant if the stock price after exercise, $S(T)^*$, exceeds the exercise price. Thus, exercise will occur if

$$\frac{S(T) + qX}{1 + q} > X$$

or

$$\frac{S(T) + qX - X - qX}{1 + q} > 0$$

---

[7]This approach was developed by Dan Galai and Meir I. Schneller, "Pricing Warrants and the Value of the Firm," *The Journal of Finance* 33, no. 5 (December 1978): 1333–1342.

TABLE 21.2

Effect of Exercise of Warrants with $30 Exercise Price

$V(T)$	$1,800	$800
$S(T)$	$ 36	$ 16
New shares issued	10	0
Total shares	60	50
New capital contributed	$ 300	0
$V(T)^*$	$2,100	$800
$S(T)^*$	$ 35	$ 16

which means $S(T) > X$. Thus, the exercise decision of the warrant holder is the same as that of a call holder. The value of the warrant at expiration is

$$W(T) = Max(0,S(T)^* - X)$$
$$= \frac{1}{1 + q}Max(0,S(T) - X)$$
$$= \frac{1}{1 + q}C(T)$$

This means the value of the warrant today is simply

$$W(t) = \frac{C(t)}{1 + q} \qquad (21.7)$$

So the warrant is like $1/(1 + q)$ calls. Thus, if the condition of European exercise is met, we can value the warrant by using the Black-Scholes model and then dividing the computed value by $1 + q$.

Consider the following example. A firm has assets valued at $1,000, no debt, and 50 shares outstanding, which means each share is worth $20. The risk-free interest rate is 8 percent. The firm issues 10 warrants that have an exercise price of $30 and expire in 5 years. The expected standard deviation of the stock's return is .4.

If we used the Black-Scholes model to determine the value of a 5-year call option on the stock with an exercise price of $30, a stock price of $20, a risk-free rate of .08, and a standard deviation of .4, we would obtain a value of $6.87.[8] The value of q is $10/50 = .2$. Thus we would divide $6.87 by 1.2 and obtain $5.73 as the value of the warrant.

Now let us consider what happens at the time of exercise. Table 21.2 contains the results of two outcomes. The first shows the results if the warrants are exercised, while the other presents the results if the warrants expire unexercised. In the first case, the value of the firm is at $1,800 when the warrants expire. This means that the stock price before the warrants are exercised is $36. Recall that warrant holders will exercise under

---

[8]As a check on your knowledge of the Black-Scholes option pricing model, you should determine that you would get this same value, subject to variation due to round-off error.

TABLE 21.3

Warrant Price Movements Relative to Stock Price Movements

$V(t) = 1,000; N_s = 50; N_w = 10; S(t) = 20; r = .08; X = 30; T - t = 5; \sigma = .4$

	10.00	15.00	20.00	25.00	30.00
Stock price	10.00	15.00	20.00	25.00	30.00
Warrant price	1.24	3.18	5.73	8.71	11.98
Percentage change in stock price	-50.00	-25.00	.	25.00	50.00
Percentage change in warrant price	-78.36	-44.50	.	52.01	109.08

the same conditions that holders of ordinary calls will exercise. Since $36 is greater than the exercise price of $30, the warrant holders will exercise. Thus, the firm will issue 10 new shares, and the warrant holders will contribute $300 of new capital. The firm will now be worth $2,100 and will have 60 shares of stock outstanding so each share will be worth $35. If the firm is worth only $800 at expiration, the stock price will be only $16 so the warrant holders will not exercise.

Warrants offer investors significant leverage because for a small initial investment, the holder of a warrant can earn very large rates of return from smaller stock price increases as shown in Table 21.3 for our sample warrant. A stock price of $20 is the base, and we demonstrate what happens to warrant price changes when we have stock price movements 5 and 10 points in both directions. Note that the percentage price change for the warrant is always greater than the percentage price change for the stock. This is the leverage effect of the warrants that is essentially the same as the leverage effect in ordinary options.

Additional information about the valuation of warrants can be obtained from other sources such as *Value Line Convertibles* which provides opinions about the values of many warrants. A sample page from Value Line's evaluation and analysis of warrants in Figure 21.5 contains the British Petroleum warrants we looked at earlier (line 21). The warrants were selling for 0.08 (column 23). Column 26 indicates that Value Line believes that the warrants are overvalued by about 90 percent. Columns 27 through 30 indicate the expected percentage price changes for given stock percentage price changes. Additional information is contained in other columns.

OTHER TYPES OF WARRANTS

Recently, a number of other innovative warrants have been introduced including *currency exchange warrants* that allow investors to acquire a specific number of U.S. dollars at specified exchange rates for a non-U.S. currency. For example, the Student Loan Marketing Association (Sallie Mae) has issued warrants that allow the holder to purchase $50 for a specific number of Japanese yen. If the dollar strengthens against the yen, the warrants would increase in value. These instruments, like index options, usually are exercised by means of a cash settlement. Sallie Mae will be obligated to provide U.S. dollars and receive yen in payment. Obviously Sallie Mae faces some risk and it usually hedges that risk by trading in the currency futures or options market.[9]

---

[9]For a case study of the Sallie Mae currency exchange warrants, see Richard J. Rogalski and James K. Seward, "Corporate Issues of Foreign Currency Warrants," *Journal of Financial Economics* 30, no. 2 (December 1991): 347–366.

FIGURE 21.5   **Warrant Analysis from** *Value Line Convertibles*

#	Footnote	Name of Warrant	Price of Warrant / Perf. Rank	Rel. Volatility (%)	Over(+) Under(−) Valued (%)	+50%	+25%	−25%	−50%	Tangible Value	Premium (%)	Per Share Cost of Warrant	I.V. Grade	Usable Sec. Description	Price	Hedge Rank	Hedge Ratio
1	1	ACTV Warrants	1.00 ◇-	210	+155	+20	+15	-50	-75	NONE	62	1.00	J			F	71
2	2	ADT Ltd. Warrant	1.38 ◇2	230	-20	+145	+65	35	-70	NONE	18	1.38	E			C+	37
3	3	AM International wt	0.13 -	230	+25	+60	+30	-40	-70	NONE	20	0.13	E			D	27
4	4	Airship Intn'l A wt	0.19 ◇-	710	-45	+295	+135	-35	-60	0.12	6	0.19	H			A	53
5	5	Airship Intn'l B wt	0.19 -	400	-50	+180	+75	-12	-40	NONE	15	0.19	H			A	30
6	6	All American Semi 97 A w	0.55 -	185	+1	+85	+40	-35	-65	0.24	24	0.56	F			C	63
7	7	All American Semi 97 B w	0.38 -	200	-20	+115	155	30	-50	NONE	28	0.38	F			B	47
8	8	Allou Health B 94 wt	1.50 ◇-	330	-23	+130	+60	-30	-60	NONE	24	1.50	H			B	43
9	9	Alpha 1 Biomedicals B wt	3.50 -	470	-25	+105	+50	-24	-50	NONE	33	3.50	H			A	50
10	10^	ALZA 1993 wt	31.75 ◇2	170	+0	+75	+35	-35	-65	31.63	0	31.75	D			C-	96
11	11	Amax Gold wt	1.94 -	190	-7	+105	+45	-35	-65	NONE	19	1.94	E			C	32
12	12	American Exploration wt	0.56 ◇-	750	+6	+180	+75	-55	-85	0.13	15	0.56	H			C	51
13	13	Anacomp Inc. wt	1.63 3	270	-9	+85	+40	-30	-60	1.29	11	1.63	I			C	73
14	14	Astrotech Int'l 1993 wt	1.00 ◇-	310	+4	+130	+55	-45	-75	NONE	20	1.00	I			C-	41
15		Atlas Corp wt	2.38 ◇5	160	+60	+35	+21	-40	-70	NONE	54	2.38	H			F	64
16	15^	Baker Hughes 1995 wt	2.38 1	260	-50	+235	+95	-23	-55	NONE	10	2.38	F			A	25
17	16	Bamberger 96 Wt	0.31 -	220	+30	+55	+30	-40	-70	NONE	31	0.31	H			F	42
18	^	Bank of New York wt	5.63 1	240	-50	+210	+85	-14	-45	NONE	13	5.63	B			A	29
19	17^	BankAmerica 1997 wt	26.00 4	165	+2	+80	+40	-40	-70	25.38	1	26.00	H			D	93
20	18	Biogen wt	11.00 ◇5	240	+22	+65	+30	-40	-70	2.75	35	11.00	D			C	67
21		British Petrol wt	0.08 ◇3	995	-90	+995	+800	+19	-70	NONE	0	0.08	C			A	4
22	19	BSN Corp 1996 wt	0.38 -	260	-10	+215	+90	-50	-85	NONE	6	0.38	H			A	17
23	20	California Micro Devices	0.50 -	860	-70	+275	+110	+35	+11	NONE	13	0.50	F			C	36
24	21	Candela Laser 2000 wt	6.63 -	240	+22	+90	+35	-35	-65	3.13	35	6.63	H			F	80
25		Canyon Resources wt	0.75 -	220	-8	+90	+40	-30	-60	NONE	32	0.75	G			C	47
26	22	Cellular Tech Serv 95 w	1.75 -	410	-40	+165	+75	20	50	NONE	23	1.75	H			A	44
27	^	Centocor Wt	9.75 5	290	+2	+85	+40	-35	-65	2.00	32	4.88	H			C	120
28	23	Chemex Pharm Mar 94 Wt	0.25 ◇-	500	-45	+170	+70	13	-45	NONE	9	0.25	H			A	16
29	24	Chemex Pharm Oct 94 Wt	2.25 -	260	+180	+15	+12	50	-80	NONE	82	2.25	H			F	91
30	25^	Chiron (Cetus wt)	0.63 ◇3	550	-40	+270	+105	-40	-75	NONE	4	2.08	I			A	4
31	26	Credit Depot 1996 wt	0.88 -	290	-45	+170	+75	-19	-50	NONE	19	0.88	F			A	38
32	27	DVI Financial 1996 wt	1.25 -	190	-60	+215	+90	-1	-30	NONE	15	1.25	G			A	31
33	28	Data Switch 95 wt	0.50 -	260	+14	+60	+30	-35	-65	NONE	35	0.50	J			A	15
34	29	Deprenyl Animal Health wt	0.88 -	220	+15	+80	+40	-15	-75	NONE	27	0.88	H			D	13
35	30	Embrex 96 wt	1.25 -	290	-9	+85	+40	30	-60	NONE	DC	1.25	H			C+	40
36	31	Enquirer/Star Warrant	2.13 -	210	-55	+260	+110	-15	-45	NONE	13	2.13	E	0S97	64.00	A	36
37	32	ENZON Inc wt	1.50 -	430	-30	+120	+55	-24	-55	NONE	19	1.50	H			A	31
38		Executone Info Warrant	0.38 ◇-	380	-2	+95	+45	-35	-65	0.06	29	0.38	H			C	57
39	33	Genesco Feb 1993 wt	0.25 ◇31	880	-40	+690	+225	-55	-90	NONE	4	0.25	H			A	24
40	34	Genesco Oct 1993 wt	0.13 ◇4	710	-7	+490	+165	-70	-95	NONE	2	0.13	H			A	10
41	35	Genetics Institute wt	7.75 -	995	75	+575	+385	+85	+15	22.39	-25	7.75	I			A	109
42	36	Genzyme Corp 1994 wt	24.88 -	200	+10	+70	+35	-35	-65	21.25	9	24.88	H			D	84
43		Go Video 95 wt	1.00 -.	330	+12	+60	+30	-35	-65	NONE	38	1.00	H			D	49
44	37^	Hanson PLC wt	3.13 3	220	-40	+260	+110	-35	-65	1.25	10	3.13	B			A	49
45	38	Hanson B 97 wt	0.38 5	210	+80	+145	+65	-65	-90	NONE	10	0.38	B			F	24
46	39^	Hasbro 94 wt	3.25 ◇3	195	+15	+100	+45	-45	-80	2.74	7	13.00	H			D	20
47	40	Hinderliter wt	0.13 ◇-	250	+995	-11	+4	-60	-90	NONE	66	0.13	J			F	77
48	41	Hotel Investors 1996 wt	0.02 -	160	-3	+120	+55	-40	-75	NONE	2	0.02	G			C	3
49	42	Hycor Biomedical 98 wt	1.75 -	250	+0	+85	+40	-35	-70	31	1	1.75	H			C+	49
50	43	IMRE Corp. wt	1.50 -	330	+25	+50	+25	-35	-65	NONE	63	1.50	H			F	75

WARRANT EVALUATION · **WARRANT ANALYSIS** · **V-21** · WARRANTS

Column headings: Footnote (21), Name of Warrant; Price of Warrant (23); Performance Rank (24); Relative Volatility % (25); Over(+) Under(−) Valued % (26); Warrant's Projected % Change for these changes in the price of the underlying security: +50% (27), +25% (28), −25% (29), −50% (30); Tangible Value (31); Per Share Cost of Warrant — Premium % (32), (33); I.V. Grade (34); Usable Security Data — Description (35), Price (36); Hedge Rank (37); Hedge Ratio (38).

Source: *Value Line Convertibles,* September 7, 1992, (New York: Arnold Bernhard & Co., Inc.). Reprinted by permission of Value Line Publishing.

CONVERTIBLE SECURITIES

A *convertible security* gives the holder the right to convert one type of security into a stipulated amount of another type at the investor's discretion. Typically, but not invariably, the security is convertible into common stock, but it could be converted into preferred stock or into a special class of common stock. The most popular convertible securities are convertible bonds and convertible preferred stock. Convertibles exhibit some characteristics of a bond and other characteristics of the security they are convertible into. Convertible issues generally are subordinated to the firm's other debt.

Like warrants, convertibles are usually offered to attract investors to a bond issue. For example, many firms can issue straight debt, that is, bonds that are not convertible. Adding the convertible feature makes the debt more attractive. Many years ago it was thought that firms that issued convertibles were generally lower-quality firms that made their bonds convertible to make it more attractive. In recent years, the popularity of derivative securities has made convertible debt financing attractive to many high quality firms.

CHARACTERISTICS OF CONVERTIBLE BONDS

As an example of a typical convertible bond, consider an issue offered by Amoco that matures in the year 2013, carries a coupon of $7\frac{3}{8}$ percent, with interest paid semi-annually on March 1 and September 1. It has a face value of $1,000 and can be converted into 19.048 shares of Amoco common stock. This value, 19.048, is called the *conversion ratio*. Alternatively, when the face value of $1,000 is divided by the conversion ratio of 19.048, it gives $52.50, which is called the *conversion price*. A convertible can be thought of as an ordinary bond with a call option attached which allows the bondholder to buy 19.048 shares of stock by simply tendering the bond. As of September 1992, the bonds were priced at $114.25, whereas the stock was priced at $51.75 and was paying a dividend of $2.20 per year. The bonds are callable after September 1, 1995, at a price of 102.210 which means that the firm can retire the bonds any time after that date by paying the investor $1,022.10 for each $1,000 face value.

ADVANTAGES TO ISSUING FIRMS

Issuing convertible bonds is considered attractive for a company for several reasons. By attaching the convertible feature, a firm can often get a *lower interest rate* on its debt. The bondholders are, in effect, substituting the certain stream of interest payments for the uncertainty of the growth prospects of the firm. If a firm performs well after the issuance of the convertibles, the convertible bondholders will be able to gain by converting their bonds into the now-more-valuable stock.

Another advantage of convertibles is that they represent *potential common stock*. The bondholder may decide to convert the bond or the firm can make it possible to force conversion in the future by including a call feature on the bonds. This future common stock feature may be desirable for a firm that currently needs equity capital for an investment but does not want to issue common stock immediately because of the potential dilution before the investment begins generating earnings. After the investment begins generating earnings, the stock price should rise above the conversion value, and the firm can force conversion by calling the bond. We will discuss forced conversion later.

ADVANTAGES TO INVESTORS

As noted, convertible bonds have special features that typically allow them to have coupon rates below what you would expect on the basis of the quality of the issue. The fact is, *they provide the upside potential of common stock and the downside protection of a bond.* The upside potential occurs because the convertible contains an option to buy the stock by simply surrendering the bond. If the stock price increases, the convertible bond gains in value due to the increased value of the stock into which it can be converted.

The convertible bond has downside protection because, irrespective of what happens to the stock, the price of the bond will not decline below what it would be worth as a straight bond. In other words, if the firm's performance deteriorated somewhat and the stock price fell, the convertible would fall in price, but unless it became likely that the firm could not make the interest payments, the convertible's price would not fall as much. Thus, it has downside protection because in the worst case, it will act like an ordinary bond.

Another plus is that the convertible usually has a higher current yield than the underlying common stock. For example, the Amoco bond is convertible into 19.048 shares of stock which means that the total dividends on the stock would be 19.048 ($2.20) = $41.91. In contrast, the bond pays $7\frac{3}{8}$ percent interest, which is $73.75.

An advantage that has been lost is the potential for leverage on convertible bonds. Prior to the 1970s, investors could buy convertibles on margin at about the same rate at which they could borrow on straight debt (about 80 percent). This capability made it possible to invest in convertibles with little cash and use the interest on the bond to offset part of the interest on the loan. Currently, however, the margin on convertible bonds is the same as the margin on common stocks.

VALUATION OF CONVERTIBLE BONDS

Because a convertible bond is actually a combination of a bond and a call option on the common stock, it is necessary to consider both aspects of the security. First, as a straight bond, what should be its yield and implied price? This analysis will indicate your *downside risk* if the stock were to decline to the point where the security had value only as a straight bond.

The value of the convertible as a bond is called its *bond* or *investment value.* To determine the bond value, you must determine the bond's required yield if it had no conversion feature attached. A simple, but not always feasible, way to do this is to identify a nonconvertible bond with similar characteristics issued by the company. The most comparable straight issue of Amoco is its $8\frac{5}{8}$s of 2016. These bonds are priced at $109\frac{1}{4}$ for a yield of 7.73 percent. Let us round this off and assume that the convertible as a straight bond would yield 7.75 percent and have a maturity of 21 years. Using these assumptions, the bond value of the Amoco convertible would be

$$\text{Bond value} = \sum_{t=1}^{2n} \frac{C_t/2}{(1 + i/2)^t} + \frac{P_p}{(1 + i/2)^{2n}}$$

$$= 36.875 \sum_{t=1}^{2n} \frac{1}{(1 + .0075/2)^t} + \frac{1000}{(1 + .0775/2)^{42}}$$

$$= 36.875 \,(20.5793) + 1000 \,(.2026)$$

$$= 758.86 + 202.60 = 961.46$$

At the present time, the convertible as a straight bond would not sell for less than $961.46. You should compare this value to the current market price of the convertible to determine the downside price risk of the bond (also referred to as the *investment premium*). In this case this is

$$\frac{\$1,142.50 - \$961.46}{\$1,142.50} = 15.85\%$$

This is a measure of your downside risk assuming that the bond's yield would not change if the firm's performance deteriorated. This is probably true over a range of stock prices. If, however, the stock price fell substantially because of a perceived threat of bankruptcy, then the bond's required yield would rise and its investment value would fall.

Next we need to compute the bond's *conversion value,* which is the value of the common stock that the bond can be converted into, as follows: 19.048 (51.75) = $985.73. Obviously the conversion value is linearly related to the stock price. The value of the convertible bond must exceed the conversion value or the bond value, whichever is larger. Thus, as a minimum we can say that

$$\text{Minimum price of convertible} = \text{Max(Bond value, Conversion value)}$$

In this case, the minimum value is the conversion value of $985.73, which exceeds the bond value of $961.46.

The market value of the convertible will typically be higher than its minimum value except at maturity. This premium exists because of the option to convert the bond into stock. The difference between the market value of the convertible and its minimum value is the value of the option to convert. This premium over its minimum value (conversion value) is called the *conversion premium* and is calculated as

$$\text{Conversion premium} = \frac{\text{Market price} - \text{Minimum (conversion) value}}{\text{Minimum (conversion) value}}$$

For the Amoco convertible, the conversion premium is

$$\frac{\$1,142.50 - \$985.73}{\$985.73} = 15.90\%$$

This indicates that the option value adds 15.9 percent to the minimum value of the bond.

Another useful measure for a convertible bond is the *conversion parity price.* This is defined as

$$\text{Conversion parity price} = \frac{\text{Market price of convertible bond}}{\text{Conversion ratio}}$$

For our bond, this is

$$\frac{\$1,142.50}{19.048} = \$59.98$$

The conversion parity price indicates that if the bond were purchased and immediately converted, the effective price paid for the common stock would be $59.98 compared to the current stock price of $51.75. Obviously, this is fairly far from the current stock price. When it gets closer, conversion may be imminent. Of course, the conversion parity price should never be below the current stock price or someone could buy the convertible, immediately convert it and sell the stock for a risk-free profit.

Another factor that is considered to be important when evaluating convertible bonds is the *payback* or *breakeven time,* which measures how long the higher interest income from the convertible bond compared to the dividend income from the common stock must persist to make up for the price of the bond relative to its conversion value (i.e., the conversion premium). The calculation is as follows:

$$\text{Payback} = \frac{\text{Bond price} - \text{Conversion value}}{\text{Bond income} - \text{Income from equal investment in common stock}}$$

The dividend yield on the stock is $2.20/$51.75 = .0425. If you invested $1,142.50 in stock (which is the current cost of the bond) you would receive dividends of $1,142.50 (.0425) = $48.56 per year. Thus, the payback would be

$$\frac{\$1,142.50 - \$985.73}{\$73.75 - \$48.56} = 6.22^{10}$$

Like its counterpart in capital budgeting analysis, the payback is not a discounted cash flow method, so it does not properly incorporate the time value of money. However, it can serve as a useful indicator of the relative attractiveness of a convertible along with other characteristics. Generally, it is preferable to have a short payback that is shorter than the first call date, which is not true in this case because the bond is callable in only 3 years.

Figure 21.6 illustrates the factors involved in the value of a convertible bond. The horizontal axis plots the value of the firm which establishes an upper bound for the value of a convertible since it cannot sell for more than the firm's assets. Thus, there is a line bisecting the plane and the value of the convertible must be below that line. Note that the line for the bond value is relatively flat for a wide range of firm values because higher firm values do not increase the value of the bond because the bondholders receive only their promised payments. In contrast, at fairly low firm values the value of the convertible drops off since bankruptcy becomes more likely. Conversion value rises directly with the value of the firm. This graph shows that for low firm values, the bond value will be the minimum value of the convertible, and for high firm values, the conversion value will be the minimum value of the convertible. Finally, the line for the value of the convertible shows that when the firm value is low, the convertible will act more like a bond, trading for only a slight premium over the bond value. Alternatively, when firm values are high, the convertible will act more like a stock, selling for only a slight premium over the conversion value. In the fairly wide middle range, the convertible will trade as the hybrid security that acts somewhat like a bond and somewhat like a stock.

---

[10]As noted, this calculation assumes that you would use the $1,142.50 to buy 22.077 shares of stock at $51.75 a share ($1,142.50/51.75). An alternative assumption is that your choice is to convert the bond into 19.048 shares of stock and receive dividends of $41.91 (19.048 × $2.20). In this case, the estimated breakeven time would be: $156.77/31.84 = 4.92 years.

FIGURE 21.6   **Value of Convertible Bond**

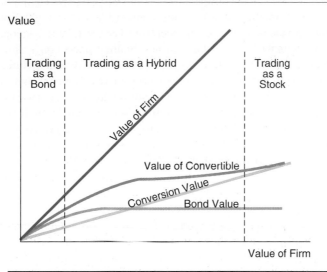

CONVERTIBLE BONDS AND OPTION THEORY

Because convertible bonds have many of the characteristics of call options, it is possible in theory to replicate convertible bonds with straight bonds and call options or warrants. However, it is not a simple matter to apply the option pricing formula to value the option contained in a convertible bond. The characteristics of the convertible bond make the formula not strictly applicable without some added complexities that we will not cover here. However, you should still be able to use some of your knowledge of options to assist you in understanding the option value of the convertible. For example, if the stock price rises, the option is worth more. If the volatility of the underlying stock rises, the option is worth more. The role of the exercise price is played by the conversion price so the higher the conversion price, the less valuable is the option. Generally, with a longer time to expiration, the option is worth more, but you must remember that the time to expiration can also affect the bond value as well (recall the typical upward sloping yield curve). Likewise, the risk-free rate is positively related to the option value, but it also affects the bond's yield, so the overall effect is difficult to see.[11]

FORCING
CONVERSION

Although most convertible bonds are callable, the firm will never call a bond selling for less than its call price. As soon as it reaches its call price, the firm should call the bond. In reality, firms often wait until the bond is selling for significantly more than its

---

[11]For a more thorough analysis of how convertibles can be valued using option pricing theory, see Jonathan E. Ingersoll, Jr., "A Contingent Claims Valuation of Convertible Securities," *Journal of Financial Economics* 4, no. 4 (May 1977): 289–322; and Michael J. Brennan and Eduardo S. Schwartz, "Analyzing Convertible Bonds," *Journal of Financial and Quantitative Analysis* 15, no. 4 (November 1980): 907–929.

call price before calling it.[12] Under these conditions, investors will have an incentive, as noted earlier, to convert the bond into stock that is worth more than what they would receive from the call price. Some convertibles even have stepped-up conversion prices that provide an even greater incentive to convert. With a stepped-up conversion price, the number of shares that can be obtained upon conversion (the conversion ratio) decreases according to a specific schedule. With this feature, it may be advisable to convert just before the conversion price increases. Firms may also be able to encourage conversion by increasing the dividends on the stock because one reason investors defer conversion is the higher income from interest than from dividends.

In some cases, firms face the problem that the convertible is never converted. This may occur because the conversion premium is too high or the stock price does not increase enough to induce conversion or allow the firm to force conversion. This is called *overhanging*. In contrast, when conversion occurs, there is *dilution*.

SOURCES OF
INFORMATION ON
CONVERTIBLES

Information on many convertible bonds can be obtained from reference books on ordinary bonds such as *Standard & Poor's Bond Guide* and *Moody's Bond Record*. Merrill Lynch publishes a monthly statistical report, *Convertible Securities,* that contains extensive data on many convertible bonds and preferred stocks. You can also obtain information on convertibles as well as warrants from *Value Line Convertibles*. Figure 21.7 presents the information page from a typical issue. The Amoco issue is found on line 33. Notably, most of the information used in our analysis is contained on line 33 in addition to Value Line's evaluation of the common stock. Figure 21.8 contains Value Line's analysis of the convertible bond. It considers the convertible undervalued by about 3 percent (column 28). Columns 29 through 32 indicate how the convertible price would change for various changes in the stock price. Additional information about the convertible bond's projected performance is provided in the remaining columns.

CONVERTIBLE
PREFERRED
STOCK

Convertible preferred stock is similar to convertible bonds; it is a combination of preferred stock and common stock. Beyond the conversion privilege, however, these issues typically have the following characteristics:

1. They are cumulative but not participating (the dividend cumulates if it is not paid, but the holders do not participate in earnings beyond the dividend).
2. They have no sinking fund or purchase fund.
3. They have a fixed conversion rate.
4. There is generally no waiting period before conversion can take place.
5. The conversion privilege does not expire.[13]

As pointed out by Pinches, most convertible preferred stock was issued in connection with mergers as a way of providing income and yet not diluting the common equity of the acquiring firm. Although preferred stock and convertible preferred stock have not

[12]See Jonathan E. Ingersoll, Jr., "An Examination of Corporate Call Policies on Convertible Securities," *The Journal of Finance* 32, no. 2 (May 1977): 463–478. Almost all of the convertible issues he studied were called later than the theoretical optimal time.

[13]George E. Pinches, "Financing with Convertible Preferred Stock, 1960–1967," *The Journal of Finance* 25, no. 1 (March 1970): 53–63; Ronald W. Melicher, "A Comment on Financing with Convertible Preferred Stock, 1960–1967," *The Journal of Finance* 26, no. 1 (March 1971): 148–149; and George E. Pinches, "Financing with Convertible Preferred Stock: 1960–1967: Reply," *The Journal of Finance* 26, no. 1 (March 1971): 150–151.

FIGURE 21.7   **Convertible Information from *Value Line Convertibles***

| V-2 COMMON | | | | | | CONVERTIBLE FACTS | | | | | | | | | | | | | | | |

(Column headers)

| | | PERFORMANCE RANK | RELATIVE VOLATILITY (%) | YIELD (%) | | CURRENT YIELD (%) | YIELD TO MATURITY (%) | PAYMENT DATES | CONVERSION RATIO | BREAK EVEN TIME (MOS) | HEDGE RANK | RATIO | ISSUE SIZE | CALL PRICE * | VALID UNTIL | IF COMMON IS ($) | FOR THIS # OF DAYS | INDUSTRY CV PAGE REF | EXCHANGE SYMBOL | |
| EXCHANGE SYMBOL | PRICE | | | | | | | | | | | | | | | | | | | |

Symbol	Ex	Price	Rank	Vol	Yield	Cur Yld	YTM	Dates	Conv Ratio	BE	HR	Ratio	Issue	Call Price	Valid Until	Common $	# Days	Industry Pg	Exch Sym
AESC	O	19.75	-	65	4.1	7.9	9.7	Ms15	24.691	NMF	C	90	50.00	NCB	3/15/95	FCP 105.000		Ind Sv 181	O
BMD	A	21.50	3	115	.8	5.0	4.0	Jd15	72.727	NMF	C	665	61.84	105.425	6/14/93			MedSup	N BMD.F
AM	N	0.63	-	170	NIL	NMF	PFD	FMAN15	2.985	NMF	B	235	3.450	25.800	2/14/93			PrcIns	N AMPr
AMP	N	55.50	5	110	NIL	NIL	6.4		5.769	NMF	C-	29	1300	44.931	3/15/93	103.29 20/30		AirTrn 149	NA AMC.F
AMA	A	8.25	-	155	NIL	9.9	12.4	Jj15	55.127	46	C+	107	60.00	NCB	1/14/93	FCP 106.525		Drug 352	A
AMD	N	10.13	3	160	NIL	8.2		PFD MJSD15	1.987	65	C	107	0.345	51.500	3/14/93			Semicn 170	N AMDPr
ADV	N	5.00	3	150	NIL	10.2	10.8	Ms15	73.706	68	C+	158	21.83	103.600	3/15/93			Broker 162	N ADV.F
AWT	A	10.38	3	140	NIL	9.7	10.2	Mn15	33.330	72	C	124	100.0	NCB	5/14/93	FCP 105.600		AirTrn	O AWTCG
ABF	A	13.25	5	135	2.3	7.6	8.9	fA15	28.169	NMF	C	27	115.0	NCB	8/21/94	FCP 104.900		AirTrn	N
ALK	N	17.50	5	100	1.1	NIL	8.1		12.396	NMF	C-	44	345.0	39.621	4/17/93	41.58 20/30		AirTrn	N ALKB.F
ALK	N	17.50	5	100	1.1	8.4	9.0	Jd15	29.762	60	C	97	66.61	104.810	6/14/93			AirTrn	N ALKA.F
ALK	N	17.50	5	100	1.1	NIL	9.2	Jd15	35.398	NMF	C	100	14.63	102.325	6/14/93			AirTrn	O
AIN	N	14.63	5	100	2.4	6.5	8.4	Ms15	38.083	90	C	125	135.0	NCB	3/14/96	FCP 91.545		Mchnry	N
ABSB	O	16.13	3†	145	-	6.8	8.3	J12	38.417	74	C	200	25.00	102.500	6/11/93			Broker	O *EURO*
AAL	N	24.63	3	90	4.1	10.5	10.7	Ao15	25.641	74	C	17	60.20	103.670	4/14/93			Ins Dv 365	O
ALN	N	22.25	3	130	.9	6.3		PFD FMAN	1.000	43	C-	69	2.300	25.700	5/14/93			AutoPt 141	N ALNPrA
ALNT	O	0.91	-	130	NIL	NMF	NMF	Mn15	25.157	NMF	A	24	39.20	103.625	5/14/93			Cmptrs 204	O ALNGC
ALWS	N	5.75	3	150	NIL	8.1	8.5	Jd	83.770	69	C-	490	30.00	105.075	5/31/93			Ind Sv	N ALWSG
AA	N	64.63	4†	95	2.5	5.2	3.7	May27	16.129	60	C-	107	150.0	103.000	5/26/93			Mining 174	O *EURO*
AZA	N	46.63	1	120	NIL	NIL	5.1		8.652	74	C-	78	0.859	26.572	12/21/92	39.76 20/30		Drug 162	A AZAL.A
AMX	N	17.88	3	120	4.5	7.0		PFD MJSD	1.310	NMF	C	57	0.235	50.000				Mining	N AMXPrB
AWAQC	O	0.47	-	135	NIL	NMF	NMF	Jj	95.200	NMF	A	45	48.00	108.050	12/31/92			AirTrn 269	O AWAIO
AWAQC	O	0.47	-	135	NIL	NMF	NMF	fA	74.074	NMF	A	114	37.35	102.325	7/31/93			AirTrn 269	O AWAGUC
AWAQC	O	0.47	-	135	NIL	NMF	NMF	Ao	71.429	NMF	A	139	36.15	103.000	3/31/93			AirTrn 269	O AWAHOC
ABIG	O	20.13	3	95	3.0	4.9	3.3	May27	50.955	83	C	250	40.51	101.000	5/26/93	25.51 30		Ins Dv 276	O *EURO*
AMB	N	46.13	2	85	3.8	3.5	0.4	S8	34.483	0	C	320	10.04	116.951	9/7/93	37.70 20/30		Tobaco	O *EURO*
AMB	N	46.13	2	85	3.8	4.5	3.0	Apr 11	25.317	NMF	C-	160	200.0	NCB	4/11/95	FCP 100.000		Tobaco 189	O *EURO*
AMB	N	46.13	2	85	3.8	6.7	5.6	Mar5	18.801	96	C-	88	150.0	NCB	3/5/94	FCP 105.338		Tobaco 189	O *EURO*
AMB	N	46.13	2	85	3.8	4.8	1.1	June15	35.273	NMF	C-	335	43.87	103.875	6/14/93			Tobaco	O *EURO*
AXP	N	20.88	3	105	4.8	7.4	7.8	Jd15	22.883	NMF	C	84	59.60	NCB	6/14/94	FCP 103.250		FinlSv 237	N Y F
ASC	N	36.75	3	100	1.9	7.0	6.7	mS15	22.222	51	C	104	175.0	NCB	9/14/94	FCP 104.531		Groc	N AHC.F
ADD	N	0.44	-	150	NIL	NMF	NMF	aO	46.512	NMF	A	52	135.0	NCB	10/15/93	FCP 105.250		RetStr 367	N ADS.F
AN	N	51.75	4†	55	4.3	6.5	6.2	mS	19.048	75	C	116	498.9	NCB	9/1/95	FCP 102.210		Petrol 141	N ANC.F
AAC	N	13.25	2	195	NIL	13.2	13.2	Jj15	57.143	76	C-	415	23.23	100.000	1/15/02			Cmptrs 261	N AAF.F
APC	N	30.75	2†	105	1.0	6.4	5.8	M9	31.573	25	C	173	79.97	104.900	3/8/93			Petrol	O *EURO*
APC	N	30.75	2†	105	1.0	5.8	5.8	Mn15	29.240	39	C	180	100.0	104.375	5/14/93			Petrol	O APD.F
ANDP	O	6.50	-	135	7.7	13.2	14.9	aO15	61.856	NMF	C+	155	9.900	103.150	10/14/92			Electr	O
APA	N	20.25	3	105	1.4	6.3	4.5	aO	52.138	30	C-	320	150.0	NCB	10/1/93	FCP 104.286		Petrol	N ACP.F
ALG	N	11.25	3	80	2.5	NIL		PFD MJSD15	1.747	NMF	C-	48	2.600	51.500	3/14/93			NatGas	N ALGPrA
AS	N	6.38	2	140	NIL	8.8		PFD MJSD	1.270	90	C-	70	1.697	40.000				Steel 174	N ASPr
AS	N	6.38	2	140	NIL	10.2		PFD JAJO	2.220	80	C	65	0.999	50.450	6/30/93			Steel 174	N ASPrA
ARW	N	20.75	1	160	NIL	6.2		PFD FMAN	1.524	NMF	C	153	2.800	25.780	4/30/93			Electr 374	N ARWPr
ARW	N	20.75	1	160	NIL	8.7	8.8	fA	28.736	58	C	108	30.00	100.000	8/1/03			Electr 164	A ARWD.A
ARV	N	27.63	2	100	2.5	6.8		PFD MJSD31	1.754	33	C	103	2.070	NCB	9/29/92	FCP 52.625		AutoPt 156	N ARVPr
ASH	N	23.25	4	70	4.3	7.8	8.2	jJ	19.478	NMF	C	57	153.7	104.725	6/30/93			Petrol 181	N ASC.F
ATC	A	1.25	-	175	NIL	10.8	16.2	Ap29	61.302	93	C	78	75.00	101.000	4/28/93			Cmptrs	O *EURO*
AAME	O	1.06	-	135	NIL	11.3	18.0	Mn15	91.408	92	C	0	30.00	104.000	5/14/93			Ins Dv	O AAMEG
ADIE	O	1.38*	-	110	NIL	NMF	NMF	Mn	28.881	NMF	A	15	30.00	102.800	4/30/93			AutoPt 133	O ADIEG
AUD	N	43.13	2	80	1.1	NIL	5.3		6.461	NMF	C-	22	805.0	NCB	2/20/96	FCP 43.641		Sftwre 132	N AD.F
AVT	N	28.00	3	100	2.1	7.9	8.1	jj	19.231	97	C-	44	100.0	101.600	9/30/92			Electr 136	N AVI.F
AVT	N	28.00	3	100	2.1	6.5	6.7	Ao15	23.256	84	C	111	115.0	103.000	4/14/93			Electr 204	N AVT.F
BBTF	O	29.13	2	80	3.0	5.3	2.7	Mjsd15	56.338	1	C-	515	34.40	102.625	3/14/93			Bank	O BBTFG
BRE	N	31.88	3	45	7.5	8.8	8.7	Jd	32.258	45	C	164	46.88	100.950	5/31/93			REIT 021	N BRP.F
BSN	A	6.13	-	90	2.9	11.7	15.4	Ao15	64.103	55	C+	54	11.00	101.110	4/14/93			Rec	A BSNA.A
JBAK	O	14.25	3	180	.4	6.5	5.9	Jd	62.016	37	C+	325	65.00	NCB	6/2/95	FCP 104.375		Apprl	O
BLY	N	1.63	3	175	NIL	NMF		PFD FMAN	2.000	NMF	B	80	0.694	52.000	1/31/93			Htl/Gm 190	O
BLY	N	1.63	3	175	NIL	NMF	NMF	mS15	34.495	NMF	B	159	23.59	100.000	9/15/98			Htl/Gm 190	N BLY.F
BLY	N	1.63	3	175	NIL	NMF	NMF	jD15	30.600	NMF	B	320	85.61	103.300	12/14/92			Htl/Gm 190	N BLZ.F
BBCM	O	6.75	-	175	NIL	NMF		PFD MJSD31	1.275	70	C-	199	22.12	102.700	3/31/93			Bank	O BBCMG
ONE	N	43.13	2	95	3.0+	5.5		PFD MJSD31	1.275	63	C-	82	5.000	NCB	4/15/93	FCP 52.100		Bank 149	O BONEO
BAC	N	42.88	3	110	3.0	5.6		PFD FMAN31	1.007	91	C-	70	5.000	NCB	5/31/95	FCP 51.950		Bank 149	O
BFL	N	8.75	-	100	NIL	9.5	10.1	aO	45.126	73	C-	215	15.82	101.800	9/30/92			S & L	N RFL.F
BKB	N	20.38	2	145	NIL	7.7	7.8	Jd15	42.699	22	C	260	95.28	103.100	12/14/92			Bank 309	O
BK	N	42.13	3	115	3.6	6.0	4.2	fA15	25.575	69	C-	153	250.0	NCB	8/15/96	FCP 103.750		Bank 218	N BK.F
BBI	N	35.38	3	115	3.7	5.9		PFD MJSD31	1.887	69	C-	124	2.000	NCB	4/15/96	FCP 52.250		Bank	N BBIPIA

Source: Value Line Convertibles, September 7, 1992, (New York: Arnold Bernhard & Co., Inc.). Reprinted by permission of Value Line Publishing.

FIGURE 21.8 **Convertible Analysis from *Value Line Convertibles***

CONVERTIBLE EVALUATION | **CONVERTIBLE ANALYSIS** | **V-3**

VALUE LINE CONVERTIBLES — September 7, 1992

BONDS & PFDS

	Footnote [23]	Name of Convertible [24]	Price [25]	Performance Rank [26]	Relative Volatility (%) [27]		Over (+) Under (−) Valued (%) [28]	Projected % Change for these changes in the price of the underlying security: +50% [29]	+25% [30]	−25% [31]	−50% [32]	Conversion Value [33]	Premium (%) [34]	Stock Market Risk [35]	Bond Market Risk [36]	I.V. Grade [37]	Investment Value [38]	Premium (%) [39]	Change per point: In Common [40]	In Interest Rates [41]
1	1	AES Corp 6.5s2002	82.00	-	50	1	+1	+13	+6	-5	-8	48.76	68	15+	35	F	73	12	0.82	4.10
2		A.L. Labs 7.75s2014	154.63	◇2	105	2	-1	+50	+25	-21	-40	156.36	1	105+	0	F	72	115	7.73	0.00
3	2	AM International $2.00	1.88	◇-	140	3	-3	+50	+24	-16	-25	1.87	1	130+	10	K	NMF	NMF	0.00	0.00
4	3~	AMR 0s2006	43.38	5	125	4	+4	+20	+9	-10	-16	32.02	35	40+	85	E	34	28	0.43	6.94
5	4	Advanced Medical 7.25s2002	73.50	-	70	5	-6	+14	+5	+0	-2	45.48	62	25+	45	G	71	4	0.74	3.68
6	5~	Advanced Micro Devices $3 Dep	36.38	2	95	6	+2	+14	+7	-8	-15	20.12	81	45+	45	F	28	30	1.09	2.18
7		Advest Group Inc 9s2008	88.00	2	95	7	-5	+11	+4	+0	+0	36.85	139	15+	80	H	90	-2	1.76	5.28
8	6	Air & Water Tech 8s2015	82.25	3	70	8	+1	+8	+4	-4	-7	34.58	138	20+	50	F	74	11	0.82	5.76
9		Airborne Freight 6.75s2001	88.25	4↓	30	9	+0	+3	+1	-1	-1	37.32	136	5+	25	D	87	1	0.00	5.30
10	7~	Alaska Air Group 0s2006	34.75	5	110	10	+1	+13	+6	-5	-9	21.69	60	20+	90	E	31	12	0.35	5.56
11	8~	Alaska Air Group 6.875s2014	82.00	4	60	11	-3	+16	+7	-3	-6	52.08	57	20+	40	E	75	9	0.82	5.74
12	~	Alaska Air Group 7.75s2010	89.00	5↓	60	12	-6	+20	+8	-1	-3	61.95	44	25+	35	E	84	6	0.00	6.23
13	9	Albany Int'l 5.25s2002	80.50	4	50	13	-3	+17	+7	-4	-7	55.70	45	25+	25	E	73	10	0.81	4.02
14	10	Alex Brown 5.75s2001	84.50	3↑	90	14	+1	+22	+10	-9	-17	61.95	36	55+	35	G	64	32	1.69	2.54
15	11~	Alexander & Alexander 11s2007	104.60	1	5	15	+1	+3	+1	-1	-1	63.14	66	5+	0	D	104	-1	0.00	0.00
16	12	Allen Group $1.75 A	27.63	◇3	95	16	+4	+25	+13	-15	-25	22.25	24	70+	25	F	17	63	0.55	1.11
17		Alliant Comp 7.25s2012	5.00	-	160	17	-6	+5	+2	+0	+0	2.28	119	5+	155	K	NMF	NMF	0.00	0.00
18		Allwaste 7.25s2014	90.00	4↓	80	18	+7	+8	+5	-12	-18	48.17	87	40+	40	F	68	32	5.40	5.40
19	13~	Aluminum Co of Amer 6.25s02	120.50	◇5↓	65	19	+7	+30	+13	-16	-25	104.23	16	55+	10	C	84	43	1.21	3.62
20	14~	ALZA 0s2010	40.50	◇1	115	20	+0	+50	+25	-21	-35	40.34	0	100+	15	E	22	84	0.81	1.22
21	~	Amax Inc $3.00	43.00	3	60	21	+1	+12	+6	-6	-11	23.42	84	25+	35	D	36	19	0.43	3.87
22	15	America West 11.5s2009	7.88	◇-	190	22	-3	+4	+1	+0	+0	4.46	76	5+	185	L	NMF	NMF	0.00	0.00
23		America West Air 7.75s2010	5.75	◇-	200	23	-9	+12	+4	+0	+0	3.47	66	15+	185	L	NMF	NMF	0.00	0.00
24		America West Air 7.5s2011	5.75	◇-	200	24	-9	+14	+5	+0	+0	3.35	72	20+	180	L	NMF	NMF	0.00	0.00
25	16	Amer Bankers Ins Grp 5.75s2001	118.00	2	40	25	-3	+30	+14	-7	-12	102.55	15	40+	0	E	100	18	1.18	0.00
26	17~	American Brands 5.375s2003	153.50	◇1↑	75	26	-3	+55	+30	-20	-30	159.05	-3	75+	0	C	100	53	3.07	0.00
27	18~	American Brands 5.75s2005	128.00	2	55	27	-1	+35	+17	-12	-20	116.77	10	50+	5	C	93	38	1.28	1.28
28	~	American Brands 7.625s2001	113.25	2	45	28	+3	+21	+9	-9	14	86.72	31	30+	15	C	94	20	1.13	4.53
29	19~	American Brands 7.75s2002	161.50	◇2	75	29	-1	+50	+25	-24	-35	162.70	-1	75+	0	C	94	72	3.23	0.00
30	20~	Amer Exp(Alleghany)6.5s2014	88.00	3	55	30	+1	+11	+5	-5	-9	47.77	84	20+	35	D	77	14	0.88	7.04
31	~	American Stores 7.25s2001	104.25	2	60	31	-3	+25	+11	-7	-13	81.67	28	40+	20	E	85	23	1.04	4.17
32	21~	Ames Dept Strs 7.5s2014	2.63	◇-	195	32	-4	+18	+2	+0	+0	2.04	29	25+	170	L	NMF	NMF	0.00	0.00
33	~	Amoco 7.375s2013	114.25	4↑	55	33	-3	+35	+15	-11	20	98.57	16	30+	25	E	79	45	1.14	4.57
34	22	Anacomp 13.875s2002	105.50	4↓	40	34	+5	-4	-2	-5	-5	17.86	491	15+	25	H	100	5	4.22	1.06
35	23~	Anadarko (Burlington) 7s2004	109.50	1↑	70	35	-2	+35	+15	-9	-16	97.09	13	55+	15	D	87	26	1.09	3.29
36	~	Anadarko Petroleum 6.25s2014	107.00	2↑	75	36	+1	+30	+14	-12	-22	89.91	19	55+	20	D	75	43	2.14	5.35
37		Andersen Group 10.5s2002	79.50	-	80	37	-9	+18	+5	+0	+0	40.21	98	25+	55	G	88	-10	2.39	4.77
38	24	Apache 7.5s2000	120.00	3	70	38	+3	+30	+14	-13	-21	105.58	14	55+	15	E	88	36	3.50	3.60
39	25~	Arkla $3.00 A	38.63	4↓	50	39	-1	+9	+4	-3	-5	19.65	97	10+	40	D	36	7	0.39	3.86
40	~	Armco $2.10	23.88	3	90	40	+4	+5	+3	-7	-11	8.10	195	20+	70	H	20	19	0.72	1.43
41	~	Armco $4.50	44.25	2↑	90	41	+3	+2	+1	-4	-6	14.15	213	10+	80	H	41	8	0.89	2.66
42	26	Arrow Elec $1.9375 Dep--CALLED	31.13	◇-x	165	42	-2	+50	+25	-24	-50	31.62	-2	165+	0	H	15	107	1.56	0.00
43		Arrow Electronics 9s2003	103.00	1	90	43	+0	+13	+6	-5	-8	59.63	73	35+	55	H	92	12	1.03	4.12
44	27	Arvin Industries $3.75	55.13	◇1	80	44	+1	+30	+14	-12	-19	48.45	14	50+	30	E	41	34	1.10	2.76
45	28~	Ashland Oil 6.75s2014	86.25	3	45	45	+1	+8	+4	-4	-6	45.29	90	10+	35	D	79	9	0.86	6.90
46	29	Atari 5.25s2002	48.50	-	100	46	-4	+2	+1	+0	+0	7.66	533	5+	95	I	50	-3	0.97	2.91
47		Atlantic American 8s97	71.00	-	55	47	-9	+0	+0	+0	+0	9.72	631	0+	55	I	78	-9	0.00	2.84
48		Autodie 7s2011	7.00	-	180	48	-5	+5	+1	+0	+0	3.97	76	5+	175	K	NMF	NMF	0.42	0.28
49	30~	Automatic Data Proc 0s2012	36.88	2↓	30	49	-3	+20	+8	-4	8	27.86	32	20+	10	B	33	12	0.00	0.74
50	31~	Avnet Inc 8s2013--CALLED	100.88	◇-	35	50	+8	+2	+2	-5	-7	53.85	87	10+	25	C	93	8	0.00	8.07
51	~	Avnet Inc 6s2012	93.00	2	55	51	+2	+18	+9	-8	-14	65.12	43	30+	25	C	75	24	0.93	5.58
52		BB&T Finl 8.75s2005	164.25	◇2	70	52	+0	+50	+25	-22	-35	164.08	0	70+	0	D	99	66	4.93	0.00
53		BRE Properties 9.5s2008	108.00	◇1	25	53	-2	+45	+19	-5	-6	102.82	5	25+	0	D	101	7	1.08	1.08
54		BSN Corp 7.75s2001	66.00	-	95	54	-6	+7	+2	+0	+0	39.26	68	5+	90	I	67	-1	0.66	3.30
55	32	Baker (J) 7s2002	108.50	2	100	55	-5	+30	+14	-7	-14	88.37	23	80+	20	E	83	31	2.17	3.26
56	33~	Bally Mfg $4.00 D	32.50	◇-	170	56	+3	+3	+2	-4	-7	9.25	251	20+	150	L	NMF	NMF	0.98	0.65
57	~	Bally Manufacturing 6s98	79.00	◇-	155	57	+5	-2	+0	-5	-6	15.95	395	15+	140	L	NMF	NMF	1.58	1.58
58	~	Bally Manufacturing 10s2006	99.25	◇-	175	58	+7	-6	-2	-6	-7	14.15	601	25+	150	L	NMF	NMF	2.98	1.99
59		Baltimore Bancorp 6.75s2011	65.00	-	100	59	+4	+7	+4	-7	-11	25.84	152	30+	70	H	54	20	1.95	3.90
60	~	Banc One $3.50 C	63.50	2	70	60	+3	+30	+14	-14	-24	54.98	15	55+	15	C	43	48	0.64	3.81
61	~	BankAmerica $3.25 G	58.25	3	75	61	+4	+25	+13	-13	-23	47.03	24	55+	20	D	39	49	0.58	3.50
62	34	BancFlorida Finl 9s2003	94.38	-	65	62	+8	+2	+1	-10	-14	39.49	139	15+	50	G	78	21	2.83	4.72
63	~	Bank of Boston 7.75s2011	101.00	◇2	90	63	+1	+30	+14	-12	-21	87.00	16	75+	30	F	73	38	3.03	4.04
64	~	Bank of New York 7.5s2001	125.00	3	75	64	+2	+30	+14	-12	-20	107.73	16	60+	15	D	91	37	1.25	3.75
65	~	Barnett Bks $4.50 A	76.25	3	70	65	+6	+30	+14	-15	-24	66.75	14	65+	5	D	53	44	0.76	1.53

Source: *Value Line Convertibles,* September 7, 1992, (New York: Arnold Bernhard & Co., Inc.). Reprinted by permission of Value Line Publishing.

been a major source of new financing, there are a number of convertible preferred issues outstanding for the interested investor.

Because convertible preferred stock is a hybrid security involving both preferred and common stock, the valuation analysis involves two steps. Consider a typical convertible preferred issue such as Cummins Engine, which pays an annual dividend of $3.50. The stock is rated BAA3 by Moody's and BBB by Standard & Poor's; it is listed on the NYSE and is convertible into .649 shares of common stock. The common stock is selling for $52 a share, and the convertible preferred stock is $46 a share.

In terms of a pure preferred stock issue, it has some downside risk. Currently most straight preferred stock issues are yielding 8 to 9 percent, whereas the yield on the Cummins convertible is 7.6 percent. Using the conservative 9 percent figure indicates that its price as a straight preferred stock price should be about $38.89 ($3.50/.09). This is about 15 percent lower than its current market price of $46. Assuming an 8 percent yield, the value of the preferred stock would be $43.75, which is about 5 percent less than the current market value. These percentages below the market value are a measure of the stock's downside risk. It appears that the convertible preferred stock is selling based on its option value because there is a fairly substantial conversion premium. Specifically, the conversion value of the stock is $33.75 (.649 × $52), compared to the market price of the convertible preferred stock of $46. You can also derive a conversion parity price for the convertible preferred stock by dividing the current market price by the conversion ratio. In this case, the conversion parity is $70.88 ($46/.649).

You should examine the income relationship between the common stock and the preferred stock. The common stock was paying an annual dividend of $2.20 a share, which indicates a dividend yield of 4.23 percent ($2.20/$52). In contrast, the preferred stock pays an annual dividend of $3.50, indicating a 7.6 percent yield ($3.50/$46).

INDEXED AND OTHER HYBRID SECURITIES

As described above, a hybrid security, like a convertible bond, is a combination of more than one security. For example, a convertible bond is a hybrid of a stock and a bond or it can be viewed as a combination of a bond and a call option. In recent years, financial managers and investment bankers have gained an increased understanding of derivative securities and have created new securities that contain optionlike features. This process of creating innovative securities that offer new payoffs to investors is called *financial engineering*, which typically requires a deep understanding of the technical aspects of security and derivative pricing. In addition, it requires marketing skills to determine what types of payoffs investors want.

Literally hundreds of new types of securities have been launched since the mid-1980s. Excellent reviews of these securities and their implications for the performance of the market are found in articles by Finnerty, Merton, and Miller.[14] Space limitations prevent us from covering but a few of these innovative hybrid securities.

One class of securities is structured so that their payoffs are tied to an index of a particular market. An example is Standard & Poor's Indexed Notes, called SPINs, that

---

[14]John D. Finnerty, "An Overview of Corporate Securities Innovation," *Journal of Applied Corporate Finance* 4, no. 4 (Winter 1992): 23–39; Robert C. Merton, "Financial Innovation and Economic Performance," *Journal of Applied Corporate Finance* 4, no. 4 (Winter 1992): 12–22; Merton H. Miller, "Financial Innovation: Achievements and Prospects," *Journal of Applied Corporate Finance* 4, no. 4 (Winter 1992): 4–11.

were first issued in 1986 by Salomon Brothers.[15] They are 4-year bonds offering a 2 percent coupon. At maturity, they pay off a $1,000 principal plus the excess of the S&P 500 index value over the initial value of the index times a predetermined multiplier computed as follows: The initial value of the S&P 500 index was 270.38 and the multiplier was 3.6985, which is equal to 1,000/270.38.

SPINs are like an ordinary coupon bond plus 3.6985 European call options on the S&P 500 index with an exercise price of 270.38. Unlike ordinary call options, they are not traded on an options exchange, so the payoff promise is subject to default in the event of financial problems at Salomon Brothers. To value the SPIN, you should find the value of an ordinary 4-year, 2 percent coupon bond and add the value of 3.6985 European call options on the S&P 500 index at an exercise price of 270.38.

A variation of the SPIN was the market indexed CD issued by Chase Manhattan bank in 1987 and subsequently by many other banks. This ordinary CD pays a guaranteed rate of interest and a percentage of the return on the S&P 500.[16] This instrument is like a zero coupon bond with a specified number of European calls on the S&P 500, with an exercise price determined by the original level of the S&P 500, the guaranteed return, and the percentage of the S&P 500 return that it offers.

In 1991 the Republic of Austria issued SIGNs, which stands for Stock Index Growth Notes. These securities had original maturities of $5\frac{1}{2}$ years and pay off $10 plus the return on a $10 investment in the S&P 500. If we assume that X is the predetermined exercise price and $S(T)$ is the S&P 500 at expiration, then the SIGNs pay $10 + 10[Max(0,(S(T) - X)/X)]$. For example, if the exercise price is 350 and the S&P 500 ends up at 362, then the S&P 500 ended up 3.43 percent higher than the exercise price. In this example, the SIGN would pay $10 + 10(.0343) = 10.343. These SIGNs can be shown to be equivalent to a zero coupon bond with a face value of $10 and $10/X$ European calls on the S&P 500 with an exercise price of X.

Many other securities issued with similar characteristics are called *equity derivatives* because their performance is tied to the stock market. However, it is not necessary to have their performance linked to the stock market. For example, in June 1986 Standard Oil issued notes whose payoffs were determined by the price of oil. Specifically, the notes paid $1,000 plus 170 times the excess of the price of a barrel of oil over $25 at maturity except the notes would not pay any excess over $40.[17] These securities can be treated as a zero coupon bond with a face value of $1,000, 170 long calls on oil with an exercise price of $25, and 170 short calls on oil with an exercise price of $40. This is equivalent to a vertical spread discussed in Chapter 20.

These illustrations are brief introductions to the world of innovative securities created by financial engineers. The valuation of these securities pose interesting and complex problems for investors. These simple illustrations show that they can often be valued by modeling their returns as a bond and a certain number of options. However, sometimes the payoffs are more complicated. For example, if any of these securities

---

[15]See K. C. Chen and R. Stephan Sears, "Pricing the SPIN," *Financial Management* 19, no. 2 (Summer 1990): 36–47.

[16]See Don M. Chance and John B. Broughton, "Market Index Depository Liabilities: Analysis, Interpretation and Performance," *Journal of Financial Services Research* 1, no. 4 (1988): 335–352.

[17]See Phelim P. Boyle and Stuart M. Turnbull, "Pricing and Hedging Capped Options," *Journal of Futures Markets* 9, no. 1 (1989): 41–54.

permitted its holder to exercise the option component early it would require an application of American option pricing theory, which we saw in Chapter 20 is much more complex. Investors face many other complications in valuing these hybrid instruments. However, their existence is certainly good for investors because they increase the opportunities available to investors. Although the new securities are more complex and difficult to understand, an investor can always choose not to hold them, so the availability of these securities does not make anyone worse off and will benefit some investors and make them better off.

SUMMARY

The richness of option pricing theory manifests itself in this chapter as we saw that there are many securities that have the characteristics of options. First, we observed that the equity of a firm with zero coupon debt could be viewed as an option written by the bondholders on the assets of the firm. This approach enhances our understanding of the valuation of equity and debt because it demonstrates that the limited liability feature of equity is simply a put option granted by the bondholders.

We examined warrants, which are options written by firms and are similar to ordinary calls, except that they tend to have longer original maturities and when they are exercised it increases the number of shares of the firm. Under some simplifying assumptions, it was shown that we can value warrants similar to the Black-Scholes valuation of ordinary calls. We also considered newly created warrants that are written on alternative currencies and the stock indexes of other countries.

We examined convertible bonds, which can be exchanged for a certain number of shares of common stock so these securities can be viewed as ordinary debt plus options to buy common stock. It was demonstrated that they will behave like a bond when the firm is performing poorly, and somewhat like a stock when the firm is performing well. Convertibles can be priced using some principles derived from option theory, but the direct application of an option pricing model to convertibles is considerably more complex. In addition, there is convertible preferred stock, which is preferred stock that likewise has a call option so that it can be converted into common stock.

We also looked at a number of new hybrid securities that represent a small sampling of recent creations of financial engineers. These hybrid securities typically contain a bond with a certain number of call options that provide payments based on the performance of a stock-market index or a commodity price.

All of these investment instruments provide additional investment opportunities. The analysis and valuation of these instruments is complex, but they add the potential for an improved risk–return profile and should not be ignored when constructing diversified global portfolios.

QUESTIONS

1. Explain how and under what conditions the stock of a firm is like a call option.

2. What are the major differences between a warrant and a call option?

3. Identify the factors that influence the value of a warrant.

4. What condition must exist at expiration for the holder of a warrant to decide to exercise it?

5. The Baron Corporation debentures are rated Aa by Moody's and are selling to yield 9.30 percent. The firm's subordinated convertible bonds are rated A by Moody's and are selling to yield 8.20 percent. Explain how this phenomenon could exist.

6. Describe what is meant by the upside potential of convertible bonds. Why do convertible bonds also provide downside protection?

7. Assume a convertible bond's conversion value is substantially above par. Why would the bondholder continue holding the bond rather than converting?

8. Describe how a firm forces conversion. What conditions must exist?

9. Explain what is meant by the payback or breakeven time for a convertible bond and why you would want a high or low payback value.

10. Explain how equity derivatives are typically constructed.

PROBLEMS

1. A corporation has assets worth $1,000,000 and a single zero coupon bond issue outstanding that has a face value of $350,000. The debt is due in 2 years. The assets have a standard deviation of .42, and the risk-free interest rate is 7.6 percent.
   a. Determine the value of the stock.
   b. Determine the value of the bonds.
   c. Determine the yield on the bonds.
   d. Calculate the value of the put option that the stockholders have that represents the value of their limited liability.

2. A firm has 100,000 shares of stock outstanding priced at $35. It has no debt. The firm issues 10,000 warrants, each allowing the purchase of one share of stock at a price of $50. The warrants expire in 5 years. The standard deviation of the stock is .34, and the risk-free rate is 5.2 percent.
   a. Estimate the value of the warrants.
   b. Determine the price of the stock at expiration assuming the warrants were exercised if the value of the firm is $5,200,000.
   c. Reconsider the information in parts a and b. Determine the percentage increase in the value of the warrants from the value you obtained in part a and the value of the warrant at expiration, which you obtained in b. Compare this to the percentage change in the price of the stock and explain your results.

3. The College Corporation has an 8 percent subordinated convertible debenture outstanding that is due in 10 years. The current yield to maturity on this A-rated bond is 5 percent. The current yield on nonconvertible A-rated bonds is 10 percent. This bond is convertible into 21 shares of common stock and is callable at 106 of par, which is $1,000. The company's $10 par-value common stock is currently selling for $54.
   a. What is the straight-debt value of this convertible bond, assuming semiannual interest payments?
   b. What is the conversion value of this bond?
   c. At present, what would be the minimum value of this bond?
   d. At present, could the College Corporation get rid of this convertible debenture? If it can, discuss specifically how it would do so.

4. Extractive Industries has debentures outstanding (par value $1,000) that are convertible into the company's common stock at a price of $25. The convertibles have a coupon interest rate of 11 percent and mature 10 years from today. Interest is payable semiannually, and the convertible debenture is callable with a 1-year interest premium.
   a. Calculate the conversion value if the stock price is $20 per share.
   b. Calculate the conversion value if the stock price is $28 per share.
   c. Calculate the straight-bond value, assuming that nonconvertible bonds of equivalent risk and maturity are yielding 12 percent per year compounded semiannually.
   d. Assume the stock price is $28. The convertible is selling for $1,225. Calculate the conversion parity price.

    e. Using the information in part d, calculate the conversion premium.

    f. Using the information in part d and the fact that the stock is paying a dividend of $1.25, calculate the payback for the convertible bond.

5. Sitting next to Dan at a business luncheon, Rachel explained, "I bought American Desk at $20 a share and it's gone to $40." Dan said, "You would have done better to buy American's warrants, as I did."

    a. Why did Dan say this?

    b. The exercise price of American Desk warrants is $18. Dan purchased the warrants for $4 each when American Desk's stock price was $20 a share. Each warrant entitles Dan to purchase one share of American stock. Assuming the original $2 time value of the warrant dropped to $1, what is the current price of the warrant?

    c. Calculate Rachel's percentage gain.

    d. Calculate Dan's percentage gain when the stock price is $40 and the time value of the warrant is $1.

6. The common stock of Apex Corporation is currently selling at $12 per share, whereas Apex's warrants, which have 5 years until expiration, are selling at $3 and permit the purchase of a share of common stock at $11 per share. By the end of the year you expect the time value on the warrants to have decreased by 20 percent and the following probability distribution to exist for the stock:

Probability	Price
.10	10
.30	13
.40	16
.15	19
.05	25

    a. Given the probability distribution, what is the expected stock price?

    b. Given the probability distribution, what is the expected warrant price?

    c. If average expectations are met, what would be your annual return from an investment in the stock?

    d. If average expectations are met, what would be your annual return from an investment in the warrants?

7. XYZ bank issues a hybrid security called Market Index Notes (called MINs) based on the performance of the S&P 500 index but which also pay off a promised amount as a minimum. The notes have a 1-year maturity and promise to pay off $100 plus one-half the difference between the S&P 500 at the end of the year and 350.

    a. Calculate the value of this note at expiration if the S&P 500 ends up at 358.

    b. Calculate the value of this note at expiration if the S&P 500 ends up at 347.

    c. Find the value of the MINs today (1 year prior to maturity) if the continuously compounded risk-free rate is 6 percent and the standard deviation of the S&P 500 is .18. The S&P 500 is currently at 351.

REFERENCES

Black, Fischer, and John Cox. "Valuing Corporate Securities: Some Effects of Bond Indenture Provisions." *The Journal of Finance* 31, no. 2 (May 1976).

Black, Fischer, and Myron Scholes. "The Pricing of Options and Corporate Liabilities." *Journal of Political Economy* 81, no. 2 (May-June 1973).

Boyle, Phelim P., and Stuart M. Turnbull. "Pricing and Hedging Capped Options." *Journal of Futures Markets* 9, no. 1 (1989).

Brennan, Michael J., and Eduardo S. Schwartz. "Analyzing Convertible Bonds." *Journal of Financial and Quantitative Analysis* 15, no. 4 (November 1980).

Chance, Don M., and John B. Broughton. "Market Index Depository Liabilities: Analysis, Interpretation and Performance." *Journal of Financial Services Research* 1, no. 4 (1988).

Chen, K. C., and R. Stephan Sears. "Pricing the SPIN." *Financial Management* 19, no. 2 (Summer 1990).

Chen, K. C., R. Stephan Sears, and Manuchehr Shahrokhi. "Pricing Nikkei Put Warrants: Some Empirical Evidence." *Journal of Futures Markets* 15, no. 3 (Fall 1992).

Finnerty, John D. "An Overview of Corporate Securities Innovation." *Journal of Applied Corporate Finance* 4, no. 4 (Winter 1992).

Galai, Dan, and Meir I. Schneller. "Pricing Warrants and the Value of the Firm." *The Journal of Finance* 33, no. 5 (December 1978).

Geske, Robert. "The Valuation of Compound Options." *Journal of Financial Economics* 3, no. 1 (March 1979).

Geske, Robert. "The Valuation of Corporate Liabilities as Compound Options." *Journal of Financial and Quantitative Analysis* 12, no. 4 (November 1977).

Hull, John. *Options, Futures and Other Derivative Instruments.* 2nd ed. Englewood Cliffs, N.J.: Prentice-Hall, 1993.

Ingersoll, Jonathan E., Jr. "A Contingent Claims Valuation of Convertible Securities." *Journal of Financial Economics* 4, no. 4 (May 1977).

Ingersoll, Jonathan E., Jr. "An Examination of Corporate Call Policies on Convertible Securities." *The Journal of Finance* 32, no. 2 (May 1977).

Kim, Moon, and Allan Young. "Rewards and Risk from Warrant Hedging." *Journal of Portfolio Management* 6, no. 4 (Summer 1980).

Melicher, Ronald W. "A Comment on Financing with Convertible Preferred Stock, 1960–1967." *The Journal of Finance* 26, no. 1 (March 1971).

Merton, Robert C. "Financial Innovation and Economic Performance." *Journal of Applied Corporate Finance* 4, no. 4 (Winter 1992).

Merton, Robert C. "On the Pricing of Corporate Debt: The Risk Structure of Interest Rates." *The Journal of Finance* 29, no. 2 (May 1974).

Miller, Merton H. "Financial Innovation: Achievements and Prospects." *Journal of Applied Corporate Finance* 4, no. 4 (Winter 1992).

Pinches, George E. "Financing with Convertible Preferred Stock, 1960–1967." *The Journal of Finance* 25, no. 1 (March 1970).

Pinches, George E. "Financing with Convertible Preferred Stock: 1960–1967: Reply." *The Journal of Finance* 26, no. 1 (March 1971).

Ritchie, J. C., Jr. "Convertible Securities and Warrants," in *The Handbook of Fixed Income Securities.* 3d ed., edited by Frank J. Fabozzi (Homewood, Ill.: Dow Jones-Irwin, 1991).

Ritchken, Peter. *Options: Theory, Strategy, Applications.* (Glenview, Ill.: Scott, Foresman, 1989.)

Rogalski, Richard J., and James K. Seward. "Corporate Issues of Foreign Currency Exchange Warrants." *Journal of Financial Economics* 30, no. 2 (December 1991).

Young, Robert A. "Convertible Securities: Definitions, Analytical Tools and Practical Investment Strategies," in *The Financial Analysts Handbook.* 2d ed., edited by Sumner N. Levine (Homewood, Ill.: Dow Jones-Irwin, 1988).

APPENDIX 21A   CONVERTIBLE GLOSSARY

Bond equivalent   *See* Fixed income equivalent

Bond value   *See* Investment value

Breakeven time   The time required for the added income from the convertible to offset the conversion premium. Also referred to as *payback period.*

"Busted" convertibles   *See* Fixed income equivalent

Call provisions   Indenture provisions describing the date, price, and other circumstances under which the issuer may redeem a convertible.

Conditional call   *See* Provisional call

Conversion premium   The excess of the market value of the convertible over its equity value if immediately converted into common stock. Typically expressed as a percentage of the equity value.

Conversion price (or exercise price)   The price at which common stock can be obtained by surrendering the convertible instrument at par value.

Conversion ratio   The number of shares of common stock for which a convertible security may be exchanged.

Conversion value   *See* Equity value

Equity equivalent   A convertible with price behavior dominated by changes in the common stock price, with relatively little sensitivity to changes in interest rates.

Equity value   The value of the convertible security if converted into common stock at the stock's current market price. Also referred to as *parity* or *conversion parity.*

Fixed income equivalent   A convertible with price behavior dominated by changes in interest rates, with relatively little sensitivity to changes in common stock price.

Floor value   *See* Investment value

Forced conversion   If an issuer attempts to redeem a convertible for cash by issuing a call, and if the equity value exceeds the redemption price, the investor is "forced" to convert into common stock in order to obtain the higher equity value.

Hard call   A convertible that does not have any provisional call feature is said to have *hard call* protection.

Initial premium   The conversion premium at the time a new convertible security is offered.

Investment value   The price at which a debenture would have to sell as a straight debt instrument. Also referred to as *bond value* or *floor value.*

Investment value premium   The difference between a convertible's market price and its investment value, expressed as a percentage of investment value.

Parity (or conversion parity)   *See* Equity value

Payback   *See* Breakeven time

Point premium   The conversion premium expressed as *points,* or the dollar price difference between the market price of the convertible and its equity value.

Provisional call   Indenture provision that permits the company to call a convertible security prior to the stated call date if the common stock price rises above a preset level. Typically expressed as a percentage (such as 140 percent or 150 percent) of the specified conversion price.

Unit offering   A combination of notes and warrants that is issued as a unit but may subsequently be traded either separately or as a unit. Also referred to as *synthetic convertibles.*

Yield advantage   The difference between the current yield of the convertible bond and the current yield of the common stock.

Yield to first call   Rate of return at the current price, assuming the issue is called at the first call date and at its call price.

Yield to first put   Rate of return at the current price, assuming the issue is called at the first put date and at its put price.

Source: Luke D. Knecht and Michael L. McCowin, "Valuing Convertible Securities," Harris Trust and Savings Bank (1986). Reprinted with permission.

CHAPTER 22   # FUTURES

In this chapter we will answer the following questions:

- What are the differences between forward and futures contracts?
- What was the reason for the original commodity futures contracts and the most recent foreign currency, interest rate, and stock index futures?
- What are some of the similarities and differences between stock trading and futures trading?
- What are the major futures exchanges, what futures contracts do they trade, and what is their relative trading volume?
- What information is contained in newspaper quotations on futures?
- What are the basic characteristics of interest rate futures contracts?
- What are the major characteristics of stock index futures contracts?
- How can an investor use futures contracts to create a long or short hedge?
- When hedging with futures contracts, what is meant by basis risk, cost of carry, and cross hedging?
- What is involved in using the portfolio approach to determine the appropriate hedge ratio?
- What is involved in using the price-sensitivity approach to determine the optimal hedge ratio?
- What are the specific steps involved in hedging the delivery of a crop?
- How would you hedge a long position in Treasury bonds?
- How would you hedge a long position in a stock portfolio?
- How could you speculate with futures?
- How would you do a Treasury bill arbitrage?
- What would you do to carry out a stock index arbitrage?
- What are the major economic functions of futures markets?
- Based on a number of empirical studies, what have been the returns experienced by those involved in futures trading?

Chapter 9 contained a presentation on the basic principles of futures pricing. In this chapter we begin with a brief discussion of how forward contracts differ from futures contracts. This is followed by an historical review of the futures markets that began with commodity futures and has added foreign currency, interest rate, and stock index futures. Also, we provide a perspective of this market by considering the similarities and differences between stock trading and futures trading, and a description of the major futures exchanges and the contracts traded.

Following this institutional background, we describe the basic characteristics of the very popular interest rate and stock index futures contracts. Because one of the major uses of futures contracts is hedging, we consider how to create both a long and short hedge including how to determine the optimal hedge ratio. We also discuss specific examples of hedging crops, Treasury bonds, and stock portfolios and consider how to do Treasury bill and stock index arbitrage. The chapter concludes with a discussion of the economic function of futures markets and a review of empirical studies on the rates of returns from futures trading.

FORWARD VERSUS FUTURES CONTRACTS

In Chapter 9, we introduced forward and futures contracts as two types of *derivative* instruments. *Forward* contracts are agreements between two parties whereby one party contracts to buy an asset from another party at a later date at a price agreed upon today. For many years there were forward markets only for foreign currencies and a few commodities. Recently forward contracting has become widespread among large, multinational corporations because forward contracts can be tailored to serve highly specialized needs. Because forward markets operate on a relationship of trust between the two parties with little, if any, collateral, these forward markets are not available to many firms and most individual investors.

Futures markets, on the other hand, are accessible to numerous individual and institutional investors. A futures contract has many of the characteristics of a forward contract: it is an agreement between two parties for one party to buy an asset from the other at a later date at a price agreed upon today. However, one difference is that a futures contract is a liquid instrument. In contrast, when an investor enters into a forward contract, he or she makes a commitment to carry out the purchase and sale of the asset at expiration. The point is, although it is possible in some cases to write a new, offsetting forward contract, both of the contracts must be completed. For example, suppose you buy a forward contract to buy 100 ounces of gold at $450 an ounce in 3 months. This obligates you to buy the gold at $450 an ounce in 3 months. Let us say 2 months later you wish to get out of this contract. You could then search for someone willing to buy gold in 1 month and sell that person a forward contract at a price of $447 an ounce. One month later when both contracts expire, you use the first contract to buy gold at $450 an ounce and the second contract to sell it at $447 an ounce. While you effectively liquidated your first contract, you actually had to complete both transactions. If you had been involved in futures contracts, you could simply have sold a similar contract on the futures exchange which would have automatically offset your prior contract and incurred the gain or loss immediately. Futures exchanges have the following requirements: all parties can trade only the specific contracts available on the exchange; all parties must deposit margin money, and all paper gains and losses are settled up each day. Given these rules, not everyone can participate in futures trading. Also, losses are potentially infinite and some financial resources must be available to cover losses before one is allowed to trade.

A BRIEF
HISTORY OF
FUTURES
TRADING

Futures trading evolved to meet the need for spreading the purchase and sale of seasonal commodities throughout the year. In the 1840s Chicago was becoming a major center for commodity transactions from midwestern farms. However, because most crops are harvested around the same time of the year, Chicago found itself deluged with crops in the fall, prices fell, and many farmers dumped their nearly worthless crops in Lake Michigan rather than trying to sell them. Later, when supplies were depleted, prices rose sharply. To rectify this situation, the Chicago Board of Trade was formed to trade what were then called *to-arrive* contracts. These contracts worked as follows. In July a farmer could enter into a contract to sell his wheat at a fixed price for delivery at a later date which means that in July the farmer has agreed to deliver the wheat in March of the following year and receive a price agreed upon in July. The farmer could store the wheat on or near the farm until it was time to deliver it in Chicago. These contracts enabled farmers to know the prices they would receive in the future and spread out the delivery and supply of the crop over a longer period of time which helped remove drastic seasonal price fluctuations.

Subsequently, some investors found that these contracts were attractive speculative instruments. For example, a member of the Chicago Board of Trade could buy wheat for future delivery, thereby speculating on the price of wheat at the delivery date. The availability of numerous speculators willing to take the risk from the farmer was, and still is, the most important benefit of futures markets.

Over the years many additional features were added to the futures markets. A clearinghouse was established in the 1920s to handle the paperwork and to take the other side of every trade which guaranteed that all parties would be paid. Margin deposits and the daily settling up were important features that made futures trading accessible to a wide range of individuals and institutions.

A significant change in the history of futures markets occurred in 1971 when foreign exchange rates were allowed to float freely without the intervention of governments. In response to this, in 1972 the Chicago Mercantile Exchange created futures contracts on foreign currencies, which were the first futures contracts that were not on physical commodities.[1] In 1975 they introduced *interest rate futures,* which were futures contracts on money, which was dubbed "the ultimate commodity." Interest rate futures are contracts to trade fixed-income securities at a later date. In 1982 they created another innovative financial futures contract, the *stock index futures.* Over the years trading in financial futures has far surpassed trading in commodity futures.

FUTURES
MARKETS

As in options markets, futures markets offer a central marketplace, a clearing corporation, standardization of expiration dates and contract sizes, and the availability of a secondary market. Futures markets also specify the terms and conditions of delivery and features such as maximum permissible price moves during a trading session. These features serve to make futures contracts useful devices for adjusting an investor's level of risk. We will explore some of the ways in which futures contracts can be used to manage risk later. For now, however, let us examine some differences between what we learned about stock trading and how futures trading is similar yet different.

---

[1] Foreign currency futures are covered in Chapter 23.

SIMILARITIES AND
DIFFERENCES IN
STOCK AND
FUTURES
TRADING
PRACTICES

Both stock and futures markets operate on highly organized exchanges in contrast to other assets such as real estate, antiques, coins, or stamps, which have highly fragmented trading markets on a geographic basis. Trading on a given exchange is limited to specified stocks or assets. Just as the New York, Tokyo, and London stock exchanges allow only trading in listed stocks, the futures exchanges limit trading to specified assets, such as commodity futures, interest rate futures, currency futures, and stock index futures. Only members can trade on an exchange (stock or futures) for themselves or as a broker for others. The mechanics of buying and selling stocks or futures contracts are quite similar. In both cases, you give an order to a local broker, who sends it to the floor of the exchange where an exchange member executes the order through the stock specialist or in the appropriate futures pit.[2] The types of orders on the exchanges are similar. In both markets, you can use market orders, stop orders, and limit orders. Because they have highly organized exchanges and communication networks, both stock and futures markets are quite liquid. This ability to turn investments into cash very quickly at a fairly certain price contrasts sharply with many other investments. In both markets some investors base their decisions on the fundamentals of supply and demand; others are technicians who use charts and depend mainly on past price movements for indications of future price movements.

Stock and futures markets, however, have some rather significant differences. Buyers of stock acquire ownership, but buyers of futures contracts are not entitled to ownership of the underlying assets until and unless they decide to accept delivery at expiration. Taking delivery rarely occurs as most futures traders use the liquidity of the market to sell their contracts before expiration.

There is much greater leverage in futures trading than in stocks. Although the current margin requirement on stocks is 50 percent, the requirements on futures are stated in dollar amounts and average between 3 and 6 percent. More leverage is not only available but also is universally used in futures trading, in contrast to stocks where only a small proportion of trading is done on margin. As a result, there are differences in the volatility of rates of return, with futures returns being far more volatile. In addition, not all common stocks are eligible for margin trading, whereas all futures contracts can be bought on margin.

There are interest charges on the money borrowed to acquire stocks, but there is not a finance charge on the difference between the price of a futures contract and the margin for a futures contract. This is because the futures contract is a *deferred-delivery contract,* so the payment of the price is deferred until the delivery date of the contract. In fact, what is referred to as margin in futures trading is really a good-faith deposit to protect the futures broker and is somewhat like a down payment on the purchase of the asset.

Although a commission is charged for the purchase and another is charged for the sale of stocks or bonds, commissions for *both* the purchase and the sale of the futures contract are paid at the initiation of the contract. The commissions on futures are a stated dollar cost per contract and tend to be a smaller percentage of the total price of the contract than for stocks.

[2]A futures pit is an octagonal multitiered facility on the trading floor where members stand and execute orders through a process called *open outcry.* Traders shout out their bids and offers and consummate their trades face-to-face.

Stock prices are free to fluctuate without limit. For many futures contracts, there is a daily limit on the price change allowed. Once a given contract reaches this limit, trading in it cannot take place beyond the limit price until the next day.

The stock market has a clearing corporation but there are dealers on the buying and the selling side of the trade who are responsible for their customers. In the futures market, the clearing corporation actually takes the other side in all transactions, either buying or selling directly. After the transaction, each party reports to the clearinghouse, which makes sure that the orders match and charges each broker accordingly. Once this is done, the brokers have liability only to the clearing corporation, not to each other. When a trader subsequently executes an offsetting trade to close out a position, the clearing corporation records the fact that one transaction was offset with another and is thereby closed out. In the stock market, you specifically sell the stock you bought or buy the stock you sold short to complete a transaction.

Performance on a futures contract—delivery as well as payment—is guaranteed by the clearing corporation for the particular futures contract. In upholding this guarantee, the clearing corporation marks a contract to market at the end of every trading day, thus ensuring that its obligations are limited by the maximum daily price change in the unusual event of default. Specifically, if the futures price has moved in favor of the customer during the day, his or her account is credited with the amount of the price change. Similarly, any unfavorable price change is debited to the customer's account. The customer is required to keep a minimum amount of margin, called maintenance margin, typically about 75 percent of the initial margin. A margin call is triggered when the margin in the commodity account falls to the level of the maintenance margin as a result of the daily resettlement. On top of the exchange-imposed margins, brokerage houses could ask for additional margins from their clients depending on the clients' creditworthiness, the volatility of futures prices, and competition.

Thus, the daily mark-to-market practice of futures trading generates many cash flows for futures traders before the contract delivery date. When futures prices rise, contract buyers accumulate cash in their futures account in the interim, but they are required to pay a higher price than they originally agreed to at the final settlement of their long position. In contrast, contract sellers experience many margin calls and cash outflows when futures prices rise. However, they receive a higher settlement price at the time of closing their short position. At final settlement, the aggregate cash receipt of the seller and net cash payment by the buyer are identical to the originally specified price. The daily mark-to-market practice of futures trading has altered only the timing of these cash flows. Further, the clearinghouse has a zero net position at all times, because for every contract buyer there is a seller.

Regular stock trading has no daily marking-to-market of customer positions. Margin trading in stocks is typically marked-to-market daily, though this is not required. In addition, margin trading accounts for only about 3 percent of all trades on the New York Stock Exchange.

Although there are organized stock and futures exchanges, there are no specialists *per se* on futures exchanges. When a trade is desired, members of the futures exchange simply go to the appropriate pit, make it known that they have an order, and all interested traders respond.

When investors want to sell a stock short, they must specifically designate it as a short sale; it cannot be done on a downtick (a decrease); investors must wait until there is a trade at an uptick (an increase) or a zero uptick (a trade with no price change when the last price change was an uptick). There is no such tick requirement for selling short futures; you simply sell a contract you did not buy previously.

Many of these differences produce a different typical holding period for the two investment alternatives. The holding period for agricultural contracts tends to be somewhat short-term, although it may occasionally be as long as a year, or even slightly longer. The holding period for financial futures will vary from interest rate futures that are typically about one month to Eurodollar futures that have delivery periods extending to several years. In contrast, stocks can be held indefinitely, and the average holding period is probably close to a year.

The normal unit of trading is also different. In stocks, the normal unit of trading is a round lot, which is almost always 100 shares. Futures are traded on the basis of contracts, which differ between commodities. A corn contract covers 5,000 bushels, a gold contract covers 100 troy ounces, a Treasury bond contract covers $100,000 face value of Treasury bonds, and a Eurodollar contract covers $1,000,000 face value of Eurodollars. Futures contracts also have fixed delivery months specified by the sponsoring exchanges. Some contracts, such as T-bond futures, have quarterly delivery cycles, and many agricultural commodity futures mature at irregular intervals that vary from a month to more than a year. T-bill futures contracts require delivery during the three business days after the Wednesday following the third Monday of the delivery month. The T-note and T-bond futures permit delivery during the entire delivery month. The futures exchanges also specify the place of delivery. In addition some futures contracts do not actually permit delivery but instead use a cash settlement procedure in which one party simply pays cash to the other. In the stock market, most delivery takes place by book entry, which swaps cash for a claim on a certain number of shares.

Trading in stocks is regulated by the SEC, whereas futures trading is regulated by the Commodity Futures Trading Commission (CFTC). The futures exchanges are required to obtain approval from the CFTC before introducing a new futures contract. Also, there are limits on the number of contracts that any one trader can hold in order to prevent possible corners and squeezes. Further, the CFTC requires larger traders to file periodic trading reports.

Finally, there are important differences in the taxation of profits and losses on stocks and futures positions. Speculative futures transactions are subject to a mark-to-market rule at the end of the year which means that all accumulated gains on futures by year-end are taxable whether the contract has been closed or not. Profits are considered to be 60 percent capital gains and 40 percent ordinary income. Hedgers, however, have their futures transactions taxed as 100 percent ordinary income, and they are exempt from the year-end mark-to-market rule.

FUTURES EXCHANGES AND CONTRACTS

Although the Chicago Board of Trade is the oldest futures exchange, there are many other futures exchanges in the United States and quite a few more in the rest of the world. Table 22.1 lists the U.S. futures exchanges and provides a few details about them.

While the Chicago Board of Trade (CBOT) remains the largest futures exchange, it is rivaled by the Chicago Mercantile Exchange (CME). Although the CBOT spe-

TABLE 22.1   **U.S. Futures Exchanges**

Chicago Board of Trade (CBOT). Referred to as "The Board of Trade." The world's oldest and largest futures exchange. The primary exchange for futures on agricultural commodities, and a major market for trading in financial futures, particularly on intermediate and long-term Treasury securities.

Chicago Mercantile Exchange (CME). Referred to as "The Merc." The second largest futures exchange. Originally specialized in livestock futures, but now most trading is in stock index, interest rate, and foreign currency futures through its subsidiaries, the Index and Option Market and the International Monetary Market.

Commodity Exchange (COMEX). Referred to as "Comex." The primary market for metal futures.

Coffee, Sugar, and Cocoa Exchange (CSCE). Located in New York. Specializes in coffee, sugar, and cocoa.

Kansas City Board of Trade (KCBT). Specializes in grain and has a small volume in stock index futures, where it was the first exchange to offer such trading.

MidAmerica Commodity Exchange (MCE). Referred to as "The MidAm." Trades scaled-down versions of many of the contracts on the Chicago Board of Trade and Chicago Mercantile Exchange.

Minneapolis Grain Exchange (MGE). Small volume of trading in grain futures.

New York Cotton Exchange (NYCTN). Specializes in cotton and orange juice, which trades on its subsidiary, the Citrus Associates, and has a small volume of trading in currency and financial futures on its subsidiary, the Financial Instruments Exchange (FINEX).

New York Futures Exchange (NYFE). Referred to as "NYFE (pronounced 'Nife')." Created out of the New York Stock Exchange. Specializes in stock index futures and has a small volume of trading in a commodity futures index and in Treasury bond futures.

New York Mercantile Exchange (NYMEX). Referred to as "NYMEX." The primary market for energy futures.

Philadelphia Board of Trade (PBT). Created out of the Philadelphia Stock Exchange. Has a small volume of trading in currency futures.

Twin Cities Board of Trade (TCBT). Created out of the Minneapolis Grain Exchange. Has a very small volume of trading in currency futures.

cializes in grains, its biggest contract is its highly successful U.S. Treasury bond futures, which was launched in 1977 and has the largest volume of any futures contract. The CME originally specialized in livestock futures, but the bulk of its current volume comes from numerous successful futures contracts on foreign currencies, stock indexes, and the Eurodollar. The third largest exchange is the New York Mercantile Exchange (NYMEX) which specializes in futures on energy products such as crude oil, gasoline, and heating oil. Trading in these contracts has exploded in recent years, because NYMEX's contracts have enabled firms to hedge the extremely volatile energy market. A listing of the currently available contracts with their exchanges is provided in Table 22.2.

Futures exchanges are highly competitive. Although exchanges attempt to distinguish their products from those of other exchanges, they compete intensively in being the first to initiate a contract. New futures contracts are frequently introduced, but the majority of them fail to attract much volume. This does not mean that futures markets are failures, but simply that there is a limited amount of speculative interest and most of it is concentrated in the established stock index and interest rate contracts. Finally, many futures exchanges also have trading in options on futures contracts which are options to buy or sell futures contracts. They will be discussed in Chapter 23.

VOLUME OF   Figure 22.1 illustrates the volume of trading in futures contracts since 1977. Financial
TRADING   contracts like stock index and interest rate futures have the most volume followed by

TABLE 22.2

Futures Contracts Available on U.S. Exchanges (as of July 1992)

Agriculture	Metals/Wood
Corn (CBOT, MCE)	Copper (COMEX)
Oats (CBOT)	Gold (COMEX, CBOT)
Soybeans (CBOT, MCE)	Platinum (NYMEX)
Soybean Meal (CBOT, MCE)	Palladium (NYMEX)
Soybean Oil (CBOT)	Silver (COMEX, CBOT, MCE)
Wheat (CBOT, KCBT, MGE, MCE)	Lumber (CME)
Feeder Cattle (CME)	**Energy**
Live Cattle (CME, MCE)	
Hogs (CME, MCE)	Heating Oil (NYMEX)
Pork Bellies (CME)	Unleaded Gasoline (NYMEX)
Broilers (CME)	Liquid Propane (NYMEX)
Cocoa (CSCE)	Natural Gas (NYMEX)
Coffee (CSCE)	Crude Oil (NYMEX)
World Sugar (CSCE)	
Domestic Sugar (CSCE)	
Cotton (NYCTN)	
Orange Juice (NYCTN)	
CRB Index (NYFE)	
Diammonium Phosphate (CBOT)	
Rough Rice (MCE)	

Financial	Currency
Treasury Bonds (CBOT, MCE)	Japanese Yen (CME, MCE)
6½- to 10-Year Treasury Notes (CBOT)	German Mark (CME, MCE)
5-Year Treasury Notes (CBOT)	Canadian Dollar (CME)
2-Year Treasury Notes (CBOT)	British Pound (CME, MCE)
30-Day Interest Rates (CBOT)	Swiss Franc (CME, MCE)
Treasury Bills (CME)	Australian Dollar (CME)
1-Month Eurodollars (CME)	U.S. Dollar Index (NYCTN)
3-Month Eurodollars (CME)	French Franc (PBT)
Municipal Bond Index (CBOT)	Mark/Yen Cross Rate (CME)
S&P 500 Index (CME)	
Nikkei 225 Stock Average (CME)	
NYSE Composite Index (NYFE)	
Major Market Index (CBOT)	
5-Year Interest Rate Swaps (CBOT)	
Value Line Stock Index (KCBT)	
S&P 400 MidCap Index (CME)	

currencies, the energy/wood category,[3] metals, and agriculturals. Clearly financials, currencies, and energy have experienced substantial growth that reflects their importance in the increasing globalization of commerce.

Figure 22.2 illustrates the distribution of trading volume across exchanges. The Chicago Board of Trade has about 43 percent of the volume, and the Chicago Mercantile Exchange has about 33 percent. The New York Mercantile Exchange has about 12 percent, but no other exchange has more than 5 percent.

FUTURES
QUOTATIONS

Figure 22.3 presents an example of the futures quotation page from *The Wall Street Journal.* Suppose you were considering buying a corn futures contract. The listing shows that the contract trades at the Chicago Board of Trade (CBT, using the *WSJ*'s

---

[3]Virtually all of the volume is in energy products.

FIGURE 22.1   **Volume of Futures Contracts by Category**

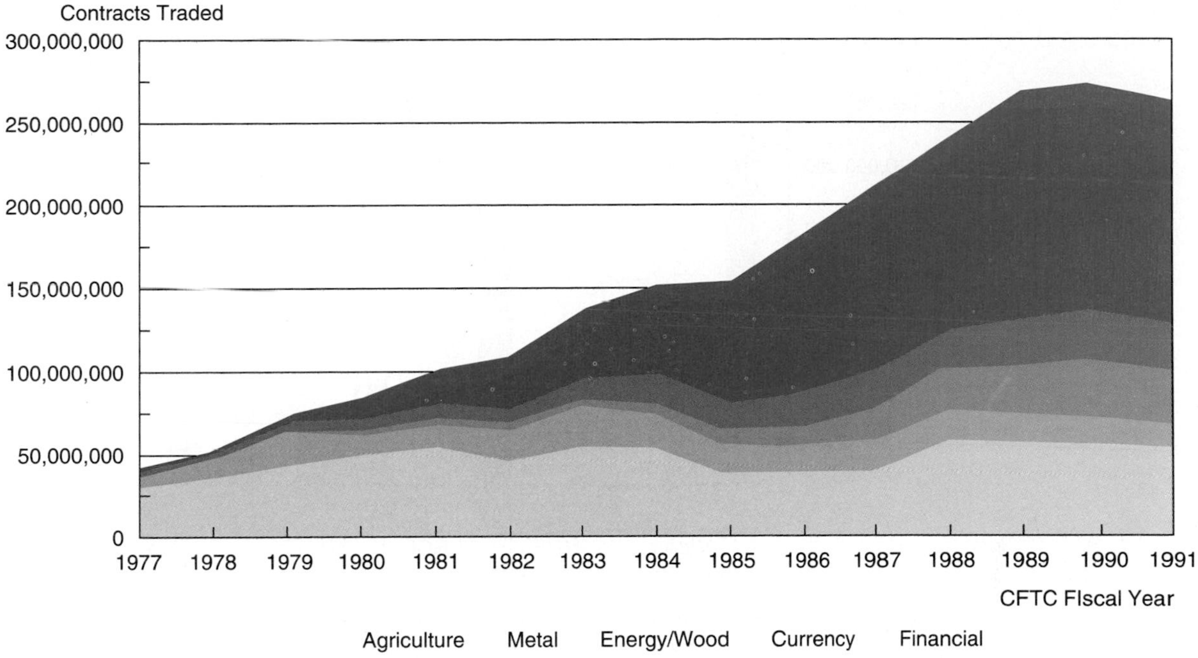

Agriculture   Metal   Energy/Wood   Currency   Financial

Source: CFTC 1991 Annual Report.

abbreviation) and trades in units of 5,000 bushels. The price quoted is in cents per bushel. The September contract on the first line opened at 239 cents per bushel, had a high of 241½ cents per bushel, and a low of 239 cents per bushel. The settlement price, which is roughly the closing price, is the price at which contracts are marked-to-market and it was 241¼ cents per bushel. The settlement price was up by 1¼ cents per bushel over the previous day. During the lifetime of the September 1993 contract, its high was 271½ and its low was 217¾. The open interest, which is the number of contracts currently outstanding, is 64,448. At the bottom of each listing for the commodity is summary information on the overall volume, the volume the previous day, and the overall open interest.

The right column of the figure contains the stock index futures contracts. If you were interested in the S&P 500 futures you would see that it trades at the Chicago Mercantile Exchange (CME), and its price is 500 times the index. The September contract opened at 449.70, which means the value of the contract was actually $500 × 449.70 = $224,850. The high during the day was 450.80, the low was 447.45, and the settlement price was 448.95, which was down .65 from the previous day. During its lifetime, the September contract had a high of 458.55 and a low of 391.00. Its open interest was 175,931 contracts. At the bottom of the S&P 500 listing there is information on volume and open interest. There is also information about the actual S&P 500 index, which closed at 449.27.

The lower column of the figure contains information on interest rate futures. The Treasury bond contract on the Chicago Board of Trade is for $100,000 face value of

FIGURE 22.2

Volume of Futures Trading by Exchange

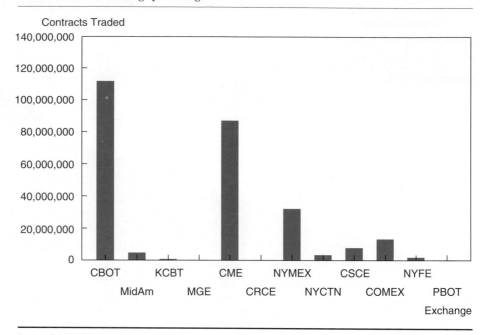

Source: CFTC 1991 Annual Report.

FIGURE 22.3

Futures Quotations from *The Wall Street Journal*

Source: Futures Prices, *The Wall Street Journal,* August 4, 1993. Copyright © 1993 Dow Jones & Company, Inc. Reprinted by permission of *The Wall Street Journal.* All rights reserved worldwide.

Treasury bonds and the price quote is in 32nds of 100 percent of face value. For example, the settlement price of the September 1993 contract is $115^{24}/_{32}$. This is an actual price of $(115 + {^{24}/_{32}})/100 \times \$100,000 = \$115,750$, which is up $^{11}/_{32}$ from the previous day. The seventh and eighth columns are yields on 15-year, 8 percent government bonds that would be implied by the settlement prices. This information is given as a guide to interpreting a price of $115^{24}/_{32}$. Some traders find it easier to think of it in terms of a yield of 6.573 percent, but it should be emphasized that unlike a bond, a futures contract does not have a yield. The final column contains the open interest and the bottom line below the Treasury bond futures listing contains volume and open interest information on all contracts.

DIFFERENT
TYPES OF
FUTURES
CONTRACTS

COMMODITY
FUTURES

In this category we include contracts on agricultural products as well as metals and other natural resources such as oil. Each type of contract typically has a variety of deliverable grades. For example, there are several types of wheat. For other commodities such as oil and gold, purity requirements must be met before the commodity can be delivered. The contract also specifies which grades of a commodity are acceptable for delivery and where delivery takes place.

Most commodity futures (and in fact, most futures in general) seldom are terminated in delivery. The liquidity of the futures market enables futures traders to execute offsetting positions, and this is exactly how most trading is done.

As we found in Chapter 9, a futures price is determined by the spot price and the cost of carry. In fact our equation was

$$F(t, T) = S(t) + C(t,T)$$

where:

$F(t, T)$ = the price of a futures today (at time t) that expires at time T
$S(t)$ = the spot price today
$C(t, T)$ = the cost of carry from today until expiration

The cost of carry includes the cost of storage and any interest lost on tying up $S(t)$ dollars in the asset until time T less any cash payments the asset makes. For commodities, the cost of storage is particularly significant. The costs of actually storing 5,000 bushels of corn or 1,000 barrels of oil can be quite substantial. However, these assets do not make any cash payments. Thus, the cost of carry is simply the storage costs plus the interest.[4]

The storability of commodities varies. Assets such as gold and oil are storable for a virtually infinite period of time. Grains are storable for a fairly long period of time but not forever. Some commodities, such as frozen concentrated orange juice and cattle, have quite limited storability. When commodities cannot be stored at all, pricing them according to the cost of carry model becomes impossible. However, most of the trading volume is in contracts with expirations that are shorter than the period of storability.

---

[4]We derived this result without regard to the transaction costs that keep this relationship from holding exactly as stated here. Transaction costs create a band around the cost of carry futures price, within which arbitrage profits cannot be earned.

Occasionally the futures price will be less than the spot price for storable commodities. This implies that the cost of carry is negative! This phenomenon is difficult to explain. Some have argued that there is an implicit return to owning a commodity during a period of low supply. This additional return, which is really nothing more than a higher current spot price resulting from tight supplies, is often called the *convenience yield*. It is viewed as the premium one earns from having the commodity on hand when supplies are tight.

Commodity futures trading differs from financial futures trading in the matter of short selling the underlying commodity. Although stocks and Treasury bonds can be sold short, there are no facilities in the commodity business for borrowing the commodity and selling it to someone else. As a result of the inability to sell short, the cost of carry relationship can be somewhat one-sided. For example, suppose the futures price falls below the spot price plus the cost of carry. For an asset that can be sold short, one would buy the futures and sell short the asset. At expiration, the holder of the futures contract would take delivery and then use the asset to cover the short position.[5] This would earn an arbitrage profit and tend to drive the futures price back to the spot price plus the cost of carry. This type of transaction, as well as the opposite transaction where you would buy the asset and sell a futures, is called *pure arbitrage*.

For commodities that cannot be sold short, there are limits to the pressure that would drive the futures price up from below the cost of carry price. Without short selling, the only type of arbitrage transaction that can be done is if someone holding the asset sells it and buys a futures, then replaces it at expiration by taking delivery. This transaction also earns an arbitrage profit and is referred to as *quasi arbitrage*. However, this transaction is not necessarily executed often enough to push the futures price back to the cost of carry price, perhaps because the holders of the commodities are reluctant to temporarily remove the asset from their inventories.

INTEREST RATE
FUTURES

An interest rate futures is a contract on a fixed-income security. The most widely traded contracts are on Treasury bonds and bills and on Eurodollars. The Treasury bond contract calls for delivery of a U.S. Treasury bond that will not mature or be called for 15 years from the expiration. The contract stipulates that the bond has an 8 percent coupon. However, there are not always 8 percent coupon bonds available. Thus, the contract allows the delivery of bonds of any coupon. The price of the contract is based on the assumption that an 8 percent coupon bond will be delivered. If a bond with a higher (lower) coupon is delivered, the person accepting delivery is paid a higher (lower) price.

Because a number of bonds are eligible for delivery, identifying the underlying spot asset is somewhat difficult. Traders use a technique designed to identify which bond is the *cheapest to deliver* but it is widely recognized that conditions change and the cheapest-to-deliver bond will change. In any case, however, the futures is priced by using the currently cheapest-to-deliver bond as the spot asset. The cost of carry is simplified because there are essentially no costs in storing a Treasury bond except the opportunity cost of your money which is usually computed as the rate on repurchase

---

[5]However, as noted earlier, many contracts permit a variety of similar but slightly different grades to be delivered. The delivery decision is always made by the holder of the short position. Therefore, the holder of the futures faces the risk that the commodity delivered is not exactly the one that was sold short in the spot market.

agreements. This so-called *repo rate* is the cost of borrowing money by pledging a government security as collateral. The cost of carry must be reduced because Treasury bonds pay coupons, which reduces the opportunity cost of the funds tied up.

Treasury bond futures pricing is further complicated by the variety of delivery options held by the holder of the short position. This includes the right to deliver any bond meeting the 15-year requirement and also to deliver any day during the delivery month. If the coupon exceeds (is less than) the opportunity cost, the holder of the short position will tend to make delivery late (early) in the month. Also, because the futures market closes at 3:00 in the afternoon and the spot market stays open until around 5:00, during the delivery month the short holder can watch for a price decline in the spot market between 3:00 and 5:00 and earn a profit by making delivery. Also, because the futures contract ceases trading around the third week of the month, but delivery can be done the final week if there is a sharp drop in spot prices during that last week, the short holder can realize a nice profit by making delivery. These options tend to reduce futures price and including them into the pricing of the contract is quite complex.

Treasury bill futures permit delivery of a 90-, 91-, or 92-day Treasury bill. Their prices are quoted by computing discounts from par value on a 360-day-a-year basis. For example, if a T-bill futures is quoted at a price of 92, it has a discount of 8 percent and an actual price of $100 - 8(90/360) = 98$ per $100 face value. Because the face value is $1,000,000, the quoted price of 92 is actually $980,000. Each basis point move in the price, say from 92 to 92.01, changes the overall price by $25. They are priced fairly easily by the cost of carry model.

Treasury bill futures began in 1976 and were for many years the leading futures contract on a short-term interest rate before being surpassed by the Eurodollar futures contract, which was begun in 1981. A Eurodollar is a dollar deposited in a foreign bank or a foreign branch of an American bank. Eurodollar deposits are out from under U.S. regulations, and do not incur exchange rate risk. The rate on Eurodollar deposits is called the *London Interbank Offer Rate (LIBOR)*. The Eurodollar futures contract specifies that upon expiration the futures price is set to the LIBOR rate that day.[6] There is no delivery; the final settlement is in cash. Since Eurodollar futures prices are quoted like T-bill futures prices, a price of 92 is really $980,000. Ninety-day Eurodollar futures are available in maturities up to almost 7 years. In addition there is a contract on 30-day Eurodollars.

Unfortunately, Eurodollar futures pricing is somewhat complex because there is no secondary market for Eurodollar deposits. Assume that you buy a 180-day Eurodollar deposit and sell a 90-day futures, expecting to form a perfect hedge for 90 days. The next day the deposit will have 179 days, the next day 178, and so on. Typically banks quote Eurodollar deposits only in maturities of multiples of 30 days. Thus, it is difficult to get quotes for the actual spot rate on deposits with 179, 178, or 177 days.[7] Without knowledge of the spot rate, pricing the contract by the cost of carry model is difficult. As a matter of practice, most traders simply interpolate based upon the surrounding quotes.

Eurodollar futures have been extremely successful because the rates on many business loans are tied to the LIBOR rate so there was a need for an instrument whose price

---

[6]It is actually an average of LIBOR rates quoted by many banks.

[7]These are called *off-the-run* quotes. They are sometimes available but are not widely disseminated.

trades in line with the LIBOR rate. In addition, the market for swaps, caps, floors, and interest rate options has grown dramatically, and many institutions hedge and arbitrage instruments using the Eurodollar futures.[8]

STOCK INDEX FUTURES

Stock index futures contracts are based on the level of a stock index. As discussed in Chapter 4, there are several price-weighted and value-weighted market indexes. The most popular stock index futures is the CME's S&P 500 futures, which is value-weighted index. Because the Dow Jones Company successfully fought the efforts of the Chicago Board of Trade to launch a futures contract on the Dow Jones Industrial Average, there are no futures contracts on the most widely followed market index. In response, the CBOT created a similar index called the Major Market Index that includes 20 stocks and it is priced-weighted like the DJIA.[9]

Stock index futures contracts are fairly easily priced using the cost of carry model. The cost of carry is essentially the opportunity cost of the funds tied up minus the dividends on the underlying stocks in the index. It is assumed, however, that all the dividends over the life of the contract are known up front. Of course, for narrow indexes such as the Major Market Index, predicting the dividends is easy compared to broad-based stock indexes such as the S&P 500. However, most traders assume that the dividend stream is fairly stable from period to period. Stock index futures contracts are usually available with expirations every 3 months. Most of the volume is concentrated in the nearby expiration contract.

If a stock index futures price deviates from the cost of carry formula, it is possible to earn an arbitrage profit by buying the stock and selling the futures or selling short the stock and buying the futures. This type of transaction, which is called *index arbitrage,* has become extremely important and controversial in recent years. It is illustrated later in this chapter.

HEDGING

Hedging is a transaction that involves taking long and short positions in two separate markets to reduce risk. Typically a hedger holds an exposed position in one market, usually the spot market. If the hedger's position would be harmed by a decrease in the spot price, the spot position is said to be *long* which occurs if the hedger holds the asset. However, if a firm anticipates selling a bond issue at a later date, it, too, is effectively long because a decrease in the price of the bond will be harmful. The investor who wishes to reduce the risk and enters into a hedge, which involves taking a short position in a futures contract, has entered into a *short hedge.* As long as the futures and spot prices move together, a price decrease will lead to a loss in the spot market, but because the investor is short in futures, it will lead to a gain in the futures market. These gains and losses are expected to at least partially offset each other. In contrast, if the price rises in the spot market, it will probably rise in the futures market and result in a loss for the futures contract and this will at least partially offset the gain in the spot market.

If the investor's spot position will be harmed by price increases, he or she is effectively short in the spot market. This could occur by a simple short sale or by the investor

---

[8]These instruments are covered in Chapter 23.

[9]As noted in Chapter 20, the AMEX trades options on the Major Market Index. In the fall of 1993, the futures contract was transferred from the CBOT to the CME.

committing to purchase an asset at a later date. In either case the investor might wish to enter into a *long hedge,* which involves the purchase of futures contracts. If the price increases, the spot market loss will be at least partially offset by a gain in the futures market. If the price decreases, a spot market gain will be at least partially offset by a loss in the futures market.

Let us consider a simple position in which the investor owns one unit of the spot asset worth $S(t)$. The futures price is $F(t,T)$. If the investor wishes to hedge, he or she might sell a single futures. Assume the position is held to expiration, at which time, the investor can either deliver the asset or buy back the futures just before expiration (at which time its price will equal the spot price), and sell the asset in the spot market. Ignoring transaction costs, the results are the same in either case. We will assume that the futures is offset at expiration. Before subtracting the cost of carry on the asset, the profit from the short hedge held to expiration is

$$S(T) - S(t) - [F(T,T) - F(t,T)]$$

Because $S(T) = F(T,T)$, the profit becomes

$$F(t,T) - S(t)$$

Thus, when the position is opened, the short hedger knows exactly what the profit will be. Note that, if the futures and spot prices are aligned by the cost of carry model, the profit will equal the cost of carry. Thus, this risk-free transaction will earn a return that will cover the carrying costs and provide the hedger with a return equivalent to the risk-free rate.

Many hedges are not held to expiration. Suppose $S(t^*)$ is the spot price and $F(t^*,T)$ is the futures price at time t^*, which is after today (t) but before expiration (T). Then, the profit from the short hedge closed out at t^* is

$$S(t^*) - S(t) - [F(t^*,T) - F(t,T)]$$

Thus, the profit is the excess of the change in the spot price over the change in the futures price. If the futures and spot prices line up according to the cost of carry model, the profit should be simply the cost of carry from t to t^*. However, in practice, futures and spot prices do not always behave as specified by the cost of carry model which introduces the concept of *basis risk.*

The *basis* is defined as the spot price minus the futures price as follows: $B(t) = S(t) - F(t,T)$. We can define the basis at any other point in time by simply replacing the t with a time indicator. When the hedge is held to expiration, the basis is $B(T) = S(T) - F(T,T) = 0$. When the hedge is closed before expiration, the basis is $B(t^*) = S(t^*) - F(t^*,T)$. Thus, when the hedge is closed out at t^*, the profit is

$$-B(t) + B(t^*)$$

In other words, it is the change in the basis. If prices do not behave according to the cost of carry model, the hedger faces *basis risk*. If the basis increases, called *strengthening,* the hedger gains because the long spot position either increases more or decreases less than the short futures position. If the basis decreases, called *weakening,* the short hedger is hurt, because the long position either decreases more or increases less than the short futures position.[10] If the position is held to expiration, the basis goes to zero and there is no basis risk. In this case, the hedger knows at the outset what the profit will be. If prices conform to the cost of carry model, there is also no basis risk and the hedge will always return the cost of carry.

The success of a hedge is contingent on the futures and spot prices moving together. Assume that you are long a portfolio of corporate bonds but there are no corporate bond futures so you decide to hedge your portfolio with a Treasury bond futures contract. Corporate and Treasury bonds will generally move in the same direction, but they are in no way linked through arbitrage. Thus, the spot price of corporate bonds and the futures price of Treasury bond futures will not necessarily line up according to the cost of carry.[11] Such a hedge is called a *cross hedge* and carries greater basis risk. Still, as long as their prices move in the same direction, the hedge will reduce the risk of holding the corporate bond portfolio.

Finally, many futures traders execute spread transactions, which are quite similar to hedges. Recall that we learned in Chapter 20 that a futures spread can be executed by buying a futures with one expiration and selling one with another expiration. For example, a long hedger who buys the spot asset and sells a futures expiring in 2 months agrees to deliver the spot asset in 2 months and receive the futures price. A spreader who buys a 2-month futures and sells a 4-month futures agrees to buy the spot asset in 2 months at the 2-month futures price and sell the asset in 4 months at the 4-month futures price. Spreads are often executed as a hedge of a single futures position. Instead of taking an opposite position in the spot market, the spreader takes an opposite position in an otherwise identical futures contract, expiring at a different time. For a large physical commodity, such as 200,000 pounds of cattle, it is much easier to do a futures transaction than a spot transaction.[12]

DETERMINING THE HEDGE RATIO

When undertaking a hedge, it is important to determine the appropriate number of futures contracts for each unit of the spot asset. This number of futures contracts per unit of spot asset is called the *hedge ratio.* If the futures contract is on the spot asset, the process is simple: one simply sells enough futures so that the entire spot position can be delivered. In general, however, this perfect match will not be the case, and the objective of the hedge ratio is to balance the volatility of the spot position with the futures position. If one owns one unit of the spot asset and its price changes by ΔS, then one would want h units of the futures so that $h\Delta F$ would equal ΔS. Simply assuming that the futures and spot positions have equivalent volatility is somewhat naive and, in fact, is called a *naive hedge ratio,* which is typically not appropriate. The following subsections discuss some alternative approaches to determining the hedge ratio.

---

[10]These results are reversed for a long hedge.

[11]However, holding maturity, coupon, and other features constant, corporate and Treasury bonds would behave generally according to a spread between their yields that reflects their differences in default risk.

[12]Actually in nearly every case, it is easier and less costly to do a futures transaction than a spot transaction.

THE PORTFOLIO
APPROACH TO
DETERMINING
THE HEDGE RATIO

The portfolio approach to determining the hedge ratio does not distinguish between hedging and speculation. It assumes that the basic motivation for futures trading is the same as that for trading stocks and bonds which is to obtain the maximum possible return for a given level of risk. Given the investor's risk preference, an optimal combination of spot and futures positions is determined. Under this approach, both the hedger and speculator pursue the same goals, but derive different combinations of spot and futures positions.

Define the dollar return on a portfolio of one unit of a spot asset and h units of futures as

$$E(DR) = \Delta S + h\Delta F$$

The variance of the dollar return on the portfolio is

$$\sigma^2(DR) = \sigma^2_{\Delta S} + h^2\sigma^2_{\Delta F} + 2h\sigma_{\Delta S,\Delta F}$$

where:

$\sigma^2_{\Delta S}$ = **the variance of expected spot price changes**

$\sigma^2_{\Delta F}$ = **the variance of expected futures price changes**

$\sigma_{\Delta S,\Delta F}$ = **the covariance of spot and futures price changes**

In the Markowitz mean-variance portfolio analysis, the holder of the portfolio seeks to maximize Q:

$$Q = E(DR) - \lambda\sigma^2(DR)$$

where λ is the risk aversion parameter, which represents the investor's relative feelings about expected return versus risk. Assuming risk aversion, λ is positive. The expression Q represents the utility of the investor's chosen combination of expected return and risk. If we maximize Q, we find the value of h that achieves the greatest possible utility. This is accomplished by differentiating Q with respect to h, setting the derivative to zero and solving for h.[13] The solution is

$$h = \frac{E(\Delta F)}{2\lambda\sigma^2_{\Delta F}} - \frac{\sigma_{\Delta S,\Delta F}}{\sigma^2_{\Delta F}} \tag{22.1}$$

Note that there are two components to the hedge ratio. The first component, called the *speculative component,* specifies that some portion of the futures position is based on the expectation of the futures price change. This speculative component is smaller, the greater the investor's risk aversion (λ) and the greater the risk of the futures ($\sigma^2_{\Delta F}$). The second component, called the *hedging component,* will be negative assuming that the futures and spot have a positive covariance. Note that it is equal to minus once times the covariance between the futures and spot price changes divided by the variance of the

---

[13]One additional step is to take the second derivative and verify that it is positive, which it is.

futures price change which is the beta coefficient of a regression of the spot price change on the futures price change.

For a risk-averse investor, the above formula gives the number of futures contracts, *h,* needed to properly hedge your spot position. Note, too, that the speculative component can swamp the hedge component, meaning that the so-called hedger actually goes long in both the spot and futures markets. Given the special case in which the futures price is not expected to change, the investor takes no speculative position and does only the pure hedge. If the futures and spot price changes are not correlated at all, the hedging component disappears and the investor takes only a speculative position because the futures adds nothing to the risk of the portfolio, so the investor speculates in futures by going long if the futures price is expected to increase and goes short if the futures price is expected to decrease.

Unfortunately, applying the portfolio approach to hedging is difficult because it is not easy to determine an investor's λ. Using the approach taken by Johnson, Stein, and Ederington, it is assumed that the objective is to minimize risk, which is equivalent to assuming an infinite value of λ.[14] Then the hedge ratio becomes

$$h = -\frac{\sigma_{\Delta S, \Delta F}}{\sigma^2_{\Delta F}} \tag{22.2}$$

which is simply the hedging component. If the relationship between the futures and spot prices remains stable over time, it is possible to estimate the hedge ratio by a regression of historical spot price changes on historical futures price changes wherein the coefficient of determination (R^2) from the regression serves as a measure of hedging effectiveness. Specifically, it measures the risk reduced by hedging relative to the risk of the original unhedged position. For example, an R^2 of .52 means that the hedge eliminated 52 percent of the risk of an unhedged position. In the special case in which the asset is a stock portfolio and the futures is on the market portfolio, the appropriate hedge ratio is simply the portfolio's beta relative to the market index.

Peck employed the portfolio model to examine whether a routine system of optimal hedging of expected egg production in the former shell egg futures market of the Chicago Mercantile Exchange succeeded in stabilizing producer income during the 1971 to 1973 period.[15] She found that the average optimal hedge ratios of hedges lasting 1 to 5 months ranged from 55 to 90 percent of production; the longer the hedge horizon, the higher the optimal hedge ratio. Note that the results obtained from using a naive hedge of one unit of the futures for every unit of the spot compared favorably with the optimal hedging strategy.

Ederington also examined the effectiveness of the portfolio approach to hedging interest rate futures.[16] Using weekly data over the period from January 1976 to De-

---

[14]See Leland L. Johnson, "The Theory of Hedging and Speculation in Commodity Futures," *Review of Economic Studies* 27 (1959–1960): 139–160; Jerome L. Stein, "The Simultaneous Determination of Spot and Futures Prices," *American Economic Review* 51, no. 5 (December 1961): 1012–1025; and Louis H. Ederington, "The Hedging Performance of the New Futures Market," *Journal of Finance* 34, no. 1 (March 1979): 157–170.

[15]Anne E. Peck, "Hedging and Income Stability: Concepts, Implications, and an Example," in *Selected Writings on Futures Markets,* edited by Anne E. Peck (Chicago: Chicago Board of Trade, 1977), 237–250.

[16]Ederington, "Hedging Performance."

cember 1977, he examined the hedging performance of futures contracts on Government National Mortgage Association (GNMA) pass-through certificates, T-bills, wheat, and corn. Although the GNMA contract no longer trades, it was the first financial futures contract. He found that for the GNMA futures, the variance-minimizing hedge ratio of a 2-week hedge involving the nearby futures contract was about 80 percent of the spot position which means the hedger should have traded futures with a face value equal to 80 percent of the par value of the cash GNMAs. Such a hedge reduced the price variability of the unhedged spot GNMA portfolio by 66 percent which was quite comparable to the effectiveness of wheat and corn futures hedges. The results for the T-bill futures contract were not quite as effective, but Franckle showed that these results could be improved by adjusting the hedge ratio through time.[17]

PRICE-SENSITIVITY APPROACH TO HEDGING WITH INTEREST RATE FUTURES

With the portfolio approach to hedging it is necessary to estimate the covariance between the spot and futures price changes to establish the optimal hedge ratio but this relationship may be unstable and, therefore, difficult to estimate. This is particularly true for fixed-income securities because as they move through time, their volatility changes. Therefore, it is more important to estimate their volatility over the hedge horizon than over the past. Fortunately, this estimation problem can be overcome by the *price-sensitivity approach,* which estimates the hedge ratio as the volatility of the spot position divided by the volatility of the futures position. This ratio of relative volatilities is captured by the durations of the spot and futures positions.[18]

Because the objective is to have the spot and futures volatility offset, we can set up the equation

$$\Delta S + h\Delta F = 0$$

This implies that

$$h = -(\Delta S/\Delta F) \cong -(dS/dF) \tag{22.3}$$

We know from the discussions in Chapter 14 on bond durations that the price volatility of a bond is related to its duration. For simplicity, assume that the term structure of interest rates is flat over the hedging horizon and the term structure experiences a small parallel shift. This enables us to express the relationship between price volatility and yield volatility of a bond using Macaulay's duration. For a small change in the bond's yield, the spot price change can be represented as

$$dS = -D(S)SdR(S)/R(S)$$

[17]Charles T. Franckle, "The Hedging Performance of the New Futures Market: Comment," *Journal of Finance* 35, no. 5 (December 1980): 1273–1279.

[18]See Robert W. Kolb and Raymond Chiang, "Immunizing Bond Portfolios Using Interest Rate Futures," *Financial Management* 10, no. 4 (Autumn 1981): 72–79.

where $D(S)$ is the duration of the spot asset being hedged and $R(S)$ is one plus the spot bond's yield. We can capture the duration of the futures by using a similar equation that reflects the price sensitivity of the bond underlying the futures contract.[19] We have

$$dF = -D(F)FdR(F)/R(F)$$

where $D(F)$ is the duration of the bond underlying the futures and $R(F)$ is one plus the yield on the bond underlying the futures. Assuming a single interest rate that drives the interest rates on all bonds, let R equal one plus that rate. The sensitivity of the spot and futures prices to a small change in this rate is given by

$$dS/dR = -D(S)SdR(S)/(R(S)dR)$$
$$dF/dR = -D(F)FdR(F)/(R(F)dR)$$

Substituting these results into Equation 22.3, we obtain

$$h = \frac{-D(S)SR(F)}{-D(F)FR(S)} \tag{22.4}$$

In other words, the hedge ratio is the ratio of the spot duration to the futures duration times the ratio of the spot price to the futures price times the ratio of one plus the futures yield to one plus the spot yield.

Although the price-sensitivity approach has some limitations, it is considered a fairly accurate method. Its use of duration to capture the volatility emphasizes the importance of current volatility, as reflected in the duration, instead of past volatility.

Gay, Kolb and Chiang tested the effectiveness of the price sensitivity hedge ratio by hedging a random sample of New York Stock Exchange bonds using the nearby T-bond futures contract during the period 1979 to 1980.[20] They compared the performance of the following alternative hedge strategies, assuming an investment of $1 million in a bond at the end of the hedge horizon: (1) do not hedge the planned investment, (2) buy ten T-bond futures contracts with a total face value of $1,000,000 (Naive Strategy 1), (3) buy ($1,000,000/future price) T-bond futures contracts (Naive Strategy 2), and (4) buy T-bond futures contracts as indicated by the price-sensitivity hedge ratio (Price-Sensitivity Strategy). The dollar performance of these alternative strategies showed that the price-sensitive strategy produces the minimum absolute wealth change (i.e., the minimum absolute difference between the actual and the expected bond prices). The results indicated that the price-sensitivity strategy reduced the variability of the unhedged position by 73 percent, which is greater than the risk reduction produced by any of the naive strategies.

SOME HEDGING EXAMPLES

A farmer who has planted a crop faces the risk that the price of the crop will fall below the level required to cover the cost. Futures contracts can be used to protect against loss. By selling a futures contract, the farmer commits to delivering the crop at a later

---

[19]This will, of course, be the currently cheapest-to-deliver bond.

[20]Gerald Gay, Robert Kolb, and Raymond Chiang, "Interest Rate Hedging: An Empirical Test of Alternative Strategies," *Journal of Financial Research* 6, no. 3 (Fall 1983): 187–197.

HEDGING THE
DELIVERY OF A
CROP

date at a price agreed upon today. In fact, the farmer can establish the final selling price of the crop long before the crop has even been planted.

Table 22.3 shows an example of how a farmer puts on a hedge during the growing season. In mid-July the farmer anticipates a harvest of 10,000 bushels of corn in late August and the price of the September futures is $3.32 a bushel. Since each corn futures contract covers 5,000 bushels, if the farmer sells two contracts, he or she will have locked in a price of $3.32 per bushel *if* the position is held to expiration. Because the farmer must harvest the crop at its optimal harvest time, the futures expiration and required delivery date do not necessarily coincide with the date when the harvested corn will be available for delivery. Thus, when the corn is available, the farmer buys back the futures and delivers the corn to the spot market. This procedure will not lock in $3.32 a bushel, but it will come fairly close if the positions are closed out near the expiration.

Thus, in July the farmer sells two futures contracts. On September 5, the corn is ready for delivery and is worth $3.18 on the spot market. The futures price is at $3.19, near but not quite equal to the spot price. The farmer buys back the futures contract at $3.19, netting a profit in the futures market of $1,300. This profit effectively increases the revenue from the sale of the corn. Thus, the farmer gets a total of $31,800 + $1,300 = $33,100 for the corn, an effective price of $3.31 per bushel. The farmer benefited from the hedge because the price of corn fell (as indicated by the fall in the futures price) and yet the effective sale price of the corn was very near the futures price of $3.32 in July. Had prices risen, there would have been a loss on the futures that would have partially offset any gains from a rising spot price. In this instance, the farmer would have forgone the added gain from a price rise to reduce the uncertainty of the final selling price. The sense of regret that the hedge was done when the price turned out to increase could cause some farmers to avoid using the futures market as a means to hedge some or all of their crop. When they do not hedge, however, they are acting

TABLE 22.3

Hedging the Delivery of a Crop

Intent: Sell futures contracts to lock in the price at which a crop to be harvested later will be sold.

Spot	Futures
Jul. 15: Farmer anticipates the harvest of 10,000 bushels of corn in late August and is concerned that the price of corn in early September will be insufficient to cover production costs.	Sells two September corn futures contracts covering 10,000 bushels of corn at a price of $3.32 a bushel.
Sep. 5: The spot price of corn turns out to be $3.18. The corn can be sold for 10,000($3.18) = $31,800.	The spot price converges to $3.19, approximately the futures price, and the farmer buys back the futures contract for a profit on the contract of 10,000($3.32 − $3.19) = $1,300.

Conclusion: The farmer sold the crop for $3.18 per bushel or $31,800, but also gained $1,300 on the futures transaction. Thus, the total revenue was $33,100, making the effective price $3.31. When the futures contract was sold in July, the farmer was attempting to lock in a selling price of $3.32. The only reason the effective price was actually $3.31 is that the farmer chose to close out the position before the contract had officially expired. If he had waited until expiration, the spot and futures prices would have been equal.

TABLE 22.4

Hedging a Long Position in Treasury Bonds

Intent: Sell futures contracts against a long position in Treasury bonds to hedge an unexpected increase in interest rates.

Spot	Futures
Nov. 1: You own $1 million of 21-year, $8\frac{3}{8}$ percent Treasury bonds priced at 82–17, yielding 10.45 percent. Your portfolio value is $825,312.50.	Sell ten March Treasury bond futures at a price of 80–09. The basis is $2\frac{8}{32}$ ($82\frac{17}{32}$ − $80\frac{9}{32}$).
Mar. 3: You sell the $8\frac{3}{8}$ percent bonds at 70–26 to yield 12.31 percent. Your portfolio value is $708,125. This is a loss of $11\frac{23}{32}$ per bond or $117,187.50 overall.	Buy ten March Treasury bond futures at 66–29. This is a gain of $13\frac{12}{32}$ per contract or $133,750. The basis is now $3\frac{29}{32}$ ($70\frac{26}{32}$ − $66\frac{29}{32}$).

Conclusion: The overall transaction resulted in a gain in the value of the portfolio. The loss of $117,187.50 was offset by a gain on the futures transaction of $133,750 for a net gain of $16,562.50. Another way of looking at the gain is the strengthening of the basis of $3\frac{29}{32}$ that resulted from the futures price decreasing more than the spot price. Because the position is long spot and short futures, the overall position benefits from the stronger basis. The basis went from $2\frac{8}{32}$ to $3\frac{29}{32}$ for an increase of $1\frac{21}{32}$, which is $16,562.50, the overall gain.

like speculators in the commodity, because, by definition, they are long the commodity that they are growing.

Because of uncertainty about the size of the harvest, transaction and margin costs, and differential price movements, it is seldom possible to hedge a position completely. There can be substantial uncertainty about the size of a crop. A drought can cause the hedge to cover more output than the farmer produces, whereas a surplus can cause the hedge to cover only a small proportion of a crop. In addition, although there will be commission and margin costs that will add to the loss or detract from the gain, these costs will be small compared to the potential gain or loss on the crop.

On the other side of the farmer's position is quite likely a corn futures trader at the CBOT who buys corn futures from the farmer. However, the trader may not want the risk of an exposed long position, so he or she may sell the position to a commodity processor. For example, if we assume that Kellogg's, a major manufacturer of cereal, is concerned that the corn it will buy in September will rise in price, its risk is just the opposite of that of the farmer. Kellogg's could buy futures to stabilize the price it pays for the corn in September so that the futures market would serve as an efficient mechanism for the reallocation of risk among market participants (i.e., the farmer and the processor).

HEDGING A LONG POSITION IN TREASURY BONDS

Bond portfolio managers face the risk of changes in interest rates. Table 22.4 illustrates the case of a bond portfolio manager concerned about an increase in interest rates. To keep things fairly simple, assume that the portfolio consists entirely of $1 million of the same issue, a 21-year Treasury bond with $8\frac{3}{8}$ percent coupon, 10.45 percent yield, and a price of $82\frac{17}{32}$ percent of par. If we assume that the futures contract is based on this particular bond, the spot bond, we do not need to adjust the hedge ratio to reflect their volatilities.[21] We will simply use $1,000,000 face value of futures to hedge the

---

[21]We could just as easily assume that this is a standard CBOT Treasury bond futures contract in which the 21-year, $8\frac{3}{8}$ percent coupon bond is the cheapest-to-deliver.

TABLE 22.5	**Hedging a Long Position in a Stock Portfolio**	

Intent: Sell futures contracts against a long position in a stock portfolio to hedge against an unexpected drop in the stock market.

Spot	Futures
Jan. 16: You own a stock portfolio worth $1.5 million. The portfolio beta is 1.3.	Sell 12 March S&P 500 futures at a price of 335.25. At a multiple of $500 per contract, the futures position is 12(335.25)($500) = $2,011,500.
Mar. 3: The stock portfolio has declined to a value of $1.3 million, a loss of $200,000.	Buy 12 March S&P 500 futures at a price of 308.45. The futures position is 12(308.45)($500) = $1,850,700. The futures transaction results in a gain of $160,800.

Conclusion: The overall transaction resulted in a loss of $200,000 − $160,800, or $39,200. However, the futures hedge reduced the loss, which would have been $200,000 without the hedge. The spot portfolio lost about 13 percent of its value, whereas the futures price fell by about 8 percent. Thus, the beta of 1.3 actually understated the movement of the portfolio relative to the market.

$1,000,000 face value of bonds which calls for ten $100,000 face value futures contracts.[22]

The appropriate contract, the March futures, is selling for 80–09 ($80\frac{9}{32}$) which is a price of 80.28125 percent of par or $80,281.25 per contract. Note that the basis is $2\frac{8}{32}$ ($82\frac{17}{32}$ − $80\frac{9}{32}$).

When we close the position, the bonds have fallen in price to $70\frac{26}{32}$, which is equivalent to a portfolio value of $708,125. Concurrently, the futures price fell to $66\frac{29}{32}$, or $66,906.25 per contract. The bonds lost $117,187.50 in the spot market but you gained $133,750 in the futures market for a net gain of $16,562.50 which can be seen as the change in the basis. The original basis was $2\frac{8}{32}$ but when the hedge was terminated it was $3\frac{29}{32}$. Recall that a long hedge benefits from a strengthening basis which in this case reflected a gain of $1\frac{21}{32}$, which is equivalent to 1.65625 or $16,562.50 overall.

Had prices moved the other direction, the spot bonds would have shown a gain and the futures position would have had a loss. The bond portfolio manager would probably have regretted doing the hedge, but giving up gains is the cost of hedging while the greater certainty of the final selling price of the bonds is the benefit.

On the opposite side of the transaction was probably a futures trader on the Chicago Board of Trade. He or she could have acquired the futures but might choose to sell it to another party. Outside of the exchange floor, there might be firms that anticipate buying Treasury bonds at a later date and wish to buy futures to lock in the purchase price. Again, we see that the futures market helps market participants reallocate risk.

HEDGING A LONG POSITION IN A STOCK PORTFOLIO

Table 22.5 illustrates a transaction in which you are the holder of $1.5 million stock portfolio and execute a hedge using stock index futures to protect the portfolio. In this case, it is quite important that you take into account the fact that the stock portfolio and the stock index futures contract might not have the same price volatility. For example, assume that your portfolio has a beta of 1.3. Because the stock index futures

---

[22]If we could not make these assumptions, we would need to use the price-sensitivity formula or the portfolio theory approach to find the correct hedge ratio.

and the market portfolio would have approximately the same volatility, the stock portfolio is about 30 percent more volatile than the futures. This means that you would need to use more contracts to cover this additional volatility. In addition, this futures contract is cash settled to an index level, so it is not possible to make delivery which means that you need to figure the dollar amount of stock index futures to hedge $1.5 million of stock.

The appropriate hedge ratio is found by using the portfolio approach. However, if the stock index futures is based on the same index that is used to determine the beta, then the hedge ratio will be nearly identical to the beta. In other words, the beta is the hedge ratio which makes sense because a stock portfolio that is approximately 30 percent more volatile than the market, will require approximately 30 percent more stock index futures for every dollar in the spot market. The actual number of contracts to use, thus, is 1.3 times the dollar spot position, or $1.5 million(1.3) = $1.95 million. The appropriate futures contract is the March contract, and it sells for 335.25. Each contract has a multiplier of $500, making the actual price equal to $167,625. Thus, the number of contracts is $1,950,000/$167,625 = 11.63, which is rounded off to 12.

Because you want to protect the stock portfolio against a loss, you sell futures. On January 16, you sell 12 futures, establishing a short position of $2,011,500 in the futures market. On March 3, you close out your position. At that time the portfolio has fallen to $1.3 million, a loss of $200,000. The futures price has fallen to 308.45. You buy the 12 contracts back at a price of 308.45($500) = $154,225 per contract for a total of $1,850,700. Thus, the futures transaction netted a gain of $160,800. This reduced the loss on the spot stock transaction to $39,200.

The hedge was not perfect because the stock portfolio and the stock index futures do not move perfectly in line with the beta. The spot stock portfolio fell about 13 percent and the futures price fell only 8 percent. Thus, the spot price moved by a factor of more than 1.6 times the futures price. This example illustrates that hedging is not an exact science; some guesswork is required to determine the best hedge ratio. Nevertheless, as long as the spot and futures prices move in the same direction, however imperfectly, even the use of a single futures contract will reduce any losses from a fall in the value of the stock portfolio.

Of course, if the stock market had risen, the stock portfolio would have shown a gain and the futures transaction would have produced a loss. Again, this is the cost of hedging; potential gains are given up to minimize the volatility of the value of the spot position.

SPECULATION

Although risk is inherent in all aspects of business operations, those who want to reduce their risks can do so by hedging. However, risk is never eliminated from the economy; it must be assumed by another party, namely, the speculator. Therefore, in this section, let us consider some speculative transactions using futures.

Suppose you have been following the market for hogs, and based on your analysis, you are pessimistic about the future price of hogs. Hog futures are traded on the Chicago Mercantile Exchange (CME) and the standard contract is 30,000 pounds. In November you decide to sell three July hog contracts that are selling for 44.00 (44 cents a pound). This means each contract's price is $13,200 ($0.44 x 30,000), and the total value of the three contracts is $39,600. If the margin requirement is $5,940, you will deposit this with the broker who deposits it in the clearinghouse. In this instance, a one-cent change in the price of hogs changes your three contract position by $900 (.01 × 90,000 pounds). Assume you put in a stop-gain order at 48 cents, which means that you want to buy three contracts to offset your prior sale if hog futures reach this price. You will recall from Chapter 3 that with this order it is not certain that you will pay 48 cents, but it should be fairly close.

Assume that prices increase, your stop-gain order is executed, and you buy three contracts at 48.5 cents a pound in February. Your return would be as follows:

Sale of three July contracts at $.44/lb.	= $39,600
(you deposit $5,940)	
Purchase of three July hog contracts at .485	= $43,650
Gross Loss	= ($ 4,050)
Less estimated round-trip commission	$ 90
($30/contract)	
Loss before interest on variable margins	$ 4,140
Rate of return on the initial margin	
subject to interest on variable margin:	

$$(\$4,140)/\$5,940 = -69.7\%$$

In this instance, hogs increased in price by 10.2 percent, and you experienced a negative rate of return of almost 70 percent on your investment in 3 months. The risks of speculating in futures should be obvious, but speculators are motivated by the potential rewards, which can be seen by having the price change in the other direction.

You may have already heard stories about wildly speculative activity in the Chicago futures pits. Whenever someone wants to make a point about excessive risk taking, the futures pits are used although such examples are misleading. Recall that the farmer who does not use the futures market to hedge is speculating on the price of the crop. The farmer is taking no less, and perhaps more, risk than the Chicago futures traders. The role of futures speculators is to willingly take the risk that the farmer and other hedgers wish to remove. Their image as a wild speculator is inaccurate and ignores the fact that by assuming the risk that others want to eliminate, speculators play an important role in our economy.

ARBITRAGE

The romantic myth of the arbitrageur as the clever and daring financial genius, risking millions of dollars on rapid transactions, executed at the push of a button, is somewhat exaggerated. The fact is, most arbitrageurs take very little risk because arbitrage in its purest form is a risk-free transaction. Although completely risk-free arbitrage is somewhat rare, the actual transactions are typically very close to the textbook examples and the risk is, thus, quite low.

In Chapter 9 and also in Chapter 20 on options, we discussed arbitrage transactions, whereby identical assets were selling for different prices. We discussed examples where an arbitrageur could buy the lower-priced asset and sell the higher-priced asset, netting a risk-free profit equal to the difference in their prices. Recall that by "identical assets," we do not simply mean IBM trading in New York and IBM trading in London. We

TABLE 22.6

Treasury Bill Arbitrage

Intent: Use a long position in Treasury bills and a short position in Treasury bill futures to create a synthetic Treasury bill offering a greater return than the actual Treasury bill of the same maturity.

Spot		Futures
Today:	You have 45 days to invest your money at the risk-free rate. Currently, 45-day T-bills are selling at a discount rate of 3.15. The price of the bills is $100 - 3.15(45/360) = 99.60625$ per 100 face value. Annualizing this rate gives a return of $(100/99.60625)^{(365/45)} - 1 = .0325$. There is a bill with a 135-day maturity selling at a discount of 3.20. Its price would be $100 - 3.20(135/360) = 98.80$ per 100 face value. Buy $1,000,000 face value of this bill.	Sell 1 Treasury bill futures contract with $1,000,000 face value that expires in 45 days. It is quoted at a discount of 3.19. This is a price of $100 - 3.19(90/360) = 99.2025$ per 100 face value.
Expiration:	The 135-day bill now has 90 days to go. Deliver it to fulfill your obligation on the futures contract.	On delivery of the bill, you will receive the current spot price plus the profit on your futures, an effective price of the original futures price of 99.2025.

Conclusion: The net effect is that you bought a Treasury bill at a price of 98.80 per 100 face value and sold it 45 days later at a price of 99.2025 per 100 face value. This is an annualized return of $(99.2025/98.80)^{(365/45)} - 1 = .0335$. This synthetic 45-day T-bill, thus, offers a return of 10 basis points above the actual T-bill.

saw that a European put plus the stock is identical to a European call plus a risk-free bond. Also, we found that a long position in the spot asset and a short position in a futures on the asset is risk-free; thus, a risk-free bond should sell for the same price.

When otherwise identical combinations of assets have different prices, the arbitrageurs go to work and the combined actions of many arbitrageurs bring the prices back in line. In this manner, arbitrageurs contribute to making the market more efficient; prices are fair and capital is allocated more efficiently when claims on identical streams of returns are priced equivalently.

Not all arbitrage is executed by the romantic international arbitrageur as shown by the following example of a portfolio manager with spare cash.

TREASURY BILL ARBITRAGE

The following example illustrated in Table 22.6 assumes you have a sum of money that can be invested at the risk-free rate for 45 days, after which time you will need the money to make payments or purchase new securities. The current rate on Treasury bills maturing in 45 days is 3.15 percent. Remember that this is a discount rate so every $100 of face value of T-bills will cost $100 - (3.15)(45/360) = 99.60625$. Thus, your rate of return from investing 99.60625 for 45 days after which you receive 100 is $(100/99.60625)^{(365/45)} - 1 = .0325$.

Because of your knowledge of the opportunities available in the futures market, you estimate that you can do better than this. There is a 135-day T-bill available with a discount rate of 3.20, giving it a price of $100 - (3.20)(135/360) = 98.80$ per $100 face value. Assume that you buy this 135-day T-bill and sell a futures contract that

TABLE 22.7

Stock Index Arbitrage

Intent: Use a long position in a portfolio identical to the S&P 500 and a short position in the S&P 500 futures to earn a return greater than the risk-free rate.

Spot	Futures
Today: The S&P 500 stock index is at 348.34. The Treasury bill rate is 3.5 percent and the S&P dividend yield is 3.1 percent. You own a large stock portfolio identical to the S&P 500.	The S&P 500 futures contract expiring in 90 days is priced at 349.75. Its theoretical fair value is $348.34(1 + (.035/4) - (.031/4)) = 348.69$. You sell futures with a face value equivalent to the value of the stock portfolio.
Expiration: At expiration, the S&P 500 index is at 345.5. You earned dividends of $348.34(.031/4) - 2.70$. Had you invested the 348.34 in the risk-free asset, you would have earned $348.34(.035/4) = 3.05$ in interest. Thus, you effectively invested $348.34 + 3.05 = 351.39$. You sell the stocks for a loss of $351.39 - 345.5 - 2.70 = 3.19$.	Your futures contract expires and is settled up at the S&P 500 index of 345.5 for a gain of $349.75 - 345.5 = 4.25$.

Conclusion: The net effect is that you bought stock for 351.39, earned 2.70 in dividends and sold it at 345.5 for a loss of 3.19; however, you made a gain in the futures market of 4.25, for an overall gain of 1.06. This equals the amount by which the original futures price (349.75) exceeded its theoretical fair value (348.69). The same profit is earned regardless of the value of the S&P 500 index at expiration. Another way of looking at it is that you bought the stock for 348.34, earned 2.70 in dividends and effectively sold the stock for 349.75, the spot price of 345.5 plus the futures profit of 4.25. Thus, your 90-day return was .01179 [$(349.75 - 348.34 + 2.70)/348.34$], which annualizes to 4.7 percent (using a 360-day year for simplicity). This is a risk-free return and exceeds the risk-free rate of 3.5 percent.

expires in 45 days which is quoted at a discount of 3.19, which implies a price of $100 - (3.19)(90/360) = 99.2025$.[23]

The futures expires 45 days later, whereupon your 135-day bill is now a 90-day bill which you deliver to fulfill the requirement of your futures contract. You receive the current spot price plus the profit on the futures. We do not need to determine the current spot price because the effective sale price for the spot asset is the original futures price. Thus, you receive an effective price of 99.2025 on delivery. The net effect is that you bought a T-bill at 98.80 per $100 face value and sold it 45 days later at 99.2025. This provides an annualized return of $(99.2025/98.80)^{(365/45)} - 1 = .0335$.

By purchasing a 135-day T-bill and selling a futures on a 90-day T-bill that expires in 45 days, you have created a synthetic 45-day T-bill that just happens to pay 10 basis points more than the prevailing T-bill. Of course, your transaction costs would have to be covered and you must move quickly because other investors will see this opportunity and rush to do this transaction, which will bring the rates on the actual and synthetic T-bills back in line.

STOCK INDEX ARBITRAGE

Now suppose you are a portfolio manager who holds a portfolio that is identical to the S&P 500. Consider the example in Table 22.7, which shows the S&P 500 is at 348.34. You can view your portfolio as a hypothetical position in a certain number of "shares"

---

[23]Remember that because the futures contract is on a 90-day T-bill, the discount is computed over 90 days.

of the S&P 500, each worth 348.34. The current T-bill rate is 3.5 percent and the S&P stocks have a combined dividend yield of 3.1 percent. Based on your understanding of the cost of carry formula, you determine that an S&P 500 futures contract expiring in 90 days should be worth

$$348.34[1 + (.035/4) - (.031/4)] = 348.69$$

Note that the spot price (348.34) is increased by the T-bill rate minus the dividend rate. The T-bill rate minus the dividend yield is the cost of carry. Because the rates are quoted on an annual basis, we divide them by 4 (using a 360-day year for simplicity). The actual S&P 500 futures contract, however, is selling for 349.75, which is 1.06 higher than its cost of carry price. Thus, you should sell the overpriced futures.

Now let us say at expiration that the S&P 500 index is at 345.5, which implies that your portfolio lost value. You earned dividends of 348.34(.031/4) = 2.70 for each "share" of the S&P 500. Had you invested the 348.34 in the risk-free asset, you would have had 348.34(.035/4) = 3.05 in interest. Thus, by the expiration date your investment outlay is really 348.34 + 3.05 = 351.39. You sell the stocks for a loss of 3.19 (351.39 − 345.5 − 2.70 in dividends). Your futures expires and is settled up at the S&P 500 index value of 345.5 for a gain of 349.75 − 345.5 = 4.25.

Thus, the overall transactions can be summarized as follows:

Bought stock	− 351.39
Earned dividends	+ 2.70
Sold stock	+ 345.50
Futures profit	+ 4.25
Total	+ 1.06

Note that this amount, 1.06, is the difference between the original stock index futures price and its value as determined by the cost of carry formula. An alternative view is to consider that you bought the stock for 348.34, collected 2.70 in dividends, and sold the stock for 349.75. This is a return of (349.75 − 348.34 + 2.70)/348.34 = .01179 for 90 days. Annualizing to a 360-day year gives 4.7 percent, which beats the risk-free T-bill rate of 3.5 percent by a large margin.

This type of trade is a variation of a trade called *stock index arbitrage.* Typically a stock index arbitrage transaction is done by someone not already owning the S&P 500 portfolio. In this case, you already owned the portfolio and used the mispricing on the futures to earn a risk-free return in excess of the risk-free rate. The combined actions of all arbitrageurs will, of course, bring prices back in line so that this transaction should earn approximately the risk-free rate.

Stock index arbitrage has had an exciting and controversial history. Because of its connection with portfolio insurance and program trading, we will defer a further discussion of this transaction until Chapter 23. At this point, you should recognize that as a portfolio manager you should always seek to earn the highest return for a given level of risk. If you can earn a risk-free return in excess of the prevailing risk-free rate by using futures, you should be ready to do so quickly before others grab these opportunities.

ECONOMIC
FUNCTIONS OF
FUTURES
MARKETS

In this chapter we have considered numerous examples of futures transactions and have alluded to the benefits of having these markets. At this point, we will examine in a little more detail the important role that futures play in our economy.

Futures markets are said to provide *price discovery*. An example of this is when the futures price is an unbiased estimate of the expected future spot price. For example, suppose a 5-month futures contract on orange juice is selling for $1.14 a pound. If the futures price is unbiased, the futures market is predicting that orange juice will sell in the spot market for $1.14 a pound. Although futures prices are not necessarily unbiased, relatively high futures prices relative to current spot prices are an indication that those involved with this commodity expect high spot prices in the future. Farmers can use futures prices as a guide in making planting decisions. Also, futures markets serve a price discovery function by consolidating the information from diverse spot markets. For example, live cattle are auctioned in spot markets all around the country. There is no single spot market, and it is difficult to identify exactly the spot market price. However, in many cases the price of a soon-to-expire futures contract serves as a good gauge of the spot price. In markets where the spot price can be identified, the relationship among futures prices, spot prices, and carrying costs provide useful information for firms that deal in the commodity.

The presentation of numerous hedging examples indicate that futures markets provide an efficient means of *managing risk*. Some parties who must assume certain risks (e.g., the farmer) oftentimes find that they wish to temporarily reduce or increase their level of risk. Futures markets provide an efficient means of allowing this transfer of risk between parties. Futures contracts have very low transaction costs and require very little capital to trade. Thus, they play an important role in aiding our financial markets allocate capital and risk. By making the market more efficient, prices are fairer to all producers, investors, and firms.

THE RETURNS
TO FUTURES
TRADING

An important question for investors is whether trading futures is profitable. If futures markets are risky, then there should be positive returns on average to speculative futures traders. At the same time, the CAPM holds that only the systematic risk and not the total price risk is relevant. The systematic risk (the beta) of a futures contract is measured by the covariance of the futures price change with the return on the market portfolio divided by the variance of the market return. Because the futures contract requires no initial investment of funds but only good-faith margin deposits, the futures contract is not a part of the market portfolio of all assets. In addition, the futures' beta is close to zero, so the expected return from trading the futures contract should be close to zero.[24] To make consistent profits on futures positions, traders must be able to forecast prices more accurately than other market participants.

In a study of corn, wheat, and soybean futures during the 1952 to 1967 period, Dusak found that futures betas and semimonthly returns were close to zero.[25] Bodie and Rosansky examined quarterly returns on 23 commodity futures contracts for the

---

[24]Because there is no outlay of money for the futures, the expected return from a futures position with zero systematic risk is zero and not the risk-free rate.

[25]Katherine Dusak, "Futures Trading and Investor Returns: An Investigation of Commodity Market Risk Premiums," *Journal of Political Economy* 81, no. 4 (December 1973): 1387–1406.

period 1950 to 1976.[26] The futures' returns are computed assuming that the investor used Treasury bills to post 100 percent margin. The annual rates of return presented in Table 22.8 indicate that the mean and standard deviation of returns on an equally weighted commodity futures portfolio are comparable to those on common stocks. The futures' returns have low to negative correlations with returns on T-bills, long-term government bonds, and common stocks, indicating the diversification potential of commodity futures contracts. The study revealed that a portfolio with 60 percent in common stocks and 40 percent in commodity futures has about the same mean rate of return as common stocks, but the standard deviation of such a portfolio is only two-thirds that of a pure common stock portfolio. Further, there was positive correlation of commodity futures returns with the rate of inflation which means that commodity futures were a better hedge against inflation than common stocks. The results in Table 22.9 indicate that the mean annual returns on most commodity futures are positive but relatively volatile. Many of the betas of future contracts were negative and close to zero indicating that the systematic risk of commodity futures is relatively small.

The diversification potential of futures has resulted in increased attention in recent years to the recognition of futures as a distinct asset class. More portfolio managers are beginning to consider allocating a portion of their portfolios to a diversified combination of futures contracts.

SUMMARY

In this chapter we saw how futures contracts evolved, how futures trading is different from stock trading and we compared the characteristics of commodity, interest rate, and financial futures contracts. The important role that futures play in enabling investors to manage risk was demonstrated with a discussion of hedging. Some hedging, speculative, and arbitrage transactions were illustrated.

We saw that futures contracts play an important role in the economy by revealing information about the prices of their underlying assets, by facilitating low-cost risk transferral from hedgers to speculators, and by making prices conform more closely to the efficient markets model. We also found that futures exhibited low to sometimes negative correlation with the market portfolio. As a result, they can be an attractive component of well-diversified investment portfolios.

QUESTIONS

1. What was the original purpose of futures contracts? What were futures contracts originally called?
2. Discuss two ways in which trading futures and trading common stocks are similar.
3. Discuss two ways in which trading futures and trading common stocks are different.
4. What are the most active types of futures contracts? Why do you think these types of futures are so active?
5. Discuss the applicability of the cost of carry formula to the pricing of a commodity futures contract.
6. How would you go about pricing a futures on a long-term bond?

---

[26]Zvi Bodic and Victor I. Rosansky, "Risk and Return in Commodity Futures," *Financial Analysts Journal* 36, no. 3 (May-June 1980): 27–39.

TABLE 22.8 **Distributions of Annual Rates of Return on Alternative Investments, 1950-1976**

Series	Mean[a]	Standard Deviation	Correlation Matrix			
			Commodity Futures	Long-Term Government Bonds	Treasury Bills	Inflation
A. Nominal Returns (percent per year)						
Common stocks	13.05	18.95	-.24	-.10	-.57	-.43
Commodity futures	13.83	22.43		-.16	.34	.58
Commodity futures with Treasury bills					.20	.03
Long-term government bonds	2.84	6.53				.76
U.S. Treasury bills	3.63	1.95				
Rate of inflation	3.43	2.90				
B. Real Returns[b] (percent per year)						
Common stocks	9.58	19.65	-.25	.14	.18	-.54
Commodity futures	9.81	19.44		-.36	-.48	.48
Commodity futures with Treasury bills					.46	-.38
Long-term government bonds	-.51	6.81				-.75
U.S. Treasury bills	.22	1.80				
C. Excess Returns[c] (percent per year)						
Common stocks	9.42	20.12	-.20	.08	—	-.48
Commodity futures	9.77	21.39		-.26	—	.52
Long-term government bonds	-.79	6.43			—	-.20

[a]The mean annual loss is defined as the sum of the annual losses (negative rates of return) divided by the number of years in which losses occurred.

[b]The real rate of return, R, is defined by: $1 + R = \dfrac{1 + R_n}{1 + i}$, where R_n = the nominal rate of return; i = the rate of inflation as measured by the proportional change in the Consumer Price Index.

[c]The excess return is the difference between the nominal rate of return and the Treasury bill rate.

Source: Zvi Bodie and Victor I. Rosansky, "Risk and Return in Commodity Futures," *Financial Analysts Journal* 36, no. 3 (May–June 1980): 27–39. Reprinted by permission of the Financial Analysts Journal.

TABLE 22.9

Distributions of Annual Rates of Return on 23 Commodity Futures Contracts (percent per year): 1950–1976

Commodity	Arithmetic Mean	Standard Deviation	Standard Error	Beta (Standard Error of beta)
Wheat	3.181	30.745	5.917	−.370 (.296)
Corn	2.130	26.310	5.063	−.429 (.247)
Oats	1.681	19.492	3.751	.000 (.194)
Soybeans	13.576	32.318	6.220	−.266 (.317)
Soybean oil	25.839	57.672	11.099	−.650 (.558)
Soybean meal	11.870	35.599	6.851	.239 (.351)
Broilers	13.065	39.202	13.860	−1.692 (.395)
Plywood	17.968	39.962	16.314	.660 (.937)
Potatoes	6.905	42.111	8.104	−.610 (.400)
Platinum	.641	25.185	7.594	.221 (.411)
Wool	7.436	36.955	7.120	.307 (.362)
Cotton	8.937	36.236	6.974	−.015 (.360)
Orange juice	2.515	31.771	10.047	.117 (.557)
Propane	68.260	202.088	71.449	−3.851 (3.788)
Cocoa	15.713	54.630	11.391	−.291 (.589)
Silver	3.587	25.622	7.106	−.272 (.375)
Copper	19.785	47.205	9.843	.005 (.492)
Cattle	7.362	21.609	6.238	.365 (.319)
Hogs	13.280	36.617	11.579	−.148 (.641)
Pork bellies	16.098	39.324	11.352	−.062 (.618)
Egg	−4.741	27.898	5.369	−.293 (.271)
Lumber	13.070	34.667	13.101	−.131 (.768)
Sugar	25.404	116.215	24.232	−2.403 (1.146)

Source: Zvi Bodie and Victor I. Rosansky, "Risk and Return in Commodity Futures," *Financial Analysts Journal* 36, no. 3 (May-June 1980): 27–39. Reprinted by permission of the *Financial Analysts Journal.*

7. How are stock index futures priced? What kind of trade is done if they are incorrectly priced?

8. Discuss the portfolio theory approach to hedging.

9. Discuss the price-sensitivity approach to hedging. What types of futures contracts could it be used with?

10. What are the primary economic functions of futures markets?

11. Why should futures contracts be considered as distinct investments and not just hedging instruments?

PROBLEMS

1. Based on the settlement price listed in *The Wall Street Journal,* compute the total price of a soybean contract for delivery in 6 months (or a length of time close to this). Assuming you buy one contract, compute the amount of money credited to your margin account if the price rises by 1 percent the following day.

2. Using *The Wall Street Journal,* assume you buy a stock index futures contract on the S&P 500 index at the settlement price. Suppose the margin is $6,000. When you later sell the contract, the price is 5 percent higher. Determine your rate of return.

3. Suppose the spot price of gold is 348.60 per ounce. A futures contract that expires in 132 days has a price of 353.90.
   a. If the futures price is deemed to be correct, what is the cost of carry on gold?
   b. If the risk-free interest rate is 1.17 percent for 132 days, what is the estimated cost of storing gold for 132 days?

4. Suppose the spot price of a commodity is 100 and the futures price is 104. Answer the following questions, assuming you do a short hedge.
   a. If the position is held to expiration and the spot price is at 96, what is the profit before considering carrying costs and transaction costs?
   b. If the position is closed out prior to expiration when the spot price is 98 and the futures price is 101, what is the profit before considering carrying costs and transaction costs?
   c. If the position is closed out before expiration and the basis goes to 6, what is the profit before considering carrying costs and transaction costs?

5. Suppose you are a coffee dealer and anticipate the purchase of 75,000 pounds of coffee in 3 months. You are concerned that the price of coffee will rise, so you buy coffee futures. Each contract covers 37,500 pounds so you buy two contracts. The futures price is 55.95 cents per pound. Three months later the actual price of coffee turns out to be 58.56 cents per pound and the futures price is 59.2 cents per pound. Determine the effective price at which you purchased the coffee.

6. *CFA Examination III (June 1983)* In February 1983, the United American Company is considering the sale of $100 million in 10-year debentures that will probably be rated AAA like the firm's other bond issues. The firm is anxious to proceed at today's rate of 10.5 percent.

   As Treasurer, you know that it will take about 12 weeks (May) to get the issue registered and sold. Therefore, you suggest that the firm hedge the pending bond issue using Treasury bond futures contracts. (Each Treasury bond contract is for $100,000.)

   Explain how you would go about hedging the bond issue, and describe the results, assuming that the following two sets of future conditions actually occur. (Ignore commissions and margin costs, and assume a 1-to-1 hedge ratio.) Show all calculations. (15 minutes)

	Case 1	Case 2
Current Values—February 1983		
Bond rate	10.5%	10.5%
June 1983 Treasury bonds	78.875	78.875
Estimated Values—May 1983		
Bond rate	11.0%	10.0%
June 1983 Treasury bond futures	75.93	81.84
Present Value of a $1 Annuity		
10 years at 10.5 percent	6.021	6.021

7. Suppose you hold a $25 million stock portfolio that has a beta of 1.12. You would like to protect it against loss over the next 3 months by selling an S&P 500 futures contract, which currently is selling for 418.20. Three months later the stock portfolio is worth $23.5 million and the futures is at 397.29. Find the rate of return on the hedge (ignore transaction costs and dividends). Compare this rate of return with the rate of return you would have experienced without the hedge.

8. A stock index futures contract expiring in about 3 months is currently priced at 352.50. The index itself is at 353. If the T-bill rate is 3.24 percent and the dividend yield is 4 percent, determine whether the futures is correctly priced. If not, recommend a trade.

REFERENCES

Bodie, Zvi, and Victor I. Rosansky. "Risk and Return in Commodity Futures." *Financial Analysts Journal* 36, no. 3 (May-June 1980).

Chance, Don M. *An Introduction to Options and Futures.* 2d ed. Fort Worth: The Dryden Press, 1992.

Chicago Board of Trade. *Commodity Trading Manual.* Chicago: Chicago Board of Trade, 1989.

Duffie, Darrell. *Futures Markets.* Englewood Cliffs, N.J.: Prentice-Hall, 1989.

Dusak, Katherine. "Futures Trading and Investor Returns: An Investigation of Commodity Market Risk Premiums." *Journal of Political Economy* 81, no. 4 (December 1973).

Ederington, Louis H. "The Hedging Performance of the New Futures Market." *The Journal of Finance* 34, no. 1 (March 1979).

Franckle, Charles T. "The Hedging Performance of the New Futures Market: Comment." *The Journal of Finance* 35, no. 5 (December 1980).

Gay, Gerald D., Robert Kolb, and Raymond Chiang. "Interest Rate Hedging: An Empirical Test of Alternative Strategies." *Journal of Financial Research* 6, no. 3 (Fall 1983).

Johnson, Leland L. "The Theory of Hedging and Speculation in Commodity Futures." *Review of Economic Studies* 27 (1959–1960).

Kolb, Robert W. *Understanding Futures Markets.* 3d ed. Miami: Kolb Publishing, 1991.

Kolb, Robert W., and Raymond Chiang. "Immunizing Bond Portfolios Using Interest Rate Futures." *Financial Management* 10, no. 4 (Autumn 1981).

Peck, Anne E. "Hedging and Income Stability: Concepts, Implications, and an Example." In *Selected Writings on Futures Markets,* edited by Anne E. Peck. Chicago: Chicago Board of Trade, 1977.

Peck, Anne E. *Selected Writings on Futures Markets.* Chicago: Chicago Board of Trade, 1977.

Siegel, Daniel R., and Diane F. Siegel. *Futures Markets.* Chicago: The Dryden Press, 1990.

Stein, Jerome L. "The Simultaneous Determination of Spot and Futures Prices." *American Economic Review* 51, no. 5 (December 1961).

Teweles, Richard J., and Frank J. Jones. *The Futures Game.* 3d ed. New York: McGraw-Hill, 1987.

CHAPTER 23   ADVANCED TOPICS ON OPTIONS
AND FUTURES

In this chapter we will answer the following questions:

- What are options on futures and what happens when you exercise one?
- What is involved in pricing options on futures?
- How does the model for pricing straight options differ from the model for pricing options on futures?
- What are options on foreign currency and how are they quoted in the paper?
- What are the major factors that must be considered when pricing currency derivatives?
- How can you hedge foreign currency risk with currency futures?
- How can you hedge foreign currency risk by entering into a currency swap?
- What are interest rate options and how do you compute the gain or loss from these options?
- What are interest rate floors, caps, and collars?
- What is entailed in an interest rate swap and why do investors get involved with them?
- What is portfolio insurance, what is its purpose, and how does it work?
- What is program trading, what is its purpose, and how is it implemented?
- What happened with program trading during the stock market crash of 1987?
- What are circuit breakers on the stock exchange?

We have mentioned many times that the financial markets have an enormous propensity to innovate and create new instruments that meet the needs of clients with highly specialized risk-management problems. These new derivative instruments can be used by investors to modify a portfolio's return–risk possibilities. Because derivative markets have low transaction costs it makes portfolio adjustments easier and less expensive. In this chapter we will look at three general classes of derivative instruments: options on futures, foreign currency derivatives, and interest rate agreements. We will conclude by examining a strategy called portfolio insurance and a procedure called program trading. Both portfolio insurance and program trading have been controversial in recent years, and we will explore that issue at the conclusion of this chapter.

OPTIONS ON
FUTURES

An important innovation in the financial markets during 1982 was the reintroduction of options on futures which are called *futures options* and *commodity options*. These instruments had existed in this country previously but were banned due to some scandals. Thus, when the Commodity Futures Trading Commission (CFTC) allowed them to be traded again, it was done on a limited basis. Originally, only a few contracts were permitted, but the program was a complete success, and many more contracts have been added.

The owner of a call (put) on a futures has the right, but not the obligation, to buy (sell) a futures contract at a fixed price. These options can be European or American, though most are American and are based on specific underlying futures contracts. For example, assume that in August there is an option to buy a December Major Market Index futures with an exercise price of 350. If the option is exercised, the owner of the call establishes a long position in the December futures contract at 350 which is equivalent to buying the futures at a price of 350. If we assume that when the option is exercised the futures price is 352, then the call holder receives a long position in the futures at 350 and this futures contract is immediately marked to market at 352, which gives the call holder a credit of 2. Margin on the futures must be deposited as usual. The writer of the call establishes a short futures position at 350 that is marked to 352 and the writer is charged 2. The exercise of a put establishes a short futures position for the owner and a long futures position for the writer.

Some of the contracts have the options expire at the same time the futures expires; others have the options expire as much as a month earlier than the futures. The options and the underlying futures contract trade side by side on a futures exchange in contrast to options on stocks, which do *not* trade side by side with the underlying stocks. This side by side trading makes it easy to execute arbitrage transactions between the options and the futures which makes the market more efficient. In addition, because there are options on commodity futures, but not options on commodities themselves, these options allow investors to take option positions based on expected price movements in commodities.

A SAMPLE
QUOTATION

Figure 23.1 contains a sample of the price quotation for options on futures taken from *The Wall Street Journal*. The quotes are grouped by type of instruments (agricultural, interest rate, and index). Below the name of the commodity is an indication of the size of the contract. For example, one S&P 500 contract is priced at $500 times the premium. The premium of the August 450 call is shown as 3.20. Thus, the total price paid for the contract is $3.20(500) = $1,600. That contract permits the purchase of the August S&P 500 futures at a price of 450. The futures price is not indicated but can be found on the pages containing futures prices, which are usually located near the futures options quotes.

The September 114 T-bond futures option quote is shown as 2-01, which is 2 and 01/64 or 2.0156. Based on a contract size of $100,000, the actual price would be $2,015.60. The September 675 soybean option is priced at 36¾ cents per bushel or .3675. Based on a contract size of 5,000 bushels, the price would be $0.3675(5000) = $1,837.50.

FIGURE 23.1

Options on Futures Quotations from *The Wall Street Journal*

```
AGRICULTURAL                    INTEREST RATE                    INDEX
CORN (CBT)                      T-BONDS (CBT)                    S&P 500 STOCK INDEX (CME)
  5,000 bu.; cents per bu.        $100,000; points and 64ths of 100%   $500 times premium
Strike  Calls—Settle  Puts—Settle  Strike  Calls—Settle  Puts—Settle  Strike  Calls—Settle  Puts—Settle
Price  Sep  Dec  Mar  Sep  Dec  Mar  Price  Sep  Dec  Mar  Sep  Dec  Mar  Price  Aug  Sep  Oct  Aug  Sep  Oct
220    21  29½  36   ¼   1¾   2     112  3-53  3-43  3-45  0-05  1-06  2-13   440  10.25 12.45  ....  1.30  3.55  5.30
230   12¼  21¾  28   1½   4    4     114  2-01  2-30  2-41  0-17  1-54  3-09   445   6.30  8.95 11.60  2.35  5.00  6.80
240    6  15⅞  21½   5   8⅜   7½    116  0-45  1-33  1-55  0-60  2-57  ....    450   3.20  5.90  8.60  4.25  6.95  8.75
250    3  11⅝  16  12¼   14  11½    118  0-08  0-55  1-15  2-26  4-14  ....    455   1.30  3.65  6.05  7.35  9.65  ....
260   1¼   8⅜  13   20  20¾  17½    120  0-01  0-29  0-51  ....  5-51  ....    460   0.45  1.95  4.05 11.50 12.95  ....
270    ½   6⅛  9¾  39¼  28½  ....   122  0-01  0-14  0-32  ....  ....  ....    465   0.15  1.00  2.50 16.15  ....  ....
Est vol 5,000  Mon 6,621 calls 2,470 puts   Est. vol. 40,000;               Est vol 6,534   Mon 997 calls 4,747 puts
Op int Mon    129,024 calls 63,045 puts     Mon vol. 17,907 calls; 20,685 puts   Op int Mon    33,525 calls 95,995 puts
SOYBEANS (CBT)                   Op. int. Mon 298,743 calls; 275,704 puts   GSCI (CME)
  5,000 bu.; cents per bu.       T-NOTES (CBT)                     $250 times GSCI nearby index
Strike  Calls—Settle  Puts—Settle   $100,000; points and 64ths of 100%   Strike  Calls—Settle  Puts—Settle
Price  Sep  Nov  Jan  Sep  Nov  Jan  Strike  Calls—Settle  Puts—Settle  Price  Aug  Oct  Dec  Aug  Oct  Dec
650    57   66  72½  1½   11   16   Price  Sep  Dec  Mar  Sep  Dec  Mar   175   .50  ....  ....  1.00  ....  ....
675   36¾   52   60    6   22  27½   111  2-14  2-12  ....  0-04  1-00  ....   176  ....  4.10  ....  ....  3.10  ....
700   21¾  41½   49  16½  35½   42   112  1-23  1-38  1-43  0-13  1-26  ....   177  ....  ....  ....  ....  ....  ....
725   12¾   33   40  32½   52  56½   113  0-43  1-08  ....  0-33  1-59  ....   178  ....  3.20  5.60  3.50  4.20  1.40
750   7½  26½  33½  51½  70¼  ....   114  0-16  0-48  ....  1-06  ....  ....   179  .0000  ....  ....  ....  ....  ....
775   4½  21½   28  73½   90  ....   115  0-05  0-31  ....  1-58  ....  ....   180  .0000  2.50  4.60  5.50  5.50  5.40
Est vol 10,000  Mon 9,210 calls 4,232 puts   116  0-01  0-19  ....  ....  ....  ....   Est vol 0      Mon 858 calls 845 puts
Op int Mon    130,549 calls 62,439 puts     Est vol 11,865  Mon 5,318 calls 7,605 puts   Op int Mon    2,899 calls 2,882 puts
SOYBEAN MEAL (CBT)               Op int Mon    73,921 calls 117,855 puts
  100 tons; $ per ton            MUNICIPAL BOND INDEX (CBT)
Strike  Calls—Settle  Puts—Settle   $100,000; pts. & 64ths of 100%
Price  Sep  Oct  Dec  Sep  Oct  Dec  Strike  Calls—Settle  Puts—Settle
200   25.20 24.25 23.80  .10  .50  1.00  Price  Sep  Dec  Mar  Sep  Dec  Mar
210   15.50 15.50 15.80  .25  1.50  2.75   99   ....  2-28  ....  ....  0-39  ....
220   7.00  9.25 11.40  2.00  5.50  8.25  100   1-55  1-48  ....  0-14  0-59  ....
230   3.00  6.00  8.00  7.60 12.10 14.75  101   1-07  1-13  ....  0-29  1-22  ....
240    .75  3.70  5.85 16.25 20.00 22.60  102   0-36  0-51  ....  0-58  1-60  ....
250    .40  2.75  4.40 25.25  ....  ....  103   0-16  0-32  ....  ....  2-40  ....
Est vol 1,750   Mon 1,707 calls 370 puts  104   0-06  ....  ....  ....  ....  ....
Op int Mon    19,309 calls 12,718 puts    Est vol 231       Mon 4 calls 0 puts
                                          Op int Mon     4,940 calls 4,770 puts
```

Source: "Futures Options Prices," *The Wall Street Journal,* August 4, 1993. Copyright © 1993 Dow Jones & Company, Inc. Reprinted by permission of The Wall Street Journal. All Rights Reserved Worldwide.

SOME FUNDAMENTALS OF PRICING OPTIONS ON FUTURES

Although options on futures are priced much like options on spot assets, there are some important differences. For American options, or for European options on the expiration day, the intrinsic value is

$$C(T) = Max(0, F(T) - X) \text{ for calls} \qquad (23.1)$$
$$P(T) = Max(0, X - F(T)) \text{ for puts}$$

These formulas should look quite familiar. Compared to options on spot assets, we use the futures price in place of the spot price. The minimum values for European options are

$$c(t) \geq Max(0, (F(t) - X)(1 + r)^{-(T-t)}) \qquad (23.2)$$
$$p(t) \geq Max(0, (X - F(t))(1 + r)^{-(T-t)})$$

Note that the intrinsic value of an American call or put is higher than the minimum value of the European call or put.[1] As a result, an American call on a futures might be exercised early. A deep-in-the-money call option behaves much like the underlying asset, moving one-for-one with the price of the asset. If the call is on the futures, the

---

[1] This is because the present value of $F(t) - X$ is less than $F(t) - X$.

call holder can exercise it and establish a futures at no cost, thus, freeing up the funds invested in the call. If the call were on the asset, however, exercise of the call would require establishing a position in the asset, which ties up funds. In other words, since the futures does not require an initial outlay of funds it may be preferable to give up the call and take the position in the futures.

It is also possible to establish a put-call parity rule for European options on futures as follows

$$p(t) = c(t) - (F(t) - X)(1 + r)^{-(T-t)} \tag{23.3}$$

Note the similarity to put-call parity for the option on the asset. If we assume the futures and the option expire at the same time and also assume no dividends on the asset. Then we know that $F(t) = S(t)(1 + r)^{(T-t)}$. Substituting this result for $F(t)$ above we obtain

$$p(t) = c(t) - S(t) + X(1 + r)^{-(T-t)}$$

This is put-call parity for options on the asset. This substitution can also be made on the lower bounds for options on futures to obtain the lower bounds for options on the spot asset. In short, when the options are European and expire the same time as the futures, then options on the spot asset and options on the futures are equivalent instruments. This makes sense because if you buy a European option on the futures and it expires the same day as the futures contract, then at expiration the futures contract you buy or sell immediately becomes the spot asset. This is equivalent to an option on the spot asset.

Some tests of whether futures option prices conform to these conditions were conducted by Ball and Torous.[2] They examined gold, the German mark, and sugar futures options during the early to mid-1980s and found few cases in which the bounds were violated. These results were confirmed by Bailey for the gold market in the 1983 to 1984 period.[3]

A MODEL FOR PRICING OPTIONS ON FUTURES

Recall that for European options on assets, we used the Black-Scholes model to price the options. For European options on futures, a similar model developed by Black is used.[4] The model contains the same assumptions as the Black-Scholes model and resembles that model in many ways. The formulas for both calls and puts are as follows:

$$c(t) = e^{-r(T-t)}[F(t)N(d_1) - XN(d_2)]$$
$$p(t) = e^{-r(T-t)}[X(1 - N(d_2)) - F(t)(1 - N(d_1))]$$
$$d_1 = \frac{\ln(F(t)/X) + (\sigma^2/2)T}{\sigma\sqrt{T}} \tag{23.4}$$
$$d_2 = d_1 - \sigma\sqrt{T}$$
$$N(\cdot) = \text{cumulative normal probability}$$

---

[2]Clifford A. Ball and Walter N. Torous, "Futures Options and the Volatility of Futures Prices," *The Journal of Finance* 41, no. 4 (September 1986): 857–870.

[3]Warren Bailey, "An Empirical Investigation of the Market for Comex Gold Futures Options," *The Journal of Finance* 42, no. 5 (December 1987): 1187–1194.

[4]See Fischer Black, "The Pricing of Commodity Contracts," *Journal of Financial Economics* 3, nos. 1, 2 (January-March 1976): 167–179.

TABLE 23.1

Calculation of Black Futures Option Values

$F(t) = 82; X = 80; r = .07; T = 55/365 = .1507; \sigma = .3$

$$c(t) = e^{-r(T-t)}[F(t)N(d_1) - XN(d_2)]$$

$$p(t) = e^{-r(T-t)}[X(1 - N(d_2)) - F(t)(1 - N(d_1))]$$

$$d_1 = \frac{\ln(F(t)/X) + (\sigma^2/2)T}{\sigma\sqrt{T}}$$

$$d_2 = d_1 - \sigma\sqrt{T}$$

$N(\cdot) = $ cumulative normal probability

Calls

$$d_1 = \frac{\ln(82/80) + ((.3)^2/2)(.1507)}{.3\sqrt{.1507}}$$

$$= \frac{.0247 + .0068}{.1165} = .27$$

$$N(.27) = .6064$$

$$d_2 = .27 - .3\sqrt{.1507} = .15$$

$$N(.15) = .5596$$

$$c(t) = e^{-.07(.1507)}[82(.6064) - 80(.5596)] = 4.91$$

Puts

$$1 - N(.27) = 1 - .6064 = .3936$$

$$1 - N(.15) = 1 - .5596 = .4404$$

$$p(t) = e^{-.07(.1507)}[80(.4404) - 82(.3936)] = 2.93$$

In computing an option value, the first noticeable difference is in the calculation of d_1. The interest rate does not appear in the Black model, whereas it does appear in the Black-Scholes model. This is because the holder of a futures contract does not expect to earn the risk-free rate since no funds are tied up. The holder of the spot asset expects to earn the risk-free rate. The formula for $c(t)$ also differs only slightly from the Black-Scholes formula so it is possible to view these as equivalent formulas. Without going into the math, it can be shown that if you substitute $S(t)(1 + r)^{(T-t)}$, the cost of carry formula for the futures price, for $F(t)$ in the Black formula, you would obtain the Black-Scholes formula. Provided that the futures is priced by the cost of carry formula, an option on the asset and an option on the futures will have the same prices.[5]

Table 23.1 illustrates how the Black model can be used to calculate the price of options on futures in which the futures price is 82, the exercise price is 80, the risk-free rate is 7 percent, the options expire in 55 days, and the standard deviation of the futures price is .3. The normal probability table from Appendix D is used in the same manner as when pricing options on the asset.

The pricing of American options on futures is quite complex, and we will not cover the models used to capture the early exercise premium on both calls and puts.[6] Whaley

---

[5]This, of course, is contingent on the assumptions that the options are European and expire the same time the futures expire.

[6]An analysis of the differences between American and European options on spot assets and options on futures is contained in Menachem Brenner, Georges Courtadon, and Marti Subrahmanyam, "Options on the Spot and Options on Futures," *The Journal of Finance* 40, no. 5 (December 1985): 1303–1317.

tested one of these models on the S&P 500 futures options and found that the models provided numerous opportunities for floor traders and those with low transaction costs to earn abnormal returns.[7] However, for the general public with higher transaction costs, the arbitrage opportunities were quite limited. Bailey found that a sophisticated model that incorporated changing interest rates performed quite well in pricing gold futures options contracts in the period 1983 to 1984.[8]

FOREIGN CURRENCY DERIVATIVES

Throughout this book, we have discussed global investing and the added risk–return opportunities available because of exchange rate changes. As noted earlier, when you invest in Japanese stocks or bonds, you must consider not only the typical business, financial, and liquidity risks, but also the added uncertainty due to exchange rate changes that can work for or against you.

The currency of a given country is just as much a commodity as that country's output of wheat, gold, or sugar. It is an asset just as much as the equity and debt of firms residing in that country. When people "invest" in a foreign currency, they convert the domestic currency to that foreign currency and while holding that currency they would be earning that country's risk-free rate. When the holding period is over, investors can then convert the currency back into their own currency at a conversion rate that is uncertain, in the same way that the future price of a stock is uncertain.

The international financial markets constitute a vast network of institutions and governments trading currencies and securities across borders. The currency market is particularly well-developed. During a trip you may have obtained a small amount of foreign currency from a local bank or a foreign currency exchange at an airport. Although you executed an international transaction, the size of your transaction is quite insignificant compared to the many billions of dollars worth of currency transactions made daily. These large currency trades accommodate the needs of firms and governments conducting business with firms and governments in other countries.

SAMPLE QUOTATIONS

The spot market for currencies is an informal network of financial institutions that deal in large volumes of currencies by trades arranged by telephone or wire. Figure 23.2 illustrates the currency spot quotations that appear in *The Wall Street Journal*. Most major currencies of countries that operate a capitalist system are included. However, many of these currencies do not freely float with respect to other currencies but the rates are established either by government order or their central bank intervenes to keep the exchange rate at a given level. Note that for most of the major trading partners of the United States, a spot and several forward rates are quoted. Recall that the forward rates represent transactions agreed upon today that will take place in the future.

For the example day (August 3, 1993) the spot price of the German mark was $0.5860, which means that 1,000,000 German marks (indicated as DM1,000,000),[9] would be DM1,000,000($0.5860/DM) = $586,000. In the third column the same quote is inverted. A price of $0.5860 can be quoted as 1/.5860 = 1.7065 marks per dollar.

---

[7]Robert E. Whaley, "Valuation of American Futures Options: Theory and Empirical Evidence," *The Journal of Finance* 41, no. 1 (March 1986): 127–150.

[8]Bailey, "An Empirical Investigation."

[9]The DM stands for deutschemarks.

FIGURE 23.2   **Currency Spot Quotations from *The Wall Street Journal***

EXCHANGE RATES

Tuesday, August 3, 1993

The New York foreign exchange selling rates below apply to trading among banks in amounts of $1 million and more, as quoted at 3 p.m. Eastern time by Bankers Trust Co., Telerate and other sources. Retail transactions provide fewer units of foreign currency per dollar.

Country	U.S. $ equiv. Tues.	Mon.	Currency per U.S. $ Tues.	Mon.
Argentina (Peso)	1.01	1.01	.99	.99
Australia (Dollar)	.6902	.6915	1.4489	1.4461
Austria (Schilling)	.08328	.08315	12.01	12.03
Bahrain (Dinar)	2.6518	2.6518	.3771	.3771
Belgium (Franc)	.02745	.02715	36.43	36.83
Brazil (Cruzeiro)	.0000143	.0000145	70000.02	69017.02
Britain (Pound)	1.5025	1.5010	.6656	.6662
30-Day Forward	1.4988	1.4972	.6672	.6679
90-Day Forward	1.4927	1.4915	.6699	.6705
180-Day Forward	1.4859	1.4848	.6730	.6735
Canada (Dollar)	.7749	.7751	1.2905	1.2902
30-Day Forward	.7742	.7745	1.2916	1.2912
90-Day Forward	.7731	.7733	1.2935	1.2931
180-Day Forward	.7711	.7714	1.2968	1.2964
Czech. Rep. (Koruna)				
Commercial rate	.0339789	.0340368	29.4300	29.3800
Chile (Peso)	.002541	.002551	393.48	391.95
China (Renminbi)	.174856	.174856	5.7190	5.7190
Colombia (Peso)	.001468	.001469	681.15	680.88
Denmark (Krone)	.1482	.1463	6.7492	6.8360
Ecuador (Sucre)				
Floating rate	.000529	.000529	1889.00	1889.00
Finland (Markka)	.17210	.17097	5.8106	5.8491
France (Franc)	.16855	.16711	5.9330	5.9840
30-Day Forward	.16756	.16610	5.9680	6.0205
90-Day Forward	.16678	.16526	5.9960	6.0510
180-Day Forward	.16593	.16437	6.0265	6.0840
Germany (Mark)	.5860	.5851	1.7065	1.7090
30-Day Forward	.5841	.5832	1.7121	1.7148
90-Day Forward	.5810	.5800	1.7212	1.7241
180-Day Forward	.5771	.5760	1.7328	1.7361
Greece (Drachma)	.004174	.004219	239.60	237.00
Hong Kong (Dollar)	.12897	.12896	7.7537	7.7545
Hungary (Forint)	.0105697	.0105496	94.6100	94.7900
India (Rupee)	.03212	.03212	31.13	31.13
Indonesia (Rupiah)	.0004771	.0004771	2096.04	2096.04
Ireland (Punt)	1.4100	1.4073	.7092	.7106
Israel (Shekel)	.3553	.3480	2.8142	2.8735
Italy (Lira)	.0000627	.0006245	15947.44	1601.36
Japan (Yen)	.009579	.009574	104.39	104.45
30-Day Forward	.009579	.009574	104.40	104.46
90-Day Forward	.009581	.009576	104.37	104.43
180-Day Forward	.009599	.009594	104.18	104.23
Jordan (Dinar)	1.4661	1.4661	.6821	.6821
Kuwait (Dinar)	3.3162	3.3162	.3016	.3016
Lebanon (Pound)	.000579	.000579	1728.50	1728.50
Malaysia (Ringgit)	.3905	.3906	2.5605	2.5600
Malta (Lira)	2.5126	2.5126	.3980	.3980
Mexico (Peso)				
Floating rate	.3210273	.3210273	3.1150	3.1150
Netherland (Guilder)	.5208	.5199	1.9203	1.9233
New Zealand (Dollar)	.5518	.5510	1.8123	1.8149
Norway (Krone)	.1355	.1354	7.3806	7.3879
Pakistan (Rupee)	.0336	.0336	29.75	29.75
Peru (New Sol)	.5077	.5103	1.97	1.96
Philippines (Peso)	.03636	.03636	27.50	27.50
Poland (Zloty)	.00005745	.00005712	17405.00	17507.00
Portugal (Escudo)	.005788	.005618	172.78	177.99
Saudi Arabia (Riyal)	.26631	.26631	3.7550	3.7550
Singapore (Dollar)	.6194	.6190	1.6145	1.6155
Slovak Rep. (Koruna)	.0303306	.0301023	32.9700	33.2200
South Africa (Rand)				
Commercial rate	.2985	.2976	3.3505	3.3603
Financial rate	.2222	.2215	4.5000	4.5150
South Korea (Won)	.0012396	.0012398	806.70	806.60
Spain (Peseta)	.007181	.007029	139.25	142.27
Sweden (Krona)	.1247	.1240	8.0206	8.0622
Switzerland (Franc)	.6656	.6686	1.5025	1.4957
30-Day Forward	.6646	.6675	1.5047	1.4981
90-Day Forward	.6631	.6661	1.5080	1.5013
180-Day Forward	.6619	.6647	1.5107	1.5045
Taiwan (Dollar)	.037509	.037123	26.66	26.94
Thailand (Baht)	.03960	.03960	25.25	25.25
Turkey (Lira)	.0000882	.0000877	11336.00	11400.00
United Arab (Dirham)	.2723	.2723	3.6725	3.6725
Uruguay (New Peso)				
Financial	.241721	.241721	4.14	4.14
Venezuela (Bolivar)				
Floating rate	.01100	.01093	90.92	91.50
	– – –			
SDR	1.39939	1.38915	.71460	.71986
ECU	1.11950	1.10940	....	....

Special Drawing Rights (SDR) are based on exchange rates for the U.S., German, British and Japanese currencies. Source: International Monetary Fund.

European Currency Unit (ECU) is based on a basket of community currencies.

On that same day, the 30-day forward rate for marks was $0.5841, which means that you could have entered into an agreement to buy DM1,000,000 in 30 days at a price of $584,100. Of course, these quotations should not be interpreted as precise since they are based on a sampling of banks and represent large transactions. Moreover, there is a bid and ask spread that does not show in these rates.

In 1972, the Chicago Mercantile Exchange began trading futures based on the currencies of the leading trading partners of the United States. Though the currency futures market is not as large as the over-the-counter currency forward market, it is, nonetheless, quite active. Figure 23.3 presents a sample of the quotations from *The Wall Street Journal* for currency futures. At the present time, the Japanese yen, German deutschemark, Canadian dollar, British pound, Swiss franc, and Australian dollar trade on the CME. In addition, there is a contract based on an index of the U. S. dollar. The most active trading is in the yen and mark contracts.

FIGURE 23.3   **Currency Futures Quotations from *The Wall Street Journal***

```
                    CURRENCY
                                   Lifetime      Open
           Open  High Low Settle Change High Low Interest
     JAPAN YEN (CME)–12.5 million yen; $ per yen (.00)
Sept  .9575 .9607 .9552 .9581 – .0003 .9608 .7945 75,893
Dec   .9580 .9612 .9563 .9589 – .0003 .9615 .7970  4,001
Mr94  .9620 .9620 .9620 .9611 – .0003 .9620 .8700    327
     Est vol 22,160; vol Mon 27,993; open int 80,255, +3,118.
     DEUTSCHEMARK (CME)–125,000 marks; $ per mark
Sept  .5830 .5861 .5807 .5835 + .0001 .6720 .5709149,794
Dec   .5765 .5813 .5765 .5789 + .0002 .6650 .5657  6,744
Mr94  .5745 .5765 .5745 .5758 + .0002 .6205 .5646     93
     Est vol 60,662; vol Mon 82,084; open int 156,643, –7,408.
     CANADIAN DOLLAR (CME)–100,000 dlrs.; $ per Can $
Sept  .7745 .7750 .7732 .7743 + .0008 .8335 .7515 37,202
Dec   .7722 .7730 .7716 .7724 + .0008 .8310 .7470  1,557
Mr94  .7710 .7710 .7702 .7705 + .0008 .7860 .7550    646
June  .7682 .7682 .7682 .7684 + .0008 .7805 .7515    382
Sept  ....  ....  ....  .7662 + .0008 .7740 .7555    143
     Est vol 5,093; vol Mon 10,938; open int 39,930, +6,733.
     BRITISH POUND (CME)–62,500 pds.; $ per pound
Sept 1.4980 1.5046 1.4912 1.4970 – .0030 1.5800 1.3980 26,427
Dec  1.4918 1.4954 1.4850 1.4886 – .0032 1.5670 1.3930    915
     Est vol 15,817; vol Mon 22,580; open int 27,428, –2,380.
     SWISS FRANC (CME)–125,000 francs; $ per franc
Sept  .6675 .6690 .6627 .6644 – .0041 .7100 .6380 41,349
Dec   .6642 .6665 .6610 .6627 – .0041 .7050 .6400  3,068
     Est vol 26.618; vol Mon 31,902; open int 44,501, –2,008.
```

Source: "Currency," *The Wall Street Journal,* August 4, 1993. Copyright © 1993 Dow Jones & Company, Inc. Reprinted by permission of The Wall Street Journal. All Rights Reserved Worldwide.

The price quotations are read much like the futures price quotations previously covered. A yen contract is for 12.5 million yen with the current settlement price of the September yen contract equal to $0.9581. However, because there are so many yen in a dollar, it is understood that there are two decimal places preceding the price. Thus, the actual price is $.009581. For a full contract, the price is ¥12,500,000($.009581/¥) = $119,762.50. The remaining contracts are interpreted as they appear; the settlement price of the September mark contract is $0.5835/DM.[10]

Figure 23.4 presents the sample quotations for currency options from *The Wall Street Journal.* Foreign currency options are traded on the Philadelphia Stock Exchange. Contracts trade on the Australian dollar, British pound, Canadian dollar, German mark, Japanese yen, the French franc, and Swiss franc (the latter two are not shown in the figure). Note that there are both European and American versions of these options as indicated in the figure.[11] The American versions are more actively traded.

The price quotations are laid out much like those of options on stocks. Let us consider the British pound (American style) September 150 call option which grants the right to buy 31,250 British pounds by the expiration day in September at a price of $1.50/£. Since the call price is 2.25 cents per pound or $0.0225, this one contract would cost £31,250($0.0225/£) = $703.125.

---

[10]This is not true in the spot and forward markets for British pounds. The traditional quote is in terms of pounds per dollar, not dollars per pound. This is due to the fact that the British pound was for many years the primary currency of international transactions. It was supplanted by the U. S. dollar, but the custom of quoting pounds in terms of dollars remains in the spot and forward markets, though not in the futures market.

[11]Recall that European means that the option can be exercised only on the expiration day, whereas American means that the option can be exercised any time prior to expiration as well.

FIGURE 23.4 **Currency Options Quotations from *The Wall Street Journal***

PHILADELPHIA OPTIONS
Tuesday, August 3, 1993

	Calls Vol. Last	Puts Vol. Last
Australian Dollar		69.01
50,000 Australian Dollars-European Style.		
70 Dec	1 1.07	... ...
50,000 Australian Dollars-cents per unit.		
68 Aug	... ...	25 0.21
69 Aug	200 0.51	... ...
69 Sep	1 0.94	5 1.09
70 Aug	... ...	20 1.29
70 Sep	2 0.50	... ...
70 Sep	5 1.06	... ...
71 Dec	2 0.84	... ...
British Pound		150.09
31,250 British Pounds-European Style.		
150 Aug	... ...	1 1.10
152½ Aug	64 0.30	... ...
155 Aug	... ...	16 4.92
31,250 British Pounds-European units.		
145 Aug	1 5.10	... ...
31,250 British Pounds-cents per unit.		
142½ Sep	... ...	50 0.28
145 Dec	50 6.42	... ...
147½ Aug	39 2.73	120 0.35
147½ Sep	39 3.45	50 1.20
150 Aug	50 1.20	50 1.23
150 Sep	180 2.25	... ...
150 Dec	8 4.15	16 4.95
152½ Aug	50 0.49	2 2.55
155 Dec	100 1.95	... ...
160 Sep	... ...	2 9.82
Canadian Dollar		77.47
50,000 Canadian Dollars EOM-cents per unit.		
77½ Aug	300 0.44	300 0.34
50,000 Canadian Dollars-cents per unit.		
77 Aug	... ...	6 0.10
77 Sep	... ...	200 0.33
78 Sep	... ...	8 0.87
ECU		113.03
62,50 European Currency Units-cents per unit.		
114 Sep	16 0.70	... ...
French Franc		168.27
250,000 French Francs-10ths of a cent per unit.		
15¾ Dec	... ...	73 1.82
16 Sep	10 8.70	250 0.95
16 Dec	... ...	24 2.46
16¼ Sep	... ...	760 1.16
16½ Aug	... ...	7090 0.42
16½ Sep	... ...	250 1.80
16½ Dec	... ...	2 4.48
16¾ Aug	2 1.30	... ...
16¾ Sep	360 2.28	40 2.70
17 Sep	120 1.10	10 4.28
17 Dec	80 2.90	... ...
250,000 French Francs-European Style.		
16 Dec	... ...	4 2.64
16½ Sep	... ...	2342 1.52

	Calls Vol. Last	Puts Vol. Last
16½ Dec	... ...	2420 4.12
16¾ Sep	... ...	2342 2.70
16¾ Dec	... ...	2420 5.44
17 Aug	2500 0.38	... ...
17 Sep	3529 1.66	3000 4.34
17¼ Sep	3478 1.00	... ...
17¾ Sep	44 0.30	... ...
GMark-JYen		61.20
62,500 German Mark-Japanese Yen cross.		
58 Dec	... ...	4 0.78
61 Aug	4 0.70	... ...
62½ Sep	20 0.45	... ...
65 Dec	310 0.42	... ...
German Mark		58.55
62,500 German Marks EOM-cents per unit.		
57 Aug	... ...	500 0.20
58 Sep	... ...	1500 0.98
58½ Aug	... ...	20 0.81
62,500 German Marks-European Style.		
57 Sep	... ...	5 0.32
58 Dec	... ...	4 1.63
59 Aug	239 0.28	... ...
59 Sep	5 0.68	... ...
59½ Aug	375 0.15	... ...
62,500 German Marks-cents per unit.		
55 Dec	7 3.59	110 0.52
56 Aug	... ...	7 0.04
56 Sep	... ...	20 0.18
56 Dec	... ...	31 0.94
57 Aug	100 1.60	1510 0.06
57 Sep	1 1.75	492 0.36
57 Dec	... ...	142 1.15
57½ Aug	1 1.24	... ...
57½ Sep	18 1.39	... ...
58 Aug	333 0.85	1253 0.19
58 Sep	237 1.14	89 0.68
58 Dec	51 1.70	360 1.64
58½ Aug	734 0.52	284 0.41
58½ Sep	59 0.84	11 0.92
59 Aug	1294 0.27	32 0.62
59 Sep	2 0.61	541 1.18
59 Dec	5 1.26	3 3.26
59½ Sep	25 0.12	5 1.10
59½ Sep	128 0.35	1 1.47
60 Sep	75 0.30	2 1.99
61 Sep	20 0.19	6 2.78
66 Sep	... ...	14 7.49
Japanese Yen		95.77
6,250,000 Japanese Yen EOM-100ths of a cent per unit.		
95 Sep	250 2.30	450 1.51
6,250,000 Japanese Yen-100ths of a cent per unit.		
87 Dec	... ...	15 0.33
91 Sep	... ...	20 0.30
91 Dec	... ...	2 0.97
91½ Aug	... ...	152 0.07

	Calls Vol. Last	Puts Vol. Last
91½ Sep	... ...	52 0.36
92 Dec	... ...	7 1.26
93 Aug	... ...	150 0.19
93 Sep	... ...	5 0.66
93½ Aug	... ...	54 0.26
93½ Sep	... ...	5 0.80
94 Aug	... ...	90 0.36
94 Sep	... ...	8 0.94
94½ Aug	... ...	70 0.58
94½ Sep	... ...	20 1.08
95 Aug	80 1.39	1700 0.64
95½ Aug	1 1.27	... ...
96 Aug	90 0.92	10 1.13
96 Sep	20 1.58	10 1.69
97 Aug	1550 0.57	... ...
97 Sep	8 1.22	... ...
97 Dec	2 2.25	... ...
98 Aug	50 0.33	... ...
99 Dec	1 1.60	... ...
100 Sep	5 0.44	... ...
102 Dec	30 0.86	... ...
6,250,000 Japanese Yen-European Style.		
92 Dec	... ...	4 1.26
96 Aug	3 0.90	... ...
97½ Sep	3 1.01	... ...
Swiss Franc		66.50
62,500 Swiss Francs EOM.		
66½ Aug	... ...	10 0.83
62,500 Swiss Francs-European Style.		
65 Sep	... ...	6 0.44
66½ Aug	... ...	6 0.50
67 Sep	6 0.83	... ...
69 Sep	6 0.27	... ...
69½ Aug	6 0.03	... ...
71½ Aug	6 0.01	... ...
62,500 Swiss Francs-cents per unit.		
65 Aug	... ...	1 0.11
65 Sep	... ...	33 0.49
65 Dec	... ...	4 1.39
65½ Aug	... ...	1000 0.10
66 Aug	10 0.82	... ...
66 Dec	... ...	10 1.82
66½ Aug	... ...	12 0.50
67 Aug	2 0.40	... ...
67½ Aug	1000 0.28	... ...
67½ Sep	70 0.65	... ...
68 Sep	... ...	60 2.00
68 Dec	1 1.30	... ...
69 Sep	5 0.24	... ...
69 Dec	... ...	1 3.63
78 Dec	30 0.07	... ...

Call Vol 29,589   Open Int ... 707,269
Put Vol 43,528   Open Int ... 618,279

There are also options on foreign currency futures that trade at the Chicago Mercantile Exchange, alongside the futures that they are based on.

PRICING CURRENCY DERIVATIVES

Under the basic assumptions we have made since Chapter 9,[12] a futures contract and a forward contract are equivalent so we can price forwards and futures the same way. In practice there are differences between the two as discussed in Chapter 22, but the differences are fairly small, and we can proceed without concern that the differences will interfere with our understanding of these markets.[13]

---

[12]Specifically, we mean that interest rates are constant. In Chapter 9 we showed that this is sufficient to make forward prices equal futures prices.

[13]Empirical tests reveal that the differences are quite small. See Bradford Cornell and Marc R. Reinganum, "Forward and Futures Prices: Evidence from the Foreign Exchange Markets," *The Journal of Finance* 36, no. 5 (December 1981): 1035–1045.

Suppose one unit of the foreign currency costs $S(t)$ dollars. Assume that you buy one unit of the currency at $S(t)$ dollars while simultaneously selling a futures contract at the price $F(t)$. While you hold the position you are losing interest on the $S(t)$ dollars at the risk-free rate, r. However, while you hold the currency you earn interest at the foreign risk-free rate, r_f. If you hold the position to expiration, the transaction is riskless because you bought the currency for $S(t)$ and sold it for $F(t)$, a rate that is known at the beginning of the transaction. Your investment of $S(t)$ dollars and the forgone interest means that you will have effectively invested $S(t)(1 + r)^{(T-t)}$ dollars in the currency by time T. However, you will have accumulated interest in the foreign asset at rate r_f. Thus, the total investment at T in the currency is

$$S(t)(1 + r)^{(T-t)}(1 + r_f)^{-(T-t)}$$

This should equal the futures price, $F(t)$. Thus, the futures pricing model is

$$F(t) = S(t)(1 + r)^{(T-t)}(1 + r_f)^{-(T-t)} \tag{23.5}$$

For example, assume that the spot price of the Swiss franc is \$0.77, the U. S. interest rate is 3.2 percent, the Swiss interest rate is 8.6 percent, and the futures contract expires in 82 days. Then $T - t = 82/365 = .2247$ and the futures price should be

$$F(t) = .77(1.032)^{.2247}(1.086)^{-.2247} = .7612$$

When the foreign interest rate is higher than the domestic interest rate, the futures (or forward) price is less than the spot price. In such a case, the currency is said to be selling at a *forward discount*, which implies that by holding the foreign currency the investor receives a higher interest rate than by holding the domestic currency. Therefore, the price at which an investor can contract to sell the currency in the future is discounted to compensate for this higher interest.

The model presented here to describe the relationship between currency spot and forward or futures prices is called *interest rate parity*. The idea is, if the forward or futures price does not equal the formula price, then an arbitrage transaction can be executed in which offsetting positions are taken in the spot or forward/futures market. This transaction, which is called *covered interest arbitrage,* is similar to stock index arbitrage, which is based on deviations from the stock index futures pricing model. If you treat the currency as a stock index and the foreign interest rate as the dividends on the component stocks of the index, then you will see that these two models are equivalent. In fact, interest rate parity is comparable to the foreign currency market's cost of carry model.

Numerous studies have examined whether actual forward and futures prices conform to interest rate parity. Transaction costs and restrictions on the flow of capital make testing more difficult as discussed in Levi.[14] For all practical purposes, however, interest rate parity is such a widely recognized paradigm that we can safely accept it.

Since currencies are similar to other assets that have cash flows, we can see that all our previous results for futures and options apply to foreign currency futures and

---

[14]Maurice D. Levi, *International Finance,* 2d ed. (New York: McGraw-Hill, 1990).

options. All the boundary conditions and our put-call parity relationship will hold with the spot price replaced by the spot exchange rate, discounted by the foreign interest rate.[15] To price a European foreign currency option, we make a slight adjustment to the Black-Scholes formula.[16] The formula is

$$c(t) = S(t)e^{-r_f(T-t)}N(d_1) - Xe^{-r(T-t)}N(d_2)$$
$$p(t) = Xe^{-r(T-t)}(1 - N(d_2)) - S(t)e^{-r_f(T-t)}(1 - N(d_1))$$
$$d_1 = \frac{\ln(S(t)e^{-r_f(T-t)}/X + (r + \sigma^2/2))T}{\sigma\sqrt{T}}$$
$$d_2 = d_1 - \sigma\sqrt{T}$$
$$N(\cdot) = \text{cumulative normal probability}$$

(23.6)

The only difference with our basic version of the Black-Scholes model is that the spot exchange rate discounted by the foreign interest rate is used instead of the stock price.[17]

Table 23.2 presents a sample calculation of an option on a foreign currency. The option values seem small but that is only because the spot exchange rate and exercise price are quoted in cents per unit of currency.

The foreign currency options market has been tested extensively to determine if there are violations of conditions that are sufficient to generate arbitrage profits. Bodurtha and Courtadon examined the boundary conditions and put-call parity for over 50,000 option trades in the period 1983 to 1984. The results show that prices conform quite closely to the boundary conditions.[18] The authors also tested foreign currency option pricing models on a data set of over 20,000 trades in the 1983 to 1985 period. Although prices seem to conform to the model, it appeared that more sophisticated models were required to price foreign currency options as effectively as the models price equity and index options.[19] Fortunately, for our purposes we do not need such extreme accuracy.

HEDGING FOREIGN CURRENCY RISK

Suppose you plan to take a trip next summer to England and expect to spend the equivalent of about $2,500 dollars while in England. Assume a pound currently costs $1.92, which means that your expected expenses are $2,500/($1.92/£) = £1,302. Assuming no significant inflation in the United Kingdom before your trip, this would be your expected expense total. However, if the pound strengthens against the dollar, the price of a pound in terms of dollars will rise. Suppose your worst case estimate is a price of $2.00/£, which means that the £1,302 will cost £1,302($2.00/£) = $2,604. Between now and the time of the trip you are exposed to the risk of an increase in the value of the pound so that you effectively have a short position in pounds or a long

[15]For a specific exposition of these principles, see J. Orlin Grabbe, *International Financial Markets,* 2d. ed. (New York: Elsevier Science Publishing, 1991).

[16]Mark B. Garman and Steven W. Kohlhagen, "Foreign Currency Option Values," *Journal of International Money and Finance* 2, no. 3 (1983): 231–237.

[17]Note that both the risk-free domestic and foreign interest rates must be expressed as continuously compounded rates.

[18]See James Bodurtha and Georges Courtadon, "Efficiency Tests of the Foreign Currency Options Market," *The Journal of Finance* 41, no. 1 (March 1986): 151–162.

[19]James Bodurtha and Georges Courtadon, "Tests of an American Option Pricing Model on the Foreign Currency Options Market," *Journal of Financial and Quantitative Analysis* 22, no. 2 (June 1987): 153–167.

TABLE 23.2

Calculation of Foreign Currency Option Values

$S(t) = .7764; X = .80; r = .032; r_t = .081; T = 83/365 = .2274; \sigma = .06$

$$c(t) = S(t)e^{-r_f(T-t)}N(d_1) - Xe^{-r(T-t)}N(d_2)$$

$$p(t) = Xe^{-r(T-t)}(1 - N(d_2)) - S(t)e^{-r_f(T-t)}(1 - N(d_1))$$

$$d_1 = \frac{\ln(S(t)e^{-r_f(T-t)}/X) + (r + (\sigma^2/2))T}{\sigma\sqrt{T}}$$

$$d_2 = d_1 - \sigma\sqrt{T}$$

$N(\cdot) = $ cumulative normal probability

Calls

$$d_1 = \frac{\ln(.7764e^{-.081(.2274)}/.80) + (.032 + ((.06)^2/2))(.2274)}{.06\sqrt{.2274}}$$

$$= \frac{-.0484 + .0077}{.0286} = -1.42$$

$$N(-1.42) = 1 - N(1.42) = 1 - .9222 = .0778$$

$$d_2 = -1.42 - .06\sqrt{.2274} = -1.45$$

$$N(-1.45) = 1 - N(1.45) = 1 - .9265 = .0735$$

$$c(t) = .7764e^{-.081(.2274)}(.0778) - .80e^{-.032(.2274)}(.0735) = .00093.$$

Puts

$$1 - N(-1.42) = 1 - .0778 = .9222$$

$$1 - N(-1.45) = 1 - .0735 = .9265$$

$$p(t) = .80e^{-.032(.2274)}(.9265) - .7764e^{-.081(.2274)}(.9222) = .0329.$$

position in dollars. In contrast, while you are in England, your money is in pounds, so you are long pounds and short dollars, which implies that you are exposed to the risk of a rising dollar.

The risk of possibly having to pay an extra $104 in expenses because of the strong pound may or may not seem like much. For firms involved in large transactions, the potential losses from a similar change in exchange rates are quite large and can make otherwise profitable transactions unprofitable. Thus, many firms use the currency forward, futures, and options markets to hedge against the exchange rate risk.

Table 23.3 presents an example of a hedge of a foreign currency risk. A U. S. importer agrees to buy industrial equipment from a British firm. Payment of £250,000 will be made at a later date. Based on the current exchange rate of $1.798, the dollar cost of the equipment will be $449,500. This transaction is similar to your trip because the U. S. firm must pay out pounds at a later date by purchasing pounds at whatever the exchange rate is on that future day. Thus, it is effectively short pounds and long dollars. To take advantage of an increase in the price of a pound, the importer buys four December pound futures contracts that are selling for $1.7864. Each contract covers 62,500 pounds. Recall that a long futures contract is equivalent to an agreement to buy the commodity (pounds) at the futures price ($1.7864) at expiration. Thus, the importer is trying to lock in a price of £250,000($1.7864) = $446,600.

On December 10, the importer has to purchase the pounds. The spot rate is $1.6840, which means that the pounds actually fell in value and the importer effectively pays £250,000($1.6840) = $421,000 for the equipment. The futures price turned out to be $1.6850. So the importer sells the four futures contracts, taking a loss of

TABLE 23.3

Hedging a Foreign Currency Risk

Intent: Hedge a future purchase of British pounds.

Spot	Futures
Jun. 5: U.S. importer agrees to buy £250,000 of industrial equipment on December 10. Current cost, based on the spot exchange rate of $1.7980/£, is $449,500. The importer is concerned about an increase in the value of the pound relative to the dollar.	Purchases four December British pound futures at $1.7864. This is designed to lock in an effective selling price of £250,000($1.7864) = $446,600.
Dec. 10: The spot exchange rate turns out to be $1.6840. The equipment is purchased at a cost in dollars of £250,000($1,684/£) = $421,000.	Sells four December British pound futures at $1.6850 for a loss on the futures of £250,000($1.7864 − $1.685) = $25,350.

Conclusion: The importer had to pay an effective amount of $421,000 + $25,350 = $446,350 or $446,500/£250,000 = $1.786. This is very close to the original futures price. The difference occurred because the hedge was not held to expiration so there was some basis risk. Note that the British pound weakened so the price of the equipment in the spot market fell, and there was a loss in the futures market. In this example, the importer would have been better off not hedging but, of course, did not know that before the fact.

£250,000($1.7864 − $1.6850) = $25,350. Thus, the effective price of the equipment was the actual price of $421,000 plus the loss on the futures contract of $25,350, for a total of $446,350, which is quite close to the price that the importer attempted to lock in by selling the futures. The only reason there is a difference is that the futures contract was not quite held to expiration.

Had the importer known that the futures price would have fallen, he or she would have chosen not to hedge. However, since the importer obviously did not know that ahead of time, the hedge made it possible to proceed with the transaction knowing that the effective price of the equipment would be near $446,600. The inability to capture gains from the fall in the price of the equipment is the cost of hedging.

There are many other types of hedges involving foreign currencies. Suppose the importer were bidding on a contract with a foreign government which specifies that the foreign government will pay a fixed amount of cash in its currency. Thus, although the contractor is exposed to a decline in the value of the currency, this can be hedged by selling a futures on the currency. However, if the bid is not won, then the contractor has a short position in a futures on that currency, which is equivalent to going short the currency and is extremely risky. If it were certain that the contract would be won, then the contractor would be long the currency and should short the currency futures.

In the case of firms bidding on foreign contracts, an option can be used to more effectively hedge. By buying a put on the currency, the contractor would pay an insurance premium, the put price, for the ability to sell the currency at a fixed price in dollars. If the bid is lost, the contractor still holds the put but at worst loses the put premium. The contractor is not exposed to large losses from a significant drop in the value of the currency as would happen with a short futures position.

CURRENCY SWAPS

One of the more popular and useful devices for hedging foreign currency risk is the currency swap, which was invented in 1981, and now constitutes a significant portion of all currency hedging transactions. Basically a *currency swap* is a transaction in

TABLE 23.4

Creating a Synthetic Dollar Bond with a Deutschemark-Denominated Bond and a Currency Swap

Scenario: A portfolio manager wishes to buy a AAA-rated 3-year bond. The yield on such bonds is currently about 8 percent. The manager finds a highly rated German firm that is offering 3-year bonds with a coupon of 10 percent. The manager arranges a currency swap in which the deutschemarks can be exchanged for dollars at a rate of DM1.5/$. The bond, selling at par, is priced at DM7 million. The current exchange rate is DM1.4475/$. The manager buys the bond by purchasing DM7 million for DM7,000,000/(DM1.4475/$) = $4,835,924.

Coupon payments at the end of each of the 3 years:

The manager receives DM700,000 and swaps them into DM700,000/(DM1.5/$) = $466,667.

Principal payment of DM7,000,000 at the end of the third year:

The manager receives DM7,000,000 and swaps them into DM7,000,000/(DM1.5/$) = $4,666,667.

Net results:

The manager effectively paid $4,835,924 and received three annual payments of $466,667 and a final principal payment of $4,666,667. The yield on a bond making these payments is

$$4,835,924 = 466,667(1 + y)^{-1} + 466,667(1 + y)^{-2} + 466,667(1 + y)^{-3} + 4,666,667(1 + y)^{-3}$$

Solving for y gives

$$y = 8.58\%$$

This is much better than the 8% yield on a domestic bond of equivalent characteristics.

which two parties agree to exchange currencies at a given rate over a period of time which means that it is identical to a series of forward contracts.

A currency swap is typically created by a swap dealer who stands between two parties. Party A currently receives cash flows in currency X but would like to receive cash flows in currency Y. Party B currently receives cash flows in currency Y but would like to receive cash flows in currency X. The swap dealer arranges for A to pay it in currency X. The dealer then pays B in currency X. B agrees to pay the dealer in currency Y and the dealer pays A in currency Y. The end result is that A receives cash flows in currency Y and B receives cash flows in currency X. A and B do this transaction because other transactions they are engaged in expose them to risks or patterns of cash flows that they do not desire. Dealers earn a profit by building in a spread in the rates at which they promise to make payments. Dealers can be exposed to risk, however, and may choose to do some hedging themselves.

Let us consider how a currency swap could be used by a portfolio manager. Table 23.4 illustrates a case where a portfolio manager buys a bond denominated in a foreign currency and uses a swap to convert the foreign cash flows to U. S. dollar cash flows. The net effect will be that the yield on the bond is higher than the yield on an otherwise equivalent U. S. dollar-denominated bond.

The portfolio manager finds that yields on AAA-rated 3-year bonds are around 8 percent in the U. S. market. A German firm offers an equivalent bond with a coupon of 10 percent that is selling at par. The manager knows that the German interest rate is higher because interest rates are higher in general in Germany; however, the swap market offers an opportunity to capture some additional returns. A swap dealer offers to swap all future cash flows at a rate of DM1.5 per dollar. The current exchange rate is DM1.4475 per dollar. There will be three coupons and one principal payment with the coupons spaced a year apart. The face value and price of the bond is DM7,000,000.

The portfolio manager buys the bond by purchasing DM7,000,000 for 7,000,000/ 1.4475 = $4,835,924. At the end of each of the 3 years, the bond pays DM700,000 (10 percent of 7 million), which are then paid to the swap dealer who pays the manager 700,000/1.5 = $466,667. When the bond matures, the manager receives DM7,000,000 and swaps it into 7,000,000/1.5 = $4,666,667. Thus, the manager effectively purchased a bond with the following cash flows:

$$
\begin{array}{cccc}
 & & & \$4,666,667 \\
+\$466,667 & +\$466,667 & +\$466,667 \\
\end{array}
$$

$-\$4,835,924$

We can solve for the yield on a bond with these cash flows as follows:

$$4,835,924 = 466,667(1 + y)^{-1} + 466,667(1 + y)^{-2}$$
$$+ 466,667(1 + y)^{-3} + 4,666,667(1 + y)^{-3}$$

The answer is $y = 8.58$ percent which is more than 50 basis points higher than the 8% yield available on an equivalent domestic bond.

Here the currency swap was used to convert a bond denominated in a foreign currency into an equivalent domestic bond. The increase in yield could not always be expected to occur because in an efficient market, we would not expect such opportunities to arise often. Still, currency swaps continue to be used because yield pickups are not necessarily the only reason to use a currency swap. For example, a portfolio manager holding a foreign bond may simply find that his or her portfolio needs to be temporarily restructured to pay off in dollars instead of marks. In such a case, the swap permits a low-cost rearrangement of cash flows without any arbitrage profits. The use of currency swaps has increased greatly over the years, so it seems unlikely that arbitrage opportunities, which should decrease as the market matures, are the sole reason for their popularity.

Currency swaps preceded interest rate swaps that we will cover a little later. Before doing so, we will examine some new popular interest rate instruments.

INTEREST RATE AGREEMENTS

The decade of the 1980s witnessed a revolution in the development of techniques for managing interest rate risk. Financial and portfolio managers began to increasingly rely on over-the-counter products to manage the risk of interest rate fluctuations. These products were all basically variations of forwards and options that took on slightly different characteristics so that they were customized to the specific needs of the user. This is in sharp contrast to exchange-traded products, which are standardized, meaning that users must accept the specific expiration dates, exercise prices, and so on that are available on the exchange.

In this section, we will examine interest rate options; interest rate floors, caps, and collars; and interest rate swaps.

INTEREST RATE OPTIONS

Although options on fixed-income instruments have existed for many years, they have been based on the price of an instrument and not the interest rate. For example, assume a 1-year pure discount bond with the price based on a discount rate that is quoted on a 360-day per year basis. If the discount rate is 10 percent, the price of a bond with a $100 face value will be $100 − (10)(360/360) = $90. If there is a call option on a 6-month bond expiring in 180 days with an exercise price of 92, the call will expire if the bond price goes to 92 or above in 180 days. If the bond goes to 92, then its annualized discount rate would be the value of x in the following equation:

$$100 - x(180/360) = 92$$

In this equation, x would be 16. If the annualized discount rate went to 16 percent or below at the end of the 6-month period, the call would expire in-the-money. This can be viewed as a put on the interest rate with a strike of 16 percent. If the interest rate goes to 16 percent or below in 6 months, the put expires in-the-money. The put on the interest rate and the call on the bond price are equivalent instruments.

Interest rate options of this type are widely used by financial and portfolio managers to speculate on movements in interest rates or to hedge the purchase or issuance of fixed-income securities. The interest rate is usually the LIBOR rate.

Consider an interest rate option on the rate on 90-day Eurodollar deposits. The option is on $5 million face value of Eurodollars. The exercise price is stated in terms of an interest rate, and we will call it the *strike* or *exercise rate* of 9.5%. The option premium is $7,500. The value of the option at expiration is

$$\$5,000,000(90/360)Max(0,\text{LIBOR} - .095)$$

For example, suppose LIBOR ends up at 9 percent. Then the option expires worth

$$\$5,000,000(90/360)Max(0,.09 - .095) = 0$$

Thus, the profit would be a loss of $7,500, the premium. If LIBOR ends up at 11 percent, the option expires worth

$$\$5,000,000(90/360)Max(0,.11 - .095) = \$18,750$$

Thus, the profit would be $18,750 − $7,500 = $11,250.

Figure 23.5 presents a graph of the profit from this interest rate call for a range of LIBORs at expiration. If you have not already noticed, a call on an interest rate is profitable if interest rates increase. This is in contrast to an ordinary call on the price of a bond. Typically one thinks of a call as a bullish strategy and when an investor is bullish on interest rates, it means that interest rates are expected to decrease. In contrast, an interest rate call is a *bearish* strategy because it is done in anticipation of an interest rate increase.

Figure 23.6 is an example of an interest rate put with the same terms and conditions as the call we examined. However, the premium is $6,875. The put pays off according to the formula

$$\$5,000,000(90/360)Max(0,.095 - \text{LIBOR})$$

FIGURE 23.5   **Profits to Buyer of Call on 90-Day LIBOR**

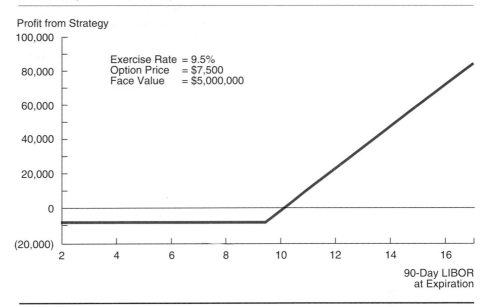

FIGURE 23.6   **Profits to Buyer of Put on 90-Day LIBOR**

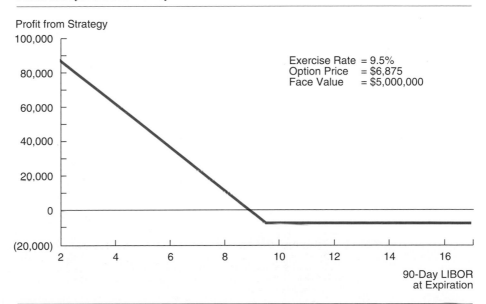

For example, if LIBOR ends up at 10 percent, the put expires worth

$$\$5,000,000(90/360)Max(0,.095 - .10) = 0$$

The profit is a loss of \$6,875. If LIBOR ends up at 8 percent, the put expires worth

$$\$5,000,000(90/360)Max(0,.095 - .08) = \$18,750$$

The profit is $\$18,750 - \$6,875 = \$11,875$. Note that an interest rate put is a strategy that is bullish on interest rates.

Pricing interest rate options has received a lot of attention in the academic literature. Because of the difficulty of specifying a mathematical model to evaluate interest rates there has been substantial controversy, and academics have competed to create the best model. Most of the models are quite complex although you can get a basic introduction to interest rate option pricing with a simple model in an article by Pitts.[20] For a slightly more advanced treatment, see Ho and Abrahamson.[21]

Although interest rate puts and calls can be used to speculate or hedge against interest rate changes, there are several variations of interest rate options that are widely used.

INTEREST RATE FLOORS, CAPS, AND COLLARS

Interest rate floors, caps, and *collars* have been quite popular among financial and portfolio managers. An interest rate *floor* is a series of interest rate put options, an interest rate *cap* is a series of interest rate call options, and an interest rate *collar* is a combination of a long floor and a short cap.

Suppose you were involved in a financial arrangement wherein you receive interest payments over a period of several years that are not known in advance and are determined by future interest rates. A common arrangement would be a banker making a loan with the interest rate adjusted according to a rate such as LIBOR. An investor might encounter this situation with a floating rate security. These are arrangements a banker or investor would undertake if interest rates were expected to increase. However, market conditions and expectations change and what looked like a good investment could change into a very poor investment. For a banker, declining interest rates would be costly, and yet the banker cannot simply call in the loan. The portfolio manager holding the floating rate security could sell it, but this could entail transaction costs and the recognition of a substantial loss due to a price decline. Sometimes the market for customized interest rate agreements will offer an attractive alternative to selling the security.

Table 23.5 illustrates a case that assumes you hold a 3-year floating rate note that has a par value of \$5,000,000 and is priced at par. Payments are made twice a year with interest determined by the LIBOR rate that was in effect on the previous interest payment date. The amount of interest is computed by counting the number of days since

---

[20]Mark Pitts, "The Pricing of Options on Debt Securities," *Journal of Portfolio Management* 9, no. 2 (Winter 1985): 41–50.

[21]Thomas S. Y. Ho and Allen A. Abrahamson, "Options on Interest Sensitive Securities," in *Financial Options: From Theory to Practice,* edited by S. Figlewski, W. L. Silber, and M. G. Subrahmanyam (Homewood, Ill.: Business One Irwin, 1990), 314–356.

TABLE 23.5

Constructing an Interest Rate Floor

Scenario: You hold a 3-year floating rate note with face and par values of $5,000,000. Payments are made twice a year with interest computed based on the LIBOR rate that was in effect at the date of the previous interest payment. Concerned that interest rates will fall over the life of the bond, you purchase an interest rate floor. The floor has a strike of 10.75 percent, meaning that any time the coupon rate is set at lower than 10.75 percent, the floor will make a payment of

$5,000,000(number of days since last interest payment/360)$Max(0,.1075 - $ LIBOR)

The payment will occur on the day the interest is owed. The floor has an up-front cost of $30,000.

Schedule of Payments (based on the stream of LIBOR rates as indicated in column 3; these are not known beforehand)

Time	Number of Days	LIBOR	Interest Payment	Principal Payment	Floor Payment	Total Payments
0	.	10.75	$ 0	$ 0	$ 0	$ 0
1	183	10.20	273,229	0	0	273,229
2	182	9.75	257,833	0	13,903	271,736
3	183	10.66	247,813	0	25,417	273,230
4	182	11.00	269,461	0	2,275	271,736
5	183	11.75	279,583	0	0	279,583
6	182	11.30	297,014	5,000,000	0	5,297,014

the last payment date. The current LIBOR rate is 10.75, and there are 183 days before the first interest payment. Thus, the first interest payment will be

$$\$5,000,000(183/360)(.1075) = \$273,229$$

All subsequent interest payments will be

$$\$5,000,000(\text{number of days since last interest payment date}/360)$$
$$(\text{LIBOR on last interest payment date})$$

On the last interest payment date, the principal of $5,000,000 is repaid.

If you are concerned that the LIBOR rate may fall over the next 3 years, you can buy an interest rate floor that has an exercise rate of 10.75 percent. Thus, at each interest payment date the floor will pay off

$$\$5,000,000(\text{number of days since last interest payment}/360)Max$$
$$(0,.1075 - \text{LIBOR on last interest payment date})$$

The cost of the floor is $30,000, which is paid up front.

Of course, you do not know the future LIBOR rates. Table 23.5 presents a scenario in which LIBOR rates initially fall and then begin to rise. The floor makes no payment on the first interest payment date (time 0) because the interest rate is the exercise rate. On the second interest payment date (time 1), LIBOR is 10.20 percent which means that the floor is in-the-money and will make a payment on the next interest payment date of

$$\$5,000,000(182/360)Max(0,.1075 - .1020) = \$13,903$$

On the third payment date (time 2), the LIBOR rate is 9.75 so the floor will make a payment on the next interest payment date of

$$\$5,000,000(183/360)Max(0,.1075 - .0975) = \$25,417$$

On the fourth payment date (time 3) LIBOR is 10.66 percent so the floor will pay off again on the next interest payment date. However, the floor does not pay off on the last two interest payment dates because the interest rate was above 10.75 percent at the two preceding interest payment dates.

The overall effect of the floor is to place a lower bound on the net interest received on the security. The interest payment made by the borrower changes with the LIBOR rate. The floor kicks in whenever the LIBOR rate falls below 10.75 percent. The actual interest payment and the floor payment combine to ensure that the lowest interest payment is $271,736. Thus, a floor works like a series of interest rate puts, with each put expiring on a specific payment date.

Just as someone can place a minimum on the amount of interest received, someone can place a maximum on the amount of interest paid. This is accomplished by an interest rate cap, which is a series of interest rate calls. If you are obligated to make periodic interest payments over a period of time based upon future interest rates, you can place a maximum on the amount of these payments by buying a cap. For example, in the previous example we bought a floor on the 6-month LIBOR rate over a 3-year period in order to place a floor under the interest payments received from a floating rate note. If we look at the same problem from the perspective of the issuer of the floating rate security, we can envision that the institution might want to cap its payments at the LIBOR rate of 10.75 percent by buying a cap that costs an up-front premium of $37,500. Table 23.6 illustrates the payments on the floating rate security and the cap payments over the 3-year period.

The cap payoff at any time is found as

$$\$5,000,000(\text{number of days since last interest payment date}/360)Max$$
$$(0,\text{LIBOR on last interest payment date} - .1075)$$

Notice that the cap does not make a payment until time 5 because prior to time 4, the LIBOR rate was always at or below 10.75 percent. At time 4 the LIBOR rate went to 11 percent and at time 5 the LIBOR rate went to 11.75 percent. The cap payment at time 5 is computed as

$$\$5,000,000(183/360)Max(0,.11 - .1075) = \$6,354$$

The cap payment at time 6 is computed as

$$\$5,000,000(182/360)Max(0,.1175 - .1075) = \$25,278$$

TABLE 23.6

Constructing an Interest Rate Cap

Scenario: You have previously issued a 3-year floating rate note with face and par values of $5,000,000. Payments are made twice a year with interest computed based on the LIBOR rate that was in effect at the date of the previous interest payment. Because you are concerned that interest rates will rise over the life of the bond, you purchase an interest rate cap. The cap has a strike value of 10.75 percent, meaning that any time market interest rates move so that the coupon rate is set at higher than 10.75 percent, the cap will make a payment of

$5,000,000(number of days since last interest payment date/360)Max(0,$LIBOR$ - .1075)$

The payment will occur on the day the interest is owed. The cap has an up-front cost of $37,500.

Schedule of Payments (based on the stream of LIBOR rates as indicated in column 3; these are not known beforehand)

Time	Number of Days	LIBOR	Interest Payment	Principal Payment	Cap Payment	Total Payments
0	.	10.75	$ 0	$ 0	$ 0	$ 0
1	183	10.20	273,229	0	0	273,229
2	182	9.75	257,833	0	0	257,833
3	183	10.66	247,813	0	0	247,813
4	182	11.00	269,461	0	0	269,461
5	183	11.75	279,583	0	6,354	273,229
6	182	11.30	297,014	5,000,000	25,278	5,271,736

The effect of the cap is to make the maximum interest payment effectively be $273,229. The firm would need to weigh the value of an initial payment of $37,500 against the certainty of a maximum interest payment of $273,229.

Because a portfolio manager deals primarily with the management of assets, the purchase of a cap would not be of much value. The manager would be more likely to buy a floor, whereas someone who deals more with obtaining financing (e.g., a corporate treasurer) would be more likely to buy a cap. When a portfolio manager considers the purchase of a floor, its cost is a significant factor in deciding whether the certainty of minimum interest payments is worthwhile. The purchase of the floor permits the portfolio manager to earn higher returns as a result of higher interest rates. However, the manager who is willing to give up the higher returns that come with higher interest rates can reduce and even eliminate the up-front cost.

When we examined the purchase of a cap it was noted that someone has to sell the cap. In other words, someone must be willing to give up the gains from higher interest rates and be compensated in the form of an initial upfront payment. If the portfolio manager *bought* a floor with a strike of 10.75 percent at a cost of $30,000 and *sold* a cap with a strike of 10.75 percent and received an up-front payment of $37,500, the manager would collect a net payment of $7,500 and, as a result, give up all gains from rising interest rates, but not incur any losses from falling interest rates. A common arrangement is for the portfolio manager to sell a cap at a strike rate such that the up-front payment received for selling the cap exactly offsets the up-front payment made to acquire the floor. This will enable the manager to capture some of the gains from rising interest rates. This arrangement, thus, will establish a maximum and minimum interest rate on the security.

TABLE 23.7   **Constructing a Zero-Cost Collar**

Scenario: You buy a 3-year floating rate note with face and par values of $5,000,000. Payments are made twice a year with interest computed based on the LIBOR rate that was in effect at the date of the previous interest payment. Because you are concerned that interest rates will decline over the life of the bond, you purchase an interest rate floor with a strike of 10.75 percent, meaning that any time the coupon rate is set at lower than 10.75 percent, the floor will make a payment of

$5,000,000(number of days since last coupon payment date/360)$Max(0, .1075 - \text{LIBOR})$

The payment will occur on the day the interest is owed. The floor has an up-front cost of $30,000. Because you are not concerned with capturing gains from rising interest rates, you decide to sell a cap with a strike of 10.95 percent. The premium received will be $30,000, which is enough to offset the cost of the floor. Thus, any time the coupon rate is set higher than 10.95 percent, you will be required to make a payment of

$5,000,000(number of days since last coupon payment date/360)$(\text{LIBOR} - .1095)$

The payment will occur on the day the interest is owed. Thus, by giving up all gains if the LIBOR rate rises above 10.95 percent and capturing all gains if the LIBOR falls below 10.75 percent, the transaction has no up-front cost.

Schedule of Payments (based on the stream of LIBOR rates as indicated in column 3; these are not known beforehand)

Time	Number of Days	LIBOR	Interest Payment	Principal Payment	Cap Payment	Floor Payment	Total Payments
0	.	10.75	$ 0	$ 0	$ 0	$ 0	$ 0
1	183	10.20	273,229	0	0	0	273,229
2	182	9.75	257,833	0	0	13,903	271,736
3	183	10.66	247,813	0	0	25,417	273,230
4	182	11.00	269,461	0	0	2,275	271,736
5	183	11.75	279,583	0	1,271	0	278,312
6	182	11.30	297,014	5,000,000	20,222	0	5,276,792

The purchase of a floor and the sale of a cap is called a *collar*. When the premiums on the cap and floor offset each other, it is called a *zero-cost collar*. Suppose in our example the portfolio manager who holds the floating rate security buys the floor described above and sells a cap with a strike of 10.95 percent. The premium on the cap is $30,000, which offsets the premium on the floor. Table 23.7 presents the results from this zero-cost collar for the same interest rates as in the previous two examples.

The cap and floor payments are determined precisely as they were before except that the strike on the cap is 10.95 percent. Note that the total interest payments (the regular interest payments plus the cap and floor payments) have a maximum of $278,313 and a minimum of $271,736. This is the same minimum for the floor example, but the maximum is higher because the cap has a strike of 10.95 percent. Within 10.75 percent and 10.95 percent, the total interest payments will vary.

This is necessarily an introductory discussion of interest rate floors, caps, and collars. For more information see Abken; Stapleton and Subrahmanyam; and Briys, Crouhy and Schöbel.[22]

---

[22]Peter Abken, "Interest-Rate Caps, Collars and Floors," *Federal Reserve Bank of Atlanta Economic Review* 72, no. 6 (November-December 1989): 2–24; Richard C. Stapleton and Marti G. Subrahmanyam, "Interest Rate Caps and Floors," in *Financial Options: From Theory to Practice,* edited by S. Figlewski, W. L. Silber, and M. G. Subrahmanyam (Homewood, Ill.: Business One Irwin, 1990); and Eric Briys, Michel Crouhy, and Rainer Schöbel, "The Pricing of Default-Free Interest Rate Caps, Floors and Collars," *The Journal of Finance* 46, no. 5 (December 1991): 1879–1892.

INTEREST RATE
SWAPS

Earlier in this chapter we discussed currency swaps where an agreement was made in which one party would make payments in one currency and receive payments in another. This agreement typically involves a swap dealer who had another party on the other side of the transaction whose needs approximately offset the needs of the first party. Currency swaps preceded interest rate swaps by a few years, but interest rate swaps are now more commonplace and have a greater dollar volume.

While there are numerous interest rate swaps, the most common is the *plain vanilla* or *generic swap* that involves a swap of fixed payments for floating-rate payments. For example, assume that one party has issued a floating-rate security that makes payments determined by a floating index such as LIBOR. Floating-rate liabilities are risky because the borrower bears the risk of rising interest rates that could prove disastrous. It is possible that the firm or government that issued a floating-rate security might prefer to make fixed-rate payments, while other parties might have the opposite position wherein they are required to make fixed payments but would prefer floating-rate payments. This might be the case if the party held assets that had floating-rate coupons. If it had floating-rate liabilities and floating-rate assets, the interest payments it makes would tend to move up and down with the interest payments it receives. Obviously if the parties could get together, they could work out a private arrangement that would be mutually beneficial. However, in most cases an intermediary is needed, which is the function of the swap dealer, a firm that arranges swaps between other firms.

When the swap market was young, firms typically made cash payments to establish swap positions, but that practice is less common now. Currently, swaps are like a series of forward contracts where a fixed rate at which interest will be paid is established, and no money changes hands up front. Party A might agree to make fixed payments to the swap dealer who agrees to make floating payments to A. A, who was probably making floating payments on a loan, has effectively converted payments from floating to fixed. The dealer who is taking a number of these positions may have some net risk exposure to interest rate changes that he may choose to take or may hedge the risk with interest rate options, caps, floors, forward contracts, or exchange-traded options or futures.

In the following example, illustrated in Table 23.8, you are a portfolio manager who holds a 4-year fixed-rate bond with a 5.3 percent coupon and a face value of $10,000,000. The bond makes semiannual interest payments, and you expect rising interest rates. As you have learned, you can do a number of different things to take advantage of rising interest rates. If your holding period is greater than the duration of your portfolio, you would benefit from rising interest rates.[23] Also, you could buy interest rate calls, sell interest rate puts, or numerous other strategies including simply selling this bond and replacing it with a floating-rate bond. Let us assume that you find that a swap could be arranged at fairly low cost that would convert your fixed-rate bond to the equivalent of a floating-rate bond. A swap dealer offers to pay you floating-rate interest based on the 6-month LIBOR rate, while you pay the dealer fixed-rate interest at 6 percent per year. The payments are made on the bond coupon dates on the face amount of $10,000,000, which is called the *notional principal*.

[23]This statement, which appears inconsistent with previous discussions, is based upon the notion that with duration and maturity less than your investment horizon, the bonds will mature before your horizon so you will not suffer the price risk related to an increase in interest rates but you will benefit from the higher reinvestment rate.

TABLE 23.8

Constructing an Interest Rate Swap

Scenario: You hold a 4-year fixed rate coupon bond with a face value of $10,000,000, making semiannual interest payments at a rate of 5.3 percent annually. You anticipate a gradual increase in interest rates over the next 4 years. You would like to modify the structure of the bond so that it would benefit from rising interest rates. One way to do this would be to convert it to a floating-rate bond. You go to a swap dealer who offers to pay you floating-rate interest based on the 6-month LIBOR rate on the previous interest payment day while you pay the dealer fixed-rate interest at a rate of 6 percent per annum. Payments will be made on the dates on which the bond makes its coupon interest payments.

Thus, on every interest payment date you will receive from your current bond $10,000,000(.053/2) = $265,000. You will pay $10,000,000(.06)(number of days since last interest payment date/360) to the swap dealer and will receive $10,000,000(LIBOR)(number of days since last interest payment date/360).

Schedule of Payments (based on the stream of LIBOR rates as indicated in column 3; these are not known beforehand)

Time	Number of Days	LIBOR	Interest Payment	Principal Payment	Floating Swap Payment	Fixed Swap Payment	Total Cash Flow
0	.	3.50	$0	$0	$0	$0	$0
1	183	3.64	265,000	0	177,917	305,000	137,917
2	182	4.31	265,000	0	184,022	303,333	145,689
3	183	5.10	265,000	0	219,092	305,000	179,092
4	182	5.83	265,000	0	257,833	303,333	219,500
5	183	6.61	265,000	0	296,358	305,000	256,358
6	182	6.72	265,000	0	334,172	303,333	295,839
7	183	7.03	265,000	0	341,600	305,000	301,600
8	182	7.33	265,000	10,000,000	355,406	303,333	10,317,073

Thus, on the interest payment date you will receive on the bond you hold:

$$\$10,000,000(.053/2) = \$265,000$$

You will pay to the swap dealer:

$$\$10,000,000(.06)(\text{number of days since last interest payment date}/360)$$

This amount will be either $303,333 or $305,000, with the variance due to the different number of days (182 or 183) between interest payment dates. The swap dealer will pay you

$$\$10,000,000(\text{LIBOR})(\text{number of days since last interest date}/360)$$

Thus, the total cash flow you receive will be

$$\$265,000 + \$10,000,000(\text{LIBOR} - .06)(183 \text{ or } 182/360)$$

Obviously you do not know the future course of interest rates. Table 23.8 illustrates the payments under one scenario in which rates increase.

At time 0, the LIBOR rate is 3.5 percent. There are 183 days until the next interest payment date. Thus, you will pay $305,000 on the next interest payment date and receive

$$\$10,000,000(.035)(183/360) = \$177,917$$

from the swap dealer. Thus, your total cash inflow is $265,000 − $305,000 + $177,917 = $137,917. The remaining total payments are shown in the final column. Note that the initial payments are lower than the interest payment on your current bond, but as interest rates get higher the payments increase, and they exceed what you would receive on your fixed-rate bond. You have effectively converted this fixed-rate bond into a floating-rate bond.

A swap is nothing more than a series of forward or futures contracts wherein one party will make payments at a fixed rate and receive payments at a floating rate. That party has entered into a series of long interest rate forward contracts and benefits if rates rise. The other party agrees to make floating payments and receive fixed payments and will benefit if rates fall because he is essentially short a series of interest rate forward contracts. Generally, the fixed rate on swaps is determined by observing the futures prices of Eurodollar contracts.

While this is an example of the fixed-for-floating swap, there are a number of other types of swaps. For example, a *basis swap* is an exchange where one party makes floating-rate payments based on one index (such as LIBOR), and the other party makes floating-rate payments based on another index (such as the Treasury bill rate). Alternatively one set of payments could be made quarterly and the other made semiannually. Another common arrangement is a combination of a currency and interest rate swap. For example, one party would make fixed payments in one currency to another party, who in turn would make floating payments in a different currency to the first party.

The tremendous growth of the swaps market has raised questions about the purpose of swaps and the potential risk to the financial system. One of the critical issues is default risk because the payments that each party promises to the other are not guaranteed. If one party defaults, it could cause the other party to default on other transactions. While the potential for defaults to ripple through the economy has been of some concern, the default risk is actually somewhat less than might otherwise appear. The payment arrangements specify that the two parties determine the net payment that one party owes the other. In other words, if Party A owes the dealer $900,000 and the dealer owes Party A $1,050,000, then the dealer simply pays Party A $150,000. Thus, if the dealer defaults, Party A is not out $1,050,000 but rather only $150,000. With each party absorbing some of the other's credit risk, the default risk is reduced, although the default risk is not eliminated. The fact is, one party may greatly subsidize the other, particularly if the credit quality of one party drops considerably after the swap is arranged. However, the overall risk is not the same as for a one-way credit transaction with a borrower and a lender.

For those wanting to know more about swaps, there is a growing body of literature. Several recent books devote considerable space to the discussion of swaps.[24] A treatment of some of the issues and applications of interest rate swaps is found in Wall and Pringle; Goodman; and Einzig and Lange.[25]

PORTFOLIO INSURANCE

Hedging strategies are designed to reduce risk. Investors who want to reduce risk and also be in a position to benefit from price moves in their favor can use an option strategy that is designed to do just that, called *portfolio insurance*. The idea was that an investor could insure that a portfolio achieved a minimum rate of return. If the market moved, the portfolio would be able to participate in the advance but at the cost of earning less than if the insurance had not been purchased. To illustrate, suppose an investor has $100 to invest over a single period, and the S&P 500 index is currently at 90.97 with the risk-free rate at 10.52 percent per period. The investor wants to guarantee a minimum rate of return of 5 percent over the period; that is, the investor wants to insure the portfolio will be worth $105 ($100 × 1.05).

One way to achieve the goal is to design a *protective put strategy* as discussed in Chapter 20. To implement this the investor buys one share in the S&P 500 portfolio for $90.97 and uses the remaining $9.03 to buy one unit of a European put option with an exercise price equal to the insured floor of $105.[26] For convenience assume a zero dividend rate over this period. At expiration, if the S&P 500 index is at or below $105, the investor exercises the put to realize the insured floor of $105. If the index value exceeds $105, the put expires worthless, but the value of the insured portfolio exceeds $105. Thus, the protective put strategy insures the portfolio against downside risk, but also retains the benefit of upside potential.

There is certainly a cost associated with portfolio insurance. The insurance premium is the cost of the put of $9.03, and this amount is forgone regardless of whether the put is exercised. If the put expires worthless, the premium is lost, which means the investor participates in only a portion of the upward move in the portfolio because the gain is partially offset by the premium cost.[27]

An alternative portfolio insurance strategy is known as a *fiduciary call*. Following put-call parity, a European call on the S&P 500 index with an exercise price of 105 and a term of one period is worth $4.99 (90.97 + 9.03 − 105/1.1052). In this strategy, an investor would purchase one call on the index and invest the remaining $95.01 in a

[24]John F. Marshall and Kenneth R. Kapner, *Understanding Swap Finance* (Cincinnati: South-Western Publishing, 1990); Clifford W. Smith, Jr., Charles W. Smithson, and D. Sykes Wilford, *Managing Financial Risk* (Grand Rapids: Harper Business, 1990); Clifford W. Smith, Jr., and Charles W. Smithson, *The Handbook of Financial Engineering* (Grand Rapids: Harper Business, 1990); and John F. Marshall and Vipul K. Bansal, *Financial Engineering* (Boston: Allyn and Bacon, 1992).

[25]Larry D. Wall and John J. Goodman, "Interest Rate Swaps: A Review of the Issues," *Federal Reserve Bank of Atlanta Economic Review* (1988): 22–40; Laurie S. Goodman, "The Use of Interest Rate Swaps in Managing Corporate Liabilities," *Journal of Applied Corporate Finance* 2, no. 4 (Winter 1990): 35–47; and Robert Einzig and Bruce Lange, "Swaps at Transamerica: Applications and Analysis," *Journal of Applied Corporate Finance* 2, no. 4 (Winter 1990): 48–58.

[26]Two things must be said here. One is that buying one share of the S&P 500 portfolio actually means to construct a portfolio of the 500 stocks that replicates the index. Obviously it would take more than $90.97 to do this. We simply scale everything for the example. Second, the price of the index and the price of one put is the amount of wealth invested. If the index costs $90.97 and the put is at $11, the investor must invest $101.97.

[27]For an analysis of the cost of portfolio insurance, see Richard J. Rendleman, Jr., and Richard W. McEnally, "Assessing the Costs of Portfolio Insurance," *Financial Analysts Journal* 43, no. 3 (May-June 1987): 27–37.

risk-free asset. At expiration, this portfolio would have a minimum value of $105 (95.01 × 1.1052). If the index value exceeds 105, then the investor could use $105 to exercise the call and buy a share of the index. Thus, both the protective put and the fiduciary call strategies produce identical end-of-period payoffs.

In practice, these portfolio insurance strategies are not feasible because the options needed are sometimes available only as American options, which means paying a higher price for the unnecessary early exercise privilege, and the terms and conditions of listed options may not meet the needs of investors. However, an investor could construct synthetic European options by following *dynamic hedging strategies* that consist of a risky asset such as a stock portfolio and a hedge asset such as a T-bill. For example, a European put option on a stock portfolio can be synthetically created by shorting some stock and investing the proceeds in the T-bill. The proportion of funds allocated to the risky asset and the T-bill are determined by the Black-Scholes European put option pricing formula and are continuously revised to ensure that the synthetic protective put replicates the actual protective put. As stock prices rise, some T-bills are sold and the proceeds are used to buy more shares. As stock prices fall, additional shares are sold short and the proceeds invested back into T-bills.

To be more explicit, recall the Black-Scholes formula for the price of a European put:

$$p(t) = Xe^{-r(T-t)}[1 - N(d_2)] - S(t)[1 - N(d_1)]$$

A protective put would be worth $p(t) + S(t)$. Adding $S(t)$ to both sides and simplifying algebraically gives

$$p(t) + S(t) = Xe^{-r(T-t)}[1 - N(d_2)] + SN(d_1)$$

The right-hand side indicates that we should buy the quantity $e^{-r(T-t)}[1 - N(d_2)]$ T-bills having a face value of X and hold $N(d_1)$ shares of stock. Such a portfolio will replicate one put and one share of stock although these proportions constantly change so revisions must be made. Following a similar approach we could construct a fiduciary call.

It is also possible to insure a portfolio by using futures instead of T-bills. Selling futures on a portion of the portfolio is equivalent to converting that portion of the portfolio to a risk-free asset. The combination of stock and the implicit risk-free asset is weighted so that the portfolio replicates a protective put.[28] Explanations of the dynamics of portfolio insurance are found in Rubinstein and in O'Brien.[29]

PROGRAM TRADING

In Chapter 22 we discussed the strategy called index arbitrage, in which a stock portfolio that replicates a stock index and a stock index futures are simultaneously traded to exploit an opportunity when the futures price does not conform to the price given

[28]For an explanation of the procedure to do this, see Chapter 14 of Don M. Chance, *An Introduction to Options and Futures*, 2d ed. (Fort Worth: The Dryden Press, 1992).

[29]Mark Rubinstein, "Alternative Paths to Portfolio Insurance," *Financial Analysts Journal* 41, no. 4 (July-August 1985): 42–52; and Thomas J. O'Brien, "Portfolio Insurance Mechanics," *Journal of Portfolio Management* 14, no. 3 (Spring 1988): 40–47.

FIGURE 23.7   **Program Trading on the New York Stock Exchange,** *The Wall Street Journal*

PROGRAM TRADING

NEW YORK – Program trading for the week ended July 30 accounted for 10%, or an average of 25.3 million daily shares, of New York Stock Exchange volume.

Brokerage firms executed an additional 2.7 million daily shares of program trading away from the Big Board, mostly on foreign markets. Program trading is the simultaneous purchase or sale of at least 15 different stocks with a total value of $1 million or more.

Of the program total on the Big Board, 37.4% involved stock-index arbitrage, up from 32% the prior week. In this strategy, traders dart between stocks and stock-index options and futures to capture fleeting price differences.

Some 49.4% of program trading was executed by firms for their own accounts or principal trading, while 42.6% was for their customers. An additional 8% was designated as customer facilitation, where firms use principal positions to facilitate customer trades.

Of the five most active firms, Salomon Brothers, Cooper Neff, and First Boston executed all or most of their program trading for their own accounts, while Morgan Stanley did most of its program trading for its customers. Nomura Securities split its program trading between its own account and those of its customers.

NYSE PROGRAM TRADING

Volume (in millions of shares) for the week ending July 30,, 1993

Top 15 Firms	Index Arbitrage	Derivative-Related*	Other Strategies	Total
Morgan Stanley	....	....	22.0	22.0
Salomon Brothers	15.0	....	5.4	20.4
Nomura Securities	5.6	0.4	11.6	17.6
Cooper Neff	....	11.3	2.2	13.5
First Boston	4.2	1.0	2.8	8.0
Bear Stearns	0.7	....	5.6	6.3
Spears Leeds	4.9	....	....	4.9
W&D Securities	0.1	....	4.2	4.3
Kidder Peabody	2.6	....	1.1	3.7
UBS Securities	3.2	....	0.3	3.5
Susquehanna	2.5	....	0.5	3.0
LIT America	2.5	....	....	2.5
Daiwa Securities	1.1	0.3	1.0	2.4
PaineWebber	0.3	....	1.6	1.9
Thomas Williams	1.7	....	....	1.7
OVERALL TOTAL	**47.3**	**13.1**	**66.0**	**126.4**

*Other derivative-related strategies besides index arbitrage
Source: New York Stock Exchange

Source: "Program Trading," *The Wall Street Journal,* August 6, 1993. Copyright © 1993 Dow Jones & Company, Inc. Reprinted by permission of The Wall Street Journal. All Rights Reserved Worldwide.

by the cost of carry model. To implement such a trade requires the purchase or sale of an enormous quantity of stock at one time and the adjustments necessary to maintain an insured portfolio also require trading large amounts of stock at one time. This has led to a new form of trading called *program trading.*

Program trading is often implemented by a computer so it has sometimes been called *computerized trading.* The role of the computer is actually fairly minor since it only makes the calculations that determine that such a trade should be made after which a network of computers sends signals to the appropriate parties that result in the trade executions. The New York Stock Exchange has facilitated the rapid execution of trades by its Designated Order Turnaround system, called DOT, and its successor, called the Super DOT system. These systems link member firms' trading desks directly to the exchange floor.

The NYSE has defined program trading as any portfolio strategy involving the simultaneous or nearly simultaneous purchase or sale of 15 or more stocks with a total value of $1 million or more.[30] The NYSE requires that these trades be reported to it and requires all index arbitrage trades to be reported. Figure 23.7 illustrates *The Wall Street Journal*'s report on program trading, which appears each Friday. Although program trading increased dramatically from the middle to late 1980s, the crash of 1987 changed people's attitudes about this strategy.

---

[30]For a discussion of the differences between program trading, portfolio insurance, and index arbitrage, see Joanne M. Hill and Frank J. Jones, "Equity Trading, Program Trading, Portfolio Insurance, Computer Trading and All That," *Financial Analysts Journal* 44, no. 4 (July-August 1988): 29–38.

PROGRAM
TRADING AND THE
1987 CRASH

Program trading and derivatives in general have been attacked for aggravating price volatility in the wake of the October 1987 stock market crash. Briefly, the enormous trading activity during October 19 and 20, 1987 swamped the electronic order-processing and information-display capabilities of the stock markets, which led to recurrent episodes of disconnected spot and futures markets. As a result, the S&P 500 futures was trading at well below its theoretical fair value, even though interest rates exceeded the dividend yield on the index. As you know, given this set of conditions, traders will want to buy the futures contract and sell the underlying stocks. On top of this mechanical disruption, the uptick short-sale rule reduced index-arbitrage trading, which would have brought the two markets back in line. The dramatic stock price moves meant that portfolio insurers needed to make very large trades to get their portfolios to the right proportions of stock and T-bills or stock and futures. These large trades, however, were not prompted by panic selling by insurers and did not imply that the insurers foresaw bad times ahead. They were simply the adjustments required by the formulas the insurers were using. However, many investors saw these large trades as information motivated and feared that large institutions knew something they did not know which sent the entire market into a state of panic and everyone was selling. These events led to the allegation that instead of providing protection against market movements, program trading and portfolio insurance *caused* a dramatic increase in stock-market volatility.

Numerous studies examined the causes of the crash, and we cannot truly identify who, if anyone, is to blame. Market movements like the crash of 1987 and another less severe crash that occurred in 1989 are often a consequence of a sudden break in the euphoria that sometimes dominates investor sentiment for a long time. Obviously, program trading can cause rapid movements in prices, but it seems unlikely that it could start a crash. A widely cited study on the crash by Roll found that the crash was truly international in scope.[31] It was shown that the U.S. market had the fifth smallest decline of 23 markets. In countries in which program trading is widely used, there was strong evidence that the decline was *less* severe which implies that program trading may have had a *stabilizing* effect.

The reasons for the crash have often been given as (1) the lack of harmony in operating procedures in the stock and futures markets, (2) the lack of coordination in the regulation of these markets, (3) a failure of the stock exchange order-processing mechanism, and (4) the undercapitalization of specialists on the stock exchange. These points continue to be controversial and the debate over who should regulate the various stock and futures markets is still a hot one and causes continuing tension between the futures and stock markets and the regulators. In response to the concerns about volatility, the futures and stock markets have instituted some limitations on program trading. *Circuit breakers* were installed, which force trading and order reporting to change if large and rapid price movements occur, and the NYSE instituted limitations to the use of the Super DOT system by institutions during fast markets.[32] Finally, there was a

---

[31]Richard Roll, "The International Crash of October 1987," in *Black Monday and the Future of Financial Markets,* edited by R. W. Kamphuis, Jr., R. C. Kormendi, and J. W. H. Watson (Homewood, Ill.: Irwin, 1989). This paper was also published in the *Financial Analysts Journal* 44, no. 5 (September–October, 1988): 19–35.

[32]A review of the issues involving circuit breakers is found in James T. Moser, "Circuit Breakers," *Federal Reserve Bank of Chicago Economic Perspectives* 14, no. 5 (September–October 1990): 2–13.

tremendous amount of bad publicity associated with program trading and portfolio insurance that led many firms to simply stop doing it.

Unfortunately, limiting program trading and portfolio insurance may be throwing the baby out with the bath water. There is little scientific evidence that they cause serious, if any, damage to the market and, in fact, they may be quite beneficial. The debate goes on.[33]

SUMMARY

In this chapter we have examined a number of new and widely used derivatives products. Options on futures are ordinary put and call contracts that grant the right to buy or sell a futures contract and they trade side by side with the underlying futures. Because there are no exchange-traded options on commodities, options on futures are the only way to take option positions based on anticipated movements in commodities. However, they are also quite popular when the underlying futures is on bonds or a stock index. Their basic pricing principles and applications are similar to those of options on spot assets, but some differences, such as the early exercise condition, are quite significant.

Foreign currencies trade in the form of spot, forward, futures, options, and swaps. The foreign currency spot and forward markets are over-the-counter markets involving large trades between creditworthy institutions and governments. Foreign currency futures have traded on the Chicago Mercantile Exchange since the early 1970s while foreign currency options trade on the Philadelphia Stock Exchange. Forwards and futures are priced by interest rate parity, the foreign exchange market's equivalent of the cost of carry model. Foreign currency options that are European-style (exercisable only at expiration) are priced with a variation of the Black-Scholes model. A currency swap is an agreement between two parties for one party to make payments in one currency to the other party, who in turn makes payments to the first party in a different currency.

Interest rate agreements are private over-the-counter transactions. Interest rate options are options in which the payoffs are determined not by the price of an underlying instrument but by an interest rate so they can be used to hedge or speculate on interest rate movements. An interest rate floor is a series of interest rate puts that is usually employed to protect a position against declining interest rates. An interest rate cap is a series of interest rate calls that is used to protect a position against rising interest rates. An interest rate collar combines an interest rate floor with a short interest rate cap to reduce or even eliminate the cost of the floor. Interest rate swaps are contracts involving the exchange of cash flows between two parties. They often consist of an agreement in which one party makes fixed-rate cash flows to another party, who in turn makes floating-rate cash flows to the first party. Swaps can be viewed as a series of forward contracts.

Finally, we discussed portfolio insurance, whereby a portfolio is positioned such that an investor can have a guaranteed minimum return by holding a put or by exchanging the portfolio for calls and T-bills. It is generally implemented by holding stock and T-bills or stock and futures. To implement portfolio insurance strategies and index

---

[33]For additional discussion and insight on this topic, see Merton H. Miller, *Financial Innovation and Market Volatility* (Cambridge, MA: Blackwell, 1991), and *Market Volatility and Investor Confidence,* Report to the Board of Directors of the New York Stock Exchange, Inc. (June 7, 1990).

arbitrage, it is often necessary for firms to trade large amounts of stock at one time. These trades are often initiated by instructions from a computer and are referred to as program trading. Unfortunately, derivatives and program trading have been accused of increasing stock market volatility and some restrictions have been placed on their usage. These issues, however, continue to be debated and examined.

Financial innovation, through the creation of new products and strategies, is a natural response to change in an increasingly complex and interconnected financial world. The creativity of firms and individuals in the investment community will certainly lead to more new products and services in the future. We have touched on a few here and you will definitely encounter many more as you plan and implement your investments.

QUESTIONS

1. How do options on futures differ from options on spot assets?

2. How is the pricing of options on futures different from the pricing of options on the spot asset? Assume the options are European and that the futures and options expire simultaneously.

3. What types of derivatives trade on foreign exchange rates? Where do they trade?

4. What is the foreign currency market's version of the cost of carry model?

5. What type of transaction is executed if foreign currency futures and spot prices are misaligned?

6. Compare the method of pricing (European) foreign currency options with the method of pricing (European) options on spot assets.

7. Describe a situation where a foreign currency futures hedge would be appropriate. Describe a situation where a foreign currency option hedge would be appropriate.

8. How do interest rate options differ from options on interest-sensitive securities?

9. What methods can be used to hedge against a series of exposures to interest rate movements?

10. How is a fixed-for-floating rate swap like other derivative contracts we have studied?

11. What is program trading and portfolio insurance and why are they controversial?

PROBLEMS

1. Determine the prices of call and put options on futures if the futures price is 86, the exercise price is 80, the risk-free rate is 7.8 percent, the standard deviation is .26, and the options expire in 62 days.

2. Determine the prices of call and put options on a foreign currency if the spot exchange rate is $0.59, the exercise price is $0.55, the domestic risk-free rate is 4.5 percent, the foreign risk-free rate is 9.2 percent, the standard deviation is .22, and the options expire in 37 days.

3. What should the forward rate be for a 90-day foreign currency contract if the exchange rate is $0.21, the domestic risk-free rate is 3.8 percent, and the foreign interest rate is 8.6 percent?

4. Suppose a portfolio manager knows that in approximately 90 days, he will receive a payoff from a zero coupon German bond in the amount of DM10,000,000. The current spot rate for the German mark is $0.6826/DM. A futures contract expiring in a little more than 90 days has a price of $.6687. Describe the transaction involved in hedging this risk. Determine how the hedge turned out if the manager closes out the hedge when the spot rate is $0.6599 and the futures price is $0.6581.

5. Suppose in the previous problem the portfolio manager simply arranged a one-time currency swap in which he agreed to pay DM10,000,000 to the swap dealer who promised to pay dollars at the rate of DM1.52/$. What would have been the effective outcome of this transaction? What are the risks to the portfolio manager and the swap dealer?

6. Consider interest rate calls and puts on the 90-day LIBOR rate. The option is on $1,000,000 face value and the exercise rate is 10 percent. Find the value at expiration of the following options under the given conditions.
   a. A call where LIBOR is at 10.8 percent at expiration.
   b. A put where LIBOR is at 10.8 percent at expiration.
   c. A call where LIBOR is at 9.3 percent at expiration.
   d. A put where LIBOR is at 9.3 percent at expiration.

7. A bank makes a 1-year loan with payments to be made four times a year. The loan is for $500,000. On the first day of each quarter, the interest rate for the quarter is set at the LIBOR rate on that day. Then at the end of the quarter, interest is paid based on that rate and the number of days in the quarter. There are 91, 92, 90, and 92 days in the respective quarters. The bank enters into a floor that pays off whenever the LIBOR rate falls below 7 percent. The current LIBOR rate is 7 percent and the LIBOR rates on the first day of each remaining quarter turn out to be 6.8 percent, 6.6 percent, and 7.1 percent. Find the bank's cash flows from the loan and the floor. The principal is repaid on the last interest payment date.

8. A portfolio manager holds a floating-rate bond that will make two more interest payments and then its final principal payment of $20,000,000. The manager previously entered into a zero-cost collar consisting of a floor at 9 percent and a cap at 9.5 percent. The next interest payment will occur in 183 days and will be at a rate of 9.9 percent. The final interest payment will be 182 days after that and will be at a rate of 8.7 percent. Find the payments from the bond and the collar.

9. A firm has entered into a swap on $5,000,000 notional principal. The firm pays a fixed rate of 8 percent on payment dates spaced 90 days apart. There are four payments left, with the next payment occurring 90 days from now. The firm receives payments based on the LIBOR rate. Determine the four remaining payments if the LIBOR rates on which those payments are computed are 8.7 percent, 7.2 percent, 7.7 percent, and 8.4 percent.

REFERENCES

Abken, Peter. "Interest-Rate Caps, Collars and Floors," *Federal Reserve Bank of Atlanta Economic Review* 72, no. 6 (November-December 1989).

Bailey, Warren. "An Empirical Investigation of the Market for Comex Gold Futures Options." *The Journal of Finance* 42, no. 5 (December 1987).

Ball, Clifford A., and Walter N. Torous. "Futures Options and the Volatility of Futures Prices," *The Journal of Finance* 41, no. 4 (September 1986).

Black, Fischer. "The Pricing of Commodity Contracts." *Journal of Financial Economics* 3, nos. 1, 2 (January-March 1976).

Bodurtha, James, and Georges Courtadon. "Efficiency Tests of the Foreign Currency Options Market." *The Journal of Finance* 41, no. 1 (March 1986).

Bodurtha, James, and Georges Courtadon. "Tests of an American Option Pricing Model on the Foreign Currency Options Market." *Journal of Financial and Quantitative Analysis* 22, no. 2 (June 1987).

Briys, Eric, Michel Crouhy, and Rainer Schöbel. "The Pricing of Default-Free Interest Rate Caps, Floors and Collars." *The Journal of Finance* 46, no. 5 (December 1991).

Chance, Don M. *An Introduction to Options and Futures.* 2d ed. Fort Worth: The Dryden Press, 1992.

Cornell, Bradford, and Marc R. Reinganum. "Forward and Futures Prices: Evidence from the Foreign Exchange Markets." *The Journal of Finance* 36, no. 5 (December 1981).

Einzig, Robert, and Bruce Lange. "Swaps at Transamerica: Applications and Analysis." *Journal of Applied Corporate Finance* 2, no. 4 (Winter 1990).

Figlewski, Stephen, William L. Silber, and Marti G. Subrahmanyam, eds. *Financial Options: From Theory to Practice.* Homewood, Ill.: Business One Irwin, 1990.

Garman, Mark B., and Steven W. Kohlhagen. "Foreign Currency Option Values." *Journal of International Money and Finance* 2, no. 3 (1983).

Goodman, Laurie S. "The Use of Interest Rate Swaps in Managing Corporate Liabilities." *Journal of Applied Corporate Finance* 2, no. 4 (Winter 1990).

Grabbe, J. Orlin. *International Financial Markets.* 2d ed. New York: Elsevier Science Publishing, 1991.

Hill, Joanne M., and Frank J. Jones. "Equity Trading, Program Trading, Portfolio Insurance, Computer Trading and All That." *Financial Analysts Journal* 44, no. 4 (July-August 1988).

Ho, Thomas S. Y., and Allen A. Abrahamson. "Options on Interest Sensitive Securities." In *Financial Options: From Theory to Practice,* edited by S. Figlewski, W. L. Silber, and M. G. Subrahmanyam. Homewood, Ill.: Business One Irwin, 1990.

Hull, John. *Options, Futures and Other Derivative Instruments.* 2nd ed. Englewood Cliffs, N.J.: Prentice-Hall, 1993.

Kamphuis, Robert W., Roger C. Kormendi, and J. W. Henry Watson, eds. *Black Monday and the Future of Financial Markets.* Homewood, Ill.: Irwin, 1989.

Levi, Maurice D. *International Finance.* 2d ed. New York: McGraw-Hill, 1990.

Marshall, John F., and Vipul K. Bansal. *Financial Engineering.* Boston: Allyn and Bacon, 1992.

Marshall, John F., and Kenneth R. Kapner. *Understanding Swap Finance.* Cincinnati: South-Western Publishing, 1990.

Miller, Merton H. *Financial Innovation and Market Volatility.* Cambridge, MA: Blackwell, 1991.

Moser, James T. "Circuit Breakers." *Federal Reserve Bank of Chicago Economic Perspectives* 14, no. 5 September-October 1990.

O'Brien, Thomas J. "Portfolio Insurance Mechanics." *Journal of Portfolio Management* 14, no. 3 (Spring 1988).

Pitts, Mark. "The Pricing of Options on Debt Securities." *Journal of Portfolio Management* 9, no. 2 (Winter 1985).

Rendleman, Richard J., Jr., and Richard W. McEnally. "Assessing the Costs of Portfolio Insurance." *Financial Analysts Journal* 43, no. 3 (May-June 1987).

Roll, Richard. "The International Crash of October 1987." In *Black Monday and the Future of Financial Markets,* edited by R. W. Kamphuis, Jr., R. C. Kormendi, and J. W. H. Watson. Homewood, Ill.: Irwin, 1989.

Rubinstein, Mark. "Alternative Paths to Portfolio Insurance." *Financial Analysts Journal* 41, no. 4 (July-August 1985).

Smith, Clifford W., Jr., and Charles W. Smithson. *The Handbook of Financial Engineering.* Grand Rapids: Harper Business, 1990.

Smith, Clifford W., Jr., Charles W. Smithson, and D. Sykes Wilford. *Managing Financial Risk.* Grand Rapids: Harper Business, 1990.

Stapleton, Richard C., and Marti G. Subrahmanyam. "Interest Rate Caps and Floors." In *Financial Options: From Theory to Practice,* edited by S. Figlewski, W. L. Silber, and M. G. Subrahmanyam. Homewood, Ill.: Business One Irwin, 1990.

Wall, Larry D., and John J. Pringle. "Interest Rate Swaps: A Review of the Issues." *Federal Reserve Bank of Atlanta Economic Review* (1988).

Whaley, Robert E. "Valuation of American Futures Options: Theory and Empirical Evidence." *The Journal of Finance* 41, no. 1 (March 1986).

CHAPTER 24

INVESTMENT COMPANIES

In this chapter we will answer the following questions:

- What is an investment company and how is one started?
- Who manages the investment company portfolio and how are the managers compensated?
- How do you compute the net asset value (NAV) for an investment company?
- What is the difference between a closed-end and an open-end investment company?
- What is the difference between the NAV and market price for a closed-end fund?
- What is the growth pattern for open-end investment companies?
- What is the difference between a load and a no-load open-end fund?
- What is a 12b-1 plan fund and how does it affect an investor in such a fund?
- What are fund management fees, how do they affect fund investors, and how do they influence fund management companies?
- What are money market funds and what has been their growth pattern?
- What are the two major means of fund distribution and what has been the pattern of growth for each approach?
- Given the breakdown of all funds by investment objectives, which groups have experienced relative growth or decline?
- What has been the risk-adjusted performance of domestic equity mutual funds relative to alternative market indexes?
- What has been the risk-adjusted performance of international stock funds and bond funds relative to appropriate market indexes?
- Beyond overall performance, what has been the ability of fund managers to correctly time the market and perform in a consistent manner?
- Given a desire to have a personal portfolio manager perform certain functions for you, how do investment companies help fulfill these needs?
- What are some of the major sources of information on the current and historical performance of funds and the costs associated with buying and owning investment companies?

Up to this point in the book, we have discussed how to analyze the aggregate market, alternative industries, and individual companies as well as their stocks and bonds in order to build a portfolio that is consistent with your investment objectives. The current section has centered on alternative instruments such as options, warrants, convertibles, and futures that provide additional risk–return possibilities beyond those available from a straight stock–bond portfolio. This chapter introduces another investment opportunity: investment companies that sell shares in portfolios of stocks, bonds, or some combination of securities. Investment companies can make up part of a larger portfolio along with investments in individual stocks and bonds, or investment companies can be your total portfolio.

Studies of efficient capital markets have indicated that few individual investors outperform the aggregate market averages. This makes managed investment companies an appealing alternative to direct investments because they provide several services. Many different types of investment companies offer a wide variety of alternative investment instruments with a range of risk and return characteristics.

The initial sections in this chapter explain investment companies with examples and discuss the management organizations for investment company groups. The following section breaks investment companies into major types based on how they are traded in the secondary market and how they charge for their services. The next section divides investment companies into types based on their investment objectives and the types of securities in their portfolios. This section outlines some very interesting alternatives ranging from unusual types of instruments to securities from around the world.

To choose among almost 3,000 investment companies available, you need to understand how to evaluate their performance. After discussing some major studies of what features are important and how to examine them, we consider the implications of these results for investors. We conclude the chapter with a presentation on some sources of information on investment companies emphasizing how these sources of information can help you to make an investment decision that considers the growing availability of investment companies that invest in stock and bonds from around the world.

WHAT IS AN INVESTMENT COMPANY?

An *investment company* invests a pool of funds belonging to many individuals in a portfolio of individual investments such as stocks and bonds. As an example, an investment company might sell 10 million shares to the public at $10 a share for a total of $100 million. If this common stock fund emphasized blue-chip stocks, the manager would invest the proceeds of the sale ($100 million less any commissions) in the stock of such companies as American Telephone and Telegraph, Standard Oil, IBM, Xerox, and General Electric. Therefore, each individual who bought shares of the investment company would own a percentage of the investment company's total portfolio.

The value of these shares depends on what happens to the investment company's portfolio of stocks. With no further transactions, if the total market value of the stocks in the portfolio increased to $105 million, then each original share of the investment company would be worth $10.50 ($105 million/10 million shares). This per-share value is the *net asset value (NAV)* of the investment company. It equals the total market value of all its assets divided by the number of fund shares outstanding.

MANAGEMENT OF INVESTMENT COMPANIES

The investment company is typically a corporation that has as its major assets the portfolio of marketable securities referred to as a fund. The management of the portfolio of securities and most of the other administrative duties are handled by a separate *investment management company* hired by the board of directors of the investment company. This legal description oversimplifies the typical arrangement. The actual management usually begins with an investment advisory firm that starts an investment company and selects a board of directors for the fund. Subsequently this board of directors hires the investment advisory firm as the fund's portfolio manager.

The contract between the investment company (the portfolio of securities) and the investment management company indicates the duties and compensation of the management company. The major duties of the investment management company include investment research, the management of the portfolio, and administrative duties such as issuing securities and handling redemptions and dividends. The management fee is generally stated as a percentage of the total value of the fund and typically ranges from one-quarter to one-half of 1 percent, with a sliding scale as the size of the fund increases.

To achieve economies of scale, many management companies start numerous funds with different characteristics. The variety of funds allows the management group to appeal to many investors with different risk–return preferences. In addition, it allows investors to switch among funds as economic or personal conditions change. This "family of funds" promotes flexibility and also increases the total capital the investment firm manages.

CLOSED-END VERSUS OPEN-END INVESTMENT COMPANIES

Investment companies begin like any other company—someone sells an issue of common stock to a group of investors. An investment company, however, uses the proceeds to purchase the securities of other publicly held companies rather than buildings and equipment. An open-end investment company (often referred to as a *mutual fund*) differs from a closed-end investment company (typically referred to as a *closed-end fund*) in the way each operates *after* the initial public offering.

CLOSED-END INVESTMENT COMPANIES

A *closed-end investment company* operates like any other public firm. Its stock trades on the regular secondary market, and the market price of its shares is determined by supply and demand. Such an investment company typically offers no further shares and does not repurchase the shares on demand. Thus, if you want to buy or sell shares in a closed-end fund, you make transactions in the public secondary market. The shares of many of these funds are listed on the NYSE. No new investment dollars are available for the investment company unless it makes another public sale of securities. Similarly, no funds are withdrawn unless the investment company decides to repurchase its stock, which is quite unusual.

The closed-end investment company's net asset value (NAV) is computed twice daily based on prevailing market prices for the securities in the portfolio. The *market price* of the investment company shares is determined by the relative supply and demand for the investment company stock in the public, secondary market. When you buy or sell shares of a closed-end fund, you pay or receive this market price plus or minus a regular trading commission. You should recognize that *the NAV and the market price of a closed-end fund are almost never the same!* Over the long run, the market price of these shares have historically been from 5 to 20 percent below the NAV (i.e., they sell at a discount to NAV). Figure 24.1 is a list of closed-end stock funds, including

FIGURE 24.1 **Closed-End Stock and Bond Funds**

CLOSED-END FUNDS

Closed-end funds sell a limited number of shares and invest the proceeds in securities. Unlike open-end funds, closed-ends generally do not buy their shares back from investors who wish to cash in their holdings. Instead, fund shares trade on a stock exchange. The following list, provided by Lipper Analytical Services, shows each fund's stock exchange (American, Chicago, NYSE, OTC, Toronto), the per-share net asset value of its portfolio, the closing price of its stock, and the percentage difference between the market price and the NAV (often called the premium or discount). For equity funds, the final column provides 52-week returns based on market prices plus dividends. For bond funds, the final column shows the past 12 months' income distributions as a percentage of the current market price.

Friday, July 30, 1993

Fund Name	Stock Exch	NAV	Market Price	Prem /Disc	52 week Market Retu.
General Equity Funds					
Adams Express	N	20.89	20⅞	− 0.1	18.4
Baker Fentress	N	21.82	18¼	− 16.4	7.0
Bergstrom Capital	A	88.09	96	+ 9.0	− 8.8
Blue Chip Value	N	7.86	8¼	+ 5.0	12.9
Central Securities	A	16.51	14⅞	− 9.9	49.9
Charles Allmon Tr	N	10.64	9⅞	− 7.2	4.4
Engex	A	11.68	9½	− 18.7	15.2
Gabelli Equity Tr	N	e11.02	10⅝	− 3.6	9.7
General American	N	24.92	23¼	− 6.7	− 7.3
Inefficient Mkt	A	11.42	9¾	− 14.6	1.8
Jundt Growth	N	14.75	14⅜	− 2.5	1.8
Liberty All-Star	N	10.54	11	+ 4.4	9.6
Morgan Gren Sm Cap	N	N/A	10½	N/A	1.8
NAIC Growth	O	N/A	11¼	N/A	16.4
Specialized Equity Funds					
ASA Limited	N	cv51.00	49	− 3.9	27.9
Alliance Glob Env	N	10.59	9⅛	− 13.8	− 6.4
Anchor Gold & Curr	C	6.59	6	− 9.0	20.0
BGR Prec Metals	T	cy14.40	13¼	− 8.0	76.7
C&S Realty Income	A	8.84	9½	+ 7.5	33.5
Central Fd Canada	A	c5.02	5⅝	+ 12.1	38.7
Counsellors Tandem	N	18.30	15¾	− 13.9	22.2
Delaware Gr Div	N	14.60	14½	− 0.7	N/A
Dover Regional Fin	O	7.73	7⅝	− 1.4	45.2
Duff Phelps Ut Inc	N	a10.37	10¾	+ 3.7	9.8
Emerging Mkts Tel	N	15.81	17	+ 7.5	16.9
First Financial	N	17.74	15⅞	− 10.5	52.4
Global Health Sci	N	11.09	9¾	− 12.1	− 20.6
H&Q Healthcare Inv	N	17.05	16⅞	− 1.0	− 20.2
World Equity Funds					
Americas All Seas	O	5.01	4 1/16	− 18.9	− 12.5
Argentina	N	10.11	10¾	+ 6.3	− 4.3
Asia Pacific	N	13.27	16½	+ 24.3	33.4
Austria	N	8.52	9	+ 5.6	16.3
Brazil	N	c18.75	16⅝	− 11.3	1.6
Brazilian Equity	N	c13.29	12	− 9.7	9.3
Chile	N	33.61	31¼	− 7.0	− 12.5
China	N	N/A	15¾	N/A	9.0
Clemente Global Gr	N	c10.70	9⅜	− 12.4	14.2
Emerging Mexico	N	c16.55	17	+ 2.7	22.8
Europe	N	11.30	11⅝	+ 2.9	1.1
European Warrant	N	c10.35	10⅝	+ 2.7	62.7
First Australia	A	11.45	9¾	− 14.8	10.1
First Iberian	A	7.11	6¾	− 5.1	2.1
First Israel	N	13.94	12⅞	− 7.6	N/A
First Philippine	N	15.70	13½	− 14.0	21.0
France Growth	N	11.45	11⅞	+ 3.7	23.8
GT Greater Europe	N	12.57	11⅝	− 7.5	22.4
Germany Fund	N	10.54	12¾	+ 21.0	18.0
Germany, Emerging	N	8.27	7⅞	− 4.8	3.0
Germany, Future Fd	N	14.10	13¾	− 2.5	5.0
Germany, New Fund	N	11.90	11⅜	− 4.4	2.7
Greater China	N	14.15	15⅛	+ 6.9	14.2
Convertible Sec's. Funds					
American Cap Conv	N	a24.69	22¾	− 7.9	24.1
Bancroft Conv	A	23.87	21⅝	9.4	18.7
Castle Convertible	A	27.49	26⅜	− 4.1	28.2
Ellsworth Cv Gr&In	A	10.06	9¼	− 8.1	19.5
Lincoln Natl Conv	N	c19.97	19⅛	− 4.2	23.9
Putnam Hi Inc Conv	N	9.49	10⅛	+ 6.7	18.8
TCW Conv Secs	N	N/A	10⅛	N/A	18.5
Dual-Purpose Funds					
Conv Holdings Cap	N	13.80	10½	− 23.9	39.4
Conv Holdings Inc	N	9.36	11	+ 17.5	− 1.3
Gemini II Fund Cap	N	22.00	18⅝	− 15.3	29.3
Gemini II Fund Inc	N	a9.73	12½	+ 28.5	12.2
Hampton Util Cap	A	c18.38	17 1/16	− 7.2	23.3
Hampton Util Inc	A	c50.11	52 5/16	+ 4.4	9.1
Quest Value DP Cap	N	27.88	26	− 6.7	26.0
Quest Value DP Inc	N	11.62	13½	+ 16.2	9.7

Fund Name	Stock Exch	NAV	Market Price	Prem /Disc	12 Mo Yield 6/30/93
Bond Funds					
1838 Bd-Debenture	N	22.49	24¼	+ 7.8	7.6
2002 Target Term	N	c14.71	14½	− 1.4	N/A
ACM Govt Inc	N	11.54	11½	− 0.3	8.3
ACM Govt Oppty	N	9.90	9⅞	− 0.3	7.9
ACM Govt Secs	N	a11.56	11⅛	− 3.8	9.2
ACM Govt Spectrum	N	9.85	9½	− 3.6	9.1
ACM Mgd Income	N	10.52	11¼	+ 6.9	9.7
AIM Strategic Inc	A	9.60	9	− 6.3	6.3
All-American Term	N	c15.22	15	− 1.4	N/A
Alliance Wld Dlr	N	19.52	19	− 2.7	N/A
Alliance Wld Dlr 2	N	N/A	15	N/A	N/A
Amer Adj Rate '95	N	c9.72	9¾	+ 0.3	6.4
Amer Adj Rate '96	N	c9.56	9⅝	+ 0.7	6.7
Amer Adj Rate '97	N	c9.63	9¾	+ 1.2	7.0
Amer Adj Rate '98	N	c9.67	9⅝	− 0.5	7.0
Amer Adj Rate '99	N	c9.63	9½	− 1.3	N/A
Amer Govt Income	N	c8.88	9⅝	+ 8.4	8.9
Amer Govt Port	N	c11.10	12	+ 8.1	9.6
Amer Govt Term Tr	N	c9.76	10⅝	+ 8.9	8.8
Amer Oppty Income	N	c10.76	11⅞	+ 10.4	9.8
Amer Str Income	N	c15.73	16⅜	+ 4.1	8.3
World Income Funds					
ACM Mgd Multi-Mkt	N	9.80	9⅛	− 6.9	9.2
BlckRk North Amer	N	c12.57	12¼	− 2.5	10.1
Dreyfus Str Govt	N	11.04	11⅝	+ 5.3	7.8
Emer Mkts Inc	N	17.52	17½	− 0.1	N/A
Emer Mkts Inc II	N	14.35	15¼	+ 6.3	N/A
First Australia Pr	A	a10.32	10⅞	+ 5.4	10.1
First Commonwealth	N	a13.54	13¼	− 2.1	9.1
Global Government	N	7.98	7⅝	− 4.4	11.4
Global Income Plus	N	9.68	9⅝	− 0.6	7.4
Global Yield	N	8.75	8⅝	− 1.4	9.6
Kleinwort Ben Aust	N	a10.67	9¾	− 8.6	8.1
Lat Am Dollar Inc	N	15.20	15½	+ 2.0	N/A
M Stan Em Mkt Debt	N	14.05	15	+ 6.8	N/A
Strategic Glob Inc	N	14.65	14¼	− 2.7	7.9
Templeton Gl Govt	N	a8.36	8½	+ 1.7	8.0
Templeton Gl Inc	N	8.50	8⅛	− 4.4	9.2
National Muni Bond Funds					
ACM Muni Secs Inc	N	14.18	14¼	+ 0.5	N/A
Amer Muni Income	N	c14.18	14⅞	+ 4.9	N/A
Amer Muni Tm II	N	c11.20	10⅝	− 5.1	5.9
Amer Muni Tm III	N	c10.45	10⅜	− 0.7	N/A
Amer Muni Tm Tr	N	c11.43	11⅛	− 2.7	6.0
Apex Muni	N	10.35	10¾	+ 3.9	7.7
BlckRk Ins 2008	N	N/A	15	N/A	N/A
BlckRk Ins Muni	N	N/A	10¼	N/A	6.1
BlckRk Inv QualMun	N	N/A	14	N/A	N/A
BlckRk Muni Target	N	N/A	10½	N/A	6.0
Colonial Hi Inc Mu	N	a8.84	9⅛	+ 3.2	7.5
Colonial Inv Gr Mu	N	11.14	12¼	+ 10.0	7.0
Colonial Mu Inc Tr	N	a7.91	8½	+ 7.5	7.6
Dreyfus Muni Inc	A	10.30	10¾	+ 4.4	6.5
Dreyfus Str Munis	N	10.33	10⅞	+ 5.3	6.9
Dreyfus Strat Muni	N	10.05	10½	+ 4.5	6.5
Duff Phelps Ut T-F	N	15.84	16½	+ 4.2	5.9
InterCap Ins M Inc	N	14.14	14¾	+ 4.3	N/A
InterCap Ins Mu Bd	N	16.16	17¼	+ 6.7	7.4
InterCap Ins Mu Tr	N	16.13	16⅛	+ 0.0	6.9
Single State Muni Bond					
BlckRk CA Ins 2008	N	N/A	14⅞	N/A	N/A
BlckRk CA Inv Qual	A	N/A	14⅝	N/A	N/A
BlckRk FL Ins 2008	N	N/A	15	N/A	N/A
BlckRk FL Inv Qual	A	N/A	14¾	N/A	N/A
BlckRk NJ Inv Qual	A	N/A	14½	N/A	N/A
BlckRk NY Ins 2008	N	N/A	15	N/A	N/A
BlckRk NY Inv Qual	A	N/A	14⅝	N/A	N/A
Dreyfus CA Mu Inc	A	9.79	10	+ 2.1	6.2
Dreyfus NY Mu Inc	A	10.44	11	+ 5.4	5.6
InterCap CA Ins	N	14.01	15⅝	+ 11.5	N/A
MA Hlth & Educ	A	14.06	15¼	+ 8.5	N/A
Minn Muni Income	A	c14.11	15⅛	+ 7.2	N/A
Minn Muni Tm Tr	N	c10.95	11⅜	+ 3.9	5.7

Source: "Closed-End Funds," *Barron's*, August 2, 1993.

TABLE 24.1

Number of Closed-End Fund Initial Public Offerings and New Funds Raised

Year	Number of Funds	Amount Raised
1981	1	$ 62 million
1982	0	—
1983	4	58 million
1984	4	106 million
1985	3	614 million
1986	28	5 billion
1987	34	9 billion
1988	66	20 billion
1989	39	9 billion
1990	38	6 billion
1991	43	11 billion
1992	98	18 billion

Source: Thomas J. Herzfeld Advisors, Inc., P.O. Box 161465, Miami, Florida 33116. Reprinted by permission of Thomas J. Herzfeld Advisors, Inc.

general equity funds, specialized equity funds, world equity funds and convertible, security, and dual-purpose funds, quoted in *Barron's*. This figure also contains a listing of closed-end bond funds including world income funds, national municipal bond funds, and single state municipal bond funds.

Table 24.1 indicates the dramatic growth in the number and value of closed-end stock funds based upon the sale of new fund issues from 1981 to 1992. Another indicator of growth is that as of 1986, there were 8 diversified common stock funds and 18 specialized and convertible funds listed in *Barron's*. By 1992 the number had grown to 56 general and specialized equity funds, 56 world equity funds, and 16 convertible securities and dual-purpose funds. The growth of bond funds has been even more dramatic. After many years of relative stability, the number of bond funds listed in *Barron's* has increased from about 20 in 1986 to 268 in 1992 including 112 regular bond funds, 16 world income funds, 95 national municipal bond funds, and 45 single state municipal bond funds. We discuss several international bond funds later in the chapter.

Some observers expect the growth of closed-end funds to slow down because of the substantial discounts on these issues.[1] Besides the long-run discount of market price to NAV, these funds seem to suffer short-run discounts following their initial public offerings (IPOs). As discussed in Chapter 6, numerous studies have shown that prices of most individual stock IPOs experience positive abnormal returns within a day after the offering. In contrast, studies of closed-end fund IPOs show fairly stable prices initially, which then drift to a discount over a 4-month period. This unusual pattern prompted an SEC study of the question.[2] Notably, several of the affected funds are the individual non-U.S. country funds (e.g., Japan, Korea, Germany, Italy, Spain, Thailand, Mexico) that we discuss later in the chapter.

---

[1]Michael Siconolfi, "Launching of Closed-End Funds May Ease," *The Wall Street Journal,* November 30, 1987, 33.

[2]Michael Siconolfi, "SEC Studies Closed-End Fund 'Mystery,'" *The Wall Street Journal,* May 23, 1988, 31; and Kathleen Weiss, "The Post Offering Performance of Closed-End Funds," *Financial Management* 18, no. 3 (Autumn 1989): 57–67.

At the time of the quotes in Figure 24.1, most of the funds were selling at discounts to their NAV. This typical relationship has prompted the following questions from investors. Why do these funds sell at a discount? Why do the discounts differ between funds? What are the returns available to investors from funds that sell at large discounts? This final question arises because an investor who acquires a portfolio at a price below market value (i.e., below NAV) expects a dividend yield above the average. Still, the total rate of return on the fund depends on what happens to the discount during the holding period. If the discount relative to the NAV declines, the investment should generate positive excess returns. If the discount increases, the investor will likely experience negative excess returns. The analysis of these discounts remains a major question of modern finance.[3]

CLOSED-END FUND INDEX

The interest in closed-end funds has led a firm that specializes in these funds (Thomas J. Herzfeld Advisors) to create an index that tracks the market price performance of the following 17 U.S. closed-end funds that invest principally in U.S. equities. The following is a list of the funds in the average:

- The Adams Express Company
- Baker, Fentress and Company
- Bergstrom Capital Corporation
- Blue Chip Value Fund, Inc.
- Central Securities Corporation
- The Charles Allmon Trust, Inc.
- Engex, Inc.
- The Gabelli Equity Trust, Inc.
- General American Investors Company, Inc.
- The Inefficient-Market Fund, Inc.
- Liberty All-Star Equity Fund
- Morgan Grenfell SMALLCap Fund, Inc.
- Royce Value Trust
- The Salomon Brothers Fund, Inc.
- Source Capital Inc.
- Tri-Continental Corporation
- The Zweig Fund, Inc.

All of the funds are listed on either the NYSE or AMEX, and one trades on NASDAQ. The price-weighted index is based on fund market values rather than NAVs. In addition to its market price index, Herzfeld also computes the average discount from NAV. The

---

[3]Studies over the years include Kenneth Boudreaux, "Discounts and Premiums on Closed-End Funds: A Study in Valuation," *Journal of Finance* 28, no. 2 (June 1973): 515–522; Rex Thompson, "The Information Content of Premiums and Discounts on Closed-End Fund Shares," *Journal of Financial Economics* 6, no. 23 (June/Sept. 1978): 151–186; Charles Lee, Andrei Shleifer, and Richard Thaler, "Investor Sentiment and the Closed-End Fund Puzzle," *Journal of Finance* 46, no. 1 (March 1991): 76–110; and Michael Barclay, Clifford Holderness, and Jeffrey Pontiff, "Private Benefits from Block Ownership and Discounts on Closed-End Funds," *Journal of Financial Economics* 33, no. 3 (June 1993): 263–292. For a discussion of bond funds, see Malcolm Richards, Donald Fraser, and John Groth, "The Attractions of Closed-End Bond Funds," *Journal of Portfolio Management* 8, no. 2 (Winter 1982): 56–61. For a discussion of performance and opportunities in closed-end funds, see Thomas J. Herzfeld, "Battered Beauties?" *Barron's,* August 13, 1990; Thomas J. Herzfeld, "Finding Value in Closed-End Funds," *Investment Advisor,* July, 1990.

FIGURE 24.2   **Herzfeld Closed-End Fund Average**

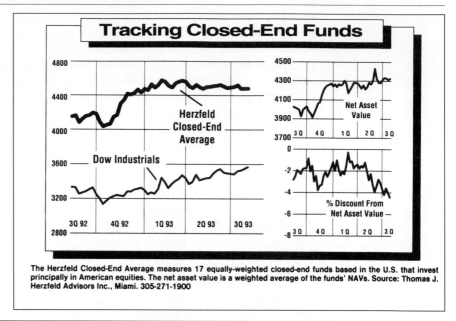

The Herzfeld Closed-End Average measures 17 equally-weighted closed-end funds based in the U.S. that invest principally in American equities. The net asset value is a weighted average of the funds' NAVs. Source: Thomas J. Herzfeld Advisors Inc., Miami. 305-271-1900

Source: *Barron's,* August 2, 1993. Copyright © 1993 Dow Jones & Company, Inc. Reprinted by permission of Barron's. All Rights Reserved Worldwide.

graph in Figure 24.2, which is updated weekly in *Barron's,* indicates that the average discount from NAV changes over time, with major effects on the market performance of the index. As an example, during the third quarter of 1993 the average discount was increasing to a value in excess of 4 percent. As a result, the performance of the Herzfeld closed-end average was relatively flat during a period when the DJIA was increasing steadily.

OPEN-END
INVESTMENT
COMPANIES

Open-end investment companies are funds that continue to sell and repurchase shares after their initial public offerings. They stand ready to sell additional shares of the fund at the NAV, with or without sales charge, or to buy back (redeem) shares of the fund at the NAV, with or without redemption fees.

Open-end investment companies, or mutual funds, have enjoyed substantial growth since World War II, as shown by the figures in Table 24.2. Clearly, open-end funds account for a substantial portion of assets invested, and they provide a very important service for almost 54 million accounts.

LOAD VERSUS NO-LOAD OPEN-END FUNDS
One distinction between open-end funds is whether they charge a sales fee for share sales. The offering price for a share of a *load fund* equals the NAV of the share plus a sales charge, which is typically 7.5 to 8.0 percent of the NAV. A fund with an 8 percent

TABLE 24.2

Open-End Investment Companies: Number and Value of Assets: 1945–1992

	Number of Reporting Funds	Assets ($Billions)		Number of Reporting Funds	Assets ($Billions)
1945	73	$ 1.3	1969	269	$ 48.3
1946	74	1.3	1970	361	47.6
1947	80	1.4	1971	392	55.0
1948	87	1.5	1972	410	59.8
1949	91	2.0	1973	421	46.5
1950	98	2.5	1974	416	34.1
1951	103	3.1	1975	390	42.2
1952	110	3.9	1976	404	47.6
1953	110	4.1	1977	427	45.0
1954	115	6.1	1978	444	45.0
1955	125	7.8	1979	446	49.0
1956	135	9.0	1980	458	58.4
1957	143	8.7	1981	486	55.2
1958	151	13.2	1982	539	76.8
1959	155	15.8	1983	653	113.6
1960	161	17.0	1984	820	137.8
1961	170	22.8	1985	1,071	251.7
1962	169	21.3	1986	1,356	424.2
1963	165	25.2	1987	1,781	453.8
1964	160	29.1	1988	2,109	472.3
1965	170	35.2	1989	2,253	553.9
1966	182	34.8	1990	2,362	568.5
1967	204	44.7	1991	2,603	808.6
1968	240	52.7	1992	2,984	1,056.3

Note: Does not include money market and short-term bond funds.

Sources: *1975 Mutual Fund Fact Book, 1981 Mutual Fund Fact Book,* and *1993 Mutual Fund Fact Book,* Investment Company Institute, Washington, D.C. Reprinted by permission of Investment Company Institute.

sales charge (load) would give an individual who invested $1,000 shares that are worth $920. Such funds generally charge no redemption fee, which means the shares can be redeemed at their NAV. These funds are typically quoted with a NAV and an offering price. The NAV price is the redemption price, and the offering price equals the NAV divided by 1.0 minus the percent loads. As an example, if the NAV of a load fund with an 8 percent load is $8.50 a share, the offering price would be $9.24 ($8.50/0.92). The 74-cent differential is really 8.7 percent of the NAV. The load percentage typically declines with the size of the order.

A *no-load fund* imposes no initial sales charge so it sells shares at their NAV. Some of these funds charge a small redemption fee of about one-half of 1 percent. In *The Wall Street Journal,* quotes for these no-load funds list bid prices as the NAV with the designation "NL" (no-load) for the offering price.

A number of no-load funds have been established in recent years. *The Wall Street Journal* lists more than 350 no-load funds, and *Barron's* lists more than 800. A directory of no-load funds is available from an industry association.[4]

---

[4]No-Load Mutual Fund Association, Inc., 11 Penn Plaza, New York, NY 10001. The cost of the directory is $10.

Between the full-load fund and the pure no-load fund, you can find several important variations. The first is the *low-load fund,* which imposes a front-end sales charge when you buy the fund, but it is typically in the 3 percent range rather than 7 to 8 percent. Generally, low-load funds are used for bond funds or equity funds offered by management companies that also offer no-load funds. For example, almost all the Fidelity Management funds were no-load prior to 1985, but several of their newer funds have carried a low load of 3 percent. Alternatively, some funds that previously charged full loads have reduced their loads.

The second major innovation is the *12b-1 plan,* named after the 1980 SEC rule that permits it. This plan permits funds to deduct as much as 1.25 percent of average net assets *per year* to cover distribution costs, such as advertising, commissions paid to brokers, and general marketing expenses. A large and growing number of no-load funds are adopting these plans, as are a few low-load funds. You can determine if a fund has a 12b-1 plan only by reading the prospectus or using an investment service that reports charges in substantial detail.

Finally, some funds have instituted *contingent, deferred sales loads.* They charge you a sales fee when you sell the fund if you have held it for less than some time period, perhaps 3 or 4 years.

FUND MANAGEMENT FEES

In addition to selling charges (loads or 12b-1 charges), all investment firms charge *annual management fees* to compensate the professional managers of the fund. Such a fee is typically a percentage of the average net assets of the fund varying from about 0.25 to 1.00 percent. Most of these management fees are on sliding scales that decline with the size of the fund. For example, a fund with assets under $1 billion might charge 1 percent, whereas one with assets over $1 billion might charge 0.50 percent.

These management fees are a major factor driving the creation of new funds. More assets under management generate more fees, but the costs of management do not increase at the same rate as the assets managed because there are substantial economies of scale in managing financial assets. Once you have established the research staff and management structure, the incremental costs do not rise in line with the assets under management. For example, the cost of managing $1 billion of assets is definitely not twice the cost of managing $500 million.

TYPES OF INVESTMENT COMPANIES BASED ON PORTFOLIO MAKEUP

COMMON STOCK FUNDS

Some funds invest almost solely in common stocks, whereas others invest in preferred stocks, bonds, and so forth. Within this category of common stock funds, you find wide differences in emphasis, including funds that focus on growth companies, small cap stocks, companies in specific industries (e.g., Chemical Fund, Oceanography Fund), certain classes of industry (e.g., Technology Fund) or even geographic areas (such as the Northeast Fund). Different common stock funds can suit almost any taste or investment objective. Therefore, you must decide whether you want a fund that invests only in common stock; then you must consider the type of common stock you desire.

BALANCED FUNDS

Balanced funds diversify outside the stock market by combining common stock with fixed-income securities, including government bonds, corporate bonds, convertible bonds, or preferred stock. The ratio of stocks to fixed-income securities will vary by fund, as stated in each fund's prospectus.

TABLE 24.3

Statistics on Money Market Funds

	Total Number of Funds	Total Accounts Outstanding	Average Maturity (Days)	Total Net Assets ($Millions)
1974	15	n.a.	n.a.	1,715.1
1975	36	208,777	93	3,695.7
1976	48	180,676	110	3,685.8
1977	50	177,522	76	3,887.7
1978	61	467,803	42	10,858.0
1979	76	2,307,852	34	45,214.2
1980	96	4,745,572	24	74,447.7
1981	159	10,282,095	34	181,910.4
1982	281	13,101,347	37	206,607.5
1983	307	12,276,639	37	162,549.5
1984	329	13,556,180	43	209,731.9
1985	348	14,425,386	42	207,535.3
1986	360	15,653,595	40	228,345.8
1987	389	16,832,666	31	254,676.4
1988	432	17,630,528	28	272,293.3
1989	463	20,173,265	38	358,719.2
1990	508	21,577,559	41	414,733.3
1991	553	21,863,351	50	449,713.6
1992	585	21,770,692	51	448,719.4

Source: *1993 Mutual Fund Fact Book,* Investment Company Institute, Washington, D.C. Reprinted by permission of Investment Company Institute.

BOND FUNDS

Bond funds concentrate on various types of bonds to generate high current income with minimal risk. Similar to common stock funds, their investment policies differ. Some funds concentrate on U.S. government or high-grade corporate bonds, others hold a mixture of investment-grade bonds, and some concentrate on high-yield (junk) bonds. Management strategies can also differ ranging from buy-and-hold to extensive trading of the bonds in the portfolio.

In addition to government, mortgage, and corporate bond funds, a change in the tax law in 1976 caused the creation of numerous municipal bond funds. These funds provide investors with monthly interest payments that are exempt from federal income taxes, although some of the interest may be subject to state and local taxes. To avoid the state tax, some municipal bond funds concentrate on bonds from specific states, such as the New York Municipal Bond Fund, which allows New York residents to avoid most state taxes on the interest income.

MONEY MARKET FUNDS

Money market funds were initiated during 1973 when short-term interest rates were at record levels. These funds attempt to provide current income, safety of principal, and liquidity by investing in a diversified portfolio of short-term securities such as Treasury bills, banker certificates of deposit, bank acceptances, and commercial paper. They are typically no-load funds and impose no penalty for withdrawal at any time. They typically allow holders to write checks against their account.[5] Table 24.3 documents the

---

[5]For a list of names and addresses of money market funds, write to Investment Company Institute, 1775 K Street N.W., Washington, DC 20006. A service that concentrates on money market funds is *Donoghue's Money Letter,* 770 Washington Street, Holliston, MA 01746. An analysis of performance is contained in Michael G. Ferri and H. Dennis Oberhelman, "How Well Do Money Market Funds Perform?" *Journal of Portfolio Management* 7, no. 3 (Spring 1981): 18–26.

significant growth of these funds. Changes in their growth rate are usually associated with investor attitudes toward the stock market. When investors are bullish toward stocks, they withdraw funds from their money market accounts to invest; when they are uncertain, they shift from stocks to the money funds. Because of the interest in money market funds, Monday editions of *The Wall Street Journal* provide a special section within the mutual fund section titled "Money Market Funds."

BREAKDOWN
BY FUND
CHARACTERISTICS

Table 24.4 groups funds by their method of sale and by investment objectives. The two major means of distribution are (1) by a sales force and (2) by direct purchase from the fund or direct marketing. Sales forces would include brokers such as Merrill Lynch, commission-based financial planners, or dedicated sales force such as those of IDS Financial. Almost all mutual funds acquired from these individuals charge sales fees (loads), from which the salespeople are compensated.

Investors purchase shares of directly marketed funds through the mail, telephone, bankwire, or an office of the fund. These direct sales funds typically impose a low sales charge or none at all. Without any sales fee, they have to be sold directly because a broker has no incentive to sell a no-load fund. As seen in Table 24.4, the division between these two major distribution channels is currently about 62 to 32 percent in

TABLE 24.4

Total Net Assets by Fund Characteristics ($Millions)

	1989		1990		1991		1992	
	Dollars	**Percent**	**Dollars**	**Percent**	**Dollars**	**Percent**	**Dollars**	**Percent**
Total net assets	$553,870.9	100.0	$568,516.9	100.0	$808,581.8	100.0	$1,056,310.0	100.0
Method of Sale								
Sales force	376,016.9	67.9	380,779.4	67.0	516,791.0	63.9	659,466.7	62.4
Direct marketing	154,769.8	27.9	163,169.2	28.7	251,873.2	31.2	341,588.0	32.3
Variable annuity	20,975.8	3.8	23,328.5	4.1	38,397.2	4.7	53,776.0	5.1
Not offering shares	2,108.5	0.4	1,239.8	0.2	1,520.4	0.2	1,479.3	0.2
Investment Objective								
Aggressive growth	37,209.0	6.7	35,395.2	6.2	63,287.3	7.8	83,365.3	7.9
Growth	66,078.8	11.9	68,151.4	12.0	104,963.0	13.0	133,175.3	12.6
Growth and income	91,362.2	16.5	86,903.3	15.3	129,498.1	16.0	168,321.0	15.9
Precious metals	4,089.3	0.7	3,122.5	0.5	2,866.1	0.4	2,143.8	0.2
International	9,888.3	1.8	14,323.5	2.5	19,084.8	2.4	22,916.5	2.2
Global equity	13,697.0	2.5	13,465.9	2.4	17,285.7	2.1	22,987.4	2.2
Flexible portfolio	4,142.6	0.8	6,701.1	1.2	9,978.3	1.2	14,836.8	1.4
Balanced	13,519.0	2.4	12,837.7	2.3	20,206.9	2.5	31,865.2	3.0
Income equity	22,925.2	4.2	22,266.7	3.9	29,281.2	3.6	42,466.5	4.0
Income—mixed	15,190.8	2.8	18,857.5	3.3	25,620.5	3.2	34,720.7	3.3
Income—bond	13,465.1	2.4	15,913.2	2.8	27,501.2	3.4	39,742.6	3.8
Option/income	3,804.3	0.7	2,159.8	0.4	1,378.0	0.2	0.0	0.0*
U.S. government income	81,400.7	14.7	75,613.2	13.3	96,918.9	12.0	120,067.4	11.4
Ginnie Mae	28,209.3	5.1	28,993.6	5.1	37,653.1	4.7	57,513.4	5.4
Global bond	3,063.2	0.6	12,411.3	2.2	27,217.2	3.4	31,633.5	3.0
Corporate bond	11,676.6	2.1	12,284.2	2.2	15,513.5	1.9	20,033.3	1.9
High-yield bond	28,492.4	5.1	18,868.0	3.3	26,126.2	3.2	34,258.6	3.2
Long-term municipal bond	64,450.6	11.6	70,739.1	12.4	88,349.9	10.9	110,846.4	10.5
Long-term state municipal bond	41,206.4	7.4	49,509.7	8.7	65,851.9	8.1	85,416.3	8.1

*As of January 1992 Option/Income was combined with Income-Equity Funds.

Sources: *1992 Mutual Fund Fact Book, 1993 Mutual Fund Fact Book,* Investment Company Institute, Washington, D.C. Reprinted by permission of Investment Company Institute.

favor of the sales force method, although there has been a steady shift toward direct marketing.

The breakdown by investment objective indicates the response by the investment companies to a shift in investor emphasis. The growth of an alternative investment objective category reflects the overall growth of the industry, but also the creation of new funds in response to the evolving demands of investors. Therefore, although aggressive growth, growth, and growth and income funds have continued to grow and maintain their percentages, categories such as international, global equity, income bonds, municipal bonds, and global bonds have also shown significant growth.[6] Also, although the sale of stock funds has increased, the number and the total outstanding value of bond and income funds have exceeded the value of equity funds.

PERFORMANCE OF INVESTMENT COMPANIES

A number of studies have examined the historical performance of mutual funds because these funds reflect the performance of professional money managers, and data on the funds are available for a long period. Two of the three major portfolio evaluation techniques (which we will discuss in Chapter 26) were derived in connection with studies of mutual fund performance.

ANALYSIS OF OVERALL PERFORMANCE

A study by Sharpe evaluated the performance of 34 open-end mutual funds.[7] For the total period, only 11 of the 34 funds outperformed the DJIA. Further, comparing the ranks of the funds between the first and second half of the sample period led Sharpe to conclude that past performance was not the best predictor of future performance.

An examination of the relationship between performance and the expense ratio indicated that good performance was associated with low expense ratios. Finally, analysis of *gross* performance, with expenses added back to the returns, indicated that 19 of the 34 funds did better than the DJIA. This led to the conclusion that the average mutual fund manager selected a portfolio at least as good as the DJIA, but after deducting the operating costs of the fund, most achieved *net* returns below those of the DJIA.

Jensen evaluated 115 open-end mutual funds with results that indicated that, on average, the funds earned 1.1 percent less per year than they should have earned for their level of risk.[8] Analysis of gross returns with expenses added back indicated that 42 percent did better than the overall market on a risk-adjusted basis, whereas the analysis of net returns indicated that only 34 percent of the funds outperformed the market. The gross returns indicate the forecasting ability of the funds, because these results do not penalize the funds for operating expenses (only brokerage commissions). Jensen concluded that, on average, these funds could not beat a buy-and-hold policy.

A comment by Mains questioned several of Jensen's estimates, which apparently biased the results against mutual funds.[9] After adjusting for these biases, he contended

---

[6]International funds consider only investing in non-U.S. stocks or bonds, whereas global funds can invest in securities from anywhere in the world, including the United States.

[7]William F. Sharpe, "Mutual Fund Performance," *Journal of Business* 39, no. 1, Part 2 (January 1966): 119–138.

[8]Michael C. Jensen, "The Performance of Mutual Funds in the Period 1945–1964," *Journal of Finance* 23, no. 2 (May 1968): 389–416.

[9]Norman E. Mains, "Risk, the Pricing of Capital Assets, and the Evaluation of Investment Portfolios: Comment," *Journal of Business* 50, no. 3 (July 1977): 371–384.

that the net returns indicated neutral performance, whereas the gross returns indicated that most fund managers outperformed the market.

Carlson examined the overall performance of mutual funds with emphasis on the effects of the market series used for comparison and the time period.[10] The results depended heavily on which market series were used: the S&P 500, the NYSE composite, or the DJIA. For the total period, most fund groups outperformed the DJIA, but only a few had gross returns better than the S&P 500 or the NYSE composite. Using net returns, *none* of the groups outperformed the S&P 500 or the NYSE composite. Analysis of the factors that determined performance indicated consistency over time for return or risk alone but no consistency in the risk-adjusted performance. Less than one-third of the funds that performed above average during the first half did so in the second half. A more recent study by Lehmann and Modest found substantial differences between benchmarks, but also concluded that average performance was consistently inferior to the overall market performance.[11]

All of the early studies were concerned with evaluating the performance of funds that concentrated in domestic (U.S.) equities. Given the growing tendency toward global investing, several authors have examined the performance of international equity funds. In addition, we noted the substantial growth of bond funds, which has prompted an analysis of bond fund performance.

Cumby and Glen examined the performance of 15 U.S.-based internationally diversified funds for the period 1982 to 1988 compared to the Morgan Stanley world equity index and a U.S. index.[12] Using two risk-adjusted performance measures they found no evidence that the funds, either individually or collectively, provided investors with performance that surpasses that of a broad international index during the sample period. Bailey and Lim examined the performance of country funds (e.g., France, Germany, Korea, Spain) with the emphasis on the ability to use these funds to attain international diversification.[13] They found that country fund returns often resembled domestic U.S. stock returns more than returns from foreign stock portfolios, which means that these funds would not provide the benefits of diversification normally expected.

Blake, Elton, and Gruber examined the performance of bond mutual funds using several models and samples.[14] They found that overall and for subcategories of bond funds that the bond funds underperformed relevant bond indexes. Because the underperformance was about equal to the management fees, it is suggested that pre-expenses these funds performed about equal to the indexes. They also found no evidence that you could use past performance to predict future performance.

---

[10]Robert S. Carlson, "Aggregate Performance of Mutual Funds, 1948–1967," *Journal of Financial and Quantitative Analysis* 5, no. 1 (March 1970): 1–32.

[11]Bruce N. Lehmann and David M. Modest, "Mutual Fund Performance Evaluations: A Comparison of Benchmarks and Benchmark Comparisons," *Journal of Finance* 42, no. 2 (June 1987): 233–265.

[12]Robert E. Cumby and Jack D. Glen, "Evaluating the Performance of International Mutual Funds," *Journal of Finance* 45, no. 2 (June 1990): 497–522.

[13]Warren Bailey and Joseph Lim, "Evaluating the Diversification Benefits of the New Country Funds," *Journal of Portfolio Management* 18, no. 3 (Spring 1992): 74–80.

[14]Christopher R. Blake, Edwin J. Elton, and Martin J. Gruber, "The Performance of Bond Mutual Funds," *The Journal of Business* 66, no. 3 (July 1993): 371–403.

Cornell and Green examined the performance of low-grade (high yield) bond funds for a total period of 1960 to 1989 and two subperiods 1960 to 1976 and 1977 to 1989.[15] Their results indicated that for the total period the returns on low-grade bond funds were about equal to the return on high-grade bonds. Because of the difficulty of measuring risk, they settled on a two-factor model that allowed for the impact of interest rates and stock returns. After adjusting for risk measured by this two-factor model they concluded that the returns on low-grade bonds were not statistically different from the returns on high-grade bonds.

IMPACT OF FUND OBJECTIVES

An investor considering buying a fund needs to know whether its performance is consistent with its stated objective. For example, does the performance of a balanced fund reflect less risk and lower return than an aggressive growth fund? To answer this question, several studies have examined the relationship between funds' stated objective and their measures of risk and return.

McDonald examined the overall performance of a sample of mutual funds relative to their stated objectives: (1) maximum capital gain, (2) growth, (3) income and growth, (4) balanced, and (5) income.[16] The results revealed a positive relationship between stated objectives and measures of risk, with risk measures increasing as objectives become more aggressive. The study also found a positive relationship between return and risk. The analysis of risk-adjusted performance indicated that the funds with the more aggressive objectives outperformed the more conservative funds during this period.

Martin, Keown, and Farrell examined mutual funds representing five investment objectives (aggressive growth, growth, growth and income, income, and other).[17] They found definite differences in the abnormal variability for the funds in alternative classifications.

MARKET TIMING ABILITY

As noted on several occasions, one way to achieve superior performance is to do a good job of market timing wherein you invest aggressively prior to strong markets and restructure into very conservative portfolios prior to weak or declining markets. Can mutual fund managers do this on your behalf? Several studies have examined the ability of mutual funds to time market cycles and react accordingly. That is, can fund portfolio managers increase the relative volatility of their portfolios in anticipation of a bull market and reduce its volatility prior to a bear market?

Several studies indicated that the funds were not able to time market changes and change risk levels accordingly.[18] Veit and Cheney using four different schemes to define bull and bear markets, concluded that mutual funds do not successfully alter their risk

---

[15]Bradford Cornell and Kevin Green, "The Investment Performance of Low-Grade Bond Funds," *Journal of Finance* 46, no. 1 (March 1991): 29–48.

[16]John G. McDonald, "Objectives and Performance of Mutual Funds, 1960–1969," *Journal of Financial and Quantitative Analysis* 9, no. 3 (June 1974): 311–333.

[17]John D. Martin, Arthur J. Keown, Jr., and James L. Farrell, "Do Fund Objectives Affect Diversification Policies?" *Journal of Portfolio Management* 8, no. 2 (Winter 1982): 19–28.

[18]Jack L. Treynor and Kay K. Mazuy, "Can Mutual Funds Outguess the Market?" *Harvard Business Review* 44, no. 4 (July-August 1966): 131–136; Frank J. Fabozzi and Jack C. Francis, "Mutual Fund Systematic Risk for Bull and Bear Markets," *Journal of Finance* 34, no. 5 (December 1979): 1243–1250.

characteristics *consistently* with timing strategies.[19] In fact, no change occurred in the characteristic lines over the market cycle.

Kon and Jen examined the ability of mutual funds to change portfolio composition to take advantage of market cycles and the ability to select undervalued securities.[20] Although many of the funds experienced a significant change in risk during the test period, implying superior timing ability, no individual fund was able to *consistently* generate superior results. Shawky found that risk was consistent with fund objectives, but overall performance results indicated that most funds had inferior performance although the funds appeared to have improved the diversification of their portfolios.[21]

Two studies examined the overall market forecasting and the specific stock selection ability of fund managers. Chang and Lewellen tested for market timing ability and found little market forecasting going on or, if any was being done, it was overwhelmed by other portfolio decisions.[22] They found neither skillful market timing nor clever security selection. The authors concurred with the conclusion of prior studies that mutual funds cannot outperform a passive investment strategy.

Henriksson considered a total period and two subperiods to test the ability to enjoy consistent success.[23] The results showed little evidence of market timing ability, and the results for each fund for the two periods were independent. They found that managers could not forecast large changes, and those who were good at stock selection apparently had negative market timing ability. Chan and Chen analyzed the timing performance of 19 mutual funds that were called asset allocation funds.[24] They found no evidence that these funds demonstrated market timing abilities. Also, an analysis of the total performance of these funds suggested relatively poor performance compared to the benchmark portfolio.

CONSISTENCY OF PERFORMANCE

Although several studies have considered consistency along with overall performances, some studies have concentrated on it. Klemkosky examined rankings of risk-adjusted performance for adjacent 2-year periods and for the two 4-year periods.[25] The results indicated some consistency between the 4-year periods, but relatively low consistency between the adjacent 2-year periods. The author concluded that investors should not use past performance to predict short-run future performance.

Dunn and Theisen examined institutional portfolios over a 10-year period to determine what proportion of managers were consistently successful.[26] A test of whether

[19]E. Theodore Veit and John M. Cheney, "Are Mutual Funds Market Timers?" *Journal of Portfolio Management* 8, no. 2 (Winter 1982): 35–42.

[20]Stanley J. Kon and Frank C. Jen, "The Investment Performance of Mutual Funds: An Empirical Investigation of Timing, Selectivity, and Market Efficiency," *Journal of Business* 52, no. 2 (April 1979): 263–289.

[21]Hany A. Shawky, "An Update on Mutual Funds: Better Grades," *Journal of Portfolio Management* 8, no. 2 (Winter 1982): 29–34.

[22]Eric C. Chang and Wilbur G. Lewellen, "Market Timing and Mutual Fund Investment Performance," *Journal of Business* 57, no. 1, part 1 (January 1984): 57–72.

[23]Roy D. Henriksson, "Market Timing and Mutual Fund Performance: An Empirical Investigation," *Journal of Business* 57, no. 1, part 1 (January 1984): 73–96.

[24]Anthony Chan and Carl R. Chen, "How Well Do Asset Allocation Mutual Fund Managers Allocate Assets?" *Journal of Portfolio Management* 18, no. 3 (Spring 1992): 81–91.

[25]Robert C. Klemkosky, "How Consistently Do Managers Manage?" *Journal of Portfolio Management* 3, no. 2 (Winter 1977): 11–15.

[26]Patricia C. Dunn and Rolf D. Theisen, "How Consistently Do Active Managers Win?" *Journal of Portfolio Management* 9, no. 4 (Summer 1983): 47–50.

managers tend to remain in the same quartile over time concluded that historical results give little help in explaining future results. The authors concluded that historical performance should be given very little weight when selecting a manager. Ang and Chua examined the consistency of performance of funds with different objectives and found that, although various funds met their stated objectives, they did not do it consistently.[27]

What functions would you want your own personal portfolio manager to perform for you? The list would probably include:

1. Determine your risk–return preferences and develop a portfolio that is consistent with them.
2. Diversify your portfolio to eliminate unsystematic risk.
3. Maintain your portfolio diversification and your desired risk class while allowing flexibility so you could shift between alternative investment instruments as desired.
4. Attempt to achieve a risk-adjusted performance that is superior to aggregate market performance. As noted, this can be done either by consistently selecting undervalued stocks or by superior asset allocation that is properly timed for markets around the world. Some investors may be willing to sacrifice diversification for superior returns in limited segments of their portfolios.
5. Administer the account, keep records of costs, provide timely information for tax purposes, and reinvest dividends if desired.

Although most of the performance studies reviewed only risk-adjusted performance, all of these functions should be considered in order to put performance into perspective. Therefore, let us consider each of these functions and discuss how mutual funds fulfill them.

Mutual funds do not determine your risk preference. However, once you determine your risk–return preferences, you can choose a mutual fund from a large and growing variety of alternative funds designed to meet almost any investment goal. Recall that the empirical studies indicated that the funds were generally consistent in meeting their stated goals for investment strategies, risk, and returns.

Diversifying your portfolio to eliminate unsystematic risk is one of the major benefits of mutual funds. They provide *instant diversification*. This is especially beneficial to small investors who do not have the resources to acquire 100 shares of 10 or 12 different issues required to reduce unsystematic risk. By initiating an investment in a fund with about $1,000 you can participate in a portfolio of securities that is correlated about 0.90 with the market portfolio, which means that it is about 90 percent diversified. Although diversification varies among funds, typically about three-quarters of the funds have a correlation with the market above 0.90. Therefore, most funds provide excellent diversification, especially if they state this as an objective.

The third function of your portfolio manager is to maintain the diversification and your desired risk class. It is not too surprising that mutual funds have generally maintained the stability of their correlation with the market because few change the makeup

---

[27]James S. Ang and Jess H. Chua, "Mutual Funds: Different Strokes for Different Folks?" *Journal of Portfolio Management* 8, no. 2 (Winter 1982): 43–47.

of reasonably well-diversified portfolios substantially. There is strong evidence regarding the consistency of the risk class for individual funds even when there was inconsistency in risk-adjusted performance.

Mutual funds have met the desire for flexibility to change investment instruments by the initiation of numerous funds within a given management company. Typically, investment groups such as T. Rowe Price or Fidelity Investments will allow you to shift among their funds without a charge simply by calling the fund. Therefore, you can shift among an aggressive stock fund, a money market fund, and a bond fund for much less than it would cost you in time and money to buy and sell numerous individual issues.

The fourth function is to provide risk-adjusted performance that is superior to the aggregate market, which implies that it is superior to a naive buy-and-hold policy. You will probably not be surprised that the funds do not fulfill this function very well. The evidence indicates that, on average, fund managers' results in selecting undervalued securities or timing the market are about as good as, or only slightly better than, the results of a naive buy-and-hold policy. This conclusion is based on *gross* returns. Unfortunately, the evidence from *net* returns, which is what you as an investor would receive, indicates that most funds do not do as well as a naive buy-and-hold policy. The shortfall in performance of about 1 percent a year roughly matches the average cost of research and trading commissions.

In response to these findings, several investment management firms have started index funds based on the philosophy, "if you can't beat them, join them." These *market index funds* do not attempt to beat the market, but merely try to match the composition, and therefore, the performance of some specified market index such as the S&P 500 Index. Because these index funds have no research costs and minimal trading expenses, their returns have typically correlated with the chosen indexes at rates in excess of .99 with very low expenses. Also, their management fees are substantially below those charged by active managers.[28]

Although institutions have used index funds for many years, such funds have not generally been available for individual investors. This changed during 1989 when several major investment company sponsors, such as Fidelity Management, initiated such funds. Currently six or seven equity index funds are available.

If you want to find a superior fund, the news is not very good. The only funds to perform consistently over time are the inferior funds. Apparently, if a fund performs poorly because of excessive expenses, it will probably continue to do so. Such funds should be avoided. The overall point is that you should not expect to enjoy consistently superior risk-adjusted performance from an investment in a mutual fund.

The final function of a portfolio manager is account administration. This is another significant benefit of most mutual funds, because they allow automatic reinvestment of dividends with no charge and consistently provide records of total cost. Further, each year they supply statements of dividend income and capital gain distribution that can be used to prepare tax returns.

In summary, as an investor, you probably want your portfolio manager to perform a set of functions. Typically, mutual funds can help you accomplish four of the five

---

[28]For a discussion of the reasoning behind these index funds (both economic and legal) and the early development, see A. F. Ehrbar, "Index Funds—An Idea Whose Time Is Coming,"*Fortune,* June 1976, 146–148.

functions at a lower cost in terms of time and money than doing the work on your own. Unfortunately, this convenience and service costs about 1 percent a year in terms of performance.

SOURCES OF
INFORMATION

Because there is a wide variety of types of funds available, you should examine the performance of various funds over time to derive some understanding of their goals and management philosophies. Daily quotations for numerous open-end funds appear in *The Wall Street Journal*. These quotations and the information provided has been enhanced dramatically since 1992 when the *Journal* began providing historical returns and rankings for alternative periods each day. A description of what is provided is shown in Figure 24.3.

A comprehensive weekly list of quotations with data on dividend income and capital gain for the previous 12 months is carried in *Barron's*. In addition, *Barron's* publishes quarterly updates on the performance of a number of funds over the previous 10 years. As shown earlier in Figure 24.1, *Barron's* lists closed-end stock and bond funds with their current net asset values, current market quotes, and the percentage of difference between the two figures.

A major source of comprehensive historical information is an annual publication issued by Arthur Wiesenberger Services entitled *Investment Companies*. This book contains statistics for over 600 mutual funds arranged alphabetically. It describes each major fund including a brief history, investment objectives and portfolio analysis, statistical history, special services available, personnel, advisors and distributors, sales charges, and a chart of the value of a hypothetical $10,000 investment over 10 years. Figure 24.4 shows a sample page for the Nicholas II, Inc. fund. The Wiesenberger book also contains a summary list with annual rates of return and price volatility measures for a number of additional funds.

Wiesenberger has two other services. Every 3 months the firm publishes *Management Results,* which updates the long-term performance of more than 400 mutual funds, arranged alphabetically and grouped by investment objective. The firm's monthly publication, *Current Performance and Dividend Record,* reports the dividend and short-run performance of more than 400 funds, listed alphabetically with objectives indicated.[29]

Another source of analytical historical information on funds is *Forbes*. This bi-weekly financial publication typically discusses individual companies and their investment potential. In addition, the magazine's August issue contains an annual survey of mutual funds. A sample page in Figure 24.5 demonstrates the survey reports on annual average 10-year returns and last 12 month returns. The survey also provides information regarding each fund's yield, its sales charge, and its annual expense ratio. Notably, they include a separate section on foreign stock funds as shown.

Business Week publishes a "Mutual Fund Scoreboard." Figure 24.6 contains a sample of this scoreboard for open-end fixed-income funds. The magazine publishes a comparable one for closed-end, fixed-income funds and equity funds. Besides information on performance (both risk-adjusted performance and total return), sales charges

---

[29]These services are currently published by Wiesenberger Investment Companies Services, Warren, Gorham and Lamont, 210 South St., Boston, MA 02111.

MUTUAL FUND QUOTATIONS

What These Listings Provide...

		NASD DATA			LIPPER ANALYTICAL DATA			
Monday	Inv. Obj.	NAV	Offer Price	NAV Chg.	%Ret YTD	Max Initl Chrg.	Total Exp Ratio	..
Tuesday	Inv. Obj.	NAV	Offer Price	NAV Chg.	YTD	Total Return 4 wk	1 yr	Rank
WEDNESDAY	**Inv. Obj.**	**NAV**	**Offer Price**	**NAV Chg.**	**YTD**	**Total Return 13 wk**	**3 yr***	**Rank**
Thursday	Inv. Obj.	NAV	Offer Price	NAV Chg.	YTD	Total Return 26 wk	4 yr*	Rank
Friday	Inv. Obj.	NAV	Offer Price	NAV Chg.	YTD	Total Return 39 wk	5 yr*	Rank

* Annualized

EXPLANATORY NOTES

Mutual fund data are supplied by two organizations. The daily Net Asset Value (NAV), Offer Price and Net Change calculations are supplied by the National Association of Securities Dealers (NASD) through Nasdaq, its automated quotation system. Performance and cost data are supplied by Lipper Analytical Services Inc.

Daily price data are entered into Nasdaq by the fund, its management company or agent. Performance and cost calculations are percentages provided by Lipper Analytical Services, based on prospectuses filed with the Securities and Exchange Commission, fund reports, financial reporting services and other sources believed to be authoritative, accurate and timely. Though verified, the data cannot be guaranteed by Lipper or its data sources and should be double-checked with the funds before making any investment decisions.

Performance figures are on a total return basis without regard to sales, deferred sales or redemption charges.

INVESTMENT OBJECTIVE (Inv. Obj.) – Based on stated investment goals outlined in the prospectus. The Journal assembled 27 groups based on classifications used by Lipper Analytical in the daily Mutual Fund Scorecard and other calculations. A detailed breakdown of classifications appears at the bottom of this page.

NET ASSET VALUE (NAV) – Per share value prepared by the fund, based on closing quotes unless noted, and supplied to the NASD by 5:30 p.m. Eastern time.

OFFER PRICE – Net asset value plus sales commission, if any.

NAV CHG. – Gain or loss, based on the previous NAV quotation.

TOTAL RETURN – Performance calculations, as percentages, assuming reinvestment of all distributions. Sales charges aren't reflected. Percentages are annualized for periods greater than one year. For funds declaring dividends daily, calculations are based on the most current data supplied by the fund within publication deadlines. A YEAR TO DATE (YTD) change is listed daily, with results ranging from 4 weeks to 5 years offered throughout the week. See chart on this page for specific situation.

MAXIMUM INITIAL SALES COMMISSION (Max Initl Chrg) – Based on prospectus; the sales charge may be modified or suspended temporarily by the fund, but any percentage change requires formal notification to the shareholders.

TOTAL EXPENSE RATIO (Total Exp Ratio) – Shown as a percentage and based on the fund's annual report, the ratio is total operating expenses for the fiscal year divided by the fund's average net assets. It includes all asset based charges such as advisory fees, other non-advisory fees and distribution expenses (12b-1).

RANKING (R) – Funds are grouped by investment objectives defined by The Wall Street Journal and ranked on longest time period listed each day. Performance measurement begins at either the closest Thursday or month-end for periods of more than one year. Gains of 100% or more are shown as a whole number, not carried out one decimal place. A=top 20%; B=next 20%; C=middle 20%; D=next 20%; E=bottom 20%.

QUOTATIONS FOOTNOTES

e-Ex-distribution. f-Previous day's quotation. s-Stock split or dividend. x-Ex–dividend.

p-Distribution costs apply, 12b-1 plan. r-Redemption charge may apply. t–Footnotes p and r apply.

NA-Not available due to incomplete price, performance or cost data. **NE**-Deleted by Lipper editor; data in question. **NL**-No Load (sales commission). **NN**-Fund doesn't wish to be tracked. **NS**-Fund didn't exist at start of period.

k-Recalculated by Lipper, using updated data. i-No valid comparison with other funds because of expense structure.

FIGURE 24.4   Sample Page from *Investment Companies*

NICHOLAS II, INC.

Nicholas II is a diversified open-end management investment company pursuing long-term growth of capital through a portfolio of common stocks with growth potentia!. Securities are not purchased with a view to rapid turnover or to obtain short-term trading profits. The fund is one of five managed by Nicholas Company, Inc.

At the close of 1989, the fund was 85.7% invested in common stocks, of which the major portion was in five industry groups: industrial products & services (11.9% of net assets); consumer products (10.1%); insurance (9.3%), and banks and health care (each 9.0%). The five largest individual common stock holdings were Chambers Development (4.3% of net assets), International Dairy Queen (3.0%), Block Drug and Marshall & Ilsley (each 2.5%), and Hamilton Oil (2.2%). The rate of portfolio turnover during the latest fiscal year was 8.2% of average assets. Unrealized appreciation in the portfolio at calendar year-end amounted to 25.3% of net assets.

Special Services: An open account provides for accumulation and dividend reinvestment. The fund offers a prototype Individual Retirement Account (IRA) plan and has available a master Keogh or self-employed IRA plan.

Statistical History

					AT YEAR-ENDS					ANNUAL DATA			
	Total Net Assets ($)	Number of Share-holders	Net Asset Value Per Share ($)	Yield (%)	Cash & Gov't	% of Assets in		Income Div-idends ($)	Capital Gains Distribu-tion ($)	Expense Ratio (%)	Offering Price ($)	
Year						Bonds & Pre-ferreds	Com-mon Stocks				High	Low
1989	404,423,252	35,116	20.16	1.5	14	—	86	0.312	0.669*	0.74	21.99	17.95
1988	361,084,568	35,467	17.98	1.9	7	—	93	0.335	0.08	0.77	18.72	15.63
1987	339,942,160	38,211	15.69	2.0	17	1	82	0.245	1.303*	0.74	21.52	14.19
1986	293,041,669	31,334	16.22	2.5	3	2	95	0.42	0.513	0.79	18.62	15.59
1985	232,693,089	25,898	15.54	1.0	39	—	61	0.163	0.061	1.11	15.73	11.69
1984	16,373,024	1,600	11.79	0.8	26	—	74	0.093	0.186	1.85	11.79	9.71
1983	2,612,530	200	10.33	NM	41	—	59	—	—	—	10.33	9.95

Note: Initially offered 10/17/83 at $10.00 per share.
* Includes short-term gains of $0.186 in 1984; $0.028 in 1985; $0.005 in 1987; $0.005 in 1989.
NM. Not meaningful; not a full year.

Directors: Albert O. Nicholas, Pres.; Melvin L. Schultz; Richard Seaman; Robert H. Bock.

Investment Adviser: Nicholas Company, Inc. Compensation to the Adviser is at an annual rate of .75 of 1% of the first $50 million of average net asset value, .6 of 1% of the next $50 million and .5 of 1% on assets in excess of $100 million.

Custodian & Transfer Agent: First Wisconsin Trust Company, Milwaukee, WI.

Distributor: Nicholas Company, Inc., 700 N. Water St., Milwaukee, WI 53202.

Sales Charge: None; shares are offered at net asset value. Minimum initial purchase is $1,000 with $100 the subsequent minimum.
Distribution Plan (12b-1): None.
Dividends: Investment income and net realized capital gains, if any, are distributed in December.
Shareholder Reports: Issued quarterly. Fiscal year ends September 30. The current prospectus was effective in January.
Qualified for Sale: In all states.
Address: 700 N. Water St., Milwaukee, WI 53202.
Telephone: (414) 272-6133.

An assumed investment of $10,000 in this fund, with capital gains accepted in shares and income dividends reinvested, is illustrated below. The explanation in the introduction to this section must be read in conjunction with this illustration.

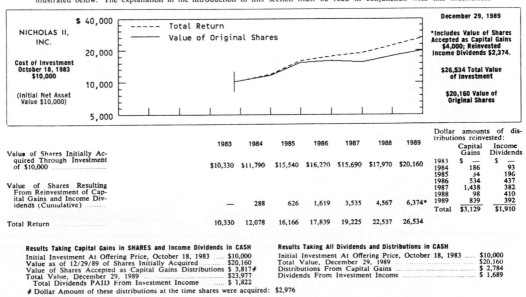

	1983	1984	1985	1986	1987	1988	1989
Value of Shares Initially Acquired Through Investment of $10,000	$10,330	$11,790	$15,540	$16,220	$15,690	$17,970	$20,160
Value of Shares Resulting From Reinvestment of Capital Gains and Income Dividends (Cumulative)	—	288	626	1,619	3,535	4,567	6,374*
Total Return	10,330	12,078	16,166	17,839	19,225	22,537	26,534

Dollar amounts of distributions reinvested:

	Capital Gains	Income Dividends
1983	$ —	$ —
1984	186	93
1985	34	196
1986	534	437
1987	1,438	382
1988	98	410
1989	839	392
Total	$3,129	$1,910

Results Taking Capital Gains in SHARES and Income Dividends in CASH
Initial Investment At Offering Price, October 18, 1983 ...... $10,000
Value as of 12/29/89 of Shares Initially Acquired $20,160
Value of Shares Accepted as Capital Gains Distributions $ 3,817#
Total Value, December 29, 1989 ..... $23,977
    Total Dividends PAID From Investment Income ...... $ 1,822
 # Dollar Amount of these distributions at the time shares were acquired: $2,976

Results Taking All Dividends and Distributions in CASH
Initial Investment At Offering Price, October 18, 1983 ...... $10,000
Total Value, December 29, 1989 ..... $20,160
Distributions From Capital Gains ..... $ 2,784
Dividends From Investment Income ..... $ 1,689

FIGURE 24.5   **Sample Fund Rating Page from *Forbes***

Stock funds

FORBES grades stock funds against the three latest market cycles of the S&P 500. To be graded, a fund must have been in existence for at least two of the market cycles—that is, since June 30, 1983. This table covers funds that have at least $25 million in assets and at least 12 months of performance history. Each fund's name is followed by that of its distributor; the table of distributors at the end of the fund survey has phone numbers. Closed-end funds have no distributor; they can be bought and sold in the secondary market and are traded just like common stock. For information on a closed-end fund contact your stock broker. Balanced funds, global stock funds and foreign stock funds are graded separately against different benchmarks; see pages 152, 158 and 160.

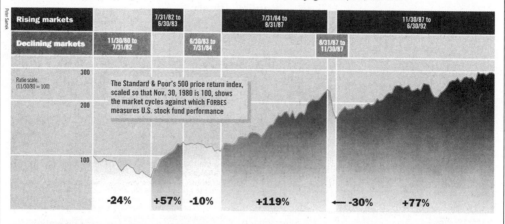

Performance		Fund/distributor	———Total return———		Yield	———Assets———		Maximum	Annual
UP markets	DOWN markets		Annual average 11/80 to 6/92	Last 12 months		6/30/92 ($mil)	% change 92 vs 91	sales charge	expenses per $100
		Standard & Poor's 500 stock average	14.1%	13.4%	3.0%				
		Forbes stock fund composite	12.3%	14.0%	1.8%				$1.27
		AAL Capital Growth Fund/AAL	—*	14.2%	2.0%	$458	105%	4.75%	*$1.28a*
		AARP Growth–Capital Growth/Scudder	—*	16.0	0.8	390	82	none	1.17
		AARP Growth–Growth & Income/Scudder	—*	18.1	3.3	654	96	none	0.96
D	D	ABT Growth & Income Trust/ABT	9.1%	8.9	2.3	83	–6	4.75	*1.27*
∎A	∎D	ABT Invest–Emerging Growth/ABT	—*	24.4	none	26	32	4.75	*1.59*
F	A	ABT Utility Income Fund/ABT	10.8	13.4	5.1	140	–1	4.75	*1.24*
B	C	Acorn Fund/Acorn	13.7	22.9	1.1	1,199	24	†	0.71
C	B	Adams Express/closed-end	12.3	11.4	2.7	635	6	NA	0.46
		Addison Capital Fund/Addison	—*	9.7	1.4	31	9	3.00	*2.09*
		Advantage Growth Fund/Advest	—*	14.9	0.2	50	57	4.00b	*2.10*

∎ Fund rated for two periods only; maximum allowable grade A.   *Fund not in operation for full period.   †Closed to new investors.   §Distributor may impose redemption fee, with proceeds reverting to other fund shareholders.   *Expense ratio is in italics if the fund has a shareholder-paid 12b-1 exceeding 0.1% pending or in force.*   a: Net of absorption of expenses by fund sponsor.   b: Includes back-end load that reverts to distributor.   NA: Not applicable or not available.

Source: "Annual Fund Ratings—Stock Funds/Foreign Stock Funds," *Forbes,* August 31, 1992, pp. 123, 160. Copyright © Forbes, Inc., 1992. Reprinted by permission of FORBES magazine.

FIGURE 24.5 (continued)

Foreign stock funds

The benchmark for measuring foreign stock funds is the dollar-denominated index from Morgan Stanley Capital International Perspective that tracks the price performance of over 1,000 stocks in Europe, Australia and the Far East. Many of these foreign markets declined during the 12 months ended in June: Measured in local currencies, the Morgan Stanley index was off 13.3%. But the dollar was also weak during this period—for example, it fell 15.7% against the German mark and 8.5% against the yen—and this worked to the advantage of U.S. investors. The dollar-denominated Morgan Stanley index shows a 12-month loss of only 2.5%. To be listed below, a fund must be based in the U.S., have at least $25 million in assets and have at least a full year of performance history.

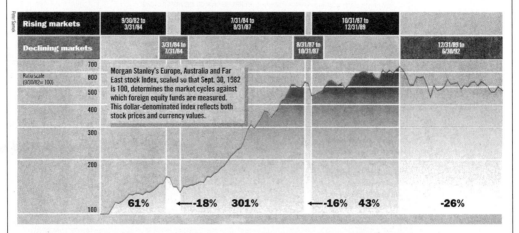

Performance		Fund/distributor	Total return		Yield	Assets		Maximum sales charge	Annual expenses per $100
UP markets	DOWN markets		Annual average 9/82 to 6/92	Last 12 months		6/30/92 ($mil)	% change 92 vs 91		
		Morgan Stanley Capital Intl EAFE index	19.3%	–0.7%	1.9%				
		Forbes foreign stock fund composite	14.1%	8.5%	1.4%				$1.72
B	C	Alliance International Fund-A/Alliance	17.5%	7.5%	0.5%	$186	–15%	5.50%	$1.82
		Alliance New Europe Fund-A/Alliance	—*	23.4	0.2	104	–19	5.50	2.24
D	D	ASA Limited/closed-end	4.4	–4.7	5.9	405	–10	NA	0.66
		Asia Pacific Fund/closed-end	—*	29.7	0.8	134	13	NA	1.92
		Austria Fund/closed-end	—*	–7.3	none	81	–9	NA	1.83
		Axe Core International ADR/USF&G	—*	–0.4	0.5	26	–2	†	1.79
		Bartlett Capital–Value Intl/Bartlett	—*	23.9	2.2	25	22	none	2.00
		Brazil Fund/closed-end	—*	3.2	none	173	2	NA	2.15
		Chile Fund/closed-end	—*	54.6	1.0	218	40	NA	1.75
		CoreFund–International Growth/Fairfield	—*	4.8	none	42	106	none	0.91a

■ Fund rated for two periods only; maximum allowable grade A. *Fund not in operation for full period. †Closed to new investors. *Expense ratio is in italics if the fund has a shareholder-paid 12b-1 exceeding 0.1% pending or in force. a: Net of absorption of expenses by fund sponsor. b: Includes back-end load that reverts to distributor. NA: Not applicable or not available.

Source: "Annual Fund Ratings—Stock Funds/Foreign Stock Funds," *Forbes,* August 31, 1992, pp. 123, 160.

FIGURE 24.6 **Mutual Fund Scoreboard**

HOW TO USE THE TABLES

BUSINESS WEEK RATING

Ratings measure risk-adjusted performance. This shows how well a fund performed relative to other funds and relative to the level of risk it took. Risk-adjusted performance is determined by subtracting a fund's risk-of-loss factor (see below) from its historic total return. Performance calculations are based on the five-year time period between Jan. 1, 1988, and Dec. 31, 1992. For rating purposes, funds are divided into two groups: municipal bond funds and all other funds. Ratings are based on a normal statistical distribution within each group and awarded as follows

♠ ♠ ♠	Superior performance
♠ ♠	Very good performance
♠	Above-average performance
AVG	Average performance
♥	Below-average performance
♥ ♥	Poor performance
♥ ♥ ♥	Very poor performance

RISK

The risk-of-loss factor is the potential for losing money in a fund, calculated as follows: The monthly Treasury bill return is subtracted from the fund's total return for each of the 60 months in the rating period. When a fund has not performed as well as

Treasury bills, the result is negative. The sum of these negative numbers is then divided by the number of months in the period. The result is a negative number, and the greater its magnitude, the higher a shareholder's risk of loss.

PERFORMANCE COMPARISON

The tables provide performance data over three time periods. Here are equivalent total return figures for the Lehman Brothers Government/Corporate Bond and Municipal Bond indexes during those periods:

	GOVT./CORP.	MUNI.
1992	7.6%	8.8%
Three-year avg. (1990-92)	10.6%	9.4%
Five-year avg. (1988-92)	10.7%	9.8%

FUND CATEGORIES

The tables group funds in one of five categories, based on assets: Corporate, Government, Municipal, International, and Convertible.

SALES CHARGE

The cost of buying a fund, commonly called the "load." Most funds take loads out of initial investments, and for BW rating purposes performance is reduced by the amount of these charges. Loads on withdrawals can take two forms. Deferred charges decrease over time usually ending after shares have been owned five years. Redemption fees are imposed whenever investors sell their shares. Funds with none of these charges are called "no-load."

EXPENSE RATIO

Fund expenses for 1992 as a percentage of average net assets. The measures show how much shareholders pay for fund management. Footnotes indicate 12(b)-1 plans, which allocate shareholder money for distribution costs.

TOTAL RETURN

A fund's net gain to investors, including reinvestment of dividends and capital gains at month-end prices.

YIELD

The income a fund earned on its portfolio investments during 1992, expressed as a percentage of the fund's yearend net asset value per share.

MATURITY

The average maturity of the securities in a fund's portfolio, weighted according to the market value of those securities.

TREND

A fund's relative performance during the five 12-month periods from Jan. 1, 1988, to Dec. 31, 1992. The boxes read from left to right, and the level of green shows how the fund performed relative to others during the period: ■ for the top quartile; ▨ for the second quartile; ▤ for the third quartile; and ☐ for the bottom quartile. An empty box indicates that a fund is not rated for that time period.

TELEPHONE NUMBERS

See the index on page 117.

	RATING	SIZE		FEES		PERFORMANCE			PORTFOLIO		TREND
		ASSETS $ MIL.	% CHG. 1991-92	SALES CHARGE (%)	EXPENSE RATIO (%)	TOTAL RET. (%) 1 YR.	3 YRS.	5 YRS.	YIELD	MATURITY (YEARS)	5-YEAR ANALYSIS

CORPORATE

	RATING	ASSETS $ MIL.	% CHG. 1991-92	SALES CHARGE (%)	EXPENSE RATIO (%)	1 YR.	3 YRS.	5 YRS.	YIELD	MATURITY (YEARS)	5-YEAR ANALYSIS
AARP HIGH-QUALITY BOND	♥	413.1	76	No load	1.13	6.2	9.7	9.9	6.2	10.9	
AIM HIGH-YIELD(C) (a)	♥	324.5	25	4.75	1.19†	18.6	15.3	13.2	11.2	8.9	
AIM INCOME(C) (b)	♥	218.8	-6	4.75	1.00†	7.4	9.5	10.2	7.6	16.5	
AMERICAN CAPITAL CORPORATE BOND	AVG	186.3	-2	4.75	1.00†	8.5	10.7	9.7	7.8	19.1	
AMERICAN CAPITAL HIGH-YIELD INVEST. A	♥ ♥ ♥	401.1	11	4.75	1.06†	17.4	11.8	6.8	11.8	7.7	
AMERICAN HIGH-INCOME		454.7	60	4.75	0.94†	14.3	14.8		9.2	6.7	
BABSON BOND L	♠	145.0	26	No load	0.98	8.0	10.2	10.2	7.6	13.5	
BARTLETT CAPITAL FIXED-INCOME	♠	134.0	-18	No load	1.00	6.9	9.1	9.6	6.1	6.8	
BERNSTEIN INTERMEDIATE DURATION		544.2	30	No load	0.67	7.7	10.6		6.3	15.6	
BERNSTEIN SHORT DURATION PLUS		537.8	19	No load	0.66	6.4	9.0		5.4	9.3	
BOND FUND OF AMERICA	♠	3917.3	37	4.75	0.77†	11.3	11.6	11.2	8.0	9.3	
COLONIAL HIGH-YIELD SECURITIES A	♥ ♥	346.5	16	4.75	1.32†	21.2	14.1	10.9	10.3	7.4	
COLONIAL INCOME A	AVG	149.3	2	4.75	1.25†	8.7	9.8	9.9	8.5	8.7	
COLONIAL STRATEGIC INCOME A	AVG	436.9	3	4.75	1.16	9.8	9.4	10.9	9.6	3.2	
COLUMBIA FIXED-INCOME SECURITIES	♠	262.6	27	No load	0.66	8.0	11.0	11.0	7.0	6.3	
COMPASS CAPITAL FIXED-INCOME		182.9	24	3.75	0.88	7.7	10.1		6.8	9.8	
COMPASS CAPITAL SHORT/INTERMEDIATE		169.6	37	3.75	0.87	6.6	9.0		6.5	3.3	
DEAN WITTER HIGH-YIELD SECURITIES	♥ ♥ ♥	454.5	7	5.50	0.77	24.4	7.6	3.4	16.5	8.1	
DEAN WITTER INTERMEDIATE INCOME		200.3	67	5.00**	1.67†	6.8	8.3		7.3	7.8	
DELAWARE DELCHESTER (c)	♥ ♥	802.9	515	4.75	1.08†	17.2	13.9	11.0	11.5	6.6	
DODGE & COX INCOME		136.3	42	No load	0.64	7.8	10.9		7.0	11.2	
DREYFUS A BONDS PLUS	AVG	522.9	12	No load	0.88	8.2	10.4	10.9	7.2	16.9	
DREYFUS STRATEGIC INCOME	AVG	165.9	156	3.00	0.85†	9.0	11.1	11.6	7.5	15.0	

*Includes redemption fee. **Includes deferred sales charge. †12(b)-1 plan in effect. ‡Not currently accepting new accounts or deposits. §New fund, less than 12 months' total return. NA = Not available. NM = Not meaningful. (a) Formerly CIGNA High-Yield Fund. (b) Formerly CIGNA Income Fund. (c) Formerly Delaware Group Delchester H/Y Bond II.

DATA: MORNINGSTAR INC.

(including those for 12b-1 plans), expenses, and portfolio yield and maturity, an accompanying table contains telephone numbers for all the funds.

United Business Service Company publishes a semimonthly report called *United Mutual Fund Selector.* Each issue contains several articles on specific mutual funds or classes of mutual funds, such as municipal bond funds. In the first issue of each month, a four-page supplement entitled "Investment Company Performance Comparisons" gives recent and historical changes in NAV for load and no-load funds.[30]

Morningstar is a relatively new information service for mutual funds but has become well-known and very well-regarded. It provides a number of services for mutual fund investors. Its basic service is "Morningstar Mutual Funds," which provides a very informative one-page sheet that evaluates the performance of open-end mutual funds (1,240 funds). An example sheet for a fund is included as Figure 24.7. This sheet provides up-to-date information on the fund's objective and its risk-adjusted performance relative to an appropriate benchmark. There is also an analysis of performance and investment strategy based upon an interview with the fund manager. The one-page sheet is best described as a *Value Line* sheet for a mutual fund. A similar service evaluates 268 closed-end funds.

In addition the firm publishes an annual source book that provides a year-end profile of 2,400 open-end funds, a source book for 370 closed-end funds, a monthly performance report (similar to the stock guide) on 2,500 mutual funds, and an annual reference publication of the elite 500 open and closed-end funds.[31]

GLOBAL INVESTMENT COMPANIES

As discussed throughout this text, you should give very serious thought to global diversification of your investment portfolio. Funds that invest in non-U.S. securities are generally called *foreign funds.* More specific designations include either *international funds* or *global funds.* International funds include only non-U.S. stocks from countries such as Germany, Japan, Singapore, and Korea. Global funds contain both U.S. and non-U.S. securities. Ideally, a global fund should invest in a large number of countries. Both international and global funds fall into familiar categories: money funds, long-term government and corporate bond funds, and equity funds. In turn, an international equity fund might limit its focus to a segment of the non-U.S. market, such as the European Fund or Pacific Basin Fund, or to a single country such as Germany, Italy, Japan, or Korea.

Although most global or international funds are open-end funds (either load and no-load), there are a significant number that are closed-end funds, including most of the single country funds. These funds have opted to be closed-end because they are not subject to major investor liquidations that require the sale of stocks in the portfolio on an illiquid foreign stock exchange. Because of the growth and popularity of foreign funds, most sources of information include separate sections on foreign stock or bond funds.

SUMMARY

An investment company can be defined as a pool of funds from many individuals that is invested in a collection of individual investments such as stocks, bonds, and other publicly traded securities. Investment companies can be classified as closed-end or

---

[30]This service is available from United Business Service Company, 210 Newbury St., Boston, MA 02116.

[31]These services are available from Morningstar, 53 West Jackson Boulevard, Chicago, IL 60604.

FIGURE 24.7   **Sample Page from Morningstar Mutual Funds**

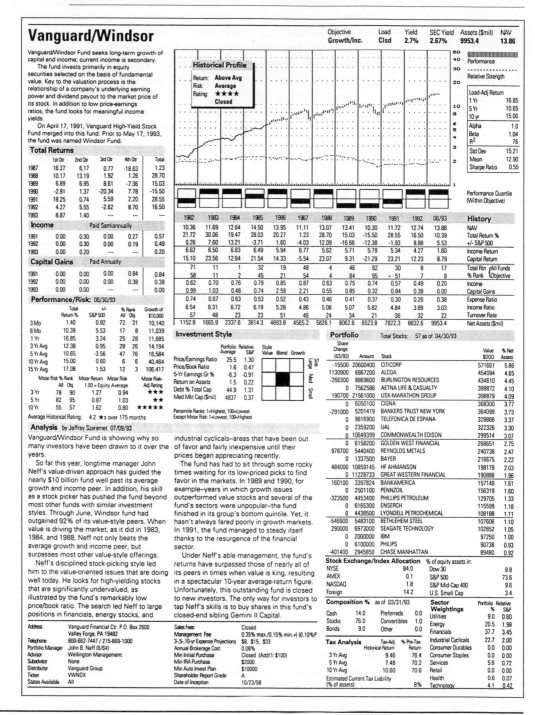

open-end; the latter can have either load or no-load funds. A wide variety of funds are available, so you can find one to match almost any investment objective or combination of objectives.

Numerous studies have examined the historical performance of mutual funds. Most found that less than half the funds matched the risk-adjusted net returns of the aggregate market. The results with gross returns generally indicated average risk-adjusted returns about equal to the market's, with about half of the funds (more than half for some studies) outperforming the market.

Although the returns received by the average individual investor on funds managed by investment companies will probably not be superior to the average results for a specific U.S. or international market, several other important services are provided by investment companies. Therefore, you should give serious consideration to these funds as an important alternative to investing in individual stocks and bonds in the United States or worldwide.

QUESTIONS

1. How do you compute the net asset value of an investment company?

2. Discuss the difference between an open-end investment company and a closed-end investment company.

3. What two prices are provided for a closed-end investment company? What is the typical relationship between these prices?

4. What is the difference between a load fund and a no-load fund?

5. What are the differences between a common stock fund and a balanced fund? How would you expect their risk and return characteristics to compare?

6. Why might you buy a money market fund? What would you want from this investment?

7. Do you care about how well a mutual fund is diversified? Why or why not?

8. Discuss why the stability of a risk measure for a mutual fund is important to an investor. Are mutual funds' risk measure generally stable?

9. Should the performance of mutual funds be judged on the basis of return alone or on a risk-adjusted basis? Discuss why, using examples.

10. Define the net return and gross return for a mutual fund. Discuss how you would compute each.

11. As an investor in a mutual fund, discuss why net returns or gross returns are relevant to you?

12. As an investigator evaluating how well mutual fund managers select undervalued stocks or project market returns, discuss whether net or gross returns are more relevant.

13. Based on the numerous tests of mutual fund performance, you are convinced that only about half of the funds do better than a naive buy-and-hold policy. Does this mean you would forget about investing in investment companies? Why or why not?

14. You are told that Fund X experienced *above-average* performance over the past 2 years. Do you think it will continue over the next 2 years? Why or why not?

15. You are told that Fund Y experienced consistently *poor* performance over the past 2 years. Do you think it will continue over the next 2 years? Why or why not?

16. You see advertisements for two mutual funds indicating that they have investment objectives that are consistent with yours.

a. How would you get a quick view of these two funds' performance over the past 2 or 3 years?

b. Where would you find more in-depth information on the funds, including addresses so you can write for prospectuses?

PROBLEMS

1. Suppose ABC Mutual fund had no liabilities and owned only four stocks as follows:

Stock	Shares	Price	Market Value
W	1,000	12	$12,000
X	1,200	15	18,000
Y	1,500	22	33,000
Z	800	16	12,800
			$75,800

The fund began by selling $50,000 of stock at $8.00 per share. What is its NAV?

2. Suppose you are considering investing $1,000 in a load fund that charges a fee of 8 percent, and you expect your investment to earn 15 percent over the next year. Alternatively, you could invest in a no-load fund with similar risk that charges a 1 percent redemption fee. You estimate that this no-load fund will earn 12 percent. Given your expectations, which is the better investment and by how much?

3. In *Barron's,* look up the NAVs and market prices for five closed-end funds. Compute the difference between the two values for each fund. How many are selling at a premium to NAV? How many are selling at a discount to NAV? What is the overall average premium or discount? How does this compare to the Herzfeld chart published in *Barron's* that tracks the average discount on these funds over time?

REFERENCES

Anderson, Seth Copeland. "Closed-End Funds vs. Market Efficiency." *Journal of Portfolio Management* 13, no. 1 (Fall 1986).

Blake, Christopher, Edwin J. Elton, and Martin J. Gruber. "The Performance of Bond Mutual Funds." *The Journal of Business* 66, no. 3 (July 1993).

Brealey, Richard A. "How to Combine Active Management with Index Funds." *Journal of Portfolio Management* 12, no. 2 (Winter 1986).

Chang, Eric C., and Wilbur G. Lewellen. "Market Timing and Mutual Fund Investment Performance." *Journal of Business* 57, no. 1, part 1 (January 1984).

Cornell, Bradford, and Kevin Green. "The Investment Performance of Low-Grade Bond Funds." *Journal of Finance* 46, no. 1 (March 1991).

Cumby, Robert E., and Jack D. Glen. "Evaluating the Performance of International Mutual Funds." *Journal of Finance* 45, no. 2 (June 1990).

Henriksson, Roy D. "Mutual Timing and Mutual Fund Performance: An Empirical Investigation." *Journal of Business* 57, no. 1, part 1 (January 1984).

Martin, John D., Arthur J. Keown, Jr., and James L. Farrell. "Do Fund Objectives Affect Diversification Policies?" *Journal of Portfolio Management* 8, no. 2 (Winter 1982).

Richards, Malcolm, Donald Fraser, and John Groth. "The Attractions of Closed-End Bond Funds." *Journal of Portfolio Management* 8, no. 2 (Winter 1982).

Simonds, Richard R. "Mutual Fund Strategies for IRA Investors." *Journal of Portfolio Management* 12, no. 2 (Winter 1986).

Thaler, Richard. "Investor Sentiment and the Closed-End Fund Puzzle." *Journal of Finance* 46, no. 1 (March 1991).

Veit, E. Theodore, and John M. Cheney. "Are Mutual Funds Market Timers?" *Journal of Portfolio Management* 8, no. 2 (Winter 1982).

Weiss, Kathleen. "The Post Offering Performance of Closed-End Funds." *Financial Management* 18, no. 3 (Autumn 1989).

APPENDIX 24A   MUTUAL FUNDS GLOSSARY

This glossary is divided into three parts: (A) general terms used in the mutual fund industry, (B) specific terms for types of mutual funds, and (C) a description of alternative retirement plans, each of which can include mutual funds.

A. GENERAL TERMS

Accumulation (periodic payment) plan An arrangement through which an investor can purchase mutual fund shares periodically in large or small amounts, usually with provisions for the reinvestment of income dividends and capital gains distributions in additional shares.

Adviser The organization employed by a mutual fund to give professional advice on the management of its assets.

Asked (offering) price The price at which you can purchase a mutual fund's shares equal to the net asset value per share plus, at times, a sales charge.

Automatic reinvestment The option available to mutual fund shareholders whereby fund income dividends and capital gains distributions are automatically put back into the fund to buy new shares and thereby build up holdings.

Bid (redemption) price The price at which a mutual fund redeems (buys back) its shares, usually equal to the net asset value per share.

Bookshares A modern share recording system that eliminates the need for mutual fund share certificates but gives fund shareowners records of their holdings.

Broker-dealer (dealer) A firm that retails mutual fund shares and other securities to the public.

Capital gains distributions Payments, usually annual, to mutual fund shareholders for gains realized on the sale of the fund's portfolio securities.

Capital growth An increase in the market value of a mutual fund's securities that is reflected in the NAV of its shares. Maximizing this factor is a long-term objective of many mutual funds.

Closed-end investment company An investment company that issues only a limited number of shares, which it does not redeem (buy back). Instead, closed-end shares are traded in securities markets at prices determined by supply and demand.

Contractual plan A program for the accumulation of mutual fund shares in which the investor agrees to invest a fixed amount on a regular basis for a specified number of years. A substantial portion of the sales charge applicable to the total investment is usually deducted from early payments.

Conversion (exchange) privilege A provision that enables a mutual fund shareholder to transfer an investment from one fund to another within the same fund group, sometimes with a small transaction charge, if needs or objectives change.

Custodian The organization (usually a bank) that holds the securities and other assets of a mutual fund in custody and safekeeping.

Diversification The policy of spreading investments among a number of different securities that do not have similar return patterns to reduce the risks inherent in investing.

Dollar-cost averaging Investing equal amounts of money at regular intervals regardless of whether the stock market is moving upward or downward. This reduces average share costs in periods of lower securities prices and number of shares purchased in periods of higher prices.

Exchange privilege *See* Conversion privilege.

Income dividends Payments to mutual fund shareholders of dividends, interest, and short-term capital gains earned on the fund's portfolio after deduction of operating expenses.

Investment adviser *See* Adviser.

Investment company A corporation, trust, or partnership in which investors may pool their money to obtain professional management and portfolio diversification of their investments. Mutual funds are the most popular type of investment company.

Investment objective The goal, such as long-term capital growth or current income, that an investor or a mutual fund pursues.

Load *See* Sales charge.

Management fee The compensation an investment company pays to the investment adviser for its services. The average annual fee is about 0.5 percent of fund assets.

Mutual fund An investment company that pools money from shareholders and invests in a variety of securities, including stocks, bonds, and money market securities. A mutual fund ordinarily stands ready to buy back (redeem) its shares at their current net asset value, which depends on the market value of the fund's portfolio of securities at the time. Mutual funds generally continuously offer new shares to investors.

Net asset value (NAV) per share The market value of an investment company's total assets (securities, cash, and any accrued earnings) after deducting liabilities, divided by the number of shares outstanding.

No-load fund A mutual fund selling its shares at net asset value without adding sales charges.

Open-end investment company The more formal name for a mutual fund, which derives from the fact that it continuously offers new shares to investors and redeems them (buys them back) on demand.

Payroll deduction plan An arrangement offered by some employers through which an employee may accumulate shares in a mutual fund. Employees authorize the employer to deduct specific amounts from their salaries at stated times and transfer the proceeds to the designated fund or funds.

Periodic payment plan *See* Contractual plan.

Prospectus A booklet describing the mutual fund and offering its shares for sale. It contains information required by the Securities and Exchange Commission on such subjects as the fund's investment objective and policies, services, investment restrictions, officers and directors, procedures for buying or redeeming shares, its charges, and its financial statements.

Qualified retirement plan A private retirement plan that meets the rules and regulations of the Internal Revenue Service. Contributions to a qualified retirement plan are generally tax deductible, and earnings on these contributions are tax sheltered until retirement.

Redemption price The amount per share the mutual fund shareholder receives when cashing in shares (also known as *bid price*). The value of the shares depends on the fund's NAV at the time.

Reinvestment privilege A provision of most mutual funds by which an investor can automatically reinvest a shareholder's income dividends and capital gains distributions in additional shares.

Sales charge An amount charged to purchase shares in most mutual funds sold by brokers or other members of a sales force. Typical charges range from 4 to 8.5 percent of the initial investment. The charge is added to the net asset value per share to determine the offer price.

Short-term funds An industry designation for money market and short-term municipal bond funds.

Transfer agent The organization employed by a mutual fund to prepare and maintain records relating to the accounts of fund shareholders.

12b-1 fee A fee charged by some funds, named after the SEC rule that permits it. Such fees pay for distribution costs, such as advertising, or for brokers' commissions. The fund's prospectus details 12b-1 charges that apply.

Underwriter (principal underwriter) The organization that acts as the distributor of a mutual fund's shares to broker-dealers and the public.

Unit investment trust An investment company that purchases a fixed portfolio of income-producing securities to create a trust and sells units in the trust through brokers.

Variable annuity A contract under which an annuity is purchased with a fixed amount of money that is converted into a varying number of accumulation units. At retirement, the annuitant is paid a fixed number of monthly units, which are converted into varying amounts of money. The value of both accumulation and annuity units varies with the performance of a portfolio of equity securities.

Variable life insurance An equity-based life insurance policy in which the reserves of which may be invested in common stocks. The death benefit is guaranteed never to fall below the face value, but it would increase if the value of the securities were to increase. This kind of policy may have no guaranteed cash-surrender value.

Voluntary plan A flexible accumulation plan that states no definite time period or total amount to be invested.

Withdrawal plans A mutual fund provision that allows shareholders to receive payments from their investments at regular intervals. These payments typically are drawn from the fund's dividends and capital gains distributions, if any, and from principal, as needed. Many mutual funds offer these plans.

B. TYPES OF MUTUAL FUNDS

Aggressive growth funds A fund that seeks maximum capital gains as its investment objective. Current income is not a significant factor. Some may invest in stocks on the fringe of the mainstream, such as those in fledgling companies, new industries, companies fallen on hard times, or industries temporarily out of favor. They may also use specialized investment techniques such as option writing. The risks are obvious, but the potential for significant reward should be greater.

Balanced funds A fund with, generally, a three-part investment objective: (1) to conserve the investors' principal, (2) to pay current income, and (3) to increase both principal and income. The fund aims to achieve this by owning a mixture of bonds, preferred stocks, and common stocks.

Corporate bond funds Like an income fund, this type of fund seeks a high level of income. It does this by buying bonds of corporations for the majority of the portfolio. Some part of the portfolio may be in U.S. Treasury and other government bonds.

Flexible portfolio funds A fund that invests in common stocks, bonds, money market securities, and other types of debt securities. The portfolio may hold up to 100 percent of any one of these types of securities or any combination of them, depending on market conditions.

Global bond funds A fund that invests in bonds issued by companies from countries worldwide, including the United States.

Global equity funds A fund that invests in the stocks of both U.S. companies and foreign companies.

GNMA (Ginnie Mae) funds A fund that invests in government-backed mortgage securities of the Government National Mortgage Association. To qualify for this category, the majority of the fund's portfolio must always be invested in mortgage-backed securities.

Growth A fund that invests in the common stock of more settled companies, but again, with the primary aim of increasing the value of its investments through capital gains rather than a steady flow of dividends.

Growth and income funds A fund that invests mainly in the common stock of companies with longer track records—companies that combine the expectation of higher share values and solid records of paying dividends.

High-yield bond funds A fund that invests predominantly in bonds rated below investment grade. In return for a generally higher yield, investors bear greater risk than more highly rated bonds require.

Income-bond funds A fund that invests in a combination of government and corporate bonds to generate income.

Income equity funds A fund that invests primarily in stocks of companies with good dividend-paying records.

Income-mixed funds A fund that seeks a high level of current income, often by investing in the common stock of companies that have good dividend-paying records. Often corporate and government bonds are also part of the portfolio.

International funds A fund that invests in the stocks or bonds of companies located outside the United States.

Long-term municipal bond funds A fund that invests in municipal bonds issued by local governments, such as cities and states, which use the money to build schools, highways, libraries, and the like. Because the federal government does not tax the income earned on most of these securities, the fund can pass the tax-free income through to shareholders.

Long-term state municipal bond funds A fund that invests predominantly in long-term municipal bonds issued within a single state. The issues are exempt from both federal income tax and state taxes for residents of the same state.

Money market mutual funds A fund that invests in the short-term securities sold in the money market. (Large companies, banks, and other institutions also invest their surplus cash in the money market for short periods of time.) In the entire investment spectrum, these are generally the safest, most stable securities available. They include Treasury bills, certificates of deposit of large banks, and commercial paper (short-term IOUs of large corporations).

Option/income funds A fund that seeks a high current return by investing primarily in dividend-paying common stocks on which call options are traded on national securities exchanges. Current returns generally consist of dividends and premiums from writing call options, but other sources include short-term gains from asset sales that may be required to satisfy exercised options and profits from closing purchase transactions.

Short-term bond funds A fund that invests in securities sold in the money market, such as those of large companies, banks, and municipal securities with relatively short maturities. Other institutions also invest their surplus cash in the municipal money market for short periods of time, known as *tax-exempt money market funds.* In the entire investment spectrum, these are generally the safest, most stable securities.

Short-term state municipal bond funds A fund that invests in municipal securities from a single state with relatively short maturities. Such issues are exempt from state taxes for residents of the same state.

U.S. government income funds A fund that invests in a variety of government securities including U.S. Treasury bonds; federally guaranteed, mortgage-backed securities; and other government issues, including agency securities.

C. RETIREMENT PLANS

Federal income tax laws permit the establishment of a number of types of tax-deferred retirement plans, each of which may be funded with mutual fund shares.

Corporate and self-employed retirement plans A tax-qualified pension and profit-sharing plan that can be established by corporations or self-employed individuals. Changes in the tax laws have made retirement plans for corporate employees essentially comparable to those for self-employed individuals. Contributions to a plan are tax deductible and earnings accumulate on a tax-deferred basis. The maximum annual amount that may be contributed to such a contribution plan on behalf of an individual is limited to the lesser of 25 percent of the individual's compensation or $30,000.

Individual retirement accounts Any wage earner under the age of $70\frac{1}{2}$ may set up an individual retirement account (IRA) and may contribute as much as 100 percent of his or her compensation each year up to $2,000. Income on these contributions are tax deferred until withdrawal. The amount contributed each year may be wholly or partially tax deductible. Under the Tax Reform Act of 1986, all taxpayers not covered by employer-sponsored retirement plans can continue to take the full deduction for IRA contributions. Those who are covered or who are married to someone who is covered must have an adjusted gross income of no more than $25,000 if they are single or $40,000 if they are married and filing jointly to take the full deduction. The deduction is phased out for incomes for single people between $25,000 and $35,000 and for married people who file jointly between $40,000 and $60,000. An individual who qualifies for an IRA and has a spouse who either has no earnings or elects to be treated as having no earnings may contribute up to 100 percent of his or her income or $2,250, whichever is less.

Simplified employee pension (SEPs) An employer-sponsored plan that may be viewed as an aggregation of separate IRAs. In a SEP, the employer contributes up to $30,000 or 15 percent of compensation, whichever is less, to an individual retirement account maintained for the employee.

Section 403(b) plan Section 403(b) of the Internal Revenue Code permits employees of certain charitable organizations and public school systems to establish tax-sheltered retirement programs. These plans may be invested in either annuity contracts or mutual fund shares.

Section 401(k) plans A particularly popular type of plan that may be offered by either corporate or noncorporate entities. A 401(k) plan is a tax-qualified profit-sharing plan that includes a "cash or deferred" arrangement that permits employees to have a portion of their compensation contributed to a tax-sheltered plan on their behalf or paid to them directly as additional taxable compensation. An employee may elect to reduce his or her taxable compensation with contributions to a 401(k) plan, where those amounts will accumulate tax free. The Tax Reform Act of 1986 established new, tighter antidiscrimination requirements for 401(k) plans and curtailed the amount of elective deferrals that may be made by all employees. Nevertheless, 401(k) plans remain excellent and popular retirement savings vehicles.

PART VII

EXTENSIONS AND APPLICATION OF ASSET PRICING AND PORTFOLIO MODELS

The two chapters in this final section of the book consider important topics on asset pricing and performance evaluation.

In Chapter 25 we return to the asset pricing models and consider the effect of changing some of the assumptions of the models. More important, we review the numerous studies that have empirically tested the CAPM and generated divergent results, including a fairly recent one that casts serious doubt on the basic model. We also revisit the "benchmark problem," which contends that it is not possible to use this model to analyze portfolio performance because the market portfolio typically used is clearly incomplete.

This chapter also includes a review of the APT model and how it differs from the CAPM. This is followed by a discussion of numerous studies that have tested the usefulness of this model compared to the CAPM. Again, the results are mixed in terms of supporting the model and there are some who even question whether it is possible to test this model because the factors cannot be identified.

We conclude the book with a chapter dealing with the evaluation of portfolio performance. After a discussion of what is required of a portfolio manager, we review in detail the major risk-adjusted portfolio performance models and consider how they relate to each other. This is followed by a demonstration of their use with a sample of mutual funds.

As always, it is important to be able to understand potential problems with a technique or models. Therefore, we consider potential problems with the measures including a review of Roll's benchmark problem and its effect on these performance models. It is demonstrated that this problem has become more significant with the growth of global investing. Finally, because the factors that determine success in bonds differ from what is important in equities, we review and evaluate several alternative models used to evaluate the performance of bond portfolio managers.

CHAPTER 25

EXTENSIONS AND TESTING OF ASSET PRICING THEORIES

In this chapter we will answer the following questions:

- What happens to the capital market line (CML) when you assume that there are differences in the risk-free borrowing and lending rates?
- What is a zero-beta asset and how does its use impact the CML?
- What happens to the security market line (SML) when you assume transactions costs, heterogeneous expectations, different planning periods, and taxes?
- What are the major questions considered when empirically testing the CAPM?
- What are the empirical results from tests that examine the stability of beta?
- How do published estimates of beta compare?
- What are the empirical test results of studies that examine the relationship between systematic risk and return?
- What other variables besides beta have had a significant impact upon returns?
- What is the theory and practice regarding the "market portfolio" and how does this difference relate to the benchmark problem?
- Assuming that there is a benchmark problem, what variables are affected by it?
- What are the major assumptions *not* required by the APT model compared to the CAPM?
- How do you test the APT by examining anomalies found with the CAPM?
- What are the empirical test results related to the APT?
- Why do some authors contend that the APT model is untestable?
- What are the concerns related to the multiple factors of the APT model?

Chapters 7 and 8 contained a detailed introduction to Markowitz portfolio theory and the capital asset pricing model (CAPM) so that these concepts could be used in the subsequent valuation chapters. In turn, this chapter considers several extensions of the CAPM, relaxes some of the assumptions, and examines the impact of these changes on the model. More important, we discuss the empirical tests of the theory. As we will discuss, some of the early results supported the predictive ability of the model but also raised some questions, including a contention by Roll that it is not possible to test the model. We will also discuss in some detail the recent study by Fama and French that raises serious questions about the relationship between beta and rates of return.

In Chapter 8 we also discussed a well-regarded alternative asset pricing model, the arbitrage pricing theory (APT), developed by Stephen Ross. Again, we will discuss the empirical tests of the theory. The empirical tests of this alternative theory yields mixed results, and it has been suggested that this theory is likewise untestable.

RELAXING THE ASSUMPTIONS

In Chapter 8 several assumptions were set forth related to the CAPM. In this section, we discuss the impact on the capital market line (CML) and the security market line (SML) when we relax several of these assumptions.

DIFFERENTIAL BORROWING AND LENDING RATES

One of the first assumptions of the CAPM was that investors could borrow and lend any amount of money at the risk-free rate. As noted, it is reasonable to assume that investors can *lend* unlimited amounts at the risk-free rate by buying government securities (e.g., T-bills). In contrast, one may question the ability of investors to borrow unlimited amounts at the T-bill rate, because this rate is usually lower than the prime rate and most investors must pay a premium relative to the prime rate when borrowing money. For example, when T-bill rates are yielding 6 percent, the prime rate will probably be about 8 percent, and most individuals would have to pay about 9 percent to borrow at the bank.

The effect of this differential is that there will be two different lines going to the Markowitz efficient frontier, as shown in Figure 25.1. The segment $RFR - F$ indicates the investment opportunities available when an investor combines risk-free assets (i.e., lending at the RFR) and Portfolio F on the Markowitz efficient frontier. It is not possible to extend this line any further if it is assumed that you cannot borrow at this risk-free rate to acquire further units of Portfolio F. If it is assumed that you can borrow at R_b,

FIGURE 25.1   **Investment Alternatives When the Cost of Borrowing Is Higher Than the Cost of Lending**

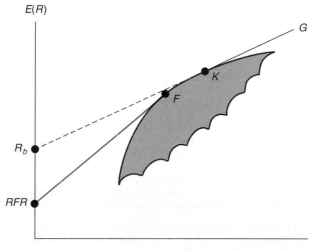

Risk (standard deviation σ)

the point of tangency from this rate would be on the curve at point *K*. This indicates that you could borrow at R_b and use the proceeds to invest in Portfolio K to extend the CML along the line segment *K–G*. Therefore, the CML is made up of *RFR–F–K–G*— that is, a line segment (*RFR–F*), a curve segment (*F–K*), and another line segment (*K–G*). This implies that you can either lend or borrow, but the borrowing portfolios are not as profitable as when it was assumed that you could borrow at the *RFR*. In this instance, because you must pay a borrowing rate that is higher than the *RFR*, your net return is less—that is, the slope of the borrowing line (*K–G*) is below that for *RFR–F*.[1]

ZERO-BETA MODEL

If the market portfolio (*M*) is mean-variance efficient (i.e., it has the lowest risk for a given level of return among the attainable set of portfolios), an alternative model, derived by Black, that does not require a risk-free asset can be used.[2] Specifically, within the set of feasible alternative portfolios, there will be several portfolios where the returns are completely uncorrelated with the market portfolio; the beta of these portfolios with the market portfolio is zero. From among the several zero-beta portfolios, you would select the one with minimum variance. Although this portfolio does not have any systematic risk, it does have some unsystematic risk. The availability of this zero-beta portfolio will not affect the CML, but it will allow construction of a linear SML, as shown in Figure 25.2. In the model, the intercept is the expected return for the zero-beta portfolio. Similar to the proof in Chapter 8, the combinations of this zero-beta portfolio and the market portfolio will be a linear relationship in return and risk because the covariance between the zero-beta portfolio (R_z) and the market portfolio is zero. Assuming that the return for the zero-beta portfolio is greater than that for a risk-free asset, the slope of the line through the market portfolio would not be as steep. The equation for this zero-beta CAPM line would be

$$E(R_i) = E(R_z) + B_i [E(R_m) - E(R_z)]$$

Obviously, the risk premiums for individual assets would be a function of the beta for the individual security and the market risk premium:

$$[E(R_m) - E(R_z)]$$

Some of the empirical results discussed in the next section support this model with its higher intercept and flatter slope. Alternatively, several studies have specifically tested this model and had conflicting results. Specifically, studies by Gibbons and by Shanken rejected the model.[3] In contrast, the results of a study by Stambaugh supported the zero-beta CAPM.[4]

---

[1] For a detailed discussion of this, see Michael Brennan, "Capital Market Equilibrium with Divergent Borrowing and Lending Rates," *Journal of Financial and Quantitative Analysis* 4, no. 1 (March 1969): 4–14.

[2] Fischer Black, "Capital Market Equilibrium with Restricted Borrowing," *Journal of Business* 45, no. 3 (July 1972): 444–445.

[3] Michael Gibbons, "Multivariate Tests of Financial Models: A New Approach," *Journal of Financial Economics* 10, no. 1 (March 1982): 3–28; and Jay Shanken, "Multivariate Tests of the Zero Beta CAPM," *Journal of Financial Economics* 14, no. 3 (September 1985): 327–348.

[4] Robert Stambaugh, "On the Exclusion of Assets from Tests of the Two-Parameter Model: A Sensitivity Analysis," *Journal of Financial Economics* 10, no. 4 (November 1982): 237–268.

FIGURE 25.2   **Security Market Line with Zero-Beta Portfolio**

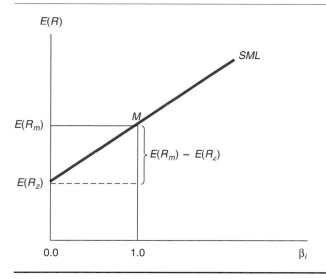

TRANSACTION COSTS

The basic assumption is that there are no transaction costs, so investors will buy or sell mispriced securities until they again plot on the SML. For instance, if a stock plots above the SML, it is underpriced (its $E(R)$ is greater than justified by its risk level). As a result, investors should buy it and bid up its price until its $E(R)$ is in line with its risk—that is, until it plots on the SML. The point is, with transaction costs, investors will not correct all mispricing, because in some instances the cost of buying and selling the security will offset any potential excess return. Therefore, securities will plot very close to the SML but not exactly on it. Thus, the SML will be a band of securities, as shown in Figure 25.3, rather than a single line. Obviously, the width of the band is a function of the amount of the transaction costs. In a world with a large proportion of purchases and sales by institutions at pennies per share and with numerous discount brokers available for individual investors, the band should be quite narrow.

The existence of transaction costs also will affect the extent of diversification by investors. In Chapter 8, there was a discussion of the relationship between the number of stocks in a portfolio and the variance of the portfolio (see Figure 8.3). Initially the variance declined rapidly, approaching about 90 percent of complete diversification with about 15 to 18 securities. An important question is how many securities must be added to derive the last 10 percent. Clearly, the existence of transaction costs would indicate that at some point the additional cost of diversification relative to its benefit would be excessive for most investors, especially when you consider the costs of monitoring and analyzing the added securities.

HETEROGENEOUS EXPECTATIONS AND PLANNING PERIODS

If all investors have different expectations about risk and return, each would have a unique CML and/or SML, and the composite graph would be a set of lines with a breadth determined by the divergence of expectations. If all investors had similar information and background, the band would be reasonably narrow.

FIGURE 25.3   **Security Market Line with Transaction Costs**

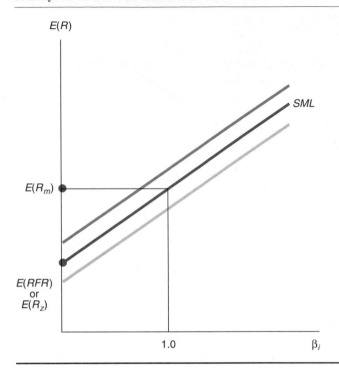

The impact of *planning periods* is similar. Recall that the CAPM is a one-period model, and the period employed should be the planning period for the individual investor. Thus, if you are using a one-year planning period, your CML and SML could differ from mine, which assumes a one-month planning period.

TAXES

The rates of return that we normally record and that were used throughout the model were pretax returns. In fact, the actual returns for most investors are affected as follows:

$$E(R_i)(AT) = \frac{(P_e - P_b) \times (1 - T_{cg}) + (Div) \times (1 - T_i)}{P_b}$$

where:

$R_i(AT)$ = **after-tax rate of return**
P_e = **ending price**
P_b = **beginning price**
Div = **dividend paid during period**
T_{cg} = **tax on capital gain or loss**
T_i = **tax on ordinary income**

Clearly, the tax rates differ between individuals and also institutions. Hence, for many institutions that do not pay taxes, the original pretax model is correctly specified—that is, T_{cg} and T_i take on values of zero. Alternatively, if investors have heavy tax burdens, this could cause major differences in the CML and SML among investors depending on their marginal tax rates.[5] Several recent studies have examined the effect of the differential taxes on dividends versus capital gains. Although most of the studies have indicated that this tax difference has had an impact, the evidence is not unanimous.[6] Obviously, the tax legislation in 1986 that equated the taxes on gains and on dividends could affect future results.

EMPIRICAL TESTS OF THE CAPM

When we discussed the assumptions of capital market theory, we pointed out that a theory should not be judged on the basis of its assumptions, but on *how well it explains the relationships that exist in the real world*. When testing the CAPM, two major questions should concern us. The first involves the stability of the measure of systematic risk (beta). Because beta is our principal risk measure, it is important to know whether past betas can be used as estimates of future betas. Also, what do we know about the published estimates of beta? The second question is basic to the theory: *Is there a positive linear relationship as hypothesized between beta and the rate of return on risky assets?* More specifically, how well do returns conform to the following SML equation:

$$E(R_i) = RFR + \beta_i(R_m - RFR)$$

Some specific questions might include

- Does the intercept approximate the *RFR* that prevailed during the period?
- Was the slope of the line positive? Was it consistent with the slope implied by the risk premium ($R_m - RFR$) that prevailed during the test period?

We will consider these two major questions in turn.

STABILITY OF BETA

Numerous studies have examined the stability of beta and generally reached similar conclusions. Levy examined weekly rates of return for 500 NYSE stocks on the NYSE and concluded that the risk measure was *not* stable for individual stocks over fairly short periods (52 weeks).[7] Alternatively, the stability of the beta for *portfolios* of stocks increased dramatically. Further, the larger the portfolio of stocks (e.g., 25 or 50 stocks) and the longer the period (over 26 weeks), the more stable the beta of the portfolio was. Specifically, the correlation of the betas for 50-stock portfolios over 26-week periods

---

[5] For a detailed consideration of this, see Fisher Black and Myron Scholes, "The Effects of Dividend Yield and Dividend Policy on Common Stock Prices and Returns," *Journal of Financial Economics* 1, no. 1 (March 1979): 1–22; and Robert Litzenberger and K. Ramaswamy, "The Effect of Personal Taxes and Dividends on Capital Asset Prices: Theory and Empirical Evidence," *Journal of Financial Economics* 7, no. 2 (June 1979): 163–196.

[6] Elton, Edwin, Martin Gruber, and Joel Rentzler, "A Single Examination of the Empirical Relationship Between Dividend Yields and Deviations from the CAPM," *Journal of Banking and Finance* 7, no. 1 (March 1983): 135–146; Roger Gordon and David Bradford, "Taxation and the Stock Market Valuation of Capital Gains and Dividends: Theory and Empirical Results," *Journal of Public Economics* 14, no. 4 (October 1980): 109–136; Merton Miller and Myron Scholes, "Dividends and Taxes: Some Empirical Evidence," *Journal of Political Economy* 90, no. 4 (December 1982): 1118–1141; and William Christie, "Dividend Yield and Expected Returns," *Journal of Financial Economics* 28, no. 1 (November-December 1990): 95–125.

[7] Robert A. Levy, "On the Short-Term Stationarity of Beta Coefficients," *Financial Analysts Journal* 27, no. 6 (November-December 1971): 55–62.

averaged above 0.91. Also, the betas tended to regress toward the mean. Specifically, high-beta portfolios tended to decline over time toward unity (1.00), whereas low-beta portfolios tended to increase over time toward unity. A study by Blume for the period 1926 to 1962 provided very similar results.[8]

Fielitz examined the impact of the number of randomly selected securities on the systematic risk of the portfolio and found substantial stability of risk with eight securities.[9] Porter and Ezzell examined the correlation of average betas over contingent periods and found no increase in the correlations as the average size of the portfolio increased.[10] Tole examined the standard deviation of the betas for portfolios of different sizes and concluded that there was substantially greater stability in beta as the portfolio size increased.[11] He also contended that the benefit of larger portfolios extends beyond 100 stocks in the portfolio.

Another factor that apparently affects the stability of beta is how many months are used to estimate the original beta and the test beta. Baesel found that the stability of the individual betas increased as the length of the estimation period increased.[12] Altman, Jacquillat, and Levasseur found similar results using French data.[13] Roenfeldt, Griepentrog, and Pflamm (RGP) examined the relationship between the length of the base period and the test period.[14] RGP compared betas derived from 48 months of data to subsequent betas for 12, 24, 36, and 48 months. The 48-month betas were not good for estimating subsequent 12-month betas, but were quite good for estimating 24-, 36-, and 48-month betas.

Theobald derived a set of analytical expressions that explained the Baesel empirical results and also partially explained the findings of Roenfeldt, Griepentrog, and Pflamm regarding the improved stability as the period was lengthened.[15] Theobald contended that the optimal length could be over 120 months assuming the beta did not shift during the period. Chen concluded that the *ordinary least square (OLS)* estimate of portfolio betas would be biased if individual betas were unstable, so he suggested a Bayesian approach to estimating these time-varying betas.[16]

Carpenter and Upton considered the influence of the trading volume on beta stability and found small differences in the betas derived.[17] They contended that the predictions

[8] Marshall E. Blume, "On the Assessment of Risk," *Journal of Finance* 26, no. 1 (March 1971): 1–10.

[9] Bruce Fielitz, "Indirect versus Direct Diversification," *Financial Management* 3, no. 4 (Winter 1974): 54–62.

[10] R. Burr Porter and John R. Ezzell, "A Note on the Predictive Ability of Beta Coefficients," *Journal of Business Research* 3, no. 4 (October 1975): 365–372.

[11] Thomas M. Tole, "How to Maximize Stationarity of Beta," *Journal of Portfolio Management* 7, no. 2 (Winter 1981): 45–49.

[12] Jerome B. Baesel, "On the Assessment of Risk: Some Further Considerations," *Journal of Finance* 29, no. 5 (December 1974): 1491–1494.

[13] Edward Altman, B. Jacquillat, and M. Levasseur, "Comparative Analysis of Risk Measures: France and the United States," *Journal of Finance* 29, no. 5 (December 1974): 1495–1511.

[14] Rodney L. Roenfeldt, Gary L. Griepentrog, and Christopher C. Pflamm, "Further Evidence on the Stationarity of Beta Coefficients," *Journal of Financial and Quantitative Analysis* 13, no. 1 (March 1978): 117–121.

[15] Michael Theobald, "Beta Stationarity and Estimation Period: Some Analytical Results," *Journal of Financial and Quantitative Analysis* 16, no. 5 (December 1981): 747–757.

[16] Son-Nan Chen, "Beta Nonstationarity, Portfolio Residual Risk, and Diversification," *Journal of Financial and Quantitative Analysis* 16, no. 1 (March 1981): 95–111.

[17] Michael D. Carpenter and David E. Upton, "Trading Volume and Beta Stability," *Journal of Portfolio Management* 7, no. 2 (Winter 1981): 60–64.

of betas were slightly better using the volume-adjusted betas. This impact of volume on beta estimates is related to the discussion in Chapter 6 on the small-firm effect that noted that the estimated beta for low-volume securities was biased downward.

To summarize, individual betas were generally volatile over time whereas portfolio betas were stable. Also, it is important to use at least 36 months of data to estimate beta and be conscious of volume.

COMPARABILITY OF PUBLISHED ESTIMATES OF BETA

In contrast to deriving your own estimate of beta for a stock, you may want to use a published source for speed or convenience, such as Merrill Lynch's *Security Risk Evaluation Report* (published monthly) and the *Value Line Investment Survey*. Although the methods of computation differ for these two estimates, both services use the following market model equation:

$$R_i = RFR + \beta_i R_m + E_t$$

Notably, they differ in the data employed. Specifically, Merrill Lynch estimates the beta using *60 monthly observations* and the S&P 500 as the market proxy, whereas the *Value Line* estimates beta using *260 weekly observations* and employs the NYSE composite series as the market proxy. They both use an adjustment process because of the regression tendencies, and their adjustment equations differ slightly.

Given these relatively minor differences, one would probably expect the published betas to be quite comparable. Statman examined the betas for 195 firms for a comparable five-year period and found the following relationship between the adjusted betas:[18]

Merrill Lynch Adjusted Beta = 0.127 + 0.879 Value Line Adjusted Beta

These results are not consistent with equality. Notably, the R^2 was only .55 and did not indicate any systematic bias in the differences. When he examined 19 portfolios of 10 stocks each, the coefficient of determination was almost the same as for individual stocks (.54 versus .55). These results imply a small but significant difference in beta estimates.

Reilly and Wright examined over 1,100 securities for three nonoverlapping periods and confirmed the difference in beta found by Statman.[19] They also indicated that the reason for the difference was the alternative time intervals (i.e., weekly versus monthly observations). Also, they found that the security's market value affected both the size and the direction of the interval effect. Therefore, when estimating beta or using a published source, you must consider the interval used and the firm's relative size.

---

[18] Meir Statman, "Betas Compared: Merrill Lynch vs. Value Line," *Journal of Portfolio Management* 7, no. 2 (Winter 1981): 41–44.

[19] Frank K. Reilly and David J. Wright, "A Comparison of Published Betas," *Journal of Portfolio Management* 14, no. 3 (Spring 1988): 64–69.

RELATIONSHIP
BETWEEN
SYSTEMATIC
RISK AND
RETURN

The ultimate question regarding the CAPM is whether it is useful in explaining the return on risky assets. Specifically, is there a positive linear relationship between the systematic risk and the rates of return on these risky assets? Sharpe and Cooper found a positive relationship between return and risk, although it was not completely linear (i.e., they found that the returns increased with risk class except for the highest risk classes, where the returns leveled off and declined slightly).[20]

Douglas examined the relationship by analyzing a systematic risk variable and a variance of return measure relative to return.[21] The results indicated intercepts that were larger than the prevailing risk-free rates. Further, although the coefficient for the total risk variable was generally significant, the coefficients for the systematic risk variables were typically *not* significant.

Miller and Scholes noted that the Douglas results could be caused by errors in measuring stock betas.[22] Unsystematic risk and betas are highly correlated, and the distribution of returns for the stocks were very skewed. These problems were not able to fully explain the Douglas results.

Because of the statistical problems with individual stocks, Black, Jensen, and Scholes examined the risk and return for portfolios of stocks and found a positive linear relationship between monthly excess return and portfolio beta, although the intercept was higher than the zero value expected.[23] Figure 25.4 contains some charts from this study, which reflect the following results: most of the measured SMLs had a positive slope, the slopes change between periods, the intercepts are not zero, and the slopes likewise change between periods.

Fama and MacBeth examined the relationship between the rates of return during a given month and betas, a beta-squared variable (to test for linearity), and a measure of unsystematic risk during the prior month.[24] Although the monthly results varied over time, the overall results supported the CAPM. The intercept was about equal to that implied by the *RFR*, the systematic risk coefficient was positive and significant, and neither of the coefficients for beta squared or unsystematic risk were significant.

EFFECT OF
SKEWNESS

Beyond the analysis of return and beta, several authors have also considered the impact of skewness on expected returns. You will recall from your statistics course that skewness reflects the presence of too many large positive or negative observations in a distribution. A normal distribution is referred to as symmetric, which means that there is balance between positive and negative observations. In contrast, if a return distribution has positive skewness, it means that there is an abnormal number of large positive price changes.

---

[20] William F. Sharpe and Guy M. Cooper, "Risk–Return Classes of New York Stock Exchange Common Stocks: 1931–1967," *Financial Analysts Journal* 28, no. 2 (March-April 1972): 46–54. A subsequent study that considered yield tilting portfolios confirmed many of these results. See William F. Sharpe and Howard B. Sosin, "Risk, Return, and Yield: New York Stock Exchange Common Stocks: 1928–1969," *Financial Analysts Journal* 32, no. 2 (March-April 1976): 33–42.

[21] G. W. Douglas, "Risk in the Equity Markets: An Empirical Appraisal of Market Efficiency," *Yale Economic Essays* 9, no. 1 (1969): 3–48.

[22] Merton H. Miller and Myron Scholes, "Rates of Return in Relation to Risk: A Re-Examination of Some Recent Findings," in *Studies in the Theory of Capital Markets,* edited by Michael Jensen (New York: Praeger, 1972).

[23] Fischer Black, Michael Jensen, and Myron Scholes, "The Capital Asset Pricing Model: Some Empirical Tests" in *Studies in the Theory of Capital Markets,* edited by Michael Jensen (New York: Praeger, 1972).

[24] Eugene Fama and R. MacBeth, "Risk, Return and Equilibrium: Empirical Tests," *Journal of Political Economy* 81, no. 2 (May-June 1973): 453–474.

FIGURE 25.4   **Average Excess Monthly Rates of Return Compared to Systematic Risk During Alternative Time Periods**

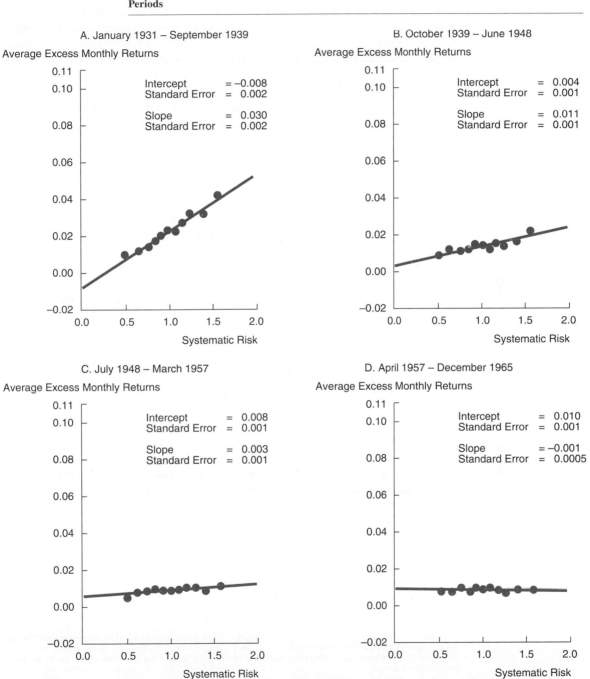

A. January 1931 – September 1939

Average Excess Monthly Returns

Intercept = −0.008
Standard Error = 0.002

Slope = 0.030
Standard Error = 0.002

Systematic Risk

B. October 1939 – June 1948

Average Excess Monthly Returns

Intercept = 0.004
Standard Error = 0.001

Slope = 0.011
Standard Error = 0.001

Systematic Risk

C. July 1948 – March 1957

Average Excess Monthly Returns

Intercept = 0.008
Standard Error = 0.001

Slope = 0.003
Standard Error = 0.001

Systematic Risk

D. April 1957 – December 1965

Average Excess Monthly Returns

Intercept = 0.010
Standard Error = 0.001

Slope = −0.001
Standard Error = 0.0005

Systematic Risk

Source: Fischer Black, Michael Jensen, and Myron Scholes, "The Capital Asset Pricing Model: Some Empirical Tests" in *Studies in the Theory of Capital Markets,* edited by Michael Jensen (New York: Praeger, 1972). Reprinted with permission.

Investigators considered skewness as a means to possibly explain the prior results wherein the model appeared to underprice low-beta stocks (so investors received returns above expectations) and overpriced high beta stocks (so investors received returns lower than expected). McEnally found results such as these, but also found that high-beta stocks had high positive skewness.[25] These results might be explained by investors who prefer stocks with high risk and high positive skewness that provide an opportunity for very large returns.

Kraus and Litzenberger examined this relationship more formally by testing a CAPM with a skewness term and found results that confirmed that investors are willing to pay for positive skewness.[26] They conclude that their three-moment CAPM corrects for the apparent mispricing of high- and low-risk stocks encountered with the standard CAPM. Subsequent testing of the model by Friend and Westerfield derived mixed results, but the importance of skewness was supported in studies by Sears and Wei and most recently by Lim.[27]

EFFECT OF SIZE, P/E, AND LEVERAGE

We know from our discussion in Chapter 6 dealing with the efficient markets hypothesis (EMH) that there has been extensive analysis of the size effect (the small-firm anomaly) and the P/E effect. Both of these variables were shown to have an inverse impact on returns after taking account of the CAPM. One could interpret these results as implying that these variables (size and P/E) are additional risk factors that need to be considered along with beta (similar to the skewness argument). Specifically, the reasoning would be that expected returns are a positive function of beta and a negative function of relative size, wherein investors require higher returns from relatively small firms. Investors would have a similar requirement for stocks with relatively low P/E ratios.

An analysis by Bhandari finds that financial leverage (measured by the debt/equity ratio) also helps explain the cross section of average returns even when both beta and size are considered.[28] This would imply a multivariate CAPM with three risk variables: beta, size, and financial leverage.

EFFECT OF BOOK-TO-MARKET VALUE: THE FAMA-FRENCH STUDY

The most recent study to examine the viability and usefulness of the CAPM is probably the most damaging not only because of the depth of the analysis, but also because one of the authors, Eugene Fama, has been a great supporter of the CAPM. The purpose of the study by Fama and French was to evaluate the joint roles of market beta, size, E/P, financial leverage, and the book-to-market equity ratio in the cross section of average returns on the NYSE, AMEX, and NASDAQ stocks.[29] Some of the earlier

[25] Richard McEnally, "A Note on the Return Behavior of High Risk Common Stocks," *Journal of Finance* 29, no. 2 (May 1974): 199–202.

[26] Alan Kraus and Robert Litzenberger, "Skewness Preference and the Valuation of Risky Assets," *Journal of Finance* 31, no. 4 (September 1976): 1085–1094.

[27] Irwin Friend and Randolph Westerfield, "Co-Skewness and Capital Asset Pricing," *Journal of Finance* 35, no. 4 (September 1980): 897–914; R. Stephen Sears and John Wei, "The Structure of Skewness Preferences in Asset Pricing Models with Higher Moments," *Financial Review* 23, no. 1 (February 1988): 25–38; and Kian-Guan Lim, "A New Test of the Three-Moment Capital Asset Pricing Model," *Journal of Financial and Quantitative Analysis* 24, no. 2 (June 1989): 205–216.

[28] Laxims Chand Bhandari, "Debt/Equity Ratio and Expected Common Stock Returns: Empirical Evidence," *Journal of Finance* 43, no. 2 (June, 1988): 507–528.

[29] Eugene F. Fama and Kenneth French, "The Cross Section of Expected Stock Returns," *Journal of Finance* 47, no. 2 (June 1992): 427–465.

studies (including Fama-MacBeth) had found a significant positive relationship between returns and beta. In contrast, this study finds that the relationship between beta and the average rate of return disappears during the more recent period 1963 to 1990, even when beta is used alone to explain average returns. In contrast, univariate tests between average returns and size, leverage, E/P, and book-to-market equity (BE/ME), indicate that all of these variables are significant and have the expected sign.

In the multivariate tests, the results contained in Table 25.1 show that the negative relationship between size and average returns is robust to the inclusion of other

TABLE 25.1

Average Slopes (*t*-Statistics) from Month-by-Month Regressions of Stock Returns on β, Size, Book-to-Market Equity, Leverage, and E/P: July 1963 to December 1990

Stocks are assigned the post-ranking β of the size-β portfolio they are in at the end of June of year t. BE is the book value of common equity plus balance-sheet deferred taxes, A is total book assets, and E is earnings (income before extraordinary items, plus income-statement deferred taxes, minus preferred dividends). BE, A, and E are for each firm's latest fiscal year ending in calendar year $t - 1$. The accounting ratios are measured using market equity ME in December of year $t - 1$. Firm size ln(ME) is measured in June of year t. In the regressions, these values of the explanatory variables for individual stocks are matched with returns from the CRSP tapes from the University of Chicago for the months from July of year t to June of year $t + 1$. The gap between the accounting data and the returns ensures that the accounting data are available prior to the returns. If earnings are positive, E(+)/P is the ratio of total earnings to market equity and E/P dummy is 0. If earnings are negative, E(+)/P is 0 and E/P dummy is 1.

The average slope is the time-series average of the monthly regression slopes for July 1963 to December 1990, and the *t*-statistic is the average slope divided by its time-series standard error.

On average, there are 2267 stocks in the monthly regressions. To avoid giving extreme observations heavy weight in the regressions, the smallest and largest 0.5% of the observations on E(+)/P, BE/ME, A/ME, and A/BE are set equal to the next largest or smallest values of the ratios (the 0.005 and 0.995 fractiles). This has no effect on inferences.

β	ln(ME)	ln(BE/ME)	ln(A/ME)	ln(A/BE)	E/P Dummy	E(+)/P
0.15 (0.46)						
	−0.15 (−2.58)					
−0.37 (−1.21)	−0.17 (−3.41)					
		0.50 (5.71)				
			0.50 (5.69)	−0.57 (−5.34)		
					0.57 (2.28)	4.72 (4.57)
	−0.11 (−1.99)	0.35 (4.44)				
	−0.11 (−2.06)		0.35 (4.32)	−0.50 (−4.56)		
	−0.16 (−3.06)				0.06 (0.38)	2.99 (3.04)
	−0.13 (−2.47)	0.33 (4.46)			−0.14 (−0.90)	0.87 (1.23)
	−0.13 (−2.47)		0.32 (4.28)	−0.46 (−4.45)	−0.08 (−0.56)	1.15 (1.57)

Source: Eugene F. Fama and Kenneth French, "The Cross Section of Expected Stock Returns," *Journal of Finance* 47, no. 2 (June 1992): 439. Reprinted by permission of the Journal of Finance.

TABLE 25.2   **Average Monthly Returns on Portfolios Formed on Size and Book-to-Market Equity; Stocks Sorted by ME (Down) and then BE/ME (Across): July 1963 to December 1990**

In June of each year t, the NYSE, AMEX, and NASDAQ stocks that meet the CRSP-COMPUSTAT data requirements are allocated to 10 size portfolios using the NYSE size (ME) breakpoints. The NYSE, AMEX, and NASDAQ stocks in each size decile are then sorted into 10 BE/ME portfolios using the book-to-market ratios for year $t - 1$. BE/ME is the book value of common equity plus balance-sheet deferred taxes for fiscal year $t - 1$, over market equity for December of year $t - 1$. The equal-weighted monthly portfolio returns are then calculated for July of year t to June of year $t + 1$.

Average monthly return is the time-series average of the monthly equal-weighted portfolio returns (in percent).

The All column shows average returns for equal-weighted size decile portfolios. The All row shows average returns for equal-weighted portfolios of the stocks in each BE/ME group.

Book-to-Market Portfolios

	All	Low	2	3	4	5	6	7	8	9	High
All	1.23	0.64	0.98	1.06	1.17	1.24	1.26	1.39	1.40	1.50	1.63
Small-ME	1.47	0.70	1.14	1.20	1.43	1.56	1.51	1.70	1.71	1.82	1.92
ME-2	1.22	0.43	1.05	0.96	1.19	1.33	1.19	1.58	1.28	1.43	1.79
ME-3	1.22	0.56	0.88	1.23	0.95	1.36	1.30	1.30	1.40	1.54	1.60
ME-4	1.19	0.39	0.72	1.06	1.36	1.13	1.21	1.34	1.59	1.51	1.47
ME-5	1.24	0.88	0.65	1.08	1.47	1.13	1.43	1.44	1.26	1.52	1.49
ME-6	1.15	0.70	0.98	1.14	1.23	0.94	1.27	1.19	1.19	1.24	1.50
ME-7	1.07	0.95	1.00	0.99	0.83	0.99	1.13	0.99	1.16	1.10	1.47
ME-8	1.08	0.66	1.13	0.91	0.95	0.99	1.01	1.15	1.05	1.29	1.55
ME-9	0.95	0.44	0.89	0.92	1.00	1.05	0.93	0.82	1.11	1.04	1.22
Large-ME	0.89	0.93	0.88	0.84	0.71	0.79	0.83	0.81	0.96	0.97	1.18

Source: Eugene F. Fama and Kenneth French, "The Cross Section of Expected Stock Returns," *Journal of Finance* 47, no. 2 (June 1992): 446. Reprinted by permission of the Journal of Finance.

variables. Further, the positive relation between BE/ME and average returns also persists when the other variables are included. Interestingly, when both of these variables are included the book-to-market value ratio (BE/ME) has the consistently stronger role in explaining average returns. The joint effect of size and BE/ME are shown in Table 25.2. The top row shows the univariate results and confirms the positive relationship between return versus the book-to-market ratio. The left-hand column shows the negative relationship between return and size. The body of the table shows that even within a size class, the returns increase with the BE/ME ratio. Similarly, within a BE/ME decile, there is generally a negative relationship for size. Hence, it is not surprising that the single highest average return is in the upper, right-hand corner (1.92), which is the portfolio with the smallest size, highest BE/ME stocks.

The authors conclude that for the period 1963 to 1990 size and book-to-market equity capture the cross-sectional variation in average stock returns associated with size, E/P, book-to-market equity, and leverage. Moreover, of the two variables, the book-to-market equity seems to be the more powerful and appears to subsume E/P and leverage.[30]

---

[30] A prior study that documented the importance of the BE/ME ratio was Barr Rosenberg, Kenneth Reid, and Ronald Lanstein, "Persuasive Evidence of Market Inefficiency," *Journal of Portfolio Management* 11, no. 3 (Spring 1985): 9–17. The relationship was confirmed in the Japanese market in Louis K. Chan, Yasusho Hamao, and Josef Lakonisok, "Fundamentals and Stock Returns in Japan," *Journal of Finance* 46, no. 5 (December 1991): 1739–1764.

SUMMARY OF
CAPM RISK–
RETURN
EMPIRICAL
RESULTS

Most of the early evidence regarding the relationship between rates of return and systematic risk for portfolios indicated support for the CAPM. Still, the evidence was not without question because it was found that the intercepts were generally higher than implied by the *RFR* that prevailed, which is either consistent with a zero-beta model or the existence of higher borrowing rates. In a search for other variables that could explain the above-expected return for low-beta stocks and the below-expected returns for high-beta stocks, additional variables were considered. Several studies indicated support for including the third moment of the distribution (skewness) as a variable, with the understanding that investors preferred positive skewness and were willing to accept lower average rates of return for the opportunity for very large returns, and positive skewness and high betas were correlated.

The efficient markets literature has provided extensive evidence that both size and the P/E ratio were also variables that could help explain cross-sectional returns in addition to beta. More recently studies have also found that financial leverage and the book-to-market value of equity ratio has explanatory power as related to returns beyond beta.

A recent study is most damaging because it considers most of the other variables suggested and concludes that during the recent period 1963 to 1990, beta was not related to average returns on stocks when included with other variables, but was not even significant when considered alone. Moreover, the two variables that were dominant were size and the book value to market value ratio, which was even stronger than size although both variables were significant.

THE MARKET
PORTFOLIO:
THEORY VERSUS
PRACTICE

Throughout our presentation of the CAPM, we noted that the market portfolio included *all* the risky assets in the economy. Further, in equilibrium, the various assets would be included in the portfolio in the proportion of their market value. Therefore, this market portfolio should contain not only stocks and bonds, but also real estate, options, art, stamps, coins, foreign stocks and bonds, and so on, with weights equal to their relative market value.

Although this concept of a market portfolio is reasonable in theory, it is difficult, if not impossible, to implement when testing or using the CAPM. The easy part is getting a stock series for the NYSE, the AMEX, and major world stock exchanges, such as Tokyo, London, and Germany. There are stock series for the OTC market, too, but these series are generally incomplete. Also, as noted in Chapter 4, there is a growing number of world stock indexes. There are also some well-regarded U.S. bond series available (e.g., from Merrill Lynch, Salomon Brothers, and Lehman Brothers) and also several world bond series (e.g., from J.P. Morgan, Salomon Brothers, and Merrill Lynch). Because of the difficulty in deriving series that are available monthly in a timely fashion for the numerous other assets mentioned, most studies have limited themselves to using a stock or bond series alone. In fact, the vast majority of studies have chosen the S&P 500 series or some other NYSE stock series that is obviously limited to only U.S. stocks, which constitutes less than 20 percent of a truly global risky asset portfolio. At best, it was assumed that the particular series used was highly correlated with the true market portfolio.

Most academicians recognized this potential problem, but they assumed that the deficiency was not serious. Several articles by Roll, however, concluded that, on the

FIGURE 25.5   **Differential Performance Based on an Error in Estimating Systematic Risk**

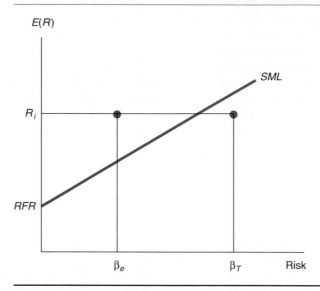

contrary, the use of these indexes as a proxy for the market portfolio had very serious implications for tests of the model and especially for using the model when evaluating portfolio performance.[31] Roll referred to it as a *benchmark error*, because the practice is to compare the performance of a portfolio manager to the return of an unmanaged portfolio of equal risk—that is, the market portfolio adjusted for risk would be the benchmark. Roll's point is that if the benchmark is mistakenly specified, you cannot measure the performance of portfolio managers properly. A mistakenly specified market portfolio can have two effects. First, the beta computed for alternative portfolios would be wrong because the market portfolio used to compute the portfolio's systematic risk is inappropriate. Second, the SML derived would be wrong because it goes from the *RFR* through the improperly specified *M* portfolio. Figure 25.5 shows an example where the true portfolio risk (β_T) is underestimated (β_e), possibly because of the proxy market portfolio used in computing the estimated beta. As shown, the portfolio being evaluated may appear to be above the SML using β_e which would imply superior management. If, in fact, the true risk (β_T) is greater, the portfolio will shift to the right and be below the SML, which would indicate inferior performance.

Figure 25.6 indicates that the intercept and slope will differ if (1) there is an error in selecting a proper risk-free asset and (2) if the market portfolio selected is not the correct mean-variance efficient portfolio. Obviously, it is very possible that, under these

[31] Richard Roll, "A Critique of the Asset Pricing Theory's Tests," *Journal of Financial Economics* 4, no. 4 (March 1977): 129–176; Richard Roll, "Ambiguity when Performance Is Measured by the Securities Market Line," *Journal of Finance* 33, no. 4 (September 1978): 1051–1069; Richard Roll, "Performance Evaluation and Benchmark Error I," Journal of Portfolio Management 6, no. 4 (Summer 1980): 5–12; and Richard Roll, "Performance Evaluation and Benchmark Error II," *Journal of Portfolio Management* 7, no. 2 (Winter 1981): 17–22. This discussion draws heavily from these articles.

FIGURE 25.6

Differential SML Based on Measured Risk-Free Asset and Proxy Market Portfolio

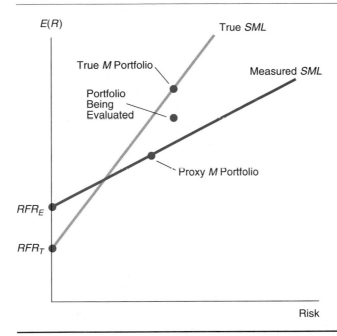

conditions, a portfolio judged to be superior relative to the first SML (i.e., it plotted above the measured SML), could be inferior relative to the true SML (i.e., it would plot below the true SML).

Roll contends that a test of the CAPM requires an analysis of whether the proxy used to represent the market portfolio is mean-variance efficient (on the Markowitz efficient frontier), and whether it is the true optimum market portfolio. Roll showed that, if the proxy market portfolio (e.g., the S&P 500 index) is mean-variance efficient, it is mathematically possible to show a linear relationship between returns and betas derived with this portfolio. Unfortunately, this is not a true test of the CAPM, because you are not working with the true SML (see Figure 25.7).[32]

In summary, the concern is that an incorrect market proxy will affect the beta risk measures, as well as the position and slope of the SML that is used to evaluate portfolio performance. In general, the errors will tend to overestimate the performance of portfolio managers, because the proxy used for the market portfolio is probably not as efficient as the true market portfolio, so the slope of the SML will be underestimated.

Roll's benchmark problems, however, do not invalidate the value of the CAPM as *a normative model of asset pricing;* they only indicate a problem in *measurement* when

---

[32] A demonstration of the effect of going from a U.S. equity benchmark to a world equity benchmark is contained in Frank K. Reilly and Rashid A. Akhtar, "A Demonstration of the Effect of the Benchmark Error Problem," University of Notre Dame Working Paper (June 1993). Some of the results were included in Chapter 8.

FIGURE 25.7   **Differential SML Using Market Proxy That Is Mean-Variance Efficient**

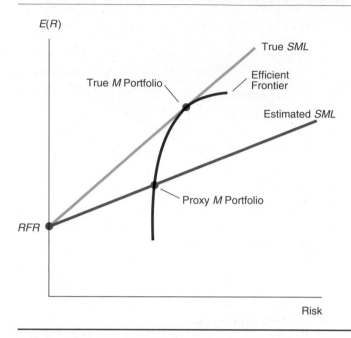

attempting to test the theory and when using this model for evaluating portfolio performance. Therefore, it is necessary to develop a better market portfolio proxy and/or adjust the portfolio performance measures to reflect this measurement problem (see Chapter 26).

ARBITRAGE PRICING THEORY (APT)

At this point we have discussed the basic theory of the CAPM, the impact of changing some of its major assumptions, the empirical evidence that does and does not support the theory, and its dependence on a market portfolio of all risky assets. In addition, the model assumes that investors have quadratic utility functions and that the distribution of security prices is normal (symmetrically distributed), with a variance term that can be estimated.

The tests of the CAPM indicated that the beta coefficients for individual securities were not stable, but the portfolio betas generally were stable assuming long enough sample periods and adequate trading volume. There was mixed support for a positive linear relationship between rates of return and systematic risk for portfolios of stock, with most of the recent evidence indicating the need to consider additional risk variables or a need for different risk proxies. In addition, several papers by Roll criticized the tests of the model and the usefulness of the model in portfolio evaluation because of its dependence on a market portfolio of risky assets that is not currently available.

Consequently, the academic community has considered an alternative asset pricing theory that is reasonably intuitive and also requires only limited assumptions. This *arbitrage pricing theory (APT)*, developed by Ross in the early 1970s and initially published in 1976, has three major assumptions:[33]

1. Capital markets are perfectly competitive.
2. Investors always prefer more wealth to less wealth with certainty.
3. The stochastic process generating asset returns can be expressed as a linear function of a set of K factors or indexes (to be described).

Equally important, the following major assumptions are *not* required: (1) quadratic utility function, (2) normally distributed security returns, and (3) a market portfolio that contains all risky assets and is mean-variance efficient. Obviously, if such a theory is able to explain differential security prices, it would be considered a superior theory to the CAPM because it is simpler (i.e., it requires fewer assumptions). Prior to discussing the empirical tests of the model, we will provide a brief review of the basics of the model. The following review of the APT model is very similar to the discussion in Chapter 8. It is repeated here for the reader's convenience.

As noted, the theory assumes that the stochastic process generating asset returns can be represented as a K factor model of the form

$$R_i = E_i + b_i \delta_i + b_{i2} \delta_2 + \ldots + b_{ik} \delta_k + \epsilon_i \text{ for } i = 1 \text{ to } N$$

where:

R_i = return on asset i during a specified time period, $i = 1, 2, 3, \ldots m$

E_i = expected return for asset i if all of the factors or indexes have zero changes

b_{ik} = reaction in asset i's returns to movements in the common factor K or index K.

δ_k = a set of common factors or indexes with a zero mean that influences the returns on all assets

ϵ_i = a unique effect on asset i's return (i.e., a random error term that, by assumption, is completely diversifiable in large portfolios and has a mean of zero)

N = number of assets

Two terms require elaboration: δ_k and b. As indicated, δ terms are the *multiple* factors expected to have an impact on the returns of *all* assets. Examples of these factors might include inflation, growth in GNP, major political upheavals, or changes in interest rates. The APT contends that there are many such factors that affect returns, in contrast to the CAPM, where the only relevant risk variable is the covariance of the asset with the market portfolio.

Given these common factors, the b_{ik} terms determine how each asset reacts to a particular common factor. To extend the earlier example, although all assets may be affected by growth in GNP, the impact (i.e., reaction) to a factor will differ. For example, stocks of cyclical firms will have larger b_{ik} terms for the "growth in GNP" factor than noncyclical firms, such as grocery chains. Likewise, you will hear discussions about

---

[33] Stephen Ross, "The Arbitrage Theory of Capital Asset Pricing," *Journal of Economic Theory* 13, no. 2 (December 1976): 341–360; Stephen Ross, "Return, Risk, and Arbitrage," in *Risk and Return in Finance,* edited by I. Friend and J. Bicksler (Cambridge: Ballinger, 1977), 189–218.

interest-sensitive stocks. All stocks are affected by changes in interest rates, but some stocks experience larger impacts. For example, an interest-sensitive stock would have a b_k for interest of 2.0 or more, whereas a stock that is relatively insensitive to interest rates would have a b_k of 0.5. Other examples of common factors include inflation, exchange rates, and interest rate spreads. Notably, when we apply the theory, *the factors are not identified.* That is, when we discuss the empirical studies, the investigators will note that they have found three, four, or five factors that affect security returns, but *they will give no indication of what these factors represent.*

Similar to the CAPM model, it is assumed that the unique effects (E_i) are independent and will be diversified away in a large portfolio. The APT assumes that, in equilibrium, the return on a zero-investment, zero-systematic-risk portfolio is zero when the unique effects are diversified away. This assumption and some theory from linear algebra implies that the expected return on any asset i (E_i) can be expressed as

$$E_0 = \lambda_0 + \lambda_1 b_{i1} + \lambda_2 b_{i2} + \ldots + \lambda_k b_{ik},$$

where:

λ_0 = the expected return on an asset with zero systematic risk where $\lambda_0 = E_0$

λ_1 = the risk premium related to each of the common factors—for example, the risk premium related to interest rate risk factor ($\lambda_i = E_i - E_0$)

b_i = the pricing relationship between the risk premium and asset i—that is, how responsive asset i is to this common factor K

For example, if we assume that the risk premium related to interest rate sensitivity is .02 and a stock that is sensitive to interest rates have a β_k, (where K is interest rate sensitivity) of 2.0, this means that this factor would cause the stocks expected return to increase by 4 percent ($K = 2.0 \times .02$). Consider the following example of two stocks and a two-factor model.

K_1 = changes in the rate of inflation. The risk premium related to this factor is 1 percent for every 1 percent change in the rate ($\lambda_2 = .01$).

K_2 = percent growth in real GNP. The average risk premium related to this factor is 2 percent for every 1 percent change in the rate of growth ($\lambda_2 = 0.02$).

λ_o = the rate of return on a zero-systematic risk asset (zero beta: $b_{oj} = 0$) is 3 percent ($\lambda_o = .03$).

The two assets (X, Y) have the following response coefficients to these factors:

b_{x1} = the response of asset X to changes in the rate of inflation is 0.50 ($b_{x1} = .50$). This asset is not very responsive to changes in the rate of inflation.

b_{y1} = the response of asset Y to changes in the rate of inflation is 2.00 ($b_{y1} = 2.00$).

b_{x2} = the response of asset X to changes in the growth rate of real GNP is 1.50 ($b_{x2} = 1.50$).

b_{y2} = the response of asset Y to changes in the growth rate of real GNP is 1.75 ($b_{y2} = 1.75$).

These response coefficients indicate that if these are the major factors influencing asset returns, asset Y is a higher risk asset, and therefore, its expected return should be greater. The overall expected return equation will bc

$$E_i = \lambda_0 + \lambda_1 b_{i1} + \lambda_2 b_{i2}$$
$$= .03 + (.01)b_{i1} + (.02)b_{i2}$$

Therefore:

$$E_x = .03 + (.01)(0.50) + (.02)(1.50)$$
$$= .065 = 6.5\%$$
$$E_y = .03 + (.01)(2.00) + (.02)(1.75)$$
$$= .085 = 8.5\%$$

If the prices of the assets do not reflect these expected returns, we would expect investors to enter into arbitrage arrangements whereby they would sell overpriced assets short and use the proceeds to purchase the underpriced assets until the relevant prices were corrected. The point is, given these linear relationships, it should be possible to find an asset or a combination of assets with equal risk to the mispriced asset, yet provide a higher expected return.

EMPIRICAL TESTS
OF THE APT

Although the APT is relatively new (any academic theory less than twenty years old is considered new), it has undergone numerous empirical studies. Before we begin discussing the empirical tests, remember the earlier caveat that when applying the theory, we do not know what the factors generated by the statistical model represent. This becomes a major point in some discussions of test results.

ROLL-ROSS STUDY

The Roll and Ross test followed a two-step procedure:[34]

1. Estimate the expected returns and the factor coefficients from time-series data on individual asset returns.
2. Use these estimates to test the basic cross-sectional pricing conclusion implied by the APT. Specifically, are the expected returns for these assets consistent with the common factors derived in Step 1?

Roll and Ross tested the following pricing relationship:

H_0: There exist nonzero constants $(E_0, \lambda_i, \ldots \lambda_k)$ such that
$$E_1 - E_0 = \lambda_1 b_{i1} + \lambda_2 b_{i2} + \ldots + \lambda_k b_{ik}.$$

The specific b_i coefficients were estimated using factor analysis. The authors pointed out that the estimation procedure was generally appropriate for the model involved, but there is very little known about the small sample properties of the results. Therefore, they emphasized the tentative nature of the conclusions.

The data file was daily returns for the period July 1962 through December 1972. Stocks were put into 42 portfolios of 30 stocks each (1,260 stocks) by alphabetical order. The estimation of the factor model indicated that the maximum reasonable number of factors was five. The factors derived were applied to all 42 portfolios, with

---

[34] Richard Roll and Stephen A. Ross, "An Empirical Investigation of the Arbitrage Pricing Theory," *Journal of Finance* 35, no. 5 (December 1980): 1073–1103.

the understanding that the importance of the various factors might differ among port-folios (e.g., the first factor in Portfolio A might not be first in Portfolio B).

Assuming a risk-free rate of 6 percent ($\lambda_0 = .06$), the subsequent analysis indicated that there were at least three important pricing factors, but probably not more than four. Further, the weight on the first two factors was quite heavy with changes in relative weights for the remaining three factors. When they allowed the model to estimate the risk-free rate (λ_0), only two factors were consistently significant, which indicated that the earlier estimate of three factors may have been an overestimate.

A subsequent test examined an alternative specification that related returns to a security's own variance, which should not affect expected return if the APT is valid, because a security's diversifiable component would be eliminated by diversification, and the nondiversifiable components should be explained by the factor loadings. The test analyzed returns against the five factors plus the security's own standard deviation. The initial results indicated that the security's own standard deviation was statistically significant, which was evidence against the APT. Subsequently, when they adjusted the results for skewness, they found that the security's own standard deviation was insignificant, which supports the APT.

Finally, they tested whether the three or four factors that affect Group A were the same as the factors that affect Group B. The analysis involved testing for cross-sectional consistency by examining whether the λ_0 terms for the 42 groups are similar. The results yielded no evidence that the intercept terms were different, although the test was admittedly weak. The authors concluded that the evidence generally supported the APT, but acknowledged that these initial tests were weak.

EXTENSIONS OF THE ROLL-ROSS TESTS

Cho, Elton, and Gruber tested the model by examining the number of factors in the return-generating process that were priced.[35] Because the APT model contends that more factors affect stock returns than are implied by the CAPM, they examined different sets of data to determine what happened to the number of factors priced in the model compared to prior studies that found between three and five significant factors. They simulated returns using the zero-beta CAPM with betas derived from Wilshire's fundamental betas and with betas derived from historical data. They found that five factors were required using the Roll-Ross procedures. The results using historical betas implied six factors were necessary, whereas the Wilshire fundamental betas indicated a need for three factors.

The authors concluded that even when returns are generated by a two-factor model, two or three factors are required to explain the returns. These results would support using the APT model because it allows for the consideration of these additional factors, which is not possible with the classical CAPM.

Dhrymes, Friend, and Gultekin (DFG) reexamined the techniques used in prior studies and contended that these techniques have several major limitations.[36] Although the division of the total sample of stocks into numerous portfolios of 30 stocks was

---

[35] D. Chinhyung Cho, Edwin J. Elton, and Martin J. Gruber, "On the Robustness of the Roll and Ross Arbitrage Pricing Theory," *Journal of Financial and Quantitative Analysis* 19, no. 1 (March 1984): 1–10.

[36] Phoebus J. Dhrymes, Irwin Friend, and N. Bulent Gultekin, "A Critical Re-Examination of the Empirical Evidence on the Arbitrage Pricing Theory," *Journal of Finance* 39, no. 2 (June 1984): 323–346.

necessary because of computer limitations, this practical constraint produced results that differed from large sample results, especially for the total sample of over 1,000 stocks. Specifically, they found *no* relationship between the "factor loading" for groups of 30 stocks and a group of 240 stocks.

DFG also noted that it is not possible to identify the actual number of factors that characterize the return-generating process. Applying the model to portfolios of different size indicated that the number of factors changed. For example, for 15 securities it is a two-factor model; for 30 securities, a three-factor model; for 45, a four-factor model; for 60, a six-factor model; and for 90, a nine-factor model. Also, with multiple factors it was difficult to know which of them were significant in explaining the returns.

Roll and Ross acknowledged that the factors differ with 30 stocks versus 240, but contended that the important consideration is whether the resulting estimates are *consistent*, because it is not feasible to consider all of the stocks together.[37] When they tested for consistency it was generally supported.

They point out that the number of factors is a secondary issue compared to how well the model explains the return-generating process compared to alternative models. Also, one would *expect* the number of factors to increase with the sample size, because more potential relationships would arise (e.g., you would introduce industry effects). The relevant question is, how many are significant in a diversified portfolio?

Dhrymes, Friend, Gultekin, and Gultekin repeated the prior tests for larger groups of securities.[38] They found that when they increased the number of securities in each group (30, 60, and 90 securities), both the number of factors that entered the model and the number of significant ("priced") factors increased, although most factors are not "priced." These results confirmed the DFG results. In addition, they found that the unique or total standard deviation for a period was as good at predicting returns in a subsequent period as the factor loadings. Also, the number of time-series observations affected the number of factors discovered. Finally, the number of observations and the group size of securities affected the model's intercept. These findings are not favorable to the empirical relevance of APT, because they indicate extreme instability in the relationships and suggest that the risk-free rate implied by the model depends on group size and the number of observations. Also the relative usefulness of the total standard deviation is discouraging.

THE APT AND ANOMALIES

An alternative set of tests of the APT is how well it explains anomalies that are not explained by a competing model. Two anomalies considered are the small-firm effect and the January anomaly.

Reinganum addressed the APT's ability to account for the differences in average returns between small firms and large firms.[39] Reinganum contended that this anomaly, which could not be explained by the CAPM, should be explained by the APT if the APT was to be considered a superior theory or an empirical replacement for the CAPM.

---

[37] Richard Roll and Stephen Ross, "A Critical Re-Examination of the Empirical Evidence on the Arbitrage Pricing Theory: A Reply," *Journal of Finance* 39, no. 2 (June 1984): 347–350.

[38] Phoebus J. Dhrymes, Irwin Friend, Mustofa N. Gultekin, and N. Bulent Gultekin, "New Tests of the APT and Their Implications," *Journal of Finance* 40, no. 3 (July 1985): 659–674.

[39] Marc R. Reinganum, "The Arbitrage Pricing Theory: Some Empirical Results," *Journal of Finance* 36, no. 2 (May 1981): 313–321.

Reinganum's test is conducted in two stages:

1. During Year Y-1, factor loadings are estimated for all securities, and securities with similar factor loadings are put into common control portfolios that should have similar risk characteristics. (The author tests models with three, four, and five factors.) During Year Y, excess security returns are derived for each control portfolio from the daily returns of the individual stocks in the portfolio. Assuming that all stocks within a control portfolio have equal risk according to the APT, they should have similar average returns and the average excess returns should be zero.

2. Given the excess returns during Year Y, all the stocks were ranked on the basis of their market value at the end of Year Y-1, and the excess returns of the firms in the bottom 10 percent of the size distribution were combined (equal weights) to form the average excess returns for Portfolio MV1. Similarly, nine other portfolios were formed, with MV10 containing excess returns for the largest firms.

Under the null hypothesis, the ten portfolios should possess identical average excess returns and these excess returns should be insignificantly different from zero. If the ten portfolios do not have identical average excess returns, this evidence would be inconsistent with the APT.

The ranking procedure described in Step 2 was done annually because the market values change, and firms are added and deleted. As stated, the APT would be supported if the average excess returns for the ten portfolios equaled zero.

The test results were *clearly inconsistent with the APT.* Specifically, the average excess returns of the ten portfolios were not equal to zero for either a three-, four-, or five-factor model. The small-firm portfolio, MV1, experienced a positive and statistically significant average excess return, whereas Portfolio MV10 had a statistically significant negative average excess return. The mean difference in excess returns between the small and large firms was about 25 percent a year. Also, the mean excess returns of MV1 through MV10 were perfectly inversely ordered with firm size.

Reinganum also tested for significant differences between individual portfolio returns and the difference between the high and low portfolio each year. Both tests confirmed that the low-market-value portfolios outperformed the high-market-value portfolios regardless of whether excess returns were derived from the three-, four-, or five-factor model. The author concluded that these results did not support the APT, but he acknowledged that the analysis involved a joint test of several hypotheses implicit in the theory and that it was not possible to pinpoint the error.

A subsequent study by Chen supported the APT model compared to the CAPM and provided evidence related to the small-firm effect that was contrary to Reinganum.[40] Prior to discussing the tests, the author contended that problems caused by the need for a limited sample and the existence of multiple factors were related to the *testing* of the theory and should not reflect on the theory itself. The analysis employed 180 stocks and five factors. A comparison of the cross-sectional results indicated that the first factor was highly correlated with beta. Chen's test of the two models for

---

[40] Nai-fu Chen, "Some Empirical Tests of the Theory of Arbitrage Pricing," *Journal of Finance* 38, no. 5 (December 1983): 1393–1414.

performance measurement was based on the contention that if the CAPM does not capture all the information related to returns, this remaining information will be in the residual series. In turn, if the APT can provide factors to explain these residual returns, it would be superior. He concluded that the CAPM was misspecified and that the missing price information was picked up by the APT.

The final tests examined whether some major variables have explanatory power after the factor loadings from the APT model. If so, it would cause one to reject the APT. The two variables considered based on prior CAPM studies were a stock's own variance and firm size. The results of the own-variance test supported the APT because a stock's own variance had no explanatory power net of factor loadings. Similarly, the results of tests of firm size indicated that firm size had no explanatory power after adjusting for risk based on factor loadings. Again, these results are in contrast to the earlier results by Reinganum.

APT AND THE JANUARY EFFECT

Given the January anomaly wherein returns in January are significantly larger than in any other month, Gultekin and Gultekin tested the ability of the APT model to adjust for this anomaly.[41] The APT model was estimated for each month and risk premia were *always* significant in January, but rarely priced in other months. It was concluded that the APT model, like the CAPM, can explain the risk–return relation only in January, which indicates that the APT model does not explain this anomaly any better than the CAPM.

Burmeister and McElroy estimated a linear factor model (LFM), the APT, and a CAPM.[42] They found a significant January effect that was not captured by any of the models. When they went beyond the January effect, however, they rejected the CAPM in favor of the APT.

THE APT AND INFLATION

A paper by Elton, Gruber, and Rentzler extended the APT to consider the impact of inflation on asset returns.[43] After deriving an equilibrium model of real returns, they assumed the inflation factor was not priced, so employed the APT model, and compared the results to prior inflation-adjusted CAPM models. They contended that it was important to develop APT models with statistically identifiable factors that had economic meaning such as inflation and growth in real GNP.

THE SHANKEN
CHALLENGE TO
TESTABILITY OF
THE APT

Similar to Roll's critique of the CAPM, a set of papers by Shanken challenged whether the APT can be empirically verified.[44] Rather than questioning specific tests or methods, Shanken questioned whether the APT is more susceptible to testing than the CAPM based on the usual empirical test that determines whether asset returns conform

[41] Mustofa N. Gultekin and N. Bulent Gultekin, "Stock Return Anomalies and the Tests of APT," *Journal of Finance* 42, no. 5 (December 1987): 1213–1224.

[42] Edwin Burmeister and Marjorie B. McElroy, "Joint Estimation of Factor Sensitivities and Risk Premia for the Arbitrage Pricing Theory," *Journal of Finance* 43, no. 3 (July 1988): 721–733.

[43] Edwin Elton, Martin Gruber, and Joel Rentzler, "The Arbitrage Pricing Model and Returns on Assets under Uncertain Inflation," *Journal of Finance* 38, no. 2 (May 1983): 525–537.

[44] Jay Shanken, "The Arbitrage Pricing Theory: Is It Testable?" *Journal of Finance* 37, no. 5 (December 1982): 1129–1140.

to a K factor model. A problem is, if returns are not explained by such a model, it is not considered a rejection of the model; however, if the factors do explain returns, it is considered support. Also, it is contended that APT has no advantage because the factors need not be observable, which means that equivalent sets of securities may conform to different factor structures. Therefore, the empirical formulation of the APT may yield different implications regarding the expected returns for a given set of securities. Unfortunately, this implies that the theory cannot explain differential returns between securities, because it cannot identify the relevant factor structure that explains the differential returns. This need to identify the relevant factor structure that affects asset returns is similar to the CAPM benchmark problem. In summary, before you can test the CAPM you must identify and use the true market portfolio, whereas you must identify the relevant factor structure that affects security returns before you can test the APT.

Dybvig and Ross replied by suggesting that the APT is testable as an equality rather than the "empirical APT" proposed by Shanken.[45] Shanken responded that what has developed is a set of equilibrium APT pricing models that are testable, but the original arbitrage based models ("APT") are not testable as originally specified.[46]

ALTERNATIVE TESTING TECHNIQUES

Beyond these articles that were concerned with prior tests, several articles have proposed other statistical techniques for testing the APT model. Jobson proposes that the APT be tested using a multivariate linear regression model.[47] Brown and Weinstein propose an approach to estimating and testing asset pricing models employing a bilinear paradigm.[48] A number of subsequent papers have proposed new or improved methodologies for testing the APT.[49]

SUMMARY

When we relax several of the major assumptions of the CAPM, the required modifications are reasonably minor and do not change the overall concept of the model. Empirical studies have indicated stable portfolio betas, especially when enough observations were used to derive the betas and there was adequate volume. Although most of the early tests confirmed the expected relationship between returns and systematic risk, with allowance for the zero-beta model, several more recent studies have indicated

---

[45] Philip H. Dybvig and Stephen A. Ross, "Yes, the APT is Testable," *Journal of Finance* 40, no. 4 (September 1985): 1173–1188.

[46] Jay Shanken, "Multi-Beta CAPM or Equilibrium APT?: A Reply," *Journal of Finance*, 40 no. 4 (September 1985): 1189–1196.

[47] J. D. Jobson, "A Multivariate Linear Regression Test for the Arbitrage Pricing Theory," *Journal of Finance* 37, no. 4 (September 1982): 1037–1042.

[48] Stephen J. Brown and Mark I. Weinstein, "A New Approach to Testing Asset Pricing Models: The Bilinear Paradigm," *Journal of Finance* 38, no. 3 (June 1983): 711–743.

[49] Among the papers are Chinhyang Cho, "On Testing the Arbitrage Pricing Theory: Inter-Battery Factor Analysis," *Journal of Finance* 39, no. 5 (December 1984): 1485–1502; Gregory Connor and Robert Korajczyk, "Risk and Return in an Equilibrium APT: Applications of a New Test Methodology," *Journal of Financial Economics* 21, no. 2 (September 1988): 255–290; Robert McCulloch and Peter Rossi, "Posterior, Predictive, and Utility-Based Approaches to Testing the Arbitrage Pricing Theory," *Journal of Financial Economics* 28, no. 1 and 2 (November-December 1990): 7–38; Ravi Shakla and Charles Trzcinka, "Sequential Tests of the Arbitrage Pricing Theory: A Comparison of Principle Components and Maximum Likelihood Factors," *Journal of Finance* 45, no. 5 (December 1990): 1541–1564; and Punect Handa and Scott C. Linn, "Arbitrage Pricing with Estimation Risk," *Journal of Financial and Quantitative Analysis* 28, no. 1 (March 1993): 81–100.

that the univariate beta model needed to be supplemented with additional variables that considered skewness, size, P/E, leverage, and the book value/market value ratio. The most recent study by Fama and French went beyond supplementing beta and contended that during the period 1963 to 1990 that beta was not relevant by itself or when supplemented. In their study the most significant variables were book-to-market value (BE/ME) and size.

Another problem has been raised by Roll who contends that it is not possible to empirically derive a true market portfolio, so it is not possible to test the CAPM model properly or to use the model to evaluate portfolio performance.

Ross subsequently devised an alternative asset pricing model (the APT) with fewer assumptions that does not require a market portfolio. The results from the empirical tests of the APT have thus far been mixed. Also, Shanken contends that the nature of many of the tests are such that it is impossible to reject the theory.

In conclusion, it is probably safe to assume that both the CAPM and APT will continue to be used to price capital assets. Coincident with their use will be further empirical tests of both theories, the ultimate goal being to determine which theory does the best job of explaining current and future returns. Notably, the APT model requires fewer assumptions and considers multiple factors to explain the risk of an asset, in contrast to the single-factor CAPM.[50]

QUESTIONS

1. In the empirical testing of the CAPM, what are two major questions of concern? Why are they important?

2. Briefly discuss why it is important for beta coefficients to be stationary over time.

3. Discuss the empirical results relative to beta stability for individual stocks and portfolios of stocks.

4. Why is the stability of beta for portfolios of stocks considered more relevant than that of individual stocks?

5. In the tests of the relationship between systematic risk (beta) and return, what are you looking for?

6. Draw an ideal SML. Based on the early empirical results, what did the actual risk–return relationship look like relative to the ideal relationship implied by the CAPM?

7. According to the CAPM, what assets are included in the market portfolio, and what are the relative weightings? In empirical studies of the CAPM, what are the typical proxies used for the market portfolio?

8. Assuming that the empirical proxy for the market portfolio is not a good proxy, what factors related to the CAPM will be affected?

9. Some studies related to the efficient market hypothesis generated results that implied additional factors beyond beta that should be considered when attempting to estimate expected returns. What are these other variables and why should they be considered?

10. According to the Fama-French study, what are the variables you should consider when attempting to select a cross section of stocks? Does it appear that you should use only one of them or multiple factors? Explain.

---

[50] For a discussion of how these models relate to each other, see William F. Sharpe, "Factor Models, CAPMs, and the APT," *Journal of Portfolio Management* 11, no. 1 (Fall 1984): 21–25.

11. What are the major assumptions required by the APT? What are some critical assumptions of the CAPM that are *not* required by the APT?

12. Briefly discuss one study that does not support the APT. Briefly discuss a study that supports the APT.

13. Briefly discuss why Shanken contends that the APT is not testable.

14. *CFA Exam III (1986)*
     Multifactor models of security returns have received increased attention. The arbitrage pricing theory (APT) probably has drawn the most attention and has been proposed as a replacement for the capital asset pricing model (CAPM).
     a. Briefly explain the primary differences between APT and CAPM. (5 minutes)
     b. Identify the *four* systematic factors suggested by Roll and Ross that determine an asset's riskiness. Explain how these factors affect an asset's expected rate of return. (10 minutes)

PROBLEMS

1. Given the following results, indicate what will happen to the beta for Stock E, relative to the market proxy, compared to the beta relative to the true market portfolio:

| | Yearly Rates of Return | | |
Year	Stock (percent)	Market Proxy (percent)	True Market (percent)
1	10	8	6
2	20	14	11
3	−14	−10	−7
4	−20	−18	−12
5	15	12	10

Discuss the reason for the differences in measured beta. Does the relationship suggested appear reasonable? Why or why not?

2. Draw the implied SMLs for the following two sets of conditions:
    a. $RFR = .07; R_m(S + P\ 500) = .16$
    b. $R_z = .09; R_m(\text{True}) = .18$

    Under which set of conditions would it be more difficult for a portfolio manager to be superior?

3. Using the graph and equations from Problem 2, which of the following portfolios would be superior?
    a. $R_a = 11\%; \beta = .09$
    b. $R_b = 14\%; \beta = 1.00$
    c. $R_c = 12\%; \beta = -.40$
    d. $R_d = 20\%; \beta = 1.10$

    Does it matter which SML you use?

4. Draw the security market line for each of the following conditions:
    a. (1) $RFR = .08$ R_m (proxy) $= .12$
        (2) $R_z = .06$ R_m (true) $= .15$
    b. Radius Tire has the following results for the last six periods. Calculate and compare the betas using each index.

Period	Return of Radius (percent)	Proxy Specific Index (percent)	True General Index (percent)
1	29	12	15
2	12	10	13
3	−12	−9	−8
4	17	14	18
5	20	25	28
6	−5	−10	0

    c. If the current period return for the market is 12 percent and for Radius is 11 percent, are superior results being obtained?

5. Under the following conditions, what are the expected returns for Stocks J and L?

$$\lambda^0 = .05 \qquad b_{J1} = 0.80$$
$$K_1 = .02 \qquad b_{J2} = 1.40$$
$$K_2 = .04 \qquad b_{L1} = 1.60$$
$$b_{L2} = 2.25$$

REFERENCES

Bhandari, Lami Chand. "Debt/Equity Ratio and Expected Common Stock Returns: Empirical Evidence." *Journal of Finance* 43, no. 2 (June 1988).

Black, Fischer. "Capital Market Equilibrium with Restricted Borrowing." *Journal of Business* 45, no. 3 (July 1972).

Black, Fischer, Michael Jensen, and Myron Scholes. "The Capital Asset Pricing Model: Some Empirical Tests" In *Studies in the Theory of Capital Markets,* edited by Michael Jensen. New York: Praeger, 1976.

Brown, Stephen J., and Mark I. Weinstein. "A New Approach to Testing Asset Pricing Models: The Bilinear Paradigm." *Journal of Finance* 38, no. 3 (June 1983).

Campbell, John Y., and John Ammer. "What Moves the Stock and Bond Markets? A Variance Decomposition for Long-Term Asset Returns." *Journal of Finance* 48, no. 1 (March 1993).

Chen, Nai-fu, Richard Roll, and Stephen A. Ross. "Economic Forces and the Stock Market." *Journal of Business* 56, no. 3 (July 1986).

Cho, D. Chinhyung, Edwin J. Elton, and Martin J. Gruber. "On the Robustness of the Roll and Ross Arbitrage Pricing Theory." *Journal of Financial and Quantitative Analysis* 19, no. 1 (March 1984).

Dhen, Nai-Fu. "Some Empirical Tests of the Theory of Arbitrage Pricing." *Journal of Finance* 38, no. 5 (December 1983).

Dhrymes, Phoebus J., Irwin Friend, and N. Bulent Gultekin. "A Critical Re-Examination of the Empirical Evidence on the Arbitrage Pricing Theory." *Journal of Finance* 39, no. 2 (June 1984).

Elton, Edwin, Martin Gruber, and Joel Rentzler. "The Arbitrage Pricing Model and Returns on Assets under Uncertain Inflation." *Journal of Finance* 38, no. 2 (May 1983).

Fama, Eugene, and Kenneth R. French. "The Cross Section of Expected Stock Returns." *Journal of Finance* 47, no. 2 (June 1992).

Handa, Punect and Scott C. Linn. "Arbitrage Pricing with Estimation Risk." *Journal of Financial and Quantitative Analysis* 28, no. 1 (March 1993).

Huberman, Gur. "Arbitrage Pricing Theory: A Simple Approach." *Journal of Economic Theory* 28, no. 1 (October 1982).

Ingersoll, J. E., Jr. "Some Results in the Theory of Arbitrage Pricing." *Journal of Finance* 39, no. 4 (September 1984).

Lehmann, B. N., and D. M. Modest. "The Empirical Foundations of the Arbitrage Pricing Theory." *Journal of Financial Economics* 21, no. 3 (September 1988).

Miller, Merton H., and Myron Scholes. "Rates of Return in Relation to Risk: A Re-Examination of Some Recent Findings." In *Studies in the Theory of Capital Markets,* edited by Michael Jensen. New York: Praeger, 1976.

Reinganum, Marc R. "The Arbitrage Pricing Theory: Some Empirical Results." *Journal of Finance* 36, no. 2 (May 1981).

Reinganum, Marc R. "A New Empirical Perspective on the CAPM." *Journal of Financial and Quantitative Analysis* 16, no. 4 (November 1981).

Roll, Richard. "A Critique of the Asset Pricing Theory's Tests." *Journal of Financial Economics* 4, no. 4 (March 1977).

Roll, Richard. "Ambiguity when Performance is Measured by the Securities Market Line." *Journal of Finance* 33, no. 4 (September 1978).

Roll, Richard. "Performance Evaluation and Benchmark Error I." *Journal of Portfolio Management* 6, no. 4 (Summer 1980).

Roll, Richard. "Performance Evaluation and Benchmark Error II." *Journal of Portfolio Management* 7, no. 2 (Winter 1981).

Roll, Richard, and Stephen A. Ross. "An Empirical Investigation of the Arbitrage Pricing Theory." *Journal of Finance* 35, no. 5 (December 1980).

Roll, Richard, and Stephen A. Ross. "A Critical Reexamination of the Empirical Evidence on the Arbitrage Pricing Theory: A Reply." *Journal of Finance* 39, no. 2 (June 1984).

Rosenberg, Barr, Kenneth Reid, and Ronald Lanstein. "Persuasive Evidence of Market Inefficiency." *Journal of Portfolio Management* 11, no. 3 (Spring 1985).

Ross, Stephen A. "The Arbitrage Theory of Capital Asset Pricing." *Journal of Economic Theory* 13, no. 2 (December 1976).

Ross, Stephen A. "Risk, Return and Arbitrage." In *Risk and Return in Finance*, edited by I. Friend and J. Bicksler. Cambridge: Ballinger, 1977.

Shanken, Jay. "The Arbitrage Pricing Theory: Is It Testable?" *Journal of Finance* 37, no. 5 (December 1982).

Shanken, Jay. "Multivariate Proxies and Asset Pricing Relations." *Journal of Financial Economics* 18, no. 1 (March 1987).

Sharpe, William F. "Factor Models, CAPMs, and the APT." *Journal of Portfolio Management* 11, no. 1 (Fall 1984).

Stambaugh, Robert F. "On the Exclusion of Assets from Tests of the Two-Parameter Model: A Sensitivity Analysis." *Journal of Financial Economics* 10, no. 4 (November 1982).

Tiemann, J. "Exact Arbitrage Pricing and the Minimum-Variance Frontier." *Journal of Finance* 43, no. 2 (June 1988).

Evaluation of Portfolio Performance

In this chapter we will answer the following questions:

- What are the major requirements that clients want from their portfolio managers?
- What can a portfolio manager do to attain superior performance?
- What is the Treynor portfolio performance measure?
- What is the Sharpe portfolio performance measure?
- What is the critical difference between the Treynor and Sharpe portfolio performance measures?
- What is the Jensen portfolio performance measure and how does it relate to the Treynor measure?
- How do you determine if a portfolio being evaluated is above or below the SML when using the Treynor measure?
- When evaluating a sample of portfolios, how do you determine how well diversified they are?
- What is the bias found regarding the composite performance measures?
- What is the Fama portfolio performance measure and what information does it provide beyond the other measures?
- How do the various performance measures relate to each other in terms of rankings?
- What is the Roll "benchmark error" problem and what are the two factors that are affected when computing portfolio performance measures?
- What is the impact of global investing on the significance of the benchmark error problem?
- How do bond portfolio performance measures differ from equity portfolio performance measures?
- In the Wagner and Tito bond portfolio performance measure, what is the measure of risk used?
- What are the components of the Dietz, Fogler, and Hardy bond portfolio performance measure?
- What are the sources of return in the Fong, Pearson, and Vasicek bond portfolio performance measure?
- What are customized benchmarks?

- What are the important characteristics that any benchmark should possess including customized benchmarks?

Investors are always interested in evaluating the performance of their portfolios. It is both expensive and time-consuming to analyze and select securities for a portfolio, so an individual, company, or institution must determine whether this effort was worth the time and money invested in it. Investors who manage their own portfolios should evaluate their own performance just as those who pay one or several professional money managers must. In the latter case, it is imperative to determine whether the investment performance justifies the cost of the service.

This chapter outlines the theory and practice of evaluating the performance of an investment portfolio. In the initial section we consider what is required of a portfolio manager. We need to pinpoint what to look for before we discuss techniques used to evaluate portfolio managers.

In section two, we begin with a brief discussion of how performance was evaluated before portfolio theory and the CAPM were developed. The rest of this section contains a detailed discussion of three portfolio performance evaluation techniques that consider return and risk (referred to as *composite performance measures* because they consider both return and risk).

The third section demonstrates these composite measures by applying them to gauge the performance of a selected sample of mutual funds. This demonstration includes an analysis of how these measures relate to each other. You should recognize that although there is some redundancy among the measures, each of them provides some unique perspectives, so they are best viewed as complementary measures. We will also consider a fourth measure that evaluates the components of performance. Because some observers have contended that these three composite measures of performance are biased in favor of low-risk portfolios, we will examine their arguments and the evidence for and against these contentions.

Section four includes a discussion of factors to consider when applying these measures. This includes consideration of the work of Roll that questioned any evaluation technique that depends on the CAPM and a market portfolio. This controversy is referred to as the *benchmark problem*. We also discuss why this benchmark problem becomes larger when you begin investing globally. Notably, it affects both your measures of risk and your portfolio performance measures. We also discuss studies that have evaluated how reliable the composite measures are at predicting future performance.

In the final section, we recognize that the factors that determine the performance of a bond portfolio differ from those that affect common stocks. Therefore, we consider several models developed to evaluate the performance of bond portfolios.

WHAT IS REQUIRED OF A PORTFOLIO MANAGER?

We have two major requirements of a portfolio manager:

1. The ability to derive above-average returns for a given risk class
2. The ability to completely diversify the portfolio to eliminate all unsystematic risk

In terms of return, the first requirement is obvious, but the necessity of considering *risk* in this context was not generally apparent prior to the 1960s, when work in portfolio theory showed its significance. In modern theory, superior risk-adjusted returns can be derived through *either* superior timing or superior security selection.

An equity portfolio manager who can do a superior job of predicting the peaks or troughs of the equity market can adjust the portfolio's composition to anticipate market trends, holding a completely diversified portfolio of high-beta stocks through rising markets and favoring low-beta stocks and money market instruments during declining markets. Bigger gains in rising markets and smaller losses in declining markets would give the portfolio manager above-average risk-adjusted returns.

A fixed-income portfolio manager with superior timing ability would change the portfolio's duration in anticipation of interest rate changes by increasing the duration of the portfolio in anticipation of falling interest rates and reducing the duration of the portfolio when rates are expected to rise. If properly executed, this bond portfolio management strategy would likewise provide superior risk-adjusted returns.

As an alternative strategy, a portfolio manager and his or her analysts could try to consistently select undervalued stocks or bonds for a given risk class. Even without superior market timing, such a portfolio would experience above-average risk-adjusted returns.

The second factor to consider in evaluating a portfolio manager is the ability to diversify completely. As noted in Chapter 8, the market rewards investors only for bearing systematic (market) risk. Unsystematic risk is not considered when determining required returns because it can be eliminated in a diversified market portfolio. Investors consequently want their portfolios completely diversified, which means that they want the portfolio manager to completely eliminate unsystematic risk. The level of diversification can be judged on the basis of the correlation between the portfolio returns and the returns for a market portfolio. A completely diversified portfolio is perfectly correlated with the fully diversified market portfolio.

These two requirements of a portfolio manager are important because some portfolio evaluation techniques take into account one requirement and not the other. Other techniques implicitly consider both factors but do not differentiate between them.

COMPOSITE
PORTFOLIO
PERFORMANCE
MEASURES

PORTFOLIO
EVALUATION
BEFORE 1960

At one time investors evaluated portfolio performance almost entirely on the basis of the rate of return. They were aware of the concept of risk, but they did not know how to quantify or measure it, so they could not consider it explicitly. Developments in portfolio theory in the early 1960s showed how to quantify and measure risk in terms of the variability of returns. Still, because no single measure combined both return and risk, it was necessary to consider the two factors separately as researchers had done in several early studies.[1] Specifically, these investigators grouped portfolios into similar risk classes based on a measure of risk such as the variance of return and then compared the rates of return for alternative portfolios directly within these risk classes.

This section describes in detail the three major composite equity portfolio performance measures that combine risk and return performance into a single value. We describe each measure and what it is meant to do and then demonstrate how to compute

---

[1]Irwin Friend, Marshall Blume, and Jean Crockett, *Mutual Funds and Other Institutional Investors* (New York: McGraw-Hill, 1970).

it and interpret the results. Also, we directly compare two of the measures and discuss how they differ and why they would rank portfolios differently.

TREYNOR PORTFOLIO PERFORMANCE MEASURE

Treynor developed the first composite measure of portfolio performance that included risk.[2] He postulated two components of risk: risk produced by general market fluctuations, and risk resulting from unique fluctuations in the securities in the portfolio. To identify risk due to market fluctuations, he introduced the *characteristic line,* which defines the relationship between the rates of return for a portfolio over time and the rates of return for an appropriate market portfolio, as we discussed in Chapter 8. He noted that the slope of the characteristic line measures the *relative volatility* of the portfolio's returns in relation to returns for the aggregate market. As we know from Chapter 8, this slope is the portfolio's beta coefficient. A higher slope (beta) characterizes a portfolio that is more sensitive to market returns and has greater market risk.

Deviations from the characteristic line indicate unique returns for the portfolio relative to the market. These differences arise from the returns on individual stocks in the portfolio. In a completely diversified portfolio, these unique returns for individual stocks should cancel out. As the correlation of the portfolio with the market increases, unique risk declines and diversification improves. Because Treynor was not interested in this aspect of portfolio performance, he gave no further consideration to the measure of diversification.

TREYNOR'S COMPOSITE PERFORMANCE MEASURE

Treynor was interested in a measure of performance that would apply to all investors regardless of their risk preferences. Building on developments in capital market theory, he introduced a risk-free asset that could be combined with different portfolios to form a straight portfolio possibility line. He showed that rational, risk-averse investors would always prefer portfolio possibility lines with larger slopes because such high-slope lines would place investors on higher indifference curves. The slope of this portfolio possibility line (designated T) is equal to[3]

$$T = \frac{R_i - RFR}{\beta_i}$$

where:

R_i = the average rate of return for portfolio i during a specified time period

RFR = the average rate of return on a risk-free investment during the same time period

β_i = the slope of the fund's characteristic line during that time period (this indicates the portfolio's relative volatility)

As noted, a larger T value indicates a larger slope and a better portfolio for all investors, regardless of their risk preferences. Because the numerator of this ratio ($R_i - RFR$) is the *risk premium* and the denominator is a measure of risk, the total expression indicates

---

[2]Jack L. Treynor, "How to Rate Management of Investment Funds," *Harvard Business Review* 43, no. 1 (January-February 1965): 63–75.

[3]The terms used in the formula differ from those used by Treynor but are consistent with our earlier discussion. Also, our discussion is concerned with general *portfolio* performance rather than being limited to mutual funds.

the portfolio's *risk premium return per unit of risk.* All risk-averse investors would prefer to maximize this value.

Note that the risk variable beta measures systematic risk and indicates nothing about the diversification of the portfolio. It *implicitly assumes* a completely diversified portfolio, which means that systematic risk is the relevant risk measure.

Comparing a portfolio's T value to a similar measure for the market portfolio indicates whether the portfolio would plot above the SML. You calculate the T value for the aggregate market as follows:

$$T_m = \frac{R_m - RFR}{\beta_m}$$

In this expression β_m equals 1.0, which is the market's beta, and it indicates the slope of the SML. Therefore, a portfolio with a higher T value than the market portfolio would plot above the SML. This would indicate superior risk-adjusted performance.

DEMONSTRATION OF COMPARATIVE TREYNOR MEASURES

To understand how to use and interpret this measure of performance, consider an example. Assume that during the most recent 10-year period, the average annual total rate of return (including dividends) on an aggregate market portfolio such as the S&P 500 was 14 percent ($R_m = 0.14$) and the average nominal rate of return on government T-bills was 8 percent ($RFR = 0.08$). Assume that, as administrator of a large pension fund that has been divided among three money managers during the past 10 years, you must decide whether to renew your investment management contracts with all three money managers. To do this, you must measure how they have performed.

A later section will show how the numbers have been derived. For now, assume you are given the following results.

Investment Manager	Average Annual Rate of Return	Beta
W	0.12	0.90
X	0.16	1.05
Y	0.18	1.20

On the basis of this information, you can compute T values for the market portfolio and for each of the individual portfolio managers as follows:

$$T_m = \frac{0.14 - 0.08}{1.00} = 0.060$$

$$T_w = \frac{0.12 - 0.08}{0.90} - 0.044$$

$$T_x = \frac{0.16 - 0.08}{1.05} = 0.076$$

$$T_y = \frac{0.18 - 0.08}{1.20} = 0.083$$

FIGURE 26.1   **Plot of Performance on SML (T Measure)**

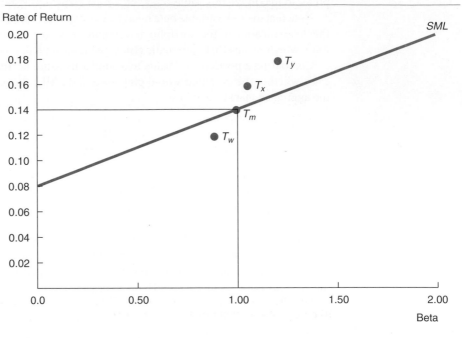

These results would indicate that investment manager W not only ranked the lowest of three managers, but did not do as well as the aggregate market did. In contrast, both X and Y beat the market portfolio, and manager Y performed somewhat better than manager X. In terms of the SML, both of their portfolios plotted above the line, as shown in Figure 26.1.

Very poor performance or very good performance with very low risk can yield negative T values. An example of poor performance would be a portfolio with both an average rate of return below the risk-free rate and a positive beta. As an example, in the preceding case assume that a fourth portfolio manager, Z, had a portfolio beta of 0.50, but an average rate of return of only 0.07. The T value would be

$$T_z = \frac{0.07 - 0.08}{0.50} = -0.02$$

Obviously, this performance would plot below the SML in Figure 26.1.

A portfolio with a *negative* beta and an average rate of return above the risk-free rate of return would likewise have a negative T value. In this case, however, it would indicate very exemplary performance. As an example, assume that portfolio manager G invested heavily in gold mining stocks during a period of great political and economic uncertainty. Because gold typically has a negative correlation with most stocks, this portfolio's beta could be negative. If you were examining this portfolio after gold prices increased in value as a result of the uncertainty, you might find excellent returns.

Assume that our gold bug portfolio G had a beta of -0.20 and yet experienced an average rate of return of 10 percent. The T value for this portfolio would then be

$$T_g = \frac{.10 - 0.08}{-0.20} = -0.100$$

Although the T value is -0.100, you can see that if you plotted these results on the graph, it would indicate a position substantially above the SML in Figure 26.1.

Because negative betas can yield T values that give confusing results, it is preferable either to plot the portfolio on an SML graph or to compute the expected return for this portfolio using the SML equation and then compare this expected return to the actual return. This comparison will tell you whether the actual return was above or below expectations. In the preceding example for portfolio G, the expected return would be

$$
\begin{aligned}
E(R_g) &= RFR + \beta_i\,(R_m - RFR) \\
&= 0.08 + (-0.20)\,(0.06) \\
&= 0.08 - 0.012 \\
&= 0.068
\end{aligned}
$$

Comparing this expected (required) rate of return of 6.8 percent to the actual return of 10 percent shows that portfolio manager G has done a superior job.

SHARPE PORTFOLIO PERFORMANCE MEASURE

Sharpe likewise conceived of a composite measure to evaluate the performance of mutual funds.[4] The measure followed closely his earlier work on the capital asset pricing model (CAPM), dealing specifically with the capital market line (CML).

The Sharpe portfolio performance measure (designated S) is stated as follows:

$$S_i = \frac{R_i - RFR}{SD_i}$$

where:

S_i = **Sharpe portfolio performance measure for portfolio** i
R_i = **the average rate of return for portfolio** i **during a specified time period**
RFR = **the average rate of return on risk-free assets during the same time period**
SD_i = **the standard deviation of the rate of return for portfolio** i **during the time period**

This composite measure of portfolio performance is clearly similar to the Treynor measure, but it seeks to measure the *total risk* of the portfolio by including the standard deviation of returns rather than considering only the systematic risk by using beta. Because the numerator is the portfolio's risk premium, this measure indicates the *risk premium return earned per unit of total risk*. In terms of capital market theory, this portfolio performance measure uses total risk to compare portfolios to the CML, whereas the Treynor measure examines portfolio performance in relation to the SML.

---

[4]William F. Sharpe, "Mutual Fund Performance," *Journal of Business* 39, no. 1, Part 2 (January 1966): 119–138.

DEMONSTRATION OF COMPARATIVE SHARPE MEASURES

The following examples use the Sharpe measure of performance. Again assume that $R_m = 0.14$ and $RFR = 0.08$. Suppose you are told that the standard deviation of the annual rate of return for the market portfolio over the past 10 years was 20 percent ($SD_m = 0.20$). Now you want to examine the performance of the following portfolios:

Portfolio	Average Annual Rate of Return	Standard Deviation of Return
D	0.13	0.18
E	0.17	0.22
F	0.16	0.23

The Sharpe measures for these portfolios would be as follows:

$$S_m = \frac{0.14 - 0.08}{0.20} = 0.300$$

$$S_d = \frac{0.13 - 0.08}{0.18} = 0.278$$

$$S_e = \frac{0.17 - 0.08}{0.22} = 0.409$$

$$S_f = \frac{0.16 - 0.08}{0.23} = 0.348$$

The D portfolio had the lowest risk premium return per unit of total risk, failing even to perform as well as the aggregate market portfolio. In contrast, portfolios E and F performed better than the aggregate market: portfolio E did better than portfolio F.

Given the results for the market portfolio during this period, it is possible to draw the CML. If we then plot the results for portfolios D, E, and F on this graph, as shown in Figure 26.2, we see that portfolio D plots below the line, whereas the E and F portfolios are above the line, indicating superior risk-adjusted performance.

TREYNOR VERSUS SHARPE MEASURE

The Sharpe portfolio performance measure uses the standard deviation of returns as the measure of risk, whereas the Treynor performance measure employs beta (systematic risk). The Sharpe measure, therefore, evaluates the portfolio manager on the basis of both rate of return performance and diversification.

For a completely diversified portfolio, one without any unsystematic risk, the two measures would give identical rankings, because the total variance of the completely diversified portfolio is its systematic variance. Alternatively, a poorly diversified portfolio could have a high ranking on the basis of the Treynor performance measure, but a much lower ranking on the basis of the Sharpe performance measure. Any difference in rank would come directly from a difference in diversification.

FIGURE 26.2 | **Plot of Performance on CML (S Measure)**

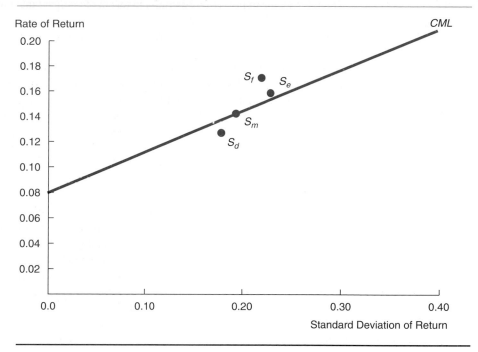

Therefore, these two performance measures provide complementary but different information, and both measures should be used. If you are dealing with a group of portfolios that are well-diversified, as most mutual funds, the two measures will provide very similar rankings.

JENSEN
PORTFOLIO
PERFORMANCE
MEASURE

The Jensen measure is similar to the measures already discussed because it is based on the capital asset pricing model (CAPM).[5] All versions of the CAPM calculate the expected one-period return on any security or portfolio by the following expression:

$$E(R_j) = RFR + \beta_j\,[E(R_m) - RFR]$$

where:

$E(R_j)$ = **the expected return on security or portfolio** j
RFR = **the one-period risk-free interest rate**
β_j = **the systematic risk (beta) for security or portfolio** j
$E(R_m)$ = **the expected return on the market portfolio of risky assets**

The expected return and the risk-free return differ for different periods. Consequently, we are concerned with the time series of expected rates of return for security j or

[5]Michael C. Jensen, "The Performance of Mutual Funds in the Period 1945–1964," *Journal of Finance* 23, no. 2 (May 1968): 389–416.

portfolio j. Moreover, assuming that the asset pricing model is empirically valid, you can express the expectations formula in terms of *realized* rates of return as follows:

$$R_{jt} = RFR_t + \beta_j [R_{mt} - RFR_t] + U_{jt}$$

This equation indicates that the realized rate of return on a security or portfolio during a given time period should be a linear function of the risk-free rate of return during the period, plus a risk premium that depends on the systematic risk of the security or portfolio during the period plus a random error term.

Subtracting the risk-free return from both sides, we have

$$R_{jt} - RFR_t = \beta_j [R_{mt} - RFR_t] + U_{jt}$$

This indicates that the risk premium earned on the jth security or portfolio j is equal to β_j times a market risk premium plus a random error term. In this form, you would not expect an intercept for the regression if all assets and portfolios were in equilibrium.

Alternatively, certain superior portfolio managers who could forecast market turns or consistently select undervalued securities would earn higher risk premiums than those implied by this model. Specifically, superior portfolio managers would have consistently positive random error terms because the actual returns for their portfolios would consistently exceed the expected returns implied by this model. To detect and measure this superior performance, you need to allow for an intercept (a nonzero constant) that measures any positive or negative difference from the model. Consistent positive differences would cause a positive intercept, whereas consistent negative differences (inferior performance) would cause a negative intercept. With an intercept or nonzero constant, the earlier equation becomes

$$R_{jt} - RFR_t = \alpha_j + \beta_j [R_{mt} - RFR_t] + U_{jt}$$

In this equation, the α_j value indicates whether the portfolio manager is superior or inferior in market timing and/or stock selection. A superior manager would have a significant positive α value because of the consistent positive residuals. In contrast, an inferior manager's returns would consistently fall short of expectations based on the CAPM model giving consistently negative residuals. In such a case, the nonzero constant α_j would be a significant negative value.

The performance of a portfolio manager who had no forecasting ability but was not clearly inferior would equal that of a naive buy-and-hold policy. In the equation, because the rate of return on such a portfolio would typically match the returns that you expect on the basis of the CAPM, the residual returns would generally be randomly positive and negative. This would give a constant term that would differ insignificantly from zero, indicating that the portfolio manager basically matched the market on a risk-adjusted basis.

Therefore, the α_j represents how much of the rate of return on the portfolio is attributable to the manager's ability to derive above-average returns adjusted for risk. Superior risk-adjusted returns indicate that the manager is good at predicting market turns and/or selecting undervalued issues for the portfolio.

APPLYING THE JENSEN MEASURE

The Jensen measure of performance requires that you use a different *RFR* for each time interval during the sample period. For example, to examine the performance of a fund manager over a 10-year period using yearly intervals, you must examine the fund's annual returns less the return on risk-free assets for each year, and relate this to the annual return on the market portfolio less the same risk-free rate. This contrasts with the Treynor or Sharpe composite measure of performance, which examine the *average* returns for the total period for all variables (the portfolio, the market, and the risk-free asset).

Also, like the Treynor measure, the Jensen measure does not evaluate the ability of the portfolio manager to diversify, because it calculates risk premiums in terms of systematic risk. As noted earlier, to evaluate the performance of a group of well-diversified portfolios such as mutual funds, this is probably a fairly legitimate assumption. Jensen's analysis of mutual fund performance showed that complete diversification was a fairly reasonable assumption because the funds typically correlated with the market at rates above 0.90.

APPLICATION OF PORTFOLIO PERFORMANCE MEASURES	To demonstrate how to apply these measures, we selected 20 open-end mutual funds and used monthly data for the 5-year period from 1988 to 1992. The monthly rates of return for the first fund (Aim Constellation Fund) and the S&P 500 are contained in Table 26.1. The total rate of return for each month is computed as follows:

$$R_{it} = \frac{EP_{it} + Div_{it} + Cap.Dist._{it} - BP_{it}}{BP_{it}}$$

where:

$$R_{it} = \text{the total rate of return on fund } i \text{ during month } t$$
$$EP_{it} = \text{the ending price for fund } i \text{ during month } t$$
$$Cap.Dist._{it} = \text{the capital gain distributions made by fund } i \text{ during month } t$$
$$Div_{it} = \text{the dividend payments made by fund } i \text{ during month } t$$
$$BP_{it} = \text{the beginning price for fund } i \text{ during month } t$$

These return computations do not take into account any sales charges by the funds. Given the monthly results for the fund and the aggregate market (as represented by the S&P 500), you can compute the composite measures presented in Table 26.2.

The arithmetic average annual rate of return for Aim Constellation Fund was 26.40 percent versus 15.71 percent for the market (26.40 versus 15.71), and the fund's beta was greater than 1.00 (1.351). Using the average rate of T-bills of 6.20 percent as the *RFR*, the Treynor measure for the Aim Constellation Fund (T_i) was substantially greater than the comparable measure for the market (T_m) (14.949 versus 9.508). Likewise, the standard deviation of returns for Aim Constellation was greater than the market's (20.67 versus 13.25). Even with the higher standard deviation, the Sharpe measure for the fund (S_i) was larger than the measure for the market (S_m) (0.977 versus 0.717).

Finally, a regression of the fund's annual risk premium ($R_{it} - RFR_t$) and the market's annual risk premium ($R_{mt} - RFR_t$) indicated a positive intercept (constant) value of

TABLE 26.1

Example of Computation of Portfolio Evaluation Measures Using Aim Constellation Fund, Inc.

	R_{it}	R_{mt}	RFR_t	$R_{it} - RFR_t$	$R_{mt} - RFR_t$
Jan. 1988	−1.00	4.27	0.49	−1.49	3.78
Feb. 1988	9.50	4.70	0.47	9.03	4.23
Mar. 1988	0.60	−3.02	0.47	0.13	−3.49
Apr. 1988	3.50	1.08	0.49	3.01	0.59
May 1988	−2.00	0.78	0.52	−2.52	0.26
Jun. 1988	12.00	4.64	0.54	11.46	4.10
Jul. 1988	−3.00	−0.40	0.50	−3.50	−0.90
Aug. 1988	−5.00	−3.31	0.53	−5.53	−3.84
Sep. 1988	4.50	4.24	0.54	3.96	3.70
Oct. 1988	0.00	2.73	0.61	−0.61	2.12
Nov. 1988	−3.00	−1.42	0.64	−3.64	−2.06
Dec. 1988	3.80	1.81	0.67	3.13	1.14
⋮	⋮	⋮	⋮	⋮	⋮
⋮	⋮	⋮	⋮	⋮	⋮
Jan. 1992	2.10	−1.86	0.32	1.78	−2.18
Feb. 1992	1.60	1.28	0.32	1.28	0.96
Mar. 1992	−3.00	−1.96	0.34	−3.34	−2.30
Apr. 1992	−5.00	2.91	0.32	−5.32	2.59
May 1992	0.70	0.54	0.31	0.39	0.24
Jun. 1992	−5.00	−1.45	0.31	−5.31	−1.76
Jul. 1992	6.00	4.03	0.27	5.73	3.76
Aug. 1992	−3.00	−2.02	0.26	−3.26	−2.28
Sep. 1992	3.70	1.15	0.25	3.45	0.90
Oct. 1992	6.20	0.36	0.24	5.96	0.12
Nov. 1992	8.20	3.37	0.26	7.94	3.11
Dec. 1992	4.00	1.31	0.27	3.73	1.04
Mean	26.40	15.71	6.20		
Standard Deviation	20.67	13.25	0.50		
Beta	1.351				
S_i	0.977				
S_m	0.717				
T_i	14.949				
T_m	9.508				
Jensen Intercept	0.610				
Beta j	1.355				
R^2_{lm}	0.752				

0.610, but it was not statistically significant. If this intercept value had been significant, it would have indicated that Aim Constellation's risk-adjusted annual rate of return averaged about .61 percent above the market.

TOTAL SAMPLE RESULTS

Analysis of the overall results in Table 26.2 indicate that they are generally consistent with the findings of earlier studies. Our sample was rather casually selected because we intended it for demonstration purposes only. The mean annual return for all the funds was quite close to the market return (15.45 versus 15.71). Considering only the rate of return, 7 of the 20 funds outperformed the market.

The R^2 for a portfolio with the market can serve as a measure of diversification. The closer the R^2 is to 1.00, the more completely diversified the portfolio is. The

TABLE 26.2 **Performance Measures for 20 Selected Mutual Funds (Based on Monthly Total Returns, 1988–1992)**

	Average Annual Rate of Return	Standard Deviation	Beta	R^2	Treynor	Sharpe	Jensen
Aim Constellation Fund, Inc.	26.40	20.67	1.351	0.751	14.949 (6)	0.977 (7)	0.610 (2)
Dean Witter Developing Growth Fund	13.72	9.51	0.594	0.605	5.650 (19)	0.332 (19)	−0.430 (20)
Dreyfus Growth Opportunity Fund	13.22	14.20	0.905	0.713	7.764 (15)	0.495 (16)	−0.134 (15)
Fasciano Fund, Inc.	17.66	12.53	0.757	0.641	15.144 (5)	0.915 (8)	0.355 (5)
Fidelity Magellan Fund	18.46	14.32	1.048	0.941	11.699 (10)	0.856 (9)	0.192 (9)
Fidelity Puritan Fund	15.24	9.12	0.645	0.878	14.029 (7)	0.992 (6)	0.240 (8)
Gabelli Asset Fund	17.42	9.51	0.594	0.686	18.888 (2)	1.180 (4)	0.463[a] (4)
Guardian Park Avenue Fund	16.04	12.91	0.828	0.723	11.883 (9)	0.762 (11)	0.160 (10)
IDS Mutual Fund	11.88	9.17	0.662	0.916	8.584 (13)	0.620 (13)	−0.053 (12)
Income Fund of America, Inc.	14.68	6.98	0.458	0.758	18.504 (3)	1.216 (2)	0.342[a] (6)
Investment Company of America Fund	16.88	10.68	0.785	0.948	13.615 (8)	1.000 (5)	0.296[a] (7)
Janus Venture Fund	22.54	13.45	0.889	0.768	18.374 (4)	1.215 (3)	0.657[a] (1)
Kemper Technology Fund	13.70	17.05	1.106	0.739	6.780 (17)	0.440 (18)	−0.253 (17)
Lindner Dividend Fund	15.06	5.64	0.227	0.285	39.064 (1)	1.573 (1)	0.555[a] (3)
Oppenheimer Fund	12.42	12.32	0.818	0.818	7.603 (16)	0.505 (15)	−0.149 (16)
Putnam Fund for Growth and Income A	14.26	9.77	0.700	0.902	11.514 (11)	0.825 (10)	0.117 (11)
Templeton World Fund	12.86	12.32	0.810	0.810	8.224 (14)	0.541 (14)	−0.100 (14)
T. Rowe Price Growth Stock Fund	12.94	14.49	1.033	0.893	6.525 (18)	0.465 (17)	−0.258 (18)
Value Line Special Situations Fund	11.00	17.53	1.033	0.609	4.651 (20)	0.274 (20)	−0.418 (19)
Vanguard Wellington Fund	12.66	10.20	0.745	0.939	8.668 (12)	0.634 (12)	−0.053 (13)
Mean	15.45	12.12	0.799	0.766	12.606	0.791	0.107
S&P 500	15.71	13.25	1.000	1.000	9.508	0.717	0.000
90-Day T-Bill Rate	6.20	0.50					

[a]significant

average R^2 for our sample was not very high at 0.766, and the range was quite large, from 0.284 to 0.948. This indicates that many of the funds were not well-diversified. Of the 20 funds, 11 had values less than 0.80.

The two risk measures (standard deviation and beta) likewise show a wide range, but are generally consistent with expectations. Specifically, 8 of the 20 funds had larger standard deviations than the market, and the mean standard deviation was smaller (12.12 versus 13.25). Only 6 of the funds had a beta above 1.00; the average beta was 0.799.

Alternative measures ranked the performance of individual funds very consistently. Using the Sharpe or the Treynor measure, 11 of the 20 funds had a value that was better than the market. The Jensen measure indicated that 11 of the 20 had positive intercepts, but only 5 of the positive intercepts were statistically significant (none of the negative intercepts were significant). The mean values for the Sharpe and Treynor measures were greater than the figure for the aggregate market. These results indicate that, on average, and without considering transaction costs, this sample of funds had results that were slightly better than the market during this time period.

You should analyze the individual funds and consider each of the components: rate of return, risk (both standard deviation and beta), and the R^2 as a measure of diversification. One might expect the best performance by funds with low diversification, because these funds are apparently attempting to beat the market by being unique in their selection or timing. This is apparently true for the top performing funds such as Lindner Dividend Fund and Gabelli Asset Fund and also some unsuccessful funds that had poor diversification but unfortunately low returns such as Value Line Special Situations Fund.

POTENTIAL BIAS OF ONE-PARAMETER MEASURES

Friend and Blume pointed out that, theoretically, the three composite measures of performance should be independent of alternative measures of risk because they are *risk-adjusted* measures.[6] An analysis of the relationship between the composite measures of performance and two measures of risk (standard deviation and beta) for 200 random portfolios from the NYSE indicated a significant *inverse* relationship (the risk-adjusted performance of low-risk portfolios was better than the comparable performance for high-risk portfolios). The results for the Jensen performance measure are contained in Figure 26.3.

Subsequently, Klemkosky examined the relationship between composite performance measures and risk measures using actual mutual fund data in contrast to the random portfolio data used by Friend and Blume.[7] Beyond the three composite measures, the author derived two measures that computed the excess return above the risk-free rate relative to the semistandard deviation and relative to the mean absolute deviation as risk measures. The results indicated a positive bias—that is, a *positive* relationship between the composite performance measures and the risk involved. This was especially true for the Treynor and Jensen measures. The performance measures that used the mean absolute deviation and the semistandard deviation as risk proxies were less biased than the three standard performance measures. It was concluded that although a bias might exist, one could not be certain of its direction.

COMPONENTS OF INVESTMENT PERFORMANCE

Subsequent to the work by Treynor, Sharpe, and Jensen, Fama suggested a somewhat finer breakdown of performance.[8] Fama's evaluation model likewise assumes that the returns on managed portfolios can be judged relative to those of naively selected portfolios with similar levels of risk. The technique uses the simple one-period version of the two-parameter model, all the perfect market assumptions, and derives the *ex ante* market line, which indicates the following equilibrium relationship between expected return and risk for any security *j*:

$$E(\hat{R}_j) = R_f + \left[\frac{E(\hat{R}_m) - R_f}{\sigma(\hat{R}_m)} \right] \frac{Cov(\hat{R}_j, \hat{R}_m)}{\sigma(\hat{R}_m)}$$

$Cov(R_j, R_m)$ is the covariance between the returns for security *j* and the return on the market portfolio. This equation indicates that the expected return on security *j* is the

[6]Irwin Friend and Marshall Blume, "Measurement of Portfolio Performance under Uncertainty," *American Economic Review* 60, no. 4 (September 1970): 561–575.

[7]Robert C. Klemkosky, "The Bias in Composite Performance Measures," *Journal of Financial and Quantitative Analysis* 8, no. 3 (June 1973): 505–514.

[8]Eugene F. Fama, "Components of Investment Performance," *Journal of Finance* 27, no. 3 (June 1972): 551–567.

FIGURE 26.3

Scatter Diagram of Jensen's Performance Measure[a] on Risk: January 1960 to June 1968

Performance

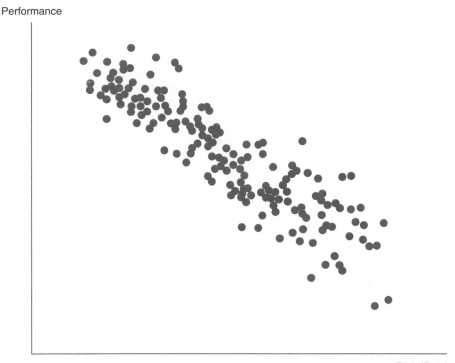

Risk (Beta)

[a]Using log relatives.

Source: Irwin Friend and Marshall Blume, "Measurement of Portfolio Performance under Uncertainty," *American Economic Review* 60, no. 4 (September 1970): 567. Reprinted by permission.

riskless rate of interest, R_f, plus a risk premium that is $[E(\tilde{R}_m) - R_f]/\sigma(\tilde{R}_m)$, called the *market price per unit of risk,* times the risk of asset j, which is $[Cov(\tilde{R}_j, \tilde{R}_m)]/\sigma\tilde{R}_m)$.

This market line relationship should hold for portfolios as well as for individual assets. This *ex ante* model assumes completely efficient markets in which prices fully reflect all available information. Assuming a portfolio manager believes that the market is not completely efficient and that he or she can make better judgments than the market can, then an *ex post* version of this market line can provide a benchmark for the manager's performance. Given that the risk variable, $Cov(R_j, R_m)/\sigma(R_m)$, can be denoted β_x, the *ex post* market line is as follows:

$$R_x = R_f + \left(\frac{R_m - R_f}{\sigma(R_m)}\right)\beta_x$$

This *ex post* market line provides the benchmark used to evaluate managed portfolios in a sequence of more complex measures.

FIGURE 26.4

An Illustration of the Performance Measures

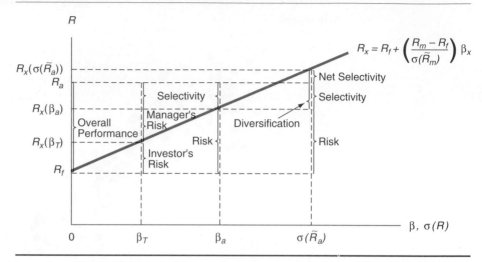

Source: Eugene F. Fama, "Components of Investment Performance," *Journal of Finance* 27, no. 3 (June 1972): 588. Reprinted by permission.

EVALUATING SELECTIVITY

You can measure the return due to selectivity as follows:

$$\text{Selectivity} = R_a - R_x(\beta_a)$$

where:

> R_a = **the return on the portfolio being evaluated**
> $R_x(\beta_a)$ = **the return on the combination of the riskless asset f and the market portfolio m that has risk β_x equal to β_a, the risk of the portfolio being evaluated**

As shown in Figure 26.4, selectivity measures how well the chosen portfolio performed relative to a naively selected portfolio of equal risk. This measure indicates any difference from the *ex post* market line and is quite similar to Treynor's measure.

Also, you can examine *overall performance* in terms of selectivity (just considered) and the returns from assuming risk as follows:

$$\begin{aligned}
\text{Overall} \\
\text{Performance} &= \text{Selectivity} + \text{Risk} \\
[R_a - R_f] &= [R_a - R_x(\beta_a)] + [R_x(\beta_a) - R_f]
\end{aligned}$$

As shown in Figure 26.4, overall performance is the total return above the risk-free return and includes the return that *should* have been received for accepting the portfolio risk (β_a). This expected return for accepting risk (β_a) is equal to $[R_x(\beta_a) - R_f]$. Any excess over this expected return is due to selectivity.

EVALUATING DIVERSIFICATION

The difference between the Treynor and the Sharpe measures is that Treynor uses systematic risk (β_i) and Sharpe uses total risk (σ_i). As noted earlier, if a portfolio is completely diversified and, therefore (by definition) does not have any unsystematic risk, then its total risk will equal its systematic risk, and the two techniques will give equal rankings. However, if a portfolio manager attempts to select undervalued stocks and, in the process, gives up some diversification, it is possible to measure the added return necessary to justify this diversification decision. The portfolio's *gross selectivity* is made up of *net selectivity* plus *diversification* as follows:

$$\overset{\text{Selectivity}}{R_a - R_x(\beta_a)} = \text{Net Selectivity} + \overset{\text{Diversification}}{R_x(\sigma(R_a)) - R_x(\beta_a)}$$

or

$$\text{Net Selectivity} = R_a - R_x(\beta_a) \overset{\text{Selectivity} - \text{Diversification}}{- R_x(\sigma(R_a)) - R_x(\beta_a)}$$
$$= R_a - R_x[\sigma(R_a)],$$

where:

$R_x\,\sigma(R_a)$ = the return on the combination of the riskless asset f and the market portfolio m that has return dispersion equivalent to that of the portfolio being evaluated

Therefore, the diversification measure indicates the *added return* required to justify any loss of diversification in the portfolio. The term emphasizes that diversification is the elimination of all unsystematic variability. If the portfolio is completely diversified so that total risk (σ) is equal to systematic risk (β), then the $R_x(\sigma(R_a))$ would be the same as $R_x(\beta_a)$, and the diversification term would equal zero.

Because the diversification measure is always positive, net selectivity will always be equal to or less than gross selectivity. The two will be equal when the portfolio is completely diversified.[9] If the investor is not concerned with the diversification of the portfolio, this particular breakdown will not be important, and only selectivity will be considered.

EVALUATING RISK

Assuming that the investor has a target level of risk for the portfolio equal to β_T, the overall performance due to risk (the total return above the risk-free return) can be assessed as follows:

$$\overset{\text{Risk}}{[R_x(\beta_a) - R_f]} = \overset{\text{Manager's Risk}}{[R_x(\beta_a) - R_x(\beta_T)]} + \overset{\text{Investor's Risk}}{[R_x(\beta_T) - R_f]}$$

[9]In Figure 26.4, which is taken from the original Fama article, the required return due to diversification *is* larger than the return due to selectivity, so the net selectivity value would be a negative value.

where:

$R_x(\beta_T)$ = **the return on the naively selected portfolio with the target level of market risk (β_T)**

If the portfolio risk is equal to the target risk ($\beta_a = \beta_T$), then there is no manager's risk. If there is a difference between β_a and β_T, then the manager's risk is the return the manager must earn due to the decision to accept risk (β_a), which is different from the risk desired by the investor (β_T). The investor's risk is the return expected because the investor stipulated some positive level of risk. This evaluation is possible only if the client has specified a desired level of market risk, which is usually the case with pensions and profit-sharing plans. Generally, it is not possible to compute this measure for *ex post* evaluations, because the desired risk level is typically not available.

APPLICATION OF FAMA MEASURES

Several of these components of performance can be used in *ex post* evaluation, as shown in Table 26.3. Overall performance is the return derived above the risk-free return (i.e., the return above 6.20 percent as shown in Table 26.2). All of these mutual funds experienced positive overall performance. Next, determine how much the portfolio (fund) *should* receive for its systematic risk using the following expected return equation for this period (15.71 percent is the return on the S&P 500 during this period, as shown in Table 26.2):

$$E(R_i) = 6.20 + \beta_i(15.71 - 6.20)$$
$$= 6.20 + \beta_i(9.51)$$

The required return for risk is simply the latter expression: $\beta_i(9.51)$. The required return for risk for Aim Constellation Fund was $1.351(9.51) = 12.85$ percent (its total required return is $6.20 + 12.85 = 19.05$). The return for selectivity is the difference between overall performance ($26.40 - 6.20 = 20.20$) and the required return for risk (12.85). If the overall performance exceeds the required return for risk, the portfolio has experienced a positive return for selectivity. The results indicate that Aim Constellation had an average annual return of 7.35 percent for selectivity ($20.20 - 12.85$). Fourteen funds had positive returns for selectivity. In contrast, several funds had positive overall performance, but their required return for risk exceeded this figure, giving them negative returns for selectivity (e.g., Kemper Technology Fund).

The next three columns indicate the effect of diversification on performance. The diversification term indicates the required return for not being completely diversified (i.e., having total risk above systematic risk). If a fund's total risk is equal to its systematic risk, then the ratio of its total risk to the market's total risk will equal its beta. If this is not the case, then the ratio of the fund's total risk for the fund relative to the market will be greater than its beta, which implies that there is an added return required because of incomplete diversification. For Aim Constellation, the ratio of total risk was

$$\frac{\sigma_i}{\sigma_m} = \frac{20.67}{13.25} = 1.56$$

TABLE 26.3   Components of Performance for 20 Selected Mutual Funds (Based on Monthly Total Returns, 1988–1992)

	Average Rate of Return	Standard Deviation	Beta	R^2	Overall Performance	Risk	Selectivity	Diversification	Net Selectivity
Aim Constellation Fund, Inc.	26.40	20.67	1.351	0.751	20.20	12.85	7.35	1.99	5.36 (2)
Dean Witter Developing Growth Fund	13.72	22.68	1.331	0.605	7.52	12.66	−5.14	3.62	−8.76 (20)
Dreyfus Growth Opportunity Fund	13.22	14.20	0.905	0.713	7.02	8.61	−1.59	1.59	−3.17 (16)
Fasciano Fund, Inc.	17.66	12.53	0.757	0.641	11.46	7.20	4.26	1.79	2.47 (8)
Fidelity Magellan Fund	18.46	14.32	1.048	0.941	12.26	9.97	2.29	0.31	1.98 (9)
Fidelity Puritan Fund	15.24	9.12	0.645	0.878	9.04	6.13	2.91	0.41	2.49 (7)
Gabelli Asset Fund	17.42	9.51	0.594	0.686	11.22	5.65	5.57	1.18	4.39 (4)
Guardian Park Avenue Fund	16.04	12.91	0.828	0.723	9.84	7.87	1.97	1.39	0.57 (11)
IDS Mutual Fund	11.88	9.17	0.662	0.916	5.68	6.30	−0.62	0.29	−0.90 (13)
Income Fund of America, Inc.	14.68	6.98	0.458	0.758	8.48	4.36	4.12	0.65	3.47 (5)
Investment Company of America Fund	16.88	10.68	0.785	0.948	10.68	7.47	3.21	0.20	3.01 (6)
Janus Venture Fund	22.54	13.45	0.889	0.768	16.34	8.45	7.89	1.20	6.69 (1)
Kemper Technology Fund	13.70	17.05	1.106	0.739	7.50	10.52	−3.02	1.72	−4.74 (18)
Lindner Dividend Fund	15.06	5.64	0.227	0.285	8.86	2.16	6.70	1.89	4.81 (3)
Oppenheimer Fund	12.42	12.32	0.818	0.818	6.22	7.78	−1.56	1.06	−2.62 (15)
Putnam Fund for Growth and Income A	14.26	9.77	0.700	0.902	8.06	6.66	1.40	0.36	1.05 (10)
Templeton World Fund	12.86	12.32	0.810	0.810	6.66	7.70	−1.04	1.14	−2.18 (14)
T. Rowe Price Growth Stock Fund	12.94	14.49	1.033	0.893	6.74	9.82	−3.08	0.58	−3.66 (17)
Value Line Special Situations Fund	11.00	17.53	1.033	0.609	4.80	9.82	−5.02	2.76	−7.78 (19)
Vanguard Wellington Fund	12.66	10.20	0.745	0.939	6.46	7.08	−0.62	0.24	−0.86 (12)
S&P 500	15.71	13.25							
90-Day T-Bill Rate	6.20	0.50							

TABLE 26.4

Correlations Among Alternative Portfolio Performance Measures

	Treynor	Sharpe	Jensen	Fama
Treynor	—			
Sharpe	.97	—		
Jensen	.96	.94	—	
Fama (net selectivity)	.97	.98	.94	—

This ratio of total risk compares to the fund's beta of 1.351, indicating that the fund is not completely diversified, which is consistent with its R^2 of 0.751. The fund's required return given its standard deviation is

$$R_i = 6.20 + 1.56 (9.51)$$
$$= 21.04$$

Recall that the fund's required return for systematic risk was 19.05 [6.20 + 1.351(9.51)]. The difference of 1.99 (21.04 − 19.05) is the added return required because of less than perfect diversification. This fairly large required return for diversification is in contrast to Fidelity Magellan Fund, which has an R^2 with the market of 0.941 and a required return for diversification of 0.31 percent.

This required return for diversification is subtracted from the selectivity return to arrive at net selectivity. Aim Constellation had a return for selectivity of 7.35 percent and net selectivity of 5.36 percent. This indicates that, even accounting for the added cost of incomplete diversification, the fund's performance was above the market line. Thirteen funds had positive net selectivity returns.

RELATIONSHIP AMONG PERFORMANCE MEASURES
Table 26.4 contains the matrix of the rank correlation coefficients among the measures. Although the various measures provide alternative insights regarding performance, *the overall ranks are very similar.* Notably, the Treynor measure appears to have the strongest relationship with the other performance measures.

FACTORS THAT
AFFECT USE OF
PERFORMANCE
MEASURES

These performance measures are only as good as their data inputs. You need to be careful when computing the rates of return to take proper account of all inflows and outflows. More importantly, you should use judgment and be patient in the evaluation process. It is not possible to evaluate a portfolio manager on the basis of a quarter or even a year. Your evaluation should extend over several years and cover at least a full market cycle. This will allow you to determine whether the manager's performance differs during rising and declining markets.[10] Beyond these general considerations, there are several specific factors that you should consider when using these measures.

Although we discussed Roll's contentions regarding the measurement problem in Chapter 25, we should recall the problem at this point, discuss the implications of a

---

[10]In this regard, see Robert C. Kirby, "You Need More than Numbers to Measure Performance," paper presented at Institute of Chartered Financial Analysts Seminar, Chicago, April 2, 1976. For a formal presentation related to the importance of the time element, see Mark Kritzman, "How to Detect Skill in Management Performance," *Journal of Portfolio Management* 12, no. 2 (Winter 1986): 16–20.

global capital market on this problem, and put it in perspective. As noted, all the equity portfolio performance measures we have discussed are derived from the CAPM. They assume the existence of a market portfolio at the point of tangency on the Markowitz efficient frontier. Theoretically, the market portfolio is an efficient, completely diversified portfolio because it is on the efficient frontier. We also noted that this market portfolio must contain all risky assets in the economy so that it will be completely diversified. Finally, all components are market-value weighted.

The problem arises in finding a real-world proxy for this theoretical market portfolio. As noted previously analysts typically use the Standard & Poor's 500 Index as the proxy for the market portfolio because it contains a fairly diversified portfolio of stocks, and the sample is market-value weighted. Unfortunately, it does not represent the true composition of the market portfolio. Specifically, it includes *only* common stocks and most of them are listed on the NYSE. Notably, it *excludes* many other risky assets that theoretically should be considered such as numerous AMEX and OTC stocks, foreign stocks, foreign and domestic bonds, real estate, coins, precious metals, stamps, and antiques.

This lack of completeness has always been recognized, but it was not highlighted until several articles by Roll detailing the problem with the market proxy and pointing out its implications for measuring portfolio performance.[11] Although a detailed discussion of Roll's critique will not be repeated here, we need to consider his major problem with the measurement of the market portfolio, which he refers to as a *benchmark error*.

When evaluating portfolio performance, various techniques employ the market portfolio as the benchmark, and we use the market portfolio to derive our risk measures (betas). Roll showed that if the proxy for the market portfolio is not a truly efficient portfolio, then the SML using this proxy may not be the true SML, the true SML could have a higher slope. In such a case, a portfolio that plotted above the SML derived using a poor benchmark could actually plot below the SML that uses the true market portfolio. Also, the beta could differ from that computed using the true market portfolio. For example, if the "true" beta were larger than the beta computed using the proxy, the true position of the portfolio would shift to the right.

BENCHMARK
ERRORS AND
GLOBAL
INVESTING

The concern with the benchmark error increases with global investing. The studies on international diversification discussed in Chapter 2 state clearly that adding non-U.S. securities to the portfolio universe almost certainly will move the efficient frontier to the left because including foreign securities reduces risk. You will recall that this reduction in risk continues as you add countries that have less economic interaction with the United States, such as some Asian and third-world countries. Also, some of these additions increase the expected returns of the universe so that the efficient frontier moves up as well as leftward. The point is, the efficient frontier will almost certainly change when you invest in foreign securities.

[11]Richard Roll, "A Critique of the Asset Pricing Theory's Tests," *Journal of Financial Economics* 4, no. 4 (March 1977): 129–176; Richard Roll, "Ambiguity When Performance Is Measured by the Securities Market Line," *Journal of Finance* 33, no. 4 (September 1978): 1051–1069; Richard Roll, "Performance Evaluation and Benchmark Error I," *Journal of Portfolio Management* 6, no. 4 (Summer 1980): 5–12; and Richard Roll, "Performance Evaluation and Benchmark Error II," *Journal of Portfolio Management* 7, no. 2 (Winter 1981): 17–22.

The extent of the shift in the efficient frontier depends on the relationships among countries, and these relationships will change dramatically in the coming decade. Because our trade with European and Asian countries will continue its rapid growth from recent years, the interdependence of our economies and the correlation of our financial markets should increase. Also, individual European countries have become more interdependent after 1992, when numerous barriers to trade and travel in the European Economic Community were eliminated. A paper by Brinson and Fachler discusses the performance measurement problem for non-U.S. equities, while a subsequent paper by Brinson, Diermeier, and Schlarbaum describe a multiple markets index (MMI) that includes U.S. stocks and bonds, non-U.S. stocks, non-dollar bonds, venture capital, and real estate.[12]

A DEMONSTRATION OF THE GLOBAL BENCHMARK PROBLEM

To demonstrate the impact of the benchmark problem in an environment of global capital markets, a paper by Reilly and Akhtar shows what happens to the individual measures of risk (beta) and the SML when the world equity market is employed.[13] Table 26.5 contains the parameters of the characteristic line for the 30 stocks in the Dow Jones Industrial Average (DJIA) using the S&P 500, which is the typical proxy, and the Morgan Stanley World Stock Index, which is a market value weighted index that contains stocks from around the world. The major differences are reflected in the betas and the R^2 of the regression lines. Specifically in 29 of the 30 cases, the beta was *smaller* when measured against the world index than against the S&P 500 Index, and the average beta (1.030 vs. 0.786) was about 24 percent lower. The impact is also reflected in the R^2, which was likewise almost always lower with the world index and had an average (0.470 vs. 0.274) that was 42 percent smaller. These results imply a fairly significant impact on the individual measures of risk with a clear tendency for a decline in the measure. You will recall from the discussion in Chapter 8 that beta is equal to the covariance between an asset and the market portfolio divided by the variance of the market portfolio. It is shown that the world portfolio has a lower variance than the S&P 500 (as expected), but the covariance was much lower, which caused the decline in beta.

The effect of the benchmark on the SML can be seen from the results in Table 26.6 and the plot of alternative security market lines in Figure 26.5. The results in Table 26.6 reflect widely divergent performance during the 5-year period that includes the 1987 market crash. The geometric mean annual rates of return for the alternative country stock markets adjusted to the U.S. dollar ranged from 7.03 percent for Germany to 15.22 percent in the United States. Similarly, the risk-free rates (the authors used the T-bill rates in all countries except Japan which does not issue T-bills) ranged from 5.48 percent in Japan to 11.41 in the United Kingdom.

[12]Gary P. Brinson and Nimrod Fachler, "Measuring Non-U.S. Equity Portfolio Performance," *Journal of Portfolio Management* 11, no. 3 (Spring 1985): 73–76. It discusses the problems with developing an appropriate index and considers market selection (country) and stock selection within countries. The multiple markets index (MMI) is described in Gary P. Brinson, Jeffrey J. Diermeier, and G. G. Schlarbaum, "A Composite Portfolio Benchmark for Pension Plans," *Financial Analysts Journal* 42, no. 2 (March-April, 1986): 15–24. This index is also discussed with changes in asset weights in, Roger G. Ibbotson and Gary P. Brinson, *Global Investing* (New York: McGraw-Hill, 1993): 18–19.

[13]Frank K. Reilly and Rashid A. Akhtar, "A Demonstration of the Benchmark Error Problem in a Global Environment." (University of Notre Dame, July 1993).

TABLE 26.5

Parameters of the Characteristic Lines for the Dow Jones 30 Industrials, Monthly Data: 1987–1991

Stock	Standard Deviation	S&P 500			World		
		Intercept	Beta	R^2	Intercept	Beta	R^2
Allied-Signal	7.396	−0.69	0.988	0.469	−0.22	0.583	0.163
Alcoa	8.893	0.27	1.119	0.416	0.79	0.691	0.159
AMEX	9.569	−1.87	1.253	0.451	−1.31	0.809	0.188
AT&T	6.914	0.31	0.829	0.378	0.54	0.740	0.302
Bethlehem Steel	13.531	0.61	1.477	0.314	1.04	1.311	0.247
Boeing	8.466	0.64	1.195	0.524	1.15	0.802	0.236
Caterpillar	9.214	−0.40	1.008	0.315	−0.06	0.830	0.213
Chevron	6.472	0.09	0.667	0.280	0.33	0.524	0.173
Coca-Cola	6.722	1.66	0.972	0.550	1.98	0.808	0.380
Disney	8.015	0.42	1.311	0.704	0.89	1.025	0.430
Du Pont	7.255	−0.02	1.046	0.547	0.41	0.738	0.272
Eastman Kodak	6.137	−0.59	0.784	0.430	−0.25	0.511	0.182
Exxon	4.579	0.28	0.570	0.407	0.46	0.469	0.276
General Electric	7.123	−0.05	1.200	0.746	0.43	0.853	0.377
General Motors	7.933	−0.95	0.974	0.397	−0.13	0.977	0.399
Goodyear	11.397	−0.10	1.110	0.250	0.30	0.856	0.148
IBM	6.719	−1.02	0.732	0.312	−0.78	0.607	0.215
International Paper	8.656	0.07	1.219	0.522	0.46	1.016	0.362
McDonald's	6.452	0.19	0.998	0.629	0.56	0.761	0.366
Merck	6.244	1.66	0.865	0.504	1.96	0.685	0.316
Minnesota M&M	6.180	0.09	0.912	0.573	0.44	0.668	0.308
JP Morgan	8.275	0.08	1.086	0.453	0.54	0.744	0.213
Philip Morris	7.060	1.63	0.977	0.503	1.99	0.738	0.287
Procter & Gamble	6.361	0.76	0.862	0.483	1.10	0.616	0.247
Sears	7.715	−1.00	1.177	0.612	−0.59	0.939	0.390
Texaco	6.876	0.50	0.654	0.238	0.68	0.605	0.204
Union Carbide	8.771	−0.89	1.015	0.352	−0.64	0.963	0.317
United Technologies	8.608	−0.64	1.427	0.723	−0.08	1.028	0.376
Westinghouse	8.454	−1.57	1.193	0.523	−0.99	0.688	0.175
Woolworth	9.489	−0.27	1.282	0.480	0.19	0.990	0.286
Means	7.849		1.030	0.470		0.786	0.274

Source: Frank K. Reilly and Rashid A. Akhtar, "A Demonstration of the Benchmark Error Problem in a Global Environment," (University of Notre Dame, July 1993).

The resulting SMLs are shown in Figure 26.5 and show that the German and Japanese lines would have been relatively easy to outperform, and the U.S. line that employed the S&P 500 would have been the most difficult benchmark. As one would expect, the world market line was above both Germany and Japan but below the United States. Again the important point is, the specific benchmark series used can have a significant effect on the SML used to evaluate portfolio performance.

IMPLICATIONS OF THE BENCHMARK PROBLEMS

Several points are significant regarding this benchmark criticism. First, the benchmark problems noted by Roll, which are increased with global investing, do *not* negate the value of the CAPM as a *normative* model of equilibrium pricing; the theory is still viable. The problem is one of *measurement* when using the theory to evaluate portfolio performance.

TABLE 26.6   **Domestic and Exchange Rate Adjusted Annual and Geometric Mean Rates of Return for Stock Market Indexes: 1987–1991**

Location	1987	1988	1989	1990	1991	Geometric Mean
United States (S&P500)						
Domestic	2.03	12.40	27.25	−6.56	26.31	15.22
Government bond yield	8.38	8.85	8.50	8.55	7.86	8.43
T-Bill	5.83	6.67	8.11	7.51	5.41	6.70
Japan (Nikkei)						
Domestic	14.48	39.86	29.04	−38.72	−3.63	4.06
Adjusted	49.45	35.40	12.26	−35.19	4.88	9.08
Government bond yield	4.21	4.27	5.05	7.36	6.53	5.48
T-Bill	N/A	N/A	N/A	N/A	N/A	N/A
United Kingdom (FT500)						
Domestic	4.59	5.35	29.91	−13.19	17.30	7.83
Adjusted	33.08	0.97	15.94	3.81	13.62	12.94
Government bond yield	9.48	9.36	9.58	11.08	9.92	9.88
T-Bill	9.25	9.78	13.05	14.08	10.96	11.41
Germany (FAZ)						
Domestic	−37.32	29.33	34.75	−18.61	6.18	−1.15
Adjusted	−9.99	14.45	41.44	−7.98	4.75	7.03
Government bond yield	5.84	6.10	7.09	8.88	8.63	7.30
T-Bill	3.28	3.62	6.28	8.10	8.33	5.90
World (Morgan Stanley)						
Domestic	32.62	13.22	11.76	−11.70	16.65	11.57
Adjusted	14.35	21.18	14.44	−18.43	8.46	8.46
Government bond yield	N/A	N/A	N/A	N/A	N/A	N/A
T-Bill	6.22	6.56	8.40	9.07	7.70	7.58

Source: Frank K. Reilly and Rashid A. Akhtar, "A Demonstration of the Benchmark Error Problem in a Global Environment," (University of Notre Dame, July 1993).

FIGURE 26.5   **Security Market Lines for S&P500, Nikkei, FT500, FAZ, World: 1987–1991**

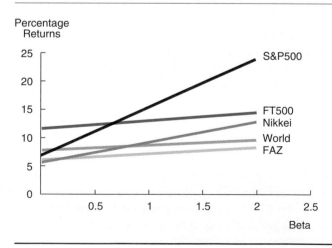

You need to find a better proxy for the market portfolio or to adjust measured performance for benchmark errors. In fact, Roll made several suggestions to help overcome this problem.[14] From Chapter 4, we know that new comprehensive stock-market and bond-market series are being developed that will be available as market portfolio proxies. Finally, the multiple markets index (MMI) developed by Brinson, Diermeier, and Schlarbaum and maintained monthly by Brinson Partners, Inc. is a major step toward a truly comprehensive world market portfolio.

Alternatively, you might consider giving greater weight to the Sharpe portfolio performance measure because it does not depend so heavily on the market portfolio. Recall that this measure relates excess return to the *standard deviation* of return, that is, to total risk. Although this evaluation process generally uses a benchmark portfolio as an example of an unmanaged portfolio for comparison purposes, the risk measure for the portfolio being evaluated does not directly depend on a market portfolio. Also, recall that the portfolio rank from the Sharpe measure typically correlates very highly with the ranks derived from alternative performance measures (see Table 26.4).

RELIABILITY OF PERFORMANCE MEASURES
Another concern is how reliably these measures rank managers and indicate their ability to significantly outperform the market. When French and Henderson examined the performance measures under ideal conditions, the results indicated that when you eliminate the random noise, these measures of performance do an excellent job of ranking portfolios consistently with their true ranking.[15] At the same time, the random noise in stocks and portfolio data complicates detecting performance that is statistically superior or inferior to the market portfolio. The fact is, a manager must be much better or worse than average before a difference shows up. This difficulty in projecting future performance based on past performance is consistent with the results discussed for mutual funds in Chapter 24.

EVALUATION OF BOND PORTFOLIO PERFORMANCE
As discussed, the analysis of risk-adjusted performance for equity portfolios started in the late 1960s following the development of portfolio theory and the capital asset pricing model (CAPM). The common stock risk measures have been fairly simple—either total risk (the standard deviation of returns) or systematic risk (betas). No such development has simplified analysis for the bond market, where there are numerous and complex factors that can influence portfolio returns. One reason for this lack of development of bond portfolio performance measures was that prior to the 1970s most bond portfolio managers followed buy-and-hold strategies, so their performance probably did not differ much. A reason for this buy-and-hold strategy is that interest rates were very stable, so one could gain little from the active management of bond portfolios.

---

[14]Richard Roll, "Performance Evaluation and Benchmark Error II," *Journal of Portfolio Management* 7, no. 2 (Winter 1981): 17–22. Several more recent papers on this topic include Jeffrey V. Bailey, "Are Manager Universes Acceptable Performance Benchmarks?" *Journal of Portfolio Management* 18, no. 3 (Spring 1992): 9–13; and Richard C. Grinwold, "Are Benchmark Portfolios Efficient?" *Journal of Portfolio Management* 19, no. 1 (Fall 1992): 34–40.

[15]Don W. French and Glenn V. Henderson, Jr., "How Well Does Performance Evaluation Perform?" *Journal of Portfolio Management* 11, no. 2 (Winter 1985): 15–18.

The environment in the bond market changed dramatically in the 1970s, and especially in the 1980s, when interest rates increased dramatically and also became more volatile. This created an incentive to trade bonds, and this trend toward more active management led to substantially more dispersed performance by bond portfolio managers. This dispersion in performance in turn created a demand for techniques that would help investors evaluate the performance of bond portfolio managers.

As with the equity market, the critical questions are: (1) How did performance compare among portfolio managers relative to the overall bond market? and (2) What factors explain or contribute to superior or inferior bond portfolio performance? In this section, we present several attempts to develop bond portfolio performance evaluation systems that consider multiple-risk factors.[16]

A BOND MARKET LINE

Wagner and Tito attempted to apply asset pricing techniques to the evaluation of bond portfolio performance.[17] A prime factor needed to evaluate performance properly is a measure of risk such as the beta coefficient for equities. This is difficult to achieve because a bond's maturity and coupon have a significant effect on the volatility of its prices.

You know from our discussion in Chapter 14 that an appropriate composite risk measure that indicates the relative price volatility for a bond compared to interest rate changes is the bond's *duration*. Using this as a measure of risk, the authors derived a bond market line much like the security market line used to evaluate equity performance. Duration simply replaces beta as the risk variable. The bond market line in Figure 26.6 is drawn from points defined by returns on Treasury bills to the Lehman Brothers Government-Corporate Bond Index rather than the S&P 500 index.[18] The Lehman Brothers Index gives the market's average annual rate of return during some common period, and the duration for the index is the value-weighted duration for the individual bonds in the index.

Given the bond market line, this technique divides the portfolio return that differs from the return on the Lehman Brothers Index into four components: (1) a policy effect, (2) a rate anticipation effect, (3) an analysis effect, and (4) a trading effect. When the latter three effects are combined, they are referred to as the *management effect*. These effects are portrayed in Figure 26.7.

The *policy effect* measures the difference in the expected return for a given portfolio because of a difference in policy regarding the duration of this portfolio compared to the duration of the Lehman Brothers Index. It is assumed that the duration of an unmanaged portfolio would be equal to the Lehman Brothers Index.[19] The duration

---

[16]An overview of this area and a discussion of the historical development is contained in H. Gifford Fong, "Bond Management: Past, Current, and Future," in *The Handbook of Fixed-Income Securities,* 3d ed., edited by Frank Fabozzi (Homewood, Ill., Business One-Irwin, 1991).

[17]Wayne H. Wagner and Dennis A. Tito, "Definitive New Measures of Bond Performance and Risk," *Pension World* (May 1977): 17–26; and Dennis A. Tito and Wayne H. Wagner, "Is Your Bond Manager Skillful?" *Pension World* (June 1977): 10–16.

[18]As you know from the presentation in Chapter 4, it would be equally reasonable to use a comparable bond-market index series from Merrill Lynch, Salomon Brothers, or the Ryan Index.

[19]Notably, the duration of the various bond-market indexes has changed over time (i.e., the duration of the corporate bond series has declined, whereas the duration of the government bond series has increased slightly). For a presentation and discussion of this phenomenon, see Frank K. Reilly, Wenchi Kao, and David J. Wright, "Alternative Bond Market Indexes," *Financial Analysts Journal* 48, no. 3 (May-June 1992): 44–58.

FIGURE 26.6   **Specification of Bond Market Line Using Lehman Brothers Bond Index**

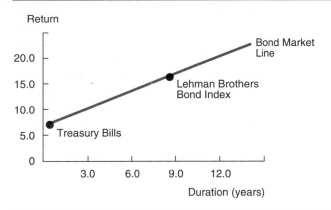

Source: Dennis A. Tito and Wayne H. Wagner, "Definitive New Measures of Bond Performance and Risk," *Pension World* (June 1977). Reprinted with permission.

FIGURE 26.7   **Graphic Display of Bond Portfolio Performance Breakdown**

Manage effect is the improvement in investment performance of a passive strategy through active bond management. It is the difference between total bond portfolio return and the expected return at the long-term average duration.

Trading effect is the result of the current quarter's trading, either through effective trade-desk operation or short-term selection abilites. It is the difference between total management effect and the effects attributable to analysis and interest rate anticipation.

Policy effect is the difference between long-term duration of a bond portfolio and the duration of a bond market index resulting from long-term investment policy. Measured as the return at the long-term average less the return on the Lehman Brothers Index.

Analysis effect, attributable to the selection of issues with better than average long-term prospects, is the difference between the actual return of the buy-and hold portfolio at the beginning of the quarter and the expected return of that buy-and-hold portfolio.

Bond market line is a straight line drawn through the return/duration of treasury bills and the return/duration of the Lehman Brothers Index.

Interest rate anticipation effect is attributable to changes in portfolio duration resulting from attempts to profit from and ability to predict bond market movements. It is the difference between the expected return at the actual portfolio duration and the expected return at the long-term duration.

Buy-and Hold portfolio is the composition of the portfolio at the beginning of the quarter. Used to differentiate between trading gains secured within a quarter and long-term analysis gains.

Duration, a measure of the average time to receipt of cash flows from an investment. It is a measure of the sensitivity of a bond's price to changes in interest rates.

Actual Return on Portfolio

Actual Return on Buy-and-Hold Portfolio

Long Term

Lehman Brothers Index

Expected Return on Buy-and-Hold Portfolio

Expected Return at Actual Duration of Portfolio

Treasury Bills

Rate of Return

Duration

Source: Dennis A. Tito and Wayne H. Wagner, "Definitive New Measures of Bond Performance and Risk," *Pension World* (June 1977). Reprinted with permission.

for a portfolio being evaluated that differs from the index duration indicates a basic policy decision regarding relative risk (measured by duration), and there should be a difference in expected return consistent with that risk policy decision. As an example, assume that the duration-return for the Lehman Brothers Index is 9.0 years and 8.25 percent. If your portfolio has a duration of 9.5 years, according to the prevailing bond market line, your return should be about 8.60 percent. In this example, the policy effect would be 0.5 years and 0.35 percent (35 basis points). Specifically, the higher duration implies that your portfolio should have a higher average return of 0.35 percent (this positive relationship assumes the typical upward-sloping yield curve).

Given the expected return and duration for this long-term portfolio, all deviations from the index portfolio are referred to as *management effects,* which are composed of (1) an interest rate anticipation effect, (2) an analysis effect, and (3) a trading effect.

The *interest rate anticipation effect* attempts to measure the differential return from changing the duration during this period compared to the portfolio's long-term duration. You would hope that the manager would increase the duration of the portfolio during periods of declining interest rates in an effort to increase the price volatility (price appreciation) of your portfolio, and reduce the duration (price volatility) of the portfolio during periods of rising interest rates to minimize the price decline. Therefore, you would determine the duration of the actual portfolio during the period and compare this to the duration of the long-term portfolio. Then you would determine the difference in expected return for these portfolios and their two durations using the bond market line. As an example, assume that the duration for the long-term portfolio is 9.5 years, which implies an expected return of 8.60 percent, and that the prevailing duration for the portfolio that is being evaluated is 10.0 years, which implies an expected return of 9.00 percent using the bond market line. Therefore, the rate anticipation effect during this period is 0.40 percent (9.00 − 8.60).

The difference between this expected return based on the portfolio's duration and the actual return for the portfolio during this period is a combination of an analysis effect and a trading effect. The *analysis effect* is the differential return attributable to acquiring bonds that are temporarily mispriced relative to their risk. To measure the analysis effect, you should compare the *expected* return for the portfolio held at the beginning of the period (using the bond market line) to the *actual* return of this same portfolio. If the actual return is greater than the expected return, it implies that the portfolio manager acquired some underpriced issues that became properly priced and provided excess returns during the period. For example, if the portfolio at the beginning of the period had a duration of 10 years, this might indicate that the portfolio's expected return was 9.00 percent for the period. In turn, if the actual return for this buy-and-hold portfolio was 9.40 percent, it would indicate an analysis effect of +0.40 percent (40 basis points).

Finally, the *trading effect* occurs due to short-run changes in the portfolio during the period. It is measured as the residual after taking account of the analysis effect from the total excess return based on duration. As an example, assume that the total actual return is 10.50 percent with a duration of 10.0 years. The prevailing bond market line indicates an expected return of 9 percent for a portfolio of 10 years duration. Thus, the combination of the analysis and trading effect is 1.50 percent (10.50 − 9.00). Previously we determined that the analysis effect was 0.40 percent, so the trading effect must be 1.10 percent (1.50 − 0.40). In summary, for this portfolio manager, the actual return was 10.50 percent, compared to a return for the Lehman Brothers Index of 8.25 percent. This total excess of 2.25 percent would be divided as follows:

- 0.35 percent policy effect due to higher long-term duration
- 0.40 percent interest rate anticipation effect due to increasing the duration of the current portfolio above the long-term portfolio duration
- 0.40 percent analysis effect—the impact of superior selection of individual issues in the beginning portfolio
- 1.10 percent trading effect—the impact of trading the issues *during* the period

This technique breaks down the return based on the duration as a comprehensive risk measure. The only concern is that *it does not consider differences in the risk of default.* Specifically, the technique does not differentiate between an AAA bond with a duration of 8 years and a BAA bond with the same duration. This could clearly affect the performance. A portfolio manager that invested in BAA bonds, for example, could experience a very positive analysis effect simply because the bonds were lower quality than the average quality implicit in the Lehman Brothers Index. The only way to avoid this would be to construct differential market lines for alternative ratings or construct a benchmark line that matches the quality makeup of the portfolio being evaluated.[20]

DECOMPOSING PORTFOLIO RETURNS

Dietz, Fogler, and Hardy set forth a technique to decompose the bond portfolio returns into maturity, sector, and quality effects.[21] The total return for a bond during a period of time is composed of a known *income effect* (due to normal yield-to-maturity factors) and an unknown *price change effect* (due to an interest rate effect, a sector/quality effect, and a residual effect). It is graphed as follows:

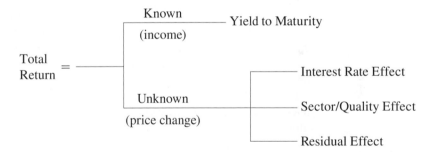

The *yield-to-maturity (income) effect* is the return an investor would receive if nothing had happened to the yield curve during the period. That is, the investor would receive the interest income, a price change relative to par, and any price change due to the passage of time and the shape of the yield curve.

The *interest rate effect* measures what happened to each issue because of changes in the term structure of interest rates during the period. Each bond is valued based on the Treasury yield curve at its maturity and takes account of its normal premium relative

[20]This problem is briefly discussed in Frank K. Reilly and Rupinder Sidhu, "The Many Uses of Bond Duration," *Financial Analysts Journal* 36, no. 4 (July-August 1980): 58–72.

[21]Peter O. Dietz, H. Russell Fogler, and Donald J. Hardy, "The Challenge of Analyzing Bond Portfolio Returns," *Journal of Portfolio Management* 6, no. 3 (Spring 1980): 53–58.

to Treasury yields. Assume a normal risk premium spread of 30 basis points and that yields on Treasury bonds with the maturity of your bond go from 8.50 percent to 9.25 percent. To determine the interest rate effect, you would compute the value of your bond at 8.80 percent (8.50 + 0.30) and at 9.55 percent (9.25 + 0.30) and then compute the price change. This is the price change caused by a change in market interest rates.

The *sector/quality effect* measures the expected impact on the returns because of the sector of the bonds (corporates, utilities, financial, GNMA, etc.) and also the quality of the bonds (Aaa, Aa, A, Baa). The authors determined the average impact of these sets of variables by deriving a matrix of sector/quality returns for all bonds on the Telstat pricing tapes as follows (i.e., you would fill in this table with the appropriate yields):

	Sector/Quality Returns (Value-Weighted)			
	Aaa	Aa	A	Baa
Corporates				
Utilities				
Financial				
Telephone				
Foreign				
GNMA				
Agencies				

Given this matrix, you can determine what happened to bonds in each cell after taking account of the yield to maturity and the interest rate effect. As an example, during a given period you might find that an average Aa utility had negative excess returns of −0.50 percent after taking account of the yield to maturity and the interest rate effect, whereas an A corporate bond experienced a comparable positive excess return of 0.30 percent. Therefore, the sector/quality effect would be −0.50 and 0.30 for these sets of bonds.

The *residual effect* is what remains after taking account of the three prior factors— yield to maturity, interest rate effect, and the sector/quality effect. It is computed as follows:

$$\text{Total Return} = \text{Yield to Maturity Effect} + \text{Interest Rate Effect} + \text{Sector/Quality Effect} + \text{Residual}$$

The presence of a consistently large positive residual would indicate superior bond selection capabilities. Specifically, a positive residual indicates that after taking account of all market effects from interest rate changes and sector/quality, it is still possible the bond manager has helped provide positive returns due to bond selection. Alternatively, large positive interest rate effects during periods of declining interest rates and small negative interest rate effects during periods of rising interest rates would indicate a bond manager with good skills at interest rate anticipation. Consistently positive sector/quality effects would indicate the ability to make proper allocations and to anticipate shifts in this area over time.

For a given portfolio, you should prepare a time-series plot of these alternative effects to determine the strengths and weaknesses of your bond portfolio manager. Also, these results net of transaction costs and taxes should be compared to the results for a static portfolio (i.e., assume that you buy and hold the beginning portfolio). Finally, these results should be compared to the performance of a broad bond-market index, which would be considered an unmanaged portfolio.

ANALYZING SOURCES OF RETURN

Fong, Pearson, and Vasicek proposed a performance evaluation technique that likewise divides the total returns into several components that affect bond returns.[22] Their intent was to measure total realized return and attribute the return to its sources (i.e., what factors contributed to the total return?). The first breakdown divides the total return (R) between the effect of the external interest rate environment (I), which is beyond the control of the portfolio manager, and the contribution of the management process (C). Thus:

$$R = I + C$$

In turn, I is broken down into two parts. The first is the *expected* rate of return (E) on a portfolio of default-free securities assuming no change in forward rates (i.e., no change in future one-period rates). This expected return is also referred to as the *market's implicit forecast*. The second component of I is U, the *unexpected* return on the Treasury index that is due to actual changes in forward rates. Thus:

$$I = E + U$$

As an example, assume that at the beginning of a quarter the expected annual return on a portfolio of Treasury bonds is 11 percent. (This expected return assumes no change in the term structure of bonds during this year.) At the end of the year, you determine that the actual return on this portfolio of Treasury bonds was 11.75 percent. This would imply an E of 11 percent and a U of .75 percent.

In turn, C (the management contribution) is composed of three factors:

- M = return from maturity management
- S = return from spread/quality management
- B = return attributable to the selection of specific securities

The return from *maturity management, M,* is determined by how well the portfolio manager changes maturity (duration) in anticipation of interest rate changes. The component is measured by computing the default-free price of every security (at the beginning and end of the period) based on the spot rate for its maturity, as indicated by the Treasury yield curve. The total return over the evaluation period is derived from these prices, while maintaining all actual trading activity. Given this total return based on maturity yields, subtract the actual return on the Treasury index (determined earlier to be 11.75 percent) to arrive at the maturity return. As an example, if the total return

[22]Gifford Fong, Charles Pearson, and Oldrich Vasicek, "Bond Performance: Analyzing Sources of Return," *Journal of Portfolio Management* 9, no. 3 (Spring 1983): 46–50.

for the portfolio based on the pricing computations was 12.25 percent, the maturity management return would be 0.50 percent, assuming the Treasury index return of 11.75 percent.[23]

The *spread/quality management* component indicates the effect on return due to the manager's selection of bonds from various sectors and quality. It is measured by pricing each bond at the beginning and end of the period using the yields that are appropriate for its specific sector and quality and then computing the rate of return given these prices. This total return less the return for Treasury bonds, considering the maturity effect (determined to be 12.25 percent), indicates the return attributable to sector/quality selection. Assuming this sector/quality pricing indicates a total return of 12.0 percent, it would imply a negative 0.25 percent for sector/quality management (12.00 − 12.25).

The *selectivity component* (B) is the remaining return. It is attributable to the selection of specific bonds after considering the maturity and sector/quality decisions—specifically, what individual bonds were selected to carry out these decisions. It is measured as the difference between the actual total return on the portfolio and the prior total return that considered maturity and sector/quality. Continuing our example, if the actual total return on the portfolio was 13.00 percent, the selectivity component would be 1.00 percent, because the return for maturity and sector/quality above was 12.00 percent. To summarize the results:

$$R = \left(\frac{E + U}{I} \right) + \left(\frac{M + S + B}{C} \right)$$

where:

E =	expected Treasury yield	11.00
U =	unexpected Treasury yield	.75
M =	maturity management	.50
S =	spread/quality management	(.25)
B =	selectivity	1.00
	Total return	13.00

This analysis would indicate that the portfolio manager was quite good at maturity (duration) decisions and at selecting individual bonds but did not do well in terms of sector/quality decisions. As before, you should do a similar breakdown for some market index series as a basis of comparison to an unmanaged portfolio. Also, you would want to examine these components over time to determine any consistent strengths or weaknesses for the portfolio manager.

CONSISTENCY OF PERFORMANCE

Numerous investigators have documented performance inconsistency for managers of equity portfolios. (These studies are discussed in Chapter 24.) Kritzman considered this question for bond managers by examining the ranking for 32 bond managers

---

[23]A subsequent article suggests a possible refinement of the maturity management effect by considering the separate effect of duration, convexity, and yield curve "twist." See Gifford Fong, Charles Pearson, Oldrich Vasicek, and Theresa Conroy, "Fixed-Income Portfolio Performance: Analyzing Sources of Return," in *The Handbook of Fixed-Income Securities,* 3d ed., edited by Frank J. Fabozzi (Homewood, Ill.: Business One Irwin, 1991).

employed by AT&T.[24] He divided a 10-year period into two 5-year periods, determined each manager's percentile ranking in each period, and correlated the rankings. The results revealed *no relationship* between performance in the two periods. A further test likewise revealed *no relationship* between past and future performance even among the best and worst performers. Based on these results, Kritzman concluded that it would be necessary to examine something besides past performance to determine superior bond portfolio managers.

REQUIRED CHARACTERISTICS OF BENCHMARKS

Earlier in this chapter and in an earlier chapter, there was a reference to the benchmark problem as related to finding a proxy for the theoretical market portfolio, especially given the trend toward global capital markets. Concurrent with this search for a global market portfolio, there has also been a search for appropriate *customized benchmarks* that reflect the specific styles of alternative managers. Bailey, Richards, and Tierney consider this to be a critical need of pension plans and endowments who hire multiple managers with widely divergent styles.[25] They point out that if a broad market index is used rather than a specific benchmark portfolio, it is implicitly assumed that the portfolio manager does not have an investment style, which is quite unrealistic. Also it does not allow the plan sponsors to determine *if* the money manager is being consistent with his or her stated investment style. The authors contend that the following basic characteristics should be possessed by any useful benchmark:

- *Unambiguous.* The names and weights of securities comprising the benchmark are clearly delineated.
- *Investable.* The option is available to forgo active management and simply hold the benchmark.
- *Measurable.* It is possible to calculate the return on the benchmark on a reasonably frequent basis.
- *Appropriate.* The benchmark is consistent with the manager's investment style or biases.
- *Reflective of current investment opinions.* The manager has current investment knowledge (be it positive, negative, or neutral) of the securities that make up the benchmark.
- *Specified in advance.* The benchmark is constructed prior to the start of an evaluation period.

If a benchmark does not possess all of these properties, it is considered flawed as an effective management tool. One example of a flawed benchmark is the use of the median manager from a broad universe of managers or even a limited universe of managers. This criticism is spelled out in detail by Bailey, who argues that the manager universe is inadequate on almost every specified characteristic.[26]

---

[24]Mark Kritzman, "Can Bond Managers Perform Consistently?" *Journal of Portfolio Management* 9, no. 4 (Summer 1983): 54–56.

[25]Jeffrey V. Bailey, Thomas M. Richards, and David E. Tierney, "Benchmark Portfolios and the Manager/Plan Sponsor Relationship," *Current Topics in Investment Management* (New York: Harper & Row, 1990). For a discussion of who shall construct a customized benchmark, see Jeffrey V. Bailey and David E. Tierney, "Gaming Manager Benchmarks," *Journal of Portfolio Management* 19, no. 4 (Summer 1993): 37–40.

[26]Jeffrey V. Bailey, "Are Manager Universes Acceptable Performance Benchmarks?" *Journal of Portfolio Management* 18, no. 3 (Spring 1992): 9–13. For a general discussion of what to look for in a benchmark, see Jeffrey V. Bailey, "Evaluating Benchmark Quality," *Financial Analysts Journal* 48, no. 3 (May-June 1992): 33–39.

In summary, because of a growing desire not only to evaluate aggregate performance, but also to be able to identify what factors contribute to superior or inferior
performance, benchmarks must be selected at two levels: (1) a *global* level that contains
the broadest mixture of risky assets available from around the world, and (2) a fairly
specific level that is consistent with the management style of an individual money
manager (i.e., a customized benchmark). When searching both levels, the set of characteristics suggested by Bailey, Richards, and Tierney should be kept in mind.

SUMMARY

The first major goal of portfolio management is to derive rates of returns that equal or
exceed the returns on a naively selected portfolio with equal risk. The second goal is
to attain complete diversification. Several techniques have been derived to evaluate
equity portfolios in terms of both risk and return (composite measures) based on the
CAPM. The Treynor measure considers the excess returns earned per unit of systematic
risk. The Sharpe measure indicates the excess return per unit of total risk. Jensen
likewise evaluated performance in terms of the systematic risk involved and showed
how to determine whether the difference in risk-adjusted performance (good or bad)
is statistically significant. The application of these evaluation techniques to 20 mutual
funds indicated the importance of considering both risk and return, because there was
a wide range of total risk, systematic risk, and diversification. Additional work in equity
portfolio evaluation has been concerned with models that indicate what components
of the management process contributed to the results. A model by Fama divided the
composite return into measures related to total risk, systematic risk, diversification,
and selectivity, in addition to measuring overall performance. The rank correlations
among the alternative portfolio performance measures were extremely high, about
0.97.

Friend and Blume contended that there was an inverse relationship between the risk
of the portfolio and its composite performance, whereas Klemkosky indicated a completely different bias. Therefore, it appears that some biases may exist, but their direction is unknown and they would seldom change the rankings.

Roll challenged the validity of all techniques that assume a "market portfolio" that
theoretically includes all risky assets when actually investigators use a proxy such as
the S&P 500 that is limited to U.S. common stocks. This criticism does not invalidate
the normative asset pricing model, only its application because of measurement problems related to the proxy for the market portfolio. It is demonstrated that the measurement problem is increased in an environment where global investing is the norm. The
good news is that more comprehensive indexes are feasible and one has been developed
by Brinson Partners.

Although the techniques for evaluating equity portfolio performance have been in
existence for almost 35 years, comparable techniques for examining bond portfolio
performance were initiated only about 10 years ago. Notably, the evaluation models
for bonds typically consider separately the several important decision variables related
to bonds: the overall market factor, the impact of maturity-duration decisions, the
influence of sector and quality factors, and the impact of individual bond selection. A
study indicated a lack of consistency over time for a sample of bond managers similar
to results for equity managers.

In conclusion, investors need to evaluate their own performance and the performance of hired managers. The various techniques discussed provide theoretically justifiable measures that differ slightly. Although there was high rank correlation among the alternative measures, *all the measures should be used,* because they provide different insights regarding the performance of managers. Finally, an evaluation of a portfolio manager should be done many times over *different market environments* before a final judgment is reached regarding the strengths and weaknesses of a manager.[27]

The chapter ended with a further discussion on benchmarks that noted the dual need for comprehensive global benchmarks and numerous specific benchmarks or customized benchmarks that will allow plan sponsors to evaluate the factors that contribute to superior or inferior performance and the consistency of style for alternative managers.

QUESTIONS

1. Assuming you are managing your own portfolio, discuss whether you should evaluate your own performance. What would you compare your performance against?

2. What are the two major factors that should be considered when evaluating a portfolio manager? What should the portfolio manager be trying to do?

3. What can a portfolio manager do to derive superior risk-adjusted returns?

4. What is the purpose of diversification according to the CAPM?

5. How can you measure whether a portfolio is completely diversified? Explain why this measure makes sense.

6. Define and discuss the Treynor measure of portfolio performance.

7. Define and discuss the Sharpe measure of portfolio performance.

8. Why is it suggested that both the Treynor and Sharpe measures of performance be employed? What additional information is provided by a comparison of the rankings achieved using the two measures?

9. Define the Jensen measure of performance, and discuss whether it should produce results similar to those from the Treynor or the Sharpe methods.

10. Define overall performance in the Fama model. Assume a fund had an overall performance figure of 5 percent. Discuss whether this means the manager is superior.

11. A fund had an overall performance value of -0.50 percent using the Fama performance technique. Discuss whether the manager of this fund could have experienced a positive selectivity value and under what conditions.

12. Define Fama's diversification term. Under what conditions will this term equal zero?

13. Define net selectivity. If a portfolio had a negative selectivity value, could it have a positive *net* selectivity measure? Under what conditions?

14. A portfolio has an R^2 with the market of 0.95 and a selectivity value of 2.5 percent. Discuss whether you would expect the portfolio to have a positive net selectivity value.

---

[27]For a general discussion of portfolio evaluation, see Peter O. Dietz and Jeannette R. Kirschman, "Evaluating Portfolio Performance," in *Managing Investment Portfolios,* 2d ed., edited by John L. Maginn and Donald L. Tuttle (Boston: Warren Gorham and Lamont, 1990). For a recent detailed discussion of the equity portfolio evaluation techniques, see Ray Shulka and Charles Trzcinka, "Performance Measurement of Managed Portfolios," in *Financial Markets, Institutions and Investments* (New York: New York University Salomon Center, Vol. 1, no. 4, 1992).

15. Assuming that the proxy used for the market portfolio is not a good proxy, discuss the potential problem with the measurement of portfolio beta. Show by an example the effect on a portfolio evaluation graph if the measured beta is significantly lower than the true beta.

16. Assuming that the market proxy is a poor proxy, show an example of the potential impact on the security market line (SML) and demonstrate with an example how a portfolio that was superior relative to the proxy SML line could be inferior when compared to the true SML.

17. Show with a graph the effect global investing should have on the aggregate efficient frontier. Discuss the effect of this on the world SML and individual betas?

18. It is contended that the derivation of an appropriate model for evaluating the performance of a bond portfolio manager is more difficult than an equity portfolio evaluation model because there are more decisions required. Discuss some of the specific decisions that need to be considered when evaluating the performance of a bond portfolio manager.

19. Briefly describe what you are trying to measure in the following cases:
    a. The interest rate effect (i.e., market effect)
    b. The maturity effect (duration)
    c. The sector/quality effect
    d. The selection effect

20 Which of the effects in Question 19 are under the control of the bond portfolio manager?

21. *CFA Examination III (1981)*
    Richard Roll, in an article on using the capital asset pricing model (CAPM) to evaluate portfolio performance, indicated that it may not be possible to evaluate portfolio management ability if there is an error in the benchmark used.
    a. In evaluating portfolio performance, *describe* the general procedure, with emphasis on the benchmark employed. [5 minutes]
    b. Explain what Roll meant by the benchmark error and identify the specific problem with this benchmark. [5 minutes]
    c. Draw a graph that shows how a portfolio that has been judged as superior relative to a "measured" security market line (SML) can be inferior relative to the "true" SML. [10 minutes]
    d. Assume that you are informed that a given portfolio manager has been evaluated as superior when compared to the DJIA, the S&P 500, and the NYSE Composite Index. Explain whether this consensus would make you feel more comfortable regarding the portfolio manager's true ability. [5 minutes]
    e. While conceding the possible problem with benchmark errors as set forth by Roll, some contend this does not mean the CAPM is incorrect, but only that there is a measurement problem when implementing the theory. Others contend that because of benchmark errors, the whole technique should be scrapped. Take and defend one of these positions. [5 minutes]

22. *CFA Examination III (1982)*
    During a quarterly review session, a client of Fixed Income Investors, a pension fund advisory firm, asks Fred Raymond, the portfolio manager for the company's account, if he could provide a more detailed analysis of their portfolio performance than simply total return. Specifically, the client had recently seen a copy of an article by Deitz, Fogler, and Hardy on the analysis of bond portfolio returns that attempted to decompose the total return into the following four components:
    a. Yield-to-maturity effect
    b. Interest rate effect

c. Sector/quality effect
d. Residual

Although he does not expect you to be able to provide such an analysis this year, he asks you to explain each of these components to him so he will be better prepared to understand such an analysis when you do it for his company's portfolio next year. Explain each of these components. [20 minutes]

PROBLEMS

1. Assume that during the past 10-year period the risk-free rate was 8 percent, and three portfolios had the following characteristics:

Portfolio	Return	Beta	σ
A	.13	1.10	.14
B	.11	0.90	.10
C	.17	1.20	.20

Compute the T value for each portfolio, and indicate which portfolio had the best performance. Assume the market return during this period was 12 percent; how did these managers fare relative to the market?

2. Given the standard deviations specified in Problem 1, compute the Sharpe measure of performance for the three portfolios. Is there any difference in the ranking achieved using the Treynor versus the Sharpe measure? Discuss the probable cause.

3. The portfolios identified below are being considered for investment. During the period under consideration, $R_f = .07$.

Portfolio	Return	Beta	σ_i
P	.15	1.0	.05
Q	.20	1.5	.10
R	.10	.6	.03
S	.17	1.1	.06
Market	.13	1.0	.04

a. Compute the Sharpe measure of each portfolio and the market portfolio.
b. Compute the Treynor measure of each portfolio and the market portfolio.
c. Rank the portfolios using each measure.

4. You have decided to undertake an evaluation of the performance of the Cirrus International Fund (CIF) for your Investment Club. After collecting the following data:

$$R_a = 0.15$$
$$R_f = 0.05$$
$$B_a = 1.20$$
$$R_m = 0.10$$

a. Draw the security market line.
b. Calculate CIF's overall performance.

c. Calculate CIF's selectivity.

d. Calculate CIF's risk.

5. Reggie Portmus has made a performance evaluation of his bond holdings. He has misplaced some of the values and has asked for your help in calculating the remaining ones. At present he holds 10-year AA, 5-year A, and 25-year B bonds, and the following information has been recovered:

I =	external interest rate environment	11.00
E =	expected return	10.00
U =	unexpected return	?
M =	maturity	.2 percent/year in the first 5 years, and .1 percent/year thereafter
S =	spread/quality	− .2 percent/rank (AAA, AA, A, BBB, etc.)
B =	specific selection	.25, .50, .75, respectively
C		?
R		?

REFERENCES

Bailey, Jeffrey, V. "Evaluating Benchmark Quality." *Financial Analysts Journal* 48, no. 3 (May-June 1992).

Bailey, Jeffrey V., Thomas M. Richards, and David E. Tierney. "Benchmark Portfolios and the Manager/Plan Sponsor Relationship." *Current Topics in Investment Management.* New York: Harper and Row, 1990.

Bailey, Jeffrey V. and David E. Tierney. "Gaming Manager Benchmarks." *Journal of Portfolio Management* 19, no. 4 (Summer 1993).

Brinson, Gary P., and Nimrod Fachler. "Measuring Non-U.S. Equity Portfolio Performance." *Journal of Portfolio Management* 11, no. 3 (Spring 1985).

Brinson, Gary P., Jeffrey J. Diermeier, and G. G. Schlarbaum. "A Composite Portfolio Benchmark for Pension Plans." *Financial Analysts Journal* 42, no. 2 (March-April 1986).

Chen, N., T. E. Copeland, and D. Mayers. "A Comparison of Single and Multifactor Portfolio Performance Methodologies." *Journal of Financial and Quantitative Analysis* 22, no. 4 (December 1987).

Dietz, Peter O., H. Russell Fogler, and Donald J. Hardy. "The Challenge of Analyzing Bond Portfolio Returns." *Journal of Portfolio Management* 6, no. 3 (Spring 1980).

Dietz, Peter O., and Jeannette R. Kirschman. "Evaluating Portfolio Performance." In *Managing Investment Portfolios,* 2d ed., edited by John L. Maginn and Donald L. Tuttle. Boston: Warren Gorham and Lamont, 1990.

Fama, Eugene. "Components of Investment Performance." *Journal of Finance* 27, no. 3 (June 1972).

Fong, Gifford, Charles Pearson, Oldrich Vasicek, and Theresa Conroy. "Fixed-Income Portfolio Performance: Analyzing Sources of Return." In *The Handbook of Fixed-Income Securities,* 3d ed., edited by Frank J. Fabozzi. Homewood, Ill.: Business One Irwin, 1991.

Grinwold, Richard C. "Are Benchmark Portfolios Efficient?" *Journal of Portfolio Management* 19, no. 1 (Fall 1992).

Jensen, Michael C. "Risk, the Pricing of Capital Assets, and the Evaluation of Investment Portfolios." *Journal of Business* 42, no. 2 (April 1969).

Roll, Richard. "A Critique of the Asset Pricing Theory's Tests." *Journal of Financial Economics* 4, no. 4 (March 1977).

Roll, Richard. "Ambiguity When Performance Is Measured by the Securities Market Line." *Journal of Finance* 33, no. 4 (September 1978).

Sharpe, William F. "Mutual Fund Performance." *Journal of Business* 39, no. 1, Part 2 (January 1966).

Shulka, Ray, and Charles Trzcinka. "Performance Measurement of Managed Portfolios." New York: New York University Salomon Center, *Financial Markets, Institutions, and Investments,* Vol. 1, no. 4, 1992).

Treynor, Jack L. "How to Rate Management of Investment Funds." *Harvard Business Review* 43, no. 1 (January-February 1965).

Williams, Arthur III. *Managing Your Investment Manager—The Complete Guide to Selection, Measurement, and Control.* Homewood, Ill.: Dow Jones-Irwin, 1986.

How to Become a Chartered Financial Analyst

As mentioned in the section on career opportunities, the professional designation of Chartered Financial Analyst (CFA) is becoming a significant requirement for a career in investment analysis and/or portfolio management. For that reason, this section presents the history and objectives of the Institute of Chartered Financial Analysts and general guidelines for acquiring the CFA designation. If you are interested in the program, you can write to the Institute for more information.

The Institute of Chartered Financial Analysts (ICFA) was formed in 1959 in Charlottesville, Virginia. The CFA candidate examinations were first offered in 1963. The ICFA, along with the Financial Analysts Federation, form the Association for Investment Management and Research (AIMR).

The Institute of Chartered Financial Analysts (ICFA) was organized to enhance the professionalism of those involved in various aspects of the investment decision-making process and to recognize those who achieve a high level of professionalism by awarding the designation of Chartered Financial Analyst (CFA).

The basic missions and purposes of the AIMR/ICFA are

- To develop and keep current a "body of knowledge" applicable to the investment decision-making process. The principal components of this knowledge are financial accounting, economics, both fixed-income and equity securities analysis, portfolio management, ethical and professional standards, and quantitative techniques.
- To administer a study and examination program for eligible candidates, the primary objectives of which are to assist the candidate in mastering and applying the body of knowledge and to test the candidate's competency in the knowledge gained.
- To award the professional CFA designation to those candidates who have passed three examination levels (encompassing a total of 18 hours of testing over a minimum of three years), who meet stipulated standards of professional conduct, and who otherwise are eligible for membership in the ICFA.
- To provide a useful and informative program of continuing education through seminars, publications, and other formats that enable members, candidates,

and others in the investment constituency to be more aware of and to better utilize the changing and expanding body of knowledge.
- To sponsor and enforce a *Code of Ethics and Standards of Professional Conduct* that apply to enrolled candidates and to all members.

A college degree is necessary to enter the program. A candidate may sit for all three examinations without having had investment experience *per se* or having joined a constituent Society of the Financial Analysts Federation. However, after passing the three examination levels, the CFA Charter will not be awarded unless or until the candidate

- has at least three years of experience as a financial analyst, which is defined as a person who has spent and/or is spending a substantial portion of his/her professional time collecting, evaluating, and applying financial, economic, and related data to the investment decision-making process, and
- has applied for membership or is a member of a constituent Society of the Financial Analysts Federation, if such a Society exists within 50 miles of the candidate's principal place of business.

The curriculum of the CFA study program covers:

1. Ethical and Professional Standards
2. Financial Accounting
3. Economics
4. Fixed-Income Securities Analysis
5. Equity Securities Analysis
6. Portfolio Management
7. Quantitative Techniques

Members and candidates are typically employed in the investment field. From 1963 to 1991, over 13,000 charters have been awarded. More than 13,000 individuals currently are registered in the CFA Candidate Program. If you are interested in learning more about the CFA program, the Institute has a booklet that describes the program and includes an application form. The address is Institute of Chartered Financial Analysts, P.O. Box 3668, Charlottesville, Virginia 22903.

Source: Reprinted with permission from The Financial Analysts Federation and The Institute of Chartered Financial Analysts, Charlottesville, Virginia.

CODE OF ETHICS AND STANDARDS OF PROFESSIONAL CONDUCT

THE STANDARDS OF PROFESSIONAL CONDUCT

I.   Obligation to Inform Employer of Code and Standards
The financial analyst shall inform his employer, through his direct supervisor, that the analyst is obligated to comply with the Code of Ethics and Standards of Professional Conduct, and is subject to disciplinary sanctions for violations thereof. He shall deliver a copy of the Code and Standards to his employer if the employer does not have a copy.

II. Compliance with Governing Laws and Regulations and the Code and Standards

A. Required Knowledge and Compliance
The financial analyst shall maintain knowledge of and shall comply with all applicable laws, rules, and regulations of any government, governmental agency, and regulatory organization governing his professional, financial, or business activities, as well as with these Standards of Professional Conduct and the accompanying Code of Ethics.

B. Prohibition Against Assisting Legal and Ethical Violations
The financial analyst shall not knowingly participate in, or assist, any acts in violation of any applicable law, rule, or regulation of any government, governmental agency, or regulatory organization governing his professional, financial, or business activities, nor any act which would violate any provision of these Standards of Professional Conduct or the accompanying Code of Ethics.

C. Prohibition Against Use of Material Nonpublic Information
The financial analyst shall comply with all laws and regulations relating to the use and communication of material nonpublic information. The financial analyst's duty is generally defined as to not trade while in possession of, nor communicate, material nonpublic information in breach of a duty, or if the information is misappropriated.

Duties under the Standard include the following: (1) If the analyst acquires such information as a result of a special or confidential relationship with the issuer or others, he shall not communicate the information (other than within the relationship), or take investment action on the basis of such information, if it violates that relationship. (2) If the analyst is not in a special or confidential relationship with the issuer or others, he shall not communicate or act on material nonpublic information if he knows, or should have known, that such information (a) was disclosed to him, or would result in a breach of a duty, or (b) was misappropriated.

If such a breach of duty exists, the analyst shall make reasonable efforts to achieve public dissemination of such information.

D. Responsibilities of Supervisors
A financial analyst with supervisory responsibility shall exercise reasonable supervision over those subordinate employees subject to his control, to prevent any violation by such persons of applicable statutes, regulations, or provisions of the Code of Ethics or Standards of Professional Conduct. In so doing the analyst is entitled to rely upon reasonable procedures established by his employer.

III. Research Reports, Investment Recommendations and Actions

A. Reasonable Basis and Representations
1. The financial analyst shall exercise diligence and thoroughness in making an investment recommendation to others or in taking an investment action for others.
2. The financial analyst shall have a reasonable and adequate basis for such recommendations and actions, supported by appropriate research and investigation.
3. The financial analyst shall make reasonable and diligent efforts to avoid any material misrepresentation in any research report or investment recommendation.
4. The financial analyst shall maintain appropriate records to support the reasonableness of such recommendations and actions.

B. Research Reports
1. The financial analyst shall use reasonable judgment as to the inclusion of relevant factors in research reports.
2. The financial analyst shall distinguish between facts and opinions in research reports.
3. The financial analyst shall indicate the basic characteristics of the investment involved when preparing for general public distribution a research report that is not directly related to a specific portfolio or client.

C. Portfolio Investment Recommendations and Actions
The financial analyst shall, when making an investment recommendation or taking an investment action for a specific portfolio or client, consider its appropriateness and suitability for such portfolio or client. In considering such matters, the financial analyst shall take into account (1) the needs and circumstances of the

---

*Masculine personal pronouns, used throughout the Code and Standards to simplify sentence structure, shall apply to all persons, regardless of sex.

client, (2) the basic characteristics of the investment involved, and (3) the basic characteristics of the total portfolio. The financial analyst shall use reasonable judgment to determine the applicable relevant factors. The financial analyst shall distinguish between facts and opinions in the presentation of investment recommendations.

D. Prohibition Against Plagiarism

The financial analyst shall not, when presenting material to his employer, associates, customers, clients, or the general public, copy or use in substantially the same form material prepared by other persons without acknowledging its use and identifying the name of the author or publisher of such material. The analyst may, however, use without acknowledgement factual information published by recognized financial and statistical reporting services or similar sources.

E. Prohibition Against Misrepresentation of Services

The financial analyst shall not make any statements, orally or in writing, which misrepresent (1) the services that the analyst or his firm is capable of performing for the client, (2) the qualifications of such analyst or his firm, (3) the investment performance that the analyst or his firm has accomplished or can reasonably be expected to achieve for the client, or (4) the expected performance of any investment.

The financial analyst shall not make, orally or in writing, explicitly or implicitly, any assurances about or guarantees of any investment or its return except communication of accurate information as to the terms of the investment instrument and the issuer's obligations under the instrument.

F. Fair Dealing with Customers and Clients

The financial analyst shall act in a manner consistent with his obligation to deal fairly with all customers and clients when (1) disseminating investment recommendations, (2) disseminating material changes in prior investment advice, and (3) taking investment action.

IV. Priority of Transactions

The financial analyst shall conduct himself in such a manner that transactions for his customers, clients, and employer have priority over personal transactions, and so that his personal transactions do not operate adversely to their interests. If an analyst decides to make a recommendation about the purchase or sale of a security or other investment, he shall give his customers, clients, and employer adequate opportunity to act on this recommendation before acting on his own behalf.

V. Disclosure of Conflicts

The financial analyst, when making investment recommendations, or taking investment actions, shall disclose to his customers and clients any material conflict of interest relating to him and any material beneficial ownership of the securities or other investments involved that could reasonably be expected to impair his ability to render unbiased and objective advice.

The financial analyst shall disclose to his employer all matters that could reasonably be expected to interfere with his duty to the employer, or with his ability to render unbiased and objective advice.

The financial analyst shall also comply with all requirements as to disclosure of conflicts of interest imposed by law and by rules and regulations of organizations governing his activities and shall comply with any prohibitions on his activities if a conflict of interest exists.

VI. Compensation

A. Disclosure of Additional Compensation Arrangements

The financial analyst shall inform his customers, clients, and employer of compensation or other benefit arrangements in connection with his services to them which are in addition to compensation from them for such services.

B. Disclosure of Referral Fees

The financial analyst shall make appropriate disclosure to a prospective client or customer of any consideration paid or other benefit delivered to others for recommending his services to that prospective client or customer.

C. Duty to Employer

The financial analyst shall not undertake independent practice for compensation or other benefit in competition with his employer unless he has received written consent from both his employer and the person for whom he undertakes independent employment.

VII. Relationships with Others

A. Preservation of Confidentiality

A financial analyst shall preserve the confidentiality of information communicated by the client concerning matters within the scope of the confidential relationship, unless the financial analyst receives information concerning illegal activities on the part of the client.

B. Maintenance of Independence and Objectivity

The financial analyst, in relationships and contacts with an issuer of securities, whether individually or as a member of a group, shall use particular care and good judgment to achieve and maintain independence and objectivity.

C. Fiduciary Duties

The financial analyst, in relationships with clients, shall use particular care in determining applicable fiduciary duty and shall comply with such duty as to those persons and interests to whom it is owed.

VIII. Use of Professional Designation

The qualified financial analyst may use, as applicable, the professional designation "Member of the Association for Investment Management and Research", "Member of the Financial Analysts Federation", and "Member of the Institute of Chartered Financial Analysts", and is encouraged to do so, but only in a dignified and judicious manner. The use of the designations may be accompanied by an accurate explanation (1) of the requirements that have been met to obtain the designation, and (2) of the Association for Investment Management and Research, the Financial Analysts Federation, and the Institute of Chartered Financial Analysts, as applicable.

The Chartered Financial Analyst may use the professional designation "Chartered Financial Analyst", or the abbreviation "CFA", and is encouraged to do so, but only in a dignified and judicious manner. The use of the designation may be accompanied by an accurate explanation (1) of the requirements that have been met to obtain the designation, and (2) of the Association for Investment Management and Research, and the Institute of Chartered Financial Analysts.

IX. Professional Misconduct

The financial analyst shall not (1) commit a criminal act that upon conviction materially reflects adversely on his honesty, trustworthiness or fitness as a financial analyst in other respects, or (2) engage in conduct involving dishonesty, fraud, deceit or misrepresentation.

INTEREST TABLES

TABLE C.1   Present Value of $1: PVIF $= 1/(1 + k)^t$

Period	1%	2%	3%	4%	5%	6%	7%	8%	9%	10%	12%	14%	15%	16%	18%	20%	24%	28%	32%	36%
1	.9901	.9804	.9709	.9615	.9524	.9434	.9346	.9259	.9174	.9091	.8929	.8772	.8696	.8621	.8475	.8333	.8065	.7813	.7576	.7353
2	.9803	.9612	.9426	.9246	.9070	.8900	.8734	.8573	.8417	.8264	.7972	.7695	.7561	.7432	.7182	.6944	.6504	.6104	.5739	.5407
3	.9706	.9423	.9151	.8890	.8638	.8396	.8163	.7938	.7722	.7513	.7118	.6750	.6575	.6407	.6086	.5787	.5245	.4768	.4348	.3975
4	.9610	.9238	.8885	.8548	.8227	.7921	.7629	.7350	.7084	.6830	.6355	.5921	.5718	.5523	.5158	.4823	.4230	.3725	.3294	.2923
5	.9515	.9057	.8626	.8219	.7835	.7473	.7130	.6806	.6499	.6209	.5674	.5194	.4972	.4761	.4371	.4019	.3411	.2910	.2495	.2149
6	.9420	.8880	.8375	.7903	.7462	.7050	.6663	.6302	.5963	.5645	.5066	.4556	.4323	.4104	.3704	.3349	.2751	.2274	.1890	.1580
7	.9327	.8706	.8131	.7599	.7107	.6651	.6227	.5835	.5470	.5132	.4523	.3996	.3759	.3538	.3139	.2791	.2218	.1776	.1432	.1162
8	.9235	.8535	.7894	.7307	.6768	.6274	.5820	.5403	.5019	.4665	.4039	.3506	.3269	.3050	.2660	.2326	.1789	.1388	.1085	.0854
9	.9143	.8368	.7664	.7026	.6446	.5919	.5439	.5002	.4604	.4241	.3606	.3075	.2843	.2630	.2255	.1938	.1443	.1084	.0822	.0628
10	.9053	.8203	.7441	.6756	.6139	.5584	.5083	.4632	.4224	.3855	.3220	.2697	.2472	.2267	.1911	.1615	.1164	.0847	.0623	.0462
11	.8963	.8043	.7224	.6496	.5847	.5268	.4751	.4289	.3875	.3505	.2875	.2366	.2149	.1954	.1619	.1346	.0938	.0662	.0472	.0340
12	.8874	.7885	.7014	.6246	.5568	.4970	.4440	.3971	.3555	.3186	.2567	.2076	.1869	.1685	.1372	.1122	.0757	.0517	.0357	.0250
13	.8787	.7730	.6810	.6006	.5303	.4688	.4150	.3677	.3262	.2897	.2292	.1821	.1625	.1452	.1163	.0935	.0610	.0404	.0271	.0184
14	.8700	.7579	.6611	.5775	.5051	.4423	.3878	.3405	.2992	.2633	.2046	.1597	.1413	.1252	.0985	.0779	.0492	.0316	.0205	.0135
15	.8613	.7430	.6419	.5553	.4810	.4173	.3624	.3152	.2745	.2394	.1827	.1401	.1229	.1079	.0835	.0649	.0397	.0247	.0155	.0099
16	.8528	.7284	.6232	.5339	.4581	.3936	.3387	.2919	.2519	.2176	.1631	.1229	.1069	.0930	.0708	.0541	.0320	.0193	.0118	.0073
17	.8444	.7142	.6050	.5134	.4363	.3714	.3166	.2703	.2311	.1978	.1456	.1078	.0929	.0802	.0600	.0451	.0258	.0150	.0089	.0054
18	.8360	.7002	.5874	.4936	.4155	.3503	.2959	.2502	.2120	.1799	.1300	.0946	.0808	.0691	.0508	.0376	.0208	.0118	.0068	.0039
19	.8277	.6864	.5703	.4746	.3957	.3305	.2765	.2317	.1945	.1635	.1161	.0829	.0703	.0596	.0431	.0313	.0168	.0092	.0051	.0029
20	.8195	.6730	.5537	.4564	.3769	.3118	.2584	.2145	.1784	.1486	.1037	.0728	.0611	.0514	.0365	.0261	.0135	.0072	.0039	.0021
25	.7798	.6095	.4776	.3751	.2953	.2330	.1842	.1460	.1160	.0923	.0588	.0378	.0304	.0245	.0160	.0105	.0046	.0021	.0010	.0005
30	.7419	.5521	.4120	.3083	.2314	.1741	.1314	.0994	.0754	.0573	.0334	.0196	.0151	.0116	.0070	.0042	.0016	.0006	.0002	.0001
40	.6717	.4529	.3066	.2083	.1420	.0972	.0668	.0460	.0318	.0221	.0107	.0053	.0037	.0026	.0013	.0007	.0002	.0001	*	*
50	.6080	.3715	.2281	.1407	.0872	.0543	.0339	.0213	.0134	.0085	.0035	.0014	.0009	.0006	.0003	.0001	*	*	*	*
60	.5504	.3048	.1697	.0951	.0535	.0303	.0173	.0099	.0057	.0033	.0011	.0004	.0002	.0001	*	*	*	*	*	*

*The factor is zero to four decimal places.

TABLE C.2

Present Value of an Annuity of $1 Per Period for n Periods:

$$PVIFA = \sum_{t=1}^{n} \frac{1}{(1+k)^t} = \frac{1 - \dfrac{1}{(1+k)^n}}{k}$$

Number of Payments	1%	2%	3%	4%	5%	6%	7%	8%	9%	10%	12%	14%	15%	16%	18%	20%	24%	28%	32%
1	0.9901	0.9804	0.9709	0.9615	0.9524	0.9434	0.9346	0.9259	0.9174	0.9091	0.8929	0.8772	0.8696	0.8621	0.8475	0.8333	0.8065	0.7813	0.7576
2	1.9704	1.9416	1.9135	1.8861	1.8594	1.8334	1.8080	1.7833	1.7591	1.7355	1.6901	1.6467	1.6257	1.6052	1.5656	1.5278	1.4568	1.3916	1.3315
3	2.9410	2.8839	2.8286	2.7751	2.7232	2.6730	2.6243	2.5771	2.5313	2.4869	2.4018	2.3216	2.2832	2.2459	2.1743	2.1065	1.9813	1.8684	1.7663
4	3.9020	3.8077	3.7171	3.6299	3.5460	3.4651	3.3872	3.3121	3.2397	3.1699	3.0373	2.9137	2.8550	2.7982	2.6901	2.5887	2.4043	2.2410	2.0957
5	4.8534	4.7135	4.5797	4.4518	4.3295	4.2124	4.1002	3.9927	3.8897	3.7908	3.6048	3.4331	3.3522	3.2743	3.1272	2.9906	2.7454	2.5320	2.3452
6	5.7955	5.6014	5.4172	5.2421	5.0757	4.9173	4.7665	4.6229	4.4859	4.3553	4.1114	3.8887	3.7845	3.6847	3.4976	3.3255	3.0205	2.7594	2.5342
7	6.7282	6.4720	6.2303	6.0021	5.7864	5.5824	5.3893	5.2064	5.0330	4.8684	4.5638	4.2883	4.1604	4.0386	3.8115	3.6046	3.2423	2.9370	2.6775
8	7.6517	7.3255	7.0197	6.7327	6.4632	6.2098	5.9713	5.7466	5.5348	5.3349	4.9676	4.6389	4.4873	4.3436	4.0776	3.8372	3.4212	3.0758	2.7860
9	8.5660	8.1622	7.7861	7.4353	7.1078	6.8017	6.5152	6.2469	5.9952	5.7590	5.3282	4.9464	4.7716	4.6065	4.3030	4.0310	3.5655	3.1842	2.8681
10	9.4713	8.9826	8.5302	8.1109	7.7217	7.3601	7.0236	6.7101	6.4177	6.1446	5.6502	5.2161	5.0188	4.8332	4.4941	4.1925	3.6819	3.2689	2.9304
11	10.3676	9.7868	9.2526	8.7605	8.3064	7.8869	7.4987	7.1390	6.8052	6.4951	5.9377	5.4527	5.2337	5.0286	4.6560	4.3271	3.7757	3.3351	2.9776
12	11.2551	10.5753	9.9540	9.3851	8.8633	8.3838	7.9427	7.5361	7.1607	6.8137	6.1944	5.6603	5.4206	5.1971	4.7932	4.4392	3.8514	3.3868	3.0133
13	12.1337	11.3484	10.6350	9.9856	9.3936	8.8527	8.3577	7.9038	7.4869	7.1034	6.4235	5.8424	5.5831	5.3423	4.9095	4.5327	3.9124	3.4272	3.0404
14	13.0037	12.1062	11.2961	10.5631	9.8986	9.2950	8.7455	8.2442	7.7862	7.3667	6.6282	6.0021	5.7245	5.4675	5.0081	4.6106	3.9616	3.4587	3.0609
15	13.8651	12.8493	11.9379	11.1184	10.3797	9.7122	9.1079	8.5595	8.0607	7.6061	6.8109	6.1422	5.8474	5.5755	5.0916	4.6755	4.0013	3.4834	3.0764
16	14.7179	13.5777	12.5611	11.6523	10.8378	10.1059	9.4466	8.8514	8.3126	7.8237	6.9740	6.2651	5.9542	5.6685	5.1624	4.7296	4.0333	3.5026	3.0882
17	15.5623	14.2919	13.1661	12.1657	11.2741	10.4773	9.7632	9.1216	8.5436	8.0216	7.1196	6.3729	6.0472	5.7487	5.2223	4.7746	4.0591	3.5177	3.0971
18	16.3983	14.9920	13.7535	12.6593	11.6896	10.8276	10.0591	9.3719	8.7556	8.2014	7.2497	6.4674	6.1280	5.8178	5.2732	4.8122	4.0799	3.5294	3.1039
19	17.2260	15.6785	14.3238	13.1339	12.0853	11.1581	10.3356	9.6036	8.9501	8.3649	7.3658	6.5504	6.1982	5.8775	5.3162	4.8435	4.0967	3.5386	3.1090
20	18.0456	16.3514	14.8775	13.5903	12.4622	11.4699	10.5940	9.8181	9.1285	8.5136	7.4694	6.6231	6.2593	5.9288	5.3527	4.8696	4.1103	3.5458	3.1129
25	22.0232	19.5235	17.4131	15.6221	14.0939	12.7834	11.6536	10.6748	9.8226	9.0770	7.8431	6.8729	6.4641	6.0971	5.4669	4.9476	4.1474	3.5640	3.1220
30	25.8077	22.3965	19.6004	17.2920	15.3725	13.7648	12.4090	11.2578	10.2737	9.4269	8.0552	7.0027	6.5660	6.1772	5.5168	4.9789	4.1601	3.5693	3.1242
40	32.8347	27.3555	23.1148	19.7928	17.1591	15.0463	13.3317	11.9246	10.7574	9.7791	8.2438	7.1050	6.6418	6.2335	5.5482	4.9966	4.1659	3.5712	3.1250
50	39.1961	31.4236	25.7298	21.4822	18.2559	15.7619	13.8007	12.2335	10.9617	9.9148	8.3045	7.1327	6.6605	6.2463	5.5541	4.9995	4.1666	3.5714	3.1250
60	44.9550	34.7609	27.6756	22.6235	18.9293	16.1614	14.0392	12.3766	11.0480	9.9672	8.3240	7.1401	6.6651	6.2402	5.5553	4.9999	4.1667	3.5714	3.1250

TABLE C.3 Future Value of $1 at the End of *n* Periods: $FVIF_{k,n} = (1 + k)^n$

Period	1%	2%	3%	4%	5%	6%	7%	8%	9%	10%	12%	14%	15%	16%	18%	20%	24%	28%	32%	36%
1	1.0100	1.0200	1.0300	1.0400	1.0500	1.0600	1.0700	1.0800	1.0900	1.1000	1.1200	1.1400	1.1500	1.1600	1.1800	1.2000	1.2400	1.2800	1.3200	1.3600
2	1.0201	1.0404	1.0609	1.0816	1.1025	1.1236	1.1449	1.1664	1.1881	1.2100	1.2544	1.2996	1.3225	1.3456	1.3924	1.4400	1.5376	1.6384	1.7424	1.8496
3	1.0303	1.0612	1.0927	1.1249	1.1576	1.1910	1.2250	1.2597	1.2950	1.3310	1.4049	1.4815	1.5209	1.5609	1.6430	1.7280	1.9066	2.0972	2.3000	2.5155
4	1.0406	1.0824	1.1255	1.1699	1.2155	1.2625	1.3108	1.3605	1.4116	1.4641	1.5735	1.6890	1.7490	1.8106	1.9388	2.0736	2.3642	2.6844	3.0360	3.4210
5	1.0510	1.1041	1.1593	1.2167	1.2763	1.3382	1.4026	1.4693	1.5386	1.6105	1.7623	1.9254	2.0114	2.1003	2.2878	2.4883	2.9316	3.4360	4.0075	4.6526
6	1.0615	1.1262	1.1941	1.2653	1.3401	1.4185	1.5007	1.5869	1.6771	1.7716	1.9738	2.1950	2.3131	2.4364	2.6996	2.9860	3.6352	4.3980	5.2899	6.3275
7	1.0721	1.1487	1.2299	1.3159	1.4071	1.5036	1.6058	1.7138	1.8280	1.9487	2.2107	2.5023	2.6600	2.8262	3.1855	3.5832	4.5077	5.6295	6.9826	8.6054
8	1.0829	1.1717	1.2668	1.3686	1.4775	1.5938	1.7182	1.8509	1.9926	2.1436	2.4760	2.8526	3.0590	3.2784	3.7589	4.2998	5.5895	7.2058	9.2170	11.703
9	1.0937	1.1951	1.3048	1.4233	1.5513	1.6895	1.8385	1.9990	2.1719	2.3579	2.7731	3.2519	3.5179	3.8030	4.4355	5.1598	6.9310	9.2234	12.166	15.916
10	1.1046	1.2190	1.3439	1.4802	1.6289	1.7908	1.9672	2.1589	2.3674	2.5937	3.1058	3.7072	4.0456	4.4114	5.2338	6.1917	8.5944	11.805	16.059	21.646
11	1.1157	1.2434	1.3842	1.5395	1.7103	1.8983	2.1049	2.3316	2.5804	2.8531	3.4785	4.2262	4.6524	5.1173	6.1759	7.4301	10.657	15.111	21.198	29.439
12	1.1268	1.2682	1.4258	1.6010	1.7959	2.0122	2.2522	2.5182	2.8127	3.1384	3.8960	4.8179	5.3502	5.9360	7.2876	8.9161	13.214	19.342	27.982	40.037
13	1.1381	1.2936	1.4685	1.6651	1.8856	2.1329	2.4098	2.7196	3.0658	3.4523	4.3635	5.4924	6.1528	6.8858	8.5994	10.699	16.386	24.758	36.937	54.451
14	1.1495	1.3195	1.5126	1.7317	1.9799	2.2609	2.5785	2.9372	3.3417	3.7975	4.8871	6.2613	7.0757	7.9875	10.147	12.839	20.319	31.691	48.756	74.053
15	1.1610	1.3459	1.5580	1.8009	2.0789	2.3966	2.7590	3.1722	3.6425	4.1772	5.4736	7.1379	8.1371	9.2655	11.973	15.407	25.195	40.564	64.358	100.71
16	1.1726	1.3728	1.6047	1.8730	2.1829	2.5404	2.9522	3.4259	3.9703	4.5950	6.1304	8.1372	9.3576	10.748	14.129	18.488	31.242	51.923	84.953	136.96
17	1.1843	1.4002	1.6528	1.9479	2.2920	2.6928	3.1588	3.7000	4.3276	5.0545	6.8660	9.2765	10.761	12.467	16.672	22.186	38.740	66.461	112.13	186.27
18	1.1961	1.4282	1.7024	2.0258	2.4066	2.8543	3.3799	3.9960	4.7171	5.5599	7.6900	10.575	12.375	14.462	19.673	26.623	48.038	85.070	148.02	253.33
19	1.2081	1.4568	1.7535	2.1068	2.5270	3.0256	3.6165	4.3157	5.1417	6.1159	8.6128	12.055	14.231	16.776	23.214	31.948	59.567	108.89	195.39	344.53
20	1.2202	1.4859	1.8061	2.1911	2.6533	3.2071	3.8697	4.6610	5.6044	6.7275	9.6463	13.743	16.366	19.460	27.393	38.337	73.864	139.37	257.91	468.57
21	1.2324	1.5157	1.8603	2.2788	2.7860	3.3996	4.1406	5.0338	6.1088	7.4002	10.803	15.667	18.821	22.574	32.323	46.005	91.591	178.40	340.44	637.26
22	1.2447	1.5460	1.9161	2.3699	2.9253	3.6035	4.4304	5.4365	6.6586	8.1403	12.100	17.861	21.644	26.186	38.142	55.206	113.57	228.35	449.39	866.67
23	1.2572	1.5769	1.9736	2.4647	3.0715	3.8197	4.7405	5.8715	7.2579	8.9543	13.552	20.361	24.891	30.376	45.007	66.247	140.83	292.30	593.19	1178.6
24	1.2697	1.6084	2.0328	2.5633	3.2251	4.0489	5.0724	6.3412	7.9111	9.8497	15.178	23.212	28.625	35.236	53.108	79.496	174.63	374.14	783.02	1602.9
25	1.2824	1.6406	2.0938	2.6658	3.3864	4.2919	5.4274	6.8485	8.6231	10.834	17.000	26.461	32.918	40.874	62.668	95.396	216.54	478.90	1033.5	2180.0
26	1.2953	1.6734	2.1566	2.7725	3.5557	4.5494	5.8074	7.3964	9.3992	11.918	19.040	30.166	37.856	47.414	73.948	114.47	268.51	612.99	1364.3	2964.9
27	1.3082	1.7069	2.2213	2.8834	3.7335	4.8223	6.2139	7.9881	10.245	13.110	21.324	34.389	43.535	55.000	87.259	137.37	332.95	784.63	1800.9	4032.2
28	1.3213	1.7410	2.2879	2.9987	3.9201	5.1117	6.6488	8.6271	11.167	14.421	23.883	39.204	50.065	63.800	102.96	164.84	412.86	1004.3	2377.2	5483.8
29	1.3345	1.7758	2.3566	3.1187	4.1161	5.4184	7.1143	9.3173	12.172	15.863	26.749	44.693	57.575	74.008	121.50	197.81	511.95	1285.5	3137.9	7458.0
30	1.3478	1.8114	2.4273	3.2434	4.3219	5.7435	7.6123	10.062	13.267	17.449	29.959	50.950	66.211	85.849	143.37	237.37	634.81	1645.5	4142.0	10143.
40	1.4889	2.2080	3.2620	4.8010	7.0400	10.285	14.974	21.724	31.409	45.259	93.050	188.88	267.86	378.72	750.37	1469.7	5455.9	19426.	66520.	•
50	1.6446	2.6916	4.3839	7.1067	11.467	18.420	29.457	46.901	74.357	117.39	289.00	700.23	1083.6	1670.7	3927.3	9100.4	46890.	•	•	•
60	1.8167	3.2810	5.8916	10.519	18.679	32.987	57.946	101.25	176.03	304.48	897.59	2595.9	4383.9	7370.1	20555.	56347.	•	•	•	•

*FVIFA > 99.999

TABLE C.4

Sum of an Annuity of $1 Per Period for n Periods:

$$FVIFA_{k,n} = \sum_{t=1}^{n}(1+k)^{t-1} = \frac{(1+k)^n - 1}{k}$$

Number of Periods	1%	2%	3%	4%	5%	6%	7%	8%	9%	10%	12%	14%	15%	16%	18%	20%	24%	28%	32%	36%
1	1.0000	1.0000	1.0000	1.0000	1.0000	1.0000	1.0000	1.0000	1.0000	1.0000	1.0000	1.0000	1.0000	1.0000	1.0000	1.0000	1.0000	1.0000	1.0000	1.0000
2	2.0100	2.0200	2.0300	2.0400	2.0500	2.0600	2.0700	2.0800	2.0900	2.1000	2.1200	2.1400	2.1500	2.1600	2.1800	2.2000	2.2400	2.2800	2.3200	2.3600
3	3.0301	3.0604	3.0909	3.1216	3.1525	3.1836	3.2149	3.2464	3.2781	3.3100	3.3744	3.4396	3.4725	3.5056	3.5724	3.6400	3.7776	3.9184	4.0624	4.2096
4	4.0604	4.1216	4.1836	4.2465	4.3101	4.3746	4.4399	4.5061	4.5731	4.6410	4.7793	4.9211	4.9934	5.0665	5.2154	5.3680	5.6842	6.0156	6.3624	6.7251
5	5.1010	5.2040	5.3091	5.4163	5.5256	5.6371	5.7507	5.8666	5.9847	6.1051	6.3528	6.6101	6.7424	6.8771	7.1542	7.4416	8.0484	8.6999	9.3983	10.146
6	6.1520	6.3081	6.4684	6.6330	6.8019	6.9753	7.1533	7.3359	7.5233	7.7156	8.1152	8.5355	8.7537	8.9775	9.4420	9.9299	10.980	12.135	13.405	14.798
7	7.2135	7.4343	7.6625	7.8983	8.1420	8.3938	8.6540	8.9228	9.2004	9.4872	10.089	10.730	11.066	11.413	12.141	12.915	14.615	16.533	18.695	21.126
8	8.2857	8.5830	8.8923	9.2142	9.5491	9.8975	10.259	10.636	11.028	11.435	12.299	13.232	13.726	14.240	15.327	16.499	19.122	22.163	25.678	29.731
9	9.3685	9.7546	10.159	10.582	11.026	11.491	11.978	12.487	13.021	13.579	14.775	16.085	16.785	17.518	19.085	20.798	24.712	29.369	34.895	41.435
10	10.462	10.949	11.463	12.006	12.577	13.180	13.816	14.486	15.192	15.937	17.548	19.337	20.303	21.321	23.521	25.958	31.643	38.592	47.061	57.351
11	11.566	12.168	12.807	13.486	14.206	14.971	15.783	16.645	17.560	18.531	20.654	23.044	24.349	25.732	28.755	32.150	40.237	50.398	63.121	78.998
12	12.682	13.412	14.192	15.025	15.917	16.869	17.888	18.977	20.140	21.384	24.133	27.270	29.001	30.850	34.931	39.580	50.894	65.510	84.320	108.43
13	13.809	14.680	15.617	16.626	17.713	18.882	20.140	21.495	22.953	24.522	28.029	32.088	34.351	36.786	42.218	48.496	64.109	84.852	112.30	148.47
14	14.947	15.973	17.086	18.291	19.598	21.015	22.550	24.214	26.019	27.975	32.392	37.581	40.504	43.672	50.818	59.195	80.496	109.61	149.23	202.92
15	16.096	17.293	18.598	20.023	21.578	23.276	25.129	27.152	29.360	31.772	37.279	43.842	47.580	51.659	60.965	72.035	100.81	141.30	197.99	276.97
16	17.257	18.639	20.156	21.824	23.657	25.672	27.888	30.324	33.003	35.949	42.753	50.980	55.717	60.925	72.939	87.442	126.01	181.86	262.35	377.69
17	18.430	20.012	21.761	23.697	25.840	28.212	30.840	33.750	36.973	40.544	48.883	59.117	65.075	71.673	87.068	105.93	157.25	233.79	347.30	514.66
18	19.614	21.412	23.414	25.645	28.132	30.905	33.999	37.450	41.301	45.599	55.749	68.394	75.836	84.140	103.74	128.11	195.99	300.25	459.44	700.93
19	20.810	22.840	25.116	27.671	30.539	33.760	37.379	41.446	46.018	51.159	63.439	78.969	88.211	98.603	123.41	154.74	244.03	385.32	607.47	954.27
20	22.019	24.297	26.370	29.778	33.066	36.785	40.995	45.762	51.160	57.275	72.052	91.024	102.44	115.37	146.62	186.68	303.60	494.21	802.86	1298.8
21	23.239	25.783	28.676	31.969	35.719	39.992	44.865	50.422	56.764	64.002	81.698	104.76	118.81	134.84	174.02	225.02	377.46	633.59	1060.7	1767.3
22	24.471	27.299	30.536	34.248	38.505	43.392	49.005	55.456	62.873	71.402	92.502	120.43	137.63	157.41	206.34	271.03	469.05	811.99	1401.2	2404.6
23	25.716	28.845	32.452	36.617	41.430	46.995	53.436	60.893	69.531	79.543	104.60	138.29	159.27	183.60	244.48	326.23	582.62	1040.3	1850.6	3271.3
24	26.973	30.421	34.426	39.082	44.502	50.815	58.176	66.764	76.789	88.497	118.15	158.65	184.16	213.97	289.49	392.48	723.46	1332.6	2443.8	4449.9
25	28.243	32.030	36.459	41.645	47.727	54.864	63.249	73.105	84.700	98.347	133.33	181.87	212.79	249.21	342.60	471.98	898.09	1706.8	3226.8	6052.9
26	29.525	33.670	38.553	44.311	51.113	59.156	68.676	79.954	93.323	109.18	150.33	208.33	245.71	290.08	405.27	567.37	1114.6	2185.7	4260.4	8233.0
27	30.820	35.344	40.709	47.084	54.669	63.705	74.483	87.350	102.72	121.09	169.37	238.49	283.56	337.50	479.22	681.85	1383.1	2798.7	5624.7	11197.9
28	32.129	37.051	42.930	49.967	58.402	68.528	80.697	95.338	112.96	134.20	190.69	272.88	327.10	392.50	566.48	819.22	1716.0	3583.3	7425.6	15230.2
29	33.450	38.792	45.218	52.966	62.322	73.639	87.346	103.96	124.13	148.63	214.58	312.09	377.16	456.30	669.44	984.06	2128.9	4587.6	9802.9	20714.1
30	34.784	40.568	47.575	56.084	66.438	79.058	94.460	113.28	136.30	164.49	241.33	356.78	434.74	530.31	790.94	1181.8	2640.9	5873.2	12940.	28172.2
40	48.886	60.402	75.401	95.025	120.79	154.76	199.63	259.05	337.88	442.59	767.09	1342.0	1779.0	2360.7	4163.2	7343.8	22728.	69377.	•	•
50	64.463	84.579	112.79	152.66	209.34	290.33	406.52	573.76	815.08	1163.9	2400.0	4994.5	7217.7	10435.	21813.	45497.	•	•	•	•
60	81.669	114.05	163.65	237.99	353.58	533.12	813.52	1253.2	1944.7	3034.8	7471.6	18535	29219.	46057.	•	•	•	•	•	•

*FVIF > 99,999

STANDARD NORMAL PROBABILITIES

z	0.00	0.01	0.02	0.03	0.04	0.05	0.06	0.07	0.08	0.09
0.0	.5000	.5040	.5080	.5120	.5160	.5199	.5239	.5279	.5219	.5359
0.1	.5398	.5438	.5478	.5517	.5557	.5596	.5636	.5675	.5714	.5753
0.2	.5793	.5832	.5871	.5910	.5948	.5987	.6026	.6064	.6103	.6141
0.3	.6179	.6217	.6255	.6293	.6331	.6368	.6406	.6443	.6480	.6517
0.4	.6554	.6591	.6628	.6664	.6700	.6736	.6772	.6808	.6844	.6879
0.5	.6915	.6950	.6985	.7019	.7054	.7088	.7123	.7157	.7190	.7224
0.6	.7257	.7291	.7324	.7357	.7389	.7422	.7454	.7486	.7517	.7549
0.7	.7580	.7611	.7642	.7673	.7704	.7734	.7764	.7794	.7823	.7852
0.8	.7881	.7910	.7939	.7967	.7995	.8023	.8051	.8078	.8106	.8133
0.9	.8159	.8186	.8212	.8238	.8264	.8289	.8315	.8340	.8365	.8389
1.0	.8413	.8438	.8461	.8485	.8508	.8531	.8554	.8577	.8599	.8621
1.1	.8643	.8665	.8686	.8708	.8729	.8749	.8770	.8790	.8810	.8830
1.2	.8849	.8860	.8888	.8907	.8925	.8943	.8962	.8980	.8997	.9015
1.3	.9032	.9049	.9066	.9082	.9099	.9115	.9131	.9147	.9162	.9177
1.4	.9192	.9207	.9222	.9236	.9251	.9265	.9279	.9292	.9306	.9319
1.5	.9332	.9345	.9357	.9370	.9382	.9394	.9406	.9418	.9429	.9441
1.6	.9452	.9463	.9474	.9484	.9495	.9505	.9515	.9525	.9535	.9545
1.7	.9554	.9564	.9573	.9582	.9591	.9599	.9608	.9616	.9625	.9633
1.8	.9641	.9649	.9656	.9664	.9671	.9678	.9686	.9693	.9699	.9706
1.9	.9713	.9719	.9726	.9732	.9738	.9744	.9750	.9756	.9761	.9767
2.0	.9772	.9778	.9783	.9788	.9793	.9798	.9803	.9808	.9812	.9817
2.1	.9821	.9826	.9830	.9834	.9838	.9842	.9846	.9850	.9854	.9857
2.2	.9861	.9864	.9868	.9871	.9875	.9878	.9881	.9884	.9887	.9890
2.3	.9893	.9896	.9898	.9901	.9904	.9906	.9909	.9911	.9913	.9916
2.4	.9918	.9920	.9922	.9925	.9927	.9929	.9931	.9932	.9934	.9936
2.5	.9938	.9940	.9941	.9943	.9945	.9946	.9948	.9949	.9951	.9952
2.6	.9953	.9955	.9956	.9957	.9959	.9960	.9961	.9962	.9963	.9964
2.7	.9965	.9966	.9967	.9968	.9969	.9970	.9971	.9972	.9973	.9974
2.8	.9974	.9975	.9976	.9977	.9977	.9978	.9979	.9979	.9980	.9981
2.9	.9981	.9982	.9982	.9983	.9984	.9984	.9985	.9985	.9986	.9986
3.0	.9987	.9987	.9987	.9988	.9988	.9989	.9989	.9989	.9990	.9990

Name Index

SUBJECT INDEX

A, AA, AAA bonds, 451
Abnormal rate of return, 202–204
Academic journals, for investment analysis information, 185–186
Accounting changes, impact of, 220
Accounting principles
   foreign, 361
   U.S. and foreign, 363–364
Accounting statements, non-U.S., 359–361
Accrued interest basis, 476
Active bond portfolio strategies, 537–550
   contingent procedures as, 565–570
ADRs. See American Depository Receipts
Advance-decline diffusion index, 729–731
Agency bond quotes, 476–478
Agency issues, 448, 456–459
Aggregated coefficients model, 212
Aggregate economic analysis, information sources and, 164–168
Aggregate financial ratios, international, 365–366
Aggregate operating profit margin, estimating, 598–601
Aggregate security-market analysis, information sources and, 168–174
Aggregate stock/bond-market index, 132
Aggressive growth funds, 907
Aim Constellation Fund, performance of, 953–954, 960–962
American Depository Receipts (ADRs), 58, 99
American Municipal Bond Assurance Corporation (AMBAC), 460
American options, 298, 754
   pricing, 775–778, 847
American Stock Exchange (AMEX), 58, 59 , 89, 90, 91–93
   options trading on, 754

AMEX Fact Book, 139
AMEX Market Value Index, 139
Analysis. See Fundamental analysis; Technical analysis
Analysis effect, 970
Annual reports, 175–178
Antiques, 64
   data on, 69–71, 82
Approximate promised yield (APY), 489–491
APT. See Arbitrage pricing theory
Arbitrage, 297, 835–838
   commodity futures and, 822
   covered interest, 854
   index, 824
   stock index, 837–838
   Treasury bill, 836–83
Arbitrage pricing theory (APT), 268, 288–291, 915
   anomalies and, 935–937
   CAPM and, 930–938
   inflation and, 937
   and January effect, 937
   Shanken challenge and, 937–938
Arithmetic mean, 9
Art, 64, 69–71, 72
Arthur Wiesenberger Services, 895, 897
Asset allocation
   global decision for, 409–438
   and global portfolio, 378, 549–551, 554
Asset-backed securities (ABS), 461, 463
Asset pricing models, 267–295
   extensions and testing of, 914–942
Asset return and risk, 68–69
Assets
   financial, 52
   Fortune 500 and, 611
   real, 52
   risk-free, 270–274
   spot prices of, 309–310
   stock, debt, and, 786
   undervalued and overvalued, 282–285
   world allocation of, 432–435
Asset turnover, 338
At-the-money, 298
Austria, SIGNs of, 804

Autocorrelation tests of independence, 199
Automatic adjustment, 137

Bahns (German bonds), 459
Balanced funds, 62, 886, 907
Balance sheets, 323, 324
   non-U.S., 359
Bank of Japan (BOJ), 469
Bank rate, 105
Bankruptcy. See Insolvency
Banks, publications of, 165–166
Bar charts, 736, 739
Barron's, 136, 168. See also Investment companies
   Confidence Index of, 725–727
   mutual fund information from, 895
Basis risk, 825–826
Basis swap, 869
Bayer, company analysis of, 692, 693
B, BB, BBB bonds, 451
BE/ME ratio. See Book-to-market value, ratio
Bearer bond, 444
Bear market. See Technical analysis
Bear spread, 768
Benchmark error, 928–929
   global portfolio performance measurement and, 963–965
   implications of, 965–967
Benchmark issue, 454
Benchmarks, bond portfolio performance and, 975–976
Beta, 967. See also Capital asset pricing model (CAPM)
   comparability of estimates, 921
   risk and, 288, 292
   stability of, 919–921
   Treynor portfolio measure and, 948
   of Walgreen's stock, 676–678
"Big Bang," and London Stock Exchange, 112, 121–22
Bills. See Treasury bills
Black-Scholes option pricing

model, 576, 771–775, 784–785
   options on futures pricing and, 848–850
Block houses, 115
Block trades, 115–116
Bond funds, 61, 887
   closed-end, 881
Bond indexes
   correlation among monthly, 155
   global, 151–152
Bond market
   global, 44
   global structure of, 446–451
   portfolio risk in global, 48–49
   technical analysis of, 742–743
Bond-market efficiency, 577–578
Bond-market indicator series, 150–152
Bond market line, 968–971
Bond portfolio performance
   benchmarks and, 975–976
   consistency of, 974–975
   decomposing returns and, 971–973
   evaluating, 967–976
   sources of return and, 973–974
Bond portfolio strategies, 534–585
   active, 537–550, 565–571
   matching fund techniques as, 551–564
   passive, 535–537
Bond prices, interest rates and, 424
Bond price volatility, 513–516
   and duration, 520–522
   and trading strategies, 516
Bond quotes
   interpreting, 474–476
   sources of, 473–474
Bond ratings, 28n
   financial ratios and, 366–367
Bonds. See also Currency swaps
   alternate issues of, 451–453
   calculating future prices, 494–496
   callable, 528–530